HOTELS & RESTAURANTS IN BRITAIN

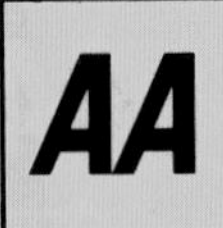

Consultant Editor: I M Tyers, FHCIMA, FTS, MCFA
Editor: Michael Buttler
Designer: Gerry McElroy

Gazetteer: Compiled by the Publications Research Unit of the Automobile Association in co-operation with the Hotels Inspectorate
Maps: Prepared by the Cartographic Services Unit of the Automobile Association
Cover Picture: Stonefield Castle Hotel

Head of Advertisement Sales: Christopher Heard
Tel 0256 20123 (ext 2020)
Advertisement Production: Karen Weeks
Tel 0256 20123 (ext 3525)
Advertisement Sales Representatives:
London, East Anglia, East Midlands, Central Southern and South East England, Edward May
Tel 0256 20123 (ext 3524) or 0256 467568
South West, West, West Midlands, Bryan Thompson
Tel 0272 393296
Wales and North of England, Arthur Williams
Tel 0222 620267
Scotland Tel 0256 20123 (ext 2020)

Filmset by: Turnergraphic Ltd, Basingstoke, Hampshire
Colour section printed by J.B. Shears and Sons Ltd, Basingstoke, Hampshire
Printed and bound in Great Britain by
Chorley and Pickersgill Ltd, Leeds

Every effort is made to ensure accuracy, but the publishers do not hold themselves responsible for any consequences that may arise from errors or omissions. Whilst the contents are believed correct at the time of going to press, changes may have occurred since that time or will occur during the currency of this book. The up to date position may be checked through AA regional offices.

Published by The Automobile Association, Fanum House, Basingstoke, Hampshire RG21 2EA

ISBN 0 86145 380 8

AA Reference 59530

May be redeemed in accordance with the conditions overleaf at any of the establishments whose gazetteer entry shows the symbol Ⓥ

The Voucher Worth £1

May be redeemed in accordance with the conditions overleaf at any of the establishments whose gazetteer entry shows the symbol Ⓥ

The Voucher Worth £1

May be redeemed in accordance with the conditions overleaf at any of the establishments whose gazetteer entry shows the symbol Ⓥ

The Voucher Worth £1

May be redeemed in accordance with the conditions overleaf at any of the establishments whose gazetteer entry shows the symbol Ⓥ

The Voucher Worth £1

May be redeemed in accordance with the conditions overleaf at any of the establishments whose gazetteer entry shows the symbol Ⓥ

The Voucher Worth £1

May be redeemed in accordance with the conditions overleaf at any of the establishments whose gazetteer entry shows the symbol Ⓥ

The Voucher Worth £1

May be redeemed in accordance with the conditions overleaf at any of the establishments whose gazetteer entry shows the symbol Ⓥ

The Voucher Worth £1

May be redeemed in accordance with the conditions overleaf at any of the establishments whose gazetteer entry shows the symbol Ⓥ

The Voucher Worth £1

May be redeemed in accordance with the conditions overleaf at any of the establishments whose gazetteer entry shows the symbol Ⓥ

The Voucher Worth £1

May be redeemed in accordance with the conditions overleaf at any of the establishments whose gazetteer entry shows the symbol Ⓥ

Conditions
A copy of AA Hotels and Restaurants in Britain 1987 must be produced with this voucher.
Only one voucher per person or party accepted.
Not redeemable for cash. No change given.
The voucher will not be valid after 31st December, 1987.
Use of the voucher is restricted to when payment is made before leaving the hotel or restaurant premises.
The voucher will only be accepted against hotel accommodation at full tariff rates or to restaurant bills over £5 excluding VAT and any service charge.

Conditions
A copy of AA Hotels and Restaurants in Britain 1987 must be produced with this voucher.
Only one voucher per person or party accepted.
Not redeemable for cash. No change given.
The voucher will not be valid after 31st December, 1987.
Use of the voucher is restricted to when payment is made before leaving the hotel or restaurant premises.
The voucher will only be accepted against hotel accommodation at full tariff rates or to restaurant bills over £5 excluding VAT and any service charge.

Conditions
A copy of AA Hotels and Restaurants in Britain 1987 must be produced with this voucher.
Only one voucher per person or party accepted.
Not redeemable for cash. No change given.
The voucher will not be valid after 31st December, 1987.
Use of the voucher is restricted to when payment is made before leaving the hotel or restaurant premises.
The voucher will only be accepted against hotel accommodation at full tariff rates or to restaurant bills over £5 excluding VAT and any service charge.

Conditions
A copy of AA Hotels and Restaurants in Britain 1987 must be produced with this voucher.
Only one voucher per person or party accepted.
Not redeemable for cash. No change given.
The voucher will not be valid after 31st December, 1987.
Use of the voucher is restricted to when payment is made before leaving the hotel or restaurant premises.
The voucher will only be accepted against hotel accommodation at full tariff rates or to restaurant bills over £5 excluding VAT and any service charge.

Conditions
A copy of AA Hotels and Restaurants in Britain 1987 must be produced with this voucher.
Only one voucher per person or party accepted.
Not redeemable for cash. No change given.
The voucher will not be valid after 31st December, 1987.
Use of the voucher is restricted to when payment is made before leaving the hotel or restaurant premises.
The voucher will only be accepted against hotel accommodation at full tariff rates or to restaurant bills over £5 excluding VAT and any service charge.

Conditions
A copy of AA Hotels and Restaurants in Britain 1987 must be produced with this voucher.
Only one voucher per person or party accepted.
Not redeemable for cash. No change given.
The voucher will not be valid after 31st December, 1987.
Use of the voucher is restricted to when payment is made before leaving the hotel or restaurant premises.
The voucher will only be accepted against hotel accommodation at full tariff rates or to restaurant bills over £5 excluding VAT and any service charge.

Conditions
A copy of AA Hotels and Restaurants in Britain 1987 must be produced with this voucher.
Only one voucher per person or party accepted.
Not redeemable for cash. No change given.
The voucher will not be valid after 31st December, 1987.
Use of the voucher is restricted to when payment is made before leaving the hotel or restaurant premises.
The voucher will only be accepted against hotel accommodation at full tariff rates or to restaurant bills over £5 excluding VAT and any service charge.

Conditions
A copy of AA Hotels and Restaurants in Britain 1987 must be produced with this voucher.
Only one voucher per person or party accepted.
Not redeemable for cash. No change given.
The voucher will not be valid after 31st December, 1987.
Use of the voucher is restricted to when payment is made before leaving the hotel or restaurant premises.
The voucher will only be accepted against hotel accommodation at full tariff rates or to restaurant bills over £5 excluding VAT and any service charge.

Conditions
A copy of AA Hotels and Restaurants in Britain 1987 must be produced with this voucher.
Only one voucher per person or party accepted.
Not redeemable for cash. No change given.
The voucher will not be valid after 31st December, 1987.
Use of the voucher is restricted to when payment is made before leaving the hotel or restaurant premises.
The voucher will only be accepted against hotel accommodation at full tariff rates or to restaurant bills over £5 excluding VAT and any service charge.

Conditions
A copy of AA Hotels and Restaurants in Britain 1987 must be produced with this voucher.
Only one voucher per person or party accepted.
Not redeemable for cash. No change given.
The voucher will not be valid after 31st December, 1987.
Use of the voucher is restricted to when payment is made before leaving the hotel or restaurant premises.
The voucher will only be accepted against hotel accommodation at full tariff rates or to restaurant bills over £5 excluding VAT and any service charge.

Contents

Preface

Dr Johnson's words in 1776 ring equally true today: 'There is nothing which has yet been contrived by man, by which so much happiness is produced as by a good tavern or inn'.

On this basis, our inspectors are finding an increased amount of happiness in the country. They report that the standards of accommodation are improving in hotels right across Britain. Hotels are offering more attractive decor, greater comfort and significantly more private bathrooms. Nevertheless, however luxurious a hotel may be, however excellent the food offered, a visit can be made or marred by the service offered. We find that the idea of *offering* service is disappearing in some hotels. When we ask for it, the staff will frequently reply that it is available. Yet they did not anticipate their guest's needs and offer service.

Whilst hoteliers sometimes complain that it is difficult to attract and retain the right men and women, it does seem that those employers who care about the welfare of their staff can overcome these problems. Indeed, we are very pleased to see the opportunities for young people to work in the hotel industry, although suitable training is all-important. Many employers find that a newcomer with the right personality is an asset to a business. Experience and a guiding hand can soon remedy any initial deficiencies and, from the customer's point of view, cheerful and friendly service may be more important than absolute correctness. But the staff's attitudes towards the guests will also be influenced by the examples they see around them. The more visible the manager or proprietor can be in the hotel, the better, particularly in making guests feel at home.

An atmosphere of welcome and hospitality does not cost money, and it is shortsighted to cut down on the time that must be spent imparting these necessary skills and attitudes to staff. We are all too familiar with the bored receptionist who is more interested in polishing her fingernails and watching the clock than in rising with a smile to greet the arriving guests, and we know the reluctant porter who stands with folded arms while you struggle with your luggage; the head waiter who lurks outside his dining room but considers himself above the obligation to provide service; the chambermaid who uses the towel of the departing guest to clean the bath, washbasin, tooth-glass and the cup and saucer from the make-it-yourself tea equipment. We would also wish for more personal farewells, particularly from the hotel management when guests depart.

Of course, the customer who wishes to enjoy the full facilities and the elaborate 24 hour service offered by one of the splendid five star palaces must be prepared to pay accordingly. At the other end of the scale, should the guest be prepared to carry his own bag, clean his own shoes, make his own tea, serve himself in the restaurant and sleep in a standard size bedroom with standard furniture and standard decor — all factors which must have reduced the running costs of that particular hotel — he is entitled to expect a commensurately lower charge. In both cases, however, the guest wants value for money — a concept which is difficult to define, but you know when you have found it!

Guests who are disappointed with a hotel very often cite small details which may seem unimportant, but create a bad impression. The good hotelier can find out many of these irritations for himself by arranging, over a period of time, to sleep in every different type of bedroom in his hotel (or delegating responsible staff in the larger establishments). This will show up the shower that either scalds or chills, the ventilator that sounds like Concorde; the missing shelf for bathroom toiletries (so that the electric shaver must be balanced with the tooth-glass on the curved top of the cistern); the bedside light switch that is just out of reach; the bedside table too small for the tea tray; the radio system that broadcasts all three channels at once; the all night lift three feet from your pillow; rattling windows and banging fire doors; the badly lit dressing table mirror. Our plea is to make hotel bedrooms more 'user friendly', with special attention paid to soundproofing, a cause of a rising number of complaints.

That it is possible to provide a warm welcome, and achieve high standards of hospitality, facilities and service, while still running a profitable business is demonstrated by the number of establishments that have won our approval and earned special awards. Red Stars and merit awards for hotels, and rosettes for food and service in restaurants are used by the AA to highlight establishments which our inspectors have recommended as being of special merit. Details of these awards are given on pages 39-50.

The emergence of the fine, personally managed country house hotels is also very encouraging. We are proud to have been the first to find and recognise these hotels. Conventional hotels had done away with so many services and become so impersonal that there was bound to be a reaction — perhaps some things had to get worse in order that others could be better! Certainly these hotels meet a very definite need in the way they have restored some of the traditional personal services and, provided cheerful and friendly services rather than just cold professionalism. Some — though not all, by any means — are expensive but often no more so than other, less pleasant hotels, while some of the lower classified ones are very reasonable. Human nature being what it is, however, not everyone enjoys them. We often use the phrase 'like being a personal guest', but this can lead to uncertainty as to how to behave; should you dress up for the evening when perhaps the hostess may appear looking tired and drawn after cooking dinner? Such questions you must answer for yourself. Those who prefer to stay in the anonymity of a large modern hotel can always do so, but it is interesting to note that an increasing number of business people think it worth their while to dine out of town to enjoy the high standards and relaxing atmosphere of these lovely Country House hotels. We hope there are very many more of them to come; we also wonder why some of the individually owned hotels in towns and cities cannot strive for the same high standards. We would certainly like to boost our Red Star list with more hotels of that type.

Brillat-Savarin, the 19th century gastronome-philosopher, observed that a restaurateur would inevitably be successful 'if he possesses sincerity, order and skill'. The intelligent professionalism which these qualities produce are indeed the ingredients of a winning formula. But the misinterpreters of Cuisine Nouvelle, who have done so much to destroy its original concept, should take note of these words. Lighter style food with excellent preparation and presentation has great merit. But miniscule portions, ineptly prepared and served cold at above average prices are to be condemned.

There has been a resurgence of real skill among many British chefs, and the catering colleges continue to do good work, but considerably more effort is still needed, not only to train more craftsmen, but also to imbue them with that sense of artistry that raises a competent cook into a great one.

We have been criticised in the past for the strong views we have expressed on many facets of the catering industry. We make no apology for this. It is our objective to give praise where we feel it is due and to censure when necessary and appropriate. We are grateful to readers whose comments have helped us to improve the presentation of this guide, and to hoteliers and restaurateurs who have co-operated so willingly in providing the information on which it is based.

If it helps potential customers to find a hotel or restaurant to suit their requirements, and at the same time encourages further improvement of standards in British hotels and restaurants, it will have achieved its aim.

I. M. Tyers

I M Tyers
FHCIMA, FTS, MCFA
Executive Manager
AA Hotel and Information Services

"Comments Please"

Tell us what you think of this book and you can obtain the 1988 edition at a substantial discount. We try to tailor our books to meet our readers' needs and this questionnaire will help us keep in touch with what you find interesting and useful. Please tell us what your comments are and return the completed questionnaire (no stamp needed) to us by 31 October 1987, to the following address:

Automobile Association
Department PMD (HRG)
Freepost
Basingstoke RG21 2BR

Everyone who replies will be entitled to a special discount on the 1988 edition of this guide. An order form will be sent shortly before publication date, but answering this questionnaire imposes no obligation to purchase. All answers will be treated in confidence.

---

1. How did you acquire this guide?

AA shop ☐
Bookshop ☐
Mail Order ☐
Other (please specify) ______

For use at
Home ☐
Office ☐ *Please tick*

---

2. Are you an AA member ☐

male? ☐
female? ☐

Under 21? ☐
21–30? ☐
31–45? ☐
46–65? ☐
over 65? ☐

---

3. Your occupation ______

---

4. Do you have any previous editions of this guide?

1984 ☐ 1985 ☐ 1986 ☐

---

5. Please indicate your usage of this guide:

	Hotels		**Restaurants**	
	Business	**Pleasure**	**Business**	**Pleasure**
4 times a week	☐	☐	☐	☐
3 times a week	☐	☐	☐	☐
Twice a week	☐	☐	☐	☐
Once a week	☐	☐	☐	☐
Once a fortnight	☐	☐	☐	☐
Once a month	☐	☐	☐	☐

---

6. How many people, apart from yourself, have consulted this guide (including those in your home and place of work)?

male ☐ female ☐

7. Do you use the 'Atlas' Section? Yes ☐ No ☐

8. How many times have you travelled overseas in the past year?
Staying at **HOTEL** ☐ **CAMPSITE** ☐

9. How many nights have you spent in hotels in the UK during the past year?

1 ☐ 2-7 ☐ 8-14 ☐ More ☐

10. Do you own more than one home? Yes ☐ No ☐

Do you own the house you live in? Yes ☐ No ☐

11. Your car
Type.............................. year..................................

12. What is yor daily newspaper? ....

13. Which of the following credit cards do you use?
Access ☐ American Express ☐ Diners ☐ Visa ☐

14. Do you find the Money-Off Vouchers useful? Yes ☐ No ☐

15. Did the Money-Off Vouchers affect your decision to buy this book?
Yes ☐ No ☐

16. What would you like us to improve in the guide?

____

____

____

Please *print* your name and address here if you would like us to send you an order form for the 1988 guide.

Name..

Address..

....

HOTELS TO KEEP YOU FIT

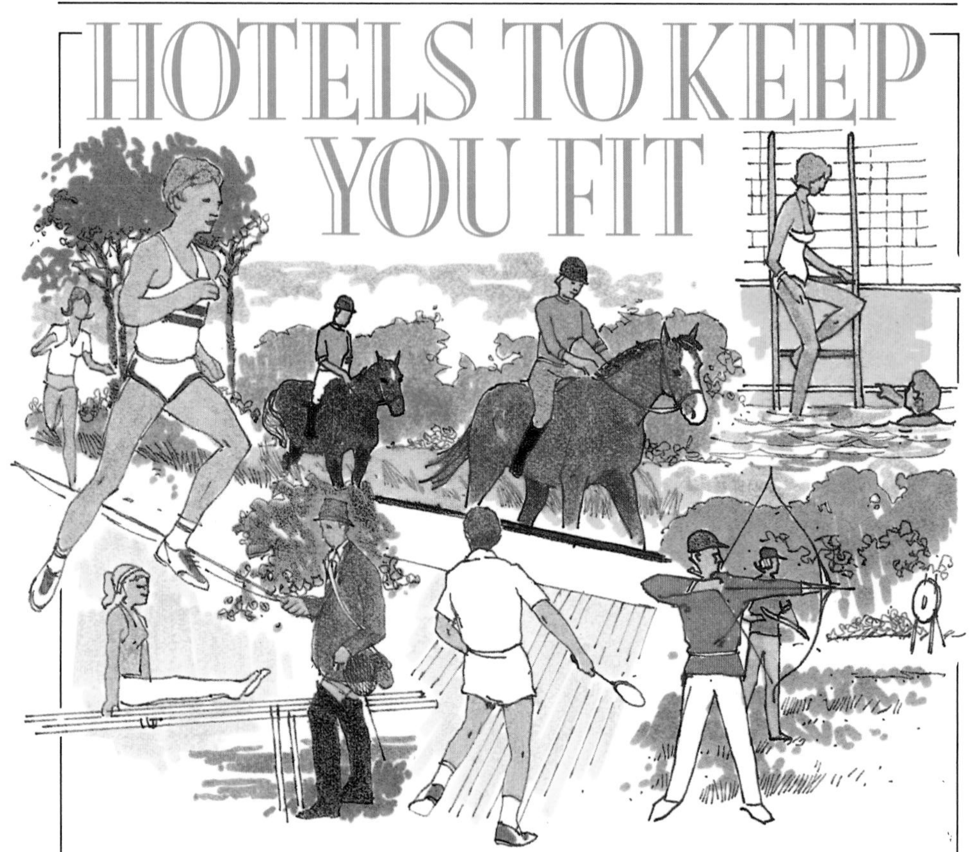

Hotels are certainly latching on to the leisure boom. Well over £20 million a year is being spent on adding new sports and leisure facilities or on improving existing ones, and the best now offer a dazzling range of attractions, beautifully designed and good for you as well.

Our inspectors in trying to come to terms with all the rich food they eat, have selected 30 hotels which boast superb sports and leisure facilities. We believe these to be the best in Britain, although there are many hundreds of others which have sports facilities, including a swimming pool at the very least. The gazetteer section of this book shows exactly which facilities are available at every AA recommended hotel, and this will provide a guide for every keep fit enthusiast. In addition, a separate listing of hotels with sporting and leisure facilities (Reference HR200) is available from the Hotels Department of the AA (Regional Headquarters or Head Office).

GLENEAGLES

AUCHTERARDER

This very famous hotel has superb facilities for almost every interest. There are four top class golf courses in a wonderful setting with a comfortable club house and a professional's shop. There are also tennis courts (grass and all weather), croquet lawns and lawn bowls. The glass domed Country Club houses a very attractive luxury swimming pool, incorporating a whirlpool bath, and overlooked by a restaurant and bar area. There are hot tubs outside the swimming pool and the complex also includes squash courts, billiard rooms, saunas, Turkish bath as well as a children's games area. An additional attraction is the availability of clay pigeon shooting, and the hotel can also arrange fishing and shooting on request.

BARNHAM BROOM HOTEL GOLF AND COUNTRY CLUB

BARNHAM BROOM

This friendly, modern hotel in the Norfolk countryside has its par 72 golf course as its focus and main attraction with a resident professional and modern teaching school. Tuition is also available in squash by English international, Alex Cowie; four squash courts are available, one with glass back. Tennis enthusiasts have three all weather tennis courts available to them, and there is a heated pool in which to relax. The Health Club offers a trimnasium, a sauna and a solarium. All the information and details are particularly well presented here, and there is a good range of pursuits which the hotel can organise for you off-site. These include fishing, riding, clay pigeon shooting, water sports, archery and even hot air ballooning.

MOLLINGTON BANASTRE

CHESTER

Considerable investment has gone into a new leisure centre at this well established hotel, and the result is most attractive. The focus is a smart swimming pool, overlooked by a bar and restaurant area. A feature of the bar is a selection of non-alcoholic cocktails which are delicious. Spread around the pool are a gymnasium, squash courts, a beauty therapist, a whirlpool bath, and saunas in the changing rooms. The squash courts can be adapted to cater for other sports such as battington (a version of badminton), volley ball and (from America) whalleyball. Table tennis is also available, while outdoors there is a croquet lawn and softball tennis court.

GLOUCESTER HOTEL AND COUNTRY CLUB

GLOUCESTER

One feature making this hotel unusual in England at least, is its attraction of an artificial ski slope. This has proved very popular with its ski tows and après ski bar. Another great draw, however, is the demanding 18 hole golf course and floodlit driving range. There are plenty of other activities available as well, from squash in one of the six courts, snooker using one of the three tables, or skittles in one of the two nine-pin alleys. In addition, there are further snooker and pool tables in the complex itself. The fitness fanatic has the facilities of a multigym at his or her disposal and relaxation is provided by the sauna, solarium, whirlpool bath and outdoor hot tub.

IMPERIAL

HYTHE

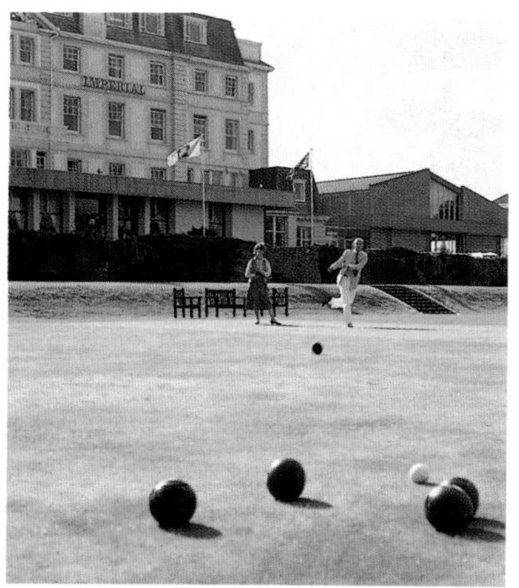

The sheer range of facilities available at this hotel is quite remarkable. We counted sixteen different activities it is possible to pursue on the hotel premises, and there are several others which can be organised off-site. Many of the activities are well geared to children and families, such as Karting and the Scalextric layout. There is a very attractive swimming pool area, squash courts, a trimnasium with qualified attendants, sauna, massage and sunbed room. Out of doors are tennis courts (four grass and two all weather), a golf course, croquet lawn, badminton court and a sports area for cricket or rounders.

PILLAR HOTEL

GREAT LANGDALE

Set in spectacular Lake District scenery is the modern (but tastefully designed) Pillar Hotel and Country Club. It includes an extensive suite of leisure facilities, which are most attractive to use. The swimming pool is decorated in tropical style and adjoins a bar and restaurant where light meals are available. There are also saunas, whirlpool baths, massage and sunbed facilities. For the more energetic, however, squash courts and a well equipped gymnasium are available. In its splendid setting, a variety of outdoor pastimes can be organised including canoeing, riding, sailing and wind surfing as well as all kinds of mountain activities, fishing and even archery, while a trim-trail has been set out in the hotel grounds.

SELSDON PARK

SANDERSTEAD

If you see flamingoes squawk and move their necks while you relax by the exotic pool in the new Tropical Leisure Complex at Selsdon Park you are not dreaming. They may not be real, but they certainly add to the atmosphere in this attractive complex. Upstairs in the water tower is a health suite with whirlpool bath, sauna, solarium and a mini-gym with carefully chosen equipment, while the more energetic have two squash courts available. Outside, there are 200 acres of grounds in which to relax, and these include a fine golf course, floodlit tennis courts and a croquet lawn. Riding stables are nearby and can be used by guests at a special rate.

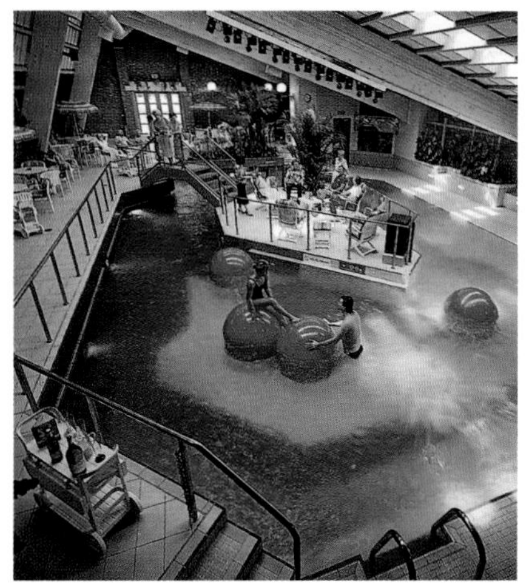

IMPERIAL

TORQUAY

This luxurious hotel has a good range of impressive sports and leisure facilities. It has two swimming pools, one indoor (with adjacent whirlpool bath) and one out, and a very well equipped gymnasium where guests can have a specially tailored fitness programme worked out for them. There is also a beauty salon with a variety of facilities and treatments, including sunbed, sauna, massage, aromatherapy, physiotherapy and chiropody. There are two squash courts and, outside, two tennis courts, a croquet lawn and putting green. Overlooking the indoor pool is a health food bar where wholesome meals are served.

TURNBERRY

TURNBERRY

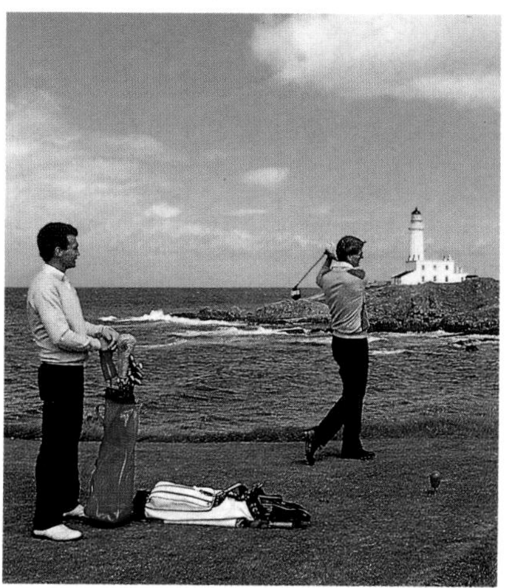

Every golf enthusiast has heard of Turnberry with its championship courses and most people stay here for this reason. However, it does have a variety of top class facilities for those who want to pursue other activities. There is a small gymnasium where a qualified attendant will advise those wishing to use the equipment, although it is tempting to relax in the luxurious swimming pool or in the sauna nearby. There are also two billiard tables, and table tennis and darts are available, while outdoors there are two hard tennis courts and riding stables. Tuition in many of the sports is available. In 1985, the hotel organised their own Highland Games, and this was a great attraction.

BELFRY

WISHAW

The Brabazon par 73 golf course at the Belfry was the scene of the 1985 Ryder Cup and epitomises one of the hotel's major attractions. Golfing enthusiasts know the hotel well, and it caters for them with this and also another par 70 course and floodlit driving range. However, a variety of other sporting and leisure facilities have been developed, and these include a very attractive swimming pool with lots of greenery and lounging chairs, two saunas, two solariums and a steam room. There are tennis courts, three squash courts, a small trimnasium and a large room with four billiard tables. A full scale beauty parlour is also available for guests at an extra charge. And in the grounds, three jogging routes have been set out.

FOREST HILLS
ABERFOYLE

An outstanding sporting feature of this hotel is the curling rink which is a full size three quarter lane rink. Adjoining it is a pleasant swimming pool, billiard room and fitness room, while badminton and squash are also available. The hotel grounds run down to Loch Ard, on which water sports are available.

REDWOOD LODGE
BRISTOL

The extensive facilities of a private country club are available to hotel residents and they include indoor and outdoor pools, 17 squash courts, 6 badminton courts, 7 tennis courts, 18 snooker tables as well as a multi-gym, saunas and solarium. Golf can be arranged nearby.

CAMBRIDGESHIRE MOAT HOUSE
BAR HILL

An 18 hole championship golf course is a major attraction of this hotel, which also has a putting green, and has laid out three joggers routes round the outside of the course. There is also a fine indoor pool, three squash courts and two all-weather tennis courts.

POST HOUSE
CAMBRIDGE

This relatively new hotel has a good range of indoor leisure facilities, including a large indoor pool, with spa bath and saunas, a fully equipped gymnasium and an outdoor jogging track.

FRENSHAM POND
CHURT

This country hotel in a beautiful setting has opened a small sports and leisure complex which is very attractive. As well as two squash courts and a gym, there is a very modern sunbed, and a small pool which features a water jet, to provide maximum exercise. A variety of other sporting activities can be arranged by the hotel.

—Lord Daresbury—

DARESBURY

The sports and leisure complex linked to this hotel has opened relatively recently and is very smart. There is an attractive indoor pool, overlooked by a bar and refreshment area, as well as a squash court, gymnasium, sauna and steam room and popular sun bed. Pride of place, though, must go to the billiard room which houses two tables.

Carlton Highland

EDINBURGH

This hotel has been totally refurbished and a new leisure centre, the Carlton Club has been opened. Situated beneath the hotel it is very spacious and includes a heated pool, a large snooker room with four tables and two pool tables, a very well equipped gymnasium, two squash courts and a large aerobics/dance studio, yoga and games room. In addition, there are saunas, solaria, steam rooms and massage facilities.

—Loch Rannoch—

KINLOCH RANNOCH

This hotel is part of the Loch Rannoch timeshare estate which includes a wide range of sporting activities to which guests have access. Notable is the floodlit ski slope and there are also watersports, an indoor pool, gymnasium, spa bath and solarium, as well as a squash court.

—Great Danes—

MAIDSTONE

A relatively small but ambitious leisure centre at this hotel involves an indoor pool complex with mini-gym, spa bath and refreshment area. Outside are floodlit tennis courts, a putting green, croquet lawn and children's play area. The games room contains two full size snooker tables, two pool tables and other amusements.

—Whitewater—

NEWBY BRIDGE

Guests at this well refurbished Lake District hotel have access to the leisure facilities incorporated into the adjoining timeshare development. The name behind this leisure complex is Champneys which indicates that there is an elaborate beauty therapy centre. The focus of the complex is a most attractive pool, with windows on to the foaming River Leven. There are also two squash courts and an exercise room, while the changing rooms contain saunas.

MOAT HOUSE

OXFORD

This new leisure complex includes an indoor swimming pool with a swim-on-the-spot wave machine, spa pool, saunas and sunbed, as well as a fitness room, two squash courts and three full size snooker tables. The tiled areas all have underfloor heating.

TAL

PENNAL

The timeshare development surrounding this hotel enables guests to have access to a range of very high quality leisure facilities, including a health spa run by Champneys, indoor and outdoor pools, two squash courts, a tennis court and a trim trail. There is also a sauna, solarium, children's adventure playground, croquet, badminton and tennis.

BROUGHTON PARK

PRESTON

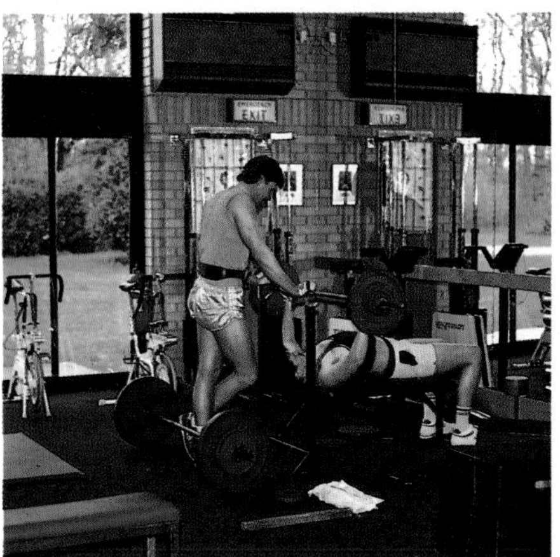

The leisure centre attached to this hotel is named Drakes and has very good facilities for fitness training. There are two gymnasia (one for men, the other for women) and these are comprehensively equipped with an instructor regularly available. Saunas and sunbeds are found in the changing rooms and the good size, attractive pool is overlooked by a bar and Drakes Restaurant.

ST PIERRE PARK

ST PETER PORT CHANNEL ISLANDS

This good, modern hotel is in a most attractive setting, which is used to the full for its splendid 9 hole golf course, designed by Tony Jacklin. There is also a driving range, as well as three tennis courts and croquet lawn. An indoor games room includes darts, pool and table tennis, while the heated indoor pool is large and attractively designed. The Health Club includes exercise room, saunas, solaria, spa baths and massage facilities.

CREST

SOUTH MIMMS HERTFORDSHIRE

An attractive new sports centre has been built at this hotel, and it includes a small pool with a children's pool and whirlpool bath, as well as a small exercise one, two saunas and two sunbeds. We were impressed by the well designed changing rooms.

TELFORD HOTEL, GOLF AND COUNTRY CLUB

TELFORD, SHROPSHIRE

In a fine setting overlooking Ironbridge Gorge, this hotel boasts a testing 18 hole golf course, as well as a large indoor swimming pool with a sauna, four squash courts and three snooker tables.

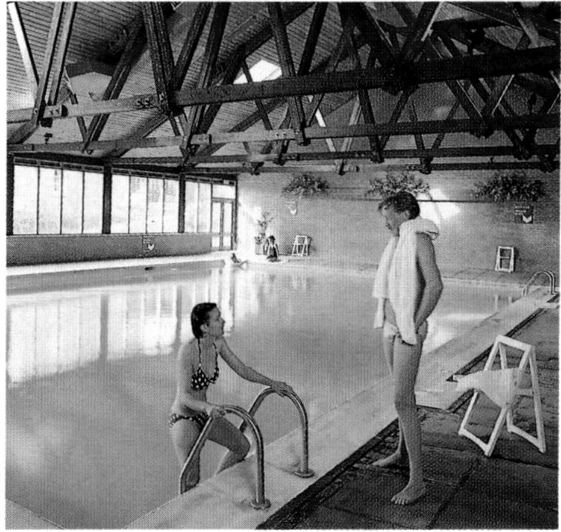

PALACE

TORQUAY, DEVON

This large and imposing hotel is set in splendid gardens, and has a good range of sporting and leisure facilities. There are six tennis courts, four of them outdoors, a nine hole golf course, and two swimming pools, the indoor one being very luxurious. The large sports hall which houses the indoor tennis courts can be used for badminton or for other purposes and the hotel also has two squash courts, two full sized billiard tables, and a good children's games room and play area.

BISHOPSTROW HOUSE

WARMINSTER

This elegant nineteenth century Georgian style mansion has been a Red Star hotel for some years now, offering elegant, comfortable accommodation as well as very good food. It also offers excellent facilities for the sportsman, including a fine indoor tennis court as well as an outdoor court among the 27 acres of grounds. These grounds extend to the River Wylye where fishing is available. There are also swimming pools, one outdoors and one very stylish indoor pool.

GEORGE WASHINGTON

WASHINGTON TYNE & WEAR

The main focus of this hotel's sporting facilities lies in its two golf courses, one of 18 holes, one of 9, in addition to which there is a driving range, jackpot golf, a golf shop and a professional. Indoors there are two squash courts and a heated swimming pool, which is set close to the multi-gym, sauna and spa bath. Close by is a snooker hall with four tables and one pool table.

HAWKSTONE PARK

WESTON UNDER REDCASTLE, SHROPSHIRE

This specialist golfing hotel is famous as the home of Sandy Lyle (his father is the professional here) and it has two courses. In addition, a wide range of other activities can be pursued, including tennis, croquet, snooker, table tennis and darts. There is a gymnasium with sauna and solarium, an outdoor swimming pool, and riding can be arranged nearby.

I arrived at the hotel at 4.45pm. It is a large, quite modern hotel with pretensions to luxury. At reception I am greeted by an unsmiling girl who is only concerned about how I am going to pay. I ask for a porter who takes my cases up to my room. After quickly unpacking, I come down for a cup of tea, and then set out to walk through the hotel. While it is quiet I have the chance to see all the parts of the hotel, good and bad, I get a mental picture of its layout, and I look at the bars and restaurants. This takes about an hour, and I return to my room to write up reports on places I have visited earlier in the day. About 7pm I order a light snack to be sent to the room, and it comes in good time. It is not very exciting, though, and rather insipid.

It is now 8pm, and I go down to test the restaurant. They have a relatively new chef, whose cooking I was keen to try. I ordered dishes that would test his skills and the meal was quite good, apart from the fact that they forgot to bring the new potatoes I ordered. After dinner I looked in the other bars and in the reception lobby, before returning to my room to start writing the report on the hotel.

Around midnight I came down to the reception lobby again to see how busy it was and had a brief chat with the night porter. Back in my room, I waited until 1am before testing the night service by ringing down for some sandwiches and hot chocolate. They came about 1.20am and after trying them, I retired to bed.

I was awakened at 7.30 by the morning call I had ordered, but the morning tea I asked for did not arrive. I also wanted to test the room service of cooked breakfast, but I was told that only Continental breakfast was available. I did not want that, and I came downstairs to eat breakfast in the restaurant.

It was self service with a very wide choice, but unfortunately, food in this type of restaurant can often go cold, which was what I found in this case. I also had to ask for my cup to be changed because it had not been cleaned properly. I finished breakfast quite quickly because I wanted to get on with my formal inspection of the hotel. I normally inspect a reasonable proportion of the bedrooms, and as this hotel had about 500 bedrooms in total, I planned to

24 HOURS IN A HOTEL INSPECTOR'S LIFE

see about 50 of them, distributed around the hotel.

I had my luggage taken to the car and then I settled my bill. Then I asked to see the General Manager, but was told he was unavailable. I explained who I was and that I wanted to see around the hotel, and before long the staff had arranged for me to be conducted round. I did eventually see the General Manager, but discovered that he was so busy he could not see me until later in the afternoon. I shall have to come back to see him.

The Food and Beverage manager then conducted me around the hotel. We started at the top and saw some of the best rooms, many of which have been only recently decorated. Then we saw a selection of the other rooms, most of which were of not nearly so high a standard as the ones I saw first. I looked all round the bedrooms, tested the lights and television to check that they worked properly, looked at the tea and coffee making equipment to see if it had been properly cleaned and stocked up. I also noted the state of the furniture, the carpets and the curtains. Then I looked in the bathrooms to see what condition the towels were in, how clean the bath and basins had been kept and to assess the general state of cleanliness.

The tour of the fifty or so bedrooms took about 1 ½ hours, and I must have walked about 2 miles! At the end I looked at the kitchens and the public lavatories. My inspection of the hotel was now complete, and since I could not discuss my findings with the General Manager until later, I left to inspect a restaurant in the meantime.

The restaurant was a smart Italian Restaurant about 50 minutes drive from the hotel. The traffic was heavy and the journey took longer than I planned. When I arrived I was greeted in a friendly fashion and ordered a soft drink while I considered the menu. Again, I had to choose dishes that would show the chef's ability and I chose to start with a Spaghetti Napolitana to see how well the pasta was cooked. Before sitting down, however, I had to look through the wine list, even though I would not drink any wine with my meal. I noted that it contained over 70 wines from a good variety of countries, and I memorised the prices of the cheapest and the most expensive, as well as the existence of any chateau bottled wines or good vintages.

As I ate the first course I watched how other diners were treated, saw how professional the service was. My main course also had a tomato sauce, and I chose it so that I could see if the same sauce was used as I had on my starter. I was pleased to see it had a different sauce. I tasted some of my vegetables first to see if they were freshly cooked — the beans had been re-heated. I discussed the dishes with the waiter, partly for my own interest, partly to test his knowledge of the menu.

When the sweet trolley was brought, I asked if any of the dishes had been home made, and found that they had not. I asked for a zabaglione to be made for me, and this came quickly. It was quite well prepared. I ordered coffee, and as soon as I had finished, I paid and left, after looking at the toilet to assess its cleanliness. The meal, although perfectly adequate, was not of the standard required for a rosette award, but I was happy to re-appoint the restaurant in its present classification.

It was now time to return to the hotel to meet the General Manager. I had quite a long list of notes made during my inspection in the morning, which I wanted to discuss with him. Several matters needed attention, and the hotel in general needed smartening up. I was also concerned as to its classification, since the rating it currently has leads people to expect more than it actually offers. We spend about 1 ½ hours in discussion, at the end of which I receive some assurances about improvements that will be made.

After I leave the hotel, I must write a full report for the Hotel Appointments Committee, and write letters to the General Manager and another to the owner of the hotel, confirming all the points we discussed. I then look forward to visiting a new restaurant in the evening for an initial inspection.

The day has been long and tiring, and I did not get much sleep last night. I have been frustrated that I could not do as much as I wanted in the day — time had been wasted in having to return to the hotel for the discussion with the General Manager. I could have spent this time better writing reports or visiting another hotel. Discussions with the hotel management have not been easy, but I hope that I will have contributed to the improvement of its general standards. I am also pleased that the Italian restaurant I visited at lunchtime is still up to standard. One thing I can be sure is that tomorrow will be completely different.

WHO ARE THE AA HOTEL INSPECTORS?

The AA has the largest team of full-time inspectors of any of the British hotel and restaurant guides. The inspectors themselves probably have the most detailed and varied job of any of the other inspection teams because of the large number of places they visit, and the detail into which they are required to report.

Like any team of people they have a fascinating mix of backgrounds and interests. Some have worked for the AA for a very long time, and bring the interests of the consumer to their task of inspecting hotels and restaurants. Others have a background in the hotel and catering industry, and this guides their assessment of standards. All of them receive training as part of their job, and all have to judge hotels and restaurants by the same standards which have evolved over the years to meet the needs of today's hotel and restaurant users.

The inspectors stay unannounced in hotels, and visit restaurants anonymously, but make themselves known to hoteliers for discussion of the star rating. They frequently use assumed names, so this survey will not help the anxious hotelier to identify the AA inspector, although it will show the variety of talents and interests that come together to form the most comprehensive, thorough and reliable assessments of any of those made of Britain's hotels.

Ron Bartley has been an AA hotel inspector for 23 years. Although he has no formal catering training, he has studied food and wine, particularly through the Wine Education Trust exams. In his spare time he regularly skates on thin ice as the Deputy Chairman of the National Skating Association. He also does a lot of cooking in his spare time.

Alan Bilton has been with the AA for over 40 years, 24 of them as an AA inspector. His activities are well publicised through television programmes and magazine articles, but his enthusiasm for big band jazz may not be so well known.

James Blackwood is a rugby player who has been a hotel inspector for 9 years. He is also one of the marathon runners in the AA inspection team and sometimes trains while staying in hotels.

Andrew Brownlee has been with the AA for some time and has been a hotel inspector for 25 years. He spent several years before that in New Zealand, but now enjoys the variety and challenge of inspecting hotels and restaurants in Britain.

James Chassels has a background of hotel management and has been a hotel inspector with the AA for 14 years. He is fond of sailing and skiing and enjoys seeing the way different hotels are run. His one regret about this otherwise absorbing job is the extent to which it keeps him away from his young family.

Fred Chrystal's abiding passion is fishing, particularly for salmon or trout, which is very difficult to fit into the life of regular hotel inspections. He has been with the AA since leaving school and for the past 12 years has been a hotel inspector.

David Coley has been with the AA for most of his working life, and has been a hotel inspector since 1968. During his time he has seen a great improvement in hotel standards and finds satisfaction in his role in assisting this improvement. When time permits, he enjoys a game of cricket or a spell of gardening.

Jill Dowling has recently joined the ranks of the AA hotel inspectors, having been to catering college, followed by jobs in hotels in Wales, Norway and Scotland. She has also worked as a stewardess with a shipping line, and in the catering section of a department store. She has a personal enthusiasm for cookery, and in the short time she has been an inspector has been generally impressed with the standards of the accommodation she has seen.

Perry Edwards comes from a family who ran a hotel and he worked in hotel management after service in the RAF. He is a keen sportsman, and is captain of a local cricket team. He finds great interest in the variety of different people who work in the hotel and catering industry and welcomes opportunities to assist them in improving standards.

Jerry Ellingham has been a hotel inspector for ten years and before that had worked as a chef and in hotel management. He also has experience in industry and in insurance, though his main interest is in the hotel trade and its improvement, combined with a love of music and his hobby of making violins.

Jean Ferguson has hotel and catering qualifications, and has worked in hotels in Manchester, Scotland and Italy. She has also run a Youth Training Scheme teaching hotel catering. She has been an AA hotel inspector for two years and is keen to do what she can to boost the image of the industry.

Leonard Furber has spent most of his career working in the hotel and catering industry, and the last seven years have been with the AA as hotel inspector. He is a family man who, like all of the inspectors, enjoys helping hoteliers to improve standards.

Nicola Geering has qualifications in catering and had worked in a hotel before joining the AA. She has been a hotel inspector for seven years and enjoys swimming and the theatre, as well as being keen on woodland conservation.

Jill Hellens has been working in the inspection team for six years and worked in other areas of the AA before becoming an inspector. She is a keen keep-fit enthusiast, taking part in cross country running, which helps to offset some of the penalties of being an inspector.

Jeff Hodgson has been a hotel inspector for nine years, but worked for some time before that on the administrative side of the AA hotel department. He enjoys the independent life that inspectors have, but when he is at home, he plays darts for his local pub.

Brian Jones worked in the hotel business for 22 years as a manager and also as a proprietor before becoming an inspector about a year ago. He was once amused to watch a hotelier who assumed that one of the other guests was the real inspector, and treated the wrong man accordingly.

Maurice Lear has been with the AA for a good deal of his working life, and for the last eleven years has been a hotel inspector. He enjoys travel, particularly motoring holidays on the continent, but also gets much satisfaction from his ability to help hoteliers improve standards.

Leon le Gallois is the AA's only French-born hotel inspector and he has worked in catering management in Paris and London's West End. He worked in the Mirabelle, and was chef and manager at Isow's Restaurant. He also ran one of London's best known night clubs before joining the AA four years ago.

Don Lewis has been a hotel inspector for four years, having gained experience in other areas of the AA. He is a keen sportsman enjoying running and soccer. He likes the variety of challenges which inspectors have to meet, although he does not like being away from home so much.

Who are the AA Hotel Inspectors

Sandra MacArthur is the AA's newest inspector, coming from a job with a hotel as conference co-ordinator. She finds the work of a hotel inspector is more thorough than she expected, and believes it is very satisfying.

Bill Phillips has been an AA hotel inspector for 20 years. He is a keen sportsman and a former county rugby player. He also enjoys marathon running, and actually took part in a recent London Marathon, while staying at the Ritz Hotel carrying out a hotel inspection!

David Robertson has been a hotel inspector for five years, having worked before that in another part of the AA. He is a keen fly fisherman, but does not have much opportunity to combine this interest with hotel inspections. He particularly enjoys the variety of people and places he encounters during the course of his work.

Sally Rudge had spent some years working on the administrative side of the AA regional hotel department before she became an inspector ten years ago. She enjoys the independence and variety of an inspector's life, but admits to finding it lonely at times. When she is at home she likes to entertain friends in her old cottage which she is renovating.

David Sims has catering qualifications as well as a batchelor of arts degree, and became a hotel inspector 8 years ago. He enjoys helping hotels to gain publicly recognised standards, and in his limited spare time is trying to renovate a Victorian house.

Ian Steel spent twelve years in hotel management before becoming an AA hotel inspector four years ago. Like several of the inspectors he is a keen jogger and participates in half-marathons. He enjoys the life of an inspector, although he complains that he does not often get a good night's sleep.

Richard Stirling ran a small hotel and restaurant with his parents until seven years ago when he achieved his ambition of becoming a hotel inspector. His formal qualifications are a useful additional background in helping assess the variety of hotels which all inspectors see.

Janet Summersgill has a degree in catering systems and won a scholarship to Pennsylvania University to study the subject further. She has also worked in hotels and as a catering manager in a sports centre and in the staff canteen of a department store. She became an AA hotel inspector two years ago and finds the challenges continuously interesting.

John Tromans has worked with the AA for many years, the last fourteen of which have been as a hotel inspector. He enjoys the freedom and independence the life offers, particularly when it gives him the opportunity to follow his hobby of bird watching.

Elaine Walker has been an AA hotel inspector for nine years and before that had worked in other departments of the AA. She has always had an interest in cooking and enjoys the responsibility the job offers for making accurate assessments of hotel quality and grading.

Colin Williams has been a hotel inspector for ten years, although he gained a great deal of background knowledge before that through working on the administrative side of the AA regional hotel department. He enjoys the aspect of the job which enables him to advise hoteliers on the standards required to achieve AA recognition.

Ron Wilson joined the AA in 1954 and has been a hotel inspector for the last sixteen years. He enjoys meeting hoteliers and likes to see the improvement in standards. In his spare time he enjoys art and sketching.

Christopher Wright Experience gained in hotel management with one of the country's foremost hotel groups, as well as further experience in industrial catering, gives him a balanced and experienced judgement in assessing hotels for the AA. His personal interests include wine and cooking, and he finds great satisfaction in helping hoteliers improve their establishments.

Jayne Wyatt has been an inspector for nearly two years, and has qualifications in hotel management. She finds the job can be lonely, although it has its rewards when she sees hotels which have successfully improved their standards.

David Young has a background of and qualifications in hotel management, and he has been an AA hotel inspector for just over a year. He is very interested in food and wine and is studying to become a Master of Wines.

Chief Inspector This person remains anonymous. His is the job of testing and assessing the best hotels and restaurants in the country. He joined the AA 17 years ago and after nearly 18 years in hotel management, during which he managed several hotels up to Four Star standard. He trained in the West End, and has a considerable personal as well as professional interest in cooking.

Appointing Hotels

The AA does not appoint all hotels automatically. The first approach must come from the hotel concerned, contacting the AA to request appointment. The application is then dealt with by the inspection department in the appropriate regional office (Twickenham, Bristol, Birmingham, Manchester or Glasgow). A short time later, one of the hotel inspectors will stay at the hotel, not announcing him or herself until after the bill has been settled the following morning. From the moment the inspector arrives, he or she will be watching how the hotel is run. How friendly is the greeting on arrival? Is any help offered with luggage? Is the hotel layout explained? Are there any outstanding aspects of the welcome? What is the bedroom like? All aspects of the bedroom are surveyed and reported on.

Later on, the inspector will go down to the dining room for dinner. Through the evening the inspector will be watching the way the meal is served, and assessing the quality of the cooking. How are the other guests treated? Does anyone ask if the meal was enjoyed? After dinner, the inspector will sit in the lounge surveying the way everyone is treated and looking out for any special touches of hospitality.

During the stay, an opportunity is taken to test as many as possible of the hotel's facilities. After what is hopefully a good night's sleep, the inspector will come down to breakfast, once again carefully watching everything that is going on. Finally, having packed, prepared to leave and settled the bill, the inspector announces him or herself to the hotel manager or proprietor. During their stay, inspectors complete a detailed report form on the hotel, and this can be used during subsequent discussion. The inspector then tours the hotel, looking at the bedrooms, all the other public rooms of the hotel and the kitchens.

The discussion with the manager or proprietor will then explain what star rating is to be recommended, together with any shortcomings that were found. Where these are serious, a time limit is usually set for their rectification, and there is then a follow-up inspection. If the work required is not carried out, the relevant star rating will not be awarded. In most cases, both parties agree that the work needed is desirable and will be an improvement. In only a very few cases do proprietors resent this assessment and reject our advice.

Following the inspector's visit a report is made up and submitted to the regional headquarters. It may be that the hotel has some outstanding characteristics which should earn the hotel a special award. If the hospitality and welcome was exceptionally good, a special award could be made for this. Other awards could be earned for the food, or for fine quality bedrooms, or for better than expected lounges, sitting rooms and other public areas. A very few superb hotels (77 in this guide) earn Red Star awards for all round excellence. These do not have to be the very expensive, luxury hotels. Red Stars are earned in all star categories.

If there are any uncertainties about the hotel's operation, its classification or its potential awards, a further visit (also anonymous) will be arranged. Once all details of the classification of the hotel have been decided, they are sent to the Hotel Appointment Committee which meets regularly at the AA national headquarters in Basingstoke. When this committee has agreed the star rating, the hotel is then officially 'AA Appointed'. Any recommendations for special awards, including Red Stars, are studied by the Chief Inspector, who also carries out independent anonymous inspections. These awards are given for one year only, and are re-assessed at the end of that time, so no hotel can afford to rest on its laurels.

Should a hotel change ownership, this results automatically in its loss of AA appointment, until the new owners choose to re-apply. Sometimes new owners will change substantially the way the hotel is run, and there is thus a chance to re-assess the quality and rating of the hotel. Every encouragement is given for improving standards.

Each edition of this hotel and restaurant guide is completely different from the one before. Many new hotels are added, some are dropped. More hotels earn special awards for merit of some kind. In every instance the decision is the result of a careful, thorough and rigorous assessment by a team of professional inspectors backed up by a detailed set of standards, applied consistently across the country.

HOW MANY STARS

The number of stars indicates the type of hotel and its level of luxury. Contrary to popular belief, it does not provide a precise indication of overall quality; the merit ratings ***H***, ***B*** and ***L***, and, of course, the Red Star awards are used for that purpose. In other words, a three star hotel is not necessarily better than a two star hotel, it just differs in its level of appointments, and the range and scope of the facilities it provides.

To receive AA appointment at all, the hotel must meet minimum criteria, although merely meeting these criteria, does not guarantee appointment.

1. There must be at least six letting bedrooms, suitably decorated and big enough to give the guest reasonable freedom of movement. They must be furnished with:

   a) modern, comfortable beds, 6'3" long (for adults); 3' wide (single) or 4'6" (double) with the headboards. A double bed must have access from either side.

   b) good quality bedding

   c) washbasin with mirror (suitably lit), hot and cold running water, fresh soap, quality tumbler, adequate size hand and bath towels for each occupant; towel rail

   d) electric shaver point within reach of suitably lit mirror

   e) power point for other electrical appliances

   f) dressing table or vanitory unit, adequately lit with mirror and stool

   g) bedside or bedhead table, cabinet or shelf for all beds

   h) chair for single room; two chairs (or chair and comfortable stool) for double room.

   i) wardrobe with adequate hangers (or other open hanging space of adequate height, provided in bedroom entrance area/lobby); drawers and shelves

   j) thick curtains, blinds or shutters with curtains

   k) means of securing door from inside and outside

   l) indication of how to obtain emergency assistance at night

   m) hotel telephone charges to be displayed.

2. The hotel must be in good decorative order inside and out, maintain a high degree of safety, security and cleanliness, and abide by statutory regulations regarding fire precautions, hygiene and various price display orders.

3. The total obligatory charge for intended accommodation must be provided either in advance or on arrival.

4. Residents and would-be guests must have ready access throughout the day and evening (and at other times by arrangement).

5. There must be a good standard of furnishing and equipment, convenient to use and maintained in good order.

6. Service must be prompt and courteous.

7. Payphone (with degree of privacy) must be situated in the public area of the hotel.

8. Public areas, corridors and stairs must be adequately lit.

9. There must be service of all meals to residents every day of the week. A priced menu must be available inside and outside the restaurant. There must be individual tables for each guest or party in at least one restaurant.

10. There must be warm bathrooms (general or en suite) with towel rail, bath mat, soap receptacle, hook, stool or chair or lidded w.c.

11. There must be arrangements for early morning call/alarm.

12. There must be arrangements for early departure, including providing refreshments.

Providing these criteria are met, the inspector then assesses the hotel for its possible star rating.

One Star ★

Hotels and inns, generally of small scale, with good facilities and furnishings, and adequate bath and lavatory arrangements. Meals are provided for residents, but may not always be available to non-residents. Other requirements are:

Reception facilities available daytime and evening (bell for summoning assistance when desk not staffed).

Porterage available on request.

Sufficient seating in a lounge or foyer area, which may contain a bar.

If licensed, a bar or lounge service of alcoholic drinks.

Light refreshments for residents and their guests in public areas; hot beverages in the morning and afternoon and as required throughout the evening (floor dispensers or Coffee Shop acceptable).

Cooked full breakfast with a choice of hot dishes (partial self service acceptable).

Dinner served for a reasonable period with last orders no earlier than 7.00 p.m.

Bedrooms to meet minimum standards defined, adequately lit with means of controlling a light from each bed, adequately heated.

Service of early morning tea, or provision of full range of equipment, including teapot and sufficient materials, safely and conveniently situated. NB only liquid milk acceptable.

Room service of lunch, dinner, refreshments in case of illness.

For rooms without private facilities, there should be a conveniently situated warm bathroom or shower room for every six bedrooms. There should also be a lavatory for every six bedrooms, and on each floor with three or more bedrooms there must be a lavatory.

In addition there must be lavatory facilities in public areas for non-residents (shared facilities with residents permitted).

Shoe cleaning service availability must be advertised, free machine or provision of materials.

Food at lunch/dinner/high tea must be correctly prepared from good raw materials and provided in clean and comfortable surroundings. 'Fast food' type operations are not acceptable, but carvery-type restaurants, coffee shops and steak bars which provide substantial dishes are acceptable. Lunch or dinner may have an element of self service.

Two Stars ★★

Hotels offering a higher standard of accommodation than One Star with the following additional requirements:

Writing table in lounge or bedroom.

Colour television in lounge or, by prior arrangement, in bedrooms.

Dinner served for a reasonable period, with last orders no earlier than 7.30 p.m.

Bedrooms to contain, in addition to other requirements, luggage stand or equivalent, reading light for each bed, with switch accessible to each occupant, and radio available on request unless TV is provided free of charge.

At least 1/5th of the bedrooms must have an en suite bath or shower and lavatory.

Lavatory facilities for non-residents must include separate facilities for ladies and gentlemen with hot and cold water, soap and towels (or hot air dryers).

Three Stars ★★★

Well appointed hotels with more spacious accommodation than Two Stars, with the following additional requirements:

Reception facilities must be readily available daytime and evening, with reception office or counter away from bar.

Sufficient seating in a lounge or foyer area, separate from a bar and without TV.

Writing table in a lounge without TV, or writing table (or its equivalent) in every bedroom, with stationery provided.

Colour television in a separate room, or, by prior arrangement in bedrooms.

Dinner served for a reasonable period with last orders no earlier than 8.30 p.m. A cold meal should be available later by prior arrangement.

Bedroom furnishings to be of a generally higher standard and including a full length mirror, on/off heating controlled by the guest, a means of calling for service during daytime and evening and a radio available on request in bedroom unless TV is provided free of charge.

Advertised availability of continental breakfast in bedrooms.

Two-thirds of bedrooms to provide private facilities. A minimum of one third must have baths.

Passenger lift must be provided when, in order to reach the bedrooms from the main entrance, guests would need to use more than two inter-floor stairways.

Meals must normally be available for chance callers.

Four Stars ★★★★

Exceptionally well appointed hotels offering a high standard of comfort and service. The following requirements are in addition to those for Three Stars:

Reception facilities available at all hours and tended by uniformed staff.

Sufficient, comfortable seating in a lounge or quiet area, without TV.

Writing room, or writing table (or its equivalent) in every bedroom with stationery provided.

Colour television in every bedroom.

Bar or lounge service of alcoholic drinks with cocktail facilities.

Light refreshments available in public areas for residents and non-residents without going to the bar.

Cooked full breakfast with a choice of hot dishes.

Dinner served for a reasonable period with last orders no earlier than 9.00 p.m.

Very comfortable and spacious bedrooms with a superior standard of furnishings and equipment; supplementary heating on request at no extra charge; telephone operating day and night; radio in every bedroom.

Advertised service of tea/coffee on request.

Advertised availability of breakfast room service of set cooked breakfast.

Room service of cold meal, including provision of hot soup during hours of lunch and dinner. Light refreshments 24 hours a day.

All bedrooms to provide private facilities; A minimum of 2/3 rds of them must have baths.

Private suites to be available.

Laundry service (48 hour), weekends excepted. Facilities for pressing clothes.

More spacious public rooms and some recreational facilities would be expected, together with a more extensive range and scope of catering facilities.

Five Stars ★★★★★

Luxury hotels offering the highest international standard. In addition to all the requirements for Four Stars, there are a number of further requirements:

Public rooms with an atmosphere of luxury. Light refreshments available for residents at all hours, and for non-residents throughout the day and evening, without going to the bar.

Writing table (or equivalent) in every bedroom with stationery provided.

A la carte breakfast with full service.

Dinner served for a reasonable period, with last orders no earlier than 9.30 p.m.

Luxurious bedrooms with fully adjustable heating.

Tea/coffee service to bedrooms to be provided.

A la carte breakfast room service.

Full floor service of hot meals at all reasonable hours.

All bedrooms to have bathrooms, a reasonable proportion of which should additionally provide a shower.

Separate lavatory facilities for ladies and gentlemen non-residents, with attendants.

Shoe cleaning service available.

Laundry service (24 hour), weekends excepted.

Valet service.

Availability of staff to drive guests' cars to and from garages.

Staff such as linkmen and pages in uniform.

Storage room for luggage.

At lunch and dinner a very high standard of food and service.

Desirable additional facilities, according to location, style and type of hotel; bookstall, bidet, dancing, direct dial telephones, flower shop, games room for children, gymnasium, hairdressing salon for ladies and gentlemen, luggage lift, movies, private function rooms, recreational facilities, sauna bath, solarium, telex facilities for guests, theatre reservation, travel bureau, typewriting, photocopying and translation facilities.

NB *In provincial Five Star hotels, some of the services are provided on a more informal and restricted basis than in London Five Star hotels.*

As with any set of criteria for grading, some hotels may possess some of the facilities or services required for a higher grading. Equally, the provision of extra facilities, unless accompanied by a commensurate rise in quality, will not necessarily guarantee an increase in classification.

All AA appointed hotels are granted a star rating. Additional awards are available to distinguish hotels that are special in some way.

Country House Hotels

Highlighted by a special symbol, these are hotels where a relaxed, informal atmosphere and personal welcome prevail. They are often secluded and, even though they may not be in the heart of the countryside, they are quiet. Hotels attracting frequent conferences or functions where noise or loud music is evident are not normally granted this classification. Some of the facilities may differ from those found in urban hotels of the same star rating.

H — Hospitality Awards

Where the hospitality, welcome, friendliness and quality of service is significantly better than expected in the particular star classification, the hotel is given the *H* award.

B — Bedroom Award

Where the bedrooms are of a significantly higher standard than is generally found in the particular star classification, the *B* award is given.

L — Award for lounges, bars and public areas
Where the sitting rooms, lounges, bars and other public areas are of a significantly higher standard than is generally found in the particular star classification, the *L* award is given.

Any hotel may earn more than one of these awards, and those that earn all three, *H*, *B* and *L*, are highlighted in a boxed panel in the gazetteer.

Rosettes

The rosette award is used to highlight hotels and restaurants where it is judged that the food and service can be especially recommended.

❀ The food is of a higher standard than is expected for its classification.

❀❀ Excellent food and service, irrespective of its classification.

❀❀❀ Outstanding food and service, irrespective of its classification.

Red Stars

This is the AA's supreme award and is given to hotels which are of outstanding merit within their classification.

Finding out about a hotel

Firstly, look at the star rating. That will tell you all about the type of hotel it is and what sort of facilities it has. Secondly, look for the subjective awards it may have. If it shows *H*, *B*, *L* or all three, some aspects of the hotel will be of a very high standard. If you enjoy good food, look for a rosette award. If you like peace and quiet, look for the Country House hotel symbol. If you are looking for a hotel with outstanding merit at any star classification, seek out one of the extra-special Red Star hotels. These hotels are identified in the gazetteer, and are indexed separately on pages 39-50. Finally, read the brief description provided. It is impossible to illustrate all aspects of any hotel in a brief space, but the description will provide a good indication of what to expect.

Good Restaurant Guide

The AA first implemented the system of rosette awards, for hotels only, in 1955 and extended it to restaurants in 1967. Every year, increasing resources go into inspecting and assessing restaurants, with, this year, much greater detail being given about recommended restaurants, especially those which have received rosette awards.

The principles by which we recognise good food in the hotels and restaurants we recommend are relatively straightforward, although judging a matter as subjective as food is not without its perils. Fundamentally, however, we only consider the standard of food in Britain and Ireland. We do not try to make comparisons with standards in any other country.

Eating out is very popular and food writers often have large followings. Many have their favourite types of food and restaurateurs — perhaps influenced by the hospitality they receive or by the need to produce a good story. We believe that the judgement of food is as difficult and controversial as the judgement of music. Comparing Mozart, Brahms and Beethoven, for example, can anyone say which of them should receive two or three rosettes for their music. Even now, expert musicians hold varying opinions about the relative merits of these masters.

Food and cooking are particularly susceptible to changing fads and fashions. In part, of course, this adds to its interest and excitement, but we have to be as catholic and as tolerant as possible. We must recognise good food wherever we find it, irrespective of type or fashion, and we must apply consistent standards in all parts of the country.

TWO ROSETTES are awarded where the standard of food is excellent, but without reaching the heights of the three rosetted establishments. This year we have been able to renew the two rosette award to ten establishments. Pierre Koffman of the recently enlarged and refurbished **Tante Claire** has two rosettes and we believe they should succeed in earning three next year. Other establishments receiving two rosettes, this year for the first time are **Intercontinental Hotel, London W1 for Le Soufflé** restaurant where Peter Kromberg's talented cooking has improved so much in recent years; **Rue St Jacques, London W1** where Gunter Schlender seems to have found his feet and cooks here far better than he ever did at Carriers; and finally a new two rosette award goes to **Pool Court at Pool in Wharfedale, West Yorkshire,** where Michael Gill must be one of the most enthusiastic restaurateurs in the country. We are watching a number of other chefs who are steadily improving and refining their cooking, particularly David Wilson of the **Peat Inn** in Scotland who is showing great promise and from whom we are hoping for very good things.

We give rosette awards for especially good food. **THREE ROSETTES** are awarded to restaurants or hotels where the food is quite outstanding, and supported by an appropriate level of service. Very few establishments gain these awards. This year, we are pleased to renew the three rosette award to **Le Gavroche, London W1** and also particularly satisfied to have seen the steady improvement over the years of Raymond Blanc of **Le Manoir aux Quat' Saisons, Great Milton** where we can award him three rosettes.

We approach the award of **ONE ROSETTE** somewhat differently from the others, which are for out and out excellence. In this case we recognise that the public have different needs, and to meet those needs we have evolved what has so far proved to be a successful system. We select hotels and restaurants that provide better food than our members would expect from their star or knife and fork classification, and we award them one rosette. Inevitably this involves a considerable range of standards. For example a Two Star hotel →

← which received a rosette award indicates that the food there is of a much higher standard than other Two Star hotels. Likewise a Four Star hotel with a rosette provides food of a higher standard than other Four Star hotels. But the food in the Two Star hotel could not sensibly be equated to that provided in the Four Star hotel. We find we award more single rosettes than other guides, but from the letters we receive, our present system appears to please our readers. We would, nevertheless, be very interested to hear from anyone who differs and thinks we should change our system.

The number of establishments that receive a single rosette award this year is 200, 40 of which are new awards. These new awards were almost equally divided amongst restaurants and hotels, three of them going to fine Red Star hotels, **Hunstrete House, Hunstrete; Esseborne Manor, Hurstbourne Tarrant** and the new Red Star hotel, **South Lodge at Lower Beeding.**

We have carried out a survey around the country to report on notable new arrivals or improvements which have earned a rosette.

London

Two restaurants appearing for the first time in this guide, have won rosette awards immediately on their appearance. They are **L'Hippocampe,** SW6 where chef Philippe Levney creates the most artistically delicate seafood dishes using the freshest of produce. The other new London restaurant of note is **Tourment d'Amour,** in Covent Garden, WC2 which is an intimate French restaurant with a good fixed price menu. **Chez Nico,** in Queenstown Road, SW8 was in the process of change when we went to press last year, and we are very pleased to award Philip Britten a rosette this year. A popular and well established restaurant which also gains a rosette this year is **Gay Hussar,** Greek Street, W1. Two major hotels earn their rosettes for the first time this year, **Park Lane,** W1 and **Dukes,** SW1.

South East England

A new restaurant of note in this area this year is the **Plough** at Clanfield, Oxfordshire, a most attractive Cotswold building where Paul Barnard produces delicious food in an elegant setting. Three restaurants in the area have earned their first rosettes, **Pebbles,** Aylesbury run by the Dorchester trained Susan and David Cavalier, **The Starr,** Great Dunmow, in a lovely 14th century restaurant where chef Jones produces some of the best food in Essex and the **Poussin,** Brockenhurst. Two hotels have also gained rosette awards, the **County** at Canterbury making this city something of a gastronomic centre in East Kent, and the beautiful 17th century **Flitwick Manor,** with its elegant Brooks restaurant.

South West England and Wales

Devon and Dorset feature predominantly in our list of establishments earning a rosette for the first time. In Dorset, the delightful small hotel **Stock Hill House** at Gillingham has been bought by Peter and Nita Hauser, who gained such a high reputation for their food at Aval du Creux, Sark, Channel Islands, and they are producing fine food in a most appealing hotel. At **Plumber Manor,** Sturminster Newton, Brian Prideaux-Brune has earned his first rosette this year for his good Anglo/French cooking, while a new restaurant in Devon gaining a rosette is **Lewtrenchard Manor,** Lewtrenchard. In Wales, a rosette award has been won by the **Three Cocks Hotel,** Three Cocks, Powys, an attractive stone hotel near the village where good, imaginative cooking is available.

Midlands and East Anglia

Birmingham is well off for good restaurants, and this year sees the addition of a fine newcomer, **Sloans** near Edgbaston. The chef, John Daniels is only 23, but he was Student of the Year in 1981, and shows great promise today. In Bakewell, Derbyshire, **Fischers** earns its first rosette for Max Fischer who brings excellent cooking, especially of fish, to this pretty town. Over in East Anglia, Sam Chalmers already has a devoted following, and he has opened **Chimneys Restaurant** in a lovely timber framed building in the centre of Long Melford, Suffolk. He cooks in the modern style using the best quality ingredients, and well deserves our rosette. In Uppingham, the tiny **Lake Isle Hotel** has already impressed us with its high quality of accommodation, and now David Whitfield earns a rosette for some excellent French style cooking.

Northern England

Two new restaurants in Northern England earn a rosette at their first appearance in this guide. **Fisherman's Lodge** in Newcastle-upon-Tyne is an excellent seafood restaurant offering memorable meals. Another is **The High Moor** in Wrightington, Lancashire, close to the M6. A 17th century farmhouse has been converted to a fine restaurant, where James Sines produces splendid food in the modern style. There are two new rosette awards in Cumbria, **Rampsbeck Hotel,** Watermillock on the shores of Ullswater, where a very high standard of French classical cuisine is provided, and **Uplands Country House Hotel,** Cartmel, where Tom and Diana Peter have their delightful hotel and restaurant in which Tom Peter's inventive cooking can be sampled. Across the border in Yorkshire is the **Brompton Forge** Restaurant, at Brompton by Sawdon, near Scarborough, where we have found attractively presented and generous dishes at good value for money. Near Manchester Airport is **Moss Nook** Restaurant, a popular little French restaurant where Pauline and Derek Harrison offer a tantalising choice of imaginative dishes.

Scotland

Quite a large number of establishments in Scotland (33 hotels and 12 restaurants) earn rosette awards this year. **Inverlochy Castle,** as last year, earns a double rosette, and the following seven Red Star hotels have also been awarded a single rosette: **Cromli House, Dunblane, Arisaig House,** Arisaig; **Greywalls,** Gullane; **Ardanaiseig,** Kilchrenan; **Airds,** Port Appin; **Chapeltown House,** Stewarton, and **Balcraig House,** Perth. The most notable new Scottish entry to the guide, earning a rosette for the first time this year is **Humnavoe Restaurant,** in Stromness, Orkney. This must also be the most remote restaurant award in the guide this year. No visitor to Orkney should miss this fine restaurant where Denis Moylan prepares splendid meals using local produce. The Orcadian Young Musician of the Year, Peter Pratt, entertains here with his fiddle music. Other hotels and restaurants earning a rosette for the first time this year are: **Sunlaws House,** Kelso, **Roman Camp Hotel,** Callander where the Swiss owners put their own individual stamp on dishes using local produce; **Loch Duich Hotel,** Ardelve; **Polmaily House,** Drumnadrochit; **Factor's House,** Fort William (a new entry to this guide, earning ***H, B*** and ***L*** awards as well as the rosette, and run by the son of Mrs Greta Hobbs at Inverlochy Castle); **Cross Hotel,** Kingussie; **Portsonachan Hotel,** Portsonachan, where Christopher Trotters' imaginative cooking is recognised; and **Nivingston House,** Cleish.

Inspecting Restaurants

The basis for assessment and classification of restaurants is different from that applied in the cases of hotels. A restaurant does not need to apply for inspection and subsequent inclusion in this guide. Our inspectors visit restaurants anonymously, and convey their recommendations to the Restaurant Appointment Committee.

Initially, restaurants are selected in a number of ways, perhaps from their reputation, perhaps by recommendation and occasionally by request. Even before a full inspection is made, an initial survey will be done to see whether the restaurant is likely to meet AA requirements. If it does, one of our inspectors eats there and reports in detail on his findings, what he ate and what the service was like. If there is any doubt about the restaurant's classification, as many further inspections as necessary are carried out until the matter is decided.

Should the food be so good that a rosette award is considered, a further visit will certainly be made by another inspector, and for two and three rosette awards, several visits will be made in total, before the final decision is made. The inspectors never announce who they are, but they observe all aspects of the restaurant during their visit. The food is obviously the most important thing, and they will take care to order the dishes which best show the chef's potential. They will try to find out how knowledgeable the waiters are, and they will memorise the main features of the wine list, even though they seldom drink any with their meals.

They will also note how proficient the service is, and watch how the other customers are treated. The quality of the table appointments is also noted, as are the style of the decor and the cleanliness of the toilets. Only if all these aspects are satisfactory will the restaurant gain the 'Knife and fork' award, and the number of these awards depends on the degree of sophistication of the restaurant concerned. The main requirements for the five basic classifications of restaurants are shown in the table below.

The AA recommends 1100 restaurants in Britain. This is, naturally, only a small proportion of the total and represents our view of the best places in the country. At the same time we recognise that many people eat out for the enjoyment of the occasion, and our inspectors always consider how *enjoyable* it is to eat in the restaurant concerned. They also look for *value for money,* a nebulous concept, but one which they try to define with reference to the clientele the restaurant attracts. Finally, they judge a restaurant by what it sets out to do and the standards it aims to achieve.

The basic requirements for all recommended restaurants are:

1. The dishes should be well cooked and presented, using fresh ingredients
2. A high standard of cleanliness throughout
3. Prompt and courteous service
4. Pleasant ambience, decor and facilities
5. Adequate washing and lavatory facilities and facilities for hats and coats
6. Open at least five days a week for lunch or dinner during the year or season
7. Menus available with prices shown
8. Value for money

	X	XX	XXX	XXXX	XXXXX
Type and style of restaurant.	Simple restaurant both in cuisine and decor.	Restaurant with higher standard of service, decor, furnishings and amenities. Small bar generally available.	Restaurant with much higher standard of service and decor. Usually, a bar lounge is available.	Exceptionally well appointed restaurant normally only found in London and larger cities.	The height of luxury and good living, comparable with the best London five star hotels. Much more seating than other types.
Cuisine	Choice of interesting dishes; wine list with choice of red and white wines. If not licensed, customers can bring their own wine.	More ambitious menu in range of type of dishes. Wine list should contain one or two vintage clarets or burgundies.	Extensive, more elaborate menu with a number of house specialities.	Menu should offer good choice of correctly prepared food for each course including classical dishes and fresh vegetables. Extensive wine list with selection of domaine and chateaux bottled wines.	Any dish within reason should be available on request. Most dishes cooked to order. Wine list should include fine examples from all major areas and great vintages from the last 20 years.

He always travelled in the best company.

After all, who else offered him the versatility of their charge card, the security of their travellers cheques and the help and experience of over 1400 travel agent and representative offices worldwide? He never left home without them.

American Express Europe Limited, incorporated with limited liability in the State of Delaware, U.S.A.

Britain's Best Hotels

Red Stars are awarded to a select few hotels that are of outstanding merit within their star classification. This list has increased substantially since last year (by 14) and now totals 77 hotels. Those new to the list this year are: Lovelady Shield Hotel, Alston; Eastwell Manor Hotel, Ashford; Gleneagles Hotel, Auchterarder; Cavendish Hotel, Baslow; Royal Crescent Hotel, Bath; Netherfield Place Hotel, Battle; Kennel Holt Hotel, Cranbrook; Ashwick House Hotel, Dulverton; Cromlix House Hotel, Dunblane; Lansdowne Hotel, Leamington Spa; South Lodge Hotel, Lower Beeding; Rookery Hall Hotel, Nantwich; Cringletie House Hotel, Peebles; Minffordd Hotel, Tal-y-Llyn; Calcot Manor Hotel, Tetbury; Old Vicarage Hotel, Witherslack; Langley House Hotel, Wiveliscombe. All these Red Star hotels listed below offer friendly hospitality, fine food, comfort and beautiful surroundings that are quite out of the ordinary.

RED STAR HOTELS

Avon		
Bath	★★★★	Royal Crescent
Bath	❀★★★	Priory
Freshford	❀★★★🌲	Homewood Park
Hunstrete	❀★★★🌲	Hunstrete House
Thornbury	❀★★★🌲	Thornbury Castle
Buckinghamshire		
Aston Clinton	★★★	Bell Inn
Cheshire		
Chester	★★★★	Chester Grosvenor
Nantwich	★★★🌲	Rookery Hall
Cumbria		
Alston	★★🌲	Lovelady Shield
Borrowdale	★★★★	Lodore Swiss
Brampton	❀★★🌲	Farlham Hall
Grasmere	❀★★★🌲	Michael's Nook
	❀★	White Moss House
Pooley Bridge	❀❀★★★🌲	Sharrow Bay
Watermillock	★🌲	Old Church
Windermere	❀❀★★	Miller Howe
Witherslack	★🌲	Old Vicarage
Derbyshire		
Baslow	★★★	Cavendish
Devon		
Barnstaple	★★🌲	Downrew House
Chagford	❀★★★🌲	Gidleigh Park
Gittisham	★★🌲	Combe House
Heddon's Mouth	★★🌲	Heddon's Gate
Whimple	★★🌲	Woodhayes
Dorset		
Poole	★★★	Mansion House
Essex		
Dedham	❀★★★🌲	Maison Talbooth
Gloucestershire		
Buckland	❀★★★🌲	Buckland Manor
Cheltenham	❀★★★🌲	Greenway
Tetbury	★★★🌲	Calcot Manor
Hampshire		
Hurstbourne Tarrant	❀★★🌲	Esseborne Manor
New Milton	❀❀★★★★🌲	Chewton Glen
Hereford and Worcester		
Abberley	❀★★★🌲	Elms
Broadway	★★★★	Lygon Arms
Kent		
Ashford	❀★★★★🌲	Eastwell Manor
Cranbrook	★★🌲	Kennel Holt
Leicestershire		
Oakham	❀❀★★★🌲	Hambleton Hall
London		
SW1	★★★★★	Berkeley
	★★★★	Goring
	★	Ebury Court
SW3	❀★★★★	Capital
W1	★★★★★	Claridge's
	❀❀★★★★★	Connaught
	❀★★★★★	Dorchester
	★★★★	Athenaeum
	★★★★	Brown's
WC2	❀★★★★★	Savoy
Northumberland		
Powburn	❀★★🌲	Breamish House
Oxfordshire		
Kingham	★★	Mill
Milton Gt	❀❀❀★★★🌲	Le Manoir aux Quat' Saisons
Woodstock	❀★★	Feathers
Somerset		
Dulverton	★★🌲	Ashwick House
Ston Easton	★★★🌲	Ston Easton Park
Taunton	❀★★★★	Castle
Wiveliscombe	★	Langley House
Sussex		
Battle	★★★🌲	Netherfield Place
East Grinstead	❀★★★🌲	Gravetye Manor
Lower Beeding	❀★★★🌲	South Lodge
Rushlake Green	★★★🌲	Priory Country House
Warwickshire		
Leamington Spa	❀❀★★★🌲	Mallory Court
	★	Lansdowne
Warminster	★★★★🌲	Bishopstrow House
Yorkshire		
York	❀★★★	Middlethorpe Hall

Channel Islands		
St Saviour, Jersey	❀★★★★🌲	Longueville Manor

WALES

Gwynedd		
Llandudno	★★★🌲	Bodysgallen Hall
	★★	St Tudno
Tal-y-Llyn	★	Minffordd

SCOTLAND

Borders		
Peebles	★★🌲	Cringletie House
Central		
Dunblane	❀★★★🌲	Cromlix House
Grampian		
Banchory	★★★🌲	Banchory Lodge
Highland		
Arisaig	❀★★★🌲	Arisaig House
Fort William	❀❀★★★★🌲	Inverlochy Castle
Lothian		
Gullane	❀★★★🌲	Greywalls
Strathclyde		
Eriska	★★★🌲	Isle of Eriska
Kilchrenan	❀★★★🌲	Ardanaiseig
Port Appin	❀★★	Airds
Stewarton	❀★★★🌲	Chapeltoun House
Tayside		
Auchterarder	★★★★★	Gleneagles
Perth	❀★★★🌲	Balcraig House

Special Awards

Out of the total of over 5,000 hotels and restaurants in this guide, 844 have received special awards of one kind or another.

One, two or three rosettes are awarded for very good cooking in either hotels or restaurants. The highest accolade of three rosettes is given this year to only two restaurants in Britain. The letters (DO) indicate that the rosette award applies to dinner only.

H, B, L A number of hotels have earned special commendation from our inspectors for either particularly friendly hospitality, unusually good bedrooms or above average lounges, bars and public areas. These are subjective awards denoted by the appropriate red letter. 43 hotels have been awarded ***H, B*** and ***L,*** and these noteworthy hotels are highlighted in the gazetteer by a boxed panel.

All Red Star hotels are also included in this list.

England

AVON

Alveston	★★★	Alveston House	— — L
Bath	★★★★	Royal Crescent	Red Stars
	★★★	Lansdown Grove	H — —
	★★★	Priory	❀ Red Stars
	X	Clos du Roy	❀ — — —
Bristol	★★★★	Grand	— B —
	XX	Les Semailles	❀ — — —
Farrington Gurney	★★	Country Ways	H B L
Freshford	★★★ ⌂	Homewood Park	❀ Red Stars
Hunstrete	★★★ ⌂	Hunstrete House	❀ Red Stars
Lympsham	★★ ⌂	Batch Farm	H — L
Thornbury	★★★ ⌂	Thornbury Castle	❀ Red Stars
Weston-Super-Mare	★★★	Grand Atlantic	— — L
	★★★	Royal Pier	H — —
Winterbourne	★★★	Grange	— B —

BEDFORDSHIRE

Bedford	★★★	Woodlands Manor	H — —
Dunstable	★★★	Old Palace Lodge	— B —
Flitwick	★★★ ⌂	Flitwick Manor	❀ — B —
Woburn	XXX	Paris House	❀ — — —

BERKSHIRE

Burghfield	XX	Knights Farm	❀(DO) — — —
Bray	XXXX	Waterside	❀❀ — — —
Elcot	★★★	Elcot Park	— B —
Kintbury	XX	Dundas Arms	❀(DO) — — —
Maidenhead	★★★★	Fredrick's	❀ — — —
Streatley	★★★	Swan	— — L
Swallowfield	★★	Mill House	— B —
Windsor	★★★★	Oakley Court	— B L
Yattendon	★★	Royal Oak	H — —

BUCKINGHAMSHIRE

Aston Clinton	★★★	Bell Inn	❀ Red Stars
Aylesbury	X	Pebbles	❀ — — —
Beaconsfield	★★★	Bellhouse	— B —
Gerrards Cross	★★	Ethorpe	— B —

CAMBRIDGESHIRE

Duxford	★★★	Duxford Lodge	— — L
Ely	X	Old Fire Engine House	❀ — — —
Six Mile Bottom	★★★	Swynford Paddocks	— B —

CHESHIRE

Altrincham	★★★	Bowdon	H — —
Chester	★★★★	Chester Grosvenor	Red Stars
	★★★	Mollington Banastre	H — —
Handforth (Manchester Airport)	★★★★	Belfry	❀ H — —
Knutsford	★★★	Cottons	— B —
Marple	★	Springfield	— B —
Nantwich	★★★ ⌂	Rookery Hall	❀ Red Stars
Sandbach	★★★	Chimney House	— B —
Tarporley	★★ ⌂	Willington Hall	— B —
Wilmslow	★★★	Stanneylands	❀ H — —

CORNWALL

Bodinnick	★	Old Ferry Inn	— — L
Bude	★	Camelot	— — L
	★	Penarvor	— — L
Cawsand	★★	Criterion	— — L
Constantine Bay	★★★	Treglos	H — L
Crantock	★★	Fairbank	H — —
Falmouth	★★★	Falmouth	— — L
	★★★	Greenbank	— — L
	★★★ ⌂	Penmere Manor	H B L
	★★★	Royal Duchy	— B —
	★★★	St Michael's	H — L
	★★	Carthion	H — L
	★★	Crill House	H B —
	★★	Lerryn	H — —
Fowey	★★	Marina	H — —
Golant	★★	Cormorant	H B L
Harlyn Bay	★	Polmark	— — L
Helford	XX	Riverside	❀(DO) — — —
Helland Bridge/Bodmin	★★★ ⌂	Tredethy Country	H — —
Helston	★ ⌂	Nansloe Manor	— — L
Lamorna Cove	★★★ ⌂	Lamorna Cove	H — L
Mawgan Porth	★★	Tredragon	H — —
Mawnan Smith	★★★ ⌂	Meudon	H — L
Mount Hawke	★	Tregarthen Country Cottage	H B L
Mousehole	★★	Lobster Pot	— — L
Newquay	★★★	Bristol	H — L
	★★★	Glendorgal	H — L
	★★★	Trebarwith	— — L
	★★★	Windsor	— — L
	★★	Whipsiderry	H — L
	★	Trevone	— — L
Pendoggett	★★	Cornish Arms	H — —
Penzance	★★★ ⌂	Higher Faugan	— — L
	★	Estoril	H — —
	★	Tarbert	H — L
Perranporth	★	Beach Dunes	H — —
Perranuthnoe	★	Ednovean	H — L
Port Gaverne	★★	Port Gaverne	H — —
Portloe	★★	Lugger	H B —
Portscatho	★★	Gerrans Bay	H — —
	★★ ⌂	Roseland House	H — —

Ruan High Lanes	★★	Hundred House	—	—	L
St Agnes	★	Sunholme	H	—	—
St Austell	★★★★	Carlyon Bay	H	—	—
	★★♣	Boscundle Manor	—	—	L
St Ives	★★★	Garrack	H	—	—
	★★	Boskerris	H	—	L
	★	Ocean Breezes	H	—	—
St Mawes	★★★	Idle Rocks	—	—	L
Sennen	★★	Tregiffian	—	—	L
Talland Bay	★★★♣	Talland Bay	—	B	L
Tintagel	★★	Atlantic View	H	—	—
Veryan	★★★	Nare	—	—	L

CUMBRIA

Alston	★★♣	Lovelady Shield	Red Stars		
Ambleside	★★★	Rothay Manor ❀(DO)	H	B	L
	★★	Kirkstone Foot	H	B	L
	★★♣	Nanny Brow	H	—	—
	★★	Wateredge	—	—	L
Bassenthwaite	★★♣	Overwater Hall	H	—	L
	★★	Pheasant Inn	—	—	L
Borrowdale	★★★★	Lodore Swiss	Red Stars		
	★★★	Borrowdale	H	—	—
Braithwaite	★★	Ivy House	H	—	L
Brampton	★★♣	Farlam Hall ❀(DO)	Red Stars		
Cartmel	✕✕	Uplands ❀(DO)	—	—	—
Crosby on Eden	★★♣	Crosby Lodge	H	—	—
Faugh	★★★	String of Horses	—	B	—
Glenridding	★★★	Ullswater	—	—	L
Grange Over Sands	★★♣	Graythwaite Manor	—	—	L
Grasmere	★★★♣	Michael's Nook ❀(DO)	Red Stars		
	★★★	Swan	—	B	L
	★★	Oak Bank	H	—	—
	★★	Grasmere	H	—	—
	★	White Moss House ❀(DO)	Red Stars		
Hawkshead	★★★♣	Tarn Hows	—	—	L
Kendal	★★	Garden House	—	B	—
Keswick	★★	Grange	—	B	—
	★★★♣	Underscar	H	—	L
	★	Crow Park	—	B	—
	★	Latrigg Lodge	—	B	—
	★	Priorholm	H	—	—
Longtown	★♣	March Bank ❀(DO)	H	—	—
Loweswater	★★♣	Scale Hill	—	—	L
Mungrisdale	★	Mill	H	—	—
Newby Bridge	★★★	Whitewater	—	B	—
Penrith	★★★	North Lakes Gateway	—	B	—
Pooley Bridge	★★★♣	Sharrow Bay ❀❀	Red Stars		
Ravenstonedale	★★	Black Swan	H	—	—
Temple Sowerby	★★	Temple Sowerby House	H	B	L
Watermillock	★★★♣	Leeming House	H	B	L
	★★	Rampsbeck ❀(DO)	—	—	—
	★♣	Old Church	Red Stars		
Wetheral	★★★	Crown	—	B	—
Windermere	★★★♣	Langdale Chase	H	—	L
	★★★	Wild Boar	H	—	L
	★★♣	Holbeck Ghyll	—	B	L
	★★♣	Lindeth Fell	H	B	—
	★★♣	Linthwaite	H	B	L
	★★	Miller Howe ❀❀(DO)	Red Stars		
	★★	Royal	H	—	—
	★	Cedar Manor	H	—	—
	★	Willowsmere	H	—	—
	✕	Porthole Eating House ❀(DO)	—	—	—
Witherslack	★♣	Old Vicarage	Red Star		

DERBYSHIRE

Bakewell	★★♣	Croft Country House	—	B	L
	★★	Milford House	H	—	—
	✕	Fischer's ❀	—	—	—
Baslow	★★★	Cavendish	Red Stars		
Buxton	★★	Grove	—	—	L
Derby	★★	Gables	H	—	—
Draycott	★★★	Tudor Court	—	—	L
Matlock	★★★♣	Riber Hall	—	B	—
Rowsley	★★★	Peacock	—	B	L

DEVON

Ashburton	★★♣	Holne Chase	H	—	—
Barnstaple	★★♣	Downrew House	Red Stars		
Burrington	★★★♣	Northcote Manor	H	—	—
Chagford	★★★♣	Gidleigh Park ❀	Red Stars		
	★★★♣	Great Tree	H	B	—
	★★★♣	Mill End	H	—	L
	★★★♣	Teignworthy	H	—	L
	★★	Easton Court	—	—	L
Clawton	★★♣	Court Barn Country House	H	—	L
Dartmouth	✕✕	Carved Angel ❀	—	—	—
Ebford	★★	Ebford House	H	—	—
Ermington	★★	Ermewood House	—	B	—
Exeter	★★★	Buckerell Lodge	H	B	—
	★★★	St Olave's Court	H	—	—
Gittisham	★★♣	Combe House	Red Stars		
Gulworthy	✕✕✕	Horn of Plenty ❀	—	—	—
Hawkchurch	★★★	Fairwater Head	H	—	—
Haytor	★★★♣	Bel Alp	H	—	—
Heddon's Mouth	★★♣	Heddon's Gate	Red Stars		
Holbeton	★★★♣	Alston Hall	H	—	L
Honiton	★★★♣	Deer Park	H	—	—
Hope Cove	★★	Cottage	H	—	—
	★★	Lantern Lodge	—	—	L
Instow	★★★	Commodore	—	B	L
Kingsbridge	★★★♣	Buckland-Tout-Saints	—	—	L
Lewtrenchard	✕✕	Manor ❀(DO)	—	—	—
Lifton	★★★	Arundel Arms	H	—	—
Lynton	★★★	Lynton Cottage	—	—	L
	★	Chough's Nest	—	B	—
	★	Seawood	—	—	L
Martinhoe	★♣	Old Rectory	H	B	L
Moretonhampstead	★★♣	Glebe House	H	—	—
	★★	White Hart	—	B	—
Newton Abbot	★	Hazlewood House	H	—	—
Ottery St Mary	✕✕	Lodge ❀(DO)	—	—	—
Plymouth	✕	Chez Nous ❀	—	—	—
Salcombe	★★★	Soar Mill Cove	H	—	—
	★★★	Bolt Head	H	—	—
	★★★	Tides Reach	H	B	L
	★★	Castle Point	H	—	—
	★★	Grafton Towers	H	—	—
Sidmouth	★★★★	Victoria	H	—	—
	★★★	Riviera	H	—	L
	★★★	Westcliff	H	—	—
Stoke Gabriel	★★♣	Gabriel Court	H	—	—
Teignmouth	★★	Glendaragh	H	—	—
	★	Drakes	—	B	—
Thurlestone	★★	Furzey Close	H	—	—
Torquay	★★★	Homers	H	B	L
	★★★	Kistor	H	—	L
	★★★	Livermead Cliff	H	—	L
	★★★	Livermead House	H	—	—
	★★★	Nepaul	H	—	L
	★★★	Toorak	—	—	L
	★★	Balmoral	—	—	L
	★★♣	Orestone House	H	B	—

Location	Rating	Establishment	Rosettes	H	B	L
	★	Windsurfer		—	B	—
Totnes	★★	Bourton Hall	❀(DO)	—	—	—
Whimple	★★♣	Woodhayes		Red Stars		
Wilmington	★★	Home Farm		H	—	—
Woodford Bridge	★★★	Woodford Bridge		—	B	L
Woolacombe	★★	Atlantic		—	B	—
	★★	Devon Beach		H	B	—
	★	Crossways		H	—	—

DORSET

Location	Rating	Establishment	Rosettes	H	B	L
Bournemouth & Boscombe	★★★	Cumberland		—	—	L
	★★★	Heathlands		—	—	L
	★★★	Langtry Manor		—	B	—
	★★★	Wessex		—	B	L
	★★	Belvedere		H	—	—
	★★	Elstead		—	—	L
	★★	Hinton Firs		—	—	L
	★★	Mansfield		—	B	—
	★	Arlington		H	—	—
	✕	Provence	❀(DO)	—	—	—
Bridport	★	Roundham House		H	—	—
Charmouth	★★	Queens Armes		H	—	L
Christchurch	★★	Fisherman's Haunt		H	—	—
Corfe Castle	★★	Morton's House		—	B	L
Gillingham	★★	Stock Hill House	❀	H	—	L
Lyme Regis	★★★	Mariners		H	—	—
Poole	★★★	Mansion House		Red Stars		
	✕✕	Le Chateau	❀	—	—	—
Sherborne	★★	Half Moon		—	B	—
Studland	★★★	Knoll House		—	—	L
Sturminster Newton	✕✕	Plumber Manor	❀(DO)	—	—	—
Swanage	★★★	Grand		H	—	L
	★★★	Pines		H	—	—
Wareham	★★★	Priory		—	B	L
	★★	Kemps Country House		—	—	L
Winterbourne Abbas	★★	Whitefriars		H	—	L

CO DURHAM

Location	Rating	Establishment	Rosettes	H	B	L
Bishop Auckland	★★	Park Head		H	B	—
Durham	★★★	Ramside Hall		—	B	—
Middleton in Teesdale	★★	Teesdale		H	B	—
Romaldkirk	★★	Rose & Crown		—	B	—

ESSEX

Location	Rating	Establishment	Rosettes	H	B	L
Clacton-on-Sea	★★	King's Cliff		—	B	—
Coggeshall	★★★	White Hart		H	B	—
Dedham	★★★♣	Maison Talbooth (& Le Talbooth)	❀	Red Stars		
Dunmow, Gt	✕✕	Starr	❀(DO)	—	—	—
Frinton-on-Sea	★★	Maplin		H	—	—
	★	Rock		H	—	—

GLOUCESTERSHIRE

Location	Rating	Establishment	Rosettes	H	B	L
Berkeley	★★	Old School House		H	—	—
Bibury	★★★	Swan		—	—	L
Bourton-on-the-Water	★★	Old Manse		H	—	L
Nr Broadway (Worcs)	★★★	Dormy House		H	B	—
Buckland	★★★♣	Buckland Manor	❀	Red Stars		
Cheltenham	★★★♣	Greenway	❀	Red Stars		
	★★	Prestbury House		—	B	L
Cirencester	★★★	King's Head		H	—	—
	★★★	Stratton House		—	—	L
Lower Slaughter	★★★♣	Manor		—	B	—
Moreton-in-Marsh	★★★	Manor House		—	—	L
Painswick	★★★	Painswick		—	B	L
Stow on the Wold	★★★♣	Wyck Hill House		—	B	L
	★★	Old Farmhouse		—	B	—
	★★	Unicorn Crest		—	B	—
Stroud	★★★♣	Burleigh Court		H	—	—
Tetbury	★★★♣	Calcot Manor		Red Stars		
	★★★	Snooty Fox		H	B	L
Tewkesbury	★★	Tudor House		—	B	—
Upper Slaughter	★★★♣	Lords of the Manor		—	—	L

HAMPSHIRE

Location	Rating	Establishment	Rosettes	H	B	L
Andover	★★	Danebury		—	B	—
Brockenhurst	✕✕	Le Poussin	❀(DO)	—	—	—
Fareham	★★	Red Lion		—	B	—
Fordingbridge	✕	Three Lions	❀	—	—	—
Grayshott	✕	Woods	❀	—	—	—
Hurstbourne Tarrant	★★♣	Esseborne Manor	❀(DO)	Red Stars		
Liphook	✕✕	Lal Quila	❀	—	—	—
Lymington	★★★♣	Passford House		—	B	L
Lyndhurst	★★★♣	Parkhill House	❀	—	—	L
	★★	Pikes Hill Forest Lodge		—	—	L
New Milton	★★★★♣	Chewton Glen	❀❀	Red Stars		
Portsmouth & Southsea	★★★★	Holiday Inn		—	B	—
	★★	Keppel's Head		—	B	—
Rotherwick/Basingstoke	★★★★♣	Tylney Hall		H	B	L
Southampton	★★★	Southampton Park		—	—	L
	✕✕	Kohinoor	❀	—	—	—
	✕	Golden Palace	❀	—	—	—
Wickham	★★	Old House	❀	—	B	—
Winchester	★★★♣	Lainston House		—	B	L

HEREFORD & WORCESTER

Location	Rating	Establishment	Rosettes	H	B	L
Abberley	★★★♣	Elms	❀	Red Stars		
Belbroughton	✕✕✕	Bell	❀	—	—	—
Broadway	★★★★	Lygon Arms		Red Stars		
	★★★	Dormy House		H	B	—
	★★♣	Collin House		H	—	—
Bromsgrove	✕✕✕	Grafton Manor	❀	—	—	—
Corse Lawn	✕✕✕	Corse Lawn House	❀	—	—	—
Droitwich	★★	St Andrews		H	—	—
Ledbury	★★♣	Hope End	❀(DO)	H	B	L
Malvern	★★★♣	Cottage in the Wood		—	—	L
	★★	Walmer Lodge	❀(DO)	—	—	—
	✕✕	Croque en Bouche	❀	—	—	—
Pershore	★★	Avonside		—	—	L
Ross-on-Wye	★★★	Chase		H	—	—
	★★★	Pengethley		H	B	—
Worcester	★★	Ye Olde Talbot		—	B	—
	✕✕	Brown's	❀	—	—	—

HERTFORDSHIRE

Location	Rating	Establishment	Rosettes	H	B	L
Chipperfield	★★	Two Brewers Inn		—	—	L
St Albans	★★★	Noke Thistle		—	B	L

HUMBERSIDE

Location	Rating	Establishment	Rosettes	H	B	L
Althorpe	★★	Lansdowne House		—	B	—

KENT

Location	Rating	Establishment	Rosettes	H	B	L
Ashford	★★★★♣	Eastwell Manor	❀	Red Stars		
Canterbury	★★★★	County	❀	—	—	—
	✕✕	Restaurant Seventy-Four	❀	—	—	—
Cranbrook	★★♣	Kennel Holt		Red Stars		

Special Awards

Place	Rating	Establishment	Rosettes	H	B	L
Dover	★★★	Dover Motel		H	B	—
Faversham	✕✕	Read's	❀	—	—	—
Goudhurst	★★	Star & Eagle		—	B	—
Hadlow	★★	Leavers Manor		—	B	—
	✕	La Cremaillere	❀	—	—	—
Ightham	✕✕	Town House	❀(DO)	—	—	—
Sevenoaks	★★	Sevenoaks Park		—	—	L
Tunbridge Wells	★★★	Spa		—	—	L
	★★	Russell		H	B	—
Westerham	★★★	Kings Arms		—	B	—

LANCASHIRE

Place	Rating	Establishment	Rosettes	H	B	L
Burnley	★★★	Oaks		—	B	—
Chorley	★★★	Shaw Hill Golf & Country Club		—	B	—
Lytham St Annes	★★★	Grand Crest		—	B	—
Wrightington	✕✕	High Moor	❀	—	—	—

LEICESTERSHIRE

Place	Rating	Establishment	Rosettes	H	B	L
Oakham	★★★♣	Hambleton Hall	❀❀	Red Stars		
Quorn	★★★★	Quorn Country		H	B	—
Rothley	★★★	Rothley Court		—	—	L
Uppingham	★	Garden House (formerly Central)		H	—	—
	★	Lake Isle	❀	—	B	—

LINCOLNSHIRE

Place	Rating	Establishment	Rosettes	H	B	L
Market Rasen	★★★	Limes		H	—	—
Stamford	★★★	George of Stamford		H	B	

LONDON (POSTAL DISTRICTS)

Place	Rating	Establishment	Rosettes	H	B	L
EC2	✕✕✕	Le Poulbot	❀(LO)	—	—	—
N1	✕	Anna's Place	❀	—	—	—
NW3	★★★★	Holiday Inn		—	B	—
	✕✕	Keats	❀(DO)	—	—	—
SW1	★★★★★	Berkeley		Red Stars		
	★★★★★	Hyatt Carlton Tower		—	—	L
	★★★★★	Hyde Park		—	B	—
	★★★★	Dukes	❀	H	B	—
	★★★★	Goring		Red Stars		
	★★★★	Stafford		H	—	—
	★★★	Royal Horseguards		—	—	L
	★★★	Rubens		—	—	L
	★	Ebury Court		Red Star		
	✕✕	Gavvers	❀(DO)	—	—	—
	✕✕	Ken Lo's Memories of China	❀	—	—	—
	✕✕	Mazarin	❀(DO)	—	—	—
	✕✕	Mijanou	❀	—	—	—
	✕✕	Salloos	❀	—	—	—
	✕	Ciboure	❀	—	—	—
SW3	★★★★	Capital	❀	Red Stars		
	★★★	Basil Street		H	—	L
	✕✕✕✕	Waltons	❀	—	—	—
	✕✕	English Garden	❀	—	—	—
	✕✕	English House	❀	—	—	—
	✕✕	Tante Claire	❀❀	—	—	—
	✕	Ma Cuisine	❀	—	—	—
	✕	Dan's	❀	—	—	—
SW5	✕	Reads	❀	—	—	—
SW6	✕✕	Gastronome One	❀	—	—	—
	✕	L'Hippocampe	❀	—	—	—
	✕	Perfumed Conservatory	❀	—	—	—
SW7	★★★	Rembrandt		—	—	L
	✕	Hilaire	❀(DO)	—	—	—
SW8	✕✕	L'Arlequin	❀❀	—	—	—
	✕✕	Chez Nico	❀	—	—	—
W1	★★★★★	Claridge's		Red Stars		
	★★★★★	Connaught	❀❀	Red Stars		
	★★★★★	Dorchester (Terrace Room)	❀	Red Stars		
	★★★★★	Grosvenor House		—	—	L
	★★★★★	Inn on the Park		—	B	L
	★★★★★	Inter-Continental (Le Soufflé)	❀❀	—	—	—
	★★★★★	Ritz		—	—	L
	★★★★	Athenaeum		Red Stars		
	★★★★	Brown's		Red Stars		
	★★★★	Holiday Inn (Marble Arch)		—	B	—
	★★★★	Park Lane (Bracewell's Restaurant)	❀	—	—	L
	★★★	Berners		—	B	—
	★★★	Chesterfield		—	—	L
	★★★	Clifton Ford		—	—	L
	✕✕✕✕	Le Gavroche	❀❀❀	—	—	—
	✕✕	Au Jardin des Gourmets	❀	—	—	—
	✕✕	Gay Hussar	❀	—	—	—
	✕✕	Odins	❀	—	—	—
	✕✕	Rue St Jacques	❀❀	—	—	—
	✕	Yungs	❀(DO)	—	—	—
W2	★★★★	Royal Lancaster		—	—	L
W8	✕✕	La Ruelle	❀	—	—	—
WC2	★★★★★	Savoy (Savoy Restaurant)	❀	Red Stars		
	✕✕✕✕	Inigo Jones	❀❀	—	—	—
	✕✕✕	Boulestin	❀	—	—	—
	✕✕	Poons of Covent Garden (King St)	❀	—	—	—
	✕✕	Tourment d'amour	❀	—	—	—
	✕	Poons (Leicester St)	❀	—	—	—

LONDON, GREATER

Place	Rating	Establishment	Rosettes	H	B	L
Heathrow Airport	★★★★	Holiday Inn		—	B	—
	★★★★	Sheraton		—	—	L
	★★★	Berkeley Arms		—	B	—
Richmond upon Thames	✕✕	Lichfields	❀	—	—	—
Surbiton	✕✕	Chez Max	❀	—	—	—
Sutton	✕	Partners 23	❀	—	—	—

MANCHESTER, GREATER

Place	Rating	Establishment	Rosettes	H	B	L
Manchester Airport	✕✕	Moss Nook	❀	—	—	—

MERSEYSIDE

Place	Rating	Establishment	Rosettes	H	B	L
Birkenhead	★★★	Bowler Hat		—	B	—

NORFOLK

Place	Rating	Establishment	Rosettes	H	B	L
Brockdish	✕✕	Sheriff House	❀	—	—	—
Bunwell	★★♣	Bunwell Manor		—	—	L
Cromer	★★	Cliff House		—	—	L
Grimston	★★★♣	Congham Hall	❀	H	B	L
Shipdham	★★♣	Shipdham Place		H	B	L
Watton	★★	Clarence House		H	—	—
Weybourne	★★	Maltings		—	—	L
Witchingham, Gt	★★♣	Lenwade House		—	—	L
Yarmouth, Gt	★★★	Cliff		H	—	—
	★★	Imperial		—	B	—

NORTHAMPTONSHIRE

Place	Rating	Establishment	Rosettes	H	B	L
Horton	✕✕	French Partridge	❀	—	—	—
Roade	✕	Roadhouse	❀	—	—	—

NORTHUMBERLAND

Place	Rating	Establishment	Rosettes	H	B	L
Berwick upon Tweed	★★	Browns		H	—	—
Blanchland	★★	Lord Crewe Arms		—	B	—
Hexham	★★	County		H	B	—

Place	Rating	Hotel/Restaurant			
Longhorsley	★★★★	Linden Hall	H	B	L
Powburn	★★♣	Breamish House	❀(DO) Red Stars		
Seahouses	★★	Beach House	H	—	—

NOTTINGHAMSHIRE

Place	Rating	Hotel/Restaurant			
Edwinstowe	★★	Forest Lodge	—	B	—
Nottingham	★★★	Savoy	H	—	—
	★★★	Waltons	—	—	L
Retford (East)	★★★	West Retford	—	—	L

OXFORDSHIRE

Place	Rating	Hotel/Restaurant			
Abingdon	★★	Upper Reaches	—	B	—
Chesterton	XX	Woods	❀—	—	—
Clanfield	XXX	Plough	❀—	—	—
Dorchester on Thames	★★	George	—	B	—
Faringdon	★★	Faringdon	—	B	—
Kingham	★★	Mill	Red Stars		
Milton, Gt/Oxford	★★★♣	Le Manoir aux Quat'Saisons	❀❀❀ Red Stars		
Minster Lovell	★★	Old Swan	—	B	—
North Stoke	★★★	Springs	—	B	—
Oxford	XX	Le Petit Blanc	❀—	—	—
Thame	★★★	Spreadeagle	H	—	—
Woodstock	★★★	Bear	—	B	—
	★★	Feathers	❀ Red Stars		

SHROPSHIRE

Place	Rating	Hotel/Restaurant			
Brimfield	X	Poppies	❀—	—	—
Ludlow	★★★	Feathers	H	B	L
Oswestry	★★♣	Sweeney Hall	—	—	L
Shifnal	★★★	Park House	H	—	—
Worfield	★★♣	Old Vicarage	—	B	—

SOMERSET

Place	Rating	Hotel/Restaurant			
Bilbrook	★★	Dragon House	H	—	L
Bridgwater	★★	Walnut Tree Inn	—	B	—
Dulverton	★★★♣	Carnarvon Arms	—	—	L
	★★♣	Ashwick House	Red Stars		
Dunster	★★	Exmoor House	—	—	L
Hatch Beauchamp	★★	Farthings Country House	H	B	L
Minehead	★★★	Northfield	H	—	L
Montacute	★★	Kings Arms	—	B	—
Porlock	★★	Oaks	H	—	—
Shipham	★★♣	Daneswood House	H	—	—
Simonsbath	★★♣	Simonsbath House	H	B	L
Somerton	★★★	Lynch Country House	H	B	L
Ston Easton	★★★♣	Ston Easton Park	Red Stars		
Taunton	★★★★	Castle	❀ Red Stars		
	★★	Falcon	H	B	—
Watchet	★★	Downfield	—	—	L
Wells	★★★	Swan	—	B	—
	★★	Crown	H	—	—
Wheddon Cross	★★♣	Raleigh Manor	H	—	—
Williton	★★	White House	❀(DO)—	—	—
Wiveliscombe	★	Langley House	Red Star		
Yeovil	★★★	Manor Crest	—	B	—

STAFFORDSHIRE

Place	Rating	Hotel/Restaurant			
Newcastle Under Lyme	★	Deansfield	H	—	—
Rangemore	★★♣	Needwood Manor	H	—	L
Waterhouses	XX	Old Beams	❀—	—	—

SUFFOLK

Place	Rating	Hotel/Restaurant			
Aldeburgh	★★★	Brudenell	H	—	—
Brome	★★	Oaksmere	—	B	L
Bury St Edmunds	★★★	Angel	H	B	L
Fressingfield	X	Fox and Goose	❀—	—	—
Hintlesham	XXX	Hintlesham Hall	❀—	—	—
Ipswich	★★★	Belstead Brook	—	B	—
	★★★	Marlborough	❀H	B	—
Lavenham	★★★	Swan	—	—	L
Long Melford	XX	Chimneys	❀—	—	—
Newmarket	★★	Rosery Country House	H	—	—
Woodbridge	★★★♣	Seckford Hall	—	—	L

SURREY

Place	Rating	Hotel/Restaurant			
Bagshot	★★★★♣	Pennyhill Park	—	B	—
Churt	★★★	Frensham Pond	—	—	L
Dorking	★★★★	Burford Bridge	—	—	L
Haslemere	★★★	Lythe Hill	—	—	L
	XX	Morels	❀—	—	—
Limpsfield	XX	Old Lodge	❀—	—	—
Staines	★★	Thames Lodge	—	B	—
Weybridge	★★★	Ship Thistle	—	B	—

SUSSEX, EAST & WEST

Place	Rating	Hotel/Restaurant			
Alfriston (E)	★★★	Deans Place	—	—	L
Ashington (W)	★★	Mill House	H	B	—
Battle (E)	★★★♣	Netherfield Place	Red Stars		
Bosham (W)	★★	Millstream	—	B	—
Brighton & Hove (E)	★★★	Courtlands	—	B	—
	★★	Granville	—	B	—
	★★	Whitehaven	—	B	L
Chilgrove (W)	XX	White Horse Inn	❀—	—	—
Climping (W)	★★★♣	Bailiffscourt	—	B	—
Cuckfield (W)	★★★	Ockenden Manor	—	B	—
Eastbourne (E)	★★★★	Cavendish	—	—	L
	★★★	Lansdowne	—	—	L
East Grinstead (W)	★★★♣	Gravetye Manor	❀ Red Stars		
Goodwood/ Chichester (W)	★★★	Goodwood Park	—	B	—
Herstmonceux (E)	XX	Sundial	❀—	—	—
Lower Beeding/ Horsham (W)	★★★♣	South Lodge	❀ Red Stars		
Pulborough (W)	★	Chequers	—	B	L
	X	Stane Street Hollow	❀—	—	—
Rushlake Green (E)	★★★♣	Priory Country House	Red Stars		
Rusper (W)	★★★	Ghyll Manor	—	B	—
Storrington (W)	XXX	Manleys	❀—	—	—
Thakeham (W)	★★★	Abingworth Hall	❀H	—	—
Wadhurst (E)	★★♣	Spindlewood	❀—	—	—
Worthing (W)	★★★	Beach	H	—	L

TYNE & WEAR

Place	Rating	Hotel/Restaurant			
Newcastle Upon Tyne	★★★★	Gosforth Park	—	B	—
	XXX	Fisherman's Lodge	❀—	—	—

WARWICKSHIRE

Place	Rating	Hotel/Restaurant			
Alderminster	★★★★	Ettington Park	❀H	B	—
Ettington	★★♣	Chase Country House	❀(DO)H	B	—
Leamington Spa	★★★♣	Mallory Court	❀❀ Red Stars		
	★	Lansdowne	Red Stars		
Rugby	★★	Dun Cow	H	—	—
Stratford-upon-Avon	★★★★	Welcombe	H	—	L
Warwick	XX	Randolph's	❀—	—	—

WEST MIDLANDS

Place	Rating	Hotel/Restaurant			
Balsall Common	★★	Haigs	H	—	—

Town	Classification	Establishment	Rosettes	H	B	L
Birmingham	★★★★	Plough & Harrow		H	B	—
	★★	Wheatsheaf		—	B	—
	✕✕✕	Sloans	❀	—	—	—
	✕✕	Chung Ying	❀	—	—	—
	✕✕	Rajdoot	❀	—	—	—
Oldbury	✕✕	Jonathans'	❀	—	—	—
Solihull	★★	Saracens Head		—	B	—
Walsall	★★★	Barons Court		—	B	—

WILTSHIRE

Town	Classification	Establishment	Rosettes	H	B	L
Corsham	★★★	Rudloe Park		—	B	—
Ludwell	★	Grove House		—	—	L
Malmesbury	★★★	Old Bell		H	—	—
	★★★ 🌲	Whatley Manor		—	B	L
Marlborough	★★★	Ivy House		H	—	—
	★★	Merlin		H	—	—
Melksham	★★★ 🌲	Beechfield House	❀	—	B	L
	★★	Conigre Farm		H	—	—
	★★	Kings Arms		H	B	—
Trowbridge	★	Hilbury Court		—	B	—
Warminster	★★★★ 🌲	Bishopstrow House		Red Stars		

YORKSHIRE (NORTH, SOUTH & WEST)

Town	Classification	Establishment	Rosettes	H	B	L
Appleton-Le-Moors (N)	★★ 🌲	Dweldapilton Hall		H	—	L
Arncliffe (N)	★★ 🌲	Amerdale House		—	—	L
Ayton, Gt (N)	★★★ 🌲	Ayton Hall	❀	H	B	L
Bolton Abbey (N)	★★★	Devonshire Arms		—	—	L
Brompton by Sawdon (N)	✕	Brompton Forge	❀(DO)	—	—	—
Crathorne (N)	★★★★ 🌲	Crathorne Hall		—	—	L
Doncaster (S)	★★	Regent		—	B	—
Halifax (W)	★★★	Holdsworth House		—	B	—
Harrogate (N)	★★★	Hospitality Inn		—	B	—
	★★★	Studley		—	B	—
	★	Gables		—	B	—
Hawes (N)	★★	Simonstone Hall		—	—	L
Helmsley (N)	★★★	Black Swan		H	B	L
	★★	Pheasant		—	B	L
Holywell Green (W)	★★	Rock Inn		—	B	—
Hovingham (N)	★★	Worsley Arms		—	—	L
Hunmanby (N)	★★	Wrangham House		H	B	L
Ilkley (W)	★★	Rombalds		H	—	—
	★	Grove		—	B	—
	✕✕✕	Box Tree	❀❀(DO)	—	—	—
Kildwick (W)	★★★	Kildwick Hall		—	B	—
Kirkby Fleetham (N)	★★★ 🌲	Kirkby Fleetham Hall		H	B	L
Lastingham (N)	★★ 🌲	Lastingham Grange		H	—	—
Markington (N)	★★★ 🌲	Hob Green		—	B	L
Masham (N)	★★ 🌲	Jervaulx Hall		H	—	—
Northallerton (N)	★★★ 🌲	Solberge Hall		—	—	L
Nunnington (N)	✕✕	Ryedale Lodge	❀(DO)	—	—	—
Pickering (N)	★★	White Swan		—	B	—
Pool in Wharfedale (W)	✕✕✕	Pool Court	❀❀(DO)	—	—	—
Ripon (N)	★★	Bridge		H	B	—
Scarborough (N)	★★ 🌲	Wrea Head		—	—	L
Settle (N)	★★	Royal Oak		—	B	—
Sheffield (S)	★★★	St. George		H	—	L
Staddlebridge (N)	✕✕	McCoys	❀(DO)	—	—	—
Thirsk (N)	★	Sheppards		H	—	—
Wentbridge (W)	★★★ 🌲	Wentbridge House		H	—	—
Whitwell on the Hill (N)	★★★ 🌲	Whitwell Hall		—	—	L
York (N)	★★★	Fairfield Manor		—	B	L
	★★★	Middlethorpe Hall	❀	Red Stars		
	★★	Town House		—	—	L

ISLES OF SCILLY

Town	Classification	Establishment	Rosettes	H	B	L
Tresco, Old Grimsby	★★★	Island	❀	H	—	—

ISLE OF WIGHT

Town	Classification	Establishment	Rosettes	H	B	L
Bembridge	★★ 🌲	Elm Country		—	B	L
	★★	Highbury		—	B	L
Ryde	★★	Biskra House		—	B	—
St Lawrence	★★	Rocklands		H	—	—
Seaview	★★	Seaview	❀	—	—	—
Shanklin	★★	Belmont		—	B	—
Ventnor	★★	Bonchurch Manor		H	B	L
	★★	Highfield		—	B	—
	★ 🌲	Madeira		—	—	L

CHANNEL ISLES

Town	Classification	Establishment	Rosettes	H	B	L
L'Etacq, Jersey	★★★	Lobster Pot		—	B	—
Rozel Bay, Jersey	★★ 🌲	Château la Chaire		—	—	L
St Helier, Jersey	★★★★	Grand (Victoria's)	❀	—	—	—
	★★	Savoy		—	—	L
St Lawrence, Jersey	★★★	Little Grove		H	—	L
St Peter Port, Guernsey	★★★	La Frégate	❀	—	—	—
St Saviour, Jersey	★★★★ 🌲	Longueville Manor	❀	Red Stars		

Wales

CLWYD

Town	Classification	Establishment	Rosettes	H	B	L
Colwyn Bay	★★★	Norfolk House		—	—	L
	★★★	Hotel 70°		—	—	L
Holywell	★★	Stamford Gate		—	B	—
Llanarmon Dyffryn Ceiriog	★★★	Hand		H	—	—
Llangollen	★★	Tyn-y-Wern		H	—	—

DYFED

Town	Classification	Establishment	Rosettes	H	B	L
Aberystwyth	★★	Court Royale		—	B	—
Crugybar	★★ 🌲	Glanrannel Park		H	—	—
Hebron	★	Preseli		H	—	—
Llandeilo	★★★	Cawdor Arms		—	B	—
Manorbier	★★	Castle Mead		H	—	—
St Clears	★★	Forge		—	B	—
Tenby	★★	Atlantic		—	—	L
	★	Harbour Heights		H	—	—
Whitland	★	Waungron Farm		H	B	—

GLAMORGAN (MID, SOUTH & WEST)

Town	Classification	Establishment	Rosettes	H	B	L
Bridgend (M)	★★★	Heronston		—	B	—
Cardiff (S)	✕	La Chaumiere	❀	—	—	—
Langland (W)	★★	Langland Court		—	B	—
Porthcawl (M)	★★	Maid of Sker		—	B	—
Swansea (W)	★★★	Ladbroke		H	—	—
	★★	Beaumont		H	—	—
	★	Windsor Lodge		H	B	L

GWENT

Town	Classification	Establishment	Rosettes	H	B	L
Abergavenny	★★	Llanwenarth Arms		—	B	—
Chepstow	★★	Castle View		H	—	—
Langstone	★★	New Inn		—	B	—
Llanddewi Skirrid	✕	Walnut Tree	❀	—	—	—
Llangybi	★★★★	Cwrt Bleddyn		H	—	—

Newport	★★★	Kings		H	—	—
Usk	★★	Glen-yr-Afon		—	—	L
Whitebrook	★★	Crown at Whitebrook	❀	H	—	—

GWYNEDD

Aberdovey	★★★♣	Plas Penhelig		—	—	L
	★★	Penhelig Arms		—	—	L
Abersoch	★★★♣	Porth Tocyn	❀(DO)	H	—	L
	★★	Deucoch		—	B	—
	★★	Neigwl		H	—	—
Bangor	★★	Telford		H	—	—
Beddgelert	★	Tanronen		—	—	L
Betws-y-Coed	★★	Park Hill		H	—	—
Bontddu	★★★	Bontddu Hall		—	—	L
Criccieth	★	Henfaes		H	—	—
Deganwy	★★	Bryn Cregin Garden		—	B	L
Llanbedr	★★	Ty Mawr		H	—	—
Llandderfel	★★★♣	Palé Hall		—	B	L
Llandudno	★★★♣	Bodysgallen Hall		Red Stars		
	★★★	Empire		—	B	L
	★★	Bromwell Court		—	B	—
	★★	Chatsworth House		—	—	L
	★★	Dunoon		—	—	L
	★★	St Tudno		Red Stars		
	★	Fairhaven		—	B	—
	★	Gwesty Leamore		H	—	—
	★	Min-y-Don		H	—	—
	★	Sunnymede		—	B	L
Llanwnda/ Caernarfon	★★★	Stables		—	B	—
Pennal	★★★	Talgarth Hall		—	B	—
Talsarnau	★★♣	Maes y Neuadd		—	—	L
Tal-y-Llyn	★	Minffordd		Red Star		

POWYS

Brecon	★★	Wellington		—	B	—
Crickhowell	★★	Bear		H	—	—
	★★♣	Gliffaes		—	—	L
Glasbury	★★	Llwynaubach Lodge		H	—	—
Llanfyllin	★★♣	Bodfach Hall		—	B	L
Llangammarch Wells	★★★♣	Lake		H	—	L
Llangynog	★	New Inn		—	B	—
Machynlleth	★★♣	Plas Dolguog		—	—	L
Presteigne	★★	Radnorshire Arms		—	B	L
Three Cocks	★	Three Cocks	❀(DO)	—	—	L

Scotland

BORDERS

Dryburgh	★★★♣	Dryburgh Abbey		—	—	L
Ettrick Bridge	★★♣	Ettrick Shaws		H	—	—
Greenlaw	★★♣	Purves Hall		H	—	L
Kelso	★★★♣	Sunlaws House	❀(DO)	—	B	L
Peebles	★★★	Hydro		H	—	—
	★★♣	Cringletie House		Red Stars		
St. Boswells	★★	Buccleuch Arms		—	—	L

CENTRAL

Blair Drummond	✕	Broughton's Country Cottage	❀(DO)	—	—	—
Callander	★★★♣	Roman Camp	❀	—	B	L
	★	Bridgend House		H	—	L
	★	Lubnaig		—	B	L
Dunblane	★★★♣	Cromlix House	❀(DO)	Red Stars		
Grangemouth	★★★	Grange Manor		H	—	—
Lochearnhead	★	Lochearnhead		—	—	L
	★	Mansewood		H	B	—
Strathblane	★★★	Country Club		—	B	—

DUMFRIES AND GALLOWAY

Annan	★★	Queensberry Arms		—	B	—
	★★	Warmanbrie		—	B	—
Auchencairn	★★★♣	Balcary Bay		H	—	L
Beattock	★★	Auchen Castle		H	—	L
Canonbie	★	Riverside	❀(DO)	H	B	L
Eskdalemuir	★★	Hart Manor		H	—	—
Gatehouse of Fleet	★★★★	Cally Palace		—	—	L
Moffat	★★	Beechwood Country House		—	B	—
Newton Stewart	★★★♣	Kirroughtree	❀(DO)	H	B	L
	★★	Creebridge House		H	—	—
Portpatrick	★★♣	Knockinaam Lodge	❀	H	B	L
	★	Mount Stewart		H	—	—
Rockcliffe	★★★♣	Barons Craig		—	—	L
Ruthwell	★♣	Kirklands		—	B	L
Stranraer	★★★	North West Castle Hotel		—	—	L
Wamphray	★	Red House		H	—	—

FIFE

Aberdour	★★	Woodside		—	—	L
Anstruther	✕✕	Cellar	❀	—	—	—
Cupar	✕	Ostlers Close	❀	—	—	—
Dunfermline	★★★	Keavil House		—	B	—
Glenrothes	★	Rescobie		H	—	L
Peat Inn	✕✕	Peat Inn	❀	—	—	—
St Andrews	★★★★	Rusacks Marine		—	—	L
	★★★	Rufflets		H	B	L
	★★★	St Andrews Golf		—	B	—

GRAMPIAN

Aberdeen	★★★	Caledonian Thistle		—	B	—
	★★★	New Marcliffe		—	—	L
Aboyne	★★	Birse Lodge		H	B	—
Ballater	★★	Darroch Learg		—	B	L
Banchory	★★★♣	Banchory Lodge		Red Stars		
	★★★♣	Raemoir		H	B	L
Fordyce	★	Hawthorn	❀(DO)	—	—	—
Elgin	★★★	Mansion House		H	B	—
Kildrummy	★★★♣	Kildrummy Castle	❀(RO)	H	B	L
Old Rayne	★	Lodge		H	—	—
Peterhead	★★★	Waterside Inn		—	B	—
Rothes	★★★♣	Rothes Glen		—	B	L

HIGHLAND

Achnasheen	★★♣	Ledgowan Lodge		H	—	L
Ardelve	★	Loch Duich	❀(DO)	H	—	L
Arisaig	★★★♣	Arisaig House	❀(DO)	Red Stars		
	★★	Arisaig		H	—	—
Balmacara	★★	Balmacara		—	—	L
Banavie	★★	Moorings		—	—	L
Cannich	★★♣	Cozac		H	—	L
Drumnadrochit	★★♣	Polmaily House	❀(DO)	H	B	L
Dulnain Bridge	★★♣	Muckrach Lodge		H	—	—
Duror	★★	Stewart		—	—	L
Fort Augustus	★★	Caledonian		H	—	—
	★★	Lovat Arms		H	—	—
Fort William	★★★★♣	Inverlochy Castle	❀❀	Red Stars		
	★	Factors House	❀(DO)	H	B	L
Glenborrodale	★★	Clan Morrison		H	—	—
	★★♣	Glenborrodale Castle		—	B	L
Grantown on Spey	★★	Garth		H	—	L
Invermoriston	★★	Glen Moriston Arms		—	B	—
Inverness	★★★★♣	Culloden House		H	B	—
	★★★	Kingsmills		—	B	L
	★★♣	Dunain Park		H	B	L

Place	Rating	Establishment				
Kentallen	★★♣	Ardsheal House	❀(DO)	H	B	L
Kingussie	★	Osprey	❀(DO)	H	—	—
	✕	Cross	❀(DO)	—	—	—
Letterfinlay	★★	Letterfinlay Lodge		H	—	L
Lochinver	★★	Culag		H	—	L
Melvich	★★	Melvich		—	B	—
Muir of Ord	★★♣	Ord House		—	—	L
Nairn	★★	Clifton	❀(DO)	H	B	L
Newtonmore	★	Ard na Coille	❀(DO)	H	—	—
Onich	★★	Lodge on the Loch		H	—	L
	★★	Onich		—	B	—
Plockton	★★	Haven		H	—	L
Scourie	★★	Scourie		H	—	L
Skye, Isle of						
Harlosh	★	Harlosh	❀(DO)	H	—	—
Isle Ornsay	★★♣	Kinloch Lodge	❀(DO)	H	—	L
Knock	★★	Toravaig House		H	—	—
Skeabost Bridge	★★★♣	Skeabost House		—	—	L
Uig	★★	Uig		—	B	—
Strathpeffer	★	Holly Lodge	❀(DO)	H	—	L
Talladale	★	Loch Maree		H	—	—
Ullapool	★★	Ceilidh Place		—	B	L
	★★	Harbour Lights		—	—	L
Whitebridge	★★♣	Knockie Lodge	❀(DO)	H	B	L

LOTHIAN

Place	Rating	Establishment				
Bonnyrigg	★★★★♣	Dalhousie Castle		—	—	L
Dirleton	★★★	Open Arms		H	—	—
Dunbar	★★	Bayswell		H	—	—
Edinburgh	★★★	Barnton Thistle		—	B	L
	★★★	Crest		—	—	L
	★★★	Donmaree		—	—	L
	★★★	Howard		—	B	L
	★★★	King James Thistle		—	B	—
	★★★	Roxburghe		—	B	L
Gullane	★★★♣	Greywalls	❀	Red Stars		
	✕	La Potiniere	❀	—	—	—
Humbie	★★★	Johnstounburn House		H	—	L
Uphall	★★★♣	Houston House		—	B	—

ORKNEY ISLES

Place	Rating	Establishment				
Stromness	✕✕	Hamnavoe	❀(DO)	—	—	—

STRATHCLYDE

Place	Rating	Establishment				
Appin	★★	Invercreran House		—	—	L
Colonsay, Isle of						
Scalasaig	★	Colonsay		H	B	L
Connel	★★	Ossians		—	—	L
Dunoon	★★	Enmore		H	—	—
	★★	Firpark		—	B	L
Eriska	★★★♣	Isle of Eriska		Red Stars		
Giffnock	★★★	Macdonald Thistle		—	B	—
Gigha, Isle of	★★	Gigha		H	—	L
Glasgow	★★★★	Holiday Inn		—	B	—
	★★★	Tinto Firs Thistle		—	B	—
	✕✕✕	Fountain	❀	—	—	—
	✕✕	The Buttery	❀	—	—	—
Islay, Isle of						
Port Ellen	★	Dower House		H	B	—
Kilchrenan	★★★♣	Ardanaiseig	❀(DO)	Red Stars		
	★★★♣	Taychreggan		H	—	L
Kilfinan	★★	Kilfinan	❀(DO)	H	B	—
Knipoch	★★★	Knipoch		—	B	L
Langbank	★★★♣	Gleddoch House	❀	—	B	—
Mull, Isle of						
Tobermory	★	Tobermory		—	—	L
	★	Ulva House		H	B	—
Port Appin	★★	Airds	❀(DO)	Red Stars		
Portsonachan	★★	Portsonachan	❀(DO)	H	—	—
Rhu	★★★	Rosslea Hall		—	—	L
Skelmorlie	★★★♣	Manor Park		—	B	L
Stewarton	★★★♣	Chapeltoun House	❀	Red Stars		
Tarbert	★★★	Stonefield Castle		H	—	—
	★	West Loch	❀(DO)	—	—	—
Troon	★★	Piersland House		—	—	L
	✕	Campbell's Kitchen	❀(DO)	—	—	—
Turnberry	★★★★	Turnberry		H	—	L

TAYSIDE

Place	Rating	Establishment				
Arbroath	★★★	Letham Grange		—	—	L
Auchterarder	★★★★★	Gleneagles		Red Stars		
Auchterhouse	★★★♣	Old Mansion House		—	B	—
Blairgowrie	★★♣	Altamount House		—	—	L
	★★★♣	Kinloch House	❀(DO)	H	—	L
Bridge of Cally	★	Bridge of Cally		—	B	L
Cleish	★★★♣	Nivingston House	❀	H	B	—
Crieff	★★♣	Cultoquhey House		H		—
	★	Gwydyr		—	B	—
Dunkeld	★★★♣	Dunkeld House		—	B	L
Glencarse	★★	Newton House		H	—	—
Glenfarg	★★	Bein Inn		H	—	—
Glenshee	★★♣	Dalmunzie		—	—	L
Killiecrankie	★★	Killiecrankie	❀(DO)	H	B	—
Kinclaven	★★★♣	Ballathie House		—	—	L
Kirkmichael	★★	Log Cabin		H	—	—
	★★	Aldchlappie		—	B	—
Meigle	★★♣	Kings of Kinloch		H	—	—
Perth	★★★♣	Balcraig House	❀(DO)	Red Stars		
	★★★	Royal George		—	—	L
	✕✕	Coach House	❀	—	—	—
Pitlochry	★★★	Atholl Palace		—	—	L
	★★	Birchwood		H	—	—
	★★	Burnside		H	—	L
	★★	Craigard		H	—	—
	★★♣	Pine Trees		—	—	L
Strathtummel	★★♣	Port-an-Eilean		H	B	—

WESTERN ISLES

Place	Rating	Establishment				
Harris, Isle of						
Scarista	★★♣	Scarista House	❀(DO)	H	B	L
Lewis, Isle of						
Stornoway	★★★	Caberfeidh		—	B	—

Hotel Groups

Key to abbreviations and central reservation telephone numbers (where applicable)

Special corporate rates are available at hotel companies marked with an *, through the facilities of business travel accounts with the AA Business Travel Service.

Bookings may be made via the AA Travel Agencies shown below

Company	Abbreviations	Telephone
Alloa Brewery Co Ltd	Alloa Brewery	
*Anchor Hotels & Taverns Ltd	Anchor	Farnborough (Hants) (0252) 517517
Berni Inns Ltd	Berni	01-636 8787
Best Western	Best Western	01-541 0033
Brend & Sons Ltd	Brend	Barnstaple (0271) 74173
Consort Hotels Ltd	Consort	York (0904) 643151
*Commonwealth Holiday Inns of Canada Ltd	Holiday Inns	01-722 7755
*Crest Hotels Ltd	Crest	01-236 3242
De Vere Hotels Ltd	De Vere	Warrington (0925) 35471
*Embassy Hotels	Embassy	01-581 3466
Exec Hotels	Exec Hotel	
Forestdale Hotel Group	Forestdale	
Frederic Robinson Ltd	Frederic Robinson	
Great British Hotels (Anchor, GW and Swallow Groups). See details under Anchor, GW Hotels and Swallow		
GW Hotels Ltd	GW Hotels	Warrington (0925) 35471
Golden Oak Inns Ltd	Golden Oak	
Guestaccom	Guestaccom	
*Hilton International Hotels Ltd		01-580 8197
*Holiday Inn International	Holiday Inns	01-722 7755
Home Brewery Co Ltd	Home Brewery	
Hotel Representative Incorporated for Berkeley, Claridges, Connaught, Savoy, Hyde Park, London; Royal Crescent, Bath, Avon; Lygon Arms, Broadway, Worcs; Grosvenor, Chester; Chewton Glen, New Milton, Hants		01-583 3050/Freephone 0800 181123
*Hyatt Hotels Worldwide		01-580 8197
Inter-Hotels	Inter-Hotels	01-373 3241
Kingsmead Hotels Ltd	Kingsmead	Reading (0734) 302925
*Ladbroke Hotels Ltd	Ladbroke	01-734 6000 (business) Watford (0923) 38877 (leisure)
Matthew Brown Manor Houses Ltd	Matthew Brown	
*Mount Charlotte Hotels Ltd	Mount Charlotte	01-837 4315
Norscot Hotels plc/Clan Hotels Ltd	Norscot/Clan Hotel	
Novotel International	Novotel	
Paten & Co Ltd	Paten	
Prestige Hotels	Prestige	01-741 9164
Quality Hotels Ltd	Quality	Freephone 0800-444444
*Queens Moat House Ltd	Queens Moat	Harrogate (0423) 52644
*Rank Hotels Ltd	Rank	01-262 2893
Relais et Châteaux Hotels	Relais et Châteaux	
Scottish Highland Hotels	Scottish Highland	041-332 6538
*Stakis Organisation	Stakis	01-930 0342 & 041-332 4343
*Swallow Hotels Ltd	Swallow	Sunderland (0783) 294666
*Thistle Hotels (Scottish & Newcastle Breweries)	Thistle	01-937 8033
Toby Restaurants Ltd	Toby	
Trusthouse Forte Hotels Ltd	Trusthouse Forte	01-567 3444
Whitbread & Co	Whitbread	
Wolverhampton & Dudley Breweries Ltd	Wolverhampton & Dudley	

Automobile Association

Bookings for hotels belonging to groups marked * can be made through AA Travel Agencies. The telephone numbers of the principal ones are given below. For a full list of AA Travel Agencies consult the *AA Members' Handbook* or Yellow Pages.

Birmingham	021-643 3373	Glasgow	041-204 0911
Bristol	Bristol (0272) 290992	London (City)	01-623 4152
Cheadle Hulme	061-485 8551	London (West End)	01-930 2462

Hours Mon—Fri 9am—5pm; Sat 9am—12.30pm. Closed Sun.

How to use the Guide

Accommodation details. The first figure shows the number of letting bedrooms. Where rooms have *en suite* bath or shower and WC, the number precedes the appropriate symbol.

Annexe — bedrooms available in an annexe are noted only if they are at least of the same standard as those in the rest of the hotel. Facilities may not be the same as in the main building however, and it is advisable to check the nature of the accommodation and the tariff before making a reservation. In some hotels, accommodation is only available in an annexe.

⅍ — number of bedrooms for non-smokers.

fb — family bedrooms.

CTV — this may mean televisions permanently in bedrooms or available on request from the hotel management. Check when making reservations.

✗ — no dogs allowed into bedrooms. Some hotels may restrict the size of dogs permitted and the rooms into which they may be taken. Hotels which do not normally accept dogs may accept guide dogs. Generally dogs are not allowed in the dining room. Check when booking the conditions under which pets are accepted.

T — direct dial facilities available from bedrooms. Many hotels impose a surcharge for calls made from bedrooms, so check before making the call. A public telephone is usually available in the hotel hallway or foyer.

Prices — prices given have been provided by the hotelier and restaurateur in good faith and are indications rather than firm quotations. Check current prices before booking. See also page 805.

Town Name listed in gazetteer in strict alphabetical order including London. This is followed by the county or region. This is the administrative county, or region, and not necessarily part of the correct postal address. Towns on islands (not connected to the mainland by a bridge) are listed under the island name. With Scottish regions or islands, the old county name follows in italics. The **map reference,** which follows denotes, first, the map page number. Then follow grid reference; read 1st figure across 2nd figure vertically within the appropriate square.

Restricted service. Some hotels, while remaining open operate a restricted service during the less busy months. This may take the form of a reduction in meals served, accommodation available, or in some cases both.

Hotel facilities. For key to symbols see inside front cover.

☾ — All hotels employing a night porter are shown thus except 4 and 5 star hotels, all of which have night porters on duty.

🚌 — No coaches. This information is published in good faith from information supplied by the establishments concerned. Inns, however have well-defined legal obligations towards travellers and it is for the customer to take up with the proprietor or the local licensing authority.

nc — hotels listed accommodate children of all ages unless a minimum age is given (eg nc4), but they may not necessarily be able to provide special facilities, nc by itself indicates 'no children'. For very young children, check before booking about such provisions as cots and high chairs and any reductions made.

👪 — establishments with special facilities for children, which will include baby sitting service or baby intercom system, playroom or playground, laundry facilities, drying and ironing facilities, cots, high chairs and special meals. Some hotels offer free accommodation to children provided they share the parent's room.

♿ — disabled people accommodated. Information has been supplied by the hotel proprietor and it is advisable to check before booking. Further details for disabled people will be found in AA *Travellers' Guide for the Disabled* available from AA offices, free to members, £2.25 to non-members. Intending guests with any form of disability should notify proprietors so that arrangements can be made to minimise difficulties, particularly in the event of an emergency.

KEY TO TOWN PLANS

- ═══ Roads with restricted access
- ✝ Churches
- [i] Tourist Information centre
- [AA] AA Centre
- [P] Car parking
- ③ Hotel and restaurant
- ★ Red Star hotel
- Built up area (shown on London plans only)
- [4 2m] Distance to hotels from edge of plan
- **AYR 6m** Mileage to town from edge of plan

SAMPLE ENTRY

The entry is fictitious

BEESTON
Derbyshire
Map **15** NJ90

★★*BL* **Red Lion** The Square (GB Hotels) ☎ (0685) 8276
Telex no 739619

RS Nov—Mar

Attractive old coaching inn with comfortable, pretty bedrooms.
19rm(14⇌5fh) Annexe: 5rm(8fb)
CTV in all bedrooms ® ✈ **T**
sB&B⇌fh£16.50—£24.50
dB&B⇌fh£31—£49 **B**

Lift ☾ CTV 100P 3⌂ ⛟ CFA ▭
nc3yrs ♿

⛫ English & French **V** ⛉ ☕ Lunch £3—£4.50 Tea 85p—£1.40 High Tea £2.75—£6 Dinner £8.25—£11 &alc Wine £4.20 Last dinner 9pm

Credit cards 1 2 3 4 5 Ⓥ

Hotel name, address and telephone number with classification and merit symbols (see page 27 for key). When establishments' names are shown in ***italics*** the particulars have not been confirmed by the management. Within towns the order is red stars, then black by alphabetical listing each classification in descending star order. Hotels precede restaurants. **Company owned hotels** and marketing consortia are shown using abbreviations (key on page 53). Before its name is shown in the guide a company must own at least five AA appointed hotels, or a hotel must be affiliated to one of the following marketing consortia. Best Western, Consort, Exec Hotels, Guestaccom, Inter-Hotels, Prestige, Relais et Châteaux and Pride of Britain. The **telephone exchange** quoted is that of the town heading. Where not, the name of the exchange is given after the ☎ symbol and before the dialling code and number. In some areas, numbers are likely to be changed during the currency of this book. In case of difficulty check with the operator. When making a reservation by **telex** it is advisable to specify which hotel you wish to book with as some hotels (particularly those in groups) use a central telex service.

Meals. Details of the style of food served and likely price ranges are given.

V — a choice of vegetarian dishes available (but check before booking).

⛉ ☕ — morning coffee or afternoon tea are served to chance callers. All 4 and 5 star hotels serve morning coffee and, normally, afternoon tea to residents. Tea can vary from a pot of tea to a full tea with light refreshments.

Prices See page 805.

Payment details

- 1 — Access/Euro/Mastercard accepted (but check current position when booking)
- 2 — American Express
- 3 — Barclaycard/Visa
- 4 — Carte Blanche
- 5 — Diners
- Ⓥ — Hotel or restaurant accepts AA Money-Off Vouchers as detailed on first page of book.

Gazetteer

The gazetteer gives locations and details of AA-appointed hotels and AA-appointed restaurants, listed in alphabetical order of place names throughout Great Britain, Channel Islands and Isle of Man. Locations on Islands are listed under the appropriate Island heading but the gazetteer text also gives cross-references. A useful first point of reference is to consult the location maps which show where AA appointed establishments are situated.
NB *There is no map for Isles of Scilly*

ABBERLEY
Hereford & Worcester
Map **7** SO76

★★★

★★★ ELMS, ABBERLEY
(on A443) (Prestige)
☎ Great Witley (029921) 666
Telex no 337105

This lovely Queen Anne house with a later wing extension is approached along an avenue of lime trees through part of the 12 acres of lovely gardens and grounds. These contain facilities for croquet, putting and tennis and also a notable herb garden. These herbs, together with other produce from the kitchen plot are put to good use in the kitchen by Chef Andreas Antona who shows sufficient skill in the modern style of cooking to justify our rosette. You will be well attended to in the elegant, candle-lit Brooke Room Restaurant by staff who are politely professional. The friendly service is typical of the rest of the staff, imbued by the manageress, Miss Rita Mooney, with the idea that the guest comes first. Bedrooms can vary in size but they are mostly adequate and provided with a plethora of extras, including fruit, sherry, books and wall safes. The public areas are smartly arranged and include the library/bar as well as the sitting rooms, either side

of the hall. Lots of flowers, open fires, comfortable seating and magazines as well as antiques and appropriate ornaments add to the attractions of this captivating country house.

18rm (17 1) Annexe: 9 (3fb) 1 CTV in all bedrooms **T** S% sB&B £51 dB&B £69
☾ 100P 6 croquet, putting *xmas*
English & French **V** S% Lunch £10.95 Tea fr£1.50 Dinner £17&alc Wine £8 Last dinner 9pm
Credit cards 1 2 3 4 5 V

ABBOTSBURY
Dorset
Map **3** SY58

★★Ilchester Arms 9 Market St
☎ (0305) 871243
Closed Xmas

This old English coaching inn, recently refurbished but retaining its character, offers attractively decorated bedrooms and a first-floor lounge with wide views. The food is well prepared and served.

8rm (6) Annexe: 2 CTV in all bedrooms ® sB&B £16—£18 dB&B £30—£32 dB&B £32—£35
35P nc14yrs
V ✱ Bar lunch £2.90—£9 Dinner £9.50alc Wine £3.80 Last dinner 9pm
Credit cards 1 3

ABERDARON
Gwynedd
Map **6** SH12

★★*Ty Newydd* ☎ (075886) 207
RS Dec—Jan

Three storey hotel in centre of Aberdaron, with direct access to the beach.

14rm (8 1) (2fb) CTV in 12 bedrooms TV in 2 bedrooms
CTV 8P 2
Mainly grills Last dinner 9pm

ABERDEEN
Grampian *Aberdeenshire*
Map **15** NJ90
See also Aberdeen Airport **See plan**

★★★★Bucksburn Moat House
Old Meldrum Rd, Bucksburn (3m N A947) (Queens Moat) ☎ (0224) 713911
Telex no 73108 Plan **2** *C8*

Hotel with a modern external appearance and pleasant, comfortable interior.

98 (14fb) CTV in all bedrooms ® **T** sB £58.40 dB £73.10 (room only)
Lift ☾ 165P CFA (heated) Disco Sat *xmas*
S% Lunch £10—£11&alc Tea £1.25 High Tea £3—£6.50 Dinner £10—£11&alc Wine £5.50 Last dinner 10.30pm
Credit cards 1 2 3 4 5

★★★★Skean Dhu Altens Souter Head Rd, Altens (3m S off A956) (Mount Charlotte) ☎ (0224) 877000 Telex no 739631 Plan **15** *E1*

A spacious hotel, standing on the main route to Aberdeen Harbour. Some bedrooms have views across the city towards the coast.

221 (70fb) CTV in all bedrooms ® **T** S% ✱ sB fr£51 dB fr£59
Lift ☾ 500P CFA heated
International **V** ✱ Lunch fr£8.50 Tea fr£1.20 High Tea fr£3.90 Dinner fr£9.85 Wine £5.25 Last dinner 10.45pm
Credit cards 1 2 3 4 5 V

★★★*B* Caledonian Thistle 10 Union Ter (Thistle) ☎ (0224) 640233
Telex no 73758 Plan **3** *D5*

Modernised facilities and tastefully furnished bedrooms are features of this granite faced Victorian building in the city centre.

77 (8fb) 2 in 2 bedrooms CTV in all bedrooms ® **T** ✱ sB £50—£70 dB £58—£82 (room only)
Lift ☾ 25P sauna bath solarium
International ✱ Bar lunch £3.95 Dinner fr£12&alc Wine £7
Last dinner 9.30pm
Credit cards 1 2 3 4 5 V
See advertisement on page 60

★★★Imperial Stirling St (Swallow)
☎ (0224) 589101 Telex no 73365
Plan **9** *D4*
Closed Xmas Day, New Years Day & 2 Jan
RS Xmas eve & New Years eve

Quietly situated near city centre, this popular hotel has attractive carvery restaurant.

109rm (27 76) CTV in all bedrooms ® **T** S% ✱ sB&B £40—45 dB&B £54—£60
Lift ☾
V S% ✱ Lunch fr£3.75&alc Dinner fr£8.75&alc Wine £5.50 Last dinner 9.45pm
Credit cards 1 2 3 5

★★★*L* New Marcliffe 51-53 Queen's Rd (Best Western) ☎ (0224) 321371 Telex no 73225 Plan **10** *A4*
Closed 1 & 2 Jan

Tasteful conversion of two granite buildings has created a small, elegant hotel with an almost club-like atmosphere. The bedrooms are attractive and well-equipped.

27 (4fb) 1 CTV in all bedrooms ® **T** S% sB&B £26—£52 dB&B £28—£56
☾ CTV 72P →

A

Aberdeen

1 Atlantis Sea Food✕
2 Bucksburn Moat House ★★★★
3 Caledonia Thistle ★★★
6 Gerard's ✕✕✕
7 Gloucester ★★
8 Gordon ★★
9 Imperial ★★★
10 New Marcliffe ★★★
12 Pinocchio ✕✕
13 Poldino's ✕
14 Shish Mahal ✕
15 Skean Dhu Altens ★★★★
16 Stakis Treetops ★★★
17 Trattoria Luigi's ✕✕

Scottish & French V Lunch S% Lunch £4.50—£8.50&alc Tea £1.50—£3.00 Dinner £8.50—£15&alc Wine £6 Last dinner 10pm

Credit cards 1 2 3 5 V

★★★**Stakis Treetops** 161 Springfield Rd (Stakis) ☎(0224) 313377 Telex no 73794 Plan **16** *A2*

This modern hotel is nicely situated in attractive landscaped grounds in the western residential area of the city.

109(3fb) 1 in 12 bedrooms CTV in all bedrooms ® T S% sB&B £55—£60 dB&B £70—£75

Lift ☾ ##350P CFA ✽ heated sauna bath solarium gymnasium *xmas*

Scottish & Continental V Lunch fr£6.50 Tea fr£1 Dinner fr£10.50 Wine £5 Last dinner 10pm

Credit cards 1 2 3 4 5

★★**Gloucester** 102 Union St (Embassy) ☎(0224) 641095 Telex no 73711 Plan **7** *D5*

City centre hotel with modern facilities.

76rm(28 48)(6fb) CTV in all bedrooms ® sB £40—£41.50 dB £60—63 (room only)

Lift ☾ *xmas*

V Lunch £4.75&alc Tea 75p—£2 High Tea £4.50—£5.50 Dinner £9&alc Wine £4.45 Last dinner 8.45pm

Credit cards 1 2 3 5 V

★★**Gordon** Wellington Rd (Alloa Brewery) ☎(0224) 873012 Plan **8** *E1*

Small business and commercial hotel near East Tullos industrial estate.

26rm(3 14) CTV in all bedrooms ® T ✱B&B fr£22 B&B fr£26 dB&B fr£30 dB&B fr£36

☾100P ✽

Mainly grills V ✱ Lunch £8&alc Tea £1.40—£1.90 Wine £3.90 Last dinner 9.30pm

Credit cards 1 2 3 4 5

✕✕✕**Gerard's** 50 Chapel St ☎(0224) 639500 Plan **6** *B4*

There is a Provincial house atmosphere to this friendly French restaurant with its conservatory bar to the rear.

Closed Sun →

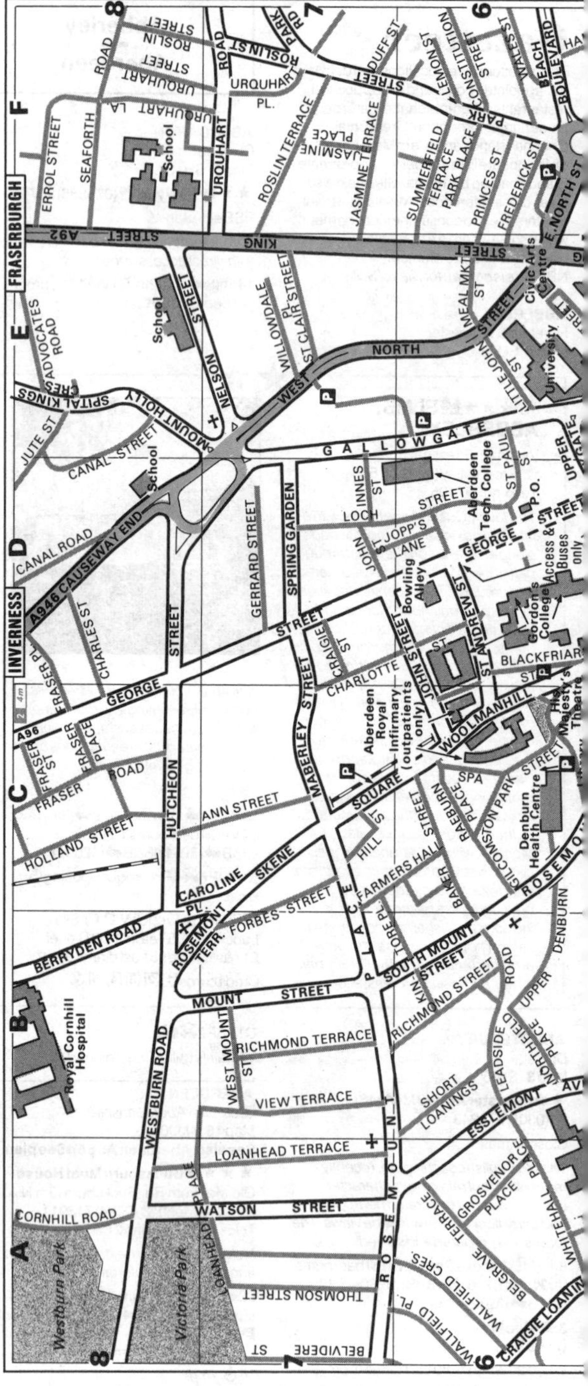

A

Central Aberdeen
© The Automobile Association 1985
Blaikies Quay
Harbour Offices
Jamieson's Quay
P & O Ferry Terminal
Fish Market
Victoria Bridge
River Dee
Wellington Bridge
Wellington Suspension Bridge
Pedestrians only
Railway Station
Bus Station
Trinity Centre
Freightliner Terminal
Town House
Justice Market
ABC Cinema
Provost Ross's House
Music Hall
St Mary of the Assumption Cathedral
Capitol Cinema
Christ's College
Bon Accord Swimming Pool
Odeon Cinema
Fonthill Maternity Home
Aberdeen College of Commerce
Nellfield Cemetery
School
UNION STREET
MARKET STREET
VICTORIA BRIDGE
SOUTH COLLEGE STREET
BON-ACCORD STREET
HOLBURN STREET
GREAT SOUTHERN ROAD
WHINHILL ROAD
FONTHILL ROAD
POLMUIR ROAD
RIVERSIDE DRIVE
ALBYN PLACE
FORFAR, DUNDEE
BRAEMAR
ALFORD
A92
A93
A944
A956
A9103

French V 80 seats Lunch £4.35—£4.95&alc Dinner fr£10.85&alc Wine £6.95 Last dinner 11pm

Credit cards 1 2 3 4 5

××***Pinocchio*** 58—60 Justice Mill Ln ☎(0224) 584599 Plan **12** *B4*

This city-centre restaurant has a trattoria-style atmosphere.

Italian 60 seats Last dinner 11pm

Credit cards 1 2 3 5

××**Trattoria Luigi's** 4 Bridge St ☎(0224) 590001 Plan **17** *D4*

Closed Sun

Italian V 80 seats Lunch £2.50—£5.50&alc Dinner £12—£15&alc Wine £7 Last dinner 11pm

Credit cards 1 2 3 4 5

×**Atlantis Sea Food** 145 Crown St ☎(0224) 591403 Plan **1** *D3*

A live lobster tank is a feature of this small seafood restaurant, which offers some expensive speciality dishes.

Closed Sun, Xmas & New Year

V 34 seats Lunch £20alc Dinner £20alc Wine £7 Last dinner 10pm 10P

Credit cards 1 2 3 5

×**Poldino's** 7 Little Belmont St ☎(0224) 647777 Plan **13** *D5*

A modern Italian restaurant in quiet back street near the city centre.

Closed Sun, Xmas Day & New Years Day

Italian V 80 seats Lunch £4.10—£4.70&alc Dinner £11alc Last dinner 10.45pm

Credit cards 1 2 3 5

×**Shish Mahal** 468 Union St ☎(0224) 643339 Plan **14** *B4*

This large, first floor Indian restaurant is remarkable for its small pool and fountain. Cheap lunch and supper menus are available.

Indian V 100 seats * Lunch £1.50—£4.50&alc Dinner £4.50—£9.95&alc Wine £6.95 Last dinner 11.30pm

Credit cards 1 2 3 5 V

Aberdeen — Aberdour

ABERDEEN AIRPORT

Grampian *Aberdeenshire*
Map **15** NJ81

★★★★ **Holiday Inn** Riverview Dr, Farburn, Dyce (Holiday Inns) ☎Aberdeen (0224) 770011 Telex no 739651

Standing close to the airport, this modern hotel has an attractive swimming pool and leisure area; the restaurant and bar feature an unusual ceiling design.

154 (68fb) in 10 bedrooms CTV in all bedrooms T sB £72—£73 dB £85—£90 (room only)

200P CFA (heated) sauna bath solarium gymnasium disco Fri & Sat live music & dancing Thu *xmas*

French S% Lunch £12.25 Tea £1.55 High Tea £5—£7 Dinner £12.25&alc Wine £6.25 Last dinner 10.30pm

Credit cards 1 2 3 4 5

★★★★ **Skean Dhu** Argyll Rd (adjacent to main entrance 1m N of A96) (Mount Charlotte) ☎(0224) 725252 Telex no 739239

Hotel with restaurant overlooking the enclosed courtyard which houses the swimming pool.

149 (48fb) CTV in all bedrooms ® T S% * sB fr£51 dB fr£59 (room only)

300P CFA (heated) Live music & dancing Thu-Sat

European V S% * Lunch fr£8.05&alc Tea £1.95 High Tea fr£1.50 Dinner fr£10&alc Wine £5.25 Last dinner 11pm

Credit cards 1 2 3 5 V

★★★ **Skean Dhu Dyce** Farburn Ter, Dyce (off A947) (Mount Charlotte) ☎Aberdeen (0224) 723101 Telex no 73473

A comfortable and modern hotel that is busy and popular.

Annexe: 220 CTV in all bedrooms ® T S% * sB&B fr£47.25 dB&B fr£52.50

300P CFA squash sauna bath solarium gymnasium Cabaret Sun mthly

French V S% * Lunch £3.25—£12&alc Tea 80p—£1.90 High Tea £3.25—£12 Dinner £9.50&alc Wine £5.25 Last dinner 10.45pm

Credit cards 1 2 3 5 V

ABERDOUR

Fife *Fife*
Map **11** NT18

★★*L* **Woodside** High St ☎(0383) 860328

The public areas of this beautifully renovated hotel feature woodwork from the Mauritania and the ornately decorated captain's cabin from HMS Orontes. Bedrooms are comfortable and the staff attentive.

21rm (16 5) (3fb) CTV in all bedrooms * sB&B £35 dB&B £45 ® T 30P Live music & dancing Sat

* Lunch £7.50&alc Tea £1.20 Dinner £10&alc Last dinner 9.45pm

Credit cards 1 2 3 5

★**Fairways** Manse St ☎(0383) 860478

Cosy hotel with an attractive restaurant.

10rm (2) (2fb) CTV in 3 bedrooms ® S% * sB&B £16 sB&B £22.50 dB&B £18—£29 dB&B £25—£35

CTV 12P

S% * Bar lunch £4.50—£5.50 Dinner £5.50—£7.50 Wine £4.50 Last dinner 9pm

Credit cards 1 2 3 V

××**La Toscana** Shore Rd ☎(0383) 860414

This cheery Italian restaurant offers light, delicate dishes prepared from good raw materials and fresh produce; it boasts a particularly fine selection of antipasti.

Closed 25 Dec & 1—2 Jan
Lunch not served Mon
Dinner not served Sun

Italian V 45 seats Lunch £5.35&alc Wine £5.95 Last dinner 9.30pm

Credit cards 1 3

ABERDOVEY
Gwynedd
Map **6** SN69

★★★ *L* **Plas Penhelig** (Inter Hotel) ☎ (065472) 676
Closed Jan & Feb
Edwardian holiday hotel, set high over Aberdovey with well tended gardens and delightful oak panelled central hall.
12rm(11🛁1🚿)(3fb) TV available in bedrooms T sB&B🛁🚿£25—£35.50 dB&B🛁🚿£38—£59 B
CTV 48P hard croquet & putting green
French V Lunch £5.75—£6.95 Tea £1.25—£1.50 Dinner fr£10.95&alc Wine £5.95 Last dinner 8.45pm
Credit cards [1] [2] [3] [5]

★★★ **Trefeddian** ☎ (065472) 213
Closed 2 Nov—29 Mar
An impressive detached hotel standing in own grounds, 1m from Aberdovey.
46🛁🚿(4fb) CTV in all bedrooms T sB&B🛁🚿£19.30—£24.30 dB&B🛁🚿£38.60—£48.60 B
Lift CTV 40P 18 (50p per day) (heated) (hard) solarium badminton pool table
English & French V Lunch £5.50 Tea £1.30 High Tea £4—£5.50 Dinner £9.25—£9.75 Wine £5.70 Last dinner 8.30pm
Credit card [1] Ⓥ

★★ *L* **Penhelig Arms** ☎ (065472) 215
Telex no 338751
Closed Xmas
Set between the hill and the sea, this small hotel provides very comfortable accommodation and good food.
11rm(4🛁7🚿) CTV in all bedrooms ® sB&B🛁🚿£16.50—£18.50 dB&B🛁🚿£33—£57 B
CTV 12P nc10yrs
V Bar lunch £2—£5 Tea £1.50—£3 Dinner £6.95—£9&alc Wine £5.50 Last dinner 9pm
Credit cards [1] [2] [3] [5]

★ **Harbour** 17 Glandovey Ter ☎ (065472) 250
Closed Oct-Feb
Victorian, family run holiday hotel in centre of resort.
6rm(1🛁4🚿)(2fb) ® sB&B£15 sB&B🛁🚿£15 dB&B£30 dB&B🛁🚿£30
CTV
V Lunch £5—£7.50&alc Tea 50p—£1.50 Dinner £5—£8.50&alc Wine £4.50 Last dinner 9pm
Credit cards [1] [3] Ⓥ

★ **Maybank** ☎ (065472) 500
Closed Nov & Feb
Small, friendly hotel overlooking beautiful harbour and providing good food.
5rm(1🛁4🚿)(2fb) TV available in bedrooms sB&Bfr£15 sB&B🛁🚿fr£17.50 dB&Bfr£29 dB&B🛁🚿fr£35 B
CTV
* Bar lunch 95p—£3.50 Dinner £9.50 Wine £5.50 Last dinner 9.30pm
Credit cards [3]

ABERFELDY
Tayside *Perthshire*
Map **14** NN84

★★ **Weem** Weem (1m NW B846) ☎ (0887) 20381
A friendly roadside inn, full of character and with an interesting history.
12rm(8🛁1🚿)(2fb) CTV in 5 bedrooms ® sB&B£13.95—£14.95 sB&B🛁🚿£14.95—£15.95 dB&B🛁🚿£30—£35
CTV 50P
V Lunch £2.75—£6.50 Tea £1.75—£2.25 High Tea £3.95—£4.75 Dinner £9.95—£13.95 Wine £5.95 Last dinner 9.30pm
Credit cards [3] [5] Ⓥ

Ailean Chraggan Weem (1m NW B846) (0887) 20346

Friendly little restaurant on the outskirts of town.

Closed 1-3 Jan

Scottish & French **V** 50 seats Lunch £5alc Dinner £12.50alc Wine £5.25 Last dinner 9pm 40P

ABERFOYLE

Central *Perthshire*
Map **11** NN50

★★★**Forest Hills** Kinlochard (3m W on B829) Kinlochard (08777) 277

Beautiful location within well landscaped grounds in the centre of a luxury development.

19rm(16)(2fb) CTV in all bedrooms ® **T** *sB&B £25—£30 dB&B £50—£60

CTV 150P & (heated) (hard) squash snooker sauna bath solarium gymnasium live music and dancing twice wkly *xmas*

Scottish, French & Italian * Lunch £4—£6 Dinner £10—£18 Wine £4.75 Last dinner 9pm

Credit cards 1 2 3 5

ABERGAVENNY

Gwent
Map **3** SO21

★★★**Angel** Cross St (Trusthouse Forte) (0873) 7121

Established town centre hotel which retains its charm and character, yet has comfortable, modern bedrooms and finally bars and restaurant.

29 (1fb) CTV in all bedrooms ® sB&B £46.50 dB&B £62.50

27P *xmas*

Last dinner 9.30pm

Credit cards 1 2 3 4 5

★★*B* **Llanwenarth Arms** Brecon Rd (0873) 810550

Perched on the bank of the River Usk, with spectacular views. The main building of this small hotel dates back to the sixteenth century. A complex of very comfortable bedrooms, most of them with river views, stands adjacent. There are two welcoming bars, and a modern restaurant.

Annexe: 18 CTV in all bedrooms ® **T** sB&B £35 dB&B £39

CTV 60P

International **V** Lunch £6.50alc Dinner £9alc Wine £4.75 Last dinner 10pm

Credit cards 1 2 3 5

ABERGELE

Clwyd
Map **6** SH97

★★**Kinmel Manor** St Georges Rd (0745) 822014

Detached Georgian hotel, with modern extension, set in its own grounds.

22rm(20 2)(3fb) CTV in all bedrooms ® **T** S% sB&B £28 dB&B £44

CTV 100P (heated) sauna bath solarium gymnasium *xmas*

English & French **V** Lunch £6.25&alc Tea 75p High Tea £1.75—£4.50 Dinner £9.75&alc Wine £5 Last dinner 10pm

Credit cards 1 2 3 4 5 V

ABERLADY

Lothian *East Lothian*
Map **12** NT47

★★**Greencraig House** (1m NE on A198) (08757) 301

8rm(5) CTV in all bedrooms ® sB&B £30—£35 sB&B £40—£45 dB&B £60—£70

20P CFA *xmas*

Scottish & French **V** Lunch fr £8.50 Tea fr £2.50 Dinner fr £14.50 Wine £5.95 Last dinner 9pm

Credit cards 1 3

★★**Kilspindle House** Main St (08757) 319

White-painted stone building with crow stepped gables and a recent extension to one side.

12rm(8 4)(1fb) ®

sB&B £18.50—£24 dB&B £34—£36

CTV 30P 3 live music and dancing Sat

V Bar lunch £1.20—£5 Tea fr £1.80 High Tea £4.50—£6 Dinner fr £8.30&alc Wine £5 Last dinner 9pm

Credit cards 1 3 V

ABERLOUR (Charlestown of Aberlour)

Grampian *Banffshire*
Map **15** NJ24

★★**Aberlour** High St (03405) 287

Friendly, homely hotel situated in the centre of this Speyside village.

19rm(14 1)(2fb) ®*sB&B £15 sB&B £16.25 dB&B £27.50

CTV 29P 4

V * Lunch £3.25—£6.95&alc Tea fr 35p High Tea £2.95—£6.25 Dinner £8.45&alc Wine £3.85 Last dinner 9pm

V

★***Lour*** The Square (03405) 224

Traditional stone Victorian hotel in the centre of this busy Speyside village.

9rm

CTV 6 billiards

Last dinner 8pm

ABERPORTH

Dyfed
Map **2** SN25

★★★**Hotel Penrallt** (0239) 810227

Closed 24 Dec—1 Jan

A comfortable country hotel with modern facilities and spacious bedrooms.

17rm(13 4)(3fb) CTV in all bedrooms ®* S% sB&B £28 dB&B £40

100P (heated) Hard

V Bar lunch fr £3 Tea fr £1.50 Dinner fr £9 Wine £3.70 Last dinner 9pm

Credit cards 1 2 3 5

★★**Highcliffe** (Exec Hotel) (0239) 810534

RS Nov—Mar

Small proprietor run hotel in an elevated position, 200 yards from two sandy beaches.

6rm(4⇌) Annexe:6⇌(3fb) TV in all bedrooms ® sB&B⇌£19—£21 dB&B⇌£34-£38 B
CTV 18P
English & French V Lunch £6.50 Tea £3.50 Dinner £8&alc Wine £4.70 Last dinner 9pm
Credit cards 1 2 3 V

★★ ***Morlan Motel*** (0239) 810611
Closed Nov—Feb
Small motel with self-catering units.
16⇌(8fb) CTV in all bedrooms ® B
12P 8
English & French V Last dinner 9pm
Credit cards 1 2 3 5

ABERSOCH
Gwynedd
Map 6 SH32

★★★ *HL* **Porth Tocyn** Bwlch Tocyn (075881) 2966
Closed Nov—wk before Etr RS Xmas & New Year
(Rosette awarded for dinner only).
Overlooking the sea, a cottagey, comfortable hotel with attractive rooms and pleasant grounds. At dinner there are some interesting English dishes using local produce, as well as home made bread, excellent soups and mouth watering desserts. The wine list is well chosen.
17⇌(1fb) CTV in all bedrooms T B
CTV P (heated) (hard)
xmas
Last dinner 9.30pm

★★★ ***Abersoch Harbour*** (Best Western) (075881) 2406
Closed 2 Nov—Feb
Prominent detached holiday hotel with small garden.
9rm(5⇌2)(2fb) 1 CTV in all bedrooms B
50P Live music & dancing Fri & Sat

French V Last dinner 9.30pm
Credit cards 1 2 3 4 5

★★★ **Riverside** (Exec Hotel) (075881) 2419
Closed Nov—Feb
Comfortable family holiday hotel, personally run and providing honest food.
12rm(7⇌3)(5fb) CTV in all bedrooms ® sB&B⇌£20—£25 dB&B⇌£40—50 B
28P (heated)
English Continental & Oriental V S% * Bar lunch £1.50—£5&alc Tea £1.50—£1.75 High Tea £3.50—£5 Dinner £12&alc Wine £5.50 Last dinner 9pm
Credit cards 1 3
See advertisement on page 64

★★ *B* **Deucoch** (Inter-Hotels) (075881) 2680
This pleasant, bright hotel overlooks Cardigan Bay; the bedrooms are well-appointed and food is good.
10rm(3⇌6)(2fb) CTV in all bedrooms ® sB&B£15.50—£30 dB&B⇌£31—£45 B
50P
Welsh English & French V Bar lunch 60p—£2.50 Tea 75p Dinner £9&alc Wine £3 Last dinner 8.30pm
Credit cards 1 2 3 5 V

★★ *H* **Neigwl** Lon Sarn Bach (075881) 2363
A small, personally run hotel close to shops and beaches.
7rm(3) Annexe:1⇌(1fb) sB&B£15—£17.50 sB&B⇌£17—£19.50 dB&B£30—£35 dB&B⇌£34—£39 B
CTV 30P *xmas*
S% Lunch £6.75 Tea £1—£2.50 Dinner £10 Wine £5.50 Last dinner 10pm
Credit cards 1 2 3 V

ABERYSTWYTH
Dyfed Map 6 SN58
★★★ **Conrah** Chancery, Ffosrhydygaled (0970) 617941 Telex no 35360 Closed 23—31 Dec
Appealing Georgian-style country mansion offers a peaceful retreat. The lounges are spacious, and the food of a commendable standard.
13rm(11⇌) Annexe:9rm(3⇌6)(1fb) CTV in all bedrooms ® T sB&B fr£31 sB&B⇌fr£34 dB&B⇌£47—£62 B
Lift 60P (heated) sauna bath croquet table tennis nc5yrs
International V Lunch £7.25—£8.75&alc Tea fr£1.50&alc Dinner fr£11.25&alc Wine £6 Last dinner 9.30pm
Credit cards 1 2 3 5
See advertisement on page 64

★★ ***Belle Vue Royal*** Marine Ter (0970) 617558
An impressive Victorian hotel on the promenade, offering friendly service from owners and local staff alike; recent upgrading of public rooms and bedrooms has not marred their traditional charm.
42rm(17⇌7)(6fb) CTV in 15 bedrooms ® B CTV 5P 8
V Last dinner 8.30pm
Credit cards 1 2 3 4 5
See advertisement on page 64

★★ **Cambrian** Alexandra Rd (0970) 612446 Closed Xmas Day
This small commercial hotel, mock Tudor in style, is opposite the railway station. Management is friendly, and the compact, modern bedrooms have been refurbished.
12rm(2⇌5)(3fb) CTV in all bedrooms ® S% sB&B£18 sB&B⇌£20 dB&B£34 dB&B⇌£38 B
V S% Lunch £4.75—£6.75&alc Tea fr75p Dinner £6.25—£8.25&alc Wine £5.25 Last dinner 9.30pm
Credit card 1 V

★★ *B* **Court Royale** Eastgate (0970) 611722
Positioned in the heart of the town yet close to the beach, this small, friendly hotel has →

recently been totally refurbished and offers a high standard of bedroom accommodation.

10rm(6🛁4🚿)(3fb) CTV in all bedrooms ® T✱sB&B🛁🚿£16—£21 dB&B🛁🚿£25—£33.50 B

2🚗 xmas

Mainly Grills V Lunch £4.75—£8.95 Tea £1.20 Dinner £4.90—£10&alc Last dinner 10pm

Credit cards 1 2 3

★★**Groves** 42—46 North Pde (Minotels) ☎(0970) 617623

Closed 24 Dec—2 Jan

A comfortable, friendly hotel set in the heart of the town and close to beaches. Owned and run by a conscientious family, it promotes commendable home cooking with imaginative menus. The bright, cosy bedrooms offer modern facilities and appointments.

12rm(5🛁7🚿) CTV in all bedrooms ® sB&B🛁🚿£21.50 dB&B🛁🚿£34 B

8P nc3yrs

Welsh English & French V Bar lunch fr£1 Dinner fr£7.25&alc Wine £4.50 Last dinner 8.30pm

Credit cards 1 2 3 5 Ⓥ

★★**Seabank** Victoria Ter ☎(0970) 617617

The small, friendly hotel is situated at the northern end of Cardigan Bay.

22rm(12🛁4🚿)(4fb) CTV in all bedrooms ® sB&B£15.50—£19 sB&B🛁🚿£19—£25 dB&B£25—£28 dB&B🛁🚿£30—£33 B

Lift

French V S% Lunch £5—£7 Tea £1—£2.50 High Tea £1.50—£3 Dinner £7—£11.50 Wine £4.80 Last dinner 8pm

Credit cards 1 2 3 5

★**Four Seasons** 50—54 Portland St ☎(0970) 612120

Closed 25 Dec—2 Jan

Small personally run hotel, with friendly service and quality food standards.

15rm(7🛁)(1fb) CTV in bedrooms ® sB&B£17.50—£23.50 sB&B🛁£22—£32 dB&B£29 dB&B🛁£37.50 B

Aberystwyth — Achnasheen

CTV 10P

English & Continental Bar lunch £1.50—£6.50 Tea £85p—£3 Dinner £8—£11 Last dinner 8.30pm

Credit cards 1 3

ABINGDON

Oxfordshire
Map **4** SU49

★★*B* **Upper Reaches** Thames St (Trusthouse Forte) ☎(0235) 22311

Converted abbey cornmill with open plan public rooms and well-equipped bedrooms.

26🛁 CTV in all bedrooms ® sB&B🛁£56 dB&B🛁£73.50 B

90P ✿ xmas

Last dinner 10pm

Credit cards 1 2 3 4 5

○ **Abingdon Lodge** Marcham Rd ☎(0235) 35333 64🛁🚿

Due to have opened July 1986.

ABOYNE

Grampian *Aberdeenshire*
Map **15** NO59

★★***Bainacoll House*** ☎(0339) 2252 Telex no 739925

Large neat hotel standing in its own grounds on the banks of the River Dee, popular with fishermen.

11rm(3🛁2🚿) ®

CTV 60P 2🚗 ✿

V Last dinner 8.30pm

Credit cards 2 3 5

★★*HB* **Birse Lodge** ☎(0339) 2253

Closed mid Oct—mid Mar

Personally run hotel set in its own grounds, popular with shooting parties and anglers.

12rm(11🛁1🚿) Annexe: 4🛁 sB&B🛁🚿£22—£25 dB&B🛁🚿£44—£50

CTV 30P ✿ putting ♿

Bar lunch fr£1.50 Tea £1.30—£2 Dinner £12 Wine £5 Last dinner 8pm

Credit cards 2 5

★★**Huntley Arms** (Consort) ☎(0339) 2101 Telex no 57515

Friendly, traditional hotel close to the field where the Aboyne Games are played.

30rm(19🛁5🚿)(4fb) ⚡ in two bedrooms ® T sB&B£19—£23 sB&B🛁🚿£23—£27 dB&B£34—£42 dB&B🛁🚿£38—£46 Continental breakfast B

☾ CTV 200P 4🚗(charged) ✿ snooker sauna bath solarium gymnasium xmas

V ⚡ Lunch £7.50—£9.50&alc Tea £4.50—£5.50 Dinner fr£12.50&alc Wine £4.50 Last dinner 9.30pm

Credit cards 1 2 3 5 Ⓥ

ABRIDGE

Essex
Map **5** TQ49

✕✕✕***Roding*** Market Pl ☎ Theydon Bois (037881) 3030

Good quality cooking and professional service are found in this 15th-century beamed restaurant.

Closed Mon & 26 Dec—early Jan

Lunch not served Sat Dinner not served Sun

English & French V 55 seats Last dinner 10pm 20P

Credit cards 1 2 3 5

ACHNASHEEN

Highland *Ross & Cromarty*
Map **14** NH15

★★*HL* **Ledgowan Lodge** (Best Western) ☎(044 588) 252

Closed Jan—16 Apr & 19 Oct—Dec

Comfortable family run hotel with a reputation for friendly atmosphere.

17rm(9🛁)(4fb) ®✱sB&B£20—£22 sB&B🛁£25—£29 dB&B£25—£39 dB&B🛁£40—£56 B

CTV 25P ✿

V ✱Lunch £5—£7.50&alc Tea 80p—£3&alc High Tea £4—£6&alc Dinner £12—£15 Wine £4.50 Last dinner 9pm

Credit cards 1 2 3 4 5 Ⓥ

ADLINGTON
Lancashire
Map **7** SD61

★**Gladmar** Railway Rd ☎ (0257) 480398

Closed Xmas Day & New Years Day

A very pleasant, small, family-run hotel standing in its own grounds; the bedrooms are well furnished and comfortable.

13rm(10🚿)(1fb) CTV in 11 bedrooms ® ✱sB&B£23 sB&B🚿£26 dB&B🚿£34 B

CTV 24P ✽

V ✱Lunch fr£3.50 Tea fr£3 Dinner fr£8.50 Wine £4.60 Last dinner 8.30pm

Credit cards 1 3

AIRDRIE
Strathclyde *Lanarkshire*
Map **11** NS76

★★**Tudor** Alexander St (Alloa Brewery) ☎ (02364) 63295

Closed 1 Jan

White painted hotel close to town centre with extensive car parking.

21rm(10🛁1🚿) CTV in all bedrooms ® sB&B£22 sB&B🛁🚿£26 dB&B£30 dB&B🛁🚿£38

☾ 50P

V Lunch £6.35—£8.50&alc Tea 75p Dinner £6.35—£8.50&alc Wine £4.45 Last dinner 9.30pm

Credit cards 1 2 3 5

✕✕**Postillion** 8—10 Anderson St ☎ (02364) 67525

Attractive restaurant housed in Staging Post Hotel, located in town centre.

Closed 1—2 Jan

Lunch not served Sat

European 68 seats Lunch fr£3.95&alc Dinner fr£5.90&alc Last dinner 10pm

Credit cards 1 2 3 5

ALCESTER
Warwickshire
Map **4** SP05

★★**Broom Hall Inn** Broom ☎ Bidford-on-Avon (0789) 773757

RS Xmas

Set in rural location, this comfortable, family-run inn dates back to the sixteenth century. It offers freshly-prepared food in both the bar and restaurant.

6rm(2🛁1🚿)(2fb) TV in 2 bedrooms CTV in 4 bedrooms sB&Bfr£15.50 sB&B🛁🚿fr£18.50 dB&Bfr£28 dB&B🛁🚿fr£31.50

80P

English & French V Bar Lunch £4.50alc Tea 80palc Dinner £10alc Wine £4.60 Last dinner 9.30pm

Credit cards 1 2 3 5

★★**Cherrytrees** Stratford Road ☎ (0789) 762505

RS 24—27 Dec

Modern motel with cedar wood chalets, popular restaurant and conference facilities.

Annexe: 22rm(18🛁4🚿)(2fb) CTV in all bedrooms ®T✱sB&B🛁🚿fr£23 dB&B🛁🚿fr£33 B

50P ✽ Live music and dancing Sat Oct-Mar

V ✱Lunch fr£4.30 Tea 55p-£2.10 High Tea fr£3.75 Dinner fr£7&alc Wine £4.80 Last dinner 9.30pm

Credit cards 1 2 3

✕✕**Rossini** 50 Birmingham Rd ☎ (0789) 762764

Italian cuisine predominates in this converted cottage on the outskirts of Alcester. At lunchtime a value-for-money table d'hôte menu is available, whilst a more extensive à la carte selection is offered in the evening.

Closed Sun & 3 wks mid summer

English & Continental 45 seats ✱Lunch £7&alc Dinner £10—£12alc Wine £5.80 Last dinner 10.30pm 20P

Credit cards 1 2 3 5

ALCONBURY
Cambridgeshire
Map **5** TL17

★★**Alconbury Hill** Alconbury Weston (1½m N on A1) ☎ Huntingdon (0480) 890807

6 miles from Huntingdon, the hotel caters for both businessman and tourist. Sports complex adjacent.

24🚿(2fb) CTV in all bedrooms ®T sB&B🚿£30 dB&B🚿£42.50 B

80P ✽ squash billiards sauna bath solarium

V Bar lunch £1.50—£5.50&alc Tea 75p Dinner £1.50—£5.50&alc Wine £3.95 Last dinner 9.45pm

Credit cards 1 2 3 V

ALDBOROUGH
Norfolk
Map **9** TG13

✕✕**Old Red Lion** ☎ Cromer (0263) 761451

This genuine small restaurant in the heart of a quiet Norfolk village offers freshly-prepared food in friendly surroundings.

Closed Mon

Dinner not served Sun

English & French V 30 seats Lunch £8.40&alc Dinner £8.75—£9.20&alc Wine £5.25 Last dinner 9.45pm 12P

Credit cards 1 3

ALDBOURNE
Wiltshire
Map **4** SU27

✕✕**Raffles** The Green ☎ Marlborough (0672) 40700

Closed Sun, 17—31 August & 25—30 Dec

Lunch not served Mon & Sat

English & French V 36 seats Lunch £12.50&alc Dinner £12.50 Wine £4.80 Last dinner 11pm Live music Fri

Credit cards 1 2 3 5

ALDEBURGH
Suffolk
Map **5** TM45

★★★*H* **Brudenell** The Parade (Trusthouse Forte) ☎ (072885) 2071

Family hotel commanding good views of the sea.

47🛁(3fb) CTV in all bedrooms ® sB&B🛁£43.50 dB&B£62.50 B

Lift ☾ 14P 6 *xmas*

Last dinner 9pm

Credit cards 1 2 3 4 5

★★★**Wentworth** Sea Front (Consort) ☎ (072 885) 2312

Closed 27 Dec—14 Jan

33rm(19⇌4⋒) CTV in all bedrooms **T** (in 3 bedrooms) sB&B£22.25—£25.50 sB&B⇌⋒£26.50—£31.25 B&B£40.25—£50 dB&B⇌⋒£52—£60 **B**

16P *xmas*

English & French. Lunch £7—£8.50&alc Tea 85p Dinner £9.75—£10.50&alc Wine £4.75 Last dinner 9pm

Credit cards 2 5

★★★**White Lion** Market Cross Pl ☎ (072 885) 2720

37rm(29⇌2⋒)(1fb) 1 CTV in all bedrooms ® ✱ sB&B£19—£23.50 sB&B⇌⋒£21.50—£28 dB&B£32—£40 dB&B⇌⋒£37—£50

Lift ☾ 15P *xmas*

English & French **V** Lunch £4.95—£6 Tea fr60p Dinner £6—£8.25&alc Wine £4.50 Last dinner 9pm

Credit cards 1 2 3 5 Ⓥ

★★**Uplands** Victoria Rd ☎ (072 885) 2420

Two storey period house with its own grounds, on main approach road.

12rm Annexe: 8rm(7⇌1⋒)(3fb) CTV in 16 bedrooms TV in 4 bedrooms ® sB&B£20—£30 sB&B⇌⋒£30 dB&B£37—£39 dB&B⇌⋒£41 **B**

CTV 22P *xmas*

V Lunch £4—£8&alc Tea fr£1.50 High Tea fr£3.50 Dinner fr£7.50&alc Wine £4.50 Last dinner 8.45

Credit cards 1 2 3 5 Ⓥ

ALDERLEY EDGE

Cheshire

Map **7** SJ87

★★★**De Trafford Arms** London Rd (GW Hotels) ☎ (0625) 583881 Telex no 629462

Commercial hotel with modern bedrooms on the southern approach to the village.

37⇌⋒(2fb) in 5 bedrooms CTV in all bedrooms ® **T** S% ✱ sB&B⇌⋒fr£44 dB&B⇌⋒fr£56 **B**

Lift ☾ 60P

International **V** S% Bar lunch fr£3 Tea fr50p Dinner fr£8.50&alc Wine £5.50 Last dinner 9.30pm

Credit cards 1 2 3 5

✕**Octobers** 47 London Rd ☎ (0625) 583942

Friendly, bistro-style restaurant with extensive blackboard menus featuring many French dishes.

Closed Sun

Lunch not served

V 66 seats Dinner £8.25&alc Wine £5.50 Last dinner 10pm 8P

Credit cards 1 3

ALDERMINSTER

Warwickshire

Map **4** SP24

★★★★ *HB* **Ettington Park** ☎ Stratford-upon-Avon (0789) 740740 Telex no 311825

Superbly refurbished Victorian Gothic mansion, offering luxurious accommodation and Michael Quinn's excellent cooking.

49⇌(5fb) 1 CTV in all bedrooms **T** sB⇌£66 dB⇌£100 (room only) **B**

Lift ☾ 90P heated (hard) snooker sauna bath solarium croquet nc 7 yrs *xmas*

V Lunch £16.50&alc Tea £2alc High Tea £7alc Dinner £23.50&alc Wine £7.50 Last dinner 10pm

Credit cards 1 2 3 5 Ⓥ

ALDERSHOT

Hampshire

Map **4** SU84

✕***Johnnie Gurkhas*** 186 Victoria Rd ☎ (0252) 28773

Popular basement restaurant producing some of the best curries in the area. The kitchen is personally supervised by Mrs Meera Karki, and tandoori specialities and Nepalese dishes are recommended. Service and atmosphere are attentive and relaxing.

Closed Xmas

Nepalese **V** 70 seats Last dinner 11.45pm

Credit cards 1 2 3 5

ALFORD

Lincolnshire

Map **9** TF47

★**White Horse** West St ☎ (05212) 2218

A typical Lincolnshire village inn dating back to the fifteenth century, there is a lively bar and modest but well-equipped bedrooms.

10rm(8⇌)(1fb) S% sB&B£16 sB&B⇌£19 dB&B£20 dB&B⇌£25 **B**

CTV 10P 3

English & French S% ✱ Lunch £3.50alc Tea £2alc Dinner £10alc Wine £4.50 Last dinner 10.30pm

Credit cards 1 3 Ⓥ

ALFRISTON

East Sussex

Map **5** TQ50

★★★ *L* **Deans Place** ☎ (0323) 870248

Closed end Dec—mid Feb

A skilfully restored and modernised Tudor manor house standing in seven acres of grounds, the hotel combines modern and well-equipped bedrooms with tastefully-furnished, extensive lounges and facilities for leisure activities.

43⇌(4fb) 1 CTV available in bedrooms ® **T** sB&B⇌£30—£40 dB&B⇌£60—£70 **B**

CTV 100P (heated) (hard) croquet table tennis *xmas*

Lunch £5.50—£7.50&alc Tea £1—£2 High Tea £3.50—£3.75 Dinner £9.50—£10.10&alc Wine £4.50 Last dinner 8.30pm

Credit cards 1 2 3

★★★**Star** (Trusthouse Forte) ☎ (0323) 870495

13th-century inn with comfortable lounges and modernised bedrooms.

32➡ CTV in all bedrooms ® sB&B➡£47.50 dB&B➡£68.50 ⊟

36P *xmas*

🍷 ☕ Last dinner 9pm

Credit cards 1 2 3 4 5

✕**Moonraker's** High St ☎ (0323) 870472

This delightful small restaurant, with oak beams, inglenook and open log fire, dates from the sixteenth century. The husband and wife team who run it offer home-made dishes and friendly service, while the extensive wine list is reasonably priced.

Closed Sun, Mon & 13 Jan—13 Feb Lunch not served

🍽 French **V** 32 seats Dinner £12.90 Wine £5.80 Last dinner 9.15pm

ALNMOUTH
Northumberland
Map **12** NU21

★★**Saddle** 24/25 Northumberland St ☎ (0665) 830476

Closed 24—27 Dec RS Sun Mar—Oct

Cosy village hotel whose proprietors take great interest in dining room and bar menus.

9rm(3➡6🚿)(1fb) CTV in all bedrooms ® sB&B➡🚿£17.50—£20 dB&B➡🚿£30—£35 ⊟

2P

🍽 International **V** 🍷 ☕ Bar lunch £4—£7 Tea £2.50—£4 Dinner £7.50—£10&alc Wine £4.50 Last dinner 9pm

Credit cards 1 3 Ⓥ

ALNWICK
Northumberland
Map **12** NU11

★★★**White Swan** Bondgate Within (Swallow) ☎ (0665) 602109 Telex no 53168

Old hotel with modern amenities.

41rm➡🚿(2fb) CTV in all bedrooms ® S% sB&B➡🚿£34.50—£38 dB&B➡🚿£52.50-£57.50 ⊟

☾ 30P ✽ *xmas*

🍽 English & French **V** 🍷 ☕ S% Lunch £5.60—£6.25 Tea 60—70p High Tea £1.50—£2.25 Dinner £9.60—£10.60&alc Wine £6 Last dinner 9pm

Credit cards 1 2 3 4 5

★★**Hotspur** Bondgate Without ☎ (0665) 602924

Closed Xmas day

Historic coaching inn with good comfortable restaurant.

28rm(17➡1🚿)(3fb) CTV in all bedrooms ® **T** sB&B£20 sB&B➡🚿£25 dB&B£36 dB&B➡🚿£43 ⊟

CTV 20P

V 🍷 ☕ Lunch £4alc Tea £1.75alc High Tea £3.50alc Dinner £8.50alc Wine £4.20 Last dinner 9pm

Credit cards 1 3

ALSAGER
Cheshire
Map **7** SJ75

★★***Manor House*** Audley Rd ☎ (09363) 78013

An above-standard restaurant and fine level of comfort are the hall-marks of this hotel, a converted 300-year-old house with natural beams.

8🚿 CTV in all bedrooms **T** ⊟

☾ 120P ✽

🍽 French **V** 🍷 ☕ Last dinner 9.30pm

Credit cards 1 2 3 5

ALSTON
Cumbria
Map **12** NY74

★★**Lovelady Shield Country House**
(see red star box opposite page)

★★**Lowbyer Manor** Hexham Rd ☎ (0498) 81230

RS Nov—Mar
Closed New Year

Converted 18th-century manor house with courtyard, and a cellar restaurant.

8rm(3➡5🚿) Annexe: 4➡ ® sB&B➡🚿£24 dB&B➡🚿£35 ⊟

CTV 14P ✽ *xmas*

V 🍷 ☕ Lunch £3.50alc Tea £1alc Dinner £9alc Wine £5

Ⓥ

★***Hillcrest*** ☎ (0498) 81251

A small, friendly hotel under the personal supervision of the resident proprietors.

11rm(2fb) ⊟

CTV 20P 3🏠 ✽ *xmas*

🍷 ☕ Last dinner 8pm

★***Victoria*** Front St ☎ (0498) 81269

A family run hotel in the market place with a friendly and informal atmosphere.

6rm(2fb) CTV in 2 bedrooms

CTV sauna bath solarium gymnasium

🍽 Mainly grills **V** 🍷 ☕ Last dinner 9.30pm

Credit cards 1 2 3 5

ALTHORPE
Humberside
Map **8** SE81

★★*B* **Lansdowne House** ☎ Scunthorpe (0724) 783369

Closed Sun

This detached Victorian building of some style and character stands in its own well laid out grounds on the edge of the village. Personally run, it provides very comfortable, well equipped bedrooms of some style and good taste. The smart, well-appointed restaurant has an adjoining lounge bar of restrained elegance.

6➡ CTV in all bedrooms ® **T** S% ✱ sB&B➡🚿£35 dB&B➡🚿£45 ⊟

60P 4🏠 ✽

🍽 English & French **V** Dinner £11.99alc Wine £5.50 Last dinner 8.30pm

Credit cards 1 2 3 5

★★

★★ LOVELADY SHIELD COUNTRY HOUSE, ALSTON

(0498) 81203

Closed mid Dec—mid Mar

Built in 1830, this is a nicely proportioned Georgian-style house set in 2½ acres of gardens by the River Nent with a tennis court and croquet lawn. It is idyllically situated in the high Pennines, and owned by Mr and Mrs Rosier who provide the warm hospitality that lifts this hotel out of the common run. They and their few staff seem to find nothing too much trouble for their guests and, on occasions, a house party atmosphere can prevail. Pleasing bedrooms are comfortable and well appointed with appropriate decoration; they are provided with hair-driers. Downstairs there is the reception/library and another larger sitting-room opposite with sumptuous chairs and traditional decor. There is also a cocktail bar, while the dining room is large with decent table appointments, again in traditional style. Good value dinners of five courses are served and the cooking could be best described as country house with French influence — Mrs

Rosier is French! Good ingredients are used and the cooking is enjoyable. The wine list is also reasonably priced. This is not one of the grander Red Star hotels, but its atmosphere is beguiling and our members have praised it highly for its delightful qualities, as well as its good value for money.

12rm(8⇌4⋔)(1fb) CTV in all bedrooms sB&B⇌⋔£22—£24 dB&B⇌⋔£44—£48 B

20P ✿ (hard)

English & French Lunch £9alc Tea £1alc Dinner fr£12 Wine £5 Last dinner 8.30pm

Credit cards 2 5 V

ALTON
Hampshire
Map **4** SU73

★★★**Swan** High St (Anchor) (0420) 83777

Attractive 16th-century former coaching inn, historically associated with the Civil War battle.

38rm(33⇌5⋔) 1 in 6 bedrooms CTV in all bedrooms ®T sB&B⇌⋔£21—£43 dB&B⇌⋔£42—£54 B

☾50P CFA

V Lunch £7—£12&alc Tea 50p Dinner £7—£12&alc Wine £6 Last dinner 9.30pm

Credit cards 1 2 3 5 V

★★***Grange*** 17 London Rd, Holybourne (0420) 86565

RS Xmas & New Year

Small hotel with well equipped bedrooms, good English home-cooking, and friendly service and atmosphere.

9rm(6⇌3⋔) Annexe: 4rm(2⇌2⋔)(1fb) CTV in 13 bedrooms ®T B

40P ✿

Last dinner 9pm

Credit cards 1 2 3 5

ALTON
Staffordshire
Map **7** SK04

★★**Bulls Head Inn** High St Oakmoor (0538) 702307

Situated in the village centre, close to the Alton Towers, the small eighteenth-century inn provides a friendly, informal atmosphere and well equipped accommodation.

6rm(3⋔)(2fb) CTV in all bedrooms ® sB&B⋔£20—£30 dB&B⋔£30

CTV 15P

V Lunch £5alc Tea £1.20alc Dinner 5.95&alc Wine £4.40 Last dinner 10pm

Credit card 3

XX ***Wild Duck Inn*** New Rd Oakamoor (0538) 702218

Large, stone inn on village outskirts.

Closed Mon Dinner not served Sun

English French & Italian 50 seats Last dinner 9pm 100P

ALTRINCHAM
Gt. Manchester
Map **7** SJ78

★★★**Ashley** Ashley Rd, Hale (De Vere) 061-928 3794 Telex no 669406

Closed Boxing Day

Modern hotel above shopping parade.

49⇌⋔ CTV in all bedrooms ®T S% sB&B⇌⋔£46—£50 dB&B⇌⋔£55—£60 B

Lift ☾ CTV 100P CFA bowling green

English & French V S% Lunch £6.50—£8&alc Tea 80p—£1 Dinner £8—£10&alc Wine £6 Last dinner 9.30pm

Credit cards 1 2 3 5

★★★ H **Bowdon** Langham Rd, Bowdon 061-928 7121 Telex no 668208

Closed Boxing day

A very capably-run and friendly hotel, quietly situated despite its proximity to Manchester Airport and several motorways.

41rm(38⇌)(1fb) CTV in all bedrooms T sB&B⇌£24—£40 dB&B⇌£38—£52 B

☾ CTV 150P CFA Live music and dancing Sat

English & French V S% Lunch £8—£9&alc Tea 80p—£1.75 Dinner £8—£9&alc Wine £5.25 Last dinner 10pm

Credit cards 1 2 3 5 V

★★★**Cresta Court** Church St (Best Western) ☎ 061-928 8017 Telex no 667242

Modern hotel with choice of restaurants.

139🛁🚿(2fb) CTV in all bedrooms ®T S% sB&B🛁🚿£21.75—£38 dB&B🛁🚿£36—£42.50 B

Lift ☾ ## 250P CFA

V ♀ ☕ Lunch £7alc Tea 55palc Dinner £8.50alc Last dinner 11pm

Credit cards [1] [2] [3] [5]

★★★**Swan** Bucklow Hill (De Vere) ☎ Bucklow Hill (0565) 830295 (for full entry see Bucklow Hill)

★★★**Woodland Park** Wellington Rd, Timperley ☎ 061-928 8631

This well-furnished, mainly commercial hotel stands in a residential area. Good food is served in a delightful dining room.

20rm(11🛁9🚿)(4fb) CTV in all bedrooms ®T ✗ ✱ sB&B🛁🚿£35 dB&B🛁🚿£48 B

☾ CTV 140P ♔

🍷 International ♀ ☕ ✱ Lunch £6.50&alc Dinner £8.95&alc Wine £5.95 Last dinner 10pm

Credit cards [1] [3]

★★**George & Dragon** Manchester Rd (GW Hotels) ☎ 061-928 9933

Large black and white hotel with modern bedrooms and newly furnished restaurant.

47rm(38🛁9🚿)(2fb) CTV in all bedrooms ®T S% sB&B🛁🚿£22—£42 dB&B🛁🚿£44—£54 B

Lift ☾ 80P

🍷 English & Continental **V** ♀ ☕ S% Lunch £7—£8 Tea £1-£1.50 Dinner £7—£10&alc Wine £5.80 Last dinner 9.45pm

Credit cards [1] [2] [3] [5]

★★**Grove Park** Park Rd, Bowdon ☎ 061-928 6191

This friendly hotel stands in a suburban setting within easy reach of motorways and airport. Its steak/kebab restaurant is renowned for its quality.

13rm(10🛁1🚿) CTV in all bedrooms ®T ✗ sB&B£15 sB&B🛁🚿£29 dB&B🛁🚿£36 B

☾ 23P

Altrincham — Alveston

🍷 International **V** Lunch £4.50—£8&alc Dinner £8.50&alc Wine £4.25 Last dinner 11.30pm

Credit cards [1] [3]

★★**Pelican Inn Motel** Manchester Rd (GW Hotels) ☎ 061-962 7414 Telex no 629462

Black and white inn with modern motel block added.

50🚿(4fb) CTV in all bedrooms ®T S% sB&B🚿£39 dB&B🚿£49 B

☾ 150P

♀ ☕ S% Bar Lunch £5.25 Tea £2.50 Dinner £8.50 Wine £5 Last dinner 9pm

Credit cards [1] [2] [3] [5]

XXX ***Le Bon Vivéur*** Wood Ln, Timperley (2m E A560) ☎ 061-904 0266

This attractive and well appointed restaurant adjoins the popular Hare and Hounds Hotel and offers an interesting choice of dishes ranging from frogs' legs cooked with Pernod and herbs to trout and almonds, all served by a smart and willing staff.

Closed Public Hols (except Xmas day lunch) Lunch not served Sat

🍷 French **V** 60 seats Last dinner 9.30pm 200P

Credit cards [1] [2] [3] [5]

XXX **Claudes** 9-11 The Old Market Pl ☎ 061-941 6807

Decorated in soft, pastel shades of pink and grey, the smart, comfortable restaurant offers a delectable range of French dishes.

Closed Mon
Lunch not served Sat
Dinner not served Sun

🍷 French **V** 85 seats Lunch fr£6.50&alc Dinner fr£10.50 Wine £6.20 Last dinner 9.30pm P

Credit cards [1] [2] [3] [4] [5]

XX ***Evergreen*** 169-171 Ashley Rd, Hale ☎ 061-928 1222

Set in the centre of Hale Village, this Cantonese Restaurant is decorated in attractive oriental style with screens and tree branches helping to create an authentic atmosphere.

Lunch not served

🍷 Cantonese **V** 76 seats Last dinner 10.15pm

Credit cards [1] [3]

XX **Hilal** 351 Stockport Rd, Timperley (2m E A560) ☎ 061-980 4090

An East Indian style restaurant standing in a row of modern shops, a good range of curries is offered, each of which is given a strength rating on the menu. The predominantly gold and brown decor is enhanced by attractive Indian pictures.

Closed 25 & 26 Dec

🍷 Indian **V** 70 seats Lunch £3.50—£4.50&alc Dinner £8.50—£9.50&alc Wine £4.40 Last dinner 11.30pm 30P

Credit cards [1] [3]

ALVELEY

Shropshire
Map **7** SO78

XX **Mill** Birds Green ☎ Quatt (0746) 780437

Closed Mon Dinner not served Sun

🍷 Italian 110 seats Lunch fr£5&alc Dinner fr£5&alc Wine £5.50 Last dinner 10.30pm 100P Live music Mons fortnightly

Credit cards [1] [2] [3] [5] Ⓥ

ALVESTON

Avon
Map **3** ST68

★★★*L* **Alveston House** ☎ Thornbury (0454) 415050 Telex no 449212

Small, comfortable Georgian house, which exudes warmth and hospitality. Major upgrading and refurbishment have been undertaken recently, resulting in an attractive Quincy's restaurant and a quite unique lounge/conservatory complex. Cooking standards are very commendable and the bedrooms are compact and well-equipped.

30⇌ CTV in all bedrooms ®T
*sB&B⇌fr£42.50 dB&B⇌fr£52.50 B
75P CFA
French V Lunch fr£11.75&alc Tea fr£1.50 Dinner fr£11.75&alc Wine £5.25 Last dinner 9.30pm
Credit cards 1 3 V

See advertisement under Bristol

★★★**Post House** Thornbury Rd (Trusthouse Forte) ☎ Thornbury (0454) 412521 Telex no 444753

Popular businessman's hotel, convenient for M4/M5, this former Tudor inn has been extended and modernised.

75⇌(21fb) CTV in all bedrooms ®
sB&B⇌£56.50 dB&B⇌£71.50 B
100P CFA (heated) *xmas*
Last dinner 10.15pm
Credit cards 1 2 3 4 5

ALWALTON
Cambridgeshire
Map **4** TL19

○ **Little Chef Lodge** A1 southbound ☎ Peterborough (0733) 231109 32⇌
Due to have opened October 1986

AMBERGATE
Derbyshire
Map **8** SK35

★**Hurt Arms** ☎ (077385) 2006

At Junction A6/A610, this small, well-maintained inn offers comfortable accommodation and informal service.

6rm(5fb) S% sB&B£14 dB&B£28
CTV 100P
S% Lunch fr£5 Wine £5 Last dinner 9pm

AMBERLEY
Gloucestershire
Map **3** SO80

★★**Amberley Inn** (Best Western) ☎ (045387) 2565

A warm and comfortable inn offering a superb view and situation.

10rm(9⇌) Annexe:4⇌(1fb) CTV in all bedrooms ®S% sB&B⇌£34—£42 dB&B⇌£42—£48 B
18P *xmas*
V S% Lunch £6—£9&alc Tea 70p Dinner £10.25—£10.75&alc Wine £5.20 Last dinner 9.30pm
Credit cards 1 2 3 V

AMBERLEY
West Sussex
Map **4** TQ01

✕'**Quins** Houghton Bridge (Close to Amberley Station 1m S of village) ☎ Bury (079881) 790
Closed Mon & Tue
Dinner not served Sun
English & Swiss V 40 seats *Lunch fr£7.50&alc Dinner £11alc Wine £5 Last dinner 9.30pm 20P nc 5yrs
Credit cards 1 2 3 4 5

AMBLESIDE
Cumbria
Map **7** NY30
See also **Elterwater** and **Langdale, Great**

★★★*HBL* **Rothay Manor**
Rothay Br ☎ (0966) 33605
Closed 4 Jan—14 Feb

Surrounded by fine mountain scenery, this family run hotel's Regency elegance, coupled with the caring and considerate service ensures an atmosphere of relaxation and comfort difficult to surpass. Dinner in the candle-lit dining room with an extensive wine list completes a most enjoyable experience.

15⇌ Annexe:3⇌(6fb) CTV in all bedrooms T sB&B⇌£47—£48 dB&B⇌£65—£77 B
30P *xmas*
English & French V Bar lunch £3.50—£6 Tea fr£3 Dinner fr£17.50 Wine £5 Last dinner 9pm
Credit cards 1 2 3 5 V

★★★**Regent** Waterhead (Consort) (1m S A591) ☎ (0966) 32254

Comfortable family owned hotel incorporating Mediterranean style wine bar.

21rm(18⇌3)(12fb)3 CTV in all bedrooms ®T S% sB&B⇌£28—£35 dB&B⇌£50—£60 B
25P (heated) *xmas*
English, French & Italian V S% Lunch £5.95—£7.95 Tea 90p—£1.75 Dinner £12—£16.50&alc Wine £4.95 Last dinner 9.15pm
Credit cards 1 3 V

See advertisement on page 72

★★★**Waterhead** Lake Rd (Best Western) ☎ (0966) 32566 Telex no 65273

Occupies a fine position overlooking the lake and mountains at Waterhead Bay.

30rm(14⇌16)(6fb) CTV in all bedrooms ®T S% sB&B⇌£24—£31 dB&B⇌£48—£62 B
50P Live music and dancing Sat (Oct—Mar) *xmas*
English & French V S% Lunch £2.95—£8.50 Tea 70p—£2 High Tea £2.15—£4.20 Dinner £10.50—£11&alc Wine £5.50 Last dinner 8.30pm
Credit cards 1 2 3 5 V

★★**Borrans Park** Borrans Rd ☎ (0966) 33454

Peacefully situated, this elegantly charming Georgian house offers comfort and a warm welcome. Good home cooking is accompanied by a fine wine list.

13rm(8⇌5)(2fb)6 CTV in all bedrooms ® *sB&B⇌£14.50—£17.50 dB&B⇌£29—£35 B
20P
*Dinner fr£8.50 Wine £4.50

★★**Elder Grove** Lake Rd (on A591 ½m S) ☎ (0966) 32504
Closed Nov—Feb

Resident proprietors provide warm, friendly atmosphere in this comfortable hotel. →

A

3→ Annexe:5rm(1⋔)(3fb) CTV in all bedrooms ® sB&B£14 sB&B→⋔£17.25 dB&B£28 dB&B→⋔fr£34.50 B

CTV 14P

V Bar lunch £2—£4 Dinner £9.50 Wine £4.75 Last dinner 7.30pm

Credit cards 1 3

★★**Fisherbeck** Old Lake Rd ☎ (0966) 33215

RS Jan

Comfortable, cheerful, family run hotel is set away from the road, overlooking its own attractive gardens.

16rm(13⋔)(2fb) CTV in 4 bedrooms ®

CTV 24P *xmas*

V Last dinner 7.30pm

Credit cards 1 3

★★**Glen Rothay** Rydal ☎ (0966) 32524

Closed mid Nov—Feb

Friendly hotel where the cooking is imaginative and the bedrooms charming.

11rm(4→7⋔)(2fb) 3 ® sB&B→⋔ £23—£26 dB&B→⋔£40—£52 B

CTV 45P *xmas*

V Bar lunch £5alc Dinner £7.95—£12.50 Wine £3.95 Last dinner 7.30pm

Credit cards 1 3 5 V

Ambleside

★★ *HBL* **Kirkstone Foot Country House** Kirkstone Pass Rd ☎ (0966) 32232

Closed 23 Dec—13 Feb

Delightful country house in a peaceful location, yet close to the village. Personally supervised by the owners, Jane and Simon Bateman, there is much for the guest to enjoy, particularly the five course dinner. Bedrooms have every modern comfort, and the lounges are also comfortable.

15rm(13→2⋔)(1fb) CTV in all bedrooms ®

T ✱ sB&B→⋔£26—£32.50 (incl dinner) dB&B→⋔£52—£75 (incl dinner)

35P nc 5yrs

V ✱ Lunch £6.95 Tea 75p Dinner £12.25 Wine £5 Last dinner 8pm

Credit cards 1 2 3 5 V

★★ *H* **Nanny Brow Country House** Clappersgate ☎ (0966) 32036

Peaceful, secluded hotel, personally supervised by the proprietors.

19rm(14→2⋔)(3fb) CTV in all bedrooms ® T sB&B£22—£29 sB&B→⋔£23—£30 dB&B£44—£50 dB&B→⋔£48—£80 B

20P snooker sauna bath solarium *xmas*

English & French V Bar lunch £2—£4 Tea £1.50—£3.50 High Tea £4—£5 Dinner £9—£11.50&alc Wine £5 Last dinner 8pm

Credit cards 1 3 V

★★**Queens** Market Pl ☎ (0966) 32206

There has been an hotel on this central site since the sixteenth century. The present building, of Lakeland slate, was constructed in 1876.

30rm(14→9⋔)(5fb) CTV in all bedrooms ® T ✱ sB&B£16—£19 sB&B→⋔£18.50—£21.50 dB&B£28—£34 dB&B→⋔£33—£39 B

2P 7 *xmas*

V ✱ Lunch £4.95 Tea £1 High Tea £3.50—£4.50 Dinner £7.50 Wine £4.95 Last dinner 10pm

Credit cards 1 3 V

★★**Riverside Hotel & Lodge** Rothay Br, Under Loughrigg ☎ (0966) 32395

Closed Dec & Jan

Very comfortable riverside hotel offering good home cooking. The Lodge (200

yards along riverbank) provides further comfortable accommodation.

10rm(4 3)Annexe:5rm(3 2)(3fb) CTV in all bedrooms ® dB&Bfr£35 dB&B fr£40

30P

Bar lunch fr£2.50 Tea fr£1 Dinner fr£9 Wine £6.15 Last dinner 8pm

Credit cards 1 3

★★**Skelwith Bridge** Skelwith Bridge (2½m W A593) (0966) 32115

This pleasantly up-dated Lakeland inn dates from the seventeenth-century and has retained some original features. It offers well-proportioned bedrooms, an

Ambleside

interesting Georgian lounge with separate TV room and a fashionable restaurant.

18rm(13 4)Annexe:6rm(5 1)(3fb) ®sB&B£15—£25 sB&B £16—£26 dB&B£30—£50 dB&B £32—£52

CTV 60P *xmas*

English & French V Lunch £5.75—£6 Dinner £9.75—£10.25 Wine £4.85 Last dinner 9pm

Credit cards 1 3

★★**Vale View** Lake Rd (Minotels) (0966) 33192

Closed Nov—Mar

An old established hotel, being modernised, yet retaining its original character.

20rm(9 4)(3fb) 1 S% *sB&B£13—£16 sB&B £15.50—£18.50 dB&B£24—£30 dB&B £29—£35

CTV 11P games room table tennis pool table

S% *Bar lunch 70p—£2.75 Dinner £9.50&alc Wine £3.60 Last dinner 7.45pm

Credit cards 1 2 3 5

★★*L* **Wateredge** Borrans Rd, Waterhead ☎ (0966) 32332

Closed Dec & Jan

A delightful hotel, originally two seventeenth-century cottages. The highest standards of decor and comfort are maintained throughout, and very good home-made meals are always served.

20rm(10🛁2🚿)(1fb) ® sB&B£19—£25 dB&B£38—£50 dB&B🛁🚿£42—£70 B

CTV 20P 🚗 ❀ nc 7yrs 🍷 ☕ Dinner £13.90—£14.90 Wine £5.95 Last dinner 8pm

Credit cards 1 3 Ⓥ

AMERSHAM
Buckinghamshire
Map **4** SU99

★★**Crown** High St (Trusthouse Forte) ☎ (02403) 21541

The accent is on comfort in this interesting Elizabethan inn with its wood panelling, inglenooks and wall paintings.

25rm(14🛁) CTV in all bedrooms ® sB&B£45.50 sB&B🛁£53.50 dB&B£61.50 dB&B🛁£69.50 B

51P *xmas*

🍷 ☕ Last dinner 9.30pm

Credit cards 1 2 3 4 5

✕✕**Kings Arms** High St ☎ (02403) 6333

This inn features oak beams and inglenook fireplaces. Market-fresh sea-food and good quality vegetables enhance the well-balanced and reliable French-style cooking, whilst the warm and friendly service is complemented by the cosy atmosphere.

Closed Mon Dinner not served Sun

🍽 English & French **V** 30 seats Lunch £13alc Dinner £13alc Wine £4.50 Last dinner 9.30pm 25P

Credit cards 1 2 3 5 Ⓥ

✕**Lam's Garden** 131 Station Rd ☎ (02403) 5505

Situated close to the railway station, the small, cosy Chinese restaurant offers an à la carte menu specialising in Peking dishes and a short menu of Szechuan dishes.

Closed Sun & 2 wks summer

🍽 Peking & Szechuan **V** 40 seats ✱ Lunch fr£3 Dinner fr£8&alc Wine £5.80 Last dinner 11.15pm 🅿

Credit cards 1 2 3 5

AMESBURY
Wiltshire
Map **4** SU14

★★**Antrobus Arms** Church St ☎ (0980) 23163

This older-style town-centre hotel is notable for its pleasant atmosphere and helpful staff. There is an attractive restaurant and a garden to the rear.

20rm(12🛁)(1fb) CTV in all bedrooms sB&Bfr£22 sB&B🛁fr£28 dB&Bfr£36 dB&B🛁fr£42 B

CTV 80P ❀

🍽 English & French **V** 🍷 ☕ Lunch £2.50alc Tea 65p—£1.20 Dinner £8.50&alc Wine £5.50 Last dinner 10pm

Credit cards 1 2 3 4 5 Ⓥ

AMLWCH
Gwynedd
Map **6** SH49

★★**Trecastell** Bull Bay (Frederic Robinson) ☎ (0407) 830651

Family run hotel overlooking Bulls Bay.

12rm(8🛁2🚿)(3fb) ® 🐕 sB&B£16—£18 sB&B🛁🚿£16—£18 dB&B£28—£30 dB&B🛁🚿£28—£30

CTV 60P 🚗 ❀ games room pool table

🍷 Lunch fr£4.75 Dinner £6.75—£8.75&alc Wine £5.20 Last dinner 8.30pm

Credit cards 1 2 3

AMMANFORD
Dyfed
Map **2** SN61

★★**Mill at Glynhir** Glyn-Hir, Llandybie (3m NE off A483)
☎ Llandybie (0269) 850672

Closed 24—28 Dec

A former 17th century mill converted into a unique small comfortable, family run hotel. Offers extensive views over the River Loughor Valley.

8rm(5🛁3🚿) Annexe: 2rm(1🛁1🚿)(3fb) CTV in all bedrooms ® ✱ sB&B🛁🚿£23 dB&B🛁🚿£46 B

20P 🚗 ❀ 🏊(heated) ⛳18 🎣 nc 11yrs

🍽 English & Continental **V** ☕ ✱ Lunch £6.50—£7.50 Dinner £10.50&alc Wine £4.75 Last dinner 8.30pm

Ⓥ

AMPFIELD
Hampshire
Map **4** SU32

★★★**Potters Heron** (Whitbread)
☎ Chandlers Ford (04215) 66611 Telex no 47459

Well-appointed hotel incorporating popular pub and grill restaurant.

60🛁🚿 1 🛏 ⚟ in 6 bedrooms CTV in all bedrooms ® T 🐕 sB&B🛁🚿£45—£52 dB&B🛁🚿£55—£65 B

☾ 200P CFA *xmas*

🍽 English & French **V** 🍷 ☕ Lunch £7.50—£11.50&alc Dinner £10—£12.50&alc Wine £5.60 Last dinner 9.45pm

Credit cards 1 2 3 5

See advertisement under Romsey

ANDOVER
Hampshire
Map **4** SU34

★★*B* **Danebury** High St (Whitbread) ☎ (0264) 23332

Here, late 16th-century origins blend with tasteful modern furnishings to create a high level of comfort. Service is extensive, well-managed and friendly.

24🛁 1 🛏 CTV in all bedrooms ® T 🐕 sB&B🛁🚿£40 dB&B🛁🚿£48 B

☾ 40P CTV *xmas*

🍽 English & French **V** ⚟ 🍷 ☕ Lunch £4.95—£5.74&alc Tea 85p—£1.90 High Tea £2.90—£3.50 Dinner £4.95—£6.50&alc Wine £5 Last dinner 9.45pm

Credit cards 1 2 3 5 Ⓥ

ANDREAS
See **Man, Isle of**

ANNAN
Dumfries & Galloway *Dumfriesshire*
Map **11** NY16

★★ *B* **Queensberry Arms** (Toby)
☎ (04612) 2024
Whitewashed, two-storey building in the centre of the town.
27rm(8🛁16🚿)(4fb) CTV in all bedrooms ® T sB&B£22 sB&B🛁🚿£25 dB&B🛁🚿£40 B
30P 6🚗 ✿ ♿ Live music and dancing wknds Cabaret mthly *xmas*
V ♡ ☕ Lunch £5.50&alc Tea fr60p High Tea £3.50—£6.50 Dinner £8.50&alc Wine £3.90 Last dinner 9.30pm
Credit cards 1 2 3 4 5

★★ *B* **Warmanbrie** ☎ (04612) 4015
Country house hotel with spacious well appointed bedrooms.
6🛁 1⊟ CTV in all bedrooms ®
✱sB&B🛁£24.50—£34
dB&B🛁£17—£30 B
25P 1🚗 ✿ ♪
✱ Bar lunch £3.70 Tea fr£1.40&alc Dinner £8.50—£11.95&alc Wine fr£4.25 Last dinner 9.30pm
Credit cards 1 2 3

★ **Corner House** High St (Mount Charlotte) ☎ (04612) 2754
This hotel caters for coach tours in summer and commercial trade in winter.
31rm(1🚿) ® ✱sB&Bfr£13 dB&Bfr£21 B
60P CTV *xmas*
Mainly grills ♡ ☕ Lunch £1.45—£3 High Tea fr£1.25 Dinner £5 Wine £4.85 Last dinner 9pm
Credit cards 1 2 3 5 Ⓥ

ANSTRUTHER
Fife
Map **12** NO50

★★★ ***Craws Nest*** Bankwell Rd
☎ (0333) 310691 Telex no 727396
An extended tourist/business hotel with an annexed wing of superior bedrooms.
31🛁 Annexe:19rm(3🛁16🚿) 2⊟ CTV in all bedrooms ® T ✗ B
☾ # ⚡ 80P ✿ billiards sauna bath solarium live music & dancing Sat *xmas*
V ♡ ☕ Last dinner 9pm
Credit cards 1 2 3 4 5

★★ **Smugglers Inn** High St ☎ (0333) 310506
The original inn dates back to 1300, and was a noted tavern in Queen Anne's time.
9rm(2🛁7🚿) sB&B🛁🚿£18—£19
dB&B🛁🚿£36—£38
CTV 12P
British & French ♡ Lunch £7.50—£8.50&alc Dinner £8.50—£10 Wine £6 Last dinner 9.30pm
Credit cards 1 2 3 5 Ⓥ

✿ ✕✕ **Cellar** 24 East Green
☎ (0333) 310378
Near the waterfront, this small restaurant with stone walls and beams is one of the finest in Fife. The service is friendly and attractive while the carefully chosen wine list complements the excellent seafood which is skilfully cooked in the modern style.
Closed Sun (in winter) & 3 days Xmas
Lunch not served Mon (in winter)
Bookings advised
French 28 seats Lunch £6alc Dinner £12—£15alc Wine £6.50 Last dinner 9.30pm nc 8yrs
Credit cards 1 2 3

APPIN
Strathclyde *Argyllshire*
Map **14** NM94

★★ *L* **Invercreran House** Glen Creran
☎ (063173) 414
Beautifully set on the hillside of a quiet, scenic glen, the small, comfortable and well-appointed modern hotel offers cheery bedrooms and tasteful lounges.
8rm(2🛁2🚿)(3fb) sB&B🛁🚿fr£30(incl dinner) dB&B🛁🚿fr£50(incl dinner) B
CTV 14P ✿
♡ ☕ Lunch fr£5&alc Tea fr£1.25 Dinner £13—£15 Last dinner 8pm
Credit cards 1 3
See advertisement on page 76

APPLEBY-IN-WESTMORLAND
Cumbria
Map **12** NY62

★★★ **Appleby Manor** Roman Rd (Best Western) ☎ (07683) 51571 Telex no 64100
A pink sandstone Victorian country house standing in extensive grounds.
12rm(8🛁)(5fb) CTV in all bedrooms ® ✗ S% sB&B£22—£24.50 sB&B🛁£30.50—£34 dB&B£38—£41 dB&B🛁£44—£49 B
40P 3🚗(£1 per night) ✿ ⊟(heated) sauna bath solarium gymnasium pool table ♿
V ☕ ⚡ S% Lunch £10—£10.50&alc Dinner £10—£10.50&alc Wine £5.50 Last dinner 9pm
Credit cards 1 2 3 5
See advertisement on page 76

★★ **Royal Oak Inn** Bongate ☎ (07683) 51463
6rm(1🛁2🚿) CTV in all bedrooms ®
✱sB&B£13.50 sB&B🛁🚿£21 dB&B£27 dB&B🛁🚿£32 B
P ♪ U
International ♡ Dinner £9.50 Wine £4.50 Last dinner 9pm
Credit cards 1 2 3
See advertisement on page 76

★★ **Tufton Arms** Market Sq, Boroughgate (Consort) ☎ (07683) 51593
18rm(15🛁)(3fb) CTV in 15 bedrooms ® sB&B£22.50 sB&B🛁£25 dB&B🛁£39.50 B CTV 30P 5🚗
V ♡ ☕ Lunch £7.50&alc Tea 75p High Tea £3.75 Dinner £8.75&alc Wine £3.75 Last dinner 9pm
Credit cards 1 3 5 Ⓥ

Invercreran House Hotel ★★ L

Glen Creran, Appin, Argyll PA38 4BJ
Tel. Appin (063 173) 414

Situated in a most attractive secluded part of the Highlands, breath-taking location, excellent views in all directions, perfect for peace, relaxation, warmth and comfort.
Luxuriously appointed, Invercreran has an allure and tranquillity entirely in keeping with its setting. Our bedrooms, reception and lounges are excellent, along with a fine reputation for exquisite food, fine wines, the atmosphere and occasion is there to be enjoyed.

The Best of Both Worlds!

The English Lakes and the Yorkshire Dales—probably the two most beautiful National Parks in Britain. Treat yourself to the best of both worlds when you *Escape to Eden* at the ***Appleby Manor Country House Hotel.*** Set in its own area of superb natural beauty, yet only minutes by car from both National Parks, you'll find yourself in the friendly atmosphere of a true country house as you enjoy a swim in the indoor Leisure Club or wine and dine in the oak-panelled restaurant. For a free colour brochure, please contact:

AA★★★

Appleby Manor Country House Hotel,
Appleby-in-Westmorland, Cumbria,
Telephone: Appleby (0930) 51571.

the Royal Oak Inn ★★

This long black and white coaching inn has been a popular place in which to stay or have a meal for many years.

Today the bedrooms are well appointed having colour TV and tea and coffee making facilities with three rooms also having private WC and shower or bath.
The Inn has a comfortable, welcoming atmosphere which suits those who want to break a long journey or who want to explore the unspoilt Eden Valley.

Bongate Appleby-in-Westmorland CUMBRIA CA16 6UN
Tel. Appleby (0930) 51463

★**Courtfield** Bongate ☎ (07683) 51394

A small homely establishment, set in three acres of gardens on the outskirts of town.

6rm Annexe:6rm(1fb) Ⓡ

CTV 30P 2 ✿

V Last dinner 8pm

Credit cards 1 3

★**White Hart** Boroughgate ☎ (07683) 51598

This 18th century, small, modernised hotel is situated in the town centre.

8rm(2)(2fb) Ⓡ

CTV 8P 3 solarium *xmas*

V Last dinner 9.30pm

Credit cards 1 3

APPLEDORE

Devon
Map **2** SS43

★★**Seagate** The Quay ☎ Bideford (02372) 72589

A pleasant, busy inn with most convivial atmosphere, overlooking the estuary.

9rm(4)(1fb) CTV in 7 bedrooms TV in 2 bedrooms Ⓡ sB&B£20—£30 sB&B£30—£35 dB&B£30—£35 dB&B£40—£45

CTV 60P Cabaret Sat *xmas*

English & Italian V Bar lunch £1.50—£6 Tea £1—£4 Dinner £6—£25 Wine £3.20 Last dinner 10.30pm

Credit cards 1 2 3 4 5 Ⓥ

Appleby-in-Westmorland — Arbroath

APPLETON-LE-MOORS

North Yorkshire
Map **8** SE78

★★ *HL* **Dweldapilton Hall** ☎ Lastingham (07515) 227

Closed Jan & Feb

The early Regency/Victorian house stands in attractively landscaped grounds at the centre of a moorland village. The public rooms are furnished in the style of the period and the comfortable bedrooms have been upgraded and restored. The atmosphere is relaxing.

12rm(10 2)(2fb) CTV in all bedrooms Ⓡ sB&B fr£24.50 dB&B fr£49

Lift CTV 30P ✿ *xmas*

V Lunch £6.50 Tea £3 Dinner £10.50&alc Wine £5 Last dinner 8pm

Credit cards 1 2 3 5 Ⓥ

ARBROATH

Tayside *Angus*
Map **12** NO64

★★★ *L* **Letham Grange** Colliston (Best Western) ☎ Gowanbank (024189) 373
Telex no 76438

Set in a 250-acre estate, this recently opened hotel offers a blend of the Victorian era and modern facilities. The charming public rooms feature sculptured ceilings and fireplaces, and the bedrooms are large and comfortable. The modern sporting facilities, due for completion in early 1986, include a four-sheet curling rink and an 18-hole golf course.

17(4fb) CTV in all bedrooms Ⓡ T sB&B fr£44 dB&B fr£59

250P ✿ snooker curling rink Live music & dancing Sat *xmas*

International V Lunch fr£6.50 Tea fr90p Dinner fr£10.50&alc Wine £4.50 Last dinner 9.30pm

Credit cards 1 2 3 4 5

★★**Hotel Seaforth** Dundee Rd ☎ (0241) 72232

This commercial hotel, close to the seafront on the south side of the town, has a snooker club on the premises.

20rm(11)(3fb) CTV in all bedrooms Ⓡ

CTV 100P 6(Charge) ✿ billiards *xmas*

V Last dinner 9pm

Credit cards 1 2 3 5

XXCarriage Room Meadowbank Inn, Montrose Rd ☎ (0241) 75755

A roadside complex which includes cafeteria, lounge and function room is the unlikely setting for this elegant Adam-style restaurant and cocktail lounge.

Closed Sun, Mon & 1st wk Jan Lunch not served Sat

French **V** 54 seats ✱ Lunch £4—£7 Dinner £10.95&alc Wine £4.95 Last dinner 9.30pm 200P

Credit cards 1 2 3 5

ARCHIRONDEL
Jersey
See Channel Islands

ARDELVE
Highland *Ross & Cromarty*
Map **14** NG82

★ *HL* **Loch Duich** ☎ Kyle (0599) 85213

Closed Nov—Mar

(*Rosette awarded for dinner only*).

An attractive little roadside hotel near Eileau Donan Castle. Mr and Mrs Stensons' genuine hospitality is matched equally by their fixed price dinners. The menu, which is changed daily, makes good use of local produce in a wholesome and homely style. The wine list is short but imaginative.

18rm(1fb)

CTV 54P 1

International Last dinner 9pm

ARDEN
Strathclyde *Dunbartonshire*
Map **10** NS38

★★★**Lomond Castle** ☎ (038985) 681

Hotel, chalet and leisure complex on banks of Loch Lomond.

21rm(16 5)(4fb) CTV in all bedrooms Ⓡ **T** sB&B £29.50—£45 dB&B £45—£65

200P (heated) (hard) sauna bath solarium gymnasium

Scottish & French **V** Lunch £8.50 Tea £2.75 Dinner £10.50&alc Wine £5.75 Last dinner 9.30pm

Credit cards 1 2 3 5

ARDENTINNY
Strathclyde *Argyllshire*
Map **10** NS18

★★**Ardentinny** (Inter Hotels) ☎ (036981) 209

Closed Jan & Feb

Good food and friendly service commend this historic hotel in a beautiful mountain setting with the gardens extending to the sea.

11rm(6 5)(1fb) CTV in all bedrooms Ⓡ sB&B £23—£30 dB&B £42—£50

CTV 30P xmas

Scottish, French & German **V** Bar lunch £2.50—£5 Tea 80p High Tea £2.50—£5 Dinner £12.50—£15 Wine £5 Last dinner 9.15pm

Credit cards 1 2 3 5

ARDEONAIG
Central *Perthshire*
Map **11** NN63

★★**Ardeonaig** South Loch Tayside ☎ Killin (05672) 400 Telex no 76163

Closed Nov—Etr RS Mar

Relaxed informal roadside inn, in quiet rural location.

14rm(10 4)(2fb) Ⓡ S% sB&B £22—£27 dB&B £44—£46

CTV 40P

Scottish, English & Continental **V** S% Bar lunch 75p—£6.50 Tea 75p—£3.75 Dinner £12.50—£15 Wine £5.50 Last dinner 8.45pm

Ⓥ

ARDLUI
Strathclyde *Dunbartonshire*
Map **10** NN31

★★**Ardlui** (Guestaccom) ☎ Inveruglas (03014) 243

A large, white-painted house whose gardens run down to shores of Loch Lomond.

11rm(2 1)(4fb) CTV in 3 bedrooms Ⓡ sB&B £16.68—£18 dB&B £30.58—£31.65 dB&B £37.45—£39.20

CTV 50P snooker

V Bar lunch £4alc Tea 60palc Dinner £10.20alc Wine £4 Last dinner 8.30pm

Credit cards 1 2 3 Ⓥ

ARDUAINE
Strathclyde *Argyllshire*
Map **10** NM80

★★★**Loch Melfort** ☎ Kilmelford (08522) 233

Closed mid Oct—Etr

Spectacular views are a feature of this popular hotel with its chalet extension.

6rm(3) Annexe: 20 Ⓡ sB&B £26—£35 sB&B £26—£35 dB&B £40 dB&B £56—£60 Continental breakfast

CTV 50P

Lunch £8&alc Tea £2&alc Dinner £15&alc Wine £6 Last dinner 8.30pm

Credit card 1

ARDVASAR
See Skye, Isle of

ARINAGOUR
See Coll, Isle of

ARISAIG
Highland *Inverness-shire*
Map **13** NM68

★★★

★★★ **ARISAIG HOUSE, ARISAIG**

Beasdale (3m E A830) (Relais et Chateaux)

☎ (06875) 622 Telex no 777279

Closed Nov—mid Apr

(Rosette awarded for dinner only)

Converted to an hotel by the Smithers family, Arisaig House retains our members' high opinion of it. Although it is a Victorian building, much of the interior is pure thirties in style. There is a small, modern bar, a comfortable morning room and a coolly elegant drawing room as well as a smart hall, all of the rooms bright with flowers and open fires when necessary. The spacious bedrooms are beautifully done with a fine sense of colour co-ordination and naturally, have extras that include fruit and yet more flowers. David Wilkinson, the son-in-law of the family, is in charge of the kitchen and he produces well cooked four-course dinners. His style is modern French although he features some Scottish dishes and he also makes good use of fine local products. You will be served here, as elsewhere in the hotel, by charming local girls who bring their own brand of good-natured friendliness to their work. The hotel is off the famous Road to the Isles, set in 20 acres of wooded grounds which provide captivating views over the Sound of Arisaig and the mountains.

14rm(13) CTV in all bedrooms **T** sB&B £35 dB&B £75—£110

16P snooker nc10yrs

Dinner fr£19.50 Wine £7 Last dinner 8.30pm

Credit card 3 Ⓥ

★★H ***Arisaig*** ☎(06875) 210
Closed Nov—Feb
A friendly, family run hotel standing on the shores of Loch Nan Ceall.
13rm(3⇌)(4fb) ®
CTV 60P ⇌ Live music & dancing wknds in season
V ⚘ ☕ Last dinner 8.30pm

ARMITAGE (near Rugeley)
Staffordshire
Map **7** SK01
XX **Old Farmhouse** ☎(0543) 490353
A roadside restaurant with a wealth of beams inside and cottage-like façade. It offers excellent value for money from a menu which offers a range of 8 or 9 items. The interesting English food is served by local waitresses who are attentive and pleasant.
Closed Mon, Dinner not served Sun.
V 100 seats ✱Lunch £5.25—£9.45 Dinner £8.95—£13.45 Wine £4.40 Last dinner 9.30pm P
Credit cards 1 2 3 5

ARNCLIFFE
North Yorkshire
Map **7** SD97
★★ L ***Amerdale House***
☎(075677) 250
Closed 2 Nov—Mar
Peaceful, very comfortable hotel with elegant rooms and fine views.
9rm(3⌂)(1fb) ®
CTV 30P ⇌ ✿
⚘ Last dinner 8.30pm
Credit cards 1 3

ARRAN, ISLE OF
Strathclyde *Bute*
Map **10**

BLACKWATERFOOT
Map **10** NR92
★★ ***Kinloch*** (Inter Hotel)
☎Shiskine (077086) 444
A two-storey hotel with a modern extension, standing on the coast overlooking Kilbrannan Sound.
49⇌(3fb) CTV in all bedrooms ®
50P CFA ✿ ▭(heated) squash sauna bath solarium ⌂ *xmas*
⚘ ☕ Last dinner 8.30pm
Credit cards 1 2 3 5

LAGG
Map **10** NR92
★★ **Lagg** (Guestaccom) ☎Sliddery (077087) 255
Attractive country inn with cosy atmosphere and good food.
17(8⇌)(3fb) ® sB&B £18—£20 sB&B⇌ £19—£21 dB&B £36—£40 dB&B⇌ £38—£42
CTV 40P ⇌ ✿ ♪ *xmas*
Scottish & French **V** ⚘ ☕ Lunch £4.50—£12 Tea fr£1.50 High Tea fr£4.50 Dinner fr£10 Wine £4.75 Last dinner 9pm

LAMLASH
Map **10** NS03
X ***Carraig Mhor*** ☎(07706) 453
Compact coffee shop restaurant serving light lunches and a most imaginative small selection at dinner.
Closed Sun, Mon, 1st 2 wks Mar & 1st 3 wks Nov
V 26 seats Last dinner 9pm

WHITING BAY
Map **10** NS02
★ **Cameronia** ☎(07707) 254
Small friendly and comfortable seafront hotel opposite sandy beach. Excellent home cooking.
6rm(2fb) ® ✖ sB&B £13—£15 dB&B £24—£28 B
CTV 6P ⇌
⚘ ☕ Bar lunch £2.50—£5 Tea £1—£2 Dinner £7&alc Wine £4.50 Last dinner 9pm

ARUNDEL
West Sussex
Map **4** TQ00
★★★ **Norfolk Arms** High St (Forest Dale) ☎(0903) 882101 Telex no 47439
An 18th century coaching inn with a central arch and also featuring an ornate staircase.
34⇌ ⅟ in 2 bedrooms CTV in all bedrooms ® **T** sB&B⇌ £32—£38 dB&B⇌ fr£46 B
14P 15⌂ table tennis pool table *xmas*
V ⚘ ☕ ⅟ Lunch £5.75—£7.75 Tea £1.20 Dinner £10.45—£15.60 Wine £4.75 Last dinner 10pm
Credit cards 1 2 3 5

★★ **Howards** Crossbush ☎(0903) 882655
This sympathetically converted Georgian house has comfortable bedrooms, a popular carvery and a French-style coffee shop. Garden and large car park available.
10⇌ CTV in all bedrooms ® **T** ✖ sB&B⇌ £28—£34 dB&B⇌ £38—£44 B
100P ⇌ ✿ nc 14yrs
⚘ ☕ Lunch £9alc Tea £1alc Dinner £10alc Wine £4.80 Last dinner 10pm
Credit cards 1 2 3 5

★ ***Burpham Country*** Old Down, Burpham (3m NE off A27) ☎(0903) 882160
This delightful country house is situated in a peaceful village overlooking the South Downs. Mrs Potter offers a warm welcome, comfortable rooms and good home cooking. Vegetarian meals are also available.
7rm ® ✖ B
CTV 12P ⇌ ✿ nc *xmas*
V ⚘ ☕ Last dinner 8.15pm
Credit card 1

ASCOT
Berkshire
Map **4** SU96
★★★★ **Berystede** Bagshot Rd (Trusthouse Forte) ☎(0990) 23311 Telex no 847707
Set in attractive grounds, this smart, well-appointed hotel continues to upgrade its bedrooms. It is popular with both conferences and private guests. →

88🛁(2fb) CTV in all bedrooms ® sB&B🛁£62.50 dB&B🛁£81 B

Lift ☾ 140P ✽ (heated) *xmas*

Last dinner 9.45pm

Credit cards 1 2 3 4 5

★★★★ **The Royal Berkshire** London Rd, Sunninghill (Ladbroke) ☎ (0990) 23322 Telex no 847280

A lovely Queen Anne house, set amid fifteen acres of lawns and beautiful trees, has been tastefully transformed into a country house hotel. Imaginative cuisine is complemented by courteous service from friendly staff.

22rm(21🛁1🚿) Annexe: 18🛁 CTV in all bedrooms ® T sB&B🛁🚿£65—£85 B

☾ 150P ✽ hard squash sauna bath putting croquet lawn *xmas*

V Lunch £15.50 Tea £1.50—£6.25 High Tea £6.25 Dinner fr£21.50&alc Wine £7.95 Last dinner 9.30pm

Credit cards 1 2 3 4 5

Ascot — Ashby-De-La-Zouch

27rm(25🛁2🚿)(7fb) 2 CTV in all bedrooms ® T sB&B🛁🚿fr£25.85 dB&B🛁🚿fr£37.85 B

Lift CTV 50P 1 (£1 per night) ✽

Mainly grills V Lunch £4.50—£5&alc Tea fr50p Dinner £5—£5.50&alc Last dinner 9.30pm

Credit cards 1 2 3 5 Ⓥ

See advertisement under Plymouth

ASHBURTON

Devon
Map **3** SX77

★★ **Dartmoor Motel** (Exec Hotel) ☎ (0364) 52232

Closed 25 Dec RS 26 Dec & 1 Jan

The modestly furnished motel-style establishment, with character bar and dining room, is used also as a main road service area.

★★ *H* **Holne Chase** (Inter Hotel) ☎ Poundsgate (03643) 471

An attractive period house in a magnificent setting with most impressive views.

13rm(8🛁3🚿)(3fb) CTV in all bedrooms ® T sB&B£17 sB&B🛁🚿£29—£33 dB&B£39—£50 dB&B🛁🚿£39—£50 B

25P 2 (charge) ✽ croquet table tennis ♿ *xmas*

V Lunch £7.75 Tea fr75p High Tea £2.50—£5 Dinner £12 Wine £4.50 Last dinner 9pm

Credit cards 1 2 3 5 Ⓥ

★★ **Tugela House** 68—70 East St ☎ (0364) 52206

Fine old country furniture enhances this owner-run town centre hotel with its popular dining room where well cooked meals are served.

6rm(2🛁2🚿) CTV in 5 bedrooms TV in 1 bedroom ✱ sB&B£15 sB&B🛁🚿£16 dB&B£30 dB&B🛁🚿£32

4 nc

English & French V Lunch £6.95alc Tea 50p Dinner £9alc Wine £4.95 Last dinner 9pm

Ⓥ

ASHBY-DE-LA-ZOUCH

Leicestershire
Map **8** SK31

★★★ **Royal Crest** Station Rd (Crest) ☎ (0530) 412833 Telex no 341629

This large Regency building beside the A453 is conveniently close to the town centre.

31rm(25🛁6🚿)(3fb) in 3 bedrooms CTV in all bedrooms ® T sB£45.05—£47.90 sB🛁🚿£47.05—£49.90 dB£55.55—£58.40 dB🛁🚿£55.55—£58.40 (room only) B

☾ 150P ✽ Live music Mon & Fri

English & French V Lunch £6.45—£9.10&alc Tea 75p High Tea £3.10—£5 Dinner £7.65—£11.50&alc Wine £5.80 Last dinner 9.45pm

Credit cards 1 2 3 4 5

✕**La Zouch** 2 Kilwardby St ☎ (0530) 412536

Simple bistro near town centre.

Closed Mon 1st wk Jan & 1st wk Jul Dinner not served Sun

V 48 seats ✱Lunch £2.25—£4.85&alc Dinner £10alc Wine £4.25 Last dinner 10pm

Credit cards 1 2 3 4 5

ASHFORD
Kent
Map **5** TR04

★★★★ **Eastwell Manor** (see red star box)

★★★**Spearpoint** Canterbury Rd, Kennington (Best Western) ☎ (0233) 36863

Set in 5 acres of parkland, hotel also features Du Vert Galant Restaurant..

36rm(30 4)(2fb) CTV in all bedrooms ®T S% ✱sB&B £44—£49 dB&B £59—£69

60P ♿

French **V** ✱Lunch £9alc Tea 65p Dinner £9alc Wine £5.25 Last dinner 9.45pm

Credit cards 1 2 3 5

See advertisement on page 82

★★★★

★★★★ EASTWELL MANOR, ASHFORD

Eastwell Park (3m N A251) (Prestige) ☎ (0233) 35751 Telex no 966281

In recent years this historic building has been transformed into a luxurious hotel, and with the affable manager, Mr Roy Yallop, now running it, the standards of hospitality have been raised to the degree where we can award Red Stars; they certainly live up to the architectural, decorative and scenic qualities of the hotel. Although there have been houses on the site since 1069, the present building dates from 1928, using materials from its predecessor — and a very fine job they have made of it. There are lovely gardens within the 3,000 acre estate situated in the North Kent Downs and you can play croquet and tennis, whilst inside there is a billiard room. There is also a helicopter pad. Inside, fine panelling and door cases, massive carved stone chimney pieces and plaster work produce an impressive atmosphere lightened by flowers, pictures and prints. There are plenty of sitting areas and the bedrooms are sumptuously furnished. At lunch there is a fixed price 'English Fayre' menu in the dining room — or you may choose a light meal on the terrace in fine weather — whilst at night there is a table d'hôte and à la carte menu in classical and modern style, which the talented Chef Anthony Blake cooks with skill. With sociable staff to look after you, your every need will be attended to and you will find the hotel an ideal spot to get away from it all.

24 CTV in all bedrooms **T** S% ✱ sB&B £55—£73 dB&B £70—£88

Lift 60P 6 (hard) snooker croquet ♿ *xmas*

S% ✱Lunch fr£11.50&alc Dinner fr£17&alc Last dinner 9.30pm

Credit cards 1 2 3 5 Ⓥ

A

Ashford — Auchterarder

ASHFORD
Surrey
London plan **5** *A2* (page **446**)

XX**Terrazza** 45 Church Rd ☎ (07842) 44887

Heathrow plan **13** *D1*

This smart, well-managed Italian restaurant features carefully prepared authentic dishes which include fresh sea-food and an antipasti trolley.

Closed Sun & Bank Hols Lunch not served Sat

Continental **V** 70 seats Lunch £11.75&alc Dinner £11.75&alc Wine £6.50 Last dinner 10.30pm

Credit cards 1 2 3 5

ASHINGTON
West Sussex
Map **4** TQ11

★★*HB* **Mill House** Mill Ln (off A24) ☎ (0903) 892426

RS 25—31 Dec

Small private hotel with attractive lawn, run by friendly proprietors, with sound cooking and excellent breakfasts.

10rm(6→2⋒) 2 CTV in all bedrooms Ⓡ available in bedrooms **T** sB£25—£30 sB→⋒£28—£33 dB£38—£40 dB→⋒£40—£45(room only)

10P

V S% Dinner £7.95—£8.95&alc Wine £5 Last dinner 9.30pm

Credit cards 1 2 3 5 Ⓥ

XX**Ashington Court** London Rd ☎ (0903) 892575

Closed Mon & 3 wks Jan
Dinner not served Sun

English & French **V** 30 seats Lunch £9.95—£10.95&alc Dinner £15.25alc Wine £5.95 Last dinner 10pm 15P

Credit cards 1 2 3 5

ASHLEY HEATH
Dorset
Map **4** SU10

★★***Struan*** Horton Rd ☎ Ringwood (04254) 3553

An attractive, white-rendered, detached property in a quiet, wooded residential area, the hotel has an attentive staff and offers a good range of well-prepared and attractively served food.

10rm(6⋒)(2fb) Ⓡ

CTV 75P

English & French **V** Last dinner 9.30pm

Credit cards 1 2 3 5

ASHTON-UNDER-LYNE
Gt Manchester
Map **7** SJ99

★★**York House** York Pl ☎ 061-330 5899

Large hotel near town centre with Victorian-style restaurant.

24rm(18→5⋒)(2fb) 1 CTV in all bedrooms Ⓡ **T** S% sB&B£28 sB&B→⋒£31—£37 dB&B→⋒£46—£50

☾30P

English & French **V** S% Lunch £8.50alc Dinner £8.50alc Wine £4.50 Last dinner 9.30pm

Credit cards 1 2 3 4 5 Ⓥ

ASKRIGG
North Yorkshire
Map **7** SD99

★★**King's Arms** Market Pl ☎ Wensleydale (0969) 50258

This is an 18th century coaching inn of great character and warmth. The comfortable, modernised bedrooms are furnished in keeping with the general style.

10rm(2→8⋒)(2fb) 4 CTV in all bedrooms Ⓡ * sB&B→⋒£16—£26 dB&B→⋒£32—£39

7P 2 *xmas*

English & French * Bar lunch £3.95—£6.95 Dinner £9.75 Wine £4.50 Last dinner 9pm

Credit cards 1 3 5 Ⓥ

ASTON CLINTON
Buckinghamshire
Map **4** SP81

★★★ **Bell Inn**
(see red star box opposite)

ATHERSTONE
Warwickshire
Map **4** SP39

★**Old Red Lion** ☎ (08277) 3156 Telex no 342817

Closed Xmas Day & Boxing Day

The small seventeenth-century coaching inn with covered courtyard, separate wine bar and buttery bar is popular with both local clientele and business people.

9rm(2→5⋒) CTV in all bedrooms Ⓡ *sB&Bfr£18 sB&B→⋒fr£21 dB&Bfr£27 dB&B→⋒fr£31

CTV 25P 5 solarium

French **V** *Lunch £2—£5&alc Tea £1&alc Dinner £7.50alc Wine £3.95 Last dinner 9.30pm

Credit cards 1 2 3 5

AUCHENCAIRN
Dumfries & Galloway *Kirkcudbrightshire*
Map **11** NX75

★★★*HL* **Balcary Bay** ☎ (055664) 217

Closed Dec & Feb

In a fine, secluded setting, this charming, family-run hotel has a friendly atmosphere and offers good food based on fresh local produce.

10rm(7→1⋒)(2fb)2 TV available in bedrooms Ⓡ sB&B£20—£23 sB&B→⋒£23—£26 dB&B£36—£40 dB&B→⋒£46—£52

CTV 50P snooker

Scottish & French Lunch £7alc Tea £2 Dinner £9.50alc Wine £3 Last dinner 9pm

Credit cards 1 3 Ⓥ

AUCHTERARDER
Tayside *Perthshire*
Map **11** NN91

★★★★★ **Gleneagles**
(see red star box opposite)

★★★

❀★★★BELL INN, ASTON CLINTON

(Relais et Chateaux) ☎ Aylesbury (0296) 630252 Telex no 83252

RS Sun eve & Mon

Gerald Harris took over this inn in 1939 and, despite the War, gained a reputation for good food that has persisted until today — it has held our Rosette award continuously since 1955. It is Michael Harris, with the help of his family, who has been in charge for many years and supervised its growth to the large operation it has become. With the help of Chef Jack Dick, high standards are maintained; cooking is mainly French and, nowadays, with a modern influence, but several of the old favourite dishes are retained. Service is polite and professional in the restaurant as it is throughout the hotel. Hotel may perhaps be a misnomer for the establishment, since, although it meets our classification requirements, residents in the public sitting rooms can be overwhelmed by restaurant customers. To compensate, however, the bedrooms, both in the main building and those around the attractive courtyard (four of which are being upgraded) across the way, have their own comfortable sitting

areas, many furnished with lovingly polished antiques. They have lovely soft furnishings, luxurious bathrooms and a great many extras including hair-driers. The 350 item wine-list deserves special commendation and there is a wine shop across the way where many of them can be bought retail.

21🛁🚿2🛏CTV in all bedrooms T S% ✱sB&B🛁🚿fr£50 dB&B🛁🚿fr£70 Continental breakfast

150P❀

🍽English & French S%✱Lunch fr£12.50&alc Dinner £36alc Wine £5 Last dinner 9.45pm

Credit cards 1 3

★★★★★

★★★★★GLENEAGLES, AUCHTERARDER

☎ (07646) 2231 Telex no 76105

This notable and internationally famous hotel, built among 600 acres in the Perthshire Hills in 1924, and it is very much in the traditional grand manner with stately columns and sumptuous furnishings. It has fine recreation facilities: four golf courses, tennis, bowls, croquet, pitch and putt and shooting, and there is a new leisure centre with swimming pool, squash court, gymnasium, three billiard tables, sauna and Turkish baths. What is comparatively recent is the high standard of hospitality now prevailing and this is due to the influence of Mr Lederer; in the short time he has been here he has transformed the attitude of the staff to one of the best in the country; cheerful, helpful, and sociable. A great deal of money has been spent re-furbishing the hotel so that the re-arrangement of the ground floor with the grand public rooms and most of the bedrooms reflect the elegance of the past. Live piano music at cocktail time and entertainment in the evenings can add to the pleasure. Catering arrangements are what you would expect but, apart from the main restaurant, the Eagle's Nest is a more intimate room for fine food. Michael Truelove from the Box Tree at Ilkley is

now the chef in charge of this room, so we are expecting great things for next year. Room service is good and you will be sure to enjoy a stay at this wonderful hotel.

254🛁🚿11🛏⚡in 12 bedrooms CTV in all bedrooms T ✈ S% sB🛁🚿£55—£70 dB🛁£90—£130 (room only) B

Lift ☾ 200P CFA ❀ ▭(heated) ⛳18 🎾(hard & grass) 🎣 squash snooker sauna bath solarium gymnasium clay pigeon shooting pool table bowls croquet pitch & putt Live music & dancing nightly 👪 ♿ *xmas*

🍽International V ☕ ☕⚡S% Lunch £17.50&alc Tea £5.95&alc High Tea £6.50alc Dinner £18.50&alc Wine £5.50 Last dinner 10pm

Credit cards 1 2 3 4 5

AUCHTERHOUSE

Tayside *Forfarshire*

Map **11** NO33

★★★🌲*B* **Old Mansion House**
☎ (082626) 366

Closed 31 Dec—7 Jan

Superior food and friendly, attentive service are priorities at this baronial mansion. There are thoughtfully equipped bedrooms, a tasteful, cosy cocktail lounge and a dining room featuring a large Jacobean fireplace and ornate plasterwork.

6rm(5🛁1🚿)(2fb) 1🛏CTV in all bedrooms ®T sB&B🛁🚿£44—£48 dB&B🛁🚿£60—£70

50P 1🚗🚌❀ ⛲(heated) 🎾(grass) squash 👪

🍽Scottish & French V ☕ Lunch £9.50—£10.50 Dinner £17alc Wine £5.95 Last dinner 9.30pm

Credit cards 1 2 3 4 5

See advertisement on page 84

AUCHTERTOOL

Fife

Map **11** NT29

★★***Camilla*** ☎ Kirkcaldy (0592) 780590

A small family-run business and tourist hotel set in a village 3½ miles west of Kirkcaldy, the Camilla has well-equipped bedrooms and offers a wide range of meals.

13🛁(2fb) CTV in all bedrooms ®T B

CTV 60P❀ Live music & dancing Sat 👪 *xmas*

🍽Scottish & French V ☕ ☕ Last dinner 9.45pm

Credit cards 1 2 3

See advertisement on page 84

AULTBEA

Highland *Ross & Cromarty*

Map **14** NG88

★★**Aultbea** ☎ (044582) 201

Closed Oct-mid Apr

Small, friendly family run hotel, delightfully set on the shore of Loch Ewe.

8rm(2🛁)(2fb) ®sB&B£10—£17.50 dB&B£20—£35 dB&B🛁£25—£40 B

CTV 30P🚌❀

🍽Cosmopolitan V ☕ ☕ Lunch £3.50—£7.50 Tea 50p—£1 Dinner £9 Wine £4 Last dinner 8pm

Credit cards 1 3 Ⓥ

★★**Drumchork Lodge** (Inter Hotel)
☎ (044582) 242

RS Nov—Feb

Comfortable, friendly, family run Highland hotel overlooking Loch Ewe.

11rm(6🛁3🚿) Annexe:3🛁(4fb) CTV in all bedrooms ®sB&B£22—£24 sB&B🛁🚿£22—£24 dB&B£42—£46 dB&B🛁🚿£42—£46

CTV 50P❀ sauna bath solarium →

Scottish & Continental Bar lunch £3—7 Tea 80p—£1 Dinner £10.50—£11 Wine £3.90 Last dinner 8pm

Credit cards 1 2 3 5 V

AUSTWICK
North Yorkshire
Map **7** SD76

★**Traddock** ☎ Clapham (04685) 224

Closed Oct—Etr

A Georgian country house of stone construction in its own grounds.

12rm(2→8⋒)(4fb) ® sB&B→⋒£15—£16 dB&B£26—£28 dB&B→⋒£28—£30 B

CTV 15P nc5yrs

Dinner fr£10 Wine £4.50 Last dinner 6.30pm

AVIEMORE
Highland *Inverness-shire*
Map **14** NH81

★★★***Badenoch*** (Toby/Consort) ☎ (0479) 810261

Conveniently situated in the Aviemore centre and offering a choice of budget or normal accommodation.

80rm(62→⋒) CTV in 61 bedrooms ® B

Lift ☾ CTV 100P CFA (heated) squash billiards sauna bath solarium gymnasium Disco 3 nights wkly Live music & dancing twice wkly *xmas*

Scottish, English and French V

Last dinner 9.15pm

Credit cards 1 2 3 4 5

★★★**Post House** Aviemore Centre (Trusthouse Forte) ☎ (0479) 810771 Telex no 75597

Modern hotel, at the rear of the Aviemore Centre, close to the dry ski-slope and convenient for the other facilities.

103→(46fb) CTV in all bedrooms ® sB&B→£45.50 dB&B→£65.50 B

Lift ☾ 140P solarium *xmas*

Last dinner 9.30pm

Credit cards 1 2 3 4 5

★★**Cairngorm** (Best Western) ☎ (0479) 810233

Closed Nov—Dec

Granite building on the main road, opposite the railway station, and adjacent to the Aviemore Centre.

23rm(12→6⋒)(3fb) CTV available in bedrooms (£2 per night) ® sB&B£18.50 sB&B→⋒£20.50 dB&B£35 dB&B→⋒£39 B

☾ CTV 25P 2 (£2 per night) pool table

Bar lunch £4alc Tea 60p—£1.50 Dinner £8.50—£12&alc Wine £5 Last dinner 9pm

Credit cards 1 2 3 5

★★**Red McGregor** Main Rd ☎ (0479) 810256

Small modern hotel in Swedish design on main road in centre of village.

28→(8fb) CTV in all bedrooms ® T S% sB&B→£18—£25 dB&B→£36—£56

☾ # CTV 65P (heated) sauna bath solarium Cabaret 4 nights wkly *xmas*

Mainly grills V Bar lunch £2—£4 Tea 95p Dinner £7.50—£12 Wine £3.95 Last dinner 10pm

Credit cards 1 3 5 V

XX**Winking Owl** ☎ (0479) 810646

Friendly, family-run restaurant and bar in converted cottage.

Closed Sun, Nov & 2wks Dec

66 seats ✱ Bar lunch £2.50—£5 Dinner £6.25—£10.10&alc Wine £4.80 Last dinner 9.30pm 50P

Credit cards 1 2 3 5

AVON
Hampshire
Map **4** SZ19

★★**Tyrrells Ford Country House** (4m S of Ringwood on B3347) ☎ Bransgore (0425) 72646

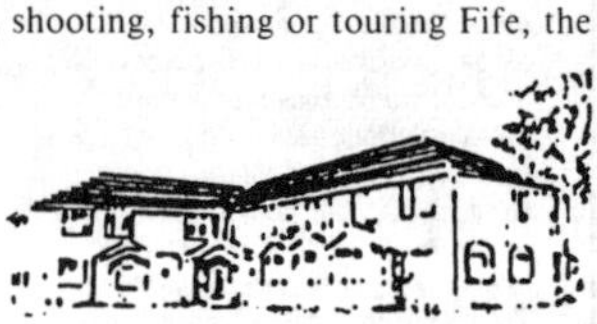

Small country house with galleried panelled rooms and coal fires, offering warm hospitality and good home cooking.

14rm(7➡7⋒)(2fb) CTV in all bedrooms ® T sB&B➡⋒£25—£35 dB&B➡⋒£45—£60 B

100P ✿ *xmas*

English & French V ✱Lunch £5.95—£7.95&alc Dinner £10.95—£11.95 Wine £4.95 Last dinner 10pm

Credit cards 1 2 3 5

See advertisement under Christchurch

AXBRIDGE
Somerset
Map **3** ST45

★★ **Oak House** The Square ☎ (0934) 732444 Telex no 449748

A fourteenth-century house in the square of this historic small town, the hotel is personally run by the proprietor with care and enthusiasm. The bedrooms have most modern amenities, but the hub of the establishment is the restaurant where imaginative, expertly-cooked dishes are cooked dishes are served accompanied by a good wine list.

11rm(7➡) CTV in all bedrooms ® ✱sB&B£20 sB&B➡£27.50 dB&B£34 dB&B➡£43 B

xmas

V ✱Lunch £7.95&alc Tea fr 70p Dinner £10.95—£14.95&alc Wine £5.95 Last dinner 10pm

Credit cards 1 2 3 4 5 V

AXMINSTER
Devon
Map **3** SY29

★★**Cedars** Silver St ☎ (0297) 32775

Converted 18th-century house near the town centre.

15rm(1➡3⋒)(2fb) CTV in 6 bedrooms TV in 2 bedrooms S% sB&B fr £10 sB&B➡⋒£12—£15 dB&B fr £20 dB&B➡⋒£22—£25 B

CTV *xmas*

V S% Lunch £3.55—£6.55 Dinner £4.75—£8.95 Wine £3.50

Credit cards 1 3 V

★★**George** Victoria Pl ☎ (0297) 32209

This coaching inn dates back to the early seventeenth century, and has an Adam fireplace and minstrels' gallery. Here George III once dined and Oliver Cromwell is reputed to have stayed.

11rm(7➡4⋒)(5fb) 1 CTV in all bedrooms ® ✱sB&B➡⋒£17—£19 dB&B➡⋒£28—£35 B

24P

V Lunch £4.25 Tea £1—£2 Dinner £6.50alc Wine £4 Last dinner 9pm

Credit cards 1 2 3 5

★★**Woodbury Park Country House** Woodbury Cross ☎ (0297) 33010

Standing in 5½-acre grounds with magnificent views across the Axe Valley, this small, family-run hotel offers tranquillity combined with discreet twentieth-century comforts.

8rm(4➡1⋒)(3fb) sB&B£11—£19 sB&B➡⋒£13—£21 dB&B£22—£28 dB&B➡⋒£26—£32 B

CTV 50P ✿ (heated) sauna bath *xmas*

V Bar lunch £4.50alc Tea 75p alc Dinner fr £5.50&alc Wine £3.75 Last dinner 9.15pm

Credit cards 1 2 3 5

AYLESBURY
Buckinghamshire
Map **4** SP81

★★**Bell** Market Sq (Trusthouse Forte) ☎ (0296) 89835

Old coaching house, situated in the centre of this market town. →

17rm(16➡1⋒)CTV in all bedrooms ® sB&B➡⋒£45.50 dB&B➡⋒£61.50 **B**

xmas

♁ Last dinner 9.30pm

Credit cards 1 2 3 4 5

> ❀✕**Pebbles** Pebble Ln
> ☎(0296) 86622
> *Small, cosy restaurant with low ceilings and wooden beams. Susan and David Cavalier bring the originality and inspiration of the new wave to the English style, French cooking here, where the prices are not excessive, though portions may be small.*
> Closed Mon, 3 wks Aug & 1 wk Xmas Lunch not served Sat Dinner not served Sun
> **V** 24 seats S% ✱Lunch £10.25&alc Dinner £18&alc Wine £4.95 Last dinner 10pm **P**
> Credit cards 1 2 3 5

AYR
Strathclyde *Ayrshire*
Map **10** NS32
See plan

★★★**Belleisle House** Belleisle Park ☎ Alloway (0292) 42331 Plan **3** *B1*

A stone mansion whose dining room which is a reproduction of the music room and Marie Antoinette's boudoir at Versailles. The bedrooms are modern and spacious.

17rm(9➡5⋒)(4fb)1⊞CTV in all bedrooms ®**T** ✱sB&B£25 sB&B➡⋒£31.50 dB&B£35 dB&B➡⋒£44 **B**

☾50P❀ ⛳ ⚑ Live music & dancing mthly ⌂ *xmas*

♈English & French **V** ♁ ☕ ✱Lunch £5.50 Tea £1.95 High Tea £4.25 Dinner £10.95&alc Wine £5.05 Last dinner 10pm

Credit cards 1 2 3 5 Ⓥ

★★★**Caledonian** Dalblair Rd (Embassy) ☎(0292) 269331 Telex no 76357 Plan **5** *C2*

Large, modern hotel with several bars and Charlie Chaplin restaurant.

118➡⋒(4fb)CTV in all bedrooms ® sB➡⋒£27 dB➡⋒£44 (room only) **B**

Lift ☾50P CFA sauna bath Live music & dancing Sat

♁ ☕ ✱Lunch fr£3.50 Dinner fr£8.50&alc Last dinner 9.15pm

Credit cards 1 2 3 5

★★★***Marine Court*** 12 Fairfield Rd ☎(0292) 267461 Plan **12** *B1*

A seaside hotel with adjoining leisure club. The Hotel provides modern facilities including in-house videos.

17rm(9➡8⋒)
Annexe: 13rm(6➡7⋒)(14fb)1⊞CTV in all bedrooms ®**T B**

☾CTV 50P ▭(heated) sauna bath solarium gymnasium *xmas*

Aylesbury — Ayr

♈French **V** ♁ ☕ Last dinner 11pm

Credit cards 1 2 3 4 5

★★★**Pickwick** 19 Racecourse Rd ☎(0292) 260111 Plan **14** *B1*

Stone mansion, dating from 1890, in residential area and popular for its value for money and good food.

15rm(10➡5⋒)(4fb)1⊞CTV in all bedrooms ®**T** ✗ sB&B➡⋒£35 dB&B➡⋒£54 **B**

☾100P ⊞ ❀

♈French **V** ♁ Bar Lunch £2—£9&alc Dinner £10.50—£12.50&alc Wine £4.25 Last dinner 9pm

Credit card 3

★★★***Savoy Park*** Racecourse Rd ☎(0292) 266112 Plan **16** *B1*

Red sandstone building standing in two acres of grounds, and located to the south of the town centre.

16rm(13➡3⋒)(5fb)CTV in all bedrooms **T B**

☾80P❀ ⌂ *xmas*

V ♁ ☕ Last dinner 8.30pm

Credit cards 1 2 3

★★★**Stakis Ayr** Burns Statue Sq (Stakis) ☎(0292) 263268 Plan **17** *D1*

A traditional style hotel, adjoining the station, providing modern facilities and services.

74➡(20fb)⊁in 10 bedrooms CTV in all bedrooms ®sB&B➡£38.90 dB&B£59.80 **B**

Lift ☾50P Disco Fri & Sat *xmas*

♈Scottish & French **V** ♁ ☕ ✱Bar lunch 75p—£4.50 Tea fr75p Dinner £8—£20 Wine £5.10 Last dinner 9.30pm

Credit cards 1 2 3 5

★★***Ayrshire & Galloway*** 1 Killoch Pl ☎(0292) 262626 Plan **1A** *C1*

RS Xmas & New Year

Commercial hotel overlooking Burns Statue Square, with attractive bars and comfortable, simple rooms.

25rm(8➡)(3fb)CTV in 8 bedrooms

☾CTV 20P disco 5 nights wkly live music & dancing 2 nights wkly

V Last dinner 8.45pm

Credit cards 1 3

★★**Balgarth** Dunure Rd, Alloway (2m S A719) (Inter Hotel) ☎(0292) 42441 Plan **2** *B1*

A red sandstone building on the edge of town with modernised rooms, attractive bars and extensive menu.

15rm(4➡7⋒)(1fb)CTV in all bedrooms ® sB&B£18 sB&B➡⋒£22 dB&B£30 dB&B➡⋒£36 **B**

CTV 80P❀ ⌂ *xmas*

♈French **V** ♁ ☕ Lunch £9.95 Tea £1—£2.10 High Tea £3.35—£5.95 Dinner £9.95&alc Wine £3.45 Last dinner 9.30pm

Credit cards 1 2 3 5

★★***Burns Monument*** Alloway (2m S on B7024) ☎(0292) 42466 Plan **4** *C1*

RS Nov—Mar

A modernised roadside inn, retaining an 'old world' character overlooking Burns Monument and the Brig O'Doon.

9rm(6➡2⋒)(2fb) ®

CTV 12P❀ ✓

V ♁ Last dinner 9.45pm

Credit cards 1 3

★★***Elms Court*** 21 Miller Rd ☎(0292) 264191 Plan **7** *C1*

This hotel provides a friendly atmosphere and good, wholesome meals.

20rm(12➡5⋒)(4fb)CTV in all bedrooms ®

☾40P

♁ ☕ Last dinner 9.30pm

Credit cards 1 3

★★**Gartferry** 44 Racecourse Rd ☎(0292) 262768 Plan **10** *B1*

Busy hotel with open fire in lounge bar. The basement houses "Captains Table" dining room and adjoining function suite.

13rm(2➡5⋒)(1fb)CTV in all bedrooms ® **T** sB&Bfr£19 sB&B➡⋒fr£24 dB&Bfr£34 dB&B➡⋒fr£38 **B**

CTV 100P❀ ⌂ *xmas*

V ♁ ☕ Lunch £4.50—£7.50&alc Tea £1.50 High Tea fr£5 Dinner fr£7.50 Wine £4 Last dinner 10pm

Credit cards 1 2 3 5

★**Aftongrange** 37 Carrick Rd ☎(0292) 265679 Plan **1** *C1*

This small, family-run hotel has a relaxed, informal atmosphere.

8rm(1➡4⋒)(2fb)CTV in all bedrooms ® ✗ sB&B£18 sB&B➡⋒£20 dB&B£29 dB&B➡⋒£31.50 **B**

30P pool table

V ♁ ☕ Lunch £3.75—£6&alc Tea fr£1 High Tea £3.50—£6 Dinner £7.50—£10&alc Wine £4 Last dinner 9pm Ⓥ

★**Fort Lodge** 2 Citadel Pl ☎(0292) 265232 Plan **8** *B3*

Red sandstone lodge dating from the 1850's standing in its own grounds near Ayr town centre.

7⋒(1fb)CTV in all bedrooms ®✗ sB&B⋒£20—£24 dB&B⋒£36—£42 **B**

CTV 12P

V Lunch £2.50—£5.75 High Tea £3.75—£6.75alc Dinner £7—£8.50 Wine £4.25 Last dinner 7pm

Credit cards 1 3

✕**Fouter's Bistro** 2A Academy St ☎(0292) 261391 Plan **9** *B3*

Situated in a narrow cobbled street, the

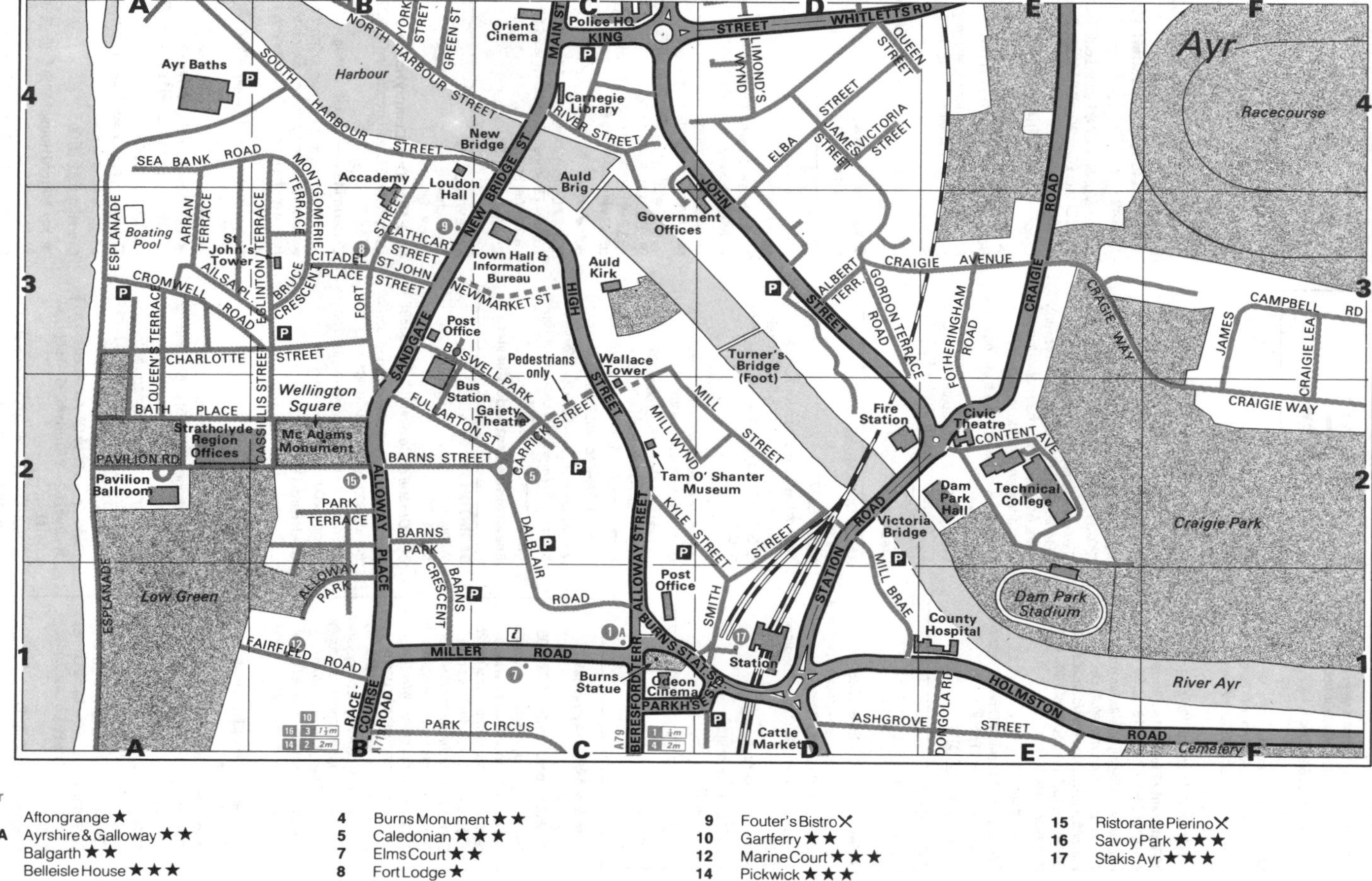

Ayr

1	Aftongrange ★	4	Burns Monument ★★	9	Fouter's Bistro ✕	15	Ristorante Pierino ✕
1A	Ayrshire & Galloway ★★	5	Caledonian ★★★	10	Gartferry ★★	16	Savoy Park ★★★
2	Balgarth ★★	7	Elms Court ★★	12	Marine Court ★★★	17	Stakis Ayr ★★★
3	Belleisle House ★★★	8	Fort Lodge ★	14	Pickwick ★★★		

Bistro's authentic atmosphere is emphasised by the old stone floor.

Closed Mon 25 & 26 Dec & 1 & 2 Jan Lunch not served Sun

French **V** 40 seats Lunch £5.75—£6.75&alc Dinner £17alc Wine £5.95 Last dinner 10.30pm Live music Thu, Fri & Sun

Credit cards 1 2 3 4 5 V

✕**Ristorante Pierino** 1A Alloway Pl ☎ (0292) 269087 Plan **15** *B2*

Popular and friendly little Italian restaurant, it is comfortable and tastefully decorated, with soft background music and candlelit tables. A good choice of pasta and veal dishes are available.

Lunch not served

European 70 seats ✱Dinner £9alc Wine £5.40 Last dinner 11pm

Credit cards 1 2 3 5

AYSGARTH
North Yorkshire
Map **7** SE08

★***Palmer Flatt*** ☎ (09693) 228

A stone built inn, converted from a pilgrim's hospice, set in beautiful Wensleydale.

11rm(2→1⋒)(1fb)2 CTV in 7 bedrooms ® B

CTV 50P 2 *xmas*

V Last dinner 9pm

Credit card 5

AYTON, GREAT
North Yorkshire
Map **8** NZ51

★★★ *HBL* **Ayton Hall**
Low Green
☎ Middlesborough (0642) 723595

This small, luxury hotel run by Melvin and Marian Rhodes is in the village centre and is said to date back to 1281, and there are links with Captain Cooke, reflected in some of the rooms. The living rooms are very elegant with antiques and open fires, while the bedrooms, some with four poster beds, contain every modern amenity. Melvin Rhodes is a very accomplished chef and produces many individually created dishes. There is also an outstanding wine list. This delightful hotel is set in six acres of landscaped grounds.

6rm(5→1⋒)(2fb)3 CTV in all bedrooms **T**
✱sB&B→⋒£50—£60
dB&B→⋒£68—£79 B

35P 2 (£5 per night) (hard) archery croquet Live music & dancing 3 nights wkly nc11yrs

International **V** ✱Lunch £8.95&alc Tea £1.50—£4.50 Dinner £13.95&alc Wine £6.95 Last dinner 9.15pm

Credit cards 1 2 3 V

Ayr — Bakewell

BABBACOMBE
Devon
See under Torquay

BABELL
Clwyd
Map **7** SJ17

✕**Black Lion Inn** ☎ Caerwys (0352) 720239

The Foster family have managed this charming sixteenth-century inn for twenty years, offering good, imaginative food in a warm and friendly atmosphere.

Closed Sun, 1st wk Nov & 1st wk Feb Lunch not served Sat

English & French 54 seats S% Lunch £7.50alc Dinner fr£15.50 Wine £5.50 Last dinner 10pm 80P

Credit cards 2 3 5

BACKFORD CROSS
Cheshire
Map **7** SJ37

★★★**Ladbroke** Backford Cross Roundabout (A41/A5117) (Ladbroke) ☎ Great Mollington (0244) 851551 Telex no 61552

Modern well furnished hotel and conference centre with attractive open plan lounges and two restaurants.

121→⋒(5fb) in 8 bedrooms CTV in all bedrooms ® **T** ✱sB→⋒£50.85—£60.85 dB→⋒£66.70—£86.70(room only) B

(150P CFA pool table tennis *xmas*

V ✱Lunch £6.50—£8.50&alc Dinner £10.50&alc Wine £5.99 Last dinner 10pm

Credit cards 1 2 3 5 V

See advertisement under Chester

BAGINTON
Warwickshire
Map **4** SP37

✕✕***Old Mill*** ☎ Coventry (0203) 303588

Converted water mill offering good food in friendly convivial surroundings.

English & French **V** 80 seats Last dinner 9.45pm 200P Live music Thu-Sat

Credit cards 1 2 3 5

BAGSHOT
Surrey
Map **4** SU96

★★★★ *B* **Pennyhill Park** College Ride (Prestige) ☎ (0276) 71774 Telex no 858841

Standing in 112 acres of magnificent gardens and parkland, this hotel retains its former country house atmosphere.

18→ Annexe: 32→ CTV in all bedrooms **T** sB→£62—£70 dB→£65—£95(room only) B

(250P (heated) (hard) sauna bath solarium *xmas*

V Lunch £16 Tea £1.50 Dinner £22alc Wine £7.50 Last dinner 10.30pm

Credit cards 1 2 3 4 5 V

★★**Cricketers** London Rd (Whitbread) ☎ (0276) 73196

Closed Xmas Day

A popular inn, with the local cricket ground at the rear.

21rm(6→11⋒) Annexe: 8→(11fb) CTV in all bedrooms ® **T** ✱sB&B£35 sB&B→⋒£40 dB&B£50 dB&B→⋒£50 B

(85P

Mainly grills ✱Lunch £6alc Tea £1alc Dinner £6alc Wine £4.55 Last dinner 10.30pm

Credit cards 1 2 3 4 5 V

✕✕**Sultans Pleasure** 13 London Rd, Bagshot Bypass ☎ (0276) 75114

Family run Turkish restaurant, featuring authentic charcoal grilled kebabs and Sasliks.

Closed Sun, Mon & 1st 2 wks Aug, Lunch not served

Turkish 60 seats ✱Dinner £13alc Wine £5.90 Last dinner 10.30pm 60P

BAINBRIDGE
North Yorkshire
Map **7** SD99

★★**Rose & Crown** Village Green (Exec Hotel) ☎ Wensleydale (0969) 50225

Original 15th-century inn, featuring an open fireplace and many old beams.

13rm(3→8⋒)(1fb)3 CTV in all bedrooms ® sB&B£16.50—£17.50 sB&B→⋒£20—21 dB&B£40—£42 dB&B→⋒£40—£42 B

80P *xmas*

V Lunch £7 Tea 60p—£3 High Tea £3.50—£5 Dinner £8.75alc Wine £4.50 Last dinner 9pm

Credit cards 1 3

BAKEWELL
Derbyshire
Map **8** SK26

★★ *BL* **Croft Country House** Great Longstone ☎ Great Longstone (062987) 278

Closed mid Jan—mid Feb & Xmas

Standing in four acres of gardens on the edge of a small village three miles north of Bakewell, this lovely old house provides well-equipped, good-quality accommodation and friendly, informal service.

8rm(3→2⋒) CTV in all bedrooms ® ✱sB&B£26—£29 sB&B→⋒£30—£34 dB&B£33—£39 dB&B→⋒£37—£44 B

Lift CTV 30P

English & French ✱Dinner £9.50 Wine £4.40 Last dinner 8pm

Credit cards 1 3 V

★★ *H* **Milford House** Mill St ☎ (062981) 2130

Closed Jan & Feb RS Nov, Dec & Mar

A fine Georgian house in a peaceful situation, close to town centre.

11rm(8⇌3⫙)CTV available in bedrooms ® ✗ sB&B⇌£18.11—£19.26 dB&B⇌£35.08—£40.82

CTV 10P 9⌂ ⚑ ✿ nc10yrs

Lunch £7.75—£8.05 (Sun only) Dinner £8.05—£9.20 Wine £5 Last dinner 7.30pm

✿✗**Fischer's** Woodhouse, Bath St ☎(062981) 2687

A comfortable little restaurant run by Max and Susan Fischer in a quiet side street is proving a considerable magnet for visitors to this picturesque town. Max cooks in a light modern manner, and provides some particularly enjoyable fish dishes. The menu changes monthly, and there is also an occasional special set menu.

Closed Mon, 24 Dec—8 Jan & 25 Aug—8 Sep Lunch not served Sat Dinner not served Sun

Continental 35 seats

*Lunch £8—£9.50 Dinner £18.50alc Wine £5.50 Last dinner 9pm nc11yrs (dinner)

Credit cards 1 2 3 5

Bakewell — Ballachulish

BALA
Gwynedd
Map **6** SH93

★★***Bala Lake*** (1m S on B4403 Llangower rd) ☎(0678) 520344

Regency hunting lodge with motel block at the rear, situated 1m from Bala.

1⇌ Annexe: 12⫙(2fb) CTV in all bedrooms ®

40P 10⌂ ⚑ ✿ ⛵ ⛳9 *xmas*

Last dinner 8.30pm

Credit cards 1 3 5

★★**Plas Coch** High St ☎(0678) 520309

Closed Xmas Day

Three-storey Victorian building located in Bala's main street.

10rm(3⇌7⫙)(4fb) CTV in all bedrooms ® sB&B⇌⫙£22—£31 dB&B⇌⫙£35 B

16P ⚑

Mainly grills Bar Lunch £1.75—£4.50 Tea £2.25 Dinner £7&alc Wine £4 Last dinner 8.30pm

Credit cards 1 2 3 5 Ⓥ

See advertisement on page 90

★★**White Lion Royal** High St (GW Hotels) ☎(0678) 520314

A former coaching inn, now a holiday hotel in the main street.

22rm(20⇌2⫙)(3fb) ® S% sB&B⇌⫙£25—£27 dB&B⇌⫙£35—£38 B

CTV 30P *xmas*

English & French **V** S% Lunch £5.25—£5.50 Tea £1—£1.50 Dinner £7.25—£7.75 Wine £5.50 Last dinner 9pm

Credit cards 1 2 3 5

BALLACHULISH
Highland *Argyllshire*
Map **14** NN05
See also **North Ballachulish**

★★★**Ballachulish** (Inter Hotel) ☎(08552) 666

Comfortable Highland hotel on the shore of Loch Leven.

Closed Nov—22 May

29rm(10⇌18⫙) 1 CTV in all bedrooms ® T ✗ S% *sB&B⇌⫙fr£27.50 dB&B fr£40 dB&B⇌⫙fr£40 B

Lift P(charged) ✿

S% Lunch fr£7 Tea fr£4 Dinner £12—£20 Last dinner 9.30pm

Credit cards 1 2 3 5

B

★★★ BL

Luxury in the heart of Wales

A country mansion built in 1870, Palé Hall is now a beautifully appointed hotel standing majestically in its own parkland setting overlooking the River Dee and at the foot of the Berwyn mountains.

Each of the individually designed bedrooms and suites has its own luxury en suite bathroom and colour TV, and two have their own private jacuzzis.

Superb cuisine complements the gracious restaurant and should you over indulge, there's a gymnasium with its plunge pool, sauna and solarium, or for the outdoor enthusiast, some excellent shooting and fishing.

Good Food Guide **Egon Ronay 70%**

Llandderfel. Bala. Gwynedd. North Wales. Tel.067-83-285

Plas Coch Hotel

BALA LL23 7AB.
Telephone: 0678 520309

A warm welcome awaits you

Situated in the centre of this picturesque market town. Private car park. Full central heating. All bedrooms with private bathrooms/shower rooms, colour TV & tea/coffee making facilities. Fully licensed hotel with good food & wine. Natural touring centre for North & Mid Wales. Bargain Breaks all year.

New Inn Hotel

Llangynog, Nr. Bala, Powys
Telephone: Pennant (069 174) 229

Your hosts: Alex, Vera & Elizabeth Williamson and Christine Lewis.

Built in 1751 of Welsh stone, the inn is set in beautiful countryside ideal for mountain climbing and walks. Situated at the foot of the Berwyn Mountains with views of the Tanat Valleys. Pony trekking available in the next village. Llangynog is situated on B4391 within easy reach of Lake Vyrnwy and Lake Bala. The waterfalls at Llanrhaedr, one of the seven wonders of Wales, are nearby. Restaurant seats 60 - private parties - coach parties, welcome by appointment - Winter Breaks available.

ALLASALLA
sle of Man
see **Man, Isle of**

ALLATER
irampian *Aberdeenshire*
Map **15** NO39
★ ★*BL* **Darroch Learg** ☎ (0338) 55443
losed Nov—Jan
he hotel, set on a tree-studded, rocky illside with a superb outlook across the River Dee, provides individually-styled edrooms, comfortable lounges and a elaxing atmosphere.
5rm(14🛁1🚿) Annexe: 8rm(3🛁2🚿)(3fb) CTV in 16 bedrooms ® S% sB&B🛁🚿£21 dB&B🛁🚿£34—£42
CTV 25P 🚗 ✿ snooker
🍷 ☕ S% Lunch £5&alc Tea £1.75 Dinner £10 Last dinner 8.30pm
Credit card [3]

ALLINLUIG
ayside *Perthshire*
Map **14** NN95
★ ★**Ballinluig Inn** ☎ (079682) 242
his small, stone, coaching inn dates from he 17th century. The public rooms retain a eriod charm, the lounge bar actually eing converted from the original stables, nd the bedrooms are furnished with nodern facilities.
rm(4🛁1🚿)(2fb)
CTV 60P 🚗 ✿
ast dinner 8pm
Credit cards [1] [2] [3] [5]

ALLOCH
trathclyde *Dunbartonshire*
Map **10** NS38
★ ★**Balloch** (Alloa Brewery)
☎ Alexandria (0389) 52579
losed 1 & 2 Jan
ttractive small hotel in the town centre on he banks of the River Leven.
2rm(6🛁)(4fb) 1📺 CTV in all bedrooms ® sB&B fr£21.45 sB&B🛁 fr£25.55 dB&B fr£33.75 dB&B🛁 fr£39.25 **B**
CTV 40P

🍽 European 🍷 ☕ ✱ Lunch 65p—£2.50 Tea 50p High Tea fr£3.75 Dinner £5.25alc Wine £3.10 Last dinner 8.30pm
Credit cards [1] [2] [3] [5]

BALMACARA
Highland *Ross & Cromarty*
Map **14** NG82
★ ★*L* **Balmacara** ☎ (059986) 283
Family run roadside hotel with fine views across Loch Alsh towards Skye.
30rm(4🛁26🚿)(3fb) sB&B🛁🚿£20—£25 dB&B🛁🚿£35—£40 **B**
CTV 30P 🎵 Live music & dancing wkly in summer
V 🍷 ☕ 🚭 Tea 75p Dinner £10&alc Wine £5.50 Last dinner 8.45pm
Credit cards [1] [3]

BALSALL COMMON
West Midlands
Map **4** SP27
★ ★*H* **Haigs** 273 Kenilworth Rd
☎ Berkswell (0676) 33004
Closed 26 Dec—4 Jan RS 1 wk Aug
Family run hotel with high standard of cooking and informal atmosphere. Near NEC and airport.
14rm(11🚿) CTV in all bedrooms ® 🐕 S% sB&B £15.50—£21.95 sB&B🚿£20—£22.95 dB&B🚿£26.25—£36.75 **B**
CTV 22P 🚗 ✿ nc4yrs
🍽 English & Continental **V** 🍷 ☕ ✱ Lunch £6.50—£7.75 Tea 50p Dinner £7.75&alc Wine £4.75 Last dinner 9pm
Credit cards [1] [2] [3] [5] Ⓥ
See advertisement under Birmingham National Exhibition Centre

BAMBURGH
Northumberland
Map **12** NU13
★ ★**Lord Crewe Arms** Front St
☎ (06684) 243
Closed 11 Nov—Mar
Comfortable, proprietor run hotel with peaceful atmosphere.
25rm(12🛁2🚿)(3fb) CTV in all bedrooms ® sB&B £20—£23 sB&B🛁🚿£25—£29 dB&B £33—£35 dB&B🛁🚿£39—£42 **B**
34P 🚗 nc5yrs
🍽 English & French 🍷 🚭 Lunch £7—£8 Tea £1—£1.20 High Tea £3.50—£6.35 Dinner £10.50—£11.50 Wine £4 Last dinner 8.30pm
Ⓥ

★ ★**Victoria** Front St ☎ (06684) 431
RS 2 Jan—15 Apr
Family run hotel, recently refurbished to offer modern bedrooms and character public rooms.
25rm(17🛁1🚿)(5fb) CTV in 10 bedrooms ® sB&B £15.75—£18.50 sB&B🛁🚿£17.95—£23.10 dB&B £29.40—£35.70 dB&B £35.70—£42 **B**
☾ CTV 8P games room *xmas*
🍷 ☕ Lunch £4—£5 Tea £1—£1.50 Dinner £7.50—£10.50 Last dinner 8pm
Credit cards [1] [2] [3] [5] Ⓥ

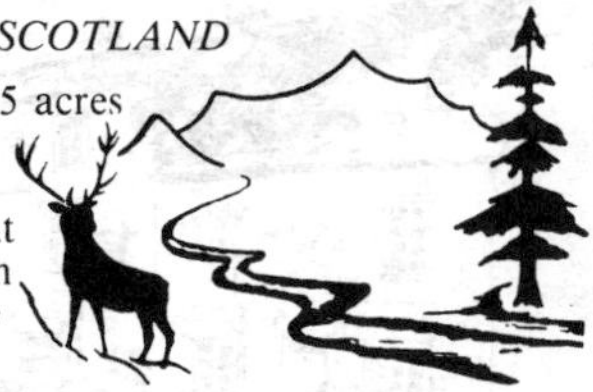

★***Sunningdale*** ☎ (06684) 334
Closed Dec & Jan
Friendly, informal hotel with comfortable accommodation and offering good value dinners.
18rm(6🛁)(3fb) **B**
CTV 16P
🍷 Last dinner 7.30pm

BAMFORD
Derbyshire
Map **8** SK28
★ ★**Marquis of Granby** Hathersage Rd
☎ Hope Valley (0433) 51206
Standing in one of Derbyshire's most attractive Peak District valleys and recently converted from a roadside inn, the hotel →

offers spacious, well-equipped bedrooms of character and historic public rooms. A cosy "village" bar and smart bar lounge adjoin the attractive restaurant, which looks out on a lawned garden.

7rm(6)(2fb) 1 CTV in all bedrooms ® * sB&B fr£22 dB&B fr£34

80P

Wine £5.50

★★**Rising Sun** Castleton Rd
☎ Hope Valley (0433) 51323

Charming roadside inn in the Hope Valley with modern comfortable accommodation and Tudor-style atmosphere.

13rm(7 1)(1fb) CTV in all bedrooms ® T sB&B fr£25 sB&B £30 dB&B fr£38 dB&B fr£42

80P 2 *xmas*

V Lunch £6.50 Tea fr75p Dinner £4.85—£8.25&alc Wine £5 Last dinner 10pm

Credit cards 1 2 3 V

BAMPTON
Devon
Map **3** SS92

★★**Bark House** Oakford Bridge (2½m W A396) ☎ Oakford (03985) 236

Closed Jan & Feb

Small and comfortable, cottage style hotel, with most congenial atmosphere.

6rm(2 2)(1fb) CTV in 5 bedrooms sB&B £12 sB&B £18 dB&B £26 dB&B £32 Continental breakfast

12P

English, American & French Lunch £5—£7.50 Tea £1 Dinner £9.25—£9.50 Wine £6.50 Last dinner 8.30pm

Credit cards 1 2 3 5

BANAVIE
Highland *Inverness-shire*
Map **14** NN17

★★*L* **Moorings** (3m from Fort William on A830) (Exec Hotel)
☎ Corpach (03977) 550

Family run modern hotel with Jacobean style dining room. Also annexe where rooms have private facilities.

Bamford — Banchory

14rm(4 1) Annexe: 3(1fb) CTV in all bedrooms ® sB&B £19.50—£24 sB&B £22—£30 dB&B £30—£34 dB&B £34—£40

CTV 25P nc10yrs

Scottish & French V Lunch £5.50&alc Tea £2—£3.50 Dinner £13&alc Wine £4.75 Last dinner 9pm

Credit cards 1 3 5 V

See advertisement under Fort William

BANBURY
Oxfordshire
Map **4** SP44

★★★**Banbury Moat House**
27-29 Oxford Rd (Queens Moat)
☎ (0295) 59361

Closed 28 Dec—2 Jan

This hotel features modern well-equipped bedrooms, with spacious bathrooms and more traditional public rooms.

52rm(51 1)(2fb) 1 CTV in all bedrooms ® T sB&B £36—£44 dB&B £48—£58

48P CFA

V S% Lunch fr£9.50&alc Tea £1.50 Dinner £12.50—£15&alc Wine £6 Last dinner 9.45pm

Credit cards 1 2 3 5 V

★★★**Whately Hall** Banbury Cross (Trusthouse Forte) ☎ (0295) 3451 Telex no 837149

The attractive stone building is set slightly back from the road in its own pleasant garden. The bedrooms vary from smart, newly-furnished ones in the original building to the more functional ones in the modern wing.

74rm(65 9) CTV in all bedrooms ® sB&B £51.50 dB&B £66.50

Lift 80P CFA *xmas*

Last dinner 9.15pm

Credit cards 1 2 3 4 5

★★**Cromwell Lodge** North Bar
☎ (0295) 59781 Telex no 83343

Pleasant, professionally run hotel with pleasant staff. Modern, well-equipped bedrooms and attractive restaurant providing good food.

32rm(29 3)(1fb) CTV in all bedrooms ® T sB&B £37—£39 dB&B £47—£49

25P

Bar lunch £4.25—£8.25 Tea 75p—£1.75 Dinner £9.95—£14.95&alc Wine £5.25 Last dinner 9.30pm

Credit cards 1 2 3 5

BANCHORY
Grampian *Kincardineshire*
Map **15** NO69

★★★ *HBL* **Raemoir**
☎ (03302) 4884

A fine 18th century mansion house in extensive wooded grounds with an annexe of special architectural interest. It's refreshing to find traditional country house values successfully combined here with modern amenities. The wood panelled lounge is a splendid room, while the bedrooms are individually decorated. Wholesome food is served in the attractive, formal dining room.

17 Annexe: 6rm(4 2)(3fb) in 3 bedrooms CTV in all bedrooms ® T sB&B £35—£40 dB&B fr£60

CTV 200P 3 (charged) (hard) boulle croquet gymnasium sauna bath clay pigeon shoot *xmas*

International V Lunch £8.50&alc Tea £1—£1.50 Dinner £14.50—£15.50&alc Wine £5.15 Last dinner 8.45pm

Credit cards 1 2 3 5 V

★★★ **Banchory Lodge**
(see red star box opposite)

B

★★★

★★★ ⚘BANCHORY LODGE, BANCHORY

☎(03302) 2625

Closed 13 Dec—28 Jan

This handsome, white-painted Georgian house stands in 12 acres of grounds on the banks of the River Dee at it's confluence with the Waters of Feugh. Leaping salmon can be seen and, as the hotel has fishing rights, it naturally attracts fisherfolk. Indeed the table in the hall with its scales often displays the catch of the day. Our members think that the irregular hours of the fishermen, adds to the informality of this exceptionally friendly hotel. Ex-farmers, Dugald and Maggie Jaffray, are the owners who created this hotel out of a near-ruin. Antiques are something of a hobby with them, and the hotel, particularly the restaurant, is furnished with good Victorian and Edwardian pieces. Lots of beautiful flowers also play their part in the generally attractive decor. Public rooms consist of a Cobbleheugh Bar, two comfortable sitting rooms, one with television, and open fires burn when necessary. Apart from fishing, other recreational facilities include table tennis, pool and a bowling green, and there is also a

shop. The main dining room gleams with polished wood and silver and provides hearty British country house cooking which features fine local fish, beef and game. This hotel is very much a favourite with our members.

24rm(23➡1⋒)(12fb)3⊟ CTV in all bedrooms ®S% ✱sB&B➡⋒£38.64 dB&B➡⋒£60.37

CTV 50P ⊞ ✿ ✔ pool table sauna bath ⌂

V ♈ ☕ S% ✱Lunch fr£6.50 Tea £3.75 Dinner £10—£14.95 Wine £4.80 Last dinner 9.15pm

Credit cards 1 2 3 4 5 Ⓥ

★★★**Tor-na-Coille** ☎(03302) 2242

Closed 24—26 Dec

A white, granite house, standing in its own wooded gardens, above the A93.

23rm(13➡10⋒)(2fb) CTV in all bedrooms ®T sB&B➡⋒£35—£40 dB&B➡⋒£50—£55 B

Lift 60P ✿ ✔ squash billiards sauna bath solarium bowling ⌂

♉Scottish & French V ♈ ☕ Bar lunch £7.50alc Tea fr85p Dinner fr£11.50 Wine £6.25 Last dinner 9.45pm

Credit cards 1 2 3 5 Ⓥ

★★***Burnett Arms*** (Consort) ☎(03302) 2545 Telex no 739925

Rough cast and granite fronted building in the main street of this pleasant, Deeside town.

17rm(4➡7⋒)(3fb) T B

CTV 40P Live music & dancing Sun

♈ ☕ Last dinner 8pm

Credit cards 1 2 3 5

BANFF
Grampian *Banffshire*
Map **15** NJ66

★★★**Banff Springs** Golden Knowes Rd (Consort) ☎(02612) 2881

A modern hotel, west of the town set on a hillside with good views over Moray Firth.

30rm(25➡5⋒)(4fb) CTV in all bedrooms ®T ✖ ✱sB&B➡⋒£27.60—£28.75 dB&B➡⋒£34 B

☾120P ⊞ ⌂ *xmas*

♉French V ♈ ☕ Bar lunch £1.30—£3.75 Tea 70p—£1.75 Dinner £8.50—£10&alc Wine £5.30 Last dinner 9pm

Credit cards 1 2 3 5 Ⓥ

★★**The County** 32 High St ☎(02612) 5353

An elegant, Georgian mansion behind weeping ash trees, set in an elevated position overlooking the Bay.

7rm(6➡)(2fb) 2⊟ CTV in all bedrooms ® T sB&B➡£23—£31 dB&B➡£32—£48 B

6P ⌂ *xmas*

♉Scottish & French V ♈ ☕ Lunch £3.25—£5.75 Tea fr£1.50 Dinner £5.75—£15.50 Wine £4.25 Last dinner 9.30pm

Credit cards 2 5 Ⓥ

★**Dounemount** ☎ Macduff (0261) 32262

RS Nov—Apr

This attractive house is attached to the farm and is located on a quiet country lane.

7rm(2⋒)(2fb) CTV in all bedrooms ® ✖ S% ✱sB&B£12.50—£13.50 dB&B£24 dB&B⋒£25

CTV 40P 2⌂ ⊞ ✿ Live music and dancing wknds

V S% ✱ Bar Lunch £1.80—£2.50&alc Dinner £7.50—£8.50 Last dinner 9pm

★**Fife Lodge** Sandyhill Rd ☎(02612) 2436

Homely and attractive small country hotel with open fires in the public rooms in cold weather.

7➡⋒(3fb) CTV in all bedrooms ®S% sB&B➡⋒£20—£22 dB&B➡⋒£27—£36 B 150P 2⌂ ✿ ⌂

V ♈ ☕ ⊁ S% Lunch £3.50—£4.50 Tea £1alc Dinner £9alc Wine £4.50 Last dinner 9pm

Credit cards 1 3

BANGOR
Gwynedd
Map **6** SH57

★★★**British** High St ☎(0248) 364911

Three-storey, commercial/tourist hotel located beside a busy road. →

52⇌(3fb) CTV in all bedrooms ® T ⊁ S% sB&B⇌£18—£20 dB&B⇌£36—£38 B
Lift ☾ CTV 50P 2⌂(£1 per night) no babies CFA♿
V ♔ S% Lunch £4—£5.50&alc Tea £1 Dinner £5.50—£8&alc Wine £3.50 Last dinner 9pm
Credit cards 1 3

★★**Railway** High St ☏(0248) 362158
Near station, this personally run hotel offers modern bedrooms and comfortable lounges and an informal, relaxed atmosphere.
20rm(8⇌6⋔) CTV in 4 bedrooms ⊁ sB&B£13.50 sB&B⇌⋔£13.50 dB&B£27 dB&B⇌⋔£27 B
CTV 20P sauna bath solarium
English & French V ♔ ☐ Lunch £4.50—£5.95 Tea fr 75p Dinner £4.75—£5.95&alc Wine £2.75 Last dinner 10pm
Credit cards 1 2 3 5 Ⓥ

★★*H* **Telford** Holyhead Rd ☏(0248) 352543
Closed 25 & 26 Dec
Good hospitality is offered by the resident owners at this comfortable, stone-built hotel, which stands on the banks of the Menai Straits, and adjacent to Telford's famous suspension bridge.
9rm(4⇌2⋔)(1fb) CTV in all bedrooms ⊁ B
CTV 12P ✿
♔ ☐ Last dinner 8.30pm
Credit cards 1 2 3

★★**Ty Uchaf** Tal-y-Bont (2m E of A55) ☏(0248) 352219
Closed 23 Dec—18 Jan
This modern, comfortable hotel, within easy reach of main line train services, prides itself on the quality of food served.
9rm(6⇌3⋔) CTV in 8 bedrooms TV in 1 bedroom ® ⊁
sB&B⇌⋔£16.50—£17.50
dB&B⇌⋔£26.50—£28.50
40P ✿ nc10yrs
V ♔ ☐ Lunch £5—£7 Tea 50p—£1 High Tea £1.50—£2.50 Dinner £7.50—£9.50&alc Wine £5 Last dinner 8.30pm
Credit cards 1 3

Bangor — Barkston

BARDON MILL
Northumberland
Map **12** NY76

★**Vallum Lodge** Military Rd, Twice Brewed ☏(04984) 248
This hotel, in a rural setting near Hadrians Wall, provides neat unpretentious accommodation.
7rm(2fb) sB&B£11—£12.50 dB&B£21—£23 B
CTV 25P ✿
Mainly Grills ♔ ☐ ⁄ Lunch £3alc Tea £2.15alc Dinner £5.75alc Wine £3.90 Last dinner 9pm

BARDSEY
North Yorkshire
Map **8** SE34

XX**Bingley Arms** Church Ln ☏Collingham Bridge (0937) 72462
One of England's oldest inns featuring English dishes and game.
Closed Mon
Lunch not served Tue-Sat Dinner not served Sun
English & French V 70 seats S% Lunch £6.50 Dinner £7.75&alc Wine £4.50 Last dinner 9.30pm 80P
Credit cards 1 3

BARFORD
Warwickshire
Map **4** SP26

★★★**Glebe** Church St ☏Warwick (0926) 624218
Tempting menus, agreeable accommodation and convivial, peaceful surroundings are offered by the Glebe Hotel, a Georgian house adjacent to the village church.
15rm(6⇌5⋔)(2fb) CTV in all bedrooms ® T ⊁ sB&B£18—£22 sB&B⇌⋔£24—£27.50 dB&B£34—£38 dB&B⇌⋔£39.50—£48 B
45P ✿ *xmas*
English & Continental V ♔ ☐ Lunch £8.75&alc Tea fr £1 Dinner fr £9.75&alc Wine £5.30 Last dinner 9.30pm
Credit cards 1 2 3 5 Ⓥ

BAR HILL
Cambridgeshire
Map **5** TL36

★★★**Cambridgeshire Moat House** (Queens Moat) ☏Crafts Hill (0954) 80555 Telex no 817141
Modern hotel with extensive sporting facilities including championship golf course.
100⇌ CTV in all bedrooms ® T
*sB&B⇌£46 dB&B⇌£59 B
☾ 200P CFA ✿ ⊡(heated) ⚑18 ℘(hard) squash sauna bath putting green disco Sat ♫ *xmas*
English & French V ♔ ☐ S% *Lunch £11.50&alc Tea £1 High Tea £1.20—£3 Dinner £11.50&alc Wine £6.15 Last dinner 10pm
Credit cards 1 2 3 4 5 Ⓥ
See advertisement under Cambridge

BARKSTON
Lincolnshire
Map **8** SK94

XX**Barkston House** ☏Loveden (0400) 50555
Sound British dishes, with fresh produce treated in a light, modern style, form the basis of the short but imaginative menu here, where the quality of food is matched by charmingly attentive service. The dining room — originally the kitchen of the pleasant eighteenth-century house — has stripped beams, complete with servants' bells, and open fireplace. The warm, country atmosphere carries through to an attractive sitting room and a large, comfortable bar. Two fine bedrooms are available for overnight guests.
Closed few days after Xmas Dinner not served Sun & Mon Lunch not served Sat
34 seats *Lunch £7.75alc Dinner £12.90alc Wine £4.95 Last dinner 9.15pm 16P
2 bedrooms available
Credit cards 1 2 3 5

BARLEY
Lancashire
Map **7** SD84

✕✕***Barley Mow*** ☎ Nelson (0282) 64293

This small, country restaurant nestles at the foot of Pendle Hill. Low ceilings and thick walls help to provide a cosy and attractive setting in which to enjoy the well-prepared and good-value menu.

Lunch not served Mon—Sat

English & French 32 seats Last dinner 10pm 15P

Credit cards 1 3

BARMOUTH
Gwynedd
Map **6** SH61

★★**Ty'r Craig** Llanaber Rd ☎ (0341) 280470

Closed Nov—Feb

Victorian mock castle with wealth of stained glass, wood panelling and decorated ceilings. Fine views of Barmouth Bay.

12rm(2⇌7⋔)(1fb)1⊠ CTV in all bedrooms ® ✗ sB&B⇌⋔£18.50 dB&B£30 dB&B⇌⋔£35 **B**

15P ⇋ ✿

Welsh, English & French Lunch fr£6.50&alc Tea fr£1.50 Dinner £7.50&alc Wine £4.95 Last dinner 8pm

Credit cards 1 3 Ⓥ

★**Bryn Melyn** Panorama Rd ☎ (0341) 280556

Closed Dec—Jan

This family-run hotel provides comfortable accommodation and occupies a commanding position over the Mawddach Estuary.

10rm(8⋔)(2fb) CTV in all bedrooms ® S% sB&B fr£15 sB&B⋔£17.50 dB&B⋔£29 **B**

CTV 10P ⇋ ✿

Bar lunch fr£2.50 Dinner £8.50—£10 Wine £4.95 Last dinner 8.30pm

Credit card 1 Ⓥ

★**Min-y-Mor** Promenade ☎ (0341) 280555

RS Oct—Mar

A detached hotel, situated on the promenade, ¼m from the town centre.

50rm(6⇌5⋔)(5fb) ✗ sB&B fr£11.50 dB&B fr£23 dB&B⇌⋔fr£27

CTV P ✿ Live music & dancing wkly in high season ♿

Lunch fr£4 Tea fr85p Dinner fr£6 Wine £3.50 Last dinner 7.30pm

Credit cards 1 3

BARNARD CASTLE
Co Durham
Map **12** NZ01

★★***King's Head*** 12/14 Market Pl ☎ Teesdale (0833) 38356

Family run hotel with comfortable well-appointed bedrooms.

20⇌(1fb) CTV in all bedrooms ® T ✗ **B**

CTV 25P

English & Continental **V** Last dinner 9pm.

Credit cards 1 2 3 5

BARNBY MOOR
Nottinghamshire
Map **8** SK68

★★★**Ye Olde Bell** (Trusthouse Forte) ☎ Retford (0777) 705121

An original 17th-century posting house whose guests have included Queen Victoria and Queen Maud of Norway.

58rm(46⇌)(1fb)2⊠ CTV in all bedrooms ® sB&B⇌£47.50 dB&B⇌£61.50 **B**

☾ 250P CFA ✿ *xmas*

Last dinner 9.45pm

Credit cards 1 2 3 4 5

BARNET
Gt London
Map **4** TQ29

✕✕***Wings*** 6 Potters Rd, New Barnet ☎ 01-449 9890

This small, family-run Chinese restaurant is very popular, featuring authentic and well-cooked Szechwan and Peking dishes and offering particularly attentive service.

Closed Mon, 2wks Jul & 25—26 Dec Lunch not served Tue

Chinese **V** 60 seats Last dinner 10.30pm **P**

Credit cards 1 2 3 5

BARNHAM BROOM
Norfolk
Map **5** TG00

★★★**Barnham Broom Hotel Golf & Country Club** (Best Western) ☎ (060545) 393 Telex no 975711

A challenging, championship-standard golf course is just one of the many leisure facilities available at this attractive modern hotel.

52⇌⋔(12fb) CTV in all bedrooms ® T sB&B⇌⋔£40—£45 dB&B⇌⋔£52—£57 **B**

☾ 200P CFA ✿ (heated) 18 (hard) squash snooker sauna bath solarium ♿

V Lunch £5—£7.50&alc Tea 60p—£1.20 Dinner £9—£9.50&alc Wine £6 Last dinner 9.30pm

Credit cards 1 2 3 5 Ⓥ

BARNSDALE BAR
South Yorkshire
Map **8** SE51

★★**TraveLodge** (A1) (Trusthouse Forte) ☎ Pontefract (0977) 620711 Telex no 557457

Situated on an A1 service area midway between London and Edinburgh, the hotel offers modern bedrooms and all the usual service area facilities.

72⇌ CTV in all bedrooms ® T sB&B⇌£31 dB&B⇌£42 **B**

☾ 120P ⇋

Mainly grills (All meals at adjacent Service Area)

Credit cards 1 2 3 4 5

BARNSLEY
South Yorkshire
Map **8** SE30

★★★**Ardsley Moat House** Doncaster Rd, Ardsley (Queens Moat) ☎ (0226) 289401 Telex no 547762

A late 18th-century house in the classical style has been enlarged and converted into an up-to-date hotel. There are spacious lounges, the attractive restaurant has an adjoining lounge bar, and there is also the smart Jopling's Bar.

62⇌(4fb)3⊠ CTV in all bedrooms ® T sB&B⇌£40 dB&B⇌£55 **B**

☾ 300P ✿ Live music and dancing Fri

English & French **V** Lunch fr£7.50&alc Tea fr£1 Dinner £9.50&alc Wine £5.50 Last dinner 10.30pm

Credit cards 1 2 3 5

★**Royal** Church St ☎ (0226) 203658

Comfortable, well-appointed hotel with spacious lounge bars and restaurant featuring local dishes.

18rm(1⇌)(1fb) CTV in all bedrooms ® sB&B£15—£22.50 sB&B⇌£16.50—£30.50 dB&B£30—£33.20 dB&B⇌£33—£37.50 **B**

CTV 5 Live music & dancing Sun

Lunch £3.99—£5.90&alc Tea 50—80p Dinner £5.90—£7.95&alc Wine £4.20 Last dinner 8.30pm

Credit cards 1 2 3 5 Ⓥ

✕✕**Brooklands** Barnsley Rd, Dodworth (2m W A628 close to M1 junct 37) ☎ (0226) 299571 Telex no 54623

Closed 25 & 26 Dec

English, French, German & Italian 184 seats Lunch £5.20—£6.20 Dinner £10.50alc Wine £2.80 Last dinner 9.30pm 300P

Credit cards 1 2 3 4 5 Ⓥ

See advertisement on page 96

BARNSTAPLE
Devon
Map **2** SS53

★★★***Barnstaple Motel*** Braunton Rd ☎ (0271) 76221

A modern, purpose-built tourist hotel in a quiet setting.

60⇌(4fb) CTV in all bedrooms ® T **B**

☾ CTV 175P 10 ⇋ ✿ (heated) sauna bath solarium gymnasium

English & French **V** Last dinner 10pm

Credit cards 1 2 3 4 5

See advertisement on page 96

Barnstaple

★★★**Imperial** Taw Vale Pde (Trusthouse Forte) ☎ (0271) 45861

All modern facilities are found in this centrally situated hotel.

56rm(55➡1⋒)(2fb) CTV in all bedrooms ®sB&B➡⋒£44.50 dB&B➡⋒£61.50 B

Lift ☾ 80P *xmas*

♈ ☕ Last dinner 9.45pm

Credit cards 1 2 3 4 5

★★★**North Devon Motel** Taw Vale (Brend) ☎ (0271) 72166 Telex no 42551

A small hotel with modern amenities, and a restaurant on the first floor.

26rm(24➡2⋒)(7fb)) CTV in all bedrooms ®sB&B➡⋒£24.73—£25.87 dB&B➡⋒£34.50—£39.10 B

☾ 80P Live music and dancing wkly

♉ English & French **V** ♈ ☕ Lunch fr£4.75&alc Tea fr75p Dinner fr£7.50&alc Wine £4.10 Last dinner 9pm

Credit cards 1 2 3 5

★★★**Roborough House** Pilton (Exec Hotel) ☎ (0271) 72354

Closed 1—18 Jan

Extended Georgian house on the edge of the town has a panoramic view over the Tew Valley. It has well furnished rooms and its restaurant is popular with local business people.

9rm(6➡3⋒)(2fb) 2⊠ CTV in all bedrooms **T** sB&B➡⋒£27.50 dB&B➡⋒£40 B

40P ⊞ ✿ *xmas*

♉ British & French **V** ✱ Lunch £6.95&alc Dinner £9.50&alc

Credit cards 1 2 3 5

★★

★★ **DOWNREW HOUSE, BARNSTAPLE**

(off unclass rd 1½m SE Bishop's Tawton A377) ☏ (0271) 42497

Closed Jan—late Mar

The worries of the world can be left behind when you enter this hotel. The warm welcome from the Ainsworths, owners of this Queen Anne gentlemen's residence, pleases all their guests who are enthusiastic in their praise of the hotel. The interior is spotlessly clean with shining brass and fresh with flowers; it is decorated with Mr Ainsworth's paintings. Recreational facilities include a fifteen hole approach golf course, croquet, swimming pool and a tennis court, and there is also a billiard and games room indoors. Children over seven are welcome so it provides for a real family holiday. Mrs Ainsworth supervises the cooking and delicious four course dinners are provided. There is an à la carte menu but, like the very large selection of packed lunches, it has to be ordered in advance. There are two sitting rooms and a tiny bar as well as the attractive dining room which overlooks the garden. The bedrooms are comfortable and nicely furnished. This is a peaceful and secluded hotel, just a few miles out of Barnstaple on the slopes of Codden Hill, and is one which our members always think very highly of.

7 Annexe: 7 CTV in all bedrooms ® in 2 bedrooms T ✱ sB&B £40.82—£56.92(incl dinner) dB&B £66.70—£82.80(incl dinner)

16P (heated) (hard) snooker solarium nc7yrs *xmas*

English & French Dinner £16.10 Wine £5.75 Last dinner 8.30pm

Ⓥ

★★**Royal & Fortescue** Boutport St (Brend) ☏ (0271) 42289 Telex no 42551

Named after King Edward VII, then Prince of Wales, who was a guest there.

61rm(33 2)(5fb) CTV in 33 bedrooms ✱sB&B£19.55 sB&B £24.15 dB&B£33.35 dB&B £39.10 B

Lift ☾ CTV 20P 6 Live music and dancing wkly *xmas*

English & French Lunch fr£3.85&alc Tea fr£1.10 Dinner fr£7.50&alc Wine £3.85 Last dinner 9pm

Credit cards 1 2 3 5

See advertisement on page 98

✕✕✕**Lynwood House** Bishop's Tawton Rd ☏ (0271) 43695

Fine food and the personal attention of the Roberts family make this restaurant an excellent choice. The businessman, be his taste in lunches light or substantial, is well catered for in the Grill Room, whilst the discerning customer might well dine in the Seafood Room.

Closed Sun & some Bank Hol Mons Lunch not served Sat

V 65 seats ✱Lunch £10alc Dinner £16alc Wine £5.50 Last dinner 10pm 25P

Credit cards 1 2 3 5 Ⓥ

BARR, GREAT
West Midlands
Map **7** SP09

★★★**Barr** Pear Tree Dr, Newton Rd (1m W of junc A34/A4041) (Best Western) ☎021-357 1141 Telex no 336406

Comfortable hotel with popular restaurant.

114🛁🚿(1fb) CTV in all bedrooms ® T ✈ S% sB&B🛁🚿£35—£40 dB&B🛁🚿£45—£50 ₿

☾220P ✽ pool room Live music and dancing Sat & Sun

♁English & Continental V ♀ ☕ S% Lunch £5.50—£6.50&alc Tea 65—75p Dinner £7.50—£8.50&alc Wine £5.25 Last dinner 10pm

Credit cards 1 2 3 4 5 Ⓥ

See advertisement under Birmingham

★★★**Post House** Chapel Ln (at junc M6/A34) (Trusthouse Forte) ☎021-357 7444 Telex no. 338497

Busy modern hotel near M5/M6. Popular business meeting place.

204🛁 CTV in all bedrooms ® T sB&B🛁£52.50 dB&B🛁£66.50 ₿

☾280P CFA ✽ ⛲ (heated)

♀ ☕ Last dinner 10pm

Credit cards 1 2 3 4 5

BARRA, ISLE OF
Western Isles *Inverness-shire*
Map **13**

TANGUSDALE
Map **13** NF60

★★**Isle of Barra** Tangusdale Beach, Castlebay (Consort) ☎Castlebay (08714) 383

Closed Oct—Apr

Modern hotel looking onto a beautiful sandy beach. The service is friendly and seafood is a speciality.

36🛁 ® S% sB&B🛁£25—£27 dB&B🛁£43—£45

1🚗 ✽ Live music & dancing weekly

♀ ☕ S% Bar lunch fr£1.50&alc Tea fr£1.50 Dinner £10.50—£12 Wine £4 Last dinner 8.50pm

Credit cards 1 2 3 4 Ⓥ

BARRHEAD
Strathclyde *Renfrewshire*
Map **11** NS45

★★**Dalmeny Park** Lochlibo Rd (Norscot) ☎041-881 9211

19th century house with gardens, on the edge of town, with open fires and Georgian-style function suite.

20rm(10🛁)(2fb) CTV in all bedrooms ® ₿

🚫🐕 ✽

♀ Lunch fr£5 Dinner £11—£14&alc

Credit cards 1 2 3 4 5 Ⓥ

See advertisement under Glasgow

BARRINGTONS, THE (near Burford)
Gloucestershire
Map **4** SP21

★★★**Inn for all Seasons** (3m W of Burford on A40) ☎Windrush (04514) 324

Closed 29 Dec—5 Jan

An ancient, small hotel with beams and exposed walls, comfortable bedrooms and a pleasant garden at the rear.

9🛁 CTV in all bedrooms ® T ✈ sB&B🛁£35 dB&B🛁£55 ₿

☾CTV 30P ✽ nc10yrs

V ♀ ☕ Lunch £6.95 Tea £1.25 Dinner £10.50 Wine £5.30 Last dinner 9.30pm

Credit cards 1 2 3

BARROW-IN-FURNESS
Cumbria
Map **7** SD16

★★★**Victoria Park** Victoria Rd (Whitbread) ☎(0229) 21159

RS 24 Dec—1 Jan

An extensively-modernised Victorian building situated just off the A590.

40rm(21🛁6🚿)(3fb) CTV in all bedrooms ® T ✈ sB&Bfr£30 sB&B🛁🚿fr£42 dB&Bfr£37 dB&B🛁🚿fr£47 ₿

☾60P Crown green bowling

♁English & French V ♀ Lunch fr£5.50 Dinner £9—£9.50&alc Wine £4.95 Last dinner 9.30pm

Credit cards 1 2 3 5

★**White House** Abbey Road ☎(0229) 27303

A commercial hotel on the main road to the town centre, the White House has lively bars and offers neat and well-equipped bedroom accommodation.

29rm(3🛁) CTV in all bedrooms ® T S% ✱sB&B£27.50 sB&B🛁£34.50 dB&B£37 dB&B🛁£42 ₿

☾60P 20🚗

♁English & French V ♀ ☕ S% ✱Lunch £5.50&alc Tea fr£2 High Tea fr£2.50 Dinner fr£7.75&alc

Credit cards 1 2 3 5

BARRY
South Glamorgan
Map **3** ST16

★★★**Mount Sorrell** Porthkerry Rd (Exec Hotel) ☎(0446) 740069

Overlooking the town and the Bristol Channel, this small, friendly commercial hotel is conveniently positioned for Cardiff or Wales International Airport.

33rm(16🛁17🚿) Annexe: 4🛁(3fb) CTV in all bedrooms ® T sB&B🛁🚿£29—£32 dB&B🛁🚿£38—£42 ₿

☾17P Disco Sat

♁Continental V ♀ Lunch £6alc Dinner £9—£9.75&alc Wine £4.50 Last dinner 10pm

Credit cards 1 2 3 4 5 Ⓥ

★★**Aberthaw House** 28 Porthkerry Rd ☎(0446) 737314

Closed 1 wk Xmas

Comfortable accommodation and home cooking of a high standard are available at this small, family-run hotel.

8rm(4🛁1🚿)(1fb) 1📺 CTV in all bedrooms ® ✱sB&Bfr£18 sB&B🛁🚿fr£20 dB&Bfr£28 dB&B🛁🚿fr£30 ₿

P 🚫🐕 solarium

♁International ♀ ☕ ✱Lunch fr£6 Dinner fr£7.50 Wine £4.35 Last dinner 10pm

Credit cards 1 3

BARTLE
Lancashire
Map **7** SD43

★★★**Bartle Hall** Lea Ln ☎ Preston (0772) 690506

Large country house in 16 acres of lawns and woodland.

12rm(7⇌5⋒)4⊞ CTV in all bedrooms ®T ✈ sB&B⇌⋒£33–£39 dB&B⇌⋒£39–£45

☾ CTV 80P ✿ ⛱ ⚲(hard)

English & French V Lunch £5.50&alc Dinner £9.50&alc Wine £6.90 Last dinner 10pm

Credit cards 1 2 3 5 Ⓥ

BARTON
Lancashire
Map **7** SD53

★★★**Barton Grange** Garstang Rd (Best Western) ☎ Preston (0772) 862551 Telex no 67392

An extended and modernised hotel set in a garden centre complex.

60rm(53⇌7⋒)(10fb) 1⊞ CTV in all bedrooms ®T ✈ S% sB&B⇌⋒£27–£45 dB&B⇌⋒£32.50–£52.50 B

Lift ☾ CTV 250P CFA ✿ (heated) *xmas*

English & French V S% Lunch fr£6.75 Tea fr75p High Tea fr£2.95 Dinner fr£9.50&alc Wine £5.95 Last dinner 10pm

Credit cards 1 2 3 5

BARTON STACEY
Hampshire
Map **4** SU44

○ **Little Chef Lodge** A303 westbound ☎ Longparish (026472) 260

20⇌⋒ Due to have opened October 1986.

BARTON UNDER NEEDWOOD
Staffordshire
Map **7** SK11

○ **Little Chef Lodge** A38 Lichfield Rd ☎ (028371) 6343

20 rms. Opened late 1985

BASILDON
Essex
Map **5** TQ78

★★★**Crest** Cranes Farm Rd (Crest) ☎ (0268) 280935 Telex no 995141

Modern hotel with well equipped, somewhat functional bedrooms, good public rooms and Fat Sams cocktail bar.

116⇌⋒ in 16 bedrooms CTV in all bedrooms ®T S% sB&B⇌⋒fr£53.95 dB&B⇌⋒fr£63.95 B

Lift ☾ CTV 90P CFA ✿ putting games room Disco nightly *xmas*

English & Continental V S% Lunch fr£8.75&alc Tea fr70p&alc Dinner fr£11.95&alc Wine £5.80 Last dinner 9.45pm

Credit cards 1 2 3 4 5

○ **Campanile** Southern arterial road (A127)

50 rms. Due to have opened by late 1986.

BASINGSTOKE
Hampshire
Map **4** SU65

★★★★ *HBL* **Tylney Hall** ☎ Hook (025672) 4881

(For full entry see Rotherwick)

★★★**Crest** Grove Rd (Crest) ☎ (0256) 468181 Telex no 858501

Modern hotel with well-equipped bedrooms, two bars and Hackwoods pantry restaurant.

86⇌⋒(7fb) in 10 bedrooms CTV in all bedrooms ®S% ∗ sB⇌⋒£49–£54 dB⇌⋒£57.50–£74(room only) B

☾ 86P CFA ♿ *xmas*

S% ∗ Lunch £7.50&alc Dinner £11.50&alc Wine £5.80 Last dinner 9.45pm

Credit cards 1 2 3 4 5

See advertisement on page 100

B

★★★**Ladbroke** (& Conference centre) Aldermaston Rbt, Ringway North (A339) (Ladbroke) ☎(0256) 20212 Telex no 858223

All bedrooms are equipped to a high standard in this modern, well-managed hotel. The Ladbroke Table features a fixed price buffet which is good value for money.

108⇌⋔(25fb)⚟in 6 bedrooms CTV in all bedrooms ®T✻sB⇌⋔£21.75—£56.50 dB⇌⋔£43.50—£70(room only) Ᵽ

Lift ☾ 150P CFA snooker *xmas*

V ♡ ☐⚟ Lunch £6.50—£8.50&alc Tea £1 Dinner £10.75—£15.&alc Wine £6 Last dinner 10pm

Credit cards 1 2 3 4 5 Ⓥ

Basingstoke

★★★**Ladbroke Lodge** Old Common Rd, Black Dam (Ladbroke) ☎(0256) 460460 Telex no 859381

The hotel is modern and well-managed, its good bedrooms equipped to a high standard. The fixed price buffet in the Hillside Restaurant represents good value for money, and service is both helpful and unpretentious.

120⇌⋔(18fb)⚟in 10 bedrooms CTV in all bedrooms ®T sB⇌⋔£50.50—£60.50 dB⇌⋔£58—£68(room only) Ᵽ

☾ 198P ✿ ▭(heated) sauna bath gymnasium *xmas*

V ♡ ☐ Wine £5.99 Last dinner 10pm

Credit cards 1 2 3 5 Ⓥ

★★**Red Lion** London St (Anchor) ☎(0256) 28525 Telex no 859504

The interior of this early-seventeenth century inn still has some old beams, but it offers modern bedrooms and a choice of good-value dining rooms.

63rm(31➡32⋒)(4fb)⊬in 7 bedrooms CTV in all bedrooms ® *sB&B➡⋒£24—£47 dB&B➡⋒£42—£57 B

Lift ☾60P

V ♈ *Lunch £5.50—£9.65alc Dinner £5.50—£9.65alc Wine £5.95 Last dinner 10.30pm

Credit cards 1 2 3 4 5 Ⓥ

◯**Audleys Wood** Alton Rd (Thistle) ☎(0256) 23286

62➡⋒ Due to open Summer 1987

BASLOW
Derbyshire
Map **8** SK27

★★★**CAVENDISH, BASLOW**

☎(024688) 2311 Telex no 547150

About 200 years old, this pleasant, stone built inn has been converted into a popular hotel with high standards of hotel keeping by Eric Marsh. It is part of the Chatsworth estate and the Duchess of Devonshire takes an interest in the decor. Two years ago an extension, the Mitford Wing, was built and, with David Milnaric and Robert Gitley, she was responsible for the superb bedrooms with their attractive, crisp, soft furnishings and containing some wooden furniture crafted in the estate workshops. Other bedrooms have been re-furbished to the same high standard and none of them overlook the road. They are well equipped with bath robes, mini bar and lots of thoughtful extras. Throughout the hotel open fires burn in winter and it is always bright with flowers. There is a welcoming hall with some seating, an intimate bar and a stylish lounge also with comfortable seating. The elegant Paxton Room is the scene of chef Buckingham's ambitious cooking. For those interested in the chef's work, there is an unusual opportunity to book a table in the kitchen. Nigel Pullar is an

amiable restaurant manager and he imbues his staff with the idea of providing friendly service — indeed an attitude that applies throughout the hotel. The garden, with delightful views, has a putting green and golf driving range.

24➡⋒ 1⊟ CTV in all bedrooms ® T ✗ *sB➡⋒£47.50—£55 dB➡⋒£57.50—£65 (room only) B

☾50P ⊭ ✿ ⟋ putting green golf net

♉Cosmopolitan V ♈ ⊒ Lunch £15.20alc Tea £1.50alc Dinner £15.20alc Wine £6.50 Last dinner 10pm

Credit cards 2 3 5

BASSENTHWAITE
Cumbria
Map **11** NY23

★★★★ ♣ **Armathwaite Hall**
☎ Bassenthwaite Lake (059681) 551

Historic building in large park with woodland, near Bassenthwaite Lake.

40rm(32➡8⋒)(4fb) 2⊟ CTV in all bedrooms T sB&B➡⋒£40—£50 dB&B➡⋒£66—£80 B

Lift ☾100P 4⌂(charge) ✿ ⊡(heated) ⌕(hard 7 ⟋ squash snooker sauna bath solarium gymnasium games room pitch & putt croquet ⊕ ♿ *xmas*

♉English & French V ♈ ⊒ Bar lunch £15—£17alc Dinner £15—£17alc Wine £5.25 Last dinner 9.30pm

Credit cards 1 2 3 5 Ⓥ

See advertisement under Keswick

★★★ **Castle Inn** ☎ Bassenthwaite Lake (059681) 401

Closed mid 2 wks Nov & Xmas

This comfortable, friendly hotel, under the same ownership for nearly thirty years, features attractive gardens and an outdoor swimming pool.

22rm(14➡4⋒)(2fb) 1⊟ CTV in all bedrooms T S% sB&B➡⋒£31—£37 dB&B➡⋒£42—£52 B

100P ✿ ⌓(heated) ⌕(grass) sauna bath solarium Live music & dancing Sat ♿

♈ ⊒ S% Lunch fr£6.75 Tea fr£1 Dinner fr£10.50 Wine £5 Last dinner 8.30pm

Credit cards 1 2 3 4 5

★★ ♣ *HL* **Overwater Hall** Ireby (2m N)
☎ Bassenthwaite Lake (059681) 566

Closed 24 Dec—20 Feb

A really warm welcome is offered by this spacious and well-appointed hotel, the building being of both architectural and historic interest.

13rm(9➡)(4fb) 3⊟ CTV in all bedrooms ® T sB&B fr£21 sB&B➡fr£23 dB&B fr£32 dB&B➡fr£36 B

25P ⊭ ✿

♉English & French ♈ ⊒ Dinner £11.50 Wine £3.85 Last dinner 8.30pm

Credit cards 1 3

★★ *L* ***Pheasant Inn*** ☎ Bassenthwaite Lake (059681) 234

Closed Xmas Day

A charming and very popular inn, the Pheasant combines abundant character with a pleasant atmosphere and good food. →

Raven Hotel ★★

Station Road, Hook,
Nr Basingstoke, Hampshire
Telephone: 025672 2541 Telex: 858901

Modernised hotel with comfortable
well equipped bedrooms.
See gazetteer under Hook

20rm(12➡1⋒)®✈
☾80P🚌✽
V🍷☕Last dinner 8.30pm
Ⓥ

BATH
Avon
Map **3** ST76 **See plan on page 103**

★★★★**Francis** Queen Sq (Trusthouse Forte) ☎(0225) 24257 Telex no 449162
Plan **2** *C3*
Comfortable accommodation and an elegant restaurant are found in this Georgian-style hotel.

Bassenthwaite — Bath

94➡CTV in all bedrooms ®sB&B➡£59 dB&B➡£78.50 B
Lift ☾72P CFA *xmas*
🍷☕Last dinner 10pm
Credit cards 1 2 3 4 5

★★★★ **Royal Crescent**
See entry on page 104

❀★★★**Priory**
See entry on page 104

★★★***Combe Grove*** Monkton Combe
Not on plan (1½m S on Exeter light traffic rd A367, and turn off at Brass Knocker Hill)
☎(0225) 834644
Secluded, owner-run hotel with fine views, popular with businessmen and tourists.
12rm(3➡9⋒)(4fb)2🛏CTV in all bedrooms ®T✈B
☾⅍100P🚌✽▭ ⛵ 🔍(grass) squash billiards sauna bath solarium gymnasium nc9yrs
V🍷☕Last dinner 9.30pm
Credit cards 1 2 3 5
See advertisement on page 105

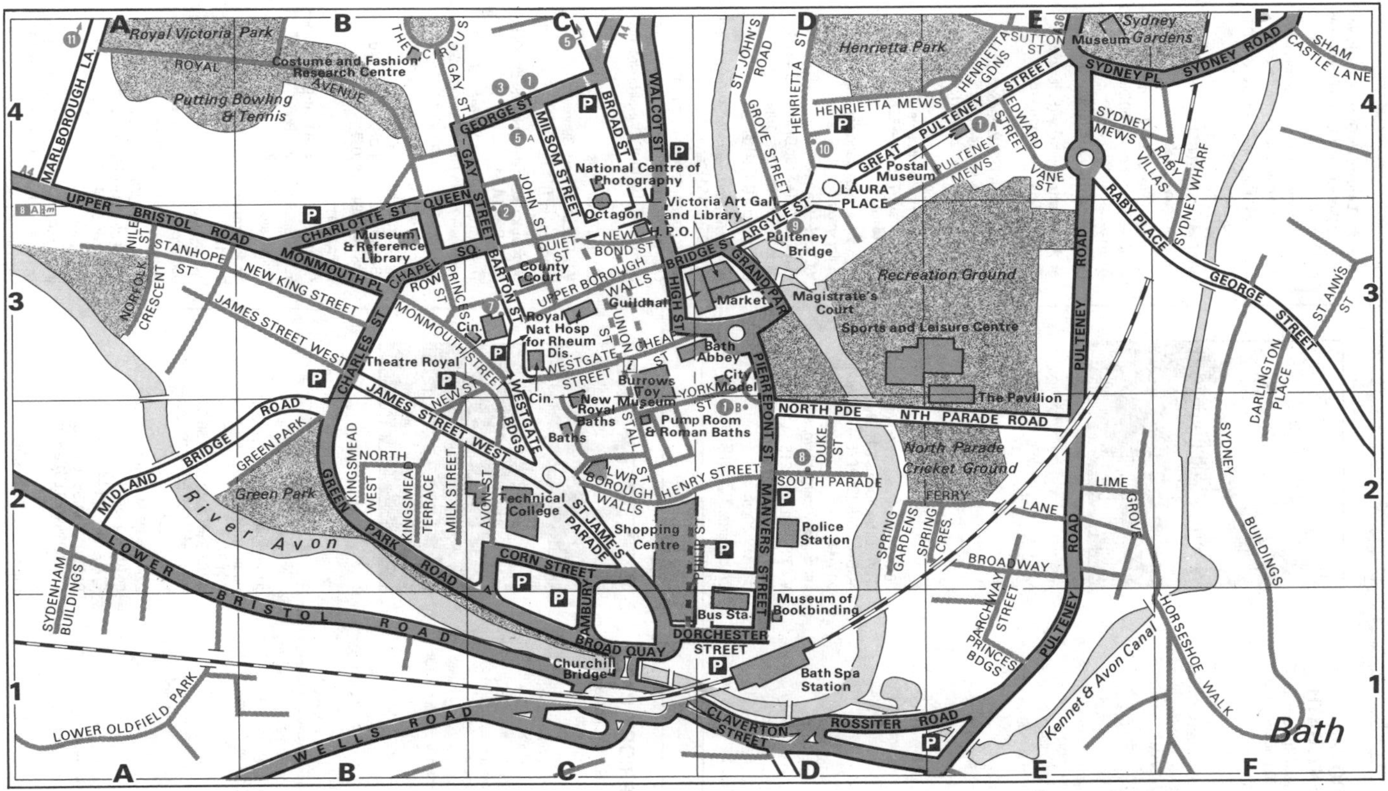

Bath

1	Clos du Roy ❀✕		**3**	Hole in the Wall ✕✕		**7**	Popjoys ✕✕✕		**9**	Rajpoot Tandoori ✕✕
1A	Dukes ✕✕		**5**	Lansdown Grove ★★★		**8**	Pratts ★★★		**10**	Redcar ★★★
1B	Fernley ★★		**5A**	Le Jardin ✕		**8A**	Priory ❀★★★		**11**	Royal Crescent ★★★★
2	Francis ★★★★									

B

★★★★

★★★★ROYAL CRESCENT, BATH

16 Royal Crescent (Prestige) ☎ (0225) 319090 Telex no 444251 Plan **11** *A4*

We have been watching this hotel closely over the years but it was not until the new manager Mr Walker made his presence felt and the standard of hospitality from the smart, courteous staff matched the superb setting of the hotel that we felt able to award Red Stars. Situated in the centre of the famous Royal Crescent, the hotel has been beautifully restored with columns, plaster and gilt ceilings, marble chimney pieces, crystal chandeliers, rich furnishings with festooned curtains, lots of good antiques including a 16th century tapestry and many oil paintings. Beside the elegant drawing room there is the bar and sun lounge overlooking the garden, which contains a Pavilion, housing annexe bedrooms and sumptuous suites. Converted last winter was the Dower House, which has now become the new restaurant, furnished and appointed in keeping with the rest of the hotel. Michael Croft, the chef, provides delicious meals in the modern style, cooking with real flair and with promise of even more to come, providing he shows more consistency. At any rate, we appreciated the food very much and, with wine from the outstanding list, you are sure to enjoy this aspect of your stay, soaking up the atmosphere of Bath's Georgian heyday.

28rm(26) Annexe: 17rm(16)6 CTV in all bedrooms **T** S%
*sB fr£68 dB £75—£275(room only)

Lift (16 (charged) *xmas*

V S% *Lunch £15—£21.50 Tea £2—£5 Dinner £27 Wine £10.50 Last dinner 9.30pm

Credit cards 1 2 3 4 5

★★★

★★★PRIORY, BATH

Weston Rd (Relais et Chateaux) ☎ (0225) 331922 Telex no 44612 Plan **8A** *A3*

This hotel with its Victorian Gothic façade stands in two acres of lovely gardens only a mile away from the city centre. This situation, and the courtesy offered by the staff — particularly the porters — make for an oasis of relaxation for the businessman or footweary tourist. The hotel, both in its public and bedrooms, is very well decorated and has delightful soft furnishings, antiques and pretty flower arrangements. The drawing room is well proportioned, sumptuously furnished and offers the elegance of Georgian Bath. There are two dining rooms which, like the drawing room, overlook the garden: one is in the appropriate Georgian style while the other is the more modern Orangery. Both are beautifully appointed, candle-lit and provide a suitable background for Michael Collom's delicious cooking. At lunch there is light fixed menu and à la carte but at dinner he provides a three-course meal priced according to the main course chosen. He cooks in the modern style and is innovative, having a sure touch with his flavouring and seasoning. The long wine list is outstanding and you are sure to find something to suit your palate and your pocket.

21rm(20 1)1 CTV in all bedrooms
T S%
*sB&B £48.30—£56.50
dB&B £88.50—£109 Continental breakfast

22P 2 (heated) croquet nc10yrs *xmas*

French S% *Lunch £12.50—£14.50 Tea £2.30 Dinner £25alc Wine £6.50 Last dinner 9.15pm

Credit cards 1 2 3 4 5

★★★*H* **Lansdown Grove** Lansdown Rd (Best Western) ☎ (0225) 315891 Telex no 444850 Plan **5** *C4*

Privately owned Georgian mansion with pretty gardens and good views of Bath.

41rm(38 3)(3fb) in 9 bedrooms CTV in all bedrooms ®**T**
sB&B £37.50—£45
dB&B £55—£66

Lift (38P 6 CFA

English & French Lunch £5.50—£7 Tea 75p—£2.50 Dinner fr£8.75 Wine £5 Last dinner 9.30pm

Credit cards 1 2 3 4 5 V

★★★**Pratts** South Pde (Forestdale) ☎ (0225) 60441 Telex no 444827 Plan **8** *D2*

Once the home of Sir Walter Scott, this recently-upgraded Georgian hotel in the city centre has a new bar and pleasant lounges.

46 1 in 2 bedrooms CTV in all bedrooms ®**T** sB&B £36—£42
dB&B fr£48

Lift (Live music and dancing Sat in winter *xmas*

V Bar lunch 95p—£2.75 Tea 75p Dinner £10.45—£15 Wine £4.75 Last dinner 10pm

Credit cards 1 2 3 5

★★★***Redcar*** Henrietta St (Kingsmead) ☎ (0225) 69151 Plan **10** *D4*

A city centre hotel forming part of a Georgian terrace.

31rm(22 4)(1fb) CTV in all bedrooms ®**T**

(12P CFA *xmas*

V Last dinner 9.30pm

Credit cards 1 2 3 5

★★**Duke's** Great Pulteney St ☎ (0225) 63512 Plan **1A** *E4*

This comfortable, city-centre hotel, personally run by the owner, provides good and extensive services.

22rm(17 3)(3fb) CTV in all bedrooms ®**T** S% sB&B £25—£30
sB&B £30—£38 dB&B £38—£40
dB&B £40—£60

xmas

S% Lunch fr£6 Tea fr£1.10 Dinner fr£7.50&alc Last dinner 8pm

Credit cards 1 3 V

★★**Fernley** North Pde ☎ (0225) 61603 Plan **1B** *D2*

The eighteenth-century, listed, stone building stands opposite the Parade Gardens, in the city centre.

47rm(27) CTV in all bedrooms ®
sB&B £25 sB&B £37 dB&B £42
dB&B £52

Lift *xmas*

V Lunch £4.50alc Tea £1alc High Tea £4.50alc Dinner £7.50alc Wine £4.50 Last dinner 9.30pm

Credit cards 1 3

B

○**Bath** Widcombe Basin
☎(0225) 338855 96

Well appointed modern hotel with attractive waterside restaurant. Open Spring 1986.

✕✕✕**Popjoys** Beau Nash House, Sawclose ☎(0225) 60494 Plan **7** *C3*

This distinguished Georgian building was once the home of Richard (Beau) Nash, and the restaurant is named after his mistress, Juliana Popjoy. Though recently refurbished, it retains its original style and offers after-dinner coffee in an elegant first-floor drawing room. The menu features interesting starters, an emphasis on fresh vegetables and exotic puddings.

Closed Sun, Mon & 3 wks New Year Lunch not served

English & French **V** 34 seats Dinner £14.50alc Wine £6.50 Last dinner 10.30pm nc 12yrs

Credit cards 1 3

✕✕ **Hole in the Wall** 16 George St ☎(0225) 25242 Plan **3** *C4*

Situated in the centre of Bath, this well-known restaurant was created from the cellars of a Georgian house. Aperitifs in the comfortable lounge will whet your appetite for a well-cooked meal served in pleasantly informal style and accompanied by an excellent wine list.

Lunch not served Sun

French **V** 45 seats Lunch £14.50 Dinner £18.50—£22 Wine £6 Last dinner 10pm

Credit cards 1 2 3 5

✕✕**Rajpoot Tandoori** 4 Argyle St ☎(0225) 66833 Plan **9** *D3*

Close to the city's Pulteney Bridge, the Rajpoot occupies what was once cellar space. Colourful decor and taped Indian music combine to create an eastern

atmosphere and you are offered a warm welcome. The attractive menu, with its careful English explanations, includes Tandoori, Mughlai and Bengali dishes, the "chef's recommendation" selections representing particularly good value.

Indian **V** 100 seats S% Dinner £7.95—£10.95&alc Wine £4.95 Last dinner 11.30pm

Credit cards 1 2 3 5

❀ ✕ **Clos Du Roy** 7 Edgar Buildings, George St ☎ (0225) 64356 Plan **1** *C4*

Small, intimate restaurant in a Georgian terrace, brightly and attractively decorated. Phillipe Roy cooks in the nouvelle cuisine style, offering some unusual and artistically presented dishes, complemented by flavoursome sauces and good crisp vegetables. The desserts are also very good and there is a well chosen wine list.

Closed Sun Mon & last wk Jan—1st wk Feb

French **V** 27 seats Lunch £7.95—£9.50&alc Dinner £18.50—£21.50&alc Wine 7.95 nc 6yrs

Credit cards 1 2 3 5

✕ **Le Jardin** 2 George St ☎ (0225) 63341 Plan **5A** *C4*

A bright, informal restaurant in the city centre, Le Jardin offers a relaxed and cordial atmosphere in which to enjoy a fairly broad range of dishes based on prime English meats and best-quality fish, all complemented by a well-balanced wine list.

Lunch not served Sun & Mon

English & French **V** 56 seats Lunch £2.65&alc Dinner fr£3.95&alc Wine £5.75 Last dinner 10.30pm

Credit cards 1 2 3

BATHGATE

Lothian *West Lothian*
Map **11** NS96

★★★ **Golden Circle** Blackburn Rd (Swallow)
☎ (0506) 53771 Telex 72606

A custom-built hotel, lying off the A7066 to the south of the town.

75rm(37 38)(2fb) CTV in all bedrooms ® S% ✱ sB&B fr£34 dB&B fr£45

Lift 100P xmas

V S% ✱ Lunch £5.95&alc Tea 80p Dinner £8.95&alc Wine £4.90 Last dinner 9.30pm

Credit cards 1 2 3 5

BATTLE

East Sussex
Map **5** TQ71

★★★

★★★ **NETHERFIELD PLACE, BATTLE**

Netherfield (3m NW B2096)
☎ (04246) 4455 Telex no 95284

Our members have been quick to tell us of the latest news of this charming hotel. A few miles from the Battle in the wooded countryside is this Georgian style building in 30 acres of parkland with the fine gardens containing a fountain and a large, walled kitchen garden. The interior is not crammed or cluttered but has been delightfully decorated and furnished and everywhere is fresh with flowers. There is an intimate bar, a gracious drawing room and another small sitting room. The dining room is panelled and comfortably furnished — there are elbow chairs and immaculate table appointments which include shaded candles and flowers. It is the scene of the owner, Michael Collier's tasty cooking for those with hearty appetites. Bedrooms are stylishly furnished, have easy chairs and are provided with flowers and fruit as well as superior toiletries. But the true delight of this hotel is the exceptionally fine hospitality; Helen and Michael Collier work well with their team of young staff to provide an entirely natural, good natured and sociable friendliness that is difficult to beat. We wish them well here and hope they succeed.

11 1 CTV in all bedrooms **T**
sB&B £35—£45
dB&B £60—£85

30P 2

French **V** ✱ Lunch £12.95&alc Tea £1.75—£4.25 Dinner £15&alc Wine £6.80 Last dinner 9.30pm

Credit cards 1 2 3 5 Ⓥ

★★ **George** High St ☎ (04246) 4466

Well managed coaching inn with some very comfortable, well-equipped bedrooms. Restaurant features English cooking and American burgers.

22rm(20 2)(4fb) 1 in 5 bedrooms CTV in all bedrooms ® **T** S% sB&B fr£22.50 dB&B fr£34.75 Continental breakfast

CTV 23P *xmas*

English & Continental Lunch £5—£7&alc Tea £1.50—£3 Dinner £9—£11&alc Wine £4.80 Last dinner 9.30pm

Credit cards 1 2 3 5 Ⓥ

See Corsham for gazetteer entry.

BAWTRY
South Yorkshire
Map **8** SK69

★★★**Crown** High St (Anchor)
☎ Doncaster (0302) 710341 Telex no 547089

An interesting old coaching inn, now modernised, and standing in the old Market Place on the Great North Road.

57 1 1 in 12 bedrooms CTV in all bedrooms ® T
*sB&B £39.50—£46.50
dB&B £49.50—£56.50 B

40P CFA xmas

English & French V *Lunch £10.50&alc Tea 65p—£1.50 Dinner £10.50&alc Wine £5.75 Last dinner 9.30pm

Credit cards 1 2 3 4 5 V

BAYHORSE
Lancashire
Map **7** SD45

★***Foxholes*** ☎ Forton (0524) 791237

The pleasant, family-run hotel with traditional-style bedrooms is set in very attractive and well-tended gardens.

10rm (1)(3fb)
CTV 50P
Last dinner 9pm

BEACHLEY
Gloucestershire
Map **3** ST59

★★**Ferry Marine** ☎ Chepstow (02912) 2474

Located next to the old ferry landing, in the shadow of the Severn Bridge.

16rm (5)(2fb) 1 CTV in all bedrooms ®
S% sB&B £22.95 sB&B £23.50
dB&B £32.95 dB&B £36.50 B

CTV 100P snooker Disco Wed Cabaret Sat xmas

V S% Lunch fr£8.95 Tea fr75p Dinner fr£8.95 Wine £4.15 Last dinner 9.30pm

Credit cards 1 2 3 5 V

See advertisement under Chepstow

BEACONSFIELD
Buckinghamshire
Map **4** SU99

★★★*B* **Bellhouse** (2m E A40) (De Vere)
☎ Gerrards Cross (0753) 887211 Telex no 848719

Busy hotel with tastefully appointed bedrooms and formal restaurant. Popular for conferences.

118 (5fb) CTV in all bedrooms ® T S%
sB&B £61—£71 dB&B £78—£91 B

Lift 405P CFA table tennis pool table Live music and dancing Fri & Sat *xmas*

V *Lunch fr£9.25&alc Tea fr95p Dinner fr£9.90 Wine £6.10 Last dinner 9.45pm

Credit cards 1 2 3 4 5

★★**Crest** Aylesbury End (Crest)
☎ (04946) 71211 Telex no 837882

RS 25, 31 Dec & 10 May

Well equipped bedrooms and open public areas are complemented by a rustic style restaurant in this busy hotel.

10rm Annexe: 28 in 3 bedrooms CTV in all bedrooms ® T S% sBfr£39.85
sB fr£50.85 dBfr£46.83
dB fr£60.85 (room only) B

90P xmas

V S% Lunch £10alc Dinner £14alc Wine £5.95 Last dinner 10pm

Credit cards 1 2 3 4 5

XXX**Santella** 43 Aylesbury End
☎ (04946) 6806

This spacious restaurant is elegantly decorated, comfortably furnished and complemented by its own bar. The Italian à la carte menu is short but provides a good range of pasta and national dishes — notably an excellent calves' liver with sage. The service, by Italian staff, is jovial and competent.

Closed Sun

Italian V 85 seats S% Lunch £10.50&alc Dinner £15alc Wine £5.50 Last dinner 11pm

Credit cards 1 2 3 4 5

X***Jasmine*** 15A Penn Rd ☎ (04946) 5335

Small Chinese restaurant with colourful Chinese lanterns and murals. Good authentic cooking with enterprising menu.

Chinese 100 seats Last dinner 11.30pm 80P

Credit cards 1 2 3 5

BEAMINSTER
Dorset
Map **3** ST40

X***Nevitt's Eating House*** 57 Hogshill St
☎ (0308) 862600

Just off the village square stands this cottage-style, stone-built restaurant where the emphasis is on good, fresh food — much of it home-made.

Closed 2 wks Jan Lunch not served Mon—Sat

English & Continental 30 seats Last dinner 10pm

Credit card 3

BEARSDEN
Strathclyde *Dunbartonshire*
Map **11** NS57

★★★**Stakis Burnbrae** Milngavie Rd (Stakis) ☎ 041-942 5951

A custom-built, modern hotel, set back from the A81 on the outskirts of the town.

18rm (17 1)(4fb) in 9 bedrooms CTV in all bedrooms ® *sB £32—£43.90
dB £40—£57.80 (room only) B

100P

*Lunch £4.95—£7.50 Tea 75p—£2.50 High Tea £2.45—£3.50 Dinner £7.50—£9.50 Wine £4.50 Last dinner 10pm

Credit cards 1 2 3 4 5 V

XX**La Bavarde** 9 New Kirk Rd
☎ 041-942 2202

Small restaurant run by friendly proprietors.

Closed Sun, Mon, 2 wks Xmas & New Year & last 3 wks Jul

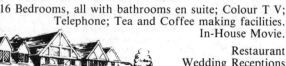

V 50 seats Lunch fr£5 Dinner £12—£15alc Wine £4.90 Last dinner 9.30pm
Credit cards 1 2 3 4 5

Amritsar Tandoori 9 Kirk Rd
041-942 7710
Closed Xmas Day & New Years Day
Lunch not served Sun
Indian **V** 100 seats Lunch £3.25—£4.95&alc Dinner £7.50alc Wine £5.25 Last dinner mdnt 10P
Credit cards 1 2 3 5 V
See advertisement under Glasgow

BEATTOCK
Dumfries & Galloway *Dumfriesshire*
Map **11** NT00

★★*HL* **Auchen Castle** (Inter Hotel)
(06833) 407
Closed 23 Dec—3 Jan
Country house style hotel set in an imposing mansion in its own grounds.
15rm(13 2) Annexe: 10 CTV in all bedrooms ® **T** sB&B £30—£32 dB&B £35—£45
CTV 35P 2 Disco Sat (Oct—Mar)
V Bar lunch 85p—£5 Tea £1—£1.50 Dinner £9—£12 Wine £5 Last dinner 9pm
Credit cards 1 2 3 4 5 V
See advertisement under Moffat

Bearsden — Beauly

★★**Beattock House** (06833) 403
This is a converted mansion, dating from 1812, that stands in 6½ acres of grounds. Children will enjoy the hotel's pets.
7rm(3)(2fb) CTV in 2 bedrooms TV in 2 bedrooms ® sB&Bfr£17.50 sB&B fr£19.50 dB&Bfr£35 dB&B fr£37
CTV 25P
V Lunch fr£5.25 Tea fr£2.15 High Tea fr£4.25 Dinner fr£9.25 Wine £5.95 Last dinner 9.30pm
Credit cards 2 3

★**Old Brig Inn & Posting House**
(06833) 401
RS Dec—Feb
Comfortable, modernised coaching inn.
9rm(1 1)(3fb) ® sB&Bfr£13.45 dB&Bfr£23.40 dB&B fr£26.90 (Continental breakfast)
CTV 20P
French **V** Lunch £3.50&alc Tea 45palc Dinner £8.50&alc Wine £3.75 Last dinner 8.30pm
Credit cards 2 3 5 V

BEAULIEU
Hampshire
Map **4** SU30

★★★**Montagu Arms** (0590) 612324
Telex no 47276
An historic coaching inn, the Montague Arms overlooks an English rose garden; bedrooms are comfortable and individually-furnished, and the haute cuisine featured in the restaurant is backed by service of a very high standard.
26 (10fb) 5 CTV in all bedrooms **T** *sB&B fr£42 dB&B £55—£73.50
40P 9 *xmas*
English & French **V** *Lunch £7.95—£9.25&alc Tea fr85p&alc High Tea £5.50alc Dinner £14.75—£24&alc Wine £6.75 Last dinner 10pm
Credit cards 1 2 3 5

BEAULY
Highland *Inverness-shire*
Map **14** NH54

★★**Priory** The Square (Inter Hotel)
(0463) 782309
Modernised hotel set in the town square.
11rm(4 7)(1fb) CTV in all bedrooms ® **T** sB&B £17.50—£23.95 dB&B £31—£40
Cabaret wkly →

V ♁ ☕ Bar lunch £1.95—£5.50 Tea 80p High Tea £3.25—£7.25 Dinner £3.25&alc Wine £3 Last dinner 9pm

Credit cards 1 2 3 5 Ⓥ

BEAUMARIS
Gwynedd
Map **6** SH67

★★**Bishopsgate House** 54 Castle St ☎(0248) 810302

Closed Xmas—Etr

Cosy, bright small hotel with pleasantly furnished public areas.

10rm(3⛀7⛆) CTV in all bedrooms Ⓡ ✱sB&B⛀⛆fr£16.50 dB&B⛀⛆fr£33 B

10P ⛝ nc5yrs

English & French V ♁ ✱Lunch £3.50—£5.50 Dinner £8.95&alc Wine £4.95 Last dinner 9pm

Credit cards 1 3 Ⓥ

★★**Bulkeley Arms** Castle St (Consort) ☎(0248) 810415 Telex no 57515

Looking over the Menai Strait, this three-storey, stone, scheduled building is close to the local shops.

41rm(34⛀7⛆)(6fb) CTV in all bedrooms **T** S% sB&B⛀⛆£21.95—£29 dB&B⛀⛆£39.95—£51.95 B

Lift 30P snooker Live music & dancing twice mthly xmas

English & French V ♁ ☕ S% Lunch £5—£8&alc Tea fr55p&alc High Tea 75p—£2&alc Dinner £8.95&alc Wine £4.95 Last dinner 9pm

Credit cards 1 2 3 5 Ⓥ

✕***Hobson's Choice*** 13—13A Castle St ☎(0248) 810323

This small, simply-appointed but pleasant restaurant offers friendly and informal service, featuring light meals at lunch time and a more extensive menu in the evening.

English & French V 100 seats Last dinner 10pm P

Credit cards 1 3

BEAUMONT
Jersey, Channel Islands
See Channel Islands

BECCLES
Suffolk
Map **5** TM49

★★**Waveney House** Puddingmoor ☎(0502) 712270

A flint-faced 16th century house, alongside the River Waveney.

13rm(1⛀4⛆)(2fb)1 CTV in all bedrooms Ⓡ**T** sB&B£27—£32 dB&B£43—£50 B

CTV 120P ✿ ♪

English & French V ♁ ☕ Lunch fr£8&alc Tea fr60p—£1.50 High Tea £3—£5 Dinner fr£8&alc Wine £4.50 Last dinner 9.30pm

Credit cards 1 2 3 4 5

BEDALE
North Yorkshire
Map **8** SE28

★★***Motel Leeming*** (1m NE junc A1/A684) ☎(0677) 23611

Part of service area complex, motel offers simple, modern accommodation.

40⛀(2fb) CTV in all bedrooms Ⓡ B

☾100P 14 ⛟

International V ♁ ☕ Last dinner 9.45pm

Credit cards 1 2 3 4 5

BEDDGELERT
Gwynedd
Map **6** SH54

★★★**Royal Goat** ☎(076686) 224

An impressive, three-storey tourist hotel, situated ¾m from Gelert's Grave.

31⛀ CTV in all bedrooms Ⓡ**T** S% sB&B⛀£24—£26 dB&B⛀£44—£48 B

Lift ☾ CTV 150P ♪ Cabaret Sat *xmas*

Welsh & French V ♁ ☕ S% Lunch £7.50—£10&alc Tea £1—£1.50 Dinner £12—£14 Wine £5.75 Last dinner 10pm

Credit cards 1 2 3 5

★**Bryn Eglwys Country House** Railbridge ☎(076686) 210

A detached Georgian house in its own grounds, about ½m from the village.

15rm(13⛀)(4fb) in 6 bedrooms Ⓡ✱ sB&B£16—£19 dB&B£30 dB&B⛀£36—£48 B

CTV 20P ⛝ ✿ *xmas*

V ♁ ☕ ✱Lunch £5.50—£6 Tea £1.25 Dinner £7—£8 Wine £4.25 Last dinner 9pm

Credit cards 1 3 Ⓥ

★*L* **Tanronen** (Frederic Robinson) ☎(076686) 3471

A two storey tourist hotel, in the centre of the village.

9rm CTV in 2 bedrooms Ⓡ sB&B£13.50 dB&B£27 B

CTV 12P 3⛟ *xmas*

V ♁ ☕ Lunch £4.50 Tea £1.50 Dinner £8.50 Wine £3.10 Last dinner 9pm

Credit cards 1 3

BEDFORD
Bedfordshire
Map **4** TL04

★★★*H* **Woodlands Manor** Green Ln, Clapham (2m N A6) ☎(0234) 63281 Telex no 825007

Set in three-and-a-half acres of its own grounds, the hotel has recently added an annexe of three superbly-appointed bedrooms, whilst a comfortable drawing room has replaced the bar. Though some of the older bedrooms are small and modestly furnished, this is in all other respects a delightful and peaceful place to stay.

16rm(8⛀8⛆) Annexe: 3⛆ CTV available in bedrooms **T** sB&B⛀⛆£41.50—£46 dB&B⛀⛆£58—£63.50 Continental breakfast B

☾P ⛝ ✿ nc7yrs

English & French V ♁ ☕ ✱Lunch £9.25—£12.75&alc Tea £1.25 Dinner £12.75&alc Wine £7.25 Last dinner 9.45pm

Credit cards 1 2 3

★★**Bedford Swan** The Embankment (Paten) ☏ (0234) 46565

A late 18th century hotel, with a new extension, in an attractive riverside position.

86⇌(4fb) 1▭ CTV in all bedrooms ®T S% sB&B⇌£39 dB&B⇌£49 B

☾CTV 70P CFA *xmas*

English & French V ☕ S% Lunch £8.45&alc Tea 70p Dinner £8.45&alc Wine £5.25 Last dinner 9.30pm

Credit cards 1 2 3 5 V

★★**De Parys** De Parys Av (Exec Hotels) ☏ (0234) 52121 Telex no 82392

Closed 1 wk Xmas

This hotel is reputed to have been built on the site of the hospitali and rectory of St John, founded in 1118 by Robert de Parys.

31rm(6⇌20⋒)(4fb) CTV in all bedrooms ® sB&B£20—£26 sB&B⇌⋒£23—£36 dB&B£28—£38 dB&B⇌⋒£28—£46 B

18P ✿

British, Asian, French & Italian V ☕ ✱Bar lunch £2.50—£5.50 Tea 95p—£1.25 Dinner £8—£12&alc Wine £4.75 Last dinner 9pm

Credit cards 1 2 3 5

BEELEY
Derbyshire
Map **8** SK26

✕✕**Devonshire Arms** ☏ Matlock (0629) 733259

A stone-built, beamed village inn with an attractive, modern restaurant extension.

Bar lunch only on Bank Hols

V 60 seats ✱Bar lunch 65p—£4.85 Dinner £8alc Wine £4.60 Last dinner 9pm 60P

Credit cards 1 2 3

BEER
Devon
Map **3** SY28

★★**Anchor Inn** ☏ Seaton (0297) 20386

RS Nov—Apr

Facing the "slip-way" to the beach, this small, traditional-looking hostelry retains the character which makes it so popular, despite complete refurbishment of the interior. Wholesome fare based on local produce is available in the dining room and a varied selection of snacks is served in the bar.

9rm(2⇌)(1fb) CTV in all bedrooms ® sB&B£18—£23 sB&B⇌£23—£27 dB&B£28—£32 dB&B⇌£32—£34 B

CTV

V ☕ Lunch £5.50—£8&alc Dinner £8alc Wine £4.20 Last dinner 9.45pm

Credit cards 1 3

★★**Dolphin** Fore St ☏ Seaton (0297) 20068

RS Nov—Mar

Modernised coaching inn where good range of food and drinks are available.

22rm(1⇌3⋒)(4fb) CTV avaiable in bedrooms ® sB&B£10.50—£17.50 sB&B⇌⋒£13.50—£20.50 dB&B£21—£35 dB&B⇌⋒£27—£41 B

CTV 60P 2🚗 Skittle alley pool table

V ☕ Lunch £4—£10.50 Tea 70p High Tea £3 Dinner £7.50 Wine £3 Last dinner 9.30pm

Credit cards 1 3 5

BEESTON
Cheshire
Map **7** SJ55

★★★**Wild Boar Inn & Restaurant** Bunbury (Embassy) ☏ Bunbury (0829) 260309 Telex no 61455

Closed 26—30 Dec

A striking Black and White building, with comfortable, well appointed bedrooms and a stylish French restaurant as well as the grill room.

Annexe: 30⇌⋒ CTV in all bedrooms ®T S% sB⇌⋒£30—£31.50 dB&B⇌⋒£40—£43(room only) B

100P ✿

French **V** ☕ ✱Lunch £9.75&alc Tea 95p Dinner £14.50&alc Wine £5.50 Last dinner 9.45pm

Credit cards 1 2 3 4 5

BEESTON
Nottinghamshire
Map **8** SK53

✕**Les Artistes Gourmands** 61 Wollerton Rd ☏ Nottingham (0602) 228288 Nottingham plan **1A** *A5*

Closed 1 wk Jan
Lunch not served Sat
Dinner not served Sun

French **V** 70 seats S% Lunch £6.90—£12.80 Dinner £9.30—£17.90 Wine £6.40 Last dinner 10.15pm 1P

Credit cards 1 2 3

BEETHAM
Cumbria
Map **7** SD47

★***Wheatsheaf*** ☏ Milnthorpe (04482) 2123

An attractive village inn, with oak beams, close to lakeland.

8rm(2⇌)(1fb) CTV in all bedrooms ®

Lift ☾ ## CTV 50P

V ☕

BELBROUGHTON
Hereford & Worcester
Map **7** SO97

✿✕✕✕**Bell Inn** Bell End ☏ (0562) 730232

The original building dates back 500 years, and has been considerably extended and refurbished. The owner and the chef offer a high standard of food well prepared and attractively presented in the Bellom Room.

Closed Mon & 1st wk Jan Lunch not served Sat Dinner not served Sun

French **V** 68 seats Lunch £9.50&alc Dinner £18.50&alc Wine £5.75 Last dinner 9.30pm 100P
nc 10yrs (Dinner)

Credit cards 1 2 3 5 V

B

BELLINGHAM
Northumberland
Map **12** NY88

★★**Riverdale Hall** (Exec Hotel) ☎(0660) 20254

Comfortable country house specialising in sporting activities.

19rm(9⇌2ⓜ)(4fb)3⊞CTV in 11 bedrooms ®**T** sB&B£13.50—£15 sB&B⇌ⓜ£20—£22 dB&B£26—£28 dB&B⇌ⓜ£37—£41 **B**

##CTV 40P ❁ ⊡(heated) ♪ sauna bath games room ⌂ *xmas*

V ♡ ⊒ Lunch £4.45—£10 Tea 45p Dinner £9.50—£10.50&alc Wine £4.05 Last dinner 9pm

Credit cards 1 2 3 5 Ⓥ

BELPER
Derbyshire
Map **8** SK34

✕✕**Remy's Restaurant Francais** 84 Bridge St ☎(077382) 2246

Attractive restaurant on 2 floors of stone terraced property.

Closed 1 wk Jan & 2 wks Aug Lunch not served Mon & Sat Dinner not served Sun

♡French **V** 27 seats ✱Lunch £8.50—£18 Dinner £12.50—£18 Wine £5.95 Last dinner 9.30pm **P** ⚟ nc 8yrs

Credit cards 2 3 5

BEMBRIDGE
Isle of Wight
See Wight, Isle of

BENLLECH BAY
Gwynedd
Map **6** SH58

★★**Bay Court** Beach Rd ☎ Tynygongl (0248) 852573

Comfortable accommodation and good food is available at this modern hotel near the beach.

18rm(2⇌1ⓜ) Annexe: 4⇌(2fb) CTV in 9 bedrooms ® in 8 bedrooms sB&B£14—£16.50 sB&B⇌ⓜ£16.50—£19 dB&B£28—£31 dB&B⇌ⓜ£33—£35 **B**

CTV 65P Live music and dancing twice wkly in summer

♡English & French **V** ♡ ⊒ Lunch £4—£7&alc Tea £1.50 High Tea £2.50 Dinner £5.50—£7.50&alc Wine £4 Last dinner 9.30pm

Credit cards 1 2 3 Ⓥ

BERKELEY
Gloucestershire
Map **3** ST69

★★**Berkeley Arms** ☎ Dursley (0453) 810291

This hotel, extensively refurbished has retained the cosy and relaxed atmosphere of the original coaching inn whilst extending and improving the bedrooms. A good range of bar meals is offered in addition to the lunch time buffet and evening set-price menus.

7⇌ CTV in all bedrooms ®✱ sB&B⇌£20—£25 dB&B⇌£35—£40 **B**

50P ❁ *xmas*

♡French **V** ♡ ⊒ ⚟ ✱Lunch £4.50—£6.50 Tea £1—£2 Dinner £4.50—£6.50&alc Wine £4 Last dinner 9.30pm

Credit cards 1 2 3

★★*H* **Old Schoolhouse — Berkeley Hotel** Canonbury St ☎ Dursley (0453) 811711

Closed 24—26 Dec

Sympathetically restored building offering spacious, comfortable bedrooms, unusual, attractive public areas, good food and friendly atmosphere.

7rm(2⇌5ⓜ) CTV in all bedrooms ®✈ sB&B⇌ⓜfr£25 dB&B⇌ⓜfr£39 **B**

15P ⊯

International Lunch £6alc Dinner £13.50 Wine £5.25 Last dinner 8.45pm
Credit cards 1 3

BERKELEY ROAD
Gloucestershire
Map **3** SO70

★★**Prince of Wales** ☎ Dursley (0453) 810474
RS 24—25 Dec
There has been an inn on this site for a hundred and fifty years, and the present-day — greatly extended — hotel offers good bedrooms, a busy bar and provision for functions.
9rm(7)(1fb) CTV in all bedrooms ®**T** S% sB&B£22—£26 sB&B£28.50—£32 dB&B£30—£35 dB&B£38.50—£41.50
120P Live music & dancing Sat
S% Lunch £5.95—£6.50 Tea 75—85p Dinner £8.50&alc Wine £4.50 Last dinner 9.30pm
Credit cards 1 2 3 5

BERKHAMSTED
Hertfordshire
Map **4** SP90

★**Swan** High St ☎ (04427) 71451 Telex no 82257
RS Xmas Day & Boxing Day
Welcoming, homely, 15th century coaching inn with wholesome food.
19rm(7 6)1 CTV in all bedrooms ®**T** sB&B£25 sB&B£28—£35 dB&B£35 dB&B£38—£45
CTV 14P 2
English & French **V** S% Lunch £5—£9.90&alc Tea 75p—£1 Dinner fr£9.90&alc Wine £4 Last dinner 10pm
Credit cards 1 3

BERWICK-UPON-TWEED
Northumberland
Map **12** NT95

★★★**King's Arms** Hide Hill (Best Western) ☎ (0289) 307454 Telex no 8811232
Impressive, stone-built hotel, forming greater part of terrace on Hide-Hill.
36rm(31 5)(3fb) 11 CTV in all bedrooms ® S% *sB&B£35 dB&B£48
snooker *xmas*
S% *Lunch £5.50 High Tea £4.50 Dinner £10.50&alc Wine £5.75 Last dinner 10pm
Credit cards 1 2 3 5 Ⓥ

★★★**Turret House** Etal Rd, Tweedmouth ☎ (0289) 307344
Elegant hotel in its own grounds with tastefully decorated open plan bar, dining room and lounge.
13rm(10 3) CTV in all bedrooms ®**T** S% sB&B£28—£32.75 dB&B£42—£48
100P
S% Lunch £6.50alc Tea £3alc Dinner 10.95alc Wine £5.95 Last dinner 9.30pm
Credit cards 1 2 3 5 Ⓥ

★★*H* **Browns** Ravensdowne ☎ (0289) 307170
Two eighteenth-century houses were converted to form this small, friendly hotel, where much of the imaginatively-cooked food is based on local recipes.
8rm(7 1)(2fb) CTV in all bedrooms ® *sB&B£18 dB&B£36
*Tea £1.75 Wine £4.10 Last dinner 9pm
Credit cards 1 2 3 4 5

★**Queens Head** Sandgate ☎ (0289) 307852
Charming character hotel with cosy lounge and bar, and large bedrooms.
6rm(4fb) CTV in all bedrooms ® sB&B£14.50—£15.50 dB&B£29—£31
xmas
Mainly grills **V** Lunch £6—£8 High Tea £4.50 Dinner £7—£10 Wine £4.50 Last dinner 9pm
Credit cards 2 3 5 Ⓥ

BETWS-Y-COED
Gwynedd
Map **6** SH75

★★★**Plas Hall** Pont-y-Pant, Dolwyddelan (3m SW A470) (Minotel/Inter Hotel) ☎ Dolwyddelan (06906) 206 Telex no 61155 Ref P5
Closed 25 & 26 Dec
16rm(15 1)(2fb) 2 CTV in all bedrooms ®**T** sB&B£21.50—£28 dB&B£43—£56
28P games room *xmas*
Welsh & French **V** Lunch fr£6.50 Tea fr£3.50 High Tea fr£3.50 Dinner £9.75&alc Last dinner 9.30pm
Credit cards 1 2 3 4 5 Ⓥ
See advertisement on page 114

★★★**Royal Oak** Holyhead Rd ☎ (06902) 219
Closed 25—26 Dec
An impressive three-storey stone hotel in the centre of the village.
27(5fb) CTV in all bedrooms **T** sB&B£35—£40 dB&B£46—£52
60P
English, French & Italian Tea 90p—£2.50 High Tea £4—£4.50 Dinner £8—£13 Wine £6 Last dinner 9pm
Credit cards 1 2 3 5

★★★**Waterloo** (Consort) ☎ (06902) 411
Closed Xmas
Modern comfortable hotel provides excellent food in Garden Room restaurant.
Annexe: 28rm(27 1)(2fb) CTV in all bedrooms ®**T** sB&B£16—£26 dB&B£33—£44
CTV 150P
International **V** Bar lunch £2.75—£3.95 Dinner £7.50—£8.50&alc Wine £4.95 Last dinner 10pm
Credit cards 1 2 3 5
See advertisement on page 114

B

★★*H* **Park Hill** Llanrwst Rd ☎ (06902) 540

Closed Dec—Jan

This small, family-run holiday hotel, overlooks the picturesque Conwy Valley. A warm and relaxed atmosphere is augmented by good home cooking.

11rm(6⇌2fh)(1fb) CTV in 1 bedroom ® sB&B£16—£17 dB&B⇌fh£34—£36 B

CTV 12P ⇌ ✽ (heated) sauna bath nc6yrs *xmas*

Welsh, English & French V ⇌ ⁄ Bar lunch fr£3.50 Tea fr70p Dinner £7.50—£8 Wine £4.50 Last dinner 7.30pm

Credit cards 1 2 3

Betws-y-Coed

★★**Ty Gwyn** ☎ (06902) 383

The sympathetically-restored, family-run coaching inn now offers attractive and individually furnished bedrooms. A relaxed, informal atmosphere and good food may be enjoyed in the character beamed bar and dining room.

12rm(1⇌7fh)(2fb)3⇌ ® sB&B£13—£18 sB&B⇌fh£17—£22 dB&B£26—£28 dB&B⇌fh£34—£40 B

CTV 12P *xmas*

English & French V ⇌ ✽Lunch £6.95—£7.95&alc Dinner £6.95—£7.95&alc Wine £4.50 Last dinner 9.30pm

Credit cards 1 3

★**Fairy Glen** ☎ (06902) 269

Closed Dec & Jan

17th century hotel by the river near Fairy Glen beauty spot. It is family run with a homely atmosphere.

10rm(5⇌)(3fb) ® sB&B£12—£16 dB&B£24—£32 dB&B⇌£28—£36 B

CTV 10P ⇌ ✽

V Lunch £3.50—£5.50 Tea 50p—£1.50 Dinner £6.50—£8.50 Wine £4 Last dinner 7.30pm

Credit cards 1 3 5 V

BEVERLEY
Humberside
Map **8** TA03

★★★**Beverley Arms** North Bar Within (Trusthouse Forte) ☎ Hull (0482) 869241 Telex no 527568

A converted and modernised Georgian building, located in the town centre.

61(2fb) CTV in all bedrooms ® sB&B£50.50 dB&B£66.50

Lift 70P *xmas*

Last dinner 9.45pm

Credit cards 1 2 3 4 5

★★★**Tickton Grange** Tickton (3m NE on A1035) ☎ Leven (0401) 43666 Telex no 527254

RS 25—29 Dec

This family-owned, Georgian country house is set in 3½ acres of gardens.

17rm(10 7)(1fb) CTV in all bedrooms ® T sB&B£46.75 dB&B£62

65P

V Lunch £10alc Tea £2.50 Dinner £10&alc Wine £7 Last dinner 9.30pm

Credit cards 1 2 3 5 V

★★***Lairgate*** 30/34 Lairgate ☎ Hull (0482) 882141

A three-storey Georgian building, situated near to the town centre.

24rm(11 7)(2fb) 1 CTV in all bedrooms ® T

CTV 20P Live music & dancing Sat

English & Continental Last dinner 9.30pm

Credit cards 1 3

BEWDLEY
Hereford & Worcester
Map **7** SO77

★★**Black Boy** Kidderminster Rd ☎ (0299) 402119

Closed Xmas Day

Friendly, 18th century inn near River Severn, with intimate bar and small, comfortable restaurant.

25rm(7 8)(2fb) CTV in 10 bedrooms *sB&B£15.90—£19.90 sB&B£21.90—£29 dB&B£29.90 dB&B£34—£39

CTV 25P

V *Bar lunch £1.75—£2.75 Dinner £7.95&alc Wine £4.20 Last dinner 8.45pm

Credit cards 1 2 3

XX**Bailiffs House** 68 High St ☎ (0299) 402691

It is fascinating to dine in this Grade I listed building dating back to 1610, with its uneven floor, exposed beams and antique furniture. The atmosphere is relaxed and the menus are imaginative.

Closed Mon Dinner not served Sun

English & French 40 seats *Lunch £7.95 Dinner £15.50 Wine £5.25 Last dinner 9.30pm

Credit cards 1 2 3

BEXHILL-ON-SEA
East Sussex
Map **5** TQ70

★**Southlands Court** Hastings Rd ☎ (0424) 210628

Quiet, old-fashioned hotel with good, simple cooking.

28rm(8 10)(3fb) CTV in 12 bedrooms ® *sB&Bfr£13.25 sB&Bfr£15.50 dB&Bfr£24.75 dB&Bfr£29

CTV 12P 5(charge) *xmas*

*Lunch fr£4 Tea fr60p Dinner fr£5 Wine £5.35 Last dinner 7.30pm

BEXLEY
Gt London
Map **5** TQ47

★★★**Crest** Black Prince Interchange, Southwold Rd (Crest) ☎ Crayford (0322) 526900 Telex no 8956539

Modern commercial hotel offering comfortable accommodation in well equipped bedrooms.

78 in 8 bedrooms CTV in all bedrooms ® S% *sB£47—£55 dB£57—£65(room only)

Lift 150P Live music & dancing Sun *xmas*

English & French V S% *Lunch fr£9.75 Tea 95p—£3 Dinner £11.50—£15&alc Wine £6.25 Last dinner 9.45pm

Credit cards 1 2 3 4 5

BIBURY
Gloucestershire
Map **4** SP10

★★★*L* **Swan** ☎ (028574) 204

Cotswold stone inn with riverside gardens. Sitting rooms are comfortable and the atmosphere charming.

23rm(22 1)(1fb) CTV in all bedrooms T sB&B£30.50 dB&B£52.50

20P 2 *xmas*

International V Lunch £10.25 Tea £1 Dinner £13.75 Wine £5.50 Last dinner 8.30pm

Credit cards 1 3

★★**Bibury Court** ☎ (028574) 337

Closed Xmas

Delightfully informal country house hotel in a beautiful setting.

16rm(15)(1fb) 10 CTV in 1 bedroom T sB&B£24 sB&B£28 dB&B£42—£48 Continental breakfast

CTV 100P

English & French Bar lunch £1—£4 Tea 80p—£1 Dinner £12—£15alc Wine £4.95 Last dinner 8.45pm

Credit cards 1 2 3 5 V

BICKLEIGH (near Tiverton)
Devon
Map **3** SS90

★★***Fisherman's Cot*** ☎ (08845) 237

A picturesque thatched building on the bank of the River Exe.

6rm(3) Annexe: 13rm(8 5)(5fb) 1 CTV in all bedrooms ®

80P

International V Last dinner 9.30pm

Credit cards 1 3

B

BIDDENDEN
Kent
Map **5** TQ83

XX Ye Maydes ☏ (0580) 291306

Skilful and imaginative cooking is found in this medieval half-timbered house.

Closed Sun, Mon, last wk Jan, last wk Aug, 1st wk Sep & last wk Oct

English & French **V** 54 seats ✻ Lunch fr£6.85&alc Dinner £14.30alc Wine £5.40 Last dinner 9.30pm

Credit cards 1 2

BIDEFORD
Devon
Map **2** SS42
See also Fairy Cross, Monkleigh & Westward Ho!

★★★ ***Durrant House*** Heywood Rd, Northam (Consort) ☏ (02372) 72361

A Georgian building with a modern extension, set on the Northam road.

58rm(56⇌2⋒)(11fb) CTV in all bedrooms ®TB

☾ # CTV 70P CFA (heated) sauna bath

Last dinner 9.30pm

Credit cards 1 2 3 5

★★ **Orchard Hill Hotel & Restaurant** Orchard Hill, Northam ☏ (02372) 72872

9rm(8⇌1⋒) CTV in all bedrooms ® sB&B⇌⋒£16—£18 dB&B⇌⋒£28—£34 B

CTV 15P ✿ nc 12yrs *xmas*

V S% Bar lunch £4.50 Tea 45p alc Dinner £7.95alc Wine £4.90 Last dinner 9pm Ⓥ

★★**Riversford** Limers Ln (Inter Hotel) ☎ (02372) 74239

Closed 20 Dec—2 Jan

This peacefully-situated, comfortable hotel has extensive views over the Torridge River. The owner and his family provide friendly service and honest home cooking.

17rm(13🛁1🚿)(9fb)2⊟ CTV in all bedrooms ® T sB&Bfr£16.45 sB&B🛁🚿£26.15 dB&Bfr£32.90 dB&B🛁🚿£40.30—£49.80 Ꞵ

CTV 20P 2🚗✽ badminton putting 🚸

Bideford

♡English & Continental **V** ♆ ☐ Lunch fr£5.40&alc Tea 90p—£1.70 Dinner fr£8.85&alc Wine £4.50 Last dinner 8.30pm

Credit cards 1 2 3 5 Ⓥ

★★**Royal** Barnstaple St (Brend) ☎ (02372) 72005 Telex no 42551

Older style hotel, situated at the eastern end of the bridge.

33rm(13🛁)(3fb) CTV in 13 bedrooms sB&B£16.68 sB&B🛁£20.13 dB&B£28.75 dB&B🛁£34.50 Ꞵ

☾ CTV 30P 10🚗 Live music and dancing wkly *xmas*

♡English & French **V** ♆ ☐ Lunch £3.50—£4.50 Tea fr50p Dinner fr£6&alc Wine £3.85 Last dinner 9pm

Credit cards 1 2 3 5

★★♣**Yeoldon House** Durrant Ln, Northam (Best Western) ☎ (02372) 74400

A comfortable, well-appointed hotel, in a peaceful situation, that enjoys fine views over River Torridge. →

B

10rm(8⇌2⋔)(3fb)1⊞CTV in all bedrooms T ✗ sB&B⇌⋔£31.50—£34.50 dB&B⇌⋔£49—£56 B

20P ⇌ ✿ *xmas*

English & Continental V ⚲ ⊐ ⚡ S% Lunch £5—£8&alc Tea 80p High Tea £2.50 Dinner £10.50—£11&alc Wine £4.75 Last dinner 9pm

Credit cards 1 2 3 5 Ⓥ

BIDFORD-ON-AVON
Warwickshire
Map **4** SP05

★★***White Lion*** High St ☎(0789) 773309

Fully modernised old riverside hotel offering guests a warm welcome.

15rm(1⇌7⋔)1⊞CTV in 14 bedrooms Ⓡ B

CTV 15P ⇌ ♩

V ⚲ ⊐ Last dinner 9pm

Credit cards 1 2

BIGBURY-ON-SEA
Devon
Map **3** SX64

★★**Seagulls** Folly Hill ☎(0548) 810331

Closed mid Oct—Etr

Cheerful, hospitable hotel with spectacular views, sheltered gardens and steps to beach.

Bideford — Billesley

10rm(5⇌5⋔)(2fb) Ⓡ S% sB&B⇌⋔£16 dB&B⇌⋔£30—£40 B

CTV 10P ⇌ ✿

English & Continental V ⚲ ⊐ ⚡ S% Bar lunch £2.50—£4 Tea 80p High Tea £1.25 Dinner £5.75—£8.50 Wine £3.25 Last dinner 8.30pm

Credit cards 1 3 Ⓥ

★**Henley** ☎(0548) 810240

Closed Oct—Etr

There are superb views of Bigbury Bay from this small country house set in its own grounds.

9rm(5⇌1⋔) Ⓡ sB&B£19 sB&B⇌⋔£21 dB&B£38 dB&B⇌⋔£42

CTV 8P ⇌ ✿ nc3yrs

Lunch fr£3 Dinner fr£7 Wine £3.25 Last dinner 7.30pm

BILBROOK
Somerset
Map **3** ST04

★★ *HL* ***Dragon House*** ☎ Washford (0984) 40215

Attractive, friendly, personally run cottage hotel with charming public rooms and comfortable, well-furnished bedrooms.

8rm(4⇌2⋔) Annexe: 2⇌(1fb) CTV in all bedrooms Ⓡ B

25P ⇌ ✿ U ⛹

English & French V ⚲ ⊐ Last dinner 9.15pm

Credit cards 1 2 3 5

★**Bilbrook Lawns** ☎ Washford (0984) 40331

This comfortable, well appointed Georgian house offers a friendly atmosphere and good food.

7rm(1⇌3⋔) Annexe: 6rm(1⇌)(2fb) CTV in 6 bedrooms TV in 7 bedrooms Ⓡ sB&B£13.50 sB&B⇌⋔£14.50—£16 dB&B£23 dB&B⇌⋔£27—£30 B

15P 1⌂ ⇌ ✿ ⛹ *xmas*

English & Continental V ⊐ ⚡ Lunch £2.75—£4.55&alc Tea £1.25 Dinner £5.50&alc Wine £3.95 Last dinner 8.45pm Ⓥ

BILLESLEY
Warwickshire
Map **4** SP15

★★★ **Billesley Manor**
☎ Stratford-upon-Avon (0789) 763737
Telex no 337105

At the time of going to press, this Elizabethan manor house was closed for repairs and major refurbishment, and it has not been possible to carry out an assessment of the merit awards. It will re-open in January 1987.

28➡4⛾CTV in all bedrooms T ✗ B
☾⅄ 150P 6⌂ ✿ (heated) ⚑9
(hard) sauna bath *xmas*
V ♉ ☕ Last dinner 9.30pm
Credit cards 1 2 3 5
See advertisement under Stratford-upon-Avon

BILLINGSHURST
West Sussex
Map **4** TQ02

✗ **Tandoori Village** 42 High St
☎ (040381) 4890

This Indian restaurant may not have the usual colourful ambience peculiar to its kind, being housed in a period building with beamed rooms, but nevertheless there is a warm, friendly atmosphere. The cooking — based mainly on dishes from Northern India — is of a very good standard.

Indian **V** 85 seats Wine £4.25 Last dinner 11pm P
Credit cards 1 2 3 5

BILLINGTON
Lancashire
Map **7** SD73

✗✗✗ **Foxfields** Whalley Rd
☎ Whalley (025482) 2556

This elegant, well-appointed restaurant stands in its own carefully-tended gardens. The menu is varied and offers some unusual dishes, one of the specialities being fresh seafood of a high quality.

Closed Mon, Bank Hol's & 3—4 days at Xmas Lunch not served Sat
French 60 seats ✱Lunch £8.50&alc Dinner £16.50alc Wine £6.50 Last dinner 9.30pm 75P nc4yrs (lunch) 8yrs (dinner)
Credit cards 1 2 3 5

BINGLEY
West Yorkshire
Map **7** SE13

★★★ **Bankfield** Bradford Rd (Embassy) ☎ Bradford (0274) 567123

A 19th century house, with modern bedroom extensions, overlooking the River Aire.

69rm(67➡2⌂)(5fb) CTV in all bedrooms ®T S% ✱sB➡⌂£37—£55 dB➡⌂£47.50—£65(room only) B
☾ 250P CFA ✿ pool table table tennis Live music & dancing Mon, Sat & Sun *xmas*
♉ ☕ S% ✱Lunch fr£8.50&alc Tea £1.05 Dinner £8.50 Wine £5.10 Last dinner 9.15pm
Credit cards 1 2 3 5
See advertisement under Bradford

★★★ ***Oakwood Hall*** Lady Ln
☎ Bradford (0274) 564123
Closed 25—28 Dec

Impressive Victorian Gothic building in quiet woodland setting. Bedrooms are well equipped and attractive dining room overlooks well kept gardens.

12rm(9➡3⌂)(1fb) 1⛾ CTV in all bedrooms ®T B
100P ✿
V ♉ Last dinner 9.30pm
Credit cards 1 2 3 4 5

BIRCH
Greater Manchester
Map **7** SD80
M62 Motorway Service Area

◯ **Granada Lodge** Between junctions 18—19
☎ 061-643 0911 40➡
Due to open summer 1987

BIRKENHEAD
Merseyside
Map **7** SJ38

★★★ ***Bowler Hat*** 2 Talbot Rd, Oxton (Best Western/Distinctive) ☎ 051-652 4931

A well-furnished and comfortable hotel, set in a residential area, offering a good standard of food and service.

29rm(27➡2⌂)(3fb) CTV in all bedrooms ®T B
☾ 40P CFA ✿ ♿ *xmas*
International ♉ ☕ Last dinner 10pm
Credit cards 1 2 3 4 5

★★ **Riverhill** Talbot Rd, Oxton
☎ 051-652 4847

This hotel is set in its own grounds, in a residential area.

10rm(7➡3⌂)(1fb) 1⛾ CTV in all bedrooms ® ✗ S% sB&B➡⌂£20—£30 dB&B➡⌂£30—£40 B
30P ✿
English, French & Italian **V** S% Lunch £7.15 Dinner £8.80 Wine £5.25 Last dinner 9.30pm
Credit cards 1 2 3 5 Ⓥ

BIRMINGHAM
West Midlands
Map **7** SP08 **See plan**
See also BIRMINGHAM AIRPORT AND BIRMINGHAM (NATIONAL EXHIBITION CENTRE)

★★★★ **Albany** Smallbrook, Queensway (Trusthouse Forte) ☎ 021-643 8171 Telex no 337031 Central plan **1** *D3*

An impressive, modern, thirteen storey building with extensive views over the city.

257➡ CTV in all bedrooms ®T sB&B➡£61 dB&B➡£77 B
Lift ☾ ## P CFA (heated) sauna bath
♉ ☕ Last dinner 11pm
Credit cards 1 2 3 4 5

★★★★ **Holiday Inn** Holiday St (Holiday Inns) ☎ 021-643 2766 Telex no 337272 Central plan **8** *B3*

International standard hotel reached from Suffolk Street Queensway before junction with Paradise Circus.

290➡(210fb) CTV in all bedrooms ®T sB➡£57.50—£65.55 dB➡£64.40—£72.45(room only) B
Lift ☾ ## 300⌂ (heated) sauna bath solarium gymnasium ♿
International **V** ♉ ☕ ⅄ ✱Lunch fr£8.95 Tea fr£1.25 Dinner fr£9.75&alc Wine £6.50 Last dinner 11pm
Credit cards 1 2 3 4 5

★★★★ **Midland** New St (Inter Hotel) ☎ 021-643 2601 Telex no 338419 Central plan **12** *D4*

A busy central hotel.

106➡ CTV in all bedrooms ® in 52 bedrooms T sB&B➡£45—£60 dB&B➡£55—£70 B
Lift ☾ P CFA
English & French ♉ ☕ Lunch £8.50—£11&alc Tea 75p Dinner £11—£12&alc Wine £5 Last dinner 10pm
Credit cards 1 2 3 4 5 Ⓥ
See advertisement on page 120

★★★★ ***HB*** **Plough & Harrow** Hagley Rd, Edgbaston (Crest) ☎ 021-454 4111 Telex no 338074 District plan **30**
RS 24 Dec—1 Jan

Prestigious hotel with individual style and modern bedrooms, whose restaurant serves interesting food.

44➡⌂ CTV in all bedrooms T S% ✱sB➡⌂£49.50—£65 dB➡⌂£77.50(room only) B
Lift ☾ 50P ✿ sauna bath
French **V** ♉ ☕ S% ✱Lunch £20alc Tea £1.75—£5 Dinner £25alc Wine £8.50 Last dinner 10.30pm
Credit cards 1 2 3 4 5

★★★ **Apollo** Hagley Rd, Edgbaston ☎ 021-455 0271 Telex no 336759 District plan **18**

Guests are offered a choice of two restaurants and comfortable accommodation in purpose-built premises at this privately-owned modern hotel.

120➡(18fb) ⅄ in 6 bedrooms CTV in all bedrooms ®T S% sB➡£44.85—£50.02 dB➡£54.05—£59.22(room only) B
Lift ☾ ## CTV 120P CFA
English & French **V** ♉ ☕ S% ✱Lunch £11.05—£12.80 Tea 75p High Tea £5 Dinner £9.75—£14.70&alc Wine £5.35 Last dinner 10.30pm
Credit cards 1 2 3 4 5 Ⓥ

★★★ **Barr** Pear Tree Dr, Newton Rd (1m W of junc A34/A4041)
☎ 021-357 1141 (Not on plan) (For full entry see **Barr, Great**)
See advertisement on page 121

★★★ **Grand** Colmore Row (Queens Moat) ☎ 021-236 7951 Telex no 338174 Central plan **6** *D5*
Closed 4 days Xmas

An old, traditional style hotel, close to city centre.

167➡(6fb) CTV in all bedrooms ®T sB&B➡£25—£55 dB&B➡£35—£65 B→

Lift ☾ P CFA ♿
🍽 English & French V 🍷 ☕ Lunch £8.30—£8.50&alc Tea £1.50 Dinner £8.30—£8.50&alc Wine £5.50 Last dinner 10pm

Credit cards 1 2 3 5

★★★**Post House** Chapel Ln, (At junc M6/A34) (Trusthouse Forte) ☎ 021-357 7444 (Not on plan) (For full entry see **Barr, Great**)

★★★**Royal Angus Thistle** St Chads, Queensway (Thistle) ☎ 021-236 4211 Telex no 336889 Central plan **16** *D6*

This modern hotel sits close to St Chads Circus, which is where the West Bromwich

Birmingham

Road (A41) meets the Birmingham Inner Ring Road. Access can also be obtained from the nearby St Chads National Car Park during the day and evening.

140rm (133🛁 7🚿) CTV in all bedrooms ® T ✱ sB🛁🚿£47—£69 dB🛁🚿£53—£75 (room only) 🅱

Lift ☾ CFA

🍽 International 🍷 ☕ ✱ Lunch £9 Dinner £9.95&alc Wine £7 Last dinner 9.30pm

Credit cards 1 2 3 4 5 Ⓥ

★★★**Strathallan Thistle** 225 Hagley Rd, Edgbaston (Thistle) ☎ 021-455 9777 Telex no 336680 District plan **33**

A striking circular building on the main thoroughfare into the city.

166🛁🚿 ⊬ in 25 bedrooms CTV in all bedrooms ® T ✱ sB🛁🚿£47—£69 dB🛁🚿£53—£75 (room only) 🅱

☾ 250P 100🚗 CFA solarium Live music & dancing Fri & Sat

🍽 International 🍷 ☕ ✱ Lunch fr£6.95&alc Dinner fr£10.50&alc Wine £7 Last dinner 10pm

Credit cards 1 2 3 4 5 Ⓥ

B

Perry Hall Hotel★★★

Kidderminster Road, Bromsgrove, Hereford & Worcs. B61 7JN.
Tel: 0527 31976

The poet A. E. Housman once lived here and his "Loveliest of trees, the cherry . . ." still stands in the secluded hotel gardens. Behind its charming ivy clad facade, Perry Hall provides all the comforts and facilities of the 20th century . . . beautifully appointed bedrooms, carefully prepared food, fine wines and conference facilities. The public areas have recently undergone major refurbishment. There is parking for 180 cars.

Embassy Hotels

BARR HOTEL

Pear Tree Drive, Newton Road, Great Barr, Birmingham B43 6HS.
Telephone: 021-357 1141 Telex: 336406

114 Bedrooms all having En Suite facilities, colour television, radio, direct dial telephone and tea/coffee making facilities.

The Partridge Restaurant offers seasonal A la Carte and Table D'hôte menus featuring fresh produce.

Conference and banqueting facilities for up to 120 guests.

Located in a peaceful suburb of Birmingham just 1½ miles from junction 7 of the M6, the hotel is a convenient base for visitors to the NEC and the West Midlands.

Royal Angus Thistle Hotel ***AA

St. Chads, Queensway, Birmingham B4 6HY. Tel: 021-236 4211. Telex: 336889.

Ideal for business or holiday visitors, the Royal Angus is conveniently located for the M1, M5 and M6 motorways and is a short drive from the National Exhibition Centre. Warwick Castle and Stratford-on-Avon are also easily accessible.

The hotel has 140 bedrooms all with private bathroom; Pemberton's Restaurant, offering the best of English cuisine, and Pemberton's bar and lounge to relax in; as well as excellent conference facilities.

For Reservations at Thistle Hotels throughout Britain, telephone: 01-937 8033.

THISTLE HOTELS

As individual as you are.

Strathallan Thistle Hotel ****AA

Hagley Road, Edgbaston, Birmingham B16 9RY. Tel: 021-455 9777. Telex: 336680.

A fine, modern hotel close to Birmingham City Centre, with easy access to the M5 and M6.

Each of the hotel's 166 bedrooms has the usual high standards of Thistle Hotels with private bathroom, direct dial telephone, TV, radio, tea and coffee making facilities.

There is also an excellent restaurant and a choice of bars, as well as extensive conference and meeting facilities.

For Reservations at Thistle Hotels throughout Britain, telephone: 01-937 8033.

THISTLE HOTELS

As individual as you are.

B

Birmingham Central

1 Albany ★★★★
4 La Capanna ✕✕
5 Chung Ying ❀ ✕✕
5A Dynasty ✕✕
6 Grand ★★★
7 Ho Tung ✕✕
8 Holiday Inn ★★★★
10 Lorenzo's ✕✕
11 Maharaja ✕
12 Midland ★★★★
13 New Happy Gathering ✕✕
15 Rajdoot ❀ ✕✕
16 Royal Angus Thistle ★★★

★★**Hotel Annabelle** 19 Sandon Rd, Edgbaston ☎ 021-429 4496 District plan **17**

This small, proprietor-run hotel can be seen from the Hagley Road (A456) barely two miles from the city centre. The bedrooms are compact, but a pleasant atmosphere is created by the friendly staff.

15rm(9fh) ⅄ in 1 bedroom TV in all bedrooms ✱ sB&B fr£26.50 sB&B fh £27.50 dB&B £48 dB&B fh £48 ℞

18P ❁ *xmas*

English & Continental **V** ♁ ☕ ✱ Lunch fr£9.50 Tea fr£3.50 High Tea fr£6 Dinner fr£9.50&alc Wine £5.50 Last dinner 9.30pm

Credit cards 1 2 3 5 Ⓥ

See advertisement on page 126

★★**Bristol Court** 250 Bristol Rd, Edgbaston ☎ 021-472 0413 District plan **20**

Closed 25 & 26 Dec

A comfortable, commercial hotel.

29rm(10➡9fh)(2fb) CTV in all bedrooms ✱ sB&B £19.55 sB&B➡fh £23 dB&B £32.20 dB&B➡fh £35.65 ℞

CTV 35P ❁ ♀

Mainly grills **V** ♁ ☕ ✱ Lunch £3—£4.50&alc Tea 90p Dinner £5.50—£6.50&alc Wine £4.80 Last dinner 8.30pm

Credit cards 1 2 3 5

★★**Cobden** 166 Hagley Rd, Edgbaston (Consort) ☎ 021-454 6621 Telex no 339715 Cobnor G District plan **21**

Closed 1 wk Xmas

Modernised hotel on main road.

210rm(25➡112fh)(24fb) CTV in all bedrooms Ⓡ **T** S% sB&B fr£24 sB&B➡fh fr£36 dB&B fr£36 dB&B➡fh fr£47 ℞

Lift ☾ 130P ❁ gymnasium

V ♁ ☕ S% Lunch fr£5.50 Tea fr£1.50 Dinner fr£8.50 Wine £5.25 Last dinner 9pm

Credit cards 1 2 3 5

★★**Meadow Court** 397 Hagley Rd, Edgbaston ☎ 021-429 2377 District plan **26**

Closed 24 Dec—1 Jan

Standing just outside the city, this friendly hotel is run by resident proprietors who →

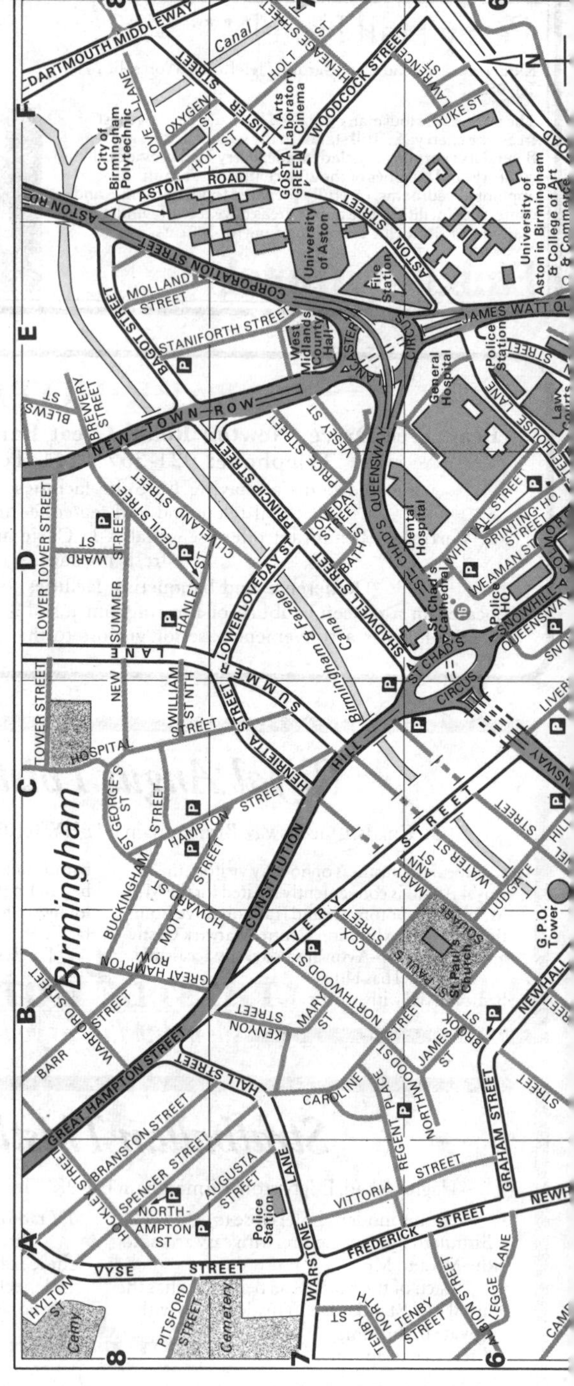

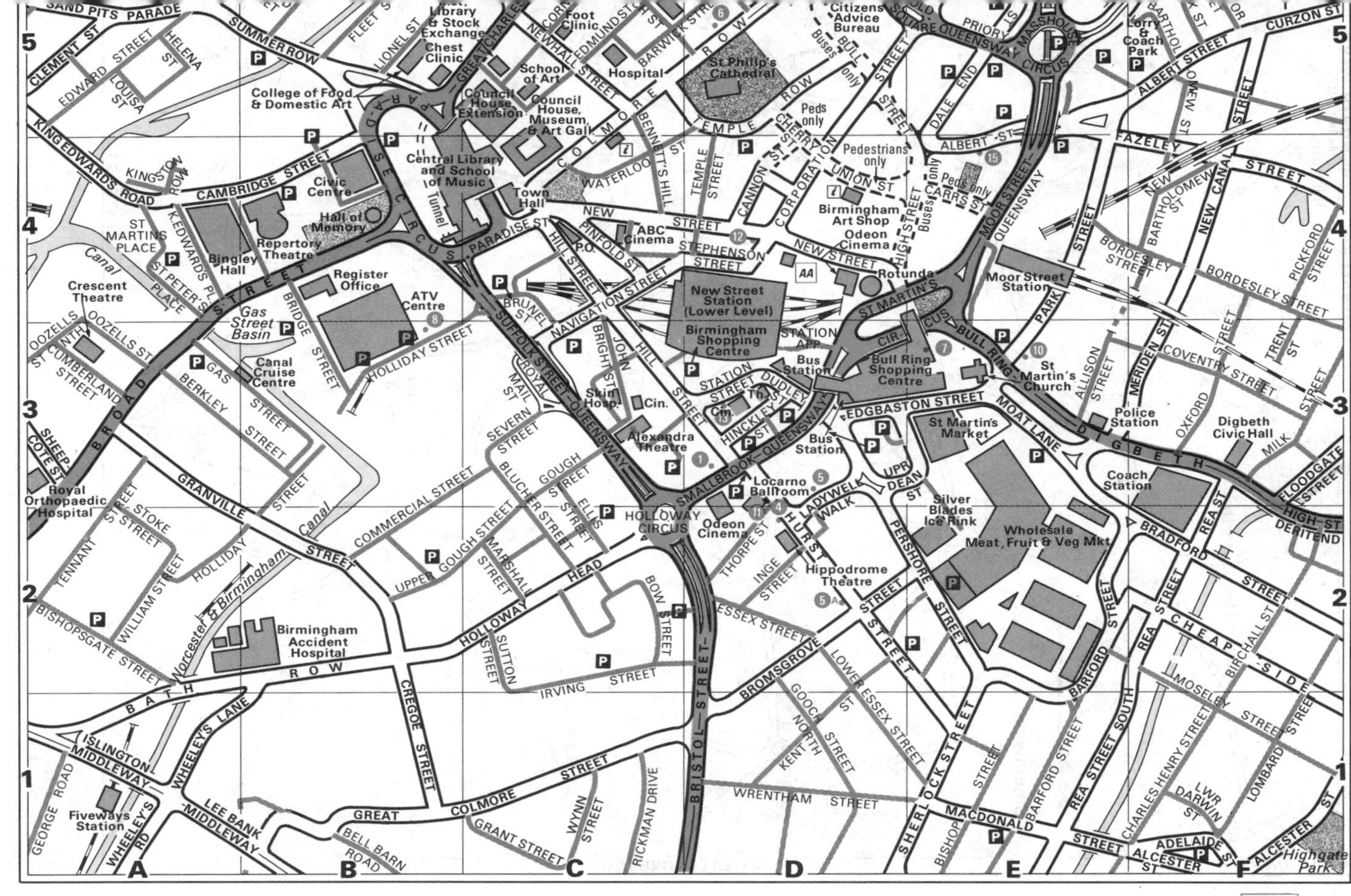

New Street Station (Lower Level)
Birmingham Shopping Centre
Bull Ring Shopping Centre
Rotunda
St Martin's Church
St Martin's Market
Moor Street Station
Digbeth Civic Hall
Police Station
Coach Station
Wholesale Meat, Fruit & Veg Mkt
Silver Blades Ice Rink
Bus Station
Hippodrome Theatre
Locarno Ballroom
Odeon Cinema
Alexandra Theatre
Skin Hosp.
ABC Cinema
Town Hall
Council House, Museum & Art Gall.
Council House Extension
School of Art
Central Library and School of Music
Library & Stock Exchange
Chest Clinic
Foot Clinic
Hospital
St Philip's Cathedral
Citizens Advice Bureau
Birmingham Art Shop
Odeon Cinema
Lorry & Coach Park
Hall of Memory
Civic Centre
Repertory Theatre
Bingley Hall
College of Food & Domestic Art
Register Office
ATV Centre
Canal Cruise Centre
Gas Street Basin
Crescent Theatre
Royal Orthopaedic Hospital
Birmingham Accident Hospital
Fiveways Station
Highgate Park
Worcester & Birmingham Canal
BRISTOL STREET
BROAD STREET
SUFFOLK STREET QUEENSWAY
SMALLBROOK QUEENSWAY
MOOR STREET QUEENSWAY
HOLLOWAY CIRCUS
HOLLOWAY HEAD
PARADISE CIRCUS
BULL RING
DIGBETH
HIGH ST DERITEND
MOAT LANE
EDGBASTON STREET
PERSHORE STREET
SHERLOCK STREET
BROMSGROVE STREET
CORPORATION STREET
NEW STREET
COLMORE ROW
GREAT CHARLES ST
NAVIGATION STREET
HILL STREET
JOHN BRIGHT ST
GRANVILLE STREET
CAMBRIDGE STREET
KING EDWARDS ROAD
SAND PITS PARADE
SUMMER ROW
GREAT COLMORE STREET
CREGOE STREET
BATH ROW
LEE BANK MIDDLEWAY
ISLINGTON MIDDLEWAY
WHEELEYS LANE
WHEELEY'S RD
GEORGE ROAD
BELL BARN ROAD
RICKMAN DRIVE
WYNN STREET
GRANT STREET
IRVING STREET
BOW STREET
SUTTON STREET
MARSHALL STREET
BLUCHER STREET
GOUGH STREET
COMMERCIAL STREET
HOLLIDAY STREET
BERKLEY STREET
GAS STREET
BRIDGE STREET
CUMBERLAND STREET
OOZELLS ST
SHEEPCOTE ST
TENNANT STREET
WILLIAM STREET
STOKE STREET
BISHOPSGATE STREET
ESSEX STREET
LOWER ESSEX STREET
GOOCH STREET
WRENTHAM STREET
KENT STREET
INGE STREET
THORPE ST
HURST STREET
LADYWELL WALK
BARFORD STREET
REA STREET SOUTH
CHARLES HENRY STREET
MOSELEY STREET
CHEAPSIDE
BRADFORD ST
REA ST
MERIDEN ST
PARK STREET
NEW CANAL STREET
FAZELEY STREET
BORDESLEY STREET
CURZON ST
ALBERT STREET
DALE END
PRIORY QUEENSWAY
MASSHOUSE CIRCUS
TEMPLE ROW
TEMPLE STREET
CANNON STREET
CHERRY ST
UNION ST
BENNETT'S HILL
WATERLOO ST
NEWHALL STREET
EDMUND ST
STEPHENSON STREET
PINFOLD ST
STATION STREET
DUDLEY ST
HINCKLEY ST
SEVERN STREET
ROYAL MAIL ST
BRUNEL ST
ST MARTINS PLACE
ST PETER'S PLACE
KINGSTON ROW
HELENA ST
LOUISA ST
CLEMENT ST
EDWARD STREET
FLEET STREET
LIONEL ST
ALCESTER ST
ADELAIDE ST
MACDONALD STREET
B

B

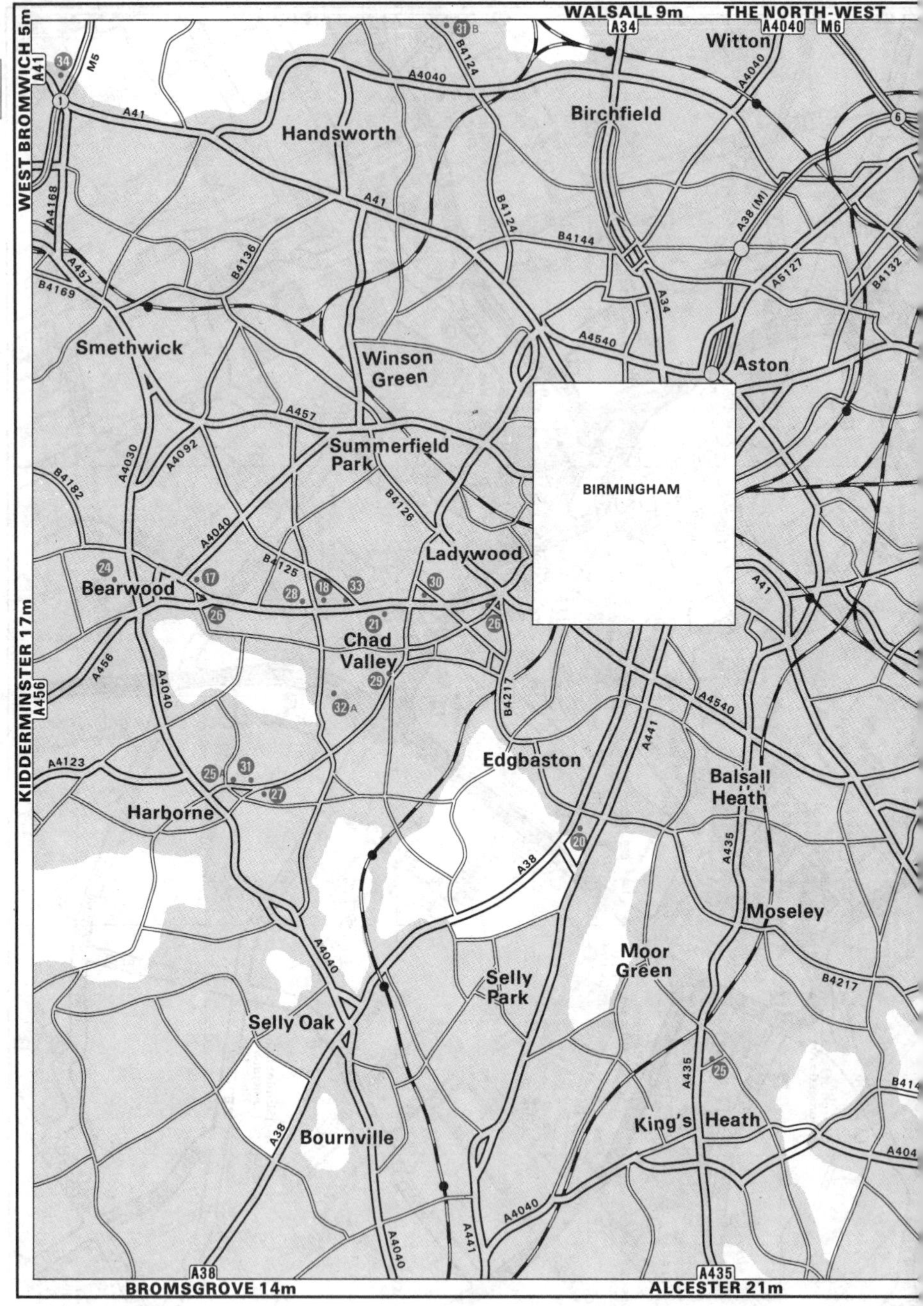

Birmingham District

17 Hotel Annabelle ★★
18 Apollo ★★★
19 Arden ★★★ *(Listed under Birmingham — National Exhibition Centre)*
20 Bristol Court ★★
21 Cobden ★★
22 Excelsior ★★★★ *(Listed under Birmingham Airport)*
23 Flemings ★★ *(Listed under Solihull)*
24 Franzi's ✕
25 Giovanni's ✕
25A Henry Wong ✕

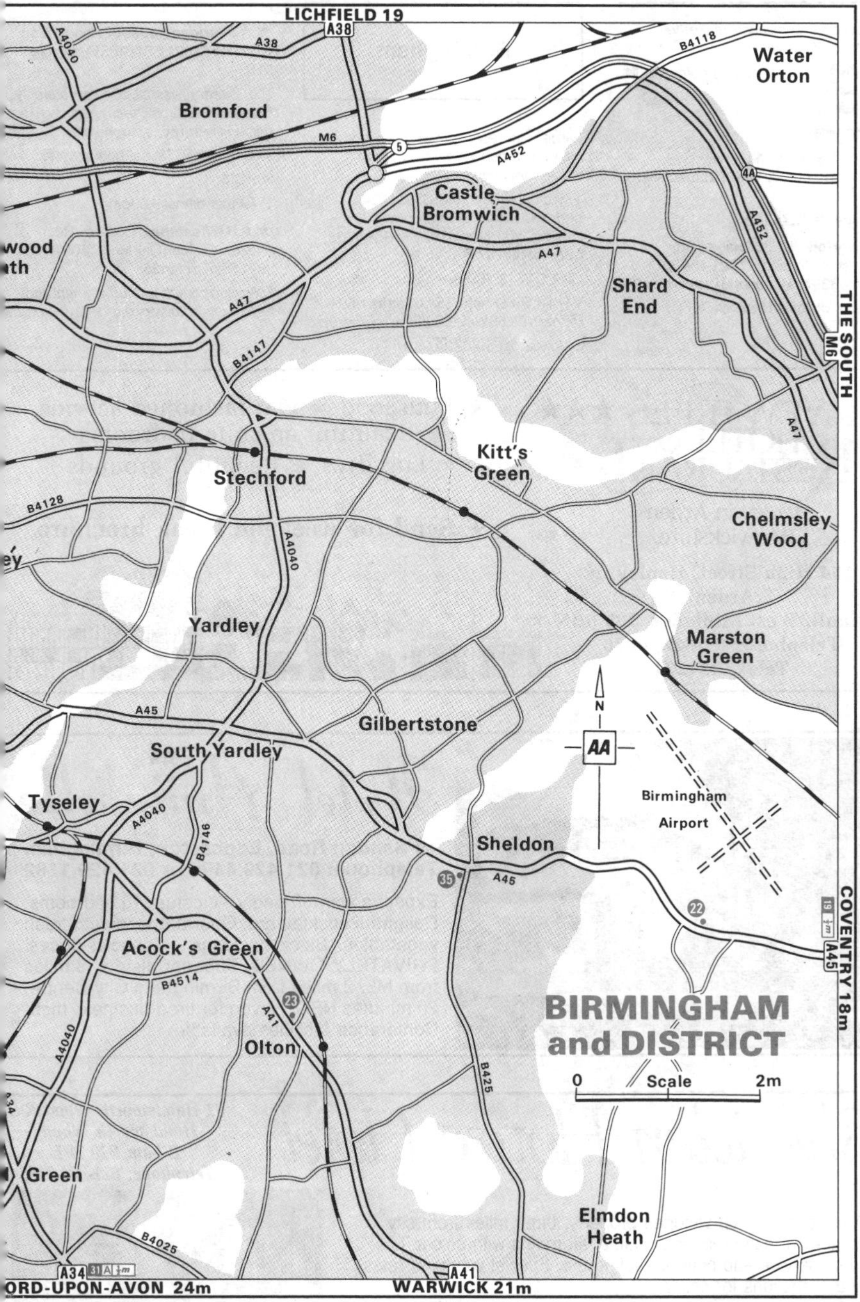

LICHFIELD 19
A38
A4040
Water
Orton
B4118
Bromford
M6
5
A452
4A
Castle
Bromwich
wood
ath
A47
Shard
End
THE SOUTH
M6
B4147
Kitt's
Green
Stechford
B4128
Chelmsley
Wood
A4040
Yardley
Marston
Green
N
AA
A45
Gilbertstone
South Yardley
Birmingham
Airport
Tyseley
A4040
Sheldon
B4146
35
A45
22
COVENTRY 18m
A45
Acock's Green
B4514
23
A41
BIRMINGHAM
and DISTRICT
Olton
B425
0
Scale
2m
Green
Elmdon
Heath
B4025
A34
31A
A41
ORD-UPON-AVON 24m
WARWICK 21m

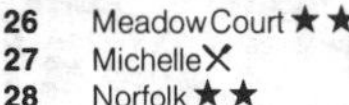

26 Meadow Court ★★
27 Michelle ✕
28 Norfolk ★★
29 Pinocchio's ✕
30 Plough & Harrow ★★★★
31 Le Provencal ✕
31A Saracens Head ★★
(See under Solihull)
31B Sheriden House ★★
32A Sloan's ✿ ✕✕✕
33 Strathallan Thistle ★★★
34 West Bromwich Moat House ★★★
(See under West Bromwich)
35 Wheatsheaf ★★

are particularly anxious to make their guests comfortable.

14rm(6⇌8⋒)CTV in all bedrooms ®T ✗ sB&B⇌⋒£32.50—£37 dB&B⇌⋒£48.65—£53

CTV 16P ⇄

♉English & French ✱Dinner £9.50—£10.50&alc Wine £6 Last dinner 8pm

Credit cards 1 2 3 5

★★**Norfolk** 257/267 Hagley Rd, Edgbaston (Consort) ☎ 021-454 8071 Telex no 339715 Cobnor G District plan **28**

Closed 1 wk Xmas/New Year

Birmingham

Large hotel, recently modernised, on busy main road offering value for money accommodation.

175rm(32⇌56⋒)(8fb) CTV in 134 bedrooms ® in 134 bedrooms T S% sB&Bfr£24 sB&B⇌⋒fr£36 dB&Bfr£36 dB&B⇌⋒fr£47 Ᵽ

Lift ☾ CTV 130P ✿ gymnasium ♿

V ♈ ☕ S% Lunch fr£5.50 Tea fr£1.50 Dinner fr£8.50 Wine £5.25 Last dinner 9pm

Credit cards 1 2 3 5

★★**Sheriden House** 82 Handsworth Wood Rd ☎ 021-554 2185 District plan **31B**

The Sheriden, a small, popular hotel only fifteen minutes from the city centre, is personally run by its proprietors.

9rm(4⋒)(2fb) CTV in all bedrooms Ᵽ

30P ⇄

♈ ☕ Last dinner 9.30pm

★★ *B* ***Wheatsheaf*** Coventry Rd, Sheldon (Golden Oak Inns) ☎ 021-743 2021 District plan **35**

Following complete refurbishment and redecoration, this once-ordinary hotel now

has some of the best-designed bedrooms in the two-star classification range, together with an eye-catching ground floor area.

100rm(16⇌84⋒)CTV in all bedrooms ®
T✗⊟
☾CTV 120P⇶
♧Last dinner 10pm
Credit cards 1 2 3

❀XXX**Sloan's** 27/29 Chad Sq, Hawthorne Rd, Edgbaston ☎021-455 7719 District plan **32A**

Tucked into the corner of a small shopping complex this French style restaurant changed hands as this guide went to press. The new owner and chef are from an equally well known Midlands restaurant, and we have every confidence that high standards will be maintained and possibly improved.

Closed Sun, Bank Hols & 2 wks Jul/Aug Lunch not served Sat

V 60 seats Last dinner 10pm

Credit cards 1 2 3 5

XX**La Capanna** Hurst St ☎021-622 2287 Central plan **4***D2*

Theatre-goers will find this Italian restaurant popular and convenient.

Closed Sun & 20 Jul—10 Aug

♧English & Italian **V** 60 seats S% Dinner £7—£12alc Wine £5 Last dinner 11pm ℙ

Credit cards 1 2 3 5 Ⓥ

❀XX**Chung Ying** 16/18 Wrottesley St ☎021-622 5669 Central plan **5***D3*

This typically Chinese restaurant on two floors is popular with Chinese families. It provides excellent Cantonese cuisine featuring many dishes seldom seen outside Hong Kong or China. It is worth asking for a translation of the daily specials which include such unusual dishes as dried squid with asparagus tips.

♧Cantonese **V** 220 seats S% Lunch £7alc Dinner £7alc Wine £4.50 Last dinner 11.45pm 10P

Credit cards 1 2 3 5

XX**Dynasty** 93/103 Hurst St ☎021-622 5306 Central plan **5A** *D2*

A smart, modern restaurant with a light, fresh decor, the Dynasty is just a few minutes' walk from the city centre and within easy reach of car parks. Many popular Cantonese dishes appear on the menu, although the emphasis is on the rather spicier Peking cuisine.

Closed 25 & 26 Dec

♧Cantonese & Pekinese **V** 120 seats ✱Lunch £5.50&alc Dinner £7&alc Wine £5.50 Last dinner 11.30pm 8P

Credit cards 1 2 3 5

Birmingham

XX***Ho Tung*** 308 Bull Ring Centre, Small Brook Ringway ☎021-643 0033 Central plan **7***E3*

A wide range of interesting dishes are briskly served in this restaurant with its modern oriental decor.

♧Cantonese 150 seats Last dinner 11pm

Credit cards 2 3 5

XX**Lorenzo's** Park St ☎021-643 0541 Central plan **10***E3*

The daily specials are often unusual in this authentically decorated Italian restaurant, with occasionally boisterous service.

Closed Sun & Public Hols Lunch not served Sat Dinner not served Mon

♧Italian **V** 70 seats Lunch £6.50&alc Dinner £16.50alc Wine £5.20 Last dinner 10.45pm ℙ

Credit cards 1 2 3 5

XX**New Happy Gathering** 43/45 Station St ☎021-643 1859 Central plan **13** *D3*

With the close proximity of the station, this Chinese restaurant is always busy, but service is quick and courteous and the food is unfailingly well prepared. In addition to the selection of set meals available here, there is a large à la carte Cantonese menu.

Closed 3 days Xmas

♧Cantonese 120 seats ✱Lunch £8.85alc Dinner £8.85alc Wine £4.50 Last dinner 11.45pm ℙ

Credit cards 1 2 3 5

❀XX**Rajdoot** 12/22 Albert St ☎021-643 8805 Central plan **15***E4*

Birmingham's premier Indian restaurant, it has maintained its elegance, along with its standards of service and its authentic cuisine, for many years. Recent additions to the menu include tandoori and massalla quail and pheasant.

Closed Xmas Lunch not served Sun & Public Hols

♧North Indian **V** 74 seats Last dinner 11.30pm

Credit cards 1 2 3 4 5

X**Franzl's** 151 Milcote Rd, Bearwood (3½m W off A4123) ☎021-429 7920 District plan **24**

The original corner shop is still recognisable in the exterior of Franzl's, but the atmosphere inside is that of a true Austrian restaurant. You can drink Austrian aperitifs in the tiny basement bar whilst choosing your meal, and the tempting descriptions on the menu — amply justified by the actual dishes — must recapture memories for anyone who has visited the country.

Closed Sun, Mon, 3 wks Aug & 25 Dec—2 Jan Lunch not served

♧Austrian **V** 35 seats ✱Dinner £11.50alc Wine £5.95 Last dinner 10.30pm

Credit cards 1 3

X**Giovanni's** 27 Poplar Rd, Kings Heath ☎021-443 2391 District plan **25**

A friendly bustling restaurant where owner Giovanni Butto and his wife have built a fine reputation for good Italian food.

Closed Sun, Mon, 3 wks for 19 Jul & 3 wks fr 24 Dec

♧English & Italian 65 seats S% Lunch fr£5.90 Dinner £10.70alc Wine £5.20 Last dinner 10.30pm ℙ

Credit cards 1 3 5 Ⓥ

X**Henry Wong** 283 High St, Harborne ☎021-427 9799 District plan **25A**

A building that once housed a bank has now been completely refurbished as a Cantonese restaurant which offers authentic, popular Chinese dishes served in a friendly and attentive manner. Set meals are available for two or more persons, and special dinners can be organised.

Closed Sun

♧Cantonese **V** 140 seats Lunch £12alc Dinner £12alc Wine £5.50 Last dinner 11pm

Credit cards 1 2 3 5

X**Maharaja** 23/25 Hurst St ☎021-622 2641 Central plan **11***D3*

This small, but extremely popular, North Indian restaurant stands close to the Hippodrome Theatre. Authentic cuisine is achieved by a subtle blending of specially-prepared herbs and spices, and, although delays are inevitable because of the individual preparation of meals, the food is well worth the wait.

Closed Sun & end Jul-beg Aug

♧North Indian **V** 65 seats Lunch £7.50&alc Dinner £7.50&alc Wine £4.50 Last dinner 11.30pm ℙ

Credit cards 1 2 3 4 5

X**Michelle** 182/184 High St, Harborne (4m W off A456) ☎021-426 4133 District plan **27**

This little restaurant and its adjoining delicatessen offer food that is uncompromisingly French. The setting is Gallic, too, with check tablecloths bright against the dark wood and tiles of the old-fashioned grocery store from which it was converted.

Closed Sun

♧French **V** 80 seats S% Lunch £3.90—£9&alc Dinner £8.20—£9.80&alc Wine £4.50 Last dinner 10pm ℙ

Credit cards 1 3

X**Pinocchio's** 8 Chad Sq, Edgbaston ☎021-454 8672 District plan **29**

An extremely popular little restaurant, Pinocchio's is set in a small, leafy square between Harborne and Edgbaston. The à la carte menu is almost exclusively →

B

Italian, and both the traditional and more unusual dishes make good use of fresh produce. Lunch times tend to be crowded, as the excellent table d'hote menu attracts shoppers and business folk alike.

Closed Sun

🍴Italian 35 seats Lunch £6.75—£7.50&alc Dinner £17.50alc Wine £5.50 Last dinner 10.30pm 25P

Credit cards 1 2 3 5

✕Le Provençal 1 Albany Rd, Harborne (4m W off A456) ☎ 021-426 2444 District plan **31**

This bright and friendly little restaurant, converted from a double-fronted shop, stands just a few yards from the village High Street. Although portions are light, a fixed-price menu with an adequate choice of dishes makes an ideal lunchtime choice, whilst the à la carte menu, with its daily specials, offers a wider range which is completed by a predominantly French wine list.

Closed Sun, Lunch not served Mon & Sat

🍴French & Swiss 50 seats S% ✱Lunch £5.80&alc Dinner £12alc Wine £6 Last dinner 10.30pm ⊁

Credit cards 1 3 5

Birmingham — Bishop Auckland

BIRMINGHAM AIRPORT

West Midlands

Map **7** SP18

★★★★**Excelsior** Coventry Rd, Elmdon (Trusthouse Forte) ☎ 021-743 8141 Telex no 338005 Birmingham District plan **22**

This luxurious building is conveniently situated at the entrance to Birmingham airport.

141🛁(3fb) CTV in all bedrooms ® sB&B🛁£53 dB&B🛁£69 Ḃ

☾#200P CFA

🍷Last dinner 10.15pm

Credit cards 1 2 3 4 5

BIRMINGHAM (NATIONAL EXHIBITION CENTRE)

West Midlands

Map **7** SP18

★★★***Arden*** Coventry Rd, Bickenhill Village, Solihull (A45) ☎ Hampton-in-Arden (06755) 3221 Telex no 337766 Elmdon G Birmingham district plan **19**

Modern motel close to complex.

46🛁 CTV in all bedrooms ® **T** Ḃ

Lift ☾ CTV 150P CFA Live music & dancing Fri & Sat

🍴French 🍷Last dinner 11pm

Credit cards 1 2 3 5

BISHOP AUCKLAND

Co Durham

Map **8** NZ22

★★***Kings Arms*** 36 Market Pl ☎ (0388) 661296

Closed Xmas & New Year

A rambling former coaching inn overlooking the market square.

13rm(12🛁1🚿)(1fb) 2⊠ CTV in all bedrooms ® ✕ Ḃ

CTV ⊁

🍴English, Asian & Continental 🍷Last dinner 9pm

Credit cards 1 2 3 5

★★***HB* Park Head** New Coundon (1m N on A688) ☎ (0388) 661727

Comfortable modernised hotel with attractive bars and good food.

8rm(6🛁2🚿) Annexe: 7🛁(3fb) 1⊠ CTV in all bedrooms ® **T** sB&B🛁🚿£22—£28 dB&B🛁🚿£30—£38 Ḃ

☾70P

🍴English & French **V** 🍷Lunch £3.10—£6.25&alc Dinner £4.50—£10.75&alc Wine £4 Last dinner 10.30pm

Credit cards 1 2 3 5

★★**Queens Head** Market Pl ☎ (0388) 603477

Old fashioned hotel in market place with excellent value carvery.

10rm(5🛁)(2fb) CTV in all bedrooms ® S% sB&B£17.50 sB&B🛁£21 dB&B£25 dB&B🛁£29 Ɓ

30P ♩ Disco Fri & Sat Live music & dancing Thu Cabaret nightly in Dec

☋English & French **V** ♈ ☕ S% Lunch £2.35—£4 Tea 60p Dinner £6—£7&alc Wine £4 Last dinner 9pm

Credit cards 1 2 3 5 Ⓥ

BISHOPBRIGGS
Strathclyde *Lanarkshire*
Map **11** NS67

✕✕**Oasis Tandoori** 4 Woodhill Rd ☎ 041-772 1073

Tandoori barbecue cooking is the speciality of this modern restaurant.

Closed 1 Jan
Lunch not served Sat—Thu

☋European & Pakistani **V** 75 seats S% ✱Lunch £6.50alc Dinner £6.50alc Wine £5.30 Last dinner 11pm 37P

Credit cards 1 2 3 5

BISHOP'S CASTLE
Shropshire
Map **7** SO38

★***Castle*** ☎ (0588) 638403

Built 1719 on old castle keep site, and occupying prominent town centre position.

8rm(1🚿)(2fb) TV available in bedrooms CTV in 1 bedroom ® Ɓ

CTV 40P ⇎ *xmas*

V ♈ Last dinner 9.30pm

Credit cards 1 2 5

BISHOP'S LYDEARD
Somerset
Map **3** ST12

✕**Rose Cottage** ☎ (0823) 432394

A small, bright restaurant in a rural setting, Rose Cottage offers pleasant, courteous service and appetising, well-cooked meals. The lunchtime menu is fairly short, but in the evening it is extended with interesting main course dishes and fresh vegetables, and vegetarian meals are available. The wine list is strong in clarets and includes some good and older vintages.

Closed Sun, Mon, 1st 2 wks Nov, & 2 wks from 24 Dec

☋French **V** 40 seats ✱Lunch £5.50alc Dinner £12alc Wine £5.50 Last dinner 9.30pm 20P ⚞

BISHOPSTEIGNTON
Devon
Map **3** SX87

★★**Cockhaven Manor** Cockhaven Rd ☎ Teignmouth (06267) 5252

RS 25 & 26 Dec

From its hillside position at the foot of Haldon Moor, the Manor has looked out over the Teign Estuary since the sixteenth century. Now tastefully and completely modernised, its quiet location off the A381 makes it particularly attractive to the tourist.

13rm(3🛁4🚿)(2fb) 4⊟ CTV in all bedrooms ® sB&B£12—£14 sB&B🛁🚿£17—£19 dB&B£24—£28 dB&B🛁🚿£34—£38 Ɓ

50P ⇎ ❃ Live music and dancing Sat

♈ Bar lunch £4.50—£7.50 Dinner £6.25—£6.75&alc Wine £4.75 Last dinner 9pm

Credit cards 1 3 Ⓥ

See advertisement under Teignmouth

BLACKBURN
Lancashire
Map **7** SD62

★★★**Blackburn Moat House** Preston New Rd (Queens Moat) ☎ (0254) 64441 Telex no 63271

Set on the ring road, this large, modern hotel provides comfortable and well-furnished accommodation.

98🛁🚿(5fb) CTV in all bedrooms ® **T** S% sB&B🛁🚿£30—£45 dB&B🛁🚿£40—£55 Ɓ

Lift ☾ 300P ❃ CFA ♿

☋English & French **V** ♈ ☕ S% Lunch £5—£5.75&alc Tea 75p—£1 Dinner £9.50—£10.50&alc Wine £6.95 Last dinner 10pm

Credit cards 1 2 3 5 Ⓥ

★★**Millstone** Church Ln, Mellor (3m NW) ☎ Mellor (025481) 3333

This stone-built hotel in the centre of Mellor village offers well-furnished bedrooms and a good restaurant.

16rm(5🛁11🚿)(2fb) CTV in all bedrooms ® **T** S% sB&B🛁🚿£36—£45 dB&B🛁🚿£48—£60 Ɓ

40P ⇎

V ♈ Lunch £6.50—£9.50 Dinner £9—£10.50&alc Wine £6.95 Last dinner 9.45pm

Credit cards 1 2 3 5

✕***English Summerhouse*** 33 Darwen St ☎ (0254) 581440

Fronted by conifers and shaded by canopies, this delightful restaurant, personally run by the owners, is a bright spot in industrial Lancashire. Refreshingly-furnished, with pot plants, lace curtains and fresh linen, it provides a pleasant setting in which to enjoy freshly-cooked dishes produced with imagination and flair.

Closed Mon
Lunch not served Tue & Wed

☋English & French **V** 60 seats Last dinner 11pm

Credit cards 1 3

BLACKPOOL
Lancashire
Map **7** SD33

★★★★**Imperial** North Prom (Quality) ☎ (0253) 23971 Telex no 677376

Imposing Victorian building overlooking sea, with spacious public areas and elegant, modern, Palm Court restaurant.

159rm(146🛁13🚿)(16fb) ⚞ in 10 bedrooms CTV in all bedrooms ® **T** ✱sB&B🛁🚿£46—£48 dB&B🛁🚿£66—£70 Ɓ

Lift ☾ 200P ⊡(heated) sauna bath solarium Disco Mon—Sat ♿ *xmas*

♈ ☕ ⚞ ✱Lunch £7 Tea 75p Dinner £9.50 Wine £4.50 Last dinner 10.30pm

Credit cards 1 2 3 5 Ⓥ

★★★★**Pembroke** North Prom ☎ (0253) 23434 Telex no 677469

Large, modern seafront hotel with spacious, comfortable lounges, swimming pool and night spot. Offers many facilities for conferences or holiday.

201🛁 CTV in all bedrooms ® **T** ✱sB&B🛁fr£43.75 dB&B🛁fr£62.50 Ɓ

Lift ☾ ### 300P ⊡(heated) sauna bath solarium gymnasium Disco Tue—Sat Live music & dancing Wed *xmas*

☋English & French **V** ♈ ☕ ✱Lunch £7.95 Tea £2.40 Dinner £8.50&alc Wine £7.50 Last dinner 10.30pm

Credit cards 1 2 3 4 5

★★★**New Clifton** Talbot Sq (Quality) ☎ (0253) 21481 Telex no 677376

Centrally sited and overlooking the sea, the hotel has well furnished bedrooms and public areas.

78rm(77🛁1🚿)(10fb) ⚞ in 12 bedrooms CTV in all bedrooms ® **T** ✱sB&B🛁🚿£36 dB&B🛁🚿£55 Ɓ

Lift ☾ Ᵽ gymnasium Disco Thu, Fri & Sat Cabaret wkly ♿ *xmas*

☋English & French **V** ♈ ☕ ⚞ Lunch £5.50&alc Tea 60p—£2 High Tea £7.95&alc Dinner £7.95&alc Wine £4.95 Last dinner 10pm

Credit cards 1 2 3 4 5 Ⓥ

★★★**Savoy** North Shore, Queens Prom (Consort) ☎ (0253) 52561 Telex no 67570

Large, impressive sea front hotel.

130rm(126🛁10🚿)(14fb) 1⊟ CTV in all bedrooms ® **T** S% sB&B£18 sB&B🛁🚿£18—£24 dB&B£36 dB&B🛁🚿£36—£44 Ɓ

Lift ☾ CTV 70P 6🚗(charge) CFA pool table *xmas*

☋English & French **V** ♈ ☕ S% Lunch £5—£6&alc Tea £1&alc High Tea £4.50&alc Dinner £8—£10&alc Wine £5 Last dinner 11.45pm

Credit cards 1 2 3 4 5 Ⓥ

★★***Carlton*** North Prom ☎ (0253) 28966

Sea front hotel with a gabled roof and modern frontage.

58rm(26🛁8🚿)(5fb) CTV in all bedrooms ® Ɓ

Lift ☾ 50P Live music & dancing Sat Cabaret Wed & Fri (summer) ♿ *xmas*

☕English & French **V** 🍷 Last dinner 8.45pm

Credit cards 1 2 3 5

★ ★ ***Chequers*** 24 Queens Prom ☎ (0253) 56431 Telex no 67570

Closed 1—14 Jan

This hotel is situated on the north shore sea front.

46rm(41🛁5🚿)(6fb) CTV in all bedrooms Ⓡ**T** 🅱

Lift ☾ CTV 27P 3🚗 ⛟ ⛪ *xmas*

☕English, French & German **V** 🍷 ☕ Last dinner 8.15pm

Credit cards 1 2 3 5

★ ★ **Claremont** 270 North Prom ☎ (0253) 293122

A large well-furnished sea front hotel.

143🛁(51fb) CTV in all bedrooms Ⓡ**T** S% sB&B🛁£17.75—£42 dB&B🛁£35.50—£53 🅱

Lift ☾ 80P CFA Cabaret wknds May—Oct *xmas*

☕International 🍷 ☕ S% Lunch £4—£4.50 Tea fr50p High Tea £3.50—£6.95 Dinner £7.50—£8 Wine £4 Last dinner 8.30pm

Credit cards 1 2 3

★ ★ **Cliffs** Queens Prom ☎ (0253) 52388 Telex no 67191

Large hotel on North shore offering good value for money.

160rm(156🛁4🚿)(35fb) CTV in all bedrooms Ⓡ**T** sB&B🛁🚿£16—£50 dB&B🛁🚿£32—£58 🅱

Lift ☾ CTV 55P Table tennis Live music and dancing nightly May—Oct Cabaret Sun May—Oct *xmas*

🍷 ☕ Lunch £4.50—£6 Tea 60p High Tea £3.75—£6 Dinner £8—£9 Wine £4.75 Last dinner 8.30pm

Credit cards 1 2 3 Ⓥ

★ ★ **Gables Balmoral** Balmoral Rd ☎ (0253) 45432 Telex no 67178

A commercial and tourist hotel with modern bedrooms, situated close to the pleasure beach.

Blackpool — Blackwood

75rm(67🛁8🚿) 1⛾ CTV in all bedrooms **T** S% sB&B🛁🚿£17.50—£28 dB&B🛁🚿£42 🅱

☾ CTV 🅿 sauna bath solarium gymnasium CFA *xmas*

🍷 ☕ ✱Bar lunch 95p—£1.50 Tea £1.75 High Tea £4.60 Dinner fr£7.90 Last dinner 9.30pm

Credit cards 1 2 3 5 Ⓥ

★ ★ **Headlands** New South Prom ☎ (0253) 41179

Closed last 2 weeks Nov

A pleasant family hotel, situated on south shore sea front.

50rm(18🛁)(12fb) ✱sB&B£14—£17 sB&B🛁£16.50—£19 dB&B£26—£30 dB&B🛁£33—£37 🅱

Lift CTV 36P 8🚗 ⛟ Table tennis *xmas*

☕ S% ✱Lunch fr£5.75 Tea fr65p Dinner £7.75 Wine £4.75 Last dinner 8.30pm

Credit cards 1 3

★ ★ **Warwick** 603—609 New South Prom (Best Western) ☎ (0253) 42192 Telex no 677334

Large, family run hotel with well furnished bedrooms.

52rm(47🛁5🚿)(10fb) CTV in all bedrooms Ⓡ**T** S% sB&B🛁🚿£21.50—£26.75 dB&B🛁🚿£37—£46

☾ CTV 30P ⛆(heated) solarium Pool table *xmas*

🍷 ☕ S% Dinner £6.95—£7.95 Wine £4.50 Last dinner 7.30pm

Credit cards 1 2 3 5

★**Kimberley** New South Prom ☎ (0253) 41184

Closed 2—15 Jan

A family hotel with modern furnishings, located on the sea front.

51rm(33🛁)(9fb) CTV in all bedrooms Ⓡ sB&B£14.50 sB&B🛁🚿£16.50 dB&B£29 dB&B🛁🚿£33

Lift ☾ CTV 25P Table tennis Live music & dancing Wed Jul-Oct *xmas*

V 🍷 ☕ Lunch £3.80 Tea 75p Dinner £4.7 Wine £3.50 Last dinner 7.30pm

Credit cards 1 3 Ⓥ

★**Revill's** 190—4 North Promenade ☎ (0253) 25768

A tall sea-front hotel close to the town centre.

50rm(22🛁3🚿)(10fb) CTV in all bedroom Ⓡ🐕 sB&Bfr£13 sB&B🛁🚿fr£15 dB&Bfr£24 dB&B🛁🚿fr£28 🅱

Lift ☾ CTV 23P snooker table tennis *xmas*

V 🍷 ☕ Bar lunch £1—£3 Tea 50—80p Dinner £5.50—£6.50 Wine £2.75 Last dinner 7.30pm

Credit cards 1 3

✕✕**White Tower** Blackpool Pleasure Beach, Promenade/Balmoral Rd ☎ (025 46710

Located in Blackpool's Pleasure Beach complex, the restaurant overlooks sea an promenade. Food of a very good standar and is served in well-furnished surroundings by professional but friendly staff.

Closed Mon & Jan Lunch not served Tue—Sat Dinner not served Sun

☕English & French 60 seats Lunch £6.50—£7 Dinner £9—£11&alc Wine £6.50 Last dinner 10.45pm 100P Live music Fri & Sat

Credit cards 1 2 3 5 Ⓥ

BLACKWATERFOOT

Isle of Arran, Strathclyde *Bute*

See **Arran, Isle of**

BLACKWOOD

Gwent

Map **3** ST19

★ ★ ★**Maes Manor** ☎ (0495) 224551

A converted country house standing in its own grounds.

10rm(8🛁🚿) Annexe: 14🛁🚿(2fb) CTV in all bedrooms Ⓡ✱sB&B£25 sB&B🛁🚿£29—£30 dB&B🛁🚿£43—£4

☾ 100P ✿

Blair Atholl

English, Welsh & French V
*Lunch £12alc Tea £1alc Dinner £12alc Wine £5.50 Last dinner 9.30pm
Credit cards 1 2 3 5

BLAIR ATHOLL
Tayside *Perthshire*
Map **14** NN86

★★**Atholl Arms** (079681) 205
A large baronial hall, complete with minstrels' gallery, provides the dining room of this sizeable, traditional hotel in its attractive Highland village setting.
RS Nov—Etr
30rm(27 3)(1fb) CTV in all bedrooms ®
60P 3 Live music & dancing 4 nights wkly in season *xmas*
V Last dinner 9.30pm
Credit cards 1 3

BLAIR DRUMMOND
Central *Stirlingshire*
Map **11** NS79

✕**Broughton's Country Cottage**
Burnbank Cottage (1m W on A873)
Doune (0786) 841897
(Rosette awarded for dinner only)
The reputation of this restaurant continues to grow. Especially noteworthy is the flair for baking—for example, a home made wholemeal loaf is left on each table at the start of the meal. The creative use of pastry is evident throughout the menu and was enjoyed in the sautéed lamb's kidneys in a pastry case, the baked salmon in pastry, and also in several of the puddings.
Closed Sun, Mon & 1 mth early Spring
Lunch not served
International V 40 seats Dinner £13.50 Wine £5.60 Last dinner 10pm 24P
Credit card 1

Tayside *Perthshire*
Map **15** NO14

★★★ *HL* **Kinloch House** (2m W A923) Essendy (025084) 237
Closed 7—28 Dec
(Rosette awarded for dinner only.)
The proprietors of this popular hotel provide a relaxed atmosphere.
13rm(8 2)(2fb) 3 ®T S%
sB&B £29.50
dB&B £38—£48
CTV 40P
V S% Bar lunch £5.70alc Dinner £12.95 Wine £4.75 Last dinner 9.30pm
Credit cards 1 2 5

Blackwood — Blandford Forum

★★ *L* ***Altamount House*** Coupar Angus Rd (0250) 3512
Closed 1 wk Oct & Jan—14 Feb
Built as a private residence in 1806, this Georgian manor has been converted by its proprietors into a comfortable hotel standing in its own gardens.
7rm(4 3)(2fb) CTV in all bedrooms ®
40P 4
Last dinner 9pm
Credit cards 1 3 5

★★***Angus*** (Consort) (0250) 2838
Telex no 76526
Busy town centre hotel with its own sporting facilities.
82rms(66)(4fb) CTV in all bedrooms ®
Lift 24P CFA (heated) squash billiards sauna bath solarium Cabaret wkly *xmas*
V Last dinner 8.30pm
Credit cards 1 2 3

★★**Rosemount Golf** Golf Course Rd, Rosemount (0250) 2604
Closed 1 Jan
A friendly, family run hotel set in its own spacious grounds close to Rosemount Golf Course.
8rm(7 1) Annexe: 4(2fb) CTV in all bedrooms ® *sB&B £17
dB&B £27—£29
70P
Lunch £3.50—£7.50 High Tea £3—£6 Dinner £8alc Wine £3.95 Last dinner 9.30pm

BLAIRLOGIE
Central *Stirlingshire*
Map **11** NS89

✕✕**Blairlogie House Hotel** Alva (0259) 61441
This charming Victorian house, set amid woods and hills, has a relaxing, country-house atmosphere. Service from both owner and staff is friendly and efficient, the public rooms are impressive and the attractive bedrooms have private bathrooms. The restaurant offers an imaginative à la carte menu based on quality local produce and game.
Dinner not served Sun
Scottish & French V 50 seats *Lunch £8alc Dinner £10alc Wine £5.80 Last dinner 9pm 20P
Credit cards 1 3

BLAKENEY
Norfolk
Map **9** TG04

★★★***Blakeney*** The Quay (Best Western) Cley (0263) 740797
Tranquilly situated on the quayside, the hotel has panoramic views towards Blakeney Point.
41rm(25 2) Annexe: 13rm(12)(4fb) CTV in all bedrooms ®T
CTV 100P CFA (heated) sauna bath solarium *xmas*
V Last dinner 9.30pm
Credit cards 1 2 3 4 5

★★**Manor** Cley (0263) 740376
Closed 7—26 Dec
Former manor house with sheltered secluded gardens.
8(1fb) CTV in all bedrooms ® S%
*sB&B £22—£26 dB&B £42—£60
60P
English & Continental V S%
*Lunch £7.35 Tea £1 High Tea £1.50 Dinner £10&alc Wine £4.05 Last dinner 8.45pm

BLANCHLAND
Northumberland
Map **12** NY95

★★ *B* ***Lord Crewe Arms***
(043475) 251
RS wkdays Jan—mid Mar
This quiet village inn was once the home of the Abbot of Blanchland, and the atmosphere of the old monastery is retained in this friendly hotel.
8rm(6 2) Annexe: 7(2fb) 1 ®T
CTV 15P *xmas*
V Last dinner 9.15pm

BLANDFORD FORUM
Dorset
Map **3** ST80

★★★**Crown** 1 West St
(0258) 56626 Telex no 418292
A Georgian building in the centre of the town near to the shops, yet with rural views.
28rm(27 1)(1fb) 1 CTV in all bedrooms ®T sB&B £32—£40
dB&B £40—£55
60P 6(£2 per night) Croquet
V Lunch fr£7.50&alc Tea fr£1 Dinner fr£8.50&alc Wine £5 Last dinner 9pm
Credit cards 1 2 3 5 Ⓥ

✕✕**La Belle Alliance** Portman Lodge, Whitecliff Mill St (0258) 52842
The restaurant stands on the edge of the town centre, housed in a spacious Victorian residence with colonnade entrance and well-appointed rooms. Service is attentive and unhurried, the dishes on the interesting short menu freshly prepared.
Lunches by arrangement Dinner not served Sun (except Bank Hols) →

French 24 seats S% Lunch £6.50—£12&alc Dinner £12.50—£15.50&alc Wine £4.95 Last dinner 9.30pm 9P ⊁ nc 6yrs

Credit cards 1 2 3 5

BLAWITH
Cumbria
Map **7** SD28

★★ **_Highfield Country_** ☎ Lowick Bridge (022985) 238

Delightful hotel overlooking Crake valley with spacious bedrooms, comfortable lounge and memorable home cooking.

11rm(8→3⋒)(1fb) CTV in 3 bedrooms ® ✈ ℞

CTV 25P ⛟ ✿ ♩ billiards ⌂ *xmas*

English, French & Italian **V** ♁ ☕ Last dinner 9pm

Credit cards 1 3

BLICKLING
Norfolk
Map **9** TG12

✕ **Buckinghamshire Arms Hotel** ☎ Aylsham (0263) 732133

A country inn adjoining Blickling Hall.

Closed 25 Dec

V 45 seats ✻ Lunch £8.50 Dinner £12.50 Wine £6 Last dinner 10pm 100P

Credit cards 1 2 3 5

BLOCKLEY
Gloucestershire
Map **4** SP13

★★ **Lower Brook House** ☎ (0386) 700286

Closed Jan

Small, comfortable personally run Cotswold village hotel, offering relaxed atmosphere, pretty bedrooms and good food.

8rm(6→2⋒)(1fb) CTV in all bedrooms ® S% ✻ sB&B→⋒£35(incl. dinner) dB&B→⋒£70—£78(incl. dinner) ℞

12P ⛟ ✿ *xmas*

♁ Bar lunch £1.75—£5.50 Dinner £13.50 Wine £5 Last dinner 9.30pm

Credit card 1

BLOFIELD
Norfolk
Map **5** TG30

✕✕ **_La Locanda_** Fox Ln ☎ Norwich (0603) 713787

Closed Sun
Lunch not served Sat

Italian 45 seats Last dinner 11pm 20P

Credit cards 1 2 3 5

BLOXHAM
Oxfordshire
Map **4** SP43

★★ **_Olde School_** Church St ☎ Banbury (0295) 720369

RS New Years Day

One-time village school with small, well-equipped bedrooms and professional restaurant.

11rm(4→7⋒) CTV in all bedrooms ® **T** ✈ ℞

CTV 50P Cabaret Fri, Sat & Sun

English & French **V** ♁ ☕ Last dinner 9.30pm

Credit cards 1 2 3 5

BLUE ANCHOR
Somerset
Map **3** ST04

★ **Langbury** ☎ Dunster (0643) 821375

RS Nov—Feb

An attractive, comfortable hotel offering attentive service and with pretty bedrooms and a well tended garden.

9rm(1→4⋒)(3fb) CTV in all bedrooms ® S% sB&B£12—£13 sB&B→⋒£16—£17 dB&B£24—£26 dB&B→⋒£27—£29 ℞

9P ⛟ ✿ ⛵

♁ S% Bar lunch fr£2 Dinner £7.50 Wine £4.80 Last dinner 7pm Ⓥ

BLUNDELLSANDS
Merseyside
Map **7** SJ39

★★★ **Blundellsands** The Serpentine (Whitbread) ☎ 051-924 6515 Liverpool plan **2** *B8*

An Edwardian red brick building situated in a quiet surburban area.

39rm(31→8⋒)(4fb) ⊁ in 7 bedrooms CTV in all bedrooms ® **T** sB&B→⋒£40 dB&B→⋒£45 ℞

Lift ☾ CTV 350P pool table

English & French **V** ♁ ☕ ✻ Lunch £6.50—£8&alc Tea fr75p High Tea £1.75—£2.75 Dinner £9.50—£10.50&alc Wine £4.95 Last dinner 9.30pm

Credit cards 1 2 3 4 5

BOAT OF GARTEN
Highland *Inverness-shire*
Map **14** NH91

★★★ **Boat** (Inter Hotel) ☎ (047983) 258 Telex no 777205

Closed Nov—21 Dec

A village centre hotel standing beside the Strathspey Railway Station overlooking golf course and close to River Spey.

36→⋒(1fb) CTV in all bedrooms ® sB&B→⋒£19—£26 dB&B→⋒£38—£48 ℞

36P CFA ✿ ⌂ *xmas*

International ♁ ☕ ⊁ S% Lunch £6.50alc Tea fr85p Dinner fr£10.50 Wine £5.95 Last dinner 9pm

Credit cards 1 2 3 4 5 Ⓥ

★★ **_Craigard_** Kinchurdy Rd ☎ (047983) 206

RS Nov—Apr except Xmas, New Year & Etr

This late-Victorian shooting lodge was converted to a hotel in 1931. It is set in 2½ acres with access to golf course.

20rm(7→1⋒)(3fb) ℞

CTV 30P 4⌂(£2 per night) ⛟ ✿

V ♁ ☕ Last dinner 8pm

Credit cards 1 2 3 5

BODINNICK
Cornwall
Map **2** SX15

★*L* **Old Ferry Inn** ☎ Polruan (072687) 237

RS Nov—Mar

A comfortably appointed historic inn with commanding views, beside the River Fowey. Sailing available.

13rm(5→1⋒)(1fb) 1⊟ CTV in 10 bedrooms ✻ sB&B£18.50—£22.50 sB&B→⋒£20.50—£22.50 dB&B£37—£45 dB&B→⋒£41—£45

CTV 10P 4⌂ ⛟

English & French ♁ ✻ Bar lunch 40p—£2.20 Tea £1.20 High Tea £3 Dinner £11.75&alc Wine £3.65 Last dinner 8.30pm

Credit card 3

BODMIN
Cornwall
Map **2** SX06

★★★ *H* **Tredethy Country** (off B3266 3m N) ☎ St Mabyn (020884) 262

(For full entry see Helland Bridge)

★★ **Hotel Allegro** 50 Higher Bore St ☎ (0208) 3480

Set on the edge of the main road, the Allegro is a small commercial hotel built around a courtyard.

12rm(3→1⋒)(2fb) CTV in all bedrooms ✈ sB&B£15 sB&B→⋒£21 dB&B£25 dB&B→⋒£31

CTV 15P ⛟

V ♁ ☕ Lunch £4.75&alc Tea 75p Dinner £4.75&alc Wine £5.20 Last dinner 9pm

Credit cards 1 2 3 5 Ⓥ

★★ **_Westberry_** Rhind St ☎ (0208) 2772

Closed Xmas & New Year

This comfortable, busy hotel, personally run and sited conveniently near to the town centre, has a pleasant cottage annexe.

15rm(7→3⋒) Annexe: 8rm(4→4⋒)(2fb) CTV in 7 bedrooms ℞

CTV 24P

♁ ☕ Last dinner 8pm

Credit cards 1 3

BOGNOR REGIS
West Sussex
Map **4** SZ99

★★★***Royal Norfolk*** The Esplanade (Best Western) ☎ (0243) 826222 Telex no 477575

Splendid Regency building facing the sea with 3 acres of lawns and gardens.

53rm(38⇌1⋔)(7fb)2⊟ CTV in all bedrooms ®T B

Lift ☾ 150P CFA ❀ ⌒ (heated) ℘(hard) Live music and dancing Sat ⌂ *xmas*

ʊ English & French **V** ♡ ⊒ Last dinner 9.30pm

Credit cards 1 2 3 4 5

★**Black Mill House** Princess Av ☎ (0243) 821945

Quiet, friendly hotel near marine gardens.

22rm(8⇌3⋔) Annexe: 4rm(6fb) CTV available in bedrooms sB&B£15.50—£21 sB&B⇌⋔£19.50—£25 dB&B£31—£42 dB&B⇌⋔£35—£46 B

CTV 12P ⊟ table tennis games room ⌂ *xmas*

ʊ English & French **V** ♡ ⊒ Lunch £4—£5 Tea fr55p Dinner £6—£7 Wine £4 Last dinner 7.30pm

Credit cards 1 2 3 5 Ⓥ

BOLLINGTON
Cheshire
Map **7** SJ97

★★★**Belgrade** Jackson Ln (Consort) ☎ (0625) 73246 Telex no 667217

A stone built hotel within its own grounds and with a modern extension.

64⇌⋔(2fb) CTV in all bedrooms ®T ✈ sB&B⇌⋔£35 dB&B⇌⋔£40

☾ 300P CFA ❀ *xmas*

ʊ French **V** ♡ ⊒ Bar lunch 85p—£3 Tea 75p Dinner £9.75&alc Wine £5 Last dinner 10.30pm

Credit cards 1 2 3 5

BOLTON
Gt Manchester
Map **7** SD70

★★★**Crest** Beaumont Rd (Crest) ☎ (0204) 651511 Telex no 635527

A modern hotel situated on the Bolton ring road close to the M61.

100⇌⋔⊬ in 25 bedrooms CTV in all bedrooms ®S% ✱sB⇌⋔fr£47 dB⇌⋔fr£57(room only) B

☾ 100P CFA *xmas*

ʊ English & French **V** ♡ ⊒⊬ ✱Lunch £5.20—£7.50&alc Tea 85—95p Dinner £11.70—£11.90&alc Wine £5.90 Last dinner 9.45pm

Credit cards 1 2 3 4 5

★★★⚘**Egerton House** Egerton (3m N A666) ☎ (0204) 57171 Telex no 635322

Family run hotel in wooded grounds with comfortable bedrooms and panoramic restaurant.

27⇌(6fb) CTV in all bedrooms ®T S% ✱sB&B⇌£44—£46 dB&B⇌£56—£58 B

CTV 80P ❀ *xmas*

ʊ International **V** ♡ ⊒ S% ✱Lunch £5.50—£7&alc Tea £2.50—£3 Dinner £8.95—£10&alc Wine £5.50 Last dinner 9.30pm

Credit cards 1 2 3 4 5

★★★**Last Drop** Hospital Rd, Bromley Cross (3m N off B6472) ☎ (0204) 591131 Telex no 635322

This modern hotel is set within a newly-built village complex, created out of former farm buildings.

73⇌⋔ Annexe: 7⇌⋔(35fb) 4⊟ CTV in all bedrooms ®T sB&B⇌⋔fr£49 dB&B⇌⋔fr£63 B

☾ 400P CFA ❀ ⊡(heated) sauna bath solarium gymnasium Disco Mon, Wed & Sun Live music & dancing Sat *xmas* →

International V Lunch £6.75—£7.50&alc Tea £1—£1.90 High Tea £2.80—£5 Dinner £8.50—£9.50&alc Wine £5.95 Last dinner 10.30pm

Credit cards 1 2 3 5

★★★**Pack Horse** Bradshawgate, Nelson Sq (De Vere) (0204) 27261 Telex no 635168

A modern commercial hotel situated in the town centre.

74 CTV in all bedrooms Ⓡ **T** S% sB&B fr£48 dB&B fr£56

Lift CFA

English & French V S% Lunch fr£7.50 Tea fr80p Dinner £9.50—£20&alc Wine £5.65 Last dinner 10pm

Credit cards 1 2 3 5

★***Broomfield*** 33—35 Wigan Rd, Deane (0204) 61570

Small, friendly hotel, west of town centre.

14rm(3 10) CTV in all bedrooms

CTV 25P 3

Last dinner 9pm

Credit cards 1 3

BOLTON ABBEY

North Yorkshire

Map **7** SE05

★★★*L* **Devonshire Arms** (Best Western) (075671) 441 Telex no 51218

Finely restored and enlarged coaching inn whose elegant mirrored restaurant features a high standard of cuisine. Friendly service and modern facilities.

38 2 CTV in all bedrooms Ⓡ **T** S% ✱sB&B fr£49.50 dB&B fr£60.50

CTV 100P *xmas*

International V S% ✱Lunch £6—£6.85 Tea 75p High Tea 90p—£2 Dinner £14.50&alc Wine £5.95 Last dinner 9.30pm

Credit cards 1 2 3 4 5 Ⓥ

See advertisement under Skipton

BONAR BRIDGE

Highland *Sutherland*

Map **14** NH69

★★**Bridge** (ExecHotel) Ardgay (08632) 204

Closed 1 & 2 Jan

Two-storey stone house situated on the main road, with views of Kyle of Sutherland.

16rm(5 5)(3fb) CTV in all bedrooms Ⓡ **T** sB&B£17—£18.50 sB&B £22.50—£25 dB&B£29—£31 dB&B £39—£42

20P

Scottish & French V ✱Bar lunch £3.50alc Tea fr80p High Tea fr£4 Dinner fr£7.50&alc Wine £4.25 Last dinner 10pm

Credit cards 1 2 3 5 Ⓥ

BONNYRIGG

Lothian *Midlothian*

Map **11** NT36

★★★★*L* **Dalhousie Castle** Gorebridge (0875) 20153 Telex no 72380

A 12th-century castle in 1,000 acres offering gracious living. The Dungeon restaurant is a delight and bedrooms are elegant with modern features.

24 (6fb) 1 CTV in all bedrooms **T** sB&B £38—£53 dB&B £59—£78

100P CFA *xmas*

Scottish & French V ✱Lunch £14alc Tea £1.50alc Dinner £16alc Wine £6.50 Last dinner 9.30pm

Credit cards 1 2 3 5 Ⓥ

BONTDDU

Gwynedd

Map **6** SH61

★★★*L* **Bontddu Hall** (034149) 661

Closed Jan—Etr RS Nov—Dec

Built in the country-house style, with 2½ acres of grounds, this hotel overlooks the Mawddach Estuary.

16rm(13 3) Annexe: 6 (6fb) 1 CTV in all bedrooms Ⓡ **T** ✱sB&B £23.50—£38.50 dB&B £47—£65

50P putting nc 3yrs

V ✱Lunch £5.50 Tea fr£1 Dinner £13&alc Wine £5.25 Last dinner 9.30pm

Credit cards 1 2 3 5 Ⓥ

BOOTLE

Merseyside

Map **7** SJ39

★★★**Park** Park Lane West, Netherton (off A5036 1m SW of junc M57/M58/A59) (Greenall Whitley) 051-525 7555 Telex no 629772 Liverpool plan **11** *D8*

Large, modern, commercial hotel, with well equipped bedrooms, and well placed for access to the motorway.

60rm(23 37) CTV in all bedrooms Ⓡ **T** S% sB&B £16.50—£37 dB&B £33—£47

Lift 250P 2 CFA

V S% Lunch £4.90—£10 Tea £1—£2 High Tea £1—£2 Dinner £5—£11 Wine £5.95 Last dinner 9.15pm

Credit cards 1 2 3 5

BOREHAM STREET

East Sussex

Map **5** TQ61

★★★**White Friars** (Best Western) Herstmonceux (0323) 832355

Closed 1—9 Jan

The ivy-clad, eighteenth century hotel, set amid the Sussex Weald, provides a homely atmosphere in its chintzy, beamed lounge and quaint though well-appointed bedrooms. Family-owned, it offers cheerful and helpful service.

13rm(8 2) Annexe: 8 (2fb) 2 CTV in all bedrooms Ⓡ **T** S% sB&B£23.50 sB&B £29.50 dB&B£41 dB&B £52

120P *xmas*

Cosmopolitan V S% ✱Lunch £6.50&alc Tea 60p Dinner £7.50&alc Wine £4.85 Last dinner 9pm

Credit cards 1 2 3 5

BOREHAM WOOD

Hertfordshire

Map **4** TQ19

★★★**Elstree Moat House** Barnet bypass (Queens Moat) 01-953 1622

RS 26 Dec—2 Jan

A pleasant thatched hotel with comfortable bars and carvery restaurant.

60 (10fb) CTV in all bedrooms Ⓡ **T** sB&B fr£51 dB&B fr£64

400P CFA Live music and dancing Sat

English & French Lunch £9.30&alc Tea fr60p High Tea fr£2 Dinner £9.30&alc Wine £5.25 Last dinner 9.45pm

Credit cards 1 2 3 4 5

BORGUE

Dumfries & Galloway *Kirkcudbrightshire*

Map **11** NX64

★★***Senwick House*** Brighouse Bay (05577) 236

Nicely furnished house in attractive well-tended gardens.

9rm(4 1)(1fb) CTV in 5 bedrooms Ⓡ

CTV 10P (hard) *xmas*

V Last dinner 9.30pm

Credit cards 2 5

BOROUGHBRIDGE

N Yorkshire

Map **8** SE36

★★★***Crown*** Horsefair (ExecHotel) (09012) 2328

Old coaching inn restored to a high standard, but without losing too much of the original character.

43 (4fb) 1 CTV in all bedrooms Ⓡ

Lift 45P sauna bath solarium *xmas*

V Last dinner 9.15pm

Credit cards 1 2 3 5

★★★**Three Arrows** Horsefair (Embassy) (09012) 2245

A Victorian country mansion standing in its own grounds.

17rm(16 1)(5fb) CTV in all bedrooms Ⓡ S% sB fr£34 dB fr£43.50 (room only)

50P *xmas*

S% Lunch fr£7 Dinner fr£10 Wine £5.50 Last dinner 9pm

Credit cards 1 2 3 4 5 Ⓥ

See advertisement under Harrogate

BORROWASH
Derbyshire
Map **8** SK43

✕✕ ***Wilmot Arms*** ☎ Derby (0332) 672222

Restaurant is in converted stable block next to 17th century inn.

Closed Sun Lunch not served Sat

☋ Continental 55 seats Last dinner 9.50pm 40P

Credit cards 1 2 3 5

BORROWDALE
Cumbria
Map **11** NY21

See also **Grange (in-Borrowdale)**, **Rosthwaite** and **Keswick**

★★★★ **LODORE SWISS BORROWDALE**

☎ (059684) 285 Telex no 64305

Closed early Nov—late Mar

This hotel standing at the edge of the lake takes its name from the notable falls which flow within the boundaries of the hotel's extensive grounds. Within the splendid granite building is a lakeland holiday hotel that offers professional standards of hotel keeping. Run by the Swiss family England with typical proficiency, the hotel offers something for everyone, young or old. There can be few places that surpass this in the recreational facilities on offer: many are mentioned below and there is also a childrens' games room, a nursery, and baby listening service. The modernised bedrooms are neat and comfortably furnished and in-house movies are provided. The attractive cocktail bar, with its ornamental fountain, is a popular rendezvous to chat with other guests, or you may relax in cushioned ease in the large lounge. Flower arrangements add their own charm. The large dining room, like the main lounge, overlooks Derwent Water and is decently appointed. A variety of attractive dishes is presented by Chef Hardiman. There is a fixed price menu of five courses, another

'gourmet' one and a Menu Surprise for two persons, while at lunch there is an à la carte menu. This remains a pleasant hotel for family holidays and offers excellent value for money.

72rm(70⇥2⌂)(10fb) CTV in all bedrooms Ⓡ T ✈ sB&B⇥⌂fr£34 dB&B⇥⌂fr£68

Lift ☾ 60P 23⌂(£1.50 per night) ⛟ ✿ ⊡/⛱ (heated) 🎾(hard) squash sauna bath solarium gymnasium Disco twice wkly in season Live music & dancing Sat ♿

☋ French & Swiss **V** ♈ ☕ Lunch £8alc Tea £3.50alc Dinner fr£13&alc Wine £5.80 Last dinner 9.30pm

Credit card 2 Ⓥ

★★★ ***H*** **Borrowdale** ☎ (059684) 224

Charming and welcoming hotel in a beautiful setting at the entrance to Borrowdale valley.

35rm(31⇥4⌂)(8fb) 5⊟ CTV in all bedrooms **T** ✱sB&B⇥⌂£14—£24 dB&B⇥⌂£26.60—£47.20 **B**

80P ⛟ ✿ *xmas*

☋ English & Continental **V** ♈ ☕ Lunch £6.95 Tea 85p Dinner £11.50 Wine £3.65 Last dinner 9.15pm

Credit cards 1 3

BOSCASTLE
Cornwall
Map **2** SX09

★★ **Bottreaux House** ☎ (08405) 231

Closed Dec & Jan

Small, comfortable hotel at the top of this picturesque harbour village.

7rm(4⇥3⌂) CTV in all bedrooms Ⓡ ✈ ✱sB&B⇥⌂£17 dB&B⇥⌂£31.50

10P ⛟ nc10yrs *xmas*

☋ English, French & Italian ♈ ⊬ Lunch fr£8&alc Dinner fr£8&alc Wine £4.75 Last dinner 9.30pm

Credit cards 1 3 Ⓥ

See advertisement on page 136

★★ **Riverside** The Harbour ☎ (08405) 216

Closed Jan—mid Feb

This small, comfortable hotel and restaurant opposite the harbour has a warm, friendly atmosphere.

10rm(7⇥3⌂) Ⓡ ✱sB&B⇥⌂£14.50 dB&B⇥⌂£29

CTV ⛟ ✿

☋ English & French **V** ✱ Lunch £4.50alc Dinner £8.50alc Wine £4.95 Last dinner 10pm

Credit card 1

See advertisement on page 136

BOSHAM
West Sussex
Map **4** SU80

★★ ***B*** **Millstream** Bosham Ln (Best Western) ☎ (0243) 573234

Small picturesque hotel, situated close to the Quay, with good service and comfortable bedrooms.

29⇥⌂(2fb) 1⊟ CTV in all bedrooms Ⓡ **T** ✱sB&B⇥⌂£32—£36 dB&B⇥⌂£52—£68 **B**

☾ CTV 40P ✿ *xmas*

☋ English & French ♈ ☕ ✱ Lunch £12alc Tea 80p—£3 Dinner £9.50—£10.50&alc Wine £5 Last dinner 9.30pm

Credit cards 1 2 3 5

BOSTON
Lincolnshire
Map **8** TF34

★★★ **New England** Wide Bargate (Anchor) ☎ (0205) 65255 Telex no 858875

This three-storey Victorian building, with its attractive public areas and comfortable, well-equipped bedrooms, is conveniently situated near to the town centre and is popular with both commercial customers and tourists.

25⇥(1fb) ⊬ in 5 bedrooms CTV in all bedrooms Ⓡ **T** ✱sB&B⇥£25—£37 dB&B⇥£38—£47 **B**

☾ 200P(charge) *xmas*

☋ Mainly Grills **V** ♈ ☕ ✱ Lunch £6.95—£10.40&alc Tea fr60p Dinner £6.95—£10.40&alc Wine £5.95 Last dinner 10pm

Credit cards 1 2 3 4 5 Ⓥ

★★ **Burton House** Wainfleet Rd ☎ (0205) 62307

Situated on the northern outskirts of the town, near the junction of the A52 with the A16, this friendly hotel provides comfortable accommodation and is popular with commercial customers.

6rm(2⇥)(1fb) CTV in all bedrooms Ⓡ sB&B£25 sB&B⇥£30 dB&B£30—£33 dB&B⇥£38—£40

100P ✿

☋ English & Italian ♈ Lunch £5.25—£16&alc High Tea £2.50—£3&alc Dinner £6.50—£11.50&alc Wine £3.95 Last dinner 9.30pm

Credit cards 1 2 3 Ⓥ

★★ **White Hart** Bridge Foot (Berni) ☎ (0205) 64877

Closed Xmas

An impressive, Regency-style building, the White Hart stands on the bank of the River Witham near the town centre, opposite the famous St Botolph's Church (the Stump). →

It has been tastefully modernised to provide comfortable bedrooms and pleasant public areas which include a choice of restaurants, each with its own bar.

31rm(7⇌2ⓜ)(2fb) CTV in all bedrooms ® ✈ sBfr£20 sB⇌ⓜ£27 dBfr£37 dB⇌ⓜ£44.50 (room only) B

☾ 40P

☺ Mainly Grills ♀ ⚡ *Lunch £7.50alc Dinner £7.50alc Wine £4.50 Last dinner 10pm

Credit cards 1 2 3 5

BOTALLACK

Cornwall
Map **2** SW33

XX Count House ☎ Penzance (0736) 788588

Ruins of former Cornish mine workings house this character restaurant.

Closed Mon, Tue & 3—4 wks Jan Lunch not served Wed—Sat Dinner not served Sun

☺ European 35 seats Lunch £6.75 Dinner £15alc Wine £4.95 Last dinner 10pm 30P

Credit cards 1 2 3 4 5

BOTHWELL

Strathclyde *Lanarkshire*
Map **11** NS75

★★ Silvertrees Silverwells Cres ☎ (0698) 852311

This is a large house in a quiet residential position, whose interior is a tasteful blend of old and modern.

7⇌ Annexe: 19⇌(1fb) 1▣ CTV in all bedrooms ® in 19 bedrooms **T** sB&B⇌£40 dB&B⇌£44—£49.50

100P ▦ ✿ ⌂

V ♀ Lunch £7.40&alc High Tea £6 Dinner £9.35&alc Wine £6.40 Last dinner 8.45pm

Credit cards 1 2 3 5 Ⓥ

BOTLEY

Hampshire
Map **4** SU51

XX Cobbett's 13 The Square ☎ (04892) 2068

Cosy 16th century cottage restaurant featuring enterprising French regional cooking with attentive friendly service.

Closed Sun Public & Bank Hols & 2 wks summer. Lunch not served Sat & Mon

☺ French **V** 45 seats Lunch £9.05 Dinner £18alc Wine £7.20 Last dinner 9.45pm 20P nc 11 yrs (Dinner)

Credit cards 1 2 3

BOTTOMHOUSE

Staffordshire
Map **7** SK05

X *Forge* Ashbourne Rd ☎ Onecote (05388) 249

Old stone inn on edge of North Staffordshire moorlands.

Closed Mon. Dinner not served Sun. Lunch not served Tue—Sat

☺ English & French 50 seats Last dinner 9.45pm 150P

BOURNE

Lincolnshire
Map **8** TF02

★★ Angel Market Pl ☎ (0778) 422346

Comfortable 16th century town centre inn with well equipped modern accommodation.

12rm(5⇌7ⓜ)(1fb) 1▣ CTV in all bedrooms ® **T** ✈ (ex guide dogs) *sB&B⇌ⓜ£23 dB&B⇌ⓜ£35 B

100P

V ♀ ☕ *Lunch £5.80 Tea 50p Dinner £10alc Wine £4.80 Last dinner 10pm

Credit cards 1 3

BOURNEMOUTH & BOSCOMBE Dorset
Map **4** SZ09
Telephone exchange 'Bournemouth'

For town plans see Key Map on page 138 or page 141 for Central Plan, page 143 for Boscombe & Southbourne Plan, or page 142 for Westbourne & Branksome plan. For additional hotels see **Christchurch, Longham** and **Poole.**

★★★★★ ***Royal Bath*** Bath Rd (De Vere) (0202) 25555 Telex no 41375 Central plan **31** *E2*

This spacious hotel stands in its own grounds overlooking the sea. Most of the bedrooms have been brought up to a very high standard and there are an ornate lounge and small library. The main restaurant is augmented by a comfortable grill room, and service throughout is pleasant and courteous.

131 1 CTV in all bedrooms **T**

Lift 120 (£2) CFA (heated) sauna bath solarium gymnasium Live music & dancing wkly *xmas*

International **V** Last dinner 11pm

Credit cards 1 2 3 4 5

★★★★ **Highcliff** West Cliff, St Michael's Rd (Best Western) (0202) 27702 Telex no 417153 Central plan **19** *C1*

In an impressive cliff-top position overlooking the sea, the hotel offers comfortable accommodation throughout. Recently-converted coastguard cottages provide fourteen additional bedrooms which are reached by a covered way from the main building.

94rm(78 16) Annexe: 14 (30fb) CTV in all bedrooms ®**T** S% sB&B £38—£45 dB&B £76—£90

Lift 85P CFA (heated) snooker sauna bath croquet Disco Mon—Sat Live music and dancing Mon—Sat *xmas*

V Lunch £6.50—£8.50&alc Tea £1.50—£3 High Tea £3.50—£6.50 Dinner £10.50—£12&alc Wine £5.25 Last dinner 9pm

Credit cards 1 2 3 5 Ⓥ

★★★★ **Palace Court** Westover Rd (0202) 27681 Telex no 418451 Central plan **26** *D2*

A balconied building of architectural interest, centrally located near the shops and opposite the Pavilion.

107 (4fb) CTV in all bedrooms ®**T** *sB&B fr£41 dB&B fr£54

Lift 100 (£1 per day) CFA sauna bath solarium gynmasium Disco 5 nights wkly *xmas*

English, French & Italian **V** *Lunch fr£7.50 Dinner fr£10.50 Wine £5.95 Last dinner 9pm

Credit cards 1 2 3 5

See advertisement on page 138

★★★ **Anglo-Swiss** Gervis Rd, East Cliff (0202) 24794 Telex no 8954665 Central plan **1** *F4*

A large hotel in an avenue of pine trees with formal service.

66rm(58 8)(10fb) CTV in all bedrooms ®**T** S% sB&B £30—£36 dB&B £50—£70

Lift CTV 65P CFA (heated) sauna bath solarium gymnasium Live music & dancing wknds & in season *xmas*

V S% Lunch £7 Tea fr50p Dinner £8—£8.50 Wine £6.50 Last dinner 8.30pm

Credit cards 1 2 3 5 Ⓥ

★★★ **Bournemouth Moat House** Knyveton Rd (Queens Moat) (0202) 293311 Telex no 47186 Boscombe & Southbourne plan **49** *B2*

Popular businessman's hotel with modern facilities.

151rm(145 6)(45fb) CTV in all bedrooms ®**T** sB&B £33—£38 dB&B £47—£57

Lift 100P (heated) snooker table tennis *xmas* →

B

English & French V Lunch £6.50—£7.50&alc Tea 60—65p High Tea £2—£2.75 Dinner £8.50—£9&alc Wine £5.10 Last dinner 9.30pm

Credit cards 1 2 3 5 V

★★★**Burley Court** Bath Rd ☎ (0202) 22824 Central plan **4** *E3*

Closed Jan

Attentive staff provide a relaxing atmosphere in this family run hotel.

41rm(31⇌1⋒)(8fb) CTV in 32 bedrooms TV in 9 bedrooms ®S% sB&B£16.50—£26 sB&B⇌⋒£25—£31.50 dB&B£33—£43 dB&B⇌⋒£40—£52.50 B

Lift ☾ CTV 45P ⌂ (heated) solarium *xmas*

Bournemouth & Boscombe

English & French S% Bar lunch £1.70—£2.70&alc Tea 85—90p Dinner £8—£9&alc Wine £5 Last dinner 8.30pm

Credit cards 1 3 V

★★★**Hotel Cecil** Parsonage Rd, Bath Hill ☎ (0202) 293336 Telex no 8954665 Cental plan **5** *E3*

Centrally situated red brick hotel, within walking distance of the shops and pier.

27rm(21⇌6⋒)(5fb) CTV in all bedrooms ®T✱sB&B⇌⋒£20—£27 dB&B⇌⋒£40—£54 B

Lift 27P Live music and dancing Sat ♿ *xmas*

French V ✱ Lunch £4.95 Tea £1 Dinner £6.50&alc Wine £5.75 Last dinner 9pm

Credit cards 1 2 3 4 5

★★★**Chesterwood** East Overcliff Dr ☎ (0202) 28057 Boscombe & Southbourne plan **51** *A1*

Closed Jan

A detached hotel on the East Cliff, offering uninterrupted sea views.

49rm(38⇌9⋒)(12fb) CTV in all bedrooms ®T sB&B£19.50—£24.45 sB&B⇌⋒£20.50—£26.05 dB&B£37—£40 dB&B⇌⋒£39—£52.10 B

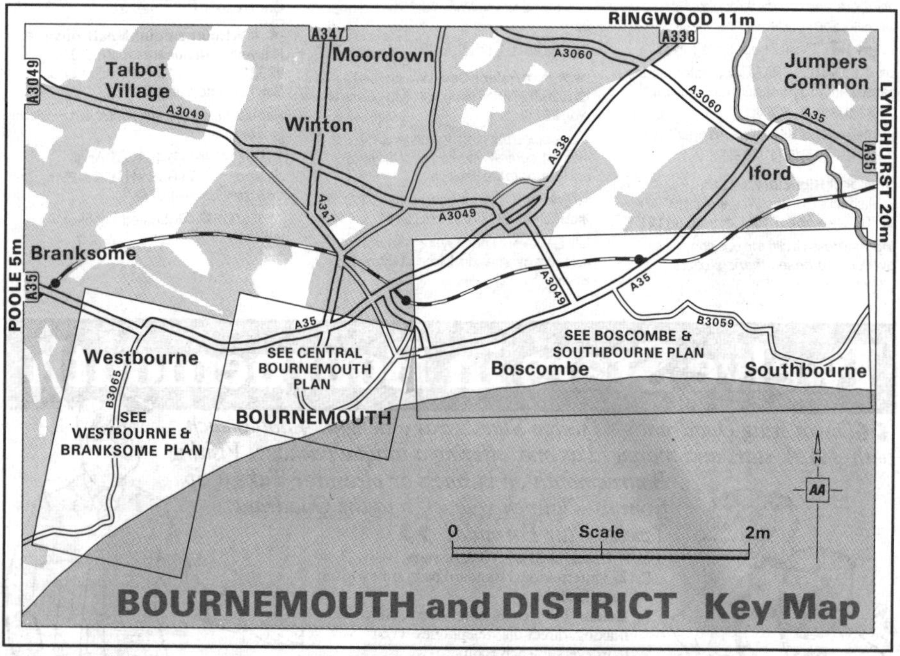

RINGWOOD 11m
A347
A338
Moordown
A3060
Talbot Village
A3049
Jumpers Common
Winton
LYNDHURST 20m
A35
Iford
A347
A3049
Branksome
POOLE 5m
A35
A3049
A35
B3059
SEE BOSCOMBE & SOUTHBOURNE PLAN
Westbourne
SEE CENTRAL BOURNEMOUTH PLAN
Boscombe
Southbourne
B3065
SEE WESTBOURNE & BRANKSOME PLAN
BOURNEMOUTH
N
AA
0 Scale 2m

BOURNEMOUTH and DISTRICT Key Map

ift ☾28P 6🚗✿ ≈ (heated) Disco wkly in
eason Live music and dancing 3 nights
vkly in season *xmas*
? Lunch £5 Tea fr55p Dinner £7.50 Wine
3.80 Last dinner 8.30pm
Credit cards [1] [3] [5]

★★★**Cliff End** Manor Rd, East Cliff
Consort) ☎ (0202) 309711 Boscombe &
Southbourne plan **53** *B1*

Modernised hotel with new wing extension and pleasant lounges.

40rm(35🛁5🚿)(15fb) CTV in all bedrooms
®T S% ✱sB&B🛁🚿£24.75
dB&B🛁🚿£49.45 B

Bournemouth & Boscombe

Lift ☾40P CFA ✿ ≈ (heated) solarium
Live music & dancing Fri & Sat (3 nights
wkly May—Sep) *xmas*
English, French & Italian V S%
✱Lunch £5.95 Tea 65p Dinner £7.75 Wine
£4.75 Last dinner 8.30pm
Credit cards [1] [2]

★★★**Cliffeside** East Overcliff Drive
☎ (0202) 25724 Boscombe &
Southbourne plan **54** *A1*

This hotel on the East Cliff has a sun terrace overlooking swimming pools and panoramic views.

64rm(46🛁13🚿)(6fb) CTV in all bedrooms
T sB&B£21—£34 sB&B🛁🚿£22—£36
dB&B£40—£68 dB&B🛁🚿£42—£70 B
Lift ☾CTV 40P CFA ≈ (heated)
snooker table tennis Disco wkly Live music
and dancing twice wkly Cabaret wkly
xmas →

French & Italian Lunch £4.75—£6.50 Tea £1—£3 High Tea £1.50—£3.50 Dinner £7.95—£9.95 Wine £4.70 Last dinner 8.30pm

Credit cards [1] [3] [V]

★★★**Hotel Courtlands** 16 Boscombe Spa Rd, East Cliff (Best Western) ☎ (0202) 302442 Telex no 41344 Boscombe & Southbourne plan **57***B1*

This is a modernised hotel with well-appointed public rooms and friendly staff, though some bedrooms require upgrading.

46rm(41➡5⋔)(10fb) CTV in all bedrooms ®**T** sB&B➡⋔£23.90—£30.70 dB&B➡⋔£41.60—£53.34 **B**

Lift ☾ 50P CFA ✿ ⛆ (heated) Live music and dancing 4 nights wkly (in season) ♿ xmas

English & French **V** Lunch £6.75 Tea 80p High Tea £3.50 Dinner £10.50&alc Wine £4.90 Last dinner 8.30pm

Credit cards [1] [2] [3] [5] [V]

★★★**Crest** The Landsdowne (Crest) ☎ (0202) 23262 Telex no 41232 Central plan **8** *F4*

A modern, purpose-built hotel of an interesting circular design.

102➡⋔ in 7 bedrooms CTV in all bedrooms **T** S% ✱sB➡⋔fr£47.95 dB➡⋔fr£68.90(room only) **B**

Lift ☾ ## CTV 78 snooker CFA *xmas*

V S% ✱Lunch fr£7.50 Tea fr75p Dinner fr£11.95&alc Last dinner 9.45pm

Credit cards [1] [2] [3] [4] [5]

★★★*L* **Cumberland** East Overcliff Dr ☎ (0202) 290722 Boscombe & Southbourne plan **57A***A1*

Closed Jan

This comfortable, purpose-built hotel, personally managed by its owners, overlooks the sea.

103➡3 CTV in all bedrooms ®**T** sB&B➡£18.22 dB&B➡£36.44 **B**

Lift ☾ CTV 75P ⛆ (heated) solarium pool table Live music and dancing 5 nights wkly in season Cabaret wkly in season *xmas*

Bournemouth & Boscombe

✱Lunch fr£5.75 Tea fr75p Dinner £8.50—£10.50 Wine £4 Last dinner 8.30pm

Credit cards [1] [2] [3] [5]

See advertisement on page 144

★★★**Durley Hall** Durley Chine Rd (Consort) ☎ (0202) 766886 Central plan **12***A2*

An imposing hotel in its own grounds set back off a quiet road.

70rm(53➡17⋔) Annexe: 10rm(9➡1⋔) (22fb) 1 CTV in all bedrooms ®**T** sB&B➡⋔£24—£38 dB&B➡⋔£48—£76 **B**

Lift ☾ 200P CFA ✿ ⛆ (heated) snooker solarium gymnasium games room Disco 3 nights wkly Live music & dancing 4 nights wkly *xmas*

English & Continental **V** Lunch £5 Tea 80p Dinner £7&alc Wine £4.45 Last dinner 8.45pm

Credit cards [1] [2] [3] [5] [V]

★★★**Durlston Court** Gervis Rd, East Cliff ☎ (0202) 291488 Central plan **13***F3*

Large hotel with spacious lounge and bar, and modern bedroom facilities.

53rm(46➡) Annexe: 6rm(5➡1⋔)(17fb) CTV in all bedrooms ®**T** sB&B£20—£25 sB&B➡⋔£30 dB&B£36—£50 dB&B➡⋔£40—£68 **B**

Lift ☾ 40P CFA ⛆ (heated) *xmas*

English & French **V** Lunch £6.50 Tea 75p Last dinner 8.30pm

Credit cards [1] [2] [3] [5]

★★★**East Anglia** 6 Poole Rd ☎ (0202) 765163 Central plan **14***A2*

Owned by the same family for twenty-seven years, this hotel is conveniently situated for the town centre.

49➡⋔ Annexe: 23rm(6➡)(12fb) CTV in all bedrooms ®**T** ✱sB&B£18.50—£23 sB&B➡⋔£25—£28 dB&B£37—£46 dB&B➡⋔£50—£56 **B**

Lift ☾ 60P CFA ⛆ (heated) sauna bath solarium *xmas*

English & French Bar lunch £4alc Tea £1alc Dinner £8—£9 Wine £5 Last dinner 8.30pm

Credit cards [1] [2] [3] [5] [V]

Bournemouth Central

1	Anglo-Swiss ★★★
1A	Arlington ★
3	Belvedere ★★
4	Burley Court ★★★
5	Hotel Cecil ★★★
6	Cliff Court ★
7	County ★★
8	Crest ★★★
9	Crusts ✕
11	Durley Grange ★★
12	Durley Hall ★★★
13	Durlston Court ★★★
14	East Anglia ★★★
16	Embassy ★★★
16A	Gresham Court ★★
17	Grosvenor ★★★
18	Heathlands ★★★
19	Highcliff ★★★★
20	Mansfield ★★
21	Marsham Court ★★★
22	Melford Hall ★★★
23	Miramar ★★★
24	New Somerset ★★
26	Palace Court ★★★★
26	La Taverna ✕✕
28	Pinehurst ★★
29	Queens ★★★
30	Hotel Riviera (West Cliff Gdns) ★★
31	Royal Bath ★★★★★
32	Royal Exeter ★★
32A	Russell Court ★★
33	St George ★★
33A	Sophisticats ✕✕
34	Sun Court ★★
36	Trouville ★★★
37	Ullswater ★
38	Wessex ★★★
39	West Cliff Hall ★★
40	Whitehall ★★
41	White Hermitage ★★★
42	Winterbourne ★★
43	Winter Gardens ★★
44	Woodcroft Tower ★★

B

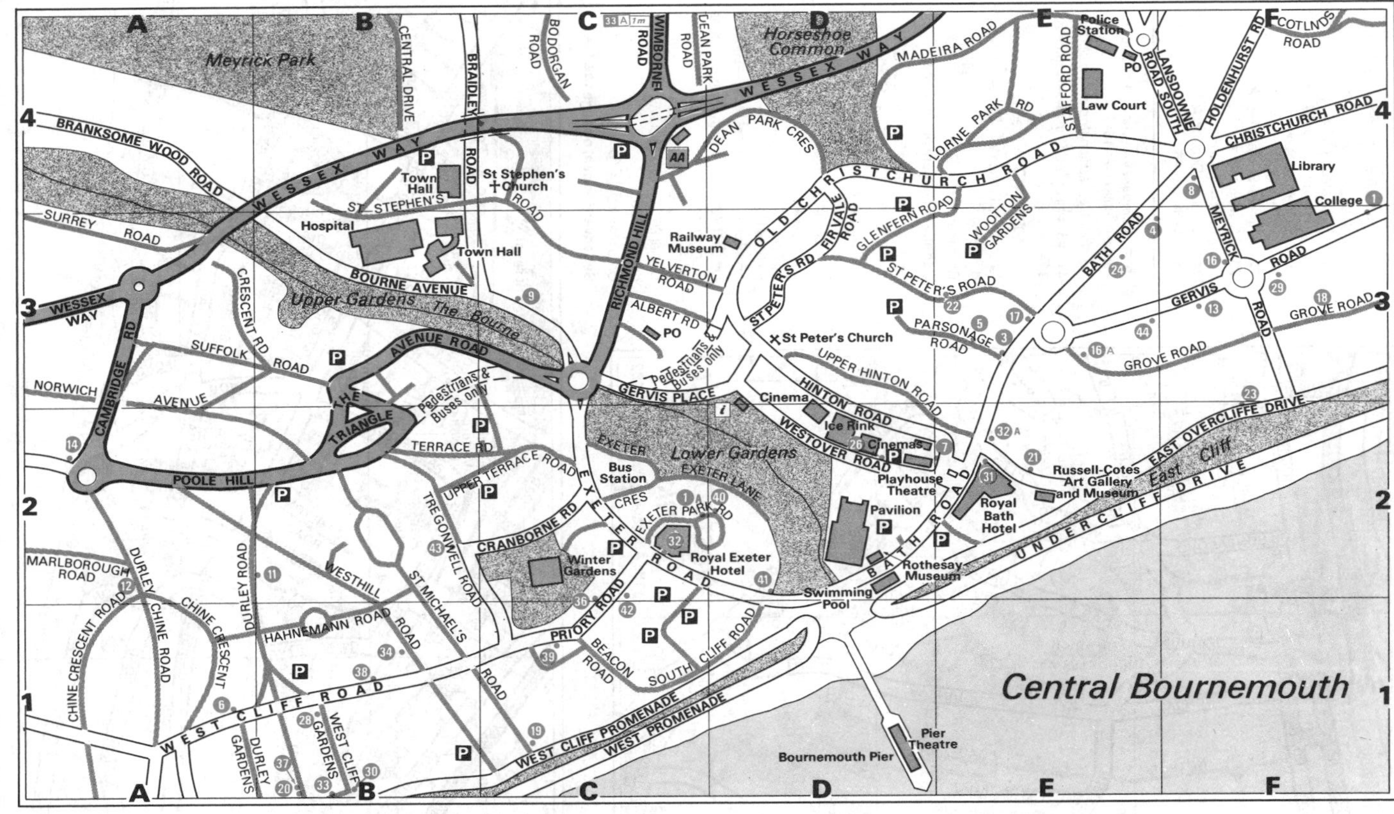

Central Bournemouth
Meyrick Park
Horseshoe Common
Upper Gardens
The Bourne
Lower Gardens
East Cliff
Bournemouth Pier
Pier Theatre
Swimming Pool
Pavilion
Rothesay Museum
Royal Bath Hotel
Russell-Cotes Art Gallery and Museum
Playhouse Theatre
Cinemas
Ice Rink
Cinema
St Peter's Church
Railway Museum
PO
Bus Station
Royal Exeter Hotel
Winter Gardens
Town Hall
St Stephen's Church
Hospital
Library
College
Law Court
Police Station
WESSEX WAY
BRANKSOME WOOD ROAD
SURREY ROAD
NORWICH AVENUE
CAMBRIDGE RD
POOLE HILL
THE TRIANGLE
AVENUE ROAD
BOURNE AVENUE
ST STEPHEN'S ROAD
BRAIDLEY ROAD
CENTRAL DRIVE
BODORGAN ROAD
WIMBORNE ROAD
DEAN PARK ROAD
DEAN PARK CRES
RICHMOND HILL
YELVERTON ROAD
ALBERT RD
GERVIS PLACE
OLD CHRISTCHURCH ROAD
ST PETER'S RD
FIRVALE ROAD
GLENFERN ROAD
ST PETER'S ROAD
PARSONAGE ROAD
UPPER HINTON ROAD
HINTON ROAD
WESTOVER ROAD
EXETER ROAD
EXETER LANE
EXETER PARK RD
EXETER CRES
BATH ROAD
UNDERCLIFF DRIVE
EAST OVERCLIFF DRIVE
GROVE ROAD
GERVIS ROAD
MEYRICK ROAD
CHRISTCHURCH ROAD
HOLDENHURST RD
LANSDOWNE ROAD SOUTH
STAFFORD ROAD
MADEIRA ROAD
LORNE PARK RD
WOOTTON GARDENS
Pedestrians & Buses only
CRANBORNE RD
TERRACE ROAD
UPPER TERRACE ROAD
TERRACE RD
PRIORY ROAD
BEACON ROAD
SOUTH CLIFF ROAD
WEST CLIFF PROMENADE
WEST PROMENADE
TREGONWELL ROAD
ST MICHAEL'S ROAD
WESTHILL ROAD
HAHNEMANN ROAD
WEST CLIFF ROAD
WEST CLIFF GARDENS
DURLEY GARDENS
DURLEY ROAD
CHINE CRESCENT
DURLEY CHINE ROAD
CHINE CRESCENT ROAD
MARLBOROUGH ROAD
CRESCENT RD
SUFFOLK ROAD

B

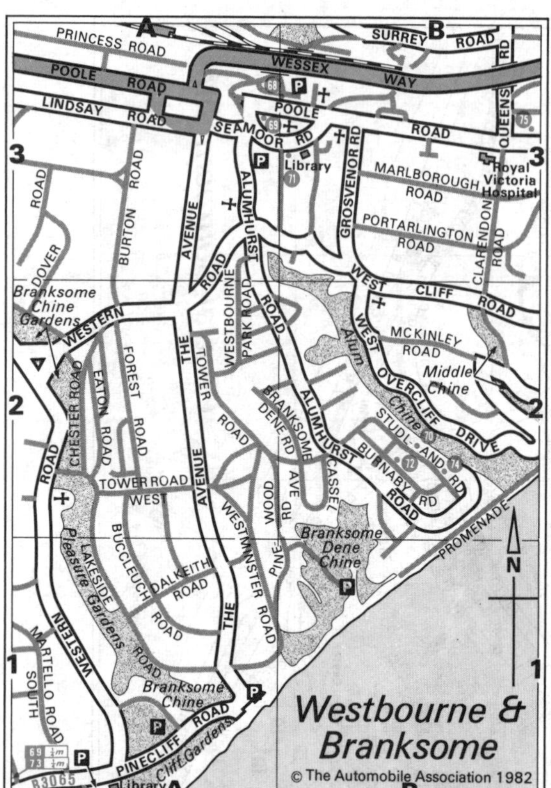

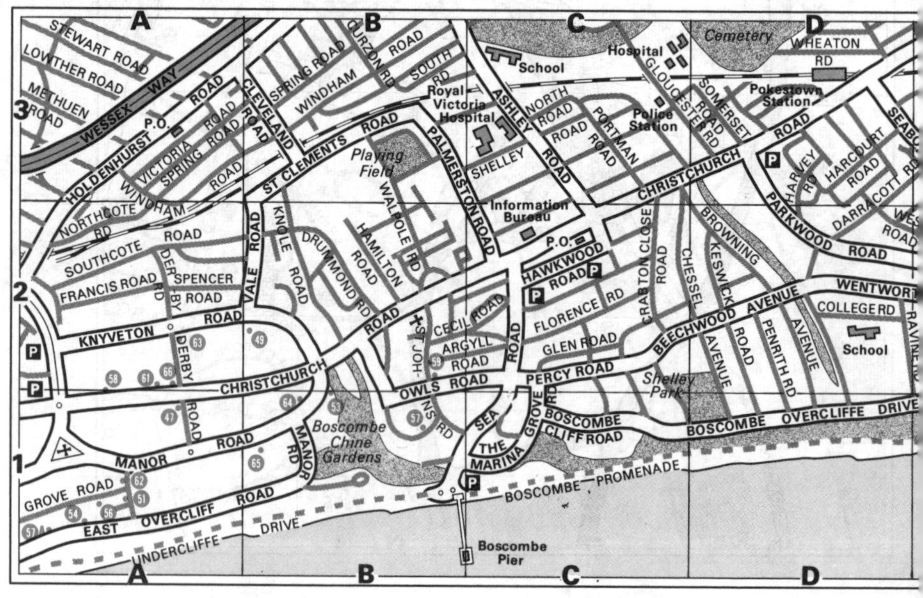

Westbourne & Branksome

68 Cadogan ★★
69 Le Chateau ✿✕✕ *(Listed under Poole)*
70 Chinehurst ★★
71 Rajkhana ✕
72 Riviera (Burnaby Rd) ★★
73 Seawitch ★★ *(Listed under Poole)*
74 Studland Dene ★★
75 Wellington ★

★★★***Embassy*** Meyrick Rd ☎ (0202) 290751 Central plan **16***F3*

Comfortable, traditional hotel near cliff top.

41rm(37⇌)(11fb) CTV in all bedrooms ® T ₿

Lift ☾ 50P CFA ≈ (heated)

English & French V Last dinner 8.30pm

Credit cards 1 2 3 5

See advertisement on page 144

★★★**Grosvenor** Bath Rd, East Cliff ☎ (0202) 28858 Central plan **17***E3*

Well equipped bedrooms, nicely furnished lounges and personal service are found in this pleasant central hotel.

40rm(33⇌3⫙)(10fb) CTV in all bedrooms ® T sB&B£22.50—£24.50 sB&B⇌⫙£24.50—£26.50 dB&B£45—£49 dB&B⇌⫙£49—£53 ₿

Lift ☾ CTV 30P sauna bath solarium games room *xmas*

Lunch £4—£5&alc Tea 40—50p Dinner £6.95—£7.25&alc Wine £4.50 Last dinner 8.30pm

Credit cards 1 3 Ⓥ

See advertisement on page 144

★★★L **Heathlands** Grove Rd, East Cliff (0202) 23336 Telex no 8954665 Central ...an **18** *F3*

...arge modern hotel in its own grounds near ...ast Cliff.

...16rm(113→3⋒)(18fb) CTV in all ...edrooms ®T ✱ sB&B→⋒£20—£27 ...B&B→⋒£40—£54 B

...ift ☾ CTV 90P CFA ✿ ⛀ (heated) sauna ...ath solarium gymnasium Disco wkly ♪ ...mas

...French V ♡ ☕ ✱ Lunch £6 Tea £1 ...inner £8 Wine £6.25 Last dinner 8.30pm

...redit cards 1 2 3 4 5

★★★B **Langtry Manor** 26 Derby Rd, ...ast Cliff ☎ (0202) 23887 Boscombe & ...outhbourne plan **63** *A2*

...ormer house of Lily Langtry is now a quiet, ...elaxing hotel.

...7rm(14→3⋒)(2fb) 4▭ CTV in all ...edrooms ®T sB&B→⋒fr£29.50 ...B&B→⋒fr£51 B

...0P ✿ *xmas*

...English & French V ♡ ☕ ⁄ ✱ Lunch ...£6 Tea fr£1 High Tea fr£4.50 Dinner ...£9.75&alc Wine £5.50 Last dinner 9pm

...redit cards 1 2 3 5

★★★ **Marsham Court** Russell Cotes Rd ...De Vere) ☎ (0202) 22111 Telex no 41420 ...entral plan **21** *E2*

...ough-cast colour-wash hotel, located on ...ast Cliff near the pier and town centre.

...0rm(72→8⋒)(16fb) CTV in all bedrooms ...®T ✗ sB&B→⋒£35—£45 ...B&B→⋒£60—£80 B

...ift ☾ 40P 40🚗(£1.50 per night) ⛀ (heated) snooker Live music and ...ancing Thu & Sat in Jul & Aug *xmas*

Bournemouth & Boscombe

V ♡ ☕ Lunch fr£8.50 Tea fr£2.75 High Tea fr£6 Dinner fr£10 Wine £6.50 Last dinner 9pm

Credit cards 1 2 3 5

★★★ **Melford Hall** St Peters Rd ☎ (0202) 21516 Central plan **22** *E3*

Large hotel with attentive staff, situated just off main shopping centre.

60rm(54→1⋒)(18fb) CTV in all bedrooms T S% sB&B£16.50—£22 sB&B→⋒£17.60—£23.65 dB&B£33—£44 dB&B→⋒£35.20—£47.30 B

Lift ☾ 55P ✿ Live music & dancing Wed & Sun Jun—Sep *xmas*

V ♡ ☕ S% Lunch £6.27—£6.93 Tea £1.45 Dinner £8.36—£9.02 Wine £5.48 Last dinner 8pm

Credit cards 1 3

★★★ **Miramar** Grove Rd ☎ (0202) 26581 Central plan **23** *F2/3*

Warm, comfortable, hotel where many rooms have fine sea views.

42rm(30→5⋒)(4fb) CTV in all bedrooms sB&B£20.70—£26.45 sB&B→⋒£25.85—£31.60 dB&B£44.40—£52.90 dB&B→⋒ £44.85—£59.80 B

Lift ☾ CTV 40P 4🚗(£2.30 per night) ▭ ✿ ♪ *xmas*

V ♡ ☕ Lunch £5.75—£6.90 Tea fr90p

Dinner £9.25—£10.50 Wine £6.20 Last dinner 8pm

Credit cards 1 2 3

★★★ ***Normandie*** Manor Rd, East Cliff ☎ (0202) 22246 Boscombe & Southbourne plan **65** *B1*

Set in quiet area near the sea, the hotel has rambling, comfortable bedrooms and attractive gardens.

58rm(47→) Annexe: 10→(7fb) CTV in all bedrooms ®T

Lift ☾ 50P ✿ ⛀ (heated) sauna bath solarium Live music & dancing Sat *xmas*

Last dinner 8.30pm

Credit cards 1 2 3

See advertisement on page 145

★★★ **Pavilion** Bath Rd (Best Western) ☎ (0202) 291266 Telex no 418253

A well appointed hotel, conveniently situated. The staff are efficient and friendly, and interesting menus are offered.

44rm(35→9⋒)(6fb) 2▭ CTV in all bedrooms ®T ✱ sB&B→⋒fr£32 dB&B→⋒fr£59

Lift ☾ 35P *xmas*

♡ ☕ Bar lunch fr£1.10&alc Tea 85p Dinner £10.50&alc Wine £4 Last dinner 8.30pm

Credit cards 1 2 3 5

★★★ **Queens** Meyrick Rd, East Cliff ☎ (0202) 24415 Telex no 418297 Central plan **29** *F3*

Large modern hotel with spacious rooms.

110rm(100→10⋒)(8fb) CTV in all bedrooms ®T sB&B→⋒£22—£28 dB&B→⋒£44—£56 B

Lift ☾ 80P 12🚗 CFA snooker Live music and dancing twice wkly ♪ *xmas*

English & French V ♡ ☕ Lunch £5.50—£6.50 Tea 70p—£1 High Tea £3—£4 Dinner £9.50—£10.50 Wine £4.75 Last dinner 9pm

Credit cards 1 3 V

See advertisement on page 145

Boscombe & Southbourne

46	Avonmore ★★
47	Avon Royal ★★
49	Bournemouth Moat House ★★★
51	Chesterwood ★★★
53	Cliff End ★★★
54	Cliffeside ★★★
55	Commodore ★
56	Cottonwood ★★
57	Hotel Courtlands ★★★
57A	Cumberland ★★★
58	Elstead ★★
59	Fircroft ★★
60	Grange ★★
61	Hartford Court ★
62	Hinton Firs ★★
63	Langtry Manor ★★★
64	Manor House ★★
65	Normandie ★★★
65A	Provence ✿✕
66	Tree Tops ★

B

★★★**Trouville** Priory Rd ☎ (0202) 22262 Central plan **36** *C2*

Closed Jan & Feb

Centrally situated hotel, adjoining Winter Gardens.

80rm(70⇌)(10fb) CTV in all bedrooms sB&B£19—£23 sB&B⇌£26—£30 dB&B⇌£38—£46

Lift ☾ 60P 5 Live music & dancing Sun Jun—Oct *xmas*

Lunch £6—£8&alc Tea 80p—£1 Dinner £8—£10&alc Wine £5 Last dinner 8.30pm

Credit cards 1 3

★★★*BL* **Wessex** West Cliff Rd ☎ (0202) 21911 Telex no 418172 Central plan **38** *B1*

Large Victorian building situated on the West Cliff near shops and seafront.

90⇌ (15fb) CTV in all bedrooms ®T sB&B⇌£32—£38 dB&B⇌£60—£70 B

Lift ☾ 300P CFA (heated) snooker sauna bath *xmas*

English & French V Lunch £5—£7 Tea 50p—£3.50 Dinner £9—£11 Wine £4.50 Last dinner 9.45pm

Credit cards 1 2 3 4 5 Ⓥ

Bournemouth & Boscombe

★★★**White Hermitage** Exeter Rd ☎ (0202) 27363 Telex no 418316 Central plan **41** *D2*

Large, central hotel with sound furnishings and pleasant, attentive staff and a range of leisure facilities.

85rm(65⇌12)(17fb) CTV in all bedrooms ®T S% *sB&B fr£31 sB&B⇌ fr£34 dB&B fr£46 dB&B⇌ fr£52 B

Lift ☾ CTV 58P CFA sauna bath solarium *xmas*

English & French S% *Lunch £4—£10 Tea fr55p High Tea £1.10—£1.50 Dinner fr£8.50&alc Wine £4.95 Last dinner 8.30pm

Credit cards 1 2 3 5

★★**Avonmore** 30 Foxholes Rd, Southbourne ☎ (0202) 428639 Boscombe & Southbourne plan **46** *G2*

Small, quiet hotel with neat bedrooms.

15rm(4⇌)(4fb) CTV available in bedrooms ® available in bedrooms sB&B£10—£12 sB&B⇌£14—£16 dB&B£18—£24 dB&B⇌£22—£28 B

CTV 10P *xmas*

English & Continental Lunch £2.95—£3.95 Tea 95p High Tea £5&alc Dinner £5&alc Wine £3.25 Last dinner 8pm

Credit cards 1 2 3 Ⓥ

★★**Avon Royal** 45 Christchurch Rd, East Cliff ☎ (0202) 292800 Boscombe & Southbourne plan **47** *A1*

Closed Jan

Attractive hotel with pleasant garden and personal service.

25rm(10⇌5)(2fb) CTV in all bedrooms ® sB&B£12—£13 sB&B⇌£15—£16 dB&B£22—£28 dB&B⇌£26—£30 B

CTV 25P Live music and dancing 3 nights wkly in season *xmas*

Bar lunch £1.50—£3 High Tea fr75p Dinner fr£6.50 Wine £4.20 Last dinner 7.30pm

★★*H* **Belvedere** Bath Rd ☎ (0202) 21080 Central plan **3** *E3*

There are views of sea and pier from this attractive hotel with its mansard roof. Run by attentive owners, it provides accommodation in neat, good bedrooms.

33rm(22⇌8)(5fb) CTV in all bedrooms ®T S% *sB&B⇌£18.50—£24 dB&B⇌£37—£48 B

Lift CTV 26P *xmas* →

B

English & Continental S% *Bar lunch £2.60—£5.30 Tea fr90p Dinner £7.50&alc Wine £3.90 Last dinner 8.30pm
Credit cards 1 2 3 5 V

★★**Cadogan** 8 Poole Rd (0202) 763006 Westbourne & Branksome plan **68** *B3*

The hotel — a gabled property with a modern extension — stands at the edge of Bournemouth, on the main road to Poole. Managed by resident owners, it offers neat bedrooms.

48rm(18 12)(5fb) 1 CTV in all bedrooms

Bournemouth & Boscombe

Lift CTV 60P nc 5yrs *xmas*

Credit cards 1 3

★★**Chinehurst** 18-20 Studland Rd, Westbourne (0202) 764583 Westbourne & Branksome plan **70** *B2*

This pleasant, family-run hotel is situated two minutes' walk from the beach, adjacent to Alum Chine, and a number of bedrooms have attractive views.

32rm(20 6)(11fb) CTV in all bedrooms sB&B £23.50—£31 dB&B £44—£58
CTV 22P *xmas*

English & Continental V Lunch £4.50—£6.50&alc Tea £1.20—£1.80&alc High Tea £3—£5&alc Dinner £7.50—£10&alc Wine £5 Last dinner 8.30pm
Credit cards 1 2 3 5 V

★ ★***Cottonwood*** Grove Rd, East Cliff
☎(0202) 23183 Boscombe & Southbourne plan **56** *A1*
A colour-washed brick building, surrounded by well-kept lawns and gardens, and overlooking the sea.
32rm(26➡6⋒)(7fb) CTV in all bedrooms ®B
Lift CTV 60P ✽ billiards *xmas*
V Last dinner 8pm
Credit card 3

★ ★**County** Westover Rd ☎(0202) 22385 Central plan **7** *E2*
Conveniently located hotel with friendly efficient service.
43rm(35➡3⋒)(11fb) CTV in all bedrooms ®sB&B£18 sB&B➡⋒£28 dB&B£32 dB&B➡⋒£42 B
Lift ☾ P Disco nightly *xmas*
V ☕ Bar lunch fr£1.50 Tea fr50p High Tea fr£1.50 Dinner fr£7 Wine £5 Last dinner 8pm
Credit cards 1 2 3

★ ★***Durley Grange*** 6 Durley Rd, West Cliff ☎(0202) 24473 Central plan **11** *B2*
Closed Dec—Feb (except Xmas & New Year)
Within short distance of Durley Chine this hotel is also near town centre.
50rm(25➡6⋒)(10fb) CTV in all bedrooms ®B

Bournemouth & Boscombe

Lift CTV 25P Cabaret twice weekly *xmas*
Last dinner 8pm
Credit cards 1 3

★ ★*L* **Elstead** 12—14 Knyveton Rd
☎(0202) 22829 Boscombe & Southbourne plan **58** *A2*
Closed 3 Oct—Apr
Well furnished hotel in quiet road.
55rm(30➡6⋒)(5fb) CTV in 29 bedrooms ®T ✱sB&B£14—£15.50 sB&B➡⋒ £17—£18.50 dB&B£28—£31 dB&B➡⋒£32—£37
Lift ☾ CTV 40P 6🚗(charge) Snooker Live music & dancing 3 nights wkly
☕ Lunch fr£4.50 Tea fr50p Dinner £6—£7.50 Wine £4.20 Last dinner 8pm
Credit card 1

★ ★**Fircroft** 4 Owls Rd, Boscombe
☎(0202) 309771 Boscombe & Southbourne plan **59** *B2*
A large Victorian building with modern extensions, set in its own grounds.
49rm(43➡6⋒)(18fb) CTV in all bedrooms sB&B➡⋒£15.50—£19 dB&B➡⋒£31—£38 B
Lift ☾ CTV 50P(charge) CFA squash Live music and dancing 3 nights wkly (in season) *xmas*
V ☕ Bar lunch £1.50—£4 Tea fr75p Dinner fr£6.50 Wine £4 Last dinner 8pm
Credit cards 1 3 Ⓥ

★ ★***Grange*** Overcliff Dr, Southbourne
☎(0202) 424228 Boscombe & Southbourne plan **60** *F1*
The frontage of this cliff-top hotel has been recently modernised.
28rm(17➡2⋒)(6fb) CTV in all bedrooms ®B
Lift ⅄ CTV 55P ✽ ♿ *xmas*
English & Italian V ☕ Last dinner 7.30pm

See advertisement on page 148

★ ★**Gresham Court** 4 Grove Rd, East Cliff ☎(0202) 21732 Central plan **16A** *E3*
Closed 29 Dec—28 Feb & 6 Nov—23 Dec
Pleasant, friendly hotel with comfortable, soundly appointed bedrooms.
34rm(15➡19⋒)(12fb) ®✱sB&B➡⋒ £18—£24 dB&B➡⋒£36—£48 B
Lift CTV 75P 5🚗(£1.50 per night) ✽ Live music & dancing wkly *xmas*
V ☕ Lunch £4.50—£6.50 Tea 40p Dinner £7—£8 Wine £4.50 Last dinner 7.30pm
Credit cards 1 2 3 Ⓥ

Bournemouth & Boscombe

★★ *L* **Hinton Firs** Manor Rd (ExecHotel) ☎ (0202) 25409 Boscombe & Southbourne plan **62** *A1*

Attentive service and well furnished lounges make this an attractive hotel.

50rm(28🛁) Annexe: 6🛁 (20fb) CTV in all bedrooms ® S% sB&B£15.50—£23 dB&B£31—£46 dB&B🛁£37—£52 B

Lift ☾ CTV 40P 🅟 ⛱ (heated) solarium Disco wkly in season Live music and dancing twice wkly in season 🚸 ♿ *xmas*

🍷 ☕ ✂ S% Bar lunch £1.50—£3 Tea 55p Dinner £6.75 Wine £4.10 Last dinner 8pm

Credit cards 1 3

★★ **Manor House** 34 Manor Rd East Cliff ☎ (0202) 36669 Boscombe & Southbourne plan **64** *B1*

Closed Nov

Attractive hotel with pleasant garden and personal attention by resident owner.

27rm(10🛁3🚿)(14fb) CTV in all bedrooms ® ✱ sB&B£13.50—£17.25 sB&B🛁🚿£15.50—£19.25 dB&B£27—£34.50 dB&B🛁🚿£31—£38.50

CTV 27P Disco 2/3 nights wkly in season *xmas*

V 🍷 ☕ ✱ Dinner £8.50 Wine £3.90 Last dinner 7.30pm

Credit cards 1 2 3 Ⓥ

★★ *B* **Mansfield** West Cliff Gds ☎ (0202) 22659 Central plan **20** *B1*

Closed 29 Dec—31 Jan

The hotel stands in a quiet road at West Cliff, an easy walk from clifftop and beach. Friendly, attentive, resident owners provide personal service, and the bedrooms are very comfortable.

29rm(18🛁11🚿)(4fb) CTV in all bedrooms ® 🐕 sB&B🛁🚿£20—£32 dB&B🛁🚿£30—£40 B

14P Live music & dancing wkly Jun—Sep *xmas*

🍴 English & French V 🍷 ☕ Lunch £4.50—£6 Tea 50p—£1 Dinner £5—£7.50 Wine £4.75 Last dinner 8pm

Credit cards 1 3 Ⓥ

★★ ***New Somerset*** Bath Rd ☎ (0202) 21983 Central plan **24** *E3*

A red brick, villa-type hotel, located on the main road opposite the shops and pier.

40rm(8🛁1🚿)(7fb) ® B

Lift ☾ CTV 22P ✿ *xmas*

🍷 ☕ Last dinner 8pm

Credit cards 1 3

★★ **Pinehurst** West Cliff Gds ☎ (0202) 26218 Central plan **28** *B1*

Closed Jan & Feb

Spacious hotel with open plan lounge and panelled bar.

76rm(38🛁20🚿)(9fb) CTV in 58 bedrooms ® sB&B£16.25—£20 sB&B🛁🚿£18.75—£22.50 dB&B£30.50—£38 dB&B🛁🚿£35.50—£43 B

Lift ☾ CTV 48P solarium table tennis pool table Live music and dancing Wed, Fri & Sat in season *xmas*

V 🍷 ☕ Lunch £5 Tea 50p Dinner £7 Wine £5 Last dinner 8.30pm

Credit card 1 Ⓥ

★★ **Riviera, Burnaby Rd,** Alum Chine ☎ (0202) 763653 Telex no 41363 Westbourne & Branksome plan **72** *B2*

Closed 3—31 Jan

White painted hotel with good facilities.

68rm(57🛁11🚿) Annexe: 9rm(3🛁6🚿) (25fb) CTV in all bedrooms S% ✱ sB&B🛁🚿£20.50—£28 dB&B🛁🚿£41—£56

Lift 60P ✿ 🏊 & ⛱ (heated) snooker sauna bath solarium Disco twice wkly Live music and dancing 5 nights wkly *xmas*

🍴 English, French & Italian 🍷 ☕ S% ✱ Lunch £4.75 Tea £1 Dinner £9.50 Wine £5.15 Last dinner 8.30pm

Credit cards 1 3

Bournemouth & Boscombe

★★**Hotel Riviera, West Cliff Gdns** ☎(0202) 22845 Central plan **30** *B1*

Closed Nov—Mar

The terrace and some bedrooms of this modern hotel have sea views.

34rm(27➡3⋔)(4fb) CTV in all bedrooms sB&B£12—£15 sB&B➡⋔£14—£17 dB&B£24—£30 dB&B➡⋔£28—£34 **B**

Lift ☾ 24P solarium *xmas*

Lunch £3—£3.50 Tea fr50p Dinner £5—£5.50 Wine £3.50 Last dinner 7.30pm

Credit card 2

★★**Royal Exeter** Exeter Rd (Berni) ☎(0202) 290566 Central plan **32** *C2*

Closed Xmas

Imposing town centre hotel, former home of Lord Tregonwell.

38➡(4fb) CTV in all bedrooms ®**T** ✱sB➡⋔£25 dB➡⋔£36 (room only)

Lift ☾ 55P

Mainly grills ✱Lunch £7.50alc Dinner £7.50alc Wine £4.50 Last dinner 10pm

Credit cards 1 2 3 5

★★**Russell Court** Bath Rd ☎(0202) 28366 Central plan **32A** *E2*

In a fine position for beach and shops, this pleasant family owned hotel provides personal friendly service. A number of bedrooms have good sea views.

69rm(26➡)(3fb) CTV in all bedrooms ® in 14 bedrooms sB&Bfr£22.50 dB&Bfr£40 dB&B➡⋔fr£46.50—£53.55 **B**

Lift ☾ 50P Disco wkly Live music and dancing 4 nights wkly Cabaret wkly *xmas*

V Bar lunch £3—£4.50 Tea 50p Dinner £6.30—£7.90 Wine £4.50 Last dinner 7.45pm

Credit cards 1 2 3 Ⓥ

★★**St George** West Cliff Gdns ☎(0202) 26075 Central plan **33** *B1*

Closed Dec—Feb

Peacefully situated on the west cliff, overlooking the bay and only ten minutes walk from the town centre and pier.

21rm(14➡7⋔)(5fb) CTV in all bedrooms ®sB&B➡⋔£14—£20.50 dB&B➡⋔£28—£41 **B**

Lift 4P nc 4yrs

V Bar lunch 75p—£2.50 Tea 60—75p Dinner £6—£10.50 Wine £4.50 Last dinner 7.30pm

Credit cards 1 3

See advertisement on page 150

★★**Studland Dene** Studland Rd, Alum Chine ☎(0202) 765445 Westbourne & Branksome plan **74** *B2*

Corner sited hotel, nestling into Alum Chine with good sea views.

30rm(14➡6⋔)(7fb) CTV in all bedrooms **T** sB&B£14—£16.50 sB&B➡⋔£16—£19 dB&B£28—£33 dB&B➡⋔£32—£38 **B**

CTV 30P Live music & dancing 3 nights wkly *xmas*

V S% Lunch £4&alc Tea 60—90p Dinner £4.50—£6&alc Wine £4.80 Last dinner 9.45pm

Credit cards 1 2 3 Ⓥ

See advertisement on page 150

★★**Sun Court** West Hill Rd ☎(0202) 21343 Central plan **34** *B1*

The detached hotel stands within a few hundred yards of Westcliff and caters competently for both holiday and commercial trade.

36rm(20➡16⋔)(4fb) CTV in all bedrooms ®**T** sB&B➡⋔£17—£21 dB&B➡⋔£34—£42 **B**

Lift ☾ CTV 50P pool table *xmas*

V Lunch £3.95 Tea 60p High Tea £3.50 Dinner £7.50&alc Wine £3.50 Last dinner 8pm

Credit cards 1 2 3 5 Ⓥ

B

★★**West Cliff Hall** 14 Priory Rd ☎(0202) 22669 Central plan **39** *C1*
Closed mid Nov—mid Mar
Well appointed hotel with efficient staff.
48rm(18🛁16🚿)(10fb) CTV in all bedrooms ®sB&B£15—£22 sB&B🛁🚿£18—£25 dB&B£28—£42 dB&B🛁🚿£34—£48
Lift CTV 34P Live music and dancing 3 nights wkly May—Oct *xmas*
Bar lunch 80p—£2 Tea fr40p Dinner fr£4 Wine £4 Last dinner 8pm
Credit cards 1 2 3 Ⓥ

★★**Whitehall** Exeter Park Rd ☎(0202) 24682 Central plan **40** *D2*
Closed 3 Nov—13 Mar
Quiet hotel near town centre and gardens.
48rm(22🛁9🚿)(5fb) CTV in all bedrooms ®T*sB&B£16.25—£20.25 sB&B🛁🚿£18—£22.25 dB&B£32.50—£40.50 dB&B🛁🚿£36—£44.50 B
Lift ☾ CTV 30P ❁
*Lunch £3.75 Dinner £6 Last dinner 8pm
Credit cards 1 2 3 5

★★**Winterbourne** Priory Rd ☎(0202) 296366 Telex no 417153 Central plan **42** *C2*
Closed 5—31 Jan
In an elevated position, with good views.

Bournemouth & Boscombe

41rm(34🛁7🚿)(12fb) CTV in all bedrooms ®T sB&B🛁🚿£19—£26.50 dB&B🛁🚿£32—£47 B
Lift 32P 2 ❁ (heated) Live music & dancing twice wkly Cabaret twice wkly *xmas*
V Bar lunch 80p—£6 Tea £1—£3 High Tea £1.95 Dinner £7.50 Wine £4.60 Last dinner 8pm
Credit cards 1 3 Ⓥ

★★**Winter Gardens** 32 Tregonwell Rd, West Cliff ☎(0202) 25769 Central plan **43** *B2*
Early 19th-century building, with public rooms overlooking well-kept gardens.
39rm(18🛁1🚿)(11fb) CTV in 26 bedrooms ®in 13 bedrooms sB&B£17—£20.50 sB&B🛁🚿£19—£22.50 dB&B£34—£41 dB&B🛁🚿£38—£45 B
Lift ☾ CTV 30P *xmas*
Lunch £4.50 Tea 75p Dinner £6.50&alc Wine £3.95 Last dinner 9.30pm
Credit card 3

★★**Woodcroft Tower** Gervis Rd, East Cliff ☎(0202) 28202 Central plan **44** E3
Standing in its own grounds, a convenient walking distance from shops, pier and the sea front.
43rm(18🛁8🚿)(4fb) CTV in all bedrooms sB&B£14—£18.90 sB&B🛁🚿£16.60—£22 dB&B£28—£37.80 dB&B🛁🚿£33.20—£44 B
Lift ☾ 40P ❁ Live music & dancing twice wkly *xmas*
Lunch £5.50 Tea 70p Dinner £7.50 Wine £4.50 Last dinner 8pm
Credit cards 1 2 3

★*H* **Arlington** Exeter Park Rd ☎(0202) 22879 Central plan **1A** *C2*
Closed Dec—Feb
In a very central position, overlooking Exeter Park, the small, personally-run hotel provides good food and friendly service.
30rm(9🛁13🚿)(4fb) ® *sB&B£17—£20 sB&B🛁🚿£19—£22 dB&B£34—£40 dB&B🛁🚿£38—£44
CTV 24P ❁
*Bar lunch 80p—£1.50 Tea fr40p Dinner fr£4.50&alc Wine £3.75 Last dinner 7.15pm
Credit cards 1 3

Bournemouth & Boscombe

B

★ **Cliff Court** 15 West Cliff Rd ☎ (0202)
5994 Central plan **6** *A1*

lodern, well-furnished hotel with personal ttention from resident owners.

3rm(18➡15⋒)(6fb) CTV in 20 bedrooms
V in 2 bedrooms ® ₽

ift CTV 38P *xmas*

♡✂ Last dinner 7.30pm

:redit card [3]

★ **Commodore** Overcliffe Dr,
outhbourne (Whitbread) ☎ (0202)
23150 Boscombe & Southbourne plan **55**
:1

\ clifftop hotel with fine views.

4rm(4fb) CTV in all bedrooms ® ✗ (ex
uide dogs) sB&Bfr£18 dB&Bfr£34 ₽

ift 20P ▤ *xmas*

♡ Lunch fr£5.50 Dinner fr£5.50 Wine
:5.20 Last dinner 9.30pm

:redit cards [1] [2] [3] [5] Ⓥ

★ **Hartford Court** 48 Christchurch Rd
☎ (0202) 21712 Boscome & Southbourne
plan **61** *A2*

This bright, pleasant, tourist and residential hotel is located within easy reach of the town centre. Bedrooms are small, but the attentive proprietors offer good value for money.

24rm(4➡3⋒)(3fb) CTV in all bedrooms ®
T S% sB&B£12.25—£13
sB&B➡⋒£14—£14.75
dB&B£24.50—£26
dB&B➡⋒£28—£29.50 ₽

CTV 25P *xmas*

V ♡ ☕ S% Lunch £4alc Tea 70palc
Dinner £5alc Wine £4 Last dinner 7pm

Credit cards [1] [3]

★ **Tree Tops** 50—52 Christchurch Rd
☎ (0202) 23157 Boscombe & Southborne
plan **66** *A2*

A large hotel on the main road between the town centre and Boscombe.

60rm(27➡10⋒)(40fb) CTV in all
bedrooms ® sB&B£13.23—£16.10
sB&B➡⋒£15.53—£18.98
dB&B£26.45—£32.20
dB&B➡⋒£31.05—£36.50 ₽

Lift CTV 36P ✿ Live music and dancing 2/3
nights wkly in season *xmas*

V ✱ Lunch £3—£4.50 Tea 70p—£1.70
Dinner £5—£5.75 Wine £3.50 Last dinner
7.30pm

Credit cards [1] [3] Ⓥ

★ **Ullswater** West Cliff Gds ☎ (0202)
25181 Central plan **37** *B1*

Closed Dec & Jan

Red brick hotel near clifftop, with friendly service.

43rm(7➡4⋒)(10fb) CTV in 11 bedrooms
® sB&B£16—£19 sB&B➡⋒£19—£23
dB&B£32—£38 dB&B➡⋒£38—£46

Lift CTV 10P snooker

♡ English & French ♡ ☕✂ Lunch
£5—£6 Tea 75p—£2 Dinner £6—£7 Wine
£4.50 Last dinner 7.15pm

Credit card [3] Ⓥ

★ ***Wellington*** 10 Poole Rd, West Cliff
☎ (0202) 768407 Westbourne &
Branksome plan **75** *B3*

Closed Nov—27 Mar (except Xmas)

There is a warm welcome from the resident owners of this Victorian hotel.

27rm(4➡8⋒)(6fb) CTV in all bedrooms ®
₽

Lift CTV 20P Disco & live music & dancing
wkly *xmas*

Last dinner 5pm

Credit cards [1] [3]

✕✕ **La Taverna** (Palace Court Hotel)
Westover Rd ☎ (0202) 27681 Telex no
418451 Central plan **26** *D2*

The interior this restaurant is attractive and well-appointed, the staff are attentive and the interesting menus soundly based on the use of good raw materials.

Closed Sun

♡ French 30 seats ✱ Lunch
£7.50—£10.50&alc Dinner
£7.50—£10.50&alc Wine £5.95 Last
dinner 10pm P(charged)

Credit cards [1] [2] [3] [5]

✕✕ **Sophisticats** 43 Charminster Rd
☎ (0202) 291019 Central plan **33A** *C4*

In a street of shops some three miles from the centre of Bournemouth, Sophisticats offers a good range of imaginative dishes — with particular emphasis on fresh fish — served in a cosy atmosphere with booth seating.

Closed Sun, Mon Feb & last 2 wks Oct
Lunch not served

♡ International **V** 32 seats Dinner £13alc
Wine £5.20 Last dinner 10pm ₱

✕ **Crusts** The Square ☎ (0202) 21430
Central plan **9** *C3*

♡ English & French **V** 50 seats ✱ Lunch
£5.95 Dinner £12.50alc Wine £5.50 Last
dinner 11pm

Credit cards [1] [3] [5]

❀✕ **Provence** 91 Belle Vue Rd,
Southbourne ☎ (0202) 424421
Boscombe & Southbourne plan **65A**
G1

(Rosette awarded for dinner only)

This pleasant, small restaurant in Southbourne is popular so book ahead. The atmosphere is bright and attractive with flowers, and the cooking is light in the modern style. Dishes are artistically presented, contrasting colours, flavours and textures, while the vegetables are lightly cooked.

Closed Sun
Lunch not served

♡ French 30 seats S% ✱ Dinner
£18alc Wine £5.45 Last dinner 10pm

Credit cards [2] [4]

✕ **Raj Khana** 43 Seamoor Rd,
Westbourne ☎ (0202) 767142
Westbourne & Branksome plan **71** *B3*

In this charming, comfortable and friendly Indian restaurant you can choose from an interesting menu featuring well-cooked, authentic dishes.

♡ Indian 40 seats ✱ Lunch £4.50—£7&alc
Dinner £4.50—£7&alc Wine £3.95 Last
dinner mdnt ₱

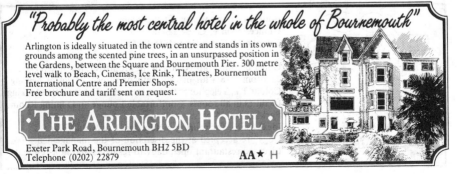

Credit cards [1] [2] [3] [5]

B

Bourton-on-the-Water — Bovey Tracey

BOURTON-ON-THE-WATER
Gloucestershire
Map **4** SP12

★★★*HL* **Old Manse** Victoria St
☎ Cotswold (0451) 20642

Closed 2 wks mid Jan

Attractive 18th-century Cotswold-stone house near River Windrush.

12rm(10 2)(1fb) CTV in all bedrooms **T** sB&B £22.50—£28.50 dB&B £35—£47 Continental breakfast

15P nc5yrs *xmas*

English & French **V** Lunch £6.95&alc Dinner £8.95&alc Wine £5.50 Last dinner 8.30pm

Credit cards 1 3

★★**Chester House Hotel & Motel** Victoria St (Minotel) ☎ Cotswold (0451) 20286

Closed Dec & Jan

Some of the rooms are in a converted row of Cotswold stone cottages, the rest are in the main hotel building.

13rm(4 5)(7fb) 1 CTV in all bedrooms ® **T** ✻ sB&B fr £20 sB&B £22—£26 dB&B fr £32 dB&B £35—£42 Continental breakfast

24P

V ✻ Lunch fr £6.95&alc Dinner fr £9.75&alc Wine £5.20 Last dinner 9.30pm

Credit cards 1 2 3 5

★★**Old New Inn** High St ☎ Cotswold (0451) 20467

Closed Xmas

Part 18th-century building with intriguing model village in the garden.

16rm(7 1)(1fb) S% sB&B fr £18 sB&B fr £20 dB&B fr £36 dB&B fr £40

CTV 25P 8 (75p per night)

✻ Lunch £4.50—£7.50 Tea fr £1.25 Dinner £9.50—£11.50 Wine £5 Last dinner 8.30pm

Credit card 3

✕ **Rose Tree** Riverside ☎ Cotswold (0451) 20635

Housed in a tall, Cotswold-stone building attractively set by the river in the centre of Bourton, the restaurant offers an imaginative menu with the emphasis on fresh food. Though space is rather limited, the decor and general atmosphere are pleasant.

Closed Mon & mid Jan—mid Feb Dinner not served Sun Lunch not served except on Suns

English & French 26 seats ✻ Sun lunch £8.95 Bar lunch £1.95—£2.95 Dinner £8.95—£14.95 Wine £5.95 Last dinner 8.30pm

Credit cards 1 2 3 5

BOVEY TRACEY
Devon
Map **3** SX87

★★**Coombe Cross** Coombe Cross (Inter Hotel) ☎ (0626) 832476

Comfortable and well appointed traditional country hotel, personally run.

25rm(22 1)(2fb) CTV in all bedrooms ® **T** S% sB&B £16.95—£19.95 sB&B £19.95—£23.95 dB&B £35—£42

CTV 27P *xmas*

V S% Bar lunch £2.95—£3.95 Tea £1.50 High Tea £2.95 Dinner £9.95 Wine £4.99 Last dinner 8pm

Credit cards 1 2 3 5 V

★★**Edgemoor** Haytor Rd ☎ (0626) 832466

Family run rural hotel with spacious reception rooms and open fires.

14rm(7)(3fb) S% sB&B fr £18.25 sB&B fr £23.75 dB&B fr £34 dB&B fr £39.75

CTV 45P 2 (£1 per night) table tennis xmas

English & Continental Bar lunch 95p—£3.90 Tea 60p High Tea £1—£2.50 Dinner £9.50—£12.75 Wine £3.95 Last dinner 8.30pm

Credit cards 1 2 3 5 V

★**Blenheim** Brimley Rd (0626) 832422

Early 20th-century small hotel set in two acres of gardens on the edge of the village.

8rm(1)(1fb) ® sB&B£14.50 sB&B£16.50 dB&B£29 dB&B£33 B

CTV 8P 1

English, Brazilian & Portugese V Bar lunch £3 Tea £1 Dinner £10 Wine £3.45 Last dinner 8pm

V

BOWMORE

Isle of Islay, Strathclyde *Argyllshire*

See **Islay, Isle of**

BOWNESS-ON-WINDERMERE

Cumbria

Map **7** SD49

Hotels are listed under Windermere

BRADFORD

W Yorkshire

Map **7** SE31

★★★★**Stakis Norfolk Gardens** Hall Ings (Stakis) (0274) 734734 Telex no 517573

This large, modern hotel stands in the city centre adjoining a multi-storey car park. Accommodation has been updated to a high standard and wedding receptions are a speciality.

126(10fb) in 12 bedrooms CTV in all bedrooms ® T sB£45 dB£60 (room only) B

Lift xmas

V Lunch £6.25 Tea £2.50 High Tea £5.50 Dinner £10.25&alc Wine £6.75 Last dinner 10pm

Credit cards 1 2 3 5

★★★**Novotel Bradford** Merrydale Rd (Novotel) (3m S adjacent to M606) (0274) 683683 Telex no 517312

The Novotel is a modern hotel situated on a trading estate adjacent to the M606 three miles south of Bradford.

136(136fb) CTV in all bedrooms T S% *sB&B£41 dB&B£52 B

Lift 140P (heated)

Continental S% *Lunch £6.50&alc Dinner £8&alc Wine £6.50 Last dinner mdnt

Credit cards 1 2 3 5 V

★★★**Victoria** Bridge St (Trusthouse Forte) (0274) 728706 Telex no 517456

Architecturally interesting hotel with tall elegant reception rooms, comfortable bedrooms and self-service carvery.

60rm(39 6) CTV in all bedrooms ® sB&B£36.50 sB&B£44.50 dB&B£52 dB&B£60 B

Lift 40P CFA

Mainly grills Last dinner 10pm

Credit cards 1 2 3 4 5

BRADWORTHY

Devon

Map **2** SS31

★**Lake Villa** (040924) 342

Dating from the fifteenth century, the delightful, old, country house hotel is surrounded by farmland.

7rm(2 3) 3 TV in all bedrooms ® S% sB&B fr£15 sB&B fr£17.50 dB&B fr£35 B

24P (hard) nc 14yrs

International V S% Bar lunch fr£1.25 Dinner £9alc Wine £4.50 Last dinner 9.30pm

See advertisement on page 154

B

B

Braintree — Bramhope

BRAINTREE
Essex
Map**5** TL72
✕**Braintree Chinese** 3 Rayne Rd
☎(0376) 24319
Large cheerful restaurant offering sound authentic Chinese cuisine.
Closed 25—27 Dec
🍷Pekinese **V** 100 seats Lunch fr£6.50 Dinner fr£12 Wine £6 Last dinner 11pm 10P
Credit cards 1 2 3 5

BRAITHWAITE
Cumbria
Map **11** NY22
★★*HL* **Ivy House** ☎(059682) 338
Closed 20 Nov—5 Mar
A 17th-century house with a Georgian wing added in 1790, quietly situated in the centre of the village.
8rm(6🛁1🚿) 2▣ CTV in all bedrooms ® ✈
dB&B£29.50 dB&B🛁🚿£32.50—£41.50
8P 1🏠 ⌗ sauna bath solarium gymnasium nc 12yrs
🍷English & French 🍸 ☕ ✂ Lunch £4.50—£5.50 Tea 95p Dinner £9.75 Wine £4.40 Last dinner 7.15pm
Credit cards 1 3 5

★★**Middle Ruddings** ☎(059682) 436
Closed 4 Jan—mid Feb
After extensive refurbishment, this is now a very comfortable and well-appointed hotel, quality being the keynote throughout.
15rm(9🛁3🚿)(2fb) 1▣ CTV in 10 bedrooms ® ✈ S% *sB&B£20.50 sB&B🛁🚿£30.75 dB&B£40.95 dB&B🛁🚿£48.30—£55 **B**
20P 2🏠(£1 per night) ⌗ ✿ *xmas*
V 🍸 ☕ ✂ S% *Lunch £6.50 Tea £1—£2.50 Dinner £9.50&alc Wine £4.50 Last dinner 8.30pm
Credit cards 1 2 3 5

BRAMHALL
Greater Manchester
Map **7** SJ88
★★★**Bramhall Moat House** Bramhall Lane South (Queens Moat) ☎061-439 8116
RS 25 Dec—1 Jan
Modern well-furnished hotel in a pleasant area.
40🛁 CTV in all bedrooms ® **T**
sB&B🛁£43—£45 dB&B🛁£54—£57 **B**
Lift ☾ ## CTV 132P ⌗ solarium ♿
🍷English & French **V** 🍸 ☕ Bar lunch £2—£4 Tea 95p—£1 Dinner £9.80—£10.50&alc Wine £4.10 Last dinner 10pm
Credit cards 1 2 3 5

✕**Belmondo** Bramhall Centre
☎061-439 6290
A colourful, lively restaurant situated in a shopping precinct, the Belmondo offers a good choice of Italian dishes and a predominantly Italian wine list; businessmen's lunches are particularly good value.
Closed Sun
🍷Italian **V** 57 seats Lunch £3.50—£4.25&alc Dinner £12.50alc Wine £4.75 Last dinner 10.30pm
Credit cards 1 2 3 5

BRAMHOPE
W Yorkshire
Map **8** SE24
★★★**Post House** Otley Rd (Trusthouse Forte) ☎ Leeds (0532) 842911 Telex no 556367
A modern hotel situated on the outskirts of Leeds.
122🛁 CTV in all bedrooms ®
sB&B🛁£55.50 dB&B🛁£73.50 **B**
Lift ☾ 220P CFA ✿ *xmas*
🍸 ☕ Last dinner 10.30pm
Credit cards 1 2 3 4 5

BRAMPTON
Cambridgeshire
Map **4** TL27

★★★***Brampton*** (junc A1/A604) (Kingsmead) ☎ Huntingdon (0480) 810434
17🛁 CTV in all bedrooms ® B
☾ 150P 18 ✽ Disco Sat *xmas*
English & French **V** ♆ ☕ Last dinner 10pm
Credit cards [1] [2] [3] [5]

★★**Grange** 115 High St ☎ Huntingdon (0480) 59516
9rm(1🛁6🚿)(1fb) CTV in all bedrooms ® **T**
✱ sB&B£24—£28.50
sB&B🛁🚿£24—£28.50
dB&B£36—£38.50
dB&B🛁🚿£36—£38.50
CTV 40P ✽
♆ ☕ Lunch £13alc Dinner £4.95—£9.10&alc Wine £4.95 Last dinner 10pm
Credit cards [1] [3] Ⓥ

BRAMPTON
Cumbria
Map **12** NY56

★★

❀★★ **FARLAM HALL, BRAMPTON, CUMBRIA**
Hallbankgate (Relais et Châteaux) (2¾m SE A689)
☎ Hallbankgate (06976) 234
Closed 1st 2wks Nov & Feb RS Nov—Jan

(Rosette awarded for dinner only)

This old mansion, originally a 17th century farmhouse, is nicely proportioned and sits in four acres of undulating grounds containing trees, stream, an ornamental lake and croquet lawn — all absolutely captivating. The Quinion family own and run it with Barry, the son, in charge of the cooking. He provides a four-course dinner which includes an array of attractive puddings laid out on the sideboard. His style is mainly traditional but there are lots of individual touches that earn him our rosette. The restaurant consists of two connecting rooms overlooking the garden, well appointed and comfortable. You will find the service throughout your stay friendly and considerate in a wholly natural way. It is this aspect that makes so many people claim that to stay here is like staying with friends. All bedrooms now have television and apart from just a few, are of good size and very well done with lots of thoughtful extras. There is a small bar, hall, lounge, and another sitting room. There are lots of pictures, china and bric-a-brac, including a collection of prettily dressed dolls, as well as an abundance of flowers.

13rm(11🛁2🚿) 1 CTV in all bedrooms sB&B🛁🚿£48—£55(incl dinner) dB&B🛁🚿£86—£120(incl. dinner) B
35P ✽ nc 5yrs
♆ ☕ Tea £1.50 Dinner £15.50 Wine £4.95 Last dinner 8pm
Credit cards [1] [2] [3]

★★***Howard Arms*** Front St ☎ (06977) 2357
Tastefully modernised 17th-century coaching inn situated in the centre of the old Market Place.
11rm(2🛁9🚿) CTV in all bedrooms
CTV 20P
V ♆ ☕ Last dinner 8.45pm
Credit cards [1] [2] [3]

★★**Sands House** The Sands ☎ (06977) 3085
Sandstone building with unusual stone and pine bedrooms, some with oak beams.
5rm Annexe: 8rm(5🛁3🚿)(3fb) CTV in 12 bedrooms ® sB&B£15 sB&B🛁🚿£20 dB&B£28 dB&B🛁🚿£35
CTV 48P ♿
V ♆ ☕ Lunch fr£4.50 Tea fr£2.25 High Tea £1.50—£4.75 Dinner £7 Wine £3.50 Last dinner 9.15pm
Credit cards [1] [2] [3] [5] Ⓥ

★★**Tarn End** Talkin Tarn (2½m S off B6413) ☎ (06977) 2340
Closed Feb
This friendly, peaceful, family-run hotel on the banks of Talkin Tarn is justifiably proud of the standard of its French haute cuisine, offering à la carte and table d'hôte menus at lunch and dinner. Breakfasts also deserve commendation, and lunchtime bar snacks are available.
6rm(2🛁2🚿) CTV in all bedrooms ® sB&B£17.50 sB&B🛁🚿£23.50 dB&Bfr£33 dB&B🛁🚿fr£44 B
70P ✽ *xmas*
French **V** ♆ ☕ Lunch £9&alc Tea £1—£3 Dinner £14.50—£16.50&alc Wine £5.25 Last dinner 9pm
Credit cards [1] [2] [3] [5]

BRANDON
Suffolk
Map **5** TL78

★★**Brandon House** High St ☎ Thetford (0842) 810171
RS Xmas Day
17rm(7🛁2🚿)(1fb) CTV in all bedrooms ®
✱ sB£26.75—£27.75
sB🛁🚿£30.75—£31.75
dB£35.50—£37.50
dB🛁🚿£40.50—£42.50(room only)
60P ✽
English & French **V** ♆ ☕ ✱ Lunch £8.35alc Tea £1.30—£1.50 Dinner £8.35alc Wine £4.75 Last dinner 8.45pm
Credit cards [1] [2] [3] [5]

BRANDON
Warwickshire
Map **4** SP47

★★★**Brandon Hall** Main St (Trusthouse Forte) ☎ Coventry (0203) 542571 Telex no 31472
A recently modernised country hotel situated in wooded grounds.
60🛁 CTV in all bedrooms ® sB&B🛁£50 dB&B🛁£66 B
☾ 250P ✽ squash *xmas*
♆ ☕ Last dinner 9.30pm
Credit cards [1] [2] [3] [4] [5]

BRANKSOME
Dorset see **Poole**

BRANSCOMBE
Devon
Map **3** SY18

✕✕**Masons Arms** ☎ (029780) 300
The fourteenth-century thatched inn nestles in a valley not far from the sea. The bar, with its slate floor and exposed beams, dates back 700 years and is built around a central fireplace. Fine food and wine are served in pleasant surroundings by friendly staff.
Lunch not served Mon—Sat
English & French **V** 46 seats 20 bedrooms available Lunch £8 Dinner £11—£14 Wine £6 Last dinner 9pm 40P
Credit cards [1] [3]

BRANSTON
Lincolnshire
Map **8** TF06

★★**Moor Lodge** ☎ Lincoln (0522) 791366
25rm(22🛁3🚿)(2fb) CTV in all bedrooms ® **T** ✱ sB&B🛁🚿£30 dB&B🛁🚿£46
100P ✽ *xmas*
International ♆ ☕ Lunch £6.50&alc Dinner £8.50&alc Wine fr£5.50 Last dinner 9.30pm
Credit cards [1] [2] [3] [5]

B

Braunton — Brent Knoll

BRAUNTON
Devon
Map **2** SS43

★★**Poyers Hotel & Restaurant** Wrafton ☎(0271) 812149

Closed Xmas & New Year

The centuries-old thatched farmhouse has a unique courtyard with bedrooms at the rear and its popular restaurant specialises in the imaginative preparation of fresh local produce.

10rm(6 4) CTV in all bedrooms ® sB&B £23—£26 dB&B £33.50—£37 B

28P

English, French, German & Italian Lunch fr£8.30&alc Dinner fr£8.30&alc Wine £5.25 Last dinner 9.30pm

Credit cards 1 2 3 5 V

BRAY
Berkshire
Map **4** SU97

XXXX
WATERSIDE, BRAY
Ferry Rd (Relais et Châteaux) ☎ Maidenhead (0628) 20691 Telex no 8813079

This year, as last, we have had reports of varied experiences again which have indicated, sadly, too little consistency for us to be able to award our highest accolade, particularly as the most criticised dishes were main ones. Some of the dishes tasted, however, revealed the highest standards; the old favourite soufflé Leonora, was a marvel for its sensitive blend of flavours; a fish course which delighted us was the fillet of brill with crayfish and scallop mousse in a delicate champagne sauce finished with cream — absoultely perfect! Among the main courses another lamb dish, germain, was much more successful than that later in the season, while the Challons duck with girofe mushrooms and honey worked beautifully. The strong point here has always been the desserts and they were highly acclaimed by everyone: soufflé, sablé biscuit with pears and bilberries with cullis of mixed fruit, as well as the now famous lemon tart, accompanied by the blackcurrant delight — a bavarois on a sponge base. Delicious savoury pastries, coffee and petit fours enhance the beginning and end of the meal. The wine list is outstanding with vintages dating back to 1918. As usual, beside the à la carte menu, there is a Menu Exceptionnel (minimum of two people) and at lunch the fixed price Menu Gastronomique is good value. You will be looked after by a team of professional staff with care and courtesy — but they have been known to 'lose their cool'! All this is in an idyllic situation on the banks of the Thames — there is a terrace where you can take an aperitif in warm weather. The fresh decor complements the surroundings and is garden like. The finest of tableware is used and the whole makes an enchanting setting for food that can occasionally reach the heights.

Closed Mon, Bank Hol's & 8 wks from 26 Dec Lunch not served Tue Dinner not served Sun from Oct—Etr

French V 70 seats S% Lunch £20&alc Dinner £35alc Wine £9.80 Last dinner 10pm 20P nc 4yrs

Credit cards 1 2 3 4 5

BRECHIN
Tayside *Angus*
Map **15** NO56

★★**Northern** Clerk St ☎(03562) 2156

Homely, commercial town centre hotel in 1890 listed building.

17rm(4 11) CTV in all bedrooms ® *sB&B £17 sB&B £23 dB&B £30 dB&B £38

CTV 30P

*Lunch £3.90—£4.60 High Tea £3.50—£6 Dinner £7.50 Wine £4.95 Last dinner 9.30pm

Credit cards 1 2 3

XX***Balbirnie Mill*** Montrose Rd ☎(03562) 4482

The restaurant, with its stone walls, high raftered ceiling, wrought iron and large log fireplace, is reminiscent of the original mill and has an almost medieval air about it. Angus beef steak, fresh fish and seafood all feature on the menu.

French V 50 seats Last dinner 9pm 200P

BRECON
Powys
Map **3** SO02

★★**Castle of Brecon** The Avenue (Consort) ☎(0874) 2551

RS Xmas

This character hotel, traditionally appointed, stands in an elevated position with views across the Usk Valley to the Brecon Beacons. A cottage annexe provides additional bedrooms in modern style.

28rm(6 3) Annexe: 12 2 CTV in all bedrooms ® T S% sB&B £28.50 dB&B £41.50 B

CTV 30P

V S% *Lunch £4.95—£8.50&alc Tea fr60p Dinner £8.50&alc Wine £4.50 Last dinner 9.30pm

Credit cards 1 2 3 4 5 V

★★*B* **Wellington** The Bulwark (Best Western) ☎(0874) 5225

A Georgian hotel in the centre of the town, the Wellington has been totally renovated to provide very comfortable bedrooms, pleasant public rooms and the attractive Dukes coffee shop, bar and bistro. The cobbled courtyard contains a few shops.

21 (1fb) CTV in all bedrooms ® T S% *sB&B £23 dB&B £40 B

xmas

Welsh, English & French V S% *Lunch £2.50—£6&alc Tea 50p&alc High Tea £2—£4.50&alc Dinner £4.75—£9.75&alc Wine £3.85 Last dinner 10.30pm

Credit cards 1 2 3

★**Lansdowne** 39 The Watton ☎(0874) 3321

This small, personally-run hotel combines character with charm and friendly service. Recent upgrading has provided comfortable bedrooms with modern private facilities.

12rm(4)(2fb) CTV in all bedrooms sB&B £14.50—£15.50 sB&B £16.50—£17.50 dB&B £23.50—£25.50 dB&B £27.50—£29.50 B

CTV 12P Live music mthly *xmas*

V Lunch £5.25alc Tea 90p—£1.10 Dinner £5.75&alc Last dinner 9.30pm

Credit cards 1 3 V

BRENDON
Devon
Map **3** SS74

★★**Stag Hunters Inn** (Minotel) ☎(05987) 222

Closed Jan—mid Mar

Pleasant, privately owned inn, in this valley village in the heart of Exmoor.

22rm(6)(2fb) 2 CTV in 6 bedrooms ® sB&Bfr£24.50 dB&Bfr£36 dB&B fr£40 B

CTV 50P *xmas*

*Bar lunch £1.50—£4.50 Tea £2.40 Dinner £10.50 Wine £4.65 Last dinner 8.30pm

Credit cards 1 2 3 5 V

BRENT KNOLL
Somerset
Map **3** ST35

★★**Battleborough Grange Country** Bristol Rd (Guestaccom) ☎(0278) 760208

Informal, pleasant country house near M5.

11rm(3🛁4🚿)2🛏CTV in all bedrooms ® 🚫 T S% *sB&B£18—£22 sB&B🛁🚿fr£22 dB&Bfr£30 dB&B🛁🚿fr£36 B

CTV 40P ✿ nc 10yrs *xmas*

English & French V ☕ *Lunch £6 Tea 60p Wine £5.40 Last dinner 9pm

Credit cards 1 2 3 5 V

See advertisement under Bridgwater

Brent Knoll — Brentwood

BRENTWOOD
Essex
Map **5** TQ59

★★★★**Brentwood Moat House** London Rd (Queens Moat) ☎(0277) 225252 Telex no 995182

Parts of this hotel — once the home of Catherine of Aragon — date back to 1520, and the panelled lounge and raftered restaurant are particularly impressive. The bedrooms, mostly in the modern chalet style, are situated around a garden.

3🛁🚿 Annexe:34🛁🚿(5fb)1🛏CTV in all bedrooms 🚫 S% sB🛁🚿£51—£58 dB🛁🚿£53—£64(room only) B

☾ 120P ✿ ♿

French V ☕ Lunch £11.50&alc(Sun only) Dinner £18.20alc Wine £6 Last dinner 10pm

Credit cards 1 2 3 5

★★★**Post House** Brook St (Trusthouse Forte) ☎(0277) 210888 Telex no 995379

Modern hotel with coffee shop and formal restaurant. →

120🛁CTV in all bedrooms ®T
sB&B🛁£57.50 dB&B🛁£71.50 B
Lift ☾ 148P CFA ✿ (heated) *xmas*
Last dinner 10pm
Credit cards 1 2 3 4 5

○ **Little Chef Lodge**
A127 ☎ (0277) 810819
20🛁
Due to have opened July 1986

BRIDESTOWE
Devon
Map **2** SX58

✕ **White Hart Inn** ☎ (083786) 318
It is advisable to make table reservations.
Closed Xmas Day & 2 wks Jan or Feb
Lunch advance bookings only 16 seats
Lunch £12—£16alc Dinner £12—£16alc
Wine £4.75 Last dinner 9pm 20P nc
Credit cards 1 2 3 5

BRIDGE
Kent
Map **5** TR16

✕ ***Anne's House*** High St ☎ Canterbury (0227) 831118
Cosy cottage style, family run restaurant. Tea rooms specialising in Fondue and Swiss cooking.
Closed Tue, Oct & Feb
Lunch not served Sun & Wed
English & Swiss **V** 30 seats Last dinner 10pm
Credit cards 1 2 3

BRIDGEFORD, GREAT
Staffordshire
Map **7** SJ82

✕✕ **Worston Mill** Worston (1m NW off A5013) ☎ Seighford (078575) 710
Imposing mill complex with family attractions, good first floor restaurant and popular carvery.
V 80 seats ✱ Lunch £5.95—£9.95&alc Dinner fr£9.95&alc Wine £4.95 Last dinner 10pm 200P Live music Tue
Credit cards 1 3

BRIDGEND
Mid Glamorgan
Map **3** SS97

★★★ *B* ***Heronston*** Ewenny (2m S B4265) ☎ (0656) 68811 Telex no 498232
Modern popular businessman's hotel with comfortable bedrooms, friendly service and good leisure facilities.
40🛁(3fb) CTV in all bedrooms ®T
☾ CTV 100P CFA (heated) sauna bath solarium gymnasium Live music & dancing Sat *xmas*
Welsh & French **V** Last dinner 10pm
Credit cards 1 2 3 4 5

★★ **Wyndham** Dunraven Pl ☎ (0656) 2080
This centrally-positioned hotel, parts of which date back to the 17th century, was recently refurbished to provide good bedrooms, restaurant and bars. The Tap Room, with its original decor, is becoming a popular venue.
28rm(25🛁) 1 CTV in all bedrooms ®T
✱sB&B£21—£22.50
sB&B🛁£27.25—£28.50
dB&B🛁£39.50—£41.50 B
☾ CTV Live music & dancing 3 nights wkly
English & French **V** Lunch £5alc Dinner £8.50alc Wine £4.50 Last dinner 10pm
Credit cards 1 2 3 5 Ⓥ

○ **Little Chef Lodge**
Sarn Park Services (eastbound M4 jct 36) (2m N A4061)
☎ 01-567 3444 40🛁
Due to open November 1986

✕✕✕ **Coed Y Mwstwr Hotel** Coychurch (3m E of Bridgend: 1m NE of Coychurch) ☎ (0656) 860621
Despite the English translation of the hotel's name being "commotion in the wood", a relaxed atmosphere prevails! Visitors to the Victorian house in its seventeen acres of woodland overlookin the Vale of Glamorgan can enjoy food of a commendably high standard backed by hospitable service.
Lunch not served Sat
Dinner not served Sun
English & French 70 seats ✱ Lunch £13.95&alc Dinner £13.95&alc Wine £6 Last dinner 10pm 60P nc 7yrs Live music Fri & Sat
Credit cards 1 2 3 4 5

BRIDGE OF ALLAN
Central *Stirlingshire*
Map **11** NS79

★★★ **Royal** Henderson St ☎ (0786) 832284 Telex no. 946240
Large building, dating from 1836, standir on the main road in the centre of the town.
33rm(25🛁) CTV in all bedrooms ®T S%
sB&B£26.50—£28.50
sB&B🛁£29.50—£31.50 dB&B£34—£4
dB&B🛁£41—£53 B
Lift ☾ 60P *xmas*
S% Bar lunch £1.15—£5.95 Tea 60—90p Dinner £10—£12.50 Wine £4.9C
Last dinner 9.30pm
Credit cards 1 2 3 4 5

BRIDGE OF CALLY
Tayside *Perthshire*
Map **15** NO15

★ *BL* **Bridge of Cally**
☎ (025086) 231
Closed Nov
This small hotel stands on the banks of the River Ardle and enjoys good views of the Perthshire countryside. Bedrooms and public rooms offer relaxed comfort and the dining room is low-ceilinged and attractive
9rm(3🛁3) sB&B£17—£18
dB&B£29—£30
dB&B🛁£31.50—£32.50
CTV 50P ✿
✱ Bar lunch £3.75—£4.50 Tea 65p—£1 Dinner £9—£10.45 Wine £4.70
Last dinner 8.30pm
Credit cards 1 3 5 Ⓥ

BRIDGNORTH
Shropshire
Map **7** SO79

★★**Falcon** St John Street, Lowtown ☎(07462) 3134

Old coaching inn in Lowtown, close to River Severn.

17rm(3➡)(4fb) CTV in all bedrooms S% sB&B£25—£30 sB&B➡£36—£40 dB&B£34—£40 dB&B➡£40—£42

200P 4🚗(charge)

🍽English & French **V** 🍷 Lunch £7.50&alc Tea 80p High Tea £2.50 Dinner £12.50&alc Wine £5.95 Last dinner 9.30pm

Credit cards 1 2 3 4 5

BRIDGWATER
Somerset
Map **3** ST33

★★*B* **Walnut Tree Inn** (North Petherton, 3m S A38) (ExecHotel) ☎(0278) 662255

Former coaching inn with quietly situated bedrooms equipped to high standard. Tourist and business hotel.

6➡ Annexe: 14➡(1fb) CTV in all bedrooms ® **T** ✗ ✱sB&B➡£29—£35 dB&B➡£40—£48 **B**

95P ✿ solarium 👪

🍽Mainly grills 🍷 ☕ Bar lunch £3.50alc Dinner £9.50alc Wine £4.10 Last dinner 9.45pm

Credit cards 1 2 3 5 Ⓥ

See advertisement on page 160

✕**Old Vicarage** 45—49 St Mary Street ☎(0278) 458891

A town-centre restaurant of considerable charm, the Old Vicarage is enthusiastically supervised by young owners. The menu is in the middle price range and includes an extensive choice of tempting puddings. →

English & French V 65 seats Lunch £10.50alc Dinner £12.50alc Wine £3.95 Last dinner 10pm 10P
Credit cards 1 2 3

BRIDLINGTON
Humberside
Map **8** TA16

★★★**Expanse** North Marine Dr
☎ (0262) 675347

A multi-storey seaside hotel built in 1937, the Expanse has been fully modernised and updated. Spacious lounges overlook the bay and Flamborough Head.

48rm(36⇌2⫪)(3fb) CTV in all bedrooms ® ✱ sB&B£21.50—£23.50 sB&B⇌⫪£24.50—£26.50 dB&B£40 dB&B⇌⫪£42—£46 B
Lift ☾ 15P 15 (charge) xmas
✱ Lunch fr£4.75 Tea 75p—£2.25 Dinner fr£7.50&alc Wine £4 Last dinner 8.30pm
Credit cards 1 2 3 5 V

★★**Monarch** South Marine Dr (Consort)
☎ (0262) 674447 Telex no 57515
Closed mid Oct—Etr

The multi-storey building overlooking South Bay provides smartly attractive public rooms and spacious, well-fitted bedrooms.

43rm(23⇌1⫪)(5fb) CTV in 24 bedrooms ✱ sB&B£17.25 sB&B⇌⫪£23.50 dB&B£31 dB&B⇌⫪£40 B
Lift ☾ CTV 10P 2 (£1 per night)
English & French V Lunch fr£4.50 Tea fr55p Dinner £7.50&alc Wine £4.20 Last dinner 9pm
Credit cards 1 2 3 5

XXOld Cooperage High St ☎(0262) 675190

Small, elegant restaurant with comfortable lounge bar.

Lunch not served Sun

🍷Indian 50 seats Lunch £3.50 Dinner £10&alc Wine £6.95 Last dinner mdnt 10P

Credit cards [1] [2] [3] [5]

BRIDPORT
Dorset
Map **3** SY49

★★★**Haddon House** West Bay (2m S off B3157 Weymouth rd) ☎(0308) 23626

Converted, modernised Regency house with stylish furnishings.

13rm(10🛁2⋔) CTV in all bedrooms ® T
*sB&B🛁⋔£27.50 dB&B🛁⋔£40 B

60P 4🚗 ♿

V 🍷 *Lunch fr£6.75 Dinner fr£8.95 Wine £4.95 Last dinner 8.30pm

Credit cards [1] [2] [3] [5]

★★**Bull** 34 East St ☎(0308) 22878

Closed 24 & 25 Dec

This sixteenth-century coaching inn stands in the centre of Bridport, managed by attentive resident owners. Its strength is its restaurant, which specialises in French food. Bedrooms are neat and traditional.

16rm(6🛁3⋔)(1fb) CTV in all bedrooms ® in 1 bedroom ✈
sB&B£13.50—£15
sB&B🛁⋔£17.50—£19.50
dB&B£29.50—£33.50
dB&B🛁⋔£31.50—£39.50 B

40P 2🚗 snooker →

English & French Lunch £5.25—£12.50 Tea 85p Dinner £6.95—£15&alc Wine £4.50 Last dinner 9.15pm

Credit cards 1 3

★★**Eype's Mouth** Eype (2m SW) ☎ (0308) 23300

Set close to the sea some two miles south west of Bridport, the hotel has fine sea views. It offers neat, small bedrooms and is run by the resident owners.

20rm(9 1)(2fb) ® *sB&Bfr£14 sB&B fr£18 dB&Bfr£26 dB&B fr£32 B

CTV 80P Live music & dancing Sat & Sun *xmas*

V *Bar lunch fr£3 Tea fr60p Dinner fr£6 Wine £4.95 Last dinner 8.30pm

Credit cards 1 2 3 5

★★***West Mead*** West Rd ☎ (0308) 22609

Mellow stone manor house in its own grounds with comfortable lounges and well-appointed bedrooms.

26rm(16 3)(7fb) CTV in 17 bedrooms ® B

CTV 100P Live music & dancing Sat

Last dinner 8.30pm

Credit cards 1 5

Bridport

★**Bridport Arms** West Bay (2m S off B3157 Weymouth rd) ☎ (0308) 22994

Colour-washed, stone, cottage-style hotel, next to the harbour and West Bay beach.

8rm(1 5)(2fb) ®
sB&B£13.50—£14.50
sB&B £14.50—£15.50
dB&B£27—£29 dB&B £29—£31 B

CTV 10P 4

Bar lunch £4.50alc Dinner £9alc Wine £4.95 Last dinner 8.45pm

Credit cards 1 3 V

★**Little Wych Country House** Burton Rd ☎ (0308) 23490

Closed Dec—Feb

Peaceful stone manor house with older style bedrooms and freshly prepared food.

6rm(2fb) 1 CTV available in bedrooms ® *sB&B£15—£16 dB&B£30—£32 B

CTV 10P 2 (hard) sauna bath solarium nc 5yrs

English & Continental V *Dinner £7.50&alc Wine £5.35 Last dinner 8.30pm

★ ***H*Roundham House** Roundham Gnds, West Bay Rd ☎ (0308) 22753

This smalll, comfortable hotel, built of Bothenhampton stone and set in its well-tended gardens, is personally run and offers good food.

8rm(4 3)(3fb) CTV in all bedrooms sB&B £15.50—£16.50 dB&B £31—£33 B

CTV 12P *xmas*

English & Continental V Lunch £4.50—£5.75 Tea 75p—£1.50 High Tea £2.50—£4.50 Dinner £7.60—£9 Wine £4.75 Last dinner 10pm

Credit card 1 V

X**Bistro Lautrec** 53 East St ☎ (0308) 56549

As implied by the name, this lower ground floor restaurant cultivates an informal atmosphere, and its comprehensive chalkboard menu offers value for money.

Dinner not served Sun (in winter)

English & French V 40 seats Lunch £5.50alc Dinner £5&alc Wine £4.90 Last dinner 10.30pm

Credit cards 1 3 5

Brightlingsea — Brighton & Hove

B

BRIGHTLINGSEA
Essex
Map **5** TM01

✕✕**Jacobe's Hall** High St ☎ (020630) 2113

An historic, timbered sea-food restaurant, complete with lobster tanks and offering personal service.

Closed Tue Dinner not served Sun

V 30 seats ✱Lunch £12alc Dinner £14alc Wine £4.50 Last dinner 9pm 40P nc8yrs

Credit cards [1] [2] [3] [5] Ⓥ

BRIGHTON & HOVE
East Sussex
Map **4** TQ30

See Brighton & Hove plans

★★★★**Dudley** Lansdowne Place, Hove (Trusthouse Forte) ☎ (0273) 736266 Telex no 87537 Hove plan **3** *C1*

Imposing hotel with well appointed lounges and modern restaurant.

80🛁 CTV in all bedrooms Ⓡ sB&B🛁£54.50 dB&B🛁£73.50 Ᵽ

Lift ☾ 15P 15🚗 CFA *xmas*

🍷 ☕ Last dinner 10pm

Credit cards [1] [2] [3] [4] [5]

★★★**Alexandra** 42 Brunswick Ter, Hove (Minotel) ☎ (0273) 202722 Telex no 877579 Hove plan **1** *C1*

RS 28 Dec—6 Jan

Well-equipped, sea front hotel with good bedrooms and limited restaurant.

63rm(61🛁2🚿)(6fb) CTV in all bedrooms Ⓡ **T** S% sB&B🛁🚿£39 dB&B🛁🚿£54.50 Ᵽ

Lift ☾ CTV Ᵽ CFA sauna bath, solarium, table tennis *xmas*

English & French **V** 🍷 ☕ S% Lunch £7.50&alc Dinner £9&alc Wine £4.99 Last dinner 9.30pm

Credit cards [1] [2] [3] [5] Ⓥ

★★★*B* **Courtlands** 22 The Drive, Hove ☎ (0273) 731055 Telex no 87574 Hove plan **2** *B2*

Comfortable, friendly hotel with well-appointed, tastefully furnished bedrooms.

52rm(44🛁6🚿) Annexe: 5🛁(3fb) CTV in all bedrooms Ⓡ available in bedrooms **T** S% sB&B🛁🚿£35—£45 dB&B£48—£60 Ᵽ

Lift ☾ CTV 26P CFA ✿ (heated) solarium games room pool table *xmas*

English & French **V** Lunch £7—£8.50&alc Tea £1.20—£1.50 Dinner £10.50—£12.50&alc Wine £6.25 Last dinner 9.30pm

Credit cards [1] [2] [3] [5]

See advertisement on page 164

★★★**Old Ship** King's Rd ☎ (0273) 29001 Telex no 877101 Brighton plan **7** *C1*

Pleasant hotel dating to 1559, with comfortable lounges and genial, traditional services.

153rm(147🛁6🚿) 1⊞ CTV in all bedrooms Ⓡ **T** S% sB&B🛁🚿fr£46 dB&B🛁🚿fr£60 Ᵽ

Lift ☾ 80🚗(charge) CFA Live music and dancing Sat *xmas*

English, French & Italian **V** 🍷 ☕ Lunch £8—£12 Tea 70p High Tea fr£2.50 Dinner fr£13&alc Wine £6.50 Last dinner 9.30pm

Credit cards [1] [2] [3] [5]

See advertisement on page 164

★★★**Royal Crescent** 100 Marine Pde ☎ (0273) 607719 Telex no 87253 Brighton plan **9** *F1*

The hotel, a Regency building of historic interest and architectural charm, is well-managed and friendly; the elegant restaurant overlooks the sea.

50🛁(4fb) 1⊞ CTV in all bedrooms Ⓡ **T** ✱sB&B🛁£30—£40 dB&B🛁£50—£60 Ᵽ

Lift ☾ **P** 8🚗(£2 per night)

🍷 ☕ Lunch £6.50alc Tea £1alc Dinner £12alc Wine £6 Last dinner 9.30pm

Credit cards [1] [2] [3] [5]

See advertisement on page 164

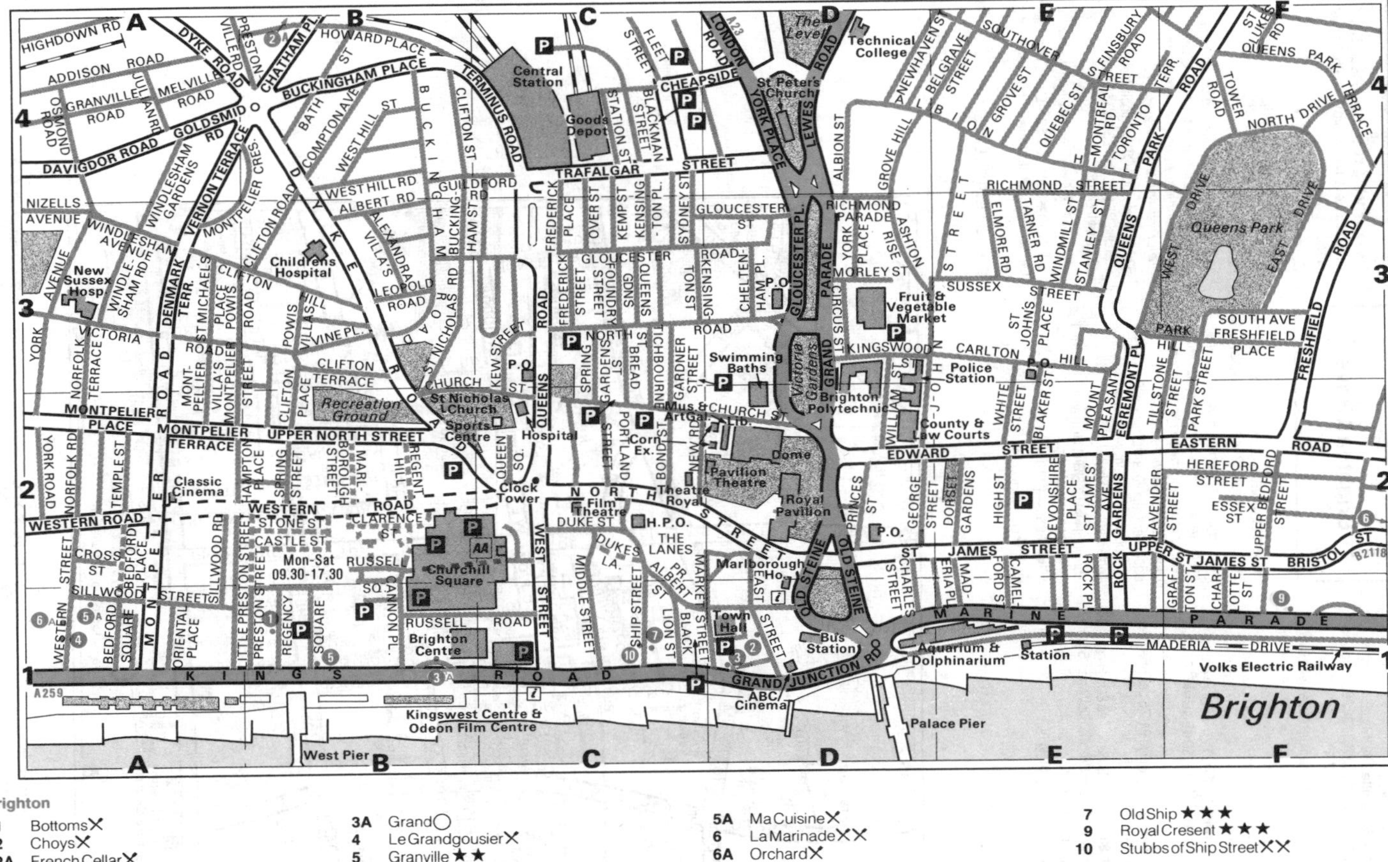

Brighton

1	Bottoms✕	3A	Grand○	5A	MaCuisine✕	7	OldShip★★★
2	Choys✕	4	LeGrandgousier✕	6	LaMarinade✕✕	9	RoyalCresent★★★
2A	FrenchCellar✕	5	Granville★★	6A	Orchard✕	10	StubbsofShipStreet✕✕
3	FrenchConnection✕						

★★★Sackville 189 Kingsway, Hove (Best Western) ☎ (0273) 736292 Telex no 877830 Hove plan **7** *A1*

An independent, sea front hotel, with well equipped old fashioned bedrooms, some with sea-views, and a well managed efficient restaurant with limited lounge accommodation.

45rm(43(bath)2(shower)) 1 CTV in all bedrooms ® **T** S% sB&B(bath)(shower)£41.50 dB&B(bath)(shower)£57.50

Lift ☾ 8 (£2.75 garage £1.75 car port per night) *xmas*

✻Lunch £8.50&alc Tea 80p High Tea fr£4.50 Dinner £8.50&alc Wine £5.30 Last dinner 9.30pm

Credit cards 1 2 3 5 V

Brighton & Hove

★★B Granville 125 King's Rd ☎ (0273) 26302 Telex no 878149 Brighton plan **5** *B1*

An elegantly-furnished, family run hotel, the Granville offers very well equipped bedrooms facing the sea (though top-floor rooms are somewhat smaller). The basement restaurant, Troggs, features French cuisine, home-made preserves and an à la carte breakfast.

25rm(24(bath)1(shower))5 CTV in all bedrooms **T** sB(bath)(shower)£47.50—£55 dB(bath)(shower)£53—£110(room only)

Lift ☾ solarium *xmas*

French **V** Lunch £6.50&alc Tea £1.80 Dinner £12.95&alc Wine £5.40 Last dinner 10.30pm

Credit cards 1 2 3 5 V

★★St Catherine's Lodge Kingsway, Hove (Inter Hotel) ☎ (0273) 778181 Telex no 877073 Hove plan **6** *A1*

The hotel has generous and comfortable public rooms and provides extensive and friendly service. Bedrooms vary, but some are furnished particularly tastefully.

53rm(38(bath))(5fb) CTV in all bedrooms S% sB&Bfr£28 sB&B(bath)£34 dB&Bfr£41 dB&B(bath)fr£49

Lift ☾ CTV 4**P** 4(charge) CFA *xmas*

S% ✻Lunch £3.50—£5.95 Tea 95p Dinner fr£8.25&alc Wine £4.50 Last dinner 9pm

Credit cards 1 2 3 5 V

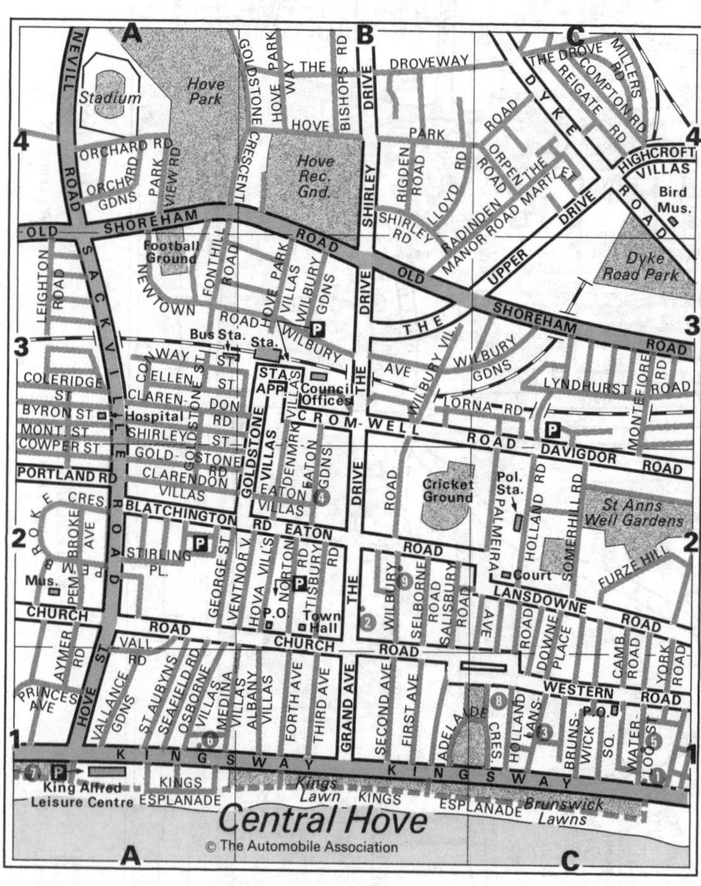

Hove

1 Alexandra ★★★
2 Courtlands ★★★
3 Dudley ★★★★
4 Eaton ✕✕✕
5 Lawrence ✕
6 St Catherine's Lodge ★★
7 Sackville ★★★
8 Vogue ✕
9 Whitehaven ★★

★★ *BL* **Whitehaven** 34 Wilbury Rd, Hove ☎ (0273) 778355 Telex no 877159 Hove plan **9** *B2*

Elegantly furnished and situated in a quiet residential area, the hotel is personally managed, offering good standards of cooking and friendly, attentive service.

17rm(11⇌6⋔)(1fb) 1⊟ CTV in all bedrooms ®**T** ✕ sB&B⇌⋔fr£40 dB&B⇌⋔fr£55 **B**

⊭ nc 8yrs *xmas*

Brighton & Hove

English & Continental **V** Bar lunch £1.50—£4.95 Tea £1—£1.50 Dinner £9.25&alc Wine £5.50 Last dinner 9.30pm

Credit cards 1 2 3 5

See advertisement on page 168

○ **Grand** King's Rd (De Vere) ☎ (0273) 21188 Brighton plan **3A** *B1*

198⇌⋔

Due to have re-opened September 1986.

○ **Ramada Renaissance** Kings Rd ☎ 01-235 5264

204⇌⋔

Expected to open May 1987

✕✕✕ **Eaton** Eaton Gdns, Hove ☎ (0273) 738921 Hove plan **4** *B2*

Long established old fashioned restaurant, with good professional service, and popular limited menu.

Closed Xmas Day & Good Fri Dinner not served Sun →

B

B

🍷International **V** 90 seats Lunch £10—£11.50&alc Dinner £13—£15.50&alc Wine £7.50 Last dinner 9.45pm 26P

Credit cards 1 2 3 5

XX La Marinade 77 St.George's Rd, Kemptown ☎ (0273) 600992 Brighton plan **6** *F2*

This very smart and well-appointed basement restaurant offers very good value for money, with professional standards of cooking and good service. Home-made desserts are a speciality.

Closed Sun, Mon, 18 Aug—5 Sep & 24 Dec—6 Jan

🍷French **V** 30 seats Lunch £6—£10 Dinner £12alc Wine £5 Last dinner 10pm P

S% Credit cards 1 2 3 5 V

XX Stubbs of Ship Street 14 Ship St ☎ (0273) 204005 Brighton plan **10** *C1*

In almost club-like surroundings, this small, elegant English restaurant is tastefully furnished and offers a menu featuring such delicacies as local lamb and roe deer. Service is efficient and has the personal touch.

Closed Feb
Lunch not served Sat—Mon

🍷English & French **V** 30 seats Lunch £8.95 Dinner £15alc Wine £5.95 Last dinner 10.30pm 10P (evenings only) no babies

Credit cards 1 2 3 5 V

X Bottoms Topps Hotel, 17 Regency Sq ☎ (0273) 729334 Telex no 877159 Brighton plan **1** *B1*

A simple English restaurant with Pauline Collins' home made dishes.

Closed Sun, Wed & 24 Dec—24 Jan Lunch not served

24 seats S% ✱Dinner £10.50 Wine £4.10 Last dinner 9.30pm P

Credit cards 1 2 3 5

X Choys 2/3 Little East St ☎ (0273) 25305 Brighton plan **2** *D2*

Popular family run Chinese restaurant featuring an extensive choice of Cantonese and Peking style dishes.

Brighton & Hove

🍷Cantonese & Pekinese **V** 100 seats S% Lunch £5—£15&alc Dinner £10—£30&alc Wine £5 Last dinner 11.15pm P

Credit cards 1 2 3

X French Cellar Basement, 37 New England Rd ☎ (0273) 603643 Brighton plan **2A** *B4*

The small, basement restaurant is comfortably furnished with reproduction antiques and features a fixed price menu which includes the house wine. The French chef/patron produces reliable, correctly-prepared dishes which include home-made soups and fresh sorbet.

Closed Sun & last 2 wks Aug

🍷French 20 seats Lunch £10alc Dinner £15—£20alc Wine £6 Last dinner 10pm P nc 9yrs (dinner)

Credit cards 1 2 3 5 V

X French Connection 11 Little East St ☎ (0273) 24454 Brighton plan **3** *D1*

A taste of France is offered in this small, cosy restaurant where well-cooked traditional dishes are accompanied by an impressive wine list.

Closed Sun, Jan & 1st wk Jul

🍷French **V** 34 seats S% ✱Lunch £8.50&alc Dinner £10.65&alc Wine £5.90 Last dinner 10pm P

Credit cards 1 2 3 5

X Le Grandgousier 15 Western St ☎ (0273) 772005 Brighton plan **4** *A1*

This small and very popular French restaurant features an interesting six-course fixed-price menu, representing excellent value for money, which is supplemented by some authentic regional dishes. Service is particularly attentive and helpful.

Closed Sun & 23 Dec—3 Jan Lunch not served Sat

🍷French 42 seats Lunch £9.45—£12.50 Dinner £9.45—£12.50 Wine £5.20 Last dinner 9pm P nc 5yrs

Credit card 2

X Lawrence 40 Waterloo St, Hove ☎ (0273) 772922 Hove plan **5** *C1*

A tiny but cosy front room restaurant featuring fixed price dishes which are imaginatively prepared.

Dinner not served Sun

🍷English & French **V** 18 seats Lunch 50p—£7&alc Dinner £15alc Wine £5.45 Last dinner 11pm P

Credit cards 1 3 V

X Ma Cuisine 43 Sillwood St ☎ (0273) 729908 Brighton plan **5A** *A1*

A Parisian "back street" atmosphere has been created in this delightful little restaurant. The reliable, good-value dishes include several based on sea-food and there are well-made fresh desserts, though the range of wines is very limited.

Closed Sun, 2 wks Spring & 2 wks Autumn Lunch not served

🍷French 24 seats ✱Dinner £6.95—£9.45 Wine £4.50 Last dinner 10pm P

Credit cards 1 2 3 5

X Orchard 33 Western St ☎ (0273) 776618 Brighton plan **6A** A1

Interesting and imaginative cooking is complemented by polite, attentive service.

Closed Sun, Mon & 23 Dec—27 Dec Lunch not served

🍷English & French 24 seats ✱Dinner £10.95 Wine £5.85 Last dinner 10pm P

Credit cards 1 2 3 4 5

X *Vogue* 57 Holland Rd, Hove ☎ (0273) 775060 Hove plan **8** *C1*

This small, plain French restaurant offers modest comfort but lots of atmosphere. The popular regional dishes are excellent value for money and the imported French ice-cream and sorbet are recommended. Service is attentive and polite. Booking advised.

Closed Mon (except Bank Hol's) Dinner not served Sun

🍷French 34 seats Last dinner 11.30pm

Credit cards 1 2 3

BRIMFIELD
Hereford & Worcester
Map **7** SO56

✻✕ **Poppies** Roebuck Inn ☎ (058472) 230

Part of the Roebuck Inn, this very popular restaurant's reputation has been built up in a short time by Carole Evans who uses only the very best produce, with many dishes featuring fresh fish, meat; vegetarian dishes are also available, and the small wine list is reasonably priced.

V 32 seats Lunch £6.95alc Dinner £6.95—£15alc Wine £4.50 Last dinner 10pm P

BRISTOL
Avon
Map **3** ST57

See plan on page 170

★★★★*B* **Grand** Broad St (Mount Charlotte) ☎ (0272) 291645 Telex no 449889 Plan **5** *D3*

Recently refurbished, this traditionally-styled hotel in the heart of the city offers very comfortable bedrooms which retain some individual charm and character, elegant public rooms and the attractive and popular Brass Nails restaurant.

178rm(163 15) CTV in all bedrooms ® **T** sB&B fr£52 dB&B fr£63 **B**

Lift 20P 25 CFA *xmas*

English & French **V** Lunch fr£8.95&alc Tea fr£1.10 High Tea fr£2 Dinner fr£9.50&alc Wine £5.95 Last dinner 10.30pm

Credit cards 1 2 3 5 V

★★★★ ***Holiday Inn*** Lower Castle St (Holiday Inns) ☎ (0272) 294281 Telex no 449720 Plan **6** *E4*

Very modern hotel in the city centre, overlooking Castle Green, and adjacent to a multi-storey car park.

284 (141fb) CTV in all bedrooms **T B**

Lift ## CFA (heated) sauna bath solarium gymnasium

English & French **V** Last dinner 10.45pm

Credit cards 1 2 3 4 5

★★★★ **Ladbroke Dragonara** Redcliffe Way (Ladbroke) ☎ (0272) 20041 Telex no 449240 Plan **8** *E2*

RS Xmas—New Year

Modern comfortable hotel with unusual restaurant set in former Bristol Glass kiln.

197 (2fb) 1 in 40 bedrooms CTV in all bedrooms ® **T** ✻ sB £60.75—£81.25 dB £78.50—£102.50 (room only) **B**

Lift 150P CFA Live music and dancing Sat in winter

English & French **V** ✻ Lunch £7.75—£8.50 Tea £1—£3 Dinner £10.95—£12.50&alc Wine £5.95 Last dinner 10pm

Credit cards 1 2 3 4 5 V

★★★ **Avon Gorge** Sion Hill, Clifton (Mount Charlotte) ☎ (0272) 738955 Telex no 444237 Plan **1** *A3*

The terrace, bar and restaurant of this hotel overlooks Avon Gorge and Brunel's suspension bridge.

81rm(74 6) 2 CTV in all bedrooms ® **T** ✻ sB&B fr£41.50 dB&B fr£55.25 **B**

Lift **P** CFA Live music & dancing Thu Fri & Sat *xmas*

English & French ✻ Lunch fr£8.25 Tea fr50p Dinner fr£8.25 Wine £5.85 Last dinner 10pm

Credit cards 1 2 3 5 V

★★★ **Crest** Filton Rd, Hambrook (6m NE off A4174) (Crest) ☎ (0272) 564242 Telex no 449376 Plan **3** *F5*

Well appointed comfortable, modern hotel near M4/M5 interchange. →

B

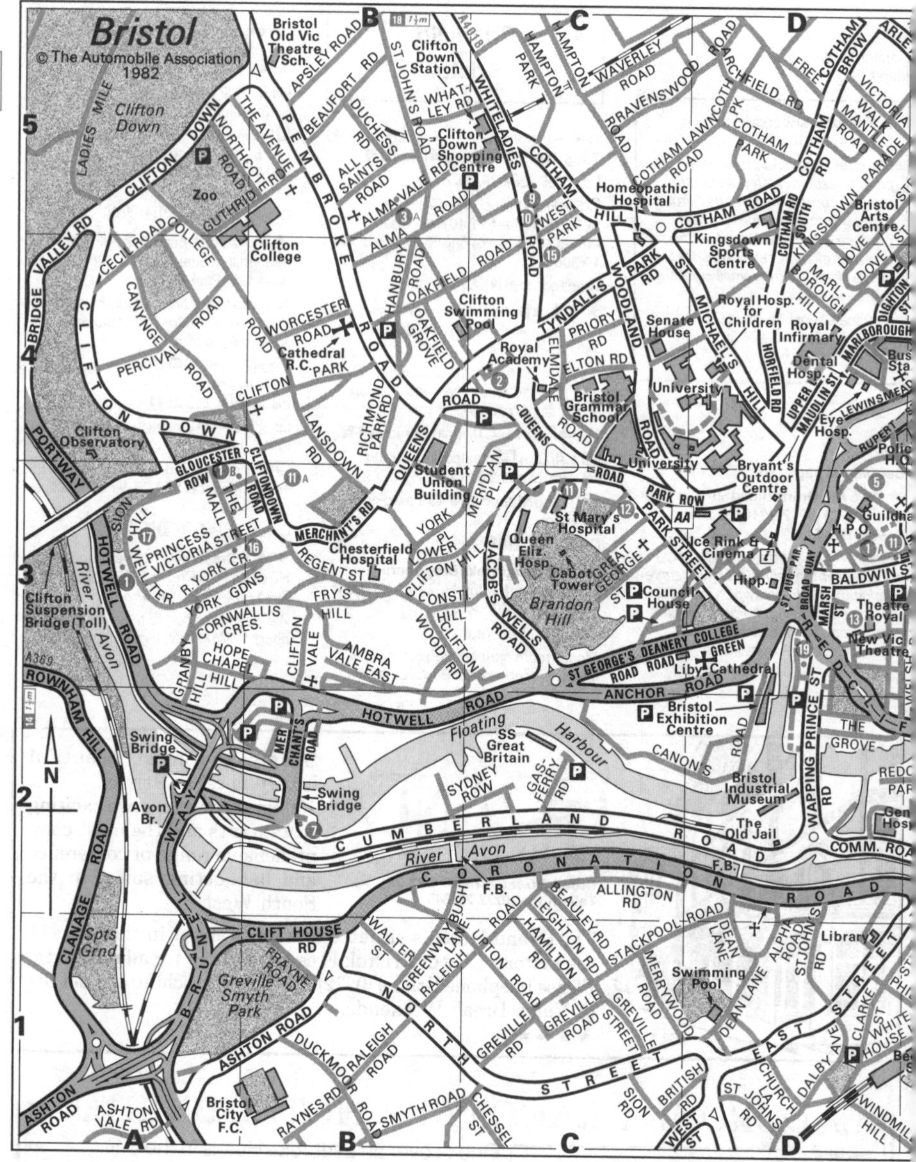

151⇔⋒✗ in 22 bedrooms CTV in all bedrooms ®T S% sB⇔⋒£57—£58.50 dB⇔⋒£67—£68.50 (room only) Ⓑ

Lift ☾ 300P CFA ❀ ▭ (heated) snooker sauna bath solarium gymnasium *xmas*

V ♀ ☕ S% Lunch fr£12.25&alc Tea fr£1.25 Dinner fr£12.25&alc Wine £6.50 Last dinner 9.45pm

Credit cards 1 2 3 4 5

See advertisement on page 172

★★★*B* **Grange** Northwoods, Winterbourne (3m N of M32 junction 1 along B4427)
(For full entry see Winterbourne)

See advertisement on page 172

★★★**Redwood Lodge** Beggar Bush Ln, Failand (2m W of Clifton Bridge on B3129) (Whitbread) ☎ (0272) 393901 Telex no 444348 Plan **14** *A2*

The comfortable new hotel on the outskirts of the city is well-placed for access to motorways. It offers extensive sports and leisure facilities, together with an attractive new restaurant and bar complex.

Annexe: 72⇔ (4fb) CTV in all bedrooms ® T ✗ sB&B⇔£45 dB&B⇔£54 Ⓑ

☾ 1000P CFA ❀ ▭ & ⛆ (heated) ⚲ (hard) squash snooker sauna bath solarium gymnasium badminton cinema (wknds only) Disco Wed & Sat Live music and dancing Thu & Fri *xmas*

B

Bristol

1	Avon Gorge ★★★
1A	Barbizon XX
1B	Bouboulina's X
2	Hotel Clifton ★★
3	Crest ★★★
3A	Edwards X
4	Ganges X
5	Grand ★★★★
6	Holiday Inn ★★★★
7	Howards X
8	Ladbroke Dragonara ★★★★
9	Malacca X
10	Mandarin X
11	Marco's XX
11A	Michel's Brasserie X
11B	Restaurant Danton XX
12	Rajdoot XX
13	Raj Tandoori X
14	Redwood Lodge ★★★
15	Restaurant du Gourmet XX
16	Rossi's Restauranti X
17	St Vincent's Rocks ★★★
18	Les Semailles ❀XX
19	Unicorn ★★★

English & French V ♁ ☕ ⊬ Lunch £7 Tea £1.50 Dinner £11 Wine £5.95 Last dinner 10pm

Credit cards 1 2 3 5

★★★**St Vincent's Rocks** Sion Hill, Clifton (Anchor) ☎ (0272) 739251 Telex no 444932 Plan **17** *A3*

Housed in a fine example of Regency architecture, this comfortable, friendly hotel looks directly onto Brunel's famous Suspension Bridge and the convivial Bridge Restaurant itself makes a pleasant location for lunch or dinner.

46rm(39➡7⋔)(3fb) ⊬ in 5 bedrooms CTV in all bedrooms ®T ✱sB&B➡⋔£44 dB&B➡⋔r£54 B

☾CTV 18P CFA

V ♁ ✱Lunch fr£8.95&alc Tea fr45p High Tea fr£4 Dinner fr£8.95 Last dinner 10pm

Credit cards 1 2 3 4 5 Ⓥ

★★★**Unicorn** Prince St (Rank) ☎ (0272) 28055 Telex no 44315 Plan **19** *D3*

Modern city centre hotel with its own multi-storey car park.

194➡⋔(29fb) CTV in all bedrooms ®T S% sB➡⋔£38.50—£44.75 dB➡⋔£52.50 (room only) B

Lift ☾ CFA *xmas*

International V ♁ ☕ S% Lunch £6.50—£6.75&alc Tea £2.75—£3.50 High Tea £2.75—£3.50 Dinner £8.95—£9.25&alc Wine £5.75 Last dinner 10pm

Credit cards 1 2 3 4 5 Ⓥ

★★**Hotel Clifton** St Pauls Rd ☎ (0272) 736882 Telex no 449075 Plan **2** *C4*

Close to city centre and University. Compact modern bedrooms, attractive "Racks" cocktail bar and restaurant on lower ground floor.

64rm(4➡36⋔) ®T S% sB&B£20 sB&B➡⋔£23.50 dB&B£29.50 dB&B➡⋔£34 B

Lift ☾ 12P

V S% Lunch £7—£8&alc Dinner £8alc Wine £4.95 Last dinner 10pm

Credit cards 1 2 3 5 Ⓥ

XX **Barbizon** 43—45 Corn St ☎ (0272) 22658 Plan **1A** *D3*

This stylish addition to Bristol's restaurants stands at the heart of the city and provides classical surroundings with its marble floor, scrolled ceilings and quality appointments. Imaginative menus are matched by friendly, conscientious service.

Closed Sun Lunch not served Sat

French V 45 seats Lunch £8.90&alc Dinner £8.90&alc Wine £5.50 Last dinner 10.45pm P (evening only)

Credit cards 1 2 3 5

XX **Restaurant Danton** 2 Upper Byron Place, The Triangle, Clifton ☎ (0272) 28314 Plan **11B** *C3*

A restaurant in the intimate tradition, the Danton provides attentive yet unobtrusive service and a French cuisine based on fresh ingredients of the best quality.

Closed Sun, 1 wk Etr & 1 wk fr Aug Bank Hol Lunch not served Sat Dinner not served Tue

French 26 seats Lunch £6—£12&alc Dinner £20alc Wine £5.50 Last dinner 11pm ₱

Credit cards 1 2 3 5 Ⓥ

XX **Restaurant du Gourmet** 43 Whiteladies Rd ☎ (0272) 736230 Plan **15** *C4*

Always a firm favourite, this convivial restaurant with personal service and an interesting range of French cuisine provides a pleasant and relaxed atmosphere.

Closed Sun, Mon & 24 Dec—1 Jan Lunch not served Sat →

🍴French **V** 75 seats Lunch £15—£20alc Dinner £15—£20alc Wine £4.95 Last dinner 11.15pm

Credit cards 1 2 3 4 5

XX Marco's 59 Baldwin St ☎ (0272) 24869 Plan **11** *D3*

Welcoming Italian restaurant with smart attentive service offering very good cooking.

Closed Sun Lunch not served Sat

🍴French & Italian **V** 80 seats Lunch £13.15alc Dinner £13.15alc Wine £4.95 Last dinner 11.15pm 🅿

Credit cards 1 2 3 5

XX Rajdoot 83 Park St ☎ (0272) 28033 Plan **12** *C3*

Atmospheric Indian restaurant with traditionally dressed staff and offering good Tandoori cooking.

Closed 25 & 26 Dec Lunch not served Sun & Public hols

🍴Indian (Punjabi) **V** 56 seats Lunch £5—£11.50&alc Dinner £9.50—£11.50&alc Wine £5.90 Last dinner 11.30pm 🅿

Credit cards 1 2 3 4 5

Bristol

❀**XX Les Semailles** 9 Druid Hill, Stoke Bishop (2m NW) ☎ (0272) 686456 Plan **18** *B5*

René Gaté and his wife Jillian continue to run this restaurant successfully, offering an interesting menu cooked in the modern style, using excellent new materials, some bought from France. Some inconsistency in standards, though, has resulted in the loss of a rosette.

Sun, Mon, Xmas Bank Hols & last 2wks Jul

🍴French 24 seats ✱Lunch £8.30—£10&alc Dinner £16alc Wine £5.90 Last dinner 10pm 🅿

Credit cards 1 3

X Bouboulina's 9 Portland St, Clifton ☎ (0272) 731192 Plan **1B** *A3*

Friendly, family-run restaurant with authentic Greek cooking and special evenings.

Closed Sun 25, 26 Dec & 1 Jan

🍴Cypriot & Greek **V** 55 seats Lunch £7.50alc Dinner £9.50—£11.95&alc Wine £4.95 Last dinner 11.30pm ⚡ Live music mthly

Credit cards 1 2 3 5 Ⓥ

X Edwards 24 Alma Vale Rd, Clifton ☎ (0272) 741533 Plan **3A** *B5*

Compact, personally run bistro, promoting imaginative and interesting dishes.

Closed Sun Lunch not served Sat

🍴International **V** 36 seats Lunch £9alc Dinner £9alc Wine £4 Last dinner 10.30pm 🅿 ⚡

Credit card 3

X Ganges 368 Gloucester Rd, Horfield ☎ (0272) 45234 Plan **4** *E5*

Well-cooked Indian dishes are accompanied by friendly service at this brightly-decorated, intimate restaurant, and its appeal seems universal.

🍴Indian **V** 52 seats S% Lunch £4—£8&alc Dinner £5—£15&alc Wine £4.60 Last dinner 11.30pm 🅿

Credit cards 1 2 3 5

X Howard's 1a Avon Cres, Hotwells ☎ (0272) 22921 Plan **7** *B2*

Near to the River Avon and to Bristol's floating harbour, this informal bistro is a perennial favourite. The keenly-priced, quality menu, simple but genial surroundings and pleasantly informal

service make eating there an enjoyable experience.

Closed Sun, Mon, 1 wk Xmas & 2 wks summer Lunch not served

English & French **V** 65 seats Dinner £12alc Wine £4.95 Last dinner 11pm Live music Sat

✕ **Malacca** 87 Whiteladies Rd ☎ (0272) 738930 Plan **9** *C5*

There is a relaxed, free and easy atmosphere in this little Malaysian restaurant, conveniently positioned close to the university and business area. The cooking is authentic and there is a garden, small but pleasant, at the back where meals can be eaten in the summer.

Closed Sun Lunch not served Sat

Malaysian **V** 60 seats Lunch £2—£6 Dinner £4—£7.50 Wine £3.45 Last dinner 11pm

S% Credit cards 1 2 Ⓥ

✕ **Mandarin** 81 Whiteladies Rd, Clifton ☎ (0272) 735095 Plan **10** *C5*

Cantonese & Pekinese **V** 65 seats Lunch £5—£18&alc Dinner £5—£18&alc Wine £4.20 Last dinner 11.30pm

Credit cards 2 3

✕ **Michel's Brasserie** 10 The Mall, Clifton ☎ (0272) 741386 Plan **11A** A3

Just like a French regional restaurant, this attractive bistro offers commendably good food plus value for money.

French 70 seats Lunch £6.45—£11.95&alc Dinner £11.95&alc Wine £5.60 Last dinner 11pm nc 10yrs (ex Sun lunch)

Credit cards 1 2 3

B

✕ **Raj Tandoori** 35 King St ☎ (0272) 291132 Plan **13** *D3*

Cosily tucked away under Bristol's famous King Street and adjacent to the Old Vic Theatre, this cellar restaurant promotes interesting Indian cuisine and in particular caters for the ethnic vegetarian.

English & Indian **V** 85 seats S% Lunch fr£3 Dinner fr£7.50&alc Wine £3.80 Last dinner mdnt

Credit cards [1] [2] [3] [5]

✕ ***Rossi's Restauranti*** 35 Princess Victoria St ☎ (0272) 730049 Plan **16** *B3*

This well-appointed restaurant stands in the heart of fashionable Clifton Village, close to the antique market. Its quality of food and service standards make it popular with the business community, and there is a comfortable, first-floor lounge for private use.

Closed Sun, Bank Hols & 2 wks mid Aug Lunch not served Sat

International **V** 45 seats Last dinner 11.30pm

Credit cards [1] [2] [3] [5]

✕ **Rupali Tandoori** 307 Two Mile Hill Rd, Kingswood (3m E off A420) ☎ (0272) 673366 Not on plan

This modestly-appointed eating establishment lays firm emphasis on good, authentic Indian cuisine and appears to attract a following with both businessmen and private clients.

Bengali **V** 36 seats S% Lunch fr£7 Wine £3.80 Last dinner 11pm P

Credit cards [1] [2] [3] [5]

BRIXHAM

Devon
Map **3** SX95

★★★ **Quayside** King St (Inter Hotel) ☎ (08045) 55751 Telex no 42962

Modernised old quayside inn overlooking the harbour, catering for both tourist and commercial trade.

32rm(22→3⋒)(6fb)2 CTV in all bedrooms Ⓡ **T** sB&B£24—£27 sB&B→⋒£30—£38 dB&B£36—£42 dB&B→⋒£48—£64 **B**

37P Live music and dancing 3 nights wkly *xmas*

Bristol — Broadstairs

English, French & German **V** Lunch £6.50—£8.50&alc Tea £2.50&alc Dinner £11—£17&alc Wine £5.75 Last dinner 9.30pm

Credit cards [1] [2] [3] [5] Ⓥ

★ **Smugglers Haunt** Church St ☎ (08045) 3050

A 400-year-old stone-built inn situated next to Brixham harbour.

14rm(4→)(2fb) Ⓡ sB&Bfr£15 sB&B→fr£17 dB&Bfr£24 dB&B→fr£27.25

CTV 6P

V Lunch £3—£4&alc Dinner fr£8&alc Wine £4.75 Last dinner 9.45pm

Credit cards [1] [2] [3]

✕ **Elizabethan** 8 Middle St ☎ (08045) 3722

Near the harbour the bow windows and continental awning of the Elizabethan make it stand out from the surrounding shops. The cosy interior is in the Tudor style and the menu offers traditional dishes based on local produce; the service is friendly and attentive.

Closed Mon Dinner not served Sun, Tue & Nov—Apr

European 30 seats Lunch £4.30—£5.75&alc Dinner £9.50alc Wine £5 Last dinner 9.30pm

Credit cards [2] [5]

BROADFORD

Isle of Skye, Highland *Inverness-shire*
See **Skye, Isle of**

BROADSTAIRS

Kent
Map **5** TR36

★★★ **Castle Keep** Kingsgate ☎ Thanet (0843) 65222

The superb, cliff-top setting of the hotel gives uninterrupted views across the sandy bay to the sea. The newly-refurbished restaurant offers à la carte and set menus featuring English and continental dishes, while the interesting wine list is reasonably priced. Bedrooms and public areas all reflect a certain comfort.

30rm(29→⋒)(6fb) CTV in all bedrooms Ⓡ sB&B£31—£36.50 sB&B→⋒£31—£36.50 dB&B£38—£43 dB&B→⋒£38—£43 **B**

CTV 100P (heated) *xmas*

English, French & Italian **V** Lunch £7.70&alc Tea £2.75 Dinner £8.25&alc Wine £5.50 Last dinner 10pm

Credit cards [1] [2] [3] [5] Ⓥ

★★ **Castlemere** Western Esp ☎ Thanet (0843) 61566

This comfortable, well-managed hotel enjoys a quiet situation facing the sea. The bedrooms, plainly decorated but well equipped, vary in size and there is a pleasantly old-fashioned feel to this very clean establishment.

37rm(26→4⋒)(5fb)2 CTV in all bedrooms Ⓡ **T** S% sB&B£18.60—£20.60 sB&B→⋒£22.10—£24.10 dB&B£35—£38 dB&B→⋒£41—£49 **B**

CTV 30P 2 (charge) *xmas*

English & French S% Bar lunch £3.30alc Dinner £8—£9.50 Wine £4.70 Last dinner 7.45pm

Credit cards [1] [3] Ⓥ

★★ **Royal Albion** Albion St ☎ Thanet (0843) 68071 Telex no 965761

19rm(17→2⋒)(3fb) CTV in all bedrooms Ⓡ **T** ✱ sB&B→⋒£32—£36 dB&B→⋒£42—£48 **B**

CTV 10P 5 (£2.50 per night) *xmas*

French **V** S% Lunch £7.50—£10&alc Dinner £10—£16&alc Wine £5 Last dinner 9.30pm

Credit cards [1] [2] [3] [4] [5]

BROADWAY
Hereford & Worcester
Map **4** SP03
See also Buckland

★★★★ **Lygon Arms**
(see red star box on next page)

★★★ **Broadway** The Green ☏ (0386) 852401
A 16th-century coaching house with modern extensions.
12rm(11⇌1⋒)
Annexe: 12rm(10⇌2⋒)(2fb) 1⊟ TV in 2 bedrooms CTV in 22 bedrooms ® T ✂ S% sB&B⇌⋒£24—£28 dB&B⇌⋒£26—£56 ₿

Broadway

30P(charge) ⊟ ✿ *xmas*
English & French ☐ ✱ Lunch fr£6.95 Tea £1—£2.50 Dinner fr£10.95&alc Wine £4.75 Last dinner 9.15pm
Credit cards 1 2 3 5

★★★*HB* **Dormy House** Willersey Hill (2m E off A44 in Gloucestershire) ☏ (0386) 852711 Telex no 338275
A former 17th-century farmhouse offering comfortable accommodation in a traditional Cotswold setting.
25⇌⋒ Annexe: 23⇌⋒(3fb) 2⊟ CTV in all bedrooms T ✂ sB&B⇌⋒£45—£55 dB&B⇌⋒£79—£90 ₿
☾ 80P CFA ✿ ⚲(hard) *xmas*
English & French V ☐ Lunch fr£12&alc Tea fr£1.75 High Tea fr£6 Dinner fr£18&alc Wine £7.50 Last dinner 9.45pm
Credit cards 1 2 3 5
See advertisement on page 176

B

★★★★

★★★★ **LYGON ARMS, BROADWAY**

(Relais et Châteaux/Prestige)
☎ (0386) 852255 Telex no 338260

This rambling inn personifies the image of England beloved by tourists and travellers, and it continues to be a major stopping place in journeys now just as it was in the 16th century. Improvements have continued over the past years and, since last year, all the bedrooms have been completely refurbished. Perhaps it is the wide variety of styles that so endears this building to its visitors who can choose to sit in comfortable lounges surrounded by the heavy timbers, huge chimney pieces and the trappings of the early period of the inn, or the more ornate and softer lines of the first floor writing room, or the Russell Room, where another of those British institutions, 'afternoon tea' is served to residents; non-residents can obtain the same standard of service in the Wine Bar just alongside the old coaching entrance. We have recently been receiving more consistent reports about the high quality of meals, and the improvement is undoubtedly due to the skill of the new Chef, Alain Dubois, whose sauces complement the carefully chosen produce so well. Reflecting British dishes as well as some in the modern style, a wider range of fish dishes is also featured. So far we have found his

main courses better than the first course and puddings, and an improvement here might well gain him a rosette. At the time of going to press, we learn that the hotel is under new ownership. We are confident that the high standards which pertain here will be maintained.

64rm(61 ⬛ ⬛)(9fb) 5 ⬛ CTV in all bedrooms **T** ✱sB&B£55—£75 sB&B ⬛ ⬛ £55—£75 dB&Bfr£85 dB&B ⬛ ⬛ £95—£105 Continental breakfast ⬛

☾CTV 150P 6 ⬛ (£5) CFA ⬛ ✿ ⬛ (hard) ⬛ *xmas*

⬛ English & French **V** ⬛ ✱Lunch £13.50&alc Tea £4.25 Dinner £19.50&alc Wine £6.75 Last dinner 9.15pm

Credit cards 1 2 3 5

★★ ⬛ *H* **Collin House** Collin Ln
☎ (0386) 858354

Closed 24, 25 & 26 Dec

Small, well restored 16th century hotel in spacious gardens, offering good food and relaxation.

7rm(5 ⬛ 1 ⬛) 2 ⬛ CTV available in bedrooms ® ⬛ sB&B£30 dB&B ⬛ ⬛ £55—£63 ⬛

CTV 32P ✿ ⬛ nc6yrs

V Bar lunch £4.50alc Dinner £11.50alc Wine £5 Last dinner 9pm

Credit cards 1 3

✕✕✕ **Hunter's Lodge** High St
☎ (0386) 853247

Almost in the centre of this picturesque village, the restaurant is a good example of the attractive 16th century Cotswold architecture. Inside, the atmosphere is intimate, with open fires, exposed beams and candlelight in the evenings. The dishes produced under the personal supervision of a Swiss chef/patron are mainly those of the French countryside and they make good use of local produce.

Closed Mon 1st 2wks Feb & 1st 2wks Aug
Dinner not served Sun

⬛ English & French **V** 50 seats ✱Lunch fr£7&alc Dinner £13—£20alc Wine £5.25 Last dinner 9.30pm 20P nc 8yrs (Dinner) Live music mthly

S% Credit cards 1 2 3 5

BROCKDISH
Norfolk
Map **5** TM27

✿✕✕ **Sheriff House** ☎ Hoxne (037975) 316

Set close to the main road, this cottage restaurant is run in a most professional manner by the Pichel-Juan family. Guests can order in advance, although a more limited menu is available to the chance caller, and there is an extensive wine list.

Closed Wed

24 seats ✱Lunch fr£7alc Dinner fr£7alc Wine £4.77 Last dinner 9.30pm P nc 14yrs

Credit cards 1 3

BROCKENHURST
Hampshire
Map **4** SU20

★★★ **Carey's Manor** Lyndhurst Rd
☎ Lymington (0590) 23551
Telex no 47442

Comfortable hotel with modern bedrooms and popular 'Jugged hare' bar.

57 ⬛ ⬛ 2 ⬛ ⬛ in 10 bedrooms CTV in all bedrooms ® **T** ✱sB&B ⬛ ⬛ fr£43.95 dB&B ⬛ ⬛ fr£63.90 ⬛

☾300P ⬛ ✿ ⬛ (heated) sauna bath solarium gymnasium Live music & dancing Fri & Sat *xmas*

⬛ English & French **V** ⬛ ✱Lunch £6.75—£8.75&alc Tea 75p High Tea £4.95—£6.95 Dinner £11.75&alc Wine £5.95 Last dinner 10pm

Credit cards 1 2 3 5

★★★**Ladbroke Balmer Lawn** Lyndhurst Rd (Ladbroke) ☎ Lymington (0590) 23116 Telex no 477649

Large imposing hotel with good facilities, located on the edge of the New Forest.

58rm(54→4⋔)(7fb) CTV in all bedrooms ®T sB&B→⋔£41.50 dB&B→⋔£60 B

Lift ☾ 90P CFA ✿ & (heated) (hard) squash sauna bath solarium gymnasium Live music & dancing Sat *xmas*

V ☕ Lunch £7.50 Tea £1.50 High Tea £1.50 Dinner £10&alc Wine £5.99 Last dinner 9.30pm

Credit cards 1 2 3 5 V

Brockenhurst

★★**Watersplash** The Rise ☎ Lymington (0590) 22344

Set in pleasant gardens and offering good accommodation with comfortable modern furnishings.

26rm (18→2⋔)(6fb) 1 CTV in 9 bedrooms sB&B£22—£24 sB&B→⋔£26—£28 dB&B£40—£44 dB&B→⋔£44—£46 B

CTV 25P 4 (charge) ✿ (heated) ♿ *xmas*

V ☕ Lunch £4.50—£8.50 Tea 80p—£1.50 High Tea £2—£4 Dinner £10.95—£16.95 Wine £5.50 Last dinner 8pm

Credit cards 1 3 V

★★**Whitley Ridge Restaurant & Country House** Beaulieu Rd ☎ Lymington (0590) 22354

Closed 2—30 Jan

Beautifully situated in the New Forest, this welcoming, family-run hotel has been refurbished to a very high standard throughout. →

B

15rm(2 6)(2fb)1 CTV in 8 bedrooms ® in 8 bedrooms S% sB&B£29 sB&B £35—£41 dB&B£43 dB&B £49—£65

CTV 20P (hard) *xmas*

European **V** Dinner £10.50&alc Wine £5.50 Last dinner 8.15pm

Credit cards 1 2 3 5 Ⓥ

★***Cloud*** Meerut Rd Lymington (0590) 22165

Closed 1st 2wks Jan

A small, family-run hotel, the Cloud offers accommodation in modest bedrooms, good plain meals in the restaurant and traditional afternoon tea served in two cosy sitting rooms.

19rm(3fb)

CTV 20P

Last dinner 8pm

✕✕Le Poussin 57-59 Brookley Rd Lymington (0590) 23063 (*Rosette awarded for dinner only*)

Closed Sun Lunch not served Mon

Patrons Alex and Caroline Aitken have brought West End standards of cuisine to this popular area of the New Forest. Their particular flair with a fixed price Gourmet menu is commendable and the attractive decor blends elegantly with the unobtrusive, attentive service.

French **V** 35 seats Lunch fr£8.95&alc Dinner £14.95—£16.95&alc Wine £5.95 Last dinner 10.30pm 5 bedrooms available

Credit cards 1 3 4

BROME
Suffolk
Map **5** TM17

★★***Brome Grange Motel*** (on A140) Eye (0379) 870456

Cottage-style roadside inn that has been converted from a farmhouse; modest rooms have been built in the courtyard.

Annexe: 22rm(20 2) CTV in all bedrooms ®**T**

100P *xmas*

English & Continental **V** Last dinner 9.30pm

Credit cards 1 2 3 5

★★*BL* **Oaksmere** Eye (0379) 870326

Enchanting Tudor/Victorian country house in 20 acres of parkland with fine gardens.

5rm(1 4) 1 CTV in all bedrooms ® *sB&B £29.50 dB&B £45—£49.50

50P

V Lunch £7.95&alc Dinner £7.95&alc Wine £5.75 Last dinner 10pm

Credit cards 1 2 3 5 Ⓥ

BROMLEY
Gt London
London plan **5** *F2* (page 447)

★★★**Bromley Court** Bromley Hill (Consort) 01-464 5011 Telex no 896310

Modernised commercial hotel with informal atmosphere and good lounges.

130 (4fb) CTV in all bedrooms ®**T** sB&B fr£42 dB&B fr£57

Lift CTV 130P CFA Live music & dancing Sat *xmas*

English, French & Italian **V** Lunch fr£8&alc Tea fr75p Dinner fr£9&alc Wine £6.25 Last dinner 9.45pm

Credit cards 1 2 3 4 5 Ⓥ

✕**Capisano's** 9 Simpson's Rd 01-464 8036

The typical Italian decor matches the good cooking and friendly hospitality.

Closed Sun, Mon & 3 wks Aug

Italian 65 seats Lunch fr£7&alc Dinner £12—£15alc Wine £5 Last dinner 11pm 10P

Credit cards 1 2 3 4

BROMPTON-BY-SAWDON
North Yorkshire
Map **8** SE98

✕**Brompton Forge** Scarborough (0723) 85409 (*Rosette awarded for dinner only*)

Once a blacksmith's forge, the picturesque restaurant stands beside the A170 not far from Scarborough. Attractively presented and generously served dishes from the table d'hôte menu make good use of fish and seafood in such specialities as salmon en croute with ginger butter and (for an extra charge) fresh lobster thermidor, but meat, poultry and game also represent good value, and the interesting wine list is well-chosen.

Closed Mon & 2 wks Feb Lunch not served Tue, Fri & Sat Dinner not served Sun

English & French **V** 70 seats *Lunch £7.50—£8&alc Dinner £11—£12.50&alc Wine £6 Last dinner 9pm 20P

BROMSGROVE
Hereford & Worcester
Map **7** SO97

★★★**Perry Hall** Kidderminster Rd. (Embassy) (0527) 31976 Due to change to 579976

A former home of poet A E Houseman, the hotel has added modern extensions. It is popular with businessmen.

55rm(38 17) CTV in all bedrooms ®**T** *sB fr£43 dB fr£57(room only)

140P CFA *xmas*

English & French *Lunch £6.25—£7.50&alc Dinner £6.25—£7.50&alc Wine £4.45 Last dinner 9.45pm

Credit cards 1 2 3 4 5

See advertisement under Birmingham

★★★**Pine Lodge** Kidderminster Rd (0527) 33033 Telex no 335072

Modern hotel in a country setting with comfortable bedrooms and reasonably priced carvery.

59rm(55⇀4⋔)(2fb)2⊞CTV in all bedrooms ®T S% sB&B⇀⋔fr£33 dB&B⇀⋔£45—£60 ⊟

CTV 300P ✽ ⌓ (heated) sauna bath solarium Disco Tue Sun

♉English & Italian ♈ ⊐ Lunch £6—£8&alc Tea £1.50 Dinner £6—£8&alc Wine £5 Last dinner 9.30pm

Credit cards 1 3 Ⓥ

❀XXX**Grafton Manor** Grafton Ln (Pride of Britain)
☎(0527) 31525

Down a long, bumpy lane, the reward is a grand manor house, once owned by the Earls of Shrewsbury, where you can dine in style. Dinner is a set price, five course meal with French country style cooking. Many unusual ingredients have their flavour enhanced by herbs from the extensive gardens. Some lovely bedrooms are available.

Lunch not served Mon—Sat

♉International 45 seats ✱Lunch £12.75 Dinner £18 Wine £6.25 Last dinner 9pm 50P nc7yrs

Credit cards 1 2 3 5

BROMYARD
Hereford & Worcester
Map **3** SO65

X**Old Penny** High St ☎(0885) 83227

Deriving its name from a mounted collection of old pennies on display there, this popular small restaurant offers value-for-money meals both at lunchtime and in the evening. The cuisine is predominantly English, with fresh vegetables and home-made sweets. Service is friendly and attentive.

Closed Mon & Tue 1st wk May & 2 wks Nov Dinner not served Sun

34 seats ✱Lunch £5.50—£6.50 Dinner £11 Wine £4 Last dinner 9pm ₱

Credit cards 1 2 3 Ⓥ

BROOK (near Cadnam)
Hampshire
Map **4** SU21

★★***Bell Inn*** ☎ Southampton (0703) 812214

Pleasant inn adjoining two golf courses on the edge of the New Forest.

12rm(8⇀) CTV in all bedrooms ®

150P ⊞ ✽ ▶18

♈ Last dinner 9.30pm

Credit cards 1 2 3 5

BRORA
Highland *Sutherland*
Map **14** NC90

★★★**Links** Golf Rd (Best Western)
☎(0408) 21225 Telex no 75242

Comfortable, friendly, recently renovated hotel beside the golf course.

26rm(23⇀)(4fb) CTV in all bedrooms ® available in bedrooms **T** sB&B£24—£30 sB&B⇀£24—£30 dB&B£41—£55 dB&B⇀£41—£55 ⊟

CTV 55P ✽

V ♈ ⊐ ⚡ Lunch £4—£11 Tea £1 Dinner £11—£12.50 Wine £4.50 Last dinner 9pm

Credit cards 1 2 3 5 Ⓥ

★★**Royal Marine** Golf Rd ☎(0408) 21252

The public rooms of this hotel still retain the atmosphere of its days as a stately home.

12rm(10⇀1⋔)(1fb) 1⊞ CTV in 5 bedrooms ®**T** sB&B⇀⋔£20—£28 dB&B⇀⋔£40—£50 ⊟

CTV 30P 6⌂(£2.50) ✽ ⊡(heated) ⅃ snooker gymnasium putting badminton pool table table tennis ⌂ *xmas*

♉Scottish & French **V** ♈ ⊐ Lunch £6.50—£8 Tea 85p High Tea £5—£8.50 Dinner £11—£14&alc Wine £5 Last dinner 9.30pm

Credit cards 1 2 3 5 Ⓥ

BROUGHTON-IN-FURNESS
Cumbria
Map **7** SD28

★★**Eccle Riggs** Foxfield Rd (Exec Hotel)
☎(06576) 398

A Victorian, stone-built house in gardens and woodland.

13rm(10⇀)(5fb) CTV in all bedrooms ® ✗ ✱sB&B£18 sB&B⇀£25 dB&Bfr£34 dB&B⇀£42 ⊟

120P ✽ ⊡(heated) ⅃ sauna bath solarium bowls ⌂ *xmas*

V ♈ Last dinner 8.30pm

Credit cards 1 2 3 5

★***Old King's Head*** Station Rd
☎(06576) 293

Old white-washed village inn.

9rm(3fb) CTV in all bedrooms ®

50P 6⌂

♈ Last dinner 7.30pm

BROXTED
Essex
Map **5** TL52

XXX**Whitehall** Church End (Pride of Britain)
☎ Bishops Stortford (0279) 850603

A delightful 12th century manor house in peaceful rural surroundings, the Whitehall offers a short à la carte menu of distinction, backed by quietly attentive service, in the relaxed atmosphere of its beamed restaurant. Four charming bedrooms are available for overnight guests.

Closed Mon & 2—20 Jan

♉French **V** 40 seats Lunch fr£13.50 Dinner fr£23.50 Wine £7.50 Last dinner 9.30pm P4 bedrooms available nc 5yrs

Credit cards 1 2 3

BROXTON
Cheshire
Map **7** SJ45

★★**Broxton Hall** Tottenhall ☎(082925) 321

A seventeenth-century black and white building is now a well-furnished and comfortable hotel run by the resident owners. →

11🛁(1fb)CTV in all bedrooms ®T
*sB&B🛁£30—£35 dB&B🛁£45—£50 B
50P ✿ xmas
🍷International ☕ Lunch £7.50 Dinner £9.50&alc Wine £5.50 Last dinner 9.30pm
Credit cards 1 2 3

BRUTON
Somerset
Map **3** ST63

✕Clogs 95 High St ☎ (0749) 812255

A medium-priced à la carte menu based on local produce and fish cooked in Dutch or Indonesian style is available in this pretty cottage restaurant.

Closed Sun, Lunch not served
🍷Dutch & Indonesian 20 seats Dinner £13alc Wine £6 Last dinner 10pm P nc 5yrs

BUCKDEN
Cambridgeshire
Map **4** TL16

★★**George** High St ☎ Huntingdon (0480) 810307 Telex no 32394

16th century coaching inn with small garden.

10rm(5🛁1🚿)(2fb) 1 CTV in all bedrooms ®T S% sB&B£22—£29 sB&B🛁🚿£31—£35 dB&B£32—£37 dB&B🛁🚿£37—£42 B
50P 3 ✿ xmas
🍷English & French **V** ☕ S% Lunch £7.25&alc Tea £1 Dinner £7.95&alc Wine £5.25 Last dinner 9.30pm
Credit cards 1 2 3 5 Ⓥ

BUCKDEN
North Yorkshire
Map **7** SD97

★**Buck Inn** ☎ Kettlewell (075676) 227

Charming Dales inn set amid beautiful scenery offering warm, friendly welcome.

10rm(2🛁1🚿)(2fb) TV in 6 bedrooms CTV in 4 bedrooms ® sB&B£11—£16 dB&B£22—£32 dB&B🛁🚿£30—£36 B
CTV 40P xmas
V ☕ Bar lunch £5alc Dinner £10alc Wine £4.15 Last dinner 9.30pm
Credit cards 1 2 3 5

BUCKFASTLEIGH
Devon
Map **3** SX76

★**Bossell House** Plymouth Rd ☎ (0364) 43294

Comfortable family holiday hotel with country house atmosphere.

11rm(1🛁4🚿)(2fb) CTV in all bedrooms ® **T** S% sB&B£14.50 sB&B🛁🚿£16.50 dB&B£29 dB&B🛁🚿£31 B
30P ✿ ⚲(hard) pool table ♿ xmas
🍷English & French **V** ☕ S% Lunch £7.95 Tea 70p Dinner £7.95&alc Wine £4.95 Last dinner 8pm
Credit cards 1 3

BUCKHURST HILL
Essex
London plan **5** *F5* (page 447)

★★**Roebuck** North End (Trusthouse Forte) ☎ 01-505 4636

Standing beside Epping Forest, the hotel contains small, elegant public rooms and well-equipped bedrooms.

23🛁 CTV in all bedrooms ®T sB&B🛁£48.50 dB&B🛁£64.50 B
45P xmas
☕ Last dinner 9.30pm
Credit cards 1 2 3 4 5

BUCKIE
Grampian *Banffshire*
Map **15** NJ46

★★**Cluny** High St ☎ (0542) 32922

Closed 1 & 2 Jan RS Jan & Dec

Victorian building on a corner site in the main square with views out to sea.

10rm(8🛁2🚿)(1fb) TV in all bedrooms ® *sB&B£10.50—£13.50 sB&B🛁🚿£13.50—£19.50 dB&B🛁🚿£27—£33 B
16P
🍷Scottish & French ☕ *Lunch £4.25 Tea 70p High Tea £3.50—£6&alc Dinner £7.50alc Wine £4 Last dinner 8.45pm
Credit cards 1 2 3 5 Ⓥ

★★**St Andrews** St Andrews Sq ☎ (0542) 31227

The small, simply-furnished hotel just outside the centre of this Moray Coast fishing town attracts both commercial and tourist trade.

12rm(3🛁1🚿)(2fb) CTV in all bedrooms ® S% sB&B£17 sB&B🛁🚿£20 dB&B£27 dB&B🛁🚿£30.50 B
CTV P
V ☕ S% Lunch fr£3.55 Tea fr£1.50 High Tea fr£4.35 Dinner fr£8.50 Wine £4.20 Last dinner 7.30pm
Credit cards 1 3

BUCKINGHAM
Buckinghamshire
Map **4** SP63

★★**White Hart** Market Sq (Trusthouse Forte) ☎ (0280) 815151

18th century traditional hotel with comfortable modernised bedrooms.

19rm(18🛁1🚿) CTV in all bedrooms ® sB&B🛁🚿£48 dB&B🛁£63.50 B
30P xmas
☕ Last dinner 10pm
Credit cards 1 2 3 4 5

BUCKLAND (near Broadway)
Gloucestershire
Map **4** SP03

★★★

❀★★★ **BUCKLAND MANOR**

☎ Broadway (0386) 852626

Closed 3—4 wks from mid Jan

This is a typical Cotswold manor house, all gables and mullioned windows, built of the golden Cotswold stone and situated in ten acres of pleasure gardens which include facilities for swimming, tennis, croquet, putting and riding; there is also a notable water garden and nut alley. Not so typical is the style in which it is run which is reminiscent of what one could have expected before 1914. Barry and Adrienne Berman are the couple who created this hotel and one that offers outstanding standards in hospitality and every other respect. Luxuriously furnished bedrooms offer every facility including fruit, flowers, Malvern Water and hairdryers. There is no bar but two sitting rooms provide ample space to relax in front of open fires when necessary. One is small but the other is a largish L-shaped room with oak strip floor and eastern carpets, stone chimney piece, oak panelling and is fresh with flowers. It is all very attractive and civilised, and conveys much of the romantic idea of a British country house. The candlelit restaurant is also beautifully furnished and appointed, and has a sound wine

list to complement the menu presented by Chef Martyn Pearn who has previously had experience at the Connaught and Claridge's. The menu is à la carte and excellent raw materials are used. The hotel is just the place to enjoy a few days break where you can feel discreetly cossetted.

11🛁(1fb) 2 CTV in all bedrooms **T** ✈ *sB&B🛁£85—£120 dB&B🛁£95—£130 B
30P ✿ (heated) ⚲(hard) U croquet putting nc 12yrs xmas
🍷International **V** ☕ *Lunch £18.50alc Dinner £18.50alc Wine £5.65 Last dinner 8.45pm
Credit cards 1 3

Buckland in the Moor — Bude

BUCKLAND IN THE MOOR
Devon
Map **3** SX77

★★ ***Buckland Hall Country House***
☎ Ashburton (0364) 52679
Comfortably-appointed, personally run hotel in a superb situation with fine views.
6rm(5🛁1🚿) CTV in all bedrooms ® ✂ ▣
20P ⊞ ✿ *xmas*
English & Continental ☕ Last dinner 8.30pm
Credit cards 1 2 3

BUCKLERS HARD
Hampshire
Map **4** SU40

★★ **Master Builders House**
☎ (059063) 253
Former home of 18th century shipbuilder, Henry Adams, this hotel overlooking the river offers warm hospitality and good home cooking.
6rm(1🛁1🚿) Annexe: 17🛁🚿 1⊞ CTV in all bedrooms ® T S% ✱sB&B£15 sB&B🛁🚿£30 dB&B£49 dB&B🛁🚿£49 ▣
45P ✿ Live music Thu *xmas*
European **V** ☕ Lunch £12alc Dinner £12alc Wine £5.30 Last dinner 9.45pm
Credit cards 1 2 3 4 5 ⓥ

BUCKLOW HILL
Cheshire
Map **7** SJ78

★★★ **Swan** (De Vere) ☎ (0565) 830295
Telex no 666911
This historic inn with modern bedroom extension is well furnished and offers extensive menu.
18🛁🚿 Annexe: 52🛁🚿(11fb) 3⊞ CTV in all bedrooms ® T S% sB&B🛁🚿£23—£49.50 dB&B🛁🚿£46—£60 ▣
☾ 200P ✿ ♿
English & French **V** ☕ S% Lunch £7.50—£8.50&alc Tea 75p Dinner £8.50—£10.75&alc Wine £4.25 Last dinner 10pm
Credit cards 1 2 3 5

BUDE
Cornwall
Map **2** SS20
See plan

★★★ **Hartland** Hartland Ter (Exec Hotel) ☎ (0288) 2509 Plan **9** *B4*
Closed mid Nov—Etr
Comfortable, family-owned hotel, occupying a favourable position, overlooking the sandy beach.
29rm(23🛁6🚿)(2fb) 3⊞ CTV in all bedrooms sB&B🛁🚿£20.70—£25.30 dB&B🛁🚿£39.10—£48.30 ▣
Lift 30P ✿ (heated) Live music and dancing 4 nights wkly *xmas*
International ☕ Lunch £6.25—£7 Tea 70p Dinner £7.25—£8.05 Wine £4.25 Last dinner 8.30pm
ⓥ

★★★ **Strand** The Strand (Trusthouse Forte) ☎ (0288) 3222 Plan **15** *C3*
Modern, well appointed commercial and family hotel by the River Neet estuary.
40rm(37🛁3🚿)(2fb) CTV in all bedrooms ®sB&B🛁🚿£39.50 dB&B🛁🚿£59.50 ▣
Lift ☾ 60P CFA
Last dinner 9pm
Credit cards 1 2 3 4 5

★★ **Grosvenor** Summerleaze Cres ☎ (0288) 2062 Plan **8** *B4*
Closed Dec & Jan
Small, terraced, comfortable hotel, 300 yards from Summerleaze Beach.
13rm(5🛁6🚿)(5fb) CTV available in bedrooms ®sB&B£12.50—£14 sB&B🛁🚿£13.50—£15 dB&B£25—£28 dB&B🛁🚿£27—£30
CTV 5P ⊞ pool table
☕ Bar lunch £1.25—£4.50 Tea fr95p Dinner £6.95 Wine £3.95 Last dinner 8pm
ⓥ

★★ **St Margaret's** Killerton Rd ☎ (0288) 2252 Plan **14** *C3*
Small comfortable hotel near town centre.
10rm(6🛁4🚿)(3fb) CTV in all bedrooms ® T S% sB&B🛁🚿£18—£22 dB&B🛁🚿£44—£46
CTV 6P ⊞ ✿ ♿ *xmas*
English & Continental **V** ☕ S% Lunch £4.25—£5.50 Tea 50p—£1.50 Dinner £6.84&alc Wine £5.25 Last dinner 8pm
Credit cards 1 3 ⓥ

★ **Bude Haven** Flexbury Av ☎ (0288) 2305 Plan **1** C5
Comfortable, privately-owned hotel in walking distance of Crooklets Beach.
11rm(4🛁3🚿)(2fb) ✂ in 11 bedrooms CTV available in bedrooms ® sB&B£11.50—£13.50 sB&B🛁🚿£13.50—£15.50 dB&B£23—£27 dB&B🛁🚿£27—£31 ▣
CTV 8P ⊞
International **V** ☕ Bar lunch £2.50 Tea 60p Dinner £6.50 Wine £4 Last dinner 7.30pm
Credit cards 1 3 ⓥ

★*L* **Camelot** Downs View Rd ☎ (0288) 2361 Plan **3** *C5*
Closed Nov—Feb
Comfortable, welcoming hotel near Crooklets Beach.
15rm(4🛁11🚿)(2fb) CTV in all bedrooms ® ✂ sB&B🛁🚿£15—£17.25 dB&B🛁🚿£30—£34.50
15P sauna bath solarium gymnasium
☕ ✂ Bar lunch £1.30—£4 Tea £1 Dinner £9 Wine £3.80 Last dinner 8pm
Credit cards 1 3 ⓥ

★ **Edgcumbe** Summerleaze Cres ☎ (0288) 3846 Plan **4** *B4*
Closed Nov—Feb
Personally run hotel specialising in family holidays.
15rm(4🚿)(8fb) ®sB&B£10.50 sB&B🚿£12.50 dB&B£20 dB&B🚿£25 ▣
CTV 10P
V Bar lunch £1.95—£3.50 Tea 40p Dinner £5.50 Wine £3.95 Last dinner 6.30pm
ⓥ

★ **Florida** 17/18 Summerleaze Cres ☎ (0288) 2451 Plan **6** *B4*
Closed Nov—Feb
Comfortable, small, terraced hotel near Summerleaze Beach and town centre.
21rm(14🚿)(6fb) ® in 20 bedrooms ✂ sB&B£11.50—£12.50 sB&B🚿£13.50—£14.50 dB&B£23—£25 dB&B🚿£27—£29 ▣
CTV 10P *xmas*
V Bar lunch £1—£2.75 Dinner £5—£6.50 Wine £3.50 Last dinner 5pm

★ **Maer Lodge** Crooklets Beach ☎ (0288) 3306 Plan **10** *B5*
Closed Nov—Feb (except Xmas)
Detached, family holiday hotel close to Crooklets Beach with fine views.
22rm(5🛁6🚿)(6fb) CTV in 8 bedrooms ® in 8 bedrooms sB&B£11—£12.50 sB&B🛁🚿£15—£16.50 dB&B£22—£25 dB&B🛁🚿£26—£29 ▣
CTV 30P ✿ pool table table tennis putting *xmas*
☕ Bar lunch 75p—£3.50 Dinner fr£6 Wine £4 Last dinner 7.30pm
Credit cards 1 2 3 5

★ **Meva Gwin** Upton ☎ (0288) 2347 Plan **11** *B1*
Closed 26 Sep—16 Apr
Family holiday hotel set midway between Bude and Widemouth Bay has glorious views of countryside and coast.
13rm(4🛁1🚿)(3fb) ® ✂ S% ✱sB&B£10—£11 sB&B🛁🚿£11.50—£13 dB&B£20—£22 dB&B🛁🚿£23—£26
CTV 44P ✿
☕ S% ✱Lunch £4.95 Tea 35p Dinner £4.95 Wine £3.50 Last dinner 7.30pm

★*L* **Penarvor** Crooklets Beach ☎ (0288) 2036 Plan **12** *B5*
Closed Nov—Feb
Owner-run hotel and restaurant only yards from Bude's famous surfing beach.
14rm(5🛁4🚿)(5fb) CTV in all bedrooms ® S% sB&B£9.80—£12.30 sB&B🛁🚿£14.70—£18.20 dB&B£19.60—£24.60 dB&B🛁🚿£29.40—£36.20 ▣
20P ✿ pool table
Bar lunch 70p—£3 Dinner £6&alc Wine £4.50 Last dinner 7.30pm
Credit cards 1 3 5 ⓥ

★ **Stamford Hill** ☎ (0288) 2709 (for full entry see Stratton)

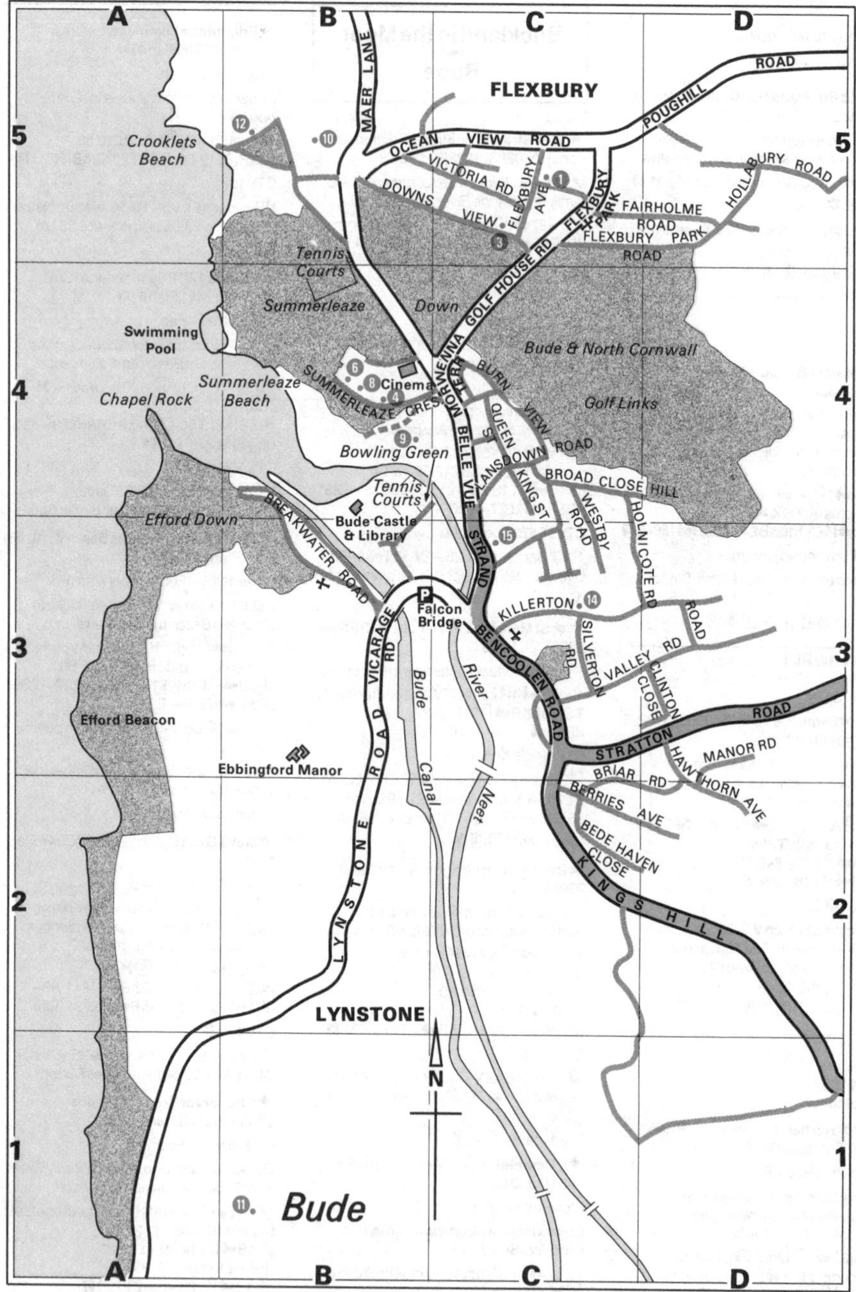

Bude

1	Bude Haven ★	8	Grosvenor ★★	12	Penarvor ★
3	Camelot ★	9	Hartland ★★★	14	St Margaret's ★★
4	Edgcumbe ★	10	Maer Lodge ★	15	Strand ★★★
6	Florida ★	11	Meva Gwin ★		

BUILTH WELLS
Powys
Map **3** SO05

★ ★***Lion*** 2 Broad St ☎ (0982) 553670

Historic inn in the centre of town, overlooking River Wye.

17rm(7🛁2🚿)(4fb) CTV in 13 bedrooms ® in 15 bedrooms **B**

CTV 14P 3🚗 *xmas*

V 🍷 ☕ Last dinner 9pm

Credit cards 1 3

★ ★***Pencerrig Country House*** Llanewedd (Consort) ☎ (0982) 553226

Standing in its own grounds with good views of the surrounding countryside, the hotel is personally managed and provides meals of a commendable standard.

27rm Annexe: 10🛁(1fb) TV in 6 bedrooms CTV in 2 bedrooms ® **B**

CTV 40P ✿ ♿ *xmas*

V 🍷 ☕ Last dinner 9pm

Credit cards 1 2 3 5

BULPHAN
Essex
Map **5** TQ68

★ ★**Ye Olde Plough House Motel** Brentwood Rd ☎ Grays Thurrock (0375) 891592 Telex no 995088

Modern chalets contrast with the central building here which is a 14th century Essex Yeoman's House.

Annexe: 75rm(55🛁20🚿)(10fb) CTV in all bedrooms ® **T** ✱sB🛁🚿fr£31 dB🛁🚿fr£38 (room only) **B**

☾ PCFA ✿ ⛱ (heated) 🎾(hard) solarium ♿

V 🍷 ☕ Lunch £7.75&alc Tea 60—80p Dinner fr£7.75&alc Wine £6 Last dinner 10pm

Credit cards 1 2 3 5

BUNGAY
Suffolk
Map **5** TM38

★***King's Head*** Market Pl ☎ (0986) 3583

13rm(3🛁1🚿) 1🛏 CTV in 5 bedrooms ® **B**

🚭 CTV 28P 🐕 Live music and dancing Sat *xmas*

V 🍷 ☕ Last dinner 9pm

Credit cards 1 2 3

✕✕***Brownes*** 20 Earshaw St ☎ (0986) 2545

Closed Sun, Mon & 2 wks Sep Lunch not served

🍽 French 36 seats Last dinner 10pm 🅿

Credit cards 1 3

BUNWELL
Norfolk
Map **5** TM19

★ ★🏠*L* **Bunwell Manor** ☎ (095389) 317

Former manor house dating back to the 16th century, set in three acres of grounds.

12rm(6🛁5🚿) CTV in 10 bedrooms TV in 2 bedrooms ® available in bedrooms **T** sB&B🛁🚿£24.50—£26.50 dB&B🛁🚿£38—£40 **B**

CTV 30P 1🚗 🐕 ✿ 🎣

🍽 English & French **V** 🍷 ☕ 🚭 Lunch £4.50—£6&alc Tea 80p—£1 Dinner £9—£10&alc Wine £4.80 Last dinner 9pm

Credit cards 1 2 3 Ⓥ

BURBAGE
Wiltshire
Map **4** SU26

★ ★**Savernake Forest** Savernake (1m NE off A346) (Best Western) ☎ Marlborough (0672) 810206

Closed 23 Dec—3 Jan

Secluded hotel with well-furnished rooms, attractive restaurant and good food.

9🛁 Annexe: 2🛁(2fb) CTV in all bedrooms ® sB&B🛁£34—£38 dB&B🛁£54 **B**

60P 🐕 ✿ 🎣

🍽 English & French 🍷 ☕ Lunch £7.50—£8.50 Dinner £11.50—£15.50 Wine £4.50 Last dinner 9.30pm

Credit cards 1 2 3 5

See advertisement under Marlborough

BURFORD
Oxfordshire
Map **4** SP21

★ ★**Cotswold Gateway** (on A40) ☎ (099382) 2148

Good tourist hotel.

12rm(2🛁)(2fb) CTV in all bedrooms ® sB&B£19.50—£25 sB&B🛁£25—£40 dB&B£25—£35 dB&B🛁£40—£46.50 **B**

60P snooker *xmas*

V 🍷 ☕ 🚭 Lunch £8.50—£12.50&alc Tea £1.50—£1.75 Dinner £9.50—£12.50&alc Wine £4.75 Last dinner 10.30pm

Credit cards 1 2 3 5

★ ★**Golden Pheasant** High St ☎ (099382) 3223 Telex no 849041

The beamed restaurant of this charming, small hotel is open and busy for most of the day, offering helpful and friendly service at breakfast, coffee time, lunch, tea and dinner.

12rm(5🛁5🚿)(2fb) 2🛏 CTV in all bedrooms ® **T** S% ✱sB&B🛁🚿£25—£30 dB&B🛁🚿£37.50—£42.50

☾ # CTV 18P 🐕 ♿ *xmas*

🍽 English & French **V** 🍷 ☕ 🚭 S% Lunch £5.95—£9.25&alc Tea £1.20—£2 High Tea £2.50—£3.50 Dinner £11.75—£15.25&alc Wine £4.25 Last dinner 9.30pm

Credit cards 1 3 Ⓥ

★**Highway** High St ☎ (099382) 2136 Telex no 838736

An ancient inn on Burford's historic High Street, the hotel is run by the proprietor and provides friendly and concerned service. Some rooms are small, but they are all charming and comfortable.

10rm(6🛁2🚿)(2fb) 1🛏 CTV in all bedrooms ® sB&B£20 sB&B🛁🚿£25 dB&B£32 dB&B🛁🚿£37 **B**

🅿 🐕 *xmas*

🍷 Bar lunch £1.90—£5.35 Dinner £10.50alc Wine £4.35 Last dinner 9pm

Credit cards 1 2 3 5

BURGHFIELD
Berkshire
Map **4** SU66

❀✕✕**Knights Farm** ☎ Reading (0734) 52366

(Rosette awarded for dinner only.)

Tucked away a mile from the village, this charming Georgian house is worth searching for, offering a high standard of honest food prepared with skill from excellent raw materials. The four-course, fixed-price menu offers a well-chosen and innovative range of dishes, the English cheeses are first-rate and a well-chosen, sensibly-priced wine list is available.

Closed Sun, Mon 2 wks Aug & 2 wks Xmas

🍽 International **V** 45 seats Lunch £11—£15 Dinner £20.50 Wine £6.95 Last dinner 9pm 30P nc 8yrs

Credit cards 1 2 3 5

BURGH HEATH
Surrey
Map **4** TQ25

★ ★**Heathside** (formerly Pickard) Brighton Rd ☎ (07373) 53355 Telex no 929908 Gatwick plan **16**

Hotel has well-equipped bedrooms and Happy Eater restaurant.

44🛁🚿(19fb) CTV in all bedrooms ® **T** sB🛁🚿£43—£51 dB🛁🚿£60—£69 (room only) **B**

☾ 180P CFA ✿ *xmas*

🍽 Mainly grills 🍷 ☕ 🚭 Lunch £5.50—£8&alc Tea £2.50 Dinner £5.50—£8&alc Wine £5 Last dinner 10pm

Credit cards 1 2 3 5 Ⓥ

BURLEY
Hampshire
Map **4** SU20

★ ★ ★🏠**Moorhill House** (Consort) ☎ (04253) 3285 Telex no 57515

Victorian country house in three acres of lawns and wooded grounds.

24rm(17🛁7🚿)(9fb) 5🛏 CTV in all bedrooms ® **T** sB&B🛁🚿£24—£30 dB&B🛁🚿£36—£50 **B**

CTV 30P 4🚗 🐕 ✿ ⛱(heated) sauna bath ♿ ♿ *xmas* →

☕English & French **V** ♆ ☕ Bar lunch £2—£3.50 Tea 65p High Tea £2.50 Dinner £8.50&alc Wine £4.75 Last dinner 8.30pm

Credit cards [1] [2] [3] [4] [5] Ⓥ

B

Burley — Burnley

BURN BRIDGE (near Harrogate)
North Yorkshire
Map **8** SE35

✕✕**Roman Court** ☎ Harrogate (0423) 879933

Closed Sun Lunch not served

☕English, French & Italian **V** 70 seats S% ✱Dinner £8.75&alc Wine £5.50 Last dinner 10.30pm 20P

Credit cards [1] [2] [3]

BURNHAM
Buckinghamshire
Map **4** SU98

★★★**Burnham Beeches** Grove Rd ☎ (06286) 3333 Telex no 946240

14🛁🚿 Annexe: 32🛁🚿(3fb) 2 ▭ CTV in all bedrooms **T** ✗ ✱sB&B🛁🚿£50—£65 dB&B🛁🚿£60—£85 **B**

☾100P ▭ ✿ 🎾(hard) croquet putting table tennis pool table ♔ *xmas*

☕English & French **V** ♆ ☕ ✱Lunch £9.50—£10.50&alc Tea 95p—£1.20 Dinner £12.50—£15&alc Wine £5.95 Last dinner 9.30pm

Credit cards [1] [2] [3] [5]

★★★**Grovefield** Taplow Common Rd ☎ (06286) 3131

This newly-opened hotel stands in peaceful surroundings and offers the comforts of home combined with an attractive restaurant serving imaginative meals.

33rm(32🛁1🚿)(1fb) CTV in all bedrooms Ⓡ **T** sB&B🛁🚿£40—£55 dB&B🛁🚿£50—£68 **B**

Lift ☾80P 5🚗 ✿

V ♆ Lunch £12—£18&alc Tea fr£1 Dinner £14—£18&alc Wine £5.25 Last dinner 10pm

Credit cards [1] [2] [3] [5]

TX: 846 873

BURNHAM MARKET
Norfolk
Map **9** TF84

✕**Fishes** Market Pl ☎ Fakenham (0328) 738588

On the ground floor of a converted period building, overlooking the Market Place.

Closed Mon & 3 wks Jan Dinner not served Sun (in winter)

48 seats Lunch £6.80—£7.95&alc Dinner £12alc Wine £4.95 Last dinner 9pm **P**

Credit cards [1] [2] [3] [5]

BURNHAM-ON-CROUCH
Essex
Map **5** TQ99

★**Ye Olde White Harte** The Quay ☎ Maldon (0621) 782106

Closed 25 & 26 Dec

Welcoming old coaching inn with comfortable bedrooms overlooking estuary.

11rm(3🛁3🚿) Annexe: 4rm(1fb) S% sB&B£14.02—£15.40 sB&B🛁🚿£20.35—£22.50 dB&B£25—£27.50 dB&B🛁🚿£31.35—£33.50

CTV 15P

V ♆ ☕ Lunch £5.95—£6.55&alc Tea 50—75p Dinner £5.95—£6.55&alc Wine £4.95 Last dinner 9pm

✕✕**Contented Sole** High St ☎ Maldon (0621) 782139

Fresh fish and French dishes impeccably served here.

Closed Sun Mon last 2 wks Jul & 22 Dec—22 Jan

☕English & French **V** 70 seats S% ✱Lunch £5.75&alc Dinner £14.50alc Wine £5.05 Last dinner 9.30pm **P**

✕***Boozles*** 4 Station Rd ☎ Maldon (0621) 783167

Small bistro style restaurant offering traditional British fare together with some less usual dishes.

Closed Mon Dinner not served Sun

☕International **V** 26 seats Last dinner 9.45pm

Credit cards [1] [3]

BURNHAM-ON-SEA
Somerset
Map **3** ST34

★★**Dunstan House** 8/10 Love Ln ☎ (0278) 784343

Attractive Georgian house with additions. The hotel is family run with friendly atmosphere and good food.

10rm(2🛁2🚿)(1fb) CTV in all bedrooms Ⓡ ✗ S% ✱sB&B£16—£19 sB&B🛁🚿£19—£20 dB&B£27—£29 dB&B🛁🚿£30—£32

CTV 40P ✿ ♔ *xmas*

☕English & French **V** ♆ ☕ ⚡ S% ✱ Lunch fr£1.50&alc Tea fr£1.50 High Tea fr£2 Dinner fr£1.50&alc Wine £3.50 Last dinner 10.30pm

Credit cards [1] [2] [3] [5]

See advertisement under Bridgwater

★★**Royal Clarence** 31 Esplanade (Minotel) ☎ (0278) 783138

Friendly, family owned and run sea front hotel with busy bars, and well equipped bedrooms.

15rm(6🛁6🚿)(2fb) CTV in all bedrooms Ⓡ **T** sB&B£13.75—£16 sB&B🛁🚿£15.75—£19 dB&B£24—£31 dB&B🛁🚿£28—£33

CTV 20P *xmas*

V ♆ ✱Lunch £3.75—£3.95&alc Tea 50p Dinner £4.95&alc Wine £4.20 Last dinner 8.30pm

Credit cards [1] [2] [3] [5] Ⓥ

See advertisement under Bridgwater

BURNLEY
Lancashire
Map **7** SD83

★★★***Keirby*** Keirby Walk ☎ (0282) 27611 Telex no 63119

Tall, modern hotel with well proportioned bedrooms and good facilities.

49🛁(3fb) CTV in all bedrooms Ⓡ Continental breakfast **B**

Lift ☾ CTV 40P 10🚘 Disco Thur, Fri, Sat & Sun

English & Continental V ☕ Last dinner 10pm

Credit cards 1 2 3 5

★★★ B **Oaks** Colne Rd, Reedley ☎ (0282) 414141 Telex no 635309

Splendid Victorian building recently converted to luxury hotel with high standards of service and incorporating good leisure complex.

32🛁🚿 1⊞ CTV in all bedrooms ®T sB&B🛁🚿£32—£56 dB&B🛁🚿£52—£70 B

☾ ## 100P ✽ (heated) squash snooker sauna bath solarium gymnasium Live music & dancing 5 nights wkly

V ☕ ✱ Lunch £5.50—£8.95 Tea £1.90 Dinner £8.95—£20

Credit cards 1 2 3 5

★★ **Rosehill House** Rosehill Av (Exec Hotel) ☎ (0282) 53931

Large, attractive, stone-built house in elevated grounds, near town centre.

20rm(9🛁11🚿)(1fb) CTV in all bedrooms ®T sB&B🛁🚿£15—£33 dB&B🛁🚿£30—£40 B

☾ 60P 2🚘 ✽

V ☕ ✱ Lunch £7.95&alc Dinner £7.95&alc Wine £5.25 Last dinner 9.30pm

Credit cards 1 2 3

BURNSALL
North Yorkshire
Map 7 SE06

★★ **Red Lion** ☎ (075672) 204

An old-world, stone-built inn on the banks of the River Wharfe in the centre of the village.

8rm Annexe: 4rm(2🛁2🚿)(2fb) CTV in 2 bedrooms ® in 4 bedrooms ✱ sB&B£17 sB&B🛁🚿£17 dB&Bfr£28 dB&B🛁🚿fr£38 B

CTV 40P

☕ S% ✱ Lunch £4.80—£5.83 Dinner £6.80—£9.60 Wine £5 Last dinner 9pm

BURNT YATES
North Yorkshire
Map 8 SE26

★★ **Bay Horse Inn & Motel**
☎ Harrogate (0423) 770230

Closed Xmas day

Comfortable, ivy clad, 18th century coaching inn, with new motel unit and well fitted bedrooms.

6🚿 Annexe: 10🚿(1fb) CTV in all bedrooms ®T sB&B🚿£18 dB&B🚿£35 B

75P

V ☕ Lunch £4.95alc Tea 75palc Dinner £8alc Last dinner 9.30pm

Credit cards 1 3

BURRINGTON
Devon
Map 2 SS61

★★★ H **Northcote Manor** (2m NW of village towards Portsmouth Arms Station & A377) (Best Western) ☎ High Bickington (0769) 60501

Closed 10 Nov—15 Mar

An 18th century building of great character where modern facilities are combined with traditional comfort.

11rm(9🛁) CTV in all bedrooms T sB&B£27—£29 sB&B🛁£27—£29 dB&B£54—£58 dB&B🛁£54—£58 B

20P ✽ *xmas*

☕ ✱ Lunch £6—£7 Tea £1—£1.50 Dinner £12—£13 Wine £5.50 Last dinner 8pm

Credit cards 1 2 3 5 Ⓥ

BURSCOUGH
Lancashire
Map 7 SD41

★★ **Briars Hall** Briars Ln, Lathom (1½m NE on A5209) ☎ (0704) 892368

8rm(5🛁2🚿) 1⊞ CTV in all bedrooms ®T sB&B£20—£25 sB&B🛁🚿£25—£32 dB&B🛁🚿£29.50—£50 B

☾ 70P ✽ *xmas*

V ☕ Wine £5 Last dinner 10pm

Credit cards 1 2 3 5

BURTON UPON TRENT
Staffordshire
Map 8 SK22

★★★ **Riverside Inn** Riverside Dr, Branston (Best Western) ☎ (0283) 63117

Large, much extended hotel in its own grounds beside River Trent.

22rm(21🛁🚿)(1fb) CTV in all bedrooms sB&B£27.50—£32.50 sB&B🛁🚿£29.50—£32.50 dB&B🛁🚿£42.50—£45 B

☾ 300P ✽ Live music & dancing mthly

English & Continental V ☕ Lunch £7.20—£8.50&alc Tea £1—£2.50 Dinner £9.85—£12.50&alc Wine £5.95 Last dinner 10pm

Credit cards 1 3

See advertisement on page 186

BURY
Gt Manchester
Map 7 SD81

★★ **Bolholt** Walshaw Rd ☎ 061-764 5239

Well furnished hotel with modern bedrooms (former residence of Earl of Harwood).

36rm(26🛁8🚿)(2fb) 1⊞ CTV in 25 bedrooms TV in 1 bedroom ®T S% ✱ sB&B£24—£30 sB&B🛁🚿£24—£30 dB&B£31—£40 dB&B🛁🚿£35—£40

CTV 170P ✽

International ☕ ✱ Lunch £4—£10 Tea £1—£2 Dinner £7.10—£10&alc Wine £4.10 Last dinner 9pm

Credit card 3

★ **Woolfield House** Wash Ln ☎ 061-764 3446

Large functional, partially modernised hotel with resident proprietor.

13rm(1🚿) TV available in bedrooms ® sB&Bfr£14 sB&B🚿fr£23 dB&Bfr£27 dB&B🚿fr£35

40P no babies

☕ ✱ Lunch fr£4.75 Tea fr60p Dinner fr£6.95 Wine £4.80 Last dinner 8.30pm

B

XX ***Normandie*** Birtle (3m NE off Rochdale rd B6222) ☎ 061-764 3869

A warm welcome, a high standard of French cooking and an excellent choice of wines are all assured at this luxurious restaurant and hotel standing high in the hills above Bury.

Closed Sun Lunch not served Sat

French **V** 60 seats Last dinner 9.45pm 70P ⊁

Credit cards [1] [2] [3] [5]

BURY ST EDMUNDS
Suffolk
Map **5** TL86

★★★ ***HBL* Angel**
(see boxed entry opposite)

★★ **Suffolk** 38 Buttermarket (Trusthouse Forte) ☎ (0284) 3995

Reconstructed ancient inn close to the 12th century Abbey.

41rm(13➧) CTV in all bedrooms ®
sB&B £39.50 sB&B➧ £47.50
dB&B £55.50 dB&B➧ £63.50 **B**

☾ 16 ⌂ *xmas*

Last dinner 9.30pm

Credit cards [1] [2] [3] [4] [5]

○ **Butterfly** (A45) ☎ (0284) 60884

50➧⋔

Due to open Spring 1987

Bury — Bushey

★★★ ***HBL* Angel** Angel Hill
☎ (0284) 3926 Telex no 81630

This fine creeper-clad hotel (an inn since 1482) is being continually improved by the Gough family. Foyer, reception and lounges have been redesigned and the bedrooms have been enlarged and made more comfortable. Staff continue to be friendly and hospitable.

36rm(35➧1⋔) 4⊟ CTV in all bedrooms **T** ✱ sB➧⋔ £25—£50
dB&B➧⋔ £50—£80 (room only) **B**

☾ 43P 7⌂ CFA

V ✱ Lunch £5.50—£11&alc Tea £1—4 Dinner £9—£11&alc Last dinner 9.30pm

Credit cards [1] [2] [3] [4] [5]

BUSBY
Strathclyde *Lanarkshire*
Map **11** NS55

★★ **Busby** 1 Field Rd ☎ 041-644 2661

Closed Xmas Day & New Years Day

Attractively situated hotel in conservation area with popular bar and function trade.

14rm(7➧7⋔)(1fb) CTV in all bedrooms ®
T ✱ sB&B➧⋔ £24—£30
dB&B➧⋔ £29.20—£36.50 **B**

Lift ☾ 40P

British & Continental **V** ✱ Lunch £5.50 Dinner £7.25&alc Wine £4.15 Last dinner 9.15pm

Credit cards [1] [2] [3] [5]

BUSHEY
Hertfordshire
Map **4** TQ19

★★★ **Ladbroke** (& Conference centre) Elton Way, Watford Bypass (A41) (Ladbroke) ☎ Watford (0923) 35881 Telex no 923422

Large, modern purpose built hotel.

163➧⋔(3fb) ⊁ in 4 bedrooms CTV in all bedrooms ® **T** ✱ sB➧⋔ fr £48.50
dB➧⋔ fr £58.50 (room only) **B**

Lift ☾ 300P CFA Live music & dancing Sat

✱ Lunch fr £10 Dinner fr £11.50 Wine £5.99 Last dinner 9.45pm

Credit cards [1] [2] [3] [4] [5] Ⓥ

See advertisement under Watford

BUTE, ISLE OF
Strathclyde *Buteshire*
Map **10**

ROTHESAY
Map **10** NS06

★**St Ebba** 37 Mountstuart Rd, Craigmore ☎(0700) 2683

Closed 11 Oct—31 Mar

On the south side of Rothesay Bay, family run hotel with views of Loch Striven and providing a comfortable homely atmosphere.

12rm(1🛁10🚿)(3fb) CTV in 7 bedrooms TV in 5 bedrooms Ⓡ sB&B£14—£15 sB&B🛁🚿£16.50—£17.50 dB&B£28—£30 dB&B🛁🚿£33—£35 B

CTV 6P

V ♀ ☕ Bar lunch £1.30—£4 Tea 50—80p Dinner £8.50—£10.50&alc Wine £4.20 Last dinner 7.30pm

Ⓥ

BUTTERMERE
Cumbria
Map **11** NY11

★★**Bridge** ☎(059685) 252

Closed Jan

Typical lakeland inn in beautiful countryside, offering congenial atmosphere.

22🛁(2fb) Ⓡ
*sB&B🛁£27—£30(incl. dinner) dB&B🛁£54—£60(incl. dinner) B

30P 🚫 *xmas*

English & French V ♀ ✗ * Bar lunch £5.35alc Dinner £10.25&alc Wine £4.75 Last dinner 9.30pm

BUXTON
Derbyshire
Map **7** SK07

★★★**Leewood** 13 Manchester Rd (A5002) (Best Western) ☎(0298) 3002 Telex no 669848

Closed 24—28 Dec

A large Georgian house standing in its own grounds, overlooking the cricket ground.

42rm(33🛁9🚿)(2fb) CTV in all bedrooms Ⓡ T sB&B🛁🚿£32—£38 dB&B🛁🚿£44—£48 B

Lift ☾ 50P CFA ✿ pool table

European ♀ ☕ Lunch £5.95—£7.50 Tea 75p—£2.50 Dinner £9.50—£10.75&alc Wine £4.50 Last dinner 9pm

Credit cards 1 2 3 5 Ⓥ

★★★**Palace** Palace Rd ☎(0298) 2001 Telex no 668169

Dating from 1870, this stately, stone, Victorian building has elegantly spacious public areas and impressive plasterwork. The large, stylish bedrooms are in process of restoration. Guests can also enjoy the well laid out gardens, the modern gymnasium and the swimming pool.

122🛁(6fb) CTV in all bedrooms Ⓡ T sB&B🛁£33 dB&B🛁£58 B

Lift ☾ 200P CFA ✿ (heated) snooker sauna bath solarium gymnasium *xmas*

English & French V ♀ ☕ Lunch £6—£7.50&alc Tea £2—£3 High Tea £4—£6 Dinner £9.50—£10.50&alc Wine £5.75 Last dinner 10pm

Credit cards 1 2 3 5 Ⓥ

★★**Buckingham** 1 Burlington Rd (Consort) ☎(0298) 70481 Telex no 57515

Two large, stone-built, Victorian houses have been combined to provide spacious public rooms and facilities suitable for small in-house conferences. The hotel is situated only a short walk from the town centre.

29rm(4🛁14🚿)(6fb) CTV in all bedrooms Ⓡ T ✗ sB&B£18—£20 sB&B🛁🚿£30—£36 dB&B£32—£36 dB&B🛁🚿£38—£42 B

Lift CTV 24P snooker *xmas* →

🏺☕ Tea fr70p High Tea fr£2.50 Dinner fr£10.45&alc Wine £6.95 Last dinner 9.30pm
Credit cards 1 2 3 5 V

★★*L* **Grove** Grove Pde (Frederic Robinson) ☎ (0298) 3804
Former coaching inn above row of shops, with attractive lounges displaying many old features, and smart restaurant featuring local and international dishes.
21rm(4🛁1🚿) CTV in all bedrooms ® *sB&B£16 sB&B🛁🚿£25 dB&B£27 dB&B🛁🚿£32 B
CTV P *xmas*
English & French V 🏺☕ Lunch £4.25—£5.25 Tea £1.35—£2.20 Dinner £5—£8.50 Wine £4.95 Last dinner 9pm
Credit cards 1 2 3 5

★**Hartington** 18 Broad Walk ☎ (0298) 2638
Closed 24 Dec—3 Jan RS Nov—Mar
Stone-built house overlooking the Pavilion gardens and a small lake.
17rm(3🛁4🚿)(3fb) CTV in 7 bedrooms sB&B£17 sB&B🛁🚿£22 dB&B£28 dB&B🛁🚿£33 B
CTV 15P♿
V Dinner £6 Wine £5.30 Last dinner 8pm
Credit card 1 V

✕**Nathaniels** 35 High St ☎ (0298) 78388
Cosy little restaurant with Victorian theme. Offers reasonably priced home made fresh food and small wine list.
Closed Mon (except Dec & Buxton Festival) & 11—21 Nov Dinner not served Sun
English & French V 50 seats Lunch £5.25—£6.50 Dinner £6.50—£10&alc Wine £4.50 Last dinner 10.30pm P
Credit cards 1 2 3 5

CAERLEON
Gwent
Map **3** ST39

✕✕***Kemeys Manor*** Bullmoor Rd ☎ Tredunnock (063349) 380
Quietly situated on the outskirts of the village, this country manor with beamed ceilings and flag-stone floors specialises in

Welsh cuisine, using fresh ingredients and honest preparation.
Closed Sun Bank Hol Mon & 1st 2 wks Jan Lunch not served Mon & Sat
Welsh & French V 60 seats Last dinner 10pm 40P
Credit cards 1 2 3

CAERNARFON
Gwynedd
Map **6** SH46

★★★*B* **Stables** (Inter Hotel) ☎ (0286) 830711
(For full entry see Llanwnda)

CAERPHILLY
Mid Glamorgan
Map **3** ST18

★★**Griffin Inn Motel** Rudry (3m E on unclass rd) ☎ (0222) 869735
Closed Xmas
The small, friendly, character inn has a rural setting and is personally owned and managed. A combination of modern, well-equipped bedrooms, good bars and a convivial restaurant make it popular with businessmen.
3rm Annexe: 20🛁(1fb) CTV in 20 bedrooms ® in 20 bedrooms T S% *sB&B🛁£18—£27.60 dB&B🛁£28—£36 B
☾ 100P (heated) Live music & dancing Sat
English & French V 🏺 *Bar lunch £3.50alc Dinner £7.85&alc Wine £4.85 Last dinner 10pm
Credit cards 1 2 3 5

CAERSWS
Powys
Map **6** SO09

★★**Maesmawr Hall** (Inter Hotel) ☎ (068684) 255
A 16th century, half-timbered, listed manor house in wooded gardens.
13rm(5🛁3🚿) Annexe: 6🛁🚿(4fb) 1 ® in 6 bedrooms *sB&B£20.25—££25 sB&B🛁🚿£22.75—£28.50 dB&B£33—£40 dB&B🛁🚿£38.75—£45 B
CTV 100P 2🚗(charge) ♿ *xmas*
V 🏺☕ *Lunch £6.60—£7.50&alc Tea £1.40—£1.80 High Tea £3.50—£8 Dinner fr£11&alc Wine £4.88 Last dinner 9pm
Credit cards 1 2 3 5 V

CALLANDER
Central *Perthshire*
Map **11** NN60

★★★*BL* **Roman Camp** ☎ (0877) 30003
Closed end Nov—early Mar RS Nov & Mar
Dating from 1625, reminiscent of a miniature château with small towers, in 20 acres of gardens bordering the River Teith. The hotel is tastefully decorated and well furnished.
11rm(9🛁2🚿)(3fb) CTV in all bedrooms ® T S% sB&B🛁🚿£35—£45 dB&B🛁🚿£49—£72 B
30P
🏺 Lunch £10—£12alc Dinner £18—£19alc Wine £5.90 Last dinner 8.55pm

★*HL* **Bridgend House** Bridgend ☎ (0877) 30130
A personally run hotel in a quiet location close to the town centre.
7rm(3🛁2🚿)(1fb) 2 CTV in 5 bedrooms ® T *sB&B£13—£26 sB&B🛁🚿£26 dB&B£20 dB&B🛁🚿£40
30P
Scottish, English & Continental 🏺☕ *Lunch £4.75—£5.75 High Tea £4.75 Dinner £9alc Wine £4.35 Last dinner 9.30pm
Credit cards 1 2 3 5 V

★*BL* **Lubnaig** Leny Feus (off A84) ☎ (0877) 30376

Closed mid Nov—Etr

Gabled, stone-built house in large lawned garden, in the village used as Tannochbrae for 'Dr Finlay's Casebook'.

6🚿 Annexe: 4🚿 (2fb) ®
sB&B🚿£14.50—£19.50
dB&B🚿£25—£35
CTV 14P ✽ nc7yrs
Bar lunch £2—£3.50 Dinner £9—£10 Wine £2 Last dinner 7.30pm
Ⓥ

★**Pinewood** Leny Rd ☎ (0877) 30111

Simply appointed, privately managed tourist hotel, set back from road.

16rm (6🛁) (2fb) ® sB&B£13.25 dB&B£23 dB&B🛁£26.50 B
CTV 30P ✽ *xmas*
Lunch £4 Tea 50p High Tea £4.25 Dinner £9.50 Wine £4.25 Last dinner 8.45pm
Credit cards 1 2 Ⓥ

★***Waverley*** Main St ☎ (0877) 30245

Privately owned, unpretentious hotel.

10rm (2fb) B
CTV Live music and dancing Fri Cabaret Sat
V Last dinner 8.30pm
Credit cards 1 3

CALNE

Wiltshire
Map **3** ST97

★★**Lansdowne Strand** The Strand ☎ (0249) 812488 Telex no 444453

Well-established hotel with attractive bars and restaurant.

19rm (12🛁 1🚿) Annexe: 5🛁 (2fb) CTV in all bedrooms ® **T** ✱ sB&B£19 sB&B🛁🚿£30—£33 dB&B£28 dB&B🛁🚿£40—£44 B
15P *xmas*
English & French **V** ✱ Lunch fr£6.50&alc Tea fr65p Dinner £7.95&alc Wine £4.90 Last dinner 9.30pm
Credit cards 1 2 3 5 Ⓥ

CALSTOCK

Cornwall
Map **2** SX46

✕**Boot Inn** ☎ Tavistock (0822) 832331

Country inn with intimate wood-panelled dining room.

V 60 seats Lunch £5.95 Dinner £10alc Wine £4.95 Last dinner 10pm 7P
Credit cards 1 2 3 5

CALVERHALL

Shropshire
Map **7** SJ63

✕***Old Jack Inn*** ☎ (094876) 235

19th century inn with friendly service and wide range of dishes and good steaks. Named after famous drinking vessel, lost around 1860.

French 70 seats Last dinner 9.30pm 45P Jazz Mon
Credit cards 1 3

CAMBERLEY

Surrey
Map **4** SU86

★★★**Frimley Hall** Portsmouth Rd (Trusthouse Forte) ☎ (0276) 28321 Telex no 858446

Fine Victorian house in 4 acres of grounds with good food and modern bedroom extension.

60rm (58🛁 2🚿) CTV in all bedrooms ® sB&B🛁🚿£53.50 dB&B🛁🚿£70 B
☾ 200P CFA ✽ *xmas*
Last dinner 9.45pm
Credit cards 1 2 3 4 5

C

CAMBRIDGE
Cambridgeshire
Map **5** TL45

★★★★**Garden House** Granta Pl, off Mill Ln (Best Western) ☎ (0223) 63421 Telex no 81463

RS 24—27 Dec

Modern hotel, set in three acres of riverside gardens, close to the city centre.

117 (4fb) CTV in all bedrooms ® T ✱ sB&B £46—£52 dB&B £66—£88 Continental breakfast

Lift 180P CFA punting *xmas*

English & Continental **V** ✱ Lunch £9.95&alc Tea £4.10 Dinner £11.75&alc Wine £6.35 Last dinner 9.30pm

Credit cards 1 2 3 5 V

★★★★**Post House** Lakeview, Bridge Rd, Impington (2½m N, on N side of rbt jct A45/B1049) (Trusthouse Forte) ☎ Histon (022023) 7000 Telex no 817123

Popular hotel with extensive leisure and conference facilities.

120 (31fb) CTV in all bedrooms ® T sB&B £58.50 dB&B £77.50

250P (heated) sauna bath solarium gymnasium *xmas*

Last dinner 10.30pm

Credit cards 1 2 3 4 5

Cambridge

★★★★**University Arms** Regent St (Inter Hotel) ☎ (0223) 351241 Telex no 817311

Traditional, family-owned hotel with spacious public rooms, modernised bedrooms. Convenient for the city centre.

115 (3fb) CTV in all bedrooms **T** S% sB&B £38 dB&B £52

Lift 75P CFA Live music and dancing Sat (Nov—Feb)

English & Continental **V** S% Lunch fr£5.50&alc Tea fr£2.70 Dinner fr£9.20&alc Wine £4.70 Last dinner 9.45pm

Credit cards 1 2 3 5

★★★**Cambridgeshire Moat House** (Queens) ☎ Crafts Hill (0954) 80555

(For full entry see Bar Hill)

★★★**Gonville** Gonville Pl ☎ (0223) 66611

Closed Xmas 4 days, except Xmas Day lunch

Conventional hotel overlooking Parker's Piece.

62 (6fb) CTV in all bedrooms ® S% sB&B fr£38 dB&B fr£46.95

Lift CTV 100P CFA

English & French **V** S% Lunch fr£6.50&alc Tea fr55p Dinner fr£8.95&alc Wine £6.50 Last dinner 9pm

Credit cards 1 2 3

★★**Arundel House** 53 Chesterton Rd ☎ (0223) 67701 Telex no 817936

Closed 25 & 26 Dec

Converted terrace on busy road, overlooking River Cam.

67rm (17 27) Annexe: 6rm (5 1) (7fb) CTV in all bedrooms ® T sB&B £19.50—£28.50 sB&B £26.50—£33.50 dB&B £30—£42.50 dB&B £33.50—£46 Continental breakfast

44P

English & French **V** Lunch £6.25&alc Tea fr55p High Tea £1—£4.25 Dinner £8.55&alc Wine £4.80 Last dinner 10pm

Credit cards 1 2 3 5 V

★**Quy Mill** Market Rd ☎ Teversham (02205) 4114

(for full entry see Stow Cum Quy)

✕**Peking** 21 Burleigh St ☎ (0223) 354755

Closed Mon & Xmas

Pekinese **V** 60 seats Lunch £5—£8alc Dinner £5—£12alc Wine £4.50 Last dinner 11pm

;AMPBELTOWN
trathclyde *Argyllshire*
lap **10** NR72

★ ★ ***Royal*** Main St ☎ (0586) 52017
'opular with both commercial trade and olidaymakers, the hotel has fine views.
6rm(8➡4⋒)(2fb) CTV in all bedrooms Ⓡ B
ift ☾ 6P 4🚗 *xmas*
♈ 🍵 Last dinner 8.30pm
;redit cards 1 2 3 5

★ **Ardshiel** Kilkerran Rd ☎ (0586) 52133
small, friendly hotel, busy with ommercial and tourist trade.
2rm(2fb) CTV in all bedrooms Ⓡ
B&B £15—£17.50 dB&B £28—£32 B
2P ✽
♈ 🍵 Lunch fr £5.50 Tea £1 alc High Tea £5 Dinner fr £9 Wine £5 Last dinner .30pm
;redit cards 1 2 3 5 Ⓥ

;ANNICH
lighland *Inverness-shire*
lap **14** NH33

★ ★ ♣ *HL* **Cozac Lodge** Glen Cannich 3m W on unclass Glen Cannich rd)
☎ (04565) 263
;losed Nov—Mar except Xmas & New 'ear
'ormer hunting lodge tastefully converted nd elegantly furnished to create a hotel of listinction.
'rm(3➡4⋒)(1fb) CTV in all bedrooms Ⓡ
;B&B➡⋒ fr £30 dB&B➡⋒ fr £46 B
12P ✽ ♪ nc8yrs *xmas*
International ♈ 🍵 Lunch fr £5.25 Tea £1.50 Dinner fr £13.50&alc Wine £4.50
.ast dinner 8.30pm
;redit cards 1 2 3

★ ★ ***Glen Affric*** ☎ (04565) 214
;losed 17 Oct—Etr
A family run, roadside hotel situated amidst nagnificent Highland scenery.
23rm(5⋒)(2fb)
;TV 30P
♈ 🍵 Last dinner 9pm

CANNOCK
Staffordshire
Map **7** SJ91

★ ★ ★ **Roman Way** Watling St, Hatherton (on A5) ☎ (05435) 72121
Large modern and busy hotel on A5 provides comfortable, well-equipped accommodation.
Annexe: 24rm(20➡4⋒)(6fb) CTV in all bedrooms Ⓡ **T** sB&B➡⋒ £30—£32 dB&B➡⋒ £39—£41 B
☾ 200P Live music and dancing Mon, Tue, Thu & Fri ♿ *xmas*
English & French **V** ♈ 🍵 Lunch fr £5.50&alc Tea fr 70p Dinner fr £5.50&alc Wine £5.75 Last dinner 10pm
Credit cards 1 2 3 5

CANONBIE
Dumfries & Galloway *Dumfriesshire*
Map **11** NY37

❀★ *HBL* **Riverside Inn**
☎ (05415) 295
Closed Xmas & 2 wks Feb
(Rosette awarded for dinner only.)
An attractively decorated and thoughtfully equipped hotel, it is now more restful since the bypass was built. It is popular with fishermen, having the River Eden flowing close by. Menus change daily, and the interesting choice of well prepared dishes justifies our rosette award.
4rm(2➡2⋒) Annexe: 2➡ CTV in all bedrooms Ⓡ ✱ sB&B➡⋒ £32—£34 dB&B➡⋒ £42—£44
30P 2🚗 ✽
Scottish & French ♈ ✱ Bar lunch £3.95 Tea fr 70p Dinner £12.50 Last dinner 8.30pm
Credit cards 1 3

CANTERBURY
Kent
Map **5** TR15

❀★ ★ ★ ★ **County** High St
☎ (0227) 66266 Telex no 965076
Cheerful staff contribute a great deal to the friendly hospitality and good atmosphere of this particularly well-appointed restaurant, where a young English chef produces an interesting range of imaginative dishes, well-prepared and attractively presented. The wine list, whilst not comprehensive, is reasonably priced.
74➡⋒(4fb) 8▭ CTV in all bedrooms Ⓡ **T** ✗ sB➡⋒ £42—£45 dB➡⋒ £53—£66 (room only) B
Lift ☾ 80P 20🚗 (£2 per night) Live music & dancing Fri & Sat
International **V** ♈ 🍵 Lunch fr £9&alc Tea fr £3 Dinner fr £12.50&alc Wine £6.50 Last dinner 10pm
Credit cards 1 2 3 4 5
See advertisement on page 192

★ ★ ★ **Chaucer** Ivy Ln (Trusthouse Forte)
☎ (0227) 464427 Telex no 965096
Largely rebuilt after the Second World War, this comfortable hotel has newly-refurbished bedrooms, well-equipped and with private facilities, and a nicely-appointed restaurant where the cooking is sound and the service friendly.
45➡ CTV in all bedrooms Ⓡ sB&B➡ £49.50 dB&B➡ £66.50 B
☾ 45P CFA *xmas*
♈ Last dinner 9.30pm
Credit cards 1 2 3 4 5

★ ★ ★ **Falstaff** St Dunstans Street (Whitbread) ☎ (0227) 462138
A 14th-century coaching inn with modern bedrooms, comfortable lounges and panelled dining room close to Westgate Tower.
25rm(21➡3⋒)(2fb) 2▭ CTV in all bedrooms Ⓡ **T** ✗ (except guide dogs) sB&B➡⋒ £38—£44 dB&B➡⋒ £50—£60 B →

☾40P *xmas*

🍽English & Continental **V** ♈ ☕ Lunch £6.50—£7&alc Tea £1—£1.50 Dinner £10alc Wine £5.10 Last dinner 9.45pm

Credit cards [1] [2] [3] [5]

★★★**Slatters** St Margarets Street (Queens Moat) ☎ (0227) 463271

Friendly modern hotel with well-equipped older style bedrooms.

30rm(26🛁)(12fb) CTV in all bedrooms Ⓡ S% sB&Bfr£30 sB&B🛁fr£43 dB&Bfr£48 dB&B🛁fr£58 🅱

Lift ☾ 26P *xmas*

🍽English & French ♈ ☕ Lunch £5.25—£5.50&alc Tea 75p—£2.75 Dinner fr£8.25&alc Wine £5 Last dinner 9pm

Credit cards [1] [2] [3] [5] Ⓥ

★★**Canterbury** 71 New Dover Rd ☎ (0227) 450551 Telex no 965809

Elegant Georgian style hotel with good standard of personal service.

27rm(12🛁15🚿)(4fb) CTV in all bedrooms Ⓡ **T** S% ✱sB&B🛁🚿fr£30 dB&B🛁🚿fr£38 🅱

Lift 40P

🍽Continental ♈ ☕ ✱Bar lunch fr£5.95 Tea fr£1.20 Dinner fr£8.50&alc Wine £4.25 Last dinner 10pm

Credit cards [1] [2] [3] [5] Ⓥ

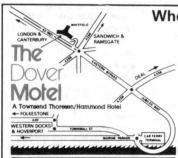

❀✕✕ **Restaurant Seventy Four** 74 Wincheap ☎ (0227) 67411

As you enter this tastefully-decorated character establishment, there is a cosy sitting area in which you can enjoy a drink before your meal or coffee after it. The atmosphere throughout the restaurant is intimate and friendly, and the standard of food, influenced by nouvelle cuisine, is high.

Closed Sun 26—30 Dec 1 wk Etr 2 wks Sep & Bank Hols

Lunch not served Sat

34 seats Lunch £9—£12 Dinner £20—£26&alc Wine £6.20 Last dinner 9.30pm 10P ⚡

Credit cards [1] [2] [3] [5]

✕✕ **Waterfield's** 5 Best Ln ☎ (0227) 450276

The restaurant, approached down a city centre cul-de-sac, has a peaceful riverside setting in what was an old glass forge. Run by the chef/patron, it boasts an ambitiously wide-ranging menu complemented by a reasonably priced wine list, friendly service and warm hospitality.

Closed Sun

Lunch not served Mon

60 seats ✱ Lunch £7.50&alc Dinner £13.50alc Wine £5 Last dinner 10.45pm Ᵽ

Credit cards [1] [2] [3]

✕ **Ristorante Tuo e Mio** 16 The Borough ☎ (0227) 61471

Closed Mon, last 2 wks Aug & 1st wk Sep Lunch not served Tue

Italian 40 seats Lunch £7&alc Wine £5 Last dinner 10.45pm Ᵽ

Credit cards [1] [2] [3] [4] [5]

CAPEL CURIG
Gwynedd
Map **6** SH75

★★ **Ty'n-y-Coed** ☎ (06904) 331

White painted hotel situated on the banks of the River Llugwy.

13 ⇌ (2fb) CTV in all bedrooms ® **T** sB&B ⇌ £18—£20 dB&B ⇌ £32—£40 Ᵽ

CTV 80P ❁ ♩ *xmas*

V ♡ ☕ Lunch £5.50—£8 Tea £1.50—£2.50 Dinner £8—£10&alc Wine £5 Last dinner 9.30pm

Credit cards [1] [2] [3]

CARBIS BAY
Cornwall
Map **2** SW53

See St Ives, Cornwall

CARDIFF
South Glamorgan
Map **3** ST17

See plan

★★★★ **Park** Park Pl (Mount Charlotte) ☎ (0222) 383471 Telex no 497195 Plan **7** *E3*

This modernised hotel in Cardiff's shopping centre is popular with business people and tourists. It offers a small lounge, well-equipped bedrooms, a choice of restaurants and the attention of pleasant and courteous staff.

108 ⇌ ⋔ (6fb) CTV in all bedrooms ® **T** S% sB&B ⇌ ⋔ fr£49 dB&B ⇌ ⋔ fr£60.50 Ᵽ

Lift ☾ 70P CFA Live music Tue—Sat ♿ *xmas*

International **V** ♡ ☕ S% Lunch fr£7.50&alc Tea 90p—£2.50 High Tea £2.50 Dinner £7.95—£9.95&alc Wine £5.95 Last dinner 11pm

Credit cards [1] [2] [3] [5] Ⓥ

★★★ **Crest** Westgate St (Crest) ☎ (0222) 388681 Telex no 497258 Plan **1** *C2*

RS Xmas

The modern, company-owned hotel stands adjacent to the National Stadium and overlooks Cardiff Castle. Its popular bars and well-equipped bedrooms attract a firm business following. →

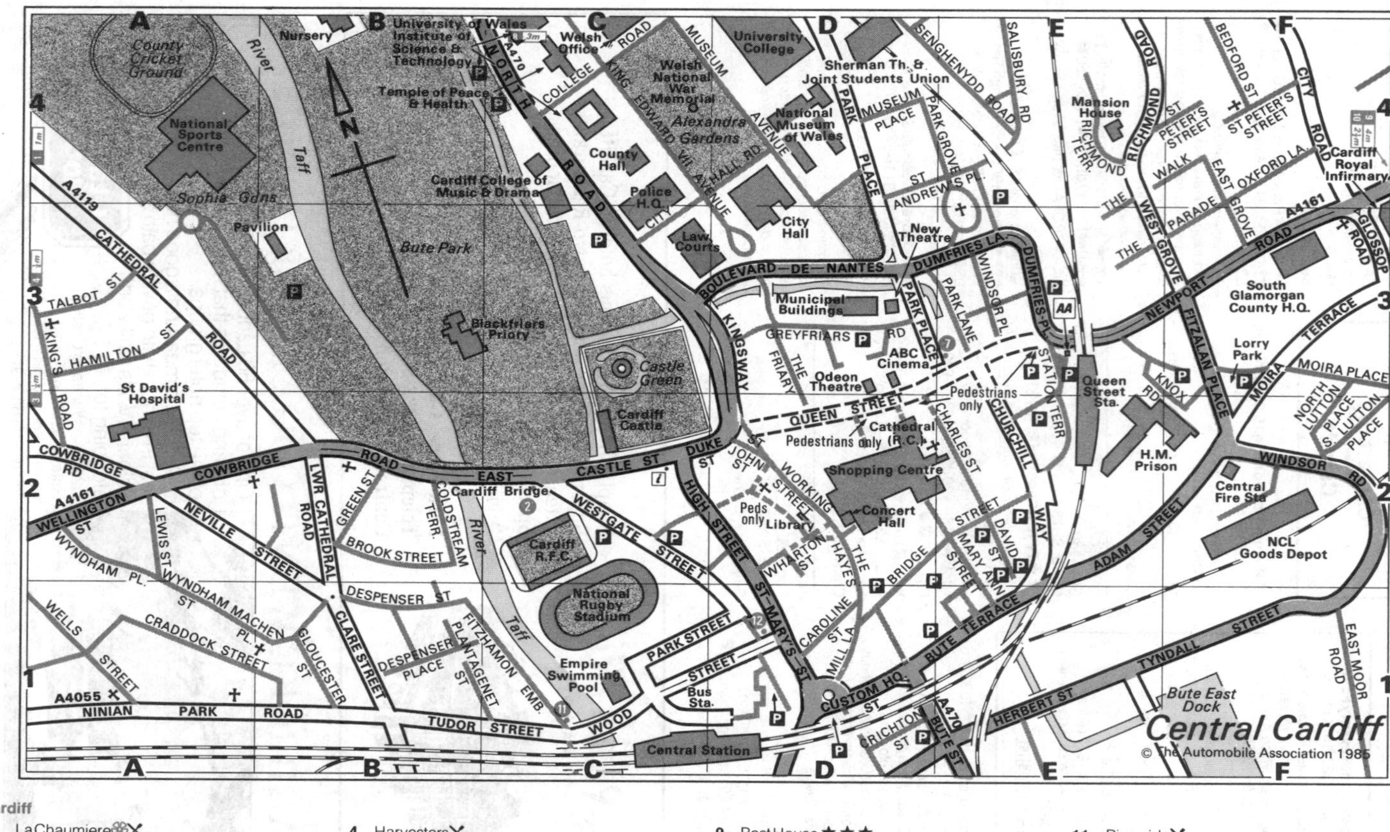

Cardiff

1 La Chaumiere ✿ ✕
2 Crest ★★★
3 Gibsons ✕
4 Harvesters ✕
7 Park ★★★★
8 Phoenix ★★
9 Post House ★★★
10 Le Provencal ✕
11 Riverside ✕
12 Royal ★★★

159 (9fb) in 16 bedrooms CTV in all bedrooms ® T
Lift (110P CFA
International V S% *Lunch £3.50—£4.50 Tea £1.50—£2.50 Dinner £10—£14.50&alc Wine £6.25 Last dinner 10pm
Credit cards 1 2 3 4 5

★★★**Post House** Pentwyn Rd, Pentwyn (Trusthouse Forte) ☎ (0222) 731212 Telex no 497633 Plan **9** *F4*
Modern hotel situated just off A48, about four miles from the city centre.
150 (41fb) CTV in all bedrooms ® sB&B £49.50 dB&B £65.50
Lift (210P CFA
Last dinner 10.30pm
Credit cards 1 2 3 4 5

★★★**Royal** St Mary's Street (Embassy) ☎ (0222) 383321 Plan **12** *D1*
Typical Victorian hotel in the city centre.
63rm(41 6)(9fb) CTV in all bedrooms ® T S% sBfr£29.50 sB fr£43 dBfr£40 dB fr£53 (room only)
Lift (CFA snooker Live music & dancing Sat *xmas*
French V S% Lunch fr£7.45&alc Tea fr95p Dinner fr£7.45&alc Wine £5.10 Last dinner 10pm
Credit cards 1 2 3 4 5 Ⓥ

★★**Phoenix** 199—201 Fidlas Rd, Llanishan ☎ (0222) 764615 Plan **8** *C4*
Privately owned hotel with business clientele.
25rm(4 16) CTV in all bedrooms ® T S% sB&B£21—£23 sB&B £26—£28 dB&B£31—£33 dB&B £35—£38
Lift (CTV 50P
V S% Lunch £6.50alc Dinner £9.50alc Wine £4.25 Last dinner 10pm
Credit cards 1 2 3 5 Ⓥ

See advertisement on page 196

★★***St Mellons Hotel & Country Club*** St Mellons (4m NE off A48) ☎ Castleton (0633) 680355 Not on plan
Closed Xmas Day
Comfortable hotel with leisure complex. Annexe rooms are very well appointed.
11 Annexe: 20 (10fb) CTV in all bedrooms ® T
(CTV 200P (heated) (hard) squash billiards sauna bath solarium gymnasium
French V Last dinner 10.30pm
Credit cards 1 2 3 5

○ **Holiday Inn** Mill Ln (Holiday Inns) ☎ (0222) 399944 182
Expected to have opened July 1986.

See advertisement on page 196

✕**La Chaumiere** Cardiff Rd, Llandaff
☎ (0222) 555319 Plan **1** *A4*
Opened last year by Cliff and Kay Morgan, already well known to us at Mr Midgley's in Usk, this charming little restaurant maintains a high standard of cuisine in the light, modern style. Meals are complemented by a short, reasonably-priced wine list, and the diner is assured of a memorable visit.
Closed Mon
Lunch not served Sat
Dinner not served Sun
French V 38 seats S% Lunch £13.50alc Dinner £14.50alc Wine £6 Last dinner 9.30pm 30P
Credit cards 1 2 5

✕**Gibsons** Romilly Cres ☎ (0222) 41264 Plan **3** *A2*
Set away from the city centre, this modest little split-level restaurant offers homely comfort and a convivial atmosphere. Its emphasis is on the presentation of imaginative, quality dishes, and it often →

promotes keenly-priced regional French evenings. Friendly and informal service is provided by a young staff.

Closed Sun

French **V** 38 seats S% Lunch £7.50—£15.50&alc Dinner £15.50&alc Wine £5.55 Last dinner 9.45pm 5P

Credit cards 1 2 3 5

X **Harvesters** 5 Pontcanna St ☎ (0222) 32616 Plan **4** *A3*

A simply-appointed, Imperial-style bistro, the restaurant offers an honest quality of food, friendly service and a warming atmosphere.

Closed Sun & 3—27 Aug Lunch not served Sat

V 46 seats Lunch £6.25—£7.80&alc Dinner £7.25—£8.20&alc Wine £4.25 Last dinner 11pm

Credit cards 1 2 3 Ⓥ

X **Le Provençal** 779 Newport Rd ☎ (0222) 778262 Plan **10** *F4*

This exceptionally popular, bright, modern bistro is situated just outside the city. The flair of its good, imaginative menus is complemented by the use of high-quality fresh produce and it is a firm favourite with local businessmen.

Closed Sun, Mon, & 1st 2 wks Aug Lunch not served Sat

French **V** 60 seats Lunch £4.40&alc Dinner £9.50alc Wine £4.90 Last dinner 10pm

Credit cards 1 2 3 5

X ***Riverside*** 44 Tudor St ☎ (0222) 372163 Plan **11** *C1*

A Cantonese restaurant, among the best of its kind in Wales.

Closed Xmas Eve & Xmas Day

Cantonese 140 seats Last dinner 11.45pm

Credit cards 1 2 3 5

CARDIGAN
Dyfed
Map **2** SN14

See also Gwbert-on-Sea

★★**Black Lion** 30 High St ☎ (0239) 612532

Originally a one-room "grogg shoppe", the Black Lion is probably one of the oldest coaching inns in Wales. Established in 1105 and upgraded by a local squire in the seventeenth century, it now offers friendly service, character bars and simple, compact, modern bedrooms.

11rm(8 3) Ⓡ

CTV *xmas*

Mainly grills Last dinner 9.30pm

Credit cards 1 2 3 4

XX **Rhyd-Garn-Wen** Croft (3m SW on A487) ☎ (0239) 612742

The hotel, a charming, small, nineteenth-century manor house, stands in its own attractive grounds near the Preseli Mountains. Personally owned and run, it serves interesting and honestly home-made food in an atmosphere of comfort and genuine hospitality. Booking is recommended, restaurant space is limited.

Closed mid Oct—Etr Lunch not served

French **V** 12 seats Dinner £13alc Wine £4.50 Last dinner 8.45pm P nc 12yrs

Credit card 1

CARFRAEMILL
Borders *Berwickshire*
Map **12** NT55

★★**Carfraemill** ☎ Oxton (05785) 200

A road-side hotel, just off the A68.

11rm(2)(2fb) CTV in all bedrooms Ⓡ T sB&B£16—£20 sB&B £20—£22 dB&B£25—£30 dB&B £30—£35

100P 4 *xmas*

Lunch £4—£8 Tea 75p High Tea £4.75 Dinner £8.75—£10.50 Wine £3.45 Last dinner 9pm

Credit cards 2 3 Ⓥ

CARLISLE
Cumbria
Map **12** NY45

★★★**Crest** Kingstown (junc 44/M6) (Crest) ☎ (0228) 31201 Telex no 64201
A modern building next to the motorway.
98⇌⋒(16fb) in 10 bedrooms CTV in all bedrooms Ⓡ ∗sB⇌⋒£44.50 dB⇌⋒£54.50 (room only) B
☾200P CFA
V ♔ ☕ ∗Lunch £6.50—£8.50 Dinner £9—£15&alc Wine £5.65 Last dinner 9.45pm
Credit cards 1 2 3 4 5

★★★***Cumbrian*** Court Sq ☎ (0228) 31951 Telex no 63287
Spacious comfortable hotel with modern bedrooms near railway station.
70rm(66⇌4⋒)(3fb) 2 CTV in all bedrooms Ⓡ B
Lift ☾60P 30 CFA
International ♔ ☕ Last dinner 9.30pm
Credit cards 1 2 3 4 5

★★★**Ladbroke Crown & Mitre** English St (Ladbroke) ☎ (0228) 25491 Telex no 64183
Conveniently situated close to both the cathedral and the castle.
78⇌⋒ Annexe: 20⇌(1fb) in 6 bedrooms CTV in all bedrooms Ⓡ ∗ sB⇌⋒£39—£49 dB⇌⋒£58—£78 (room only) B
Lift ☾ 45 CFA (heated) gymnasium ♿ *xmas*
English & French V ♔ ☕ ∗Bar lunch 80p—£4.10 Tea 65p Dinner £5.50—£14.45 Wine £6.99 Last dinner 9.45pm
Credit cards 1 2 3 4 5 V

Carlisle

★★★**Swallow Hilltop** London Rd (Swallow) ☎ (0228) 29255 Telex no 64292
Large modern hotel with very good facilities and new leisure complex.
110rm(92⇌5⋒)(6fb) CTV in all bedrooms Ⓡ S% ∗sB&B£25 sB&B⇌⋒£40.50—£41 dB&B£38 dB&B⇌⋒£52—£54 B
Lift ☾500P CFA ✿ (heated) sauna bath solarium gymnasium pool table Disco Tue Live music and dancing Sat Cabaret mthly (Oct—Apr) *xmas*
V ♔ ☕ S% ∗Lunch £6.50&alc Tea 75p Dinner £9&alc Wine £5.50 Last dinner 9.45pm
Credit cards 1 2 3 5

★★**Central** Victoria Viaduct (Greenall Whitley) ☎ (0228) 20256
This hotel stands on Carlisle's old city walls.
82rm(21⇌9⋒)(6fb) CTV in all bedrooms **T** ∗sB&B£20.50—£24.50 sB&B⇌⋒£23.50—£27.50 dB&B£33 dB&B⇌⋒£38.50 B
Lift ☾CTV 15P
V ♔ ☕ ∗Bar lunch £3.05—£3.65&alc Tea 75p Dinner £6.95 Wine £4.30 Last dinner 8.45pm
Credit cards 1 2 3 5

★★**Cumbria Park** 32 Scotland Rd ☎ (0228) 22887
Closed Xmas Day & Boxing Day
Comfortable accommodation and friendly service.
42rm(39⇌⋒)(4fb) 2 CTV in all bedrooms Ⓡ sB&B⇌⋒£24—£28 dB&B⇌⋒£32—£36
CTV 40P ✿ ♿
V ♔ ☕ Lunch £4—£7 Tea 60p—£1.50 High tea £2—£4 Dinner £8—£9.50&alc Wine £5.50 Last dinner 8pm
Credit cards 1 3 V

★★**Pinegrove** 262 London Rd ☎ (0228) 24828
Closed Xmas day
Comfortable hotel with hospitable proprietor.
20rm(8⇌)(6fb) CTV in all bedrooms Ⓡ **T** sB&B£18.50 sB&B⇌£22.50 dB&B fr£28.75 dB&B⇌fr£39
CTV 30P ✿ →

C

V Lunch £7.50—£8&alc Tea £1—£3 Dinner £7.50—£8&alc Wine £4 Last dinner 8.30pm

Credit cards 1 3

★ ***Vallum House*** Burgh Rd (0228) 21860

Closed Xmas

Informal, friendly hotel offering neat accommodation.

10rm CTV in 3 bedrooms TV in 7 bedrooms ®

CTV 50P

V Last dinner 9.30pm

Credit card 1

CARMARTHEN

Dyfed
Map **2** SN42

★★★ **Ivy Bush Royal** Spilman St (Trusthouse Forte) (0267) 235111 Telex no 48520

A popular hotel with businessmen, it is also well situated for touring in West Wales.

79 (9fb) CTV in all bedrooms ® sB&B £43.50 dB&B £59.50

Lift CTV 75P CFA sauna bath *xmas*

Last dinner 9pm

Credit cards 1 2 3 4 5

CARNFORTH

Lancashire
Map **7** SD47

★★ ***Royal Station*** Market St (0524) 732033

Town centre public house, situated close to the railway station.

12rm(5 4)(2fb) CTV in all bedrooms ®

CTV 8P 10P billiards

English, French & Italian V Last dinner 8.30pm

Credit cards 2 3 5

CARNOUSTIE

Tayside *Angus*
Map **12** NO53

★★ **Carlogie House** Carlogie Rd (0241) 53185

Closed 1st—3rd Jan

Small, well decorated, family-run hotel set within its own grounds.

11rm(1 10)(1fb) CTV in all bedrooms ® T sB&B £25 dB&B £35

CTV 150P 4

British & French V Lunch fr£7.75&alc Tea fr£1.75 High Tea fr£4 Dinner fr£7.75&alc Wine £5 Last dinner 9.30pm

Credit cards 1 2 3 5 V

★★ **Glencoe** Links Pde (0241) 53273

RS 1 Jan

Homely, family hotel overlooking golf course, offering very good value meals.

11rm(3 5)(2fb) CTV in all bedrooms T S% sB&B £16 dB&B fr£34

CTV 12P

Scottish & French S% Bar lunch £3.50—£4 Tea 70p—£2 Dinner £8—£13 Wine £5.50 Last dinner 9pm

Credit cards 1 2 3 5 V

★ **Station** (0241) 52447

Small, friendly, town centre hotel next to the station and near the beach.

9rm(2)(2fb) sB&B fr£11 dB&B fr£22 dB&B fr£28

CTV 10—12P Fri Live music & dancing mthly *xmas*

V Lunch fr£3.50 Tea 50p—£1.25 High Tea £3.50—£5 Dinner £6—£7 Last dinner 9pm

Credit cards 1 3 V

CARRADALE

Strathclyde *Argyllshire*
Map **10** NR83

★★ **Carradale** (05833) 223

Pleasant holiday hotel standing in its own gardens, next to the golf course and overlooking Kilbrannan Sound.

14rm(4 3) Annexe: 6rm(1 3)(2fb) ® S% sB&B £16—£17 sB&B £17—£18 dB&B £34—£36 dB&B £36—£38

CTV 20P squash sauna bath solarium

International V Lunch £4.50—£6.50 Tea £1.20 High Tea £3.50—£5.50 Dinner £10.50—£14.50 Wine £4.10 Last dinner 9pm

Credit cards 1 3 V

CARRUTHERSTOWN

Dumfries & Galloway *Dumfriesshire*
Map **11** NY17

★★ **Hetland Hall** (038784) 201

27rm(12 11)(4fb) in 1 bedroom CTV in all bedrooms ® T sB&B £20—£25 sB&B £28—£34 dB&B £34—£42

CTV 60P solarium gymnasium badminton court Live music & dancing Sat *xmas*

International V Lunch £4.50—£9 Tea fr 75p High Tea £3.85—£8 Dinner £8.50—£10.50&alc Wine £5 Last dinner 9.30pm

Credit cards 1 2 3 5 V

CARTMEL

Cumbria
Map **7** SD37

★★ **Aynsome Manor** (1m N on unclass rd) (044854) 276

Closed 3—25 Jan

This lovely old manor house features open fires in its comfortable lounges and serves a freshly-prepared five-course dinner of a very high standard.

11rm(9 1) Annexe: 2(2fb) 1 CTV in all bedrooms ® sB&B £30.50—£32(incl dinner) sB&B fr£32—£34.50(incl dinner) dB&B £53—£58(incl dinner) dB&B £58—£63(incl dinner)

20P *xmas*

Tea fr 70p Dinner fr£11.80 Wine £4.20 Last dinner 8.15pm

Credit cards 1 2 3

★★***Grammar*** ☎ (044854) 367
Closed Jan & Feb
Converted school-house, now a comfortable hotel overlooking the racecourse.
11⇨⋒(2fb) CTV in 2 bedrooms TV in 2 bedrooms ®ℝ
CTV 30P ✿ *xmas*
Cosmopolitan **V** Last dinner 8pm

★★***Priory*** The Square ☎ (044854) 267
RS Dec—Mar
Delightful small hotel, family owned and run, located in the town square.
9rm(5⇨)(3fb) ®ℝ
CTV 8P *xmas*
International **V** Last dinner 8.30pm
Credit card 1

✿XX**Uplands Hotel** Haggs Ln
☎ (044 854) 248
(*Rosette awarded for dinner only*)
Tom and Diana Peter were at Miller Howe, Windermere, with John Tovey for many years before opening this delightful hotel and restaurant in 1985. The four-course menu includes a tureen of home-made soup, and the range of dishes spans such old favourites as loin of lamb and the more exotic roast guinea fowl, all prepared with skill and inventiveness and accompanied by a carefully-chosen wine list.
Closed 4 Jan—12 Feb
Lunch not served Mon
30 seats Lunch £9 Dinner £15 Wine £6
Last dinner 8pm 12P
4 bedrooms available nc 10yrs
Credit cards 1 2

CASTERTON
Cumbria
Map **7** SD67
★★**Pheasant Inn** ☎ Kirkby Lonsdale (0468) 71230
Village inn with newly appointed restaurant and bedrooms.
10rm(9⇨1⋒)(1fb) 1 CTV available in bedrooms ®sB&B⇨⋒fr£19.50 dB&B⇨⋒fr£32 ℝ
CTV 60P ✿ *xmas*
V Lunch fr£5.75 Dinner fr£10.50&alc Wine £4.75 Last dinner 9.15pm

CASTLE ASHBY
Northamptonshire
Map **4** SP85
XX**Falcon Hotel** ☎ Yardley Hastings (060129) 200 Telex no 312207
V 60 seats Lunch £14.25alc Dinner £14.25alc Wine £6 Last dinner 9.45pm 60P
Credit cards 1 2 3

CASTLE CARY
Somerset
Map **3** ST63
★★***George*** High St, Market Pl ☎ (0963) 50761
Closed Xmas
A town centre inn with considerable character and offering particularly attractive accommodation.
17rm(15⇨2⋒) 1 CTV in all bedrooms ℝ
12P
English & French **V** Last dinner 9.30pm
Credit cards 1 2 3 5

C

CASTLE COMBE
Wiltshire
Map **3** ST87

★★★ **Manor House** (Best Western) ☎ (0249) 782206 Telex no 449931

A 14th-century house, with 26 acres of parkland in wooded valley. It is tastefully furnished and comfortably appointed.

13rm(10 3) Annexe: 20 (1fb) 4 CTV in all bedrooms ® **T** S% sB&B £40 dB&B £72—£89

☾ 100P (heated) (hard) xmas

English & Continental **V** Lunch £10&alc Tea fr£1 High Tea fr£3 Dinner fr£18&alc Wine £7.50 Last dinner 9pm

Credit cards 1 2 3 5

See advertisement on page 199

CASTLE DONINGTON
Leicestershire
Map **8** SK42

★★★ **Priest House Inn** Kings Mills (2m W unclass) (Inter Hotel) ☎ Derby (0332) 810649 Telex no 341995

Very old stone building by River Trent with modern, comfortable bedrooms in adjacent row of cottages.

Annexe: 15rm(5 10)(2fb) 2 CTV in all bedrooms ® **T** sB&B £32—£35 dB&B £45—£49.50

150P Live music & dancing Sat

V Lunch £3.75—£5.95&alc Tea £1.20&alc Dinner £6.50—£12.50&alc Wine £5.90 Last dinner 10pm

Credit cards 1 2 3 5 Ⓥ

★★ **Donington Manor** High St ☎ Derby (0332) 810253 Telex no 377208

Closed 27—30 Dec

Restored and modernised Regency posting house and coaching inn, catering mainly for the commercial trade.

35rm(34) Annexe: 3rm(3fb) 4 CTV in all bedrooms ® **T** * sB&B fr£27 sB&B fr£32.75 dB&B fr£34 dB&B fr£45.40

☾ CTV 50P Live music & dancing Sat in winter Cabaret wknds *xmas*

English & French S% * Lunch £4.90 Tea 45p Dinner £6.50 Last dinner 9.15pm

Credit cards 1 2 3 5

○ **Donington Thistle** East Midlands Airport (Thistle) ☎ 01-937 8033

112

Due to open early 1987.

CASTLE DOUGLAS
Dumfries & Galloway *Kirkcudbrightshire*
Map **11** NX76

★★ **Imperial** King St ☎ (0556) 2086

Neat, homely hotel in main street.

13rm(3 4) CTV in 9 bedrooms ® sB&B £15—£16 sB&B £19—£21 dB&B £29—£31 dB&B £35—£37

CTV 15P 8

V Bar Lunch £1.75—£4.50&alc Tea 55—70p High Tea £3—£7.50 Wine £4.50 Last high tea 7pm

Credit cards 1 3 Ⓥ

★★ **King's Arms** St Andrew's Street ☎ (0556) 2626

Closed New Years Day

Modernised coaching inn, standing on a corner site in this thriving market town.

14rm(5 3) CTV in 8 bedrooms S% sB&B £15—£16 sB&B £20.50—£21 dB&B £30—£32 dB&B £41—£42

CTV 17P

French **V** Bar Lunch £3.60—£4 High Tea £5—£6 Dinner £11.50—£12.50&alc Wine £5 Last dinner 8pm

Credit cards 1 2 3 5 Ⓥ

★ **Merrick** 193 King St ☎ (0556) 2173

RS Oct—Mar

Friendly hotel which forms upper storeys of main street building. Restricted drinks licence only.

6rm(2fb) CTV in 1 bedroom ® sB&B £9.50—£10 dB&B £18—£20

CTV 6P

High Tea £4—£5&alc Dinner £4.50—£6&alc Wine £4 Last dinner 8pm

Ⓥ

CASTLETON
Gwent
Map **3** ST28

★★★ **Ladbroke Wentloog Castle** (Ladbroke) ☎ (0633) 680591

Well appointed, modern hotel near M4.

54rm(34 20)(2fb) in 10 bedrooms CTV in all bedrooms ® **T** sB&B £35—£42 dB&B £42—£50

☾ 150P sauna bath Live music and dancing Thu & Sat

V Lunch £5—£12 Tea £1 High Tea £2.20 Dinner £5—£12&alc Wine £4.25 Last dinner 10.30pm

Credit cards 1 2 3 5 Ⓥ

See advertisement under Cardiff

CASTLETON
North Yorkshire
Map **8** NZ60

★★ **Moorlands** ☎ (0287) 60206

Country house on the edge of the village, with views across the Esk Valley.

10rm(1 5) sB&B fr£16 dB&B fr£32 dB&B fr£34

CTV 15P nc 2yrs

English & French Lunch fr£5.50 Tea 70—90p High Tea £3.50—£5 Dinner £11alc Wine £4.75 Last dinner 9pm

CASTLETOWN
Isle of Man
See **Man, Isle of**

CÂTEL (CASTEL)
Guernsey, Channel Islands
See **Channel Islands**

CATTAWADE
Suffolk
Map **5** TM13

✕ **Bucks** ☎ Colchester (0206) 392571

Attractively converted Victorian pub featuring friendly service and imaginatively cooked food. Notable is the 'Cameo' menu of 11 small courses which include most of the popular dishes on the menu.

Dinner not served Sun

International 28 seats S% Lunch £10—£15&alc Dinner £10—£15 Wine £4.95 Last dinner 9.45pm 50P

Credit cards 1 2 3 5 Ⓥ

CATTERICK BRIDGE
North Yorkshire
Map **8** SE29

★★ **Bridge House** ☎ Richmond (0748) 818331

Old coaching inn with character bars, impressive dining room and homely bedrooms.

17rm(4 3)(4fb) 1 CTV in all bedrooms ® **T** in 7 bedrooms * sB&B £16.50—£17.50 sB&B £25—£26.50 dB&B £27.50—£29 dB&B £35—£39

CTV 100P

V * Lunch £4.75—£8.50 Dinner £6.50—£8.50&alc Wine £6 Last dinner 9.30pm

Credit cards 1 2 3 5

CAVENDISH
Suffolk
Map **5** TL84

✕✕ **Alfonso Ristorante** ☎ Glemsford (0787) 280372

Small, family run Italian restaurant in an idyllic setting overlooking delightful village green and historic church.

Lunch not served Mon Dinner not served Sun

European **V** 30 seats Lunch £10.50alc Dinner £15alc Wine £6 Last dinner 9.30pm 20P

Credit cards 1 2 5

CAWSAND
Cornwall
Map **2** SX45

★★ *L* **Criterion** Garrett St ☎ Plymouth (0752) 822244

Small family-run hotel at the water's edge, in the village centre.

8rm(3)(1fb) CTV in all bedrooms * sB&B £14.50 sB&B £20—£25 dB&B £26—£30 dB&B £34—£37

CTV xmas

V Lunch £3.20alc Tea 60p—£1.30 High Tea £4—£7&alc Dinner £10—£16&alc Wine £4.95 Last dinner 10.30pm

Credit cards 1 3

CHADLINGTON
Oxfordshire
Map **4** SP32

★★ ***Chadlington House*** (060876) 437 Telex no 83138

Closed Jan—Feb

Delightful hotel in its own grounds with welcoming proprietors, homely rooms and good cooking.

10rm(3 6)(1fb) 1 CTV in 7 bedrooms Ⓡ B

CTV 20P 2 nc8yrs

English & French V Last dinner 8pm

Credit cards 1 3 5

CHAGFORD
Devon
Map **3** SX78

★★★ **Gidleigh Park**
(see red star box opposite)

★★★ *HB* **Great Tree** Sandy Park (2½m N on A382) (Best Western) (06473) 2491

Closed 27Dec—Jan

A 19th-century hunting lodge set in 20 acres of grounds with splendid views of the Dartmoor tors.

13 Annexe: 1 (2fb) CTV in all bedrooms Ⓡ T in 4 bedrooms sB&B £23—£29 dB&B £50—£58 B

20P 4 xmas

V Lunch £5—£6.50 Tea £1.50—£3 Dinner £10—£12 Wine £4.10 Last dinner 9pm

Credit cards 1 2 3 5 Ⓥ

★★★ *HL* **Mill End** Sandy Park (2m N on A382) (06473) 2282

Closed 18—28 Dec

Carefully converted from an old watermill, this hotel has well kept grounds set in lovely countryside.

★★★

★★★ GIDLEIGH PARK, CHAGFORD

(Relais et Chateaux) (06473) 2367

The big news here is the departure of Chef John Webber to the newly opened Cliveden Hotel and his replacement by Shaun Hill who has given up his own restaurant in Stratford on Avon. At this stage we have not seen a great deal of change: they both cook in the same modern style; perhaps some of the mixtures are less well judged but the sauces are improved with more intense flavour. As well as the usual five course dinner they now also offer a small à la carte menu featuring dishes with more expensive ingredients. To complement your meal, choose a wine from the superb wine list of more than 300 with vintages back to 1920. It is altogether a fine list but unique in its selection of American examples, and prices start reasonably. Apart from the food the hotel is notable in many respects. Mock-tudor in style, its situation in 40 acres of grounds sweeping down to the tumbling North Teign River at the edge of Dartmoor is enchanting. Nor does the interior of this charming country house let it down. The owners, Paul and Kay Henderson have dedicated themselves to the achievement of high standards and they have clearly succeeded. Sumptuous seating in the drawing room and hall, antiques, pictures, porcelain, lots of flowers and open fires when necessary, all play their part in creating an appealing ambiance — one which has a rare quality of enabling the guest to be truly relaxed (rather like the Isle of Eriska). Bedrooms are all you would expect, comfortable and provided with many extras, and this year new bedrooms have been added. The young staff deserve special mention for their obliging disposition and general amiability.

12 Annexe: 2 CTV in all bedrooms T S% *sB&B £50—£120 dB&B £50—£120 Continental breakfast B

25P croquet

French S% *Lunch fr£16&alc Tea £1.50—£4.50 Dinner £25 Wine £7 Last dinner 9.30pm

Credit cards 1 2 3 5

17rm(14 7)(2fb) CTV in all bedrooms T sB&B £24—£27.50 sB&B £25—£45 dB&B £52.50—£60

CTV 17P 4 (£1 per day)

English & French Lunch £11 Tea £1.25 Dinner £13.50 Wine £5.50 Last dinner 9pm

Credit cards 1 2 3 5

★★★ *H* **Teignworthy** Frenchbeer (2m S on unclass rd to Thornworthy) (06473) 3355

Charming stone house in lovely setting with superb views, where the owners provide a welcoming atmosphere.

6 Annexe: 3 CTV in all bedrooms T sB&B £42.50—£48.50 dB&B £67—£77 B

15P 2 (grass) sauna bath solarium nc12yrs *xmas*

Lunch £10—£20&alc Tea £1.50—£4.50 Dinner £19.50—£25 Wine £5 Last dinner 9.30pm

Credit cards 1 3 Ⓥ

C

★★*L* ***Easton Court*** Easton Cross (1½m E A382) ☎ (06473) 3469

Great care has been taken to preserve the original features of this small, thatched Tudor house whilst at the same time offering modern facilities. Several books, including Evelyn Waugh's "Brideshead Revisited", are known to have been written here.

8rm(3⇌5⋔) 1⊟ CTV available in bedrooms ®B

⅟CTV 20P ⊞ ✿ nc10yrs *xmas*

V ♱ ⊡ Last dinner 8pm

Credit cards 1 2 3 5

★★**Three Crowns** ☎ (06473) 3444

A 13th-century stone inn with busy bars, situated in the village.

17rm(8⇌2⋔)(3fb) 2⊟ CTV in 8 bedrooms ® S% sB&B£17—£20 sB&B⇌⋔£20—£25 dB&B£34—£40 dB&B⇌⋔£40—£45 B

CTV 16P 1⌂ snooker games room *xmas*

♉English & Continental V ♱ Lunch £3—£7&alc Dinner £7—£10.50&alc Wine £6.50 Last dinner 9.30pm

Credit cards 1 3

CHALE
Isle of Wight
See **Wight, Isle of**

CHALFORD
Gloucestershire
Map **3** SO80

★★**Springfield House** London Rd (on A419) ☎ Brimscombe (0453) 883555

Closed 1st 2 wks in Jan

A comfortable small hotel offering personal service and well prepared meals.

8rm(7⇌)(1fb) 2⊟ CTV in all bedrooms ® sB&B£26 sB&B⇌£28—£32 dB&B⇌£42—£46 B

20P ⊞ ✿ *xmas*

♉French V ♱ ⊡ Lunch £7—£14 Tea 75p—£1 Dinner £9—£14 Wine £4.75 Last dinner 9.30pm

Credit cards 1 2 3 Ⓥ

CHANNEL ISLANDS
Map **16**

ALDERNEY

★★**Inchalla** ☎ Alderney (048182) 3220

The hotel is small and modern, bright and comfortably appointed. À la carte and table d'hôte menus are available, the food being well cooked and presented.

12rm(8⇌) CTV in all bedrooms ® ✈
*sB&B£15.50 sB&B⇌£15.50 dB&B£31 dB&B⇌£31

8P ✿ sauna bath solarium

♱ ⊡ High Tea fr£1.50 Dinner fr£7.95&alc Wine £3 Last dinner 8pm

Credit cards 2 3

GUERNSEY
CÂTEL (CASTEL)

★★**Hotel Hougue du Pommier** Hougue du Pommier Rd ☎ Guernsey (0481) 56531 Telex no 4191664

Attractive hotel converted from old farmhouse with spacious bar and restaurant and well laid out gardens.

39rm(17⇌22⋔)(12fb) CTV in all bedrooms ® T ✈
*sB&B⇌⋔£13.50—£25 dB&B⇌⋔£27—£54

92P ✿ ⊡(heated) ⚑18 Live music Mon & Thu *xmas*

♉English & Continental V ♱ ⊡ *Bar lunch £1—£3.35&alc Tea 75p—£1.60 Dinner £6.60 Wine £3.60 Last dinner 9.45pm

Credit cards 1 3

FERMAIN BAY

★★★**Le Chalet** (Consort) ☎ Guernsey (0481) 35716

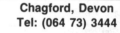

Closed 25 Oct—20 Apr

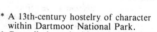

In wooded valley with views of sea, this Austrian chalet style hotel has comfortable public rooms and bedrooms.

48rm(40⇌5⋒)(3fb) CTV in all bedrooms ®T sB&B⇌⋒£18.50—£21.50 dB&B⇌⋒£31—£40 B

35P

English, Austrian & French V Lunch £7.50alc Tea £1.50—£2.50 Dinner £6.50—£8.50&alc Wine £2.75

Credit cards 1 2 3 4 5 Ⓥ

★★**La Favorita** ☎ Guernsey (0481) 35666

Closed 21 Dec—7 Feb
RS 1—20 Dec & 7—28 Feb

Attractive holiday hotel overlooking valley leading to sea. It has smart bar, open fires in lounges and modernised bedrooms.

30rm(28⇌2⋒)(6fb) CTV in all bedrooms ®T S% sB&B⇌⋒£15.50—£24 dB&B⇌⋒£31—£56

40P

V S% Bar lunch £4.50alc Tea £1 Dinner £6 Wine £2 Last dinner 9pm

Credit card 3 Ⓥ

ST MARTIN

★★★**Hotel Bella Luce** La Fosse ☎ Guernsey (0481) 38764

Closed 3 wks Jan/Feb

Once a 12th century manor house, the hotel stands quietly in its own grounds. It has a popular restaurant with a comprehensive à la carte menu, and the beamed bars are attractive.

31rm(27⇌4⋒)(9fb) CTV in all bedrooms ® available in bedrooms
*sB&B⇌⋒£16—£27.50
dB&B⇌⋒£24—£52

60P (heated) sauna bath solarium *xmas*

English, French & Continental V
*Lunch £4.15—£6.95&alc Tea 90p—£2.95&alc Dinner £6.95—£7.95&alc Wine £3.95 Last dinner 10pm

★★★**Green Acres** Les Hubits ☎ Guernsey (0481) 35711

Attractive, bright, modernised hotel in quiet setting with tidy gardens. The lounge has been refurbished and the bedrooms are being upgraded. The staff are friendly and helpful. Good value for money.

48rm(44⇌4⋒)(3fb) CTV in all bedrooms ®T dB&B⇌⋒£28—£48

75P (heated) solarium *xmas*

English & French Lunch £5 Tea 75p Dinner £7&alc Wine £3.40 Last dinner 8.30pm

Credit cards 1 3

Channel Islands, Fermain Bay — St Martin

★★★**Ronnie Ronalde's St Martin's** Les Merrienes (Best Western) ☎ Guernsey (0481) 35644

Spacious holiday hotel standing in its own grounds, offering good amenities.

51⇌(20fb) CTV in all bedrooms
sB&B⇌£23—£28.50 dB&B⇌£46—£57

Lift 300P 3(£5) CFA (heated) (hard) pool table table tennis croquet

English, Austrian & French V S% Lunch £5.50&alc Tea fr80p High Tea fr£2.50 Dinner £7.70&alc Wine £2.20 Last dinner 9pm

Credit cards 1 2 3 5

★★★***St Margaret's Lodge*** Forest Rd ☎ Guernsey (0481) 35757

White painted hotel with lawns and pool. The lounges are pleasant, and it has an attractive bar and restaurant. Within reach of the airport.

43⇌ CTV in all bedrooms ® in 10 bedrooms T B

Lift CTV 100P CFA (heated) Live music & dancing Fri *xmas*

English & French V Last dinner 9.30pm

Credit cards 1 3 5

ST PETER PORT

★★★★**Old Government House** Ann's Pl ☎ Guernsey (0481) 24921 Telex no 4191144

Long established, modernised hotel with swimming pool, basement disco and comfortable lounge. There are good views over the harbour.

74 (8fb) CTV in all bedrooms **T** ✱sB&B £23—£35 dB&B £46—£70

Lift ☾ 20P CFA (heated) Disco 6 nights wkly Live music & dancing 6 nights wkly *xmas*

English, French & Italian **V** ✱Lunch £5—£6&alc Tea fr65p Dinner fr£7.25&alc Wine £3.70 Last dinner 9.15pm

Credit cards [1] [2] [3] [5] Ⓥ

★★★★**St Pierre Park** Rohais ☎ Guernsey (0481) 28282 Telex no 4191146

Attractive modern hotel with well equipped comfortable bedrooms and smart Victor Hugo restaurant. There are many good facilities including shops and the indoor pool near the brasserie restaurant. Also many sports facilities, and, in special grounds, a lake and bird sanctuary.

133 (1fb) CTV in all bedrooms ®**T** ✱sB&B £39—£49.25 dB&B £64—£78.50 **B**

Lift ☾ 350P (heated) (hard) sauna bath solarium gymnasium croquet games room Live music & dancing nightly *xmas*

English & French **V** Lunch £6.50&alc Tea £1.50—£5 Dinner £10 Wine £4.50 Last dinner 10pm

Credit cards [1] [2] [3] [5]

★★★**La Frégate** Les Côtils ☎ Guernsey (0481) 24624

Well converted 17th century manor house overlooking sea with comfortable bedrooms, and serving good, French-style food using fresh raw materials.

13 CTV available in bedrooms ®**T**

25P nc 14yrs *xmas*

French **V** Last dinner 9.30pm

Credit cards [1] [2] [3] [4] [5]

★★★**La Collinette** St Jacques ☎ Guernsey (0481) 710331

Comfortable hotel in its own grounds in quiet part of the town. Split level restaurant provides good food. There are good self catering bungalows in the grounds.

27rm(25 2) CTV in all bedrooms ®**T** ✱sB&B £12—£25 dB&B £24—£50 **B**

CTV 25P (heated) sauna bath

English & French **V** ✱Lunch £5 Tea fr75p High Tea fr£3 Dinner fr£6.50 Wine £3.10 Last dinner 8.30pm

Credit cards [1] [2] [3] [5]

★★★**Royal** Glategny Esplanade ☎ Guernsey (0481) 23921 Telex no 4191221

Old established hotel facing sea with plush grill room and outdoor pool. Regular entertainment is provided.

78rm(71 7)(8fb) CTV in all bedrooms ✱sB&B £18.50—£29 dB&B £37—£58

Lift ☾ 100P CFA (heated) Live music & dancing 5 nights wkly *xmas*

English, French & Italian **V** ✱Lunch fr£6&alc Tea fr£1 Dinner fr£7&alc Wine £3.60 Last dinner 10.30pm

Credit cards [1] [2] [3] [5] Ⓥ

★★**Hotel de Havelet** Havelet (Consort) ☎ Guernsey (0481) 22199

Georgian style house with good views. All bedrooms have been refurbished to a good standard. Restaurant and bar in separate modern building.

32 (6fb) CTV in all bedrooms ®**T** sB&B £18.50—£23.50 dB&B £29—£45 **B**

CTV 40P *xmas*

🍽English, Austrian & French V Lunch £5.50—£10.50alc Dinner £6.50—£7.50£alc Wine £2.75 Last dinner 9.30pm

Credit cards 1 2 3 4 5

★★**Moore's** Pollet (Consort)
☎ Guernsey (0481) 24452

Tourist and commercial hotel close to the shopping centre in town.

34rm(31🛁) Annexe: 6rm(3🛁4fb) CTV in all bedrooms ® T sB&B£15.50—£21.65 sB&B🛁£16.50—£22.50 dB&B£26—£36 dB&B🛁£28—£41.50

Lift ☾ P xmas

🍽English, Austrian & French V Lunch fr£4.50 Tea fr£1 Dinner £5.50—£7.50&alc Wine £2.90 Last dinner 8.45pm

Credit cards 1 2 3 5 Ⓥ

See advertisement on page 206

XXX **Le Nautique** Quay Steps
☎ Guernsey (0481) 21714

Attractive popular converted harbour warehouse, with food (especially local fish) of high standard.

Closed Sun & 1st 3 wks Jan

🍽French 66 seats S% Lunch £13.80alc Dinner £13.80alc Wine £4.40 Last dinner 10pm P nc5yrs

Credit cards 1 2 3 5 Ⓥ

Channel Islands, St Peter Port — Beaumont

X ***Nino's Ristorante Italiano*** Lefevre St
☎ Guernsey (0481) 23052

Popular restaurant serving pasta and fish. Grill and pizza restaurant below.

Closed Sun

🍽English, French & Italian V 92 seats Last dinner 10.30pm 1P

Credit cards 1 2 3 4 5

ST SAVIOUR

★★★**L'Atlantique** Perelle Bay
☎ Guernsey (0481) 64056

Modern hotel facing sea with attractive bars and restaurants. Also good self-catering units in the grounds.

21🛁(4fb) CTV in all bedrooms ® T sB&B🛁£13—£25 dB&B🛁£26—£40 B

80P (heated)

🍽International V ✱ Lunch £3.75—£5.75 Dinner £6.75—£7.25&alc Wine £3.80 Last dinner 10pm

Credit cards 1 2 3 5

JERSEY

ARCHIRONDEL

★★**Les Arches** Archirondel Bay
☎ Jersey (0534) 53839 Telex no 4192085

An attractive holiday hotel, with modern bedrooms and good bars, overlooking the sea.

54rm(35🛁19🚿) CTV in all bedrooms T sB&B🛁🚿£16.50—£26 dB&B🛁🚿£33—£52

☾ CTV 120P (heated) (hard) Disco 6 nights wkly Cabaret wkly (in season) xmas

🍽English & Continental V Lunch £6.50—£11.50 Tea 85p—£1 Dinner £8—£16 Wine £3.50 Last dinner 8.30pm

Credit cards 1 3 4

BEAUMONT

★★**Hotel L'Hermitage** ☎ Jersey (0534) 33314 Telex no 4192170

Closed 2 Nov—15 Mar

Modest tourist hotel with some chalet-style rooms.

109rm(96🛁13🚿) CTV in all bedrooms ® ✱ sB&B🛁🚿£12.50—£19.90 dB&B🛁🚿£25—£39.80

☾ 100P (heated) sauna bath Disco, Live music & dancing Cabaret wkly nc 14yrs →

English & French Lunch £3 Tea 40p Dinner £4.50 Wine £2.50 Last dinner 8pm

C

CORBIERE

XXX Sea Crest Hotel Restaurant Petit Port ☎ Jersey (0534) 42687

Attractive, popular hotel restaurant specialising in fresh fish and Italian dishes.

Closed Mon (Nov—Mar) Dinner not served Sun (Nov—Mar)

English, French & Italian **V** 60 seats S% *Lunch £12alc Dinner £15alc Wine £3.60 Last dinner 10pm 30P

Credit cards 1 2 3 4

Channel Islands, Beaumont — Gorey

GOREY

★★★ Old Court House ☎ Jersey (0534) 54444 Telex no 4192032

Closed Nov—Mar

Old courthouse building with a modern frontage and an attractive, beamed restaurant.

58 (4fb) CTV in all bedrooms
sB&B £20.50—£29.50
dB&B £41—£59

Lift 40P (heated) sauna bath solarium Live music & dancing wkly Cabaret wkly

English, French & Italian *Lunch fr£3.50 Dinner £7.50&alc Wine £2.50 Last dinner 9pm

Credit cards 1 2 3 5

★★ Dolphin Gorey Pier ☎ Jersey (0534) 53370 Telex no 4192085

This small hotel overlooking the harbour has a popular 'Fisherman's Bar'; most bedrooms are equipped with private shower.

17rm(14⋒)(1fb) CTV in all bedrooms 🐕 S% *sB&B£15—£18 sB&B⋒£17—£20 dB&B£30—£36 dB&B⋒£34—£40 B

☾CTV P *xmas*

English & Continental V S% *Lunch £4.80—£9 Tea 60p—£1.20 Dinner £9&alc Last dinner 10pm

Credit cards 1 3 4 V

✕ **Galley** ☎ Jersey (0534) 53456

Pleasantly decorated little restaurant by the harbour, it specialises in shellfish.

Closed Jan—14 Feb Dinner not served Mon (ex Bank Hols)

English & French V 42 seats *Lunch fr£6.50&alc Dinner £13alc Wine £4 Last dinner 10.15pm P

Credit cards 1 3 5

L'ETACQ

★★★B **Lobster Pot Hotel & Restaurant** ☎ (0534) 82888 Telex no 4192605

Attractive stone building with excellent accommodation and popular restaurant.

13⇌ CTV in all bedrooms ® T 🐕 sB&B⇌£32—£46 dB&B⇌£44—£72

☾CTV 90P ✿ Live music & dancing 6 nights wkly nc 13yrs *xmas*

English, French & Italian V Lunch £6—£6.50&alc Tea £1—£2 Dinner £9.25—£10.25&alc Wine £3.75 Last dinner 10.15pm

Credit cards 1 2 3 5

Channel Islands, Gorey — St Brelade

ROZEL BAY

★★ *L* **Château La Chaire** Rozel Valley

☎ Jersey (0534) 63354

Quiet country house in wooded setting which includes some rare and exotic plants. The panelled reception hall leads to an ornate lounge. There is another panelled lounge and a comfortable dining room. The atmosphere is peaceful and informal.

14⇌⋒ CTV in all bedrooms T sB&B⇌⋒£32—£46 dB&B⇌⋒£55—£76

☾30P ✿ nc 7yrs

French V Lunch £6.50—£8.50&alc Tea 80p—£3 Dinner £8.50—£10.50&alc Wine £3.80 Last dinner 9.30pm

Credit cards 1 2 3 4 5

See advertisement on page 208

ST AUBIN

✕✕ **Old Court House Inn** St Aubin's Harbour ☎ Jersey (0534) 41156

17th century harbourside restaurant (featured in 'Bergerac') offering seafood specialities.

English & French V 56 seats S% *Bar lunch £2.50alc Dinner £15alc Wine £3.50 Last dinner 11pm P nc

ST BRELADE

★★★★ **Atlantic** La Moye, St Brelade's Bay (Best Western) ☎ Jersey (0534) 44101 Telex no 4192405

Closed Jan—7 Mar

Modern hotel in its own grounds, with sea views. It has a good restaurant and the open plan public rooms are well appointed.

46⇌ CTV in all bedrooms T 🐕 sB&B⇌£38—£59 dB&B⇌£56—£98

Lift ☾46P CFA ✿ (heated) (hard) *xmas*

International Lunch fr£7.50&alc Dinner fr£11.50&alc Wine £4 Last dinner 9.15pm

Credit cards 1 2 3 4 5

★★★★ **Hotel l'Horizon** St Brelade's Bay (Prestige) ☎ Jersey (0534) 43101 Telex no 4192281

Good, well appointed hotel at Waters edge with well equipped bedrooms. Popular Star Grill restaurant provides comprehensive menu with good fish dishes and a selection of seasonal items. There are 250 wines on the list, including one from Jersey.

104⇌⋒(7fb) 1 CTV in all bedrooms T 🐕 S% sB&B⇌⋒£35—£61 dB&B⇌⋒£70—£146 B →

C

Lift ☾ 125P CFA ⛆ ▭(heated) Live music & dancing 6 nights wkly (in season) *xmas*

♁International **V** ♁ ☕ S% Lunch £8alc Tea £1.40alc Dinner £15&alc Wine £4.20 Last dinner 9.45pm

Credit cards 1 2 3 4 5

★★★**Château Valeuse** Rue de Valeuse, St Brelade's Bay ☎ Jersey (0534) 43476

Closed Nov—Feb

Small comfortable hotel with fine view across lawns to the sea.

Channel Islands, St Brelade

26rm(18🛁5⛆) ✈

*sB&B£17.50—£22.50 sB&B🛁⛆£20.50—£25.50 dB&B£35—£45 dB&B🛁⛆£41—£51

☾ CTV 50P ⛆ ✿ ⛀ (heated) nc5yrs

♁French ♁ ☕ Lunch £4.50&alc Dinner £6&alc Wine £3.50 Last dinner 9.15pm

Credit cards 1 3

★★**Beau Rivage** ☎ Jersey (0534) 45983 Telex no 4192341

Closed Nov—Mar

Backing on to a sandy bay, this hotel has been completely modernised to provide comfortable holiday accommodation.

27🛁⛆(9fb) CTV in all bedrooms ✈ sB&B🛁⛆£18—£25 dB&B🛁⛆£22—£50

Lift ☾ 14P Disco wkly Live music & dancing 4 nights wkly

♁English, French & Italian **V** ♁ ☕ Lunch £2.50—£5&alc Tea 75p High Tea £2 Dinner £7—£10&alc Wine £3.25 Last dinner 7.30pm

Credit cards 1 3

Chateau La Chaire, Rozel Valley,
Jersey. Telephone: Jersey (0534) 63354
Telex: 449848
★★
1st Register
Château La Chaire
This beautiful country house hotel nestles in a cliffside setting in the heart of the magnificent Rozel Valley, just a few minutes walk from the quaint Rozel Bay. The Chateau is surrounded by exotic trees and shrubs in its 7 acres of terraced gardens where guests can relax and enjoy the many walks. Having recently undergone a total refurbishment of all its bedrooms the hotel now offers luxurious accommodation with ensuite facilities — some with jacuzzis. The restaurant and Rococo style lounge are furnished with antiques and this coupled with truly traditional hospitality, service and fine food and wine, now offers a truly relaxing country house atmosphere whether for a weekend away or a holiday.

Channel Islands, St Clements Bay — St Helier

ST CLEMENTS BAY

★★★**Hotel Ambassadeur** Greve d'Azette ☎ Jersey (0534) 24455

Closed Jan & Feb

Modernised holiday hotel overlooking sea with contemporary public rooms and nicely furnished bedrooms. There is a separate à la carte restaurant and 14 good self catering units within the hotel.

41⇌(4fb) CTV in all bedrooms *sB&B⇌£14—£26 dB&B⇌£28—£52

Lift ☾ 50P ⛵ (heated) *xmas*

English, French & Italian ♈ ☕ *Lunch £5.50—£11&alc Tea fr85p Dinner £5.50—£11&alc Wine £3.50 Last dinner 9.45pm

Credit cards 1 2 3 5 Ⓥ

XXX **Shakespeare Hotel** Samares Coast Rd ☎ Jersey (0534) 51915

Busy restaurant within Shakespeare Hotel. There is a comprehensive menu of traditional fare, and service is smart and efficient. Must book.

Closed Feb Lunch not served Mon—Sat

French **V** 130 seats Lunch £5—£8&alc Dinner £7—£8.50&alc Wine £3.20 Last dinner 10pm 50P Disco Fri & Sat

Credit cards 1 2 3 5

ST HELIER

❀★★★★**Grand** The Esplanade ☎ (0534) 22301 Telex no 4192104

(Rosette awarded for Victoria's).

Large, recently modernised hotel with good leisure facilities. Victoria's restaurant is attractive and well appointed with good selection of dishes.

116⇌ CTV in all bedrooms **T** *sB&B⇌⫿£29—£43 dB&B⇌⫿£58—£86 **B**

Lift ☾ 35P CFA ▭(heated) billiards sauna bath solarium gymnasium Live music & dancing nightly (in restaurant) & Sat in summer (in hotel) *xmas*

English & Continental **V** ♈ ☕

Credit cards 1 2 3 5

★★★**Apollo** St Saviour's Rd ☎ Jersey (0534) 25441 Telex no 4192086

Closed Sep—Apr

Popular, modern style hotel with refurbished public rooms. Good parking.

90⇌⫿(5fb) 1⊟ ⚡ in 5 bedrooms CTV in all bedrooms ®**T** ✗ sB&B⇌⫿£31—£39 dB&B⇌⫿£47—£55 **B**

Lift ☾ CTV 45P ⇌ ▭(heated) Disco twice wkly Cabaret wkly *xmas*

French ♈ ☕ S% Lunch £6alc Tea 75p—£1.25 Dinner £7—£7.50&alc Wine £3 Last dinner 9pm

Credit cards 1 2 3 4 5

★★★**Beaufort** Green St ☎ Jersey (0534) 32471 Telex no 4192160

Modern, comfortable, conveniently situated hotel popular with tourists and businesspeople. The bar has been refurbished and the bedrooms are being further upgraded.

54⇌⫿(3fb) CTV in all bedrooms ®**T** ✗ sB&B⇌⫿£36—£44 dB&B⇌⫿£52—£60 **B**

Lift ☾ CTV 24P ⇌ ▭(heated) *xmas*

French ♈ ☕ Lunch £6.50alc Tea 75p—£1.25 Dinner £7—7.50&alc Wine £3.25 Last dinner 9pm

Credit cards 1 2 3 4 5

★★★**Pomme D'Or** The Esplande ☎ Jersey (0534) 78644 Telex no 4192309

Central, modernised hotel facing harbour, and having extensive public rooms, coffee shop and carvery. Popular with businessmen.

→

C

151⇌⌂(6fb) CTV in all bedrooms ® T ⊁ S% ✱sB&B⇌⌂£29—£32 dB&B⇌⌂£48—£52 ₱

Lift ☾ ℙ Disco twice wkly (in season) Live music & dancing nighly (in season) Cabaret twice wkly (in season) *xmas*

Continental V S% Lunch £2.75—£5.25 Tea 70p High Tea £2—£3 Dinner £8.50—£10&alc Wine £3.50 Last dinner 9pm

Credit cards 1 2 3 4 5 V

C

★★**Mountview** St John's Road ☎ Jersey (0534) 78887 Telex no 4192341

Closed 16 Nov—19 Mar

An attractive holiday hotel providing pleasant service.

35rm(15⇌20⌂)(2fb) CTV in all bedrooms S% ✱sB&B⇌⌂£19—£28 dB&B⇌⌂£28—£46

Lift ☾ 12P

English & French ✱Lunch fr£5 Tea 60p—£2.50 Dinner fr£7.50 Wine £4 Last dinner 8pm

Credit cards 1 3 V

★★**Royal Yacht** The Weighbridge ☎ Jersey (0534) 20511 Telex no 4192085

Overlooking harbour, hotel has Victorian style carvery, attractive bars and good bedrooms.

45rm(18⇌27⌂) CTV in all bedrooms T sB&B⇌⌂£19.25—£22 dB&B⇌⌂£38.50—£44

Lift ☾ CTV ℙ *xmas*

English, French & Italian Lunch £5.50&alc Tea £1 Dinner £8.50&alc Wine £4.75 Last dinner 8.30pm

Credit cards 1 2 3 4

★★*L* **Hotel Savoy** Rouge Bouillon ☎ Jersey (0534) 27521

Closed Nov—Mar

Traditional hotel, well appointed and spacious. Tourist and commercial trade.

61rm(53⇌8⌂)(1fb) CTV in all bedrooms T ⊁ S% ✱sB&B£15.50—£19.50 dB&B⇌⌂£31—£39

Lift ☾ 50P (heated) Live music twice wkly

English, French & Italian V S% ✱Lunch £4.50&alc Tea 65p Dinner £6.50&alc Wine £3 Last dinner 8.30pm

Credit cards 1 V

✕✕ **Mauro's** 37 La Notte St ☎ Jersey (0534) 20147

Popular restaurant offering French and Italian dishes, seafood predominating. There are daily specialities, and the service is prompt and efficient.

Closed Sun & 4 Jan—1 Feb

French & Italian V 48 seats S% Lunch £6—£10&alc Dinner £10—£12.50&alc Wine £4 Last dinner 10.30pm ℙ

Credit cards 1 2 3 4 5 V

Channel Islands, St Helier — Chapeltown

✕ **La Buca** The Parade ☎ Jersey (0534) 34283

Small, bright, Italian restaurant serving good, well prepared mostly Italian and some English dishes. There are daily and weekly specialities. Service is impressive. Must book.

Closed Wed & 25 Dec—1 Jan

Continental V 65 seats ✱Lunch fr£4&alc Dinner fr£8&alc Last dinner 11.30pm ℙ

Credit cards 1 2 3 4 5

ST LAWRENCE

★★★*HL* ***Little Grove*** Rue de Haut ☎ Jersey (0534) 25321

This delightful hotel has been refurbished to a very high standard. The elegant restaurant offers very good food.

14rm(11⇌3⌂)(10fb) 3 CTV in all bedrooms T ₱

☾ 48P (heated) *xmas*

French Last dinner 9.30pm

Credit cards 1 2 3 4 5

ST SAVIOUR

★★★★

★★★★ **LONGUEVILLE MANOR, ST SAVIOUR, JERSEY**

(off St Helier/Grouville Rd A3) (Relais et Châteaux) ☎ Jersey (0534) 25501 Telex no 4192306

This attractive Norman-style mansion has had, since its conception in 1948, three generations of the Lewis family to have lovingly and sympathetically restored this former manor house into one of Europe's leading hotels. It is now geared to provide the facilities and services for today's climate but, whether a tourist or businessman, a visit to Longueville is a memorable and thoroughly relaxing experience. One of the family, or their manager Simon Dufty, always seem to be in attendance to ensure that, with their friendly staff, guests' needs are fulfilled without undue fuss. Mrs Lewis and her daughter-in-law are the brains behind the often dramatic but extremely tasteful colour schemes. The public rooms and bedrooms are not only provided with every modern facility but also with a genuine feeling of warmth. In addition to the luxuriously appointed lounges there is a well designed swimming pool with full service and a charming, mature, garden of 5 acres for gentle exercise during the warmer weather. Longueville also enjoys a coveted Rosette for its high standard of food and Chef William Dicken presides over the kitchen, which provides innovative, well cooked food, dramatically presented. The most recent addition to the hotel is the luxuriously appointed garden suite and the Lewis's plans for the current winter are to build an extension, not to increase the number of bedrooms but allow for increased spaciousness and comfort in the existing ones.

34⇌ 1 CTV in all bedrooms T S% sB&B⇌£44—£50 dB&B⇌£75—£115 ₱

Lift ☾ P (heated) nc 7yrs *xmas*

French V Lunch £12.50&alc Tea £1.50alc Dinner £16&alc Wine £4.25 Last dinner 9.30pm

Credit cards 1 2 3 4 5 V

SARK

✕✕ **Aval Du Creux Hotel** Harbour Hill ☎ (048183) 2036

Set in wooded grounds atop Harbour Hill, this friendly restaurant with its picture windows offers delicious, well cooked food.

Closed Oct—Etr

International V 35 seats ✱Lunch £5.50&alc Dinner £9&alc Wine £3.75 Last dinner 8.30pm ℙ

Credit cards 1 3

CHAPELTOWN

South Yorkshire
Map **8** SK39

★★★**Staindrop Lodge** Lane End ☎ Sheffield (0742) 846727

A nineteenth-century building of some architectural interest, standing in its own grounds in a quiet area of Sheffield, has been suitably converted into an up-to-date hotel where the interesting international menu and good-value wine list are complemented by friendly family service.

13rm(11⇌2⌂) CTV in all bedrooms ® T ⊁ ✱sB&B⇌⌂£30 dB&B⇌⌂£42 ₱

60P *xmas*

Last dinner 9.30pm

Credit cards 1 2 3 4 5

CHARLBURY
Oxfordshire
Map **4** SP31

★★**The Bell at Charlbury** Church St ☎(0608) 810278

Set in an unspoilt village, this picturesque, Cotswold-stone hotel offers comfortable and well-equipped bedrooms, each individually decorated to a high standard, complemented by a rustic bar and cosy restaurant.

10rm(3→⋔) Annexe:4→ CTV in all bedrooms **T** ✱ sB&B£27.50 sB&B→⋔£31 dB&B£39.50 dB&B→⋔£43 **B**

CTV 30P ✱

✱ Lunch £8.95&alc Tea 75p Dinner £10.95&alc Wine £4.95 Last dinner 10pm

Credit cards 1 2 3 5

Charlbury — Charlecote

CHARLECOTE
Warwickshire
Map **4** SP25

★★★**Charlecote Pheasant Country** (Best Western) ☎ Stratford-upon-Avon (0789) 840200

Stratford upon Avon plan **4** *C2*

A 17th-century farmhouse has been tastefully restored to provide an attractive hotel. You are advised to book for the carvery restaurant as it is very popular.

Annexe: 22rm(10→12⋔)(4fb) 5 CTV in all bedrooms ® **T** S% sB&B→⋔£32—£34 dB&B→⋔£42—£44 **B**

→

C

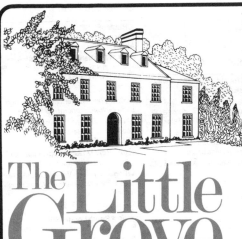

Lift ☾CTV 120P(charge) ✿ (heated) (hard) snooker sauna bath solarium gymnasium

English & Continental V S% Lunch £6.80&alc Tea fr£1.20 Dinner £8.60&alc Wine £4.70 Last dinner 9.45pm

Credit cards 1 2 3 5 V

CHARLWOOD
Surrey
Map **4** TQ24

Hotels are listed under Gatwick Airport

CHARMOUTH
Dorset
Map **3** SY39

★★**Charmouth House** The Street ☎(0297) 60319

Character hotel with neat bedrooms and oak style bar.

11rm(3)(2fb) CTV in 5 bedrooms ® *sB&B£15 sB&B£16.50 dB&B£30 dB&B£33 B

CTV 30P ✿ (heated) sauna bath

*Bar lunch £4alc Dinner £8.50alc Wine £4.25 Last dinner 9.30pm

Credit cards 3 V

★★**Fernhill** ☎(0297) 60492

Friendly, relaxing hotel serving well prepared food with extensive menu.

15rm(5 3)(6fb) ® sB&B£19—£21 sB&B £21—£23 dB&B£38—£42 dB&B £42—£46 B

CTV 50P ✿ (heated) squash *xmas*

English & Continental V Bar lunch £2—£6 Dinner £10—£11.50&alc Wine £5 Last dinner 8.45pm

Credit cards 1 3 V

See advertisement under Lyme Regis

★★*HL* **Queen's Arms** The Street ☎(0297) 60339

Closed Dec—2nd wk Feb RS Sun

Rendered, colour-washed hotel, once visited by Catherine of Aragon, Charles II and Edward VII.

11rm(5 4) 1 CTV in all bedrooms ® T sB&B£17—£21 sB&B £17—£21 dB&B£34—£42 dB&B £34—£42 B

CTV 25P ✿ nc4yrs

English & French V Bar lunch £4alc Dinner £9alc Wine £4.50 Last dinner 8.45pm

Credit cards 1 3

★★**White House** 2 Hillside, The Street (on A35) ☎(0297) 60411

The small, attractive, white-painted hotel has a well-appointed interior and a restaurant which provides well-prepared meals.

6(1fb) CTV in all bedrooms ® T *sB&B£18.50—£24.50 dB&B£37—£49 B

12P nc4yrs

Dinner £10.50—£12.50&alc Wine £4.65 Last dinner 9pm

Credit cards 1 3

See advertisement under Lyme Regis.

★**Sea Horse** Higher Sea Ln ☎(0297) 60414

An 18th-century house standing in one acre of grounds with a secluded walled garden and views of the sea and the hills.

8rm(3) Annexe: 2rm(1)(3fb) ® sB&B£11—£14.50 sB&B£12.75—£16.25 dB&B£22—£29 dB&B£25.50—£32.50

CTV 12P ✿ *xmas*

Lunch fr£3.50 Tea fr50p High Tea fr£3.50 Dinner fr£6.50 Wine £3.90 Last dinner 7.45pm

Credit cards 1 3

CHARNOCK RICHARD
Lancashire
Map **7** SD51

★★**Hunters Lodge Motel** Preston Rd ☎Coppull (0257) 793011

The small, family-run motel features a good restaurant and well-equipped bedrooms.

23rm(4 19) CTV in all bedrooms ® T *sB&B £21.75—£29.75 dB&B £29.75—£37 B

100P ✿ CFA

Cosmopolitan V *Lunch £5.50—£6.50 Tea 60—65p High Tea £5.50—£6.50 Dinner £10.50alc Wine £5.95 Last dinner 10pm

Credit cards 1 2 3 5 V

CHARNOCK RICHARD (M6 Motorway Service Area) Lancashire
Map **7** SD51

★★**TraveLodge** Mill Ln (Trusthouse Forte) ☎Coppull (0257) 791746 Telex no 67315

The restaurant is situated in the adjacent service area and provides mainly grills.

103 CTV in all bedrooms ® sB&B£33 dB&B£44 B

☾

Mainly Grills

Credit cards 1 2 3 4 5

CHEADLE HULME
Gt Manchester
Map **7** SJ88

✕**Cheshire Tandoori** 9, The Precinct ☎061-485 4942

Colourful restaurant featuring delicately spiced dishes.

Closed Sun

Indian V 40 seats Lunch £2.50—£7.95&alc Dinner £5.75—£7.95&alc Wine £4.25 Last dinner 11.30pm 100P

Credit cards 1 2 3 5 V

CHEDDAR
Somerset
Map **3** ST45

★**Gordons** Cliff St ☎(0934) 742497

Closed Xmas & New Year
RS Feb

This small, friendly, owner-run hotel with simple bedrooms is conveniently situated near the Cheddar Gorge.

11rm(2) Annexe: 1(2fb) CTV in 1 bedroom TV in 11 bedrooms ® *sB&B£11—£13 sB&B£13—£25 dB&B£20—£24 dB&B£26—£30 B

CTV 10P ✿ (heated)

*Lunch £5.95alc Dinner £5.95alc Wine £4.25 Last dinner 9pm

Credit cards 1 5

CHELFORD
Cheshire
Map **7** SJ87

★★**Dixon Arms** Knutsford Rd ☎Macclesfield (0625) 861313

Closed 24 Dec—1 Jan

A well-furnished village pub, the Dixon Arms offers a very good standard of accommodation and meals that can be highly recommended.

10(2fb) CTV in all bedrooms ® T sB&B fr£36 dB&B fr£44

100P ✿ bowling green CFA

English & French *Bar lunch fr£3&alc Tea fr60p Dinner fr£8.50&alc Wine £4.50 Last dinner 10pm

Credit cards 1 3 4 5 V

CHELMSFORD
Essex
Map **5** TL70

★★★**Pontlands Park Country** West Hanningfield Rd, Great Baddow ☎(0245) 76444 Telex no 995411

RS Sat & Sun

A country house hotel with well equipped bedrooms and modern health centre.

18(3fb) 1 in 11 bedrooms CTV in all bedrooms T S% sB&B£52 dB&B£67 B

☾ ## 60P ✿ (heated) sauna bath solarium gymnasium *xmas*

English & French V Lunch £11alc Tea £1.25alc Dinner £15alc Wine £6 Last dinner 9.45pm

Credit cards 1 2 3 5

★★★**South Lodge** 196 New London Rd ☎(0245) 264564 Telex no 99452

Busy hotel with compact well equipped bedrooms.

26 Annexe: 16(3fb) CTV in all bedrooms ® T S% sB £43.50—£45 dB £52.50—£54 (room only) B

☾ CTV 50P(charge)

V S% Lunch £9.50&alc Tea £1—£2.50 Dinner £9.50&alc Wine £5.75 Last dinner 9.30pm

Credit cards 1 2 3 5

★★**County** Rainsford Rd ☎ (0245) 266911
Closed 27—30 Dec
Busy commercial hotel with modern bedrooms.
31rm(22⇌7⌒) Annexe: 23rm(7⇌)(1fb) CTV in 36 bedrooms ® T sB&B£21 sB&B⇌⌒£32.50—£37 dB&B£36 dB&B⇌⌒£50—£52.50 B
☾CTV 80P
English & French V ♀ ☕ Lunch £6.50—£7&alc Tea 65p Dinner £7.75—£9&alc Wine £5.25 Last dinner 9pm
Credit cards 1 2 3 5

Chelmsford — Cheltenham

CHELTENHAM
Gloucestershire
Map **3** SO92
See also Cleeve Hill

★★★★**Golden Valley Thistle** Gloucester Rd (Thistle) ☎ (0242) 32691 Telex no 43410
Modern well appointed hotel with extensive conference facilities.
98⇌⌒(20fb) ⊁ in 10 bedrooms CTV in all bedrooms ® T ✱ sB⇌⌒£48—£65 dB⇌⌒£58—£75 (room only) B
Lift ☾ 280P CFA ✿
International ♀ ☕ ✱ Lunch fr£8.75&alc Dinner fr£11.50&alc Wine £7 Last dinner 9.30pm
Credit cards 1 2 3 4 5 Ⓥ

★★★★**Queen's** Promenade (Trusthouse Forte) ☎ (0242) 514724 Telex no 43381
A comfortable hotel, impressively situated overlooking gardens. →

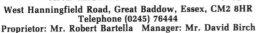

C

77🛁(3fb) CTV in all bedrooms Ⓡ sB&B🛁£59 dB&B🛁£77 B
Lift ☾ 32P CFA *xmas*
🍷 ☕ Last dinner 9.45pm
Credit cards [1] [2] [3] [4] [5]

★★★

❀★★★♣ GREENWAY, CHELTENHAM
Shurdington (Pride of Britain)
☎ (0242) 862352
Telex no 437216
Closed 28 Dec—5 Jan RS Sat & Bank Hols

An important change has taken place here: a Canadian company has bought this hotel and another, but have retained Tony Elliott, the previous owner, as managing director of both of them (as well as any others they may buy). So far there has been no deterioration of standards and we believe that Red Stars are still justified. Other news is the extension to the well appointed candlelit restaurant, the scene of William Bennett's imaginative cooking. Lunch is informal, but then and at dinner there is a fixed price menu — four courses for dinner. The young staff are obliging and friendly so you will be sure to enjoy your meals here. Bedrooms vary in size but are individually decorated and furnished and equipped to a high standard. In addition, some new bedrooms are being constructed. Besides the restaurant on the ground floor are the hall and lounge with a handsome old press, and the chic drawing room with an intimate bar connecting with it. Open fires and flowers add their charm to those of antiques and porcelain. A notable feature is the medieval carved overmantle in one of the private meeting rooms. All this is in a most attractive Elizabethan manor house in its own grounds just two and a half miles south of the town.

11🛁 Annexe: 8🛁 1▣ CTV in all bedrooms **T** ✂ S% sB&B🛁£65—£80 dB&B🛁£90—£115 B
50P ⛟ ✿ croquet nc7yrs *xmas*
🍷 French **V** S% Lunch £13alc Dinner £21alc Wine £6 Last dinner 9.30pm
Credit cards [1] [2] [3] [4] [5]

★★★Carlton Parabola Rd ☎ (0242) 514453 Telex no 43310
Traditional hotel with well equipped bedrooms, situated near the town centre.
49🛁 CTV in all bedrooms Ⓡ **T** S% sB&B🛁🚿£38 dB&B🛁🚿£50.50 B
Lift ☾ 30P CFA *xmas*
V 🍷 ☕ S% Lunch £8&alc Tea 60p Dinner £9.50&alc Wine £4 Last dinner 9pm
Credit cards [1] [2] [3] [5]

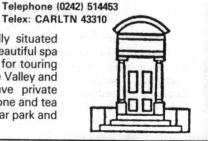

★★★Hotel De La Bere Southam (3m NE A46) (Best Western) ☎ (0242) 37771 Telex no 43232
Well modernised historic hotel with good restaurants and nicely refurbished bedrooms.
32rm (30🛁 2🚿) Annexe: 10🛁 5▣ CTV in all bedrooms Ⓡ **T** S% sB&B🛁🚿£37.50—£45 dB&B🛁🚿£54—£74 Continental breakfast B
☾ 200P CFA ✿ ⛆ (heated in summer only) 🎾 (hard) squash sauna bath solarium gymnasium indoor tennis badminton *xmas*
🍷 International **V** 🍷 ✱ Lunch £6.75—£10.75 Dinner £12.95&alc Wine £5.85 Last dinner 9.45pm
Credit cards [1] [2] [3] [5]

★★★Wyastone Parabola Rd ☎ (0242) 516654
A comfortable, small proprietor-run hotel.
13rm (5🛁 8🚿) (2fb) 1▣ CTV in all bedrooms Ⓡ **T** ✂ S% sB&B🛁🚿£37—£44 dB&B🛁🚿£53—£58 B
25P ⛟ snooker
🍷 Continental **V** 🍷 ☕ S% Lunch £9.50—£10.50&alc Tea £1.50—£2.50 Dinner £9.50—£10.50&alc Wine £5 Last dinner 9.30pm
Credit cards [1] [2] [3] [5] Ⓥ

★★George St George's Rd (Best Western) ☎ (0242) 35751 Telex no 437262
Traditional-style town hotel offering good value meals.
41rm (29🛁 4🚿) (3fb) CTV in all bedrooms Ⓡ **T** S% sB&B£23.50—£24.50 sB&B🛁🚿£28.50—£29.50 dB&B£33—£35 dB&B🛁🚿£41—£43.50 B
☾ CTV 15P 4⌂ (garage £5 per day) *xmas*
V 🍷 S% Lunch £4.40—£5.50 Dinner £8.50—£9.50 Wine £7 Last dinner 10pm
Credit cards [1] [2] [3] [5]

★★ *BL* Prestbury House The Burgage, Prestbury (2m NE A46) ☎ (0242) 529533
Closed 10 days Xmas, 4 days Etr, 1st 2 wks Aug & Bank Hols
Peacefully situated, personally run period house with fine first floor lounge and gracious restaurant offering good food and service.
10rm (8🛁) (2fb) CTV in all bedrooms Ⓡ S% ✱ sB&B🛁fr£34.16 dB&B🛁fr£45.54
40P ⛟ ✿
🍷 English & French **V** S% ✱ Lunch £11.38—£14.29 Dinner £12—£14.95&alc Wine £6.25 Last dinner 9pm

XX Cleeveway House Bishop's Cleeve (3m N A435) ☎ Bishop's Cleeve (024267) 2585

This well appointed country house restaurant makes commendable use of game, fish and raw materials in season.

Closed 25 Dec—2 Jan, 1 wk in summer
Lunch not served Mon
Dinner not served Sun

🍷English & French **V** 36 seats Lunch £12.50alc Dinner £12.50alc Wine £4.80 Last dinner 9.30pm P

Credit card [1]

See advertisement on page 216

Cheltenham

X La Ciboulette 24 Suffolk Rd ☎ (0242) 573449

Enthusiastically run by charming young hosts, this French restaurant augments the à la carte menu with a lunchtime table d'hôte meal that combines quality with economy, both menus being complemented by fine wines.

Closed Sun, Mon, 1 wk Xmas, 1 wk Etr & 2 wks Aug

🍷French 36 seats S% Lunch £8.70 Dinner £15alc Wine £5.60 Last dinner 10.30pm P̸

Credit cards [1] [2] [3]

X Mayflower Chinese 32 Clarence St ☎ (0242) 522426

This small, personally-run, Chinese restaurant is served by a helpful and friendly staff. The menu offers a good choice of authentic Cantonese-style dishes, cooked with care and well presented.

Closed 25—27 Dec
Lunch not served Sun →

C

Cantonese V 45 seats Lunch £2.60—£3.50&alc Dinner £8.50—£16.50&alc Wine £4.60 Last dinner 11pm

Credit cards [2] [5]

C

✕**Rajvooj Tandoori** 1 Albion St ☎(0242) 524288

"Rajvooj" is food suitable for Maharajas, Nawabs and Kings, and the bright decor, shining brassware and Indian music of this town-centre restaurant combine to create an evocative atmosphere in which to enjoy it. The dishes on offer — mainly Tandoori, Mughlai and Bengali — are helpfully described on the menu.

Closed Xmas day

Indian V 54 seats *Lunch £2.25—£4.95&alc Dinner £6.75—£8.75 Wine £4 Last dinner 11.30pm

Credit cards [1] [2] [3] [5] (V)

Cheltenham — Chenies

CHENIES

Buckinghamshire
Map **4** TQ09

★★★**Bedford Arms Thistle** (Thistle)
☎ Chorleywood (09278) 3301 Telex no 893939

Small country hotel with nice bedrooms, an attractive restaurant, good food and some unusual drinks.

10(3fb) CTV in all bedrooms **T** *sB £50—£60 dB £65—£75 (room only)
120P

French ♕ ☕ ✱ Lunch fr£15.50alc Dinner fr£17.50alc Wine £7 Last dinner 9.30pm

Credit cards 1 2 3 4 5 Ⓥ

CHEPSTOW
Gwent
Map **3** ST59

★ ★ ***Beaufort*** Beaufort Sq St Mary Street ☎ (02912) 2497 Telex no 498280

Welcoming 17th-century hotel with warm, modern bedrooms, attractive, intimate dining room and popular bars.

11rm(3🛁3🚿)(2fb) CTV in all bedrooms Ⓡ T B

15P 🚌

Mainly Grills **V** ♕ ☕ Last dinner 10pm

Credit cards 1 2 3 5

★ ★ *H* **Castle View** 16 Bridge St (Exec Hotels) ☎ (02912) 70349 Telex no 498280

Personally owned and managed, this friendly hotel is housed in an eighteenth-century building which looks directly onto Chepstow Castle. The modern bedrooms are compact but comfortable, and imaginative meals featuring fine home cooking are served in the character dining room, once the kitchen.

9rm(8🛁1🚿) Annexe: 2🛁(5fb) CTV in all bedrooms Ⓡ T sB&B🛁🚿£27—£30 dB&B🛁🚿£42—£45 B

P 🚌 ✿ *xmas*

V ♕ ⊁ Lunch £6.50—£9.50&alc Dinner £9.50&alc Wine £4.50 Last dinner 9pm

Credit cards 1 2 3 5 Ⓥ

★ ★ **George** Moor St (Trusthouse Forte) ☎ (02912) 5363

Small friendly hotel with comfortable bedrooms. →

C

15rm(14→1⋒)CTV in all bedrooms ® sB&B→⋒£46 dB&B→£59.50 B

25P *xmas*

♁ Last dinner 9.30pm

Credit cards 1 2 3 4 5

CHESTER
Cheshire
Map **7** SJ46

★★★★

★★★★CHESTER GROSVENOR HOTEL, CHESTER

Eastgate St (Prestige) ☎ (0244) 24024 Telex no 61240

Closed Xmas day & Boxing day

Built in 1865, this splendid hotel with its black and white half timbered facade, fits easily among the buildings of the famous Rows. The interior, with its elegant hall, handsome staircase and exquisite Georgian chandelier, reflects the style of the hotel. The public rooms include the lounge, busy with local people and foot weary tourists taking their ease, the club-like Arkle Bar and, in the basement, the less formal Harvey's. The elegantly appointed and comfortable restaurant provides a variety of dishes to satisfy most tastes. Paul Reid is the chef and his cooking is always above average and artistically presented. We understand that £5 million has been spent refurbishing the hotel and the effect is apparent; the bedrooms and suites are luxuriously furnished and well equipped with items like mini bars, trouser presses and other extras. Room service is good. The staff are courteously formal and you will be attended to with every consideration here.

100⋒(3fb)2⊟CTV in all bedrooms **T** ✱sB⋒£59.50—£72.50 dB⋒£75—£200(room only) B

Lift ☾ CFA ♫ Live music & dancing Sat (Oct—Apr)

☗French **V** ♁ ☕ ✱Lunch fr£9.75&alc Tea £2.25—£4.50 Dinner fr£16&alc Wine £7.50 Last dinner 10pm

Credit cards 1 2 3 4 5

★★★Abbots Well Whitchurch Rd, Christleton (Embassy) ☎ (0244) 332121 Telex no 61561

Well appointed, modern hotel, situated on the A41 south of Chester.

127→⋒(4fb)CTV in all bedrooms ®**T**S% ✱sB&B→⋒fr£43.50 dB&B→⋒fr£59.50 B

☾ ## 200P CFA ✿ Disco Sat Sep—May ♿ *xmas*

☗French **V** ♁ ☕ S% ✱Lunch £7&alc Tea 50p Dinner £11&alc Wine £5.20 Last dinner 10pm

Credit cards 1 2 3 5

★★★Blossoms St John Street (Quality) ☎ (0244) 23186 Telex no 61113

Large and elegant city centre hotel which is over 300 years old.

72→⋒(3fb)⊬ in 10 bedrooms CTV in all bedrooms ®**T** S% sB&B→⋒fr£48 dB&B→⋒fr£72 B

Lift ☾ P̸ CFA *xmas*

☗International **V** ♁ ☕ ⊬ Lunch £5.50—£8&alc Tea fr80p High tea £3—£4.50 Dinner £7.50—£9.30&alc Wine £4.50 Last dinner 9.30pm

Credit cards 1 2 3 5

★★★Ladbroke Backford Cross Rbt ☎ (0244) 851551

(For full entry see Backford Cross)

★★★*H* **Mollington Banastre** Parkgate Rd (A540) (Best Western) ☎ (0244) 851471 Telex no 61686

The converted Victorian mansion stands in its own grounds some three miles from Chester. Bedrooms are modern and comfortable, the public areas pleasantly proportioned and elegantly decorated, and the overall atmosphere is one of friendliness and hospitality. There is also a good sports/leisure centre with a swimming pool.

70→(8fb)4⊟⊬ in 5 bedrooms CTV in all bedrooms ®**T** S% sB&B→£52.50—£60 dB&B→£68—£74 B

Lift ☾ CTV 300P CFA ✿ ⊠(heated) ❦(grass) squash U sauna bath solarium gymnasium hairdressing & health & beauty salon Disco Fri & Sat Cabaret Sun (lunch) ♫ *xmas*

V ♁ ☕ S% Lunch £6—£8&alc Dinner fr£13&alc Last dinner 10pm

Credit cards 1 2 3 5

★★★Plantation Inn Liverpool Rd ☎ (0244) 374100 Telex no 61263

Closed Xmas

Large hotel in its own grounds with modern extension.

93→⋒(4fb)CTV in all bedrooms ®**T** sB&B→⋒fr£39.75 dB&B→⋒fr£58 B

Lift ☾ 150P sauna bath solarium gymnasium hairdressing salon Disco Mon—Sat ♿

☗French **V** ♁ ☕ Lunch £5—£6 Tea 50p—£1 High tea £3—£4 Dinner £8—£12&alc Wine £4.95 Last dinner 11.30pm

Credit cards 1 2 3 4 5 Ⓥ

★★★**Post House** Wrexham Rd (Trusthouse Forte) ☎ (0244) 674111 Telex no 61450
Modern hotel with spacious well-appointed bedrooms.
64⇌(2fb) CTV in all bedrooms ® T sB&B⇌£50.50 dB&B⇌£66.50 B
☾250P CFA *xmas*
Last dinner 10pm
Credit cards 1 2 3 4 5

★★★**Queen** City Rd (Trusthouse Forte) ☎ (0244) 28341 Telex no 617101
A mid-Victorian building next to the railway station and convenient for the city centre.
91⇌(5fb) CTV in all bedrooms ® sB&B⇌£49.50 dB&B⇌£65.50 B
Lift ☾130P ✽ *xmas*
Last dinner 9.30pm
Credit cards 1 2 3 4 5

★★★**Rowton Hall** Whitchurch Rd, Rowton (Consort) (2m SE A41) ☎ (0244) 335262 Telex no 61172
Standing in delightful grounds this hotel offers comfortable accommodation and a friendly atmosphere.
42⇌(4fb) 2 CTV in all bedrooms ® T sB&B⇌fr£38 dB&B⇌fr£52 B
☾CTV 200P 7 ✽
French V Lunch fr£6.50&alc Tea fr£1 Dinner fr£8.50&alc Wine £5.50 Last dinner 9.30pm
Credit cards 1 2 3 5 V

★★**Dene** Hoole Rd ☎ (0244) 21165
Large house with a modern extension situated on the A56 one mile from the city.
41rm(28⇌11ᶠ)(3fb) CTV in all bedrooms ® T sB&B£19 sB&B⇌ᶠ£27 dB&B⇌ᶠ£38 B
CTV 55P ✽
Bar lunch £2—£2.50 Tea £1 Dinner £6.50—£10&alc Wine £4.25 Last dinner 8pm V

★★**Royal Oak** Warrington Rd, Mickle Trafford (3m NE A56) ☎ (0244) 301391
36⇌ᶠ(6fb) CTV in all bedrooms ® T ✱sB&B⇌ᶠ£32.50 dB&B⇌ᶠ£46 B
☾100P
✱Lunch £5.25—£5.75&alc Dinner £5.25—£5.75&alc Wine £4 Last dinner 9.45pm
Credit cards 1 2 3 4 5

★**Green Bough** 60 Hoole Rd ☎ (0244) 26241
This pleasant, family-run, small hotel offers good food and friendly service.
11rm(2⇌6ᶠ)(2fb) CTV in all bedrooms ® S% sB&B£15—£16 sB&B⇌ᶠ£21—£22 dB&B£23—£24 dB&B⇌ᶠ£29.50—£32 B
CTV 9P
S% Bar lunch £5—£7 Dinner £6.50—£9.50 Wine £4.50 Last dinner 7pm
Credit cards 1 3

★***Ye Olde Kings Head*** 48—50 Lower Bridge St ☎ (0244) 24855
Closed 24—27 Dec
Black & white Cheshire inn (circa 1520) with beams, and plenty of character.
11rm(1fb) CTV in all bedrooms ® B
CTV 3P 6
V Last dinner 9.30pm
Credit cards 1 2 3 5

✕✕***Pippa's 'In Town'*** 58 Watergate St ☎ (0244) 313721
Located in the centre of the town, near to the famous Rows, this is a refreshingly bright restaurant with a distinctive French flavour to it. An interesting and extensive menu is complemented by efficient and friendly service.
French 65 seats Last dinner 10.15pm
Credit cards 1 2 3 5

CHESTERFIELD
Derbyshire
Map **8** SK37

★★★**Chesterfield** Corporation St (Best Western) ☎ (0246) 71141 Telex no 547492
The elegant and exciting 1920s are the theme of this transformed hotel which provides every modern facility.

1🛁⛆(8fb) CTV in all bedrooms ®T
sB&B🛁⛆£38.50—£45
dB&B🛁⛆£52—£57 B
Lift ☾60P 8🚗 CFA *xmas*
🍴International V 🍷 ☕ Lunch fr£6.05 Tea
65p Dinner fr£8.50 Wine £5.25 Last
dinner 10pm
Credit cards 1 2 3 5

★★**Portland** West Bars ☎(0246) 34502
Two-storey, half timbered, gabled hotel in town centre.
24rm(13🛁)(3fb) CTV in all bedrooms ®T
sB&B£25.75 sB&B🛁£33.50
dB&B🛁fr£42 B
☾CTV 30P
🍴Mainly grills V 🍷 Lunch £5.50alc Dinner
£8alc Wine £4.50 Last dinner 9.30pm
Credit cards 1 2 3 4 5 Ⓥ

CHESTERFORD, GREAT
Essex
Map **5** TL54
★★**Crown House** ☎ Saffron Walden
(0799) 30515
A small historic building, that also offers well-equipped, modern annexe accommodation.
3🛁 Annexe: 10🛁(1fb) 1🛏 CTV in all
bedrooms ®T ✱sB&B🛁£28.50—£50
dB&B🛁£37—£60 B
CTV 40P 🎵 Live music and dancing mthly
🐎 *xmas*
🍴English & French V🚭 ✱Lunch
fr£7.75&alc Tea fr65p Dinner fr£7.75&alc
Wine £4.50 Last dinner 10pm
Credit cards 1 3 Ⓥ
See advertisement under Cambridge

CHESTER-LE-STREET
Co Durham
Map **12** NZ25
★★★**Lumley Castle** Lumley Castle
☎(0385) 891111 Telex no 537433
Closed Xmas Day, Boxing Day & New Year's Day
Impressive 13th-century castle sympathetically converted to hotel with charming bedrooms.
12rm(8🛁3⛆)
Annexe: 42rm(33🛁6⛆)(3fb) 4🛏🚭 in 3
bedrooms CTV in all bedrooms ®T S%
sB&B£39.50—£42
sB&B🛁⛆£48.50—£52
dB&B£59.50—£65
dB&B🛁⛆£59.50—£65 B
☾100P CFA ✿ snooker sauna bath 🏠
xmas
🍴English & French V 🍷 ☕🚭 S% Lunch
fr£6.95&alc Tea 75p—£1 High tea
£3—£3.50 Dinner £10.75—£11.75 Wine
£5.95 Last dinner 9.45pm
Credit cards 1 2 3 5

Chesterfield — Chideock

CHESTERTON
Oxfordshire
Map **4** SP52

✿✕✕**Woods**
☎ Bicester (0869) 241444
This attractively-beamed, well-furnished restaurant, originally a farmhouse, stands on the peaceful outskirts of a Cotswold-style village. The Woods provide pleasant service, whilst chef Harrison's skill and lightness of touch transform first-class fresh ingredients into uncomplicated but delectable dishes, his soufflés being particularly noteworthy.
Closed Mon
Lunch not served Sat
Dinner not served Sun
🍴French V 40 seats Last dinner
10pm 25P
Credit cards 1 2 3 4 5

CHICHESTER
West Sussex
Map **4** SU80
★★★***Chichester Lodge***
Westhampnett (Consort) ☎(0243) 786351
Telex no 869127
RS Xmas
Located on the A27, this modern road-side hotel has generally acceptable bedrooms and standards of service complemented by professional management.
43🛁 CTV in all bedrooms ®T B
☾100P 6🚗 ✿ CFA 🏠
🍴French V 🍷 ☕ Last dinner 9.30pm
Credit cards 1 2 3

★★★**Dolphin & Anchor** West St
(Trusthouse Forte) ☎(0243) 785121
This hotel opposite the cathedral combines two ancient inns and has elegant décor.
54rm(49🛁5⛆) CTV in all bedrooms ®
sB&B🛁⛆£50.50 dB&B🛁£67.50 B
☾16🚗 CFA *xmas*
🍷 Last dinner 10pm
Credit cards 1 2 3 4 5

★★★*B* **Goodwood Park** (Best Western)
☎(0243) 775537
(For full entry see Goodwood)

✕✕**Aspen Tree** 149 St Pancras
☎(0243) 788724
Simple restaurant with elegant bar and spicy French food.
Closed Sun
🍴International V 39 seats Lunch
£2.50—£5&alc Dinner £10alc Wine £5 Last
dinner 10.30pm🚭
Credit cards 1 2 3 5

CHICKERELL
Dorset
Map **3** SY68
✕**Turks Head Inn** 6 East St ☎ Weymouth
(0305) 783093
Simple English food — including, generally, a Roast of the Day — is served by pleasant staff in this attractive and popular restaurant on the edge of Weymouth.
Closed Mon & 24—31 Dec Lunch not
served Sat Dinner not served Sun
🍴English & French V 48 seats Lunch
£5—£6 Dinner £9alc Wine £4.50 Last
dinner 9.30pm 80P Ⓥ

CHIDDINGFOLD
Surrey
Map **4** SU93
✕✕✕ **Crown Inn** ☎ Wormley (042879)
2255
Skilfully cooked traditional dishes supplemented by some imaginative specialities are served in the Elizabethan Restaurant and Cocktail Bar. The beautifully timbered medieval inn also has some very good bedrooms and residential amenities.
Lunch not served Mon
🍴English & French 80 seats Lunch
£12.95&alc Dinner £12.95&alc Wine £7.25
Last dinner 9.30pm 12P
Credit cards 1 2 3 5

CHIDDINGSTONE
Kent
Map **5** TQ44
✕**Castle Inn** ☎ Penshurst (0892) 870247
This historic country-inn restaurant stands in an attractive, Tudor-style village. The menu offers honest English cooking, and refreshments can be taken in the courtyard garden.
Closed Tue & Jan Lunch not served Wed
35 seats S% ✱Lunch £8.50—£20 Dinner
£16—£20&alc Wine £5.50 Last dinner
9.30pm P
Credit cards 1 2 3 5

CHIDEOCK
Dorset
Map **3** SY49
★***Clock House*** ☎(0297) 89423
Set on the main road, this thatched, cottage-style hotel is personally managed and provides sound food and simple accommodation.
3rm Annexe: 3rm(1🛁) ®
CTV 30P squash nc5yrs
V 🍷 ☕ Last dinner 10pm
Credit cards 1 3

C

C

CHILGROVE
West Sussex
Map **4** SU81

❀✕✕**White Horse Inn** ☎ East Marden (024359) 219

A small, intimate restaurant that, for years, has produced cooking of a very high standard. It has its own style of English and French cooking, accompanied by a superb wine list, probably the best in Sussex.

Closed Sun, Mon & Feb

English & French **V** 60 seats S% Lunch £13.45 Dinner £16.80 Wine £5.95 Last dinner 9.30pm 200P

Credit cards 1 2 3 4 5 Ⓥ

CHILLINGTON
Devon
Map **3** SX74

★★**Oddicombe House** ☎ Frogmore (054853) 234

Closed Nov—Etr

Standing in three acres of grounds with views of the surrounding countryside.

8rm(6) Annexe: 2rm(2fb) Ⓡ *sB&B£15.50—£18.50 sB&B£19—£22 dB&B£31—£37 dB&B£35—£40

CTV 15P

European *Lunch £6(Sunday only) Tea £1.75alc Dinner £9&alc Wine £4.80 Last dinner 8.15pm

Ⓥ

★**White House**
☎ Kingsbridge (0548) 580580

Closed Nov—Mar

The delightfully proportioned, stone, Georgian house is surrounded by an acre of formal gardens — including a croquet lawn. Personally run by the owners, it offers a warm welcome to visitors.

8rm(3 3) Ⓡ *sB&B£14 sB&B £15.50 dB&B£28 dB&B £31—£34 B

CTV 8P croquet nc 5yrs

*Bar lunch £2—£4 Tea 50—75p Dinner £6—£7 Wine £4.90 Last dinner 5pm

CHILTON POLDEN
Somerset
Map **3** ST34

✕**Wilton Farmhouse** 9 Goose Ln
☎ (0278) 722134

Charming, small restored farmhouse with galleried restaurant where freshly prepared, imaginative food is served in a friendly, relaxing atmosphere. There is also a most comfortable lounge.

Closed Sun & Mon (Sun—Thu Jan & Feb) Lunch not served

English & French **V** 36 seats Dinner £9.50alc Wine £5.20 Last dinner 9.30pm 11P

Credit cards 3 5

CHINNOR
Oxfordshire
Map **4** SP70

✕✕***Crickets*** Keens Ln ☎ Kingston Blount (0844) 53566

Tucked away off Church Lane, Crickets is a warm, comfortable restaurant with its own bar; the à la carte menu provides a good balance of classical French dishes and innovations, the emphasis being on fish, and skilled service is provided by friendly staff.

Closed Sun, Mon & 2wks Jul/Aug
Lunch not served Tue

French 100 seats Last dinner 10pm

Credit cards 1 3

CHIPPENHAM
Wiltshire
See **Sutton Benger**

CHIPPERFIELD
Hertfordshire
Map **4** TL00

★★*L* **Two Brewers Inn** The Common (Trusthouse Forte) ☎ Kings Langley (09277) 65266

Appealing 17th century inn with oak beams and open fires, yet providing well-equipped modern accommodation and sound English cooking.

20 CTV in all bedrooms ® sB&B £53.50 dB&B £69.50

25P *xmas*

Last dinner 10pm

Credit cards 1 2 3 4 5

CHIPPING CAMPDEN
Gloucestershire
Map **4** SP13

★★**Cotswold House** The Square ☎ Evesham (0386) 840330 Telex no 336810

Closed 24 Dec—2 Jan

Attractive Regency house with elegant dining room and friendly atmosphere.

18rm(12 2)(1fb) CTV in all bedrooms ✱sB&B£25 sB&B £29.50 dB&B£39 dB&B £47

12P 4(£2 per night)

English & French V ✱ Bar lunch £1—£3.50 Tea £1—£4.50 Dinner £11&alc Wine £5.50 Last dinner 9.30pm

Credit cards 1 2 3 5

★★**Noel Arms** (Exec Hotel) ☎ Evesham (0386) 840317

Cosy 14th-century inn with an open courtyard and a bowling green to the rear. Traditionally furnished bedrooms.

19rm(13 3)(1fb) 2 CTV in 17 bedrooms sB&Bfr£26.25 sB&B fr£29.95 dB&Bfr£35.50 dB&B fr£45.95

CTV 40P bowling green *xmas*

V Lunch £7&alc Dinner £11.50&alc Wine £6.95 Last dinner 9pm

Credit cards 1 3

XX**King's Arms** The Square ☎ Evesham (0386) 840256

Lunch not served except Sun

40 seats 7P 14 bedrooms available S% ✱Bar lunch 90p—£4.10 Dinner £14.02 Wine £5.25 Last dinner 9pm

Credit cards 1 3

CHIPPING NORTON
Oxfordshire
Map **4** SP32

★★**Crown & Cushion** High St (Inter Hotel) ☎ (0608) 2533

RS Sun (mid winter)

Old world 15th-century hotel with comfortable bedrooms.

17(1fb) 2 CTV in all bedrooms ® S% ✱sB&B £19.50—£29.50 dB&B £29.50—£45

21P *xmas*

English & French Lunch £6.90 Dinner £8.75—£9.75 Wine £4.95 Last dinner 9pm

Credit cards 1 2 3 5 V

★★**White Hart** High St (Trusthouse Forte) ☎ (0608) 2572

Comfortable hotel with attractive lounge and bar, both with log fires.

11rm(1) Annexe: 10rm(5) 2 CTV in all bedrooms ® sB&B£31.50 sB&B £39.50 dB&B£47.50 dB&B £55.50

CTV 10P 6 *xmas*

Last dinner 9pm

Credit cards 1 2 3 4 5

X**La Madonette** 7 Horsefair ☎ (0608) 2320

Simply decorated but well appointed, this cottage-style restaurant has more space than most of its type. A short, French, →

à la carte menu is accompanied by a good wine list, and the combination of efficient service and relaxed atmosphere makes the restaurant popular with business and social diners alike.

Closed Sun & Mon Lunch not served

French 30 seats Dinner £14alc Wine £5.10 Last dinner 9.45pm

Credit cards 1 3 5

CHIPPING SODBURY
Avon
Map **3** ST78

✕ ***Sultan*** 29 Horse St ☎ (0454) 323510

An Indian restaurant with a difference, the Sultan serves well cooked and authentic regional dishes in the comfortable and relaxed atmosphere of a traditionally-furnished Georgian house typical of this charming Cotswold market town.

Indian **V** 44 seats Last dinner 11pm

Credit cards 1 2 3

CHIPSTEAD
Surrey
Map **4** TQ25

✕✕✕ **Dene Farm** Outwood Ln
☎ Downland (07375) 52661

Closed Mon, 2 wks after Xmas & 2 wks Aug
Lunch not served Sat
Dinner not served Sun

French **V** 60 seats S% Lunch £15.75&alc Dinner £15.75&alc Wine £6.95 Last dinner 10pm 40P

Credit cards 1 2 3 5

CHIRNSIDE
Borders *Berwickshire*
Map **12** NT85

★ **Chirnside Country House**
☎ (089081) 219

Closed 25 & 26 Dec

Early Victorian country mansion with extensive grounds and a walled garden.

14rm(3)(2fb) sB&B£14—£16 dB&B£28—£30

Lift CTV 20P

Scottish & Continental Lunch fr£6 Tea fr£1.95 High Tea fr£4.25 Dinner fr£10&alc Last dinner 9pm

Credit cards 1 2 3 5

Chipping Norton — Christchurch

CHITTLEHAMHOLT
Devon
Map **2** SS62

★★★ **Highbullen** ☎ (07694) 561

The secluded hotel offers beautiful views and has excellent sports facilities, including an indoor tennis court. Furnishings are comfortable, and a good standard of food can be enjoyed in the basement restaurant.

12rm() Annexe: 18rm()(2fb) CTV in all bedrooms ® T *sB&B fr£26.50 dB&B fr£53

40P (heated) (hard) squash snooker sauna bath solarium nc 10yrs

*Lunch 75p—£2.50 Tea fr30p High tea 75p—£1.50 Dinner fr£8.50 Wine £6 Last dinner 9pm

CHOLLERFORD
Northumberland
Map **12** NY97

★★★ **George** Humshaugh (Swallow)
☎ Humshaugh (043481) 611 Telex no 53168

Ivy-clad hotel with a modern bedroom wing and riverside gardens.

54(5fb) 1 CTV in all bedrooms ® T S% sB&B fr£40 dB&B £58.50

CTV 70P (heated) sauna bath solarium pool table putting *xmas*

International **V** S% Lunch £7.70&alc Tea 80p—£2.70 Dinner £10.95&alc Wine £4.90 Last dinner 9.30pm

Credit cards 1 2 3 5

CHORLEY
Lancashire
Map **7** SD51

★★★ ***B*** **Shaw Hill Hotel Golf & Country Club** Preston Rd Whittle-le-Woods (2m N A6) Hotel situated 1m from Jct 8 M61 and 2m from M6 Jct 28.
☎ (02572) 69221

Elegant Georgian mansion in rolling parkland with own golf course. It offers a high standard of French cuisine.

18 1 CTV in all bedrooms ® T * sB&B £40 dB&B £60

CTV 200P snooker sauna bath solarium Disco mthly Live music & dancing mthly *xmas*

International **V** *Lunch £7.95—£12.50 Tea 60palc High Tea £1.45alc Dinner £9.50&alc Wine £5.50 Last dinner 9.45pm

Credit cards 1 2 3 5

★★ **Hartwood Hall** Preston Rd
☎ (02572) 69966

Closed 25—28 Dec & 1 Jan

The attractive and well furnished hotel stands on the A6 to the north of the town, and close to the M61.

10rm(1 1) Annexe: 10rm(2 8)(3fb) CTV in all bedrooms ® T S% sB&B fr£26 sB&B fr£30 dB&B fr£34 dB&B fr£40

CTV 100P Live music & dancing mthly

English & Continental *S% Lunch £3.95—£10.50 Tea 75p—£1 Dinner £6—£10.50&alc Wine £5.50 Last dinner 9pm

Credit cards 1 2 3 5 V

CHRISTCHURCH
Dorset
Map **4** SZ19

See also Avon

★★★ **Avonmouth** Mudeford (2m E off B3059) (Trusthouse Forte) ☎ (0202) 483434

Pleasant, modern riverside hotel with comfortable bedrooms and attractive restaurant.

27 Annexe: 14(3fb) CTV in all bedrooms ® sB&B £45.50 dB&B £73.50

66P (heated) *xmas*

Last dinner 8.45pm

Credit cards 1 2 3 4 5

★★★ **Waterford Lodge** 87 Bure Ln, Friars Cliff, Mudeford (2m E off B3059)
☎ Highcliffe (04252) 72948

Comfortable and quietly situated in an attractive garden, the hotel has well-appointed bedrooms and provides good food and warm hospitality.

21rm(18⇝3⌂)(10fb)CTV in all bedrooms ®T sB&B⇝⌂£21 dB&B⇝⌂£42 B
CTV 40P ✿ putting green ⌂ *xmas*
♁ ☐ Lunch £5.75&alc Tea £1.20—£1.50 Dinner £8.50 Wine £4.20 Last dinner 8.30pm
Credit cards 1 3 Ⓥ

★★**Dan Cooks** Lyndhurst Rd ☎ Highcliffe (04252) 3202
Detached, gabled Tudor style exterior. White stucco walls with dark wood insets. Pleasant restaurant.

Christchurch

20rm(2⇝16⌂)(2fb)2⊟ ⊁ in 2 bedrooms CTV in all bedrooms ®T ✕ S% *sB&B£20—£24 sB&B⇝⌂£24 dB&B⇝⌂£42 B
CTV 70P ♿ *xmas*
♁English & French V ♁ *Lunch £5.75&alc Dinner £8.50—£9.50&alc Wine £4.95 Last dinner 10pm
Credit cards 1 2 3 5 Ⓥ

★★*H* **Fisherman's Haunt** Salisbury Rd, Winkton (2½m N on B3347) ☎ (0202) 484071
Closed Xmas Day
Attractive 17th-century country house with good food, attentive service and comfortable bedrooms.
4rm(1⇝2⌂) Annexe: 15rm(13⇝)(4fb) 2⊟ CTV in all bedrooms ®T S% sB&B£17 dB&B£33 dB&B⇝⌂£36 B
CTV 100P ✿ ⌂
V ♁ ☐ Lunch £5—£5.50 Tea £1.50 Dinner £10.50alc Wine £5 Last dinner 10pm
Credit cards 1 2 3 5 Ⓥ

C

✕**Splinters** 12 Church St ☎ (0202) 483454

This bistro-style restaurant provides an intimate atmosphere in which to enjoy well-prepared and generously-served meals chosen from a menu with a French influence. Pre-dinner drinks can be taken in the pleasant bar, and there is a comfortable lounge for coffee.

Closed Sun & 25—27 Dec

French **V** 46 seats Dinner £15alc Wine £5.50 Last dinner 10.30pm nc 8yrs after 7.30pm

Credit cards ② ③ ⑤

CHURCHSTOKE
Powys
Map **7** SO29

★★**Mellington Hall** ☎ (05885) 456

Closed Nov & Feb

Impressive, Victorian stone country house set in parkland at the end of a long drive.

10rm(4🛁)(1fb) TV in 2 bedrooms ® ✱sB&B£15.50 sB&B🛁£17.50 dB&B£26.70 dB&B🛁£30.70

CTV 200P ✿ *xmas*

V ✱Lunch £3.60—£6.10 Tea fr90p Dinner £4.40—£7.45 Wine £4.50 Last dinner 9pm

---

CHURCH STRETTON
Shropshire
Map **7** SO49

★★★**Stretton Hall** All Stretton (Best Western)
☎ (0694) 723224

This 18th-century country house with its spacious grounds provides comfortable accommodation and a relaxed atmosphere.

13rm(10🛁3🚿)(1fb) CTV in all bedrooms ® **T** ✱sB&B🛁🚿fr£32 dB&B🛁🚿fr£43 **B**

60P ✿ *xmas*

English & French **V** Lunch fr£7.50 Wine £5 Last dinner 9pm

Credit cards ① ② ③ ⑤

★★**Sandford** Watling Street South
☎ (0694) 722131

Large, gabled, Edwardian house.

24rm(6🛁3🚿)(3fb) ® sB&Bfr£16.50 sB&B🛁🚿fr£18 dB&Bfr£29.50 dB&B🛁🚿fr£32.50 **B**

CTV 30P ✿ *xmas*

Lunch fr£5.25 Tea fr65p Dinner fr£6.55 Wine £4.75 Last dinner 8.30pm

Credit cards ① ③ Ⓥ

CHURT
Surrey
Map **4** SU83

★★★*L* **Frensham Pond** ☎ Frensham (025125) 3175 Telex no 858610

New management and a new team of chefs have brought great changes to this beautifully-located hotel, which also has a new leisure centre.

7🛁 Annexe: 12🛁 CTV in all bedrooms ® in 12 bedrooms **T** ✱sB&B🛁£45—£48 dB&B🛁£55—£80 **B**

100P ✿ (heated) squash sauna bath solarium gymnasium Live music and dancing Sat *xmas*

English & French **V** ✱Lunch fr£12.95&alc Dinner fr£14.50&alc Wine £5.95 Last dinner 9.30pm

Credit cards ① ② ③ ⑤

★★**Pride of the Valley** Jumps Rd (Best Western) ☎ Hindhead (042873) 5799

Quietly situated family run hotel with comfortable well equipped modern bedrooms, and good cooking.

13rm(8🛁2🚿)(2fb) CTV in all bedrooms ® **T** S% sB&B£32—£35 sB&B🛁🚿£35—£38 dB&B£42—£45 dB&B🛁🚿£44—£47 **B**

50P CFA ✿ Live music & dancing Sat mthly *xmas*

V Lunch £7.80—£8.50 Dinner £8.50—£9.50&alc Wine £5.50 Last dinner 9.45pm

Credit cards ① ② ③ ⑤ Ⓥ

CIRENCESTER
Gloucestershire
Map **4** SP00

See also Ewen

★★★**Fleece** Market Pl ☎ (0285) 68507 Telex no 437287

RS 24—26 Dec

Comfortable, well-refurbished Tudor inn with good food, and wine bar across courtyard.

22🛁🚿(2fb) 2 CTV in all bedrooms ® **T** S% sB&B🛁🚿£41—£45 dB&B🛁🚿£52—£57.50 **B**

11P

English & French **V** Lunch £6.25—£7.50&alc Tea £3.45 Dinner £12.95&alc Wine £6.50 Last dinner 9.30pm

Credit cards ① ② ③ ⑤ Ⓥ

★★★*H* **King's Head** Market Pl (Best Western) ☎ (0285) 3322 Telex no 43470

Closed 27—30 Dec

This town centre hotel, formerly a famous fourteenth-century coaching inn, provides comfortable, traditional rooms linked by rambling corridors. The cocktail bar contains a fine old oil painting.

70🛁(4fb) 2 CTV in all bedrooms **T** S% sB&B🛁£42.50—£45 dB&B🛁£54—£57 **B**

Lift 25P CFA games room *xmas*

V S% Lunch fr£7.95&alc Tea fr£2.30 Dinner fr£10.35&alc Wine £6.50 Last dinner 9pm

Credit cards ① ② ③ ④ ⑤ Ⓥ

★★★*L* **Stratton House** Gloucester Rd (A417) ☎ (0285) 61761

Elegant and traditional hotel with country house atmosphere, set in attractive walled gardens.

26rm(17🛁3🚿)(3fb) CTV available in bedrooms ® **T** S% sB&Bfr£28.50 sB&B🛁🚿fr£32.50 dB&Bfr£37.50 dB&B🛁🚿fr£42 **B**

CTV 100P ✿ croquet ♿ *xmas*

English & French V 🍷 ☕ S% Lunch £7&alc Tea 80p High Tea fr£2.50 Dinner £8.95—£9.50&alc Wine £5 Last dinner 9.45pm
Credit cards 1 2 3 4 5 V

★★**Corinium Court** Gloucester St ☎(0285) 69711
A traditional, small, proprietor-run hotel.
12rm(9→3⌂)(1fb) CTV in all bedrooms T S% sB&B£30—£38 sB&B→⌂£30—£38 dB&B£35—£48
40P ✿
V 🍷 ☕ Lunch £2—£5.50 Tea £1—£2.50 High Tea £2—£4.50 Dinner £8.50—£11&alc Wine £6.25 Last dinner 9.30pm
Credit cards 1 2 3 4 5

CLACHAN-SEIL
Strathclyde *Argyllshire*
Map **10** NM71

★**Willowburn** (Guestaccom) ☎ Balvicar (08523) 276
The small hotel, picturesquely set across the 'Atlantic Bridge' on the Isle of Seil, provides comfortable accommodation, good food and friendly service.
6rm(1→2⌂)(1fb) Ⓡ S%
*dB&B£22—£29 dB&B→⌂£25—£33 B
CTV 25P ✿ *xmas*
V 🍷 ☕ *Lunch £4alc Tea £1.20alc Dinner £7.50&alc Wine £4.40 Last dinner 9pm
Credit cards 1 2 3 5 V

C

CLACTON-ON-SEA
Essex
Map **5** TM11

★★*B* **King's Cliff** Kings Pde, Holland-on-Sea ☎(0255) 812343

Seafront hotel with comfortable well-appointed bedrooms and formal restaurant.

17rm(13⇀4⋒)(5fb) 1▭CTV in all bedrooms ®T ✕ sB&B⇀⋒£21–£23 dB&B⇀⋒£35–£38 B

☾80P 5⌂(80p) ✿ putting green Live music & dancing wknds cabaret wknds ⌂ *xmas*

☋English & French V ⚲ ▭ S% ✱Lunch £4–£5&alc Tea 65p Dinner £6.50–£7.50&alc Wine £3.85 Last dinner 9.30pm

Credit cards 1 3 Ⓥ

CLANFIELD
Oxfordshire
Map **4** SP20

❀✕✕✕ **Plough at Clanfield**
☎(036781) 222 Telex no 449848

This pretty, Cotswold-stone building, with its thoughtfully-appointed restaurant and elegant bar lounge, also offers four small but attractive bedrooms. Chef/patron Paul Bernard produces exquisite dishes full of flavour from his two fixed-price menus, and the professional service, whilst not too formal, is capable of doing justice to the better quality wines available.

☋English & French V 45 seats ✱Lunch £8.95–£10.50 Dinner £16.75–£21.75 Wine £6.50 Last dinner 9.15pm 30P 7 bedrooms available

Credit cards 1 2 3 5

CLARE
Suffolk
Map **5** TL74

★★***Bell*** Market Hill (Minotel) ☎(0787) 277741

There is some modern annexe accommodation around the courtyard of this small sixteenth-century inn. Guests can choose between the attractive, beamed dining room and a smart, informal wine bar which serves a range of local dishes.

17rm(2⇀⋒) Annexe: 11⇀(1fb) 2▭CTV in 18 bedrooms ® B

CTV 20P *xmas*

V ⚲ ▭ Last dinner 9.30pm

Credit cards 1 2 3 5

CLAVERING
Essex
Map **5** TL43

✕**Cricketer's** ☎(079985) 442

(classification awarded for dinner only)

There is a rustic air to this rather isolated but pretty village pub, which has been recently extended and refurbished to be both attractive and comfortable. The short, set-price menu of English and French dishes can be specially recommended for its first-class vegetables, and uncomplicated service is provided by good-natured staff.

☋English & French V 80 seats Lunch £5–£9 Dinner £12&alc Wine £4 Last dinner 10pm 20P

Credit cards 1 3

CLAWTON
Devon
Map **2** SX39

★★⚘*HL* **Court Barn Country House** (ExecHotel) ☎North Tamerton (040927) 219

Closed 1st 2 wks Jan RS mid Jan–Feb

Attractive, small holiday hotel with friendly atmosphere in a peaceful country setting.

8rm(4⇀2⋒)(3fb) ®sB&B£16–£21.50 sB&B⇀⋒£21.85–£29 dB&B£32–£37.50 dB&B⇀⋒£34.70–£39.60 B

CTV 12P ▭ ✿ ⌂ *xmas*

V ⚲ ▭ Lunch £3.25 Dinner £10.50&alc Wine £4.95 Last dinner 8.30pm

Credit cards 1 2 3 5

CLAYWORTH
Nottinghamshire
Map **8** SK78

★★**Royston Manor** St Peters Ln ☎Retford (0777) 817484

This lovely old Elizabethan manor house, situated on the edge of a pleasant village, stands in 4½ acres of grounds and enjoys excellent views over the surrounding countryside. Well-equipped modern bedrooms are housed in a purpose-built block about a hundred yards from the main building.

Annexe: 12rm(8⇀4⋒)(2fb) 1▭CTV in all bedrooms ®T S% sB&B⇀⋒£25–£30 dB&B⇀⋒£35–£40 B

150P ▭ ✿

V S% Lunch £5alc Dinner £9–£10.50 Wine £4 Last dinner 9.30pm

Credit cards 1 2 3 5 Ⓥ

See advertisement under Retford

CLEARWELL
Gloucestershire
Map **3** SO50

✕**Wyndham Arms** ☎Dean (0594) 33666

Delightful old village inn offering good value, fresh lunches, grills and having a small restaurant (evenings only).

Closed Xmas day & Boxing day

☋International V 50 seats Lunch £6&alc Dinner £14.50&alc Wine £4.50 Last dinner 10pm 30P

Credit card 1 Ⓥ

CLEETHORPES
Humberside
Map **8** TA30

★★★**Kingsway** Kingsway ☎(0472) 601122

Closed 25 & 26 Dec

Charming and comfortable three-storey hotel overlooking the sea.

55⇀ CTV in all bedrooms ✕ S% sB&B⇀£34.50–£41 dB&B⇀£48–£54 B

Lift ☾30P 20⌂(£1 per night) ▭

☋English & French ⚲ S% Lunch £7.50 Dinner £9.50 Wine £6.25 Last dinner 9pm

Credit cards 1 2 3 5

★★**Wellow** Kings Rd (Whitbread)
☎(0472) 695589

Standing on the southern outskirts of the town, this hotel is ideally situated for sports facilities and the beach. Comfortable and stylish bedrooms are matched by cheerful public areas which include bars, a separate residents' lounge and an attractive restaurant with a holiday theme.

10⇌(4fb) CTV in all bedrooms ®**T** ₽
80P 1🚗
Mainly grills **V** ☕ Last dinner 10pm
Credit cards [1] [2] [3]

CLEEVE HILL
Gloucestershire
Map **3** SO92

★★★**Rising Sun** (Whitbread)
☎ Bishops Cleeve (024267) 6281

Small, comfortable hotel overlooking the Cotswold countryside to the Malverns.

24⇌⋔(3fb) 1📺 CTV in all bedrooms ®**T** S% *sB&B⇌⋔£40 dB&B⇌⋔£48 ₽
56P ✿ snooker sauna bath *xmas*
V ☕ *Lunch £7.50&alc Tea £1.25 Dinner £9.95&alc Wine £4.90 Last dinner 10pm
Credit cards [1] [2] [3] [5]

See advertisement under Cheltenham

✕✕✕**Malvern View** ☎ Bishops Cleeve (024267) 2017

Attractive restaurant with bedrooms offering good choice of French style dishes. Fine views over Severn Vale.

Closed 2 wks Xmas
Lunch not served Dinner not served Sun
French **V** 40 seats S% Dinner £14 Wine £6.50 Last dinner 9.30pm 22P
Credit cards [1] [3]

See advertisement under Cheltenham

CLEISH
Tayside *Kinross-shire*
Map **11** NT09

✿★★★ *HB* **Nivingston House** (Inter Hotel) ☎ Cleish Hills (05775) 216 Telex no 946240

A delightful hotel in a peaceful location. An extensive range of dishes is offered in the charming restaurant, where the menu features good quality local produce, cooked and presented with flair.

17rm(12⇌5⋔)(2fb) 1📺 CTV in all bedrooms ®**T**
sB&B⇌⋔£38.50—£45
dB&B⇌⋔£55—£65 ₽
50P ✿ croquet
Continental **V** ☕ Lunch £10.50alc Tea £4alc Dinner £15.50alc Wine £7.50 Last dinner 9pm
Credit cards [1] [2] [3] [5]

CLEOBURY MORTIMER
Shropshire
Map **7** SO67

★★**Redfern** (Minotel) ☎(0299) 270395 Telex no 335176

This old stone and brick building at the edge of the village began life as a pub. Later, it became a private house, but now it has been converted into a pleasant little hotel offering modern, well-equipped accommodation (much of it in a purpose-built annexe).

5rm(2⇌3⋔) Annexe: 6rm(3⇌3⋔) (3fb) 1📺 CTV in all bedrooms ®**T** S%
sB&B⇌⋔£24—£26
dB&B⇌⋔£36.50—£40 ₽
20P snooker *xmas*
English & French ☕ S% Lunch £4—£6 Tea £1.50 Dinner £9.25 Wine £4.50 Last dinner 9.30pm
Credit cards [1] [2] [3] [5] Ⓥ

CLEVEDON
Avon
Map **3** ST47

★★★**Walton Park** Wellington Ter
☎(0272) 874253

Imposing hotel in its own grounds, with good views over the Bristol Channel.

35rm(24⇌3⋔)(2fb) CTV in all bedrooms ®**T** sB&B£17.95—£27.50 sB&B⇌⋔£17.95—£33 dB&B£34—£38 dB&B⇌⋔£34—£45 ₽
Lift 40P 4🚗(£1 per night) ✿ *xmas*
V ☕ Lunch £6.50—£7.95&alc Tea 70—75p&alc Dinner £8.50—£10&alc Wine £4.65 Last dinner 9pm
Credit cards [1] [2] [3] [5] Ⓥ

See advertisement on page 230

CLIFTONVILLE
Kent see **Margate**

CLIMPING
West Sussex
Map **4** TQ00

★★★ *B* **Bailiffscourt**
☎ Littlehampton (0903) 723511 Telex no 877870

The hotel enjoys a delighfully secluded location, standing in 25 acres only half a mile from the sea. Though built only fifty years ago, it is medieval in style, with stone-flagged floors and old furniture, some of its well-appointed bedrooms being reached by way of an underground tunnel. Friendly and informal service is provided.

8⇌ Annexe: 12⇌ 7📺 CTV in all bedrooms **T** S% *sB&B⇌£45—£50
dB&B⇌£65—£95 ₽
50P ✿ (hard) sauna bath solarium croquet putting nc 10yrs *xmas*
☕ S% *Lunch £9.25—£10.50 Tea £3 Dinner £13.50—£18.50alc Wine £7 Last dinner 9.45pm
Credit cards [1] [2] [3] [4] [5]

CLOVELLY
Devon
See **Horns Cross** & **Woolfardisworthy**

CLUN
Shropshire
Map **7** SO38

✕Old Post Office 9 The Square
☎(05884) 687

A former post office beside a tiny village square has been converted into a bright little restaurant reminiscent of the 1930's. Local produce and game are prepared in both British and Southern French country style, and meals, including wine, represent excellent value for money. Two comfortable bedrooms are also available.

Closed Sun, Mon & Feb
Lunch not served Nov—Mar

English, French & Italian **V** 20 seats
Lunch £6.50alc Dinner £13.50 Wine £4.75
Last dinner 9.30pm
3 bedrooms available

COATHAM MUNDEVILLE
Co Durham
Map **8** NZ22

★★★**Hall Garth** (Consort) ☎ Aycliffe (0325) 313333

Closed 22 Dec—2 Jan

Rambling, Georgian house in 56 acres of park and woodland, one mile from A1(M) and three miles from Darlington.

10rm (9 1)
Annexe: 11rm (4 6)(1fb) 4 CTV in all bedrooms ® T sB&B £34—£40 dB&B £48—£58 Continental breakfast **B**

0P ✽ (heated) (grass) sauna bath solarium putting croquet

English & French ✱Lunch £9—£10.50 Dinner £12.50—£13.50 Wine £4.25 Last dinner 9.15pm

Credit cards 1 2 3 5

COBHAM
Surrey
Map **4** TQ16

★★★**Ladbroke Seven Hills** (& Conferencentre) Seven Hills Rd (Ladbroke) ☎(0932) 64471 Telex no 929196

Situated in 23 acres of parkland.

115 Annexe: 25(5fb) in 5 bedrooms CTV in all bedrooms ®T sB&B£63—£70 dB&B£84.50—£95 B

Lift ☾ 250P CFA (hard) squash sauna bath gymnasium Live music and dancing Fri & Sat *xmas*

English & French **V** ✱Lunch £9—£10 Tea fr£1.50 Dinner £11—£12.50&alc Wine £6 Last dinner 10pm

Credit cards 1 2 3 4 5 Ⓥ

COCKERMOUTH
Cumbria
Map **11** NY13

★★★**Broughton Craggs** Great Broughton ☎(0900) 824400

Mid 19th-century manor house, comfortably modernised.

10(1fb) 1 CTV in all bedrooms ®T sB&B£28—£30 dB&B£40—£42 B

60P ✽

English & French **V** Lunch £5.50—£6.50&alc Tea £1—£2.50 Dinner £9.75—£10&alc Wine £5.50 Last dinner 9.30pm

Credit cards 1 2 3

★★★**Trout** Crown St ☎(0900) 823591

Closed Xmas Day

Modernised but retaining its 18th-century character, the Trout has private frontage to the River Derwent, with fishing rights.

23rm(184)(1fb) CTV in all bedrooms ®T sB&B£24—£25 sB&B£24—£25 dB&B£39 dB&B£39 B

☾ 75P ✽

English, French & Italian **V** Lunch fr£6.50&alc Dinner £11&alc Wine £5.50 Last dinner 9.30pm

Credit cards 1 3

★★***Allerdale Court*** Market Sq ☎(0900) 823654

RS 24 & 25 Dec

This attractive listed building, dating from the 1730's, retains its oak beams, and the original character of the hotel is also reflected by many pieces of period furniture.

25rm(146)(2fb) 2 CTV in all bedrooms ®T B

CTV

English, French & Italian Last dinner 9.30pm

Credit cards 1 2 3

★★**Globe** Main St (Consort) ☎(0900) 822126

Closed Xmas Day

This hotel is situated close to the lakes and forms an ideal touring base.

33rm(10)(3fb) ®CTV in 10 bedrooms ✱sB&B fr£20 sB&B£25 dB&B£33 dB&B£38 B

CTV 20 snooker

English & French S% ✱Lunch £3.50alc Tea £1.25alc Dinner £9.50&alc Wine £3 Last dinner 9.30pm

Credit cards 1 2 3 5

★★**Wordsworth** Main St ☎(0900) 822757

Closed Xmas day

Formerly a coaching inn, dating back to the early 17th-century.

18rm(46)(1fb) 1 CTV in all bedrooms ✱sB&B£17 sB&B£25 dB&B£28 dB&B£35 B

CTV 30P

Dinner £8 Wine £3.90 Last dinner 9.30pm

Credit cards 1 3 Ⓥ

✕**Old Court House** Main St ☎(0900) 823871

The charming little restaurant stands in the centre of the town, approached down a short flight of steps just before the river bridge. German cooking is the speciality, and an interesting and unusual table d'hôte menu is offered.

Dinner not served Sun

English & Continental **V** 36 seats Lunch £5—£7 Dinner £9.50—£12.50 Wine £3.60 Last dinner 9.30pm

COGGESHALL
Essex
Map **5** TL82

★★★***HB*** **White Hart** ☎(0376) 61654

Closed Aug & 2wks Xmas

Friendly coaching inn with modern, clean bedrooms, sound classical cooking and a very good wine list.

18rm(144)(1fb) CTV in all bedrooms **T** sB&B£35—£45 dB&B£60

CTV 20P 6

English & French **V** Lunch £20alc Dinner £20alc Wine £5.95 Last dinner 9.30pm

Credit cards 1 2 3 4 5

COLBOST
Isle of Skye, Highland *Inverness-shire*
See **Skye, Isle of**

COLCHESTER
Essex
Map **5** TL92

★★★**George** 116 High St (Queens Moat)
☎(0206) 578494

Town centre coaching inn with modern well-equipped bedrooms and carvery restaurant.

47(4fb) CTV in all bedrooms ® sB&B fr£39 dB&B fr£49 B

☾ 50P sauna bath, solarium & gymnasium *xmas* →

♁ ☕ Lunch fr£8.50 Tea fr80p Dinner fr£8.50 Wine £5.25 Last dinner 10pm
Credit cards 1 2 3 5

★★★**Marks Tey** London Rd ☎ (0206) 210001
(For full entry see Marks Tey)

★★**Kings Ford Park** Layer Rd, Layer de la Haye (2½m S B1026) ☎ (0206) 34301 Telex no 987562
Comfortable Regency house in woodland park with some modernised bedrooms.
15rm(9⇒5⋔)(2fb) 1▭ CTV in all bedrooms ® T sB&B£26.50—£31 sB&B⇒⋔£31—£37 dB&B⇒⋔£41—£55 B
CTV 200P ✿ ⚘ *xmas*
♉International V ♁ ☕ Lunch £7.50—£8.50&alc Tea 75—95p Dinner £7.50—£8.50&alc Wine £5.50 Last dinner 9.30pm
Credit cards 1 2 3 4 5

★★**Red Lion** High St (Whitbread) ☎ (0206) 577986
Closed 23—30 Dec
Popular old commercial hotel with adequate accommodation, busy bars and grill-style restaurant.
19rm(16⇒)(2fb) CTV in all bedrooms ® T sB&Bfr£28 sB&B⇒fr£38 dB&Bfr£36 dB&B⇒fr£45 B
☾ CTV P Live music and dancing Wed
♉Mainly grills V ♁ ☕ Lunch £4.65—£7.90&alc Tea 50p—£1.25 Dinner £4.65—£7.90&alc Wine £4.80 Last dinner 10pm
Credit cards 1 2 3 4 5

COLDINGHAM
Borders *Berwickshire*
Map **12** NT96

★★**Shieling** ☎ (03903) 216
Closed Nov—Feb
The small, traditional hotel stands on an elevated site overlooking beach and bay. It is well-provided with lounges, and friendly personal service is offered by the owners and their local staff.
10rm(4⇒1⋔)(1fb) ® sB&B£15 sB&B⇒⋔£17 dB&B£30 dB&B⇒⋔£34 B
CTV 15P ✿ ♿
V ♁ ☕ ⚡ Lunch £3alc Tea £2alc High Tea £3.75alc Dinner £8.50 Wine £5 Last dinner 8pm
Ⓥ

COLDSTREAM
Borders *Berwickshire*
Map **12** NT83

★***Majicado*** 71 High St ☎ (0890) 2112
Converted sandstone house dating from 1860, close to the River Tweed.
7rm(1fb) ®
CTV
V ♁ Last dinner 8.30pm

COLEFORD
Gloucestershire
Map **3** SO51

★★**Speech House** Forest of Dean (Trusthouse Forte) ☎ Dean (0594) 22607
Comfortable, friendly hotel built in 1676 as a court house for the Verderers of the Forest of Dean.
13rm(6⇒)(2fb) 3▭ CTV in all bedrooms ® sB&B£41.50 sB&B⇒£49.50 dB&B£63.50 dB&B⇒£57 B
40P ✿ *xmas*
♁ ☕ Last dinner 9.30pm
Credit cards 1 2 3 4 5

★♣**Lambsquay** ☎ Dean (0594) 33127
Closed mid wk in Dec & Jan
Peacefully situated, attractive Georgian house, offering high quality, home-produced cooking.
10rm(5⇒) 1▭ ⚡ in all bedrooms CTV in all bedrooms ® ✱ sB&B£15—£22 sB&B⇒£20—£25 dB&B£28—£38 dB&B⇒£30—£44 B
30P ⛟ ✿ nc 11yrs
V ♁ ✱ Lunch fr£9 Dinner fr£9 Wine £6.50 Last dinner 7.30pm
Credit cards 1 3

COLERNE
Wiltshire
Map **3** ST87

✕**Vineyard** ☎ Bath (0225) 742491
There are fine views over the countryside from this stone-built, cottage style restaurant, where traces of the terracing on which vines grew in the thirteenth century are still visible. Sound food is served in a pleasant atmosphere.
Closed Bank Hols
Dinner not served Sun
♉English & French V 30 seats ✱ Lunch £7.50&alc Dinner £8.50 Wine £4.45 Last dinner 9.30pm 28P ⚡
Credit cards 1 2 3 4 5 Ⓥ

COLESHILL
Warwickshire
Map **4** SP28

★★★**Coleshill** 152 High St (Whitbread) ☎ (0675) 65527
Situated close to Junction 4 of the M6, the comfortable modern hotel looks much older than it is, for materials from old buildings were cleverly used in its construction in 1982.
15rm(13⇒2⋔)(1fb) 2▭ CTV in all bedrooms ® T ✱ sB&B⇒⋔£38—£42 dB&B⇒⋔£46—£50 B
☾ 60P *xmas*
♉English & French V ♁ ☕ Lunch £6.50—£7.50&alc Tea 65p—£1.50 Dinner £8.50—£9.50&alc Wine £4.75 Last dinner 10pm
Credit cards 1 2 3 5

★★***Swan*** High St (Golden Oak Inns) ☎ (0675) 62212
Fully modernised hotel popular with business people.
34rm(23⋔) CTV in all bedrooms ® T ✕ B
CTV 120P ⛟
♁ Last dinner 10pm
Credit cards 1 2 3

COLL, ISLE OF
Strathclyde *Argyllshire*
Map **13**
ARINAGOUR
Map **13** NM26

★Isle of Coll ☎(08793) 334
Pleasant family atmosphere in this 1720 island inn.
8rm(1🚿)(2fb) CTV available in all bedrooms ®✱sB&B£14—£17.50 dB&B£24—£30 dB&B🚿£28—£35
CTV 30P✽ sauna bath solarium Live music nightly (in season) 👪
🍷 ☕ ✱Lunch £8 Tea 75p—£1.50 Dinner £9.25&alc Wine £2.95 Last dinner 8pm
Credit cards 1 3 4 5 V

COLONSAY, ISLE OF
Strathclyde *Argyllshire*
Map **10**
SCALASAIG
Map **10** NR39

★*HBL* *Colonsay* (Minotel)
☎(09512) 316
Closed Xmas Day
As you arrive at the island pier, the first building you see is the hotel and the first person you meet is its proprietor. Kevin Byane. This relaxing hospitality is reflected throughout the hotel, which has attractive bedrooms and carefully prepared set dinners, using much produce from the hotel's own gardens.
11rm(8🚿)(2fb) CTV availalble in bedrooms 𝔅
TV 32P 🚌 ✽ 👪
🍽European 🍷 ☕ Last dinner 7.30pm
Credit cards 1 2 3 5

COLVEND
Dumfries & Galloway *Kirkcudbrightshire*
Map **11** NX85

★★🏠Clonyard House ☎Rockcliffe (055663) 372
Country house with formal restaurant and lounge bar, and new ground floor wing of tasteful, contemporary bedrooms.
11rm(5🛁2🚿)(2fb) CTV in 7 bedrooms ® sB&B£12 sB&B🛁🚿£22 dB&B£24 dB&B🛁🚿£35 𝔅
CTV 25P 🚌 ✽ 👪 ♿
🍽British & French **V** 🍷 Bar lunch £3alc Dinner £9&alc Wine £4.50 Last dinner 9pm
Credit cards 1 3 V

COLWYN BAY
Clwyd
Map **6** SH87 **See plan**

Telephone numbers commencing with 2 or 3 are due to change.

★★★Hopeside Princes Dr ☎(0492) 33244 Telex no 61254 Plan **4***B2*
Closed Xmas & New Year's Eve
Detached holiday and tourist hotel near shops and beach.
19rm(13🛁6🚿)⊁in 6 bedrooms CTV in all bedrooms ®S% sB&B🛁🚿fr£20 dB&B🛁🚿fr£28 𝔅
20P nc6yrs
V 🍷 ☕ S% ✱Bar lunch fr£2.50 Tea fr£1.50 Dinner fr£8 Wine £3 Last dinner 9pm
Credit cards 1 2 3 5

★★★*L* Norfolk House Princes Dr ☎(0492) 31757 Telex no 61155 Plan **8***B2*
Personally-run tourist and business hotel in its own gardens, close to the beach and town centre.
27rm(12🛁15🚿)(3fb) CTV in all bedrooms ®sB&B🛁🚿£25—£27.50 dB&B🛁🚿£38 𝔅
Lift ☾ 40P 3🚗(charged) ✽ 👪
🍽English & French **V** 🍷 ☕ Bar lunch £1.25—£2.75&alc Tea £2alc High Tea £4.50alc Dinner £8.50alc Wine £5.10 Last dinner 9pm
Credit cards 1 2 3 4 5

★★★*L* Hotel 70° Penmaenhead (2m E A547) (Best Western) ☎(0492) 516555 Telex no 61362 Plan **5***C1*
Closed 22 Dec—5 Jan
The modern-style hotel on the clifftop is popular with businessmen, having well-appointed public rooms and spacious, comfortable bedrooms with good facilities. The restaurant commands fine views over the sea and offers speciality dishes from an Epicurean menu in addition to the basic à la carte selection. The wine list is extensive.
41🛁🚿(7fb) 1🛏 CTV in all bedrooms ®**T** S% sB&B🛁🚿£39—£45 dB&B🛁🚿£54—£66 𝔅
☾ 200P CFA Live music and dancing Sat
🍽International **V** 🍷 ☕ S% Lunch £8.95—£10.95&alc Tea £1.75—£3 Dinner £12.85—£17.85&alc Wine £7.50 Last dinner 9.30pm
Credit cards 1 2 3 4 5 V
See advertisement on page 235

★★Ashmount College Av, Rhos-on-Sea ☎(0492) 45479 Telex no 61155 Plan **1***A4*
This well-equipped, family-run hotel stands in a residential area close to the promenade.
18rm(5🛁13🚿)(4fb) CTV in all bedrooms ®**T** S% ✱sB&B🛁🚿£18—£20 dB&B🛁🚿£32—£35 𝔅
10P ♿ *xmas*
V 🍷 ☕ S% ✱Lunch £4.50 Tea £1.70 Dinner £7.50 Wine £4.40 Last dinner 8pm
Credit cards 1 2 3 5 V
See advertisement on page 234

★★Edelweiss Lawson Rd (Consort) ☎(0492) 2314 Telex no 57515 Plan **3***C1*
Detached Victorian house set in its own grounds, ½m from the beach.
25rm(19🛁6🚿)(7fb) 1🛏 CTV in all bedrooms ®sB&B🛁🚿fr£19 dB&B🛁🚿fr£34 𝔅
CTV 25P✽ sauna bath solarium games room 👪 *xmas*
🍽Welsh, English, French & Italian **V** 🍷 ☕ Lunch fr£4.50&alc Tea fr£1 High Tea fr£3.75 Dinner fr£7.50&alc Wine £4.65 Last dinner 8pm
Credit cards 1 2 5 V

Central Colwyn Bay

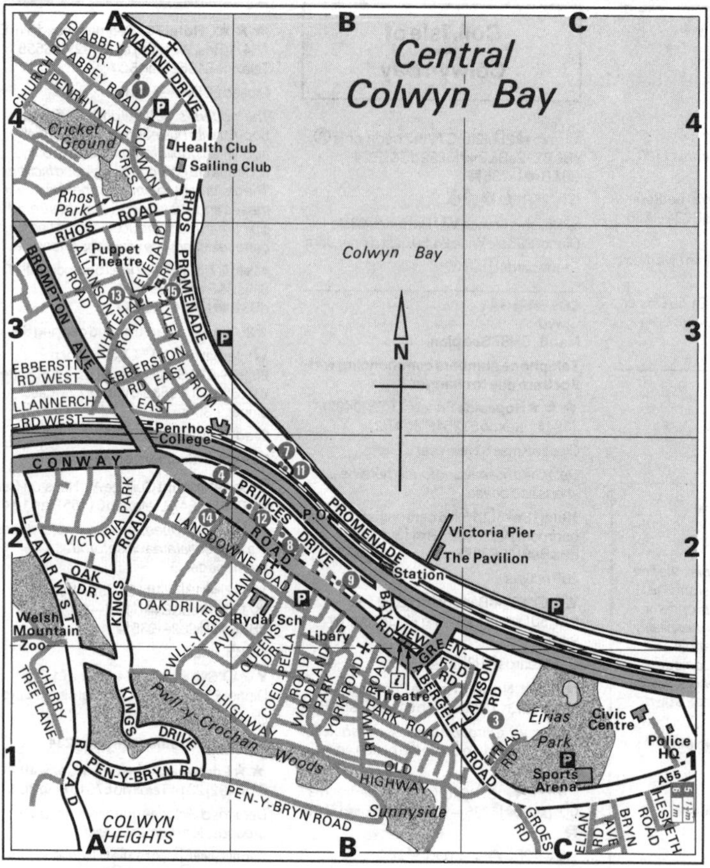

Colwyn Bay

1 Ashmount ★★
3 Edelweiss ★★
4 Hopeside ★★★
5 Hotel 70° ★★★
6 Lyndale ★★
7 Marine ★
8 Norfolk House ★★★
9 Penrhyn Suite ✕✕
11 St Enoch's ★★
12 St Margarets ★
13 Stanton House ★
14 West Point ★
15 Whitehall ★

Colwyn Bay

★★**Lyndale** 410 Abergele Rd, Old Colwyn (Guestaccom Exec Hotels) ☎ (0492) 515429 Telex no 61155 Plan **6***C1*

Modern, relaxing hotel where the Welsh chef provides imaginative, enjoyable food.

14rm(6⇌8🚿)(3fb)1▭CTV in all bedrooms ®T S% *sB&B⇌🚿£23 dB&B⇌🚿£39 Ɓ

20P

♔Welsh, English & French **V** ♡ ☕ Lunch fr£6.50 Tea fr75p High Tea fr£3.50 Dinner fr£8.50&alc Wine £5 Last dinner 9pm

Credit cards 1 2 3 Ⓥ

★★***St Enoch's*** Promenade ☎ (0492) 2031 Plan **11***B2*

Family-run with excellent collection of Welsh baronial memorabilia.

21rm(7⇌1🚿)(6fb)1▭CTV in 14 bedrooms TV in 1 bedroom ®Ɓ

CTV 6P *xmas*

♡ ☕ Last dinner 7.30pm

Credit cards 1 2 3

★**Marine** West Prom ☎ (0492) 30295 due to change to 530295 Plan **7***B2*

Closed Nov—Mar

Personally-run holiday hotel overlooking the sea with colourful terraced garden.

14rm(7🚿)(4fb) ®sB&B£14.50—£15.50 sB&B🚿£15.50—£16.50 dB&B£26—£27 dB&B🚿£27—£28 Ɓ

CTV 12P

V ♡ ☕ Lunch £4—£4.50 Dinner £5—£5.50 Wine £4.10 Last dinner 7.30pm

Credit cards 2 5 Ⓥ

C

★St Margaret's Princes Dr ☎ (0492) 2718 Plan **12***B2*

Late-Victorian hotel occupying a corner position, ½ mile from the shops and beach.

14rm(1→3⋒)(6fb) TV in all bedrooms ® sB&B£12.75 sB&B→⋒£14.75 dB&B£25.50 dB&B→⋒£29.50 **B**

CTV 10P Disco 5 nights wkly *xmas*

Lunch £3—£3.95 Tea 55p High Tea £1.50 Dinner £5—£8 Wine £4.95 Last dinner 7.30pm

Credit cards 1 3

★Stanton House Whitehall Rd, Rhos-on-Sea ☎ (0492) 44363 Plan **13***A3*

Quiet family run hotel with homely atmosphere and good home cooking.

11rm(3→)(3fb) in 2 bedrooms CTV in 1 bedroom TV in 4 bedrooms ® in 6 bedrooms sB&B£11.95—£13.95 sB&B→£13.95—£15.95 dB&B£21.95—£24.95 dB&B→£26.95—£30.95 **B**

CTV 7P *xmas*

V S% Lunch £2.50—£3.50 Tea £1—£1.50 High Tea £2—£2.95 Dinner £4.25—£4.95 Wine £4.95 Last dinner 7.30pm

Credit cards 1 3 Ⓥ

★West Point 102 Conway Rd (Minotel) ☎ (0492) 30331 Plan **14***B2*

Closed 1st 2 wks Jan

Welcoming, family-run hotel not far from sea and town centre.

14rm(3→4⋒)(3fb) ® sB&B£12—£13 sB&B→⋒£14—£15 dB&B£24 dB&B→⋒£28 **B**

CTV 12P *xmas*

English & French Lunch £3.50—£6 Tea 75p—£2.25 High Tea £5 Dinner £7—£9 Wine £4.95 Last dinner 7.25pm

Credit cards 1 3 Ⓥ

★Whitehall Cayley Prom, Rhos-on-Sea ☎ (0492) 47296 Plan **15***A3*

Closed end Oct—Etr

Bright, family-run hotel overlooking sea.

14rm(6⋒)(3fb) CTV in 7 bedrooms ® sB&B£12.50—£13.25 dB&B£25—£26.50 dB&B⋒£29—£30.50 **B**

CTV 6P nc3yrs

Bar lunch £2.50—£3 Dinner £6.50—£7 Wine £3.50 Last dinner 7pm

Ⓥ

XXPenrhyn Suite Penrhyn Rd ☎ (0492) 2738 Plan **9***B2*

New 1st floor restaurant, tastefully furnished and offering imaginative, well-cooked food. Good value for money.

Closed Mon
Dinner not served Sun

English & French **V** 50 seats Lunch £5.05—£10.85 Dinner £9.95&alc Wine £4.90 Last dinner 9.30pm

Credit cards 1 2 3 5

COLYTON

Devon
Map **3** SY29

XXOld Bakehouse Lower Church St ☎ (0297) 52518

Situated at the centre of the village, and housed in an attractive, double-fronted, stone building that was once the bakery, the tastefully-furnished restaurant has flint walls and exposed beams, whilst the lounge/aperitif bar features a copper-canopied fireplace. Morning coffee, lunch and afternoon tea are now offered in addition to the à la carte dinner menu.

Closed Mon & Jan

French 30 seats Lunch £1.25—£4.50alc Dinner £10—£12alc Wine £4.60 Last dinner 10pm 10P

Credit card 3

COMBEINTEIGNHEAD

Devon
Map **3** SX97

★★*Netherton House* ☎ Shaldon (062687) 3251

Peaceful, comfortably-appointed hotel in secluded country setting.

10rm(5→1⋒) CTV in all bedrooms ®

50P (heated) nc8yrs *xmas*

English & French Last dinner 8.45pm

Credit cards 1 2 3

COMBE MARTIN

Devon
Map **2** SS54

★★Rone House King St ☎ (027188) 3428

Closed mid Nov—mid Dec

Comfortable family run hotel offering honest home cooking.

10rm(4→4⋒)(4fb) TV in all bedrooms sB&B£10.50—£12.50 dB&B£21—£25 dB&B→⋒£26—£30 **B**

CTV 12P (heated) nc4yrs *xmas*

Bar lunch £2.95 Dinner £8 Wine £3.30 Last dinner 7.30pm

Credit card 1 Ⓥ

★Britannia Moory Meadow, Seaside ☎ (027188) 2294

Quiet, spacious hotel overlooking the sea and offering good food.

10rm(1→1⋒)(2fb) S% sB&B£13—£13.75 sB&B→⋒£15.50—£16.25 dB&B£24.50—£26 dB&B→⋒£27—£28.50 **B**

CTV 10P 2 *xmas*

S% Lunch fr£5 Tea fr50p Dinner fr£8.50 Wine £3.60 Last dinner 7.30pm

Ⓥ

COMRIE

Tayside *Perthshire*
Map **11** NN72

★★Comrie Drummond St ☎ (0764) 70239

RS Oct—Mar

A privately owned and managed ivy clad hotel.

10rm(1→5⋒) Annexe: 2→ CTV in 9 bedrooms ® S% sB&B£15 sB&B→⋒£24 dB&B£30 dB&B→⋒£48

CTV 24P nc5yrs

S% Lunch £6.50—£7.50&alc Tea £1 Dinner £9—£10&alc Wine £3.50 Last dinner 9.30pm

Ⓥ

★★Royal ☎ (0764) 70200 Telex no 76277

RS Oct—Mar

Originally a famed hostelry with royal and historic connections, the hotel is now comfortable and thoughtfully run.

9→ Annexe: 3→(3fb) 1 CTV in all bedrooms ® **T** sB&B→£19.50—£21 dB&B→£42 **B**

30P 2 *xmas*

Scottish & French **V** Lunch £5alc Dinner £11&alc Wine £4.60 Last dinner 9pm

Credit cards 1 2 3 Ⓥ

CONISTON

Cumbria
Map **7** SD39

★★Coniston Sun ☎ (0966) 41248

Closed Jan & Feb

The beautifully-situated hotel is tastefully decorated and furnished throughout. The elegantly comfortable lounge and dining room, together with many of the bedrooms, have spectacular views.

11rm(8→3⋒) 2 CTV in all bedrooms ® *sB&B→⋒£24 dB&B→⋒£40—£48 **B**

12P 3

V *Bar lunch £5alc Tea 85p—£2 Dinner £9.50—£11 Wine £5.50 Last dinner 8pm

Credit cards 1 3

★Black Bull Yewdale Rd ☎ (0966) 41335

Old world village inn dating from 16th century.

7rm(3fb) CTV in all bedrooms ® *sB&Bfr£21.25 dB&B£27.60 **B**

CTV 10P 2

English & French **V** Lunch fr£4.50 Tea fr80p High Tea fr£3.75 Dinner fr£6 Wine £5 Last dinner 6pm

Ⓥ

★Yewdale Yewdale Rd ☎ (0966) 41280

6rm(4⋒)(2fb) CTV in all bedrooms ® S% *sB&B£12.50—£14.95 sB&B⋒£14.95—£16 dB&B£25 dB&B⋒£29.95 **B**

CTV 6P

🍷☕S%✱Lunch £3.50alc Tea £2alc High Tea £3.50alc Dinner £5.50 alc Wine £4.95 Last dinner 8.30pm

Credit cards 1 3

CONNEL
Strathclyde *Argyllshire*
Map **10** NM93

★★**Falls of Lora** (Exec Hotel)
☎(063171) 483

RS Xmas—New Year

Large Victorian hotel with modern extension.

30rm(23⇌)(4fb)1⊟CTV available in bedrooms sB&B£12.50—£27.50 sB&B⇌£18.50—£37.50 dB&B£21—£37 dB&B⇌fr£25 B

☾CTV 40P 9🚗 ✿♿

Scottish & French V 🍷☕ Lunch £6.50 Tea £1.50—£3.50 Dinner £10.25 Wine £5.25 Last dinner 9.30pm

Credit cards 1 2 3 5 V

★★**Lochnell Arms** North Connel
☎(063171) 408

Small hotel with an attractive lounge and bar, patio and lochside gardens.

11rm(7⇌)(4fb) sB&B£13—£16 sB&B⇌£14—£17 dB&B£26—£32 dB&B⇌£28—£35 B

CTV 50P ✿ *xmas*

Coniston — Conwy

V 🍷☕ Lunch £5—£7 Tea 60p—£1 Dinner £10—£15 Wine £4.50 Last dinner 10pm

Credit cards 1 2 3 5 V

★★*L* **Ossians** Connel North
☎(063171) 322

Closed Oct—mid Apr

Modern hotel overlooking Loch Etive.

14rm(4⇌) ®sB&B£17.43 dB&B£34.86 dB&B⇌£36.86

CTV 50P ✿

English & French 🍷☕ Lunch £3alc Tea £1.50alc Dinner £12alc Wine £5.40 Last dinner 8pm

Credit cards 2 3

CONSTANTINE BAY
Cornwall
Map **2** SW87

★★★*HL* **Treglos** (Consort) ☎ Padstow (0841) 520727 Telex no 45795

Closed 6 Nov—11 Mar

Attractive hotel with views over rocky coastline and golfing facilities nearby.

44⇌⋒(12fb) CTV in all bedrooms T sB&B⇌⋒£22—£38 dB&B⇌⋒£42—£74

Lift ☾ 50P 8🚗(80p per day) CFA ✿ ⊠(heated) croquet nc 3yrs (in restaurant)

English & French 🍷☕ Lunch £6.95—£7.50 Tea 70p-£2 Dinner £11.25&alc Wine £4.75 Last dinner 9.30pm

Credit cards 1 3

CONWY
Gwynedd
Map **6** SH77

During the currency of this guide telephone numbers are due to change

★★★**Sychnant Pass** Sychnant Pass Rd ☎(049263) 6868 Telex no 61155

Closed Jan RS Nov—Mar

Modern well appointed hotel in beautiful surroundings, featuring Four Seasons restaurant and Columbian pine cocktail bar.

11rm(8⇌3⋒)(2fb) CTV in all bedrooms ® T sB&B⇌⋒£35—£40 dB&B⇌⋒£40—£50 B

30P ✿ sauna bath solarium *xmas*

British & French 🍷☕ Bar lunch £1.75—£3.50&alc Tea fr 90p Dinner £10.95—£14.95 Wine £5.75 Last dinner 9.30pm

Credit cards 1 2 3 5 V

See advertisement on page 238

C

C

★★**Castle** High St (Trusthouse Forte) ☎(049263) 2324

An important 19th-century coaching house, featuring a unique collection of the Victorian artist, JD Watson. The lounge has been refurbished and the bedrooms are being upgraded.

25⇌ CTV in all bedrooms ® sB&B⇌£44 dB&B⇌£62.50 B

30P *xmas*

Last dinner 9pm

Credit cards 1 2 3 4 5

★★**Castle Bank** Mount Pleasant ☎(049263) 3888

Closed Jan RS Dec & Feb

Victorian stone house standing in its own gardens, next to the castle walls.

9rm(8⋒)(3fb) CTV in all bedrooms ® sB&Bfr£16.50 dB&B⋒fr£33 B

CTV 12P

International Lunch fr£6 Dinner fr£9.50 Wine £4.50 Last dinner 8pm

Ⓥ

COODEN BEACH
East Sussex
Map **5** TQ70

★★★***Cooden Beach*** Cooden Sea Rd (Best Western) ☎ Cooden (04243) 2281 Telex no 877247

Comfortable, friendly, well managed hotel facing the sea with good leisure facilities.

32rm(24⇌5⋒)(9fb) CTV in 31 bedrooms TV in 1 bedroom ® T B

(CTV 50P 7 (charge) (heated) *xmas*

Last dinner 9.30pm

Credit cards 1 2 3 5

COOKHAM
Berkshire
Map **4** SU88

XX***Cookham Tandoori*** High St ☎ Bourne End (06285) 22584

The furnishings and decor of this smart Indian restaurant are more subdued than many. Division into three sections gives an intimate atmosphere, and a selection of well-cooked dishes from the northern regions of India are reasonably priced, though more expensive specialities are obtainable by giving 24 hours' notice.

Indian **V** 70 seats Last dinner 11pm

X***Peking Inn*** High St ☎ Bourne End (06285) 20900

This is a branch of the well-known Chef Peking restaurant in Maidenhead, and it seems to be proving just as popular. Modern and bright, with well-appointed tables, it achieves a friendly, informal atmosphere which complements the well-prepared Pekinese food. For those not familiar with the cuisine, the leave-it-to-us feast is to be recommended.

Pekinese **V** 80 seats Last dinner 11pm

COPTHORNE
West Sussex
Map **4** TQ33

Hotels are listed under **Gatwick Airport**

CORBIÉRE
Jersey, see **Channel Islands**

CORBRIDGE
Northumberland
Map **12** NY96

★**Angel Inn** Main St ☎(043471) 2119

Attractive old coaching inn with comfortable bedrooms and a wealth of mahogany panelling.

6rm CTV in all bedrooms ® *sB&Bfr£16 dB&Bfr£25

10P

*Dinner fr£4.95 Wine £3.95 Last dinner 10pm

Credit cards 1 2 3 5

★**Riverside** Main St (Guestaccom) ☎(043471) 2942

Closed Xmas—Jan

Small, comfortable hotel with neat accommodation and friendly service.

11rm(1⇌3⋒)(2fb) *sB&B£16—£17.50 sB&B⇌⋒£19.50 dB&B£24.50—£26 dB&B⇌⋒£29.50

CTV 10P

English & French *Dinner £8.95 Last dinner 8pm

XX**Ramblers Country House** Farnley (½m SE on A68) ☎(043471) 2424

The elegant, country-house restaurant has charming dining rooms, a very comfortable coffee lounge with log fire and a cheerful cocktail bar. An interesting selection of German dishes is offered, and the staff are very happy to give advice on both the menu and the wine list.

Closed Sun & Mon Lunch not served

International **V** 80 seats Dinner £9.85&alc Wine £4.90 Last dinner 10pm 30P

Credit cards 1 2 3 5

CORFE CASTLE
Dorset
Map **3** SY98

★★*BL* **Mortons House** East St ☎(0929) 480988

A comfortable, small, Elizabethan manor house, set in this historic and unspoiled village, provides bedrooms which have been converted to modern standards of comfort without losing their charm and public rooms whose original style is virtually unchanged. The restaurant serves interesting food, well cooked and presented.

7⇌ 1 CTV in all bedrooms *sB&B⇌£30—£60 dB&B⇌£40—£110

20P *xmas*

*Lunch £5.50&alc Tea 60p&alc Dinner £12&alc Wine £5.50 Last dinner 9.45pm

Credit cards 1 3

CORSE LAWN
Hereford & Worcester
Map **3** SO83

✿ ✕✕✕ **Corse Lawn House Hotel** ☎ Tirley (045278) 479
For seven years Mr and Mrs Hine have gained our rosette award with their imaginative menu, sympathetic cooking, caring staff and pleasant surroundings. Recently, bedrooms with private facilities have been made available in the Queen Anne style house.
Dinner not served Sun
English & French **V** 50 seats S% Lunch fr£10.50&alc Dinner fr£14.75 Wine £4.75 Last dinner 10pm 50P
Credit cards 1 2 3 5

CORSHAM
Wiltshire
Map **3** ST86

★★★ **Rudloe Park** Leafy Ln ☎ Bath (0225) 810555
Delightful hotel with well-appointed bedrooms, and good elegant restaurant. No dogs.
8 (2fb) 1 CTV in all bedrooms ® **T** sB&B £40—£42.50 dB&B £55—£65
70P 2 ✿ croquet nc 10yrs *xmas*
International **V** Lunch £8.50&alc Tea £1—£2 Dinner £9.75&alc Wine £7 Last dinner 10pm
Credit cards 1 2 3 4 5 V
See advertisement under Bath

★★ **Methuen Arms** High St (ExecHotel) ☎ (0249) 714867
RS Sun in winter
The town-centre hotel, located in a character building which dates back to the 1400's, has a pleasant restaurant and soundly furnished bedrooms.
18rm(13 1) Annexe: 6rm(2 4)(2fb) CTV in all bedrooms ® **T** sB&B £27.50 sB&B £33 dB&B £44 dB&B £51
60P ✿ *xmas*
English & French **V** ✱Lunch £12.90&alc Dinner £7.95—£12.90&alc Wine £4.50 Last dinner 9.30pm
Credit cards 1 3
See advertisement under Bath

★★ **Park Lane Manor** (formerly Stagecoach Motel) Pickwick ☎ (0249) 713162 Telex no 445804
Modern hotel with studio-style bedrooms and attractive bar.
21rm(20 1)(10fb) in 2 bedrooms CTV in all bedrooms ® **T** sB&B £28.75—£30.95 dB&B £45.50—£49.90
CTV 36P CFA ✿ games room *xmas*
International **V** Lunch £5—£9.75&alc Tea 60p—£1 High Tea £2.95—£5.50 Dinner £9.75—£12.50&alc Wine £5.25 Last dinner 9.30pm
Credit cards 1 2 3 5 V
See advertisement under Bath

✕✕ **Weavers Loft** High St ☎ (0249) 713982
This attractive first-floor restaurant is in the heart of the town. A warm welcome is extended by the restaurant, which is comfortably appointed and has fresh flowers on the tables. The food is imaginative, well prepared and presented, and the three menu-styles represent a range of prices.
Closed Sun Mon 1st wk Nov & 1st wk Jan Lunch not served
British & Continental **V** 40 seats Dinner £10.25—£13.50&alc Wine £5 Last dinner 9.30pm
Credit cards 1 3 5 V

COTTINGHAM
Northamptonshire
Map **4** SP89

★★ **Hunting Lodge** High St ☎ Rockingham (0536) 771370
Closed 25 & 26 Dec
This busy inn at the centre of the village is set behind a tall screen of mature trees. A car park divides the bedroom block from the main building, and rooms are of a modern design, in modular form.
Annexe: 8 CTV in all bedrooms ® **T** ✱sB&B £36 dB&B £46
CTV 250P Live music & dancing Fri & Sat
English & French ✱Lunch £9&alc Dinner £9&alc Wine £3.75 Last dinner 10.30pm
Credit cards 1 2 3 5

COVE
Strathclyde *Dunbartonshire*
Map **10** NS28

★★ ***Knockderry*** ☎ Kilcreggan (043684) 2283
Family run hotel on shores of Loch Long.
13rm(5)(1fb) ®
CTV 50P ✿ Live music & dancing Sat
V Last dinner 8.30pm
Credit cards 1 2 3 5

COVENTRY
West Midlands
Map **4** SP37

★★★★ **De Vere** Cathedral Sq (De Vere) ☎ (0203) 51851 Telex no 31380
Modern hotel with choice of bars and restaurants and large conference/ banqueting facilities.
190 (9fb) CTV in all bedrooms ® **T**
Lift ☾ 130P CFA *xmas*
International **V** S% Lunch £6 Tea 75p High Tea £3.50 Dinner £6—£9&alc Last dinner 11pm
Credit cards 1 2 3 5

★★★★ **Hotel Leofric** Broadgate (Embassy) ☎ (0203) 21371 Telex no 311193
Modern, city centre hotel with large rooms.
91 (10fb) CTV in all bedrooms ® **T** S% sB&B fr£51 dB&B fr£66
Lift ☾ CFA *xmas*
International **V** S% ✱Lunch fr£8.50&alc Dinner fr£9.50&alc Wine £5.10 Last dinner 9.45pm
Credit cards 1 2 3 4 5

★★★ ***Allesley*** Allesley Village ☎ (0203) 403272 Telex no 312549
Closed Xmas Day
Set in a quiet village on the outskirts of the city, this large, modernised hotel has sizeable function rooms for conferences and receptions.
24rm(14 2) Annexe: 13rm(3fb) CTV in 33 bedrooms ® **T**
☾ 350P Disco Tue & Wed Live music & dancing Thu—Sat
V Last dinner 10.30pm
Credit cards 1 2 3 4 5

★★★ **Chace Crest** London Rd, Willenhall (Crest) ☎ (0203) 303398 Telex no 311993
The Victorian house has a modern bedroom extension and offers a good location for small business conferences.
68 in 6 bedrooms CTV in all bedrooms ® S% ✱sB fr£52.95 dB fr£68.90 (room only)
☾ 150P ✿ Disco nightly Live music & dancing 3 nights wkly *xmas*
French **V** S% ✱Lunch £6.50—£8.50&alc Tea £1.50 High Tea £3.50—£6.95 Dinner £11.75—£13.75&alc Wine £5.80 Last dinner 9.45pm
Credit cards 1 2 3 5

★★★ **Crest** Hinckley Rd, Walsgrave (junc 2 M6) (Crest) ☎ (0203) 613261 Telex no 311292
RS Xmas
Popular roadside hotel with modern bedroom extension.
152 in 14 bedrooms CTV in all bedrooms ® **T** S% sB £47—£50.75 dB £57—£62 (room only)
Lift ☾ 250P CFA ✿ pool table Live music & dancing Sat
V S% ✱Lunch fr£9.25 Tea fr80p Dinner fr£11.50 Wine £6.15 Last dinner 9.45pm
Credit cards 1 2 3 4 5

★★★**Hylands** Warwick Rd (Best Western) ☎ (0203) 501600 Telex no 312388

RS 25 & 26 Dec (afternoon)

This hotel's proximity to the city centre and its popular carvery restaurant make it an ideal choice for businessmen.

56rm(55➡1⋔)(4fb) CTV in all bedrooms ®T sB&B➡⋔fr£36.15—£38.90 dB&B➡⋔£47.15 B

☾CTV 60P pool table

♉English & Continental ♈ ☕ ⚔ Lunch fr£6.50&alc Tea 65p Dinner fr£7&alc Wine £5.25 Last dinner 9.45pm

Credit cards 1 2 3 5

★★★**Novotel Coventry** Wilsons Ln (A444/M6 junc 3) ☎ (0203) 365000 Telex no 31545

With six squash courts and other sporting facilities, the hotel offers an energetic break to guests visiting the Midlands area.

100➡⋔(100fb) CTV in all bedrooms T S% ✱sB&B➡⋔fr£45 dB&B➡⋔fr£54.50 B

Lift ☾ ## 160P CFA ✿ ♒(heated) squash sauna bath solarium gymnasium pool table petanque Disco Fri ♿ *xmas*

♉French V ♈ ☕ S% ✱Lunch £7.50&alc Tea 85p Dinner £8.50&alc Wine £6.95 Last dinner mdnt

Credit cards 1 2 3 4 5 Ⓥ

★★★**Post House** Rye Hill, Allesley (Trusthouse Forte) ☎ (0203) 402151 Telex no 31427

Situated on the A45 and overlooking the local surroundings from its eight storeys, this hotel caters for all types of small function.

196➡(38fb) CTV in all bedrooms ®T sB&B➡£49.50 dB&B➡£63.50 B

Lift ☾ ## 177P 120🏠 CFA

♈ ☕ Last dinner 10pm

Credit cards 1 2 3 4 5

★★★***Royal Court*** Tamworth Rd, Keresley (3m NW on B4098) ☎ Keresley (020333) 4171 Telex no 312549

Closed Xmas Day

Busy hotel in 11 acres wooded grounds with carvery restaurant.

99rm(84➡12⋔)(3fb) CTV in all bedrooms ®T ✕ B

Lift ☾ 500P ✿ 🎾 Disco 5 nights wkly Live music & dancing twice wkly

♉English & French V ♈ ☕ Last dinner 11pm

Credit cards 1 2 3 5

★★**Beechwood** Sandpits Ln, Keresley (3m NW on B4098) ☎ Keresley (020333) 4243

Commercial hotel, situated in a quiet rural area.

27rm(18⋔)(1fb) CTV in all bedrooms sB&B£22 sB&B⋔£27 dB&B⋔£38 B

☾100P ✿ pool table

♉English & Continental V ♈ ✱Lunch £8 Tea 80p Dinner £8 Wine £5 Last dinner 9.30pm

Credit cards 1 2 3 5 Ⓥ

COWBRIDGE

South Glamorgan
Map **3** SS97

★★**Bear** High St ☎ (04463) 4814

This is one of the oldest coaching inns in Wales, for parts of it date from the twelfth century. Today's hotel complements the cosy, character bars and stylish, stone-vaulted restaurant with a comfortable bedroom wing.

22rm(19➡) Annexe: 16rm(10➡6⋔)(1fb) 2🛏 CTV in all bedrooms ®T ✱sB&B£22 sB&B➡⋔fr£27 dB&B➡⋔fr£37 B

100P ♿

♉English & French ♈ ☕ ✱Lunch fr£5.95 High Tea fr£1 Dinner £9alc Wine £4.75 Last dinner 10pm

Credit cards 1 2 3 5 Ⓥ

COWES
See **Wight, Isle of**

COWFOLD
West Sussex
Map **4** TQ22

✕St Peters Cottage The Street
☎(040386) 324

A 17th-century cottage houses a restaurant where a simple menu of good, honest food is served in a traditional English atmosphere.

Closed Mon & mid Sep—mid Oct Dinner not served

V 65 seats Lunch £5—£6 Wine £4.50 P
Credit cards 1 3

CRACKINGTON HAVEN
Cornwall
Map **2** SX19

★★Coombe Barton ☎St Gennys (08403) 345

Closed 18 Oct—20 Mar

Comfortable residence, part 18th century, set by the sea.

10rm(3⇌)(1fb) Ⓡ sB&B£16—£17.50 dB&B£30—£32 dB&B⇌£33—£37 B

CTV 35P

V Bar lunch £3.50alc Dinner fr £9.50&alc Wine £5.75 Last dinner 9pm

Credit cards 1 3

★★Crackington Manor ☎St Gennys (08403) 397

Closed 4 Jan—Feb

Friendly hotel on headland specialising in local produce. Welcomes families. →

15rm(6⇌2⋒)(5fb) 1▣ Ⓡ
*sB&B£18—£20 dB&B⇌⋒£40—£47 B
CTV 25P ✿ ⛆(heated) ⚲ sauna bath solarium ⌂ *xmas*
☗International V ☕ ⊐ ⊁ Bar lunch fr80p Tea fr40p Dinner fr£8.50&alc Wine £4.45 Last dinner 9pm
Credit cards 1 2 3 Ⓥ

CRAIGHOUSE
Isle of Jura, Strathclyde *Argyllshire*
See **Jura, Isle of**

CRAIGNURE
Isle of Mull, Strathclyde *Argyllshire*
See **Mull, Isle of**

CRAIL
Fife
Map **12** NO60

★**Croma** Nethergate ☏(0333) 50239
Closed Nov—Feb
Small, well maintained, family hotel with a garden at the rear, situated in a quiet, residential area.
9rm(2⇌)(2fb) sB&B£10—£12 sB&B⇌£10—£12 dB&B£20 dB&B⇌£20—£24 B
CTV 6P ✿ ⌂
V ☕ ⊐ Bar lunch £3.50—£5 Tea £2.50—£3.50 High Tea £4—£4.50 Dinner £7.50—£8 Wine £4 Last dinner 10.30pm
Ⓥ

★***Marine*** 54 Nethergate ☏(0333) 50207
Small family hotel with garden extending to waters edge.
12rm(2fb) CTV in 3 bedrooms Ⓡ B
CTV
☗Scottish, English, French & Italian V ☕ ⊐ Last dinner 9pm
Credit cards 1 3

CRANBROOK
Kent
Map **5** TQ73

★★ ♣**KENNEL HOLT, CRANBROOK**
☏(0580) 712032
Closed 23 Dec—25 Jan
Among the hop gardens and orchards of the Weald of Kent lies this delightful small hotel in 5 acres of immaculately tended gardens, with lawns, tree lined walks, rose beds and a duck pond; there is also a croquet lawn. The house is an Elizabethan manor which retains some of the original features. Mr and Mrs Cliff, the owners are a hospitable and sociable couple who have set out to create the atmosphere of a private house. Mrs Cliff used to teach Cordon Bleu cookery and her skill is apparent in the enjoyable dinners of four courses. Besides the fixed price meal there are a number of other main course items at an extra charge. Traditional services are provided such as attention to the bedrooms during the evening and your shoes will be cleaned. Bedrooms are attractively furnished and comfortable with extra touches which include hair dryers. There are two sitting rooms, both with log fires when needed, beams, a few antique pieces and comfortable seating. The sitting room at the rear is an atmospheric panelled room, with games, shelves and books. Everywhere there are lots of flowers that brighten the already spotlessly clean rooms. This is a charming little hotel which we are sure you will approve of.

★★

8rm(4⇌2⋒) 1▣ CTV in all bedrooms Ⓡ in 1 bedroom
*sB&B⇌⋒£27—£32 dB&B⇌⋒£42—£70 B
30P ⊞ ✿ nc6yrs
☗English & French ⊁ * Lunch £5alc Tea 75palc Dinner £12alc Wine £4.95 Last dinner 8pm

★★**Willesley** ☏(0580) 713555
Closed 1st wk Feb
A well run, friendly hotel, part of which dates from the 14th century, with modern, well equipped bedrooms.
16⇌(2fb) 1▣ CTV in all bedrooms Ⓡ T S% sB&B⇌£33—£35 dB&B⇌£48—£52 B
CTV 50P ✿ snooker
☗French V ☕ S% Lunch £6.45—£7 Tea 75—90p Dinner £9.70—£11.50&alc Wine £4.95 Last dinner 9.30pm
Credit cards 1 2 3 4 5

★**George** Stone St ☏(0580) 713348
The resident proprietors of this cosy Tudor Inn, once visited by Elizabeth I, provide good food and personal service.
9rm(1fb) *sB&B fr£18 dB&B£28—£30
CTV 25P
☗English & French V ☕ * Lunch fr£6.50 Dinner fr£6.50&alc Last dinner 9pm
Credit cards 1 2 3

CRANTOCK
Cornwall
Map **2** SW76

★★**Crantock Bay** West Pentire
☎(0637) 830229
Closed Nov—Mar
Beautifully situated to overlook Crantock Bay, this owner-run hotel offers good facilities.
29rm(27 1) CTV in all bedrooms Ⓡ sB&B £16—£27 dB&B £32—£54
CTV 35P Disco wkly Live music and dancing wkly
Bar lunch £1—£5 Tea 75p—£2 Dinner £7—£7.95 Wine £3.80 Last dinner 8pm
Credit card 3 Ⓥ

★★*H* ***Fairbank*** West Pentire Rd
☎(0637) 830424
Closed Nov—Mar
Small friendly family hotel in a quiet village, commanding views over the nearby coastline.
30rm(4 20)(3fb) 2 CTV in 4 bedrooms
CTV 30P Disco Tue (in season) Live music Thu (in season)
Last dinner 8pm
Credit cards 1 3 5

CRATHORNE
North Yorkshire
Map **8** NZ40

★★★★ *L* **Crathorne Hall**
☎ Stokesley (0642) 700398 Telex no 587426
Closed 1—3 Jan
Reputed to be one of the last stately homes, built 1906, it stands in 15 acres of grounds.
39rm(33 6)(2fb) 1 CTV in all bedrooms Ⓡ **T** ✱ sB&B £46 dB&B £59
CTV 200P billiards *xmas*
French **V** ✱ Lunch £7—£7.50&alc Tea 95 High Tea £4.25 Dinner £10.95—£14.50&alc Wine £7.15 Last dinner 10pm
Credit cards 1 2 3 4 5

CRAWLEY
West Sussex
Map **4** TQ23
Hotels are listed under Gatwick Airport

CREETOWN
Dumfries & Galloway *Kirkcudbrightshire*
Map **11** NX45

✕ **Henry's Seafood** Carsluith
☎(067182) 216
Set on the hillside overlooking the Solway Firth, this delightful little restaurant is renowned for first-class cooking which makes full use of quality fish, both local and from around the Scottish markets.
Closed Tue
V 36 seats
✱ Lunch £7alc Dinner £9alc Wine £5.25 Last dinner 10pm 20P

CRESSAGE
Shropshire
Map **7** SJ50

✕✕ ***Old Hall*** ☎(095289) 298
A lovely well maintained house with beautiful gardens and fine views.
Closed Mon Dinner not served Sun
English & French 45 seats Last dinner 9pm 25P
Credit cards 1 3 5

CREWE
Cheshire
Map **7** SJ75

★★★**Crewe Arms** Nantwich Rd (Embassy) ☎(0270) 213204
Large modern hotel next to the railway station. →

35rm(33➡2⋒)(2fb) CTV in all bedrooms ®T S% sB➡⋒fr£39.50 dB➡⋒fr£52(room only) B
☾250P games room CFA *xmas*
English & French V S% *Lunch £7.95&alc Tea fr£1 Dinner £7.95&alc Wine £4.45 Last dinner 9.30pm
Credit cards 1 2 3 5 V

C

CREWKERNE
Somerset
Map **3** ST40

★★**Old Parsonage** Barn St (Exec Hotels) ☎(0460) 73516

Attractive part 15th-century house with comfortable bedrooms, an attractive restaurant and good fresh cooking.

4rm(3➡1⋒) Annexe: 6rm(4➡2⋒)(2fb) CTV in all bedrooms ®T sB&B➡⋒fr£26.50 dB&B➡⋒£40—£45
☾12P
V *Lunch £6.75—£12 Dinner £6.75—£12 Wine £3.95 Last dinner 9.30pm
Credit cards 1 2 3 5 V

CRICCIETH
Gwynedd
Map **6** SH43

★★★**Bron Eifion** ☎(076671) 2385

Country house with magnificent panelled hall and gallery and well tended gardens.

19rm(13➡5⋒)(4fb) T S% *sB&B➡⋒£38—£39(incl dinner) dB&B➡⋒£76—£78(incl dinner) B
CTV 100P croquet nc 3yrs *xmas*
English & Continental S% *Lunch £6.50 Tea 75p Dinner £11 Wine £5.50 Last dinner 9pm
Credit card 1 V

★★**George IV** (Consort) ☎(076671) 2168

Late-Victorian, holiday/tourist hotel in Criccieth main street.

34rm(22➡8⋒)(7fb) CTV in all bedrooms ®sB&B£14.25—£16.75 sB&B➡⋒£16.75—£18.75 dB&B£28.50—£32.50 dB&B➡⋒£32.50—£36.50 B
Lift CTV 60P *xmas*
V *Lunch fr£4.35 Tea fr75p High Tea fr£3.75 Dinner £4.35—£6.95 Last dinner 9.15pm
Credit cards 1 3 V

★★**Gwyndy** Llanystumdwy ☎(076671) 2720

Converted 17th century farmhouse, retaining some original features, but with most bedrooms in modern annexe.

2⋒ Annexe: 8➡(4fb) CTV in 8 bedrooms ®sB&B➡⋒£14.50—£15.50 dB&B➡⋒£27.50—£29 B
CTV 20P
Lunch £4.50—£6&alc Tea fr£1.75 High Tea fr£3 Dinner £7—£9&alc Wine £5 Last dinner 9pm

Crewe — Crickhowell

★★**Lion** Y Maes ☎(076671) 2460

Detached hotel, set back from the main road, ½ mile from the beach.

40rm(12➡3⋒)(4fb) CTV in all bedrooms ®sB&B£14—£16.50 sB&B➡⋒£15.50—£18.50 dB&B£26—£31 dB&B➡⋒£29—£35 B
Lift 20P 12 solarium *xmas*
Lunch £4.25—£5.25 Tea fr70p High Tea £2.50—£2.70 Dinner £7.50—£9.50 Last dinner 8.15pm
Credit cards 1 2 3 5 V

★★**Parciau Mawr** High St ☎(076671) 2368
Closed Nov—Feb

Country house, built in 1907, set in its own grounds which include a 300-year-old barn.

7rm(2➡1⋒) Annexe: 6⋒(3fb) CTV in all bedrooms ® sB&B£16.50 sB&B➡⋒£21.50 dB&B£33 dB&B➡⋒£38 B
30P nc 5yrs
English & French Dinner £6.50 Wine £4.25 Last dinner 8pm
Credit cards 1 3 4

★★**Plas Gwyn** Pentrefelin (1m NE A497) ☎(076671) 2559

Detached Victorian hotel situated 1 mile from Criccieth.

16⋒(4fb) CTV in all bedrooms ®S% sB&B⋒£16—£17.50 dB&B⋒£32—£35
CTV 50P 4 Disco Fri & Sat
English, French & Italian V Lunch £5—£6 Tea £1.50—£2 High Tea £3—£4 Dinner £8—£10 Wine £5.25 Last dinner 9pm
Credit cards 1 2 3 5
See advertisement under Porthmadog

★***Abereistedd*** West Pde ☎(076671) 2710
Closed Oct—Feb

Detached Victorian hotel in corner position at end of promenade, ½ mile from shops.

12rm(5⋒)(2fb) ®
CTV 10P 1 nc 3yrs
Last dinner 7pm

★**Caerwylan** ☎(076671) 2547
Closed Nov—Etr

Semi-detached, Victorian sea-front hotel.

30rm(7➡) CTV in all bedrooms sB&Bfr£9 dB&Bfr£20 dB&B➡fr£23.50
Lift CTV 12(charged)
Lunch fr£3.95 Tea fr85p Dinner fr£5 Wine £4.25 Last dinner 7.30pm
V

★ *H* **Henfaes** Porthmadog Rd ☎(076671) 2396
Closed Nov—Etr

There are excellent views of sea and mountain from this large, detached hotel which provides spacious bedrooms and caring service by resident proprietors.

10➡(2fb) CTV in all bedrooms ® *sB&B➡£13.80—£14.95 dB&B➡£27.60—£29.90 B
6P 4
*Bar lunch £2.30—£2.90 Tea 30—36p Dinner £5.20—£6.10 Wine £4.60 Last dinner 7.30pm

CRICK
Northamptonshire
Map **4** SP57

★★★**Post House** (Trusthouse Forte) ☎(0788) 822101 Telex no 311107

Well equipped modern hotel close to M1 Junction 18.

96➡(17fb) CTV in all bedrooms ® sB&B➡£51.50 dB&B➡£66.50 B
☾150P CFA solarium gymnasium
Last dinner 10pm
Credit cards 1 2 3 4 5

CRICKHOWELL
Powys
Map **3** SO21

★★ *H* ***Bear*** ☎(0873) 810408

The charmingly old-fashioned inn-style hotel has cheerful character bars and an intimate restaurant serving imaginative and commendably cooked food. Bedrooms are compact, but cosy and provided with modern facilities.

12rm(3➡6⋒)(2fb) CTV in 1 bedroom B
CTV 24P 3
V Last dinner 8.45pm
Credit card 1

★★ *L* **Gliffaes** ☎ Bwlch (0874) 730371
Closed Jan—12 Mar

Set amid rare trees and shrubs in 30 acres of magnificent grounds, the distinctive hotel commands fine views of the River Usk and its wooded valley. An informal, friendly atmosphere prevails and the standard of the good home cooking is consistent. Elegant lounges and character bedrooms are well equipped with modern facilities.

19rm(15➡3⋒)(4fb) ®T S% sB&B£19.50 sB&B➡⋒£19.50 dB&B£39—£53 dB&B➡⋒£39—£53 B
CTV 35P (hard) snooker bowls croquet
S% Lunch £6.30 Tea £2.70 Dinner £9.50—£12.65 Wine £4.70 Last dinner 9pm
Credit cards 1 2 3

✕ **Glen-y-Dwr** Brecon Rd ☎(0873) 810756

This is a small restaurant, well furnished and equipped to serve a varied and

interesting menu of good food in the cosy atmosphere induced by a real log fire.
Closed Mon & 1st 2 wks Jan
French **V** 30 seats Lunch £8alc Dinner £15—£20 alc Last dinner 9pm 18P 2 bedrooms available
Credit card 1

CRICKLADE
Wiltshire
Map **4** SU19

★★**White Hart** High St Swindon (0793) 750206
Busy, personally run town centre inn with attractive lounge bar and good food.
17rm(3 3)(2fb) CTV in all bedrooms ® sB&B£24 sB&B £29 dB&B£34 dB&B £38
CTV 20P 4 Live music & dancing Thu
V Lunch £7.50&alc Tea £1 Dinner £7.50&alc Wine £5.50 Last dinner 9.30pm
Credit cards 1 2 3 5

★***Vale Inn*** High St Swindon (0793) 750223
Brick-built hotel with ornamental shutters and secluded rear patio, in town centre.
10rm(4 2) CTV in 6 bedrooms ®
CTV 16P 1
V Last dinner 9.15pm

CRIEFF
Tayside *Perthshire*
Map **11** NN82

★★***Crieff*** 47/49 East High St (0764) 2632
Small, friendly hotel with attractive wood panelled dining room. Modern and traditional facilities are blended successfully here.
11rm(3 2)(1fb) CTV in 5 bedrooms ®
CTV 12P sauna bath solarium
Last dinner 9.30pm
Credit cards 1 2 5

★★ *H* **Cultoquhey House** (0764) 3253
Closed 28 Feb—5 Apr
A homely, family-run mansion, the hotel offers sincere, friendly service and very good country house cooking.
12rm(6 6)(2fb)2 CTV in all bedrooms ®**T** *sB&B£20 sB&B £23 dB&B£39 dB&B £45 P
shooting
*Bar lunch £4.50alc Dinner £10&alc Wine £4 Last dinner 9.45pm
Credit cards 1 2 3

★★**Murray Park** Connaught Ter (0764) 3731
Well run hotel serving good food.
15rm(10)(1fb) CTV in 1 bedroom ® *sB&Bfr£20 sB&B fr£27.50 dB&Bfr£35 dB&B fr£42
CTV 50P
Scottish & French **V** *Lunch £8.50 Tea 50p Dinner £12.95&alc Wine £4.85 Last dinner 9.30pm
Credit cards 2 3 5 Ⓥ

★***George*** King St (0764) 2089
Town centre, family-run hotel, the George offers a neat, modest standard in bedroom accommodation and lounges.
30rm(4)(2fb) ®
CTV 20P Live music and dancing wkly Cabaret wkly *xmas*
Scottish, English & French Last dinner 9pm

★*B* **Gwydyr House** Comrie Rd (0764) 3277
Closed Nov—Mar
Former private mansion, overlooking MacRosty Park on the west side of Crieff.
10rm(4fb) CTV in all bedrooms ® sB&B£10.25—£11.75 dB&B£20.50—£23.50
CTV 15P
British & French Bar lunch £3.10—£6.65 Dinner £7.35&alc Wine £5.50 Last dinner 8pm
Ⓥ

★**Lockes Acre** Comrie Rd (0764) 2526
This attractive, family run hotel on the outskirts of the town enjoys a splendid outlook. Bedrooms and public areas are well-appointed, and an exemplary standard of housekeeping prevails.
7rm(4)(1fb) CTV in all bedrooms ®S% sB&Bfr£17 dB&Bfr£27 dB&B fr£36
20P golf practice net
Bar lunch fr£3 Tea fr£3 High Tea fr£5 Dinner fr£9 Wine £4.10 Last dinner 9pm
Credit cards 1 3 Ⓥ

CRINAN
Strathclyde *Argyllshire*
Map **10** NR79

★★★**Crinan** (054683) 235
Closed Nov—mid Mar
In a magnificent setting by the western end of the canal, with views across to the islands of Jura and Scarba, the restaurant specialises in what is probably the freshest seafood in Scotland.
22rm(20 2)(1fb) **T** *sB&B £33 dB&B £55—£70.50
Lift CTV 25P
*Bar lunch £3—£8 Tea £1.50 Dinner £18.50 Wine £6.50 Last dinner 9pm
Credit cards 1 3

CROCKETFORD
Dumfries & Galloway *Kirkcudbrightshire*
Map **11** NX87

★★**Galloway Arms** Stranraer Rd (055669) 240
Closed Nov
This popular family-run hotel has an attractive cottage restaurant.
12rm(9)(1fb) CTV in all bedrooms ® sB&B£17—£20 sB&B £20—£25 dB&B£34—£36 dB&B £36—£40
30P *xmas*
Scottish & French **V** Lunch £5—£7&alc Tea £1.75—£3 High Tea £3.25—£5 Dinner £10—£15&alc Wine £5.50 Last dinner 10pm
Credit cards 1 3 5 Ⓥ

★***Lockview Motel*** Crocketford Rd (055669) 281
Closed 26 Dec & 1—2 Jan
Bungalow style motel/restaurant on main road by Loch. Very comfortable bedrooms and limited lounge facilities.
7 CTV in all bedrooms ®
50P Live music & dancing Sat
Last dinner 10pm
Credit cards 1 3

CROFT-ON-TEES
North Yorkshire
Map **8** NZ20

★★★**Croft Spa** Darlington (0325) 720319
Large, pleasantly furnished hotel beside River Tees. Was TV setting for All Creatures Great and Small.
24rm(9 15)(3fb) 2 CTV in all bedrooms ®**T** sB&B £32.50—£35 dB&B £45—£50
CTV 150P snooker sauna bath solarium gymnasium *xmas*
Continental **V** S% *Lunch fr£5.95 Tea £3—£3.50 Dinner fr£9.50 Wine £5.20 Last dinner 10pm
Credit cards 1 3 5

CROMARTY
Highland *Ross & Cromarty*
Map **14** NH76

★★**Royal** Marine Ter (Exec Hotel) (03817) 217
A homely hotel with inviting log fires, and cheerful service.
10rm(3 2)(2fb) ®sB&B£14.75—£16 sB&B fr£15.75 dB&B£27.50—£29 dB&B fr£28.50
CTV 10P 2 games room
V Lunch £5—£6.50 Tea fr85p High Tea fr£5 Dinner fr£9.50 Wine £4.75 Last dinner 9pm
Credit cards 2 3 Ⓥ

✕ **Le Chardon** Church St (03817) 471
A pretty little restaurant is sited in a quiet street of this former seaport on the Black Isle. Food is innovative and well cooked.
Closed Mon
Lunch not served Tue—Sat (in winter)
25 seats Lunch £8.50 Dinner £14 Wine £4.95 Last dinner 10pm P nc 8yrs (dinner)
Credit cards 1 2 3

C

C

CROMER
Norfolk
Map **9** TG24

★★*L* **Cliff House** Overstrand Rd
☎(0263) 514094
Closed late Oct—2nd wk Apr
27rm(6⛡4⛆)(3fb)1⛝CTV in all bedrooms ®sB&B£16—£19 sB&B⛡⛆£25 dB&B£32—£38 dB&B⛡⛆£40—£56
CTV 25P✿nc 10yrs♿
V♡☕Lunch £6.50 Tea 65p High tea £4—£6 Dinner £9.50&alc Wine £4.50 Last dinner 9.30pm
Credit cards 1 2 3 Ⓥ

★★**Cliftonville** Runton Rd ☎(0263) 512543
Imposing, Victorian building with spacious lounges overlooking the sea.
46rm(10⛡4⛆)(4fb) CTV in 17 bedrooms ®in 10 bedrooms sB&B£17.50—££19.50 sB&B⛡⛆£24—£26 dB&B£35—£37 dB&B⛡⛆£48—£50 B
Lift ☾CTV 20P 2🚗(charge) snooker Live music & dancing twice wkly *xmas*
V♡☕Lunch fr£5.50 Tea fr75p Dinner fr£9 Wine £4.50 Last dinner 9pm
Credit cards 1 2 3 5 Ⓥ

★**West Parade** Runton Rd ☎(0263) 512443
Closed late Oct—mid Apr (except xmas)
30rm(4fb) ®sB&B£13—£13.50 dB&B£26—£27
CTV 22P *xmas*
V♡☕Lunch £4.50 Tea 45p Dinner £7—£7.50 Last dinner 7.45pm
Ⓥ

CROOKLANDS
Cumbria
Map **7** SD58

★★★**Crooklands** (Best Western) ☎(04487) 432
This 400-year-old inn has modern bedrooms and its restaurant forms part of a converted barn.
15⛡(1fb) CTV in all bedrooms ® ✱sB&B⛡£37—£40.50 dB&B⛡£54—£60 B
120P♪ Disco mthly *xmas*
V♡☕✱Lunch £6.50—£7.50 Tea 85p—£1 High Tea £2.50—£3.50 Dinner £11.50—£12.50&alc Wine £5 Last dinner 9.30pm
Credit cards 1 2 3 5

CROSBY-ON-EDEN
Cumbria
Map **12** NY45

★★★**Newby Grange** ☎(022873) 645
This hotel with its spacious grounds has been recently modernised to provide very comfortable bedrooms. The restaurant is especially recommended.
20rm(18⛡2⛆)(3fb) CTV in all bedrooms ® T sB&B⛡⛆£24 dB&B⛡⛆£32 B
☾CTV 200P✿⛬ *xmas*
☗International V♡☕Lunch £5&alc Tea £3 High Tea £5 Dinner £6.50—£9.50&alc Wine £4 Last dinner 10.30pm
Credit cards 1 3

★★🌲*H* **Crosby Lodge** ☎(022873) 618
Closed Xmas eve—mid Jan RS Sun
Very comfortable country house with a wealth of antique furnishings and noted for good food.
9rm(8⛡1⛆) Annexe: 2⛡(2fb) 2⛝CTV in all bedrooms sB&B⛡⛆£38—£40 dB&B⛡⛆£55—£58 B
40P⛟✿
☗English & French ♡Lunch £10.50&alc Dinner £15.75&alc Wine £4.50 Last dinner 9pm
Credit cards 2 3 5

CROSSMICHAEL
Dumfries & Galloway *Kirkcudbrightshire*
Map **11** NX76

★★🌲**Culgruff House** ☎(055667) 230
RS Oct—Etr
Baronial mansion set in secluded, wooded grounds in the heart of farming land high above the village.
15rm(4⛡)(2fb) CTV in 3 bedrooms TV in 1 bedroom sB&B£8.50—£11 sB&B⛡£15 dB&B£16—£22 dB&B⛡£30 B
CTV 50P 8🚗(40p per night)✿
V♡☕⚡Lunch £5&alc Tea 75p&alc High Tea £3.50—£4.50&alc Dinner £8&alc Wine £4.30 Last dinner 8pm
Credit cards 1 2 3 Ⓥ

CROSSWAY GREEN
Hereford & Worcester
Map **7** SO86

★**Mitre Oak** ☎Hartlebury (0299) 250352
Roadside hotel offering reasonably priced meals and accommodation.
9rm(2fb) CTV in 1 bedroom TV in 1 bedroom ®✗sB&Bfr£14 dB&Bfr£24 B
CTV 110P✿Disco twice wkly ⛬ *xmas*
☗English & French V♡⚡Lunch £3—£4.25&alc High Tea £1—£4 Dinner £5—£12&alc Wine £4.95 Last dinner 9.15pm
Credit cards 1 3 Ⓥ

CROSTHWAITE
Cumbria
Map **7** SD49

★★★**Damson Dene Cottage Hotel & Country Club** Lythe Valley (A5074) q05) (04488) 676
RS Jan & Feb
Comfortable hotel in Lythe Valley, with modernised bedrooms.
37rm(27⛡10⛆)(5fb) 1⛝CTV in all bedrooms ®T S% ✱sB&B⛡⛆£32 dB&B⛡⛆£56.50 B
☾100P✿⛶(heated) squash snooker sauna bath solarium gymnasium table tennis pool table *xmas*
V♡☕✱Lunch £5.50&alc Tea £2.50&alc Dinner £10.75&alc Wine £5.50 Last dinner 9.30pm
Credit cards 1 2 3 Ⓥ

CROWTHORNE
Berkshire
Map **4** SU86

★★★**Waterloo** Dukes Ride (Anchor) ☎(0344) 777711 Telex no 848139
Modern facilities and friendly service are found in this basically Victorian building.

58rm(35➡23⋔) 1⊟⊬ in 10 bedrooms CTV in all bedrooms ®T ✻sB&B➡⋔£47—£54 dB&B➡⋔£57—£64 B

☾120P♿

♈International **V** ♈ ☕ ✻Lunch £8.75—£9.75&alc Tea £1.50—£3.75 Dinner £9.50&alc Wine £5.95 Last dinner 10pm

Credit cards 1 2 3 4 5 Ⓥ

CROYDE
Devon
Map **2** SS43

★★**Croyde Bay House** ☎(0271) 890270

Closed late Oct—wk before Etr

Carefully managed by experienced hands, this little hotel with a cottagey atmosphere is uniquely positioned on the edge of the beach.

8rm(1➡4⋔)(2fb) CTV in 5 bedrooms ® sB&B£16—£18 sB&B➡⋔£18—£20 dB&B£24—£30 dB&B➡⋔£28—£34

CTV 16P ♪

♈French **V** ♈ ☕⊬ Bar lunch £1.50alc Tea £1.50alc Dinner £8—£9&alc Wine £4 Last dinner 8.45pm

Ⓥ

★★**Kittiwell House** St Mary's Rd ☎ (0271) 890247

Closed Feb

A Devon thatched longhouse dating from the sixteenth century has been renovated to a good standard and now provides a relaxed, congenial atmosphere and carefully cooked meals.

14rm(3➡5⋔)(2fb)3⊟ ® ✻sB&B£14—£17 sB&B➡⋔£17—£20 dB&B£28—£34 dB&B➡⋔£34—£40 B

CTV 15P ✿ *xmas*

♈ ☕ ✻Tea 45p Dinner £7&alc Wine fr£4.90 Last dinner 9.30pm

Credit cards 1 3

CROYDON
Greater London plan **5***D1* (page 000)

★★★★**Holiday Inn** 7 Altyre Rd (Holiday Inns) ☎01-680 9200 Telex no 8956268

Modern, comfortable hotel with very well equipped bedrooms, two bright, attractive restaurants and good leisure facilities.

214➡⋔(40fb) CTV in all bedrooms **T** S% ✻sB&B➡⋔£68.30 dB&B➡⋔£80.50 B

Lift ☾ ## 68P 50 ⌂ ▭(heated) squash sauna bath solarium gymnasium ♿ *xmas*

♈International **V** ♈ ☕ S% ✻Lunch £12.75&alc Tea 90p High tea £3 Dinner £10.25&alc Wine £6.95 Last dinner 10pm

Credit cards 1 2 3 4 5

★★★★**Selsdon Park** Sanderstead (3m SE off A2022) (Best Western) ☎01-657 8811

(For full entry see Sanderstead)

See advertisement on page 248

★★★**Croydon Court** Purley Way (Anchor) ☎01-688 5185 Telex no 893814

Three-storey hotel with a large modern extension at one side, close to the main Brighton road.

86➡⋔⊬ in 17 bedrooms CTV in all bedrooms ®**T** sB&B➡⋔£49.50 dB&B➡⋔£60 B

☾100P CFA

♈English & French **V** ♈ ☕⊬ Lunch £10.25&alc Tea 95palc Dinner £15&alc Wine £6.10 Last dinner 11pm

Credit cards 1 2 3 5 Ⓥ

★★**Briarley** 8/10 Outram Rd ☎01-654 1000 Telex no 943763

RS Xmas

Converted from two Victorian houses, but with an annexe of very good bedrooms, the family-run hotel is warmly welcoming.

16rm(10➡6⋔) Annexe: 10➡1⊟ CTV in all bedrooms ®**T** sB&B➡⋔£40—£45 dB&B➡⋔£50—£60 B

CTV 15P ✿ pool table

♈Mainly grills Lunch £7.50—£9&alc Dinner £7.50—£9&alc Wine £6 Last dinner 10pm

Credit cards 1 2 3 5 Ⓥ

★**Central** 3/5 South Park Hill Rd, South Croydon ☎01-688 0840

Warm, compact and simply-appointed bedrooms are complemented by a cosy dining room serving wholesome, freshly-cooked food.

24rm(8➡12⋔) 1⊟ CTV in all bedrooms ® **T** ✂ S% sB&B£23—£25 sB&B➡⋔£30—£34 dB&B➡⋔£40—£45 B

☾ CTV 30P ✿

V ♈ ☕ Lunch £5.95—£6.95 Tea £2.95—£3.25 High Tea £5.95—£6.95 Dinner £6.95—£12.95&alc Wine £2.50 Last dinner 8pm

Credit cards 1 3

✕✕✕**Château Napoleon** Coombe Ln ☎01-686 1244

Secluded Tudor beamed house with delightful panelled rooms and a friendly atmosphere.

♈French & Italian **V** 70 seats ✻Lunch £8.95&alc Dinner £9.95&alc Last dinner 10.30pm

Credit cards 1 2 3 5

✕**Le St Jacques** 1123 Whitgift Centre ☎01-760 0881

Closed Sat, Sun & Bank Hols
Dinner not served Mon—Wed

♈French 36 seats ✻Lunch £11alc Dinner £11alc Wine £6 Last dinner 10pm ₱ nc 8yrs

Credit cards 1 2 3 4 5

✕**Tung Kum** 205/207 High St ☎01-688 0748

Spacious Chinese restaurant with good selection of dishes and delightful panelled rooms and a friendly atmosphere.

Closed 25 Dec & Bank Hol Mon's

♈Cantonese 100 seats ✻Lunch £2.30—£9&alc Wine £5.40 Last dinner 11.30pm ₱

Credit cards 1 2 3 5

C

CRUDWELL
Wiltshire
Map **3** ST99

★★**Mayfield House** ☎(06667) 409

Friendly, family-run country house hotel in a quiet village. It retains its old world charm, although it has been completely modernised. It has neat bedrooms and freshly cooked food is served in the cosy dining room.

21rm(11➡6⋒) CTV in all bedrooms Ⓡ sB&B£18 sB&B➡⋒£26 dB&B£32—£39 dB&B➡⋒£39—£44 B

CTV 50P ✿

English & French Lunch fr£5.95 Tea fr65p Dinner fr£8.50&alc Wine £5.50 Last dinner 9pm

Credit cards 1 3

CRUGYBAR
Dyfed
Map **2** SN63

★★ *H* **Glanrannell Park** ☎ Talley (05583) 230

Closed Nov—Mar

Delightful country house in large grounds overlooking a small lake, offering genuine hospitality and quality home cooking.

8rm(5➡)(2fb) Ⓡ sB&B£19 sB&B➡£20.50 dB&B£32 dB&B➡£35

CTV 20P 3 ✿

Bar lunch £1.25—£3.50 Tea 70p—£2.50 Dinner £8—£10 Wine £3.50 Last dinner 8pm

Ⓥ

CUCKFIELD
West Sussex
Map **4** TQ32

★★★ *B* **Ockenden Manor** Ockenden Ln ☎ Haywards Heath (0444) 416111 Telex no 87677

Closed Xmas day night—30 Dec

This attractive manor house, parts of which date back to the sixteenth century, stands amid trees, terraced lawns and clipped hedges. Its panelled public rooms are tastefully furnished, and the bedrooms — each named after a member of the original family — are well appointed. In the restaurant, lit by a stained glass window, good food in the nouvelle cuisine style is accompanied by an extensive wine list.

10rm(9➡⋒) 9 CTV in all bedrooms Ⓡ sB&B➡⋒£42—£46 dB&B➡⋒£77—£95 Continental breakfast B

44P 1 ✿ nc 7yrs

V Lunch £12—£13.50&alc Tea £1—£5.50 Dinner £18—£21.50&alc Wine £6 Last dinner 9.15pm

Credit cards 1 2 3 5

★★ **Hilton Park** ☎ Haywards Heath (0444) 454555

Family-run country house with fine gardens overlooking South Downs.

14rm(8➡2⋒)(5fb) CTV in all bedrooms Ⓡ sB&B fr£35 sB&B➡⋒fr£38 dB&B fr£48 dB&B➡⋒fr£53

CTV 50P 2 ✿ solarium

British & French Tea fr£1.50 High tea fr£3 Dinner fr£9.50 Wine £6 Last dinner 8pm

Credit cards 1 2 3 5 Ⓥ

CULLEN
Grampian *Banffshire*
Map **15** NJ56

★★★ **Seafield Arms** Seafield St ☎(0542) 40791

Modernised, coaching inn, built 1822 by the Earl of Seafield.

24rm(21➡1⋒)(2fb) CTV in all bedrooms Ⓡ **T** sB&B£21.80—£23 sB&B➡⋒£21.80—£23 dB&B➡⋒£40—£43 B

☾ CTV 30P snooker *xmas*

Lunch £5.70—£6.60 Tea 80p—£2 High tea £4.90—£8.50 Dinner £9.90—£10.70&alc Wine £4.60 Last dinner 9.30pm

Credit cards 1 2 3 5

★★ **Cullen Bay** ☎(0542) 40432

RS Mar—Nov

Post Victorian hotel with neat bedrooms and fine views.

15rm(4➡)(1fb) TV in 8 bedrooms CTV in 4 bedrooms Ⓡ S% sB&B£17 sB&B➡£20 dB&B£42 dB&B➡£50 B

CTV 150P 4 ✿

Lunch £4.50&alc High Tea £3.50 Dinner £9.50&alc Wine £3 Last dinner 8.30pm

Credit cards 2 3 5

CULLINGWORTH
West Yorkshire
Map **7** SE03

★★★ **Five Flags** Manywells Heights (near junc A629/B6429) ☎ Bradford (0274) 834188

A large stone building in a moorland setting provides accommodation in spacious modern bedrooms and has an international-style restaurant in addition to a Taverna. There is a choice of two bars, and conference facilities are available.

26➡ CTV in all bedrooms **T** sB&B➡£24—£29 dB&B➡£32—£52 B

☾ CTV 120P

English, French, Greek & Italian **V** S% Lunch £6.25—£8.50&alc Dinner fr£11.50&alc Wine £6 Last dinner 10pm

Credit cards 1 2 3 4 5 Ⓥ

CUMBERNAULD
Strathclyde *Dunbartonshire*
Map **11** NS77

✕ ***Neelam Tandoori*** Dalshannon Farm, Condorrat ☎(02367) 20648

Smart ethnic restaurant housed in an attractively converted farmhouse.

French & Indian 140 seats Last dinner 11.30pm 70P

Credit cards 1 2 3 5

CUMNOCK
Strathclyde *Ayrshire*
Map **11** NS51

★ **Royal** 1 Glaisnock St ☎(0290) 20822

Red sandstone, two-storey hotel, dating from 1850 standing on the main road in the town centre. →

11rm(2→1⋒)(1fb) CTV in 3 bedrooms TV in 2 bedrooms sB&B£16—£18 dB&B£30—£34 dB&B→⋒£36—£40
CTV 10P

V ♈ ☕ Lunch £4.50—£6 Tea £1.50—£1.80 High Tea £4.40—£6 Dinner £8—£10 Wine £5.60 Last dinner 9pm
Credit card 1 Ⓥ

CUMNOR
Oxfordshire
Map **4** SP40

✕✕**Bear & Ragged Staff** ☎ Oxford (0865) 862329

Imaginative French and English cuisine is served in this Cotswold stone inn.

Lunch not served Sat Dinner not served Sun (in winter)

English & French 36 seats S% Lunch £17alc Dinner £17alc Wine £4.95 Last dinner 10pm 65P nc

Credit cards 1 2 3 5

CUPAR
Fife
Map **11** NO31

✕**Ostlers Close** 25 Bonnygate ☎ (0334) 55574

The small, cottage-style restaurant stands in a close of the same name at the centre of the town. Friendly service complements menus which make good use of fresh produce and Scottish meat, game and seafood.

Closed Sun Lunch not served Mon

French & Swiss **V** 30 seats Lunch £8alc Dinner £15alc Wine £5.15 Last dinner 9pm nc 6yrs

Credit cards 1 3

CWMBRAN
Gwent
Map **3** ST29

★★★***Hotel Commodore*** Mill Ln, Llanyravon (Consort) ☎ (06333) 4091

Friendly family run hotel with good standards of service.

60rm(47→11⋒)(2fb) CTV in all bedrooms

Lift ☾ CTV 250P 8 CFA Disco Fri & Sat Live music & dancing Sat Cabaret Sat *xmas*

English & French **V** ♈ ☕ Last dinner 10pm

Credit cards 1 2 3 5

★★**Cwmbran Centre** Victoria St, Oldbury Rd ☎ (06333) 72511

The modern bedrooms of this popular commercial hotel are comfortable, though compact, and there is an attractive bar on the ground floor. Service is friendly.

39rm(18⋒)(5fb) 1 in bedrooms CTV in all bedrooms ®**T** S%
sB&B£21.25—£28.50
sB&B⋒£21.25—£28.50
dB&B£28.50—£42.80
dB&B⋒£28.50—£42.80

☾ 150P sauna bath *xmas*

English, French & Italian **V** ♈ ☕ Lunch £3—£4.50&alc Tea 50p High Tea £2.50 Dinner £4—£5.95&alc Wine £4.25 Last dinner 10pm

Credit cards 1 2 3 5 Ⓥ

DALRY
Dumfries & Galloway *Kirkcudbrightshire*
Map **11** NX68

★★***Lochinvar*** Main St ☎ (06443) 210

RS Oct—Apr

The ivy clad building stands on the main street of this attractive small village.

15rm(3→)(2fb)
CTV 40P 4 nc3yrs
♈ Last dinner 7.30pm

DALTON
North Yorkshire
Map **12** NZ10

✕**Travellers Rest** ☎ Teesdale (0833) 21225

Small country inn with cosy dining room.

Closed Sun

24 seats Bar lunch £5.65alc Dinner £10.20alc Wine £4.50 Last dinner 9pm 30P

Credit cards 1 3

DALWHINNIE
Highland *Inverness-shire*
Map **14** NN68

★★**Loch Ericht** ☎ (05282) 257

RS Nov—Mar

Situated in Scotland's highest village, this modern hotel has an unusual design.

27rm(22→5⋒)(3fb) ®
sB&B→⋒£16.50—£22.50
dB&B→⋒£30—£37.50
50P

V ♈ ☕ Bar lunch £3—£6 Tea fr80p High Tea £3—£7.50&alc Dinner £4.50—£12.50&alc Wine £3.20 Last dinner 9pm

Credit cards 1 2 3 5 Ⓥ

DARESBURY
Cheshire
Map **7** SJ58

★★★**Lord Daresbury** Chester Rd (De Vere) ☎ Warrington (0925) 67331 Telex no 629330

RS 25 Dec—1 Jan

A modern purpose built hotel with good sports and leisure facilities set in pleasant Cheshire countryside, on the A56 close to junction 11 of the M56 motorway.

141→(4fb) CTV in all bedrooms ®**T**
sB&B→£56—£67 dB&B→£69—£85

Lift ☾ 450P CFA (heated) squash snooker table tennis sauna bath solarium gymnasium

English & French ♈ ☕ Lunch £9.50 Tea 70p—£1.20 Dinner £10.95&alc Wine £5.75 Last dinner 10.15pm

Credit cards 1 2 3 5

DARLINGTON
Co Durham
Map **8** NZ21

★★★★**Blackwell Grange Moat House** Blackwell Grange (Queens Moat) ☎ (0325) 460111 Telex no 587272

Standing in 15 acres of wooded parkland with a golf course, the hotel is a converted 17th century mansion to which modern bedroom wings have been added.

98→3 CTV in all bedrooms ®**T**
sB&B→£45—£55 dB&B→£59.50—£75

Lift ☾ 150P 3 CFA 18 (hard) boule Live music & dancing Sat *xmas*

International **V** ♈ ☕ Lunch £8.75&alc Tea £3.50 Dinner £8.75—£10.50&alc Wine £5.25 Last dinner 9.45pm

Credit cards 1 2 3 5

★★★**Kings Head** Priestgate (Swallow) ☎ (0325) 467612 (due to change to 380222) Telex no 587112

Victorian four-storey town centre hotel.

86→⋒(1fb) CTV in all bedrooms ®**T**
sB&B→⋒£27—£43
dB&B→⋒£48.50—£54

Lift ☾ CTV 30P CFA *xmas*

V ♈ ☕ Lunch £5—£7&alc Tea 50p—£3 High Tea £1.75—£5 Dinner £7.50—£10&alc Wine £5.50 Last dinner 9.30pm

Credit cards 1 2 3 5

★★★**Stakis White Horse** Harrowgate Hill (Stakis) ☎ (0325) 487111 Telex no 778704

The large, white, Tudor-style building has a modern bedroom wing and offers functional accommodation.

40→⋒ CTV in all bedrooms ®**T**
sB→⋒£24—£42 dB→⋒£40—£54 (room only)

Lift ☾ 150P Disco Sat *xmas*

English & French **V** ♈ ☕ Lunch £4.95—£6 Tea £1—£3.50 High Tea £3.50—£5 Dinner £4.95—£15 Last dinner 10pm

Credit cards 1 2 3 5

★**Coachman** Victoria Rd (Whitbread) ☎ (0325) 286116

Closed xmas & New Years Eve RS Bank Hols

Recently renovated and modernised 19th century building with comfortable bedrooms and attractive public areas.

25rm CTV in all bedrooms ®
sB&B£17—£22 dB&B£27—£32

☾ 6P 4 Disco Thu

♈ ☕ Lunch £8alc Tea 60—80p Dinner £8.10alc Wine £4.95 Last dinner 8.45pm

Credit cards 1 3

✕✕**Bishop's House** 38 Coniscliffe Rd ☎(0325) 286666

Built round a small, attractive courtyard, this elegant, town-centre restaurant is both comfortable and intimate. The fixed-price menus for both lunch and dinner offer interesting home-made dishes, the delicious puddings being particularly notable.

Closed Sun, Xmas—New Year & Bank Hols Lunch not served Sat

English & French 30 seats Lunch £6.50—£8 Dinner £11.50—£12.50 Wine £6.20 Last dinner 9.30pm

Credit cards 1 2 3

DARTMOUTH
Devon
Map **3** SX85

★★★**Dart Marina** Sandquay (Trusthouse Forte) ☎(08043) 2580

Comfortable, modernised hotel on the quayside with fine views of the River Dart.

35rm(26➡)(2fb) CTV in all bedrooms Ⓡ sB&B£35.50 sB&B➡£43.50 dB&B£57.50 dB&B➡£65.50 B

75P *xmas*

Last dinner 9.15pm

Credit cards 1 2 3 4 5

★★**Royal Castle** 11 The Quay ☎(08043) 2397

Dating from 1594, this quayside hotel was once a coaching inn, and the provision of modern comforts has not destroyed the atmosphere that was no doubt enjoyed by the seven reigning monarchs who have stayed here! Personally run, it offers friendly service and good food.

21rm(16➡5⋒)(4fb) 3 CTV in all bedrooms Ⓡ T ✱ sB&B➡⋒£22—£29.50 dB&B➡⋒£44—£58 B

☾8 (£1.50 per day) *xmas*

V ✱ Lunch £5.95—£6.55&alc Tea 45p—£3 High Tea £1—£3 Dinner £8.95—£11&alc Wine £3.95 Last dinner 10pm

Credit cards 1 3 Ⓥ

★★**Royle House** Mount Boone ☎(08043) 3649

Georgian house in its own grounds in an elevated position overlooking the town.

10rm(8➡) CTV in all bedrooms Ⓡ sB&B➡£25—£26.50 dB&B➡£42—£48 B

CTV 15P ✿ sauna bath solarium

V Bar lunch £3—£4 Tea £1.25—£1.50 Dinner fr£6.95&alc Wine £3.95 Last dinner 8.30pm

Credit cards 1 3 Ⓥ

See advertisement on page 252

★★**Stoke Lodge** Cinders Ln, (Stoke Fleming 2m S A379) ☎ Stoke Fleming (0803) 770523

In quiet elevated position and 1½ acres of grounds, overlooking village to the sea, this hotel offers good food and the best local produce.

24rm(17➡7⋒)(5fb) CTV in all bedrooms Ⓡ T sB&B➡⋒£19—£24.50 dB&B➡⋒£31—£39 B

50P ✿ & (heated) sauna bath solarium gymnasium table tennis putting *xmas*

English & French V Lunch £5.75—£6.25&alc Tea 65—75p Dinner £8.25—£8.95&alc Wine £5.25 Last dinner 9pm

Credit cards 1 3 Ⓥ

See advertisement on page 252

D

⊛✕✕**Carved Angel** 2 South Embankment ☎ (08043) 2465

This bright, fairly modern restaurant is situated in a fine tile-hung and balconied building on a River Dart quayside. Its open-plan kitchen means that guests can see what is going on there, and drinks are served at your table, though there is no bar. The food is very good, prepared from fresh raw materials in the Elizabeth David style with emphasis on the use of fish, and a sound wine list is available.

Closed Mon & Jan Dinner not served Sun

International **V** 34 seats S% ✱Lunch £15&alc Dinner £20—£25 Wine £6.50 Last dinner 9.30pm

DARWEN
Lancashire
Map **7** SD62

★★★**Whitehall** Springbank, Whitehall ☎ (0254) 71595

Attractive, family run hotel with modern extension, well equipped bedrooms and good restaurant.

18rm(14) CTV in all bedrooms ® **T** S% sB&B£20—£22 sB&B£33—£37.50 dB&B£45—£.50

CTV 60P 2 (heated) sauna bath solarium snooker

English & French Lunch £5—£5.50&alc Tea 50p High Tea £5—£6 Dinner £7.50&alc Wine £5 Last dinner 10pm

Credit cards 1 2 3 4 5

★***Millstone*** The Circus ☎ (0254) 72588

Tall sandstone, public house in the town centre.

9rm CTV in all bedrooms ®

billiards nc6yrs

Last dinner 8.30pm

Credit cards 1 3

DATCHET
Berkshire
Map **4** SU97

★★**Manor** Village Green (Consort) ☎ Slough (0753) 43442 Telex no 41363

Pleasant hotel, overlooking village green, with comfortable bedrooms and two bars.

30rm(17 13)(1fb) 1 CTV in all bedrooms ® **T** S% ✱sB&B£44—£49 dB&B£60—£67

25P *xmas*

English & French **V** Lunch £8—£9alc Tea 80p Dinner £10&alc Wine £5.95 Last dinner 9.45pm

Credit cards 1 2 3 5 Ⓥ

See advertisement under Windsor

DAVIOT
Highland *Inverness-shire*
Map **14** NH73

★★**Meallmore Lodge** ☎ (046385) 206

Charming family run hotel with spacious rooms and comfortable lounges.

11rm(3)(2fb) ®sB&B£16—£18 sB&B£18—£20 dB&B£32—£36 dB&B£36—£40

CTV 60P Live music & dancing wknds Cabaret wknds *xmas*

Cosmopolitan **V** Lunch £5.95—£7.95 Tea £2—£5 High Tea £4.50—£9.50 Dinner £9.95—£12.95&alc Wine £4 Last dinner 9pm

Credit cards 1 2 3 5

See advertisement under Inverness

DAWLISH
Devon
Map **3** SX97

★★★**Langstone Cliff** Dawlish Warren (1½m NE off A379 Exeter road) (Consort) ☎ (0626) 865155

Modern, family hotel set in 12 acres of grounds.

64→⋔(52fb) CTV in all bedrooms ® T sB&B→⋔£22—£25 dB&B→⋔£40—£50 B

Lift ☾ CTV 200P CFA ✿ & (heated) (hard) snooker & table tennis solarium Disco wkly in summer Live music & dancing twice wkly in summer Cabaret wkly in summer *xmas*

V Lunch £6 Tea 70p Dinner fr£8.50 Wine £5.20 Last dinner 8.30pm

Credit cards 1 2 3 5 V

★★**Charlton House** Exeter Rd ☎ (0626) 863260

Tourist and commercial hotel, set in an elevated position on the edge of town.

22rm(10→1⋔)(6fb) TV in 7 bedrooms CTV in 15 bedrooms S% sB&B£16.50—£17.50 sB&B→⋔£17.75—£19 dB&B£33—£35 dB&B→⋔£35.50—£38 B

CTV 30P ✿ (heated) games room sauna bath solarium Disco wkly Live music & dancing twice wkly *xmas*

V Lunch £4.50—£6.75&alc Tea £1—£1.30 High Tea £1.50—£3.75 Dinner £6.75—£8.25&alc Wine £4.50 Last dinner 9pm

Credit cards 1 2 3 5 V

See advertisement on page 254

DEDDINGTON
Oxfordshire
Map **4** SP43

★★**Holcombe Hotel & Restaurant** High St (Best Western) ☎ (0869) 38274

Closed 24—28 Dec

Comfortable bedrooms and an upgraded restaurant are provided by this small hotel.

15rm(10→4⋔)(1fb) CTV in all bedrooms **T** sB&B→⋔£33—£35 dB&B→⋔£43—45 B

CTV 30P ✿

English & French **V** ✱ Lunch £7.50—£11.50 Tea £1.25—£2 Dinner fr£11.50&alc Wine £5.95 Last dinner 9.30pm

Credit cards 1 2 3 5 V

See advertisement under Banbury

DEDHAM
Essex
Map **5** TM03

★★★

❀★★★ **MAISON TALBOOTH, DEDHAM**

Stratford Rd (Pride of Britain) ☎ Colchester (0206) 322367 Telex no 987083

(Rosette awarded for XXX Le Talbooth Restaurant).

This luxuriously restored Victorian country house is the work of Gerald Milsom who for many years confined his interests to Le Talbooth, an enchanting 16th century cottage on the banks of the River Stour, which now also serves as the restaurant for the hotel. They are about two thirds of a mile apart but transport to and fro can be arranged. Light meals are served at the hotel as well as breakfast in the bedrooms. These latter are mostly spacious and lavishly, almost sybaritically furnished with everything you might desire. Some are large enough to have sitting areas. Fruit, flowers and bathrobes are provided as well as a selection of drinks (not complimentary). The drawing room is in two sections and coolly chic with its colour scheme of rose and cream. Pictures and antiques add to the atmosphere as does the grand piano where a pianist occasionally performs. It is all very charming, and you will be attended to by amiable young girls. In the romantically candlelit restaurant you will also be well served by pleasant young staff.

10rm(9→1⋔)(1fb) CTV in all bedrooms **T** S% sB&B→⋔£50—£85 dB&B→⋔£65—£110 Continental breakfast

P ✿ croquet

English & French **V** Lunch fr£11.75&alc Dinner £25alc Wine £6.50 Last dinner 9.30pm

Credit cards 1 2 3 4 5

❀XXX**Le Talbooth** ☎ Colchester (0206) 323150 Telex no 987083

Flemish weavers' 16th century, timbered cottage in a delightful setting on the banks of the River Stour.

English & French **V** 80 seats ✱ Lunch fr£10.75&alc Dinner fr£21&alc Wine £6.50 Last dinner 9pm 60P

Credit cards 1 2 3 5

DEGANWY
Gwynedd
Map **6** SH77

★★*BL* **Bryn Cregin Garden** Ty Mawr Rd (Exec Hotel) ☎ (0492) 83402

Closed Jan

The exceptionally comfortable public rooms of the hotel have attractive views across its own grounds to the Conwy Estuary and Castle. →

16rm(12 4)1 CTV in all bedrooms ® T sB&B £20—£35 dB&B £28—£50

30P nc12yrs

V Bar lunch 95p—£7&alc Tea fr65p Dinner £9.50&alc Wine £4.95 Last dinner 9pm

Credit cards 1 3

★★**Deganwy Castle** Station Rd ☎(0492) 83555 Telex no 61155

From this hotel there are fine views across the Conwy estuary to Conwy Castle and the mountains of Snowdonia.

25rm(21)(3fb) 2 CTV in all bedrooms ® T S% sB&B£20—£22 sB&B £24—£26 dB&B£36—£38 dB&B £42—£48

60P

European V S% Bar lunch £1.50—£6 Tea 50—60p Dinner £9.25—£9.75&alc Wine £4.30 Last dinner 9.15pm

Credit cards 1 2 3 5 Ⓥ

DELABOLE
Cornwall
Map **2** SX08

★★***Poldark Inn*** Treligga Downs ☎ Camelford (0840) 212565

Modern, comfortable, rural hotel and restaurant.

11rm(6)(1fb) CTV in 10 bedrooms ®

70P Disco Thu nc10yrs

English & French V Last dinner 9.30pm

Credit card 2

See advertisement under Tintagel

DENBIGH
Clwyd
Map **6** SJ06

★★**Bull** Hall Sq ☎(074571) 2582

The former coaching inn is a tourist and commercial hotel in the centre of the town.

13rm(3)(4fb) *sB&B£13.75—£15.25 sB&B £15.25—£16.25 dB&B£26.50 dB&B £28

CTV 12P

V Lunch £3.50—£5.50&alc Tea fr£1.20 High Tea fr£2.50 Dinner £5.50—£7.75&alc Wine £4.50 Last dinner 9.30pm

Credit cards 1 2 3 5 Ⓥ

DENTON
Gt Manchester
Map **7** SJ99

★★★**Old Rectory** Meadow Ln, Haughton Gn ☎061-336 7516 Telex no 668615

Closed 25 Dec—1 Jan RS Sun & Bank Hol's

A friendly, hospitable, family run hotel situated in its own grounds providing good, fresh food.

26 CTV in all bedrooms ® T S% *sB&B £20—£32 dB&B £30—£45

CTV 60P nc6yrs

International V S% Lunch £8.50alc Dinner £10alc Wine £5 Last dinner 9pm

Credit card 1 Ⓥ

DERBY
Derbyshire
Map **8** SK33

★★★**Breadsall Priory** Morley (3½m N) ☎(0332) 832235

Large Elizabethan manor house in extensive grounds with golf course.

17rm(14 3)(3fb) 2 CTV in all bedrooms ® S% sB&B £36 dB&B £50

150P 18 squash snooker

English & Continental V S% Lunch £6.50—£7.50&alc Dinner £10&alc Wine £5.50 Last dinner 9.45pm

Credit cards 1 2 3 5 Ⓥ

★★★**Crest** Pasture Hill, Littleover (Crest) ☎(0332) 514933 Telex no 377081

A large, red-brick house, extensively modernised and enlarged, the Crest Hotel is usefully situated on the southern edge of the town between the A38 and the ring road. The restaurant and many of the bedrooms have good views over open fields and a golf course.

66(1fb) in 6 bedrooms CTV in all bedrooms ® T sB £49—£60 dB £60—£70(room only)

250P

International V *Lunch fr£8.50&alc Tea fr80p Dinner fr£11.50&alc Wine £6.25 Last dinner 9.45pm

Credit cards 1 2 3 4 5

★★★**International** 288 Burton Rd (Consort) ☎(0332) 369321 Telex no 377759

Large, modernised, Victorian house on the main Burton road.

41rm(39 2)(2fb) CTV in all bedrooms ® T sB £38.50 dB £46(room only)

Lift 60P Disco Fri & Sat

International V Lunch £6.50&alc Tea £1.50 High Tea £4.50 Dinner £10.50&alc Wine £6 Last dinner 10pm

Credit cards 1 2 3 5

★★★**Midland** Midland Rd ☎(0332) 45894

Adjacent to the station and dating from 1854, this is reputed to be the oldest railway hotel. Its well-equipped bedrooms and pleasant public areas make it popular with businessmen.

62rm(39) CTV in all bedrooms ® in 29 bedrooms T sB&B£24.75 sB&B £38 dB&B£31.50 dB&B £45

CTV 40P 15 CFA

V Lunch £5.25alc Tea 65—90p Dinner £7.50—£10.50 Wine £4.75 Last dinner 10pm

Credit cards 1 2 3 5

★★★**Pennine** Macklin St (De Vere) ☎(0332) 41741 Telex no 377545

Five-storey modern hotel, offering views over the city centre.

100(1fb) CTV in all bedrooms ® T *sB&B £23.50—£41 dB&B £47—£55

Lift 25P CFA *xmas*

⊖English & French V ♔ ☕ ✱Lunch £1.80—£3.50 Tea fr60p Dinner £7.25&alc Wine £6 Last dinner 9.45pm

Credit cards 1 2 3 5

★★**Clarendon** Midland Rd ☎ (0332) 365235

Late-Victorian, predominantly commercial hotel, close to the railway station.

48rm(13⇌6♒)(1fb) CTV in 29 bedrooms ®in 21 bedrooms S% ✱ sB&B£12—£16.50 sB&B⇌♒£19.50—£29.50 dB&B£22—£26.50 dB&B⇌♒£29—£38 **B**

☾ CTV 80P pool

⊖English & French V ♔ ☕ ✱Lunch fr£1.95 Tea fr£1 High Tea fr£4 Dinner fr£4.75 Wine £4.15 Last dinner 10.30pm

Credit cards 1 2 3 5 Ⓥ

★★ *H* **Gables** 119 London Rd ☎ (0332) 40633

Closed 25 Dec—1 Jan

A busy hotel near the railway station, the Gables caters mainly for commercial visitors, offering well-equipped accommodation and good, friendly service.

76rm(39⇌17♒)(6fb) CTV in all bedrooms **T** ✈ sB&B£18—£21 sB&B⇌♒£25.95—£39.95 dB&B£28.95—£31.95 dB&B⇌♒£39.95—£49.95 **B**

☾ 60P CFA ♿

V ♔ ☕ ✱Lunch fr£5&alc Tea fr75p Dinner fr£7.50&alc Wine £4.95 Last dinner 9.45pm

Credit cards 1 2 3 Ⓥ

★★**Kedleston** Kedleston Rd, Quarndon (3m NW) ☎ (0332) 559202

14rm(6⇌)(1fb) 1⊞ CTV in all bedrooms ® ✈ ✱sB&B£23—£27 sB&B⇌£25—£29.50 dB&B£29—£35.50 dB&B⇌£37—£43 **B**

100P ⛟ ⛳18

V ♔ ☕ ✱Lunch £5.25—£9&alc Tea £1.25 Dinner £8.95&alc Wine £5.75 Last dinner 9.15pm

Credit cards 1 2 3 5 Ⓥ

★***Howard*** Friar Gate ☎ (0332) 43455

Standing on the A52 north of the city centre, this large Georgian town house provides modest accommodation suitable for commercial guests.

20rm(1⇌1♒)(3fb) CTV in all bedrooms

60P Disco Mon & Thu—Sat

♔ ☕ Last dinner 8pm

Credit cards 1 2 3 5

DEREHAM (EAST)

Norfolk
Map **9** TF91

★★**King's Head** Norwich St ☎ (0362) 3842

Small 17th-century modernised inn with a walled garden.

9rm(4⇌2♒) Annexe: 5rm(2⇌3♒)(2fb) CTV in all bedrooms ®**T** sB&B£23—£24 sB&B⇌♒£23—£24 dB&B£30—£32 dB&B⇌♒£34—£36 **B**

CTV 20P 2🚗 ⚲(grass) bowling green

⊖English, French & Italian V ♔ ☕ ✱Lunch £5—£8.20&alc Tea £1 Dinner £6—£9.95&alc Wine £4.60 Last dinner 9.30pm

Credit cards 1 2 3 5 Ⓥ

★★**Phoenix** Church St (Trusthouse Forte) ☎ (0362) 2276

Modern hotel in town centre, small and with friendly service.

24⇌(1fb) CTV in all bedrooms ® sB&B⇌£44 dB&B⇌£61.50 **B**

40P *xmas*

♔ Last dinner 9.30pm

Credit cards 1 2 3 4 5

DERSINGHAM

Norfolk
Map **9** TF62

★***Feathers*** ☎ (0485) 40207

Victorian building standing in three acres of grounds on the edge of the Sandringham estate.

6rm CTV in all bedrooms ® ✈

50P ❁ nc14yrs

V ♔ Last dinner 9.30pm

Credit cards 1 3 5 Ⓥ

DEVIZES

Wiltshire
Map **4** SU06

★★**Bear** Market Pl ☎ (0380) 2444

A 16th-century coaching hotel with traditional comfort and good menu.

27rm(15⇌)(4fb) 3⊞ CTV in all bedrooms ®**T** ✱sB&B£24 sB&B⇌£28 dB&B£32 dB&B⇌£38—£45 **B**

CTV 36P (50p per day)

⊖English & Continental V ♔ ☕ ✱Lunch £7&alc Tea fr60p Dinner £8.50&alc Wine £5 Last dinner 10pm

Credit cards 1 2 3 Ⓥ

DINAS MAWDDWY

Gwynedd
Map **6** SH81

★★**Buckley Pines** ☎ (06504) 261

The family-run hotel provides comfortable accommodation and specialises in vegetarian dishes. Its setting in the Dovey Valley is particularly picturesque.

RS 22 Dec—Apr

14rm(3⇌2♒)(1fb) CTV in all bedrooms ® sB&B fr£16 sB&B⇌♒fr£20 dB&B fr£28 dB&B⇌♒fr£36 **B**

40P ♪

V ♔ ☕ ⚡ Lunch £2.60—£4 Tea 60p Dinner fr£7&alc Wine £4 Last dinner 9pm

Credit cards 1 3

DINGWALL

Highland *Ross & Cromarty*
Map **14** NH55

★★**Royal** High St ☎ (0349) 62130

Recently renovated commercial hotel on a corner site in the town centre.

20rm(10⇌2♒)(1fb) CTV in all bedrooms ®**T** sB&B£12—£15 sB&B⇌♒£15—£19 dB&B£24—£30 dB&B⇌♒£27—£33 **B**

CTV 30P Disco Fri ♫ *xmas*

V ♔ ☕ ✱Lunch £3.50—£6 Tea 75p—£1 High Tea £2.50—£7.50 Dinner £6.50—£8.50 Wine £3.25 Last dinner 9pm

Credit cards 1 3 5

D

DINNINGTON
South Yorkshire
Map **8** SK58

XX**Deans** 3 Laughton Rd, Falcon Sq ☎(0909) 562455

This restaurant has been achieved by the amalgamation and modification of two old cottages to provide attractive premises which include a beamed dining room with an adjoining lounge bar. The dishes available range from the straightforward grills and roast of the table d'hôte menu to the extended à la carte choice supplemented by the chef's daily special selection.

Closed 25—26 Dec, 1 Jan & all Bank Hol Mon's
Lunch not served Sat
Dinner not served Sun

International **V** 75 seats Lunch £5—£7&alc Dinner £10.45—£10.95&alc Wine £4.95 Last dinner 10pm 18P Live music Sun, Cabaret last Tue & Wed in mth

Credit cards 1 3

DIRLETON
Lothian *East Lothian*
Map **12** NT58

★★★*H* **Open Arms** ☎(062085) 241 Telex no 727887

Small select hotel with good food. In a picturesque setting by the village green.

7rm(6 1) CTV in all bedrooms **T** sB&B fr£45 dB&B £63—£73

CTV 60P

V Lunch £7.50—£8.50 Tea fr£1.25 Dinner £10—£17 Wine £7 Last dinner 10pm

Credit cards 1 2 3 4 5

DISLEY
Cheshire
Map **7** SJ98

★★★**Moorside** Mudhurst Ln, Higher Disley (Best Western) ☎(06632) 4151 Telex no 665170

Modern hotel standing on the edge of Lyme Park with good views.

41rm(37 4)(2fb) CTV in all bedrooms ® **T** sB £27—£50 dB £32—£70 (room only)

Lift CTV 250P CFA sauna bath solarium Live music & dancing Sat *xmas*

English & French **V** Lunch £7.50—£8.50&alc Tea 65—75p High Tea £3.50—£6 Dinner £12.50—£14&alc Wine £6 Last dinner 10pm

Credit cards 1 2 3 4 5

DISS
Norfolk
Map **5** TM18

XX**Salisbury House** 84 Victoria Rd ☎(0379) 4738

Comfortably furnished restaurant with interesting menu and good cooking.

Closed Sun, Mon, 2 wks Xmas, 1 wk Spring & 1 wk Autumn
Lunch not served

English & French **V** 30 seats *Dinner £16.50 Wine £6.75 Last dinner 9pm 10P nc 14yrs

DITTON PRIORS
Shropshire
Map **7** SO68

XX**Howard Arms** ☎(074634) 200

Remote country inn offering imaginative cuisine at reasonable prices.

Closed Mon, last wk July & 1st 2 wks Aug
Lunch not served Tue—Sat
Dinner not served Sun

English & French **V** 36 seats *Lunch £9.50—£13 Dinner £14.50—£17.50 Wine £6.15 Last dinner 9.30pm 30P

DODDISCOMBSLEIGH
Devon
Map **3** SX88

X**Nobody Inn** ☎Christow (0647) 52394

Good choice of local produce is offered in this friendly old village inn, well furnished with country antiques.

Closed Sun & Mon Lunch not served

English & Continental **V** 40 seats Dinner £9.50alc Wine £3.25 Last dinner 9.30pm 50P

Credit cards 1 3

DOLGELLAU
Gwynedd
Map **6** SH71

★★**Dolserau Hall** ☎(0341) 422522

Country house in its own rural surroundings, 1 mile from Dolgellau.

13rm(9 1)(5fb) CTV in all bedrooms ® sB&B£14—£18 sB&B £14—£18 dB&B£28—£36 dB&B £28—£36

Lift CTV 80P *xmas*

V Bar Lunch £2alc Tea £1—£2 Dinner £8alc Wine £4.50 Last dinner 9pm

Credit card 3

★★**Royal Ship** (Frederic Robinson) ☎(0341) 422209

Commercial and tourist hotel in the town centre, dating back to the 18th-century.

25rm(10 1)(7fb) CTV in 11 bedrooms ® sB&B£10—£17.75 sB&B £17.75 dB&B£20—£35.50 dB&B £35.50

Lift TV 8P 3 *xmas*

V Lunch £5 Tea £1.65 Dinner £8.75 Wine £3.10 Last dinner 9pm

Credit cards 1 3 5

DOLWYDDELAN
Gwynedd
Map **6** SH75

★★**Elen's Castle** (Guestaccom) ☎(06906) 207

Closed 10 Oct—3 Mar

18th-century coach house with spectacular views across the Lledr Valley.

10rm(3 4)(2fb) 1 CTV available in bedrooms ® *sB&B£14.70—£15.70 sB&B £16.70—£17.70 dB&B£29.40—£31.40 dB&B £32.40—£34.40

40P 3 sauna bath

*Lunch fr£1.20 Tea fr45p Dinner fr£4.90 Wine £4.20 Last dinner 7.30pm

Ⓥ

DONCASTER
South Yorkshire
Map **8** SE50

★★★**Danum Swallow** High St (Swallow) ☎ (0302) 342261 Telex no 547533

Town centre hotel recently refurbished to provide modern accommodation and an attractive first floor restaurant.

66rm(58🛁8🚿)(3fb) 1📺 ⚡ in 6 bedrooms CTV in all bedrooms Ⓡ**T** S% ✱ sB&B🛁🚿fr£42 dB&B🛁🚿fr£54 **B**

Lift ☾ 60P 25🏠 CFA *xmas*

V ☕ S% Lunch fr£7.25&alc Tea fr70p Dinner fr£8.95&alc Wine £5.25 Last dinner 9.30pm

Credit cards 1 2 3 5

★★★**Earl of Doncaster** Bennetthorpe (Anchor) ☎ (0302) 61371 Telex no 547923

Four-storey hotel of contemporary design near the town centre.

53rm(49🛁4🚿)(1fb) ⚡ in 6 bedrooms CTV in all bedrooms Ⓡ**T** S% ✱ sB&B🛁🚿£39.50 dB&B🛁🚿£49.50 **B**

Lift ☾ 80P CFA *xmas*

V ☕ S% Lunch £6.25—£9&alc Tea 50p Dinner £6.25—£9&alc Wine £5 Last dinner 10.30pm

Credit cards 1 2 3 4 5 Ⓥ

★★**Mount Pleasant** Rossington (On A638 Great North Rd, 1½m E of village) ☎ (0302) 868696 (For full details see Rossington)

★★**Punch's** Bawtry Rd, Bessacarr (Embassy) ☎ (0302) 535235

Two-storey brick building on the southern outskirts of town.

25rm(15🛁)(2fb) CTV in all bedrooms Ⓡ S% sB£16.50—£27 sB🛁£22.50—£36.50 dB£26—£35.50 dB🛁£32—£46(room only) **B**

☾ 150P ✿ *xmas*

English & French ☕ S% Lunch £7.30—£7.35&alc Tea fr85p Dinner £7.35&alc Wine £5.10 Last dinner 9.15pm

Credit cards 1 2 3 5

★★*B* **Regent** Regent Sq ☎ (0302) 64180

Closed Xmas Day & New Years Day RS Bank Hol's

Victorian town houses have been converted into this convenient hotel.

34rm(11🛁23🚿)(2fb) 2📺 CTV in all bedrooms Ⓡ**T** sB&B🛁🚿£24—£36 dB&B🛁🚿£31—£46 **B**

Lift ☾ 20P 1🏠 sauna bath

English & French **V** ☕ Lunch £3.50—£9 Tea £2—£2.50 High Tea £2 Dinner £7.50—£8.50&alc Wine £5.85 Last dinner 10pm

Credit cards 1 2 3 4 5 Ⓥ

◯ **Doncaster Moat House** Warmsworth, (Adjacent A1 (M) and A630) ☎ York (0904) 25674 78🛁🚿

Expected to open early 1987

DONNINGTON
Shropshire
Map **7** SJ71
See under Telford

DONYATT
Somerset
Map **3** ST31

✕✕**Thatcher's Pond** ☎ Ilminster (04605) 3210

Tasteful conversion of a 15th-century beamed farmhouse has resulted in a charming restaurant with a friendly and informal atmosphere. The cold buffet, with its wide range of salad items and sumptuous array of meats, is a popular choice.

Closed Mon & 24 Dec—Feb Dinner not served Sun

V 30 seats ✱ Lunch £9.20alc Dinner £11alc Wine £4.50 Last dinner 9.15pm 20P

Credit cards 1 3

Dorchester — Dorking

DORCHESTER
Dorset
Map **3** SY69

★★★**King's Arms** (Exec Hotel) ☎(0305) 65353

An 18th-century inn with bow windows over the pillared porch.

26rm(21→5⋔)(1fb) 2▭ CTV in all bedrooms ®**T** ✱ sB&B→⋔£30 dB&B→⋔£45.50 **B**

40P solarium

♕ ▭ ✱ Lunch fr£5.25&alc Tea 90p Dinner £10.25—£12.75 Wine £5.25 Last dinner 8.30pm

Credit cards 1 2 3 Ⓥ

DORCHESTER-ON-THAMES
Oxfordshire
Map **4** SU59

★★★*B***White Hart** High St ☎ Oxford (0865) 340074

Tastefully modernised 17th-century coaching inn with good bedrooms, and serving well prepared meals in the attractive beamed restaurant.

20rm(19→1⋔)(2fb) 2▭ ⊁ in 7 bedrooms CTV in all bedrooms ®**T** ⋈ S% sB&B→⋔£48—£53 dB&B→⋔£66—£72 **B**

CTV 25P ⊭

♕English & French **V** ♕ ⊁ ✱ Lunch £9—£12 Dinner £12.75&alc Wine £8.50 Last dinner 9.30pm

Credit cards 1 2 3 5

★★*B***George** High St ☎ Oxford (0865) 340404 Telex no 83147

Closed 25—30 Dec

13th-century coaching inn with warm, informal atmosphere.

11rm(9→) Annexe: 6→(1fb) 2▭ CTV in all bedrooms ®**T** ⋈ sB&B£33—£40 sB&B→£33—£40 dB&B£45 dB&B→£48—£65 **B**

CTV 80P ⊭ ✿

♕English & French **V** ♕ Lunch £15alc Dinner £10—£13.50&alc Wine £5.75 Last dinner 9.45pm

Credit cards 1 2 3 5 Ⓥ

DORKING
Surrey
Map **4** TQ14

★★★★*L***Burford Bridge** Burford Bridge, Box Hill (2m NE A24) (Trusthouse Forte) ☎(0306) 884561 Telex no 859507 Gatwick plan **2**

Well-appointed hotel with most attractive lounge and restaurant, and a variety of bedroom sizes.

48→ 1▭ CTV in all bedrooms ®**T** sB&B→£64 dB&B→£85 **B**

☾80P CFA ✿ ⌓ (heated) sauna bath *xmas*

♕ ▭ Last dinner 9.30pm

Credit cards 1 2 3 4 5

★★★**White Horse** High St (Trusthouse Forte) ☎(0306) 881138

Comfortable traditional coaching inn with well-appointed bedrooms in modern extension.

36→⋔ Annexe: 32→(1fb) CTV in all bedrooms ® sB&B→⋔£49.50 dB&B→£66.50 **B**

☾73P ⌓ (heated) *xmas*

♕ ▭ Last dinner 9.30pm

Credit cards 1 2 3 4 5

★★**Punch Bowl** Reigate Rd (Anchor) ☎(0306) 889335 Telex no 858875 Gatwick plan **18**

Overlooking Box Hill, this old inn has modern bedroom annexe.

Annexe: 29→(6fb) ⊁ in 5 bedrooms CTV in all bedrooms ® S% sB&B→£46 dB&B→£56 **B**

☾100P ✿ ♿

V ♕ ▭ S% ✱ Lunch £9.25alc Dinner £9.25alc Wine £5.95 Last dinner 10pm

Credit cards 1 2 3 4 5 Ⓥ

✕**River Kwai** 274—276 High St ☎ (0306) 889053

Very popular small restaurant combining Thai cooking with friendly service.

Closed 25, 26, 31 Dec & 1 Jan Lunch not served Mon

Thai **V** 45 seats Lunch £8.50—£12&alc Dinner £12—£15&alc Wine £5.80 Last dinner 10.45pm

Credit cards 1 3 5

DORMINGTON
Hereford & Worcester
Map **3** SO54

★**Dormington Court Country House**
☎ Hereford (0432) 850370

Parts of this old farm manor, set in one-and-a-half acres of grounds, date back to the 17th century; its friendly atmosphere offers a relaxing break.

6rm(1fb) CTV in all bedrooms ® sB&B fr £16 dB&B fr £42

CTV 20P Live music & dancing twice mthly Cabaret twice mthly *xmas*

English, Continental & Indian Lunch £8.50alc Tea £1.25alc Dinner £8.50—£9.50&alc Wine £4.75 Last dinner 9.30pm

Credit cards 1 2 3 5 Ⓥ

DORNOCH
Highland *Sutherland*
Map **14** NH78

★★★**Royal Golf** (Norscot/Clan)
☎ (0862) 810283 Telex no 75300

Closed Nov—Mar

The secluded hotel is set in its own grounds and overlooks the Royal Dornoch Golf Course.

26rm(20 3) Annexe: 8 CTV in 26 bedrooms ® in 26 bedrooms **T** sB&B £28—£45 dB&B £48—£70

50P

Bar lunch £2—£4 Dinner £16—£18 Wine £5.25 Last dinner 9pm

Credit cards 1 2 3 4 5 Ⓥ

★★**Burghfield House** ☎ (0862) 810212

Closed 18 Oct—2 Apr

Scottish, baronial-style, turreted mansion in 5½ acres of tree-studded grounds.

14rm(12 2) Annexe: 32rm(8)(8fb) CTV in 22 bedrooms ® in 40 bedrooms sB&B £18—£27 sB&B £21—£30 dB&B £36—£46 dB&B £42—£52

CTV 80P

Scottish & French Lunch fr £5 Dinner fr £12.50&alc Wine £3.95 Last dinner 8.30pm

Credit cards 1 2 3 5 Ⓥ

★★**Dornoch Castle** Castle St (Inter Hotel) ☎ (0862) 810216

Closed Nov—22 Apr

The former seat of the Bishops of Caithness, this hotel is situated in the town centre overlooking Dornoch Firth.

20rm(13 3)(3fb) CTV in 3 bedrooms ® sB&B £17.50—£19.50 sB&B £23—£26.50 dB&B £32—£38.50 dB&B £36.50—£58.50

Lift CTV 20P putting

Scottish & Continental Lunch £4—£7&alc Tea £1.70 Dinner £11.25

Credit cards 1 2 3

DORRIDGE
West Midlands
Map **7** SP17

★★***Forest*** Station Approach ☎ Knowle (05645) 2120

A well run private hotel.

12rm(10)(1fb) CTV in all bedrooms ®

60P Disco Tue

English & French **V** Last dinner 9.30pm

Credit cards 1 2 5

D

DORRINGTON
Shropshire
Map **7** SJ40

XX Country Friends (074373) 707

This 17th century, black and white timbered house has long been a landmark in the centre of the village. The interior of the restaurant has been carefully modernised and attractively decorated, whilst the menus offer imaginative and well-cooked dishes based on fresh produce.

Closed Sun Lunch not served Mon

English & French 35 seats Lunch £6.50—£9.50&alc Dinner fr£9.50&alc Wine £5 Last dinner 9pm 30P

Credit cards 2 3 5

DOUGLAS
See **Man, Isle of**

DOVER
Kent
Map **5** TR34

★★★ *HB* Dover Motel Whitfield (3m NW junc A2/A256) (0304) 821222 Telex no 965866

RS 24—27 Dec

Sound service, large, well-equipped bedrooms and a choice of restaurants which includes a conservatory-style cocktail bar are features of this well-appointed Motel.

67 (38fb) in 3 bedrooms CTV in all bedrooms ® T sB fr£42.95 dB fr£56.90 (room only)

75P

International V Lunch £2.95—£6.25&alc Tea fr85p High Tea £2.25 Dinner £10.95—£18&alc Wine £5.70 Last dinner 11pm

Credit cards 1 2 3 5

★★★ White Cliffs Esplanade (0304) 203633 Telex no 965422

Closed 24—26 Dec

Sea-front hotel with acceptable bedrooms and service, and good views of the harbour.

62rm(36 6)(7fb) CTV in all bedrooms T sB&B£25—£28 sB&B £30—£32 dB&B£42—£44 dB&B £48—£50

Lift CTV 25 (£1) Live music nightly

English & French Lunch £4.60—£6&alc Tea fr£1.25 Dinner £5.95—£6.25 Wine £5.60 Last dinner 9.30pm

Credit cards 1 2 3 4 5 V

★★ Cliffe Court 26 Marine Pde (0304) 211001

A friendly and well managed hotel adjacent to the Eastern Docks.

25rm(3 7)(4fb) 2 CTV in all bedrooms S% sB&B£21 dB&B£31 dB&B £33

CTV 20P

English, French, Italian & Spanish V S% Lunch £6.25&alc Dinner £6.50&alc Wine £4.95 Last dinner 9pm

Credit cards 1 2 3 4 5

DOWNHAM MARKET
Norfolk
Map **5** TF60

★ Crown Bridge St (0366) 382322

Closed 25 & 26 Dec

Privately owned, personally supervised 17th-century coaching inn.

10rm(5 2) CTV in 7 bedrooms ® T sB&B£15 sB&B £20 dB&B£24 dB&B £29

CTV 50P 2 nc14yrs

Mainly grills V Lunch £3.40—£6.70&alc Tea £1.20—£3.40 Dinner £4.40—£6.70&alc Wine £3.60 Last dinner 10pm

Credit cards 2 3 5

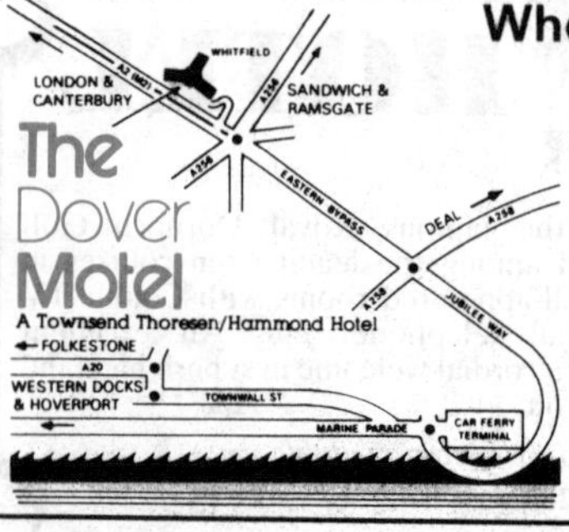

DOWN THOMAS
Devon
Map **2** SX55

★★**Langdon Court** ☎ Plymouth (0752) 862358

Modernised Elizabethan mansion on an unclassified road between Wembury and Down Thomas.

15🛁(3fb) CTV in all bedrooms ®T sB&B🛁£30 dB&B🛁£42 B

100P ❀ pool room nc5yrs

French V ♀ ☕ Dinner £12alc Wine £4.60 Last dinner 9pm

Credit cards 1 2 3 5

DRAYCOTT
Derbyshire
Map **8** SK43

★★★*L* **Tudor Court** Gypsy Ln (Best Western) ☎ (03317) 4581 Telex no 341995 Ref 423

Recently built hotel with a mock Tudor façade, standing in 8¼ acres of grounds.

30🛁⋒(8fb) CTV in all bedrooms ® *sB🛁⋒£19—£42.25 dB🛁⋒£38—£57 (room only) B

☾ 300P ❀ Disco 3 nights wkly

V ♀ ☕ *Lunch £6.25&alc Tea 75p Dinner £10.50&alc Wine £5.70 Last dinner 10.30pm

Credit cards 1 2 3 5 Ⓥ

DRIFFIELD, GREAT
Humberside
Map **8** TA05

★★★**Bell** 46 Market Pl (Best Western) ☎ (0377) 46661

This historic coaching inn, standing in the town centre, successfully combines modern facilities with its traditional features; the spacious tea rooms are popular.

14🛁 2 CTV in all bedrooms T S% sB&B🛁£33—£36.23 dB&B🛁£44.28—£47.73 B

50P squash snooker Disco Fri nc12yrs

V ♀ S% Lunch £5.50 Tea 75p Dinner £10.50alc Wine £4.50 Last dinner 9.30pm

Credit cards 1 2 3 5

★★**Wold House Country** Nafferton (3m E A166) ☎ (0377) 44242

Georgian style country house with rural views.

12rm(3🛁3⋒)(4fb) CTV in all bedrooms ® S% sB&B£17 sB&B🛁⋒£19 dB&B£27 dB&B🛁⋒£30 B

☾ CTV 40P 3 ❀ (heated) snooker

V ♀ Lunch £5.75 Tea £2 High Tea £4 Dinner £7.50—£9.50 Wine £5 Last dinner 8.30pm

Ⓥ

✕ **Queen's Head Inn** Kirkburn (3m SW on A168) ☎ (0377) 89261

Closed Mon Lunch not served Tue—Sat Dinner not served Sun

International V 32 seats *Lunch fr£5.45 Dinner £9alc Wine £4.42 Last dinner 9.30pm 50P

Credit card 5

DROITWICH
Hereford & Worcester
Map **3** SO86

★★★★**Château Impney** ☎ (0905) 774411 Telex no 336673

Closed Xmas

Extensive conference facilities are available in the stylish setting of the Château Impney, a late 19th century replica of a French château standing in 65 acres of parkland.

67rm(63🛁4⋒)(2fb) 1 CTV in all bedrooms S% *sB&B🛁⋒£36.90—£71.90 dB&B🛁⋒£73.90—£83.85 B

Lift ☾ CTV 600P CFA ❀ (hard) sauna bath, solarium, gymnasium

English & French V ♀ ☕ S% *Lunch £8.99&alc Tea fr£1.60alc Dinner £10.99—£11.99&alc Wine £5.95 Last dinner 10pm

Credit cards 1 2 3 5

★★★★**Raven** St Andrews Street ☎ (0905) 772224 Telex no 336673

Closed Xmas

Large, central hotel with many conference facilities.

55🛁(2fb) CTV in all bedrooms S% *sB&B🛁£36.90—£56.90 dB&B🛁£68.85 B

Lift ☾ CTV 250P CFA

English & French V ♀ ☕ S% *Lunch £8.99&alc Tea fr£1.60alc Dinner £10.99—£11.99&alc Wine £5.95

Credit cards 1 2 3 5

★★*H* **St Andrew's House** Worcester Rd ☎ (0905) 779677

An early Victorian house in a residential area just to the south of the town centre, the hotel is popular with locals and visitors alike.

28rm(18🛁)(2fb) CTV in all bedrooms ®T *sB&B£23.50 sB&B🛁£27.25 dB&B£38 dB&B🛁£43.60 B

48P ❀

Cosmopolitan V ♀ ☕ *Lunch £7.50&alc Tea 65p Dinner £7.50&alc Wine £3.95 Last dinner 10pm

Credit cards 1 2 3 5 Ⓥ

DRONFIELD
Derbyshire
Map **8** SK37

★★***Manor*** 10 High St ☎ (0246) 413971

RS Sun

A converted Georgian building in the centre of this ancient hamlet.

10rm(1🛁9⋒)(1fb) CTV in all bedrooms ® B

CTV 22P

V ♀ ☕ Last dinner 10pm

Credit cards 1 2 3

DROXFORD
Hampshire
Map **4** SU61

✕ ***White Horse Inn*** ☎ (0489) 877490

Popular, friendly pub, with good bar snacks and a small separate restaurant offering good, home-made plain cooking. →

Lunch not served Mon—Fri
Dinner not served Sun & Mon
26 seats Last dinner 9.30pm 25P

DRUMNADROCHIT
Highland *Inverness-shire*
Map **14** NH53
★★***Drumnadrochit*** ☎(04562) 218
Modern roadside hotel near Loch Ness Monster exhibition.
16⇌(2fb) ®
100P ✽ ♪ billiards Live music & dancing 5 nights wkly
English & Italian Last dinner 9pm
Credit cards 3 5

★★ *HBL* **Polmaily House** Milton ☎(04562) 343
Closed Mid Oct—Etr
(Rosette awarded for dinner only)
A friendly, relaxed atmosphere pervades this white painted house set in its own grounds outside the village. All rooms are attractively furnished and decorated in keeping with the style of the house and include many homely touches. Mr Parsons is an attentive host and Mrs Parsons oversees the creation of the hotel's appetising food.
9rm(7⇌)(2fb) 1 sB&B£24 sB&B⇌£35—£50 dB&B⇌£56
CTV 25P ✽ (hard) croquet lawn
International Dinner £15alc Wine £5.50 Last dinner 9.30pm
Credit cards 1 3 Ⓥ

DRYBRIDGE
Grampian *Banffshire*
Map **15** NJ46
XX **Old Monastery** (1m E off Deskford Rd) ☎ Buckie (0542) 32660
The name of this country restaurant is self-explanatory, and the dining room retains an appropriately simple style. Meals feature local seafood and game, making good use of fresh produce, and guests can enjoy fine views of the Moray coast.
Closed Sun, Mon, 3 days Xmas, 3 wks Jan & 2 wks Oct
Scottish & French 40 seats Bar lunch £6.75alc Dinner £12alc Wine £5.50 Last dinner 9pm 22P nc8yrs (restaurant) 14yrs (bar)

DRYBURGH
Borders *Berwickshire*
Map **12** NT53
★★★ *L* **Dryburgh Abbey** Newton St Boswells ☎ St Boswells (0835) 22261
This turreted mansion, dating from 1848, stands in 11 acres of parkland on the banks of the River Tweed.
28rm(13⇌7⋒)(1fb) 3 ® ✱ sB&B£21.50 sB&B⇌⋒£26.50 dB&B£36 dB&B⇌⋒£48—£65 B
CTV 160P ✽ putting xmas

Droxford — Dumfries

V Bar lunch £5.50alc Tea 75p—£2.55 Dinner £12.50&alc Wine £6 Last dinner 8.30pm
Credit cards 1 2 3 5 Ⓥ

DRYMEN
Central *Stirlingshire*
Map **11** NS48
★★★**Buchanan Arms** (Scottish Highland) ☎(0360) 60588 Telex no 778215
Modernised 18th-century coaching inn situated in the centre of this small village.
35⇌(4fb) 1 CTV in all bedrooms ®T sB&B⇌fr£39 dB&B⇌fr£62 B
(90P ✽ xmas
Scottish & French V Lunch £6.95—£7.95&alc Tea £2.50—£3 High Tea £4.75—£5.50 Dinner £11.75—£12.50&alc Wine £5.25 Last dinner 9.30pm
Credit cards 1 2 3 5 Ⓥ

DUDLEY
West Midlands
Map **7** SO99
★★**Station** Birmingham Rd (Wolverhampton & Dudley) ☎(0384) 53418
A large hotel offering a range of amenities, the Station is situated near to the town centre and within easy reach of the zoo.
29rm(9⇌2⋒)(4fb) CTV in all bedrooms ® ✱ sB&B£17.50—£21 sB&B⇌⋒£20.50—£28 dB&B£23—£28 dB&B⇌⋒£27—£32 B
Lift (CTV 100P
✱ Lunch £4.95&alc Tea 50p Dinner £5.75&alc Wine £4.30 Last dinner 9.30pm
Credit cards 1 2 3 Ⓥ

★**Ward Arms** Birmingham Rd (Wolverhampton & Dudley) ☎(0384) 52723
Large hotel with popular bar.
12rm(6⋒) CTV in all bedrooms ® sB&B£10—£15.50 dB&B£20—£26 B
CTV 100P
✱ Lunch £4.50 Dinner £4.50&alc Wine £4.30 Last dinner 8.45pm
Credit cards 1 2 3 Ⓥ

DULNAIN BRIDGE
Highland *Morayshire*
Map **14** NH92
★★ *H* ***Muckrach Lodge*** ☎(047985) 257
Formerly a shooting lodge, now a family-run hotel. Muckrach Lodge stands in 10 acres of grounds.
9rm(8⇌1⋒) CTV available in bedrooms sB&B⇌⋒£24—£27 dB&B⇌⋒£39—£44
50P 4 (50p per night) ✽

British & French Bar lunch £4alc Dinner £15 Wine £6.50 Last dinner 8.30pm

DULVERTON
Somerset
Map **3** SS92
★★★ *L* **Carnarvon Arms** Brushford (2m S on B3222) ☎(0398) 23302
Closed 7 Feb—22 Mar
Traditional sporting hotel with its own shooting and fishing facilities.
27rm(21⇌1⋒)(2fb) TV available in 16 bedrooms CTV in 11 bedrooms ® sB&B£26.75—£37 sB&B⇌⋒£28.75—£39 dB&B£53.50—£74 dB&B⇌⋒£57.50—£78 B
CTV P ✽ (heated) (hard) ♪ snooker xmas
V Lunch £6.50—£6.75&alc High Tea £3.75—£5.75 Dinner £11.50&alc Wine £4.95 Last dinner 6.30pm
Credit cards 1 2 3 5

★★ **Ashwick House**
(see red star box opposite)

★★ ***Three Acres Captain's Country*** Brushford ☎(0398) 23426
Closed Nov—Feb
Small, personally run hotel with a relaxed atmosphere and good views.
7rm(2⇌1⋒) 1 CTV in all bedrooms ®
CTV 20P ✽ ♪ nc 11yrs xmas
Last dinner 7.30pm

DUMBARTON
Strathclyde *Dunbartonshire*
Map **10** NS37
★★**Dumbuck** Glasgow Rd ☎(0389) 62148 Due to change to 34336 Telex no 778303
Popular, privately owned hotel with attractive 'old world' restaurant.
25rm(10⇌⋒)(2fb) CTV in all bedrooms ® T ✱ sB&B£22 sB&B⇌⋒£27.50 dB&B£33.50 dB&B⇌⋒£38.50
(CTV 200P ✽
V ✱ Lunch £6&alc Tea fr80p Dinner fr£8&alc Wine £4.10 Last dinner 9.30pm
Credit cards 1 2 3 5

DUMFRIES
Dumfries & Galloway *Dumfriesshire*
Map **11** NX97
★★★**Station** 49 Lovers Walk (Consort) ☎(0387) 54316 Telex no 778654
Closed New Years Day
Victorian building, progressively modernised and offering city style services and facilities.
30rm(18⇌12⋒)(2fb) CTV in all bedrooms ®T sB&B£22—£37 sB&B⇌⋒£22—£37 dB&B⇌⋒£35—£50 B
Lift (63P
V Lunch £4.75&alc Tea 90p High Tea £4.75 Dinner £10.50&alc Wine £6 Last dinner 10.30pm
Credit cards 1 2 3 5 Ⓥ

★★♣ASHWICK HOUSE, DULVERTON

(3m NW off B3223) ☎ (0398) 23868

Originally part of a large estate that was eventually sold off, this Edwardian house (1910) remains in six acres of grounds with lawns sweeping down to the water gardens above the beautiful River Barle. Now owned and run by the Sherwood family, it is just the place for a relaxing, country house holiday. The hotel has been sympathetically converted, retaining many of the original features of the house. In the galleried hall, a William Morris wallpaper is preserved, and there are several marble chimney pieces. It is well maintained and an abundance of flowers and plants add their fresh charm. The hall has a roaring wood fire and there is another drawing room and library, giving plenty of space for relaxation and quiet. The dining rooms are connected by an arched opening and overlook the gardens. They possess a fresh decor and good table appointments with lustre drop candlesticks. The fixed price menu gives a limited choice but good raw materials are soundly cooked. Some of the individually decorated bedrooms are very spacious, and they are most comfortable and well

equipped: remote controlled television, radio cassette player with cassettes, fruit, flowers, books and magazines, trouser presses, hair-driers, even talking scales; they all indicate the thought and care provided by the Sherwoods for their customers. It is an hotel with its heart in the right place, one where they will do their utmost to cater for your needs.

6➡ CTV in all bedrooms ✈ sB&B➡£26 dB&B➡£40 Ⓑ

30P ⊞ ✿ nc 12yrs *xmas*

☐ International ☐ ☐ ✂ Lunch £7 Tea £1.20—£2.50 Dinner £10 Wine £4.80 Last dinner 8.45pm

Ⓥ

★Skyline 123 Irish St ☎ (0387) 62416

Closed 1 & 2 Jan

A small homely, nicely decorated hotel in convenient central location.

6rm(2⋔)(2fb) CTV in all bedrooms Ⓡ ✈ sB&B£16 sB&B⋔£19 dB&B£28.50 dB&B⋔£34

CTV 20P

V Lunch £6 High Tea £4 Dinner £9alc Wine £4.85 Last dinner 8.45pm

★Swan at Kingholm Kingholm Quay ☎ (0387) 53756

Small hotel by the Nith Estuary, popular for its bar food.

9rm CTV in 1 bedroom TV in 5 bedrooms sB&Bfr£14 dB&Bfr£22

CTV 30P ✿

☐ Lunch £4.20alc Dinner £6.50alc Wine £3 Last dinner 8pm

Credit card 1

D

DUNBAR

Lothian *East Lothian*
Map **12** NT67

★★*H* Bayswell Bayswell Park ☎ (0368) 62225

Closed 25 Dec—mid Jan

Red sandstone building standing in own grounds overlooking sea. →

14rm(13⇌1⋔)(2fb) CTV in all bedrooms ®T sB&B⇌⋔£32—£37 dB&B⇌⋔£40—£45 B

20P ✿

S% Lunch £3&alc Dinner £10—£12&alc Wine £3.95 Last dinner 9pm

Credit cards 1 2 3

★★★

✿★★★ **CROMLIX HOUSE, DUNBLANE**

Kinbuck (3m NE B8033) (Pride of Britain) ☎ (0786) 822125

(*Rosette awarded for dinner only.*)

The finest qualities of the past century are reflected in this imposing country house, built in 1880 in a peaceful and extensive estate of 5,000 acres. The house has been in the same family ownership for 400 years and much of the original furniture, furnishings, porcelain, silver and other memorabilia still grace both the outstanding public rooms and bedrooms. The public rooms are spacious, elegantly decorated and furnished, all with large open fires and they are well provided with fresh flowers. The bedrooms are finely appointed combining space with period furniture; all have en-suite facilities ranging from modern to original, and eight of the 14 rooms have private sitting rooms; all have colour television and direct dial phones. The delightful family atmosphere is retained in the two dining rooms. There is no formal menu and dinner is discussed to meet individual guests' preferences in the elegant drawing room over pre-dinner drinks. The food is excellent, cooked in the modern manner and the chef, Stephen Frost, thoroughly deserves our rosette. While some physical improvements have been carried out, the reason we now award Red Stars is the fairly recently appointed Manager, Mr Grant Howlett. He has been very successful in imbuing his staff with the right attitude; they are welcoming and friendly, and you are now assured of fine hospitality. The hotel is run on truly private house lines so that if you elect not to have breakfast in your bedroom it is served at a communal table in the inner hall.

14⇌ CTV in all bedrooms **T** S% *sB&B⇌£55—£68 dB&B⇌£97.50—£125 B

30P 2 ✿ xmas

S% *Lunch £5.50—£13 Tea £2.50—£3.50 Dinner £18—£25&alc Wine £5.50

Credit cards 1 2 3 5

DUNBLANE
Central *Perthshire*
Map **11** NN70

DUNDEE
Tayside *Angus*
Map **11** NO33

★★★**Angus Thistle** 10 Marketgait (Thistle) ☎ (0382) 26874 Telex no 76456

Modern hotel with attractive restaurant and cocktail bar and offering alternatives of pub meals or coffee shop snacks. It has a reputation for good food.

58⇌⋔ 2 in 7 bedrooms CTV in all bedrooms ®**T** *sB⇌⋔£40—£50 dB⇌⋔£53—£65 (room only) B

Lift ☾ 20P CFA Live music & dancing Sat Cabaret Fri & Sat

International *Lunch fr£7&alc Dinner fr£10.50&alc Wine £7.50 Last dinner 9.30pm

Credit cards 1 2 3 4 5 Ⓥ

★★★**Swallow** Kingsway West, Invergowrie (3½m W off A972 Dundee Ring Road) (Swallow) ☎ (0382) 641122 Telex no 76694

Very comfortable hotel in own grounds blending modern and 19th century features, plus good leisure facilities.

69⇌(3fb) 2 CTV in all bedrooms ®**T** S% *sB&B⇌£47.50 dB&B⇌£60 B

☾ CTV 100P ✿ (heated) sauna bath solarium gymnasium xmas

English & French **V** S% *Lunch £6&alc Tea £2.75 Dinner £10.50&alc Wine £5.50 Last dinner 9.45pm

Credit cards 1 2 3 5

★★**Queen's** 160 Nethergate ☎ (0382) 22515

Friendly, traditional hotel popular with businessmen.

48rm(18⇌1⋔)(1fb) CTV in all bedrooms ®**T** *sB&B£20—£30 sB&B⇌⋔£24—£45 dB&B£34—£51 dB&B⇌⋔£38—£78 B

Lift ☾ 40P *xmas*

Scottish, French & Italian *Tea 70p—£3.50 Dinner £10.50 Last dinner 9.30pm

Credit cards 1 2 3 4 5 Ⓥ

DUNDONNELL
Highland *Ross & Cromarty*
Map **14** NH08

★★**Dundonnell** (Inter Hotel) ☎ (085483) 204

Closed Nov—Etr

A comfortable modern style hotel nicely situated on the shore of Little Loch Broom.

24rm(23⇌1⋔)(3fb) CTV in all bedrooms ®**T** sB&B⇌⋔£21.50—£27.50 dB&B⇌⋔£35—£45 B

60P

V Lunch £5—£7.50 Tea £1—£2.50 Dinner £10.50—£11.50 Wine £4.95 Last dinner 8.30pm

Credit cards 1 3 Ⓥ

DUNFERMLINE
Fife
Map **11** NT08

★★★ *B* **Keavil House** Crossford (2m W A994) (Consort) ☎ (0383) 736258 Telex no 728227

The converted fortified mansion has an elegant new bedroom wing and two attractive restaurants, the main dining room and cocktail bar being complemented by a characterful lounge bar and adjoining supper restaurant. The hotel attracts both tourist and business trade.

32rm(28⇌4⋔)(2fb) CTV in all bedrooms ®**T** sB&B⇌⋔£29—£33 dB&B⇌⋔£44 B

☾ CTV 100P ✿ (hard) *xmas*

International **V** Lunch £10alc Tea 80p—£2.25 Dinner £11—£15 Wine £4.50 Last dinner 10pm

Credit cards 1 2 3

★★★**King Malcolm Thistle** Queensferry Rd, Wester Pitcorthie (Thistle) ☎ (0383) 722611 Telex no 727721

This modern, purpose-built hotel on the south side of the town is conveniently situated for the Forth road bridge. Tastefully decorated, it offers accommodation in well-equipped bedrooms.

48⇌⋔(6fb) in 15 bedrooms CTV in all bedrooms ®**T** *sB⇌⋔£40—£47 dB⇌⋔£47—£60 (room only) B

☾ 70P ✿

International *Bar lunch £3 Dinner fr£9.50&alc Wine £7 Last dinner 9pm

Credit cards 1 2 3 4 5 Ⓥ

Dunfermline — Dunoon

★★★**Pitfirrane Arms** Main St, Crossford (½m W A994) ☎ (0383) 736132 Telex no 728265

Former coaching inn restored and greatly extended to provide modern standards.

31rm(17 14)(1fb) CTV in all bedrooms ® T sB&B £30—£42.50 dB&B £48 B

50P Disco Thu-Sun *xmas*

International V Lunch fr£6.50&alc Dinner fr£10.75&alc Wine £3.75 Last dinner 9pm

Credit cards 1 2 3

★★***Brucefield*** Woodmill Rd ☎ (0383) 722199

Converted, Victorian mansion dating from 1845 and standing in its own grounds.

9rm(5)(1fb) TV in 6 bedrooms

CTV 30P 3

Last dinner 8.30pm

Credit cards 1 2

★★**City** 18 Bridge St ☎ (0383) 722538

Town centre commercial hotel with neat, well-equipped bedrooms.

17rm(8)(2fb) CTV in all bedrooms ® T S% *sB&B £19.50—£23 sB&B £23 dB&B £30 dB&B £30—£32 B

20P

V *Lunch £4.50 Tea £1.95 High Tea £3.50—£5.95 Dinner £8.50alc Wine £4.50 Last dinner 9pm

Credit cards 1 3 V

DUNHOLME

Lincolnshire
Map **8** TF07

★★**Four Seasons** Scothern Ln ☎ Welton (0673) 60108

Restaurant/entertainment centre with a separate block of modern bedrooms.

12rm(8 4)(1fb) CTV in all bedrooms ® T sB&B £26 dB&B £38 B

200P 18 Live music and dancing Sat

V Lunch £4.95—£7.50&alc Tea £1.50—£2 Dinner £4.95—£7.50&alc Wine £4.50 Last dinner 10pm

Credit cards 1 2 3

DUNKELD

Tayside *Perthshire*
Map **11** NO04

★★**Atholl Arms** Bridgehead ☎ (03502) 219

Closed Feb

Family run traditional hotel standing by the famous bridge over the River Tay.

20rm(4)(1fb) CTV in 4 bedrooms sB&B fr£14 B

V Dinner fr£9 Last dinner 8.30pm

Credit cards 1 2 3

★***Taybank*** Tay Ter ☎ (03502) 340

RS Nov—Feb

Modest, but friendly, country inn.

6rm(1fb)

CTV 20P

Last dinner 8pm

DUNMOW, GREAT

Essex
Map **5** TL62

★★**Saracen's Head** High St (Trusthouse Forte) ☎ (0371) 3901

17th century inn, now well run hotel with cosy lounges and spacious, comfortable well-equipped bedrooms.

24 CTV in all bedrooms ® sB&B £51.50 dB&B £67.50 B

60P *xmas*

Last dinner 9.30pm

Credit cards 1 2 3 4 5

XX**Starr** Market Pl ☎ (0371) 4321
(*Rosette awarded for dinner only.*)

The rosette award is well deserved by this comfortable and attractive 14th century restaurant, which produces some of the best food in Essex from mainly local ingredients. The blackboard menu is posted in the bar, where Mr Jones enthusiastically explains the dishes, and is accompanied by an outstanding wine list.

Closed 3wks Aug & 2wks after Xmas Lunch not served Sat Dinner not served Sun

English & French V 60 seats *Lunch £9.95—£12.95 Dinner £20.25 Wine £6.35 Last dinner 9.30pm 20P

Credit cards 1 3 5

DUNNET

Highland *Caithness*
Map **15** ND27

★★**Northern Sands** ☎ Barrock (084785) 270

A small tourist hotel situated close to Dunnet Sands.

14rm(2 1)(1fb) sB&B £15—£16 sB&B £18—£19 dB&B £30—£32 dB&B £36—£38

CTV 40P

French & Italian V Bar lunch £3—£8.50 Tea 95p—£1.40 High Tea £4.95—£5.90 Dinner £9.40—£15&alc Wine £4.50 Last dinner 8.30pm

Credit card 3

DUNOON

Strathclyde *Argyllshire*
Map **10** NS17

★★***Abbeyhill*** Dhailling Rd ☎ (0369) 2204

This hillside hotel is named after an old folly resembling an abbey. It has a tidy garden and excellent views.

14rm(7 7)(3fb) CTV in all bedrooms ®

40P

Last dinner 8.30pm

Credit card 3

★★*H* **Enmore** Marine Pde, Kirn ☎ (0369) 2230

RS Nov—Feb

Friendly seafront hotel with tasteful bedrooms, interesting home cooking and some leisure facilities.

12rm(6 3)(1fb) 3 CTV in 9 bedrooms sB&B £18 sB&B £30 dB&B £36 dB&B £40—£64 B

CTV 20P squash games room

Scottish & French V Bar lunch £1—£7 Tea 75p High Tea £4.50 Dinner £13.50 Wine £4.50 Last dinner 8.30pm

Credit cards 3 5 V

See advertisement on page 266

★★*BL* **Firpark** Ardnadam (3m N A815) ☎ (0369) 6506

A small, well-appointed hotel with wood panelled drawing room and individually decorated bedrooms.

6rm(2 2) CTV in all bedrooms ® sB&B fr£17.75 sB&B fr£19.75 dB&B fr£30 dB&B fr£35

CTV 30P

Bar lunch fr£2.95 Dinner fr£5.50&alc Wine £3.95 Last dinner 9pm

Credit card 3

★★**Hunter's Quay** Marine Pde, Hunters Quay ☎ (0369) 4190

This friendly, family-run hotel stands opposite the ferry terminal, overlooking the Firth of Clyde. In its comfortable dining room the menu reflects good, imaginative cooking with an emphasis on Scottish game dishes.

18rm(8)(5fb) CTV in 2 bedrooms ® sB&B fr£16 sB&B fr£22 dB&B fr£27 dB&B fr£32 B

CTV 30P Cabaret Sun *xmas*

V Lunch fr£5 Tea fr£1 Dinner £8—£12 Wine £5 Last dinner 10pm

Credit card 1

X**Casa Santana** 10 John St ☎ (0369) 3284

The unpretentious little Spanish restaurant, easily recognised by its red-tiled roof and brown-shuttered windows, is a firm favourite with the town's American population. The tiny interior is comfortably, though simply, furnished and an abundance of Spanish curios achieve the desired atmosphere. The menu offers a choice of Spanish and European dishes. →

D

Closed Mon & 24 Dec—20 Jan

European V 26 seats Lunch £5.50—£7.50 Dinner £7.50—£9.50 Wine £6.50 Last dinner 10.30pm

Credit card 3

DUNSTABLE
Bedfordshire
Map **4** TL02

★★★B ***Old Palace Lodge*** Church St ☎ Luton (0582) 62201

Charming, ivy clad building with comfortable, tastefully-appointed bedrooms and friendly, helpful service.

50 (6fb) 2 CTV in all bedrooms T B

Lift 70P *xmas*

V Last dinner 10pm

Credit cards 1 2 3 5

★★**Highwayman** London Rd ☎ (0582) 601122 Telex no 825353

Closed Xmas day

Commercial hotel with well equipped accommodation and friendly service.

38 CTV in all bedrooms ® T S% *sB&B fr£28 dB&B fr£38 B

50P

*Bar lunch £1.55—£5.95 Tea fr65p Dinner £4.65—£7.95&alc Wine £4.50 Last dinner 9pm

Credit cards 1 2 3 5 V

Dunoon — Durham

DUNSTER
Somerset
Map **3** SS94

★★★**Luttrell Arms** High St (Trusthouse Forte) ☎ (0643) 821555

This historic, holiday and touring hotel of character, has modern amenities, and many original features.

21 4 CTV in all bedrooms ® sB&B £50.50 dB&B £66.50 B

xmas

Last dinner 9.30pm

Credit cards 1 2 3 4 5

★★*L* **Exmoor House** West St ☎ (0643) 821268

Closed Dec—Jan

This small hotel, located close to the town centre, provides comfortable lounges and friendly, attentive service by the proprietors.

6rm (1 3)(2fb) in bedrooms CTV in all bedrooms sB&B £23.50—£24.50 sB&B £26—£27 dB&B £32—£34 dB&B £37—£39 B

CTV

Tea 45p—£1.50 Dinner £9.75—£10.25 Wine £4.50 Last dinner 8pm

Credit cards 1 2 3 5 V

DUNVEGAN
Isle of Skye, Highland *Inverness-shire*
See **Skye, Isle of**

DURHAM
Co Durham
Map **12** NZ24
See also **Thornley**

★★★★**Royal County** Old Elvet (Swallow) ☎ (0385) 66821 Telex no 538238

Overlooking the river, this historic hotel has a Georgian facade and new bedroom wing.

120 (9fb) 1 CTV in all bedrooms ® T S% *sB&B fr£48.50 dB&B fr£58 B

Lift 120P sauna bath CFA *xmas*

V S% *Lunch £7.25—£7.50&alc Dinner fr£10.50&alc Wine £5.50 Last dinner 10.15pm

Credit cards 1 2 3 5

★★★**Bowburn Hall** Bowburn (3m SE junc A177/A1(M)) ☎ (0385) 770311 Telex no 537681

Standing in own grounds, hotel has well-appointed bedrooms and most attractive dining room and lounge.

19➡CTV in all bedrooms *sB&B➡fr£32 dB&B➡fr£40 B

CTV 100P ✽ ⚘

V ♁ ☕ Lunch £8.45—£10.50 Dinner £10.50&alc Wine £5.50 Last dinner 10pm

Credit cards 1 2 3 5

★★★**Bridge** Croxdale (2¼m S off A167) (Toby) ☎ (0385) 780524 Telex no 538156

Modern chalet accommodation is to be found in the courtyard behind the original inn, which houses the restaurant and bar.

46➡CTV in all bedrooms ® sB&B➡£19.50—£33 dB&B➡£29.50—£44 B

☾150P ✽

♛English & French ♁ Lunch £10&alc Dinner £6—£10&alc Wine £4.95 Last dinner 9.45pm

Credit cards 1 2 3 4 5

★★★*B* **Ramside Hall** Belmont (3m NE A690) ☎ (0385) 65282 Telex no 537681

Converted country house with spacious comfortable bars, and set in 80 acres of parkland.

35rm(31➡)(4fb) ⁄ in 12 bedrooms CTV in all bedrooms ® T *sB&Bfr£36 sB&B➡£42—£50 dB&Bfr£44 dB&B➡£52—£58 B

☾700P ✽ Disco Mon Live music and dancing Wed—Sun ⚘ ♿

V ♁ ☕ Lunch £7&alc Tea fr£2.50 Dinner fr£7.50&alc Wine £6 Last dinner 10pm

Credit cards 1 2 3 5

★★★**Three Tuns** New Elvet (Swallow) ☎ (0385) 64326 Telex no 538238

This traditional town-centre hotel has been modernised to offer comfortable accommodation, but the public areas retain the character of the original coaching inn.

54➡⋒(4fb) 1▦ CTV in all bedrooms ® sB&B➡⋒£44—£49 dB&B➡⋒£56—£60 B

☾60P CFA *xmas*

♛English & French V ♁ ☕ Lunch £4—£8&alc Tea fr£3 High Tea £4—£6 Dinner £8.50—£10&alc Wine £5.95 Last dinner 9.30pm

Credit cards 1 2 3 5

★**Redhills** Redhills Ln, Crossgate Moor ☎ (0385) 64331 Telex no 537681

The hotel is comfortable, having been modernised recently, and the restaurant can be specially recommended for its good-value menus.

6rm CTV in all bedrooms ✗ sB&Bfr£22 dB&Bfr£35 B

100P

♁ ☕ Lunch fr£5.50 Dinner fr£8 Wine £5.50 Last dinner 9.45pm

Credit cards 1 2 3 5

✕**Squire Trelawny** 80 Front St Sherburn Village (3m E off A181) ☎ (0385) 720613

This cosy, intimate restaurant has an attractive balcony-style dining area surrounded by rustic colonnades, while the tiny cocktail bar features interesting bric-à-brac from The Squire's Tuck Room. The carefully compiled menu caters for all tastes, offering a good range of house specialities as well as a comprehensive choice of grills.

Closed Mon Dinner not served Sun

V 28 seats Lunch £2.50—£4 Dinner £8—£9alc Wine £4.50 Last dinner 9.30pm 8P

DUROR

Highland *Argyllshire*
Map **14** NM95

★★*L* **Stewart** (Best Western) ☎ (063174) 268

Closed Nov—Jan

RS Feb—9 Apr

A comfortable and nicely appointed Highland hotel successfully blending modern facilities with original features.

26➡(7fb) CTV in all bedrooms ® sB&B➡£29 dB&B➡£48 B

50P ✽ sauna bath solarium ⚘

V ♁ ☕ Bar lunch £5.50alc Tea £1.50alc Dinner £12 Wine £4.95 Last dinner 8.30pm

Credit cards 1 2 3 5 Ⓥ

DUXFORD

Cambridgeshire
Map **5** TL44

★★★*L* **Duxford Lodge** Ickleton Rd ☎ Cambridge (0223) 836444 Telex no 817438

The comfortable and well-appointed hotel, once a wartime fighter base HQ, is ideally situated for visits to the Duxford War Museum and Cambridge.

11rm(10➡1⋒) Annexe: 5➡ CTV in all bedrooms ® T S% sB&B➡⋒£40—£50 dB&B➡⋒£55—£70 B

34P ✈ ✽ ⚘ *xmas*

♛English & French V ♁ ☕ Lunch £8.50—£10&alc Dinner £12.50—£15&alc Wine £5.95 Last dinner 9.30pm

Credit cards 1 2 3 5 Ⓥ

EAGLESHAM

Strathclyde *Renfrewshire*
Map **11** NS55

★★**Eglinton Arms** Gilmour St ☎ (03553) 2631

Pleasant, and popular inn in centre of picturesque village.

12➡CTV in all bedrooms ® T sB&B➡£28—£40 dB&B➡£35—£50 B

☾50P Live music & dancing Mon

♛French V ☕ * Bar lunch £2—£4 Dinner £7.95—£9.95&alc Wine £4.60 Last dinner 9.30pm

Credit cards 1 2 3 5

✕✕**Pepper Pot** Cross Keys Inn ☎ (03553) 2002

Attractive first floor restaurant facing village green.

Closed Sun

♛Scottish & French V 70 seats Lunch £6.60&alc Dinner £13 Wine £5.45 Last dinner 10pm 40P

Credit cards 1 2 3

EARLS COLNE

Essex
Map **5** TL82

✕**Drapers House** High St ☎ (07875) 2484

Historic, converted Drapers shop, with original beamed ceiling, and records dating back to Elizabethan days.

Closed Mon
Lunch not served Sat

♛English, French & Italian 80 seats S% Lunch £7alc Dinner £13alc Wine £3.90 Last dinner 10pm 20P Live music Fri

Credit cards 1 2 3 5

EARL SHILTON

Leicestershire
Map **4** SP49

★**Fernleigh** 32 Wood St ☎ (0455) 47011

Friendly, family run hotel, extended and modernised to provide comfortable accommodation.

15rm(1➡12⋒)(1fb) CTV in all bedrooms ® *sB&B£20—£25 sB&B➡⋒£20—£25 dB&B£30—£34 dB&B➡⋒£30—£34 B

CTV 100P solarium *xmas*

V ♁ ☕ * Lunch £4.95&alc Tea £1.50 Dinner £6.95&alc Wine £4.95 Last dinner 9.30pm

Credit cards 1 3 Ⓥ

EASDALE

Strathclyde *Argyll*
Map **10** NM71

★**Easdale Inn** ☎ Balvicar (08523) 256

Closed Nov—Feb

6rm(4➡)(1fb) CTV in all bedrooms sB&Bfr£16.50 dB&B£26—£30 dB&B➡£30—£35

20P ✈ ✽

♛British & French V ♁ ☕ Lunch £5alc Tea 90p alc Dinner £8alc Wine £4.50 Last dinner 8.30pm

EASINGTON

Cleveland
Map **4** NZ71

★★★♣ **Grinkle Park** (2m S off unclass rd linking A174 & A171) ☎ Guisborough (0287) 40515

20rm(14➡6⋒) 1▦ CTV in all bedrooms ® T S% sB&B➡⋒£40—£45 dB&B➡⋒£50—£55 B

CTV 130P ✽ snooker *xmas*

♛English & French V ♁ ☕ S% Lunch £6.25—£7.50&alc Tea £1.50—£2.95 Dinner £11.65—£13.50&alc Wine £4.75 Last dinner 9.30pm

Credit cards 1 2 3 5

E

EASINGWOLD
North Yorkshire
Map **8** SE56

★★***George*** Market Pl ☎ (0347) 21698
Closed Xmas Day RS 24 & 26 Dec
Originally a coaching inn, the hotel retains its character in the low-beamed public rooms despite improvements and extensions.
18rm(16⇌2⋒)(2fb) CTV in all bedrooms ® ₽
8P Live music and dancing Fri & Sat
♈ Last dinner 9pm
Credit card 3

EAST BERGHOLT
Suffolk
Map **5** TM03

✕**Fountain House** The Street ☎ Colchester (0206) 298232
Closed Mon & 1st 2wks Jan. Dinner not served Sun
32 seats Lunch £8.50 Dinner £10.50 Wine £4.95 Last dinner 9pm 12P
Credit cards 1 3

EASTBOURNE
East Sussex
Map **5** TV69
See plan

★★★★★**Grand** King Edwards Pde (De Vere) ☎ (0323) 22611 Telex no 87332 Plan **7** *D1*
Large impressive Victorian sea-front hotel.
178rm(175⇌3⋒)(10fb) 1▣ CTV in all bedrooms **T** S% ✱sB&B⇌⋒£60—£80 dB&B⇌⋒£95—£135 ₽
Lift ☾ 60P CFA ⛟ ✿ ⛆ (heated) ▭ (heated) snooker sauna bath solarium gymnasium Live music and dancing 4 nights wkly ♿ xmas
♉English & French **V** ♈ ☕ S% Lunch £12&alc Tea £1.30 Dinner £16&alc Wine £7.50 Last dinner 9.30pm
Credit cards 1 2 3 4 5 Ⓥ

★★★★*L* **Cavendish** Grand Pde (De Vere) ☎ (0323) 27401 Telex no 87579 Plan **2** *D1*
Luxury hotel in fine position.
114⇌ CTV in all bedrooms ® **T** S% sB&B⇌£46—£60 dB&B⇌£72—£100 ₽
Lift ☾ 50P snooker games room CFA Live music & dancing Sat *xmas*
♉English & French **V** ♈ ☕ S% ✱Lunch £7.50&alc Tea £1.10—£3 Dinner £12&alc Wine £6.50 Last dinner 9pm
Credit cards 1 2 3 5

★★★★**Queens** Marine Pde (De Vere) ☎ (0323) 22822 Telex no 877736 Plan **16** *D2*
Popular, family hotel with good bedrooms.
108rm(104⇌4⋒)(5fb) CTV in all bedrooms ® **T** S% sB&B⇌⋒£42—£46 dB&B⇌⋒£68—£76 ₽
Lift ☾ 50P CFA snooker Live music and dancing Sat Jun—Sep ♿ *xmas*
♉English & French ♈ ☕ S% Lunch £9&alc Tea 85p High Tea £2.50 Dinner £11&alc Wine £6.50 Last dinner 8.45pm
Credit cards 1 2 3 5

★★★**Chatsworth** Grand Pde ☎ (0323) 30327 Plan **3** *D1*
Closed Jan—mid Mar
Four-storey building with sun terrace overlooking the sea, situated between the pier and the bandstand.
45rm(14⇌30⋒)(1fb) CTV in all bedrooms sB&B⇌⋒£24.60—£26.35 dB&B⇌⋒£49.20—£59.80 ₽
Lift ☾ CTV ₱ CFA *xmas*
V ♈ ☕ Lunch £7 (Sun only) Tea fr 80p Dinner £8.25 Wine £5 Last dinner 8pm
Credit cards 1 2 3

★★★**Cumberland** Grand Pde ☎ (0323) 30342 Plan **4** *D1*
Nicely appointed hotel with enclosed sun terrace and sea views.
70rm(65⇌5⋒) CTV in all bedrooms **T** sB&B⇌⋒£32—£33.50 dB&B⇌⋒£53—£67 ₽
Lift ☾ CTV ₱ CFA *xmas*
♉English & French ♈ ☕ ✱Lunch £5.18 Tea 69p Dinner £7.50&alc Wine £4.05 Last dinner 8.15pm

★★★*L* **Lansdowne** King Edward's Pde (Best Western) ☎ (0323) 25174 Plan **10** *D1*
Closed 1—11 Jan
This well-appointed, family-run, sea front hotel stands opposite Western Lawns and close to theatres, shops and all amenities. It provides every modern facility, together with a friendly atmosphere.
136rm(86⇌16⋒)(6fb) CTV in all bedrooms ® S% sB&B£23—£30 sB&B⇌⋒£25.50—£34 dB&B£42—£54 dB&B⇌⋒£47—£61 ₽
Lift ☾ CTV 21 🏠 (£2 per day) CFA snooker Live music & dancing wkly (Jun—Sep) *xmas*
V ♈ ☕ ⚡ S% Lunch £6alc Tea £1.25 High Tea £5 Dinner £9&alc Wine £5.25 Last dinner 8.30pm
Credit cards 1 2 3 5 Ⓥ

★★★**Mansion** Grand Pde ☎ (0323) 27411 Plan **12** *D1*
Four-storey building, with enclosed sun terrace, overlooking the sea.
103rm(75⇌2⋒)(10fb) CTV in all bedrooms ® **T** ✗ sB&B£17—£22 sB&B⇌⋒£21—£28 dB&B£34—£44 dB&B⇌⋒£42—£56 ₽
Lift ☾ CTV ₱ CFA Disco wkly Live music & dancing wkly *xmas*
♉English & French **V** ♈ ☕ Lunch £5.50&alc Tea 85p High tea £1.50 Dinner £7.50 Wine £4.50 Last dinner 8.30pm
Credit cards 1 2 3 5 Ⓥ

★★★**Princes** Lascelles Ter (Inter-Hotels) ☎ (0323) 22056 Plan **15** *D1*
Closed 29 Dec—1 Feb
Four-storey, late Victorian terraced building just off the sea-front.
50rm(37⇌1⋒)(3fb) CTV in all bedrooms ® **T** sB&B£16—£22.50 sB&B⇌⋒£24.50—£27.50 dB&B£34—£43 dB&B⇌⋒£39—£55 ₽
Lift ☾ ₱ solarium pool table & table tennis CFA Live music twice wkly *xmas*

French ♀ ☕ Lunch £6 Tea £1.25 Dinner £8.50 Wine £6 Last dinner 8.15pm

Credit cards 1 2 3 5

★★★**Sandhurst** Grand Pde ☎ (0323) 27868 Plan **17** *D1*

Well-appointed, carefully run hotel overlooking the sea.

64rm(38⇌14 ⋒)(2fb) CTV in all bedrooms ® sB&B£20—£28 sB&B⇌⋒£21—£29 dB&B£40—£56 dB&B⇌⋒£42—£58 ₿

Lift ☾ P CFA Live music and dancing wkly *xmas*

Eastbourne

International ♀ ☕ Lunch fr£5.95 Dinner fr£7.50 Wine £4.95 Last dinner 8.30pm

Credit cards 1 2 3 5 Ⓥ

See advertisement on page 271

★★**Croft** 18 Prideaux Rd ☎ (0323) 642291 Plan **3A** *C3*

Quietly situated, this small, family-run hotel and restaurant offers friendly, attentive service and accommodation in well-equipped rooms of various sizes. "Le Jardin" offers an à la carte menu in addition to the table d'hôte of the hotel dining room, and the overall standard of cooking is enterprising and reliable.

9rm(8⇌)(2fb) CTV in all bedrooms ® ✱sB&B£15—£18.50 sB&B⇌£23—£28.50 dB&B⇌£34.50—£38.50

CTV P ✽ (heated) (hard) *xmas*

French ♀ ☕ ✱Lunch fr£6.75&alc Tea fr70p Dinner fr£7.50&alc Wine £5.25 Last dinner 9.45pm

Credit cards 1 2 3 4 5

See advertisement on page 271

Eastbourne

Eastbourne

1	Byrons✕		5	Downland ★		10A	Lathom ★		16	Queens ★★★★
2	Cavendish ★★★★		6	Farrar's ★★		12	Mansion ★★★		17	Sandhurst ★★★
3	Chatsworth ★★★		7	Grand ★★★★★		13	New Wilmington ★		18	West Rocks ★★
3A	Croft ★★		9	Langham ★★		14	Oban ★		19	Wish Tower ★★
4	Cumberland ★★★		10	Lansdowne ★★★		15	Princes ★★★			

★★**Farrar's** 3—5 Wilmington Gdns ☎(0323) 23737 Plan **6** *C1*

Quiet, comfortable, with satisfactory bedrooms.

42rm(24🛁6🚿)(2fb) CTV in 32 bedrooms sB&B£19—£21 sB&B🛁🚿£21—£25 dB&B£38—£40 dB&B🛁🚿£42—£50 **B**

Lift ☾ CTV 26P nc3yrs

English, French & Italian **V** Lunch £1—£5alc Tea 75p Dinner £7.50 Wine £4 Last dinner 8pm

Credit cards 1 2 3

See advertisement on page 272

Eastbourne

★★**Langham** Royal Pde ☎(0323) 31451 Plan **9** *E2*

This comfortable and well maintained hotel enjoys uninterrupted views of the sea. A high standard of management and the comfort of generous public rooms combine to make the visitor's stay a pleasant one.

83rm(46🛁6🚿) Ⓡ sB&B£16—£22 sB&B🛁🚿£19—£25 dB&B£32—£44 dB&B🛁🚿£38—£50 **B**

Lift ☾ CTV 3 (charge) Live music & dancing twice wkly (in season) Cabaret wkly (in season)

European Lunch £5.50 Tea £1.35 High Tea £3 Dinner £7.50 Wine £4.25 Last dinner 7.30pm

Credit card 3 Ⓥ

★★**New Wilmington** 25 Compton St ☎(0323) 21219 Plan **13** *D1*

Closed Dec—Feb RS Mar

Friendly, family-run hotel with comfortable, well-equipped bedrooms. →

38rm(16 12)(4fb)CTV in all bedrooms ® T sB&B£16.50—£20.50 sB&B £18—£22 dB&B£30—£38 dB&B £33—£41

Lift CTV 3 (£1.50 per day) Live music & dancing twice wkly *xmas*

English & French Bar lunch £3alc Tea fr50p Dinner £6.50—£7 Wine £4 Last dinner 7.30pm

Credit cards 1 2 3 V

E

★★**West Rocks** Grand Pde (0323) 25217 Plan **18** *D1*

Closed Nov—Mar

54rm(8 30)(5fb)CTV in all bedrooms sB&B£19 sB&B £25.50 dB&B£31 dB&B £51

Lift CTV nc 3yrs

Lunch £4&alc Tea 60p Dinner £6 Wine £3.75 Last dinner 7.30pm

★★**Wish Tower** King Edward's Pde (Trusthouse Forte) (0323) 22676 Plan **19** *D1*

This comfortable hotel occupies a prominent sea-front position.

75rm(38)CTV in all bedrooms ® sB&B£32.50 sB&B £40.50 dB&B£50.50 dB&B £58.50

Lift CTV CFA *xmas*

Last dinner 8.30pm

Credit cards 1 2 3 4 5

Eastbourne

★**Downland** 37 Lewes Rd (Minotel) (0323) 32689 Plan **5** *C3*

Closed Dec—Feb except Xmas RS Nov, Apr & May

One can enjoy good, simple, home cooking in the pinewood-furnished restaurant of this warm, compact establishment which offers a good standard of accommodation.

16rm(8 8)(4fb) 1 CTV in all bedrooms ® sB&B £17—£25 dB&B £30—£42

CTV 16P *xmas*

Lunch £2.50—£5.50 Dinner £7.50—£9 Wine £3.95 Last dinner 7.30pm

Credit cards 1 2 3 V

★**Lathom** 4—6 Howard Sq, off Grand Pde (0323) 641986 Plan **10A** *D1*

Closed Dec—Feb

The comfortable, privately-owned hotel provides nicely-appointed bedrooms and an attractive lounge. The proprietors and their team of young staff are particularly helpful.

40rm(2 13)(2fb)CTV in all bedrooms ® sB&B£15—£16.50 sB&B £17—£18.50 dB&B£30—£33 dB&B £34—£37

Lift 11P(£1.25 daily) Live music & dancing twice wkly *xmas*

V Lunch £4—£4.50 Tea 60p High Tea £2—£3.50 Dinner £5.50—£6.50 Wine £4.75 Last dinner 8pm

Credit cards 1 2 V

★**Oban** King Edward's Pde (0323) 31581 Plan **14** *D1*

Closed mid Nov—Mar

Family run sea-front hotel close to theatres and shops.

31rm(13 18)CTV in all bedrooms ® sB&B £16—£20 dB&B £32—£40

Lift CTV

V Lunch £4.50—£5.50 Tea fr60p Dinner £7—£8 Wine £4 Last dinner 7.30pm

Credit card 3 V

X**Byrons** 6 Crown St, Old Town (0323) 20171 Plan **1** *B2*

Restaurant with a romantic French air complementing the cuisine.

Closed Sun & 25—31 Dec Lunch not served Sat

French V 22 seats Lunch £7.80alc Dinner £12.50alc Wine £4.50 Last dinner 10.30pm

Credit cards 2 3 5

EAST GRINSTEAD
West Sussex
Map **5** TQ33

★★★

★★★ **GRAVETYE MANOR, EAST GRINSTEAD**

(3m SW off unclass road joining B2110 & B2028) (Relais et Chateaux)
q05) Sharpthorne (0342) 810567
Telex no 957239 Gatwick plan **14**

Beautifully situated in 1000 acres just 30 miles from London, this hotel also has 30 acres of show piece gardens designed in the English style by William Robinson more than 100 years ago. The owner, Peter Herbert, ensures that the gardens are maintained, while the kitchen plot provides for Chef Allen Garth to use to good effect in the kitchen. He cooks in the modern French style. Dishes like parfait of chicken liver, poached sea bass with langoustines, sirloin steak with red wine sauce and walnut tart have demonstrated his skill. The wine list is outstanding. The dining rooms have been furnished with more comfortable chairs. Like the rest of the interior, it is well appointed with stone floors and carpets, splendid staircase and panelling, moulded ceilings, handsome chimney pieces in wood and marble with interesting fire dogs where log fires burn in winter. All these features create the atmosphere at this fine, creeper-clad Elizabethan house, an effect which is enhanced by antiques and lots of flowers. The bedrooms, named after trees, are well up to these high standards, spotlessly clean and provided with lots of thoughtful 'extras'. Service is discreetly courteous and very smooth. Altogether it remains a unique example of gracious, country house living.

14rm(12 2) 1 CTV in all bedrooms T S% *
sB £54—£67.85
dB £73.60—£124.20(room only)
25P croquet nc 7yrs
English & French S% * Lunch £15 Dinner £25alc Wine £8 Last dinner 9.30pm

★★★ **Felbridge Hotel & Health Club** London Rd East Grinstead (0342) 26992 Telex no 95156 Gatwick plan **5**

RS Xmas

Well appointed comfortable hotel with adjacent health and leisure club.

49 (10fb) 3 CTV in all bedrooms ®

450P CFA (heated) (heated) snooker sauna bath solarium gymnasium disco 4 nights wkly

English & French S% Lunch fr£8 Dinner £10—£12.50 Wine £5.25 Last dinner 9.30pm

Credit cards 1 2 3 4 5

★★ **Woodbury House** Lewes Rd (0342) 313657 Gatwick plan **20**

Closed 25 & 26 Dec

The restaurant of this small, family-run hotel offers an enterprising menu of skilfully cooked dishes backed by friendly, attentive service, and its bedrooms are very well equipped and indvidually furnished.

6 Annexe: 1rm(1fb) 1 CTV in all bedrooms ® T * sB&B £27.50—£31 dB&B £40—£50

25P

English & French Lunch fr£9.50&alc Tea fr75p Dinner fr£9.50&alc Wine £5.25 Last dinner 10pm

Credit cards 1 2 3 4 5 V

EASTHAM
Merseyside
Map **7** SJ38

○ **Little Chef Lodge**

New Chester Rd (adjacent M53 jct 5 northbound carriageway A41)
051-327 2489

31

Opened early 1986

EAST HORNDON
Essex
Map **5** TQ68

○ **Little Chef Lodge** A127 (3m E of M25 jct 29) Brentwood (0277) 810819

20 Due to have opened July 1986

EAST HORSLEY
Surrey
Map **4** TQ05

★★★ **Thatchers** Epsom Rd (Best Western) (04865) 4291 Telex no 946240

Set in 4 acres, this hotel has modern bedrooms and imaginative cooking.

6 Annexe: 23 (1fb) 2 CTV in all bedrooms ® T sB £45.75—£52.75 dB £62—£69(room only)

90P (heated)

English & French Lunch £9.50—£11.25&alc Tea £1—£3.95 Dinner £10.50—£12.25&alc Wine £6.50 Last dinner 9.30pm

Credit cards 1 2 3 5

See advertisement under Guildford

E

EAST KILBRIDE
Strathclyde *Lanarkshire*
Map **11** NS65

★★★**Bruce** Cornwall St (Swallow) ☎ (03552) 29771 Telex no 778428

This modern, custom-built hotel forms part of the New Town complex.

84rm(32⇌52♨) CTV in all bedrooms ® S% ✱sB&B⇌♨£31.50–£43 dB&B⇌♨£39.50–£54 B

Lift ☾ 15P 25⌂ CFA Disco Sun *xmas*

International V ♔ ☕ S% ✱Lunch £5.50 Tea 85palc Dinner £8.50 Wine £5.50 Last dinner 9.45pm

Credit cards 1 2 3 5

★★★**Stuart** 2 Cornwall Way ☎ (03552) 21161 Telex no 778504

A busy new town centre is the settng for this modern hotel with pleasant, spacious public rooms and compact bedrooms.

40⇌♨(1fb) 1▭ CTV in all bedrooms ® T ✱sB&B⇌♨£35–£38 dB&B⇌♨£45–£48 B

Lift ☾ ## ₽ CTV Live music & dancing Sat ♿ *xmas*

French V ♔ ☕ Lunch £5.80&alc Tea 75palc High Tea £4.40alc Dinner £10alc Wine £4.20 Last dinner 9.30pm

Credit cards 1 2 3 5 Ⓥ

EASTLEIGH
Hampshire
Map **4** SU41

★★★**Crest** Leigh Rd, Passfield Av (Crest) ☎ (0703) 619700 Telex no 47606

RS Xmas

Attractive modern hotel with friendly service and choice of restaurants.

120⇌(10fb) ⁄ in 14 bedrooms CTV in all bedrooms ® T S% ✱ sB&B⇌£57.15–£65.15 dB&B⇌£73.30–£81.30 B

Lift ☾ ## 240P Live music & dancing Sat ♿

English & French V ♔ ☕ ⁄ ✱Lunch £8–£12 Tea £1–£2 Dinner £12.25&alc Wine £6.45 Last dinner 9.45pm

Credit cards 1 2 3 5

EAST MOLESEY
Surrey London plan **5** *B1* (page 446)

✕✕**Lantern** 20 Bridge Rd ☎ 01-979 1531

Tastefully decorated restaurant with conservatory, run by the chef-patron and his wife.

Closed Sun, Aug & Bank Hols
Lunch not served Mon & Sat

French V 50 seats ✱Lunch £11.95–£15.95&alc Dinner £12.75–£15.95&alc Wine £6.15 Last dinner 11pm ₽ nc 8yrs

Credit cards 1 2 3 5

✕**Le Chien Qui Fume** 107 Walton Rd ☎ 01-979 7150

This restaurant features imaginative French regional cooking, its blackboard specialities complemented by an excellent cheese board, and service is friendly and helpful.

Closed Sun, 11–31 Aug & Bank Hol Mon's

French 55 seats ✱Lunch £6.50&alc Dinner £15alc Wine £6 Last dinner 11pm 8P

Credit cards 1 2 3 5

EAST PORTLEMOUTH
Devon
Map **3** SX73

★★**Gara Rock** ☎ Salcombe (054 884) 2342

Closed Oct–Etr

Converted coast guard cottages with superb sea views and pleasant gardens.

28rm(16⇌5♨)(15fb) CTV in 20 bedrooms ✱sB&B£20–£24 dB&B£40–£48 dB&B⇌♨£44–£52 B

CTV 60P ▭ ✿ ≈ (heated) ⚲(hard) ⸙ Disco wkly Live music & dancing wkly ⌂

V ♔ ☕ ✱Bar lunch £1–£4.50 Tea fr 85p High Tea fr £3.50 Dinner £6.75–£14.50 Wine £4.75 Last dinner 8.45pm

Credit cards 1 3

See advertisement under Salcombe

EAST PRESTON
West Sussex
Map **4** TQ00

✕✕**Old Forge** The Street ☎ Rustington (0903) 782040

Restaurant retains Victorian character from which it was home of E. Hardy, the water colourist.

Closed Mon Dinner not served Sun

English & Continental V 75 seats ✱Lunch £5.85–£6.45&alc Wine £4.90 Last dinner 10pm 24P

Credit cards 1 2 3 4 5

EATHORPE
Warwickshire
Map **4** SP36

★★**Eathorpe Park** Fosse Way (Exec Hotel) ☎ Marton (0926) 632245

Closed Xmas night & Boxing Day

Large early-Victorian building situated amid eleven acres of woodland.

10rm(5⇌3♨)(1fb) CTV in 8 bedrooms ® sB&B£24.25 sB&B⇌♨£27.25 dB&B£31.50 dB&B⇌♨£36.50 B

CTV 200P ✿

V ♔ Lunch £7.50 Dinner £10.50 Wine £4.75 Last dinner 9.45pm

Credit cards 1 2 3 5

EBFORD
Devon
Map **3** SX98

★★*H* **Ebford House** Exmouth Rd ☎ Topsham (039287) 7658

The hotel, an attractive Georgian house set in its own grounds, is managed by friendly and attentive resident owners. Menus offer a good choice of dishes and the food is well prepared.

10rm(8⇌) CTV in all bedrooms ® sB&B£18–£25 sB&B⇌£25–£28 dB&B⇌£36–£40 B

40P ✿ sauna bath solarium gymnasium

English & French V ♔ ☕ Lunch £7.50–£12&alc Dinner £12–£14&alc Wine £5.20 Last dinner 9.30pm

Credit cards 1 2 3 Ⓥ

EDDLESTON
Borders *Peeblesshire*
Map **11** NT24

✕✕**Horse Shoe Inn** ☎ (07213) 225

Attractive country restaurant also renowned for bar meals.

Closed Xmas Day & New Years Day

International V 55 seats ✱Lunch £5.95–£7.45&alc Dinner £12.95&alc Wine £5.50 Last dinner 10pm 36P

Credit cards 1 2 3 5

EDENHALL
Cumbria
Map **12** NY53

★★**Edenhall** ☎ Langwathby (076881) 454

The hotel dining room, with its large expanse of windows, offers fine views of the garden.

31⇌(2fb) CTV in all bedrooms T ✈ sB&B⇌£20.30 dB&B⇌£32.50 B

CTV 60P ▭ ✿ *xmas*

International V ♔ ☕ Lunch £4.80&alc Tea 50p–£2.50 Dinner £7.90&alc Wine £5.25 Last dinner 9pm

Credit cards 1 2 3 5

EDINBURGH
Lothian *Midlothian*
Map **11** NT27
see plan

★★★★★**Caledonian** Princes St (Pride of Britain) ☎ 031-225 2433 Telex no 72179 Central plan **8** ***B4***

This hotel has been refurbished to a high standard and the Pompadour Restaurant — specialising in Scottish dishes — is particularly recommended. Bedrooms vary in size and style, but all are well furnished and equipped, whilst service is extremely obliging and friendly.

254rm(216⇌38♨) ⁄ in 12 bedrooms CTV in all bedrooms T ✈ S% sB⇌♨£45–£70 dB⇌♨£70–£105 (room only) B

Lift ☾ 150P CFA Live music nightly *xmas*

Scottish & French V ☕ S% Lunch fr£11.50&alc Tea £3.85alc Dinner £12.50—£25&alc Wine £6.50 Last dinner 10pm

Credit cards 1 2 3 4 5

★★★★**Carlton Highland** North Bridge (Scottish Highland) ☎ 031-556 7277 Telex no 727001 Central plan **9** *E4*

This quality hotel of character stands in the city centre.

207➡ CTV in all bedrooms Ⓡ**T** ✱sB&B➡£55—£70 dB&B➡£80—£98 **B**

Lift ☾ # CFA ▭(heated) squash snooker pool table table tennis sauna bath solarium gymnasium

Scottish & French V ☕ S% ✱Lunch £7.90—£9.95 Tea £2.50 Dinner £7.95—£9.95 Wine £5.50 Last dinner 10.30pm

Credit cards 1 2 3 4 5

★★★★**George** George St ☎ 031-225 1251 Telex no 72570 Central plan **15A** *D5*

Tastefully modernised traditional hotel with a magnificent dining room and elegant French restaurant.

195➡⋒ CTV in all bedrooms Ⓡ**T** S% ✱sB➡⋒£60.50—£82.50 dB➡⋒£88—£99(room only) **B**

Lift ☾ 26P CFA Cabaret 5 nights wkly Apr—Oct *xmas*

British & French V ☕ S% Lunch £10.75—£12&alc Tea £3.25—£4 Dinner £10.75—£12&alc Wine £6.25 Last dinner 10pm

Credit cards 1 2 3 4 5

★★★★**Ladbroke Dragonara** Bells Mills, 69 Belford Rd (Ladbroke) ☎ 031-332 2545 Telex no 727979 Central plan **21** *A5*

Old mill converted to interesting modern hotel, with good modern cooking offered in attractive waterside restaurant.

146➡⋒(3fb) CTV in all bedrooms Ⓡ**T** ✱sB➡⋒£60.50 dB➡⋒£82.50(room only) **B**

Lift ☾ 43P 36 CFA ♿ *xmas*

English, French & Italian ☕ ✱Lunch £8.75&alc Tea £1 High Tea £2.25 Dinner £7.20—£24&alc Wine £6.40 Last dinner 10.30pm

Credit cards 1 2 3 5

Edinburgh

★★★***Albany*** 39—43 Albany St ☎ 031-556 0397 Telex no 727079 Central plan **1** *E6*

Closed 24 Dec—2 Jan

The restored Georgian façade is a feature of this 'New-Town' hotel.

21rm(16➡5⋒)(2fb) CTV in all bedrooms Ⓡ Continental breakfast **B**

☾ **P**

V ☕ Last dinner 9.30pm

Credit cards 1 2 3 5

★★★*BL* **Barnton Thistle** Queensferry Rd, Barnton (Thistle) ☎ 031-339 1144 Telex no 727928 District plan **33**

Traditional building which has been modernised and extended.

50➡⋒(10fb) 1 in 10 bedrooms CTV in all bedrooms Ⓡ**T** ✱sB➡⋒£45—£53 dB➡⋒£53—£70(room only) **B**

Lift ☾ 100P sauna bath solarium Live music & dancing Sat

International ☕ ✱Lunch fr£8.50&alc Dinner fr£10.25&alc Wine £7 Last dinner 9.30pm

Credit cards 1 2 3 4 5 Ⓥ

★★★**Braid Hills** 134 Braid Rd, Braid Hills (2½m S A702) ☎ 031-447 8888 Telex no 72311 District plan **34**

A long established hotel now undergoing a phased improvement programme. Smart, colonial style foyer and cocktail bar.

67rm(42➡25⋒)(4fb) 3 CTV in all bedrooms Ⓡ**T** sB➡⋒£35—£55 dB➡⋒£56—£70(room only) **B**

☾ 38P ✿ *xmas*

Scottish & French V ☕ Lunch £6.50—£7.30&alc Tea £2.50 Dinner £8.50—£9.50&alc Wine £6.50 Last dinner 9pm

Credit cards 1 2 3 5

★★★**Bruntsfield** 69—74 Bruntsfield Pl (Best Western) ☎ 031-229 1393 Telex no 727897 Central plan **7** *B1*

A privately-owned hotel close to the city centre, the Bruntsfield has recently been completely refurbished.

54rm(46➡8⋒)(1fb) CTV in all bedrooms **T** ✱sB&B➡⋒£36—£45 dB&B➡⋒£54—£65 **B**

Lift ☾ 40P CFA *xmas*

International V ☕ Lunch £6.50—£9&alc Tea fr£1.50 High Tea £6.50—£9 Dinner £11.50—£14.50&alc Wine £5.95 Last dinner 11pm

Credit cards 1 2 3 5 Ⓥ

See advertisement on page 280

★★★*L* **Crest** Queensferry Rd (Crest) ☎ 031-332 2442 Telex no 72541 District plan **37**

Modern hotel, 1m from the city centre on the way to the Forth Road Bridge.

118rm(79➡39⋒)(8fb) CTV in all bedrooms Ⓡ**T** S% ✱sB➡⋒£56.15—£61.50 dB➡⋒£72.80—£82.30(room only) **B**

Lift ☾ 100P *xmas*

English & French V ☕ ✱Lunch £6—£8.70&alc Tea £1 High Tea £5 Dinner £10.50—£12.25&alc Wine £6.50 Last dinner 9.45pm

Credit cards 1 2 3 4 5

See advertisement on page 280

★★★*L* **Donmaree** 21 Mayfield Gdns ☎ 031-667 3641 District plan **38**

Closed Xmas & New Year

Attractively decorated in Victorian style and boasting a restaurant with a fine reputation, the hotel is particularly popular with businessmen.

9rm(5➡4⋒) Annexe: 8rm(3➡2⋒)(2fb) CTV in all bedrooms **T** sB&B➡⋒£40.25 dB&B£46 dB&B➡⋒£57.50—£63.25

☾ CTV 6P

French V S% Lunch £7.15&alc Dinner £17.50alc Wine £5.55 Last dinner 10pm

Credit cards 1 2 3 Ⓥ

E

E

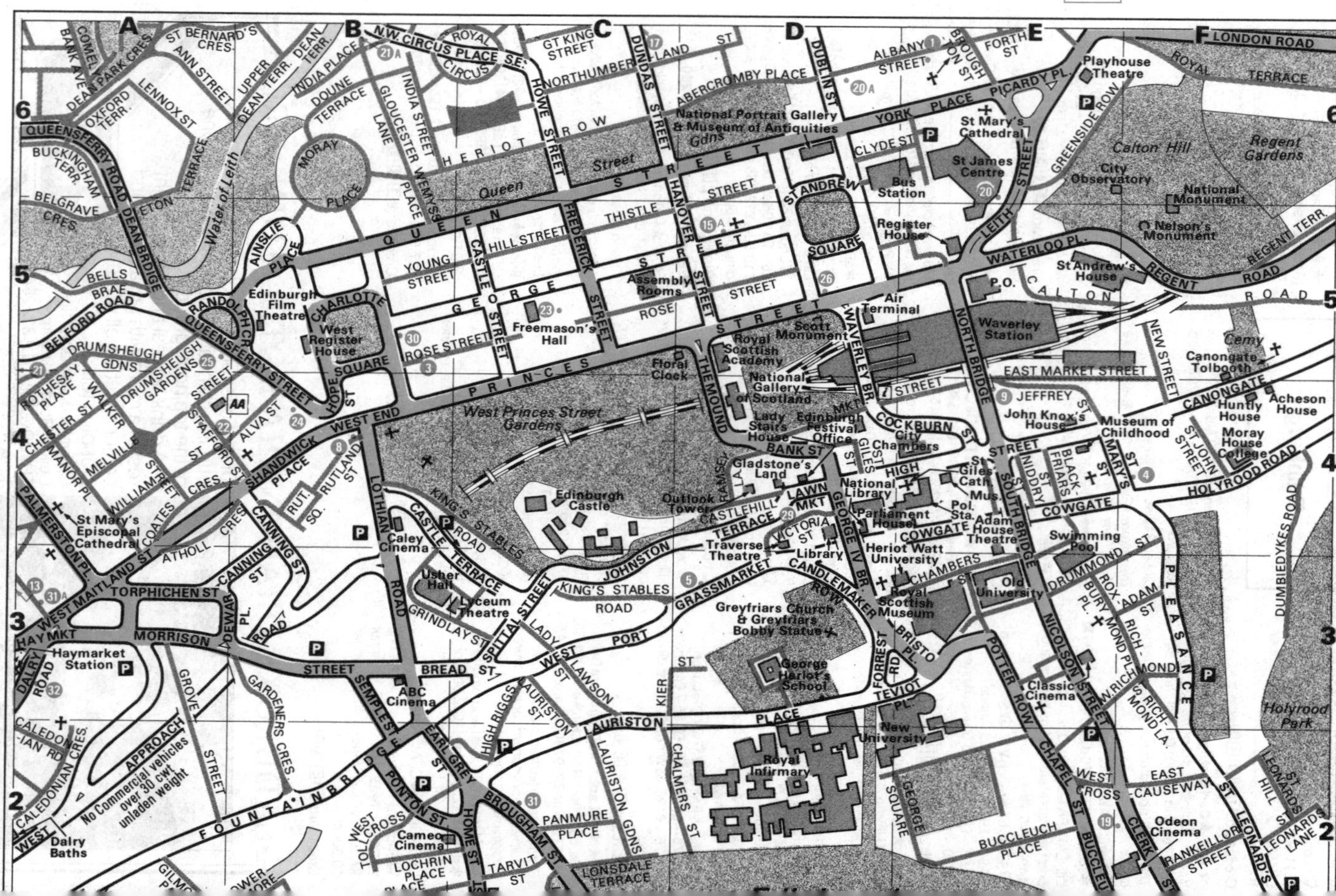

LONDON ROAD
ROYAL TERRACE
Regent Gardens
Calton Hill
National Monument
Nelson's Monument
City Observatory
Playhouse Theatre
GREENSIDE ROW
PICARDY PL.
LEITH STREET
St Mary's Cathedral
St James Centre
BROUGHTON ST
FORTH ST
ALBANY STREET
YORK PLACE
Bus Station
CLYDE ST
Register House
DUBLIN ST
ST ANDREW SQUARE
National Portrait Gallery & Museum of Antiquities
ABERCROMBY PLACE
NORTHUMBERLAND ST
DUNDAS STREET
HANOVER STREET
QUEEN STREET
Queen Street Gdns
HERIOT ROW
HOWE STREET
GT KING STREET
ROYAL CIRCUS
N.W. CIRCUS PLACE
INDIA STREET
GLOUCESTER LANE
WEMYSS PLACE
INDIA PLACE
DOUNE TERRACE
MORAY PLACE
AINSLIE PLACE
RANDOLPH CR.
QUEENSFERRY STREET
QUEENSFERRY ROAD
DEAN BRIDGE
Water of Leith
UPPER DEAN TERR.
DEAN TERR.
ANN STREET
ST BERNARD'S CRES.
LENNOX ST
ETON TERRACE
OXFORD TERR.
DEAN PARK CRES.
COMELY BANK AVE
BUCKINGHAM TERR.
BELGRAVE CRES.
BELLS BRAE
BELFORD ROAD
DRUMSHEUGH GDNS
DRUMSHEUGH GARDENS
ROTHESAY PLACE
CHESTER ST
WALKER ST
MANOR PL.
MELVILLE ST
WILLIAM ST
COATES CRES.
STAFFORD ST
ALVA ST
Edinburgh Film Theatre
CHARLOTTE SQUARE
West Register House
HOPE ST
YOUNG STREET
CASTLE STREET
HILL STREET
THISTLE STREET
FREDERICK STREET
ROSE STREET
GEORGE STREET
Assembly Rooms
Freemason's Hall
PRINCES STREET
West Princes Street Gardens
Floral Clock
THE MOUND
Royal Scottish Academy
National Gallery of Scotland
Scott Monument
WAVERLEY BR.
Waverley Station
Air Terminal
NORTH BRIDGE
WATERLOO PL.
REGENT ROAD
REGENT TERR.
P.O.
St Andrew's House
CALTON ROAD
Cemy
NEW STREET
EAST MARKET STREET
JEFFREY ST
Canongate Tolbooth
CANONGATE
Acheson House
Huntly House
Moray House College
HOLYROOD ROAD
DUMBIEDYKES ROAD
ST JOHN STREET
Museum of Childhood
John Knox's House
ST MARY'S ST
BLACKFRIARS ST
ST NIDDRY ST
COWGATE
Swimming Pool
SOUTH BRIDGE
PLEASANCE
Holyrood Park
ST LEONARDS HILL
ST LEONARD'S ST
ST LEONARD'S LANE
EAST CROSSCAUSEWAY
WEST CROSSCAUSEWAY
Odeon Cinema
RANKEILLOR STREET
CLERK ST
BUCCLEUCH ST
BUCCLEUCH PLACE
NICOLSON STREET
Classic Cinema
RICHMOND PL.
ROXBURGH PL.
DRUMMOND ST
Old University
POTTER ROW
CHAPEL ST
GEORGE SQUARE
New University
TEVIOT PL.
BRISTO PL.
FORREST RD
Royal Scottish Museum
CHAMBERS ST
Heriot Watt University
Adam House Theatre
Parliament House
National Library
St Giles Cath.
HIGH ST
COCKBURN ST
City Chambers
Edinburgh Festival Office
ST GILES ST
BANK ST
Lady Stairs House
Gladstone's Land
LAWNMKT
GEORGE IV BR.
VICTORIA ST
Library
CANDLEMAKER ROW
Greyfriars Church & Greyfriars Bobby Statue
George Heriot's School
Royal Infirmary
LAURISTON PLACE
CHALMERS ST
KIER ST
GRASSMARKET
Traverse Theatre
Outlook Tower
RAMSEY LA.
CASTLEHILL
JOHNSTON TERRACE
Edinburgh Castle
KING'S STABLES ROAD
WEST PORT
LADY LAWSON ST
LAURISTON ST
LAURISTON GDNS
PANMURE PLACE
LONSDALE TERRACE
HIGH RIGGS
SPITTAL STREET
GRINDLAY ST
Lyceum Theatre
Usher Hall
CASTLE TERRACE
Caley Cinema
LOTHIAN ROAD
BREAD ST
ABC Cinema
EARL GREY ST
BROUGHAM ST
HOME ST
TARVIT ST
PONTON ST
Cameo Cinema
LOCHRIN PLACE
WEST TOLLCROSS
SEMPLE ST
FOUNTAINBRIDGE
WEST END
SHANDWICK PLACE
RUTLAND ST
RUTLAND SQ.
CANNING ST
ATHOLL CRES.
TORPHICHEN ST
DEWAR PL.
MORRISON STREET
GARDENERS CRES.
GROVE STREET
APPROACH
No Commercial vehicles over 30 cwt unladen weight
St Mary's Episcopal Cathedral
WEST MAITLAND ST
PALMERSTON PL.
HAYMKT
Haymarket Station
DALRY ROAD
CALEDONIAN CRES.
CALEDONIAN RD
WEST APPROACH
Dalry Baths

Edinburgh

★★★ **Ellersly House** 4 Ellersly Rd (Embassy) ☎ 031-337 6888 Telex no 76357 District plan **39**

Quietly situated near city centre, with attractively refurbished bedrooms helping to retain country house atmosphere.

55rm(54⇌1⋒)(3fb) 1⊟ CTV in all bedrooms Ⓡ ✗ S% sB&B⇌⋒fr£48.50 dB&B⇌⋒fr£66 ⊟

Lift ☾ 40P ✿ croquet Live music & dancing Fri & Sat ♿ *xmas*

♉ ☕ S% Lunch £7—£11&alc Tea fr£1 Dinner fr£11&alc Wine £5 Last dinner 9pm

Credit cards 1 2 3 4 5

★★★ *BL* **Howard** Great King St ☎ 031-557 3500 Telex no 727887 Central plan **17** *C6*

Relaxing club-like atmosphere in this small hotel in Georgian New Town area.

25rm(18⇌7⋒)(2fb) CTV in all bedrooms Ⓡ **T** S% sB&B⇌⋒£45—£52 dB&B⇌⋒£65—£85 ⊟

Lift ☾ 14P CFA ⊭

♉ Lunch £7.50—£8.50 Tea £1 Dinner £12.50—£17.50 Wine £7 Last dinner 9.30pm

Credit cards 1 2 3 4 5

★★★ *B* **King James Thistle** 107 St James Centre (Thistle) ☎ 031-556 0111 Telex no 727200 Central plan **20** *E6*

Modern hotel in new shopping centre.

147⇌⋒(11fb) ⊁ in 10 bedrooms CTV in all bedrooms **T** ✱ sB⇌⋒£45—£65 dB⇌⋒£65—£95 (room only) ⊟

Lift ☾ 20P 8⌂ CFA ⊭ Live music & dancing Mon—Sat Apr—Oct Cabaret Mon—Sat Apr—Oct

♉ International ♉ ☕ ✱ Lunch fr£8.95&alc Dinner fr£11.95&alc Wine £7 Last dinner 9.45pm

Credit cards 1 2 3 4 5 Ⓥ

See advertisement on page 280

★★★ **Old Waverley** Princes St (Scottish Highland) ☎ 031-556 4648 Telex no 727050 Central plan **26** *D5*

Traditional hotel whose front rooms have fine views of the gardens and Castle.

62rm(53⇌9⋒)(12fb) 1⊟ CTV in all bedrooms Ⓡ **T** sB&B⇌⋒£30—£45 dB&B⇌⋒£50—£66 ⊟

Lift ☾ Ᵽ CFA *xmas*

V ♉ ☕ ✱ Lunch £2.65—£4.85 Tea 95p—£2.30 Dinner £6.25—£8.75&alc Wine £4.95 Last dinner 10pm

Credit cards 1 2 3 5

★★★ **Post House** Corstorphine Rd (Trusthouse Forte) ☎ 031-334 8221 Telex no 727103 District plan **49**

On western city approach and backed by Edinburgh Zoo this comfortable and spacious hotel offers fine views over the city.

207⇌(100fb) CTV in all bedrooms Ⓡ sB&B⇌£57.50 dB&B⇌£76.50 ⊟

Lift ☾ 158P CFA ♿

♉ Last dinner 10.30pm

Credit cards 1 2 3 4 5

★★★ *BL* **Roxburghe** Charlotte Sq (Best Western) ☎ 031-225 3921 Telex no 727054 Central plan **30** *B5*

In one of Edinburgh's grandest squares, stands this fine hotel designed by Robert Adam. It has a club-like atmosphere and several spacious, elegant bedrooms.

76rm(62⇌14⋒)(1fb) 1⊟ CTV in all bedrooms Ⓡ **T** S% sB&B⇌⋒£47.50—£58 dB&B⇌⋒£79—£98 Continental breakfast ⊟

Lift ☾ Ᵽ CFA

♉ French **V** ♉ ☕ Lunch £7.50—£9.50&alc Tea 95p—£3 Dinner £10.50—£12.50&alc Wine £6.50 Last dinner 10pm

Credit cards 1 2 3 5

See advertisement on page 281

★★★ **Royal Scot** 111 Glasgow Rd (Swallow) ☎ 031-334 9191 Telex no 727197 District plan **51**

Modern hotel convenient for airport.

252⇌⋒(58fb) CTV in all bedrooms Ⓡ **T** S% sB&B⇌⋒£57—£60 dB&B⇌⋒£70—£76 ⊟

Lift ☾ ## 250P CFA ⊠ (heated) sauna bath solarium gymnasium Live music and dancing Sat *xmas*

♉ International **V** ♉ ☕ S% Lunch £10.95 Dinner £10.25&alc Wine £5.90 Last dinner 10pm

Credit cards 1 2 3 4 5

★★★ ***Stakis Commodore*** West Marine Dr, Cramond Foreshore (Stakis) ☎ 031-336 1700 Telex no 727167 District plan **36**

Set in parkland overlooking Firth of Forth, hotel has a restaurant specialising in steaks.

48⇌(8fb) CTV in all bedrooms Ⓡ **T** ⊟

Lift ☾ ## CFA *xmas*

Last dinner 9.45pm

Credit cards 1 2 3 5

★★★ ***Stakis Grosvenor*** Grosvenor St (Stakis) ☎ 031-226 6001 Telex no 72445 Central plan **31A** *A3*

The recently refurbished hotel caters for business and coach markets with a choice of two attractive restaurants.

138rm(105⇌31⋒)(18fb) 1⊟ CTV in all bedrooms Ⓡ **T** ⊟

Lift ☾ ## Cabaret Sun—Fri (May—Sep) *xmas*

♉ ☕ Last dinner 10.30pm

Credit cards 1 2 3 4 5

E

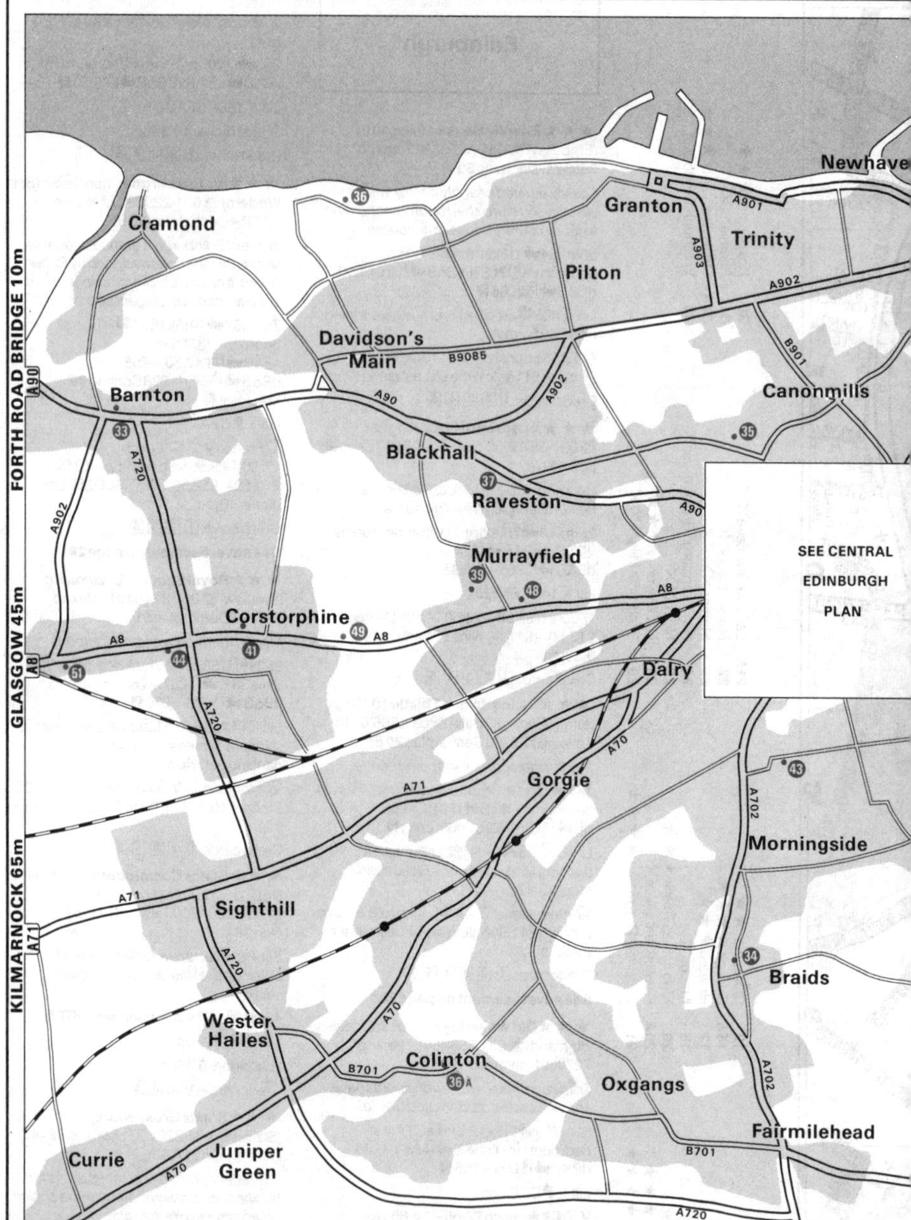

★★**Clarendon** Grosvenor St (Scottish Highland) ☎031-337 7033 Telex no 78215 Central plan **13** *A3*

Recently refurbished, the quiet, friendly hotel is situated in the attractivee West End of the city.

51rm(43⇌8⋔)(5fb) CTV in all bedrooms ®**T** sB&B⇌⋔£28—£36 dB&B⇌⋔£50—£60 **B**

Lift ☾CTV **P** Cabaret wkly *xmas*

V ♡ ☕ Lunch £3.25—£8 Tea 75p—£2.50 High Tea £3.50—£6.50 Dinner £8.50—£10&alc Wine £5.60 Last dinner 10pm

Credit cards 1 2 3 5

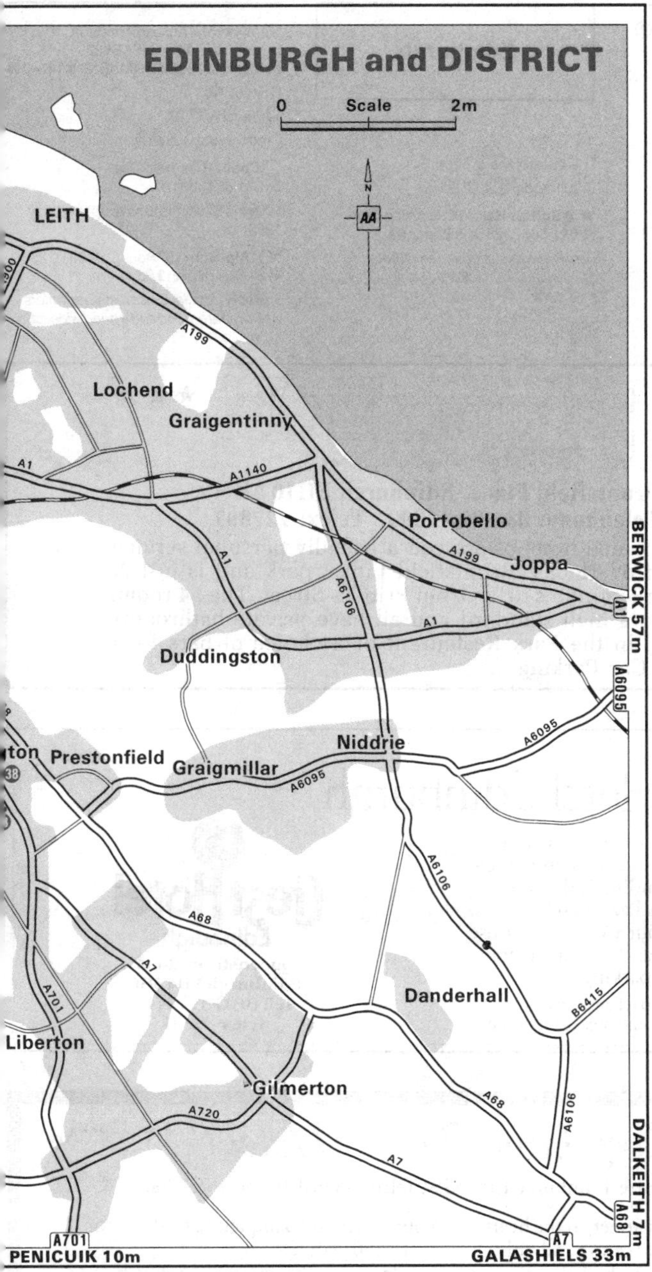

EDINBURGH and DISTRICT

0 Scale 2m

N

AA

LEITH

Lochend

Graigentinny

Portobello

Joppa

Duddingston

Prestonfield

Graigmillar

Niddrie

Danderhall

Liberton

Gilmerton

A1 A1140 A199 A6106 A6095 A68 A7 A701 A720 B6415 A900

BERWICK 57m A1

A6095

DALKEITH 7m A68

PENICUIK 10m A701

GALASHIELS 33m A7

Edinburgh District

33	Barton Thistle ★★★
34	Braid Hills ★★★
35	Chez Julie ✕
36	Stakis Commodore ★★★
36A	Champany Inn Town ✕✕
37	Crest ★★★
38	Donmaree ★★★
39	Ellersly House ★★★
41	Harp ★★
43	Iona ★★
44	Lightbody's ✕✕
47	Montgomeries at the Mansion House ✕✕
48	Murrayfield ★★
49	Post House ★★★
51	Royal Scot ★★★
53	Suffolk Hall ★★

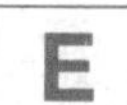

★★***Harp*** St John's Rd, Corstorphine (3½m W on A8) (Osprey) ☎ 031-334 4750
District plan **41**

Commercial hotel with compact bedrooms.

27rm(11🛁16🚿) CTV in all bedrooms ®**T**
B

☾ 40P Live music & dancing wkly *xmas*

V ♆ ☕ Last dinner 9pm

Credit cards [1] [2] [3] [5]

★★**Iona** Strathearn Pl ☎ 031-447 6264
District plan **43**

Small commercial/tourist hotel in quiet residential area. The dinner menu offers exceptional value.

→

17rm(2⇌2⋔)(2fb) CTV in all bedrooms ® T sB&B£22 sB&B⇌⋔£30 dB&B£40 dB&B⇌⋔£46

CTV 20P

V Lunch fr£5 High Tea fr£5 Dinner £8.50alc Wine £5 Last dinner 9pm

Credit cards 1 3 V

★★**Murrayfield** 18 Corstorphine Rd (Alloa) ☎ 031-337 1844 District plan **48**

The hotel stands on a busy roadside and its recently-refurbished bedrooms make it popular with tourists and businessmen alike.

22rm(7⇌2⋔) CTV in all bedrooms ® T

E

Edinburgh

CTV 40P

Last dinner 9.30pm

Credit cards 1 2 3 5

★★**Suffolk Hall** 10 Craigmillar Park ☎ 031-667 9328 District plan **53**

Family-run tourist/commercial hotel in residential suburb close to students halls of residence.

12rm(4⇌5⋔) Annexe: 4rm(5fb) CTV in 12 bedrooms ® S% sB&B£22 sB&B⇌⋔£28 dB&B£30 dB&B⇌⋔£40

CTV 16P

French V

Credit cards 1 2 3 5

○ **Capital** Clermiston Rd ☎ 031-334 3391

100⇌⋔ Expected to have opened July 1986

XX **Alp-Horn** 167 Rose St ☎ 031-225 4787 Central plan **3** *B5*

This very popular Swiss restaurant offers well-prepared food and a good wine list.

Recently extended, it now provides an optional non-smoking dining room.

Closed Sun, Mon, 2wks from Xmas Eve & 3wks end Jun/beginning Jul

Swiss 66 seats Lunch £7—£10alc Dinner £12—£15alc Wine £4.80 Last dinner 10pm P ⁄

Credit card 1

XX L'Auberge 56 St Mary's Street ☎ 031-556 5888 Central plan **4** *F4*

Friendly French restaurant with interesting menu specialising in fish.

French 60 seats ✻Lunch fr£6.75&alc Dinner £19.50&alc Wine £6.50 Last dinner 9.30pm P

Credit cards 1 2 3 5

XX *Champany Inn Town* 2 Bridge Rd, Colinton ☎ 031-441 2587 District plan **36A**

The small, superior steak restaurant is appropriately housed in a former butcher's shop. The beamed ceiling and wood panelling, together with lots of copperwork and Victorian tables, give a cottage appearance and a cosy atmosphere.

Closed Sun, 2wks fr 24 Jan

36 seats Last dinner 10pm

Credit cards 1 2 3 5

Edinburgh

XX Lancers Brasserie 5 Hamilton Pl, Stockbridge ☎ 031-332 3444 Central plan **21A** *B6*

As suggested by its name, the theme of this restaurant is the Regiment of Bengal Lancers. The thali, a traditional Bengali meal, is especially recommended, offering a selection of seven small portions of different dishes, either vegetarian or non-vegetarian.

North Indian & Bengali **V** 80 seats ✻Lunch £4.95—£5.95&alc Dinner £6.95—£9.95&alc Wine £4.05 Last dinner 11.300pm P

Credit cards 1 2 3 V

XX Lightbody's 23 Glasgow Rd ☎ 031-334 2300 District plan **44**

This little roadside restaurant on the western outskirts of the city is very busy at both lunch and dinner time. The food is wholesome and traditional, the staff friendly and attentive.

Closed Sun

British & French 54 seats ✻Lunch £5.55—£6.05&alc Dinner £10alc Wine £5.65 Last dinner 10pm 14P

Credit cards 1 2 3

XX Martins 70—72 Rose St, North Ln ☎ 031-225 3106 Central plan **23** *C5*

Tucked away off the city's famous Rose Street, the bright little restaurant has a friendly young staff who create a cheerful atmosphere. Standards are consistently good and there is usually a selection of game on the menu.

Closed Sun, Mon 26 Dec—3 Jan & 2 wks Jun/Jul Lunch not served Sat

Scottish, French & Italian **V** 25 seats ✻Lunch £7.75—£11.75 Dinner £15.95—£18 Wine £6.50 Last dinner 10pm P ⁄ nc 8yrs

Credit cards 1 2 3 5

XX *Ristorante Milano* 7 Victoria St ☎ 031-226 5260 Central plan **29** *D4*

Situated in the city's Old Town, in the shadow of the castle, this small English restaurant offers an interesting menu, friendly and attentive service and a reasonably-priced list of mainly Italian wines.

Closed Sun

Italian **V** 65 seats Last dinner 11pm

Credit cards 1 2 3 4 5

X Chez Julie 110 Raeburn Place ☎ 031-332 2827 District plan **35**

A busy little restaurant on the north side of the city, Chez Julie has a bistro-style atmosphere. Attentive service and a reasonably-priced menu of well prepared food have made it a popular rendezvous. →

E

Closed Sun

French **V** 38 seats Lunch £4.20—£5.50&alc Dinner £8—£9alc Wine £4.25 Last dinner 10pm

Credit cards 1 2 3 5

✕**Kalpna** 2—3 St Patrick Square ☎ 031-667 9890 Central plan **19** *F2*

Simply decorated restaurant offering authentic Indian vegetable cuisine.

Closed Sun

Indian Vegetarian only **V** 66 seats S% Lunch £3.50—£6.50 Dinner £5.50—£7.50&alc Wine £5.50 Last dinner 11pm

Credit cards 1 3

✕**Kweilin Cantonese** 19—21 Dundas St ☎ 031-557 1875 Plan **20A** *D6*

Booking is essential at this large restaurant, which specialises in Continental cuisine.

Closed Xmas Day, New Years Day & Chinese New Year

Cantonese 80 seats Lunch £5—£6alc Dinner £9.75&alc Wine £6 Last dinner 11.15pm Ᵽ

✕**MacKintosh's** 24A Stafford St ☎ 031-226 7530 Central plan **22** *A4*

This compact and friendly basement restaurant is designed in the style of Charles Rennie MacKintosh.

Closed Sun, 26, 27 Dec & 1, 2 Jan Lunch not served Sat

Scottish & French 30 seats Lunch £6.80—£7.80&alc Dinner £16—£20alc Wine £5.90 Last dinner 10.15pm

Credit cards 1 2 3 5

✕**New Edinburgh Rendezvous** 10A Queensferry St ☎ 031-225 2023 Central plan **24** *B4*

This traditional first-floor restaurant specialises in Pekinese dishes.

Closed Xmas Day, Boxing Day, New Years Day & Chinese New Year

Chinese **V** 135 seats ✱Lunch £2.60—£14.50&alc Dinner £2.60—£18 Wine £4.70 Last dinner 11.30pm Ᵽ

Credit cards 1 2 3 5

Edinburgh — Eggesford

✕**Shamiana** 14 Brougham St ☎ 031-228 2265 Central plan **31** *C2*

Small compact Indian restaurant, neatly decorated.

Closed Xmas Day & New Years Day Lunch not served

Kashmiri & North Indian **V** 40 seats Dinner £10alc Wine £5 Last dinner 11.30pm Ᵽ

Credit cards 1 2 3 4 5

✕**Verandah Tandoori** 17 Dalry Rd ☎ 031-337 5828 Central plan **32** *A3*

Popular, smart Indian restaurant.

Bengali & North Indian **V** 44 seats Lunch £7.50—£9.50&alc Dinner fr£7.50&alc Wine £3.95 Last dinner 11.45pm Ᵽ

Credit cards 1 2 3 Ⓥ

EDWINSTOWE

Nottinghamshire
Map **8** SK66

★★*B* **Forest Lodge** 2 Church St ☎ Mansfield (0623) 822970

Set in the heart of Robin Hood country, the 250-year-old coaching inn has a wealth of character. Bedrooms are comfortable and well equipped.

7rm(2🛁5🚿)(1fb) 1 CTV in all bedrooms ®**T** S% sB&B🛁🚿£25 dB&B🛁🚿£35 B

44P Disco Thu

International **V** S% ✱Lunch £3.95—£12.95 Dinner £3.95—£12.95&alc Wine £3.95 Last dinner 10pm

Credit cards 1 2 3 5 Ⓥ

EDZELL

Tayside *Angus*
Map **15** NO56

★★★**Glenesk** High St ☎ (03564) 319

Popular golfing hotel with access to the neighbouring course.

25rm(14🛁7🚿)(2fb) CTV in all bedrooms ®**T** sB&Bfr£25 sB&B🛁🚿fr£28 dB&Bfr£46 dB&B🛁🚿fr£52

150P 4 ✱ snooker

✱Lunch £4.50 Tea £2 High Tea £4.50 Dinner £8.50 Wine £5.50 Last dinner 8.45pm

Credit cards 2 5

★★**Central** ☎ (03564) 218

A small three-storey hotel standing in a quiet street.

20rm(3🛁9🚿)(1fb) in all bedrooms CTV in 11 bedrooms sB&B£16—£22 sB&B🛁🚿£21—£25 dB&B£26—£30 dB&B🛁🚿£32—£36 B

CTV 70P 2 snooker

V Lunch £3.50—£5 Tea £1.50—£1.75 High Tea £2.85—£6.50 Dinner £7.25—£10 Wine £4.50 Last dinner 9.30pm

Credit cards 2 3

★★**Panmure Arms** High St ☎ (03564) 420

Attractive mock Tudor hotel offering good range of bar meals. Squash can be viewed from lounge bar.

16rm(5🛁11🚿)(4fb) 1 CTV in all bedrooms **T** S% sB&B🛁🚿fr£25 dB&B🛁🚿fr£40 B

30P (heated) squash sauna bath solarium Disco wkly Live music and dancing mthly *xmas*

V S% Lunch £3.50—£7 Tea 55p High Tea £3.75 Dinner £9 Wine £4.50 Last dinner 9pm

Credit cards 1 2 3 5 Ⓥ

EGGESFORD

Devon
Map **3** SS61

★★**Fox & Hounds** (Minotel) ☎ Chulmleigh (0769) 80345

RS Jan & Feb

Privately-owned fishing hotel in its own grounds.

10rm(6🛁) Annexe: 2🛁 1 ® sB&B£12—£19 sB&B🛁£16—£19 dB&B£24—£38 dB&B🛁£32—£38 B

CTV 30P 6 ✱ Live music & dancing Fri fortnightly nc 10yrs

Lunch £5alc Tea 75palc Dinner £8.25—£9.75&alc Wine £5 Last dinner 10pm

Credit cards 1 2 3 V

EGHAM
Surrey
Map **4** TQ07

XX **La Bonne Franquette** 5 High St ☎ (0784) 39494

Cosy Anglo-French restaurant and bar, featuring seasonal dishes with a good wine selection, and efficient service.

Lunch not served Sat

French 40 seats S% Lunch £12.50&alc Dinner £20&alc Wine £7.50 Last dinner 9.30pm 15P nc 8yrs

Credit cards 1 2 3 5

EGLWYSFACH
Dyfed
Map **6** SN69

★★★ **Ynyshir Hall** ☎ Glandyfi (065474) 209

Comfortable manor house set amidst gardens next to RSPB bird sanctuary.

11rm(6 2)(1fb) 1 in 7 bedrooms **T** S% sB&B£20 sB&B £23—£25 dB&B £50 **B**

CTV 20P 1 *xmas*

English & French **V** S% Lunch £8.50&alc Tea £1.50 Dinner £15&alc Wine £4.95 Last dinner 9pm

Credit cards 1 2 3 5 V

Eggesford — Elgin

EGREMONT
Cumbria
Map **11** NY01

★★ **Blackbeck Inn** (Blackbeck 2¾m A595) ☎ Beckermet (094684) 661

A converted Georgian farmhouse with 1½ acres of paddock.

22rm(21 1) 1 CTV in all bedrooms ® **T** sB&B £32—£42 dB&B £42—£50 **B**

CTV 50P billiards

Mainly grills **V** Lunch £5.50—£6.95 Tea £1.50—£3.95 High Tea £2.25—£3.95 Dinner fr£7.50&alc Wine £4.50 Last dinner 10pm

Credit cards 1 2 3 5 V

ELCOT
Berkshire
Map **4** SU36

★★★ *B* **Elcot Park** (1m N of A4) (Best Western) ☎ Kintbury (0488) 58100 Telex no 846448

Luxurious bedrooms are complemented by elegantly furnished public rooms in a country hotel with views over the Kennet Valley. Quality cooking displays the flair and individuality of the chef, and service is professional.

19rm(17 2) Annexe: 11 (2fb) 4 CTV in all bedrooms ® **T** *sB&B £45—£55 dB&B £48—£100 **B**

40P 4 croquet *xmas*

English & French **V** Last dinner 9.30pm

Credit cards 1 2 3 5

ELGIN
Grampian *Morayshire*
Map **15** NJ26

★★★ **Eight Acres** Sheriffmill (Consort) ☎ (0343) 3077 Telex no 73347

This purpose-built hotel stands on the A96, on the western outskirts of the town. The bedrooms vary in size and are mainly functional, but those built in 1985 in conjunction with the sports and leisure complex are very tastefully appointed.

57rm(33 24)(5fb) CTV in all bedrooms **T** S% *sB&B £29.95—£33.95 dB&B £46—£55 **B**

CTV 300P CFA (heated) squash snooker sauna bath solarium gymnasium *xmas*

International S% *Bar lunch £4—£5.50 Tea 80p—£1 High Tea £6.10—£10.45 Dinner £9.95&alc Wine £4 Last dinner 9.30pm

Credit cards 1 2 3 5 V

★★★*HB* **Mansion House** The Haugh ☎ (0343) 48811

Closed 1 & 2 Jan

Elegant, skilfully restored mansion, tastefully furnished and with well equipped bedrooms. Restaurant is gaining a reputation for good cooking in the nouvelle cuisine style.

12 (1fb) 2 CTV in all bedrooms ® T S% sB&B £29.50—£37.50 dB&B £47.50—£57.50

30P

V Lunch £7alc Dinner £13alc Wine £5 Last dinner 9pm

Credit cards 1 2 3 4 5

★★**Laichmoray** Station Rd ☎ (0343) 7832

Friendly, commercial hotel with some good modern bedrooms.

34rm (10 7)(5fb) CTV in 28 bedrooms **T** sB&B £15—£17.50 sB&B £25—£27 dB&B £26—£28 dB&B £35—£40

CTV 100P snooker

V Lunch £5.25 Tea fr50p High Tea £2.25—£6.25 Dinner £8.50 Last dinner 8.45pm

Credit cards 1 2 3 5

★**St Leonards** Duff Av ☎ (0343) 7350

Homely, commercial hotel in a residential area.

17rm (6 3)(2fb) CTV in all bedrooms ® sB&B fr£18.40 sB&B fr£21.85 dB&B fr£28.75 dB&B fr£35

CTV 60P

Scottish & French **V** Lunch £4.60 Tea £1—£1.50 High Tea £3—£6 Dinner £9.20—£10.35 Wine £3.75 Last dinner 8.30pm

Credit cards 1 3 Ⓥ

✕✕**Enrico's** 15 Grey Friars St ☎ (0343) 2849

Small, friendly, Italian restaurant behind main street.

Closed Sun

French & Italian 56 seats ✱Lunch £3—£3.50&alc Dinner £8—£10alc Wine £3.60 Last dinner 9.30pm

Credit cards 1 2 3 5

Elgin — Ellon

ELIE
Fife
Map **11** NO44

★★***Golf*** Bank St ☎ (0333) 330209

22rm (9 6)(4fb) CTV in 1 bedroom

CTV 50P

Last dinner 9pm

Credit cards 1 2 3 5

ELLESMERE
Shropshire
Map **7** SJ33

★★**Grange** Grange Rd (Exec Hotel/Guestaccom) ☎ (069171) 3495

Closed 28 Dec—4 Jan

An attractive, Georgian, country house, the hotel provides comfortable, well-equipped, modern accommodation and a relaxing atmosphere. It stands in its own extensive grounds on the outskirts of the town.

13rm (11 1) Annexe: 3 (3fb) 1 CTV in all bedrooms ® T ✱sB&B fr£17 sB&B fr£25 dB&B fr£37

20P croquet *xmas*

✱Lunch fr£5.50 Tea fr£1.50 Dinner £9—£10 Wine £3.50 Last dinner 8pm

Credit cards 1 3 5 Ⓥ

★***Black Lion*** Scotland St ☎ (069171) 2418

Simple but homely accommodation is available in the small market town inn.

6rm (2fb) ®

CTV 30P 3

V Last dinner 9.30pm

Credit cards 1 2

★***Red Lion*** Church St ☎ (069171) 2632

Closed Xmas

Comfortable, homely 17th-century inn with modern accommodation.

7rm (1)(1fb)

CTV 16P billiards Disco wkly Live music and dancing wkly Cabaret wkly

Last dinner 9.30pm

ELLON
Grampian *Aberdeenshire*
Map **15** NJ93

★★★**Ladbroke** (Ladbroke) ☎ (0358) 20666 Telex 739200

The modern business hotel overlooks the town and the River Ythan.

40 (10fb) in 2 bedrooms CTV in all bedrooms ® sB&B £40—£44 dB&B £56—£60

200P CFA snooker *xmas*

Lunch £4.50—£6 Tea £1—£1.25 Dinner £9.50—£10&alc Wine £5.99 Last dinner 9.30pm

Credit cards 1 2 3 4 5 Ⓥ

★***Buchan*** ☎ (0358) 20208

Neatly appointed homely hotel in village centre close to River Ythan.

17rm (1)(3fb) CTV in all bedrooms

CTV 60P Disco 3 nights wkly

V Last dinner 6.45pm

★**New Inn** Market St ☎ (0358) 20425

Homely, commercial hotel close to the River Ythan.

12rm (3 4)(2fb) CTV in all bedrooms ® **T** S% ✱sB&B £14 sB&B £17 dB&B £26 dB&B £32

CTV 63P

V S% ✱Lunch £3.25—£4 Tea fr£1 High Tea £3.25—£4.75 Wine £4 Last high tea 7pm

Credit cards 1 2 3 5

✕**Jacobite Bistro** 41—43 Station Rd ☎ (0358) 22737

The informal little restaurant is open throughout the day for coffee and snacks in addition to its à la carte dinner menu.

Lunch not served Sun

English & French **V** 38 seats S% Lunch £4alc Dinner £9alc Wine £4.40 Last dinner 9.30pm

Credit cards 1 2 3 Ⓥ

ELTERWATER
Cumbria
Map **7** NY30

★**Britannia Inn** ☎ Langdale (09667) 210 Telex 8950511
Closed Xmas
Personally-managed, modest country inn.
10rm(1fb) CTV available in bedrooms ®
sB&B£17.25—£18.50 dB&B£34.50—£37
10P
V Bar lunch £5alc Dinner £9.75—£11.50 Wine £6 Last dinner 7.30pm
Credit cards 1 3 V

★***Eltermere*** (on unclass road between A593 & B5343) ☎ Langdale (09667) 207
Closed 5 Nov—Etr
Charming peaceful old mansion, standing in its own grounds.
14rm(3)®
16P nc5yrs
Last dinner 7.30pm

ELY
Cambridgeshire
Map **5** TL58

★★★**Fenlands Lodge** Soham Rd Stuntney (2m SE A142) ☎ (0353) 67047
Conveniently situated on the A142, this small, personal hotel offers comfortable accommodation.
Annexe: 9 CTV in all bedrooms ® T
CTV 20P Live music & dancing Sat *xmas*
International Lunch £7&alc Tea £1 High Tea £3&alc Dinner £9&alc Wine £4.45 Last dinner 10pm
Credit cards 1 2 3 5 V

✕**Old Fire Engine House** 25 St Mary's Street ☎ (0353) 2582
The 18th century house stands in the shadow of the cathedral, fronting a tiny green on the main road. Ely's fire engine was kept here at one time, and a fine portrait of it hangs in the bar. The best of fresh Fenland ingredients are the basis of an honest, simple cuisine, and you can pass through the tantalising aromas of the kitchen on your way from the oak-filled bar to the simply furnished dining room. Pictures and sculptures are on sale in two galleries.
Closed Public Hol's & 2wks fr 24 Dec
Dinner not served Sun
36 seats Lunch £9.50alc Dinner £10.50alc Wine £3.90 Last dinner 9pm 8P

EMBLETON
Northumberland
Map **12** NU22

★★**Dunstanburgh Castle** ☎ (066576) 203
The family hotel stands in rural surroundings within easy reach of the sea.
17rm(9)(3fb) ® ✱ sB&B£14.25 sB&B£16.25 dB&B£28.50 dB&B£33.50
CTV 20P 1 *xmas*
English & French ✱ Lunch £4.75—£6 Tea 95p—£2.20 Dinner £8.95 Wine £3.20 Last dinner 7.45pm
Credit cards 1 3 V

EMBOROUGH
Somerset
Map **3** ST65

★★**Court** ☎ Stratton-on-the-Fosse (0761) 232237
This busy, little country hotel, personally run by the owners, provides a good choice of menus with the emphasis on interesting dishes, fresh ingredients and careful cooking.
10rm(6 4)(2fb) 2 CTV in all bedrooms ® S%
sB&B £27.50—£28.50
dB&B £34.50—£39.50
35P *xmas*
French V Lunch fr£5.25&alc Tea fr£1.85&alc Dinner £7.50&alc Wine £4.50 Last dinner 9pm
Credit cards 1 3 V

EMSWORTH
Hampshire
Map **4** SU70

★★★*B* **Brookfield** Havant Rd ☎ (0243) 373363
Closed 24 Dec—1 Jan
Friendly well-run hotel with good bedrooms, but limited lunch facilities.
31rm(25 6) 1 CTV in all bedrooms ® T S% sB&B £36 dB&B £47
90P
English & French V Lunch £8&alc Tea 70p—£1.20 Dinner £8&alc Wine £4.95 Last dinner 9.30pm
Credit cards 1 2 3 5 V

✕**36 North St** 36 North St ☎ (0243) 375592
In this highly original first-floor cottage restaurant the customer can dine by Victorian gas light, pushing the bell on the table to summon attention. Food is carefully researched and enthusiastically stylish, with prompt service by friendly, beautifully turned-out staff.
Closed Sun & Mon
Lunch by reservation ony
V 48 seats ✱ Lunch £18alc Dinner £18alc Wine £5.95 Last dinner 11pm nc5yrs
Credit cards 1 2 3 5

ENFIELD
Greater London
Map **4** TQ39

★★★**Royal Chace** The Ridgeway ☎ 01-366 6500 Telex no 266628
Very busy commercial and conference hotel with tasteful restaurant and well-equipped bedrooms.
→

92rm(51➡41⋒)(5fb) CTV in all bedrooms ®✗ S% *sB&B➡⋒£41 dB&B➡⋒£51 Continental breakfast
☾300P CFA ⛟ ✽ ⛟
🍽English & Continental 🍽 S% *Lunch fr£8.50&alc Dinner fr£9&alc Wine £7.10 Last dinner 9.45pm
Credit cards 1 2 3 5

★★**Holtwhites** Chase Side ☎ 01-363 0124 Telex no 299670
Small privately owned hotel with friendly atmosphere.
30rm(19➡5⋒)(2fb) CTV in all bedrooms ® available in bedrooms **T** *sB&B£32.50—£42.50 sB&B➡⋒£38.50—£48.50 dB&B£48.50 dB&B➡⋒£55.50 **B**
☾CTV 30P 4🏠 nc 4yrs
V 🍽 ☕ *Lunch £12alc Tea £2—4&alc Dinner £9—£20&alc Wine £4.80 Last dinner 8pm
Credit cards 1 2 3 5 Ⓥ

✗✗***Norfolk*** 80 London Rd ☎ 01-363 0979
Old fashioned restaurant with extensive menu, using fresh materials, and pleasantly served.
Closed Sun & Bank Hols Lunch not served Sat Dinner not served Mon
🍽English & French **V** 70 seats Last dinner 10pm
Credit cards 1 2 3 4 5

EPPING
Essex
Map **5** TL40

★★★**Post House** High Rd, Bell Common (Trusthouse Forte) ☎ (0378) 73137 Telex no 81617
Hotel offers variety of types of bedroom and a good restaurant.
Annexe: 82➡ CTV in all bedrooms ®**T** sB&B➡£55 dB&B➡£69.50 **B**
☾95P CFA *xmas*
🍽 ☕ Last dinner 10.30pm
Credit cards 1 2 3 4 5

EPSOM
Surrey
Map **4** TQ26

★★**Heathside** (formerly Pickard) Brighton Rd ☎ Burgh Heath (07373) 53355
(For full entry see Burgh Heath)

✗**River Kwai** 4 East St ☎ (03727) 41475
Very good, authentic Thai dishes plus friendly service. Good value for money.
Lunch not served Sun
🍽Thai **V** 45 seats Lunch £2.90—£5.60&alc Dinner £3.50—£6.50&alc Wine £5.60 Last dinner 10.45pm 10P
Credit cards 1 3 5

ERBISTOCK
Clwyd
Map **7** SJ34

✗***Boat Inn*** ☎ Bangor-on-Dee (0978) 780143
This 16th-century building stands near the pretty church and is fronted by the River Dee. A stone-slabbed bar leads into the oak-beamed restaurant where an eloborate choice of well-cooked food is served.
Closed Mon (mid Sep—Apr) & 3wks Jan Dinner not served Sun (mid Sep—Apr)
🍽English & French 65 seats Last dinner 9.30pm 30P
Credit cards 1 2 3 5

ERISKA
Strathclyde *Argyllshire*
Map **10** NM94

★★★

★★★🌲**ISLE OF ERISKA, ERISKA**
(Prestige) ☎ Ledaig (063172) 371 Telex no 777040
Closed Dec—mid Feb
One of the first hotels to gain our Red Stars, this remains the epitome of the traditional country house style with afternoon tea with homemade cakes on arrival, a large joint carved at your table for dinner and lavish breakfasts from chafing-dishes on the sideboard, together with a house party atmosphere engendered by the owners, the Buchanan-Smiths. You cross a bridge to the island, continue along a drive bordered by trees and rhododendrons, and eventually the baronial style, granite house is revealed. 280 acres of garden, farm and moorland, offer magnificent views across the loch — where seals can sometimes be seen basking — to the Isle of Lismore. It is a happy place for naturalists, and you can play croquet or tennis, bathe or take part in various water sports. The farm provides a great deal of produce for the use of the kitchen, while the lochs and rivers are a source of the excellent fish featured on the menu. Indeed they keep an excellent table and you will enjoy very

much the six-course dinners. Naturally the bedrooms and the public rooms (hall, drawing room and library/bar) are comfortable and well done — but it is the unique atmosphere that makes this hotel so special. Besides the friendly, obliging staff, we and our members think it's unique in making guests feel truly at home.

16➡(1fb) CTV available in bedrooms ®**T** sB&B➡£73—£105(incl dinner) dB&B➡£146—£170(incl dinner)
☾P ⛟ ✽ 🎾 🎣 U croquet ♿ 🏠
Lunch £5—£20 High Tea £6 Dinner £25 Wine £5.95 Last dinner 8.30pm
Credit cards 1 2

ERMINGTON
Devon
Map **2** SX65

★★*B* **Ermewood House** Totnes Rd (Exec Hotel) ☎ Modbury (0548) 830741
Friendly, country house style hotel catering for the tourist and commercial trade.
10rm(7➡3⋒)(2fb) 1🛏 CTV in all bedrooms ®sB&B➡⋒£23—£28 dB&B➡⋒£48—£52 **B**
40P ⛟ ✽ *xmas*
🍽English & Continental **V** 🍽 ☕ Bar lunch £1.50—£7.50 Tea £1.75 Dinner £8.50&alc Wine £5 Last dinner 9.30pm
Credit cards 1 2 3 5 Ⓥ

ERSKINE
Strathclyde *Renfrewshire*
Map **11** NS47

★★★**Crest Hotel Erskine Bridge**
North Barr, Inchinnan (Crest) ☎ 041-812 0123 Telex no 777713
Purpose-built hotel on the banks of the Clyde near Erskine Bridge.
186➡(8fb)⊬ in 30 bedrooms CTV in all bedrooms ®S% sB&B➡£40—£54.44 dB&B➡£40—£70.03 **B**
Lift ☾CTV 300P ✽ CFA pitch & putt solarium gymnasium Live music and dancing Sat ♿ *xmas*
V 🍽 ☕ ⊬ Lunch £5.95—£8.95&alc Tea 55p Dinner £7.50—£11.50&alc Wine £6.25 Last dinner 9.45pm
Credit cards 1 2 3 4 5

ESHER
Surrey London plan **5** *B1*

★★**Haven** Portsmouth Rd (1m NE on A307) (Inter Hotel)
☎ 01-398 0023

The small, family-run, commercial hotel is situated beside the main road and the railway line. It provides a homely atmosphere, with compact bedrooms and a nicely appointed dining room serving good home-cooked dishes.

16rm(2➡4⋒) Annexe: 4rm(2➡2⋒) (3fb) CTV in 10 bedrooms ® in 10 bedrooms sB&B£22.50—£24 sB&B➡⋒£32.50 dB&B£34.50 dB&B➡⋒£43

CTV 20P 1🚗 ⛟ ⚘

🍷International ♣ ☕ Bar lunch £4—£5 Tea fr70p Dinner £6.50—£9.75 Wine £4.25 Last dinner 8.30pm

Credit cards [1] [2] [3] [5] Ⓥ

✕✕**Good Earth** 14—16 High St
☎ (0372) 62489

Modern Chinese restaurant specialising in regional cuisine.

🍷Chinese **V** 100 seats Lunch £10—£16&alc Dinner £10—£16&alc Wine £5 Last dinner 11.30pm ₱

Credit cards [1] [2] [3] [5]

✕***Shapla*** 34 High St ☎ (0372) 68497

A small modern well appointed Tandoori featuring authentic speciality cooking.

🍷Indian 45 seats 50P

Credit cards [1] [2] [3] [5]

ESKDALE
Cumbria
Map **7** NY10

★★**Bower House Inn** Eskdale Green
☎ (09403) 244

Closed Xmas Day

Delightful old inn nestling in the Eskdale valley.

6rm Annexe: 15➡ (4fb) ⚡ in bedrooms CTV in 15 bedrooms ®**T** sB&B£21.50 sB&B➡£23.50 dB&B£30 dB&B➡£35 **B**

60P ✿ ⟆

🍷International **V** ♣ S% Bar lunch 75p—£3.50&alc High Tea £1.50—£2 Dinner £11.50—£17&alc Wine £4.50 Last dinner 8.30pm

ESKDALEMUIR
Dumfries & Galloway *Dumfriesshire*
Map **11** NY29

★★*H* **Hart Manor** ☎ (05416) 217

Standing in a beautiful, remote situation, the attractively decorated and comfortably furnished little hotel has a deserved reputation for the standard of its food and for friendly, attentive service.

7rm(5⋒) (2fb) TV in 3 bedrooms ® sB&B£20 sB&B⋒£22.50 dB&B£36 dB&B⋒£60

TV 30P ⛟ ✿

V ♣ Bar lunch £2.90alc Dinner £10.50alc Wine £5 Last dinner 8pm

Credit card [3]

ETON
Berkshire
Map **4** SU97

✕✕**Antico** 42 High St ☎ Windsor (0753) 863977

Historic Italian restaurant with authentic cuisine.

Closed Sun & Bank Hols Lunch not served Sat

🍷Italian 65 seats S% Lunch £15—£16alc Dinner £15—£16alc Wine £5.40 Last dinner 11pm 8P nc 9yrs

Credit cards [1] [2] [3] [5]

ETTINGTON
Warwickshire
Map **4** SP24

❀★★⚘*HB* **Chase Country House** Banbury Rd ☎ Stratford-on-Avon (0789) 740000

Closed 24 Dec—3rd wk in Jan

(Rosette awarded for dinner only)

David Cunliffe's Victorian hotel has undergone many improvements lately, but the consistently high standard of its cuisine needed no such attention! British country house in style, it includes internationally known dishes transformed by his unmistakable touch — hickery-smoked rabbit or guinea fowl accompanied by his own smoked bacon, for example. Unusual English and French cheeses may be served with homemade date loaf or oatmeal biscuits, whilst desserts are creative and beautifully presented.

11rm(10➡1⋒) CTV in all bedrooms ®**T** ✈ sB&B➡⋒fr£39 dB&B➡⋒fr£51.50 **B**

50P ⛟ ✿ nc 8yrs

♣ Lunch fr£9.95 Dinner £12—£16&alc Wine £5.50 Last dinner 9pm

Credit cards [1] [2] [3] [5]

See advertisement under Stratford-upon-Avon

ETTRICKBRIDGE
Borders *Selkirkshire*
Map **11** NT32

★★⚘*H* **Ettrickshaws** (1m W off B7009)
☎ (0750) 52229

Closed mid Dec—mid Feb

Homely Victorian country mansion close to the River Ettrick in the Ettrick valley.

6➡ CTV in all bedrooms ® sB&B➡£26—£37 dB&B➡£42—£64 **B**

12P ⛟ ✿ ⟆ croquet nc 9yrs

🍷English & Continental ♣ ☕ ⚡ Lunch £3—£8 Tea fr£1.50 Dinner £13.50—£15 Wine £4.90 Last dinner 9pm

Credit cards [1] [2] [3] [5]

EVANTON
Highland *Ross & Cromarty*
Map **14** NH66

★★***Novar Arms*** ☎ (0349) 830210

Homely and informal commercial hotel in a small village.

10rm ✈

CTV 30P

🍷Mainly grills ♣ ☕ Last dinner 7.30pm

Credit card [3]

EVERCREECH
Somerset
Map **3** ST63

★★⚘**Maesmoor Glen** Shapway Ln
☎ (0749) 830369

An hospitable country house with an attractive garden.

12rm(5➡2⋒) (1fb) CTV in all bedrooms ® ✈ S% sB&B£22 sB&B➡⋒£28.50 dB&B£32 dB&B➡⋒£38.50 **B**

20P 3🚗 ⛟ ✿ 🎾(grass) croquet *xmas*

♣ ☕ S% Lunch £8 Tea £2.50 High Tea £5 Dinner £12.50 Wine £5 Last dinner 9pm

Credit cards [1] [2] [3] [5] Ⓥ

EVESHAM
Hereford & Worcester
Map **4** SP04

★★★**Evesham** Coopers Ln, off Waterside (Best Western) ☎ (0386) 49111
Telex no 339342

Closed Xmas

Standards are always improving at this family-run hotel, and comfortable accommodation plus interesting menus and a carefully-chosen wine list provide a relaxing stay for guests.

34rm(28➡5⋒) (1fb) CTV in all bedrooms ® S% ✱ sB&B➡⋒£38—£40 dB&B➡⋒£52—£55 **B**

50P ⛟ ✿ croquet putting

🍷International **V** ♣ ☕ S% Lunch £6.35—£7&alc Tea 60p Dinner £11.65alc Wine £4.80 Last dinner 9.30pm

Credit cards [1] [2] [3] [5]

★**Park View** Waterside ☎ (0386) 2639

Closed 23 Dec—4 Jan

Standing by the River Avon, the small, family-run hotel offers guests a warm welcome.

29rm(2fb) sB&B£12.50—£13.30 dB&B£25—£26.50

CTV 40P

♣ ☕ Bar lunch 90p—£2.50 Tea fr80p Dinner £6.25—£9.25 Wine £3.80 Last dinner 7pm

Credit cards [1] [3] Ⓥ

See advertisement on page 288

E

EWEN (nr Cirencester)
Gloucestershire
Map **4** SU09

★★★**Wild Duck Inn** ☎ Kemble (028577) 310

Cosy village inn with popular restaurant and pretty bedrooms.

8 (1fb) CTV in all bedrooms ® *sB&B fr£29 dB&B fr£38 Continental breakfast

CTV P Live music Fri & Sat *xmas*

English & French V Lunch fr£8&alc Tea fr75p Dinner £9.50—£11.50&alc Wine £4.95 Last dinner 9.45pm

Credit cards 1 2 3 5 V

EXEBRIDGE
Somerset
Map **3** SS92

★**Anchor Inn** ☎ Dulverton (0398) 23433

This attractive hotel is set in very pleasant gardens on the banks of the River Exe just outside Dulverton. It offers neat bedrooms and attentive service.

6rm(1)(1fb) ® *sB&B £13.50 dB&B £27 dB&B £30

CTV P

*Lunch £5&alc Dinner £8&alc Last dinner 8.30pm

Ewen — Exeter

EXETER
Devon
Map **3** SX99
See plan

★★★*HB* **Buckerell Lodge Crest** Topsham Rd (Crest) ☎ (0392) 52451 Telex no 42410 Plan **1** *C1*

A character main house dating from the 12th century has been extended and converted into a well-appointed hotel popular with businessmen. Standards of service and hospitable management are high, and a wide range of bedrooms caters for all requirements. The hotel is conveniently situated for both city and the M5 motorway.

54rm(53 1)(2fb) in 3 bedrooms CTV in all bedrooms ®T S% sB fr£44.50 dB fr£54.50(room only)

50P *xmas*

V S% Lunch £6.25—£7.25 Tea fr85p Dinner fr£12.25&alc Last dinner 9.45pm

Credit cards 1 2 3 4 5

★★★**Devon Motel** Exeter bypass, Matford (Brend) ☎ (0392) 59268 Telex no 42551 Not on plan

Situated close to the Exeter bypass, with modern extensions.

Annexe: 41rm(35 4)(3fb) CTV in all bedrooms ®T sB&B £27.60—£29.90 dB&B £34.50—£39.10

250P wkly Live music & dancing *xmas*

English & French Bar lunch £1.35—£5.75&alc Tea fr50p Dinner fr£7.40&alc Wine £5.25 Last dinner 9.15pm

Credit cards 1 2 3 5

See advertisement on page 290

★★★**Exeter Arms** Rydon Ln, Middlemoor (Toby) ☎ (0392) 35353 Plan **3A** *F2*

Modern purpose-built complex alongside primary road on outskirts of city.

37 (6fb) CTV in all bedrooms ®T (ex guide dogs) sB&B £19—£33.50 dB&B £28—£43.50

380P

V Lunch £7—£8&alc Dinner £7—£8&alc Wine £4.50 Last dinner 10.30pm

Credit cards 1 2 3 5

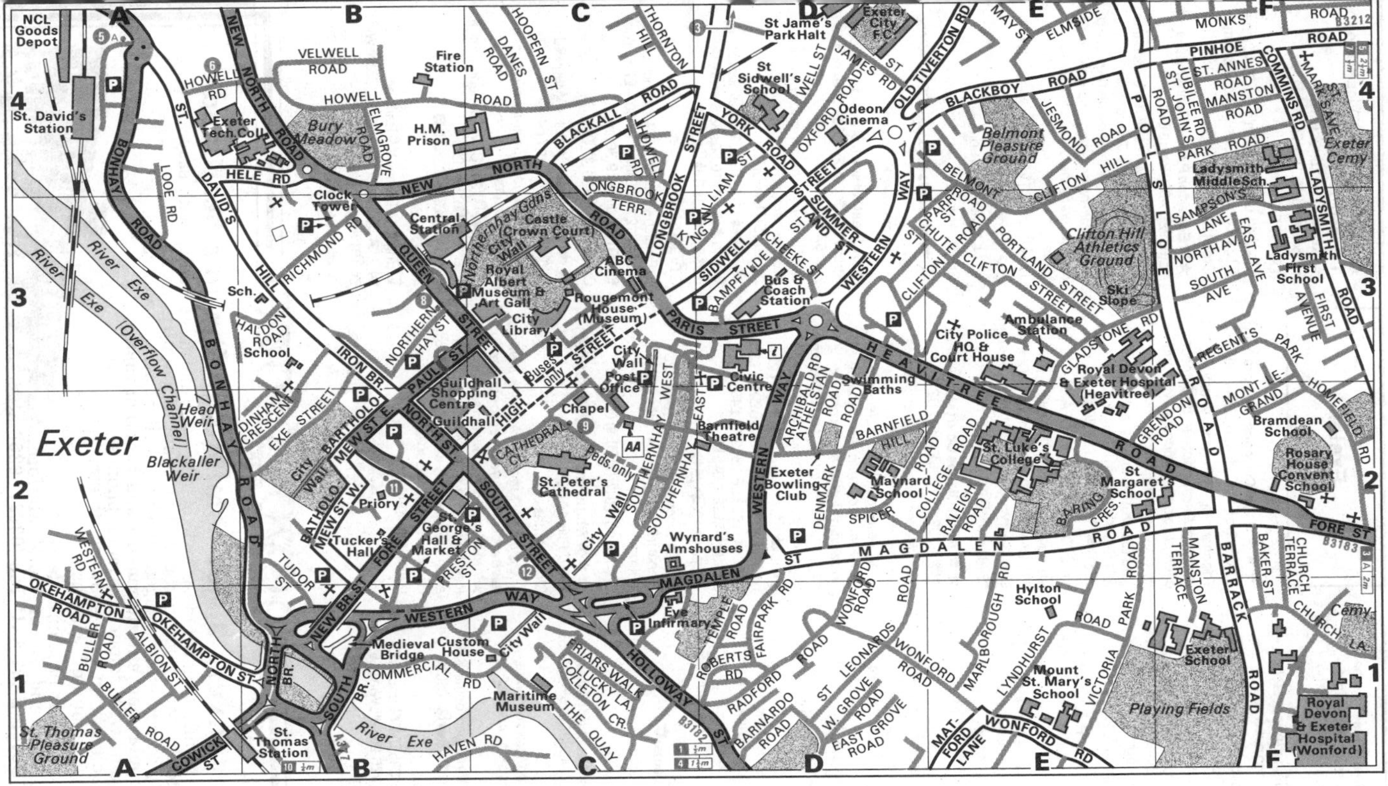

Exeter

1	Buckerell Lodge Crest ★★★
3	Edgerton Park ★★
3A	Exeter Arms ★★★
4	Exeter Moat House ★★★
5	Gipsy Hill ★★★
5A	Great Western ★★
6	Imperial ★★★
7	Red House ★★
8	Rougemont ★★★
9	Royal Clarence ★★★
10	St Andrews ★★
11	St Olaves Court ★★★
12	White Hart ★★★

E

★★★**Exeter Moat House** Topsham Road, Exeter bypass (Queens Moat) ☎ Topsham (039287) 5441 Telex no 42551 Plan **4** *C1*

The hotel bedrooms here are detached from the reception and public rooms.

44➡(1fb) CTV in all bedrooms ® **T** S% ✻sB&B➡fr£34.50 dB&B➡fr£44.50 B

☾ 100P CFA *xmas* ♿

English & French **V** Lunch £7.95&alc Tea 65p Dinner £7.95&alc Wine £4.95 Last dinner 9.45pm

Credit cards 1 2 3 5 V

★★★ **Gipsy Hill** Gipsy Hill Ln, Pinhoe (3m E on B3181) (Consort) ☎ (0392) 65252 Telex no 57515 Plan **5** *F2*

Located in a peaceful position on the edge of the city, with well appointed rooms.

20rm(19➡1⋒)(3fb) 1 CTV in all bedrooms ® **T** sB&B➡⋒fr£31 dB&B➡⋒fr£42 B

50P ✽ Live music & dancing Mon

English & French **V** Lunch £5.50&alc Dinner £7.50&alc Wine £4.50 Last dinner 9.30pm

Credit cards 1 2 3 4 5 V

★★★***Imperial*** St David's Hill ☎ (0392) 211811 Plan **6** *A4*

Built as a mansion during Queen Anne period, this hotel is situated in five acres of spacious sheltered grounds.

25rm(19➡2⋒)(1fb) CTV in all bedrooms **T** B

☾ CTV 70P 12 (charge) ✽

V Last dinner 9pm

Credit cards 1 2 3 5

★★★**Rougemont** Queen St (Mount Charlotte) ☎ (0392) 54982 Telex no 42455 Plan **8** *B3*

Recently modernised hotel in a central position, catering for the tourist and commercial trade.

68rm(64➡4⋒) CTV in all bedrooms ® **T** sB&B➡⋒fr£36.75 dB&B➡⋒fr£50 B

Lift ☾ 40P CFA *xmas*

English & French S% Lunch fr£5 Tea fr£1.75 Dinner fr£8.25&alc Wine £5.65 Last dinner 9.30pm

Credit cards 1 2 3 5 V

Exeter

★★★ **Royal Clarence** Cathedral Yard ☎ (0392) 58464 Telex no 23241 Plan **9** *C2*

The charming, 18th-century hotel, standing directly opposite the Cathedral, offers pleasant, traditional service and recently renovated accommodation.

62rm(56➡6⋒)(4fb) CTV in all bedrooms ® **T** S% ✻sB&B➡⋒£35—£40 dB&B➡⋒£52.50—£57.50 B

Lift ☾ 20P(75p per night) CFA

English & French **V** ✻Lunch £6.50&alc Tea £1.70 High Tea £4 Dinner £7.50&alc Wine £4.75 Last dinner 9.30pm

Credit cards 1 2 3 5

★★★***H*** **St Olaves Court** Mary Arches St ☎ (0392) 217736 Plan **11** *B2*

This attractive little hotel stands in a quiet road just off the city centre, facing into a small, walled garden complete with pond. Bedrooms are comfortable, and the Golsworthy Restaurant is worthy of mention, offering interesting dishes which represent excellent value for money.

8rm(3➡3⋒) Annexe: 4➡(3fb) CTV in all bedrooms ® **T** S% sB&B£21—£33 sB&B➡⋒£33 dB&B£28—£45 dB&B➡⋒£28—£45 B

☾ CTV 12P 2 ✽

V Lunch fr£6.95&alc Tea £1.25 Dinner fr£10.95 Wine £4.50 Last dinner 9.30pm

Credit cards 1 2 3 4 5 V

★★★**White Hart** 65 South St ☎ (0392) 79897 Plan **12** *C2*

Closed Xmas

One of the city's most ancient inns, the hotel has been carefully restored to equip rooms with modern facilities without sacrificing their original charm; particularly popular are the 15th-century wine room and bars. Friendly, traditional service standards prevail throughout.

61rm(41➡16⋒)(2fb) CTV in all bedrooms **T** sB&Bfr£24 sB&B➡⋒£30.25—£36.85 dB&B➡⋒£45.10—£52.80 B

Lift ☾ CTV 70P

✻Lunch £5.25&alc Tea 70p Dinner £12alc Wine £4.60 Last dinner 9.30pm

Credit cards 1 2 3 5

★★***Edgerton Park*** 84 Pennsylvania Rd ☎ (0392) 74029 Plan **3** *D4*

This small hotel with public bars is situated in a residential area. The compact bedrooms are for the most part equipped with private bathrooms or showers, and the hotel caters for the tourist and student trade.

17➡⋒(1fb) CTV in all bedrooms ® B

50P nc5yrs

V Last dinner 9pm

Credit cards 1 3

★★**Fairwinds** ☎ (0392) 832911 Not on plan

(For full entry see Kennford)

★★**Great Western** St David's Station Approach ☎ (0392) 74039 Telex no 42551 Plan **5A** *A4*

The family-run, character hotel, with its popular bars and restaurant, is situated close to St David's Station.

40rm(9➡11⋒)(1fb) CTV in all bedrooms ® S% ✻sB&B£16.50 sB&B➡⋒£19 dB&B£26 dB&B➡⋒£31 B

CTV 30P

English & French **V** Lunch £4.25 Tea £1—£1.50 Dinner £6.50—£7.50 Wine £3.90 Last dinner 9.30pm

Credit cards 1 2 3 5

★★**Red House** 2 Whipton Village Rd ☎ (0392) 56104 Plan **7** *F4*

Modern hotel in suburban location, short distance from town.

12rm(7➡5⋒)(2fb) CTV in all bedrooms ® **T** sB&B➡⋒£20—£25 dB&B➡⋒£30—£36.50 B

40P nc5yrs

English & French **V** Bar lunch £4—£4.30 Dinner £5.25—£5.75&alc Wine £4.10 Last dinner 9.30pm

Credit cards 1 2 3 5 V

★★St Andrews 28 Alphington Rd ☎ (0392) 76784 Plan **10** *B1*

Closed Xmas

Comfortable hotel with friendly atmosphere and good home cooking.

16rm(8⇌12fi)(2fb) CTV in all bedrooms ® T sB&B⇌fi£27—£30 dB&B⇌fi£38—£43 B

CTV 20P

Lunch £7alc Tea 80p—£1.10 Dinner £9alc Wine £4.75 Last dinner 8pm

Credit cards 1 2 3 V

Exeter — Exford

○Granada Lodge Junction 30, M5 Motorway, Sandgate ☎ (0392) 74044

58⇌fi Opened Summer 1986

XXOld Mill Ide (2m SW unclass rd off A30) ☎ (0392) 59480 Not on plan

Attractive old beamed restaurant offering interesting, well prepared food and some fine, rare wines.

Closed Sun, 24—26 Dec & 1 Jan

42 seats Lunch £5.45—£7.50&alc Dinner fr£10.75&alc Wine £4.95 Last dinner 9.45pm 12P

Credit cards 1 2 3

EXFORD

Somerset

Map **3** SS83

★★Crown Hotel & Restaurant ☎ (064383) 554

A 17th-century coaching inn, the Crown offers friendly service and a relaxed, convivial atmosphere in which to enjoy country pursuits. →

E

18 CTV in all bedrooms ® T sB&B £28—£38 dB&B £44—£56 B
40P U xmas
English & French V Lunch £7.50 Tea 85p Dinner £13.75 Wine £4.30 Last dinner 9.30pm
Credit cards 1 2 3 V

EXMOUTH
Devon
Map **3** SY08

★★★**Devoncourt** Douglas Av ☎ (0395) 272277
The hotel is set in four acres of sub-tropical grounds, overlooking the sea.
68 (10fb) CTV in all bedrooms ® T sB&B £27.50—£32.25 dB&B £55—£64.50 B
Lift ☾ 36P 9 (charged) CFA & (heated) (hard) sauna bath solarium gymnasium putting croquet xmas
English & French V Lunch £6&alc Tea fr90p Dinner £7.25&alc Wine £4.25 Last dinner 9.30pm
Credit cards 1 2 3

★★★**Imperial** The Esplanade (Trusthouse Forte) ☎ (0395) 274761
Stands in four acres of gardens, facing south.
58 (10fb) CTV in all bedrooms ® sB&B £45.50 dB&B £66.50 B
Lift ☾ 55P CFA (heated) (hard) sauna bath solarium xmas
Last dinner 9pm
Credit cards 1 2 3 4 5

★★★**Royal Beacon** The Beacon (Best Western) ☎ (0395) 264886
Sympathetically-modernised Georgian posting house, overlooking the sea.
32rm(30)(4fb) CTV in all bedrooms ® T S% *sB&B £23.25—£27.65 sB&B £23.25—£27.65 dB&B £46—£54 dB&B £46—£54 B
Lift 20P 10 CTV CFA snooker games room xmas
English & French V S% Lunch £5.95&alc Tea £1.85 High Tea £3 Dinner £9.25&alc Wine £5.75 Last dinner 9pm
Credit cards 1 2 3 4 5 V

★★**Barn** Foxholes Hill, off Marine Dr ☎ (0395) 274411
Friendly hotel with garden, set in an elevated position, with good sea views.
11rm(8 1)(4fb) CTV in 9 bedrooms TV in 2 bedrooms sB&B £18.50—£21.30 sB&B £18.50—£21.30 dB&B £37—£42.50 dB&B £37—£42.50 B
30P 3 (grass) croquet
Lunch £7.50alc Tea £1alc High Tea £1.50alc Dinner £11.50alc Wine £5 Last dinner 8pm

Exford — Fairy Cross

★★**Cavendish** 11 Morton Cres, The Esplanade ☎ (0395) 272528
Closed Dec—Feb except Xmas
Terraced hotel situated on the sea front with fine views and short distance to shops.
71rm(63)(4fb) sB&B £11—£13.90 sB&B £13—£15.90 dB&B £22—£27.50 dB&B £26—£31 B
Lift CTV 30P snooker Disco twice wkly Live music and dancing 3 nights wkly xmas
Lunch fr£4.50 Dinner fr£5.50 Wine £4.20 Last dinner 7.45pm
Credit cards 1 3

★★**Grand** Morton Cres, The Esplanade ☎ (0395) 263278
Closed 6 Dec—22 Dec & 3 Jan—15 Feb
Popular family hotel with views across estuary.
83rm(44 35)(5fb) CTV in 13 bedrooms TV in 70 bedrooms ® sB&B £24.15—£31.05 dB&B £43.70—£57.50 B
Lift 30P CFA snooker Live music and dancing 4 nights wkly (Feb—Nov)
V Lunch fr£6 Dinner fr£8 Wine £5.45 Last dinner 7.30pm

★★**Manor** The Beacon ☎ (0395) 272549
Terraced hotel in central location, overlooking park.
40rm(38 2)(6fb) CTV in all bedrooms sB&B £15.53—£18.40 dB&B £31.05—£36.80 B
Lift 10P 3 xmas
V Lunch £4—£4.40 Tea 55—60p Dinner £5—£5.50 Wine £4.25 Last dinner 8pm
Credit cards 1 3

★***Aliston House*** 58 Salterton Rd ☎ (0395) 274119
The Aperitif Bar of this friendly, welcoming hotel features an old, black-leaded range. Throughout, rooms are attractively decorated and the standard of service is good.
10rm(4) Annexe: 2 (1fb) CTV in 6 bedrooms ® B
CTV 16P
V Last dinner 8.30pm

XX**Guy's** The Strand ☎ (0395) 263086
The Tudor-style restaurant, with its lace covers and fresh flowers, occupies the first floor and overlooks lawns and gardens; French cuisine is served by attentive staff and a good atmosphere is assured.
Closed Sun & Feb
English & French 45 seats S% *Lunch fr£2.50 Dinner fr£10.55&alc Wine £5.95 Last dinner 9.30pm
Credit cards 1 2 3 5

FADMOOR
North Yorkshire
Map **8** SE68

X***Plough Inn*** ☎ Kirkbymoorside (0751) 31515
You must book well ahead to sample the delights of this tiny village inn on the edge of the North Yorkshire moors, where a good range of dishes is complemented by an excellent wine list.
Closed Sun, Mon, 1 wk Feb, 1 wk May & 1 wk Oct Lunch not served
English & French 25 seats Last dinner 8.30pm 15P

FAIRBOURNE
Gwynedd
Map **6** SH61

★★**Brackenhurst** ☎ (0341) 250226
Country house whose high position affords good views over the Mawddach Estuary.
10rm(1 1) TV available on request ® sB&B £13 sB&B £16 dB&B £26 dB&B £29 B
CTV 15P nc 14yrs
English & Continental Lunch £4.75 Tea £1.20 Dinner £7.25 Wine £3.50 Last dinner 8pm
Credit cards 1 3 V

FAIRFORD
Gloucestershire
Map **4** SP10

★★**Hyperion** London St ☎ Cirencester (0285) 712349
A charming small hotel in its own grounds offering pleasing service.
23rm(18 2)(5fb) CTV in all bedrooms ® T sB&B £28—£30 sB&B £30—£35 dB&B £38—£40 dB&B £40—£45 B
40P xmas
English & French V Lunch £5.50—£7.50 Tea £2—£5 Dinner £10.50—£12.50&alc Wine £5.25 Last dinner 9.30pm
Credit cards 1 2 3 5

FAIRLIE
Strathclyde *Ayrshire*
Map **10** NS25

XX**Fairlieburne House Hotel** ☎ (047556) 246
Set in gardens beside the Clyde, this hotel restaurant offers fine, imaginative food and excellent value set price menu.
Closed Mon 1st wk Feb & 1st 2 wks Oct Dinner not served Sun
French V 40 seats *Lunch £6—£10 Dinner £15.50 Wine £5.25 Last dinner 8.45pm 60P
Credit card 2

FAIRY CROSS
Devon
Map **2** SS42

★★★**Portledge** (off A39) ☎ Horns Cross (02375) 262
Closed Dec—Mar

Gracious stately home set in parkland. There is a fine galleried entrance hall and connections with Spanish Armada.

36rm(17⇌)(6fb) CTV in 1 bedroom *sB£10.50—£12.50 sB⇌£20.50—£25 dB£37—£45 dB⇌£45—£55(room only) B

CTV 40P CFA ⌘ ✽ ⇒ (heated) ⚲(hard) ♩ croquet

♉English & French **V** ♉ ☕ Lunch £3.50—£6.45 Tea £1.30—£1.75 Dinner £10.50—£12.25&alc Last dinner 8.45pm

Credit cards [1] [3] [5]

See advertisement under Bideford

FAKENHAM

Norfolk
Map **9** TF92

★★**Old Mill** Bridge St ☎ (0328) 2100

Many original features have been preserved in this attractive conversion of a former mill house. The friendly hotel now features Thai food cooked by the proprietor's wife.

9⋔ 1⊟ CTV in all bedrooms ®**T** ✈ *sB&B⋔£30 dB&B⋔£42 Continental breakfast

30P ⌘ ♩ nc

♉International ♉ ☕ Tea 40p&alc Dinner £8.50alc Wine £5.50 Last dinner 10pm

Credit cards [1] [2] [3] [5]

FALFIELD

Avon
Map **3** ST69

★★**Park** ☎ (0454) 260550

RS Sun

Rurally located small hotel offering friendly service and good food.

10rm(4⇌2⋔)(1fb) CTV in all bedrooms **T** sB£29.50—£37 sB⇌⋔£37 dBfr£41 dB⇌⋔fr£57(room only) B

100P ✽ *xmas*

♉Continental **V** ♉ Lunch £9.50alc Dinner £10.50alc Wine £7.50 Last dinner 10.15pm

Credit cards [1] [2] [3] [5]

FALKIRK

Central *Stirlingshire*
Map **11** NS87

★★★**Stakis Park** Arnot Hill, Camelon Rd (Stakis) ☎ (0324) 28331 Telex no 776502

Modern hotel complex set on outskirts of town.

55⇌⋔(3fb) ⊬ in 12 bedrooms CTV in all bedrooms ®**T** *sB⇌⋔fr£38 dB⇌⋔fr£48(room only) B

Lift ☾ CFA *xmas*

♉English & French ♉ ☕ *Lunch £4.25—£15 Tea 65p High Tea fr£5 Dinner £7.50—£20&alc Wine £3.85 Last dinner 9.45pm

Credit cards [1] [2] [3] [5]

✕**Pierre's** 140 Graham's Rd ☎ (0324) 35843.

The chef/patron's personal attention ensures a friendly atmosphere at this small restaurant.

Closed Sun, Mon, 25, 26 Dec, 1&2 Jan Lunch not served Sat

♉French 38 seats Lunch £4.25—£5.95&alc Dinner £9.50—£12.75&alc Wine £4.25 Last dinner 9.30pm 12P

Credit cards [1] [2] [3] [5] Ⓥ

FALMOUTH

Cornwall
Map **2** SW83 **See plan**

See also Mawnan Smith

★★★**Bay** Cliff Rd ☎ (0326) 312094 Telex no 45262 Plan **1** *D1*

Closed Nov—Feb

Large, traditional hotel on the sea front, overlooking Gyllynvrase beach, yet close to the town centre.

36⇌⋔(2fb) CTV in all bedrooms ®**T** S% sB&B⇌⋔£24.75—£36 dB&B⇌⋔£49.50—£72 →

F

Lift ☾50P✿sauna bath solarium nc 10yrs
♈☕S% Lunch £5.50 Tea £1—£2.50
Dinner £8 Wine £4.85 Last dinner 9.30pm
Credit cards 1 2 3 4 5 Ⓥ

★★★ *L* **Falmouth** ☎(0326) 312671
Telex no 45262 Plan **5** *D2*
Closed Xmas
Comfortable, large, modernised hotel in its own grounds on the sea front.
73🛁(8fb) 1🛏CTV in all bedrooms ®T S%
sB&B🛁£28—£50.50 dB&B🛁£56—£89
B
Lift ☾90P CFA✿ ⛱(heated) snooker
solarium ♿
☋English & French ♈☕⚡S% Lunch
£6.50&alc Tea £1—£2.50 Dinner
£11.50&alc Wine £4.85 Last dinner 10pm
Credit cards 1 2 3 4 5 Ⓥ

★★★ *L* ***Greenbank*** Harbourside
☎(0326) 312440 Telex no 45240 Plan **6** *C3*
Closed 24 Dec—1 Feb
Set beside the River Fal with its own quay, this well appointed hotel offers hospitality and character.

F

Falmouth

40rm(35🛁5⋔)(1fb) CTV in all bedrooms
®T B
Lift ☾45P 30🚗🐟
☋English & French **V** ♈ ☕ Last dinner
10pm
Credit cards 1 2 3 5

★★★ **Green Lawns** Western Ter
☎(0326) 312734 Telex no 45169 Plan **7**
B2
Closed 24—30 Dec
Built in 1920 in the style of a French château, the hotel is set in 1½ acres of terraced lawns.
41rm(36🛁3⋔)(9fb) CTV in all bedrooms
®T sB&B£18.40—£35.65
sB&B🛁⋔£31.05—£35.65
dB&B£38.24—£54.04
dB&B🛁⋔£38.24—£54.04 B

☾60P CFA✿⛱(heated) squash
sauna bath solarium gymnasium Live
music and dancing Sat ♿
☋English & French **V** ♈ ☕⚡ Lunch
£6.50—£7&alc Tea £1—£2 High Tea £2
Dinner £10&alc Wine £4.75 Last dinner
10pm
Credit cards 1 2 3 4 5 Ⓥ

★★★ **Gyllyngdune** Melville Rd
☎(0326) 312978 Plan **8** *C1*
Closed Jan
Old Georgian manor house situated in beautiful gardens overlooking the bay.
35rm(29🛁)(3fb) 3🛏CTV in all bedrooms
✱sB&B£17.50—£22.50
sB&B🛁£17.50—£22.50 dB&B£35—£51
dB&B🛁£35—£61 B
☾#35P 4🚗(charged)✿⛱(heated)
sauna bath solarium gynmasium *xmas*
☋Continental **V** ♈ ☕ Lunch £4.95 Tea
70p Dinner £7.50 Wine £4.25 Last dinner
9pm
Credit cards 1 2 3 4 5 Ⓥ
See advertisement on page 296

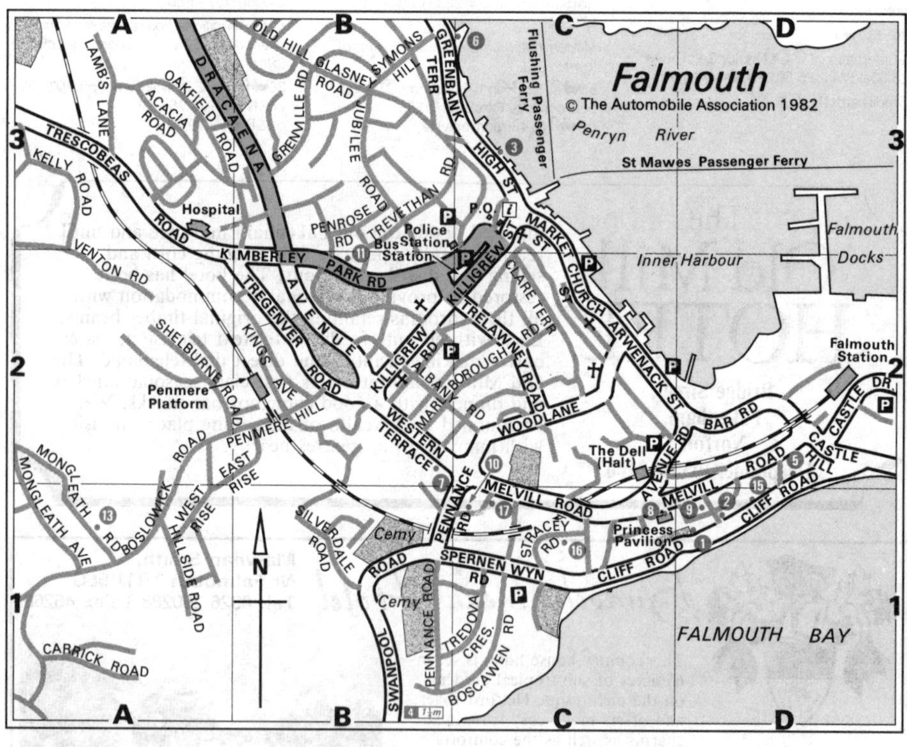

Falmouth

1 Bay ★★★
2 Carthion ★★
3 Continental ✕
4 Crill House ★★
5 Falmouth ★★★
6 Greenbank ★★★
7 Green Lawns ★★★
8 Gyllyngdune ★★★
9 Lerryn ★★
10 Melville ★★
11 Park Grove ★★
13 Penmere Manor ★★★
15 Royal Duchy ★★★
16 Hotel St Michaels ★★★
17 Somerdale ★★

★★★ *HBL* **Penmere Manor** Mongleath Rd (Best Western) ☎ (0326) 314545 Telex no 45266 Plan **13** *A1*

Closed Xmas

An attractive Georgian house with modern extensions, set in quiet, well kept grounds. It is managed by the Pope family and their helpful and pleasant staff who provide a comfortable and relaxed atmosphere. The hotel has been tastefully modernised and the comfortable bedrooms have good private facilities. Dinner is selected from an interesting, varied menu.

28rm(25 3) Annexe: 5rm(2 3)(5fb) CTV in all bedrooms ®T sB&B £26.50—£30 dB&B £44—£50 B

40P (heated) games room Bar lunch 80p—£3 Tea £1 High Tea £4 Dinner £11 Wine £4.95 Last dinner 8.30pm

Credit cards 1 2 3 5 Ⓥ

See advertisement on page 296

Falmouth

★★★ *B* **Royal Duchy** Cliff Rd (Brend) ☎ (0326) 313042 Telex no 42551 Plan **15** *D1*

Comfortable, hospitable, well-appointed hotel with good food and open sea views.

43 (10fb) CTV in all bedrooms **T** sB&B £24.15—£27.60 dB&B £36.80—£62.10 B

Lift CTV 35P (heated) sauna bath solarium Live music and dancing 3 nights wkly *xmas*

English & French Lunch fr £4.95 Tea fr 78p Dinner fr £7.50&alc Wine £4.75 Last dinner 9pm

Credit cards 1 2 3 5

See advertisement on page 297

★★★ *HL* **Hotel St Michaels** Cliff Rd (Consort) ☎ (0326) 312707 Telex no 45540 Plan **16** *D1*

Situated in four acres of prize-winning gardens that slope down to the beach. This hotel has fine views of the Cornish coastline.

60rm(45 15) Annexe: 15rm(13 2)(15fb) in 22 bedrooms CTV in all bedrooms ®T S% sB&B £24—£37 dB&B £48—£72 B

Lift 85P (heated) snooker sauna bath solarium gymnasium Disco wkly Live music and dancing twice wkly *xmas*

English & French **V** S% Lunch £6—£12&alc Tea £1—£1.50 High Tea £5 Dinner £9—£11.50&alc Wine £5 Last dinner 10pm

Credit cards 1 2 3 5

See advertisement on page 296

★★ *HL* **Carthion** Cliff Rd ☎ (0326) 313669 Plan **2** *D1*

Closed Nov—Feb

Comfortable, family owned hotel with fine views over Falmouth Bay.

18rm(12 6) CTV in all bedrooms sB&B £16—£20.50 dB&B £32—£41 B

18P nc 10yrs

English & French **V** Bar lunch 70p—£4 Tea 45p—£1 Dinner £9 Wine £4 Last dinner 8pm

Credit cards 1 2 3 5 Ⓥ

F

F

The Gyllyngdune Manor Hotel

AA ★ ★ ★

Melville Road, Falmouth, Cornwall TR11 4AR

Telephones: (0326) Management: 312978 Guests: 311479

Old Georgian manor house, romantically situated in two acres of beautiful gardens, overlooking the Bay and Estuary. Guaranteed away from traffic, but within ten minutes' walk of the town centre. Very large car park, covered space if required. Luxury indoor heated swimming pool, games room, Sauna and Solarium. Golf at Falmouth Golf Club. 95% rooms en-suite and colour TV. Every comfort with personal attention the primary consideration. Gourmet cuisine, table d'hôte, à la carte our speciality and highly recommended.

Penmere Manor Hotel

★ ★ ★ HBL

Mongleath Road, Falmouth
Tel. 0326 314545

This fine Georgian Mansion situated in 5 acres of secluded gardens and woodland is personally run by David and Rachel Pope with their son Andrew and daughter Elizabeth. Each of the attractive bedrooms are individually designed and decorated and all have private facilities en-suite, colour TV, hair dryer, clock/radio, telephone and tea/coffee making facilities. There are two residents lounges with games tables, a cellar games room, and heated outdoor swimming pool.

OUR NEW INDOOR LEISURE COMPLEX IS DUE FOR COMPLETION IN SPRING 1987

HOTEL & CONFERENCE CENTRE, Gyllyngvase Beach, Seafront, Falmouth, South Cornwall
Tel: (0326) 312707 Tlx: 45540

Spoil yourself for choice

Just look at what you get with us ...

- Indoor pool, jacuzzi, sauna & solarium
- Free squash, watersports, golf & Trimnasium
- Bath/shower in every room
- Only yards from beach
- Beautiful panoramic views
- Family suites

GLENROCK HOTELS   AA ★ ★ ★   HL

- Apartments
- Special offers & children's reductions
- 4 acres of championship gardens
- Exceptional home-cooked food
- Friendly service

★★*HB* **Crill House** Golden Bank (2½m W on unclass rd) ☎ (0326) 312994 Plan **4** *B1*

Closed end Oct—mid Mar

Small, comfortable, friendly hotel in a peaceful rural location.

11 (3fb) CTV in all bedrooms ® sB&B £21.50—£25.50

22P 1 (heated)

English & Continental Bar lunch £1—£3.50 Tea £1—£2.50 Dinner £9.25&alc Last dinner 8pm

Credit cards 1 3 5 V

Falmouth

★★*H* **Lerryn** De Pass Rd ☎ (0326) 312489 Plan **9** *D1*

Closed 7 Oct—Apr

Small hotel in quiet position near sea front.

20rm (10 10)(2fb) CTV in all bedrooms ® S% sB&B £12.50—£15.50 dB&B £22—£28

13P 2 (£9) nc6yrs

V S% Tea fr £2 Dinner £6.50—£8&alc Wine £2.10 Last dinner 8pm

★★**Melville** Sea View Rd ☎ (0326) 312134 Plan **10** *C2*

Closed Dec & Jan

Detached hotel in 2 acres of sub-tropical gardens.

22rm (4 18)(3fb) sB&B £15.95 dB&B £29.90

CTV 20P 10 (£12 per week) putting Live music and dancing Mon & Fri *xmas*

Lunch £4 Dinner £8.50&alc Wine £4.95 Last dinner 8pm

F

★★**Park Grove** Kimberley Park Rd ☎(0326) 313276 Plan **11** *B2*

Closed Nov—Mar

Friendly, comfortable, family hotel opposite the park and gardens.

17rm(15⋒)(4fb) CTV in all bedrooms Ⓡ sB&B£12.50—£15 sB&B⋒£12.50—£15 dB&B£25—£30 dB&B⋒£25—£30

25P

V ♁ ☕ Bar lunch £1—£3.50 Tea 50p—£1.50 Dinner fr£7 Wine £4.20 Last dinner 7.30pm

Credit cards 1 3 Ⓥ

Falmouth

★★**Somerdale** Seaview Rd ☎(0326) 312566 Plan **17** *C1*

Closed Xmas & Jan

Situated in a quiet, residential area, the hotel provides well-equipped bedrooms, many with en suite facilities. Special holidays include those with spring garden, golf and bowling themes.

18rm(11🛁) Annexe: 4🛁⋒(5fb) CTV in all bedrooms Ⓡ T ✖ sB&B£15.50—£17.50 sB&B🛁⋒£17.50—£19.50 dB&B£31—£35 dB&B🛁⋒£35—£39 B

13P ✿ pool table

♁ ☕ Bar lunch £1—£6 Tea 60p—£2.75 Dinner £9—£12 Wine £4.50 Last dinner 8.15pm

Credit cards 1 2 3 5 Ⓥ

✕**Continental** 29 High St ☎(0326) 313003 Plan **3** *C3*

A cellar restaurant in the centre of the town, the Continental features dishes from various parts of Europe matched by wines

F

of similar origin. Local fish figures large on the menu, and steaks are also available, together with light à la carte lunches.

Closed Sun Lunch not served

Continental **V** 45 seats Dinner £10alc Wine £5.20 Last dinner 11pm

Credit cards 2 3 5

FAREHAM
Hampshire
Map **4** SU50

★★ *B* **Red Lion** East St (Whitbread)
☎ (0329) 239611 Telex no 86204

Well-appointed coaching inn with excellent bedrooms.

33🛁(3fb) 1 CTV in all bedrooms ®T sB&B🛁fr£40 dB&B🛁fr£50

CTV 80P 3

English & Continental **V** Lunch fr£6.75&alc Dinner £10.50alc Wine £5.30 Last dinner 10pm

Credit cards 1 2 3 5 Ⓥ

FARINGDON
Oxfordshire
Map **4** SU29

★★ *B* **Faringdon** Market Pl
☎ (0367) 20536

Extensively modernised, the hotel features compact, well-equipped bedrooms and a new restaurant with set and à la carte Continental menus.

11🚿 Annexe: 1🚿(1fb) CTV in all bedrooms ®T S% ✱sB&B🚿£22–£28.50 dB&B🚿£38.50

3P

French Lunch £6.95 Tea fr85p Dinner £8.50&alc Wine £5.25 Last dinner 10pm

Credit cards 1 2 3 5 Ⓥ

✕✕ **Sinclairs** 6 Market Pl ☎ (0367) 20945

Small, pretty restaurant offering short menu of traditional dishes.

Closed Sun & Mon Lunch not served

V 34 seats Dinner £9alc Wine £4 Last dinner 9.30pm

Credit cards 1 2 3 5

FARMBOROUGH
Avon
Map **3** ST66

✕✕ **Conways** The New Inn
☎ Timsbury (0761) 70350

There is an inn-like atmosphere to this country-style restaurant with its charming dining room and bar. Both lunch and dinner menus offer a good choice, and service is friendly.

Dinner not served Sun

English & French **V** 83 seats Lunch £9.75alc Dinner £13.25&alc Wine £6.25 Last dinner 10pm 70P nc 12yrs Live music Tue–Sat & Sun lunch

Credit cards 1 3

FARNBOROUGH
Hampshire
Map **4** SU85

★★★ **Queens** Lynchford Rd (Anchor)
☎ (0252) 545051 Telex no 859637

A well appointed hotel with coffee shop and à la carte restaurant, as well as leisure centre.

110🛁🚿(4fb) in 18 bedrooms CTV in all bedrooms ®T S% ✱sB&B🛁🚿£49–£56 dB&B🛁🚿£59–£66

170P CFA (heated) sauna bath solarium gymnasium

English & French **V** ✱Lunch £6–£11&alc Tea 50p High Tea £2.50–£5 Dinner £9.95&alc Wine £5.75 Last dinner 10pm

Credit cards 1 2 3 4 5 Ⓥ

✕ **Wings Cottage Chinese** 32 Alexandra Rd, North Camp ☎ (0252) 544141

This compact, popular restaurant offers a friendly welcome and a choice between good-value set meals and the more expensive à la carte menu which includes some traditional duck specialities and a selection of stir-fry dishes, all backed by admirably attentive service.

Chinese 50 seats Lunch £15alc Dinner £15–£20alc Wine £6.50 Last dinner 10.30pm 20P

Credit cards 1 2 3 5

FARNHAM
Surrey
Map **4** SU84

★★★ **Bush** The Borough (Anchor)
☎ (0252) 715237 Telex no 858764

A 17th-century Coaching House with well equipped bedrooms, friendly, helpful staff coffee shop and restaurant.

65rm(62🛁3🚿)(2fb) 1 in 10 bedrooms CTV in all bedrooms ®
✱sB&B🛁🚿£47–£54
dB&B🛁🚿£57–£64

60P CFA *xmas*

✱Lunch fr£6.95&alc Tea fr£1.60 Dinner fr£6.95&alc Wine £5.95 Last dinner 10.30pm

Credit cards 1 2 3 4 5 Ⓥ

★★ **Bishop's Table** 27 West St (Best Western) ☎ (0252) 710222

An 18th-century Hostelry with own walled garden, country Kitchen, wine bar and intimate a la carte restaurant.

7🛁 Annexe: 9rm(7🛁)(1fb) 1 CTV in all bedrooms ® sB&B£37–£40 sB&B🛁£37–£40 dB&B£47.50–£52.50 dB&B🛁£47.50–£52.50

V Lunch £5.50–£6&alc Tea fr£1.50 Dinner £10.50–£12&alc Wine £5.25 Last dinner 9.30pm

Credit cards 1 2 3 5 Ⓥ

★★ **Trevena House** Alton Rd
☎ (0252) 716908 Telex no 946240

Closed 24 Dec–5 Jan

Hotel has comfortable, smart bedrooms, restaurant provides snack lunches and well-cooked dinners.

20rm(17🛁3🚿)(4fb) CTV in all bedrooms ®T S% sB&B🛁🚿£34–£39.50 dB&B🛁🚿£42–£49.50

30P (heated) (hard)

S% Tea £1.25 Dinner £11alc Wine £5.95 Last dinner 9.15pm

Credit cards 1 2 3 5 Ⓥ

Farnham — Felixstowe

✕✕Viceroy 23 East St ☎ (0252) 710949

This is an elegant restaurant with a refined atmosphere and silver service. The menu offers a good choice of Tandoori specialities, authentic curries and regional dishes, all well spiced and freshly cooked.

Closed Xmas day & Boxing day

Indian **V** 45 seats S% ✱ Lunch fr£7&alc Dinner £10alc Wine £5.50 Last dinner 11.30pm

Credit cards 1 2 3 4 5

✕Guishan Tandoori 53 Farnborough Rd, Heath End ☎ (0252) 22822

The small, comfortable Indian restaurant features popular regional dishes and Tandoori specialities. The atmosphere is very relaxing and the service quietly efficient.

Indian **V** 40 seats ✱ Lunch fr£5.50 Dinner fr£6 Wine £5.30 Last dinner 11.30pm 30P

Credit cards 1 2 3 5 Ⓥ

FARNLEY TYAS
West Yorkshire
Map **7** SE11

✕Golden Cock ☎ Huddersfield (0484) 661979

This restaurant is part of a charming village inn set in picturesque countryside. The menu specialises in game and in season and in fish dishes, the overall standard being high and helpings generous. Good-value house wines are supplemented by a connoisseur's list. Service is friendly and attentive, the atmosphere warm and relaxing.

Lunch not served Sat
Dinner not served Sun

English & Continental **V** 48 seats Lunch £7.95&alc Dinner £14.50&alc Wine £4.95 Last dinner 9.45pm 70P

Credit cards 1 2 3 4 5

FARRINGTON GURNEY
Avon
Map **3** ST55

★★*HBL* Country Ways
(see red box top of next column)

✕✕Old Parsonage Main St ☎ Temple Cloud (0761) 52211

This pleasant, stone-built country house contains a comfortable restaurant, well appointed with antique furnishings and gleaming silverware. There is a selection of appetising starters and well prepared traditional dishes using good materials anc fresh vegetables. The desserts are mouth-watering and the short, well-chosen wine list complements the good food.

Closed Mon, 25—28 Dec & Good Fri
Dinner not served Sun

English & French 26 seats S% Lunch £18.20alc Dinner £18.20alc Wine £5.20 Last dinner 10pm 100P

★★*HBL* Country Ways Marsh Ln ☎ Temple Cloud (0761) 52449

Closed 2wks Xmas

An attractive stone house in its own grounds overlooking rolling countryside, it has been tastefully renovated by Desmond and Susan Pow. The bedrooms are very pleasant and the beamed restaurant is most attractive. There is a choice of dishes for dinner, but lunch is only served by prior arrangement.

6rm(5➡1⋒) CTV in all bedrooms Ⓡ S% sB&B➡⋒£29.90—£35.55 dB&B➡⋒£39.75—£44.80

10P ✽ nc8yrs

V S% Lunch £7.50—£11.50 Tea £1.50—£4.50 Dinner £9.50—£12.50 Wine £4.50 Last dinner 8.30pm

Credit cards 1 2 3 5 Ⓥ

See advertisement under Wells

FAUGH
Cumbria
Map **12** NY55

★★★*B* String of Horses Inn ☎ Hayton (022870) 297

A quaint old world inn with white facade and leaded windows.

13rm(8➡5⋒)3 CTV in all bedrooms Ⓡ**T** sB&B➡⋒£38—£48 dB&B➡⋒£48—£68

CTV 50P (heated) sauna bath solarium gymnasium

English & French **V** Lunch £7alc Dinner £8.50—£12.95&alc Wine £5.50 Last dinner 10.15pm

Credit cards 1 2 3 5 Ⓥ

FAVERSHAM
Kent
Map **5** TR06

✕✕Read's Painters Forstal ☎ (0795) 535344

A sleepy village in a relatively unspoiled area of the countryside houses this pretty restaurant, which offers a warm welcome to a wide range of clients. The French menu features a balanced selection of well-prepared meat and fish dishes accompanied by a wine list that caters for most tastes.

Closed Sun & Boxing Day

French 40 seats Lunch £8.50—£10&alc Dinner £16alc Wine £5.40 Last dinner 10pm 40P

Credit cards 2 3 5

FEARNAN
Tayside *Perthshire*
Map **11** NN74

★Tigh-an-Loan (Guestaccom) ☎ Kenmore (08873) 249

RS Nov—Etr

Cosy, personally-run hotel overlooking Loch Tay.

9rm(1➡)(1fb) Ⓡ available in bedrooms sB&Bfr£14 dB&Bfr£28 dB&B➡fr£32

CTV 25P ✽

V Bar lunch £3.50alc Tea 60palc Dinner £7.50alc Wine £3.50 Last dinner 8pm

Ⓥ

FELIXSTOWE
Suffolk
Map **5** TM33

★★★★Orwell Moat House Hamilton Rd (Queens Moat) ☎ (0394) 285511

The service is friendly and hospitable at this traditional hotel.

60➡⋒(10fb) CTV in all bedrooms **T** S% ✱ sB➡⋒£42.25—£50 dB➡⋒£55.50—£65(room only)

Lift ☾ 150P 20 CFA ✽ Live music and dancing Sat

English & French **V** S% ✱ Lunch £8&alc Tea £1 Dinner £9&alc Wine £6.50 Last dinner 9.45pm

Credit cards 1 2 3 5 Ⓥ

★★Marlborough Sea Front ☎ (0394) 285621 Telex no 987047

The hotel is located on the sea front, 250 yards south of the new pier leisure complex. Recently refurbished, it provides accommodation in a range of comfortable bedrooms.

55rm(35➡)(2fb) 1 CTV in all bedrooms Ⓡ in 35 bedrooms **T** sB&B£22.50—£23.60 sB&B➡£29.75—£31 dB&B£32.50—£34.20 dB&B➡£39.50—£41.50

Lift ☾ CTV 19P *xmas*

English & French **V** ✱ Lunch £4.75—£6.75&alc Tea 50p—£1.50 Dinner £7—£7.50&alc Wine £4.50 Last dinner 9.45pm

Credit cards 1 2 3 5 Ⓥ

★★*Ordnance* 1 Undercliff Road West (Exec Hotels/Guestaccom) ☎ (0394) 273427

RS Xmas Day

11rm(4⋒)(1fb) CTV in all bedrooms Ⓡ**T**

CTV 55P

English & Continental Last dinner 10.30pm

Credit cards 1 2 3 5

★★Waverley Wolsey Gdns ☎ (0394) 282811

Closed 25 & 26 Dec

Comfortable, family run hotel adjacent to the town centre with views overlooking the bay.

12rm(9)CTV in all bedrooms ®T sB&B£27.50 sB&B£37 dB&B£42 dB&B£51.50 B

CTV 26P 1(£2 per night)

French V Lunch £4.95&alc Tea £1.50 High Tea £3.50 Dinner £7.50&alc Wine £6 Last dinner 9.30pm

Credit cards [1] [2] [3] [5] (V)

FELSTED
Essex
Map **5** TL62

XX**Boote House** Great Dunmow (0371) 820279

The cottagey lounge bar and panelled dining room of this restaurant reflect the age of the building, erected by one Mr Boote in 1686. The attentive proprietors offer a short à la carte menu of European dishes and an inexpensive set-price selection.

Closed Mon, Tue, 2wks Feb & 1st 2wks Sep Lunch served Sun only Dinner not served Sun

International **V** 70 seats Lunch £8—£12 Dinner £14—£16&alc Wine £5.40 Last dinner 10pm Live music Fri & Sat

Credit cards [1] [2] [3] [5]

FELTHAM
Greater London Plan **5** A2

X**Hyatt Peking** 82 The Centre 01-890 2648

Closed Sun & Xmas

Cantonese & Pekinese 70 seats Lunch £7.50—£9.90 Dinner £7.70—£9.90&alc Wine £4.50 Last dinner 11pm

Credit cards [1] [2] [3] [5]

FENNY BENTLEY
Derbyshire
Map **7** SK14

★★**Bentley Brook Inn** Thorpe Cloud (033529) 278

Detached gabled house on the edge of the Peak District National Park.

9rm(3)(1fb) CTV in all bedrooms ®T sB&B£20—£25 sB&B£25—£30 dB&B£30—£35 dB&B£35—£40 B

CTV 65P

V Lunch £5—£13.75 Tea 60p—£3.50 High Tea £1.95—£6.50 Dinner £8.75—£13.75 Wine £4 Last dinner 9.30pm

Credit card [1]

FENNY BRIDGES
Devon
Map **3** SY19

★**Fenny Bridges** Honiton (0404) 850218

An inn-style small hotel in own grounds beside A30.

6rm(1fb) CTV in all bedrooms ®T sB&B£14.50 dB&B£24.50 B

CTV 50P

English & French Lunch fr£5.50 Tea fr£1.45 Dinner fr£7.50 Wine £4.35 Last dinner 9.30pm

Credit cards [1] [2] [3] [5] (V)

FERMAIN BAY
Guernsey
See **Channel Islands**

FERNDOWN
Dorset
Map **4** SU00

★★★★**Dormy** New Rd (De Vere) (0202) 872121 Telex no 418301

Attractive hotel with well-appointed bedrooms, some in individual bungalows in hotel's extensive grounds.

133rm(128 5)(6fb) 2 CTV in all bedrooms ®T sB&B£55—£60 dB&B£85—£95 B →

Lift ☾CTV 200P CFA ❀ ▭(heated) ⚲(hard) squash snooker sauna bath solarium gymnasium Disco Fri (in summer) Live music and dancing Sat ♿ *xmas*

☊English & French **V** ♆ ☕ Lunch £8.50—£9&alc Tea £1—£1.50 Dinner £11—£12&alc Wine £7 Last dinner 9.30pm

Credit cards 1 2 3 4 5 Ⓥ

See advertisement under Bournemouth

★★ **Coach House Motel** Tricketts Cross (junc A31/A348) (ExecHotel) ☎ (0202) 871222

Modern hotel where all bedrooms are sited in individual units.

Annexe: 44rm(32➡12⋒) CTV in all bedrooms ®T S% sB&B➡⋒£27—£29 dB&B➡⋒£39.50—£42 B

100P CFA

☊Mainly grills ♆ ☕ Bar lunch £2.50—£7 Tea 60p Dinner £6.25—£6.75&alc Wine £5.25 Last dinner 9.30pm

Credit cards 1 2 3 5 Ⓥ

FIDDINGTON

Somerset

Map **3** SP24

✕**Baron's Table** Manor Farm ☎ Nether Stowey (0278) 732797 Telex no 46398

The charming, country-style restaurant offers a fixed price menu for dinner only, except on Sundays when a traditional roast lunch is served. Local raw materials are used in the preparation of the food, and a vegetarian dish is always available; wines are enterprisingly chosen.

Closed Mon Dinner not served Sun

☊English & French **V** 50 seats ✱Lunch £7alc Dinner £10alc Wine £4.75 Last dinner 9.30pm 30P Live music Fri

Credit cards 1 2 3 5 Ⓥ

FILEY

North Yorkshire

Map **8** TA18

✕✕**Victoria Court** The Crescent ☎ Scarborough (0723) 513237

A canopied, Victorian-style restaurant with a comfortable lounge bar overlooking the sea and a lower ground floor dining room, the Victoria serves a good range of bar meals at lunch time and a more formal menu in the evening.

V 88 seats ✱Lunch £5.95&alc Dinner £8.75&alc Wine £4.30 Last dinner 10pm ₱

FINDON

West Sussex

Map **4** TQ10

✕**Darlings Bistro** The Square ☎ (090671) 3817

Standing in the centre of the peaceful village, the small, cottage-style restaurant has simple furnishings and a cosy, friendly atmosphere. A short, interesting menu is changed frequently, and cooking is of a high standard.

Closed Mon Dinner not served Sun

☊English & French 20 seats ✱Lunch fr£6.95&alc Dinner £6.95&alc Wine £5 Last dinner 9pm ₱

Credit cards 1 2 3 5

See advertisement under Worthing

FISHGUARD

Dyfed

Map **2** SM93

★★**Cartref** High St ☎ (0348) 872430

Comfortable hotel situated in the town centre.

14rm(3➡3⋒) CTV in 6 bedrooms ✈ sB&B fr£16 sB&B➡⋒ fr£22 dB&B fr£27 dB&B➡⋒ fr£36 B

☾CTV 20P 2⌂ ⇎ nc7yrs

♆ ☕ Lunch fr£4 Tea fr80p High Tea fr£2 Dinner fr£7.50 Wine £3.80 Last dinner 8pm

Credit cards 1 3

★★***Fishguard Bay*** Goodwick ☎ (0348) 873571

Impressive building surrounded by woodland and overlooking the bay.

62rm(28➡)(6fb) 1⊟ CTV in 16 bedrooms B

Lift ☾CTV 50P CFA ❀ ⌒(heated) billiards *xmas*

☊Welsh, English, French & Italian **V** ♆ ☕ Last dinner 9.30pm

Credit cards 1 2 3 5

★**Manor House** Main St ☎ (0348) 873260

RS Oct—Apr

Set almost in the town centre, this hotel is compact and homely.

7rm(2fb) sB&B £12.50—£15 dB&B £25—£30 B

CTV ₱ ⇎

♆ ☕ Bar lunch £4.80alc Tea 90p—£1.65 Dinner £7.40alc Wine £4 Last dinner 9pm

Credit cards 1 2 3

FLAMBOROUGH

Humberside

Map **8** TA26

★★***Timoneer Country Manor*** Southsea Rd ☎ Bridlington (0262) 850219

An attractively situated country house of great style, with comfortable accommodation, friendly staff and good food.

10rm(5➡5⋒) CTV in all bedrooms ® B

200P ❀

V Last dinner 9.30pm

Credit cards 1 2 3 5

★***Flaneburg*** North Marine Rd ☎ Bridlington (0262) 850284

Closed Nov—Etr

A three-storey building on the edge of the village near the famous cliffs, this friendly hotel provides accommodation in nicely-appointed bedrooms which are complemented by comfortable publc rooms.

13rm(6⋒)(3fb) ® ✈ B

CTV 20P ❀

Last dinner 9pm

FLEET

Hampshire

Map **4** SU85

★★★**Lismoyne** Church Rd ☎ (0252) 628555

Victorian hotel in pleasant gardens, with variety of bedrooms, well-appointed public areas and popular restaurant.

40rm(29➡2⋒) CTV in all bedrooms ®T S% sB&B £30 sB&B➡⋒£40—£44 dB&B➡⋒£52 B

☾80P ❀ Live music and dancing Sat Nov—Apr ⌂

☊English & French **V** ♆ ☕ S% Lunch fr£7&alc Tea fr80p Dinner fr£8.90&alc Wine £5.10 Last dinner 9.30pm

Credit cards 1 2 3 4 5

FLEETWOOD

Lancashire

Map **7** SD34

★★★**North Euston** The Esplanade (Best Western) ☎ (03917) 6525

Mid-Victorian crescent-shaped building overlooking the sea.

57rm(34➡12⋒)(4fb) CTV in all bedrooms ®T sB&B £20 sB&B➡⋒£24 dB&B £38 dB&B➡⋒£41 B

Lift ☾60P *xmas*

♆ ☕ Lunch £5.50—£6.15&alc Dinner £8.75—£9.40&alc Wine £4.50 Last dinner 9.30pm

Credit cards 1 2 3 5

FLICHITY

Highland *Inverness-shire*

Map **14** NH62

✕***Grouse & Trout*** ☎ Farr (08083) 314

Attractive cottage restaurant with bar and craft shop.

Dinner not served Mon & Tue

50 seats Last dinner 9.30pm 100P ⚡

Credit cards 1 2 3 5

FLITWICK
Bedfordshire
Map **4** TL03

❀★★★ ***B* Flitwick Manor** Church Rd (Pride of Britain) ☎ (0525) 712242 Telex no 825562

Surrounded by delightful woodland, this beautiful 17th century house features the well-appointed, Regency-style Brooks Restaurant, mahogany-furnished and portrait-hung, which offers a good set lunch and an extensive à la carte menu cf predominantly fish dishes. Beautifully fresh and well-prepared food, a comprehensive wine list and friendly service all combine to ensure your enjoyment.

8rm(6⇌2⋒)3 CTV in all bedrooms **T** S% sB&B⇌⋒£48—£90 dB&B⇌⋒£65—£110

70P ❀ sauna bath croquet

V Lunch £12.50&alc Dinner £12.50&alc Wine £6.90 Last dinner 9.30pm

Credit cards 1 2 3 5

FLIXTON
North Yorkshire
Map **8** TA07

XX Foxhound Inn ☎ Scarborough (0723) 890301

This modernised country inn retains much of its old world charm and serves a wide selection of popular dishes at competitive prices.

English & French **V** 100 seats Lunch £6.50 Dinner £10.75alc Wine £5.25 Last dinner 10pm 120P

Credit cards 1 2 3 5

FOCHABERS
Grampian *Morayshire*
Map **15** NJ35

★★ **Gordon Arms** ☎ (0343) 820508

RS 31 Dec & 1 Jan

Friendly coaching inn with character set in small town.

10rm(9⇌) Annexe: 2⇌ CTV in all bedrooms ® **T** sB&B£24—£28 sB&B⇌£30—£35 dB&B£30—£35 dB&B⇌£40—£45 B

50P ❀ petanque

Lunch £3.50—£5 Tea £1.50—£2.50 High Tea £3.50—£5 Dinner £8.50—£12.50 Wine £3.50 Last dinner 8.45pm

Credit cards 1 2 3 5

FOLKESTONE
Kent
Map **5** TR23

★★★ **Burlington** Earl's Av ☎ (0303) 55301 Telex no 966331

Standing in pleasant gardens, this hotel has a popular restaurant and accommodation for guests in a variety of bedrooms and in well-appointed public rooms.

59⇌(6fb) CTV in all bedrooms sB&B⇌£30—£32 dB&B⇌£48—£50 B

Lift ☾ 12P ❀ snooker putting *xmas*

English & French **V** Lunch £6.50—£8.50 Tea £1.30—£1.50 Dinner fr£10.25&alc Wine £5.50 Last dinner 9.15pm

Credit cards 1 2 3 5 Ⓥ

★★★ **Clifton** The Leas (Consort) ☎ (0303) 41231

Hotel commands fine views of English Channel.

58rm(42⇌3⋒)(4fb) CTV in all bedrooms ® **T** S% ✱ sB&B£23—£24 sB&B⇌⋒£32—£33.45 dB&B£40.90 dB&B⇌⋒£48.90 B

Lift ☾ P ❀ solarium pool table table tennis *xmas*

English & French ✱ Lunch £6.50—£7&alc Tea 90p—£1 Dinner £8.50—£9&alc Wine £4.95 Last dinner 8.45pm

Credit cards 1 2 3 5 Ⓥ

★★ **Garden House** 142 Sandgate Rd (Inter Hotel) ☎ (0303) 52278

The modernised and refurbished Victorian hotel has well-equipped bedrooms, an efficiently-managed restaurant and limited lounge accommodation.

42rm(29⇌10⋒)(7fb) 1 CTV in all bedrooms ® in 10 bedrooms **T** sB&Bfr£21.50 sB&B⇌⋒fr£29.50 dB&Bfr£35 dB&B⇌⋒fr£45.50 B

Lift ☾ 16P ❀ *xmas*

French ✱ Lunch £6.25 Tea fr65p Dinner fr£8.50&alc Wine £5.25 Last dinner 8.45pm

Credit cards 1 2 3 5 Ⓥ

XX La Tavernetta Leaside Court ☎ (0303) 54955

A well-appointed, lower ground floor restaurant overlooking gardens near the sea front.

Closed Sun

French & Italian 55 seats Lunch £5.95—£6.50&alc Dinner £11alc Wine £5.50 Last dinner 10.30pm

Credit cards 1 2 3 5

X Emillo's Portofino 124A Sandgate Rd ☎ (0303) 55866

Good, modestly priced Italian cuisine.

Closed Mon

Italian **V** 55 seats ✱ Lunch £6.50&alc Dinner £12alc Wine £6.50 Last dinner 10.30pm P

Credit cards 1 2 3 5

X Paul's 2A Bouverie Road West ☎ (0303) 59697

Effective decor with cane furniture and plants. Cooking by the Chef patron.

Closed Sun

English & French **V** 44 seats ✱ Lunch £9.65alc Dinner £9.65alc Wine £5.50 Last dinner 9.30pm 20P (evenings)

Credit cards 1 3

F

FORD
Wiltshire
Map **3** ST87

★★**White Hart Inn** ☎ Castle Combe (0249) 782213

Closed Xmas eve—New Years eve

Quiet 15th-century stone inn with beams and log fires.

3⌂ Annexe: 8🛁(1fb) 4 CTV in all bedrooms ® ✗ sB&B🛁⌂£28—£31 dB&B🛁⌂£40—£44 B

CTV 100P ✿ ≈ (heated) nc 3yrs

English & French Bar lunch £1.50—£5 Dinner £10.50—£12.50 Wine £4.95 Last dinner 9.30pm

Credit card 1

FORDINGBRIDGE
Hampshire
Map **4** SU11

★★**Ashburn Hotel & Restaurant** Station Rd (Minotel) ☎ (0425) 52060

A small hotel with a modern extension, the Ashburn welcomes guests warmly to its much-improved public rooms and the well-appointed restaurant where wholesome, carefully-prepared meals are served.

25rm(9🛁)(3fb) ® sB&B fr£17.25 sB&B🛁 fr£26.75 dB&B fr£30 dB&B🛁 fr£42 B

CTV 50P ✿ ≈ (heated) table tennis

International V Lunch fr£6.75 Tea fr65p Dinner fr£9&alc Wine £5 Last dinner 9pm

Credit cards 1 3 V

✗✗**Hour Glass** Burgate ☎ (0425) 52348

Family run restaurant in quaint, thatched cottage.

Closed Sun & Mon Lunch not served

English & French 35 seats Dinner £13.50alc Wine £4.90 Last dinner 9.45pm 30P nc 12yrs

Credit cards 1 2 3 5

❀✗**Three Lions Inn** Stuckton ☎ (0425) 52489

Popular pub restaurant where the chef/patron produces good, honestly prepared food using fresh materials. The atmosphere is friendly and informal with charming, attentive staff.

Closed Mon Dinner not served Sun

International 50 seats Lunch £9.80alc Dinner £16.50alc Wine £5.50 Last dinner 9.30pm 30P nc 14yrs

Credit card 1

FORDYCE
Grampian *Banffshire*
Map **15** NJ56

❀✗**Hawthorne** Church St ☎ Portsoy (0261) 43003

(*Rosette awarded for dinner only*)

A 17th-century cottage has been tastefully restored to form a charming little country restaurant offering a homely atmosphere and personal attention. The cooking is inventive, using local produce wherever possible.

Closed Mon
Dinner not served Sun

V 32 seats ✱ Bar lunch £2.50—£5 Dinner £12alc Wine £5 Last dinner 9.30pm 14P nc 12yrs (dinner)

Credit cards 1 3

FOREST ROW
East Sussex
Map **5** TQ43

★★★**Roebuck** Wych Cross (2m S junc A22/A275) (Embassy/Consort) ☎ (034282) 3811 Telex no 957088

An early Georgian country inn with extensive gardens and views over Ashdown Forest.

31🛁⌂ CTV in all bedrooms ® sB&B🛁⌂£43 dB&B🛁⌂£58.40 B

☾ 150P *xmas*

English & French V ✱ Lunch fr£8.50&alc Tea fr60p Dinner fr£8.50&alc Wine £4.70 Last dinner 9.15pm

Credit cards 1 2 3 4 5

See advertisement under East Grinstead

FORFAR
Tayside *Angus*
Map **15** MO45

★★**Royal** Castle St ☎ (0307) 62691

Modernised hotel in the town centre, personally supervised by the owner.

20rm(13🛁5⌂)(2fb) CTV in all bedrooms ® T ✗ S% sB&B£25 sB&B🛁⌂£30 dB&B£30 dB&B🛁⌂£40—£50 B

Lift ☾ CTV 36P ≈ (heated) sauna bath solarium gymnasium Disco Fri & Sat *xmas*

British & French V S% Lunch £5—£8alc Tea £1—£1.50 High Tea £5—£7 Dinner £12alc Wine £5.50 Last dinner 10.45pm

Credit cards 2 3 5

FORRES
Grampian *Morayshire*
Map **14** NJ05

★★***Ramnee*** Victoria Road ☎ (0309) 72410

Closed Jan

Fine two-storey stone villa standing back from the main road in well-kept grounds.

15rm(5🛁4⌂) Annexe: 2⌂(2fb) CTV in all bedrooms ® ✗

50P ✿

French & Italian V Last dinner 9pm

Credit cards 1 2 3

★★**Royal** Tytler St ☎ (0309) 72617

Three-storey building, standing in a quiet area of the town opposite the market and near the station.

20rm(1🛁11⌂)(3fb) CTV in all bedrooms ® sB&B£17.75—£20 sB&B🛁⌂£21.75—£24.50 dB&B£27.50—£30 dB&B🛁⌂£35—£39 B

CTV 40P ✿ games room pool table

European V Lunch £4.20alc Tea 75palc High Tea £5alc Dinner £7alc Wine £4.90 Last dinner 8.30pm

Credit cards 1 3 V

★**Heather** Tytler St ☎ (0309) 72377

Small, pleasant family-run hotel.

7rm(1 6) Ⓡ

CTV 20P

V Last dinner 7pm

Credit card 3

FORSINARD
Highland *Sutherland*
Map **14** NC84

★★**Forsinard** (Exec Hotels/ Guestaccom) ☎ Halladale (06417) 221

Closed Nov—Etr

Comfortable modern family run Highland Hotel with special facilities for fishing, shooting and stalking.

10rm(6 2)(1fb) Ⓡ sB&B£17—£19 sB&B £21—£23 dB&B£26—£30 dB&B £36—£40 B

CTV 30P ✿

Lunch fr £8 Tea fr £1.50 High Tea fr£8 Dinner fr£10.50 Wine £3.95 Last dinner 8.30pm

Credit cards 1 3 V

FORT AUGUSTUS
Highland *Inverness-shire*
Map **14** NH30

★★*H* **Caledonian** ☎ (0320) 6256

Closed Oct—Etr

This small family run hotel is especially noted for its warm and friendly hospitality.

12rm(2 2)(2fb) sB&B£12.50—£17.50 dB&B£25—£29 dB&B £29—£33 B

CTV 20P ✿

Scottish & French V Bar lunch £3.50alc Tea fr60p High Tea fr£2 Dinner £6.50—£7.50 Wine £3.75 Last dinner 9.30pm

V

Forres — Fort William

★★ **Inchnacardoch Lodge** Loch Ness ☎ (0320) 6258 Telex no 946240

A converted hunting lodge overlooking Loch Ness.

17rm(1 5)(5fb) CTV in 12 bedrooms Ⓡ sB&B£15—£19.50 dB&B£30—£40 dB&B £45—£55

CTV 40P 2 ✿ *xmas*

International V Lunch £5.50—£7.50 Dinner £7.50—£9.50 Wine £4.85 Last dinner 9pm

Credit cards 1 2 3 5 V

★★*H* ***Lovat Arms*** ☎ (0320) 6206

Closed Nov—mid Dec

Comfortable, family run hotel with good home cooking and friendly service.

18rm(15)(3fb) Ⓡ B

CTV 50P ✿

V Last dinner 8.30pm

Credit card 3

FORTINGALL
Tayside *Perthshire*
Map **14** NN74

★★**Fortingall** ☎ Kenmore (08873) 367

RS Dec—Feb

Crow-stepped gables are a feature of this 18th century hotel with a coaching history. Set in an attractive village, it reflects a traditional standard of accommodation coupled with the personal attention of the owners.

11rm(3 1) ✱ sB&B£16 sB&B £17 dB&B£30 dB&B £34 B

CTV 20P 5 ✿ U

✱ Lunch £5.50&alc Tea £2.25&alc High Tea £4.50&alc Dinner £9.50 Wine £4.45 Last dinner 8.30pm

Credit card 3

FORTROSE
Highland *Ross & Cromarty*
Map **14** NH76

★**Royal** Union St ☎ (0381) 20236

Closed 25 Dec, 1 & 2 Jan

Small, family run hotel overlooking cathedral square.

10rm(2fb) Ⓡ sB&B£16.50—£17.50 dB&B£24—£26

CTV 10P Cabaret wkly (mid Jun—Sep)

Scottish & French V Lunch £6.30—£6.95 Tea 55—75p Dinner £8.50—£12.50&alc Wine £4.25 Last dinner 9pm

Credit cards 1 3 V

FORT WILLIAM
Highland *Inverness-shire*
Map **14** NN17

See also Banavie

★★★★ **Inverlochy Castle** (see red star box on next page)

★★★**Alexandra** The Parade ☎ (0397) 2241 Telex no 777210

Victorian building on a corner site just off the main shopping centre and close to the railway station.

87(7fb) CTV in all bedrooms Ⓡ **T** S% ✱ sB&B £21.50—£26.50 dB&B £42—£49 B

Lift 40P *xmas*

Scottish & French V S% ✱ Lunch £3.25—£6 Tea 75p—£1.50 High Tea £3.75—£4.75 Dinner £6.40—£9.75 Wine £4.30 Last dinner 8.45pm

Credit cards 1 2 3 5 V

★★★**Ladbroke** Achintore Rd (on A82) (Ladbroke) ☎ (0397) 3117 Telex no 776531

Modern, low-rise building, standing by the main road on the southern outskirts of town, with splendid views over Loch Linnhe. The bedrooms have recently been extended and refurbished to a high standard.

85 (13fb) CTV in all bedrooms Ⓡ **T** S% sB&B £28—£44.50 dB&B £42—£64.50 B →

F

★★★★

❀❀★★★★

INVERLOCHY CASTLE, FORT WILLIAM

(3m NE A82) (Relais et Châteaux)
☎ (0397) 2177 Telex no 776229

Closed mid Nov—mid Mar

In the shadow of Ben Nevis among spectacular highland scenery lies this baronial style house, built in 1863. It was the home of Mrs Grete Hobbs who eventually converted it to a magnificent hotel. The highest of standards prevail here in every respect. You pass through the lobby into the impressive Great Hall with its moulded and painted ceiling, off which are the French style drawing room with marble chimney pieces, and the two dining rooms. All is richly furnished with antiques, pictures, gilt mirrors, crystal chandeliers and fresh flowers. Bedrooms are equally beautifully done, as you would expect. There is a grand piano and, for the more energetic, billiards and table tennis. Standards of housekeeping are immaculate. Throughout the hall you will be served by friendly, attentive staff, under the able supervision of Michael Lenard, the managing director. He keeps a close eye on the service in the luxuriously appointed dining rooms, where chef François Huguet provides the best quality ingredients cooked with rare skill. Considering that he has to start each season with many new cooks, it is a wonder that he succeeds so well. Six

course luncheons are served without choice; at dinner there is a similar recommended menu, plus some other choices. He cooks in the modern French style, although ignoring some of the old favourites; the dishes are eye-catching as well as delectable. Breakfasts, too, are well thought of, as is the outstanding wine list. Mrs. Hobbs is a hostess par excellence so that to stay here is a memorable experience that can be equalled in only a very few other hotels in the country.

16 CTV in all bedrooms **T** sB&B £92 dB&B £121 Continental breakfast

☾ P2 snooker

Internatonal Lunch £14—£21alc Dinner £29alc Wine £8 Last dinner 9pm

Credit cards 1 3

Lift 160P CFA sauna bath Live music and dancing 3 nights wkly *xmas*

European **V** S% Lunch £2—£6.50 Tea 75p—£1.80 High Tea £3.50—£8 Dinner £9.75—£16&alc Wine £6.75 Last dinner 9.30pm

Credit cards 1 2 3 5

★★**Cruachan** Achintore Rd (Consort) ☎ (0397) 2022

Closed mid Oct—Feb

Large hotel overlooking Loch Linnhe with modern bedroom extension at rear. Caters for tour parties.

56rm(54)(2fb) in 15 bedrooms CTV in all bedrooms Ⓡ sB&B £17.50—£22.50 dB&B £33—£39

☾ CTV 30P snooker Cabaret Tue

V Lunch £5—£7 Tea 70—90p Dinner £9—£11&alc Last dinner 9pm

★★**Grand** Gordon Sq ☎ (0397) 2928

This pre-war three-storey hotel stands on a corner site in the shopping centre.

33(4fb) CTV in all bedrooms Ⓡ sB&B £17—£26 dB&B £30—£50 B

20P *xmas*

V Lunch fr£4.75 Tea fr65p Dinner fr£8.25 Wine £4.45 Last dinner 8.30pm

Credit cards 1 2 3 5 Ⓥ

★★**Imperial** Fraser's Sq ☎ (0397) 2040

Closed Xmas and New Year

An extended, large Victorian building, near the main shopping area and with views of Loch Linnhe.

42rm(10 6)(2fb) CTV in 12 bedrooms Ⓡ sB&B £17.50—£19.50 sB&B £20.50—£22.50 dB&B £30—£36 dB&B £36—£42 B

CTV 30P

Lunch £4—£4.50 Dinner £7.50—£9.50 Wine £4.20 Last dinner 8.15pm

Credit cards 1 3 Ⓥ

★★**Nevis Bank** Belford Rd (Best Western) ☎ (0397) 5721

Tourist and commercial hotel with well-appointed bedrooms is situated on A82 north of town, at access road to Glen Nevis.

31rm(17 14)(2fb) CTV in 30 bedrooms Ⓡ in 30 bedrooms **T** sB&B £20 dB&B £38 B

CTV 25P Cabaret twice wkly *xmas*

V Bar lunch £3.95alc Tea 60p Dinner £9.50 Wine £4.95 Last dinner 8.30pm

Credit cards 1 2 3 Ⓥ

★★**Stag's Head** High St ☎ (0397) 4144

Closed Oct—May

Converted terraced building located over shops.

45rm(8 1)(6fb) sB&B £16 sB&B £19 dB&B £30 dB&B £36 B

Lift CTV 6P nc 12yrs

V Lunch £4—£6 Tea 60p—£1 Dinner £7.50—£10.50 Wine £4.80 Last dinner 9pm

Credit cards 1 2 3 4 5

★★★❀ **Beasdale, Arisaig**
Inverness-shire PH39 4NR
Tel. Arisaig (068 75) 622

GLORIOUS WESTERN HIGHLANDS

Arisaig House which is set in many acres of mature gardens has 14 bedrooms all with private bathrooms, direct-dial telephone, and colour television; the public rooms are furnished with elegance and comfort. Here is Highland scenery at its finest and Arisaig House, built originally to the plans of Philip Webb in 1864 and now listed as being of architectural interest, is ideally situated for touring the Highlands and Islands. Its broad terraces overlook the gardens, Loch Nan Uamh and the Sound of Arisaig towards the mountains of Morven and Ardnamurchan. The resident owners, Ruth and John Smither, together with their son-in-law, chef David Wilkinson, aim to set the highest standards of service, comfort and cuisine.

See gazetteer under Arisaig.

F

IMPERIAL HOTEL

(Fort William) Inverness-shire PH33 6DW
Telephone: Fort William 0397 2040

Situated in the heart of Fort William, close to the shopping centre and with panoramic views of Loch Linnhe and the surrounding countryside. The Hotel offers the ideal base to explore and discover the beauty of the West Highlands by car or coach. It is one of the oldest established hotels in Fort William and has developed over the years a reputation for Highland hospitality and good food. The hotel has been substantially refurbished to provide quality accommodation at reasoable prices.

"Astounding Situation. Most Remarkable Hotel"

THE LODGE ON THE LOCH

In the heart of the Highlands, where mountains and Gulf Stream meet in tranquility.
Panoramic views from designer bedrooms, each with private facilities.
Renowned restaurant serving local seafood, salmon, trout and venison with home baking as well as health foods.

Creag Dhu, ONICH, By Fort William
Inverness-shire. (08553) 237
Norman, Jessie and Laurence McP Young

See gazetteer entry under ONICH

NEVIS BANK HOTEL

BELFORD ROAD, FORT WILLIAM PH33 6BY Telephone: (0397) 5721

Nevis Bank Hotel is a privately owned hotel situated on the eastern side of the town 10 minutes walk from the Main Street & Travel Centre and at the foot of the access road to Ben Nevis, Britain's highest mountain. The Hotel is famous for its Home Cooking and comfortable surroundings. Cabaret in Ceilidh Bar most weekends throughout the year.

❀★*HBL* **The Factors House**
Torlundy (2m NE A82)
☎ (0397) 5767
Closed 15 Dec—15 Mar
(Rosette awarded for dinner only)

This elegant new hotel, run by Peter Hobbs (whose family own Inverlochy Castle), is warm and welcoming. The bedrooms, though compact, are individually decorated and well furnished. Good quality produce is used on the reasonable set price menu, and features home made terrine, mousses and stews.

8rm(6➡2⋒) CTV in all bedrooms T ✗
✱sB&B➡⋒£28.75
dB&B➡⋒£57.50
30P ⇌ ✿ ᑫ(hard) ⤸ ∪
✱Tea 60p Dinner £11.50 Wine £8.50
Last dinner 9.30pm
Credit cards 1 2 3 5

FOSSEBRIDGE
Gloucestershire
Map **4** SP01

★★**Fossebridge Inn** (ExecHotel)
☎ (028572) 310
Closed Xmas

Relaxed, informal, Cotswold stone inn with comfortable bedrooms and buttery restaurant.

8rm(5➡) Annexe: 4➡ ® ✗
sB&B£20.25—£31.50 dB&B£27
dB&B➡£35—£42 B
CTV 40P ✿ ⤸ nc 10yrs
♡English & French V ♔ ☕ ✱Bar lunch £1—£5.75 Tea fr 75p Dinner £17.95&alc Wine £3.60 Last dinner 9.30pm
Credit cards 1 2 3 5

FOUR MILE BRIDGE
Gwynedd
Map **6** SH27

★★★**Anchorage** ☎ Holyhead (0407) 740168
Closed Xmas

Modern, commercial/holiday hotel situated one mile from beaches and shops.

18rm(8➡7⋒)(1fb) CTV in 17 bedrooms ® in 17 bedrooms ✗ S% sB&B£22—£24 sB&B➡⋒£24 dB&B£35 dB&B➡⋒£37 B
CTV 100P ⇌
♡British & French V ♔ ⚡ Bar lunch £4.50alc Dinner £10alc Wine £4 Last dinner 9.30pm
Credit cards 1 3

FOWEY
Cornwall
Map **2** SX15

★★★**Fowey** The Esplanade
☎ (072683) 2551

There are glorious views over Fowey Estuary to Polruan from this former railway hotel with its elegant public rooms.

29rm(15➡9⋒)(3fb) CTV in all bedrooms ®T sB&B➡⋒£23—£26 dB&B£42—£48 dB&B➡⋒£46—£52 B
Lift ☾ CTV 20P ⇌ ✿ ♿ *xmas*
♔ ☕ Lunch £10alc Tea fr 80p Dinner fr £9&alc Wine £4.50 Last dinner 8.45pm
Credit cards 1 2 3 5

★★*H* **Marina** Esplanade ☎ (072683) 3315
Closed Nov—Feb

Comfortable hotel where good food is served in the waterside restaurant.

10rm(9➡1⋒)(1fb) CTV in all bedrooms sB&B➡⋒£18—£23 dB&B➡⋒£36—£46 B
CTV P ⇌
♡English & French V ♔ ☕ ⚡ Bar lunch £1—£3 Tea 60p—£2 Dinner £10&alc Wine £4.85 Last dinner 8.30pm
Credit cards 1 2 3 4 5 Ⓥ

★★**Old Quay** Fore St ☎ (072683) 3302
Closed Dec & Jan
Waterside hotel offering friendly atmosphere and character.
13rm(7🛁2🚿)(3fb) CTV in all bedrooms ® S% sB&B£14—£15.50 dB&B£24—£27 dB&B🛁🚿£28—£31 B
CTV
S% Bar lunch £2 Tea 55p Dinner £6.50&alc Wine £4.95 Last dinner 7.45pm
Credit cards [1] [3] Ⓥ

★★**Penlee** The Esplanade ☎ (072683) 3220
RS Nov—Feb
Friendly, comfortable hotel in an elevated position with unrestricted views of the estuary and the sea.
10rm(8🛁)(4fb) 1 CTV in all bedrooms ® sB&B🛁£22—£25 dB&B🛁£34—£40 B
11P
English & Continental V Bar lunch £2.50—£3.50 Dinner £8.50—£9.50&alc Wine £4 Last dinner 9pm
Credit cards [1] [2] [3] [5] Ⓥ

★★**Riverside** ☎ (072683) 2275
RS 2nd wk Oct—Mar
Comfortable, well-situated hotel with fine views.
14rm(4🛁2🚿)(3fb) 1 CTV in 2 bedrooms sB&B£16—£22 sB&B🛁🚿£18—£24 dB&B£32—£44 dB&B🛁🚿£36—£48 B
CTV 5P 5
English & French V Bar lunch £1—£2.50 Dinner £7.50—£12&alc Wine £4 Last dinner 9pm
Credit card [1]

✕***Food For Thought*** The Quay ☎ (072683) 2221
Closed Sun, Oct—Mar (except wknds) Lunch not served
French 38 seats Last dinner 9.30pm
Credit cards [1] [3]

FOWLMERE
Cambridgeshire
Map **5** TL44

✕✕**Chequers Inn** ☎ (076382) 369
Closed Xmas Day & Boxing Day
English & French **V** 30 seats S%
*Lunch £17.50alc Dinner £17.50alc Wine £5.90 Last dinner 10pm 50P
Credit cards [1] [2] [3] [4] [5]

FOWNHOPE
Hereford & Worcester
Map **3** SO53

★★**Green Man Inn** ☎ (043277) 243
The comfortable, black and white, half-timbered inn with its attractive rear garden has been part of this quiet village since 1485.
9🛁🚿 Annexe: 5🛁🚿(3fb) 1 CTV in all bedrooms ® sB&B🛁🚿£17.50 dB&B🛁🚿£29 B
CTV 55P *xmas*
V Bar lunch 75p—£5 Tea 45p—£1.20 Dinner fr£7&alc Wine £3.50 Last dinner 9.30pm

FOYERS
Highland *Inverness-shire*
Map **14** NH42

★**Foyers** (Guestaccom) ☎ Gorthleck (04563) 216
Attractive roadside inn set on the hillside above Loch Ness 19 miles west of Inverness.
9rm(1fb) ® S% sB&B£12.50 dB&B£25
CTV 25P
S% Bar lunch 75p—£5 Tea fr70p Dinner £6 Wine £4.50 Last dinner 7.30pm
Ⓥ

FRAMLINGHAM
Suffolk
Map **5** TM26

★★**Crown** Market Hill (Trusthouse Forte) ☎ (0728) 723521
16th century inn with magnificent beamed lounges and log fires.
13rm(9🛁) 1 CTV in all bedrooms ® sB&B£39.50 sB&B🛁£49.50 dB&B£57.50 dB&B🛁£65.50 B
15P *xmas*
Last dinner 9.30pm
Credit cards [1] [2] [3] [4] [5]

✕***Market Place*** 18 Market Hill ☎ (0728) 724275
Tiny, detached cottage with fresh food catering for both the family and the discerning diner.
Closed Sun, Mon & 12 Jan—3 Feb
V 30 seats Last dinner 9.30pm
Credit cards [1] [3]

FRANKLEY
West Midlands
Map **7** SO98

○**Granada Lodge** Between junct 3-4, M5 Motorway Service Area ☎ 021-550 3131 40🛁
Opening Summer 1987

FRANT
East Sussex
Map **5** TQ53

✕**Bassets** 35 High St ☎ (089275) 635
Interesting good value fixed price menu, using local produce, in a low beamed former shop near the village church.
Closed Sun, Mon & 25—28 Dec Lunch not served
French 28 seats Dinner £13.50 Wine £4.50 Last dinner 9pm
Credit cards [1] [2] [3]

Fraserburgh — Frinton-on-Sea

F

FRASERBURGH
Grampian *Aberdeenshire*
Map **15** NJ96

★ ★ **Royal** Broad St ☎ (0346) 28524

Standing in the town centre, close to the harbour, this neatly-decorated, friendly family inn also offers accommodation to commercial guests.

16rm(8⇌)(1fb) CTV in all bedrooms Ⓡ S% sB&B£15 sB&B⇌£15 dB&B£26 dB&B⇌£26 Continental breakfast

CTV Live music & dancing twice wkly Cabaret wkly

V S% Lunch £2.25alc Tea £1alc High Tea £3.25alc Dinner £6.75alc Wine £4.70 Last dinner 9pm

Credit card 3 Ⓥ

★ ★ **Station** Seaforth St
☎ (0346) 23343

Cheap, simple meals are avaiable at this homely, family-run commercial hotel.

20rm(3⇌2⋒)(4fb) CTV in all bedrooms Ⓡ *sB&B£12 sB&B⇌⋒£16 dB&B£22 dB&B⇌⋒£24

CTV P billiards

*Lunch £2.75 High Tea £2.75—£4.74alc Dinner £5.75 Wine £4.25 Last dinner 9pm

Credit cards 1 2 3 5

★★★

❀★★★ HOMEWOOD PARK, FRESHFORD

Hinton Charterhouse (Between A36 & village) (Prestige) ☎ Limpley Stoke (022122) 3731 Telex no 444937

Closed 24 Dec—12 Jan

Our award of Red Stars last year — 'belated' say some of our members — has been popular. This is a pleasing Victorian house in ten acres of grounds which have been extensively planted and include tennis court and croquet lawns. Stephen and Penny Ross have done a super job with its conversion. There is a handsome staircase leading out of the hall, an elegant drawing room and a comfortable bar lounge. Not at all precious, the decor tends to be light and fresh with flowers and plants. There are lots of ornaments, including vases by a local artist, shelves of books and some nice pieces of furniture. Bedrooms are equally freshly decorated and comfortable with appealing soft furnishings and are well equipped with extras including a miniature of sherry. There are two important features that lift the hotel above other similar ones: first the good natured friendliness displayed by everyone; secondly the food. 'The kitchen is the heart of a good hotel'

says Stephen, and he carries out that precept in his well appointed dining rooms. He cooks in the modern style but has an individual approach, preparing excellent raw materials in an unpretentious, delicious way that earns our Rosette.

15⇌ CTV in all bedrooms T S% *sB&B⇌£40—£80 dB&B⇌£65—£95 Continental breakfast

30P

S% *Lunch £12.50—£15.50 Tea £1.50—£5.50 Dinner £16.50—£21.50 Wine £7.50 Last dinner 9.30pm

Credit cards 1 2 3 5

FRECKLETON
Lancashire
Map **7** SD42

XX **Caravela** Preston New Rd ☎ (0772) 632308

The restaurant, Continental with Portuguese overtones, is situated on the crossroads at the centre of the village. The resident proprietors serve good, well-prepared meals in a friendly atmosphere, and the surroundings are pleasant, a comfortable cocktail lounge leading into a modern restaurant decorated with pictures of sailing ships.

Closed Mon & 2 wks Summer

Lunch not served Sat

Portuguese 50 seats *Lunch fr£3.45&alc Dinner £9alc Wine £4.95 Last dinner 10.30pm 10P

Credit cards 1 3 Ⓥ

FRESHFORD
Avon
Map **3** ST75

FRESHWATER
Isle of Wight
See **Wight, Isle of**

FRESSINGFIELD
Suffolk
Map **5** TM27

❀X **Fox & Goose** ☎ (037986) 247

Booking essential.

Built in 1509 and enlarged in 1606, the attractive, mellow, brick inn is set between the village church and duckpond. Limited space makes booking advisable and also gives you time to peruse the long list of dish suggestions that will be sent to you (though there are also à la carte and table d'hôte menus). The extensive wine list repays study too.

Closed Tue & 21—28 Dec

English & French 24 seats Last dinner 9pm 30P

Credit cards 1 2 3 5

FREUCHIE
Fife
Map **11** NO20

★ ★ **Lomond Hills** Parliament Sq (Exec Hotel) ☎ Falkland (0337) 57329

Modernised and extended former coaching inn.

19rm(10⇌7⋒)(2fb) 1 CTV in 16 bedrooms TV in 3 bedrooms Ⓡ sB&B£18—£19.50 sB&B⇌⋒£20—£22.50 dB&B£28.50—£31.50 dB&B⇌⋒£31.50—£35 40P

sauna bath

English & French V Lunch £8.50—£10.50 Tea 75p—85p High Tea £5—£7.50 Dinner £9—£10.50&alc Wine £4.25 Last dinner 9.15pm

Credit cards 1 2 3 5 Ⓥ

FRINTON-ON-SEA
Essex
Map **5** TM21

★ ★ *H* **Maplin** Esplanade ☎ (02556) 3832

Closed Jan

Welcoming, family run hotel with comfortable impeccably kept bedrooms and sound home cooking.

12rm(9⇌1⋒)(2fb) CTV in all bedrooms Ⓡ T S% sB&B£24 sB&B⇌⋒£25.50 dB&B£51—£52 dB&B⇌⋒£51—£52

CTV 15P 2 (heated) nc 10yrs xmas

V S% Lunch fr£10.25&alc Tea fr60p Dinner fr£12&alc Wine £5.20 Last dinner 9.30pm

Credit cards 1 2 3 5 Ⓥ

★ *H* **Rock** The Esplanade, 1 Third Av
☎ (02556) 5173

Closed Jan

Friendly and efficiently-run family hotel with a warm welcome.

6rm(5⋔)(3fb) CTV in all bedrooms ® sB&B£21—£26 sB&B⋔£21—£26 dB&B⋔£42—£46

CTV 10P

V Lunch fr£8&alc Dinner fr£8.50&alc Wine £4.95 Last dinner 9pm

Credit cards 1 2 3 5 V

FROME
Somerset
Map **3** ST74

★★★**Mendip Lodge** Bath Rd ☎ (0373) 63223 Telex no 44832

Edwardian house with attractive public rooms and an adjoining motel bedroom block.

40⇌(8fb) CTV in all bedrooms ® sB&B⇌£34 dB&B⇌£53 Continental breakfast

60P CFA

English & Continental V Lunch fr£7&alc Tea fr85p Dinner fr£10.50&alc Last dinner 9.30pm

Credit cards 1 2 3 5

★★**George** 4 Market Pl ☎ (0373) 62584

Privately-run town centre hotel catering mainly for the business and touring trade.

15rm(4⇌)(1fb) CTV in 13 bedrooms TV in 2 bedrooms ® sB&B£22—£25 sB&B⇌£25—£29 dB&B£30—£38 dB&B⇌£36—£40

12 solarium pool table Disco nightly

V Wine £3.95 Last dinner 9pm

Credit cards 1 2 3 5

★★**Portway** The Portway ☎ (0373) 63508

Closed Xmas wk

Quiet, proprietor run hotel with well maintained bedrooms and lawned garden.

18rm(11⇌)(1fb) CTV in 11 bedrooms ® T sB&B⇌£24—£30 dB&B⇌£34.50—£41

CTV 30P

V Lunch fr£6&alc Tea fr50p Dinner fr£8.75&alc Wine £4.50 Last dinner 8.30pm

Credit cards 1 2 3 5

✕✕**Halligan's** 6 Vicarage St ☎ (0373) 64238

This small, attractive and well-appointed cottage-style restaurant, personally run by the owners, is located in a quiet lane off the town centre.

Closed Sun, Mon, last wk Feb & 1st wk Mar Lunch not served Sat

36 seats Lunch £3—£6 Dinner £12.50 Wine £5.50 Last dinner 10pm

Credit cards 1 2 3 5 V

GAINSBOROUGH
Lincolnshire
Map **8** SK88

★★**Hickman-Hill** Cox's Hill ☎ (0427) 3639

Built in the late 16th century as a school, this pleasant and comfortable hotel stands in spacious grounds on the eastern outskirts of the town.

8rm(3⇌1⋔)(1fb) CTV in all bedrooms ® T sB&B£28.50 sB&B⇌⋔£28.50 dB&B£40.50 dB&B⇌⋔£40.50

CTV 25P solarium gymnasium *xmas*

V Lunch fr£5.50 Tea fr£1.75 High Tea fr£2.95 Dinner £12alc Wine £5.50 Last dinner 9pm

Credit cards 1 3 V

GAIRLOCH
Highland *Ross & Cromarty*
Map **14** NG87

★★★**Gairloch** (Scottish Highland) ☎ (0445) 2001 Telex no 778215

Closed Nov—Mar

Three storey character hotel with fine views over Gairloch Bay.

51rm(36⇌13⋔)(3fb) ® ✱ sB&B⇌⋔£32 dB&B⇌⋔£54

Lift CTV 50P (hard) Disco Fri

Scottish & French Last dinner 9pm

Credit cards 1 2 3 5

GALASHIELS
Borders *Selkirkshire*
Map **12** NT43

★★★**Kingsknowes** Selkirk Rd ☎ (0896) 3478

Fine, tastefully decorated mansion house, retaining many country house features, particularly the friendly informal service.

11rm(8⇌2⋔)(2fb) CTV in all bedrooms ® T sB&B fr£28 sB&B⇌⋔fr£30 dB&B fr£44 dB&B⇌⋔fr£48

50P (hard)

V Lunch £9.50&alc Dinner £9.50&alc Wine £4 Last dinner 8.45pm

Credit cards 1 2 3 5

★★★ ***Woodlands House*** Windyknowe Rd (Consort) ☎ (0896) 4722 Telex no 727396

Victorian Gothic style mansion in tree studded grounds with good looking spacious rooms.

9rm(8⇌1⋔)(2fb) CTV in all bedrooms ® T

CTV 30P

Last dinner 10pm

Credit cards 1 2 3 5

★★**Abbotsford Arms** 63 Stirling St ☎ (0896) 2517

Closed Xmas & New Years Day

This Victorian hotel in a busy border town setting has been modernised to provide good bedrooms and offers pleasant, friendly service.

10rm(5⋔)(2fb) CTV in all bedrooms ® ✱ sB&B fr£14 sB&B⋔fr£17 dB&B fr£21 dB&B⋔fr£25

CTV

✱Lunch £3.50—£4 High Tea £3.50—£4 Dinner £5—£7.25 Wine £3.45 Last dinner 9pm

Credit cards 1 3 V

GANLLWYD
Gwynedd
Map **6** SH72

★**Tyn-y-Groes** ☎ (034140) 275

There is fishing available in the vicinity of this small, family-run hotel in the beautiful Mawddach Valley.

10rm(1⇌) TV in 2 bedrooms ® sB&B fr£15 dB&B fr£25 dB&B⇌fr£30

CTV 30P *xmas*

English & French V Bar lunch £2—£4 Tea 75p—£1.50 Dinner £9.50alc Wine £3.95 Last dinner 9pm

Credit cards 1 2 3 5 V

GARFORTH
West Yorkshire
Map **8** SE43

★★★**Ladbroke** (& Conference centre) Wakefield Rd, Garforth Rbt, (junc A63/A642 6m E of Leeds) (Ladbroke) ☎ Leeds (0532) 866556 Telex no 556324

Well designed modern hotel in spacious grounds with watermill theme in carvery restaurant.

142⇌(25fb) in 4 bedrooms CTV in all bedrooms ® T ✱ sB⇌£44—£54 dB⇌fr£52 (room only)

250P CFA pool table *xmas*

✱Lunch fr£8.50&alc Tea 50p—80p Dinner fr£10.25&alc Wine £4.99 Last dinner 10pm

Credit cards 1 2 3 4 5 V

See advertisement under Leeds

GARGRAVE
North Yorkshire
Map **7** SD95

★★**Anchor Inn** (Consort) ☎ (075678) 666

A stone-built country pub, whose garden leads down to the Leeds-Liverpool canal.

8rm(6⇌2⋔)(1fb) CTV in all bedrooms ® T sB&B⇌⋔£25—£28 dB&B⇌⋔£35—£38

CTV 175P

Wine £5 Last dinner 9pm

Credit cards 1 2 3 V

GARSTANG
Lancashire
Map **7** SD44

★★**Crofters** Cabus (A6) (Consort) ☎ (09952) 4128

A modern well-furnished hotel on the A6, close to Garstang.

23rm(3⇌20⋔)(4fb) CTV in all bedrooms ® T S% ✱ sB&B⇌⋔£25—£28.50 dB&B⇌⋔£29—£33.50

200P *xmas*

English & French V ✱Lunch £5.15&alc Dinner £8.50alc Wine £5.25 Last dinner 10pm

Credit cards 1 2 3 5

G

GARVE
Highland *Ross & Cromarty*
Map **14** NH36

★★**Garve** ☎ (09974) 205

Closed Nov—Mar

Large stone building set on the main road in the shadow of Ben Wyvis.

35rm(16⇢)(2fb) sB&B£14.50—£16.50 dB&B£29—£33 dB&B⇢£33 B

CTV 100P ⌂ ✿ snooker

V ♁ ☕ Lunch £3.50—£4.50&alc Tea £1—£3.50 High Tea £3.50—£4.50 Dinner £9.50—£12.50 Wine £3.50 Last dinner 9.30pm

Credit cards 1 2 3 Ⓥ

★★**Inchbae Lodge** Inchbae ☎ Aultguish (09975) 269

Comfortable, family-run hotel offering good food and located 6m W of Garve on A835.

6rm(3⇢) Annexe: 6⋒(3fb) Ⓡ sB&B£18.50—£20 sB&B⇢⋒£19.50—£20 dB&B£31—£34 dB&B⇢⋒£34

30P ✿ ♪

♕ Scottish & French ♁ ☕ Bar lunch £3.50alc Tea £1alc High Tea £3.50alc Dinner £11.50 Wine £4.20 Last dinner 9pm

GATEHOUSE OF FLEET
Dumfries & Galloway *Kirkcudbrightshire*
Map **11** NX55

★★★★*L* **Cally Palace** ☎ Gatehouse (05574) 341 Telex no 777088

Closed Nov—Feb

This tastefully-appointed and comfortable hotel, standing in tree-studded grounds overlooking the town, offers a wide range of facilities.

52⇢(22fb) 1 CTV in all bedrooms ⓇT S% sB&B⇢fr£32 dB&B⇢fr£64 B

Lift ☾ 100P ✿ (heated) (hard) sauna bath solarium putting croquet Live music & dancing Sat

V ♁ ☕ S% Lunch fr£5.50 Tea fr£1.50 Dinner fr£11.50 Wine £4.50 Last dinner 9.30pm

Credit card 3 Ⓥ

★★★**Murray Arms** (Best Western) ☎ Gatehouse (05574) 207 Telex no 8814912

An historic 17th-century posting house carefully extended to retain its traditional character.

13rm(11⇢1⋒)(2fb) CTV in all bedrooms ⓇT S% sB&B£23 sB&B⇢⋒£25—£27 dB&B⇢⋒£50—£54 B

☾ CTV 20P ✿ *xmas*

V ♁ ☕ S% Bar lunch £3—£5 Tea £1.50—£2.50 High Tea £3—£5 Dinner £11—£12.50 Wine £4.95 Last dinner 9pm

Credit cards 1 2 3 5 Ⓥ

GATESHEAD
Tyne & Wear
Map **12** NZ26

★★★**Five Bridges** High West St (Swallow) ☎ Tyneside (091) 4771105 Telex no 53534

Situated on the southern approach to Newcastle and named after the five Tyne Bridges, this is a modern hotel with a pleasantly refurbished bar and restaurant.

106⇢⋒(6fb) CTV in all bedrooms ⓇT S% sB&B⇢⋒£25—£39.50 dB&B⇢⋒£38—£50 B

Lift ☾ CTV 12P 60⌂ CFA (heated) sauna bath solarium gymnasium Live music and dancing Sat ♿ *xmas*

♕ English & Continental V ♁ ☕ S% ✱ Lunch £5—£10&alc Tea fr75p High Tea £2.70—£5.50 Dinner £9.75—£10.25&alc Wine £5.50 Last dinner 10pm

Credit cards 1 2 3 4 5

★★★**Springfield** Durham Rd (Embassy) ☎ Tyneside (091) 4774121

RS Xmas

Recently modernised to a most comfortable standard. The elegant restaurant offers a carvery as well as the standard menu.

40⇢⋒(2fb) CTV in all bedrooms ⓇT S% ✱sB&B⇢⋒£39.50—£44 dB&B⇢⋒£54.50 B

☾ 100P

V ♁ ☕ S% ✱ Lunch £4.50—£7.50&alc Tea 65p—£1.75 Dinner £7.50&alc Wine £5.10 Last dinner 9.30pm

Credit cards 1 2 3 5

GATTONSIDE
Borders *Roxburghshire*
Map **12** NT53

✕✕**Hoebridge Inn** ☎ Melrose (089682) 3082

The modern exterior of this extended farmhouse belies its rustic Italian interior, and a high standard of interesting food coupled with warmth and efficiency of service attracts many visitors to the quiet riverside village.

Closed Mon 1st 2 wks Apr, 1st 2 wks Oct Lunch not served

♕ International V 46 seats Dinner £10—£12alc Wine £5.25 Last dinner 10pm 12P

Credit card 3

GATWICK AIRPORT (LONDON)
West Sussex
Map **4** TQ24 **See plan**

★★★★***Copthorne*** Copthorne Rd, Copthorne, Crawley (on A264 2m E of A264/B2036 Rbt) ☎ Copthorne (0342) 714971 Telex no 95500 Plan **4**

16th-century farmhouse with modern amenities but retaining original charm.

223rm(177⇢46⋒)(10fb) CTV in all bedrooms ⓇT

☾ CTV 300P CFA ✿ squash billiards sauna bath solarium gymnasium ♿

♕ English & Continental V ♁ ☕ Last dinner 10.30pm

Credit cards 1 2 3 5

★★★★**Gatwick Hilton International** ☎ Crawley (0293) 518080 Telex no 877021 Plan **7**

Compact, modern hotel.

333⇢⋒(4fb) in 4 bedrooms CTV in all bedrooms T S% ✱sB&B⇢⋒£78.75—£84.75 dB&B⇢⋒£95.50—£101.50

Lift ☾ # P(charged) CFA (heated) sauna bath solarium gymnasium ♿ *xmas*

♕ Continental V ♁ ☕ ✱ Lunch £10.50—£12.50&alc Tea £4.50—£6.75 High Tea £10—£12&alc Dinner £14.50—£17.50&alc Wine £7.25 Last dinner 10.30pm

Credit cards 1 2 3 4 5

★★★**Chequers Thistle** Brighton Rd, Horley (Thistle) ☎ Horley (0293) 786992 Telex no 877550 Plan **3**

Originally a Tudor coaching house, now extended to form a modern hotel.

78⇢⋒(2fb) in 16 bedrooms CTV in all bedrooms ⓇT ✱sB⇢⋒£52—£62 dB⇢⋒£60—£70(room only) B

☾ 185P CFA ✿

♕ International ♁ ☕ ✱ Lunch fr£7.25&alc Dinner fr£10.50&alc Wine £7 Last dinner 10pm

Credit cards 1 2 3 4 5 Ⓥ

★★★**Gatwick Concorde** Church Rd, Lowfield Heath, Crawley (Queens Moat) ☎ Crawley (0293) 33441 Telex no 87287 Plan **6**

Closed Xmas

Imaginatively designed and well equipped bedrooms with some compact family bedrooms, and generally acceptable standards of cuisine.

92⇢⋒(2fb) CTV in all bedrooms ⓇT S% ✱sB⇢⋒£45.75 dB⇢⋒£61.50(room only) B

Lift ☾ # 100P(£2.25 per night) CFA ♿ *xmas*

♕ English & French V ♁ ☕ Lunch £7.50&alc Tea £1 Dinner £9.50&alc Wine £5.25 Last dinner 10pm

Credit cards 1 2 3 5

★★★**George** High St, Crawley (Trusthouse Forte) ☎ Crawley (0293) 24215 Telex no 87385 Plan **11**

Welcoming 15th century tile-hung inn with attractive dining room and coffee shop. Service is friendly and bedrooms modern.

76⇢(3fb) CTV in all bedrooms Ⓡ sB&B⇢£54.50 dB&B⇢£68.50 B

☾ 75P CFA *xmas*

♁ ☕ Last dinner 9.30pm

Credit cards 1 2 3 4 5

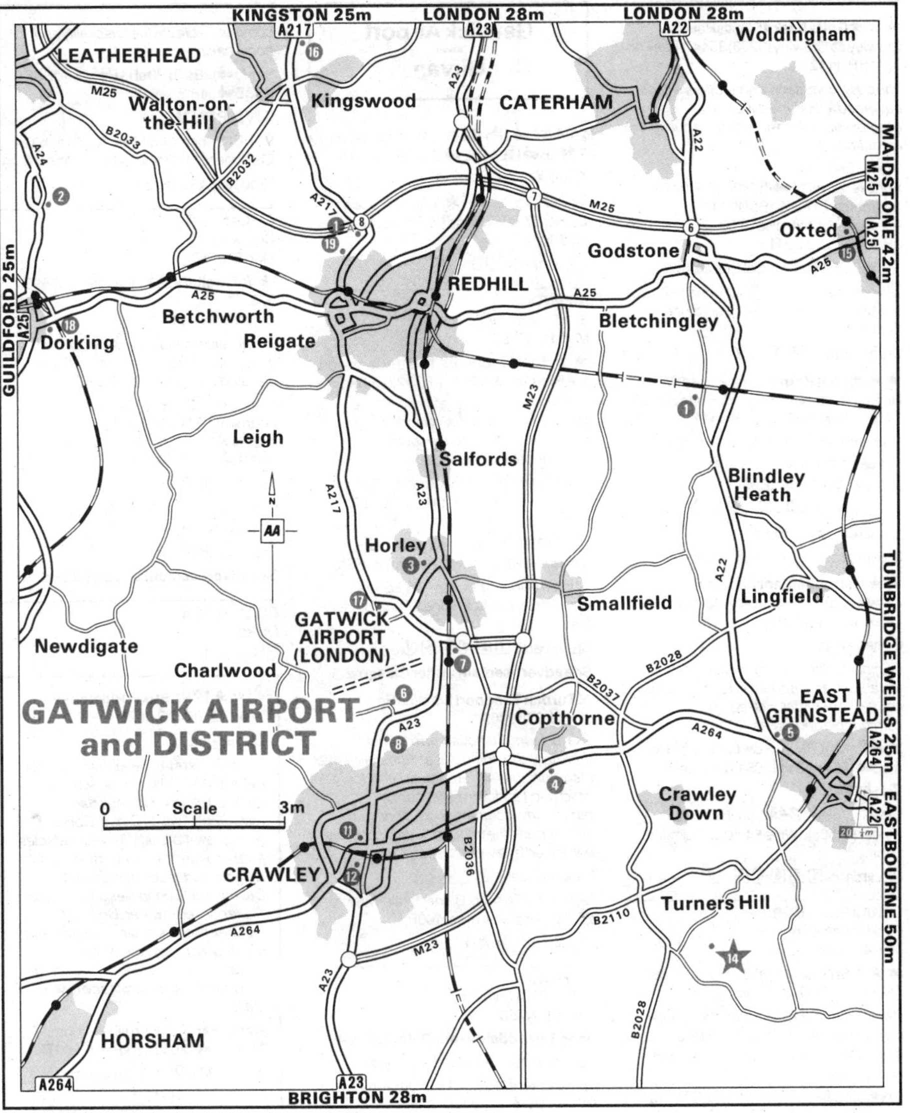

Gatwick Airport & District

1 La Bonne Auberge ✕✕ *(See under South Godstone)*

1A Bridge House ★★ *(See under Reigate)*

2 Burford Bridge ★★★★ *(See under Dorking)*

3 Chequers Thistle ★★★

4 Copthorne ★★★★

5 Felbridge Hotel & Health Club ★★★ *(See under East Grinstead)*

6 Gatwick Concorde ★★★

7 Gatwick Hilton International ★★★★

8 Gatwick Manor ★★

11 George ★★★

12 Goffs Park ★★★

14 Gravetye Manor ❀★★★ *(See under East Grinstead)*

15 Hoskins ★★ *(See under Oxted)*

16 Heathside ★★ *(See under Burgh Heath)*

17 Post House ★★★

18 Punch Bowl ★★ *(See under Dorking)*

19 Reigate Manor ★★ *(See under Reigate)*

20 Woodbury House ★★ *(See under East Grinstead)*

★★★**Goffs Park** 45 Goffs Park Rd, Crawley ☎ Crawley (0293) 35447 Telex no 87415 Plan **12**

The busy, commercial hotel offers well-equipped accommodation, a cosmopolitan atmosphere in the public areas and a choice of bars.

37rm(18⇒17⋒)
Annexe: 22rm(14⇒6⋒)(2fb) CTV in all bedrooms ® T S% sB&B£30 sB&B⇒⋒£42.50 dB&B£39 dB&B⇒⋒£59.50 **B**

☾150P CFA ✿ Disco Sat Cabaret mthly

English & French **V** Lunch £7&alc Tea 65p Dinner £7.75&alc Last dinner 9.30pm

Credit cards 1 2 3 5 Ⓥ

★★★**Post House** Povey Cross Rd, Horley (Trusthouse Forte) ☎ Horley (0293) 771621 Telex no 877351 Plan **17**

Efficient, well-managed modern hotel.

148⇒ CTV in all bedrooms ® sB&B⇒£58.50 dB&B⇒£77.50

Lift ☾350P CFA ✿ (heated) ♿

Last dinner 10.30pm

Credit cards 1 2 3 4 5

★★ **Gatwick Manor** London Rd, Crawley (Berni) ☎ Crawley (0293) 26301 Telex no 87529 Plan **8**

Closed Xmas

Original Tudor buildings house Berni restaurant, and modern extension across courtyard provides well-equipped comfortable bedrooms.

30⇒⋒(7fb) CTV in all bedrooms ® T ✱sB⇒⋒£44 dB⇒⋒£54(room only)

☾150P ✿ ♿

Mainly grills ✱Lunch £7.50alc Dinner £7.50alc Wine £4.50 Last dinner 10pm

Credit cards 1 2 3 4 5

GERRARDS CROSS

Buckinghamshire
Map **4** TQ08

★★★**Bull** (De Vere) ☎ (0753) 880368 Telex no 847747

Originally a coaching inn, this busy hotel, set in its own grounds near the station, offers a warm welcome and many of the traditional services.

98⇒(6fb) 2 in 6 bedrooms CTV in all bedrooms ® T S% sB&B⇒£50–£63 dB&B⇒£60–£85 **B**

Lift ☾220P CFA ✿

English & French **V** S% Lunch £13–£14.50 Tea £1–£1.50 Dinner £13.75–£14.50&alc Wine £6.50 Last dinner 9.30pm

Credit cards 1 2 3 5

★★ *B* **Ethorpe** Packhorse Rd (Berni) ☎ (0753) 882039

Closed Xmas

Small, commercial Berni hotel with friendly, informal atmosphere.

29rm(28⇒1⋒) 1 CTV in all bedrooms ® T sB⇒⋒£44 dB⇒⋒£56(room only)

☾80P ✿

Mainly grills ✱Lunch £7.50alc Dinner £7.50alc Wine £4.50 Last dinner 10.20pm

Credit cards 1 2 3 5

GIFFNOCK

Strathclyde *Renfrewshire*
Map **11** NS55

★★★*B* **MacDonald Thistle** Eastwood Toll Rbt, (Thistle) ☎ 041-638 2225 Telex no 779138

Modern hotel at the Eastwood Toll roundabout (A77), on the southern outskirts of Glasgow.

54⇒⋒(1fb) in 10 bedrooms CTV in all bedrooms ® T ✱sB⇒⋒£45–£55 dB⇒⋒£55–£65(room only) **B**

Lift ☾100P CFA ✿ sauna bath solarium gymnasium Live music and dancing Sat

International ✱Lunch fr£6.95&alc Dinner fr£10.95&alc Wine £7 Last dinner 10pm

Credit cards 1 2 3 4 5 Ⓥ

See advertisement under Glasgow

✕**Turban Tandoori** 2 Station Rd ☎ 041-638 0069

The restaurant is housed in a modern, brick-faced building close to the station; the menu includes all the popular items (of which the Tandoori dishes can be particularly recommended), service is attentive and the congenial atmosphere is enhanced by a wealth of pot plants.

Lunch not served

Indian **V** 70 seats Dinner £7alc Wine £5.75 Last dinner mdnt 100P

Credit cards 1 2 3

GIFFORD

Lothian *East Lothian*
Map **12** NT56

★★ **Tweeddale Arms** ☎ (062081) 240

Country hotel in an attractive village.

15rm(13⇒2⋒)(2fb) CTV in all bedrooms ® T sB&B⇒⋒£22.50–£25 dB&B⇒⋒£38–£45 **B**

xmas

V Lunch £6.50 Tea £1.95 High Tea £3.95 Dinner £9.75&alc Wine £4.50 Last dinner 9pm

Credit cards 2 3 Ⓥ

GIGHA ISLAND

Strathclyde *Argyllshire*
Map **10** NR64
(Car Ferry from Tayinloan (mainland))

★★*HL* **Gigha** ☎ (05835) 254

Closed Nov–31 Mar

This extended and modernised inn has won an architectural award; equally commendable are the hospitality and home baking.

9rm(3⇒) sB&B£20 sB&B⇒£23 dB&B£40 dB&B⇒£46

CTV 20P ✿

V Lunch £6.50 Tea £1.50 High Tea £7 Dinner £11 Wine £4.20 Last dinner 8pm

Credit cards 1 3 Ⓥ

GILLAN

Cornwall
Map **2** SW72

★★**Tregildry** ☎ Manaccan (032623) 378

Closed Nov–Etr

Imaginative menus of well-cooked dishes are offered at this family-run hotel with elevated views over Falmouth Bay.

11rm(6⇒1⋒)(2fb) CTV available in 6 bedrooms ® ✱sB&Bfr£15 sB&B⇒⋒fr£17 dB&Bfr£30 dB&B⇒⋒fr£34 **B**

CTV 20P ✿

✱Dinner £8.50&alc Wine £4.50 Last dinner 8.30pm

Credit cards 1 3

See advertisement under Helford

GILLINGHAM

Dorset
Map **3** ST82

❀★★*HL* **Stock Hill House** Wyke ☎ (07476) 3626

Closed Feb

The owners of this delightful little hotel, Peter and Nita Hauser, previously gained distinction for their Sark restaurant, Aval du Creux. Good quality raw materials, fresh vegetables and herbs are transmuted into repasts which include such delicacies as Devon Crab Quennelles and Wing of Skate cooked in Cider. Desserts feature delicious Austrian dishes, and the meal includes coffee and sweetmeats. Attractive surroundings and warm hospitality will add to your pleasure.

10rm(4⇒6⋒) CTV in all bedrooms T sB&B⇒⋒£30 dB&B⇒⋒£60 **B**

25P ✿ (heated) sauna bath solarium nc 7yrs *xmas*

English, Austrian & French **V** S% Lunch £9 Dinner £15 Wine £6.39 Last dinner 9pm

Credit cards 1 3

GIRVAN

Strathclyde *Ayrshire*
Map **10** NX19

★★ **King's Arms** Dalrymple St ☎ (0465) 3322

This family-run hotel places the emphasis on good food and friendly service, whilst golfing cocktails such as 'The Perfect Slice' are a feature of the Bunker Bar.

27rm(8⇌3⋒)(4fb) CTV in 20 bedrooms ® **T** ✗ sB&Bfr£18 sB&B⇌⋒fr£20 dB&Bfr£29 dB&B⇌⋒fr£31 **B**

40P 1⌂ snooker games room *xmas*

V ♆ ☕ Lunch £3.50alc Tea fr65p alc High Tea £4alc Dinner £8.50alc Wine £3.80 Last dinner 9.30pm

Credit cards 1 3 Ⓥ

GISBURN
Lancashire
Map **7** SD84

★★★**Stirk House** (Consort) ☎ (02005) 581 Telex no 635238

A 16th-century manor house with modern extensions, situated in the Ribble Valley.

40rm(37⇌3⋒) Annexe: 12⇌ (2fb) CTV in all bedrooms ® **T** ✗ S% sB&B⇌⋒fr£35 dB&B⇌⋒fr£49 **B**

☾ 100P CFA ✿ ⊡ (heated) squash sauna bath solarium Disco Sat *xmas*

♉ English & French ♆ S% Lunch £7—£9 Dinner fr£9&alc Wine £5.55 Last dinner 9.30pm

Credit cards 1 2 3 4 5 Ⓥ

GITTISHAM
Devon
Map **3** SY19

★★♛**Combe House**

(see red star box on next page)

GLAMIS
Tayside *Angus*
Map **15** NO34

✕✕**Strathmore Arms** ☎ (030784) 248

Nicely-appointed country restaurant and bar, in a historic village, with the famous Glamis Castle nearby.

Closed Mon (Jan—Etr) Dinner not served Sun (Jan—Etr) →

★★

★★ COMBE HOUSE, GITTISHAM

(Pride of Britain) ☎ Honiton (0404) 2756

Closed 12 Jan—26 Feb

Approached from the National Trust village up a long drive through the 3500 acres estate, this Elizabethan house stands in six acres of gardens featuring some fine trees and marvellous views. John and Thérèse Boswell, converted the hotel with a minimum of disturbance to its structure. Indeed, many of the original features remain and the hall with its dark panelling, massive chimney piece and moulded ceiling sets the scene for the rest of the house. There is the elegant drawing room and a second, more cosy, sitting room at the rear adjoining the intimate bar. The whole is appropriately furnished with antiques, paintings and prints, and fresh flowers abound. No doubt all this is the work of Thérèse Boswell, a professional artist, who has some of her own work at the hotel. It is she who has been responsible for the catering arrangements but last year Robert Doble was employed as chef. His is the modern style which he brings off to good effect. Most of the bedrooms are

spacious, all are comfortable and well equipped and include homemade biscuits and small boxes of chocolates. Traditional services are provided and the friendly attitude of the cheerful young staff make their own welcoming contribution to the pleasure of a stay here.

12 CTV in all bedrooms **T** S%
*sB&B £37—£52.50
dB&B £61—£71.50 **B**

50P 3 (charge) *xmas*

English & French **V** S% *Bar lunch fr£2.50 Tea fr£2.50 Dinner fr£17 Wine £5.90 Last dinner 9.30pm

Credit cards [1] [2] [3] [5]

G

Scottish & French 90 seats Lunch £4.20—£5.50 Dinner £8.50—£11&alc Wine £5 Last dinner 9pm 40P

Credit cards [1] [2] [3] [5]

GLANTON
Northumberland
Map **12** NU01

★ ***Red Lion*** ☎ Powburn (066578) 216

RS Dec—Feb

Standing close to the A697, this unpretentious village inn is ideally situated for touring.

6rm (1fb)

CTV 50P billiards

V Last dinner 9.30pm

GLASGOW
Strathclyde *Lanarkshire*
Map **11** NS56 **See plan**

★★★★**Albany** Bothwell St (Trusthouse Forte) ☎ 041-248 2656 Telex no 77440
Central plan **1** *B3*

Large, modern, city-centre hotel with an attractive restaurant.

258 CTV in all bedrooms ®**T**
sB&B £62 dB&B £79 **B**

Lift ☾ ## 25P CFA

Last dinner 11pm

Credit cards [1] [2] [3] [4] [5]

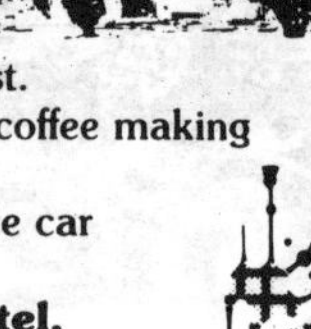

Glasgow

★★★★B **Holiday Inn Glasgow** Argyle St, Anderston (Holiday Inns) ☎041-226 5577 Telex no 776355 Central plan **7** *B2*

Centrally located 'high rise' hotel close to bus, rail and motorway, with good leisure facilities.

296→⫪(80fb)⁄ in 35 bedrooms CTV in all bedrooms **T** sB→⫪£72.05—£78.95 dB→⫪£91.20(room only) **B**

Lift ☾ # 200P (heated) squash sauna bath solarium gymnasium Live music and dancing Fri—Sun ♿ *xmas*

European **V** ♡ Lunch £6—£11.50 Tea £2 Dinner £6—£13.75&alc Wine £7.50 Last dinner 11pm

Credit cards 1 2 3 4 5

★★★★ **Hospitality Inn** 36 Cambridge St (Mount Charlotte) ☎041-332 3311 Telex no 777334 Central plan **7A** *C4*

Glasgow's largest hotel stands close to the Theatre Royal and the STV studios, providing undercover private car parking and spacious amenities.

316→ CTV in all bedrooms ®**T** S% sB&B→£31.25—£48.75 dB&B→£36.50—£54 **B**

Lift ☾ 250 CFA *xmas*

Scottish, Danish & American **V** ♡ S% Lunch fr£5.75&alc Tea fr£2.50 Dinner fr£7&alc Wine £6.25 Last dinner 11.30pm

Credit cards 1 2 3 4 5 Ⓥ

★★★★ **Stakis Grosvenor** Grosvenor Ter, Great Western Rd (Stakis) ☎041-339 8811 Telex no 776247 District plan **23**

Impressively modernised hotel which has retained its traditional character.

95→⫪(11fb) 1 CTV in all bedrooms ®**T** sB→⫪£40—£54 dB→⫪£50—£70(room only) **B**

Lift ☾ 70P

V ♡ ⁄ Lunch £5—£8 Tea 75p—£1.20 High Tea £5—£7 Dinner £6—£15&alc Wine £4.50 Last dinner 11pm

Credit cards 1 2 3 4 5

★★★ **Bellahouston Swallow** 517 Paisley Road West (Swallow) ☎041-427 3146 Telex no 778795 District plan **15**

Modern hotel on the south side of the city, close to the M8.

122→ CTV in all bedrooms ®**T** S% *sB&B→£41.50—£46.50 dB&B→£52—£56 **B**

Lift ☾ 150P CFA ♿ *xmas*

English & French **V** ♡ S% *Lunch £5.25&alc Dinner £8.50&alc Wine £5.50 Last dinner 9.30pm

Credit cards 1 2 3 5

★★★ **Crest Hotel Glasgow-City** Argyle St (Crest) ☎041-248 2355 Telex no 779652 Central plan **5** *B2*

RS 24 Dec—4 Jan

Modern city centre hotel opposite Anderston Bus Station.

121→⁄ in 15 bedrooms CTV in all bedrooms ®**T** S% sB&B→£51.95 dB&B→£66 **B**

Lift P CFA

International **V** ♡ ⁄ S% Lunch £7.60&alc Tea £1.25 High Tea £1.95 Dinner £11.15&alc Wine £5.65 Last dinner 9.45pm

Credit cards 1 2 3 4 5

★★★ **Stakis Burnbrae** Milngavie Rd, Bearsden (Stakis) ☎041-942 5951 Not on plan

(For full entry see Bearsden)

★★★ **Stakis Ingram** Ingram St (Stakis) ☎041-248 4401 Telex no 776470 Central plan **8** *D2*

Modern city centre hotel.

90→⫪(1fb)⁄ in 39 bedrooms CTV in all bedrooms ®**T** S% sB&B→⫪£35—£48.90 dB&B→⫪£42—£59.90 **B**

Lift ☾ CTV 40P CFA Live music Sat

V ♡ *Lunch £4.50 Tea 60p—80p Dinner £7.50&alc Last dinner 9.45pm

Credit cards 1 2 3 4 5 Ⓥ

★★★ **Stakis Pond** Great Western Road (Stakis) ☎041-334 8161 Telex no 776573 District plan **20**

Modern hotel in the north-west suburbs of the city.

132→⫪(6fb)⁄ in 20 bedrooms CTV in all bedrooms ®sB&B→⫪£45.90 dB&B→⫪£59.80 **B**

Lift ☾ CTV 200P ✿ (heated) sauna bath solarium gymnasium Disco Tue & Thu *xmas*

V ♡ ⁄ Lunch fr£5.98&alc Tea £1 alc Dinner fr£8.95&alc Wine £5.50 Last dinner 10pm

Credit cards 1 2 3 5

★★★B **Tinto Firs Thistle** 470 Kilmarnock Road (Thistle) ☎041-637 2353 Telex no 778329 District plan **24**

Attractively refurbished hotel on south side of city in residential area, with popular restaurant and bars.

27→⫪(2fb)⁄ in 2 bedrooms CTV in all bedrooms ®**T** ✗ *sB→⫪£45—£55 dB→⫪£55—£65(room only) **B**

☾ 46P Live music & dancing Fri

International *Lunch fr£6.50&alc Dinner fr£11.25&alc Wine £7 Last dinner 9.15pm

Credit cards 1 2 3 4 5 Ⓥ

★★ **Ewington** 132 Queens Dr, Queens Park ☎041-423 1152 District plan **16**

Friendly, traditional hotel in a terrace overlooking the park.

47rm(4→12⫪)(1fb) CTV available in bedrooms **T** S% *sB&B£18.50—£20 sB&B→⫪£21.50—£26 dB&B£33—£36 dB&B→⫪£34—£38

Lift ☾ CTV 12P

♡ S% *Lunch £4—£5 Tea £2.50—£3 High Tea £4—£4.50 Dinner £7.25—£8&alc Wine £4 Last dinner 8.30pm

Credit cards 1 2 3 5 Ⓥ

★★ **Newlands** 260 Kilmarnock Rd ☎041-632 9171 District plan **18**

Conveniently situated, small hotel, set in the southern suburbs of the city.

17→ CTV in all bedrooms ® sB&B→£17.50—£28 dB&B→£35—£52 **B**

☾ snooker

French & Italian **V** ♡ ⁄ *Bar lunch £3.25—£5&alc Tea £1—£2.50 Dinner £10 alc Wine £5.55 Last dinner 9.45pm

Credit cards 1 2 3 5

G

G

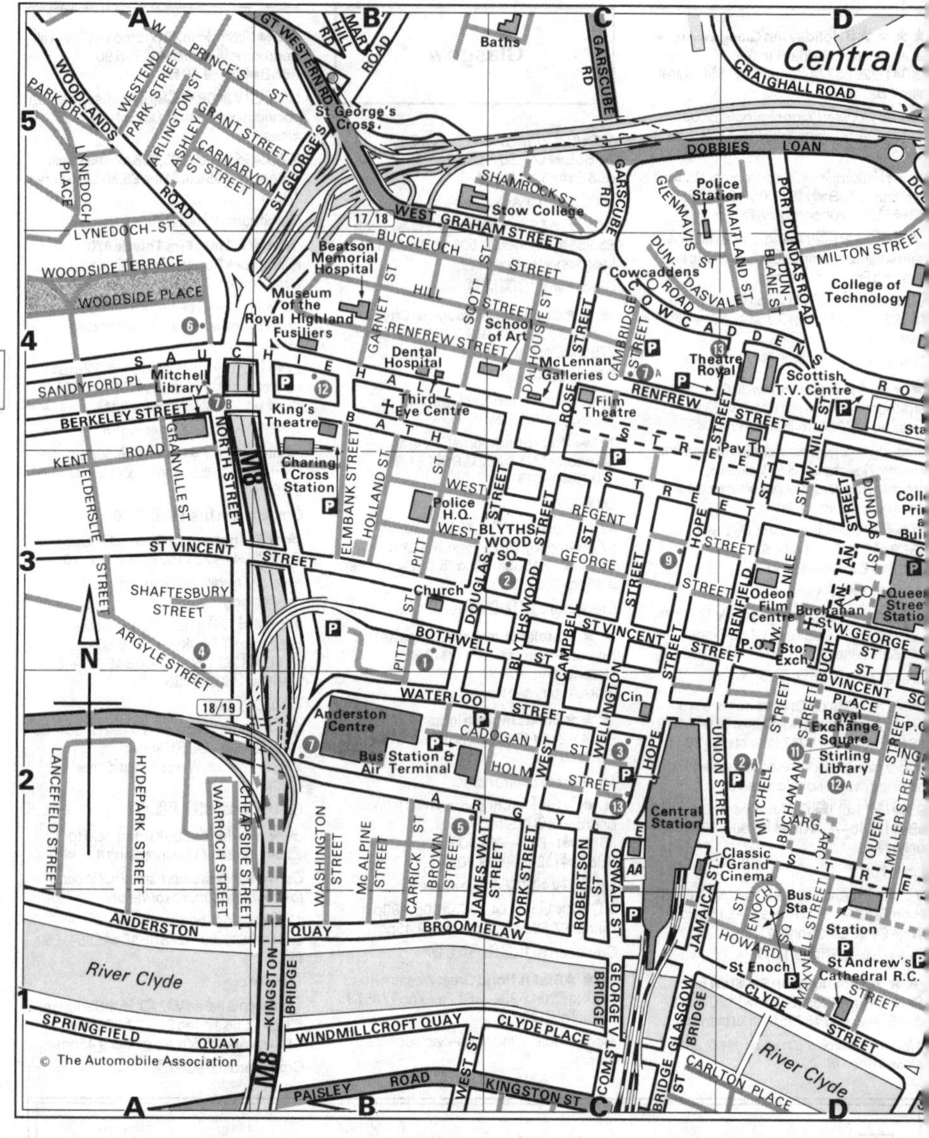

★★**Sherbrooke** 11 Sherbrooke Av, Pollokshields ☎ 041-427 4227 District plan **21**

Closed 1 & 2 Jan

Traditional red sandstone building located on south side of city with convenient access to motorway.

9rm(5🛁4🚿) CTV in all bedrooms ®**T** sB&B🛁🚿fr£31.50 dB&B🛁🚿fr£41.50 ⊞ 50P 🚐 ✿

🍽English & French **V** 🍷 ☕ Lunch fr£5.50&alc Tea fr60p High Tea fr£5 Dinner fr£8.20&alc Wine £4.65 Last dinner 8.30pm

Credit cards 1 2 3 5

★★**Wickets** 52—54 Fortrose St, Partickhill ☎ 041-334 9334 District plan **26**

Closed New Years Day

9rm(5🛁🚿)(2fb) 🚭 in 5 bedrooms CTV in all bedrooms ®**T** sB&B£29.95 sB&B🛁🚿£33.95 dB&B£39.95 dB&B🛁🚿£43.95—£49.95 ⊞

☾ 35P ✿ 👪

🍽European **V** 🍷 ☕ Lunch £5.95—£9.50&alc Tea £1.25—£2.95 High Tea £3.95—£4.95 Dinner £9.50&alc Wine £3.95 Last dinner 10.30pm

Credit cards 1 2 3 4 5 Ⓥ

✕✕✕**Ambassador** 19/20 Blythswood Sq ☎ 041-221 2034 Central plan **2** *C3*

Well appointed basement Italian restaurant.

🍽International 100 seats Lunch £7—£9&alc Dinner £10—£12&alc Wine £4 Last dinner 11pm P 🚭 Live music & dancing Fri & Sat

Credit cards 1 2 3 4 5

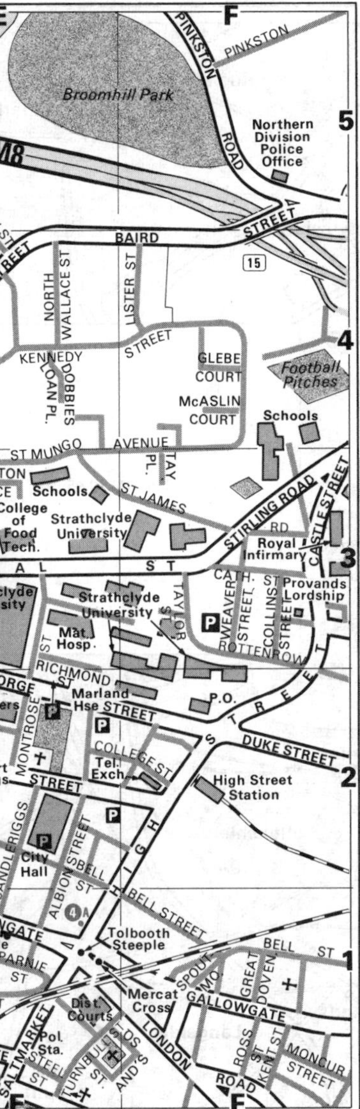

Glasgow Central

1	Albany ★★★★
2	Ambassador XXX
2A	L'Ariosto Ristorante XX
3	The Basement at Archies's X
4	Buttery ❀XX
4A	Colonial XX
5	Crest Hotel Glasgow — City ★★★
6	Fountain ❀XXX
7	Holiday Inn Glasgow ★★★★
7A	Hospitality Inn ★★★★
7B	Koh-i-Noor XX
8	Stakis Ingram ★★★
9	Peking Inn X
12	Loon Fung X
12A	Rogano XX
13	Trattoria Caruso X

❀XXX**Fountain**

(see boxed rosette entry top of column)

XX **L'Arosto Ristorante** 92—94 Mitchell St ☎ 041-221 0971 Central plan **2A** *D2*

A wide range of international and Italian dishes is offered at this very popular and authentic Italian trattoria in the city centre. Though there is a cover charge after 8.30, the dinner dance is a great attraction.

Closed Sun

Italian **V** 110 seats ✱Lunch £4.95—£7.85&alc Dinner £12alc Wine £4.80 Last dinner 11pm Live music & dancing Tue—Sat

Credit cards 1 2 3 5

❀XX**Buttery**

(see boxed rosette entry in next column)

XX**Colonial** 25 High St ☎ 041-552 1923 Central plan **4A** *E1*

Situated in one of the city's more historic areas, this established restaurant places emphasis on 'the modern taste of Scotland', introducing interesting variations on traditional dishes.

Closed Sun, 25, 26 Dec, 1—4 Jan & 18 Jul—3 Aug
Lunch not served Sat
Dinner not served Mon

French **V** 45 seats Lunch £5.95—£8.75&alc Dinner £15—£18.90&alc Wine £6 Last dinner 10.30pm nc 4yrs

Credit cards 1 2 3 5

❀XXX**Fountain** 2 Woodside Cres ☎ 041-332 6396 Central plan **6** *A4*

The restaurant, small and intimate, yet furnished in the grand, formal style, features haute cuisine in its split level dining room and tasty bar snacks in the comfortable cocktail bar. In the evening, a sophisticated singing duo helps to set the atmosphere.

Closed Sun Lunch not served Sat
Dinner not served Mon

French 58 seats ✱Lunch £9.50—£9.95&alc Dinner £13.95&alc Wine £6.50 Last dinner 11pm nc
Live music and dancing Tue—Sat

Credit cards 1 2 3 5

❀XX**Buttery** 652 Argyle St ☎ 041-221 8188 Central plan **4** *A3*

The splendour and atmosphere of a previous age has been recaptured in the extensive refurbishment of this city-centre restaurant. The predominantly French menu is adventurous, featuring such imaginative dishes as Terrine of Salmon and Sole or Feuillete of Lambs' Kidneys, all produced with creative flair and served by a capable and attentive staff.

Closed Sun Lunch not served Sat

French 50 seats S% Lunch £11.55&alc Dinner £20alc Wine £6.95 Last dinner 10pm 30P

Credit cards 1 2 3 5

XX**Kensingtons** 164 Darnley St, Pollokshields, ☎ 041-424 3662 District plan **17**

Attractively decorated ground floor restaurant.

Closed Sun & Mon Lunch not served Sat

International 30 seats S% ✱Lunch fr£7.70&alc Dinner fr£17&alc Wine £5.25 Last dinner 9.30pm P

Credit cards 1 2 3 5

See advertisement on page 322

XX**Koh-I-Noor** 235 North St ☎ 041-221 1555 Central plan **7B** *A4*

This spacious and well-appointed restaurant close to the city centre provides Mughal and Punjabi cuisine attentively served by smartly-dresssed staff. Customers have a choice of bars in which to enjoy an aperitif, whilst for special occasions a function suite can accommodate parties of up to 120.

Indian **V** 140 seats Lunch £2.50—£2.70&alc Dinner £8.50—£10&alc Last dinner mdnt
Live music Mon

Credit cards 1 2 3 5

G

G

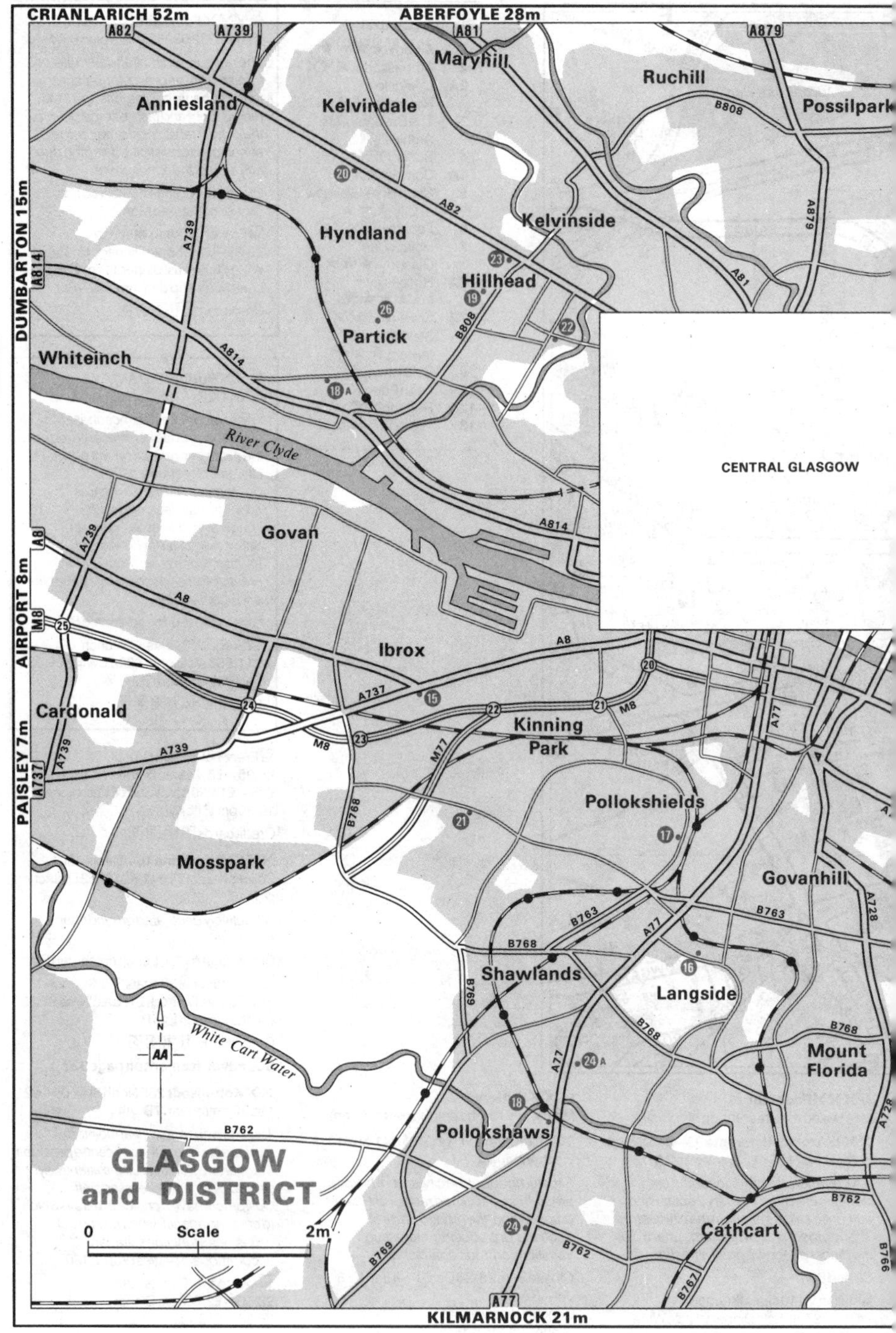
CRIANLARICH 52m
ABERFOYLE 28m
A82
A739
A81
A879
Maryhill
Ruchill
Annniesland
Kelvindale
B808
Possilpark
A82
A879
Kelvinside
DUMBARTON 15m
A814
A739
Hyndland
Hillhead
A81
Partick
B808
Whiteinch
A814
River Clyde
CENTRAL GLASGOW
A814
Govan
A8
A739
AIRPORT 8m
M8
A8
A8
Ibrox
A737
M8
Cardonald
Kinning
Park
A77
M77
M8
A739
B768
PAISLEY 7m
A737
Pollokshields
Mosspark
Govanhill
B763
A728
B763
A77
B768
Shawlands
B769
Langside
White Cart Water
B768
B768
Mount
Florida
A77
Pollokshaws
A728
B762
GLASGOW
and DISTRICT
B762
0
Scale
2m
Cathcart
B769
B762
B767
A77
KILMARNOCK 21m

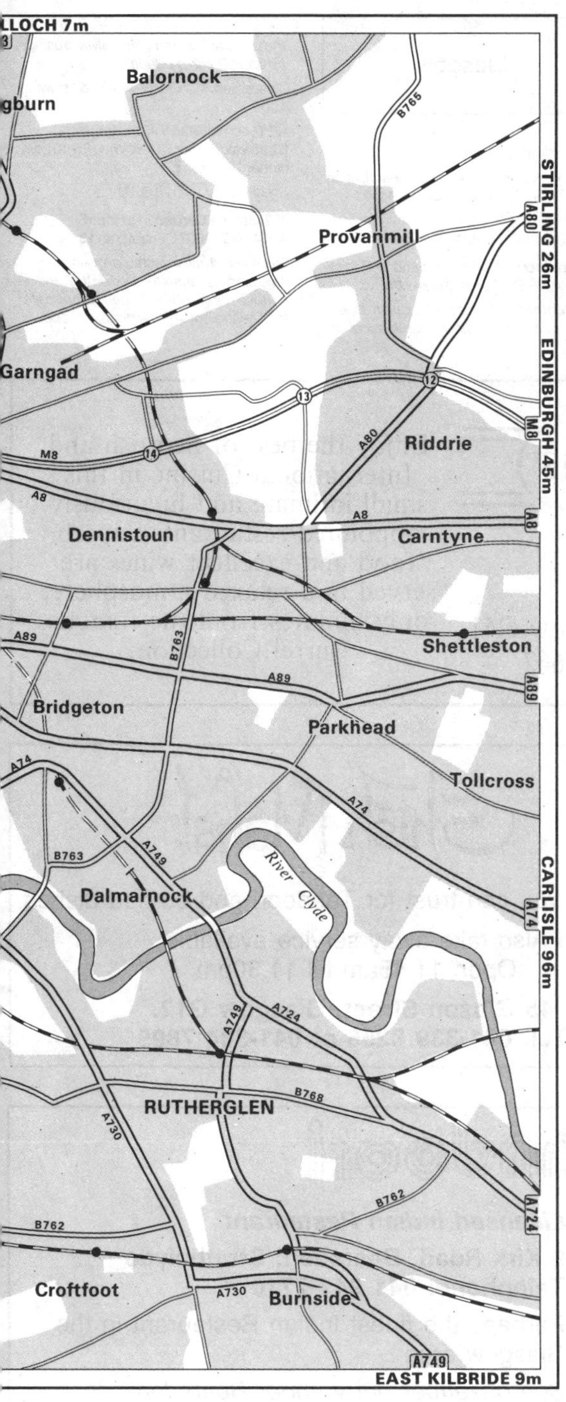

Glasgow District

15	Bellahouston Swallow ★★★
16	Ewington ★★
17	Kensingtons ✕✕
18	Newlands ★★
18A	Peppino's ✕
19	Poachers ✕✕
20	Stakis Pond ★★★
21	Sherbrooke ★★
22	Shish Mahal ✕✕
23	Stakis Grosvenor ★★★★
24	Tinto Firs Thistle ★★★
24A	Trattorio Sorrento ✕
26	Wickets ★★

✕✕**Poachers** Ruthven Ln ☎ 041-339 0932 District plan **19**

Bright, ground-floor restaurant located in a lane off the busy Byres Road and popular with business clientele.

Closed Sun

V 45 seats Lunch £8.50alc Dinner £15alc Wine £5.85 Last dinner 11pm 8P

Credit cards 1 2 3 5

✕✕**Rogano** 11 Exchange Pl ☎ 041-248 4055 Central plan **12A** *D2*

Splendidly restored in the Art Deco style of the 1930's, the city-centre restaurant retains its seafood tradition with a marine theme, though a wide range of meat dishes is also available. Its popularity at lunchtime makes booking advisable.

Closed Sun, Xmas Day, Boxing Day, New Years Day & Bank Hols

French **V** 50 seats S% Lunch £20alc Dinner £20alc Wine £6.95 Last dinner 10.30pm P

Credit cards 1 2 3 5

✕✕**Shish Mahal** 45 Gibson St ☎ 041-334 7899 District plan **22**

Popular, well appointed restaurant with tasteful modern decor, situated close to University.

English, Indian & Pakistani **V** Unlicensed No corkage charge 110 seats ✱Lunch £4&alc Dinner £10alc Last dinner 11.30pm P

Credit cards 1 2 3 4 5

See advertisement on page 322

✕**Basement at Archie's** 27 Waterloo St ☎ 041-221 0551 Central plan **3** *C2*

Not far from the Central station, this popular basement restaurant offers a reasonable variety of dishes — including a good choice of steaks — together with efficient, though unhurried, service. Tastefully decorated and comfortably furnished, it creates a relaxed atmosphere.

Closed Sun Lunch not served Sat

European 48 seats ✱Lunch £8—£14&alc Dinner £8—£14 Wine £5.55 Last dinner 10pm P

Credit cards 1 2 3 5

✕**Loon Fung** 417 Sauchiehall St ☎ 041-332 1240 Central plan **12** *B4*

A former dance hall in one of Glasgow's most famous shopping streets, this is →

G

now the largest Chinese restaurant in the city. Staff are correct and attentive, and the menu specialises in Cantonese dishes.

Cantonese **V** 120 seats Lunch fr£4.20 Dinner fr£6.50 Wine £6.30 Last dinner 11.30pm

Credit cards 1 2 3

✕Peking Inn 191 Hope St ☎ 041-332 8971 Central plan **9** *C3*

Chinese girls in pink mandarin jackets will serve your choice of Peking and Cantonese dishes in the bright, relaxing atmosphere of this spacious, city-centre restaurant where five chefs each produce their own regional specialities.

Glasgow

Closed Sun & Chinese New Year

Cantonese & Pekinese **V** 60 seats Lunch fr£3.90&alc Dinner fr£5.50&alc Wine £5.50 Last dinner 11.30pm

Credit cards 1 2 3 5 Ⓥ

✕Peppino's 11—13 Hyndland St, Partick ☎ 041-339 6523 District plan **18A**

Situated in Partick, this smart, Italian-style restaurant also offers the more classical and popular French dishes, always using the best of fresh produce.

Closed Sun, Mon, last 2 wks Jul & 1st wk Aug

French & Italian **V** 40 seats Lunch £3.95&alc Dinner £11alc Wine £5.30 Last dinner 10.30pm

Credit cards 1 2 3 4 5

✕*Trattoria Caruso* 313 Hope St ☎ 041-331 2607 Central plan **13** *C4*

This modest Italian restaurant with adjoining pizzeria is located on the northern fringe of the city centre, opposite the Theatre Royal. Reasonably-priced,

honest, Italian cuisine is efficiently served in a relaxed and informal atmosphere.

Closed Sun & 1st 2 wks Aug

Italian **V** 120 seats Last dinner 11pm

Credit cards 1 2 3 5

✕**Trattoria Sorrento** 87 Kilmarnock Rd, Shawlands ☎ 041-649 3002 District plan **24A**

This smartly-canopied and glass-fronted trattoria, tucked between two blocks of flats on the main road, has a comfortable split-level interior with a relaxed atmosphere. The tasteful decor is enhanced by trestles and hanging plants, the menu offers a good choice of Italian and Continental dishes, and the friendly staff serve generous portions!

Closed Xmas & New Year

Lunch not served Sun

French & Italian **V** 90 seats Lunch £2—£4.95&alc Dinner £5.25&alc Wine £4.50 Last dinner 11pm

Credit cards 1 2 3 5

GLASGOW AIRPORT
Strathclyde *Renfrewshire*
Map **11** NS46

★★★★**Excelsior** Abbotsinch, Paisley (Trusthouse Forte) ☎ 041-887 1212 Telex no 777733

Modern, high-rise hotel complex situated at the airport terminal.

290 (8fb) CTV in all bedrooms ® **T** sB&B £58 dB&B £76

Lift ☾ ## 35P CFA

Last dinner 10.30pm

Credit cards 1 2 3 4 5

★★★**Crest Hotel Erskine Bridge** North Barr, Inchinan ☎ 041-812 0123 (For full entry see Erksine)

★★★***Dean Park*** 91 Glasgow Rd, Renfrew (3m NE A8) (Consort) ☎ 041-886 3771 Telex no 779032

Modern hotel complex with well equipped bedrooms, popular cocktail bar and good function facilities.

Glasgow — Glastonbury

120 (9fb) CTV in all bedrooms ® **T**

☾ 200P CFA (heated) saunabath solarium gymnasium, Disco Sun Live music and dancing Fri & Sat Cabaret wkly

European **V** Last dinner 9.45pm

Credit cards 1 2 3 4 5

★★★**Glynhill** Paisley Rd, Renfrew (2m E A741) ☎ 041-886 5555 Telex no 779536

Small stone-built hotel, close to airport, with modern rooms, function suite and bars.

80 (25fb) 2 CTV in all bedrooms ® **T** S% sB&B £29—£42 dB&B £40—£52

☾ 200P CFA Live music and dancing Fri & Sat Cabaret mthly *xmas*

International **V** Lunch fr£7 Tea fr£1 Dinner £10—£12.50&alc Wine £6 Last dinner 10.30pm

Credit cards 1 2 3 5 Ⓥ

★★★**Stakis Normandy** Inchinan Rd, Renfrew (2m NE A8) (Stakis) ☎ 041-886 4100 Telex no 778897

Modern hotel adjacent to golf range, operates courtesy bus to and from airport.

142 (3fb) CTV in all bedrooms ® **T** sB&B fr£45.90 dB&B fr£59.80

Lift ☾ ## 750P (heated) sauna bath solarium gymnasium Live music & dancing Sat *xmas*

International Lunch £3.90—£5.95&alc Tea 65p Dinner £3.90—£10.95&alc

Credit cards 1 2 3 5 Ⓥ

★★***Ardgowan*** Blackhall St, Lonend, Paisley ☎ 041-887 2196

Commercial hotel not far from the town offering modest accommodation and function facilities.

17rm (7 7)(1fb) 1 CTV in all bedrooms ®

Lift ☾ CTV 40P sauna bath

V Last dinner 9.30pm

Credit cards 1 3

★★**Rockfield** 125 Renfew Rd, Paisley (2m SE off A741) (Alloa Brewery) ☎ 041-889 6182

Closed Xmas, Boxing & New Years day

A small, friendly hotel with compact rooms and good facilities, close to the airport.

20rm (8 12)(1fb) 1 CTV in all bedrooms ® **T** S% sB&B fr£29.25 dB&B fr£34.75

CTV 100P

S% ✱ Bar lunch £1.75—£2.95 Tea 50—75p Dinner £4.50—£9.50&alc Wine £3.80 Last dinner 8.30pm

Credit cards 1 3 5 Ⓥ

✕**Peking Rendezvous** 40 Old Sneddon St, Paisley ☎ 041-848 1333

Cantonese & Pekinese **V** 90 seats Lunch fr£2.95 Dinner fr£5&alc Wine £4 Last dinner 11.45pm

Credit cards 1 2 3 5

GLASTONBURY
Somerset
Map **3** ST53

★★**George & Pilgrims Hotel & Restaurant** High St (Inter Hotel) ☎ (0458) 31146

Centrally located, comfortable 15th-century hostelry, full of character.

12rm (7 3)(1fb) 4 CTV in all bedrooms ® **T** sB&B £30—£35 dB&B £46—£58

4P *xmas*

English & French **V** Lunch fr£7.50&alc Tea £1.50—£2.50 High Tea 95p—£4.50 Dinner £11.50&alc Last dinner 9.30pm

Credit cards 1 2 3 4 5 Ⓥ

✕✕**No 3** Magdalene St ☎ (0458) 32129

An attractive period house close by the Abbey ruins of this ancient town, the hotel is personally run by the owners to provide interesting menus, carefully cooked, and a thoughtfully chosen wine list.

Closed Mon Lunch not served Tue & Sat Dinner not served Sun

English & French **V** 28 seats Lunch £10.50—£19 Dinner £17—£19 Wine £5.50 Last dinner 9.30pm 8P

Credit cards 2 3 5

G

GLEMSFORD
Suffolk
Map **5** TL84

XX ***Weeks*** 31 Egremont St
☎(0787) 281573

A friendly, relaxed atmosphere pervades this converted Edwardian shop, with its comfortable lounge and fresh, attractive dining room. The menu offers a comparatively small range of dishes, but these are of good quality and well presented.

Closed Sun & Mon
Lunch not served

French 16 seats Last dinner 8.30pm 6P

GLENBORRODALE
Highland *Argyllshire*
Map **13** NM66

★★*H* **Clan Morrison** ☎(09724) 232
Closed Nov—Feb

Small family run hotel in picturesque lochside position specialising in good food.

6 Ⓡ S% *sB&B £16.65—£20.24 dB&B £33.30—£40.48
CTV 40P
V *Bar lunch £2—£5 Dinner £10alc Wine £2.50 Last dinner 8pm
Ⓥ

★★ *BL* **Glenborrodale Castle**
☎(09724) 266

Beautiful red sandstone castle dating from 1900, standing close to Loch Sunart.

19rm(5)(5fb) CTV in all bedrooms Ⓡ sB&B £45.50(incl dinner) sB&B £51.50(incl dinner) dB&B £86(incl dinner)
40P
Last dinner 9pm
Credit cards 1 2 3 4 5

GLENCAPLE
Dumfries & Galloway *Dumfriesshire*
Map **11** NX96

★★**Nith** ☎(038777) 213

Small family run hotel, set on the side of River Nith.

10rm(2 5)(1fb) CTV in 6 bedrooms TV in 4 bedrooms Ⓡ sB&B £15—£17.50 sB&B £17.50—£20 dB&B £28—£30.50 dB&B £30.50—£33
20P
V *Lunch £4alc Tea fr50p High Tea £2.80—£6.95 Dinner £7.40alc Wine £3.05 Last dinner 8.30pm
Credit card 1 Ⓥ

GLENCARSE
Tayside *Perthshire*
Map **11** NO12

★★*H* **Newton House**
☎(073886) 250

Former dower house situated on the edge of the village, bordering the main Perth to Dundee road.

7rm(4 2)(1fb) CTV in all bedrooms Ⓡ T *sB&B £27—£29 dB&B £38—£40
CTV 40P(charge) putting *xmas*
Scottish & French V Lunch £5—£8.10&alc Dinner £11.50—£12.50&alc Wine £5.60 Last dinner 9.30pm
Credit cards 1 2 3 5 Ⓥ

GLENCOE
Highland *Argyllshire*
Map **14** NN15

★★***Glencoe*** ☎ Ballachulish (08552) 245
Closed Nov—Mar

Modernised stone building at the western end of Glencoe overlooking Loch Leven.

13rm(4 1)(3fb) Ⓡ
CTV 30P
V Last dinner 9pm
Credit cards 1 2 3 5

★★***Kings House*** (1.2m SE A82)
☎ Kingshouse (08556) 259
Closed Nov—Jan

A long-established small hotel in an isolated situation of rugged beauty, it was originally a drover's inn. It is a popular stop for today's walkers who appreciate its good Scottish cuisine and warm hospitality.

21rm(12)(1fb)
CTV 70P Live music & dancing Sat
V Last dinner 8.15pm
Credit cards 1 2

GLENDEVON
Tayside *Perthshire*
Map **11** NN90

XX **Tormaukin Hotel** ☎(025982) 252

There is a great deal of country charm about this little restaurant set in a converted 18th century drover's inn. Low beamed ceilings, natural stone walls and highly polished wood create an atmosphere which is found also in the small, tastefully decorated and well equipped bedrooms. À la carte menus offer a pleasant range of international dishes with the accent on Scottish produce, all well cooked and attractively presented.

Closed Jan
International 75 seats Lunch £13.50alc Dinner £13.50alc Wine £5.95 Last dinner 9.45pm 70P
Credit cards 1 2

GLENEAGLES
Tayside *Perthshire*
Map **11** NN91 **See Auchterarder**

GLENFARG
Tayside *Perthshire*
Map **11** NO11

★★*H* **Bein Inn** ☎(05773) 216

Former drovers inn nestling in a beautiful glen, provides comfortable and modern accommodation.

9rm(7) Annexe: 4 (4fb) CTV in all bedrooms Ⓡ sB&B £20.75 sB&B £24.25 dB&B £30.75 dB&B £35—£48
60P

Scottish & French V Lunch £11alc Tea 60p High Tea £4 Dinner £11alc Wine £5.25 Last dinner 10pm

Credit cards [1] [3] (V)

See advertisement under Perth

GLENLIVET
Grampian *Banffshire*
Map **15** NJ12

★★**Minmore House** ☎ (08073) 378

An informal country house atmosphere prevails at this mansion, which has The Glenlivet Distillery as its neighbour. First class country house cooking is a feature.

10rm(9)(2fb)

P (heated) (hard)

Last dinner 9.30pm

Credit cards [1] [3]

GLENLUCE
Dumfries & Galloway *Wigtownshire*
Map **10** NX25

★**King's Arms** 31 Main St ☎ (05813) 219

Modestly-appointed but homely, the family-run hotel stands on the town's main street.

3rm(2)(1fb) ® S% sB&B£10.50 sB&B£11.75 dB&B£21 dB&B£23.50

CTV 16P Cabaret mthly

V S% Bar lunch £2—£8 High Tea £2—£8 Dinner £8.50 Wine £4.50 Last dinner 9pm

GLENRIDDING
Cumbria
Map **11** NY31

★★★*L* **Ullswater** ☎ (08532) 444
Telex no 58164

This is a spacious hotel with elegant, comfortable lounges and fine views of the lake and surrounding fells.

47rm(41 6)(7fb) 1 CTV in 10 bedrooms ® T sB&B£26 dB&B£52—£72

Lift CTV 100P CFA (grass) *xmas*

English & French V Lunch £6.95 Tea 75p—£2 High Tea £3—£5 Dinner £9.95&alc Wine £4.40 Last dinner 9pm

Credit cards [1] [2] [3] [5]

★★**Glenridding** (Best Western) ☎ (08532) 228

Closed 5 Jan—12 Feb

Hotel occupying an unrivalled position at the head of Ullswater.

45rm(34 6)(5fb) ® in 20 bedrooms sB&B fr£24 dB&B fr£42

CTV 24P Live music Thu in season *xmas*

✻ Bar lunch 75p—£3.95 Tea £1.30—£1.50 Dinner £9.50 Wine £4.75 Last dinner 8.30pm

Credit cards [1] [2] [3] [5] (V)

GLENROTHES
Fife
Map **11** NO20

★★★**Balgeddie House** Leslie
☎ (0592) 742511

Closed 1 & 2 Jan RS 25 Dec

Large privately owned mansion dating from 1936 standing on a hillside of six acres of land.

18rm(16 2) CTV in all bedrooms ® T S% sB&B£44 dB&B£60

CTV P pool table

French V S% Lunch £14.50alc Tea £1.65 Dinner £11.55&alc Wine £7.50 Last dinner 9.30pm

Credit cards [1] [2] [3]

★★★**Stakis Albany** 1 North St (Stakis)
☎ (0592) 752292

This purpose-built business hotel, off the A911 in the new town centre, was completely upgraded in 1984 to provide well-appointed bedrooms and an attractive steak-house restaurant.

29rm(15 14) 1 in 8 bedrooms CTV in all bedrooms ® T
✻ sB&B£30.25—£39.90 dB&B£50—£52.80

Lift 60P

V ✻ Lunch £4.80—£12.55 Tea 70p Dinner £4.80—£12.55 Wine £3.90 Last dinner 9.30pm

Credit cards [1] [2] [3] [5]

★★***Greenside*** High St, Leslie (2m W A911) ☎ (0592) 743453

Closed New Years Day

A commercial hotel, offering accommodation in a wing of modern bedrooms.

16rm(10)(1fb) CTV in all bedrooms ® T

CTV 50P *xmas*

V

Credit cards [1] [2] [3] [4]

★*HL* **Rescobie** Valley Dr, Leslie
☎ (0592) 742143

Secluded mansion offering country house atmosphere, comfortable lounges and first class cooking.

8rm(3) CTV in all bedrooms ® sB&B£22 sB&B£28.50 dB&B£39 dB&B£45

10P

V Lunch £3.50—£5.50 Dinner £9.50—£11&alc Wine £4.80 Last dinner 9pm

Credit cards [1] [2] [3] (V)

GLENSHEE (Spittal of)
Tayside *Perthshire*
Map **15** NO16

★★ *L* **Dalmunzie House**
☎ (025085) 224

Closed 1 Nov—20 Dec

This turretted and imposing mansion, with 9-hole private golf course and fishing, stands in a secluded position on an extensive estate. The public rooms offer style and comfort, and a warm welcome is extended by the owners.

19rm(9 1) sB&B£18—£25 dB&B£36—£50 dB&B£40—£56

Lift CTV 30P (hard) ski-ing shooting *xmas*

English & Continental V Bar lunch £1.25—£7.75 Tea £2.75alc Dinner £14alc Last dinner 9pm

Credit cards [1] [5] (V)

★**Dalrulzion Highland** ☎ Blacklunans (025082) 222

The family-run hotel has been created from a historically-interesting building that was originally a hunting lodge.

12rm(2)(3fb) ® sB&B£12—£15 sB&B£15—£18 dB&B£24—£30 dB&B£29—£35

CTV 50P Disco mthly Live music and dancing Sat Cabaret Sun *xmas*

Bar lunch £2—£5 Tea 60p High Tea £3.25—£6 Dinner £8—£9.50&alc Wine £3.75 Last dinner 9pm

Credit card [3] (V)

GLENSHIEL (SHIEL BRIDGE)
Highland *Ross & Cromarty*
Map **14** NG91

★★**Kintail Lodge** ☎ (059981) 275

RS Nov-Mar

Set at the head of Loch Duich, the small, family-run hotel provides comfortable accommodation.

11rm(5 1)(3fb) CTV available in bedrooms ® S% ✻ sB&B£19—£23 dB&B£30—£38 dB&B£42—£52

20P

Scottish & French V S% ✻ Bar lunch £2—£3.50 Tea 80p—£1.50 Dinner £10—£15 Wine £5 Last dinner 8.45pm

Credit cards [1] [3] (V)

GLOUCESTER
Gloucestershire
Map **3** SO81

★★★**Bowden Hall** Bond End Ln, Upton St Leonards (3m SE B4073)
☎ (0452) 614121

RS Xmas

Imposing hotel in its own grounds with popular carvery restaurant.

24rm(23 1)(3fb) CTV in all bedrooms ® T sB&B£33—£36 dB&B£45

250P 1 sauna bath solarium Live music and dancing Sat & Sun Cabaret Sat

G

English & French V Lunch £7.50&alc Dinner £7.50&alc Wine £5.10 Last dinner 9.30pm

Credit cards 1 2 3 5

★★★**Crest** Crest Way, Barnwood (Crest) (0452) 613311 Telex no 437273

RS 24 Dec—4 Jan

Comfortable modern hotel in quiet and convenient situation for city centre.

100(10fb) in 10 bedrooms CTV in all bedrooms ® T S% sB£51—£54 dB£61—£64 (room only)

160P CFA xmas

V S% Lunch £6—£6.50 Tea 75—80p High Tea £1.50—£2 Dinner fr£16&alc Wine £6.25 Last dinner 9.45pm

Credit cards 1 2 3 4 5

★★★**Gloucester Hotel & Country Club** Robinswood Hill (2½m SE off B4073) (Embassy) (0452) 25653 Telex no 43571

Good hotel with comfortable bedrooms in the main block. It has a feature bar, and the restaurant has comprehensive menus and a carvery. There are extensive sporting facilities including a popular dry-ski slope.

53 Annexe: 20rm(19 1)(8fb) 1 CTV in all bedrooms ® T S% *sB&B £49 dB&B £65

G

Gloucester — Glyn Ceiriog

CTV 300P squash snooker sauna bath solarium gymnasium dry-ski slope Live music & dancing Sat *xmas*

French V S% *Lunch £6.50&alc Tea fr£1.30 Dinner £9.50&alc Wine £5.50 Last dinner 10pm

Credit cards 1 2 3 4 5

★★★**Hatton Court** (formerly Tara) Upton Hill, Upton St Leonards (3m SE B4073) (Best Western) (0452) 617412 Telex no 449848

Popular Cotswold stone house, with panoramic views of the Severn Valley.

23rm(12 11) 2 CTV in all bedrooms T S% sB&B £45—£60 dB&B £65—£78

75P (heated) *xmas*

English & French V S% Lunch £9.50—£16.50 Tea £3 Dinner £9.50—£16.50

Credit cards 1 2 3 5

GLYN CEIRIOG
Clwyd
Map **7** SJ23

★★★**Golden Pheasant** (Inter Hotel) (069172) 281 Telex no 35664

Situated in a beautiful holiday and sporting valley, this old village inn has been carefully developed to provide good, comfortable accommodation.

18rm(16 2)(5fb) 4 CTV in all bedrooms ® S% sB&B £25—£31 dB&B £40—£61

45P *xmas*

Mainly grills V S% *Lunch £8.20—£12.50 Tea £1.50—£2 Dinner £12.50alc Wine £7.95 Last dinner 6pm

Credit cards 1 2 3 V

★***Glyn Valley*** (069172) 210

White-painted, Victorian, village inn, with good picture collection in lounge and bar.

9rm(5)(2fb) 1 CTV in all bedrooms ®

CTV 40P *xmas*

English & French V Last dinner 10pm

Goathland — Goodwood

GOATHLAND
North Yorkshire
Map **8** NZ80

★★**Goathland Hydro** ☎ (0947) 86296

Sedate and old-fashioned, the house boasts a wealth of solid oak furniture built by a local craftsman.

32rm(15⇌)(4fb) CTV available in bedrooms Ⓡ available in bedrooms sB&B£16.50–£19 sB&B⇌£16.50–£22 dB&B£33–£38 dB&B⇌£33–£54

CTV 20P ✿ croquet ♿

V ♈ ☕ Lunch £4.50&alc Tea 70palc High Tea £3alc Dinner £8 Wine £4 Last dinner 8pm

Credit cards 1 3 5 Ⓥ

★**Whitfield House** Darnholm (Guestaccom) ☎ Whitby (0947) 86215

Closed 7 Dec–15 Jan

A converted stone-built 'period' style cottage on the North Yorkshire moors.

10rm(2⇌3⋔)(1fb) Ⓡ sB&B£12–£13.25 dB&B£22–£24.50 dB&B⇌⋔£25.60–£28.50 **B**

CTV 10P ⇌ nc3yrs

♈ ☕ ⚡ Tea 75p–£1.50 Dinner £5.75–£8.50 Wine £3.95 Last dinner 7pm

Ⓥ

GODALMING
Surrey
Map **4** SU94

✕✕**Inn on the Lake** Ockford Rd ☎ (04868) 5575

Well-appointed hotel restaurant offering enterprising cuisine.

International **V** 50 seats ✱ Lunch £9.50–£15.50 Dinner £9.50–£15.50 Wine £5.25 Last dinner 10pm 100P Live Music Fri & Sat

Credit cards 1 2 3 5

GOLANT
Cornwall
Map **2** SX15

★★ *HBL* **Cormorant** ☎ Fowey (072683) 3426

In a splendid setting overlooking the Fowey estuary, this peaceful hotel offers tranquility with caring hospitality. The rooms have superb views of the estuary, with a spacious, comfortable lounge and finely decorated, well equipped bedrooms. Good food using fresh local produce is provided.

11⇌(1fb) CTV in all bedrooms **T** sB&B⇌£21.50–£27.50 dB&B⇌£43–£48 **B**

25P ⇌ ✿ & ⛱ (heated) *xmas*

French **V** ♈ ☕ Lunch £9.85alc Tea £1.50alc High Tea £4alc Dinner £10.25alc Wine £4 Last dinner 8.30pm

Credit card 3

GOLSPIE
Highland *Sutherland*
Map **14** NH89

★★**Golf Links** ☎ (04083) 3408

A comfortable little hotel situated beside the beach and close to the golf course.

10rm(5⇌2⋔) CTV in all bedrooms Ⓡ sB&B£15–£18.50 sB&B⇌⋔£16.50–£18.50 dB&B£30–£37 dB&B⇌⋔£33–£37 **B**

CTV 25P ⇌ ✿ ⛹ *xmas*

V ♈ ☕ Bar lunch £1–£7 Tea £2–£3 High Tea fr £6 Dinner £10–£14 Wine £4 Last dinner 8pm

Credit cards 1 2 3 5 Ⓥ

★★**Sutherland Arms** Old Bank Rd ☎ (04083) 3234

A traditional Highland hotel dating from 1808 when established as the first coaching station in Sutherland.

13rm(8⇌)(2fb) Ⓡ ✱ sB&B£8.50–£10.50 sB&B⇌£15 dB&B£17–£21 dB&B⇌£30 **B**

CTV 30P ✿ ⛹

V ♈ ✱ Lunch £3–£5 Tea £1.50 High Tea £3–£5.50 Dinner £9.50 Last dinner 9pm

Credit card 2

GOODRICH
Hereford & Worcester
Map **3** SO51

★★**Ye Hostelrie** ☎ Symonds Yat (0600) 890241

Small homely hotel with romantic façade. Popular with the locals.

7rm(1⇌2⋔)(1fb) Ⓡ S% ✱ sB&B£20 sB&B⇌⋔£22 dB&B£32 dB&B⇌⋔£34

CTV 25P ⇌ ✿

V ♈ ⚡ S% Bar lunch 95p–£5.25 High Tea 95p–£5.25 Dinner £8.50–£10.50 Wine £4.50 Last dinner 8.30pm

Ⓥ

GOODRINGTON
Devon see **Paignton**

GOODWOOD
West Sussex
Map **4** SU80

★★★ *B* **Goodwood Park** (Best Western) ☎ Chichester (0243) 775537 Telex no 869173

50⇌⋔(3fb) 1 ☐ CTV in all bedrooms Ⓡ **T** S% sB&B⇌⋔£41–£45 dB&B⇌⋔£57.50–£67.50 **B**

☾ CTV 80P ✿ ⛱ (heated) snooker sauna bath solarium gymnasium *xmas*

English & French ♈ ☕ S% Lunch £7.50–£10.50&alc Tea £2.25 High Tea £5.50 Dinner £13.50–£15.50&alc Wine £6.95 Last dinner 9.30pm

Credit cards 1 2 3 4 5 Ⓥ

G

GOOLE
Humberside
Map **8** SE72

★ ★ **Clifton** 1 Clifton Gdns, Boothferry Rd ☎ (0405) 61336

Two-storey, Edwardian building located near the town and the docks.

11rm(5⇌3⋔)(1fb) CTV in all bedrooms **T** sB&B£24—£25 sB&B⇌⋔£28—£29 dB&B£34—£36 dB&B⇌⋔£36—£38

CTV 10P

English & Continental Lunch £7.50—£12 Tea fr£1.50 Dinner £10—£16 Wine £6 Last dinner 9pm

Credit cards 1 2 3 5 V

G

GOOSNARGH
Lancashire
Map **7** SD53

✕ **Ye Horns** ☎ Broughton (0772) 865230

The restaurant, a delightful 17th century inn, specialises in English dishes, including home-made soups and roast duckling. Guests will find the atmosphere cosy and friendly — and the prices within reach of their pockets.

Closed Mon (ex Bank Hol's)

100 seats Lunch £7—£7.50 Dinner £9.50—£10 Wine £3.75 Last dinner 9.30pm 50P nc

Credit cards 1 2 3 5

GOREY
Jersey
See **Channel Islands**

GORLESTON-ON-SEA
Norfolk See **Yarmouth (Great)**

GOSPORT
Hampshire
Map **4** SZ69

★ ★ **Anglesey** Crescent Rd, Alverstoke ☎ (0705) 582157

Part of a Regency terrace, this unusual hotel provides modernised and well-appointed bedrooms. An elegant restaurant offers a wide range of à la carte dishes, many of them based on fish.

18rm(5⇌14⋔)(1fb) 1 CTV in all bedrooms ® sB&B⇌⋔fr£25 dB&B⇌⋔fr£30

CTV 3 (£2 per night) Live music twice wkly

Continental **V** Lunch fr£6.95&alc Dinner fr£7.50&alc Wine £4.85 Last dinner 10pm

Credit cards 1 2 3

GOUDHURST
Kent
Map **5** TQ73

★ ★ *B* **Star & Eagle** (Whitbread) ☎ (0580) 211512

An attractive 14th-century inn combining a homely atmosphere and good cooking.

11rm(9⇌⋔) 1 CTV in all bedrooms ® **T**

24P *xmas*

European **V** Last dinner 9.30pm

Credit cards 1 2 3 5

★ ***Green Cross Inn*** (1m W of village on A262) ☎ (0580) 211200

Closed Xmas Day & Boxing Day

Small, family-run country free house whose restaurant is furnished with antiques.

6rm(2fb) TV in all bedrooms ®

CTV 25P

Last dinner 9.30pm

Credit cards 1 2 5

GOUROCK
Strathclyde *Renfrewshire*
Map **10** NS27

★ ★ ★ **Stakis Gantock** Cloch Rd (Stakis) ☎ (0475) 34671

Modern building, situated one mile southwest of the town, with views out across the Clyde.

63⇌⋔(2fb) CTV in all bedrooms ® in 20 bedrooms sB⇌⋔£30—£42.90 dB⇌⋔£46—£60(room only)

☾ 200P CFA Live music & dancing Sat & Sun (out of season) *xmas*

Scottish, French & Italian **V** Lunch fr£4.25 Tea 90p—£2.95 High Tea fr£4.25 Dinner fr£8.25&alc Wine £3.85 Last dinner 9.15pm

Credit cards 1 2 3 5

GRANGE (In-Borrowdale)
Cumbria
Map **11** NY21

See also **Borrowdale** and **Rosthwaite**

★ ★ ***Borrowdale Gates Country House*** ☎ Borrowdale (059684) 204

Comfortable relaxing hotel with panoramic views of surrounding countryside and fells.

20rm(14⇌)(2fb) CTV in all bedrooms ®

CTV 35P *xmas*

International **V** Last dinner 8.45pm

Credit cards 1 2 3 5

GRANGEMOUTH
Central *Stirlingshire*
Map **11** NS98

★ ★ ★ *H* **Grange Manor** Glensburgh Rd ☎ (0324) 474836 Telex no 777620

A Georgian mansion has been elegantly restored to create a small business hotel, furnished and decorated throughout to a high standard and offering well-equipped bedrooms, first-class cuisine and friendly service.

7rm(5⇌2⋔) 1 CTV in all bedrooms ® **T** S% sB&B⇌⋔£39 dB&B⇌⋔£49

CTV 150P Live music & dancing Sat *xmas*

French **V** S% Lunch £5.95—£7.25&alc Tea 75p Dinner £12alc Wine £4.95 Last dinner 9.30pm

Credit cards 1 2 3 5 V

GRANGE-OVER-SANDS
Cumbria
Map **7** SD47

★ ★ ★ **Cumbria Grand** ☎ (04484) 2331

Large, stone-built hotel with spacious accommodation, set in an elevated position.

120rm(108⇌12⋔)(8fb) CTV in all bedrooms ® sB&B⇌⋔£22—£28 dB&B⇌⋔£39—£48

Lift ☾ 150P CFA ✿ ⚲(hard) snooker putting ⌂ *xmas*

⚲English & French ⚲ ☐ Lunch £3.50—£6.50 Tea 75p High Tea £3.80 Dinner £8.50—£9.50&alc Wine £5.50 Last dinner 8.45pm

Credit cards 1 2 3 4 5 Ⓥ

★ ★**Grange** Lindale Rd Station Sq ☎(04484) 3666

Large Victorian building with views across Morecambe Bay.

40rm(33➡4⋒)(6fb) CTV in all bedrooms ®T sB&B➡⋒£22—£26 dB&B➡⋒£36—£44

☾CTV 100P CFA ✿ Live music & dancing Sat ⌂ *xmas*

⚲English & Continental **V** ⚲ ☐ Lunch £4.95—£10&alc Tea £1—£2.95 High Tea £2.95—£5.50 Dinner £7—£10.75&alc Wine £4.95 Last dinner 9.30pm

Credit cards 1 2 3 Ⓥ

★ ★ *L* ***Graythwaite Manor*** Fernhill Rd ☎(04484) 2001

Large country house in beautiful grounds, with home grown produce used in restaurant.

24rm(12➡)(1fb) CTV in all bedrooms ®T ✗(ex guide dogs) **B**

18P 14 (charged) ✿ ⚲(hard)

⚲English & French **V** ⚲ ☐ Last dinner 8pm

Credit cards 1 3

★ ★**Kents Bank** Kentsford Rd (Guestaccom) ☎(04484) 2054

Pleasant house in its own grounds, in an elevated position with good views.

8rm(3➡)(1fb) TV available in bedrooms ® ✱sB&B£15 sB&B➡£17 dB&B£26 dB&B➡£30 **B**

CTV 30P pool table *xmas*

⚲Lunch £3.75&alc Dinner £8.50alc Wine £4.50 Last dinner 8.45pm

Credit cards 1 3 Ⓥ

★ ★**Netherwood** Lindale Rd ☎(04484) 2552

A large Victorian building, with some oak décor, standing in its own grounds.

23rm(15➡2⋒)(6fb) CTV in all bedrooms ®T sB&B£17—£19.50 sB&B➡⋒£18.50—£19.50 dB&B£34—£39 dB&B➡⋒£37—£39 **B**

☾CTV 60P 12 ✿ ⌂

⚲English & French **V** ⚲ ☐ Lunch £4.50—£5 Tea 70p—£2.95 High Tea £3—£4.60 Dinner £7—£7.65 Wine £4.15 Last dinner 8.15pm

★**Methven** Kents Bank Rd ☎(04484) 2031

Closed 19 Oct—28 Mar

Small detached family-run hotel overlooking Morecambe Bay.

12rm(1➡2⋒)(3fb) TV in 1 bedroom sB&B£11.25—£13.50 dB&B£22.50—£27 dB&B➡⋒£28.80—£34

Grange-over-Sands — Grantown-on-Spey

CTV 12P ✿ nc4yrs

Bar lunch £1 Dinner £5.25 Wine £3.60 Last dinner 6pm

GRANTHAM

Lincolnshire

Map **8** SK93

★ ★ ★**George** High St (Best Western) ☎(0476) 63286 Telex no 378121

Georgian inn once the home of Issac Newton.

46rms(40➡6⋒)(2fb) 2 in 10 bedrooms CTV in all bedrooms ®T S% sB&B➡⋒£39.50—£47.25 dB&B➡⋒£49.85—£57.75 **B**

☾70P *xmas*

⚲International **V** ⚲ ☐ Lunch £15alc Tea 75p High Tea £2.25—£4.50 Dinner £11.50—£15.50&alc Wine £5.75 Last dinner 9.30pm

Credit cards 1 2 3 5 Ⓥ

★ ★**Angel & Royal** High St (Trusthouse Forte) ☎(0476) 65816

Historic town centre inn, originally a hostel for Knights Templar.

28rm(17➡) CTV in all bedrooms ® sB&B£40.50 sB&B➡£48.50 dB&B£56.50 dB&B➡£64.50 **B**

☾60P *xmas*

⚲ ☐ Last dinner 10pm

Credit cards 1 2 3 4 5 590800

★ ★**Kings** North Pde ☎(0476) ~~65881~~

The hotel stands just to the north of the town centre and close to the railway line; extensive alterations were undertaken during the latter half of 1985 to enhance the ground floor.

17rm(5➡5⋒) CTV in all bedrooms ®T sB&Bfr£20 sB&B➡⋒fr£28 dB&Bfr£30 dB&B➡⋒fr£39 **B**

☾40P ✿ ⚲ Live music & dancing Fri & Sat ♿

V ⚲ ☐ Lunch £6.50&alc Tea £2 Dinner £7.95&alc Wine £4.72

Credit cards 1 2 3 5 Ⓥ

✕✕**Premier** 2—6 North Parade ☎(0476) 77855

Margaret Thatcher's childhood home and shop has been converted to form this restaurant.

Closed Mon Lunch not served Tue Dinner not served Sun

48 seats Lunch £3.75—£6.95&alc Dinner £13.95&alc Wine £4.75 Last dinner 9.30pm 4P

Credit cards 1 2 3 5

GRANTOWN-ON-SPEY

Highland *Morayshire*

Map **14** NJ02

★ ★**Ben Mhor** High St ☎(0479) 2056

Family-run stone-built hotel located in the main street.

24rm(20➡4⋒)(2fb) CTV in all bedrooms ®✱sB&B➡⋒£17.50 dB&B➡⋒£32

25P *xmas*

V ⚲ ☐ ✱Lunch £5—£6&alc Tea 90p—£1 High Tea £3.75—£5.95 Dinner £13alc Wine £4.50 Last dinner 8.30pm

Credit cards 1 3 5 Ⓥ

★ ★**Coppice** Grant Rd (Exec Hotel) ☎(0479) 2688

RS Nov—Mar

Detached two-storey stone building dating from 1890. Standing in its own grounds.

26rm(11⋒)(1fb) CTV in 11 bedrooms ®✗ ✱sB&Bfr£13 sB&B⋒fr£18 dB&Bfr£26 dB&B⋒fr£30

CTV 30P ✿

⚲ ✱Dinner fr£7 Wine £3.50 Last dinner 8pm

★ ★ *HL* **Garth** Castle Rd ☎(0479) 2836

Charming converted 18th-century house.

14rm(9➡2⋒) CTV in 10 bedrooms **T** sB&B£16 sB&B➡⋒£17.75 dB&B£28 dB&B➡⋒£31.50

CTV 10P 2 ✿ putting

⚲French **V** ⚲ ☐ ✱Bar lunch 90p—£5 Tea 60p High Tea £4—£7 Dinner fr£8 Wine £4.50 Last dinner 8.30pm

Credit cards 1 3 4 5

★ ★**Rosehall** The Square ☎(0479) 2721

Distinctive stone building standing in The Square.

14rm(4➡4⋒)(2fb) ®sB&B£14.95—£16 sB&B➡⋒£20.95—£22 dB&B£29—£31 dB&B➡⋒£31—£33

CTV 20P ⌂

V Lunch £4.50—£6 Dinner £9.20 Wine £4 Last dinner 8pm

★ ★**Seafield Lodge** Woodside Av (Minotel) ☎(0479) 2152

Closed Nov & Jan RS Dec & Feb

Comfortable, family run hotel with special facilities for fishing, shooting and curling.

14rm(3➡6⋒) CTV in all bedrooms ® sB&B£15—£17 sB&B➡⋒£19—£21 dB&B£30—£34 dB&B➡⋒£36—£40 **B**

50P ✿ putting

⚲Scottish & Swiss **V** ⚲Lunch £5.50—£6.50 Tea 80p—£1 Dinner £8.50—£10.50&alc Wine £4.50 Last dinner 9.30pm

Credit cards 1 2 3 5 Ⓥ

★**Dunvegan** Heathfield Rd ☎(0479) 2301

Closed 16—31 Oct & 20—30 Dec

Small family-run hotel in a quiet area opposite playing fields and the golf course.

9rm(5fb) sB&B£10—£12 dB&B£20—£24 **B** →

G

CTV 9P 1 (£1 per night)

V Bar lunch fr£1.15 Tea fr75p Dinner fr£7 Wine £4 Last dinner 7.30pm

Ⓥ

★Spey Valley Seafield Ave ☎ (0479) 2942

RS mid Oct—30 Dec

Attractive granite-stone hotel with a tidy garden, located in a quiet area.

19rm(6fb) ✱sB&B£12.50 dB&B£25

CTV 24P ✿

V ✱Bar lunch £2.50—£7.50 Tea £1.75—£2.50 Dinner £9 Wine £4.50 Last dinner 9.30pm

✕Craggan Mill ☎ (0479) 2288

Situated in a white-painted mill house on the western outskirts of the town, the restaurant has a rustic theme.

Closed Mon (winter) & Feb Lunch not served Oct—May

British & Italian V 60 seats Bar lunch £2—£3.25 Dinner £10alc Wine £4.25 Last dinner 10pm 30P

Credit card 3

G

GRASMERE

Cumbria

Map **11** NY30

★★★★Wordsworth ☎ (09665) 592 Telex no 65329

Delightfully placed in the village centre and surrounded by fells and meadowland, the hotel has been elegantly restored and caters for all occasions. The combination of luxurious lounge and attractive, individually-designed bedrooms makes for a distinguished and unique hotel.

35rm(34 1)(3fb) 1 CTV in all bedrooms T sB&B £29—£36 dB&B £54—£86

Lift 60P CFA ✿ (heated) sauna bath solarium games room xmas

English & French V Lunch £15alc Tea 95p—£4 Dinner £16.50—£18 Wine £5.50 Last dinner 9pm

Credit cards 1 2 3 4 5 Ⓥ

★★★Gold Rill Country House ☎ (09665) 486

Closed Dec—Feb (except Xmas)

Grantown-on-Spey — Grasmere

A comfortable hotel with a tranquil atmosphere, set on the edge of the village.

16(5fb) CTV in all bedrooms Ⓡ sB&B £34—£37 dB&B £68—£74

35P ✿ (heated) pool table putting nc5yrs *xmas*

Bar lunch £2.50—£4 Tea 85p Dinner £14 Wine £3.50 Last dinner 8.30pm

Credit cards 1 2 3 5 Ⓥ

★★★Grasmere Red Lion (Consort/Exec Hotel) ☎ (09665) 456

Closed mid Nov—mid Mar

A 200-year-old coaching inn, with a modern entrance and interior.

36rm(34 2)(5fb) CTV in all bedrooms ⓇT S% sB&B £28.50—£30.50 dB&B £42.50—£50.50

Lift 40P CFA

English & French V S% Bar lunch 95p—£4.75 Tea 80p Dinner fr£11.25 Wine £5.90 Last dinner 9pm

Credit cards 1 2 3 5 Ⓥ

★★★Prince of Wales (Mount Charlotte) ☎ (09665) 666 Telex no 65364

A large hotel standing by the lakeside in nine acres of grounds.

81rm(68 9)(7fb) 1 CTV in all bedrooms ⓇT S% ✱sB&B fr£36.75 dB&B fr£55

90P CFA ✿ *xmas*

V ✱Lunch £6.50 Tea 85p High Tea £3.50—£4.50 Dinner £9 Wine £5.50 Last dinner 9pm

Credit cards 1 2 3 5 Ⓥ

★★★*BL* Swan (Trusthouse Forte) ☎ (09665) 551

An attractive 17th century hotel, the Swan has a great deal of character and exhibits a magnificent collection of horse brasses, copper jugs, old pewter and fine china.

41rm(25)(3fb) CTV in all bedrooms Ⓡ sB&B£44.50 sB&B £52.50 dB&B£65 dB&B £73

CTV 40P ✿ *xmas*

Last dinner 8.45pm

Credit cards 1 2 3 4 5

★★*H* Grasmere Broadgate ☎ (09665) 277

Closed Dec—Feb

Very comfortable hotel, noted for its home cooking.

12rm(5 7)CTV in all bedrooms T sB&B £22—£24 dB&B £36—£40

CTV 16P ✿ croquet

English & French Bar lunch £1—£3.50 Tea 65p—£1.75 Dinner £10 Wine £3.90 Last dinner 8pm

Credit cards 1 3 Ⓥ

★★★ Michael's Nook (see red star box opposite)

★★*H* Oak Bank Broadgate ☎ (09665) 217

Closed Xmas & Jan

Very comfortable hotel where dinner can be especially recommended.

14rm(6 8)(1fb) CTV in all bedrooms T sB&B £18—£24 dB&B £36—£48

CTV 14P

English & Continental V Bar lunch £2.50—£6.50 Tea 70p alc Dinner £10alc Wine £2.95 Last dinner 7.30pm

Credit cards 1 3 Ⓥ

See advertisement on page 332

★★Rothay Garden Broadgate ☎ (09665) 334

Closed Dec & Jan RS New Year

This charming hotel, set in attractive gardens, offers pretty bedrooms and an elegant restaurant where very good food is served.

16rm(11 5)(1fb) 4 CTV in all bedrooms ⓇT sB&B £24—£28 dB&B £38—£58

30P ✿ nc5yrs

V Dinner £12.50 Wine £4.25 Last dinner 8pm

Credit cards 1 2 3 Ⓥ

See advertisement on page 332

★★★

❀★★★ **MICHAEL'S NOOK, GRASMERE**
(Pride of Britain)
☎(09665) 496 Telex no 65329
(Rosette awarded for dinner only)

Converted to a hotel in 1969 by Mr and Mrs Gifford, this hotel has become very popular with our members, not least for the excellent food provided by the chef. Lunches are by arrangement while dinner is of five courses of top quality ingredients cooked with skill. The style is mostly fashionably modern and you will be attended to in the traditionally appointed candlelit dining room, as throughout the hotel, by good natured staff. The wine list is noteworthy. The creeper-clad stone house was built in 1859 and has a solid middle class air about it as does the interior with a hall handsomely done with oak door cases, window surrounds and staircase. Mrs Gifford's flair for decor and Mr Gifford's professional knowledge of antiques, can be appreciated in the public rooms — including the elegant drawing room, another sitting room and cosy bar — and the bedrooms (including two new suites), are most attractively done. A collection of English prints, porcelain, furniture and rugs, as well as beautiful flower arrangements, (and open fires in winter), all help to create the atmosphere of a country house. The bedrooms are also well equipped, and with the provision of fruit, flowers and bathrobes you can be sure the Giffords have the best interests of their guests at heart. In the village is the Wordsworth Hotel under the same ownership whose facilities of swimming pool and solarium are available free to guests here.

11rm(10⇌1⋒)1⊟ CTV in all bedrooms **T** ✈
*sB&B⇌⋒£56—£74(incl dinner) dB&B⇌⋒£92—£190(incl dinner)

20P ⇌ ✿ croquet *xmas*

♉British & French ⁄ *Lunch £17.50alc Dinner £24alc Wine £5.40 Last dinner 7.30pm

Credit card [2]

★

❀★ **WHITE MOSS HOUSE, GRASMERE**
Rydal Water ☎(09665) 295
Closed mid Nov—mid Mar
(Rosette awarded for dinner only)

This gem of a hotel is run by the Butterworths with their daughter and her husband, Susan and Peter Dixon. It is a delightful little stone built hotel with pleasant gardens but it has gained a high reputation for its cuisine: Jean Butterworth and her son-in-law combine to achieve the highest standards of cooking; mainly in the British traditional style, and lightened by fashionably modern touches. There is no choice of the five course dinners until the puddings. The extensive wine list of mostly French wines is good and sensibly priced. Breakfasts are hearty and tea can be enjoyed by a roaring fire in the relaxing sitting room. Here and in the bedrooms there are some pieces of period furniture as well as fresh flowers. Some of the rooms can be small but their quality is high; you will be comfortable here. You can be sure of that because comfort and a warm welcome for their guests are considered important by the family here and it is kept immaculately. A marvellously peaceful and civilised hotel.

5⇌ Annexe: 2rm(1⇌1⋒) CTV in all bedrooms ✈ dB&B⇌⋒£57—£62

10P ⇌ ✿ ♩ nc 10yrs

⁄ Dinner £16.95 Wine £4.40 Last dinner 8pm

Ⓥ

✕✕ **The Dovecot** Town End ☎(09665) 268

Situated just south of Grasmere, the restaurant is housed in an old building which has been most tastefully converted to combine character and comfort. Morning coffee, afternoon tea and pre-dinner drinks are served in an attractive lounge with an open fire, whilst the choice in the dining room spans vegetarian, snack and à la carte menus including some interesting and unusual dishes.

Closed Mon, 2 wks Nov & 2 wks Jan
Dinner not served Sun

♉English & French **V** 36 seats Lunch £8.50—£11.50 Dinner £8.50—£11.50 Wine £5.10 Last dinner 9pm 8P ⁄

Credit cards [1] [2] [3] Ⓥ

GRASSINGTON
North Yorkshire
Map **7** SE06

★ **Grassington House** 5 The Square
☎(0756) 752406

Closed Nov—6 Mar

Charming, privately run village centre hotel with attractive furnishings.

12rm(1⇌5⋒) Annexe: 6rm(2fb) ®S% sB&B£17.25 sB&B⇌⋒£19.55 dB&B£29.32 dB&B⇌⋒£33.90 **B**

CTV 25P 1⌂

V ♉ ☕ S% *Bar lunch £2—£8&alc Tea £1.65—£2 High Tea £2.20—£3.25 Dinner £8.05 Wine £4.75 Last dinner 7pm

GRAVESEND
Kent
Map **5** TQ67

★★★ **Inn on the Lake** Watling St
☎Shorne (047482) 3333
(For full entry see Shorne)

GRAYS
Essex
Map **5** TQ67

★★★ **Stifford Moat House** (Queens Moat) ☎ Grays Thurrock (0375) 371451
(For full entry see North Stifford)

GRAYSHOTT
Hampshire
Map **4** SU83

❀✕**Woods** Headley Rd (1m SW B3002 off A3) ☏ Hindhead (042873) 5555

Previously a butcher's shop, Woods retains its clinical tiling and meat-racks, though it is warmly furnished with simple pine furniture and decked with fresh wild flowers. The talented Swedish chef and his Czechoslovakian wife provide a European menu of unusually combined meat and fish dishes, outstanding in quality and cooked with unfailing skill.

Closed Sun & Mon Lunch not served

French 35 seats Dinner £16.50alc Wine £4.80 Last dinner 11pm

Credit cards 1 2 3 5

GREAT
Places incorporating the word 'Great' will be found under the actual place name — eg Great Yarmouth is listed under Yarmouth

G

GREENLAW
Borders *Berwickshire*
Map **12** NT74

★★*HL* ***Purves Hall*** (4m SE off A697) ☏ Leitholm (089084) 558

Attractively furnished hotel with attentive service and fine views.

7rm(2⇌5⋒)(2fb) ®

CTV 14P ❀ (heated) (hard)

Last dinner 8.45pm

GREENOCK
Strathclyde *Renfrewshire*
Map **10** NS27

★★★**Tontine** 6 Ardgowan Sq (Best Western) ☏ (0475) 23316

Closed 26 Dec & 1 Jan

A 19th-century building with an extension wing, situated in the west end of the town.

32⇌⋒(1fb) CTV in all bedrooms ® T S% sB&B£27.50—£30 sB&B⇌£33—£36 dB&B£36—£40 dB&B⇌⋒£40—£44

☾14 ❀

Scottish & French V S% Lunch £5.65—£6&alc Tea £1.85—£2 High Tea £3.95—£4.25 Dinner £7.50—£8&alc Wine £5.50 Last dinner 9pm

Credit cards 1 2 3 4 5

GRETA BRIDGE
Co Durham
Map **12** NZ01

★★**Morritt Arms** ☏ Teesdale (0833) 27232

Old coaching inn retaining Dickensian character.

23rm(16⇌)(3fb) 4 CTV in 18 bedrooms TV in 5 bedrooms ® ✱ sB&B£21 sB&B⇌£27.50 dB&B£33 dB&B⇌£39—£45

150P 5 ❀ snooker *xmas*

English & French V ✱ Lunch £7.25&alc Tea 75p&alc Dinner fr£10.95&alc Wine £6.50 Last dinner 9pm

Credit cards 1 3 5

GRETNA
Dumfries & Galloway *Dumfriesshire*
Map **11** NY36

★★**Gretna Chase** (¼m S on B721, in England) ☏ (0461) 37517

Once a marriage house, it has now been modernised while retaining much of its original character.

9rm(3⇀2⋒)(1fb)CTV in all bedrooms ✕ sB&B£21 sB&B⇀⋒£26 dB&B£34 dB&B⇀⋒£36—£50 B

40P ✿

English & French V Lunch fr£6.50&alc Tea fr£3 High Tea fr£4 Dinner £9alc Wine £3.95 Last dinner 9.30pm

Credit cards 1 2 3 5 V

★★**Royal Stewart Motel** ☎(0461) 38210

Closed Xmas Day & New Years Day

Bungalow-style motel on the outskirts of the town.

13rm(4⇀7⋒)(2fb)CTV in all bedrooms Ⓡ S% sB&B⇀⋒£19—£22 dB&B⇀⋒£28—£32

☾25P

V S% Lunch £4.80 Dinner £7—£10.50 Wine £4 Last dinner 8.45pm

Credit cards 1 2 3 5 V

★★**Solway Lodge** Annan Rd ☎(0461) 38266

Closed 25 & 26 Dec

Small, homely hotel with chalet style annexe.

3rm(1⇀) Annexe:7⇀(1fb)CTV in all bedrooms Ⓡ sB&B⇀£16.50—£17 dB&B⇀£27—£28

CTV 25P Live music & dancing wkly

V Bar lunch 50p—£8 Tea fr60p Dinner £7—£10&alc Wine £3.40 Last dinner 9pm

Credit cards 1 2 3 5

GRIMSBY
Humberside
Map **8** TA20

★★★**Crest** St James' Sq (Crest) ☎(0472) 59771 Telex no 527741

Closed Xmas

Modern, hotel near the town centre.

131⇀ in 13 bedrooms CTV in all bedrooms Ⓡ S% ✱sB⇀£48.85—£50.95 dB⇀£58.85—£60.95(room only) B

Lift ☾ 100P CFA sauna bath Live music & dancing Sun

English & French V ✱Lunch £3.95—£4.10 Tea 85—95p High Tea fr£5.85 Dinner £11.15—£11.95&alc Wine £5.80 Last dinner 10pm

Credit cards 1 2 3 4 5

★★★**Humber Royal Crest** Littlecoates Rd (Crest) ☎(0472) 50295 Telex no 527776

Modern four-storey brick building on the outskirts of town next to the golf course.

52⇀ in 5 bedrooms CTV in all bedrooms Ⓡ S% ✱sB⇀fr£49 dB⇀fr£59(room only) B

Lift ☾ 200P CFA *xmas*

International V ✱Lunch fr£7.45&alc Tea fr70p Dinner £7.95—£12.25&alc wine £6.25 Last dinner 9.45pm

Credit cards 1 2 3 4 5

✕**Othello** 25 Bethlehem St, Old Market Pl ☎(0472) 56704

Spacious ground floor bar leads to first floor dining room, where authentic Greek cuisine is available.

Lunch not served Sun

Greek & Continental 120 seats S% Lunch £12.50alc Dinner £12.50alc Wine £5.75 Last dinner 11pm

Credit cards 1 2 3 5

GRIMSTHORPE
Lincolnshire
Map **8** TF02

✕**Black Horse Inn** ☎ Edenham (077832) 247

Large detached house in spacious grounds and gardens and set in small picturesque village.

Closed Sun, 2 wks Xmas & Bank Hols (except Etr)

V 48 seats S% Lunch £4.35—£10.95 Dinner £13.50—£25&alc Wine £7.50 Last dinner 9pm

40P nc 8yrs

Credit cards 1 2 3

GRIMSTON
Norfolk
Map **9** TF72

✿★★★ *HBL* **Congham Hall Country House** Lynn Rd (Pride of Britain) ☎ Hillington (0485) 600250 Telex no 81508

Closed 25 Dec—9 Jan

A relaxing Georgian country house which is home to the Forecast family. The food is most enterprising with good use made of local produce supplemented by the best from London's markets, and complemented by herbs from the hotel's superb garden. Dinner is of eight courses, though luncheon is more modest and features rich flavours and unusual combinations of ingredients.

11rm(10⇀1⋒) 1 CTV in all bedrooms **T** ✕ sB&B⇀⋒£50 dB&B⇀⋒£64 Continental breakfast B

☾50P 1 ✿ (heated) (hard) nc 12yrs

Lunch £9.50—£10.50&alc Dinner £21.50alc Wine £6.50 Last dinner 9.30pm

Credit cards 1 2 3 5

See advertisement under Kings Lynn

GRINDLEFORD
Derbyshire
Map **8** SK27

★★★**Maynard Arms** Main Rd ☎ Hope Valley (0433) 30321

The hotel is an attractive Victorian building set in well laid out gardens overlooking the valley of the River Derwent. There are smart, well-fitted bedrooms on the two upper floors, where a very attractive residents' lounge also takes advantage of the view; on the ground floor are a panelled public bar, separate lounge bar and well-appointed restaurant. →

G

13rm(9→2⋒)(1fb)2 four-poster CTV in all bedrooms ®T*sB&B→⋒£32—£35 dB&B→⋒£42—£50 B

70P 6 ✿ xmas

English & French V * Lunch £5.95—£7.25 Dinner £7.95—£10.50 Wine £4.95 Last dinner 9.30pm

Credit cards 1 2 3 5

GRIZEDALE
Cumbria
Map **7** SD39

★★**Grizedale Lodge** (formerly Ormandy) ☎ Hawkshead (09666) 532

Closed 3 Jan—mid Feb

Detached converted farmhouse standing in an 8000 acre forest.

6rm(2→4⋒)(2fb) CTV in all bedrooms ® sB&B→⋒£18.50 dB&B→⋒£35 B

24P *xmas*

V Lunch £6.50 Tea 80p—£1.80 Dinner £9.50 Wine £5 Last dinner 9pm

Credit cards 1 3 V

GROBY
Leicestershire
Map **4** SK50

★**Brant Inn** Leicester Rd ☎ Leicester (0533) 872703

Closed Xmas Day & Boxing Day

Large two-storey building with grounds and gardens, situated in a residential area, just off the A50 4m NW of Leicester.

10rm CTV in all bedrooms ®T* sB&B£20.50—£21.50 dB&B£35

200P ✿ Live music & dancing Thu & Sun

*Lunch £5.95—£6.45&alc Dinner £10alc Wine £5.95 Last dinner 10.30pm

Credit cards 1 3 5 V

GUERNSEY
See **Channel Islands**

GUILDFORD
Surrey
Map **4** SU94

★★★**Hogs Back** Hogs Back ☎ Runfold (02518) 2345

(For full entry see Seale)

★★**Angel** High St (Trusthouse Forte) ☎ (0483) 64555

Modernised 14th-century coaching inn with modestly furnished bedrooms, coffee shop and 13th-century Crypt Restaurant.

27→⋒CTV in all bedrooms ® sB&B→⋒£52 dB&B→⋒£71.50 B

xmas

Last dinner 9.45pm

Credit cards 1 2 3 4 5

◯**Post House** Egerton Rd (Trusthouse Forte)
☎ 01-937 8033
120→⋒ Due to open March 1987

XX**Three Kingdoms** 14 Park St
☎ (0483) 61458
Classification for dinner only.

A well managed and friendly restaurant featuring Peking cuisine.

Closed 25—28 Dec

Cantonese & Pekinese V 80 seats Lunch £3.50—£13&alc Dinner £10.50—£13&alc Wine £5.50 Last dinner 11.15pm P

Credit cards 1 2 3 5 V

X**Rum-Wong** 16—18 London Rd
☎ (0483) 36092
Here, in the Khan Tok room, you can watch Thai dancers as you recline on cushions to eat your meal from low tables in the traditional way; should your taste run to more conventional furnishings and service, however, these are available in the à la carte room.
Closed 24—26 Dec, 31 Dec, 1 Jan & 1st 2wks Aug Lunch not served Mon

Thai V 40 seats *Lunch £5—£8alc Dinner £10—£15alc Wine £6.10 Last dinner 10.30pm P

Credit cards 1 3

GUIST
Norfolk
Map **9** TF92

XX**Tollbridge** ☎ Foulsham (036284) 359

The original toll bridge stands at the end of this delightful cottage's terrace, past which flows the River Wensum. The restaurant is noted for its friendly service and value-for-money meals — a range of attractively-presented French country dishes, carefully prepared with excellent Norfolk produce and making good use of local game and fish.

Closed Sun, Mon 1st 3 wks Jan & 1st wk Oct

English & French 40 seats Lunch fr£7.50 Dinner fr£9&alc Wine £4.65 Last dinner 9.30pm 30P

Credit card 3

GULLANE
Lothian *East Lothian*
Map **12** NT48

✿★★★**Greywalls**
(see red star box opposite)

✿X**La Potinière** Main St ☎ (0620) 843214

The charming little restaurant, its interior beamed and decorated with dried flowers and framed wine labels, offers a fixed-price menu that contains no choice but changes daily. Booking is essential, as Hilary Brown's delightful French cooking is very popular.

Closed Wed, 1 wk Jun & Oct Lunch not served Sat Dinner served Sat only

French 32 seats Lunch £10.75—£11.50 Dinner £16.50 Wine £5.50 10P

X**Scott-Hamilton's** 3 Roseberry Pl
☎ (0620) 842233
The wood-panelled interior of this little restaurant with its attractive selection of pot plants creates a pleasant setting in which to enjoy a selection of French and Scottish dishes, all prepared and served to a high standard which has earned its proprietor an excellent reputation.

G

★★★

✿★★★ GREYWALLS, GULLANE

Duncar Rd (Pride of Britain) ☎ (0620) 842144 Telex no 72294

Closed Nov—14 Apr

On the ground floor of this hotel there are a number of rooms where you can take your ease: in the small bar the talk is mostly golf, and there are four other sitting rooms, one with TV. Popular is the panelled library, where you could imagine that you were in a private house since, as with some of the other rooms, the private possessions of the owners remain. Then there is the dining room in two sections which is very civilised. Andrew Mitchell is the chef and he uses good raw materials for his fixed priced meals. He can cook well but the ingredients in some of his dishes are somewhat eccentric to say the least. In any event, you should be able to find a wine to complement your meal from the long and outstanding list of 4-500 wines. Service is amiable throughout the hotel. Bedrooms vary in style and size but are comfortable and provided with the usual extras such as fruit, flowers, bathrobes and hairdryers. As most people will know, this most attractive country house was designed by Lutyens and the five

acres of gardens by Gertrude Jekyll are still immaculately kept. Tennis and croquet are available but the chief asset is the nearby Muirfield Golf Course, one of 10 courses in the vicinity.

18 1 CTV in all bedrooms T *sB&B £42—£48 dB&B £84—£94

CTV 60P (hard) croquet putting

V Lunch £7.50—£9.50 Tea £1.50—£6.50 Dinner £19.50&alc Wine £4.95 Last dinner 9.30pm

Credit cards 1 2 3

Closed Mon Lunch not served Tue

Scottish & French V 40 seats Wine £5.95 Last dinner 9.30pm

Credit cards 1 2 3

GULWORTHY
Devon
Map 2 SX47

✿XXX Horn of Plenty
☎ Tavistock (0822) 832528

This delightful restaurant, situated in a quiet location overlooking the Tamar Valley, is noted for the good English food which is created by its proprietor, Sonia Stevenson, from first-class local raw materials and accompanied by an interesting and comprehensive wine list. Accommodation is available in six well-appointed bedrooms which have recently been constructed from an old barn, and residential courses in the preparation of sauces are offered by Mr Stevenson.

Closed Thu & Xmas Day Lunch not served Fri

English & French V 60 seats Last dinner 9.30pm 30P

GUNNISLAKE
Cornwall
Map 2 SX47

★★ ***Cornish Inn*** The Square
☎ Tavistock (0822) 832475
Closed Xmas & Boxing Day

A small, country inn situated in the glorious Tamar valley.

9rm(5)(1fb) ®

CTV 25P

English & French Last dinner 9.30pm

Credit cards 1 2 3 5

GWBERT-ON-SEA
Dyfed
Map 2 SN15

★★★ **Cliff** ☎ Cardigan (0239) 613241 Telex no 48440

A family, holiday hotel with a friendly atmosphere, the Cliff stands perched on its own 30 acres of headland with fine sea views and offers a good range of facilities.

70 2 CTV in all bedrooms T S% sB&B £25—£35 dB&B £40—£55

CTV 150P CFA (heated) squash snooker Live music & dancing Wed

Welsh, English & French V Lunch fr£7.50 Tea fr80p High Tea fr£3.50 Dinner £9.25—£13.50 Wine £4.75 Last dinner 10pm

Credit cards 1 2 3 5 Ⓥ

GWITHIAN
Cornwall
Map 2 SW54

★★ **Glencoe House** 23 Churchtown Rd (ExecHotel) ☎ Hayle (0736) 752216
Closed Nov—Feb

Comfortable small friendly hotel in a quiet position yet close to the beach.

11rm(9 2)(2fb) 2 CTV in all bedrooms ® sB&B £21—£26 dB&B £38—£42

CTV 20P (heated)

English & French V Lunch £7alc Tea £3alc Dinner £9.50alc Wine £5.15 Last dinner 9.30pm

Credit cards 1 2 3 5 Ⓥ

G

HACKNESS
North Yorkshire
Map 8 SE99

★★★ ***Hackness Grange Country Hotel*** (Best Western) ☎ Scarborough (0723) 369966 Telex no 527667

An elegant country house in a superb setting, the family-run hotel offers very comfortable accommodation, a relaxing atmosphere and courteous service.

14rm(9 5) Annexe: 14rm(12 2)(4fb) 1 CTV in all bedrooms ® in 15 bedrooms T

60P (heated) (hard) nc 5yrs *xmas*

V Last dinner 8.30pm

Credit cards 1 2 3 4 5

See advertisement under Scarborough

HADDINGTON
Lothian *East Lothian*
Map 12 NT57

★★ **George** 91 High St ☎ (062082) 3372

The attractively renovated hotel, which dates back 350 years, stands at the centre of the town.

11rm(4)(2fb) CTV in all bedrooms ® T sB&B fr£23 sB&B fr£27 dB&B fr£32 dB&B fr£37

CTV 12P

Lunch fr£6 High Tea fr£4.50 Dinner fr£10 Wine £4.50 Last dinner 9pm

Credit cards 1 2 3 5

X Waterside Bistro 1—5 Waterside, Nungate ☎ (062082) 5674

A compact restaurant with a Victorian theme, the Waterside is set on the first floor of an old, converted building overlooking the River Tyne. The menu, which is mainly French, is accompanied by an interesting wine list, and quality bar meals are served downstairs.

International V 45 seats *Lunch fr£7.95&alc Dinner £11.95alc Wine £4.95 Last dinner 10pm 25P

Credit cards 1 2 3 5

Hadleigh — Halifax

HADLEIGH
Suffolk
Map **5** TM04

✕✕**Taviton's** 103 High St ☎ (0473) 822820
Closed Mon
English & French **V** 22 seats Lunch £3—£5.75 Dinner £12.50 Wine £5.50 Last dinner 9.30pm 8P ⁄
Credit cards [1] [3]

✕**Spinning Wheel** 117 High St ☎ (0473) 822175
This attractive little restaurant sits on the main road at the edge of the town. The wooden beams, dark furniture, candles and fresh flowers of its interior present a warm and comfortable atmosphere in which to enjoy a meal selected from a wide range of dishes, many of which have an Italian flavour.
Closed Boxing Day
English & Continental **V** 60 seats Lunch £5.95—£6.95&alc Dinner £8.95&alc Wine £5.30 Last dinner 10pm P ⁄ Cabaret mthly
Credit cards [1] [2] [3] [5]

H

HADLEY WOOD
Greater London
Map **4** TQ29

★★★★**West Lodge Park** Cockfosters Rd ☎ 01-440 8311 Telex no 24734
Late-Georgian building with an interesting history, standing in quiet parkland and farmland.
50⇌(2fb) 3 CTV in all bedrooms ® **T** sB&B⇌£50 dB&B⇌£63—£75 B
Lift ☾ 200P CFA ✽ putting croquet
V Lunch £11.50alc Tea 70palc Dinner £11.50alc Wine £6.75 Last dinner 9.30pm
Credit cards [1] [2] [3] [5]

HADLOW
Kent
Map **5** TQ65

★★*B* **Leavers Manor** Goose Gn ☎ (0732) 851442
Closed Jan
The elegant Georgian house offers attractively decorated bedrooms and comfortably furnished public areas; meals are soundly cooked and efficiently served.

10rm(8⇌2⚲)(2fb) CTV in all bedrooms ® **T** S% sB&B⇌⚲£30—£35.50 dB&B⇌⚲£38—£44 B
CTV P ✽ (hard)
International Tea £2 Dinner £12.50alc Wine £5 Last dinner 10.30pm
Credit cards [1] [2] [3] [5] Ⓥ

✽✕**La Crémaillère** The Square ☎ (0732) 851489
The small, family-run restaurant features separate dining areas which include a conservatory grapevine. The chef/patron's carefully prepared and authentic French dishes are served by a friendly young staff.
Closed Sun Lunch not served Sat
French 33 seats Lunch £12.50 Dinner £12.50 Wine £6 Last dinner 9pm P
Credit cards [1] [2] [3]

HALIFAX
West Yorkshire
Map **7** SE02

★★★*B* **Holdsworth House** Holdsworth, Holmfield (3m NW off A629 Keighley Rd) ☎ (0422) 240024 Telex no 51574
Closed 25 & 26 Dec
Stone-built period house dating from 1633 and standing in its own grounds.

40rm(28⇌12⋒)(1fb)4⊟CTV in all bedrooms T S% sB&B⇌⋒£39—£49 dB&B⇌⋒£49—£59 ℞

☾40P CFA ✿ ♿ *xmas*

♔ ⊏ S% Lunch £15alc Tea £1.50alc Dinner £15alc Wine £7.50 Last dinner 9pm

Credit cards 1 2 3 4 5 Ⓥ

✕**Yorkshireman** 2 Towngate, Hipperholme (2m E on A58) ☎ (0422) 206130

Three Pennine-stone cottages, dating from the 18th century, have been pleasingly modified and extended to create a restaurant which retains much of the original character and charm. The cooking is honest-to-goodness and straightforward, conserving the natural flavours of the food, and the sweet trolley is particularly good.

Lunch not served Sat Dinner not served Sun

♉English & French **V** 46 seats ✱ Lunch £5.35—£8.75&alc Dinner £8.75—£9.75&alc Wine £6 Last dinner 10pm ₱

Credit cards 1 2 3 5

HALLAND
East Sussex
Map **5** TQ41

★★**Halland Forge** (InterHotel/ExecHotel) ☎ (082584) 456 Telex no 8951994

Hotel with very clean and comfortable accommodation, also nicely appointed restaurant and coffee shop.

Annexe: 20rm(17⇌3⋒)(2fb) CTV in all bedrooms ® sB&B⇌⋒£34.50—£37.50 dB&B⇌⋒£47—£53 ℞

70P ✿ nc 5yrs

♉English & French **V** ♔ ⊏ ✂ ✱ Lunch fr£7.95&alc Tea £2 High Tea fr£5 Dinner fr£9.50&alc Wine £4.95 Last dinner 9.30pm

Credit cards 1 2 3 5 Ⓥ

Halifax — Harbertonford

HAMBLE
Hampshire
Map **4** SU40

✕✕**Beth's** The Quay ☎ Southampton (0703) 454314

This cosy and sophisticated restaurant is set in a waterfront cottage and has a tasteful lounge bar on the ground floor as well as the well-appointed first-floor dining room with its imaginative French menu.

♉English & French **V** 55 seats Lunch £9.75&alc Dinner £9.75&alc Wine £5.75 Last dinner 9.30pm 100P ✂

Credit cards 1 2 3 4 5

HAMILTON
Strathclyde *Lanarkshire*
Map **11** NS75

✕✕***Costa's*** 17—21 Campbell St ☎ (0698) 283552

Modern Greek-run restaurant offering European cuisine.

Closed Sun, 1st 3 wks Aug, Xmas Day & New Years Day

♉European 55 seats Last dinner 10.15pm ₱

Credit cards 1 2 3 4 5

HAMPTON
Greater London
London Plan **5** *A2* (page 446)

✕***Garrick's*** 75 Station Rd ☎ 01-941 3587

Closed Sun Lunch not served Sat

♉English & French **V** 80 seats Last dinner 10pm

Credit cards 1 2 3 5

HAMPTON LOADE
Shropshire
Map **7** SO78

✕✕**Haywain** (6m SE of Bridgnorth, W off A442) ☎ Quatt (0746) 780404

Popular split-level restaurant in this picturesque riverside village.

Closed Mon Lunch not served Tue—Sat Dinner not served Sun

♉English & French **V** 44 seats Sun Lunch £10 Dinner £17.50 Wine £3.50 Last dinner 9.30pm 20P

Credit cards 1 2 3 5

HANDFORTH
Cheshire
Map **7** SJ88

❀★★★★*H* **Belfry** Stanley Rd ☎ 061-437 0511 Telex no 666358

RS 26 Dec

The modern, family-run hotel provides service of a very high standard and features superb haute cuisine. A meal to suit all tastes can be ordered from an international menu, accompanied by a fine wine list. Dishes range from scampi poached in brandy and madeira with a rich cream of langoustines to noisettes of lamb with a port sauce, and all are delicious.

96rm(95⇌1⋒)(3fb) CTV in all bedrooms T ✖ sB⇌⋒£46.50 dB⇌fr£60 (room only) ℞

Lift ☾200P CFA ✿

♉International **V** ♔ ⊏ Lunch £8.50&alc Tea fr85p Dinner £9.50&alc Wine £5.50 Last dinner 10pm

Credit cards 1 2 3 5

HARBERTONFORD
Devon
Map **3** SX75

✕✕***Hungry Horse*** ☎ (080423) 441

Beamed, stone-built cottage in the centre of the village close to the river.

Closed Sun, Mon & Feb Lunch not served

♉French **V** 50 seats Last dinner 9.30pm 8P

Credit cards 1 2 3 5

H

HARDGATE
Strathclyde *Dunbartonshire*
Map **11** NS47

★★***Cameron House*** Main St
☎ Duntocher (0389) 73535

Small family-run hotel that caters especially for functions.

16rm(4→12⋒) CTV in 15 bedrooms TV in 1 bedroom **T**

Lift ☾# CTV 100P 9⌂(£1) Disco Tue, Thu, Sun Live music & dancing Tue

European **V** Last dinner 9.15pm

HARLECH
Gwynedd
Map **6** SH53
See also **Talsarnau**

★**Noddfa House** Lower Rd ☎ (0766) 780043

Stone-built hotel located under the walls of the castle and overlooking golf course.

7rm(2→)(1fb) TV available in bedrooms ® sB&B£12 dB&B£24 dB&B→£30

CTV 45P ✽ field archery nc 5yrs *xmas*

International Bar lunch £1.50—£3 Tea 50p Dinner £6.50—£7&alc Wine £3.50 Last dinner 8.30pm

Credit cards 1 3

✕**Cemlyn** High St ☎ (0766) 780425

This small, lively restaurant is situated at the centre of the village and has attractive views of the castle. The well-balanced menu is augmented by the chef's daily specialities; the atmosphere is informal and the service friendly.

Closed Oct—Etr (ex Sat until 1 Jan) Lunch not served

International **V** 34 seats Dinner £7.95—£8.95&alc Wine £4.50 Last dinner 9.30pm **P** nc 8yrs

Credit cards 2 5 Ⓥ

HARLESTON
Norfolk
Map **5** TM28

★★**Swan** The Thoroughfare ☎ (0379) 852221

11rm(8→) ® S% sB&B→£20—£22 dB&B→£29.50—£31.50

CTV 80P *xmas*

English & French ✽Lunch £4.95—£6.95 Dinner £8—£11.50 Wine £3.95 Last dinner 9.15pm

Credit cards 1 2 3

HARLOSH
Isle of Skye, Highland *Inverness-shire*
See **Skye, Isle of**

HARLOW
Essex
Map **5** TL41

★★★**Churchgate Manor** Churchgate St, Old Harlow (Best Western) ☎ (0279) 20246 Telex no 818289

Originally built in the 17th century as a chantry house, the hotel has been extended and developed to provide modern, well-equipped bedrooms in the new wing, whilst the Chantry Bar and restaurant reflect the traditional style of the original.

71→(4fb) CTV in all bedrooms ®**T** sB&B→£46.50—£55 dB&B→£53—£62

☾110P ✽ (heated) sauna bath solarium gymnasium games room *xmas*

English & French **V** Lunch £8.50&alc Tea £1—£3 Dinner £10.50&alc Wine £5.75 Last dinner 9.45pm

Credit cards 1 2 3 5 Ⓥ

★★★**Green Man** Mulberry Green, Old Harlow (Anchor) ☎ (0279) 442521 Telex no 817972

Interesting coaching inn with comfortable well-equipped bedrooms in modern annexe.

Annexe: 55→⋒(3fb) in 10 bedrooms CTV in all bedrooms ®**T** sB&B→⋒£45—£47 dB&B→⋒£55—£57

☾75P

International **V** Lunch £8.75—£10 Tea 50p—£2.50 Dinner £9.50—£10.50&alc Wine £5.95 Last dinner 10pm

Credit cards 1 2 3 5 Ⓥ

★★★**Harlow Moat House** Southern Way (Queens Moat) ☎ (0279) 22441 Telex no 81658

Large hotel with modern, motel-style bedrooms spacious public rooms which include a more formal restaurant.

120→⋒ CTV in all bedrooms ®**T** S% ✱sB&B→⋒£21.50—£43 dB&B→⋒£28—£56

☾CTV 200P Live music & dancing Sat CFA

English & French **V** S% ✱Lunch £7.75&alc Tea £1—£2 Dinner £8.95—£12.75&alc Wine £7.15 Last dinner 10.30pm

Credit cards 1 2 3 5 Ⓥ

HARLYN BAY
Cornwall
Map **2** SW87

★*L* **Polmark** (off B3276) ☎ Padstow (0841) 520206

Closed Jan

Attractive Cornish stone house in peaceful situation close to the beach.

6rm Annexe: 9rm (2fb) ✱sB&B£12.50 dB&B£25

CTV 40P ✽ (heated) putting

✱Lunch £5.70—£6 Tea £1—£1.50 Dinner £6.25—£7.50&alc Wine £4.60 Last dinner 8.30pm

Ⓥ

HAROME
North Yorkshire
Map **8** SE68
See **Helmsley**

HARPENDEN
Hertfordshire
Map **4** TL11

★★★★**Harpenden Moat House** 18 Southdown Rd (Queens Moat) ☎ (05827) 64111

This Georgian period house was once known as St Dominic's convent.

18rm(15→3⋒) Annexe: 37→ in 6 bedrooms CTV in all bedrooms ®**T** sB&B→⋒fr£46.50 dB&B→⋒fr£62

☾50P

French **V** Lunch fr£9.50&alc Tea fr£1 Dinner fr£12 Wine £6.50 Last dinner 10pm

Credit cards 1 2 3 5

★★★***Glen Eagle*** 1 Luton Rd ☎ (05827) 60271 Telex no 925859

Pleasant country-house style hotel with very good facilities.

51rm(48→3⋒)(4fb) CTV in all bedrooms

Lift ☾# 100P CFA ✽ *xmas*

English & French **V** Last dinner 10pm

Credit cards 1 2 3 5

HARRIS, ISLE OF
Western Isles *Inverness-shire*
Map **13**

SCARISTA
Map **13** NG09

✽★★ ***HBL*** **Scarista House**
☎ (085985) 238

Closed Oct—Etr

(Rosette awarded for dinner only)

A recently renovated old manse, next to the church, and with breathtaking views across the west coast of Harris. It is close to some of Scotland's most beautiful beaches and makes a peaceful, quiet haven. It is tastefully appointed and with a homely atmosphere, while the food is very well prepared and beautifully served. Bedrooms are available either in the hotel or in the cottage at the back.

7→ ®sB&B→£35—£37 dB&B→£50—£54

10P ✽ nc 8yrs

Dinner £15—£17 Wine £4.50 Last dinner 8pm

TARBERT
Map **13** NB10

★★***Harris*** ☎ Harris (0859) 2154

Closed Nov—mid Mar

Family run, Highland hotel with good home cooking in modern restaurant complex.

25rm(12→2⋒)(2fb)

CTV 25P ✽

V Last dinner 6.30pm

HARROGATE
North Yorkshire
Map **8** SE35

★★★★**Crown** Crown Pl (Trusthouse Forte) ☎ (0423) 67755 Telex no 57652

An 18th-century building near Valley Gardens and the Royal Baths.

122rm(100→22⋔) CTV in all bedrooms ® T sB&B→⋔£53 dB&B→⋔£69 B

Lift ☾ 50P CFA *xmas*

Last dinner 9.30pm

Credit cards 1 2 3 4 5

★★★★**Majestic** Ripon Rd (Trusthouse Forte) ☎ (0423) 68972 Telex no 57918

Spacious stylish and comfortable hotel with well-appointed bedrooms.

157→⋔(6fb) CTV in all bedrooms ® T sB&B→⋔£55 dB&B→⋔£71 B

Lift ☾ 180P CFA ❁ (heated) (hard) squash billiards Live music and dancing Sat (Oct–Apr) *xmas*

Last dinner 9.45pm

Credit cards 1 2 3 4 5

★★★★**Old Swan** Swan Rd ☎ (0423) 500055 Telex no 57922

This large Victorian building stands in well-kept gardens with provision for tennis and croquet, conveniently close to the Conference Centre and town facilities. Recently refurbished bedrooms are complemented by public areas of style and character and there is a choice of restaurants.

140→⋔(12fb) CTV in all bedrooms ® T S% ✱sB&B→⋔£52 dB&B→⋔£70 B

Lift ☾ 200P CFA ❁ (hard) croquet putting *xmas*

English & French V ✱Lunch £8 Tea £3.50 High Tea £6 Dinner £10.50&alc Wine £6.50 Last dinner 10pm

Credit cards 1 2 3 5

★★★**Cairn** Ripon Rd (Quality) ☎ (0423) 504005 Telex no 57792

A large, stone-built four-storey Victorian hotel, situated near the town centre.

137→(5fb) in 12 bedrooms CTV in all bedrooms ® ✱sB&B→£45 dB&B→£60 B

Lift ☾ 150P CFA ❁ (hard) gymnasium pool table croquet *xmas*

V ✱Lunch £6.95 Tea £1.85 High Tea £4.50alc Dinner £8.75&alc Wine £3.95 Last dinner 9.15pm

Credit cards 1 2 3 5

★★★**Grants** 3–7 Swan Rd ☎ (0423) 60666

Well restored Georgian town houses form this friendly hotel near conference centre. It has very well appointed bedrooms and most comfortable public rooms.

17rm(7→10⋔)(2fb) CTV in all bedrooms ® T ✱sB&B→⋔£37.50 dB&B→⋔£52 B

Lift ☾ 15P *xmas*

French V ✱Lunch fr£6.95 Tea fr65p Dinner fr£9.95&alc Wine £4.95 Last dinner 9.30pm

Credit cards 1 2 3 5

★★★**Harrogate International** Kings Rd (Queens Moat) ☎ (0423) 500000 Telex no 57575

Closed 22–28 Dec

The modern, purpose-built, multi-storey hotel stands adjacent to the Conference Centre, providing accommodation in smart, modern bedrooms and the use of a spacious reception lounge and conference facilities. The restaurant, with its popular lounge bar, offers high-quality cuisine, or guests may eat at the Orangery Coffee Shop.

214→⋔ in 17 bedrooms CTV in all bedrooms ® T sB&B→⋔£45–£47.50 dB&B→⋔£62–£65 B

Lift ☾ ## 30P 260 (charged) Live music & dancing Fri & Sat *xmas* →

H

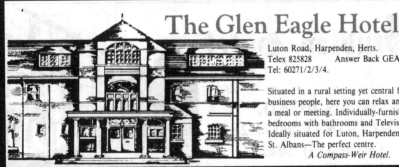

English & French V S% Lunch £7.50 High Tea £2.50—£4.50 Wine £4.95 Last dinner 8.30pm

Credit cards 1 2 3 4 5

★★★B **Hospitality Inn** Prospect Pl, West Park (Mount Charlotte) ☎ (0423) 64601 Telex no 57530

Six-storey stone built Victorian building in the town centre.

71 CTV in all bedrooms ® T ✱ sB&B fr £44.50 dB&B fr £55 B

Lift ☾ 30P CFA *xmas*

Last dinner 9.30pm

Credit cards 1 2 3 4 5 V

Harrogate

★★★ **Hotel St George** 1 Ripon Rd (Swallow) ☎ (0423) 61431 Telex no 57995

Large hotel with well-proportioned rooms, good restaurant and Lamplight Bar.

85rm (80 5) (13fb) CTV in all bedrooms ® T S% sB&B fr £52 dB&B fr £72 B

Lift ☾ 60P CFA (heated) sauna bath solarium gymnasium *xmas*

English & French V S% ✱ Lunch £7.25—£8.25 Tea £1—£1.50 Dinner £9.75—£10.75&alc Wine £5.50 Last dinner 9.15pm

Credit cards 1 2 3 5

★★★B **Studley** Swan Rd ☎ (0423) 60425 Telex no 57506

Close to all amenities, including the beautiful Valley Gardens, this attractive, comfortable and enthusiastically-run hotel prides itself on the high standard of cuisine both in the French restaurant and in the recently-opened "Shrimps", which specialises in sea food.

39 CTV in all bedrooms ® T S%
*sB&B £42—£46 dB&B £54—£60 B
Lift ☾ CTV 14P nc 8yrs
French ✱Lunch £8.60alc Dinner £8.50&alc Wine £4.75 Last dinner 10pm
Credit cards 1 2 3 4

★★**Fern** Swan Rd (Inter-Hotel) ☎ (0423) 523866 Telex no 57583
A pair of stone-built houses with forecourt gardens, near the town centre.
28rm(26)(4fb) CTV in all bedrooms ® T B
☾
French V Last dinner 9.30pm
Credit cards 1 2 3 5

★★**Green Park** Valley Dr (Consort) ☎ (0423) 504681 Telex no 57515
A three-storey stone building on a corner position and overlooking Valley gardens.
44rm(28 16)(2fb) CTV in all bedrooms ® sB&B £29 dB&B £48—£53 B
Lift ☾ 10P
V Bar lunch £2alc Tea 75—80p alc Dinner £8.75&alc Wine £4.75 Last dinner 8.30pm
Credit cards 1 2 3 5

★★**Hotel Italia** 53 Kings Rd ☎ (0423) 67404
The distinctive Victorian stone house stands in attractive gardens close to the Conference Centre. The impressive, decorative plaster ceilings of the lounge bars and restaurant are noteworthy. Bedroom accommodation is provided in an extension, conference facilities are available, and fresh food with an Italian flavour is served in a well-appointed restaurant.
27rm(3 2)(1fb) CTV in all bedrooms ® T sB&B £27.03 sB&B £28.75 dB&B £40.25 dB&B £44.85 B
CTV 18P
English & Italian Lunch £6.90 Tea £1.38 Dinner £8.63&alc Wine £6.33 Last dinner 9.30pm
Credit cards 2 3 5

★★**Russell** Valley Dr ☎ (0423) 509866
Closed 28—30 Dec
Large converted Victorian house overlooking Valley gardens.
34rm(22 12)(3fb) CTV in all bedrooms T sB&B £31.25—£34.95 dB&B £43.50—£53.50 B
Lift ☾ *xmas*
French V Bar lunch £3.65alc Dinner £10.75—£11.50&alc Wine £5.95 Last dinner 10.30pm
Credit cards 1 2 3 4 5

★★**Wessex** 22—23 Harlow Moor Dr ☎ (0423) 65890
Closed Dec
A charming small hotel converted from a pair of town houses, the Wessex overlooks the Valley Gardens and complements well-fitted bedrooms with cosy public rooms including lounge and separate bar.
13(3fb) TV in 1 bedroom CTV in 1 bedroom ® sB&B £16 dB&B £32 B
CTV 30P
Cosmopolitan V Lunch £3.50—£5&alc Tea £1—£1.80 High Tea £2.50—£4 Dinner £7.50—£9&alc Wine £4.20 Last dinner 7.30pm
Credit cards 1 3

★★**White House** 10 Park Pde (Exec Hotel) ☎ (0423) 501388
This elegant, early Victorian building overlooking part of "The Stray" retains many of the original features, including plasterwork and a rather impressive staircase. The bedrooms are well designed, with homely fittings, the restaurant is decorated in quiet good taste and there is a public lounge with separate lounge bar. Interesting antiques are dotted throughout the hotel.
14rm(8 6)(2fb) CTV in all bedrooms ® T sB&B £27—£32 dB&B £35—£43 B
CTV 10P *xmas* →

English & Continental V ☕ Lunch £3.75—£5.50&alc Tea £1.25—£2.25 High Tea £2.25—£3.25 Dinner £8.50—£10.50&alc Wine £5 Last dinner 9pm

Credit cards [1] [2] [3] [4] [5] Ⓥ

★**Alvera Court** 76 Kings Rd ☎ (0423) 505735

Comfortable small hotel with well proportioned rooms and friendly proprietors.

11rm(3 8)(4fb) CTV in all bedrooms ® * sB&B £15—£18 dB&B £30—£34

CTV 4P *xmas*

*Bar lunch fr £3 Dinner fr £7.50 Wine £3.50 Last dinner 7pm

Credit card [1]

★**Britannia Lodge** 16 Swan Rd ☎ (0423) 508482

Friendly hotel with homely accommodation, spacious public rooms and small bar.

12rm(10 2)(4fb) CTV in all bedrooms ® sB&B £22 dB&B £34—£40

CTV 6P 1

V ☕ Lunch £5.50 Tea £2 Dinner £7.50 Wine £4.50 Last dinner 6pm

Credit cards [1] [3] Ⓥ

★**Caesars** 51 Valley Drive ☎ (0423) 65818

Closed Xmas & New Year

Comfortable hotel overlooking Valley Gardens with attractive dining rooms and good bedrooms.

10rm(5 5)(4fb) TV in all bedrooms ® sB&B £23—26 dB&B £38—£40

P CTV

English & French V ☕ Bar lunch £1—£4.50 Tea £1.50—£3 Dinner £8—£13&alc Wine £3.50 Last dinner 8.45pm

Credit cards [1] [3]

Harrogate

★B **Gables** 2 West Grove Rd ☎ (0423) 505625

The converted Victorian house aptly named, stands conveniently close to the shopping area and Conference Centre. The interior is immaculate, offering a spacious and comfortable lounge with separate lounge bar and an attractive and well-appointed restaurant.

9rm(4 3) CTV in all bedrooms ® sB&B fr £21.50 dB&B fr £42

6P

☕ Tea fr 60p Dinner £7.50 Wine £4.50 Last dinner 8pm

Credit cards [1] [2] [3]

★**Young's** 15 York Rd ☎ (0423) 67336

Closed 20 Dec—2 Jan

Clean, comfortable hotel with quiet, attractive public rooms and surrounded by gardens.

15rm(10 5)(2fb) CTV in all bedrooms ® S% *sB&B £22—£25 dB&B £39—£45

CTV 18P

English & French V Bar lunch £1.50—£2.50 Tea £1.20 Dinner £8.50—£9&alc Wine £4.25 Last dinner 7pm

Credit card [1] Ⓥ

✕✕**Emilio's** 3 Ripon Rd ☎ (0423) 65267

An impressive Victorian residence opposite the Conference Centre now contains a smart restaurant specialising in fish dishes from the Iberian Peninsula, together with other Spanish favourites. From the décor and fittings one could easily imagine oneself in Spain, and the mood is enhanced by the background music. Service is by immaculately dressed and helpful waiters.

Closed Sun

Spanish V 70 seats *Lunch £5.90&alc Dinner £13.50alc Wine £4.90 Last dinner 11pm 22P

Credit cards [1] [2] [3] [5]

✕✕***Number Six*** 6 Ripon Rd ☎ (0423) 502908

Comfortable and spacious restaurant with excellent cuisine.

Closed Mon & 3 wks Aug Lunch not served

French 58 seats Last dinner 10pm 20P

Credit cards [1] [2] [3] [5]

✕✕**Oliver** 24 King's Rd ☎ (0423) 68600

Closed Sun

French V 80 seats S% *Lunch £4.99—£7.99&alc Dinner £12—£18&alc Wine £4.99 Last dinner 11pm

Credit cards [1] [2] [3]

✕✕**Shabab** 1 John St ☎ (0423) 500250

Pleasantly decorated restaurant in rich eastern colours of gold and cream, with suitably dressed and courteous staff.

Closed Xmas Day Lunch not served Sun

Indian 120 seats Last dinner 11.30pm

Credit cards [1] [2] [3] [5]

✕✕**Shrimps Seafood** Swan Rd ☎ (0423) 508111

Comfortable, intimate restaurant offering good value seafood dishes.

Closed Sun

Lunch not served Mon

French V 50 seats Lunch £2.85—£7.50&alc *Dinner £7.75—£10&alc Wine £4.95 Last dinner 11pm nc10yrs Live music Tue, Wed, Fri & Sat

Credit cards [1] [2] [3] [5]

✕**Burdekin's** 21 Cheltenham Cres ☎ (0423) 502610

This ground floor restaurant, converted from a terraced town house, is convenient for the town centre and close to the Conference/Exhibition Centre. In surroundings of quiet good taste, well-prepared food — mostly imaginative English dishes, but including an international element — is served, accompanied by an interesting wine list.

Lunch not served

English & French V 40 seats *Dinner £7.95&alc Wine £4.90 Last dinner 9.30pm nc12yrs

Credit cards [1] [2] [3]

✕**Casa Romana** 23 Cheltenham Cres ☎(0423) 68568

This unmistakably Italian restaurant has been converted from a town house and is conveniently placed for both the shopping area and the Conference Centre. Pizzas, pastas and classical Italian dishes are cooked on the premises (the viewing window into the kitchen giving you an insight on this!) and served with tangy sauces, whilst the Mediterranean atmosphere is enhanced by marble table tops and appropriate music.

English & Continental 75 seats S% Lunch £2.95—£4.95 Dinner £6.95—£12.95 Wine £4.25 Last dinner 11.30pm

Credit cards 1 3

HARROW
Greater London
London plan **5** *B5* (page 446)

★★**Cumberland** 1 St John's Rd ☎01-863 4111 Telex no 917201

Privately owned commercial hotel with informal, friendly atmosphere.

30rm(8 22) Annexe: 51rm(18 16)(5fb) CTV in all bedrooms ®T ✱sB&B£33 sB&B £42—£46 dB&B £52—£56

CTV 55P

English & French **V** S% ✱Lunch £5.99—£7.50&alc Tea 75p Dinner £9.75&alc Wine £5.20 Last dinner 9.30pm

Credit cards 1 2 3 5 V

★★**Harrow** Roxborough Bridge 12—22 Pinner Rd (Consort) ☎01-427 3435 Telex no 917898

RS Xmas

Small, friendly hotel with comfortable, well equipped bedrooms.

76rm(20 52)(4fb) 1 CTV in all bedrooms ®T sB&B£38 sB&B £42—£48 dB&B £56—£58

67P

International **V** Lunch fr£10.25&alc Tea fr£1.50 Dinner fr£10.25&alc Wine £5.95 Last dinner 9.30pm

Credit cards 1 2 3 5

★★**Monksdene** 2—12 Northwick Park Rd ☎01-427 2899 Telex no 919171

This modernised commercial hotel offers bedrooms which are fairly small but well equipped and the use of health club facilities. The atmosphere is informal and friendly.

70rm(58 5)(1fb) CTV in all bedrooms ®T S% sB&B£20—£27 sB&B £28—£35 dB&B £39—£48

CTV 60P snooker sauna bath solarium

S% Lunch £9.50alc Tea £1 Dinner £9.50alc Wine £4.75 Last dinner 10pm

Credit cards 1 2 3 5 V

✕**Old Etonian** 38 High St ☎01-422 8482

Small French restaurant providing good food.

Closed Sun & Bank Hols Lunch not served Sat

French **V** 85 seats ✱Lunch £15alc Dinner £15alc Wine £5.85 Last dinner 11pm

Credit cards 1 2 3 4 5

HARROW WEALD
Greater London
London plan **5** *B5* (page 446)

★★★**Grims Dyke** Old Redding (Best Western) ☎01-954 4227

Closed 26—29 Dec

Attractive house, once the home of W.S. Gilbert, with well-equipped bedrooms in modern annexe.

8rm(4 4) Annexe: 40 2 CTV in all bedrooms ®T S% sB&B £53.75 dB&B £71.50—£96.50

150P croquet Cabaret Sun →

H

V ♔ ☕ ⚡ S% Lunch £13.75&alc Tea £1.50—£4.75 Dinner £13.75&alc Wine £6.50 Last dinner 10pm

Credit cards 1 2 3 4 5 Ⓥ

HARTINGTON
Derbyshire
Map **7** SK16

★**Charles Cotton** ☎ (029884) 229

Situated in the centre of this popular Peak District village, the old, stone-built inn provides simple but adequate accommodation. It is named after the famous 17th century author, who lived locally.

9rm(2fb) CTV in all bedrooms ® S% sB&B fr£12.65 dB&B fr£22 ℞

CTV 50P ✿ ♪ Live music & dancing Fri Sat & Sun

V ♔ ☕ S% Lunch fr£5&alc Tea £1—£2 High Tea fr£4 Dinner fr£7 Wine £4 Last dinner 9.30pm

HARTLAND
Devon
Map **2** SS22

★**Hartland Quay** Hartland Quay ☎ (02374) 218

Closed mid Nov—mid Mar RS mid Mar—Etr

Standing beside the old harbour, the hotel was converted from the harbour master's cottage and stores.

16rm(7→1⋒)(2fb) ® in 14 bedrooms S% sB&B £12—£12.50 sB&B→⋒ £13—£13.50 dB&B £24—£25 dB&B→⋒ £26—£27

CTV 100P 16⌂ ⛵

♔ ☕ S% Bar lunch £1.50—£4.50 Tea fr45p Dinner £6—£7&alc Wine £4 Last dinner 8pm

HARTOFT END
North Yorkshire
Map **8** SE79

★★**Blacksmiths Arms** ☎ Lastingham (07515) 331

A converted moorland farmhouse dating from the 16th-century, surrounded by attractive scenery.

12rm(7→3⋒) CTV in all bedrooms ® sB&B £20—£25 sB&B→⋒ £25 dB&B £34—£40 dB&B→⋒ fr£40 ℞

CTV 80P ⊞ ✿

♛ English & French ♔ Bar lunch £1.80—£6.50 Dinner fr£9.50&alc Wine £5 Last dinner 9.15pm

Credit cards 1 3

HARWICH
Essex
Map **5** TM23

★★**Cliff** Marine Pde, Dovercourt ☎ (0255) 503345

RS Xmas

Informal sea-front hotel with some modern bedroom facilities.

Harrow Weald — Haslemere

31rm(20→4⋒)(5fb) CTV in all bedrooms ® T sB&B £23—£28 sB&B→⋒ £28 dB&B £38—£41 dB&B→⋒ £41

☾ 60P 4⌂(charged)

♔ ☕ Lunch £4.88&alc Tea fr80p High Tea fr£3.50 Dinner fr£6.84&alc Wine £4.40 Last dinner 9pm

Credit cards 1 2 3 5

★★**Tower** Main Rd, Dovercourt ☎ (0255) 504952

Closed Xmas Day & Boxing Day

In this recently converted Victorian building modern bedrooms are complemented by friendly service.

15rm(8→7⋒)(2fb) CTV in all bedrooms ® T sB&B→⋒ £27 dB&B→⋒ £44—£48 ℞

☾ CTV 50P ✿

V ♔ ☕ Lunch £6.25 Tea fr£1 Dinner fr£10alc Wine £5.65 Last dinner 10pm

Credit cards 1 2 3 5

XX**Pier** The Quay ☎ (0255) 503363 Telex no 987083

The waterfront restaurant overlooks the port of Harwich, and its decor captures an atmosphere of sea and ships. Fresh, locally-caught fish of excellent quality are matched by fine sauces, and the young staff provide informal yet efficient service.

♛ English & French **V** 130 seats Lunch £6.25—£8.50&alc Dinner £5—£12.50alc Wine £5.50 Last dinner 9.30pm 10P Live music Mon—Sat & Sun lunch

Credit cards 1 2 3 5

HASLEMERE
Surrey
Map **4** SU93

★★★**Georgian** High St ☎ (0428) 51555

Closed 24 Dec—mid Jan RS xmas day

The well-managed, 18th century hotel has an old-fashioned atmosphere, friendly service and comfortable bedrooms.

18rm(9→1⋒) Annexe: 3→(2fb) CTV in all bedrooms ® sB £25—£29 sB→⋒ £32.50—£36 dB £35—£40 dB→⋒ £40—£45(room only) ℞

20P ✿ squash sauna bath ♧

♛ English & Continental **V** ♔ ☕ Lunch £6—£7 Tea £1.50—£3 Dinner £15alc Wine £5.50 Last dinner 9.15pm

Credit cards 1 2 3 5 Ⓥ

★★★*L* **Lythe Hill** Petworth Rd (1¼m E B2131) (Prestige) ☎ (0428) 51251 Telex no 858402

Set in an attractive location, the professionally run, hotel offers tastefully furnished bedrooms and suites. A choice of restaurants is available, including L'Auberge de France (as follows). Service throughout the hotel is first-class.

38rm(34→2⋒)(8fb) 1⊟ CTV in all bedrooms ® in 32 bedrooms **T** sB&B £38 sB&B→⋒ £50—£55 dB&B £55 dB&B→⋒ £66—£93 Continental breakfast ℞

☾ 200P CFA ⊞ ✿ ♀(hard) ♪ sauna bath Live music and dancing Sat (except mid Jun—mid Sep) ♧ *xmas*

♛ English & Continental **V** ♔ ☕ Lunch £13alc Tea £1.75alc Dinner £13alc Wine £9 Last dinner 9.15pm

Credit cards 1 2 3 5 Ⓥ

XXX**L'Auberge De France** (Lythe Hill Hotel) Petworth Rd (1¼m E B2131) ☎ (0428) 51251 Telex no 858402

The service is charming, the menu is imaginative and the cooking is sound in this 600-year-old timbered building with a modern addition.

Closed Mon Lunch not served Tue

♛ French 50 seats Lunch £16alc Dinner £16alc Wine £9 Last dinner 10.30pm 200P

Credit cards 1 2 3 5

❀XX**Morel's** 25—27 Lower St ☎ (0428) 51462

Uncomplicated, honest and skilful French cuisine is featured by this main-street restaurant. Menus change monthly, and there is a sensibly chosen and priced wine list. These factors, together with the quick, formal service, make this arguably the best French restaurant in Surrey.

Closed Sun, Mon last 2 wks Feb last wk Sep & 1st wk Oct Lunch not served Sat

♛ French 43 seats ✱ Lunch £11&alc Dinner £13&alc Wine £6 Last dinner 10pm ℙ

Credit cards 1 2 3 5

X***Good Earth*** 97 Weyhill ☎ (0428) 51240

This small, comfortable Pekinese restaurant provides authentic cuisine with a good selection of chef's specialities; the menu is designed to include the best combination of regional dishes, and there are some fixed-price meals. Standards of service and cookng are good, the fresh Chinese vegetables being particularly recommended.

♛ Pekinese 60 seats

Credit cards 1 2 3 5

X**Shrimpton's of Kingsley Green** 2 Grove Cottages, Midhurst Rd ☎ (0428) 3539

In this cosy, converted 16th century cottage, the English & Continental menu is supplemented by daily special dishes.

Closed Sun Lunch not served Mon & Sat

♛ English & Continental **V** 24 seats Lunch £9alc Dinner £12alc Wine £5.75 Last dinner 10pm 4P nc 4yrs

Credit cards 1 2 3 5

Simla Tandoori 84 Weyhill ☎ (0428) 885

he specialities of this very well appointed ndian restaurant include Tandoori dishes nd some particularly good home-made auces. In summer, patrons can eat on the atio at the rear, weather permitting, and here is also a take-away service.

Closed Xmas

Indian **V** 44 seats ✱ Lunch 3.95—£4.95&alc Dinner £10—£12alc Vine £5.25 Last dinner 11.30pm

Credit cards 1 2 3 4 5

HASTINGS & ST LEONARDS
East Sussex
Map **5** TQ80

★★★**Beauport Park** Battle Rd (3m N off A2100) ☎ (0424) 51222

Set in 33 acres of parkland, the Georgian house offers tastefully-restored modern bedrooms complemented by reliable service and good standards of cooking.

23 (2fb) 1 CTV in all bedrooms ®T sB&B £38—£42 dB&B £48—£54 B

60P 4 (£1.50 per night) (heated) 18 (grass) putting *xmas*

English & French **V** Lunch £7.95—£8.50&alc Tea £1.50—£1.75 High Tea £2.50—£4.50 Dinner £9.50—£10.50&alc Wine £5.50 Last dinner 9.30pm

Credit cards 1 2 3 5

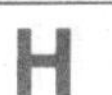

×**Roser's** 64 Eversfield Pl, St Leonards-on-Sea ☎ (0424) 712218

Once an Italian restaurant, but now under the control of a chef who specialises in imaginative French cuisine, Rösen's well-balanced menu combines a good choice of dishes including some well-made terrines and fresh sea-food. Service is particularly efficient and friendly.

Closed Sun, 1st 2 wks Jan & Bank Hol Mon's

Lunch not served Sat **V** 40 seats S% Lunch £15.50alc Dinner £15.50alc Wine £5.95 Last dinner 10.30pm Live music Sat

Credit cards 1 2 3 5

HATCH BEAUCHAMP
Somerset
Map **6** ST32

★★*HBL* **Farthing's Country House** (off A358 in village) ☎ (0823) 480664

Closed late Dec—early Jan

An attractive Georgian hotel with pleasant gardens and lawns, where Mr and Mrs Cooper look after their guests well. The rooms are comfortable, with compact, well appointed public rooms, and well equipped bedrooms. A variety of interesting dishes, nicely served and accompanied by fresh vegetables are featured at dinner.

6 CTV in all bedrooms ® sB&B £45—£55 dB&B £65—£80

25P 2 (£3) nc 10yrs

English & French Dinner £15alc Wine £6 Last dinner 9—9.30pm

Credit cards 1 3

HATFIELD
Hertfordshire
Map **4** TL20

★★★**Comet** 301 St Albans Road West (junc A1/A414) (Embassy) ☎ (07072) 65411

RS Xmas

This hotel is named after the De Havilland Comet, a model of which stands in the forecourt.

57rm(52 2)(3fb) CTV in all bedrooms ®**T** S% ✱ sB£28.50—£30 sB £45.50—£47 dB £51—£52.50 (room only)

150P

S% ✱ Lunch fr£8&alc Dinner fr£8&alc Wine £4.45 Last dinner 10pm

Credit cards 1 2 3 5

×××**Salisbury** 15 The Broadway, Old Hatfield ☎ (07072) 62220 Telex no 848259

This well-appointed, comfortable restaurant offers an interesting and appealing menu, the imaginative dishes being described in good detail. The fixed-price menu represents good value for money, as does the wine list, which complements the style of the restaurant.

Closed Mon Lunch not served Sat Dinner not served Sun

60 seats S% Lunch £9.75—£11.50&alc Dinner £19.50&alc Wine £7.25 Last dinner 9.30pm 16P

Credit cards 1 2 3 5

HATHERSAGE
Derbyshire
Map **8** SK28

★★**George** Main Rd (Whitbread) ☎ Hope Valley (0433) 50436

A 16th century coaching inn has been restored and modernised to provide a well-equipped hotel with spacious bedrooms, attractive restaurant, lounge bar and separate public bar.

18rm(16 2)(3fb) CTV in all bedrooms ®**T** sB&B £40.85 dB&B £49.45

50P *xmas*

English & French **V** Lunch £7.50&alc Tea £1—£2.50 Dinner £10alc Wine £4.75 Last dinner 9.45pm

Credit cards 1 2 3

★★**Hathersage Inn** Main St (Best Western) ☎ Hope Valley (0433) 50259

Stone-built inn on the village main street.

11rm(9 2) Annexe:3rm(1fb) 1 CTV in all bedrooms ®**T** S% sB&B fr£26 sB&B fr£34 dB&B fr£32 dB&B £45.50—£54

20P *xmas*

Lunch £6.50alc Tea fr£2.50 Dinner £9.75alc Wine £6 Last dinner 9.30pm

Credit cards 1 2 3 5

HAUGHLEY
Suffolk
Map **5** TM06

×**Old Counting House** ☎ Stowmarket (0449) 673617

Standing at the centre of the village, this cottage-style restaurant with its beams and exposed brickwork was a 16th century counting house or bank. It now deals in modest lunches and more imaginative evening meals, all making full use of fresh produce.

Closed Sun Lunch not served Sat

English & French **V** 46 seats Lunch £5—£9.25 Dinner £12.25 Wine £4.40 Last dinner 9.30pm

Credit cards 1 3

HAVANT
Hampshire
Map **4** SU70

★★★**Bear** East St (Whitbread) ☎ (0705) 486501 Telex no 869136

Town centre converted hotel with parts dating back to the 16th-century. Open-plan modern restaurant and bar.

35rm(30 5) 1 CTV in all bedrooms ®**T** (ex guide dogs) sB&B £40 dB&B £50

Lift 100P *xmas*

Mainly grills **V** Lunch £7—£8&alc Tea 80p alc Dinner £9.50—£10.50&alc Last dinner 10pm

Credit cards 1 2 3 5

HAVERFORDWEST
Dyfed
Map **2** SM91

★★**Hotel Mariners** Mariners Sq
☎(0437) 3353
Closed 26 & 27 Dec & 1 Jan
A 17th-century inn with stables and old coaching post, situated in the town centre.
29rm(20⇌4⋒) CTV in all bedrooms ®**T** sB&B£18.50—£20 sB&B⇌⋒fr£27 dB&Bfr£34 dB&B⇌⋒fr£40 **B**
☾40P
English & French **V** ⛊ ☕ ✱Lunch fr£5.25 Tea fr£1 Dinner £7.50—£8.10&alc Wine £4.95 Last dinner 9.30pm
Credit cards 1 2 3 5

HAWES
North Yorkshire
Map **7** SD88

★★***Fountain*** Market Pl ☎(09697) 206
Modernised, town centre hotel, family owned and run.
12rm(5⇌7⋒)(1fb) ®**B**
CTV 10P *xmas*
Last dinner 8.45pm

★★*L* **Simonstone Hall** Simonstone ☎(09697) 255
Delightfully restored Hall with spacious rooms and fine home cooking.
10rm(7⇌1⋒)(1fb) 1⊟ CTV available in bedrooms ®sB&B£21.50—£25.50 dB&B⇌⋒£43—£51 **B**
CTV 20P ✽ *xmas*
⛊ ☕ Lunch £6.25 Tea 75p Dinner fr£11.75&alc Wine £5.25 Last dinner 8pm
Credit cards 1 5 Ⓥ

HAWESWATER
Cumbria
Map **12** NY41

★**Haweswater** ☎ Bampton (09313) 235
This hotel offers good views of the lake and surrounding countryside.
16rm(3fb) ®S% ✱sB&B£16 dB&B£32 **B**
CTV 20P 10 ✽ *xmas*

V ⛊ ☕ S% ✱Bar lunch £2.70alc Tea 60palc Dinner £7.50alc Wine £4 Last dinner 8pm
Credit cards 1 3 5
See advertisement under Penrith

HAWICK
Borders *Roxburghshire*
Map **12** NT51

★★**Buccleuch** 1 Trinity St ☎(0450) 72368
Located close to the town centre and providing well-equipped bedrooms, the hotel is popular with businessmen.
18rm(4⇌)(1fb) CTV in all bedrooms ®**T** sB&B£16 sB&B⇌£19.50 dB&B£26 dB&B⇌£30
30P 15
⛊ Bar lunch £2.25—£4.25 Tea fr75p Dinner £7.50—£9.50&alc Wine £4.50 Last dinner 9pm
Credit card 3 Ⓥ

★★**Kirklands** West Stewart Pl (Exec Hotel) ☎(0450) 72263
Closed Xmas Day & Boxing Day RS Sun
Small well-appointed hotel with attractive dining room and thoughtfully equipped bedrooms.
6rm(2⇌1⋒) CTV in all bedrooms ® sB&B£25 sB&B⇌⋒£27 dB&B£38 dB&B⇌⋒£40 **B**
20P ✽
International **V** ⛊ Lunch £5alc Dinner £10.50alc Wine £3.50 Last dinner 9.30pm
Ⓥ

★★**Teviotdale Lodge Country** Commonside (7m S off A7) (Minotel) ☎ Teviotdale (045085) 232
Small family-run hotel in its own grounds, close to the River Teviot.
8rm(2⇌)(1fb) 1⊟ CTV in all bedrooms ® ✱sB&B£17 sB&B⇌£19.50 dB&B£29 dB&B⇌£32.50 **B**
35P ✽

⛊ ✱Bar lunch £3—£8.50 Dinner £7.50—£9.50 Wine £4.05 Last dinner 9pm
Credit cards 1 2 3 5

HAWKCHURCH
Devon
Map **3** ST30

★★★*H* **Fairwater Head** ☎(02977) 349
Closed Jan & Feb
Pleasant extended country house hotel set in its own gardens. A pianist plays during candlelit dinners on Saturdays.
14⇌ Annexe: 4⇌ CTV in all bedrooms ® **T** in 4 bedrooms S% sB&B⇌£30—£32 dB&B⇌£52—£57 **B**
28P ✽ Pianist Sat
English & French ⛊ S% Lunch £7.50 Dinner £11&alc Wine £5 Last dinner 8.30pm
Credit cards 1 3 5
See advertisement under Lyme Regis

HAWKHURST
Kent
Map **5** TQ73

★★**Tudor Arms** (Best Western) ☎(05805) 2312
This friendly little hotel offers well-equipped bedrooms and a good choice of soundly-cooked dishes.
14rm(6⇌3⋒)(1fb) 2⊟ CTV in all bedrooms ®**T** S% sB&B£22 sB&B⇌⋒£26 dB&B£43 dB&B⇌⋒£51 **B**
CTV 40P 2(£1.50 per night) ✽ (hard) *xmas*
International ⛊ ☕ S% Lunch fr£7&alc Tea fr£1 Dinner £8.50—£9&alc Wine £6.50 Last dinner 9.15pm
Credit cards 1 2 3 5
See advertisement on page 348

✕✕**Osborn House** Highgate ☎(05805) 3265
Closed Sun, Wed & Jan
Lunch not served
International **V** 24 seats ✱Dinner £14.50—£16.50&alc Wine £5.25 Last dinner 9.30pm 3P
Credit cards 1 2 3

HAWKRIDGE
Somerset
Map **3** SS83

★★ **Tarr Steps** Winsford (064385) 293

Closed mid Nov—mid Mar

12rm(6) Annexe: 3rm(2) 2 sB&B£19.50 sB&B£22.50 dB&B£39 dB&B£42

20P rough & clay pigeon shooting *xmas*

Bar lunch £5alc Tea £1.25 High Tea £5.75 Dinner £11.50 Wine £4.45 Last dinner 9.45pm

Credit cards 2 3 V

HAWKSHEAD (near Ambleside)
Cumbria
Map **7** SD39

★★★ *L* **Tarn Hows** Hawkshead Hill (09666) 330
Closed 12 Jan—13 Feb

A beautifully situated country-house hotel in 30 acres of garden and parkland.

15rm(141)(2fb) 1 CTV in all bedrooms T sB&B£20—£35 dB&B£44—£66

CTV 40P (heated) sauna bath solarium putting *xmas*

V Lunch £7alc Tea £1—£3&alc High Tea £6alc Dinner £13.50 Wine £4 Last dinner 8.30pm

Credit cards 1 2 3 5

★ **Red Lion** (09666) 213

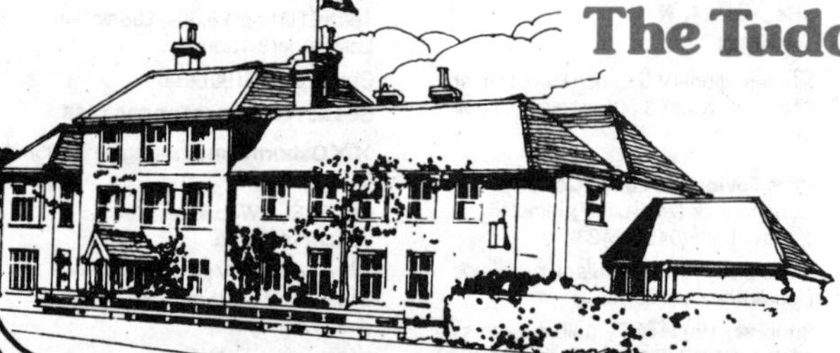

A prominent feature of the village is this 15th-century coaching inn.

8(1fb) dB&B£29.90

CTV 8P *xmas*

'English & Continental V ♆ ☐ Bar lunch
2—£4 Tea £1.50 Dinner £4—£10 Wine
.65 Last dinner 9pm

AWORTH
est Yorkshire
ap **7** SE03
★**Old White Lion** 6 West Ln ☎ (0535)
2313
one-built coaching inn standing at the top 'the main street.
2rm(4→6⋒)(1fb) TV available in edrooms sB&B£17.50 sB&B→⋒£19
3&B£27.50 dB&B→⋒£31 **B**
TV 10P 2
English, French & Italian V ♆ ☐ Lunch
.50—£4.95 Tea 75p Dinner £7.25 Wine
.20 Last dinner 9.45pm
redit cards 1 2 3 5 Ⓥ
ee advertisement under Keighley

AYDOCK
erseyside
lap **7** SJ59
★★★**Post House** Lodge Ln, Newton-
-Willows (adj to M6 junc 23) (Trusthouse
orte) ☎ Wigan (0942) 717878 Telex no
77672
arge modern hotel, convenient for the otorway and the racecourse.
8→ CTV in all bedrooms ® T
B&B→£54.50 dB&B→£70.50 **B**
130P CFA
Last dinner 10.30pm
redit cards 1 2 3 4 5

AYDON BRIDGE
orthumberland
lap **12** NY86
★★**Anchor** John Martin St (Exec Hotel)
☎ (043484) 227
riendly hotel supervised by resident proprietors.
0rm(7⋒)(2fb) CTV in 7 bedrooms ®
B&B£18—£20 sB&B⋒£22—£24
B&B£28—£30 dB&B⋒£32—£34 **B**
TV 20P pool table
♆ Bar lunch £5—£6 Dinner £9alc Wine
4.50 Last dinner 8.30pm
redit cards 1 2 3 5 Ⓥ
✕**General Havelock Inn** Ratcliffe Rd
☎ (043484) 376
The quaint dining room of this tiny High Street inn has been created from an attached barn to the rear. The proprietress attends to all the cooking, using fresh produce to prepare some interesting dishes.
Closed Mon, Tue, 1st wk Jan, 3rd wk Apr & 1st 2 wks Sep
Dinner not served Sun
English & French 30 seats Lunch
£5—£6.75&alc Dinner £12—£15 Wine
£5.40 Last dinner 8.30pm 18P

HAYLE
Cornwall
Map **2** SW53
★★**Hillside** 1 Grist Ln, Angarrack (1½m E of Hayle on unclass road off A30)
☎ (0736) 752180
Closed 23—31 Dec
Peacefully situated within a walled garden and personally run with friendly atmosphere and good food.
10rm(1→3⋒)(3fb)
sB&B£12.50—£12.95
sB&B→⋒£15—£15.75
dB&B£22.50—£24
dB&B→⋒£27—£28.50 **B**
CTV 8P
V ♆ ☐ Bar lunch £3.75alc Tea £1.75alc
High Tea £3.75—£4.50 Dinner £6.50—£7
Wine £3.75 Last dinner 7.30pm
Ⓥ
★**Penellen** Riviere Towans, Phillack
☎ (0736) 753777
RS Nov—Mar
Small, family hotel in its own grounds overlooking the beach.
11rm(5⋒)(6fb) ® dB&B⋒£12.50 (incl dinner) **B**
CTV 22P (heated)
English & Continental V ♆ ☐ Last dinner 11pm

HAYLING ISLAND
Hampshire
Map **4** SU70
★★★**Post House** Northney Rd
(Trusthouse Forte) ☎ (0705) 465011 Telex no 86620
Modern well equipped hotel overlooking the estuary.
Annexe: 96→(4fb) CTV in all bedrooms ®
T sB&B→£53.50 dB&B→£68.50 **B**
CTV 150P CFA (heated) solarium gymnasium *xmas*
♆ Last dinner 10pm
Credit cards 1 2 3 4 5
★★**Newtown House** Manor Rd
☎ (0705) 466131
Closed 24 Dec—2 Jan
Well-appointed hotel, personally run, with friendly helpful staff.
21rm(10→9⋒)(3fb) CTV in all bedrooms
® T sB&B£22—£25
sB&B→⋒£31—£34 dB&B→⋒£48—£54
B
40P (heated) (hard) sauna bath
English & French V ♆ ☐ Lunch £6&alc
Tea fr£1.50 High Tea fr£4 Dinner
£8.50&alc Wine £5.25 Last dinner 9pm
Credit cards 1 2 3 5 Ⓥ

HAY-ON-WYE
Powys
Map **3** SO24
★★**Olde Black Lion** Lion St ☎ (0497) 820841
A village inn of charm and character, personally owned and with friendly service, the hotel has cosy, comfortable bedrooms and a nice cottage restaurant offering imaginative menus and good home cooking.
6⋒ Annexe: 4rm(2→)(2fb) CTV in all bedrooms ® sB&Bfr£18.50
sB&B→⋒£27.50 dB&Bfr£35.25
dB&B→⋒£38
CTV 20P *xmas*
European V ♆ ☐ ✱Lunch
£6—£12&alc Tea £3 Dinner £6—£12&alc
Wine £4.50 Last dinner 9pm
Credit card 1
✕**Lions Corner House** Lion St ☎ (0497) 820175
A small, unpretentious restaurant, standing in the centre of this historic border town, offers good food in informal surroundings.
Closed Sun (except Bank Hols) Mon (out of season) 4 Jan—Feb
V 41 seats Lunch £5.95 Dinner £7.95&alc
Wine £4.95 Last dinner 9.30pm
Credit card 3 Ⓥ

HAYTOR
Devon
Map **3** SX77
★★★ *H* **Bel Alp House** ☎ (03646) 217
Closed Xmas RS Dec—Feb
The small, elegant country house is beautifully furnished in a style befitting its origins as an Edwardian mansion. Views over undulating South Devon countryside can be enjoyed from the well-appointed dining room and the majority of the comfortably furnished bedrooms.
9rm(7→2⋒) CTV in all bedrooms ®
sB&B→⋒£36 dB&B→⋒fr£60
Lift 20P (hard) snooker
English & French ♆ ☐ Lunch £12
Tea £1 Dinner £18 Wine £5 Last dinner 8.30pm
Credit cards 1 3
See advertisement on page 352
★★**Rock Inn** Haytor Vale ☎ (03646) 305
Busy, family-run, convivial inn, with well appointed bedrooms and good food.
9rm(5→)(2fb) CTV in all bedrooms ®
✱sB&B£11.50—£14.50
sB&B→£18.50—£25 dB&B£29
dB&B→£37—£55 **B**
CTV 6P *xmas*
English & French V ♆ ☐ ✱Bar lunch
£10—£18 Tea £2 Dinner £8.95—£25 Wine
£4.55 Last dinner 8.30pm

H

HEATHROW AIRPORT (London)

Greater London
Map **4** TQ07

See plan

★★★★**Excelsior** Bath Rd, West Drayton (adj M4 Spur at junc with A4) (Trusthouse Forte) ☎ 01-759 6611 Telex no 24525 Plan **3** *D4*

Large, well-appointed hotel opposite Heathrow Airport.

609➡(6fb) CTV in all bedrooms ® **T** sB&B➡£67 dB&B➡£81.50

Lift ☾ ## 500P CFA ⛆ (heated) sauna bath

🍷 Last dinner 10.45pm

Credit cards 1 2 3 4 5

See advertisement on page 352

★★★★***Heathrow Penta*** Bath Rd, Hounslow ☎ 01-897 6363 Telex no 934660 Plan **4** *D4*

Modern well-equipped hotel with good bedrooms and restaurant.

670➡ CTV in all bedrooms ® **T**

Lift ☾ ## 700P CFA ⛆ (heated) sauna bath solarium gymnasium Disco 3 nights wkly

International 🍷 ☕ Last dinner mdnt

Credit cards 1 2 3 4 5

★★★★*B* **Holiday Inn** Stockley Rd, West Drayton (2m N junc M4/A408) (Holiday Inns) ☎ West Drayton (0895) 445555 Telex no 934518 Plan **5** *D5*

Well-appointed hotel with spacious bedrooms and popular leisure facilities.

396➡⫿(220fb) ⊁ in 21 bedrooms CTV in all bedrooms **T** S% sB➡⫿fr£57.50 dB&B➡⫿fr£67.50 (room only) **B**

Lift ☾ ## 400P CFA ✿ ⛆ (heated) ⚑ (hard) sauna bath solarium gymnasium

V 🍷 ☕ S% Lunch fr£9.75 Dinner fr£9.75 Wine £6.95

Credit cards 1 2 3 4 5

★★★★*L* ***Sheraton—Heathrow*** Colnbrook Bypass, West Drayton (2m W A4) ☎ 01-759 2424 Telex no 934331 Plan **11** *C4*

A modern spacious and comfortably appointed transit hotel.

440➡⫿ CTV in all bedrooms **T B**

Lift ☾ ## 600P CFA ⛆ (heated) & ⛆ (heated) sauna bath solarium gymnasium Live music 5 nights wkly *xmas*

International **V** 🍷 ☕ Last dinner 11.30pm

Credit cards 1 2 3 4 5

★★★**Ariel** Bath Rd, Hayes (1½m E junc A4/A437) (Trusthouse Forte) ☎ 01-759 2552 Telex no 21777 Plan **1** *E4*

Comfortable modern circular hotel with Huntsman's Table restaurant.

177➡ CTV in all bedrooms ® sB&B➡£57.50 dB&B➡£75

Lift ☾ ## 100P CFA

🍷 ☕ Last dinner 11pm

Credit cards 1 2 3 4 5

★★★*B* **Berkeley Arms** Bath Rd, Cranford (2½m E on A4) (Embassy) ☎ 01-897 2121 Telex no 935728 Plan **2** *F4*

Conveniently located airport hotel.

40➡⫿ CTV in all bedrooms ® **T** S% ✱sB➡⫿fr£44 (room only) **B**

Lift ☾ 120P

V 🍷 ☕ S% ✱Lunch £9.25&alc Tea 90p Dinner £9.25&alc Wine £5.25 Last dinner 9.45pm

Credit cards 1 2 3 5

See advertisement on page 352

★★★**Master Robert Motel** 366 Great West Rd ☎ 01-570 6261 Plan **7** *F4*
(For full entry see Hounslow)

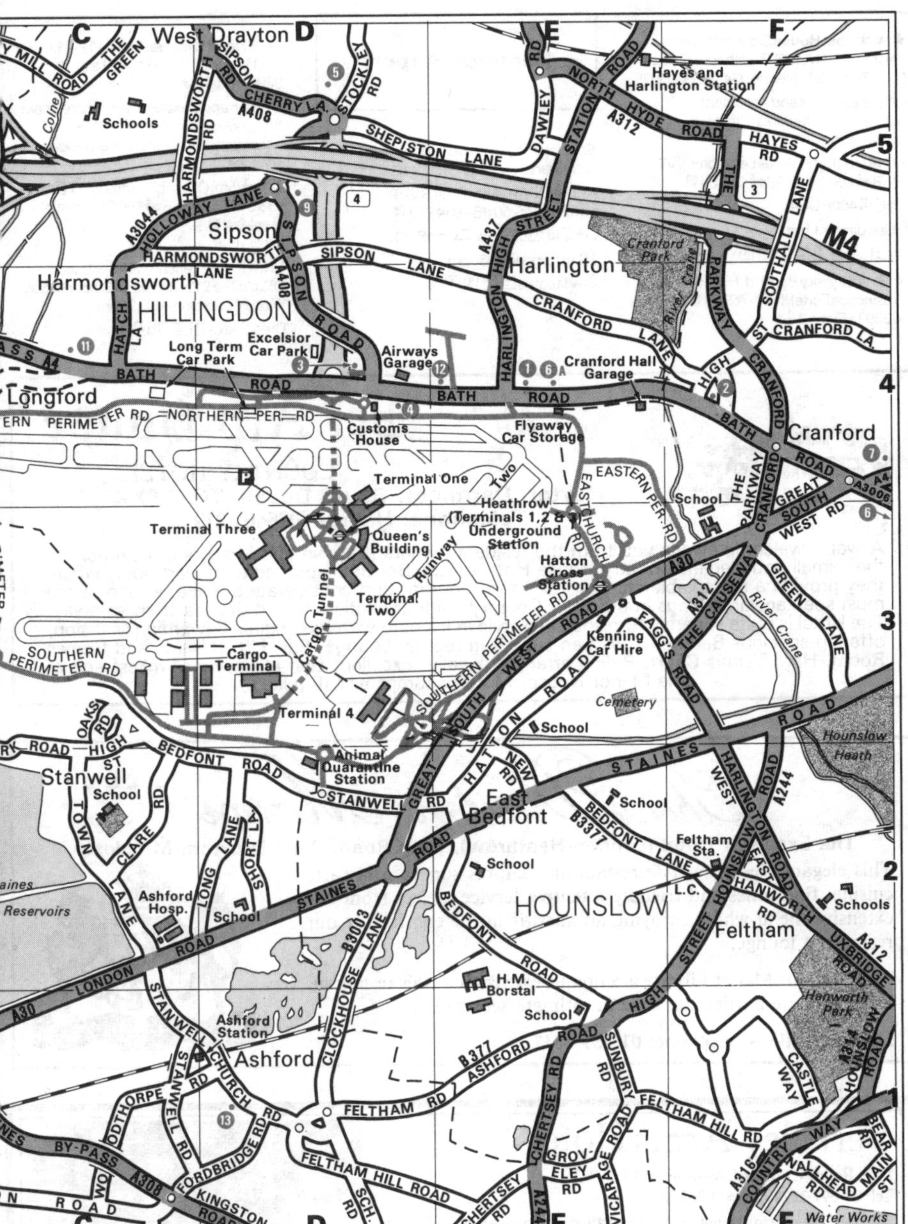

Heathrow Airport

1 Ariel ★★★
2 Berkeley Arms ★★★
3 Excelsior ★★★★
4 Heathrow Penta ★★★★
5 Holiday Inn ★★★★
6 Hounslow Chinese ✕
(See under Hounslow)
6A Hotel Ibis Heathrow ★★
7 Master Robert Motel ★★★
(See under Hounslow)
8 Thames Lodge ★★
(See under Staines)
9 Post House ★★★
11 Sheraton — Heathrow ★★★★
12 Skyway ★★★
13 Terrazza ✕✕
(See under Ashford)

★★★**Post House** Sipson Rd, West Drayton (2m N A408) (Trusthouse Forte) ☎01-759 2323 Telex no 934280 plan **9** *D5*

Large bedrooms and a choice of restaurants are features of this well-appointed hotel.

597⇌(104fb) CTV in all bedrooms ®**T** sB&B⇌£60.50 dB&B⇌£77.50 **B**

Lift ☾ ## 400P CFA

Last dinner 11pm

Credit cards 1 2 3 4 5

★★★**Skyway** Bath Rd, Hayes (Trusthouse Forte) ☎01-759 6311 Telex no 23935 Plan **12** *E4*

Spacious hotel with well-appointed restaurant.

411⇌ CTV in all bedrooms ®**T** sB&B⇌£56.50 dB&B⇌£73 **B**

Lift ☾ ## 230P CFA (heated)

Last dinner 10.30pm

Credit cards 1 2 3 4 5

Heathrow Airport

★★**Hotel Ibis Heathrow** 112—114 Bath Rd, Hayes ☎01-759 4888 Telex no 929014 Plan **6A** *E4*

Modern and inexpensive, the hotel offers basic but reasonably comfortable accommodation with a limited range of services.

244⇌(5fb) CTV in all bedrooms **T** S% sB&B⇌£42 dB&B⇌£50 Continental breakfast **B**

Lift ☾ 160P

English & French S% Lunch £8&alc Tea £1 High Tea £4 Dinner £8&alc Wine £6 Last dinner 10.30pm

Credit cards 1 2 3 4 5

H

HEBDEN BRIDGE
West Yorkshire
Map **7** SD92

★★**Hebden Lodge** New Rd (Exec Hotel)
☎(0422) 845272

This handsome, three-storey, Victorian building overlooks the "Marina" development of the canal. Its stylish bedrooms are well fitted and decorated, the lounges and bar cosy, whilst the restaurant offers unpretentious good value.

13rm(9⫚)(3fb) CTV in all bedrooms Ⓡ sB&B⫚£19.50—£21.50 dB&B⫚£39—£43 B
P *xmas*
V ☕ Lunch £1.50—£4.50 Tea fr75p High Tea £2—£4 Dinner £7.95 Wine £5 Last dinner 9.30pm
Credit cards 1 2 3 5 Ⓥ

✕✕**Sutcliffe's** Colden Row, Colden
☎(0422) 842479

Three crofters' or weavers' stone cottages set high on the moorland have been most sympathetically restored to retain mullioned windows and other original features, then tastefully decorated to provide a comfortable lounge bar and three separate dining rooms. The table d'hôte menu — largely English, but with an international element — features food which is well prepared and cooked from good, fresh ingredients.

Closed Tue (except for reservations)
Dinner not served Sun
English & French 50 seats Lunch fr£2 Dinner fr£8 Wine £5 Last dinner 9.30pm
20P
Credit cards 1 3

HEBRON
Dyfed
Map **2** SN12

★ *H* **Preseli Country House** (½m W of A478 Tenby—Cardigan rd, 8½m N of jct with A40 & 3½m S of Crymych) ☎(09947) 425
RS Oct—Apr

Cosily tucked away amidst the beautiful scenery of the Pembrokeshire National Park, this charming little country house hotel exudes hospitality. The bedrooms are individual and pretty, the lounge furnished in the traditional style and to a very high standard of comfort, whilst a small library/lounge provides a congenial haven. The restaurant serves imaginative food, freshly prepared from locally produced ingredients.

6rm(1)(2fb) in 2 bedrooms TV in 2 bedrooms CTV in 2 bedrooms Ⓡ sB&B£15—£18 sB&B£16—£18 dB&B£32—£34 dB&B£32—£34 B
CTV 30P 3 U solarium *xmas*
English & Continental **V** Lunch £6—£10&alc Tea fr£1.50 High Tea £3.50&alc Dinner £10—£12&alc Wine £5.50 Last dinner 9.30pm
Credit card 1 Ⓥ

HEDDON'S MOUTH
Devon
Map **2** SS64

★★

★★ **HEDDON'S GATE, HEDDON'S MOUTH**
☎Parracombe (05983) 313
Closed Nov—Mar

Approached along narrow hilly lanes this hotel is well worth seeking out. It is situated on a hill with captivating views over moorland, and a luxuriously wooded valley from which another runs from the sea. There are 20 acres of grounds which include the most attractive terraced gardens and a paved terrace outside the hotel itself. This was first built in 1890 but subsequent additions, although somewhat haphazard, make a not unharmonious whole. Inside there are plenty of sitting areas; comfortable sitting room, cosy library, writing room and bar. The spacious dining room has two walls of windows giving wonderful views. It is well appointed and the scene of Anne De Villes' cooking. Start the day with an ample breakfast, return for a cream tea if you feel you can manage it and, later, the five-course dinner; the style is best described as country house and is very enjoyable. Comfortable, individually styled bedrooms feature several extras including fruit and the annexe rooms have been beautifully refurbished. Anne and Bob De Ville, the owners, have improved the hotel substantially over the years. They are affable hosts so that, with their friendly, local staff enhancing the peace and quiet of the situation, you are sure to very much enjoy a relaxing stay at this good-hearted hotel.

13rm(112⫚) Annexe: 2(1fb)2 CTV in all bedrooms Ⓡ**T**
SB&B⫚£24
dB&B⫚£38.20—£48
20P nc10yrs
Bar lunch £2—£5 Tea 60p—£2.60 Dinner £15 Last dinner 8.15pm
Credit cards 1 2
See advertisement under Lynton

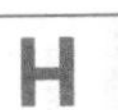

HEDGE END
Hampshire
Map **4** SU41

★★★**Botleigh Grange** (Best Western)
☎Botley (04892) 5611

The old-fashioned and secluded country hotel provides accommodation in a modern wing of individually-furnished bedrooms. There is a choice of restaurants with enterprising cooking in the Squires restaurant. Riding and hunting can be arranged with the hotel's own stables and fishing is also available.

44rm(2420⫚)(4fb) 2 CTV in all bedrooms Ⓡ**T** S% sB&B⫚£44 dB&B⫚£55—£66 B
(CTV 300P putting table tennis Disco Sat *xmas*
V S% Lunch £6.50—£8&alc Tea £1—2 High Tea £2—£3 Dinner £7—£9&alc Wine £5.50 Last dinner 10pm
Credit cards 1 2 3 5
See advertisement under Southampton

HELENSBURGH
Strathclyde *Dunbartonshire*
Map **10** NS28

★★★***Commodore*** 112 West Clyde St (Osprey) ☎(0436) 6924

Comfortable, modern hotel on seafront.

45 CTV in all bedrooms Ⓡ**T** B
Lift (200P Disco Thu *xmas*
Scottish & French Last dinner 9.30pm
Credit cards 1 2 3 4 5

HELFORD
Cornwall
Map**2** SW72

❀XX**Riverside** ☎ Manaccan (032 623) 443
(Rosette awarded for dinner only)
The beautiful, cottage-style restaurant stands in a charming creek-side village on the Helford River Estuary. The proprietors, George Perry Smith and Heather Crosbie (formerly of the Hole in the Wall, Bath) offer dishes carefully prepared from the best ingredients and complemented by an extensive wine list and good service.
Closed Nov—end Mar Lunch not served
English & French **V** 30 seats S% Dinner £25&alc Wine £7.50 Last dinner 9.30pm

H

HELLAND BRIDGE
Cornwall
Map**2** SX07

★★★ *H* **Tredethy Country** (off B3266) ☎ St Mabyn (020884) 262
Closed 25 Dec—Jan
Beautiful property, once the much-loved home of the author Prince Chula.

11rm(9 2) CTV available in bedrooms ® sB&B £21—£24 dB&B £36—£48
CTV 30P (heated) solarium nc 12yrs
English & French Lunch £6 Tea £1.20 Dinner £7.50 Wine £4 Last dinner 8.30pm
Ⓥ

HELMSDALE
Highland *Sutherland*
Map**14** ND01

★★ **Navidale House** (1m NE A9) ☎ (04312) 258
Closed Nov-Jan
RS Feb
The delightful, small hotel has breathtaking sea views and extends a warm welcome, providing a relaxed atmosphere and good food. It is an ideal base for those fishing the famed Sutherland Rivers.
11rm(1) Annexe: 9rm
sB&B£12.25—£14.50 sB&B£17.95
dB&B£24.50—£28 dB&B£36—£39
CTV 30P 1 clay pigeon shoot

International **V** Lunch £2.50—£6.50 Tea 75p High Tea £2.50—£6.50 Dinner £7—£10.50&alc Wine £4.35 Last dinner 8.30pm
Credit cards 1 2 3 Ⓥ

HELMSLEY
North Yorkshire
Map**8** SE68

★★★ *HBL* **Black Swan** Market Pl (Trusthouse Forte) ☎ (0439) 70466
A former 16th century inn well modernised and being continuously refurbished without spoiling its character. Lounges and bedrooms are recentl beneficiaries. The staff give a very high standard of service, and the food is of fine quality. There is also a delightful walled garden to the rear.
37(6fb) CTV in all bedrooms ®
sB&B £51.50 dB&B £71.50
36P *xmas*
Last dinner 9.15pm
Credit cards 1 2 3 4 5

★★★ **Feversham Arms** 1 High St (Best Western) ☎ (0439) 70766
Carefully modernised old inn providing comfort and a peaceful atmosphere.

20(6fb)2 CTV in all bedrooms ®T sB&B£37 dB&B£48—£58
30P (hard)
English, French & Spanish V Lunch £7—£10&alc Dinner £11—£15&alc Wine £4.50 Last dinner 9pm
Credit cards 1 2 3 5 V

★★**Crown** Market Sq (0439) 70297
Converted 16th-century inn overlooking the market place.
15rm(1 10)(2fb) CTV in all bedrooms ® sB&B£18.50 sB&B£20.50 dB&B£37 dB&B£41
CTV 20P 2(70p per night) *xmas*
Lunch £4.75—£5.50 Tea £1.50 High Tea £2.90—£4.70 Dinner £8.50—£9.50 Wine £3.70 Last dinner 8pm
Credit cards 1 3 V

★★**Feathers** Market Pl (0439) 70275
Closed 23 Dec—1 Jan
Local stone house, partly 14th-century and partly 17th-century, with Georgian modifications.
18rm(6 7)(3fb) CTV in all bedrooms ® S% sB&B£15 sB&B£18 dB&B£30 dB&B£36
CTV 12P
V Lunch £5.50 Tea £2 High Tea £3.50—£4.50 Dinner £9.50&alc Wine £5 Last dinner 9pm
Credit cards 1 2 3 5

Helmsley — Helston

★★*BL* **Pheasant** Harome (2½m SE unclass)
(0439) 71241
RS Jan & Feb
Newly established and converted from premises that housed the village blacksmith and a shop as well as cottages, this charming and friendly hotel overlooks the mill-stream and village pond.
11 CTV in all bedrooms ®
sB&B£18—£26 dB&B£36—£50
20P nc 12yrs
Bar lunch 85p—£3.75&alc Dinner £10.50 Wine £3.50 Last dinner 8.15pm

X**Star Inn** Harome (2½m SE unclass)
(0439) 70397
A quaint coffee loft is situated in the thatched roof of this old cruck-beamed inn. The low-beamed ceilings, uneven walls and attractive furnishings combine to create a charming atmosphere, whilst the fixed price menu offers both a good choice and value for money.
Closed Sun, Mon & Jan
English & French V 36 seats S% Bar lunch £3alc Dinner £15alc Wine £5.50 Last dinner 9.30pm P nc7yrs
Credit cards 1 2 3 5 V

HELSTON
Cornwall
Map **2** SW62

★★**Gwealdues** Falmouth Rd
(03265) 2808 due to change to 572808
Closed last wk of Dec
Small commercial hotel with friendly informal atmosphere.
15rm(4 5)(2fb) CTV in 13 bedrooms ® sB&B£17—£19 sB&B£21.50—£23 dB&B28.50—£30 dB&B£32—£36
CTV 35P nc 10yrs
Lunch £3—£3.50 Tea 50—75p Dinner £5.50—£8.50&alc Wine £5.25 Last dinner 8pm
Credit cards 1 3
See advertisement on page 356

★***Angel*** Coinage Hall St (03265) 2701
Telex no 45117
An inn of character with galleried first floor restaurant.
21rm(3fb) CTV in 17 bedrooms ® in 17 bedrooms
CTV 12P 2
V Last dinner 9.30pm
Credit cards 1 2 3 4 5
See advertisement on page 356

H

★ **_Nansloe Manor Country Hotel_** Meneage Rd ☎ (0326) 574691

Attractive and secluded small Cornish Manor, personally run as a small hotel.

6rm(3⇌)(2fb) 1⊟ CTV in 3 bedrooms Ⓡ

CTV 50P ⇌ ✽

V Last dinner 9pm

Credit cards 1 2 3 5

HEMEL HEMPSTEAD
Hertfordshire
Map **4** TL00

★★★ **Aubrey Park** Hemel Hempstead Rd ☎ Redbourn (058285) 2105
(For full entry see Redbourn)

★★★ **Hemel Hempstead Moat House** London Rd, Bourne End (Queens Moat) ☎ Berkhampsted (04427) 71241 Telex 8950511

Modern hotel in a pleasant rural situation by a watermill on the River Bulbourne.

40⇌ CTV in all bedrooms Ⓡ S%
sB&B⇌ £38.50—£39.50
dB&B⇌ £45.50—£46.50 Ⓑ

☾ 80P pool table

⊕ International **V** ♀ ☕ S% Lunch £7.25—£7.95&alc Tea 75p Dinner £7.25—£7.95&alc Wine £5.95 Last dinner 9.45pm

Credit cards 1 2 3 4 5

Helston — Henley-in-Arden

★★★ **Post House** Breakspear Way (Trusthouse Forte) ☎ (0442) 51122 Telex no 826902

Attractively decorated and furnished hotel about 2 miles from the town centre.

Annexe: 107⇌(8fb) CTV in all bedrooms Ⓡ **T** sB&B⇌ £54 dB&B⇌ £70 Ⓑ

Lift ☾ 140P CFA ✽ *xmas*

♀ Last dinner 9.45pm

Credit cards 1 2 3 4 5

HENLEY-IN-ARDEN
Warwickshire
Map **7** SP16

★★★ **Yew Trees** 154 High St (Best Western)
☎ (05642) 4636 Telex no 334264

Very well preserved Tudor hotel with landscaped gardens. The bedrooms are comfortable and the restaurant is very popular.

30rm(28⇌2⋒)(2fb) 1⊟ CTV in all bedrooms Ⓡ **T** ✱ sB&B⇌⋒ £50—£54 dB&B⇌⋒ £68—£76 Ⓑ

60P 4⌂ ⇌ ✽ nc 10yrs

⊕ English & French **V** ♀ ☕ Lunch £9—£10 Tea £3—£4.50 Dinner £12—£14&alc Wine £5.95 Last dinner 10pm

Credit cards 1 2 3 5 Ⓥ

See advertisement under Birmingham

✕✕✕ **_Beaudesert_** ☎ (05642) 2675

The family-run restaurant is housed in a single-storey building on the house on the busy A34 and offers a creative menu backed by attentive service.

Closed Mon Lunch not served Tue—Sat Dinner not served Sun

⊕ French **V** 60 seats Last dinner 10pm 40P

Credit cards 1 2 3 4 5

✕✕ **Le Filbert Cottage** 64 High St
☎ (05642) 2700

A small, black-and-white Tudor cottage in the centre of the village, the restaurant serves authentic French cuisine and has a reputation for good food and service. At lunchtime there is a choice from prix fixée or à la carte menus, both with specialities of the day.

Closed Sun & Bank Hols

⊕ French 32 seats Lunch fr£8&alc Dinner £19.50—£20 Wine £5 Last dinner 9.45pm nc 6yrs

Credit cards 1 2 3 4 5

XX***Othello*** 148 High St ☎ (05642) 3089

Though basically Italian, this restaurant also offers other continental dishes. Its generous portions and friendly staff make it a popular rendezvous.

Continental V 50 seats Last dinner 10.30pm

Credit cards 1 2 3 4 5

HENLEY-ON-THAMES
Oxfordshire
Map **4** SU78

★★★**Red Lion** ☎ (0491) 572161 Telex no 83343

Traditional style hotel with some modern comforts.

27rm(20)(4fb) 1 CTV in all bedrooms S% *sB&Bfr£28 sB&B £42—£50 dB&Bfr£50 dB&B fr£60

30P 4

English & French S% Lunch £6.50—£8.50&alc Tea 80p—£1 High Tea £1.75—£2 Dinner £8.95—£9.50&alc Wine £4.85 Last dinner 10pm

Credit cards 1 2 3 V

XX**Flohrs Hotel & Restaurant** Northfield End ☎ (0491) 573412

The tastefully decorated restaurant and bar are part of a small hotel on the edge of Henley nearest Oxford. The short, deliberately simple, à la carte menu uses quality ingredients to good effect. Accommodation is available in eight simply-furnished but modern bedrooms.

Dinner not served Sun

Continental V 40 seats *Lunch £7.90—£8.50&alc Dinner £13alc Wine £5.50 Last dinner 10pm 6P
9 bedrooms available

Credit cards 1 2 3 5

X**Restaurant Alpenhütte** 41 Station Rd ☎ (0491) 572984

This small Austrian restaurant, cheerfully decorated in traditional style, features a short menu of Austrian German dishes, including warming soups, veal, sauerkraut, pancakes and fondues. Austrian wines complement the food, service is unobtrusive, and a friendly, informal atmosphere prevails.

Henley-in-Arden — Hereford

Closed Sun
Lunch not served Mon

Austrian & German 30 seats *Lunch £11.50alc Dinner £11.50alc Wine £5.10 Last dinner 10pm

Credit cards 1 2 3 4 5

X**Antico** 49—51 Market Pl ☎ (0491) 573060

Small and well-kept, the Italian restaurant provides a short menu with a good range of pasta dishes.

Closed Sun Lunch not served Sat

Italian 45 seats S% Lunch £10—£12alc Dinner £10—£12alc Wine £4.80 Last dinner 11pm

Credit cards 1 2 3 5

X**Chef Peking** 10 Market Pl ☎ (0491) 578681

This simply decorated but striking restaurant stands in the centre of Henley and is popular with local residents. The short à la carte menu includes such regional specialities as whole steamed fish and Peking Duck (though the latter must be ordered in advance). Formal service is provided by smiling staff.

Closed 25—28 Dec

Pekinese 75 seats *Lunch £12alc Dinner £12alc Last dinner 11.15pm

Credit cards 1 2 3 5

HEREFORD
Hereford & Worcester
Map **3** SO54

★★★**Green Dragon** Broad St (Trusthouse Forte) ☎ (0432) 272506 Telex no 35491

Traditional hotel in the centre of Hereford.

88 2 CTV in all bedrooms ® sB&B £48.50 dB&B £63.50

Lift CTV 90 CFA *xmas*

Last dinner 10.30pm

Credit cards 1 2 3 4 5

★★★**Hereford Moat House** Belmont Rd (Queens Moat) ☎ (0432) 54301

Modern comfortable motel on city outskirts, whose restaurant offers varied menu.

Annexe: 32 CTV in all bedrooms ® S% *sB&B £36 dB&B £45

150P

English & French V *Lunch £6—£7&alc Tea 60p Dinner £8&alc Wine £4.75 Last dinner 9.45pm

Credit cards 1 2 3 5

★★**Castle Pool** Castle St ☎ (0432) 56321

Set in a quiet, secluded area of the city, this hotel offers guests a comfortable stay with a friendly, family atmosphere.

26 (3fb) 2 CTV in all bedrooms ® *sB&B £27 dB&B £38
Continental breakfast

10P

Continental Lunch £5 Dinner £9.25 Wine £4.20 Last dinner 9.30pm

Credit cards 1 3 5

★★**Graftonbury** Grafton Ln ☎ (0432) 56411

A large house has been considerably altered and extended to form this hotel, which now includes a small health club.

21rm(9 3)(3fb) TV in all bedrooms ®T sB&B£14—£16 sB&B £21—£23 dB&B£26 dB&B £33—£36

Lift CTV 100P sauna bath solarium gymnasium *xmas*

V Lunch £6—£7 Tea 55p Dinner fr£7.50&alc Wine £3.95 Last dinner 9.15pm

Credit cards 1 2 3 5

See advertisement on page 358

★★**Litchfield Lodge** 32 Bodenham Rd ☎ (0432) 273258

Set in a quiet, residential area half a mile from the city centre, the family-run hotel offers attentive service and a relaxed atmosphere.

9rm(1 6) CTV in all bedrooms ® *sB&B£18.50 sB&B £21.50 dB&B£28 dB&B £33 →

15P nc8yrs *xmas*

English & Continental V ✱Lunch £1—£3.60 Tea £1—£1.75 High Tea £5.50 Dinner £7.50 Wine £5.50 Last dinner 8pm

Credit cards 1 3 5 Ⓥ

★★**Merton** Commercial Rd ☎ (0432) 265925

Family-run town centre hotel with a popular, traditional, English menu.

15rm(12 ⋔) Annexe: 3rm(1fb) in 2 bedrooms CTV in all bedrooms **T** sB&Bfr£26 sB&B ⋔fr£30 dB&Bfr£36 dB&B ⋔fr£42 **B**

CTV 6P *xmas*

V Lunch £4—£10 Tea fr80p High Tea 80p—£8 Dinner £8.50—£15&alc Wine £4 Last dinner 9pm

Credit cards 1 2 3 5 Ⓥ

H

★★**The Priory** Stretton Sugwas (3m NW on A480) ☎ (0432) 760264

9rm(2 5⋔) CTV in all bedrooms

70P ✿

★★**Somerville House** 12 Bodenham Rd ☎ (0432) 273991

This large, detached house in the suburbs is popular with business people who enjoy the quiet, residential atmosphere.

10rm(2 4⋔)(1fb) TV in 4 bedrooms CTV in 6 bedrooms Ⓡ (ex guide dogs) S% sB&B£13.50—£14.50 sB&B ⋔£18—£22 dB&Bfr£27 dB&B ⋔£31.50—£33.50

CTV 12P

V S% Lunch £3.50—£5 Tea £1.50—£3 Dinner £5.50—£8&alc Wine £3 Last dinner 8pm

Ⓥ

HERSTMONCEUX
East Sussex
Map **5** TQ61

✿XX**Sundial** ☎ (0323) 832217

Set in rural, village surroundings, the elegant, country restaurant has a warm, friendly atmosphere and is personally supervised by the chef/patron and his charming French wife. The French cuisine, which specialises in fish cookery, is prepared to a very high standard.

Closed Mon, 10 Aug to 10 Sep & 23 Dec—20 Jan Dinner not served Sun

French V 60 seats ✱Lunch fr£12.50&alc Dinner fr£16.50&alc Wine £6.50 Last dinner 9.30pm 20P

Credit cards 1 2 3 5 Ⓥ

HERTFORD 0992 586791
Hertfordshire
Map **4** TL31

★★★**White Horse Inn** Hertingfordbury (1m W on A414) (Trusthouse Forte) ☎ (0992) 56791

Small, attractive inn with modern bedroom block. £70 - Single

30 CTV in all bedrooms Ⓡ sB&B £51.50 dB&B £68.50 **B**

60P ✿ *xmas*

Last dinner 10pm

Credit cards 1 2 3 4 5

XX**Marquee** 1 Bircherley Gn ☎ (0992) 558999

Standing on the river bank, this attractively appointed restaurant offers an appealing selection of English, French and other international dishes.

Closed Good Fri

International V 85 seats ✱Lunch £7.50&alc Dinner £15alc Wine £6.50 Last dinner 10.30pm 40P

Credit cards 1 2 3 4 5

HETHERSETT
Norfolk
Map **5** TG10

★★★**Park Farm** ☎ Norwich (0603) 810264

The hotel is a well-maintained Georgian house set well back from the road. A wide choice of bedrooms is offered in the main building and the annexe blocks at the rear. Friendly, family-run service and a range of leisure pursuits make it popular with tourist and businessman alike.

6 ⋔ Annexe: 26 ⋔(9fb) 8 CTV in all bedrooms Ⓡ **T** sB&B ⋔£35—£43 dB&B ⋔£45—£53 **B**

CTV 100P ✿ (heated) (hard) sauna bath solarium pool table table tennis

English & French V S% Lunch £6—£7 Tea £2—£3 High Tea £3—£4 Dinner £8—£8.50 Wine £4.50 Last dinner 9pm

Credit cards 1 2 3 4 5

HEVERSHAM
Cumbria
Map **7** SD48

★★★***Blue Bell at Heversham*** Prince's Way ☎ Milnthorpe (04482) 3159

An attractive country inn, once a vicarage, whose history dates back to 1692.

28rm(12 7⋔) CTV in all bedrooms Ⓡ **B**

CTV 104P

English & Swiss V

Credit cards 1 2 3

HEXHAM
Northumberland
Map **12** NY96

★★**Beaumont** Beaumont St ☎ (0434) 602331

Closed 26 Dec & 1 Jan RS 25 Dec

This very pleasant hotel offers an elegant restaurant, a comfortable cocktail bar and

everal well-appointed bedrooms verlooking the Abbey grounds.

0rm(4→16⋒)(2fb) 1⊟ CTV in all edrooms ® T ✗ S% ✱sB&B→⋒fr£23 B&B→⋒£33—£35 ₽

🍷 ☕ ✱Lunch fr£5.50&alc Tea £2.10 Dinner fr£6.95&alc Wine £4.95 Last dinner .45pm

Credit cards 1 2 3 4 5

★★ *HB* **County** Priestpopple ☎ (0434) 602030

Warm, comfortable, small hotel with good wholesome food.

0rm(4⋒)(3fb) CTV in all bedrooms ® T B&B£22—£24 dB&B£32—£36 dB&B⋒£32—£36 ₽

(₽

International V 🍷 ☕ Lunch £6.50—£9 Tea £2.30 High Tea £2.75—£7&alc Dinner £7.50—£12&alc Wine £4.50 Last dinner .30pm

Credit cards 1 2 3

★★ **Royal** Priestpopple (Consort) ☎ (0434) 602270

An old established inn with the original coaching arch, located in the town centre.

25rm(16→1⋒)(3fb) CTV in all bedrooms ® sB&B£18.50—£20.50 sB&B→⋒fr£27.50 dB&Bfr£37.50 dB&B→fr£41.50 ₽

25P

Scottish, English & French V 🍷 Lunch £2.50—£5.50&alc High Tea £4.50—£5.50 Dinner fr£8.50&alc Wine £4.50 Last dinner 9.30pm

Credit cards 1 2 3 5 Ⓥ

HIGHBRIDGE

Somerset

Map **3** ST34

★★ **The Sundowner** 74 Main Rd, West Huntspill 1m S on A38 ☎ Burnham-on-Sea (0278) 784766

This small, family-run hotel, standing on the main road, was originally a thatched cottage and has been completely refurbished to provide pleasant bedrooms, a comfortable bar lounge. English home cooking is served in a friendly atmosphere, and a first class breakfast is provided.

8rm(2→4⋒)(2fb) CTV in all bedrooms ® ✗ sB&B£22—£24 sB&B→⋒£22—£24 dB&B£34—£36 dB&B→⋒£34—£36

CTV 35P

Mainly grills V 🍷 ☕ ✱Lunch £4.60&alc Tea fr60p Dinner fr£4.60&alc Wine £4.75 Last dinner 9.30pm

Credit cards 1 2 3 5

✗✗ **Huntspill Villa** 82 Main Rd (West Huntspill 1m S A38) ☎ Burnham-on-Sea (0278) 782291

Lunch not served Sat & Mon
Dinner not served Sun

46 seats Lunch £12alc Dinner £12alc Wine £5 Last dinner 9.30pm 20P

Credit cards 1 2 3 5 Ⓥ

HIGH EASTER

Essex

Map **5** TL61

✗✗ **Punch Bowl** ☎ Good Easter (024531) 222

(Classification awarded for dinner only).

The isolated village setting of this charming, beamed restaurant does not deter its many customers. An informal atmosphere is created by good-natured staff who serve excellently-cooked food.

Closed Mon Lunch not served Tue—Sat
Dinner not served Sun

English & French V 66 seats ✱Lunch £8.50 Dinner £16.50&alc Wine £5.25 Last dinner 10.30pm 15P

Credit cards 1 2 3 5

HIGH HALDEN

Kent

Map **5** TQ93

✗ ***Hookstead House*** Durrant Gn ☎ (023385) 612

Improvements are still being made to the house, and it is hoped to open a public bar with its own entrance in the near future. The set-price meals represent good value, and the wine list is interesting and reasonably priced.

Closed Mon Dinner not served Sun

French 38 seats Last dinner 9.45pm 40P
2 bedrooms available

Credit cards 1 2 3 4 5

HIGH LANE

Greater Manchester

Map **7** SJ98

✗✗ **Red Lion** Buxton Rd ☎ Disley (06632) 5227

Situated alongside the A6, the inn has a good car park. Inside, a genial atmosphere is created by the attractive lighting, china and framed prints which show off the Georgian bow windows and panelled walls to advantage. The menu is interesting and the service attentive.

V 60 seats ✱Lunch £3.50—£7.25&alc Dinner £10 Wine £2.95 Last dinner 10pm 100P

Credit cards 1 2 3 5

HIGH OFFLEY

Staffordshire

Map **7** SJ72

✗✗ **Royal Oak** ☎ Woodseaves (078574) 579

Tiny village inn, comfortably modernised serving imaginative and traditional food.

Closed mid Aug & Bank Hols
Dinner not served Sun

40 seats Last dinner 9.30pm 15P

Credit cards 1 2 3 5

HIGH WYCOMBE

Buckinghamshire

Map **4** SU89

★★★ **Crest** Crest Rd, Handy Cross (Crest) ☎ (0494) 442100 Telex no 83626

New hotel with good bedrooms and interesting restaurant.

108→⋒ ⊁ in 17 bedrooms CTV in all bedrooms ® T ✗ S% sB→⋒£58.15 dB→⋒£64.30—£74.30 (room ony) ₽

(220P CFA ♿

→

H

♀French V ♀ ☕ ⁄ S% *Lunch £8.95&alc Tea 95p Dinner £11.25&alc Wine £6.15 Last dinner 10.30pm

Credit cards 1 2 3 4 5

HILFIELD
Dorset
Map **3** ST60

XX Good Hope ☎ Holnest (096321) 551

The detached, white-painted building has a good car park and pleasant garden. Service is attentive and the food very fresh, with a particularly attractive range of homemade desserts.

Closed Mon & Feb
Lunch not served Tue—Sat (Sep—May)
Dinner not served Sun

♀English & Continental **V** 30 seats *Lunch £11 alc Dinner £11 alc Wine £4.65 Last dinner 9pm 20P

Credit cards 1 2

HILLINGDON
Greater London
London plan **5** *A4* (page 446)

★★★ **Master Brewer Motel** Western Av (A40) ☎ Uxbridge (0895) 51199

Modern low-rise hotel with well equipped bedrooms.

106 ⇌ (16fb) ⁄ in 10 bedrooms CTV in all bedrooms ® **T** S% sB ⇌ £37.50—£45 dB ⇌ £37.50—£58 (room only) **B**

☾ # 200P CFA ❀

♀English & Continental **V** ♀ ☕ Lunch £6.50—£8.50&alc Tea fr £2.50 Dinner £6.50—£8.50&alc Last dinner 11pm

Credit cards 1 2 3 5

HINCKLEY
Leicestershire
Map **4** SP49

★★ ***Sketchley Grange*** Sketchley Ln, Burbage ☎ (0455) 634251

This friendly, privately-owned hotel is pleasantly situated in four acres of grounds with views of unspoilt countryside, yet is conveniently placed for the M69 and A5.

10rm (4 ⇌ 5 ⋔) (1fb) CTV in all bedrooms ® **T**

200P

High Wycombe — Hitchin

♀ ☕ Last dinner 9.45pm

Credit cards 1 2 3 5

See advertisement under Leicester

HINDHEAD
Surrey
Map **4** SU83

★★ **Devils Punch Bowl** London Rd ☎ (042873) 6565

The hotel has recently been completely refurbished to sound standards, and the public rooms include a friendly bar.

20 ⇌ ⋔ Annexe: 20 ⇌ (1fb) CTV in all bedrooms ® **T** S% *sB&B ⇌ ⋔ fr £36 dB&B ⇌ ⋔ fr £42 **B**

100P CFA

♀Mainly grills **V** ♀ ☕ S% *Lunch £7.50&alc Tea 75p—£2.50 Dinner £8.50&alc Wine £5.50 Last dinner 10pm

Credit cards 1 2 3 5

HINDON
Wiltshire
Map **3** ST93

★★ **Lamb at Hindon** ☎ (074 789) 225

Closed 25 & 26 Dec

Attractive, creeper-clad 16th-century inn with a traditional open fire in the bar.

16rm (8 ⇌ 1 ⋔) (2fb) 1 ▣ ® ✗ S% sB&B £18—£27 sB&B ⇌ ⋔ £20—£29 dB&B £36—£38 dB&B ⇌ ⋔ £40—£48 **B**

CTV 12P ❀

♀English & Continental **V** ♀ ⁄ Lunch £6.75—£9.50 Tea £1 Dinner £9.50—£11.50 Wine £4.50 Last dinner 9pm

Credit card 1

HINTLESHAM
Suffolk
Map **5** TM04

❀XXX **Hintlesham Hall**
☎ (047387) 268

An elegant example of the English country house, the hotel is set in 18 acres of parkland and has recently been refurbished and redecorated to offer a high standard of comfort. Imaginative and innovative menus show French and Far Eastern influences, the enjoyment of the food being heightened by the good wine list and the relaxed atmosphere.

Closed 26 Jan—9 Feb

Lunch not served Sat

♀English & French **V** 75 seats S% *Lunch £13.50&alc Dinner £21.50&alc Wine £6.50 Last dinner 9.15pm 50P 11 bedrooms available nc 10yrs

Credit cards 1 2 3 5

HITCHIN
Hertfordshire
Map **4** TL12

★★★ **Blakemore** Little Wymondley (2m SE A602) ☎ Stevenage (0438) 355821

Georgian style house with modern extension in large grounds.

69rm (68 ⇌ 1 ⋔) (1fb) CTV in all bedrooms ® **T** *sB&B ⇌ ⋔ £42 dB&B ⇌ ⋔ £50 **B**

Lift ☾ 150P ❀ ⌒ (heated) sauna bath Disco Sat (Oct—Apr) *xmas*

♀English & French ♀ ☕ S% *Lunch £8&alc Tea £1.25 Dinner £9.50&alc Wine £6.75 Last dinner 10pm

Credit cards 1 2 3 5

See advertisement under Stevenage

★★ **The Sun** Sun St, Town Centre (Toby) ☎ (0462) 32092

This modernised 16th-century coaching inn offers splendidly equipped bedrooms and tasteful standards of furnishing. Mr Toby's Carving-Room provides excellent value for money with its traditionally-carved English roasts and pies.

rm(13→13fi) Annexe: 6rm(2→4fi)
'V in all bedrooms ®T
sB&B→fi£33.50 dB&B→fi£43.50
P
? Wine £5 Last dinner 10pm
edit cards 1 2 3 4 5

)LBETON
evon
ap **2** SX65
★★ **HL Alston Hall** Battisborough
oss ☎ (075530) 259
e creeper-clad stone manor house, with impressive, oak-panelled hall and instrel gallery, offers comfortable edrooms, a friendly atmosphere and eshly-cooked food.
m(8→1fi) CTV in all bedrooms T ✗ S%
&B→fi£39—£48 dB&B→fi£52—£68
P ✿ (hard) *xmas*
English & French V S% Lunch
0alc Tea £1.20 High Tea £3.25 Dinner
4alc Wine £5.95 Last dinner 9.30pm
edit cards 1 2 3 5 V

)LFORD
merset
ap **3** ST14
★ **Alfoxton Park** ☎ (027874) 211
osed end Nov—end Mar
hite 18th-century house, home of poet illiam Wordsworth in 1797, set in 50 acres parkland.
→(3fb) CTV in all bedrooms ® ✗ B
P ✿ (heated) (hard) croquet
English & French Last dinner 9pm
edit cards 1 2 3 5
★ **Combe House** ☎ (027874) 382
osed Jan RS Nov, Dec & Feb
tractive 17th-century house in wooded alley, still retaining large water wheel. edrooms are well-appointed.
rm(13→)(2fb) 1 CTV available in edrooms sB&B£14.50—£18.50
&B→£18.50—£22.50 dB&B£28—£33
B&B→£30—£39 B
P ✿ (heated) (hard) sauna
ath solarium
Bar lunch £1.25—£5.50 Tea
p—£1 Dinner £8—£9 Last dinner
30pm
edit cards 1 2 3

OLKHAM
orfolk
ap **9** TF84
e also **Wells-next-the-Sea**
Victoria ☎ Fakenham (0328) 710469
compact building, constructed of local nts, and situated at the entrance to olkham Hall.
m ® sB&B£14—£18 dB&B£28—£36 B
TV 50P ✿
English & French Lunch fr£7 Dinner
£8 Wine £5.50 Last dinner 8.30pm
)

HOLLINGBOURNE
Kent
Map **5** TQ85
★★★ **Great Danes** Ashford Rd (Embassy) ☎ Maidstone (0622) 30022 Telex no 96198
Spacious, modern hotel with compact, well-equipped bedrooms.
126→(5fb) CTV in all bedrooms ®T S% sB→£47.50—£50 dB→£57.50—£60 (room only) B
Lift 500P CFA ✿ (heated) (hard) snooker sauna bath solarium gymnasium croquet pitch & putt Live music & dancing Sat (Sep—Jul) *xmas*
English & French V S% Lunch £7.50—£8.50 Tea £2.25—£2.75 High Tea £4.50—£5.50 Dinner £8.75—£10 Wine £6 Last dinner 10.45pm
Credit cards 1 2 3 4 5 V
See advertisement under Maidstone

HOLMES CHAPEL
Cheshire
Map **7** SJ76
★★ **Old Vicarage** Knutsford Rd ☎ (0477) 32041
Situated on the banks of the River Dane, this comfortable hotel has been converted from a 17th century Rectory.
3→ Annexe: 5→(1fb) CTV in all bedrooms ®T ✗ B
70P ✿
French V Last dinner 10pm
Credit cards 1 2 3 5
XX **Yellow Broom** Twemlow Green (1¾m NE A535) ☎ (0477) 33289
Country restaurant near Jodrell Bank, providing French cuisine in attractive, intimate surroundings.
Closed Mon Lunch not served Tue—Sat Dinner not served Sun
French V 50 seats Lunch £8.50alc Dinner £17—£19alc Wine £6.50 Last dinner 10pm 25P Live music mthly
Credit cards 1 2 3

HOLYWELL
Clwyd
Map **7** SJ17
★★ **B Stamford Gate** Halkyn Rd ☎ (0352) 712942
This modern hotel offers all creature comforts, and its excellent restaurant is supplied with fresh fish by the hotel's own trawler.
12→ CTV in all bedrooms ® ✗ S% sB&B→£22—£24 dB&B→£32—£34 B
100P Disco twice wkly nc1yr
International V S% Lunch £5—£6.50&alc Tea £1—£2 Dinner £7.15—£9&alc Wine £4.75 Last dinner 10pm
Credit cards 1 2 3 5 V

HOLYWELL GREEN
West Yorkshire
Map **7** SE01
★★ **B Rock Inn** ☎ Halifax (0422) 79721
Converted and extended 17th-century inn overlooking Pennine countryside.
18fi CTV in all bedrooms ®T S% sB&Bfi£23—£34 dB&Bfi£29—£44 B
100P 2 ✿ solarium Live music & dancing/cabaret Sat *xmas*
English & French V Lunch £5.50&alc Tea £3.50 Dinner £8.50&alc Wine £5.50 Last dinner 10pm
Credit cards 1 2 3 4 5 V

HONITON
Devon
Map **3** ST10
★★★ **H Deer Park** Weston (2½m W off A30) ☎ (0404) 2064
Old stone manor house, built in 1777, set in its own grounds of 26 acres.
17rm(15→) Annexe: 14→(2fb) 3 CTV in all bedrooms S% sB&B£23.50—£45 sB&B→£23.50—£45 dB&B£40—£85 dB&B→£40—£85 B
CTV 60P 4 CFA ✿ (heated) (hard) squash snooker sauna bath solarium putting croquet *xmas*
English & French V S% Lunch fr£6.50&alc Tea fr£1.50 High Tea fr£2.50 Dinner £12.50—£16&alc Wine £6 Last dinner 10pm
Credit cards 1 2 3 4 5
See advertisement on page 362
★ **Angel** High St ☎ (0404) 2829
Closed Xmas & Boxing day
Small, 17th century inn with continental awnings in town centre.
6rm(1→)(1fb) CTV available in bedrooms ® ✗ sB&B£15.50—£17.50 sB&B→£17.50 dB&B£25—£29 dB&B→£29 B
CTV 25P nc6yrs
English & Continental V Lunch £3.75—£5.70 Dinner £8.50alc Wine £4.50 Last dinner 9pm
★ **New Dolphin** High St ☎ (0404) 2377
Closed Xmas
Situated in the High Street, the inn-style hotel has pleasant, well-furnished bedrooms and simply-appointed public rooms.
10rm(4→)(2fb) CTV in all bedrooms ® ✗
CTV 12P
V Last dinner 9.30pm
Credit cards 1 3

H

HOOK
Hampshire
Map **4** SU75

★★**Raven** Station Rd ¾m N of M3 junc 5 on B3349 ☎ (025672) 4383 Telex no 858901

Standing close to the station, the hotel is a popular drinking place with home-coming commuters. Bedrooms are well appointed, though modestly furnished, and the informal staff are friendly and helpful.

46rm(28 18)(1fb) CTV in all bedrooms ® T * sB&B £44.27 dB&B £60.95 B

(100P CFA Live music and dancing Sat

Italian V Bar lunch 90p—£3 Wine £5.50 Last dinner 10pm

Credit cards 1 2 3 4 5

See advertisement under Basingstoke

XX**Whitewater House** (off A30, 1m NE) ☎ (025672) 2436

Lovely 17th century house forming select restaurant, where set lunch and dinner menus feature good home made food.

Closed Mon, Bank Hols Xmas & 2 wks Jan Dinner not served Sun

English & French V 40 seats Lunch £18alc Dinner £21alc Wine £6.30 Last dinner 9.30pm 30P nc 8yrs

Credit cards 1 2 3 5

Hook — Hope Cove

HOPE
Derbyshire
Map **7** SK18

XXX**Poachers Arms** Castleton Rd ☎ Hope Valley (0433) 20380

Attractive, well-appointed restaurant set in countryside.

Closed Xmas Day, Boxing Day & New Years Day

English & Continental V 70 seats S% Lunch £8.25—£10&alc Dinner £9.75—£11.25&alc Wine £6.25 Last dinner 9.30pm 30P

Credit cards 1 2 3 5

HOPE COVE
Devon
Map **3** SX64

★★*H* **Cottage** ☎ Kingsbridge (0548) 561555

Closed 2—30 Jan

This converted and extended cottage hotel is set in two acres of grounds with panoramic views of Hope Cove. Family-owned, it promotes high standards of hospitable service throughout, providing comfortable, traditional lounges and a well-appointed restaurant. All the bedrooms are cosy, but eight of them have recently been totally refurbished to an excellent standard

35rm(17 2)(5fb) CTV in 7 bedrooms T S% sB&B fr £13.15 dB&B £26.30—£34.70 dB&B £26.30—£62.40 B

CTV 50P Disco Sat (in season) xmas

English & French S% Lunch £6&alc Tea 90p—£1.75 Dinner £10.95&alc Wine £4.50 Last dinner 8.45pm

★★*L* **Lantern Lodge** ☎ Kingsbridge (0548) 561280

Closed Dec—Feb

Small, friendly, cliff-top hotel with tasteful lounges, good food and sheltered gardens.

17rm(13 4)(1fb) 3 ® sB&B £21—£29 dB&B £42—£58 B

CTV 17P (heated) sauna bath solarium nc 8yrs

English & French Bar lunch £1.50 Tea fr 60p Dinner fr £12 Wine £5.50 Last dinner 9pm

Credit cards 2 3

★★**Sun Bay** Kingsbridge ☎ (0548) 561371

Closed Nov—Mar

Modern hotel overlooking Hope Cove Bay

14rm(8 1)(3fb) B

CTV 14P
V Last dinner 8.15pm

★**Greystone** Kingsbridge (0548) 561233

The comfortable public rooms of the hotel have large windows giving magnificent views of Hope Cove. The substantial, home-prepared meals and friendly, informal service make for an enjoyable stay.

11rm(1fb) CTV in 1 bedroom ® sB&B£12.50 dB&B£25
CTV 15P 3 xmas
Lunch £5.75 Tea 50p Dinner £8.50 Wine £4.75 Last dinner 9.30pm
Credit cards 1 2 3

HOPTON WAFERS
Shropshire
Map **7** SO67

X**Crown Inn** Cleobury Mortimer (0299) 270372

The village, with the Crown at its centre, sits in a steep-sided valley on the eastern side of Clee Hill. Stone-built in the rugged local style and heated by open fires, the bar and restaurant offer a genuinely warm welcome beneath their heavy beams, with a comfortable background of everyday bric-à-brac. Seafood figures prominently among the interesting dishes on the menu, and daily 'specials' make use of seasonal produce.

Closed Mon (except Bank Hol's) Dinner not served Sun
English & French 50 seats Last dinner 9.30pm 40P
Credit cards 1 3

HORLEY
Surrey
Map **4** TQ24

Hotels are listed under Gatwick Airport

HORNBY
Lancashire
Map **7** SD56

★★**Castle** Main St (0468) 21204

Stone-built inn situated in the centre of the village.

Hope Cove — Horrabridge

13rm(4 4)(2fb) CTV in all bedrooms sB&B£18—£20 sB&B £22.50—£24 dB&B£28—£30 dB&B £33—£36
50P *xmas*
English & Continental V Lunch £4.75—£5.75 Tea £1.95 Dinner £8.50—£9.50&alc Wine £5 Last dinner 9.30pm
Credit cards 1 2 3 V

HORNCASTLE
Lincolnshire
Map **8** TF26

★***Bull*** Bull Ring (06582) 3331

A 16th-century inn, with a historically decorated banqueting hall, and a cobbled yard.

8rm(1)(1fb) TV in 1 bedroom ®
CTV 25P Live music & dancing/cabaret Fri/Sat
English & French V Last dinner 9.30pm
Credit cards 1 2 3 5

HORNCHURCH
Greater London
Map **5** TQ58

★★★**Ladbroke** Southend Arterial Rd (Ladbroke) Ingrebourne (04023) 46789 Telex no 897315

Modern hotel with comfortable bedrooms.

137(10fb) in 4 bedrooms CTV in all bedrooms ® T *sB £46 dB £56(room only)
170P CFA Live music & dancing Fri & Sat *xmas*
V *Lunch fr£8.50 Tea fr£1.25 Dinner fr£9.95 Wine £5.95
Credit cards 1 2 3 5

HORNING
Norfolk
Map **9** TG31

★★**Petersfield House** Lower St (0692) 630741

Set slightly back from the banks of the River Bure and surrounded by landscaped gardens, the hotel offers the solitude of a riverside retreat.

18rm(13 5)(1fb) CTV in all bedrooms T sB&B £30 dB&B £45
40P Live music and dancing Sat *xmas*
English & French V Lunch £7&alc Tea 65p Dinner fr£9&alc Wine £5.35 Last dinner 9.30pm
Credit cards 1 2 3 5

HORN'S CROSS
Devon
Map **2** SS32

★★★**Foxdown Manor** (Signed from A39 W of village) (02375) 325

Closed Jan—30 Mar

Secluded, personally-run country hotel with many facilities, in large grounds.

7rm(5 1)2 CTV in all bedrooms ® *sB&B£14—£23 sB&B £17—£26 dB&B £30—£50
30P (heated) (hard) sauna bath solarium putting croquet games room Disco Wed & Sat *xmas*
English & Continental V *Lunch fr£5.50 Tea fr60p High Tea fr£4 Dinner fr£9.75&alc Wine £4.95 Last dinner 8.45pm
Credit cards 1 2 3

HORRABRIDGE
Devon
Map **2** SX56

★★**Overcombe** (0822) 853501

RS Xmas

At this small, personally-run hotel the owners arrange programme weekends for the walker who wants to explore Dartmoor. The accommodation is comfortably furnished throughout and the bedrooms are well equipped. →

11rm(1⇛7⋒)(2fb) CTV in all bedrooms ® *sB&B£12.90 sB&B⇛⋒£15.90 dB&B£25.80 dB&B⇛⋒£28.80

CTV 13P ⇏ ✿ U ⚲

Lunch £2&alc Tea 60p—£1.20&alc Dinner £7.10&alc Last dinner 8.30pm

Credit cards 1 2 3 5

HORSFORTH
West Yorkshire
Map **8** SE23

XXX Low Hall Calverley Ln ☎ Leeds (0532) 588221

The restaurant is housed in a charming period building whose mullioned windows overlook the valley of the River Aire. Menus feature international dishes, cooked with skill and served by relaxed, professional staff; the wine list is also extremely good.

Closed Sun, Mon, 25—30 Dec & Spring Bank Hol wk Lunch not served Sat

English & French **V** 80 seats S% Lunch £8.50&alc Dinner £15.50&alc Wine £5.50 Last dinner 10pm 80P

Credit cards 1 3

HORSHAM
West Sussex
Map **4** TQ13

★★Ye Olde King's Head ☎ (0403) 53126

Closed 25 & 26 Dec

Part timbered, two-storey inn situated on Carfax. It was established in 1401, and the cellars date from the 12th century.

43rm(6⇛35⋒)(3fb) 1 ⊟ CTV in all bedrooms ® **T** sB&Bfr£32.50 sB&B⇛⋒fr£41.50 dB&Bfr£51 dB&B⇛⋒fr£51 **B**

40P ⇏ CFA

V Lunch £1.95—£6.50&alc Tea £2 High Tea £2 Dinner £8.95&alc Wine £4.95 Last dinner 9.45pm

Credit cards 1 2 3 5 V

❀★★★ **South Lodge** Brighton Rd, Lower Beeding ☎ Lower Beeding (040376) 7111

25⇛ (For full entry see Lower Beeding).

HORTON
Northamptonshire
Map **4** SP85

❀XX **French Partridge**
☎ Northampton (0604) 870033

A calm, dignified atmosphere distinguishes this family-run house where Mrs Partridge attends to the bar and takes orders whilst her husband creates carefully balanced dishes of French flair and flavour. Pastries and mousses are his specialities, but savoury dishes such as his feuillete of lambs' tongue and kidneys are becoming very popular. The predominantly French wine list includes many well-chosen regional wines and is reasonably priced.

Closed Sun, Mon 2 wks Xmas, 2 wks Etr & 3 wks Jul/Aug Lunch not served

French 46 seats S% Dinner £15 Wine £5.20 Last dinner 9pm 40P

HORTON-CUM-STUDLEY
Oxfordshire
Map **4** SP51

★★★ Studley Priory (Consort)
☎ Stanton St John (086735) 203 Telex no 23152

Closed 2—15 Jan

This unique, partly 13th century hotel in extensive, rural grounds. The cuisine is of the new, light, French style, making use of the best fresh ingredients and complemented by fine wines.

19rm(15⇛4⋒)(1fb) 2 ⊟ CTV in all bedrooms ® **T** S% sB&B⇛⋒£45 dB&B⇛⋒£63—£110 **B**

100P 2 ⇏ ✿ (grass) clay pigeon shoot *xmas*

English & French S% Lunch fr£14.50&alc Dinner fr£14.50&alc Last dinner 9.30pm

Credit cards 1 2 3 4 5

HORWICH
Greater Manchester
Map **7** SD61

★★Swallowfield Chorley New Rd
☎ (0204) 697914

Modernised, Victorian house set in its own grounds offering friendly, family atmosphere.

18rm(9⇛5⋒)(3fb) CTV in all bedrooms S% sB&B£17—£23 sB&B⇛⋒£21—£27.50 dB&B£23.50—£32.50 dB&B⇛⋒£29—£38.50 **B**

25P 2 ⇏ ✿ ⚲

S% Lunch £4.95—£6.95 Tea 75p Dinner £6.10—£7.90 Wine £4.95 Last dinner 9pm

Credit cards 1 2 3 V

HOUGHTON CONQUEST
Bedfordshire
Map **4** TL04

X Knife & Cleaver ☎ Bedford (0234) 740387

Good home cooking served in olde worlde restaurant by friendly family.

Lunch not served Sat Dinner not served Sun

V 70 seats Lunch £10alc Dinner £15alc Wine £4.95 Last dinner 9.30pm 35P

Credit cards 1 3

HOUNSLOW
Greater London
London plan **5** *B3* (page 446)

★★★Master Robert Motel 366 Great West Rd (A4) ☎ 01-570 6261 Heathrow plan **7** *F4*

Well-appointed comfortable motel with good food and pleasant staff.

Annexe: 63⇛ 6 ⊟ CTV in all bedrooms ® **T** S% sB⇛£37.50—£45 dB⇛£37.50—£58(room only) **B**

☾ 80P ✿ ⚲

Mainly grills **V** Lunch £6.50—£8.50&alc Tea fr£2.50 Dinner £6.50—£8.50&alc Wine £5.25 Last dinner 11pm

Credit cards 1 2 3 5 V

✕***Hounslow Chinese*** 261—263 Bath Rd ☎ 01-570 2161 Heathrow plan **6** *F3*

Comfortable restaurant providing well-flavoured Pekinese dishes.

Closed 25—27 Dec Lunch not served Sun

Chinese, Pekinese & Szechuan 130 seats Last dinner 11.30pm

Credit cards 1 2 3 4 5

HOVE
East Sussex
Map **4** TQ20

See Brighton & Hove

HOVINGHAM
North Yorkshire
Map **8** SE67

★★ *L* **Worsley Arms** ☎ (065382) 234

Closed 25 & 26 Dec

The hotel, a charming Georgian building at the centre of an historic village in the Howardian Hills, offers accommodation in well-fitted and restful bedrooms, comfortable, spacious lounge areas and an elegant restaurant of a reliable standard.

14 1 CTV in 1 bedroom Ⓡ in 1 bedroom sB&B £25—£28.50 dB&B £44.50—£48

CTV 50P 6 (£1)

International **V** Lunch £3—£13 Tea 85p—£3.20 High Tea £4.50—£7.50 Dinner £11.50—£14.50 Last dinner 8.45pm

Credit cards 1 3

HOW CAPLE
Hereford & Worcester
Map **3** SO63

★★ **How Caple Grange** ☎ (098986) 208

Large hotel in five acres of grounds.

26rm(18)(2fb) CTV available in bedrooms Ⓡ ✱ sB&B £23—£25 dB&B £39—£43

CTV 50P sauna bath solarium gymnasium *xmas*

Lunch fr£5 Tea fr£1.50 Dinner fr£7 Wine £5 Last dinner 9.30pm

Hounslow — Hull

HOWDEN
Humberside
Map **8** SE72

★★ **Bowmans** Bridgegate ☎ (0430) 30805

A converted merchant's residence and stables, situated in the town centre.

13rm(10)(1fb) CTV in all bedrooms Ⓡ **T** sB&B £24.95—£26.95 dB&B £41.95 dB&B £41.95

80P

English & French **V** S% Lunch fr£9.35&alc Dinner fr£9.35&alc Wine £5.40 Last dinner 9.30pm

Credit cards 1 2 3 5

★***Wellington*** 31 Bridgegate ☎ (0430) 30258

Once a Georgian coaching inn, parts of this hotel dates back to the 16th-century.

9 CTV in all bedrooms

50P sauna bath solarium

Last dinner 8pm

Credit card 1

HOWGATE
Lothian *Midlothian*
Map **11** NT25

✕✕ **Old Howgate Inn** Wester Howgate ☎ Penicuik (0968) 74244

Old coaching house reputed to have been used by pilgrims from Edinburgh.

Closed Xmas Day & New Year's Day

Danish **V** 45 seats ✱ Lunch £2—£8.50alc Dinner £2—£8.50alc Wine £5 Last dinner 10pm 36P

HUDDERSFIELD
West Yorkshire
Map **7** SE11

★★★ **George** St George's Sq (Trusthouse Forte) ☎ (0484) 25444

Large town centre hotel close to the railway station.

62rm(38) CTV in all bedrooms Ⓡ sB&B £34.50 sB&B £42.50 dB&B £45.50 dB&B £53.50

Lift ☾ 12P CFA

Last dinner 10pm

Credit cards 1 2 3 4 5

★★★ **Ladbroke** (& Conference centre) Ainley Top (Ladbroke) ☎ Elland (0422) 75431 Telex no 517346

This modern hotel provides up-to-date facilities and stands in a commanding position just off Junction 24 of the M62 motorway. There are attractive, open-plan public areas, well-equipped conference facilities and a carvery restaurant.

119 in 6 bedrooms CTV in all bedrooms Ⓡ **T** S% ✱ sB £46 dB £54 (room only)

Lift ☾ 250P CFA pool table Live music & dancing Sat Cabaret mthly *xmas*

International **V** S% ✱ Lunch £5—£7.75 Tea 65p Dinner £7—£9.95 Wine £5.99 Last dinner 10pm

Credit cards 1 2 3 5 Ⓥ

See advertisement on page 366

★★ **Huddersfield** 37—47 Kirkgate ☎ (0484) 512111 Telex no 51575

The hotel, standing close to the central ring road, has compact, well-fitted bedrooms with stylish decor, a reception lounge and nightclub access through the bistro-style restaurant. Staff are friendly and helpful.

26rm(9 17)(1fb) CTV in all bedrooms Ⓡ **T** S% sB&B £21.50—£27 dB&B £31.50—£37

Lift ☾ 30P sauna bath solarium pool table Disco 6 nights wkly Live music & dancing 4 nights wkly *xmas*

✱ Lunch £2—£4&alc Tea £1.75—£2.75 Dinner £5.95—£6.95&alc Wine £4.75 Last dinner 1am

Credit cards 1 2 3 4 5 Ⓥ

HULL
Humberside
Map **8** TA02

★★★ **Stakis Paragon** Paragon St (Stakis) ☎ (0482) 26462

A town-centre, multi-storey building in a busy shopping area, the hotel is of →

H

modern design and offers up-to-date facilities and conference areas.

125→⌂(4fb)⊬in 15 bedrooms CTV in all bedrooms ®T ✱sB&B→⌂£44.90 dB&B→⌂£54.80 ₽

Lift ☾ P CFA *xmas*

V ♁ ☕ ✱Lunch £5.25—£6.50 Tea fr65p Dinner £10.75 Last dinner 10pm

Credit cards 1 2 3 5

★★★**Crest—Humber Bridge** Ferriby High Rd ☎(0482) 645212
(For full entry see North Ferriby)

★★★**Willerby Manor** Well Ln (Consort) ☎(0482) 652616
(For full entry see Willerby)

★★**Pearson Park** Pearson Park ☎(0482) 43043
Closed Xmas

Substantial hotel overlooking the Park, with spacious public rooms and an attractive restaurant.

37rm(24→2⌂)(4fb)1⊟CTV in all bedrooms ®T sB&B£20—£24 sB&B→⌂£24—£29.50 dB&B→⌂£38—£44 ₽

☾30P♿

V ♁ ☕ Lunch £4.50alc Tea 65palc Dinner £6.85&alc Wine £4.25 Last dinner 9pm

Credit cards 1 3

H

Hull — Hungerford

✕✕**Cerutti's** 10 Nelson St ☎(0482) 28501

Originally the station-master's house on the quay-side serving the Humber Ferry, the restaurant has fine views over the river. It specialises in fish, and classical dishes are expertly served by professional staff in a friendly family atmosphere.

Closed Sun, Bank Hols & 1 wk Xmas Lunch not served Sat

V 40 seats Lunch £16alc Dinner £16alc Wine £5.25 Last dinner 9.30pm 10P

Credit card 1

HUMBIE

Lothian *East Lothian*
Map **12** NT46

★★★♣*L* **Johnstounburn House** (1m S on A6137) (Mount Charlotte) ☎(087533) 696

An attractive and comfortable 17th century house standing in its own extensive and well-tended gardens, the hotel offers attentive service and a peaceful atmosphere.

11rm(9→2⌂) Annexe: 9→⌂(3fb) CTV in all bedrooms ® in 9 bedrooms **T** ✱sB&B→⌂£30.50—£60 dB&B→⌂£61—£87.50

100P ✿ clay pigeon shooting

♔French **V** ♁ ☕ ✱Lunch £4—£10 Tea £1.50—£3 Dinner £12—£16&alc Wine £5.90 Last dinner 8.45pm

Credit cards 1 2 3 5

HUNGERFORD

Berkshire
Map **4** SU36

★★★**Bear** (Best Western) ☎(0488) 82512 Telex no 477575 (Ref 202)

RS 24—27 Dec

13th-century roadside inn, once Charles I's Civil War HQ, it has well-equipped bedrooms and imaginative cooking.

28rm(25→3⌂)(3fb) 1⊟CTV in all bedrooms ®T ✕ S% ✱sB&B→⌂£41.75—£46.75 dB&B→⌂£53.50—£58.50 ₽

75P ⛟

♁✱Lunch £10.45—£18.95&alc Dinner £13.45—£20.95&alc Wine £6.75 Last dinner 9.30pm

Credit cards 1 2 3 5

HUNMANBY

North Yorkshire
Map **8** TA07

★★*HBL* **Wrangham House** Stonegate (Guestaccom) ☎ Scarborough (0723) 891333

Closed mid Nov—Feb

Most tastefully restored former vicarage in secluded, well-kept gardens is now a very comfortable family run hotel offering every modern amenity, with traditional charm and character. The food is particularly enjoyable.

9rm(5🛁4🚿)(1fb) CTV in all bedrooms ® ✱ sB&B🛁🚿fr£28(incl dinner) dB&B🛁🚿fr£56(incl dinner) B

20P 🚗 ✿ putting nc 5yrs

✱Dinner £10.50 Wine £4.50 Last dinner 6pm

Credit cards 1 3 V

HUNSTANTON

Norfolk Map **9** TF64

★★★**Le Strange Arms** Golf Course Rd, Sea Front, Old Hunstanton (Consort) ☎ (04853) 34411

Large Victorian hotel with views of the Wash and access to the beach.

30rm(23🛁2🚿)(2fb) CTV in all bedrooms ® B

150P ✿ 🎾(grass) snooker *xmas*

V ☕ Lunch £9.25—£9.75&alc Tea £1—£1.20 High Tea £2—£2.50 Dinner £9.25—£9.75&alc Wine £4 Last dinner 8.45pm

Credit cards 1 2 3 5

★★**Lodge** Hunstanton Rd, Old Hunstanton ☎ (04853) 2896

The small, family-run hotel, located near to the well-known golf course, provides comfortable accommodation and friendly service.

15rm(6🛁9🚿)(2fb) CTV in all bedrooms ® ✱ sB&B🛁🚿£24—£29 dB&B🛁🚿£40—£55 B

70P ✿

English, French & Italian ☕ ✱Lunch £7&alc Tea £1—£3 Dinner £7&alc Wine £4.30 Last dinner 8.45pm

Credit cards 1 3 V

★***Wash & Tope*** Le Strange Ter ☎ (04853) 2250

11rm(3fb) CTV in all bedrooms ® B

CTV 12P 4🏠 *xmas*

V ☕ Last dinner 9.30pm

Credit cards 1 2 3

HUNSTRETE

Avon
Map **3** ST66

★★★

❀★★★ **HUNSTRETE HOUSE, HUNSTRETE**

Chelwood (Relais et Châteaux) ☎ Compton Dando (07618) 578 Telex no 449540

In 90 peaceful acres of grounds, which include a swimming pool, croquet lawn, tennis court and deer park, this nobly proportioned Georgian house, offers some of the best elegant country house living. John and Thea Dupays have succeeded in creating an atmosphere that exudes character and charm thanks to stunning decor, opulent furnishings, fine antiques and an abundance of flowers. The drawing room is particularly elegant and offers cushioned comfort; but there is also the library, other seating in the hall and the small cheerfully decorated bar. Bedrooms follow the same high standard and are beautifully decorated and furnished as well as being equipped with almost everything you might need, including hair-driers and trouser presses; bowls of fruit are provided in the corridors. Another charming feature is a courtyard overlooking an Italian fountain amidst the flower-filled terrace. Throughout the hotel the young staff are courteous and friendly. There are two adjoining dining rooms where Robert Elsmore, the young chef, uses excellent raw materials to provide enjoyable meals. The menu, which changes monthly, is fixed price and offers a good choice.

13🛁 Annexe: 8🛁 1▣ CTV in all bedrooms T ✱ S% sB&B🛁£72.45—£92 dB&B🛁£96.60—£138 Continental breakfast B

40P 🚗 ✿ ≈(heated) 🎾(hard) croquet nc 9yrs ♿ *xmas*

🚭 S% Lunch fr£9.20&alc Dinner £27.60—£32.20&alc Last dinner 9.30pm

Credit cards 1 2 3 4 5

HUNTINGDON

Cambridgeshire
Map **4** TL27

★★★**Brampton** ☎ (0480) 810434 (For full entry see Brampton)

★★★**George** George St (Trusthouse Forte) ☎ (0480) 53096

Sound, hotel with modern facilities.

24🛁🚿(2fb) CTV in all bedrooms ® T sB&B🛁🚿£47.50 dB&B🛁🚿£62.50 B

71P *xmas*

☕ Last dinner 9.30pm

Credit cards 1 2 3 4 5

★★★**Old Bridge** ☎ (0480) 52681 Telex no 32706

The hotel, an attractive, ivy-clad, Georgian house, stands on the ring road with the River Ouse flowing past its car park. The public rooms have some fine oak panelling, whilst the well-equipped bedrooms are individually styled. The menu is mainly British, and the skilful use of fresh produce makes the hotel a popular eating-place.

27rm(24🛁3🚿)(2fb) 1▣ CTV in all bedrooms T ✱ S% sB&B🛁🚿£46.75 dB&B🛁🚿£71 B

☾ 70P ✿ 🎣

V ☕ S% Lunch £14.75alc Tea £2.75alc High Tea £5.50alc Dinner £16.25alc Wine £6.25 Last dinner 10pm

Credit cards 1 2 3 5

HUNTLY

Grampian *Aberdeenshire*
Map **15** NJ53

★★**Castle** ☎ (0466) 2696

18th-century mansion standing in own ground of 4 acres close to Huntly Castle.

24rm(7🛁2🚿)(2fb) 1▣ ® sB&B£18—£21 sB&B🛁🚿£20.50—£25 dB&B£33—£35 dB&B🛁🚿£35.50—£37.50 B

CTV 20P 3🏠(50p per night) ✿ 🎣 putting croquet ♿

V ☕ Lunch £5.50—£7&alc Tea £1.50—£2.50 High Tea £4—£6&alc Dinner £9.50—£11&alc Wine £3.80 Last dinner 10pm

Credit cards 2 3 5 V

See advertisement on page 368

HURLEY
Berkshire
Map **4** SU88

★★**East Arms** Henley Rd ☎ Littlewick Green (062882) 3227

An 18th century inn has been modernised without loss of character to give well-appointed and comfortable bedrooms. Friendly and helpful staff create an informal atmosphere in keeping with the house.

7rm(3⇌4⋒) CTV in all bedrooms ® S% * sB&B⇌⋒£30—£35 dB&B⇌⋒£40—£45

150P ✿ Live music and dancing Sat *xmas*

English & French **V** ♡ ⊒ ⚡ *Lunch £7.50—£9.50&alc Tea 90p—£2.50 Dinner £14.15alc Wine £6.95 Last dinner 9.30pm

Credit cards 2 3 4 5

★★**Ye Olde Bell** ☎ Littlewick Green (062882) 5881 Telex no 847035

Built in 1136, this ancient inn retains much original character plus comfortable bedrooms and friendly, willing service.

10rm(9⇌1⋒) Annexe: 14rm(13⇌1⋒) 2▭ CTV in all bedrooms ® **T** S% *sB&B⇌⋒£43.30—£89.45 dB&B⇌⋒£60.75—£94.50 **B**

☾ 150P 6⌂(charge) ✿ *xmas*

English & French **V** ♡ ⊒ S% *Lunch fr£14.06&alc Tea fr£1.50&alc Dinner fr£15.20&alc Wine £7.60 Last dinner 9.45pm

Credit cards 1 2 3 4 5 Ⓥ

HURSTBOURNE TARRANT
Hampshire
Map **4** SU35

★★

✿★★♣ **ESSEBORNE MANOR, HURSTBOURNE TARRANT**

☎ (026476) 444

(Rosette awarded for dinner only)

Closed Xmas

Many of our members have been delighted with this hotel, awarded Red Stars for the first time last year. One wrote to us: "That hackneyed phrase 'like staying with friends' really applies here and the virtues of the hotel are simply staggering; I could not find any fault!" All this is a tribute to the amiable owners Messrs Harris and Birnie, who have created this little gem. As you would expect from a Red Star hotel all is beautifully clean and well maintained in this Georgian and Victorian building set in two acres of grounds in the gentle countryside of the Bourne Valley. Bedrooms vary in size but are individually decorated with great flair and provided with many little extras. The public rooms are stylishly done as well; both the Blue and Yellow sitting room, the striking little bar and the well-appointed dining room are most appealing and enjoy views of the garden. The menu is enterprising but features dishe to suit all tastes and we think that you will enjoy your meals here as much as you will the very warm hospitality.

6⇌ CTV in all bedrooms **T** ✈ *sB&B⇌£40 dB&B⇌£60

20P ▭ ✿ ⚲(hard) croquet nc9yrs

English & French ♡ ⊒ *Lunch £15alc Tea £1.35alc Dinner £15alc Wine £6.25 Last dinner 9.30pm

Credit cards 1 2 3 5 Ⓥ

HURST GREEN
Lancashire
Map **7** SD63

★★**Shireburn Arms** ☎ Stonyhurst (025486) 518
RS Boxing Day

A 17th-century coaching inn, furnished with several fine antiques.

11rm(6⇌1⋔)(1fb)1⊟ CTV in all bedrooms ®S% sB&B£19.50 sB&B⇌⋔£24—£29.50 dB&B£29.50 dB&B⇌⋔£39.50 **B**

CTV 30P 2⌂ ✽ putting

English & French **V** S% Lunch £6.95&alc Tea 60p Dinner £11.50alc Wine £5.20 Last dinner 9.30pm

Credit card [1]

HURSTPIERPOINT
West Sussex
Map **4** TQ21

X**Barrons** 120 High St, Hassocks ☎ (0273) 832183

A small country town restaurant providing simple fare including excellent home made soups.

Lunch not served Mon & Sat Dinner not served Sun

English & French **V** 40 seats Lunch £9—£12&alc Dinner £9—£12&alc Wine £4.95 Last dinner 10.30pm ℗ nc 3yrs

Credit cards [1] [3] [4]

HYTHE
Kent
Map **5** TR13

★★★★**Hotel Imperial** Princes Pde (Best Western) ☎ (0303) 67441 Telex no 965082

Imposing sea front hotel, with golf course, swimming pool and squash courts and several other sporting facilities.

83rm(81⇌2⋔)(5fb) 2⊟ CTV in all bedrooms ®T sB&B⇌⋔£38—£45 dB&B⇌⋔£70—£100 **B**

Lift ☾ 150P 10⌂(£3 per night) ✽ (heated) (hard & grass) squash snooker sauna bath solarium gymnasium croquet bowls putting table tennis Disco Sat *xmas*

English & French **V** Lunch fr£8.50&alc Tea fr£1 High Tea fr£4 Dinner fr£12.50&alc Wine £6.25 Last dinner 9pm

Credit cards [1] [2] [3] [5]

★★★**Stade Court** West Pde (Best Western) ☎ (0303) 68263 Telex no 965082

Comfortable, efficient hotel with sea views, sharing leisure facilities with Hotel Imperial.

35rm(30⇌5⋔)(4fb) in 4 bedrooms CTV in all bedrooms ®T sB&B⇌⋔£26.50—£34 dB&B⇌⋔£45—£52 **B**

Lift 12P 2⌂(charged) (heated) squash snooker sauna bath solarium gymnasium putting croquet bowling green CFA *xmas*

English & Continental **V** Lunch £5.25—£7.50&alc Tea 70—90p High Tea £2.50—£3.50 Dinner £10.50—£15&alc Wine £5.25 Last dinner 9pm

Credit cards [1] [2] [3] [5] Ⓥ

IGHTHAM
Kent
Map **5** TQ55

❀XX**Town House** ☎ Borough Green (0732) 884578
(Rosette awarded for dinner only)

The very well appointed, beamed restaurant is effectively supervised by the proprietress and offers a consistently high standard of cuisine. A good wine list accompanies the meal, and guests can relax in an elegant, comfortable lounge.

Closed Sun, Mon,, 2 wks Etr, 2 wks Aug/Sep & 2 wks Xmas Lunch served by prior arrangement

34 seats S% Lunch fr£14.50 Dinner £20—£24.50 Wine £7.25 Last dinner 9.30pm 15P nc 10yrs

Credit cards [1] [2] [3] [5]

ILFORD
Greater London
London plan **5** *F4* (page 447)

X**Da Umberto** 361 Ley St ☎ 01-553 5763

A warm, informal atmosphere and a traditionally friendly Italian greeting await the customer at this small restaurant. The menu of popular Italian dishes is supplemented by daily specials displayed on a blackboard, the standard of cuisine being very high and the presentation attractive.

Closed Sun & 20 Jul—20 Aug Lunch not served Sat

Italian **V** 40 seats Lunch £12.50alc Dinner £12.50alc Wine £4.90 Last dinner 11pm ℗

Credit cards [1] [3]

ILFRACOMBE
Devon
Map **2** SS54

★★★**Cliffe Hydro** Hillsborough Rd ☎ (0271) 63606

Privately owned and run coaching hotel with fine views of the harbour.

38rm(21⇌7⋔)(4fb) CTV in all bedrooms ®T sB&B£15—£17.50 sB&B⇌⋔£18—£22 dB&B£30—£35 dB&B⇌⋔£36—£44 **B**

Lift 8P ✽ Live music & dancing 3 nights wkly Cabaret wkly *xmas*

English & Continental **V** Lunch fr£4 Tea fr75p High Tea fr£6 Dinner fr£8 Wine £3.95 Last dinner 8.30pm

Credit card [1] Ⓥ

★★**Carlton** Runnacleave Rd (Consort) ☎ (0271) 62446
Closed Nov—Feb (except Xmas) RS Mar

Detached holiday and touring hotel with popular bar, located in the centre of town.

53rm(13⇌13⋔)(6fb) ® sB&B£14—£16 sB&B⇌⋔£15—£17 dB&B£28—£32 dB&B⇌⋔£30—£34 **B**

Lift ☾ CTV 20P Live music & dancing nightly Cabaret nightly *xmas*

✽ Lunch £2.50—£3.75 Tea 60p High Tea £1.75—£2.50 Dinner £5—£8.50 Wine £3.95 Last dinner 8pm

Credit cards [1] [2] [3] Ⓥ

★★**Elmfield** Torrs Park ☎ (0271) 63377

Closed Dec—Feb except Xmas

The peacefully-located holiday hotel, privately owned and run, offers good views from its compact bedrooms.

12rm(11⫛)(2fb) CTV in all bedrooms Ⓡ ✖ ✱sB&B£12.50 sB&B⫛£12.50—£23 dB&B⫛£23 Ⓑ

⊘ 12P ✿ *xmas*

♉ ☕ ✱Dinner £7.50&alc Wine fr£4 Last dinner 7.30pm

Credit cards 1 2 3

★★**Imperial** ☎ (0271) 62536

Closed mid Oct—Apr

Large coach and holiday hotel with views over the sea.

100rm(19→45⫛) CTV in 10 bedrooms sB&B£11—£13 sB&B⫛£15—£18 dB&B£22—£26 dB&B→⫛£30—£36

Lift ☾ CTV 12P

♉ ☕ ✱Bar lunch 85p—£2.75 Tea fr50p Dinner £6.25 Wine £4.25 Last dinner 8pm

★★♣**Langleigh Country** Langleigh Rd ☎ (0271) 62629

Closed Dec & Jan

Standing in three acres of grounds on the edge of the town, this Georgian country house was formerly the home of Admiral Down, of Nelson's fleet. Menus are interesting and varied.

6rm(4→2⫛)(3fb) ⊘ in bedrooms CTV in all bedrooms Ⓡ S% sB&B→⫛£15—£21 dB&B→⫛£32—£44

10P 🚌 ✿ solarium ⌂

♉International ♉ ☕ S% Bar lunch fr£2 Tea fr£1 High Tea fr£4 Dinner fr£8 Last dinner 8pm

★★**St Helier** Hillsborough Rd ☎ (0271) 64906

Closed Oct—Apr

Privately-owned and run holiday touring hotel with its own gardens.

25rm(15→)(6fb) CTV in all bedrooms Ⓡ sB&B£12.50—£13.50 dB&B£24—£26 dB&B→£27—£29

CTV 20P 9⌂ 🚌 ✿ pool table table tennis Disco wkly

♉Austrian, French & Italian ♉ ☕ Bar lunch £1—£3.50 Tea fr55p High Tea £2 Dinner £6—£6.50 Wine £4.20 Last dinner 8pm

Credit cards 1 3

★★**Tracy House** Belmont Rd ☎ (0271) 63933

Closed Nov

Small, secluded, privately-owned hotel.

11rm(4→4⫛)(2fb) CTV in 6 bedrooms Ⓡ sB&B£15—£16.50 sB&B→⫛£18—£19 dB&B£27—£30 dB&B→⫛£34—£39 Ⓑ

CTV 11P 1⌂(£1 per day) 🚌 ✿ solarium putting ⌂

♉English & Continental ♉ ☕ Bar lunch fr75p Tea 45—60p Dinner £7.75 Wine £4 Last dinner 8pm

Ilfracombe — Ilkley

★**Torrs** Torrs Park ☎ (0271) 62334

Closed Dec & Jan

Holiday hotel in a quiet situation, personally run by the owners.

16rm(6→6⫛)(4fb) CTV in all bedrooms Ⓡ sB&B£15.50—£16.50 sB&B→⫛£17—£18 dB&B£31—£33 dB&B→⫛£34—£36

16P 🚌 nc5yrs

♉ ☕ Lunch £4—£9 Tea £1.50—£3 High Tea £2—£4 Dinner £5—£10 Wine £3.50 Last dinner 7.30pm

Credit cards 1 2 3 4 5 Ⓥ

ILKLEY

West Yorkshire

Map **7** SE14

★★★**Cow & Calf** Moor Top ☎ (0943) 607335

Closed Xmas

Large, comfortable, stone house on the summit of Ilkley Moor, near famous Cow and Calf rocks.

17rm(9→8⫛)(1fb) 1⊟ CTV in all bedrooms Ⓡ sB&B→⫛£32—£35 dB&B→⫛£40—£45 Ⓑ

100P 🚌 ✿

♉English & French **V** ♉ Lunch £2.75—£4.25 Tea 75p Dinner £8.50alc Wine £4.95 Last dinner 9.30pm

Credit cards 1 2 3 5

★★★**Craiglands** Cowpasture Rd (Trusthouse Forte) ☎ (0943) 607676 Telex no 51137

Converted and extended 19th-century mansion on the edge of the moor.

73rm(48→5⫛) CTV in all bedrooms Ⓡ sB&B£38 sB&B→⫛£46 dB&B£55 dB&B→⫛£63 Ⓑ

Lift ☾ 200P 8⌂ CFA ✿ 🎾(hard) snooker ⌂ *xmas*

♉ ☕ Last dinner 9.30pm

Credit cards 1 2 3 4 5

★★**Greystones** 1 Ben Rhydding Rd ☎ (0943) 607408

Closed Xmas Day & New Years Day

Converted stone built residence in its own secluded grounds and gardens.

10→⫛(1fb) Ⓡ **T** ✱sB&B£22 sB&B→⫛£25 dB&B£28 dB&B→⫛£35

CTV 17P ✿

♉Dinner £8.95—£9.95 Wine £4.20 Last dinner 8.45pm

Credit cards 1 2 3 5

★★**Lister's Arms** Skipton Rd ☎ (0943) 608698

Three-storey, stone-built, coaching inn near the town centre with an attractive rear garden.

17rm(5→)(2fb) ⊘ in 1 bedroom CTV in 5 bedrooms Ⓡ ✖ sB&B fr£25 sB&B→ fr£30 dB&B fr£32 dB&B→ fr£36 Ⓑ

CTV 120P 1⌂(charge) ✿ sauna bath solarium gymnasium ⌂ *xmas*

♉English & French **V** ♉ ☕ ⊘ Lunch fr£5.25 High Tea fr£4.95 Dinner fr£9.95 Wine £4.95 Last dinner 8.45pm

Credit card 1

★★*H* **Rombalds** 11 West View, Wells Rd ☎ (0943) 603201 Telex no 51593

Personally supervised by the proprietors, this elegant, carefully-restored Georgian house stands on the edge of the moor. Dinner, where dishes range from the local to the more exotic, is particularly recommended.

22rm(11→11⫛)(5fb) CTV in all bedrooms Ⓡ **T** sB&B→⫛£36—£43 dB&B→⫛£48—£56 Ⓑ

☾ 22P 🚌 *xmas*

♉Cosmopolitan **V** ♉ ☕ Lunch £5—£12&alc Tea £1.65—£3&alc High Tea £5alc Dinner £14.20—£20&alc Wine £5 Last dinner 10pm

Credit cards 1 2 3 5 Ⓥ

★*B* **Grove** 66 The Grove ☎ (0943) 600298

Closed mid Dec—mid Jan

A Victorian town-house in a quiet position close to the central shopping area, the hotel is personally operated by the resident proprietor and provides spacious, elegantly-decorated accommodation.

6rm(2→3⫛) CTV in all bedrooms Ⓡ sB&B£18 sB&B→⫛£22—£24 dB&B£30 dB&B→⫛£34—£36

CTV 4P 🚌 nc7yrs

Lunch fr£5 Dinner fr£7.50 Wine £4 Last dinner 7.30pm

Credit cards 1 3

✿✿ ✕✕✕**Box Tree**

(see rosette box opposite)

✕**Olive Tree** 31 Church St ☎ (0943) 603150

This Greek restaurant is set in a small, fashionable shopping arcade close to the town's central car park. The à la carte menu features a good range of authentic dishes, prepared on the premises and available either individually or in a selection chosen for you, and the wine list includes some of Greek origin.

Lunch not served

♉Greek **V** 90 seats ✱Dinner £6.25—£7.95&alc Wine £5.50 Last dinner 11.30pm Ⓟ ⊘ Live music & dancing twice mthly

Credit cards 1 3 5

✕**Sabera** 9 Wells Rd ☎ (0943) 607104

The skilful use of herbs and spices in a variety of Asian dishes is the hallmark of this small Indian restaurant which stands close to the town centre.

Closed Xmas day
English & Indian V 44 seats *Lunch fr£2.25 Dinner £5alc Wine £3.75 Last dinner mdnt
Credit cards 1 2 3 5

XXX BOX TREE, ILKLEY
Church St (0943) 608484

(Rosette awarded for dinner only.)

Among the pioneers of good food, particularly out of London, it is 25 years since Malcolm Reid and Colin Long started, and that they have maintained their high standards for so long is a tribute to their high degree of dedication. The basis of their cooking style is classical and such grounding stands them in good stead when their foray takes them into the realms of modern French cuisine. The sole reputation is perfectly light, though not at the expense of flavour. This year a parfait of duck liver, with sauterne jelly was near perfect as was the roundels of monk fish in a green peppercorn sauce; consomme and fish soup have also been highly commended. Among the main course, medallions of tender, well flavoured beef Perigourdine with its rich red wine sauce, the chicken breast spiked with roquefort and the calves liver and sweetbreads with grain mustard and blackcurrant sauce demonstrate the skill and subtlety of the cooking. They also have a way with puddings which are always delectable. Brian Wonersley is the obliging man in charge and reverently takes your order while the whole brigade will serve you in a most friendly manner. There is also an outstanding wine list. From the outside the restaurant looks cottagey but that impression is belied by the rich interior: comfortable furniture, refined table appointments, oil paintings, porcelain, and objects d'art abound. You will enjoy your experience in this finest of north country restaurants.

Closed Sun & Mon Lunch not served
French 50 seats *Dinner £17.50alc Wine £7.50 Last dinner 10.15pm
S% Credit cards 1 2 3 5 V

ILMINSTER
Somerset
Map **3** ST31

★★★**Horton Cross** (04605) 2144
Modern purpose-built hotel, with easy access and car park.
23(7fb) CTV in all bedrooms ®S% * sB£27.50—£36.70 dB£39.70—£50.70(room only)
CTV 50P Live music & dancing wknds *xmas*
English & Continental V S% *Lunch £5.45&alc Dinner £7—£8.50&alc Wine £4.25 Last dinner 9.30pm
Credit cards 1 2 3 4 5

★★**Shrubbery** (Consort) (04605) 2108
The busy, owner-run, function, commercial and touring hotel offers well equipped accommodation, whilst the original 15th-century section has been carefully renovated to house the restaurant and banqueting suites. Service throughout is by pleasant and helpful staff.
13rm(8 1)(3fb) CTV in all bedrooms ® T sB&B£21—£30 sB&B£27.50—£35 dB&B£30—£35 dB&B£40—£45
100P (heated) Live music & dancing mthly
Lunch £6—£12.50&alc Tea £1.50—£2 Dinner £7.50—£15&alc Wine £5.25 Last dinner 9.30pm
Credit cards 1 2 3 4 5 V

INCHNADAMPH
Highland *Sutherland*
Map **14** NC22

★★**Inchnadamph** Assynt (05712) 202
Closed Nov—Feb
Beautifully situated Highland hotel, renowned as a quiet anglers retreat and a restful base for touring holiday makers.
28rm(7)(6fb)
30P 2
V Last dinner 7.45pm
Credit cards 1 3 5

INGATESTONE
Essex
Map **5** TQ69

★★★**Heybridge Moat House** Roman Rd (Queens Moat) (0277) 355355 Telex no 995186
22 CTV in all bedrooms T
*sB&B£39.50 dB&B£44
CTV P Live music & dancing Thu—Sat
International Last dinner 10.30pm
Credit cards 1 2 3 4 5

INGLESHAM
Wiltshire
Map **4** SU29

XX ***Inglesham Forge*** Faringdon (0367) 52298
This attractive, small, cottage-style restaurant offers an à la carte menu of mainly French dishes appropriate to business entertaining. The wine list is comprehensive, service friendly and efficient.
Closed Sun 25—30 Dec, Bank Hols & last 2 wks Aug Lunch not served Mon & Sat
French 30 seats Last dinner 9.30pm 15P
Credit cards 1 2 3 4 5

INSTOW
Devon
Map **2** SS43

★★★***BL Commodore*** Marine Pde (0271) 860347
Modern, white stucco building in its own grounds with estuary and sea views. →

20 CTV in all bedrooms ®T

CTV 100P 10 Live music & dancing Sat

English & French V Last dinner 9.30pm

Credit cards 1 2 3

INVERARAY
Strathclyde *Argyllshire*
Map **10** NN00

★**Fernpoint** Ferryland ☎ (0499) 2170

Closed Nov—wk before Etr

The oldest house in the town, featuring a spiral stair tower, the personally-run hotel offers a range of traditional Scottish fare which includes a special Scottish Dinner.

6rm(4)(4fb) ® sB&B£14—£18 dB&B£28—£40

CTV 12P

V Lunch £4.50alc Tea £1&alc High Tea £4.50alc Dinner £9.50—£20 Wine £5 Last dinner 9pm

INVERGARRY
Highland *Inverness-shire*
Map **14** NH30

★★**Glengarry Castle** ☎ (08093) 254

Closed 16 Oct—13 Apr

Ruins of Invergarry Castle are to be found in the grounds of this Victorian mansion.

28rm(24 1)(4fb) CTV in 1 bedroom ® sB&B£17.50—£19 sB&B£22.50—£24 dB&B£31—£34 dB&B£37—£40

CTV 30P 2 (hard)

V Lunch £5.25—£5.50 Tea £1—£2.20 Dinner £8.75—£9.50 Wine £4.20 Last dinner 8.15pm

Credit cards 1 3 5

INVERKIP
Strathclyde *Renfrewshire*
Map **10** NS27

★★***Langhouse*** Langhouse Rd ☎ Wemyss Bay (0475) 521211

Converted private house situated on hill overlooking the Firth of Clyde.

10rm(4)(1fb) CTV in all bedrooms ®

30P *xmas*

V Last dinner 9pm

Instow — Inverness

INVERMORISTON
Highland *Inverness-shire*
Map **14** NH41

★★ ***B*Glenmoriston Arms** Glenmoriston ☎ Glenmoriston (0320) 51206

Closed 25 Dec—3 Jan

This friendly and comfortable little hotel features good home cooking.

8rm(6) CTV in 6 bedrooms ®T *sB&B£20 sB&B£24 dB&B£31 dB&B£37

CTV 24P

Scottish & French V *Bar lunch £5.50alc Dinner £13.50alc Wine £4.95 Last dinner 8.30pm

Credit cards 1 2 3 5

INVERNESS
Highland *Inverness-shire*
Map **14** NH64
See plan

★★★★ ***HBCulloden House*** Culloden (2m E off A96) (Prestige) ☎ (0463) 790461 Telex no 75402 Plan **4** *D3*

Bonnie Prince Charlie made this house his base before the Battle of Culloden, and the spacious hotel is decorated and furnished in a style appropriate to the period. The proprietors are proud to offer traditional Scottish hospitality, the good cuisine being accompanied by a connoisseur's wine list.

20 3 CTV in all bedrooms T

P 2 (hard) billiards nc10yrs *xmas*

Scottish & French V Last dinner 9.15pm

Credit cards 1 2 3 5

★★★**Caledonian** Church St (Embassy) ☎ (0463) 235181 Telex no 75232 Plan **2** *B2*

Large, commercial and coach tour hotel.

116(4fb) CTV in all bedrooms ®T sB&B£34 dB&B£59

Lift 60P CFA

Bar lunch £3.50 High Tea £3.50—£5.50 Dinner £10—£13.50 Wine £4.55 Last dinner 9pm

Credit cards 1 2 3 5 V

★★★**Craigmonie** 9 Annfield Rd (Best Western) ☎ (0463) 231649 Telex no 946240 Plan **3** *D1*

Gabled, turreted red sandstone mansion (1832) with modern extension.

30rm(29)(4fb) 1 CTV in all bedrooms ®T sB&B£28—£36 dB&B£42—£50

Lift 60P *xmas*

French V Lunch £4.95—£6.50 Tea £1.75 Dinner £10.50—£11.50&alc Wine £5.50 Last dinner 9.30pm

Credit cards 1 2 3 5 V

See advertisement on page 374

★★★ ***BL*Kingsmills** Culcabock Rd (Swallow) ☎ (0463) 237166 Telex no 75566 Plan **11** *D1*

The well-appointed and comfortable hotel, standing in its own landscaped grounds with views of the golf course, offers a country-house style of service.

58rm(28 25)(12fb) CTV in all bedrooms ®T S% sB&B£44—£48 sB&B£44—£48 dB&B£62—£72 dB&B£62—£72

CTV 90P squash *xmas*

V Bar lunch £1.95—£7 Tea fr75p Dinner £11&alc Wine £5.50 Last dinner 9.45pm

Credit cards 1 2 3 5

★★★**Ladbroke** (& Conference centre) Nairn Rd (junction A9/A96) (Ladbroke) ☎ (0463) 239666 Telex no 75377 Plan **12** *D3*

Modern commercial, tourist and conference hotel. Many bedrooms have fine views.

118(5fb) CTV in all bedrooms ®T *sB&B£24—£48 dB&B£48—£70.50

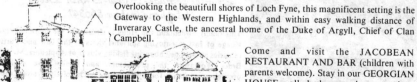

Lift 200P *xmas*

V ✿ ☕ *Lunch £3.25—£6.75 Tea fr55p Dinner £9.75&alc Wine £5.95 Last dinner 9.30pm

Credit cards 1 2 3 5 V

See advertisement on page 374

★★★**Palace** Ness Walk ☎ (0463) 223243 Telex no 777210 Plan **14** *B2*

A Victorian building, located in the town centre, is opposite the castle and next to the river.

43➡ Annexe: 41➡ (12fb) CTV in all bedrooms ® T S%
sB&B➡ £26.50—£29.50
dB&B➡ £42—£49 ℞

Inverness

Lift ☾ 40P ⛲ *xmas*

☋ Scottish & French ✿ ☕ S% Lunch £3.25—£6&alc Tea 75p—£1.50 High Tea £3.75—£4.50&alc Dinner £6.40—£9.75&alc Wine £4.30 Last dinner 8.45pm

Credit cards 1 2 3 5 V

See advertisement on page 376

★★★**Station** 18 Academy St ☎ (0463) 231926 Telex no 75275 Plan **17** *C3*

Closed 6 days Xmas

Situated in the town centre, beside the railway station, this hotel provides modern comforts whilst still retaining some of the splendour of bygone days. The lunchtime hot/cold buffet in the spacious foyer lounge is popular.

66rm(43➡ 10⋒)(6fb) CTV in all bedrooms
® T *sB&B £20—£29.50
sB&B➡⋒ £30—£44.50
dB&B➡⋒ £48—£66 ℞ →

I

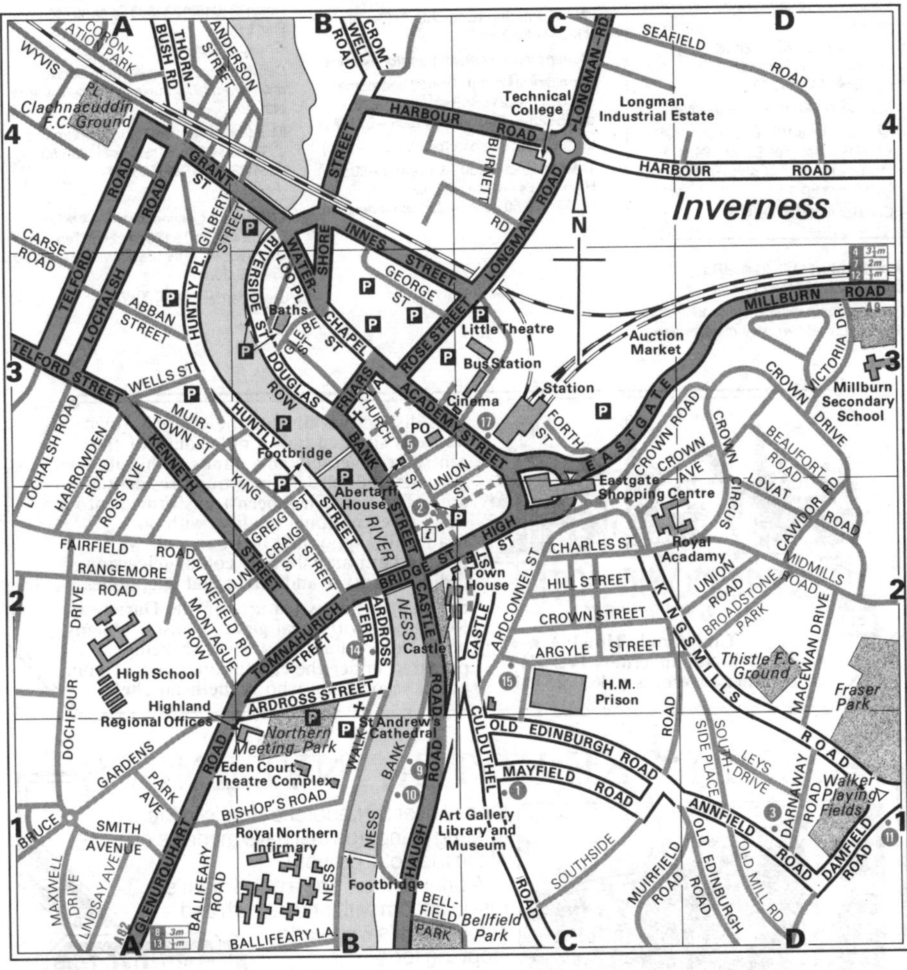

Inverness

1	Beaufort ★★	7	Drumossie ★★	12	Ladbroke ★★★
2	Caledonian ★★★	8	Dunain Park ★★	13	Loch Ness House ★★
3	Craigmonie ★★★	9	Glen Mhor ★★	14	Palace ★★★
4	Culloden House ★★★★	10	Glenmoriston ★★	15	Redcliffe ★
5	Cummings ★★	11	Kingsmills ★★★	17	Station ★★★

Lift ☾24P♿

🍽British & French **V** ⛉ ☕ Lunch fr£4 Tea fr£1.50 Dinner fr£11.50&alc Wine £7 Last dinner 9.15pm

Credit cards 1 2 3 4 5 Ⓥ

★★🌲 *HBL* **Dunain Park** ☎(0463) 230512 Plan **8** *A1*

Delightful country house in 6 acres of grounds near Loch Ness, it is run in a friendly and congenial manner by Ann and Edward Nicoll. Good country cooking is provided in the well appointed dining room, and the charming bedrooms are very thoughtfully equipped with many extras.

6rm(4➡)(2fb) 1📺 CTV in all bedrooms sB&B➡fr£22 dB&B➡£44–£72 **B**

30P 1🚗 ✿ croquet badminton

🍽International **V** ⛉ ☕ Lunch £7–£8.50&alc Tea £2.50–£4.50 Dinner £15–£17.50&alc Wine £5 Last dinner 9pm

Credit cards 1 2 3 5 Ⓥ

★★**Beaufort** 11 Culduthel Rd ☎(0463) 222897 Plan **1** *C1*

The hotel stands in its own grounds in the best area of the town, a few minutes walk

Inverness

from the centre. There is generous car parking space.

31⋒ CTV in all bedrooms **T** sB&B⋒£25–£30 dB&B⋒£40–£45 **B**

CTV 50P 6🚗 Live music Sun Cabaret Sun ♿

V ⛉ ☕ Lunch £4–£6.50 Tea £2–£2.50 High Tea £5–£8 Dinner £8.50–£15 Wine £6.50 Last dinner 10pm

Credit cards 1 2 3 5

★★**Cummings** Church St ☎(0463) 232531 Plan **5** *B3*

Modernised, commercial and tourist hotel.

38rm(6➡5⋒)(3fb) CTV in 20 bedrooms sB&B£17–£21 sB&B➡⋒£22–£26 dB&B£28–£36 dB&B➡⋒£35–£43 **B**

Lift ☾ CTV 25P Cabaret nightly (Jun–Sep)

⛉ ☕ ✱Lunch £3.50–£4 Tea 60–80p High Tea £4–£6&alc Dinner £6.50–£8.50 Wine £4.25 Last dinner 8pm

Ⓥ

★★**Drumossie** Perth Rd, Inshes (Norscot/Clan) ☎(0463) 236451 Telex no 75138 Plan **7** *D3*

Set in its own grounds on the outskirts of Inverness, this commercial-type hotel offers views over the town.

76rm(54➡22⋒)(2fb) 1📺 CTV in all bedrooms ® **T** sB&B➡⋒£27–£32 dB&B➡⋒£42–£50 **B**

☾ CTV 80P CFA ✿ Live music and dancing wkly *xmas*

⛉ Lunch fr£4.75 Dinner £10.50–£12.50 Wine £5.25 Last dinner 8.30pm

Credit cards 1 2 3 4 5 Ⓥ

★★**Glen Mhor** 10 Ness Bank (Inter Hotel) ☎(0463) 234308 Telex no 75114 Plan **9** *B1*

Closed 31 Dec–4 Jan

Conversion of Tarradale stone mansion dating from 1870, in a quiet residential area of the town.

21rm(8➡10⋒)(1fb) CTV in all bedrooms ® **T** ✱sB&B£16.50 sB&B➡⋒£32.50 dB&B£30 dB&B➡⋒£50 **B**

20P

🍽Scottish & Continental **V** ⛉ ☕ ✱Bar lunch £4.95alc Tea 75palc High Tea £5.50alc Dinner fr£12&alc Wine £4.95 Last dinner 9.30pm

Credit cards 1 2 3 5 Ⓥ

I

★★**Glenmoriston** 20 Ness Bank ☎(0463) 223777 Plan **10** *B1*

A small comfortable riverside hotel, catering for business and tourist trade.

21rm(2⇌11⋒)(1fb) 1⊟ CTV in all bedrooms ® **T** ✗ sB&B£19—£21 sB&B⇌⋒£21—£25 dB&B£35—£40 dB&B⇌⋒£40—£45

CTV 30P ⇌ ✿

British & Italian **V** ☕ ✱ Bar lunch £2.50—£5.75 Dinner £9.50—£11.50&alc Wine £5.25 Last dinner 9.30pm

Credit cards 1 3 4

★★**Loch Ness House** Glenurquhart Rd (Exec Hotel) ☎(0463) 231248 Plan **13** *A1*

The commercial hotel is situated on the outskirts of the town.

23rm(4⇌13⋒)(1fb) 2⊟ CTV in all bedrooms ® **T** sB&B£18—£19 sB&B⇌⋒£22.50—£25 dB&B£34—£37 dB&B⇌⋒£42—£45 **B**

60P ⇌ ✿ *xmas*

Scottish & French **V** ☕ Bar lunch £3.30alc Tea fr75p High Tea £6.50alc Dinner £9.50alc Wine £6 Last dinner 9pm

Credit cards 1 2 3 4 Ⓥ

★***Redcliffe*** 1 Gordon Ter ☎(0463) 232767 Plan **15** *C2*

Friendly and comfortable little family-run hotel standing close to the town centre and featuring good food.

7rm(2⇌)(2fb) CTV in all bedrooms ® **B**

CTV 8P ⇌

Last dinner 8pm

INVERSHIN

Highland *Sutherland*

Map **14** NH59

★★**Invershin** ☎(054982) 202

Closed 1st wk Jan

Simple, former drovers' inn, dating from 1908, standing in its own grounds.

10rm(4⇌1⋒) Annexe: 12rm(7⇌2⋒)(2fb) CTV in all bedrooms ® sB&B£16—£20 sB&B⇌⋒£18—£22 dB&B£32—£40 dB&B⇌⋒£36—£44 **B**

40P ✿ ∪

Inverness — Ipswich

V ☕ Lunch £5 Tea £1.75 High Tea £3—£10 Dinner £7.50—£10 Wine £4 Last dinner 9pm

Credit cards 1 3 5 Ⓥ

INVERURIE

Grampian *Aberdeenshire*

Map **15** NJ72

★**Gordon Arms** The Square ☎(0467) 20314

Small family run hotel of unusual design.

11rm(6⋒) CTV in all bedrooms ® ✱sB&B£17.95 sB&B⋒£19.95 dB&B£26.50 dB&B⋒£28.50

CTV P ⇌

Mainly grills ✱ Lunch £3.75alc High Tea £3alc Dinner £5alc Wine £3.95 Last dinner 8pm

Credit cards 1 2 3 5

✕**J.G.'s** Market Pl ☎(0467) 21378

Popular, friendly town centre restaurant.

Dinner not served Mon

V 56 seats Lunch £4.50—£7.50&alc Dinner £9—£12.50&alc Wine £4.50 Last dinner 9.30pm 20P

Credit cards 1 2 5

IPSWICH

Suffolk

Map **5** TM14

★★★*B* **Belstead Brook** Belstead Rd ☎(0473) 684241 Telex no 987674

Comfortable, hospitable hotel with country atmosphere.

26⇌⋒ Annexe: 7⇌⋒(14fb) 1⊟ in 1 bedroom CTV in all bedrooms ® **T** ✗ S% ✱sB⇌⋒£42.50—£56.50 dB⇌⋒£56.50—£65(room only) **B**

☾ 100P CFA ✿ *xmas*

V ☕ ✱ Lunch £10.50&alc Tea £1 Dinner £10.50&alc Wine £5.95 Last dinner 9.30pm

Credit cards 1 2 3 5

★★★**Ipswich Moat House** London Rd (3½m S A12) (Queens Moat) ☎ Copdock (047386) 444 Telex no 987207

Modern hotel, geared to short stay guests, with extensive function facilities.

45⇌(2fb) CTV in all bedrooms ® **T** sB&B⇌£26.50—£44 dB&B⇌£42—£60 **B**

☾ 400P ✿ *xmas*

English & Continental ☕ Lunch £5.10—£8.35 Tea fr90p Wine £6 Last dinner 9.20pm

Credit cards 1 2 3 5 Ⓥ

✿★★★*HB* **Marlborough** Henley Rd ☎(0473) 57677 Telex no 81630

This much-extended house, located in residential suburbs near the town centre, has lovely bedrooms and a well-deserved reputation for friendly, attentive hospitality. Menus offer a good selection of dishes cooked in the modern style, carefully and delicately presented, the crayfish soufflé with lobster sauce being a notable example; the table d'hôte selection at both lunch and dinner is modestly priced, and booking is recommended.

22⇌(3fb) CTV in all bedrooms **T** sB⇌£42 dB&B⇌£55(room only) **B**

☾ 60P ⇌ ✿ *xmas*

V ☕ Lunch £7.85—£10&alc Tea 80p—£2.75 Dinner £11—£15&alc Wine £7 Last dinner 9.30pm

Credit cards 1 2 3 5

★★★**Post House** London Rd (Trusthouse Forte) ☎(0473) 690313 Telex no 987150

Modern hotel complex on the southern outskirts of the town.

118⇌ CTV in all bedrooms ® **T** sB&B⇌£49.50 dB&B⇌£64.50 **B**

☾ 175P CFA ✿ (heated) *xmas*

☕ Last dinner 10pm

Credit cards 1 2 3 4 5

★★***Crown & Anchor*** Westgate St (Whitbread) ☎(0473) 58506

RS 25-31 Dec

55rm(23⇌4⋒) Annexe: 1rm(2fb) CTV in all bedrooms ®**T** ⊞

☾30P CFA

Mainly grills **V** ♈ ⊏ Last dinner 10.30pm

Credit cards 1 2 3 5

★★***Great White Horse*** Tavern St ☎(0473) 56558

Historic hotel having links with Dickens and George II.

55rm(10⇌)(1fb) 1⊞ CTV in all bedrooms ®⊞

☾CTV ⊞ *xmas*

♈ Last dinner 9.30pm

Credit cards 1 2 3 4 5

IRVINE
Strathclyde *Ayrshire*
Map **10** NS33

★★★★**Hospitality Inn** Roseholm, Annickwater (Mount Charlotte) ☎(0294) 74272 Telex no 777097

The spacious modern hotel favours a Moorish theme in its comfortable foyer lounge area. The Hawaiian Lagoon, with a pool ideal for children, is a notable feature.

128⇌⋒(44fb) CTV in all bedrooms ®**T** sB⇌⋒fr£44.50 dB⇌⋒fr£57.75 (room only) ⊞

☾200P ▭(heated) Live music Sun lunchtime *xmas*

International **V** ♈ ⊏ Lunch £9.50 Tea fr£1.25 Dinner £9.25—£15.50&alc Wine £5.50 Last dinner 11pm

Credit cards 1 2 3 5 Ⓥ

ISLAY, ISLE OF
Strathclyde *Argyllshire*
Map **10**

BOWMORE
Map **10** NR35

★★**Lochside** 19 Shore St ☎(049681) 244

Family run hotel with compact, modern bedrooms, some with good views of the bay.

7rm(2⇌) CTV in all bedrooms ®**T** ✱sB&B£20—£24 sB&B⇌fr£24 dB&B£38—£40 dB&B⇌£42—£44

V ♈ ⊏ ✱Lunch £5—£7&alc Tea £1 High Tea £3—£5 Dinner £7—£10&alc Wine £4 Last dinner 8pm

Credit cards 1 2 3

PORT ASKAIG
Map **10** NR46

★★**Port Askaig** ☎(049684) 245

Typical Highland Inn overlooking picturesque harbour. Good value special terms.

9rm(2⇌2⋒)(1fb) CTV in all bedrooms ® S% sB&B fr£18 sB&B⇌⋒fr£21 dB&B fr£34 dB&B⇌⋒fr£40 ⊞

10P 6⊞ ✽ nc6yrs

V ♈ ⊏ S% Lunch fr£6.50 Tea fr65p Dinner fr£10 Wine £4.95 Last dinner 9pm

Ⓥ

PORT ELLEN
Map **10** NR34

★***HB*** **Dower House** Kildalton (5½m E A846) ☎(0496) 2425

Closed mid Oct—Etr

Small, friendly, family run hotel with good home cooking. Located beside a small bay to the east of Port Ellen.

7rm(6⇌1⋒)(1fb) ®sB&B⇌⋒£18—£20 dB&B⇌⋒£36—£40

CTV 12P ✽

♈ ⊏ Lunch £9alc Tea fr60p alc High Tea £3alc Dinner £9alc Wine £4 Last dinner 7.30pm

ISLE OF ARRAN Strathclyde *Buteshire*
See **Arran, Isle of**

ISLE OF BARRA Western Isles *Inverness-shire*
See **Barra, Isle of**

ISLE OF BUTE Strathclyde *Buteshire*
See **Bute, Isle of**

ISLE OF COLL Strathclyde *Argyllshire*
See **Coll, Isle of**

ISLE OF COLONSAY Strathclyde *Argyllshire*
See **Colonsay, Isle of**

ISLE OF GIGHA Strathclyde *Argyllshire*
See **Gigha, Isle of**

ISLE OF HARRIS Western Isles *Inverness-shire*
See **Harris, Isle of**

ISLE OF ISLAY Strathclyde *Argyllshire*
See **Islay, Isle of**

ISLE OF JURA Strathclyde *Argyllshire*
See **Jura, Isle of**

ISLE OF LEWIS Western Isle *Ross & Cromarty*
See **Lewis, Isle of**

ISLE OF MAN See **Man, Isle of**

ISLE OF MULL Strathclyde *Argyllshire*
See **Mull, Isle of**

ISLE OF RAASAY Highland *Inverness-shire*
See **Raasay, Isle of**

ISLE OF SKYE Highland *Inverness-shire*
See **Skye, Isle of**

ISLE OF SOUTH UIST Western Isles, *Inverness-shire*
See **South Uist, Isle of**

ISLE OF WHITHORN
Dumfries & Galloway *Wigtownshire*
Map **11** NX43

★**Queen's Arms** ☎Whithorn (09885) 369

Small, family run hotel.

10rm(4⇌4⋒)(1fb) CTV in all bedrooms ® S% sB&B£13.50—£14.50 dB&B£27—£29 dB&B⇌⋒£31—£35 ⊞

12P ⊞ *xmas*

V ♈ ⊏ S% Bar lunch £1.50—£6.50 Tea £1.20—£1.50 High Tea £3.50—£7.50 Dinner £9.50—£10.50&alc Wine £4.50 Last dinner 9pm

Credit cards 2 3 5 Ⓥ

ISLE OF WIGHT Hampshire
See **Wight Isle of**

I

ISLE ORNSAY
Isle of Skye, Highland, *Inverness-shire*
See **Skye, Isle of**

ISLES OF SCILLY
See **Scilly, Isles of**

IVINGHOE
Buckinghamshire
Map **4** SP91

✕✕**Kings Head** ☎ Cheddington (0296) 668388

Formerly a 17th-century posting house for coaches using the old Roman road.

English & French **V** 55 seats Lunch £13.75&alc Dinner £13.75&alc Wine £7.25 Last dinner 9.30pm 20P

Credit cards 1 2 3 4 5

IXWORTH
Suffolk
Map **5** TL97

✕✕**Theobalds** 68 High St ☎ Pakenham (0359) 31707

Old beams and an open log fire contribute to the cosy atmosphere of a restaurant which retains little sign of its former use as a village grocery store. Menus offer a good range of imaginatively chosen and well-cooked dishes.

Closed Mon, 25—26 Dec & 1st wk Jan Lunch not served Sat Dinner not served Sun

French **V** 36 seats Sun Lunch £7.95 Dinner £13.25alc Wine £5.50 Last dinner 10pm nc 8yrs (dinner)

Credit cards 1 3

JEDBURGH
Borders *Roxburghshire*
Map **12** NT62

★★**Jedforest Country House** (3m S of Jedburgh off A68) ☎ Camptown (08354) 274

Closed 25 Dec & 1 Jan

Mansion dating from 1870, standing in 50 acres of tree-studded parkland bordering the River Jed.

7rm Annexe: 4 (2fb) CTV in 6 bedrooms Ⓡ sB&B£19.50 sB&B £25 dB&B£31 dB&B £35

CTV 100P ✽

Mainly grills Lunch £10.50 Tea fr 75p Dinner £10.50 Wine £3.50 Last dinner 8.30pm

Credit card 1

✕**Carters Rest** ☎ (0835) 63414

Standing in the shadow of the Abbey, this popular little restaurant with its Tudor decor and open kitchen is well known for its friendly, efficient service and consistently good steaks.

Closed Sun (Nov—Etr)

European **V** 100 seats Lunch £5.50—£8.50&alc Dinner £5.50—£8.50&alc Wine £5 Last dinner 9pm P

Credit cards 2 3

JERSEY
See **Channel Islands**

JEVINGTON
East Sussex
Map **5** TQ50

✕✕**Hungry Monk** ☎ Polegate (03212) 2178

Situated in a charming village, this delightful restaurant offers a unique combination of comfort, cosiness and charm. A fixed-price menu, which includes a glass of port, features fine English cookery and the whole experience is a rare delight.

Lunch not served Mon—Sat

English & French **V** 38 seats ✱ Lunch £11.50—£12.50 Dinner £12—£14 Wine £5.25 Last dinner 10.15pm 14P nc 3yrs

---

JOHN O'GROATS
Highland *Caithness*
Map **15** ND37

★★**John O'Groats House** ☎ (095581) 203

RS Oct—Feb

Said to be the most northerly house on the British mainland, it overlooks the harbour with views across Stroma to the Orkneys.

18rm (2 1)(2fb) CTV in 3 bedrooms Ⓡ ✱ sB&B£10—£13.80 sB&B £13—£17.25 dB&B£20—£27.60 dB&B £26—£34.50

CTV 20P ✽

V ✱ Bar lunch £1.30—£3 Tea 70p—£1.50 Dinner £6.50alc Wine £4 Last dinner 9pm

Credit cards 1 3 Ⓥ

★**Sea View** ☎ (095581) 220

Closed 1 & 2 Jan

Stone building standing on the roadside overlooking Pentland Firth and the isles of Stroma and Orkney.

9rm (1 1)(1fb) Ⓡ sB&B£12 sB&B £14 dB&B£24 dB&B £28

CTV 30P 2 snooker

V Lunch fr £4.50 Tea fr £1.20 High Tea fr £4&alc Dinner fr £7&alc Wine £5.75 Last dinner 8pm

Ⓥ

JOHNSTONE BRIDGE
Dumfries & Galloway *Dumfriess-shire*
Map **11** NY19

★★***Dinwoodie Lodge*** Main Rd (Guestaccom) ☎ (05764) 289

Closed Xmas Day

Lodge house on the A74, positioned at the junction for Newton Wamphray.

8rm (2)(3fb) TV in all bedrooms Ⓡ

CTV 100P ✽

V Last dinner 9.30pm

Credit cards 1 2 3 5

JURA, ISLE OF
Strathclyde *Argyllshire*
Map **10**

CRAIGHOUSE
Map **10** NR56

★★**Jura** ☎ Jura (049682) 243

The only hotel on the island, it sits beside the distillery overlooking the Bay. Service is friendly and the food is good.

17rm (4 1)(1fb) Ⓡ S% sB&B£17.50 sB&B £19 dB&B£35 dB&B £38

CTV 10P 6 ✽

S% Lunch £6 Tea £1.50alc Dinner £9.50&alc Last dinner 9pm

Credit cards 1 2 3 5

Kegworth — Kelso

KEGWORTH
Leicestershire
Map **8** SK42

★★★**Yew Lodge** 33 Packington Hill
☎(05097) 2518 Telex no 341995

Modernised, extended house near the village centre and close to the M1.

54rm(44➡10⋒)(3fb) CTV in all bedrooms ®T sB&B➡⋒£33 dB&B➡⋒£45 B

Lift ☾ 100P Disco Sat

English & French V ☕ Lunch fr£5 Tea fr75p Dinner fr£9.30 Wine £4.70 Last dinner 10pm

Credit cards 1 2 3 5 Ⓥ

KEIGHLEY
West Yorkshire
Map **7** SE04

★★**Beeches** Bradford Rd ☎(0535) 607227

Converted Victorian manor house, ½m from the town centre.

10rm(2➡) Annexe:(9⋒)(6fb) CTV in all bedrooms ® in 9 bedrooms
*sB&B£16.68—£23
sB&B➡⋒£27.03—£29.33
dB&B£32.20—£36.80
dB&B➡⋒£35.65—£39.10 B

☾ CTV 100P 2🚗 ✿ Live music & dancing wknds *xmas*

V ☕ *Lunch £4.50—£6.50 Tea £1.20 High Tea £1.75—£2.50 Dinner £6alc Wine £4.30 Last dinner 10pm

Credit cards 1 2 3 Ⓥ

KEITH
Grampian *Banffshire*
Map **15** NJ45

★★**Royal** Church Rd ☎(05422) 2528

Country town hotel set above shops.

12rm(3➡)(1fb) CTV in 3 bedrooms ® in 3 bedrooms ✗ sB&B£15—£16.50
sB&B➡£20—£22 dB&B£25—£27.50
dB&B➡£32—£35

CTV 8P 4🚗

☕ Lunch £4—£6&alc Tea £1.75—£2.25 High Tea £4—£5 Dinner £6.50—£9&alc Wine £4.50 Last dinner 8.30pm

Credit cards 1 3 5

KELSO
Borders *Roxburghshire*
Map **12** NT73

★★★***Cross Keys*** 36—37 The Square
☎(0573) 23303

Modernised coaching inn standing in a cobbled square in the town centre.

25rm(9➡9⋒)(3fb) CTV in all bedrooms ® T B

Lift ☾ CTV Disco wkly Live music & dancing mthly ♿

Scottish & Continental V ☕ Last dinner 9.30pm

Credit cards 1 2 3 5

★★★**Ednam House** Bridge St
☎(0573) 24168

Closed 24 Dec—10 Jan

The imposing Georgian mansion beside the River Tweed has long been favoured by the fishing and shooting fraternities. Attractively old-fashioned, it retains its historic character, and the emphasis is on traditional home cooking.

32rm(26➡4⋒)(4fb) T
*sB&B➡⋒£22—£26 dB&B fr£34
dB&B➡⋒£40—£48

CTV 100P 2🚗(£1 per night) ✿

☕ Lunch fr£6.30 Tea fr£2 Dinner fr£10.50 Last dinner 9pm

Credit card 3

★★★ BL **Sunlaws House** Heiton (2m SW A698) ☎ Roxburgh (05735) 331 Telex no 728147
(Rosette awarded for dinner only)

A country house set in 200 acres of ground tastefully converted by the Duke and Duchess of Roxburghe.

15 (1fb) 1 CTV in all bedrooms ® T sB&B £37—£45 dB&B £56—£70 B

50P clay pigeon shooting *xmas*

V Lunch £6.50alc Tea £3alc Dinner £13.50alc Wine £5.95 Last dinner 9.15pm

Credit cards 1 2 3 5 V

KENDAL
Cumbria
Map **7** SD59

★★★ **Woolpack** Stricklandgate (Swallow) ☎ (0539) 23852 Telex no 53168

One-time coaching inn, now a modern hotel. The Crown Bar here was once Kendal's wool auction room.

57rm (50 7)(2fb) CTV in all bedrooms ® T S% *sB&B £42 dB&B £54 B

CTV CFA *xmas*

K

Kelso — Kenilworth

V S% *Lunch £5.50—£6.50&alc Tea 65p—£2.35 Dinner £10&alc Wine £5.50 Last dinner 9.30pm

Credit cards 1 2 3 5

★★ B **Garden House** Fowl-ing Ln ☎ (0539) 31131

Closed 4 days Xmas

A delightfully furnished house standing in two acres of grounds. It is personally owned and run and provides a good standard of food and service.

10rm (8 2)(3fb) 1 CTV in all bedrooms ® T
*sB&B £27.50—£29.50 dB&B £39.50 B

40P

Wine £4.50 Last dinner 9pm

Credit cards 1 3

XXX **Riverside** Stramongate Bridge ☎ (0539) 24707

This elegantly decorated restaurant, serving well presented French style dishes.

French V 75 seats Last dinner 10pm

Credit cards 1 2 3 5

KENILWORTH
Warwickshire
Map **4** SP27

★★★★ **De Montfort** The Square (De Vere) ☎ (0926) 55944 Telex no 311012

Multi-storey hotel overlooking town with 2 restaurants and conference facilities.

95 (9fb) CTV in all bedrooms ® T S% sB&B £49.50—£52 dB&B £67—£70 B

Lift 85P CFA

English & French S% *Lunch £8.50&alc Tea £2.50 Dinner £9.75&alc Wine £6.75 Last dinner 10pm

Credit cards 1 2 3 4 5

★★★ **Chesford Grange** Chesford Bridge (½m SE jct A46/A452) (Consort) ☎ (0926) 52371 Telex no 311918

The large hotel and conference centre has comfortable bedrooms and a popular carvery-style restaurant.

106 (44fb) CTV in all bedrooms ® T sB&B £27—£43 dB&B £40—£56 Continental breakfast B

Lift 500P Disco Tue—Sat *xmas*

English & French V Lunch £7.50&alc Dinner £9&alc Wine £5.50 Last dinner 10.15pm

Credit cards 1 2 3 5 V

★★★**Kenilworth Moat House** Chesford Bridge (Queens Moat) ☎ (0926) 58331

This modern hotel on the outskirts of the town offers a choice of two restaurants, one of them being in the 'carvery' style.

48 CTV in all bedrooms Ⓡ **T** S% sB&B £24—£40 dB&B £34—£50 B

☾ 150P *xmas*

English, French & Italian **V** Lunch £7.50&alc Tea £2—£4 High Tea £2—£4 Dinner £9.50&alc Wine £4.95 Last dinner 10pm

Credit cards 1 2 3 4 5 Ⓥ

★★**Clarendon House** Old High St ☎ (0926) 57668 Telex no 311240

An old oak tree still supports part of the main roof of this charming Tudor building in the old town, and a deep well has been renovated in the cocktail bar.

32rm(23 9)(1fb) 4 CTV in all bedrooms Ⓡ **T** sB&B £27.50 sB&B £30 dB&B £38.50—£44 dB&B £46.50—£50 B

CTV 30P *xmas*

V Lunch fr£7&alc Tea fr£3.50 High Tea fr£5 Dinner fr£9.50&alc Wine £6.50 Last dinner 10pm

Credit cards 1 3 Ⓥ

XX**Diments** 121—123 Warwick Rd ☎ (0926) 53763

On the ground floor of this corner house the main restaurant serves French-style cuisine, whilst in the cellar a bistro provides less expensive dishes and an informal atmosphere.

Closed Sun, Mon, Bank Hols & 1st 3 wks Aug Lunch not served Sat

French 42 seats ✻ Lunch £5.75—£7.25&alc Dinner £11.45&alc Wine £5.75 Last dinner 10pm 12P

Credit cards 1 2 3 5

XX**Romano's** 60 Waverley Rd ☎ (0926) 57473

This successful restaurant specialises in high-quality Italian cuisine, though other dishes can be prepared on request, and the emphasis in the extensive wine list is predictably Italian too.

Closed Sun & Aug Lunch not served Sat

English & Italian 30 seats Lunch £7.50&alc Dinner £12.50alc Wine £5.50 Last dinner 10.30pm 10P

Credit cards 2 3

X**Restaurant Bosquet** 97A Warwick Rd ☎ (0926) 52463

An honest French menu is served in the intimate atmosphere of this compact restaurant.

Closed Sun Lunch not served Sat

French 26 seats Lunch fr£10.50&alc Dinner fr£10.50&alc Wine £5.90 Last dinner 9.30pm

Credit card 3

Kenilworth — Keswick

KENMORE

Tayside *Perthshire*
Map **14** NN74

★★★***Kenmore*** Village Sq ☎ (08873) 205

Historic, sporting hotel forming the focal point of the village, and set at the eastern end of Loch Tay.

24rm(23 1)Annexe:14rm(13 1) CTV in 24 bedrooms Ⓡ **T**

Lift CTV 100P *xmas*

Last dinner 9pm

Credit cards 1 2 3

KENNFORD

Devon
Map **3** SX98

★★**Fairwinds** ☎ Exeter (0392) 832911

Closed 15—31 Dec

Well-appointed tourist and commercial hotel, personally owned and run.

8rm(4 2)(1fb) in 1 bedroom CTV in all bedrooms Ⓡ sB&B £15—£19 sB&B £20—£26 dB&B £25—£35 B

8P

Dinner £5.65—£8.45&alc Wine £3.40 Last dinner 8pm

Credit cards 1 3 Ⓥ

KENTALLEN

Highland *Argyllshire*
Map **14** NN05

★★ *HBL* **Ardsheal House** ☎ Duror (063174) 227

Closed Nov—Etr

(Rosette awarded for dinner only).

In a splendid location by the shores of Loch Linnhe, this hospitable, hotel run by the Taylor family offers a warm welcome. Chef Robert Gardiner cooks in an elegant style using the best produce, and the meals are accompanied by a notable wine list.

14rm(6 4) ✻ sB&B £60—£65(incl dinner) sB&B £65(incl dinner) dB&B £80(incl dinner) dB&B £92—£114(incl dinner)

CTV (hard) snooker

International ✻ Lunch £5—£8 Tea £1 Dinner £20 Wine £6.50 Last dinner 8.30pm

Ⓥ

XX**Holly Tree** Kentallen Pier ☎ Duror (063174) 292

The restaurant reflects the charming style of the converted Edwardian railway station of which it forms a part and enjoys a beautiful setting with views over Loch Linnhe. Specialities include local seafood, home-cooked salmon, Scottish beef, venison and traditional baking.

Closed Wed (Oct—May) Mon & Tue (Nov—Etr) & 6 Jan—6 Feb

International 60 seats Lunch £7.50alc Dinner fr£12.50&alc Wine £5.25 Last dinner 9.30pm 25P

Credit cards 1 3 5

KERNE BRIDGE

Hereford & Worcester
Map **3** SO51

★★**Castle View** ☎ Symonds Yat (0600) 890329

Small coaching inn specialising in home cooking and personal service.

8rm(1 1)(1fb) Ⓡ sB&B £16.95 sB&B £19.95 dB&B £28.95 dB&B £32.95 B

CTV 50P *xmas*

English, French & Italian **V** Lunch £7alc Tea £1.50alc High Tea £3alc Dinner £7.95&alc Wine £4.25 Last dinner 10pm

Credit cards 1 2 3 5 Ⓥ

KESWICK

Cumbria
Map **11** NY22 **See plan**
See map 11 for details of other hotels in the vicinity

★★★**Derwentwater** Portinscale (Consort) ☎ (07687) 72538 Plan **3** *A5*

This large, old, lake-side house stands amid vast gardens in a tiny village near Keswick.

46rm(39 7)(2fb) CTV in all bedrooms Ⓡ sB&B £27.50—£35 dB&B £48—£60

Lift ☾ CTV 70P putting *xmas*

European Lunch £4.95—£6.95 Tea 65—80p High Tea £2.10—£4.50 Dinner £9—£9.95&alc Wine £4.25 Last dinner 9pm

Credit cards 1 2 3 5 Ⓥ

See advertisement on page 384

★★★**Keswick** Station Rd (Trusthouse Forte) ☎ (07687) 72020 Telex no 64200 Plan **6** *C3*

Charming, grand old hotel, situated in well tended grounds.

64 CTV in all bedrooms Ⓡ sB&B £45.50 dB&B £61.50 B

Lift ☾ 50P *xmas*

Last dinner 8.30pm

Credit cards 1 2 3 4 5

★★★ *HL* **Underscar Country House** Applethwaite (1m N off A591) ☎ (07687) 72469 Telex no 64354 Plan **15** *B5*

Closed 16 Dec—Jan

There are superb views from the three graceful lounges and many of the lovely bedrooms of this well-appointed hotel. High quality British food is served in the charming restaurant. →

12rm(10→2⋒)(2fb) CTV in all bedrooms ® in 6 bedrooms T sB&B→⋒£20—£32 dB&B→⋒£40—£70 B
45P 2 (£2 per night)

V Lunch fr£3.50 Tea fr£1.25 Dinner fr£15 Wine £7.25 Last dinner 8.30pm
Credit cards 1 2 5 V

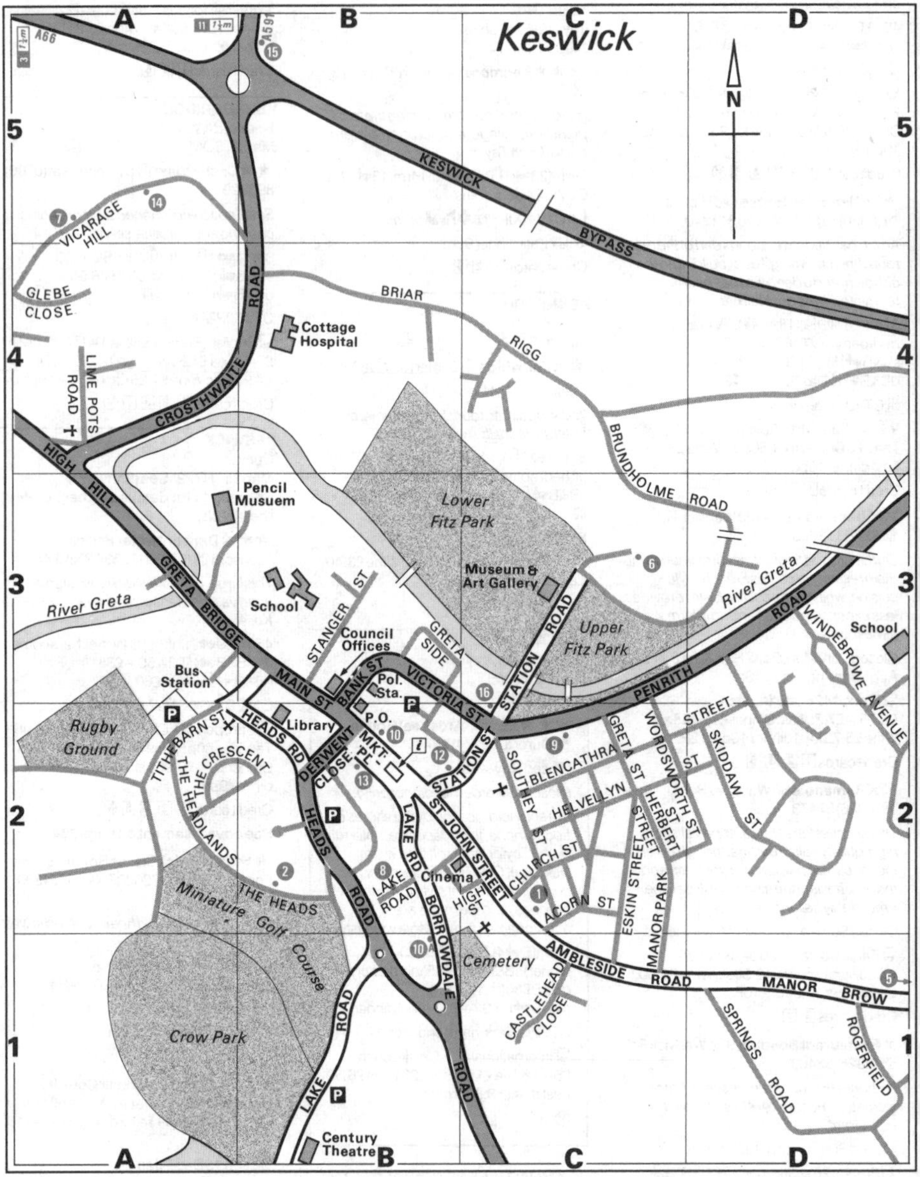

Keswick

Keswick

1	Chaucer House ★	10	Queen's ★★
2	Crow Park ★	10A	Priorholm ★
3	Derwentwater ★★★	11	Red House ★★
5	Grange Country House ★★	12	Royal Oak ★★
6	Keswick ★★★	13	Skiddaw ★★
7	Lairbeck ★★	14	Skiddaw Grove ★
8	Latrigg Lodge ★	15	Underscar Country House ★★★
9	Linnet Hill ★	16	Walpole ★★

★★*B* **Grange Country House** Manor Brow, Ambleside Rd ☎ (07687) 72500 Plan **5** *D1*

A charming, graceful and genuine country house containing many antiques, the Grange is quietly situated in its own gardens overlooking Keswick with panoramic mountain views.

11rm(3➡6⋒)(1fb) 2⊟ CTV in all bedrooms Ⓡ sB&B£17.50 dB&B➡⋒£39 **B**

12P ⇄ ✿

European ♔ ☕ ⚔ Bar lunch £4.50alc Tea 80p alc Dinner £9.50 Wine £4.90 Last dinner 8pm

Credit card 1 Ⓥ

See advertisement on page 384

★★ **Lairbeck** Vicarage Hill ☎ (07687) 73373 Plan **7** *A5*

Family hotel with clean accommodation and good home cooking.

12rm(5➡1⋒)(7fb) ✈ sB&B£13.50—£16.50 sB&B➡⋒£16—£19 dB&B£27—£33 dB&B➡⋒£32—£38

CTV 25P ⇄ ✿ ⌂

English & French ♔ ☕ Bar lunch £3.75 Tea 60p Dinner fr£8.50 Wine £4.55 Last dinner 8pm

Ⓥ

Keswick

★★ **Queen's** Main St (Exec Hotel) ☎ (07687) 73333 Plan **10** *B2*

RS Nov—Feb

Built of local stone and standing in the centre of the town, this hotel is one of the oldest in Keswick.

38rm(28➡6⋒)(12fb) CTV in all bedrooms Ⓡ T ✈ sB&B£14—£18 sB&B➡⋒£23--£25 dB&B£30—£36 dB&B➡⋒£46 **B**

Lift 18⌂ *xmas*

English & French V ♔ ☕ ⚔ Lunch fr£3.75&alc Tea £1.85alc High Tea £3.50alc Dinner £7.50alc Wine £4.35 Last dinner 8.30pm

Credit cards 1 2 3 5 Ⓥ

★★ ♣ **Red House** Under Skiddaw (on A591) ☎ (07687) 72211 Plan **11** *A5*

Closed Dec—Feb

Gabled, red painted early-Victorian country house set in 10 acres of gardens.

22rm(18➡)(6fb) Ⓡ S% sB&B£22—£23 sB&B➡fr£28 dB&B£44 dB&B➡£45—£48

CTV 25P ✿ ⌒ games room putting

V ♔ ☕ Lunch fr£4 Tea 75p—£2 High Tea £4—£5 Dinner £6—£7 Wine £4 Last dinner 8pm

Ⓥ

★★ ***Royal Oak*** Station St ☎ (07687) 72965 Plan **12** *B2*

Originating from Elizabethan times, this hotel is now a centre for business and social functions.

43rm(22➡2⋒)(4fb) CTV in all bedrooms Ⓡ T **B**

Lift ☾ 40P CFA *xmas*

♔ ☕ Last dinner 10pm

Credit cards 1 2 3 5

See advertisement on page 384

★★ ***Skiddaw*** Main St ☎ (07687) 72071 Plan **13** *B2*

Closed mid Dec—1st wk Jan

Large town centre hotel with very hospitable atmosphere and service. Bedrooms are well-appointed.

52rm(22➡1⋒)(5fb) CTV in all bedrooms Ⓡ **B**

Lift 20P ⇄ sauna bath solarium gymnasium

V ♔ ☕ Last dinner 9pm

Credit cards 1 2 3 5

See advertisement on page 385

K

★★**Walpole** Station St ☎ (07687) 72072 Plan **16** *C2*

About 100 years old and one of the finest examples of local slate work.

17rm(5⇌4⋒)(4fb) CTV in all bedrooms ® sB&B£14.75—£15.50 sB&B⇌⋒£16.75—£17.50 dB&B£29.50—£31 dB&B⇌⋒£33.50—£35

CTV 9P ⇌ games room

English & French **V** Dinner £8—£8.50&alc Wine £5.25 Last dinner 8.30pm

★**Chaucer House** Ambleside Rd ☎ (07687) 72318 Plan **1** *C2*

Closed Nov—Etr

Family-run hotel with views of Skiddaw, Cat Bells, Grisedale and Derwentwater.

30rm(4⇌9⋒)(7fb) CTV in 20 bedrooms ® sB&B£11.50—£12.50 sB&B⇌⋒£17.50 dB&B£23—£25 dB&B⇌⋒£32 **B**

CTV 25P(15p per night) ⇌

V Dinner £7&alc Wine £4.50 Last dinner 7.30pm

Credit cards 1 2 Ⓥ

★*B* **Crow Park** The Heads ☎ (07687) 72208 Plan **2** *B2*

Closed Xmas & New Year RS Dec—Feb

Large, terraced house close to the shores of Derwentwater.

Keswick

26rm(13⇌13⋒)(1fb) CTV in all bedrooms ® sB&B⇌⋒£13—£15 dB&B⇌⋒£26—£30 **B**

26P ⇌

Dinner £6.50—£8 Wine £4 Last dinner 7.30pm

Credit cards 1 3

★*B* **Latrigg Lodge** Lake Rd ☎ (07687) 73545 Plan **8** *B2*

This family-run hotel, set in a cul-de-sac near the town centre, provides accommodation of very good quality and a warm welcome; its restaurant is particularly popular.

7rm(2⇌5⋒) 1 CTV in all bedrooms ® **T** S% sB&B⇌⋒£23—£25 dB&B⇌⋒£34—£36 **B**

CTV 4P ⇌ *xmas*

English & French **V** Lunch £8alc Dinner £9&alc Wine £4.30 Last dinner 11pm

Credit cards 1 2 3 5 Ⓥ

★**Linnett Hill** 4 Penrith Rd ☎ (07687) 73109 Plan **9** *C2*

Closed Xmas

The cosy little family-run hotel has pretty bedrooms and offers a friendly welcome.

7rm(1⇌3⋒)(2fb) ® sB&B£14 dB&B£24 dB&B⇌⋒£28 **B**

CTV 8P ⇌ nc5yrs

Bar lunch £3—£5 Dinner £6&alc Wine £3.95 Last dinner 7pm

Credit cards 1 3 Ⓥ

★*H* **Priorholm** Borrowdale Rd ☎ (07687) 72745 Plan **10A** *B1*

A charming hotel with comfortable and well-appointed bedrooms, the Priorholm offers excellent meals in its elegant restaurant.

9rm(3⇌1⋒) CTV in 4 bedrooms ® S% *sB&B£10—£13 dB&B£26—£32 dB&B⇌⋒£32—£35

CTV 7P ⇌ *xmas*

International **V** *Lunch £6.50—£8&alc Tea £1—£3&alc Dinner £10.50—£11.50&alc Wine £4 Last dinner 8.30pm

Credit cards 1 3 Ⓥ

★**Skiddaw Grove** Vicarage Hill ☎ (07687) 73324 Plan **14** *A5*

Closed Nov—Feb (except New Year)

Family-run hotel with bright cheerful bedrooms and comfortable public rooms.

11rm(5⇌)(2fb) sB&B£13—£15 sB&B⇌£15—£17.50 dB&B£26—£30 dB&B⇌£30—£35

CTV 12P ⇌ nc7yrs

Lunch £4—£5 Dinner £9 Wine £3.60 Last dinner 7pm

KETTERING
Northamptonshire
Map **4** SP87

★★★**Ketterings Royal** Market Pl ☎(0536) 520732

The warm, comfortable, traditional-style hotel stands in the town centre, attracting commercial and local trade.

39rm(34🛁4🚿)(3fb) 1🛏 CTV in all bedrooms Ⓡ**T** ✱sB&B🛁🚿£35 dB&B£30 dB&B🛁🚿£46 **B**

☾CTV 36🚗 Disco Thu—Sun nc *xmas*

🍽English & French ♀ ☕ ✱Tea 50p Wine £3.50 Last dinner 10pm

Credit cards 1 2 3

★★**George** Sheep St (Paten) ☎(0536) 518620

Town centre Tudor inn with mainly commercial clientele.

45rm(24🛁)(1fb) CTV in all bedrooms Ⓡ**T** S% sB&B£26 sB&B🛁£36 dB&B£36 dB&B🛁£49 **B**

☾CTV 26P

V ♀ ☕ S% Lunch £8.95&alc Tea 70p Dinner £8.95&alc Wine £5.25 Last dinner 10.30pm

Credit cards 1 2 3 5 Ⓥ

KETTLEWELL
North Yorkshire
Map **7** SD97

★★**Racehorses** ☎(075676) 233

An 18th-century former coaching inn, situated on the riverside in village centre.

15rm(3🛁4🚿)(1fb) sB&B£19—£20 dB&B£33—£37 dB&B🛁🚿£38—£42 **B**

CTV 20P 🐕 *xmas*

Bar lunch £5alc Dinner £10—£12.50&alc Wine £4.80 Last dinner 8.30pm

Credit card 1 Ⓥ

★**Blue Bell** Middle Ln ☎(075676) 230

Village inn set close to the riverside in the heart of Wharfedale.

8rm(2🛁) CTV in all bedrooms sB&B£20—£26 dB&B£26 dB&B🛁£29 **B**

CTV 7P 🐕

♀ Bar lunch £4.20—£7.80 Dinner £7.50 Wine £5.35 Last dinner 9pm

KEYSTON
Cambridgeshire
Map **4** TL07

✕✕**Pheasant Inn** ☎ Bythorn (08014) 241

This delightfully picturesque village inn, with thatched roof and lovely old timbers, maintains all that is best in traditional English hospitality. The menu, on which game figures prominently, makes imaginative use of English and Continental country dishes and is based on first-rate produce.

Closed 25 & 26 Dec (evening)

🍽English & French 30 seats ✱Lunch £12.50 Dinner £12.50 Wine £6.50 Last dinner 10pm 30P

Credit cards 1 2 3 5

KIDDERMINSTER
Hereford & Worcester
Map **7** SO87

★★★★**Stone Manor** Stone (2m SE on A448) ☎ Chaddesley Corbett (056283) 555 Telex no 335661

RS 25 Dec (night)

The hotel stands in 24 acres of grounds just two miles from the centre of the town. Its bedrooms are comfortable, willing service is offered, and there is a popular restaurant.

23🛁(1fb) 3🛏 CTV in all bedrooms Ⓡ**T** S% sB&B🛁£46 dB&B🛁£64 **B**

☾CTV 400P CFA ✿ ⛱ 🎾(hard) Disco Tue Thu & Fri Live music Tue—Sat 🏠

🍽International **V** ♀ ☕ Lunch £7.50&alc Tea 95p Dinner £14alc Wine £5.95 Last dinner 10pm

Credit cards 1 2 3 5

★★**Gainsborough House** Bewdley Hill (Best Western) ☎(0562) 754041 Telex no 333058

Modern hotel with large banqueting facilities.

42🛁(2fb) 1🛏 ⊬ in 8 bedrooms CTV in all bedrooms Ⓡ**T** sB&B🛁£32.50—£35.75 dB&B🛁£43.50—£48.95 **B**

☾130P CFA solarium *xmas*

🍽European **V** ♀ ☕ S% ✱Lunch £5.50—£6.25 Tea 55—75p Dinner £7.50—£8.50&alc Wine £5.45 Last dinner 9.30pm

Credit cards 1 2 3 4 5

✕✕**Granary** Heath Ln Shenstone (3m SE off A450) ☎ Chaddesley Corbett (056283) 535

An English carvery restaurant with a small cocktail bar, the Granary makes good use of local produce.

Closed Mon Lunch not served Sat Dinner not served Sun

V 50 seats Lunch £6.50—£8.95&alc Dinner £11.50&alc Wine £4.95 Last dinner 9.30pm 50P

Credit cards 1 2 3 5

KILCHRENAN
Strathclyde *Argyllshire*
Map **10** NN02

★★★

✿★★★🌲**ARDANAISEIG, KILCHRENAN**

(Pride of Britain) ☎(08663) 333

Closed mid Oct—Etr

(Rosette awarded for dinner only)

Michael and Frieda Yeo are the genial hosts at this 19th century mansion and they are indefatigable in their efforts to please their guests, from thoughtful touches in the bedrooms like fruit, mineral water and sherry to, more importantly, the friendly and sociable atmosphere they engender. Built in 1834 by William Burn, a pupil of Robert Adam, it is an interesting old building in a wonderful situation right on the shore of Loch Awe, enjoying remarkable views as well as creating its own interest by the establishment of 30 acres of one of the finest gardens in Scotland. Inside, an open fire burns in the hall. There is an elegant drawing room and the library/bar which makes a suitable venue in which to chat with other guests. Then there is the smart and well appointed, candlelit dining room in which to enjoy Jeremy Brazil's good cooking. He provides a set five course dinner with a sort of à la carte list of main courses at extra prices. He cooks mostly in the traditional style with modern touches and, with the excellent raw materials — particularly

local products — you will enjoy your meals here. Bedrooms are not luxurious but, needless to say, they offer all the creature comforts you might require. Apart from the tennis, recreational facilities include a billiard room, croquet, clay pigeon shooting as well as fly and coarse fishing.

14🛁 CTV in all bedrooms **T** S% sB&B🛁£75(incl dinner) dB&B🛁£144(incl dinner) **B**

15P 🐕 ✿ 🎾(hard) 🎣 snooker croquet nc8yrs

🍽English & French ♀ ☕ ✱Lunch £11.50alc Tea £1.65—£3 Dinner £22 Wine £6.95 Last dinner 8.30pm

Credit cards 1 2 3

★★★ *HL* **Taychreggan** ☏ (08663) 211

Closed 11 Oct—12 Apr

This tastefully-appointed country house hotel is beautifully situated on the secluded shores of Loch Awe. Hospitality is warm and friendly, with bright, cheerful bedrooms and comfortable lounges, whilst the restaurant serves good food with an international flavour.

16rm(15) 1 sB&B£23—£27 sB&B£27—£31 dB&B£46—£54 dB&B£54—£86

CTV 25P

International Lunch £8 Tea fr£2 Dinner £13 Wine £5.50 Last dinner 9pm

Credit cards 1 2 3 5 V

KILCREGGAN
Strathclyde *Dunbartonshire*
Map **10** NS28

★★**Kilcreggan** ☏ (043684) 2243

Set high up overlooking gardens and River Clyde.

8rm(4 4)(2fb) sB&B£17.50—£19.50 dB&B£31—£35 B

CTV 40P

V Lunch £1.20—£3 Dinner £8—£8.50 Wine £3.75 Last dinner 8pm

Credit cards 1 2 3 5

KILDRUMMY
Grampian *Aberdeenshire*
Map **15** NJ41

★★★ *HBL* **Kildrummy Castle** (Best Western) ☏ (03365) 288
Telex no 946240
Closed 4 Jan—13 Mar
(Rosette awarded for dinner only)

An elegant Victorian mansion whose beautiful gardens contain the ruins of the original 13th century castle. The tasteful furnishings and decorations capture the traditional country house atmosphere, with good hospitality extended by the proprietor and his staff.

16rm(15 1)(3fb) 1 CTV in all bedrooms ® T sB&B£32—£35 dB&B£54—£70 B

30P snooker *xmas*

Scottish & French V Lunch £9&alc Tea £1.25 Dinner £14.50&alc Wine £6 Last dinner 9pm

Credit cards 1 2 3 4 5 V

KILDWICK
West Yorkshire
Map **7** SE04

★★★ *B* **Kildwick Hall** ☏ Cross Hills (0535) 32244

Elegantly furnished Jacobean manor house overlooking the valley.

12rm(10 2) 2 CTV in all bedrooms T S% *sB&B£28.50—£55 dB&B£28.50—£87 B

CTV 60P *xmas*

French V S% *Lunch £4.95—£10.50&alc Tea £1.25—£2.50alc Dinner £13.95&alc Wine £7.25 Last dinner 10pm

Credit cards 1 2 3 5 V

See advertisement under Skipton

KILFINAN
Strathclyde *Argyll*
Map **10** NR97

★★ *HB* **Kilfinan**

(see overleaf for entry) →

❀★★HB **Kilfinan** ☎ (070082) 201
(Rosette awarded for dinner only)
This charming, black and white family-run hotel guarantees you a warm welcome. Bedrooms are elegant, with many useful extras, and you are assured of a memorable meal in the well-appointed dining room.
11➡(1fb) CTV in all bedrooms ®T
sB&B➡£28 dB&B➡£42—£48
20P ✿
Scottish & French **V** Bar lunch £5alc Tea £2alc Dinner £14.50&alc Wine £4 Last dinner 9pm
Credit cards 1 2 3 5

KILLEARN
Central *Stirlingshire*
Map **11** NS58
★★**Black Bull** (Alloa Brewery) ☎ (0360) 50215
Small country town inn, dating from 1880, with a garden at the rear.
13rm(7➡) 1 ®T sB&B£20 sB&B➡fr£23.75 dB&Bfr£31 dB&B➡fr£37
CTV 40P ✿
European ✱ Lunch £6.50alc Tea fr50p High Tea fr£3.75 Dinner £6.50alc Wine £3.20 Last dinner 8.30pm
Credit cards 1 2 3 5

KILLIECRANKIE
Tayside *Perthshire*
Map **14** NN96

❀★★HB **Killiecrankie** ☎ Pitlochry (0796) 3220
Closed mid Oct—Etr
(Rosette awarded for dinner only)
Warm and caring service has always been offered by this delightful country hotel, and now that the A9 no longer passes its front entrance guests can also enjoy a peaceful, quiet environment. Duncan and Jennifer Hattersley-Smith personally show guests to their attractive bedrooms, and a comfortable lounge on the first floor is provided with colour TV, books, games and magazines. Bar meals are popular (and are served in the restaurant also at lunchtime), but the consistently good evening meals are a special treat.
12rm(5➡6⋒)(2fb)
sB&B£17.35—£21.70
sB&B➡⋒£19.85—£24.20
dB&B£34.70—£43.40
dB&B➡⋒£39.70—£48.40
CTV 30P ✿ croquet putting
V Bar lunch £2—£5 Tea 75p—£1 Dinner £12.50—£13.50 Wine £3.80 Last dinner 8.30pm

KILLIN
Central *Perthshire*
Map **11** NN53
★★**Bridge of Lochay** ☎ (05672) 272
Closed 8 Nov—11 Apr
An 18th-century drovers' inn on the outskirts of town, near River Lochay.
17rm(4➡3⋒)(1fb) ®
sB&B£13.50—£14.50 dB&B£25.50—£28 dB&B➡⋒£29—£32
CTV 35P 3 ✿
British & Continental **V** Lunch £4.50—£5.50 Tea £1.75 Dinner £8.50 Wine £4.75 Last dinner 9.15pm

★★***Killin*** (Best Western) ☎ (05672) 296
The courthouse that originally stood on this site was replaced by the present hotel which stands by the River Lochay.
30rm(7➡3⋒)(2fb)
Lift CTV 50P 8 ✿ billiards Live music and dancing twice mthly in season *xmas*
V Last dinner 9.30pm
Credit cards 1 2 3 5

★★**Morenish Lodge** Loch Tayside ☎ (05672) 258
Closed mid Oct—mid Apr
Conversion of traditional shooting lodge, overlooking Loch Tay.
12rm(4➡4⋒)(1fb) 2 ® sB&B£17 sB&B➡⋒£20 dB&B£28 dB&B➡⋒£34
CTV 24P ✿ nc4yrs
Bar lunch £4alc Dinner £9—£11 Wine £4.50 Last dinner 8pm
Credit cards 1 3

★**Falls of Dochart** Main St ☎ (05672) 237
Closed Nov—16 Apr
Informal hotel situated in the main street.
9rm(1➡)(2fb) sB&B£10.50 sB&B➡£14.50 dB&B£20 dB&B➡£25
CTV 25P 2
Scottish & Continental **V** Lunch £4 High Tea £4—£7.50 Dinner £6.75—£10.50&alc Wine £4 Last dinner 8.30pm
Credit cards 1 3 Ⓥ

KILMARNOCK
Strathclyde *Ayrshire*
Map **10** NS43
★★★**Howard Park** Glasgow Rd (Swallow) ☎ (0563) 31211 Telex no 53168
Modern hotel on outskirts of town provides limited public areas but good food and efficient service.
46➡⋒(6fb) CTV in all bedrooms ®S%
sB&B➡⋒£38 dB&B➡⋒£48.50
Lift ☾ CTV 250P *xmas*
International **V** S% Lunch £5.75 Tea 60p High Tea £3.25 Dinner £8.15&alc Wine £4.75 Last dinner 9.30pm
Credit cards 1 2 3 4 5 Ⓥ

✕✕**Caesar's** 108—112 John Finnie St ☎ (0563) 25706
One of the town's most popular restaurants, Caesar's is easily recognised by its smart, canopied windows. Its modern interior features a dark colour scheme which contrasts effectively with the white quarry-tiled floor. Lunch is a carvery-style meal, but à la carte and gourmet menus are efficiently served at dinner.
British & French **V** 60 seats Lunch £5—£10&alc Dinner £13&alc Wine £6.95 Last dinner 9.45pm Disco Fri & Sat
Credit cards 1 2 3 4 5

✕✕***Fisher*** 5 Kilmaurs Rd, Crosshouse (2m W A71) ☎ (0563) 26284
This attractive restaurant and lounge bar is named after John Fisher, the local pit-boy who rose to high office in Australia. The French-style food, freshly prepared and with an emphasis on grills, is competitively priced and there is a relaxed, friendly atmosphere.
Dinner not served Mon
French 60 seats Last dinner 9.30pm 20P
Credit cards 1 2 3 5

KILMARTIN
Strathclyde *Argyllshire*
Map **10** NR89
✕**Cairn** ☎ (05465) 254
Popular, and with an established reputation for good food and friendly service, the restaurant is simple in style, the candlelit tables and cobblestone bar adding to the cosy intimacy of its atmosphere.
Closed Mon—Thu (Nov—Mar)
40 seats ✱ Lunch £7alc Dinner £10alc Wine £4.70 Last dinner 10pm 25P nc 10yrs
Credit cards 2 3 5

KIMBOLTON
Cambridgeshire
Map **4** TL06
✕**La Côte d'Or** High St ☎ Huntingdon (0480) 861587
The oak floor, low beams and exposed brickwork of this terraced cottage in the main street create an old world atmosphere in which to enjoy some really good French country cooking.
Closed Tue Xmas Day & New Years Day
Dinner not served Sun
French **V** 30 seats Lunch £4.25—£7.50&alc Dinner £16.50&alc Wine £5.95 Last dinner 9.15pm nc 6yrs
Credit cards 1 3 Ⓥ

KINCLAVEN
Tayside *Perthshire*
Map **11** NO13
★★★L **Ballathie House** (Best Western) ☎ Meikleour (025083) 268 Telex no 727396

Closed 2 Jan—27 Feb RS Dec

The gabled and turreted Victorian mansion is set in an extensive, tree-studded estate overlooking the River Tay. Bedrooms vary in size and style, and lounges are impressive, with ornately moulded ceilings and Italian carved-marble fireplace.

22rm(19⇌3⋒) Annexe: 12rm(11⇌)(3fb) 2⊟ CTV in 22 bedrooms TV in 12 bedrooms ® T sB&B£26.50—£40 sB&BsB&B⇌⋒£26.50—£40 dB&B⇌⋒£44—£72 B

50P CFA ✿ ↖(hard) ♪ croquet putting ♿

Scottish & French ♆ ☐ Lunch £8.20—£9 Tea 75p—£5&alc Dinner £12.50—£15&alc Wine £5.20 Last dinner 9.30pm

Credit cards 1 2 3 5

KINCRAIG
Highland *Inverness-shire*
Map **14** NH80

★***Suie*** ☎ (05404) 344

RS in winter

Converted stone-built house standing in its own grounds overlooking Cairngorms.

6rm(2fb)

⊁30P ⇌ ✿ ♪ nc5yrs

♆ ☐ Last dinner 7pm

KINGHAM
Oxfordshire
Map **4** SP22

★★

★★MILL HOTEL, KINGHAM

☎ (060871) 8188 Telex no 849041

This is a refreshingly unpretentious little hotel, clean and bright with lots of flowers. Since last year it has been improved by enlarging the elegant, candlelit dining room and building on an attractive and comfortable sitting room off the traditional beamed bar. The owners, John and Val Barnett, create a convivial atmosphere and their staff are pleasant and cheerful. Modern bedrooms are smartly done, provided with colour televisions, radios, telephones and good toiletries. The new chef has introduced more flair to his modern-style cooking so that the restaurant is becoming increasingly popular with local customers. A little improvement in skill could win him a rosette next year. This was an old mill, mentioned in the Domesday Book, and the millstream still flows through the garden. The hotel is built of Cotswold Stone in seven acres of grounds. While the interior boasts some old features like beams, flagstone floors, fireplace and baker's oven, modern conveniences have not been forgotten. It is most attractively decorated with charming soft furnishings and some nice old pieces of country furniture. It has proved most popular with our members.

20rm(19⇌1⋒)(1fb) 1⊟ CTV in all bedrooms ® T ⊁ sB&B⇌⋒£25—£28 dB&B⇌⋒£40—£46 B

60P ⇌ ✿ ♪ nc5yrs *xmas*

English & French **V** ♆ ☐ Lunch £6.95—£8.95&alc Tea £1.50 High Tea £3—£3.50 Dinner £13.95&alc Wine £5.95 Last dinner 9.45pm

Credit cards 1 2 3 4 5 Ⓥ

Kingsbridge — Kingskerswell

KINGSBRIDGE
Devon
Map **3** SX74

★★★ *L* **Buckland-Tout-Saints**
Goveton (2½m NE on unclass rd) (Best Western) ☎ (0548) 3055 Telex no 42513
Closed Jan RS Feb
Elegant Queen Anne house set in 27 acres of parkland and garden. Comfortable bedrooms and attractive public rooms.
13rm(11 2) 1 CTV in all bedrooms **T**
sB&B £39.50—£55.50
dB&B £45—£60
20P 10 (charged) ✿ croquet mini golf *xmas*
English & French Lunch £15.50—£17.50&alc Tea £1—£4 High Tea £3.50—£5.50 Dinner £15.50—£17.50 Wine £5.50 Last dinner 9pm
Credit cards 1 2 3 4 5

★★ **Kings Arms** Fore St (Exec Hotel)
☎ (0548) 2071
Historical coaching inn located in terraced shopping area of old town.
12rm(7) 9 ® S% sB&Bfr£20.50 sB&B fr£23 dB&Bfr£35 dB&B fr£42
CTV 40P (heated) nc8yrs
V S% Lunch £1.95—£4 Dinner £8.50—£9.50 Wine £4.50 Last dinner 9.30pm
Credit cards 1 3

★★ **Rockwood** Embankment Rd
☎ (0548) 2480
Closed 25 & 26 Dec
Small villa with new extension overlooking estuary.
6rm(4 2)(2fb) TV in all bedrooms ®
sB&B £14.50—£16.50
dB&B £29—£33
CTV 5P 3
English & Continental **V** Lunch £8.50&alc Dinner £8.50&alc Wine £4.50 Last dinner 9.30pm
Credit cards 1 3 Ⓥ

★★ **Vineyard** Embankment Rd
☎ (0548) 2520
Closed Nov—Etr
Standing in its own grounds overlooking the estuary, the attractive, Grade II listed Regency villa offers bright, comfortable bedrooms and character public rooms.
11rm(7 4)(4fb) CTV available in 3 bedrooms S% ✱sB&B £15—£20
dB&B £30—£40
CTV 18P 1 ✿
Cosmopolitan ✱ Bar lunch £1.20—£5 Tea 45p alc Dinner £10—£12 Wine £4.25 Last dinner 8.30pm

KINGSKERSWELL
Devon
Map **3** SX86

★★ **Bickley Mill Inn** Stoneycombe
☎ (08047) 3201
Closed 15 Jan—15 Feb
The restaurant and bars, set in the beautiful, wooded Stonycombe valley and housed in a one-time flour mill that dates back to 1294, are full of old world charm. Bedrooms have been tastefully modernised to a good standard of comfort.
9 CTV in all bedrooms ®
✱sB&B £16—£18
dB&B £25—£28
80P ✿ nc12yrs *xmas*
English & Continental ✱ Lunch £8&alc Dinner £8&alc Last dinner 9.45pm
Credit card 3

✕✕✕ **Pitt House** ☎ (08047) 3374
In this charming, 16th century, thatched cottage Thomas Fairfax was entertained in 1646, and William of Orange dined here in 1668. Today's visitor, too, can dine in rooms with exposed beams and open log fires, enjoying attentive service and cuisine in the best French tradition.
Closed Sun & mid Jan—mid Feb Lunch not served Sat
French & Swiss **V** 35 seats Lunch £6—£12&alc Dinner £10.50—£16&alc Wine £5.10 Last dinner 9.30pm 25P
Credit cards 1 2 3 5 Ⓥ

KING'S LYNN

Norfolk
Map **9** TF62

★★★**Duke's Head** Tuesday Market Pl (Trusthouse Forte) ☎ (0553) 774996 Telex no 817349

Busy commercial hotel dating from 1685, with modern accommodation in new wing.

72➡(3fb) CTV in all bedrooms ® sB&B➡£48.50 dB&B➡£65.50 B

Lift ☾ 50P CFA *xmas*

♈ Last dinner 9.30pm

Credit cards 1 2 3 4 5

King's Lynn

★★***Hotel Mildenhall*** ☎ (0553) 775146

Closed Xmas Day

Commercial hotel overlooking small park.

46rm(18➡) Annexe: 8➡(3fb) CTV in all bedrooms ® T B

Lift ☾ CTV 50P Live music & dancing Sat Cabaret Sat

English & Continental ♈ Last dinner 9.15pm

Credit cards 1 2 3 5

★★**Stuart House** Goodwins Rd (Minotel/Exec Hotel) ☎ (0553) 772169 Telex no 817209

Closed 24 Dec—2 Jan

19rm(11➡⋒) Annexe: 2rm(6fb) CTV in all bedrooms ® T sB&B£20—£30 sB&B➡⋒£25—£29.50 dB&B£34—£35 dB&B➡⋒£35—£39.50 B

CTV 21P

European ♈ Bar lunch £1.25—£5 Tea 75p—£1 Dinner £7.95—£9&alc Wine £3.95 Last dinner 8.30pm

Credit cards 1 3 5

K

★★*Tudor Rose* 11 St Nicholas Street ☎(0553) 762824
RS Sun
Town centre hotel, parts of which date to Tudor times.
13rm(2→5⋒)(1fb) CTV in all bedrooms T ✈ B
CTV P xmas
V ☕ Last dinner 9.30pm
Credit cards 1 2 3

○**Butterfly** Hardwick Narrows ☎(0553) 771707
50→⋒ Due to have opened October 1986

○**Rising Lodge** Knightshill Village, South Wooton ☎(0553) 675566
9→⋒ Due to have opened August 1986

KINGSTEIGNTON
Devon
Map **3** SX87

✕**Thatchers** Crossley Moor Rd ☎ Newton Abbot (0626) 65650
Very much a family-run concern, with a relaxed atmosphere and friendly service, the small, 15th-century, thatched cottage restaurant offers lunch and dinner menus based on honest home cooking. In addition, there is a light table d'hôte lunch menu which is changed every day and represents good value.
Closed Tue Dinner not served Sun
V 28 seats Lunch £4.50—£6alc Dinner £11—£14alc Wine £5.35 Last dinner 9.30pm 20P
Credit cards 1 2 3 5

KINGSTON UPON THAMES
Greater London Plan **5** *B2*

○**Kingston Lodge** Kingston Hill (Anchor) ☎01-541 4481
64→⋒ Due to have opened June 1986

KINGSWINFORD
West Midlands
Map **7** SO88

★★*Summerhill House* Swindon Rd (Golden Oak Inns) ☎(0384) 295254
Busy hotel in quiet surroundings with large function suite.
10rm(3⋒) ® ✈ B
CTV 200P
☕ Last dinner 10pm
Credit cards 1 2 3

KINGUSSIE
Highland *Inverness-shire*
Map **14** NH70

★*Columba House* Manse Rd ☎(05402) 402
Closed Nov & Dec RS Jan—Apr
Originally the manse now a small friendly hotel run by resident proprietor. The hotel has a restricted license.
6rm(2⋒) Annexe: 1→(1fb) ® B
CTV 10P ✿
Scottish & French ☕ Last dinner 7.30pm

King's Lynn — Kinross

✿★*H* **Osprey** Ruthven Rd ☎(05402) 510
Closed Nov—27 Dec
(Rosette awarded for dinner only)
Friendly and characterful, the small, family-run hotel has a reputation for its food, the emphasis being on home cooking and baking with fresh Scottish produce and good raw materials. Dinner consists of a set main course augmented by a more-than-adequate choice of starters and puddings. Dishes are prepared with skill and enthusiasm by Mrs Reeves, whilst her husband makes an admirable host in the dining room.
8rm(1→2⋒)(1fb) sB&B£12—£16 dB&B£24—£32 dB&B→⋒£34—£44 B
CTV 10P
Scottish, English & French V ☕ Tea £1.50—£3 Dinner £11—£13 Wine £4.90 Last dinner 8pm
Credit cards 1 2 3 5 V

★*Silverfjord* Ruthven Rd ☎(05402) 292
Comfortable little hotel near station.
7rm(1→)(1fb) ®
CTV 12P ✿ ♿
V ☕ Last dinner 8.30pm
Credit card 3

✿✕**The Cross** High St ☎(05402) 762
(Rosette awarded for dinners only)
This small, cottage-style hotel stands on the main street of the popular Speyside town. On arrival, you will be offered aperitifs in the snug lounge area by the proprietor, Tony Hadley, and menu and comprehensive wine list will be discussed in detail before you move to the friendly atmosphere of the small, intimate restaurant area. The delicious dishes produced by Ruth Hadley make full use of local produce, their effectiveness lying in the skilful blending of flavours.
Closed Mon & 1—24 Dec
Lunch not served
V 24 seats Dinner £12alc Wine £3.50 Last dinner 10pm P nc 8yrs

KINLOCHBERVIE
Highland *Sutherland*
Map **14** NC25

★★★**Kinlochbervie** (Exec Hotel) ☎(097182) 275
RS mid Nov—Etr
This comfortable, modern hotel stands in a delightful position overlooking the harbour. Personally supervised by the owners, it specialises in Cordon Bleu cookery.
14→ CTV in all bedrooms ® T sB&B→£21—£55 dB&B→£32—£65 B
30P
☕ Bar lunch £3.75—£7 Tea £1 High Tea £5.50—£8.50 Dinner £15.95—£17.95 Wine £5.40 Last dinner 8.30pm
Credit cards 1 2 3 4 5 V

KINLOCHEWE
Highland *Ross & Cromarty*
Map **14** NH06

★**Kinlochewe** (Guestaccom) ☎(044584) 253
Closed Dec-Mar
A comfortable little hotel with friendly atmosphere and ideally situated for fishing and hill walking.
10rm(1→1⋒)(1fb) ✱sB&B£20 dB&B£32 dB&B→⋒£38
CTV 20P
V ☕ ✱Bar lunch £3.95—£4.45 Tea £2.30 High Tea £3.95 Dinner £11.50—£13.90 Wine £4.95 Last dinner 8pm
Credit cards 1 3

KINLOCH RANNOCH
Tayside *Perthshire*
Map **14** NN65

★★*Dunalastair* ☎(08822) 323
RS Nov—Apr
Charming old world hotel with wood panelled dining room.
23rm(10→)(4fb) ®
CTV 40P 3 ♿
☕ Last dinner 8.30pm
Credit cards 1 3

★★**Loch Rannoch** ☎(08822) 201
Impressive, late 19th-century hillside hotel with views of Loch Rannoch.
13→⋒ CTV in all bedrooms ® T S% sB&B→⋒£25—£32.50 dB&B→⋒£40—£65 B
☾40P ✿ (heated) (hard) squash snooker sauna bath solarium gymnasium dry ski-slope Disco wkly Live music and dancing wkly *xmas*
International V ☕ S% Lunch £2.50—£8&alc Tea 75p High Tea £4—£6&alc Dinner £10.75—£13.75&alc Wine £4.95 Last dinner 10pm
Credit cards 1 2 3 5 V

KINROSS
Tayside *Kinross-shire*
Map **11** NO10

★★★**Green** 2 The Muirs (Best Western) ☎(0577) 63467 Telex no 76684
Fully-modernised, former coaching inn standing in six acres of gardens.
45rm(39→6⋒)(6fb) CTV in all bedrooms T sB&B→⋒£38—£42 dB&B→⋒£52—£56 B
☾60P ✿ (heated) squash sauna bath solarium gymnasium curling rink Live music and dancing wkly CFA

Scottish & French Bar lunch
£2.50—£10 Tea £2.50—£3 High Tea
£2.50—£10 Dinner £12—£15&alc Wine
£6.10 Last dinner 9.30pm
Credit cards 1 2 3 4 5

★★★**Windlestrae** The Muirs ☎ (0577) 63217

Extensively refurbished, the former restaurant is now a comfortable hotel with 14 attractive bedrooms and a striking split-level lounge bar.

18 (3fb) CTV in all bedrooms ® T sB&B £25—£35 dB&B £35—£48 B

#60P 1 sauna bath *xmas*

International V Lunch £6.50—£7.95&alc Tea 95p—£1.25 Dinner £9.50—£12.50&alc Wine £4.60 Last dinner 9.30pm

Credit cards 1 2 3 5 V

○**Granada Lodge** M90 Motorway Service Area off junction 6 ☎ (0577) 63123

Expected to open Summer 1987

XX***Kirklands Hotel*** High St ☎ (0577) 63313

Once a coaching house, this friendly, personally-owned little restaurant stands in the centre of the town and features an attractive and reasonably-priced menu.

French 36 seats Last dinner 9.15pm 26P

Credit cards 2 3

KINTBURY
Berkshire
Map **4** SU36

XX**Dundas Arms** ☎ (0488) 58263

(*Rosette awarded for dinner only*)

A sensibly-chosen, mainly French menu with consistently high standards of cuisine is offered by this smart, cosy, international restaurant, which forms part of a popular pub. Its desirable location, quiet, comfortable lounge, cheerful service and good wine list make it a popular choice with local people.

Closed Sun, Mon & Xmas—New Year

English & French 36 seats *Lunch £8.50—£9.50 Dinner £12.50—£14&alc Wine £6.50 Last dinner 9.15pm 50P

Credit cards 1 2 3 5

KINVER
Staffordshire
Map **7** SO88

XXX**Berkleys (Piano Room)** High St ☎ (0384) 873679

The elegant piano room offers an extensive menu, while simpler fare is served in the ground floor restaurant.

Closed Sun Lunch not served

French 38 seats Dinner £16 Wine £5.25 Last dinner 10pm 12P Live music Fri & Sat

Credit cards 1 2 3 5

KIRBY MISPERTON
North Yorkshire
Map **8** SE77

★★**Beansheaf Restaurant Motel** Malton Rd ☎ (065386) 614

RS Mon

The established and noteworthy restaurant, set in rural surroundings, has added an accommodation wing and now offers well-equipped bedrooms, charmingly fitted out with pine furniture and modern fabrics.

12rm (1 11) 1 CTV in all bedrooms ® T S% sB&B £14.50—£21.50 dB&B £25—£30

CTV 60P *xmas*

English & Continental V Lunch £4.50—£4.80 Dinner fr £8&alc Wine £4.25 Last dinner 9.30pm

Credit card 3

KIRKBY FLEETHAM
North Yorkshire
Map **8** SE29

★★★ *HBL* **Kirkby Fleetham Hall** ☎ Northallerton (0609) 748226
Charming Georgian country house in 30 acres of splendid grounds, this friendly hotel, supervised by David and Chris Grant, offers delightfully furnished rooms and most interesting food, served in the attractive dining room overlooking the lake.
15 3 CTV in all bedrooms **T** S% sB&B £48 dB&B £64—£82
40P *xmas*
S% Lunch £8.50 (Sun only) Dinner £15.50 Wine £6 Last dinner 9.15pm
Credit cards 2 3

KIRKBY LONSDALE
Cumbria
Map **7** SD67

★★★ ***Royal*** Main St (Minotel) ☎ (0468) 71217
One-time coaching inn, now a well-furnished hotel, opposite the town square.
22rm (15 1)(1fb) 1 CTV in all bedrooms ® **T**
CTV 35P Live music twice wkly
V Last dinner 10pm
Credit cards 1 2 3 5

★**Red Dragon Inn** Main St ☎ (0468) 71205
RS Dec—Feb
Town centre inn offering modest accommodation.
8rm (1fb) sB&B £11 dB&B £20
CTV 6P 2
Bar lunch £2.20—£2.80 High Tea £2.20—£2.80 Dinner £5 Wine £3.80 Last dinner 7.30pm

KIRKBY MOORSIDE
North Yorkshire
Map **8** SE68

★★ ***George & Dragon*** Market Pl ☎ (0751) 31637
Closed 24—26 Dec
Welcoming 13th-century inn with modern bedrooms in converted stables.
14rm (10 4) Annexe: 9rm (5 1)(3fb) CTV in 18 bedrooms TV in 2 bedrooms ® in 22 bedrooms **T**
25P nc5yrs
International **V** Last dinner 9.30pm
Credit cards 1 3

KIRKBY STEPHEN
Cumbria
Map **12** NY70

★★ **King's Arms** Market St (Whitbread) ☎ (07683) 71378
Closed 25 Dec
Modernised 18th-century inn situated on the main street of this small town.
9rm (1 1)(1fb) ® in 3 bedrooms sB&B £18.50 sB&B £22.50 dB&B £30 dB&B £37.50
CTV 4P 6
Lunch £5.75 Dinner fr £6 Last dinner 9pm
Credit cards 1 3

KIRKCALDY
Fife
Map **11** NT29

★★★ **Dean Park** Chapel Level ☎ (0592) 261635
Closed 1 & 2 Jan
Two miles to the north of the town, off the A910, this business hotel offers modern bedrooms, a formal restaurant and limited lounge facilities. An annexe in the grounds comprises 12 compact, modern bungalows.
20 Annexe: 12 (5fb) CTV in all bedrooms ® **T** S% ✱ sB&B £33.50 dB&B £50
100P snooker sauna bath *xmas*
International **V** ✱ Lunch £5.25&alc Tea £1.50—£2.50 High Tea £2.50—£5.50 Dinner £8.50&alc Wine £4.20 Last dinner 9.45pm
Credit cards 1 2 3 4 5

★★ **Station** 4 Bennochy Rd ☎ (0592) 262461
Victorian hotel near to town centre opposite railway station.
34rm (5 8)(2fb) CTV in 9 bedrooms **T** ✱ sB&B fr £16 sB&B fr £22 dB&B fr £28 dB&B fr £36
CTV 25
V ✱ Bar lunch fr £3.50 Tea fr 60p High Tea £3.50—£4.50 Dinner £5.50—£8.50 Wine £4.50 Last dinner 9pm
Credit cards 1 2 3 5 Ⓥ

XXX **Oswald Room** (Dunnikier House Hotel) Dunnikier Park ☎ (0592) 268393
There is a pleasant and relaxing atmosphere to this restaurant, set in an Adam-style mansion which stands in Dunnikier Park, to the north of the town.
Dinner not served Sun
French & Italian **V** 50 seats Lunch £10.50&alc Dinner £10.50&alc Wine £5.50 Last dinner 9.45pm 100P
Credit cards 1 2 3 5

X **Shabab Tandoori** 274 High St ☎ (0592) 204166
Situated on the ground floor of a modern building at the east end of the busy High Street, the restaurant specialises in aromatically-spiced Indian food complemented by friendly and attentive service. The small fountain, with constantly changing coloured lights playing on its waters, is an unusual feature.
Indian **V** 64 seats Lunch £1.50—£5&alc Wine £4.75 Last dinner 11.30pm 10P
Credit cards 1 2 3 5

KIRKCOLM
Dumfries & Galloway *Wigtownshire*
Map **10** NX06

★★ **Knocknassie House** Ervie (3½m W off B738) ☎ (0776) 854217
Early 19th-century stone mansion in open countryside.
7rm (1 1)(2fb) TV in 5 bedrooms CTV in 2 bedrooms ® ✱ sB&B fr £13.50 sB&B fr £15 dB&B fr £27 dB&B fr £30
CTV 30P golf snooker
✱ Lunch £3—£5&alc Tea £2—£2.50&alc High Tea £4—£5&alc Dinner £5—£12&alc Wine £4.70 Last dinner 9pm

★ ***Corsewall Arms*** Main St ☎ (0776) 853228
Friendly hotel in small village.
11rm (1 1)(1fb)
CTV 20P
V Last dinner 8pm

KIRKCUDBRIGHT
Dumfries & Galloway *Kirkcudbrightshire*
Map **11** NX65

★★ **Selkirk Arms** High St ☎ (0557) 30402
18th-century two-storey inn, where Robert Burns wrote the 'Selkirk Grace'.
15rm (4 2) Annexe: 11rm (4)(5fb) CTV in 12 bedrooms ®
sB&B £15—£17.50
sB&B £17.50—£20.50
dB&B £30—£35 dB&B £35—£41
CTV 5P 16 *xmas*
V Lunch £3.50—£6.75&alc Tea £1.25—£2.95 High Tea £3.95—£4.95 Dinner £9.50&alc Wine £4.95 Last dinner 9.30pm
Credit cards 1 2 3 5 Ⓥ

X ***Ingle*** St Mary St ☎ (0557) 30606
Sitting in the centre of a picturesque fishing village, this unpretentious little restaurant is a real find in an area of Scotland sadly lacking in good eating houses. The proprietors are always on hand to maintain the standard and athenticity of the simply-prepared food, whilst the atmosphere of a country inn is created by stoneclad walls, woodwork and dimmed lighting.
Closed Mon & Feb Lunch not served
Italian 40 seats Last dinner 9.30pm
Credit cards 1 2 3 5

KIRKHILL
Highland *Inverness-shire*
Map **14** NH54

★ ***Bogroy*** (Located at junction A862/B9164) ☎ Drumchardine (046383) 240
RS Oct—Mar
The small, friendly, family-run hotel on the A862 about six miles from Inverness.

9rm(1fb) ✈ ⊞
200P
♔ ☕ Last dinner 8pm
Credit cards 1 2 3

KIRK LANGLEY
Derbyshire
Map **8** SK23

★★**Meynell Arms** Ashbourne Rd (Guestaccom) ☎ (033124) 515
Standing on the A52 just north of Derby and offering comfortable accommodation, this popular hotel was built in 1776 as a Georgian manor farm house.
10rm(4⇌1⋔)(2fb) 2⊟ CTV in all bedrooms ®sB&B£20—£22 sB&B⇌⋔£25 dB&B£33 dB&B⇌⋔£40 ⊞
100P ✽
V ♔ ☕ Lunch £6—£7 Tea 50p Dinner £6&alc Wine £5.50 Last dinner 9.30pm
Credit cards 1 2 3 5

KIRKMICHAEL
Tayside *Perthshire*
Map **15** NO06

★★*B* **Aldchlappie** ☎ Strathardle (025081) 224
Comfortable, attractively modernised, personally managed hotel.
6rm(5⇌)(1fb) ®sB&B£14—£16 dB&B⇌£32—£36 ⊞
CTV 20P 4⌂ ✽ ♪ nc 5yrs
♔ ☕ Lunch £4.50 Tea 50p—£1.50 Dinner £9.50—£11 Wine £4.40 Last dinner 9.30pm
Ⓥ

★★*H* **Log Cabin** (Exec Hotel) ☎ Strathardle (025081) 288 Telex no 76277
Closed mid Nov—mid Dec
Attractive log-built hotel, set 900 feet up amongst heather and pine forest.
13rm(7⇌6⋔)(5fb) ®S% sB&B⇌⋔£32.50—£38.50(incl dinner) dB&B⇌⋔£65—£77(incl dinner) ⊞
CTV 60P ✽ ♪ shooting ski-ing keep fit equipment ♿ *xmas*
V ♔ ☕ ⚡ S% Bar lunch £4alc Tea 75p alc Dinner £12.50alc Wine £5.25 Last dinner 9pm
Credit cards 1 2 3 5 Ⓥ

★**Strathlene** ☎ Strathardle (025081) 347
Small family-run hotel whose emphasis is on hospitality and good food.
7rm(1⇌)(2fb) ®S% sB&B£11—£12 sB&B⇌£13—£14 dB&B£22—£24 dB&B⇌£24—£26 ⊞
CTV 3P 🚌
V ♔ ☕ Bar lunch £2.50—£9.70 Tea 95p—£1.45 Dinner £9.50 Wine £3.90 Last dinner 8.30pm
Credit cards 1 2 3 Ⓥ

KIRKWALL
See **Orkney**

KIRKWHELPINGTON
Northumberland
Map **12** NY98

★★**Knowesgate** Knowesgate (Inter-Hotels) ☎ Otterburn (0830) 40261
Modern hotel complex.
16rm(8⇌8⋔) CTV in all bedrooms ®T S% sB&B⇌⋔£25—£30 dB&B⇌⋔£40—£46 ⊞
100P games room
V ♔ ☕ ⚡ Bar lunch £2—£7&alc Tea £2—£2.50&alc High Tea £2.50—£6&alc Dinner £9.50&alc Wine £4.10 Last dinner 9pm
Credit cards 1 2 3 5

KNARESBOROUGH
North Yorkshire
Map **8** SE35

★★★**Dower House** Bond End (Best Western) ☎ Harrogate (0423) 863302 Telex no 57453
Closed 25 Dec
Evidence can still be seen of the Tudor origins of this impressive building, although the hotel is now substantially modernised, with up-to-date facilities. Privately operated, it is nicely placed between the town centre and the river and its stylish restaurant overlooks well-kept gardens.
16rm(11⇌3⋔) Annexe: 4rm(3⇌1⋔)(2fb) CTV in all bedrooms ® in 4 bedrooms T ✱sB&Bfr£28 sB&B⇌⋔fr£30 dB&B£37.50 dB&B⇌⋔£47.50—£62.50 ⊞
☾ 100P ✽ 🏠
V ♔ ☕ ⚡ ✱ Lunch £6.95—£13.30&alc Tea 85p Dinner £9.25—£15.75 Wine £5.75 Last dinner 9pm
Credit cards 1 2 3 5

★★**Mitre** Station Rd ☎ Harrogate (0423) 863589
A Georgian-type building set in a picturesque part of town.
7rm(1⇌5⋔) CTV in all bedrooms ®T sB&B⇌⋔£25 dB&B⇌⋔£35 ⊞
CTV Ᵽ *xmas*
♔ English & French V ♔ ✱ Lunch £4alc Tea £2alc Dinner £8.50alc Wine £4.35 Last dinner 10pm
Credit cards 1 2 3 5 Ⓥ

KNIGHTWICK
Hereford & Worcester
Map **3** SO75

★**Talbot** ☎ (0886) 21235
A half-timbered inn, standing on the banks of the River Teme, offers friendly service and tempting menus in both bar and restaurant.
10rm(5⇌2⋔)(1fb) ®S% sB&B£14.25 sB&B⇌⋔£16.80 dB&B£22—£25.75 dB&B⇌⋔£32.50—£36.25
CTV 50P ✽ ♪ squash sauna bath
V ♔ ☕ S% Lunch £8.50alc Tea 80p alc Dinner £10alc Wine £4.25 Last dinner 9.45pm
Credit cards 1 3

KNIPOCH
Strathclyde *Argyllshire*
Map **10** NM82

★★★*BL* **Knipoch** (6m S of Oban) ☎ Kilninver (08526) 251
Closed Jan
The modernised and extended Georgian house is beautifully situated, overlooking Loch Feochan. Spacious bedrooms are tastefully furnished and thoughtfully equipped, lounges elegant and relaxing with leather armchairs and open fires.
21⇌⋔(2fb) CTV in all bedrooms T ✈ sB&B⇌⋔£40—£45 dB&B⇌⋔£80—£90 ⊞
40P ✽
♔ European ♔ Bar lunch £8alc Dinner £23.50 Wine £4.50 Last dinner 9.30pm
Credit cards 1 2 3 5

KNOCK
Isle of Skye, Highland *Inverness-shire*
See **Skye, Isle of**

KNOWLE
West Midlands
Map **7** SP17

★★***Greswolde Arms*** High St (Golden Oak Inns) ☎ (05645) 2711
Elegant hotel in the centre of the village.
19rm(6⋔) CTV in all bedrooms ® ✈ ⊞
CTV 100P
♔ Last dinner 10pm
Credit cards 1 2 3

KNUTSFORD
Cheshire
Map **7** SJ77

★★★*B* **Cottons** Manchester Rd ☎ (0565) 50333 Telex no 669931
This well-designed and thoughtfully-appointed hotel provides very good bedrooms and suites, public areas based on a New Orleans theme (as is the well-prepared food), and an indefinably special quality of service.
60⇌(8fb) 1⊟ CTV in all bedrooms ®T S% sB&B⇌£55—£63 dB&B⇌£65—£80 ⊞
Lift ☾ CTV 160P ⊡(heated) sauna bath solarium gymnasium
♔ English, Creole, French & New Orleans V ♔ ☕ S% Lunch fr£8&alc Tea fr£2.50 Dinner fr£10&alc Wine £6.55 Last dinner 9.45pm
Credit cards 1 2 3 5

★**Rose & Crown** King St ☎ (0565) 52366
Former coaching inn, built in 1647 and restored in 1923, but retaining its original Tudor style.
16rm(2➡3⋔)(4fb) 1⊞ CTV in all bedrooms ®T sB&B£18—£24 sB&B➡⋔£23—£29 dB&B£28—£34 dB&B➡⋔£33—£39
25P ⊞
♕English & American **V** ♕Lunch £4alc Dinner £7alc Wine £4.70 Last dinner 10pm
Credit cards 1 2 3 Ⓥ

✕✕***La Belle Èpoque*** 60 King St ☎ (0565) 3060
Set in an Italian-style building, and virtually a shrine to Art Nouveau, this first-class French restaurant provides an excellent setting in which to enjoy expertly prepared and attractively presented food. The bar contains Chinese Chippendale chairs and Venetian glass, while the Edwardian-style restaurant features Gaudez's bronze statue Faucheur. Service is friendly and professional, the wine list extensive.
Closed Sun, Bank Hols & 1st wk Jan Lunch not served
♕French **V** 85 seats Last dinner 10pm ⚡
Credit cards 1 2 3 4 5

K

✕✕**David's Place** 10 Princess St ☎ (0565) 3356
The cuisine offered at this cosy, charmingly old-fashioned, High Street restaurant is mainly French, though menus do include Italian and other international specialities. Guests can enjoy a pre-dinner drink in the small, brick-walled bar with its open fire before going into one of the two dining rooms, where candlelit tables create an intimate atmosphere.
Closed Sun
♕International 70 seats ✱Lunch £6—£17alc Dinner £10.50&alc Wine £4.80 Last dinner 10pm ₱
Credit cards 1 2 3

KYLE OF LOCHALSH
Highland *Ross & Cromarty*
Map **13** NG72

★★★**Lochalsh** Ferry Rd ☎ Kyle (0599) 4202 Telex no 75318
Closed Xmas wk
Situated in a prominent position, with fine views across the Kyle of Lochalsh to Skye.
40rm(38➡)(4fb) CTV in all bedrooms ®T S% sB&B£25—£46 sB&B➡⋔£25—£46 dB&B➡⋔£50—£95
Lift ☾ 30P 6⌂ ✿ motor boat
♕Scottish & French **V** ♕ ☕ S% Lunch £4.25—£8 Tea £1.50—£1.75 Dinner £14.50&alc Wine £8.25 Last dinner 9pm
Credit cards 1 2 3 4 5

KYLESKU
Highland *Sutherland*
Map **14** NC23

★**Kylesku** ☎ Kylestrome (097183) 231
End Oct—Mar
The simple, homely hotel stands beside the now-obsolete ferry ramp; its restaurant features freshly-caught seafood at very reasonable prices.
7rm ®✱sB&B£12 dB&B£24
CTV 12P ⊞ ♪
♕ ☕ ✱Bar lunch £4alc Tea 60p alc Dinner £10alc Wine £4.50 Last dinner 8pm
Credit card 1 Ⓥ

LACEBY
Humberside
Map **8** TA20

★★★***Oaklands*** Barton St ☎ Grimsby (0472) 72248
The converted Victorian country house stands in its own grounds surrounded by agricultural land. The original rooms have been supplemented by two modern extensions, and the restaurant and lounges have been restored to retain some original features.
49rm(47➡2⋔)(3fb) 1⊞ CTV in all bedrooms ®T
☾ 200P CFA ✿ ⊟(heated) sauna bath solarium Live music & dancing wkly ⛹
♕English & Continental ♕ ☕ Last dinner 9.30pm
Credit cards 1 2 3 5

LACOCK
Wiltshire
Map **3** ST96

✕**Sign of the Angel** ☎ (024973) 230
The restaurant, which offers some bedroom accommodation, is a charming, 15th century, half-timbered building set at the centre of the lovely National Trust village. Beneath the old beams of the two dining rooms, where open log fires burn during the winter months, traditional roasts and game dishes are served with excellent fresh vegetables and a choice of several excellent starters and desserts, all complemented by a very good wine list.
Closed 23 Dec—2 Jan
Lunch not served Sat
Dinner not served Sun
40 seats ✱Lunch £10—£12.50 Dinner £16.50 Wine £6 Last dinner 8.15pm 2P

LAGG
Isle of Arran, Strathclyde *Bute*
See **Arran, Isle of**

LAIRG
Highland *Sutherland*
Map **14** NC50

★★★**Sutherland Arms** (Scottish Highland) ☎ (0549) 2291 Telex no 778215
Closed Nov—Mar
Stone-built hotel with views over the River Shin and dam.
25rm(18➡2⋔)(3fb) ®sB&B£29 sB&B➡⋔£32 dB&B£48 dB&B➡⋔£54 ⊞
CTV 30P ✿ ⛹ ♿
V ♕ ☕ Bar lunch £2—£5 Tea 75p—£1.50 Dinner £10—£10.50 Wine £5.60 Last dinner 8.30pm
Credit cards 1 2 3 5

LAMLASH
Isle of Arran, Strathclyde *Bute*
See **Arran, Isle of**

LAMORNA COVE
Cornwall
Map **2** SW42
★★★ *HL* **Lamorna Cove** (Inter Hotel) ☎ Penzance (0736) 731411
Closed Dec & Jan
Comfortable character hotel with well appointed bedrooms, in attractive Lamorna Valley.
19rm(15 4)(3fb) 1 CTV in all bedrooms **T** ✱ sB&B £27—£38 dB&B £34.95—£45.95
Lift 30P ✿ (heated) sauna bath solarium
V Wine £5 Last dinner 7.30pm
Credit cards 1 2 3 5 V

LAMPETER
Dyfed
Map **2** SN54
★★★ **Falcondale Country House** ☎ (0570) 422910
RS Sun Nov—Mar
Well appointed family run hotel in most attractive grounds.
22rm(7 15)(8fb) CTV in all bedrooms ® **T** sB&B £28 dB&B £36
Lift CTV 60P ✿ *xmas*

International **V** Lunch £8.50 Tea £3 Dinner £8.50&alc Wine £4.95 Last dinner 9.30pm
Credit cards 1 3
See advertisement on page 398

★★ **Black Lion Royal** High St ☎ (0570) 422172
RS Sun
This old coaching inn has pleasant bedrooms and convivial bars.
15rm(6 1)(2fb) CTV in all bedrooms ® sB&B £16 sB&B £18 dB&B £27 dB&B £30
CTV 50P ✿ Disco Wed Fri Sat *xmas*
English & French **V** Lunch £5—£6.75&alc Dinner £6.75—£7.25&alc Wine £4.25 Last dinner 9pm
Credit cards 1 3 V
See advertisement on page 398

LAMPHEY
Dyfed
Map **2** SN00
★★★ **Court** (Best Western) ☎ (0646) 672273 Telex no 48587
Imposing small country house with comfortable bedrooms and small leisure complex.
22rm(21 1)(6fb) 4 CTV in all bedrooms **T** S%
sB&B £29.50—£37.50
dB&B £42.50—£53.50
100P CFA ✿ (heated) sauna bath solarium gymnasium *xmas*
S% Lunch £6.95—£10.50 Tea 90p—£3 Dinner £10.50&alc Wine £5.95 Last dinner 9.30pm
Credit cards 1 2 3 5 V
See advertisement under Pembroke

LANARK
Strathclyde *Lanarkshire*
Map **11** NS84
✕✕ **Ristorante La Vigna** 40 Wellgate ☎ (0555) 4320
This small, street-level restaurant with tasteful appointments specialises in Italian cuisine supported by a good range of mainly Italian wines and very friendly, attentive service.
Lunch not served Sun
Italian **V** 40 seats Lunch £15alc Dinner £15alc Wine £6.15 Last dinner 10.45pm
Credit cards 1 2 3 5

LANCASTER
Lancashire
Map **7** SD46

★★★★**Post House** Waterside Park, Caton Rd (close to junc 34 M6) (Trusthouse Forte) ☎ (0524) 65999 Telex no 65363

Modern, well furnished riverside hotel with very comfortable bedrooms.

117 (23fb) CTV in all bedrooms ®T sB&B £54.50 dB&B £70.50 B

Lift ☾ 180P ✽ (heated) sauna bath solarium gymnasium ♿ *xmas*

Last dinner 10.30pm

Credit cards 1 2 3 4 5 Ⓥ

LANGBANK
Strathclyde *Renfrewshire*
Map **10** NS37

❀★★★ *B* **Gleddoch House**
(see rosette box in next column)

Lancaster — Langho

❀★★★ *B* **Gleddoch House**
☎ (047554) 711 Telex no 779801

Closed 26—27 Dec & 1—2 Jan

Once the home of a Clydeside shipping magnate, the hotel has splendid view northward across the River Clyde and Dumbarton towards Ben Lomond. Despite extension and modernisation, the house retains a graciously calm atmosphere. A sports club adjoining the hotel offers golf, squash, snooker and horse riding. Innovative meals prepared by Charles Price, fast establishing himself as one of Scotland's leading chefs, are served in the spacious restaurant.

20 1 CTV in all bedrooms ®T sB&B £59—£66 dB&B £78—£95 B

☾ 100P ✽ 18 squash U snooker sauna bath *xmas*

Scottish & French **V** Lunch £8.25—£11.50&alc Dinner £19.50&alc Wine £6.75 Last dinner 9pm

Credit cards 1 2 3 4 5 Ⓥ

LANGDALE, GREAT
Cumbria
Map **11** NY30

★★★**Pillar** Langdale Estate
☎ (09667) 302 Telex no 65188

In a beautiful setting, this new hotel offers very good accommodation and extensive leisure facilities.

36 (19fb) CTV in all bedrooms ®T sB&B £58—£68 dB&B £70—£82 B

☾ 200P ✽ (heated) squash U sauna bath solarium gymnasium Disco Wed & Sat *xmas*

English & French **V** Lunch £1.95—£5.50&alc Dinner £4.95—£17&alc Wine £6.45 Last dinner 10pm

Credit cards 1 2 3 5

LANGHO
Lancashire
Map **7** SD73

XXX**Northcote Manor** Northcote Rd
☎ Blackburn (0254) 40555 Telex no 635359

This comfortable country house forms an attractive hotel and restaurant. The mainly British menu features expertly prepared food with friendly, efficient service. →

L

Closed Mon, 25, 26 Dec & 1 Jan Lunch not served Sat

English & French V 70 seats Lunch £6.25—£7.50&alc Dinner £17alc Wine £6 Last dinner 9.30pm 50P Live music Fri & Sat

Credit cards 1 2 3 5

LANGHOLM
Dumfries & Galloway *Dumfriesshire*
Map **11** NY38

★★**Eskdale** Market Pl (Minotel) ☎ (0541) 80357

Built on the site of the former King's Arms Inn, a famous coaching hostelry.

15rm(5)(2fb) in 3 bedrooms CTV in all bedrooms ® sB&B£14.50—£15.50 sB&B£16—£17.50 dB&B£26—£27 dB&B£28.50—£30 B

CTV 10P solarium gymasium *xmas*

Lunch £5alc Dinner £8.75alc Wine £4.30 Last dinner 9.30pm

Credit cards 1 3

★**Crown** High St ☎ (0541) 80247

Homely family run hotel in town centre.

8rm(1fb) CTV in all bedrooms ® sB&B£13.50 dB&B£26

4P

Bar lunch £2.50—£5 Dinner £5—£10 Wine £4.50 Last dinner 9pm

Credit cards 1 3

L

Langho — Langland Bay

★**Holmwood House** Holmwood Dr (off B709) ☎ (0541) 80211

Neatly-appointed, Victorian house, situated on the edge of a housing estate.

7rm(1 1)(1fb) ® sB&B£12.50 sB&B£14 dB&B£22 dB&B£25

CTV 25P

S% Lunch fr£4 Tea fr£1.50 High Tea fr£4 Dinner fr£6.50&alc Wine £4 Last dinner 9.30pm

LANGLAND BAY
West Glamorgan
Map **2** SS68
See also **Mumbles** and **Swansea**

★★★**Osborne** Rotherslade Rd (Embassy) ☎ Swansea (0792) 66274 due to change to (0792) 366274

Popular hotel on clifftop, offering warm and friendly service.

36rm(29)(2fb) CTV in all bedrooms ® T S% sB&B£30—£40 sB&B£42.50—£45 dB&B£45—£53 dB&B£53—£60 B

Lift 40P

Welsh, English & French V S% *Lunch fr£5.50&alc Tea 75p—£2.20 Dinner fr£8.10&alc Wine £4.45 Last dinner 8.45pm

Credit cards 1 2 3 4 5 V

See advertisement under Swansea

★★***Brynfield Manor*** Brynfield Rd ☎ Swansea (0792) 66208

Small country house style hotel with friendly service and commendable food.

12rm(6)(2fb) CTV in 10 bedrooms ® B

CTV 35P

V Last dinner 9.30pm

Credit cards 1 2 3

★★*B* **Langland Court** Langland Court Rd (Best Western) ☎ Swansea (0792) 61545 Telex no 498037

The small, personally-run hotel has received major upgrading recently and now offers very comfortable, modern bedrooms, well equipped and individually decorated. In the wood-panelled dining room you can rely on quality cooking standards and prompt, friendly service, whilst outside there are attractive small gardens with good views over Swansea Bay.

16 Annexe: 5(7fb) 1 in 1 bedroom CTV in all bedrooms ® T sB&B£30—£40 dB&B£40—£60 B

40P 6🚗(£1.50)✿croquet ♤

🍷English & Continental **V** 🍷Bar lunch £3.50—£5.50 High Tea £8.50—£9.50(summer only) Dinner £8.50—£11&alc Wine £5 Last dinner 9.30pm

Credit cards [1] [2] [3] [5] Ⓥ

★**Ael-y-Don** ☎ Swansea (0792) 66466 due to change to (0792) 366466

Closed Nov—Feb

A small family-run hotel with sea views.

15rm(1🛁5🚿)(4fb) Ⓡ✗ sB&B£14—£15 sB&B🛁🚿£15—£16 dB&B£28—£30 dB&B🛁🚿£30—£32 **B**

CTV 12P 3🚗✿ nc 5yrs

🍷✗Lunch £4.50—£5 Dinner £4.95—£5.50 Wine £3.95 Last dinner 7.30pm

Ⓥ

LANGSTONE

Gwent
Map **3** ST38

★★*B* ***New Inn Motel*** (Golden Oak Inns) ☎ Newport (063341) 2426

Conveniently sited just off the M4 north-east of Newport, this comfortable small motel has quality bedrooms and popular restaurant and bar facilities.

36rm(3🛁33🚿)(1fb) CTV in all bedrooms ⓇT✗**B**

CTV 200P

Langland Bay — Largs

🍷Last dinner 10pm

Credit cards [1] [2] [3]

LANREATH

Cornwall
Map **2** SX15

★★**Punch Bowl Inn** ☎ (0503) 20218

Closed Nov—Mar

Early 17th-century, former coaching inn and smugglers' haunt, whose sign was painted by Augustus John.

18rm(11🛁2🚿)(2fb) 4🛏 CTV in all bedrooms Ⓡ sB&B£12—£15.25 sB&B🛁🚿£15.25—£18.50 dB&B£24—£30.50 dB&B🛁🚿£30.50—£37

CTV 50P 2🚗(£1 per night) ✿

V 🍷Bar lunch £5alc High Tea £5alc Dinner £7.95&alc Wine £3.80 Last dinner 9.30pm

Credit cards [1] [3]

See advertisement under Looe

LARGS

Strathclyde *Ayrshire*
Map **10** NS25

★★**Elderslie** John St, Broomfields ☎ (0475) 686460

Closed Xmas & Boxing day

A 19th-century building on Largs sea-front, commanding magnificent views.

25rm(9🛁4🚿) Ⓡ sB&B£19.50 sB&B🛁🚿£22 dB&B£39 dB&B🛁🚿£44 **B**

CTV 30P ✿ ♤

🍷Lunch £5.50—£7.50 High Tea £4.25 Dinner £8.50—£10.50 Wine £4.50 Last dinner 8.30pm

Credit cards [1] [2] [3] [5] Ⓥ

★★**Springfield** Greenock Rd ☎ (0475) 673119

Resort hotel with continental-style dining room. Many bedrooms have sea views.

45rm(3🛁28🚿)(5fb) CTV available sB&B£16 sB&B🛁🚿£19 dB&B£27.50 dB&B🛁🚿£34

Lift CTV 80P Live music & dancing twice wkly *xmas*

🍷Scottish & French 🍷Lunch £3.25—£5 High Tea £4—£10.50 Dinner £8&alc Wine £2.95 Last dinner 8pm

Credit cards [1] [2] [3] [5]

LARKFIELD
Kent
Map **5** TQ65
★★★**Larkfield** London Rd (Anchor)
☎ West Malling (0732) 846858 Telex no 957420
Professional, well managed hotel with modern, well appointed bedrooms, an à la carte restaurant and welcoming staff.
52rm(48⇌4ⓕ)1⊟⚡in 5 bedrooms CTV in all bedrooms ®T
sB&B⇌ⓕ£43.50—£50.50 dB&B⇌ⓕ£53 B
☾95P CFA ❀ *xmas*
English & French V ♀ ☕⚡ Lunch £8.95&alc Tea 75p Dinner £9.95&alc Wine £5.95 Last dinner 10pm
Credit cards 1 2 3 5 Ⓥ

✕✕✕**Wealden Hall** 773 London Rd
☎ West Malling (0732) 840259
Franco Italian cuisine served in attractive wooden beamed surroundings.
French & Italian 60 seats ✱Lunch £7.95&alc Dinner £9.50&alc Last dinner 10.30pm 20P
Credit cards 1 2 3 5

LASTINGHAM
North Yorkshire
Map **8** SE79
★★ *H* **Lastingham Grange**
☎ (07515) 345
Closed mid Dec—Feb
A 17th-century house of local stone, with extensive gardens, to which a wing was added during the last century.
12⇌(2fb) CTV in all bedrooms ®T
✱sB&B⇌£33.75 dB&B⇌£61 B
30P 2 ❀
V ♀ ☕⚡✱Lunch £6.50—£8.25 Tea £1.95—£2.25 Dinner £11.50—£11.75 Wine £3.75 Last dinner 8.30pm
Credit cards 2 5

LAUDER
Borders *Berwickshire*
Map **12** NT54
★★**Black Bull** Market Pl ☎ (05782) 208
The personally-run hotel, formerly a coaching inn, stands on the main road of the town.
13rm(5ⓕ)(2fb) ®S% sB&Bfr£17 sB&Bⓕfr£18 dB&Bfr£34 dB&Bⓕfr£36
Lift ☾ ## CTV 30P(charge) ❀ *xmas*
V ♀ ☕ S% Lunch fr£5&alc Tea fr£2 High Tea £4—£5&alc Dinner £8.50—£10.60&alc Wine £5 Last dinner 9.30pm

LAUNCESTON
Cornwall
Map **2** SX38
★★**White Hart** Broad St (Best Western)
☎ (0566) 2013
Former coaching inn with modern facilities.
25rm(15⇌5ⓕ)(2fb) CTV in 20 bedrooms ®in 20 bedrooms T sB&B£14.50 sB&B⇌ⓕ£17 dB&B£26 dB&B⇌ⓕ£32 B
CTV 25P CFA snooker *xmas*
V ♀ ☕ Lunch £5.25 Tea £1.25 High Tea £2.75 Dinner £8 Wine £4.25 Last dinner 9.45pm
Credit cards 1 2 3 4 5 Ⓥ

LAVENHAM
Suffolk
Map **5** TL94
★★★ *L* **Swan** High St (Trusthouse Forte)
☎ (0787) 247477
Four picturesque Tudor houses with beamed ceilings, make up this fine hotel.
48⇌ CTV in all bedrooms ®
sB&B⇌£52.50 dB&B⇌£72 B
CTV 60P ❀ *xmas*
♀ ☕ Last dinner 9.45pm
Credit cards 1 2 3 4 5

LEA *near Matlock*
Derbyshire
Map **8** SK35

✕**Coach House** ☎ Dethick (062984) 346
Forming the heart of an interesting complex set on high ground above the Derwent Valley just south of Matlock, the comfortable country restaurant occupies the old stables and tack rooms of a 75-year-old model farm. The farm's Jersey herd supplies the restaurant kitchen with dairy produce, their ice cream being particularly noteworthy.
Dinner not served Sun
British & French **V** 38 seats Lunch £1—£2.25&alc Dinner fr£8.50&alc Wine £4.50 Last dinner 9.45pm 40P

LEAMINGTON SPA (ROYAL)
Warwickshire
Map **4** SP36

★★★**Manor House** Avenue Rd (Anchor) ☎ (0926) 23251 Telex no 311653
Large hotel near station with choice of restaurants and ample conference facilities.
53rm(48 5)(2fb) in 6 bedrooms CTV in all bedrooms ®**T** *sB&B £43 dB&B £53 **B**
Lift ☾ 100P 2 CFA *xmas*
V Lunch fr£5.25 Tea 50p High Tea £3.90 Dinner £9.25 Wine £5.95 Last dinner 10pm
Credit cards 1 2 3 5

★★★

★★★ MALLORY COURT, LEAMINGTON SPA

Harbury Ln, Bishop's Tachbrook (2m S off A452) (Relais et Châteaux)
☎ (0926) 30214 Telex no 317294
Closed 26 Dec—1 Jan

This handsome stone house was built in the twenties and stands in 10 acres of delightful gardens with terraced water gardens; there is a croquet lawn and a squash court as well as the swimming pool. All is immaculately kept, from the reception rooms to the luxurious bedrooms. The former consist of the fresh looking drawing room and the more masculine one with bookshelves. Both feature open fires in season and the house is fresh with lovely soft furnishings and flowers. The two panelled dining rooms are extremely well appointed. Jeremy Mort and Alan Holland are the owners who have created this elegant hotel and they ensure that you will be well looked after by the cheerful and friendly young staff. It is Alan Holland who supervises the kitchen. Breakfasts are excellent; at lunch there is a shorter menu, but at dinner he serves a 3-course meal priced according to the main course chosen. The style is modern French but British dishes are not forgotten, particularly puddings, so that there is something for everyone. Their mousselines and parfaits are flavoursome, sauces are delicate allowing the flavour of the fish or meat to come through, yet zestful; vegetables have been described as near perfect, while puddings such as passion fruit soufflé with orange sorbet and treacle tart have been thought quite delightful. You will also be able to find something to please you from the long wine list.

9 (1fb) 1 CTV in all bedrooms **T** S% dB&B £72—£115 Continental breakfast
50P 6 (£2 per night) squash nc12yrs
French S% Lunch £16.50 Tea £6.25 Dinner £28.75 Wine £6.75 Last dinner 9.45pm
Credit cards 1 2 3

★★★**Falstaff** 20 Warwick New Rd
☎ (0926) 312044
Neat Victorian house with attractive wood-faced modern extension and a small garden.
54rm(28 23)(3fb) 2 CTV in all bedrooms ®**T** S% sB&B £26—£35 dB&B £50 **B**
Lift ☾ 80P CFA *xmas*
English & French **V** S% Lunch £5—£8&alc Tea 50p Dinner £8—£9&alc Wine £5.45 Last dinner 9.15pm
Credit cards 1 2 3 4 5

★★★**Regent** 77 The Parade (Best Western) ☎ (0926) 27231 Telex no 311715
Traditional, town centre hotel.
80 (7fb) 1 CTV in all bedrooms ®**T** sB&B £37.25—£51 dB&B £51.25—£76.50 **B**
Lift ☾ CTV 70P 30 CFA *xmas*
English, French & Italian S% Lunch fr£7.35 Tea fr£1 Dinner fr£10 Wine £5 Last dinner 10.45pm
Credit cards 1 2 3 5

★★***Abbacourt*** 40 Kenilworth Rd
☎ (0926) 311188
Large converted house, popular with business people.
21rm(3 6) CTV in 11 bedrooms TV in 10 bedrooms ® **B**
CTV 27P
Continental **V** Last dinner 9.30pm
Credit cards 1 2 3 5

★★**Angel** 143 Regent St
☎ (0926) 881296
Standing near to the town centre, the Regency-style hotel has half-timbered interior decor and a select, friendly restaurant.
16 (4fb) CTV in all bedrooms ®**T** (ex guide dogs)
sB&B £29.50—£33.50
dB&B £34.50—£39.50 **B**
☾ 40P
English & French **V** S% Lunch fr£6.25&alc Tea 75p Dinner £8.95—£10&alc Wine £5.50 Last dinner 9.45pm
Credit cards 1 2 3

★★**Beech Lodge** Warwick New Rd
☎ (0926) 22227
A large, Victorian, private house, standing on the main road to Warwick just west of the town centre, has been converted to provide comfortable modern accommodation suitable for both commercial and tourist trade.
13rm(6) CTV in 6 bedrooms ®
sB&B £23.25 sB&B £27.50 dB&B £37 dB&B £42 **B**
CTV 14P nc4yrs
English & French Bar lunch £4alc Tea £3alc Dinner £9alc Wine £5.50 Last dinner 7.30pm
Credit cards 1 3
See advertisement on page 404

★**Lansdowne**
(see red star box on next page)

LECHLADE
Gloucestershire
Map **4** SU29

✕**Weylands** 6 Oak St ☎ Faringdon (0367) 52587
Accurately described by the proprietor as a "continental kitchen", this tiny but charming restaurant serves good, interesting food complemented by a short but sound wine list and friendly service — the whole representing excellent value for money.
Continental **V** 18 seats S% Lunch £5.95—£7.50&alc Dinner £10.50alc Wine £4.75 Last dinner 10pm

LECKMELM
Highland *Ross & Cromarty*
Map **14** NH19

★**Tir-Aluinn** ☎ Ullapool (0854) 2074
Closed 30 Sep—20 May
Country house hotel quietly situated on the shores of Loch Broom. →

L

★LANSDOWNE, LEAMINGTON SPA

87 Clarendon St ☎ (0926) 21313
Telex no 337556

RS 26 Dec—12 Jan

We have received many commendations for this hotel but have been slow to award Red Stars because it is so dissimilar to most of our others. But if you take it for what it is: a comfortable, small hotel at a very reasonable cost, we do not think you will be disappointed. It is owned and professionally run by David and Gillian Allen who seem to care for their guests in the most amiable manner. Very helpful, they make you feel at ease. One or two bedrooms are rather small but they are comfortable and quite well equipped for the hotel's classification. On the ground floor there is a small lounge with TV and bar, and the traditionally furnished dining room — where you will enjoy wholesome decently cooked food. The building is Regency period, situated just off the town centre, so that

it is suitable for business people as well as tourists.

10rm(1➡2⋒)(1fb) ✈
sB&B£19.95—£22.85
sB&B➡⋒£26.85—£29.50
dB&B£31.90—£32.90
dB&B➡⋒£33.90—£34.90 ₿
CTV 8P ⊞ nc 5yrs
English, French & German **V**
Lunch £7.95 Dinner £9.65 Wine £5.65 Last dinner 8.30pm
Credit card 1

16rm(3➡)(3fb) sB&B£12.65 sB&B➡£14
dB&B£25.30 dB&B➡£28
CTV 30P ⊞ ✽ ♿
V Bar lunch £1.50—£3 Tea £1
Dinner £5.75 Wine £3.50 Last dinner 8pm

L

LEDBURY
Hereford & Worcester
Map **3** SO73

★★★**Feathers** High St ☎ (0531) 5266

Friendly, attentive service is a feature of this attractive hotel, housed in an Elizabethan building at the heart of the town. The Quills Restaurant offers both an interesting à la carte and a grill menu.

11➡(1fb) CTV in all bedrooms Ⓡ**T**
sB&B➡£33—£35 dB&B➡£49.50 ₿
☾30P 15 ⊞ squash *xmas*
English & French **V** Lunch £8.20—£8.45 Tea 80p Dinner £8.20&alc Wine £4.90 Last dinner 9.30pm
Credit cards 1 2 5 Ⓥ

✽★★ *HBL* **Hope End Country House** Hope End (2½m NE unclass)
☎ (0531) 3613

Closed Dec—Feb & Mon & Tue
(Rosette awarded for dinner only)

A beautifully restored house in idyllic countryside. This hotel offers peace and comfort, yet a convenient touring base. The fine cooking uses best home grown produce and rare English cheeses are a speciality. The style is French and English country cooking, and there is an extensive, good value wine list. Hotel is closed Monday night and Tuesday night.

5➡ Annexe: 2➡ CTV in 1 bedroom
Ⓡ✈ S% dB&B➡£58—£66 ₿
10P ⊞ ✽ nc 14yrs ♿
S% Dinner £18alc Wine £4 Last dinner 8.30pm
Credit cards 1 3

★★**Royal Oak** The Southend ☎ (0531) 2110

RS Xmas Day

Built in 1643, but boasting comfortable modern bedrooms, this fine old coaching inn stands in the main street of the town.

8rm(4⋒)(1fb) CTV in 5 bedrooms Ⓡ✈
✱sB&B£14—£25 sB&B⋒£25
dB&B£25—£34.50 dB&B⋒£34.50
CTV 4P 4 ⊞ snooker
V ✱Bar lunch £1.50—£4 Dinner £6—£7alc Wine £3.75 Last dinner 9.30pm
Credit cards 1 3

★★**Verzons** Trumpet (3m W A438)
☎ Trumpet (053183) 381

Comfortable, country hotel with a popular restaurant.

7rm(3➡1⋒)(1fb) CTV in all bedrooms Ⓡ
S% sB&B£15—£17 sB&B➡⋒£19—£20
dB&B£23—£25 dB&B➡⋒£28—£32 ₿
CTV 40P ⊞ ✽
English & French **V** Lunch £6.50—£7.50&alc Tea £1alc High Tea £3alc Dinner £6.50—£7.50&alc Wine £4.80 Last dinner 10pm
Credit cards 1 2 3 5 Ⓥ

LEE
Devon
Map **2** SS44

★★★**Lee Bay** Lee Bay (Best Western)
☎ Ilfracombe (0271) 63503

Peacefully set in a craggy cove, this family holiday and conference hotel has gracious public rooms and attractive bistro and bar.

50➡(25fb) 1⊟ CTV in all bedrooms Ⓡ**T**
✱sB&B➡£26.45—£28.75
dB&B➡⋒£52.90—£57.50
☾100P ✽ ⛆(heated) U snooker sauna bath solarium gymnasium Live music and dancing 3 nights wkly *xmas*
English & French **V** ✱Lunch £3—£6.50 Tea 90p—£1.50 High Tea £3.50 Dinner £11.50&alc Wine £5.60 Last dinner 9.30pm
Credit cards 1 2 3 5 Ⓥ

★★ Lee Manor Country House Hotel & Restaurant Lee Bay (3m W on unclass road) ☎ Ilfracombe (0271) 63920

Closed Nov—Mar RS Xmas & New Year

Originally a 19th-century country house, Lee Manor was subsequently restored as a fine replica of a Tudor mansion, one example of the conversion being the minstrels' gallery that stands above a dining room where good food can be enjoyed in front of the huge log fire.

12rm (6 9) 1 CTV in 3 bedrooms TV in 9 bedrooms ® ✱ sB&B £17—£22 dB&B £30—£52

20P nc 12yrs *xmas*

English & Continental ✱ Lunch £6.50 Dinner £8.50&alc Wine £4.95 Last dinner 9pm

LEEDS
West Yorkshire
Map **8** SE33

★★★★ **Ladbroke Dragonara** Neville St (Ladbroke) ☎ (0532) 442000 Telex no 557143

Modern tower-block hotel in the centre of Leeds, next to the railway station.

234rm (205 29) (3fb) in 30 bedrooms CTV in all bedrooms ® T ✱ sB £52.50—£70 dB £76—£90 (room only) B

Lift ☾ ## 80P CFA ♿

Lee — Leeds

French V Lunch £7.50—£10 Tea £2 Dinner £10.95—£18&alc Wine £6 Last dinner 10pm

Credit cards 1 2 3 5 V

★★★★ **Queen's** City Sq (Trusthouse Forte) ☎ (0532) 431323 Telex no 55161

Impressive eight-storey building with a Portland stone façade adjoining the City station.

205rm (183) CTV in all bedrooms ® sB&B £53 dB&B £74 B

Lift ☾ 20P CFA sauna bath

Last dinner 10pm

Credit cards 1 2 3 4 5

★★★ **Crest** The Grove ☎ (0532) 826201

(For full entry see Oulton)

★★★ **Ladbroke** (& Conferencentre) Garforth Rbt ☎ (0532) 866556

(For full entry see Garforth)

See advertisement on page 406

★★★ ***Merrion*** Merrion Centre (Kingsmead) ☎ (0532) 439191 Telex no 55459

This smart, comfortable, modern, city-centre hotel provides stylish bedrooms. The Starlets Restaurant has an attractive Victorian Music Hall theme and offers an imaginative à la carte menu.

120 (4fb) CTV in all bedrooms ® T (ex guide dogs) B

Lift ☾ 100 CFA Live music & dancing Fri & Sat Cabaret Fri & Sat *xmas*

V Last dinner 10.30pm

Credit cards 1 2 3 5

★★★ **Metropole** King St (Trusthouse Forte) ☎ (0532) 450841 Telex no 557755

Victorian central hotel with modern bedrooms and carvery style restaurant.

114rm (70 6) CTV in all bedrooms ® sB&B £37.50 sB&B £45.50 dB&B £53.50 dB&B £61.50 B

Lift ☾ 28P CFA

Last dinner 10.15pm

Credit cards 1 2 3 4 5

★★★ **Stakis Windmill** Mill Green View Seacroft (Stakis) ☎ (0532) 732323

The modern hotel features well-appointed bedrooms and a restaurant which is one of the popular Stakis Steakhouses, offering an interesting menu with daily variation. →

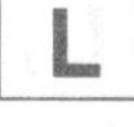

100⇌⫛✗ in 10 bedrooms CTV in all bedrooms ® T ✗(ex guide dogs) S% sB⇌⫛£45.90—£48.90 dB⇌⫛£57.80—£61.80(room only) B
Lift ☾ ## 200P ♿ *xmas*
English, French & Italian S% Lunch £5.95—£6.55 Tea 70p—£1.25 Dinner £10.75 Last dinner 10pm
Credit cards 1 2 3 4 5

★**Hartrigg** Shire Oak Rd, Headingley (2½m NW A660) ☎ (0532) 751568
Large, Edwardian house with lawns, gardens and mature trees in a quiet position on northern side of town.
30rm(2fb) ® sB&B£18.97 dB&B£29.32 CTV 12P 3
Dinner £6.61 Last dinner 7.30pm
Credit cards 1 2 3 Ⓥ

XXX**La Terrazza** Minerva House, 16 Greek St ☎ (0532) 432880
Situated in the business area, the smart Italian restaurant offers high standards of cuisine and service and features a mirrored wall, views of the kitchen and a comfortable bar where guests can enjoy a drink as they order their meal.
Closed Sun, Bank Hols, 25, 26 Dec & 1 Jan Lunch not served Sat
Italian **V** 90 seats Lunch fr£7.25&alc Dinner £7.25&alc Wine £5.90 Last dinner 11.30pm P
Credit cards 1 2 3

L

Leeds — Leek

XX**Mandalay** 8 Harrison St ☎ (0532) 446453
A wide range of interesting and authentic Asian dishes is available at this busy town-centre restaurant. Drinks are served and orders taken in a comfortable lounge area with low, deep seating.
Closed Sun
Lunch not served Sat
Indian **V** 95 seats S% ✱Lunch £4.75&alc Dinner £10.50—£11.50&alc Wine £5.95 Last dinner 11.15pm 5P Live music Fri & Sat
Credit cards 1 2 3 5

XX**Shabab** 2 Eastgate ☎ (0532) 468988
Located in the town centre, a first floor restaurant with pleasing Indian decor and atmosphere features authentic dishes making traditional use of spices and herbs. The à la carte menu covers a wide range but is divided up to make choice easier, and Indian waiters, colourfully dressed in national costume, offer helpful and courteous service.
Closed Xmas Day
Lunch not served Sun
Indian 80 seats Last dinner 11.30pm P
Credit cards 1 2 3 5

X***Rules*** 188 Selby Rd ☎ (0532) 604564
The smart, cosy, one-room restaurant, set in a small shopping development near Temple Newsham Park, serves a French and international cuisine prepared with skill and imagination.
Closed Mon Lunch served Sun only
French **V** 40 seats Last dinner 10pm 20P
Credit cards 1 2 3 5

LEEK
Staffordshire
Map **7** SJ95

★★**Jester at Leek** 81 Mill St ☎ (0538) 383997
RS Sun
A century ago this modern and popular hotel, standing on the A523 to the north of the town centre, was a small inn and adjoining cottages.
14rm(10⇌⫛)(3fb) CTV in all bedrooms ® S% sB&B£15.50—£19.50 sB&B⇌⫛£19.50—£21.50 dB&Bfr£26.50 dB&B⇌⫛£29.50—£32.50 B
80P Disco Sat
V ✗ Lunch £5alc Tea £2.50alc High Tea £4alc Dinner £10alc Wine £4.25 Last dinner 9.30pm
Ⓥ

LEEMING BAR
North Yorkshire
Map **8** SE28

★★**Motel Leeming** ☎ Bedale (0677) 23611
(For full entry see Bedale)

★**White Rose** ☎ Bedale (0677) 22707
Modest, clean roadside hotel.
12rm(2→10⋒) CTV in all bedrooms ®**T**
sB&B→⋒£16–£18 dB&B→⋒£28–£32
30P ✿ ⛫
V ☥ ☕ Lunch £4–£5.50&alc Dinner £7.95–£9.95&alc Wine £5.95 Last dinner 9.45pm
Credit cards [1] [2] [3] [5] Ⓥ

LEICESTER
Leicestershire
Map **4** SK50

★★★★**Grand** Granby St (Embassy)
☎ (0533) 555599 Telex no 342244
Impressive Victorian city-centre building standing on the main A6.
93rm(85→8⋒) CTV in all bedrooms ®**T**
S% sB&B→⋒£45 dB&B→⋒£58 **B**
Lift ☾ 120P CFA ♿
♉European ☥ ☕ S% Lunch £5.95–£7.95&alc Tea £3.75 Dinner £5.95–£7.95 Wine £5.10 Last dinner 9.30pm
Credit cards [1] [2] [3] [4] [5] Ⓥ

Leeming Bar — Leicester

★★★★**Holiday Inn** St Nicholas Circle (Holiday Inns) ☎ (0533) 531161 Telex no 341281
Large, modern, purpose-built hotel close to the city centre.
188→⋒)(108fb) ⚟ in 54 bedrooms CTV in all bedrooms **T** sB→⋒fr£50.80 dB→⋒fr£59.10(room only) **B**
Lift ☾ ♯ CFA ▭(heated) sauna bath gymnasium ♿
♉International **V** ☥ ☕ ⚟ Lunch £7.25–£9&alc Tea 75p–£1.25 Dinner £15alc Last dinner 10.15pm
Credit cards [1] [2] [3] [4] [5]

★★★**Belmont** De Montfort St (Best Western) ☎ (0533) 544773 Telex no 34619
Closed 24 Dec–2 Jan
Large Victorian house close to the A6, ½m south of the city centre.
40rm(31→3⋒) Annexe: 21rm(15→)(5fb) CTV in all bedrooms ®**T** **B**
Lift ☾ 30P CFA
♉English & French **V** ☥ ☕ ⚟ Lunch fr£8&alc Tea £1 Dinner fr£10&alc Last dinner 9.50pm
Credit cards [1] [2] [3] [5] Ⓥ

★★★**Eaton Bray** Abbey St ☎ (0533) 50666 Telex no 342434
72→⋒(4fb) CTV in all bedrooms ®**T** S% sB&B→⋒£44 dB&B→⋒£52 **B**
Lift ☾ 250 ⌂ *xmas*
V ☥ ☕ ⚟ S% Lunch £4.95–£7.95&alc Tea £1–£1.50 Dinner £7.95–£9.25&alc Wine £4.95 Last dinner 10pm
Credit cards [1] [2] [3] [5] Ⓥ

★★★**Ladbroke** Humberstone Rd (Ladbroke) ☎ (0533) 20471 Telex no 341460
Closed Xmas
Sited close to the city centre, this large, multi-storey, purpose-built hotel provides well-equipped modern accommodation and extensive conference and function facilities.
218→(3fb) ⚟ in 22 bedrooms CTV in all bedrooms ®**T** S%
sB&B→£43.50–£48.50
dB&B→£61–£71 **B**
Lift ☾ 25 ⌂
☥ ☕ S% Lunch £6.50alc Tea £2.50alc High Tea £6alc Dinner fr£9.50&alc Wine £6.25 Last dinner 10.30pm
Credit cards [1] [2] [3] [4] [5] Ⓥ

★★★**Leicester Forest Moat House** Hinckley Rd, Leicester Forest East (Queens Moat) ☎(0533) 394661

Closed 24—28 Dec

Attractive modern building on the A47, with a predominantly commercial trade.

31 ⇌ fi CTV in all bedrooms ® S% * sB&B ⇌ fi £18—£38 dB&B ⇌ fi £30—£46 B

☾ 180P ✿ Putting

English & French **V** S% *Lunch £5.25—£11.95&alc Tea £1.25—£2.50 Dinner £8.50&alc Wine £5.75 Last dinner 9.45pm

Credit cards 1 2 3 5 Ⓥ

★★★**Leicestershire Moat House** Wigston Rd, Oadby (3m SE A6) (Queens Moat) ☎(0533) 719441

29 ⇌ (3fb) ⅟ in 3 bedrooms CTV in all bedrooms ® **T** S% sB&B ⇌ £36.50—£40 dB&B ⇌ £46.50—£52 B

Lift ☾ 190P CFA ✿ Live music & dancing wkly *xmas*

English & French **V** S% Lunch £5.50—£7.50 Tea £1—£1.30 High Tea £3—£6 Dinner £7.50—£14 Wine £5.50 Last dinner 9.45pm

Credit cards 1 2 3 5 Ⓥ

Leicester — Leigh

★★★**Post House** Braunstone Lane East (Trusthouse Forte) ☎(0533) 896688 Telex no 341009

Modern, purpose-built complex, located 2 miles from the city and close to the M1.

172 ⇌ CTV in all bedrooms ® **T** sB&B ⇌ £50.50 dB&B ⇌ £63.50 B

Lift ☾ 102P CFA *xmas*

Last dinner 10pm

Credit cards 1 2 3 4 5

★**Rowans** 290 London Rd ☎(0533) 705364

Closed 23 Dec—4 Jan

Large Victorian house on the A6, 1m south of the city.

15rm (1fb) CTV in 3 bedrooms TV in 10 bedrooms ® in 4 bedrooms S% sB&B£15.50—£20 dB&B£22—£27

CTV 15P

English, French & Italian Bar lunch £1—£2 Dinner £6.50&alc Wine £3.95 Last dinner 7pm

Credit card 1 Ⓥ

XXX***Manor*** Glen Parva Manor, The Ford, Little Glen Rd, Glen Parva (3m SW on A426) ☎(0533) 774604

A 16th-century manor house with later additions, approximately three miles from the city centre.

Closed Sun Lunch not served Sat

English & French **V** 85 seats Last dinner 10pm 40P

Credit cards 1 2 3

XXX***White House*** Scraptoft Ln ☎(0533) 415951

Lunch not served Sat
Dinner not served Sun

French **V** 140 seats Last dinner 9.30pm 150P

Credit cards 1 2 3 5

LEIGH

Greater Manchester
Map **7** SJ69

★★★**Greyhound** Warrington Rd (Embassy) ☎(0942) 671256

Large public house with a modern motel block at the rear.

54 ⇌ fi CTV in all bedrooms ® **T** S% sB ⇌ fi £45 dB ⇌ fi £58 (room only)

Lift ☾ ## 250P

English & French **V** S% *Lunch fr£7.35 Tea fr60p Dinner fr£7.35 Wine £5.50 Last dinner 9.45pm

Credit cards 1 2 3 4 5 Ⓥ

L

LEIGHTON BUZZARD
Bedfordshire
Map **4** SP92

★★★**Swan** High St ☎(0525) 372148
Telex no 825562

The carefully restored 18th century inn stands at the centre of the old market town and offers comfortable, well equipped accommodation with pleasant service.

34➡(2fb) CTV in all bedrooms ®T
*sB&B➡£44—£55 dB&B➡£54—£65 B

8P Live music Fri & Sat

V ☕ *Lunch £8.50—£9.50 Tea 75p—£1 Dinner £12.50—£13.50&alc Wine £5 Last dinner 9.30pm

Credit cards 1 2 3 5 V

LEISTON
Suffolk
Map **5** TM46

★**White Horse** Station Rd ☎(0728) 830694

Built in the 1700's, the inn had ties with smuggling through several of its early landlords; nowadays it provides comfortable accommodation enhanced by traditional hospitality.

9rm(1➡)(1fb) ®sB&B£18—£19.50 dB&B£26.50—£29.50 dB&B➡£29.50—£32 B

CTV 14P Disco mnthly Live music & dancing mnthly *xmas*

English & French V ☕ Lunch £3.50—£7 Tea fr75p High Tea £3—£5 Dinner £7—£10.50&alc Wine £3.95 Last dinner 9.30pm

Credit cards 1 3 V

LELANT DOWNS
Cornwall
Map **2** SW53

XX**Watermill** Mill Hill (½m from jct A30/A3074) along unclass rd towards Lelant Downs) ☎ Penzance (0736) 755019

French **V** 50 seats Lunch £6—£10&alc Dinner £10—£12&alc Wine £4.90 Last dinner 9.45pm 34P

Credit cards 1 2 3 5

LEOMINSTER
Hereford & Worcester
Map **3** SO45

★★★**Talbot** West St (Best Western) ☎(0568) 2121

The cruck-framed hotel, parts of which date from 1470, will please both individual and conference guests with its period furniture, log fires and relaxed atmosphere.

28rm(17➡8⋒)(1fb) 1 CTV in all bedrooms ® S% *sB&B£23—£30 sB&B➡⋒£23—£30 dB&B£42—£46 dB&B➡⋒£42—£46 B

30P *xmas*

V ☕ *Lunch £4.50—£6.50 Tea 60p Dinner £7—£13&alc Wine £4.50 Last dinner 9.30pm

Credit cards 1 2 3 5

★★**Royal Oak** South St (Minotel) ☎(0568) 2610

This old coaching inn has been modernised in a sympathetic manner, the lounge bar still retaining its beams and panelling. An interesting range of real ales is served.

20rm(19➡1⋒)(3fb) 1 CTV in all bedrooms ®
*sB&B➡⋒£19.50—£22.50 dB&B➡⋒£32—£42 B

CTV 26P Disco Fri—Sat Live music & dancing Fri—Sat Cabaret monthly

V ☕ *Lunch £4.95—£8&alc Tea £1.90 High Tea £2.20—£3.20 Dinner £3.95—£8&alc Wine £4.15 Last dinner 9.30pm

Credit cards 1 2 3 5 V

XX***Wheelbarrow Castle*** ☎(0568) 2219

Old manor farmhouse with large country restaurant offering freshly prepared local produce. Including home smoked meat and fish.

English & Continental **V** 60 seats Last dinner 9.30pm 30P Live music Sat

Credit cards 1 2 3

LERWICK
See **Shetland**

L'ETACQ
Jersey
See **Channel Islands**

LETHAM
Fife
Map **11** NO31

★★★**Fernie Castle** ☎(033781) 381
Telex no 295141

RS 6 Jan—16 Mar

Modernised castle with thoughtfully equipped bedrooms, popular with business people and tourists.

16rm(6➡10⋒)(2fb) 1 CTV in all bedrooms ®T sB&B➡⋒£32.50—£45 dB&B➡⋒£49.50—£75

CTV 80P

Scottish & French V ☕ Lunch £10—£17.50&alc Tea £1.50 Dinner £12.50—£20&alc Wine £4.25 Last dinner 9.30pm

Credit cards 1 2 3 5 V

LETHAM
Tayside *Angus*
Map **15** NO54

★★★**Idvies House** ☎(030781) 787
Telex no 76252

6➡(1fb) 1 CTV in all bedrooms ®T S% sB&B➡£30 dB&B➡£35—£45 B

60P squash

V ☕ S% Lunch fr£7&alc High Tea £4.50—£6.50 Dinner £9—£12&alc Wine £5.50 Last dinner 9.30pm

Credit cards 1 2 3 5 V

LETTERFINLAY
Highland *Inverness-shire*
Map **14** NN29

★★*HL* **Letterfinlay Lodge** (off A82) ☎ Invergloy (039784) 222

A friendly and comfortable family-run hotel delightfully situated overlooking Loch Lochy.

15rm(2➡3⋒)(4fb) S% sB&B£18—£22 sB&B➡⋒£20—£25 dB&B£36—£44 dB&B➡⋒£40—£50 B

CTV 100P *xmas*

→

L

V ⚘ ☕ S% Bar lunch £1.80—£8&alc Tea 90p—£1.20 Dinner £11—£12.50 Wine £3 Last dinner 9pm

Credit cards 1 2 3 5 Ⓥ

LETTERSTON
Dyfed
Map **2** SM92

★★**Brynawelon** (Best Western) ☎ (0348) 840307

Closed Dec & Jan

Conveniently positioned adjacent to the A40 south of Fishguard, this proprietor-run motel provides comfortable and well-equipped bedrooms.

25rm(22 3)(1fb) CTV in all bedrooms ®T

CTV 120P

V ⚘ Wine £4 Last dinner 9pm

LEVENS near Kendal
Cumbria
Map **7** SD48

★★**Heaves** (off A6, ½m from junc with A591) ☎ Sedgwick (0448) 60396

Closed 4 days at Xmas

Georgian residence, featuring an Adam style staircase, set in its own grounds.

16rm(5 1)(3fb) TV in 5 bedrooms ® in 5 bedrooms **T** sB&B£14—£15 sB&B £15—£17 dB&B£28—£30 dB&B £30—£34

Unlicensed CTV 24P snooker

⚘ ☕ Lunch £4—£4.50 Tea £1—£1.50 Dinner £5.50—£6 Last dinner 8pm

Credit cards 1 2 3 5

L

LEWES
East Sussex
Map **5** TQ41

★★★**Shelleys** High St (Mount Charlotte) ☎ (0273) 472361

Its comfortable, skilfully-restored public rooms elegantly furnished with antiques, the gracious, Georgian-style hotel makes an ideal base for visits to Glynebourne.

21 2 CTV in all bedrooms **T** sB&B fr£44.50 dB&B fr£68

25P 1 (£5) CFA *xmas*

English & Continental **V** ⚘ ☕ Lunch £9—£10&alc Tea 90p—£1 Dinner £10—£11&alc Wine £5.95 Last dinner 9.15pm

Credit cards 1 2 3 5 Ⓥ

★★**White Hart** High St (Best Western) ☎ (0273) 474676

Famous coaching inn with bedroom annexe. Good food is complemented by friendly service.

19rm(15) Annexe: 14(2fb) 2 CTV in 29 bedrooms **T** S% sB&B£25—£27 sB&B £31—£36 dB&B£36—£38 dB&B £52—£55

CTV 45P

V ⚘ ☕ S% Lunch £6.50&alc Tea £1.95 Dinner £6.50&alc Wine £4.80 Last dinner 10.15pm

Credit cards 1 2 3 5 Ⓥ

Letterfinlay — Leyland

✕**Kenwards** Pipe Passage, 151A High St ☎ (0273) 472343

Imaginative English cooking served in this converted loft in a 16th-century building.

Closed Sun & Mon Lunch by reservation only

25 seats S% ✱Lunch £12.50alc Dinner £12.50alc Wine £6.30 Last dinner 9.30pm

Credit card 2

LEWIS, ISLE OF
Western Isles *Ross & Cromarty*
Map **13**

SHAWBOST
Map **13** NB24

✕**Raebhat House** ☎ (085171) 205

(Appointment granted for dinner only)

Homely little cottage restaurant of charm and character.

English & French **V** Unlicensed no corkage charge 45 seats Dinner £9.50—£11&alc Last dinner 10pm 25P

Ⓥ

STORNOWAY
Map **13** NB43

★★★*B* **Caberfeidh** (Best Western) ☎ (0851) 2604 Telex no 75505

A purpose built hotel on northern edge of town.

40 CTV in all bedrooms ®**T** sB&B £40—£44 dB&B £55

Lift CTV 80P Disco wkly Live music & dancing wkly

V ⚘ ☕ Lunch £7 Tea £1.50 Dinner £12.50—£15 Wine £5 Last dinner 9.30pm

Credit cards 1 2 3 5 Ⓥ

★★★**Seaforth** James St ☎ (0851) 2740

Large, friendly hotel which also contains a cinema.

56(6fb) CTV in 30 in bedrooms ✱sB&B £29.50—£30.50 dB&B £43—£44

Lift CTV 30P CFA snooker cinema Disco wkly

⚘ ☕ Lunch fr£4.75 Tea fr60p Dinner £9.25&alc Wine £5 Last dinner 9.30pm

Credit cards 1 2 3 Ⓥ

LEWTRENCHARD
Devon
Map **2** SX48

✕✕**Lewtrenchard Manor**
☎ Lewdown (056683) 256

This interesting manor house is being renovated to become a country house hotel. While this process is going on, and although bedrooms are available, it is especially notable for its food. The chef, Peter Hayes, comes from the Waterside at Bray, and prepares meals to a very high standard. A range of interesting dishes is offered and they are all well presented.

Lunch not served Mon—Sat

French 40 seats Lunch £13.50 Dinner £15.50—£18.50 Wine £6 Last dinner 9.30pm 30P 11 bedrooms available nc12yrs (in bedrooms)

Credit cards 1 2 3

LEYBURN
North Yorkshire
Map **7** SE19

★**Golden Lion** Market Pl ☎ Wensleydale (0969) 22161

10rm(5)(5fb) CTV in all bedrooms ® S% sB&B£12—£17 sB&B £17 dB&B£24—£26 dB&B £38—£40

Lift CTV squash sauna bath solarium gymnasium

V ⚘ ☕ S% Lunch £2.60—£5&alc Tea fr£1.50 High Tea fr£2.50 Dinner £4—£7.50&alc Wine £4.30 Last dinner 9pm

Ⓥ

LEYLAND
Lancashire
Map **7** SD52

★★★**Ladbroke** (& Conference centre) Leyland Way (Ladbroke) ☎ (0772) 422922 Telex no 677651

A modern hotel situated at junction 28 of the M6.

93(9fb) in 6 bedrooms CTV in all bedrooms ®**T** sB £48—£58 dB £59.50—£69.50 (room only)

CTV 200P CFA *xmas*

European **V** ⚘ ☕ Lunch £7.75—£8.25 Dinner £9.95—£10.25&alc Wine £5.99 Last dinner 10pm

Credit cards 1 2 3 5

★★★**Pines** Clayton-le-Woods (1m S of M6 jct 29 on A6) ☎ Preston (0772) 38551 Telex no 677584

Closed 24 & 25 Dec

A well-furnished, late Victorian house with modern extensions.

25 CTV in all bedrooms ®**T** S% sB&B £25.30—£37.95 dB&B £44.25—£50.60

130P squash solarium pool table Live music & dancing Fri

V ♁ ☕ S% Lunch £6.33&alc Tea fr80p Dinner £11.95&alc Wine £4.75 Last dinner 9.30pm

Credit cards 1 2 3 5

LICHFIELD

Staffordshire
Map 7 SK10

★★★**George** Bird St (Embassy) ☎ (0543) 414822

Large Georgian inn near Cathedral. (The nearby Swan Hotel, under same ownership, is used as an annexe.)

39rm(35 4)(3fb) CTV in all bedrooms ®T S% *sB £42 dB £50 (room only) B

☾ 40P CFA *xmas*

Cosmopolitan V ♁ ☕ S% *Lunch £6.75—£7.75&alc Tea 85p Dinner £9.25&alc Wine £4.45 Last dinner 10pm

Credit cards 1 2 3 4 5

★★★**Little Barrow** Beacon St ☎ (0543) 414500

Popular central hotel with modern, well-equipped bedrooms.

24 CTV in all bedrooms T *sB&B £35 dB&B £45 B

☾ CTV 70P

Continental V ♁ *Lunch £6.50&alc Tea 70p Dinner £9.50—£12&alc Wine £6.50 Last dinner 9.30pm

Credit cards 1 2 3 5

★★**Angel Croft** Beacon St ☎ (0543) 258737

Closed Xmas RS Sun

Rich brown brick Georgian house, with one acre of grounds, situated close to the Cathedral.

13rm(3 5)(1fb) 1 CTV in all bedrooms ®T *sB&B£21—£26 sB&B £25—£32 dB&B£31—£37 dB&B £36—£45 B

CTV 60P

V ♁ ☕ *Lunch £5.75—£11 Tea fr80p Dinner £7.50—£11.50 Wine £5 Last dinner 8.45pm

Credit cards 1 3 5 V

Leyland — Limpley Stoke

★★**Fradley Arms** Rykneld St (Fradley, on A38, 3m NE) ☎ Burton-on-Trent (0283) 790186

Small Georgian inn beside A38, offering friendly service.

6 (1fb) CTV in all bedrooms ®T S% *sB&B £30—£35 dB&B £40—£45 B

CTV 100P Live music & dancing Sun *xmas*

English & French V ♁ ☕ S% Lunch £6—£9&alc Tea £1—£2 Dinner £6—£9&alc Wine £4.95 Last dinner 9.30pm

Credit cards 1 2 3 5 V

LIFTON

Devon
Map 2 SX38

★★★*H* **Arundell Arms** (Best Western) ☎ (0566) 84666

Closed 5 days Xmas

Friendly, personally run coaching inn with good food, plus excellent shooting and fishing facilities.

24rm(17 5) CTV in all bedrooms ®T sB&B£23.50 sB&B £33 dB&B£47 dB&B £53—£56 B

80P CFA games room

English & French ♁ ☕ Lunch £8&alc Tea fr£1.25 Dinner £13—£13.50&alc Wine £5.75 Last dinner 9pm

Credit cards 1 2 3 5

See advertisement under Launceston

★★**Lifton Cottage** ☎ (0566) 84439

A small, family-run hotel of character, with an attractive atmosphere.

12rm(4)(3fb) CTV in all bedrooms ® sB&B£13—£15.50 sB&B £18.50 dB&B£25 dB&B £30.50

15P solarium

V ♁ *Lunch £4.50—£7.25&alc Dinner £7.25&alc Wine £4.75 Last dinner 9pm

Credit cards 1 2 3 5 V

LIMPLEY STOKE near Bath

Wiltshire
Map 3 ST76

★★★**Cliffe** Crowe Hill (Best Western) ☎ (022122) 3226

Closed 31 Dec—15 Jan

This country house hotel near the railway commands good views over a wooded valley. Rooms have good facilities (access to three of them being from outside the hotel), and the "Coterie" Restaurant offers à la carte and table d'hôte menus.

12rm(11 1)(3fb) 1 CTV in all bedrooms ®T sB&B £28—£38 dB&B £49—£68 B

40P (heated) nc 3yrs

English & Continental V ♁ ☕ Lunch £8—£11 Tea £1.20—£1.50 Dinner £11—£13&alc Wine £6 Last dinner 9pm

Credit cards 1 2 3 5 V

See advertisement under Bath

★★**Limpley Stoke** (Consort) ☎ (022122) 3333 Telex no 57515 (Attn 13)

Approached up a private road, this country house is situated in the heart of the River Avon valley.

54rm(42 12)(5fb) 3 CTV in all bedrooms ®S% *sB&B £28—£30 dB&B £40.50—£43.50 B

Lift CTV 60P CFA

♁ *Bar lunch £1.30—£5 Dinner £8.50—£8.95&alc Wine £4.50 Last dinner 8.30pm

Credit cards 1 2 3 5

See advertisement under Bath

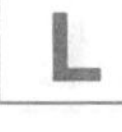

LIMPSFIELD
Surrey
Map **5** TQ45

❀✕✕ **Old Lodge** High St ☎ Oxted (08833) 2996

An unassuming exterior belies the true quality of this unusual, beamed restaurant where modern French cuisine is skilfully created and served by professional staff.

Closed Mon, Good Fri & 1st 2 wks Jan Lunch not served Sat Dinner not served Sun

French **V** 52 seats Last dinner 9pm 50P

Credit cards 1 2 3 4 5

LINCOLN
Lincolnshire
Map 7 SK97
See also **Washingborough**

★★★★ **White Hart** Bailgate (Trusthouse Forte) ☎ (0522) 26222 Telex no 56304

Early Georgian house with a late Victorian façade, standing in the shadow of Lincoln Cathedral.

51 (1fb) CTV in all bedrooms ® sB&B £55.50 dB&B £72.50

Lift CTV 25P 35 CFA *xmas*

Last dinner 9.45pm

Credit cards 1 2 3 4 5

★★★ **Eastgate Post House** Eastgate (Trusthouse Forte) ☎ (0522) 20341 Telex no 56316

Large modern hotel near Cathedral.

71 (1fb) CTV in all bedrooms ® **T** sB&B £52.50 dB&B £70.50

Lift 110P CFA *xmas*

Last dinner 10pm

Credit cards 1 2 3 4 5

★★ **Barbican** St Mary's Street ☎ (0522) 28374

17rm (10) (2fb) CTV in all bedrooms ® **T** ✱sB&B £23 sB&B £30 dB&B £34 dB&B £44

nc

Mainly grills ✱Lunch £7.25alc Dinner £7.25alc Wine £4.60 Last dinner 10pm

Credit cards 1 2 3 5

★★ ***Castle*** Westgate ☎ (0522) 38801

Lovely old building, built as a school in 1852, tastefully modernised and converted.

15 Annexe: 6 CTV in all bedrooms ®

21P nc5yrs

Continental Last dinner 9.30pm

Credit cards 1 2 3

★★ ***Duke William*** 44 Bailgate ☎ (0522) 33351

Closed Xmas Day

Located a few minutes' walk from the cathedral, the comfortable and friendly hotel has been an inn since 1791.

11rm (4) (2fb) TV in 11 bedrooms ® **T**

12P

V Last dinner 9.30pm

Credit cards 1 2 3 5

★★ **Four Seasons** Scothern Ln ☎ Welton (0673) 60108

(For full entry see Dunholme)

★★ **Grand** St Mary's Street ☎ (0522) 24211

Modernised, city-centre hotel in the business area, convenient for all the transport terminals.

50rm (43 7) (2fb) CTV in all bedrooms ® **T** sB&B £32 dB&B £44

40P

English & French **V** Lunch £5.70—£8.90&alc Tea fr £1.50 High Tea fr £5 Dinner £7.90—£11&alc Wine £4.95 Last dinner 10pm

Credit cards 1 2 3 5

★★ **Hillcrest** 15 Lindum Ter (Guestaccom) ☎ (0522) 26341

A former Victorian rectory with rose gardens standing in a quiet road north-east of the city centre, the hotel provides comfortable, well-equipped rooms and has good views over part of the city.

15rm (10) (4fb) CTV in all bedrooms ® sB&B £21 sB&B £26 dB&B £30 dB&B £36

8P

International Bar lunch £4alc Tea 70palc Dinner £7.50alc Wine £5.25

Credit cards 1 3 Ⓥ

★★ **Loudor** 37 Newark Rd, North Hykeham (3m SW A46) ☎ (0522) 680333

A small, attractive house has been completely remodelled and enlarged to create a compact, modern hotel where personal attention ranks high.

9rm (2 8) Annexe: 1rm (1fb) CTV in all bedrooms ® ✱sB&B £25—£28 dB&B £36—£40

15P *xmas*

English & French **V** ✱Lunch £9.50alc Tea fr £1 Dinner £7.95alc Wine £3.95 Last dinner 9.30pm

Credit cards 1 2 3 5 Ⓥ

★★ **Moor Lodge** ☎ (0522) 791366

(For full entry see Branston)

✕ **White's** The Jews House, 15 The Strait ☎ (0522) 24851

Fresh produce, cooked in the modern light style, is served here in one of Britain's oldest houses.

Closed Mon & 2 wks after New Year

French **V** 28 seats Lunch £2.50—£10 Dinner £10—£30 Wine £4 Last dinner 9.45pm

Credit cards 1 2 3

LINLITHGOW
Lothian *West Lothian*
Map **11** NS97

✕✕✕ ***Champany*** (2m NE off A904) ☎ Philipstoun (050683) 4532

Attractive, circular restaurant specialising in fine grills.

Closed 24 Dec—13 Jan
Dinner not served Sun
V 48 seats Last dinner 10pm 70P
Credit cards 1 2 3 5

LIPHOOK
Hampshire
Map **4** SU83

✿XX **Lai Quilla** 15 The Square ☎(0428) 722095
The modern Indian restaurant provides polite and efficient service, whilst its Tandoori specialities and authentic curries are among the best to be found in the south east.
Indian 48 seats *Lunch £6alc Dinner £7alc Wine £6.95 Last dinner 11.30pm
Credit cards 1 2 3 5

LISKEARD
Cornwall
Map **2** SX26

★★ **Country Castle** Station Rd ☎(0579) 42694
Closed Nov RS Jan
Charming hotel offering friendly service and fine views.
11rm(5 2)(2fb) CTV in all bedrooms ® *sB&B£15 sB&B £22 dB&B£28 dB&B £42—£48
60P croquet boules
English & French **V** *Lunch £4.50—£8alc Tea fr£1alc Dinner £7.50—£8.50&alc Wine £4.50 Last dinner 8pm
Credit cards 1 3 V

★★ **Lord Eliot** Castle St ☎(0579) 42717
Small hotel built around the character house of a one-time country landlord.
16rm(2 4)(1fb) CTV in 10 bedrooms S% *sB&B£15—£20.50 sB&B £15—£23 dB&B£30.50—£43 dB&B £30.50—£46
CTV 75P Disco Fri & Sat Live music & dancing Fri & Sat Cabaret Fri & Sat *xmas*
English & French **V** S% Lunch £3—5&alc Tea £1 High Tea £3 Dinner £4—£5.75&alc Wine £3.95 Last dinner 9.30pm
Credit card 1

★★ ***Webbs*** The Parade ☎(0579) 43675
Pleasant Georgian-style hotel within this Chester town.
15rm(10) 1 CTV in 10 bedrooms ® **T**
CTV 14P

LITTLEBOROUGH
Greater Manchester
Map **7** SD91

★ ***Sun*** Featherstall Rd ☎(0706) 78957
Small, friendly public house with satisfactory bedrooms.
8rm(1fb) ®
CTV 8P
Last dinner 9.30pm
Credit cards 1 2 3 5

LITTLE STAUGHTON
Bedfordshire
Map **4** TL16

X ***Crown Inn*** ☎ Colmworth (023062) 260
French cuisine and friendly service are offered by the cosy restaurant of this charming inn. Located in a quiet rural area, it is popular with local people.
Closed Sun
French 24 seats Last dinner 9pm 20P
Credit card 2

LIVERPOOL
Merseyside
Map **7** SJ39
See plan See also **Blundellsands** and **Bootle**

★★★★ **Atlantic Tower Thistle** Chapel St (Thistle) ☎051-227 4444 Telex no 627070 Plan **1** *B5*
A distinctive example of modern architecture, the hotel offers well- →

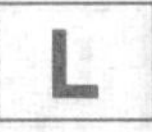

furnished bedrooms and some excellent suites. There are fine views across the River Mersey.

226🛁⋒(6fb) ⚡in 18 bedrooms CTV in all bedrooms ®T ✱sB🛁⋒£47—£57 dB🛁⋒£58—£70(room only) B

Lift ☾ ## 60P 45🚗 CFA Live music and dancing Sat Cabaret Fri & Sat

International ☕ ✱Lunch fr£9.50&alc Dinner fr£9.50&alc Wine £7 Last dinner 9.30pm

Credit cards [1] [2] [3] [4] [5] [V]

★★★★*Liverpool Moat House*
Paradise St (Queens Moat) ☎051-709 0181 Telex no 627270 Plan **9** *C4*

Modern, purpose-built hotel close to city centre.

258🛁⋒(212fb) CTV in all bedrooms **T** B

Lift ☾ ## 1000P CFA (heated) sauna bath solarium gymnasium ♿

English & French ☕ Last dinner 10.30pm

Credit cards [1] [2] [3] [4] [5]

★★★★St George's St John's Precinct, Lime St (Trusthouse Forte) ☎051-709 7090 Telex no 627630 Plan **12** *D4*

This large, modern and well-furnished hotel stands in the heart of the city, opposite Lime Street station.

155🛁 CTV in all bedrooms ®T sB&B🛁£52 dB&B🛁£67 B

Lift ☾ P CFA

☕Last dinner 10pm

Credit cards [1] [2] [3] [4] [5]

★★★Crest Hotel Liverpool—City
Lord Nelson St (Crest) ☎051-709 7050 Telex no 627954 Plan **4** *E5*

Tall, modern, city-centre hotel overlooking Lime Street Station.

160🛁(2fb) ⚡in 12 bedrooms CTV in all bedrooms ®T S% sB&B🛁fr£48.75 dB&B🛁fr£64.50 B

Lift ☾ ## CTV 200P CFA Live music & dancing Thu *xmas*

V ☕ ⚡ S% Bar lunch £1—£5 Tea £2.50—£5 Dinner £11.15&alc Wine £5 Last dinner 9.45pm

Credit cards [1] [2] [3] [4] [5]

Liverpool

1 Atlantic Tower Thistle ★★★★
2 Blundellsands ★★★ *(See under Blundellsands)*
4 Crest Hotel Liverpool — City ★★★
6 Grange ★★
7 Green Park ★★
8 Lau's ✕✕
9 Liverpool Moat House
11 Park ★★★ *(See under Bootle)*
12 St George's ★★★★
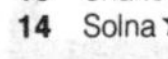
13 Shaftesbury ★★
14 Solna ★

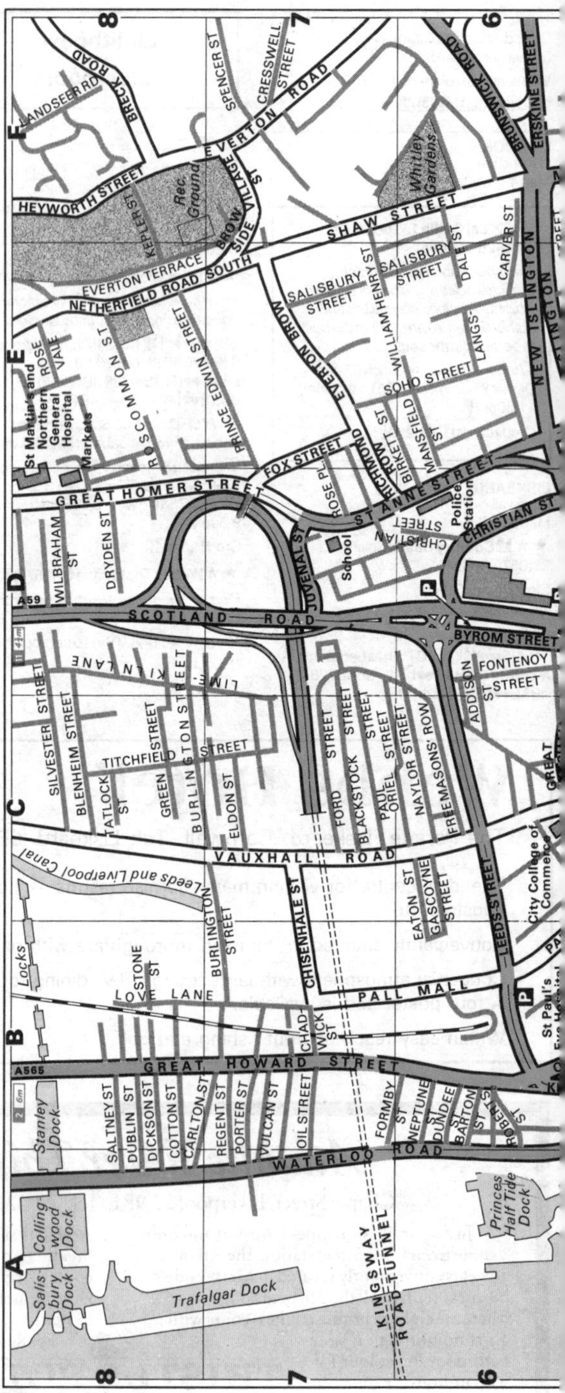

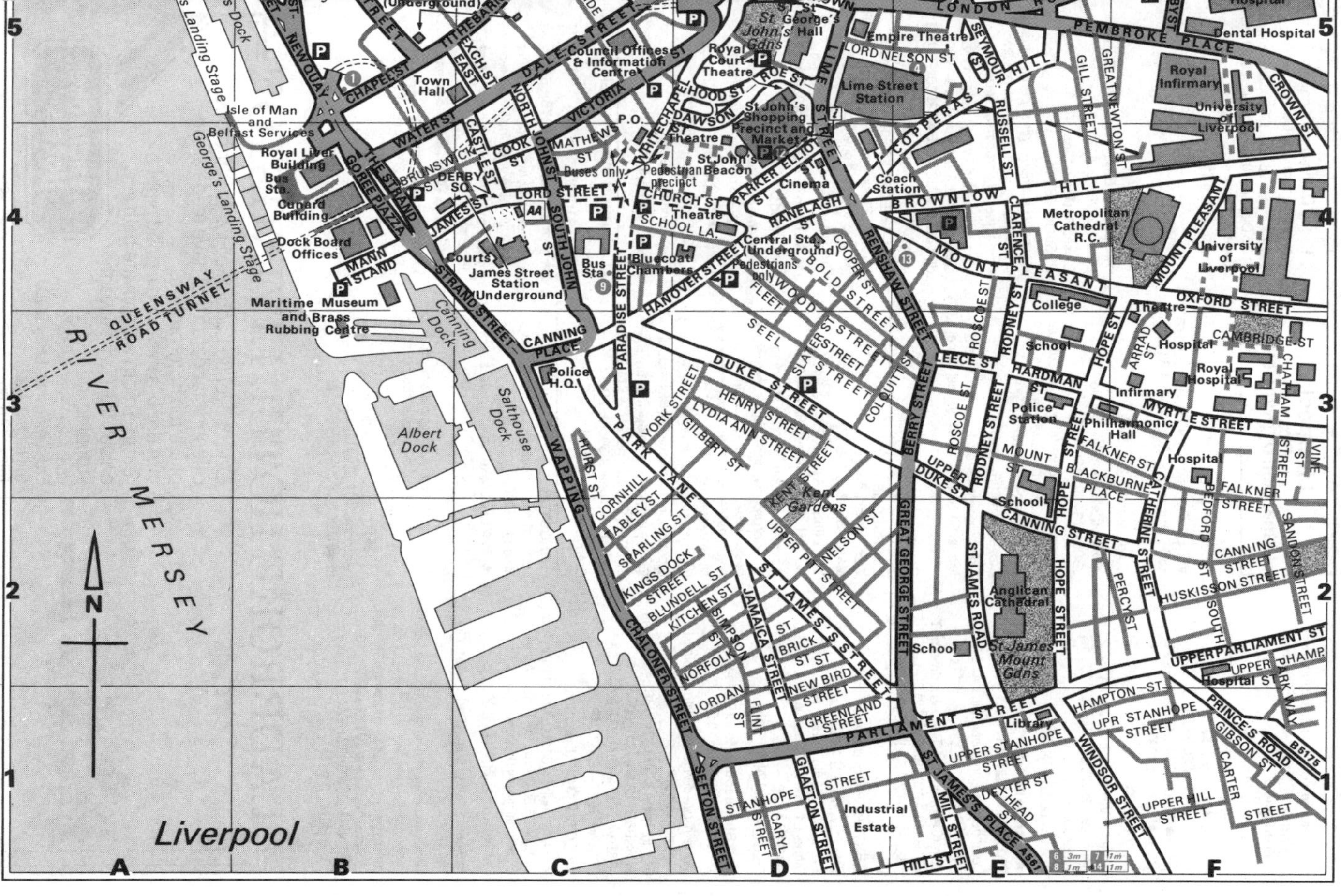
Liverpool
RIVER MERSEY
QUEENSWAY ROAD TUNNEL
George's Landing Stage
Isle of Man and Belfast Services
Royal Liver Building
Cunard Building
Dock Board Offices
Maritime Museum and Brass Rubbing Centre
Canning Dock
Albert Dock
Salthouse Dock
Town Hall
Council Offices & Information Centre
Lime Street Station
Empire Theatre
St George's Hall
St John's Gdns
Royal Court Theatre
St John's Shopping Precinct and Market
St John's Beacon
Pedestrian precinct
Central Sta. (Underground)
James Street Station (Underground)
Bluecoat Chambers
Coach Station
Metropolitan Cathedral R.C.
University of Liverpool
Royal Infirmary
Dental Hospital
Philharmonic Hall
Police Station
Police H.Q.
Kent Gardens
Anglican Cathedral
St James' Mount Gdns
Industrial Estate
PEMBROKE PLACE
LONDON RD
MOUNT PLEASANT
LIME STREET
RENSHAW STREET
BERRY STREET
GREAT GEORGE STREET
HOPE STREET
CANNING STREET
CATHERINE STREET
UPPER PARLIAMENT ST
PARLIAMENT STREET
PRINCE'S ROAD
WINDSOR STREET
ST JAMES'S PLACE
ST JAMES ROAD
ST JAMES'S STREET
DUKE STREET
HANOVER STREET
PARK LANE
WAPPING
STRAND STREET
THE STRAND
GOREE PIAZZA
NEW QUAY
DALE STREET
VICTORIA STREET
WATER ST
CASTLE ST
LORD STREET
SOUTH JOHN ST
NORTH JOHN ST
PARADISE STREET
SCHOOL LA.
BOLD STREET
SEEL STREET
CHALONER STREET
SEFTON STREET
JAMAICA STREET
GRAFTON STREET
MILL STREET
CANNING PLACE
A
B
C
D
E
F
1
2
3
4
5

★★**Grange** Holmfield Road, Aigburth (Best Western) ☎051-427 2950 Telex no 298928 Plan **6** *E1*

Standing in its own grounds, four miles from the city centre in a surburban area.

25rm(20⇌2⋒)(1fb) 3⊟ CTV in all bedrooms ® **T** ✱ sB&B£15—£21 sB&B⇌⋒£20—£30 dB&B£25—£31 dB&B⇌⋒£32—£40 Ɓ

CTV 50P ✿

French **V** ✱ Lunch (Sun only) £6.25 Dinner £9—£9.75&alc Wine £5.10 Last dinner 9pm

Credit cards 1 2 3 5 Ⓥ

★★**Green Park** 4/6 Greenbank Dr ☎051-733 3382 Plan **7** *F1*

Detached, red-brick building, close to Sefton Park.

23rm(6⇌8⋒)(4fb) CTV in all bedrooms **T** sB&B£13—£19 sB&B⇌⋒£16—£23 dB&B£24—£27.50 dB&B⇌⋒£26—£32 Ɓ

☾ # CTV 25P ✿ games room

Mainly grills **V** Lunch £4.75—£5.25&alc Tea 50p High Tea £1.25 Dinner £4.75—£5.25&alc Wine £3.85 Last dinner 9.30pm

Credit cards 1 2 3 5 Ⓥ

★★**Shaftesbury** Mount Pleasant ☎051-709 4421 Plan **13** *E4*

Modern, city-centre hotel with a mainly commercial trade.

67rm(24⇌5⋒)(3fb) CTV in 46 bedrooms **T** ✱ sB&B£12.50—£19.50 sB&B⇌⋒£17—£24 dB&B£25—£28 dB&B⇌⋒£27—£32.50 Ɓ

Lift ☾ CTV ✿ CFA Disco Sun

V Lunch £4.55&alc Tea £1 High Tea £4.50—£6.50 Dinner £5.70&alc Wine £5.50 Last dinner 9.30pm

Credit cards 1 2 3 4 5 Ⓥ

★**Solna** Ullet Rd Sefton Park ☎051-733 1943 Plan **14** *E1*

Large, detached house overlooking Sefton Park.

20rm(10⇌) Annexe: 18rm(2⇌10⋒)(11fb) CTV in all bedrooms ® **T** S% sB&B£16.10 sB&B⇌⋒£23.70 dB&B£27.60 dB&B⇌⋒£32.20 Ɓ

☾ 60P 2⌂ Disco Wed

V S% Lunch £4.95 Tea £2 High Tea £5.95 Dinner £5.95&alc Wine £4.65 Last dinner 9pm

Credit cards 1 2 3 5 Ⓥ

✕✕**Lau's** Rankin Hall, 44 Ullet Rd ☎051-734 3930 Plan **8** *E1*

Delicious food served in spacious, ornate Pekinese style surroundings and overlooking Sefton Park.

Closed Sun & 25—26 Dec

Pekinese **V** 450 seats Lunch £5alc Dinner £8.50alc Wine £4.50 Last dinner 11pm 55P

Credit cards 1 2 3 5

LIVERSEDGE

West Yorkshire
Map **7** SE12

✕✕**Lillibets** Ashfield House, 64 Leeds Rd ☎Heckmondwike (0924) 404911

A converted country house, standing in 2-3 acres of grounds and landscaped gardens beside the A62, features a smart, comfortable lounge bar and an elegantly stylish restaurant.
(Lunch by reservation only)

Closed Sun, 1 wk Xmas & 2 wks end Jul

English & French 40 seats ✱ Lunch £7.50—£10.50 Dinner £10—£11.95 Wine £5.50 Last dinner 9.30pm 22P

Credit cards 1 2 3 5

LIVINGSTON

Lothian *West Lothian*
Map **11** NT06

★★★**Ladbroke** Almondvale East (Ladbroke) ☎(0506) 31222 Telex no 727680

The modern hotel has spacious bedrooms and open-plan public areas incorporating a carvery restaurant.

114⇌⋒(18fb) in 6 bedrooms CTV in all bedrooms ® **T** sB⇌⋒£49—£59 dB⇌⋒£67—£77 (room only) Ɓ

☾ 170P ✿ (heated) sauna bath gymnasium pool table Cabaret Sat

V Lunch £6.25—£7.50&alc Tea £1.75 Dinner £10.25&alc Wine £5.99 Last dinner 9.45pm

Credit cards 1 2 3 5

LIZARD

Cornwall
Map **2** SW71

★★**Housel Bay** Housel Cove ☎The Lizard (0326) 290417

Closed 31 Dec—4 Jan
RS 5 Jan—28 Feb

House of Victorian origin superbly situated in cliffside grounds. Breathtaking views from all the public rooms & gardens.

27rm(10⇌3⋒) CTV in 5 bedrooms ® sB&B£12—£16 sB&B⇌⋒£15—£20 dB&B£24—£32 dB&B⇌⋒£30—£48 Ɓ

CTV 20P 4⌂(charge) ✿ *xmas*

V Lunch £5.50—£6.50 Tea £1.50—£2 High Tea £4—£5 Dinner £8&alc Wine £3.90 Last dinner 9pm

Credit cards 1 2 3 Ⓥ

★★***Lizard*** ☎The Lizard (0326) 290456

Closed mid Oct—Mar

Family-run inn in the centre of the village with busy bars catering for local trade.

8rm(1⇌2⋒)(2fb) ®

CTV 20P 2⌂(£2 per night)

Last dinner 9.15pm

Credit cards 1 3

LLANARMON DYFFRYN CEIROG

Clwyd
Map **7** SJ13

★★★***H* Hand** ☎(069176) 666

A 16th-century, two storey hotel in the village, with shooting and fishing facilities.

14⇌(1fb) CTV in 1 bedroom sB&B⇌£32 dB&B⇌£50 Ɓ

CTV 30P ✿ (hard) *xmas*

English & Continental **V** Lunch fr£8.95 Tea fr£1.60 Dinner fr£11.95 Wine £5.75 Last dinner 9pm

Credit cards 1 2 3 Ⓥ

★★**West Arms** (Minotel) ☎ (069176) 665

Country hotel, over 400 years old, situated in a small picturesque village 950ft above sea level.

13rm(6→)(1fb) 1🛏 ✱ sB&B£17 dB&B£34 dB&B→£37 ₿

CTV 30P ✿ ♩ *xmas*

♕ ☕ ✱ Lunch £7.50 Tea £1.25 High Tea £3.50 Dinner £9.50—£10.50 Wine £4.75 Last dinner 9pm

Credit cards 1 2 3 5 Ⓥ

LLANBEDR
Gwynedd
Map **6** SH52

★★🌲**Cae Nest Hall** ☎ (034123) 349

Closed Jan

15th-century stone house in wooded grounds with comfortable lounge, modestly furnished bedrooms, and offering some Welsh regional dishes.

10rm(3→2⋒)(2fb) CTV in all bedrooms ® S% sB&B£14.75—£16.75 dB&B£29.55—£33.55 dB&B→⋒£36—£40 ₿

CTV 12P ⚡ ✿ *xmas*

☕ British & Continental **V** ♕ S% Lunch £6—9 Dinner £9&alc Wine £4.50 Last dinner 9.30pm

Credit card 3 Ⓥ

Llanarmon Dyffryn Ceirog — Llanberis

★★*H* **Ty Mawr** ☎ (034123) 440

Comfortable, personally run hotel, with good home cooking.

10rm(4→6⋒)(2fb) CTV in all bedrooms ® sB&B→⋒£17—£18 dB&B→⋒£34—£36 ₿

CTV 20P ⚡ ✿

V ♕ ☕ Bar lunch £1.50—£3.50&alc Tea £1.50—£2 High Tea £2—£4 Dinner £8—£10&alc Wine £5 Last dinner 8.45pm

LLANBEDROG
Gwynedd
Map **6** SH33

★★**Bryn Derwen** ☎ (0758) 740257

Closed 31 Dec

Pebble-dashed Edwardian house in the village set in its own grounds, with sea views.

12rm(9→)(9fb) CTV in 10 bedrooms sB&B£16—£23 sB&B→£17—£30 dB&B£26—£40 dB&B→£34—£50 ₿

CTV 20P ✿ ♘ *xmas*

V ♕ ☕ Lunch £6.95—£8.80&alc Tea £1.20—£1.50&alc High Tea £4.65—£5.12&alc Dinner £10—£14.30&alc Wine £4.28 Last dinner 8pm

Credit cards 1 3 Ⓥ

LLANBERIS
Gwynedd
Map **6** SH56

★**Gallt-y-Glyn** Caernarfon Rd ☎ (0286) 870370

Part 17th-century, roadside hotel.

10rm(1fb) ✗ ✱ sB&B£16 dB&B£28—£29.75

CTV 14P ⚡ *xmas*

Bar lunch £1.50—£2.50 Dinner £8—£10 Wine £4 Last dinner 8pm

Credit cards 1 2 3 5

See advertisement on page 418

✕✕**Y Bistro** Glandwr, 43—45 Stryd Fawr ☎ (0286) 871278

Set at the heart of this very Welsh village this restaurant successfully combines an essentially Welsh atmosphere with the refinements of French cooking. Dining room and cocktail bar are comfortably furnished and have a real fire.

Closed Sun (except Bank Hol's) & 3 wks Jan

Lunch by reservation only

V 50 seats Dinner £10—£16 Wine £5 Last dinner 9.30 P ⁄

Credit cards 1 2 3 5

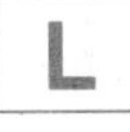

LLANDDERFEL
Gwynedd
Map **6** SH93

★★★ *BL* **Palé Hall** ☎ (06783) 285
Telex no 677584

Standing in its own parkland, the mellow stone country house has been beautifully restored to provide an elegant restaurant, an attractive bar, and a fine panelled lounge whose adjoining room has a painted, domed ceiling. Bedrooms are furnished to a very high standard and have good facilities, whilst the bath in the Victoria Suite is the very one that Queen Victoria used when she visited the house!

17 (2fb) 1 CTV in all bedrooms **T**
*sB&B £40 dB&B £55–£70
Lift 150P sauna bath solarium gymnasium *xmas*
V Lunch £8.50 Tea £1.25–£3.50 Dinner £15&alc Wine £5 Last dinner 9.30pm
Credit cards 1 2 3 5

See advertisement under Bala

Llandderfel — Llandrindod Wells

LLANDDEWI SKYRRID
Gwent
Map **3** SO31

Walnut Tree Inn (3m NE of Abergavenny) ☎ Abergavenny (0873) 2797

This intriguingly small country restaurant is a perennial favourite. In the cheerful, homely surroundings of the snug dining room, pleasantly informal service from knowledgable, local staff complements the high standard of cooking to be sampled in such tempting dishes as Smoked Salmon Bavarois or Supreme of Guinea Fowl with Truffles.

Closed Sun
French & Italian **V** 45 seats 30P

LLANDEILO
Dyfed
Map **2** SN62

★★★ *B* **Cawdor Arms** ☎ (0558) 823500

Elegant, very comfortable Georgian house offering good quality food.

16 2 CTV in all bedrooms
*sB&B £33 dB&B £48.50–£53.50
8P
British & French *Lunch £11.50alc Tea 90p&alc Dinner £13.50 Wine £5.45 Last dinner 9.30pm
Credit cards 1 2 3 5

LLANDOGO
Gwent
Map **3** SO50

★★ **Old Farmhouse** ☎ Dean (0594) 530303

4 Annexe: 16 (4fb) CTV in 8 bedrooms ® in 16 bedrooms **T** in 16 bedrooms sB&B £20 sB&B £25 dB&B £30 dB&B £35
CTV 100P *xmas*
English & French **V** Lunch £8.50&alc Tea 60p Dinner £8.50&alc Wine £2.25 Last dinner 9.30pm
Credit cards 1 3 Ⓥ

LLANDRINDOD WELLS
Powys
Map **3** SO06

★★★ **Hotel Metropole** Temple St (Best Western) ☎ (0597) 2881 Telex no 35237

Spacious town centre hotel offering a relaxed atmosphere and attentive service.

L

121rm(114🛁7🚿)(2fb)CTV in all bedrooms T in 48 bedrooms S% *sB&B🛁🚿£31.50—£34.50 dB&B🛁🚿£49.50—£52 B
Lift ☾CTV 150P xmas
V ☕ *Lunch fr£8.50 Tea £1.75—£1.95 Dinner fr£10.50 Wine £4.95 Last dinner 9pm
Credit cards 1 2 3 4 5 V

LLANDUDNO
Gwynedd
Map **6** SH78
See plan

★★★

★★★ **BODYSGALLEN HALL, LLANDUDNO**
(on A470 Llandudno link road) (Prestige) ☎ Deganwy (0492) 84466 Telex no 617163
Plan **2** *E1*

Bodysgallen Hall was originally built in the 14th Century as a watchtower to help in the defence of Conwy Castle, but was enlarged in Elizabethan and Jacobean times, before being extensively converted to this fine hotel. It is set in splendid grounds whose pleasure gardens include the notable Knot Garden, rock-garden with cascade and walled rose garden. Tennis and croquet are available. The interior conveys a great sense of history with a panelled hall and a stone chimney-piece with open fire; the Jacobean drawing-room on the first floor is also panelled and has a stone chimney-piece surmounted by over-mantles with two coats of arms from previous family owners. There are also the cosy bar and the peaceful library. Antiques abound and all is enlivened with bright soft furnishings and flowers. The comfortably furnished bedrooms are well-equipped with trouser presses and other items such as home-made biscuits, flowering plants and Malvern water. The restaurant is dignified and well-appointed with elegant table settings.

Food is provided from a fixed price menu and is enjoyable. So too, is the service — our members always commend the courteous smiling way in which the friendly staff attends you. This is very much a hotel for the collector of country houses.

19🛁 Annexe:9🛁(3fb)1 CTV in all bedrooms ® in 9 bedrooms T S% sB&B🛁£55.50—£65.50 dB&B🛁£76—£106 B
☾70P 1 (hard) croquet Live music Sat nc 8yrs xmas
V ☕ Lunch £7.37—£9.35 Tea £1.54—£3.85 Dinner £16.50—£18.15&alc Wine £6.60 Last dinner 9.45pm
Credit cards 1 2 3 5 V

★★★*BL* **Empire** Church Walks ☎ (0492) 79955 Telex no 617161 Plan **11** *B4*
Closed Xmas & New Year
Comfortable privately run hotel furnished to high standard offering excellent facilities and good food.
56🛁(9fb) 2 CTV in all bedrooms ® T S% sB&B🛁£27.50—£37.50 dB&B🛁£45—£65 B
Lift ☾30P 6 CFA & (heated) sauna bath solarium Live music and dancing Sat
V ☕ S% Lunch £7.50 Tea £1.25 Dinner £11.50 Wine £6 Last dinner 9.30pm
Credit cards 1 2 3 5

★★★ **Gogarth Abbey** West Shore ☎ (0492) 76211 Plan **14** *A3*
Closed 23 Dec—24 Jan
Holiday hotel set on to the Great Orme, facing the West Shore.
41rm(33🛁6🚿)(5fb) CTV in all bedrooms ® sB&B🛁🚿£20—£30 dB&B🛁🚿£40—£60 B
CTV 40P (heated) sauna bath solarium croquet putting Live music & dancing wkly in season
☕ Lunch £6—£9 Tea £1—£3 High Tea £3—£6 Dinner £10—£14&alc Wine £4.50 Last dinner 8.30pm
Credit cards 1 2 3

★★★ **Imperial** Promenade (Best Western) ☎ (0492) 77466 Telex no 61606 Plan **18** *C3*
Impressive six storey Victorian hotel close to the shops.
135rm(100🛁2🚿)(5fb) in 2 bedrooms CTV in all bedrooms ® T *sB&B🛁🚿£21—£25 dB&B🛁🚿£42—£50 B
Lift ☾35P CFA snooker sauna bath solarium gymnasium Disco 6 nights wkly Live music and dancing 3 nights wkly Cabaret nightly *xmas*
V ☕ S% *Lunch £5—£6 Tea 60p—75p High Tea £4—£4.50 Dinner £8.50—£9.50&alc Wine £4.75 Last dinner 8.30pm
Credit cards 1 2 3 5 V

★★★ **Marine** Vaughan St (Trusthouse Forte) ☎ (0492) 77521 Plan **19** *C3*
Public areas and bedrooms are being upgraded in this Victorian sea-front hotel, which attracts a popular tourist trade.
76rm(53🛁)(5fb) CTV in all bedrooms ® sB&B£30.50 sB&B🛁£38.50 dB&B£45.50 dB&B🛁£53.50 B
Lift ☾28P CFA *xmas*
☕ Last dinner 9pm
Credit cards 1 2 3 4 5

★★ **St Tudno**
(see red star box on next page)

★★ **Belle Vue** North Pde ☎ (0492) 79547 Plan **1A** *C4*
Modern hotel overlooking sea provides well appointed accommodation and good food.
16rm(9🛁7🚿) CTV in all bedrooms ® sB&B🛁🚿£14—£18 dB&B🛁🚿£28—£36 B
Lift *xmas*
French V ☕ Lunch £5.50—£6.50 Tea £1—£2 High Tea £2—£4 Dinner £6.50—£8.50&alc Wine £4.50 Last dinner 9pm
Credit card 1 V

★★*B* **Bromwell Court** Promenade ☎ (0492) 78416 Plan **4** *E3*
RS Nov—Feb
This small, family-run hotel is equipped with all modern facilities and has a quiet, relaxing atmosphere.
11rm(3🛁6🚿)(2fb) CTV in all bedrooms ® T sB&B🛁🚿£17—£18.50 dB&B£28—£32 dB&B🛁🚿£32—£36 B
nc
V ☕ Lunch £6—£6.50 Tea £1.50—£3.50 Dinner £9—£11.50 Wine £5.25
Credit cards 1 3 V

★★*L* **Chatsworth House** Central Prom ☎ (0492) 79421 Plan **6** *C3*
Modernised Victorian-fronted holiday hotel, on seafront and near shops.
56rm(46🛁10🚿)(18fb) CTV in all bedrooms ® sB&B🛁🚿£16.50—£24.50 dB&B🛁🚿£31—£55.50 B
Lift ☾CTV 10P (heated) sauna bath solarium games room Live music & dancing nightly *xmas*
☕ Lunch £5.95 Tea £2.45 Dinner £7.95 Wine £6 Last dinner 8.30pm
Credit cards 1 3
See advertisement on page 420

★★ **ST TUDNO, LLANDUDNO**

North Parade ☎ (0492) 74411 Plan **31** *B4*

Closed 20 Dec—22 Jan

Janette and Martin Bland's hotel continues to please our members. Martin supervises the kitchen while Janette seems to be everywhere with her cheerful, outgoing friendliness. This cheerfulness is reflected in the bright decor, particularly in the reception area in the coffee lounge, through which you pass to the stunning, air-conditioned, garden-like dining room: with green and white trellis wallpaper set off by handpainted Chinois panels; with lime coloured bamboo chairs and lots of hanging plants, the illusion is complete. Here you can start the day with a hearty breakfast and at dinner sample the five-course meal. The style is eclectic but includes Welsh dishes. There is an attractive bar and a non-smoking sitting room, both of which have a Victorian air without the usual Victorian heaviness. Bedrooms can be compact, but they are prettily decorated and provided with many items not indicated by the hotel's classification, including a quarter bottle of sparkling wine. The Blands have imbued their staff with their own spirit of hospitality so that aspect will not be the least memorable part of your stay.

21rm(19→2⋒)(4fb) ⁄ in 2 bedrooms CTV in all bedrooms ® **T** sB&B→⋒£25—£42.50 dB&B→⋒£36—£70 **B**

Lift 4P 3⌂(£2.50) ⛟ ▭(heated)

International **V** ♁ ☕ ⁄ Lunch £4.95—£8.25 Tea £1 Dinner £14.25 Wine £5.80 Last dinner 9.30pm

Credit cards [1] [3] Ⓥ

★★*L* **Dunoon** Gloddaeth St ☎ (0492) 77078 Plan **10** *B3*

Closed Nov—mid Mar

Good, comfortable accommodation is provided by this centrally-situated, family run hotel.

56rm(47→5⋒) Annexe: 14→(22fb) CTV in all bedrooms ® sB&B£12.50—£15 sB&B→⋒£14—£19 dB&B→⋒£26—£38 **B**

Lift CTV 24P solarium ♿

♁ ☕ S% Lunch £5—£6 Tea 75p—£1 Dinner £7—£8&alc Wine £3.75 Last dinner 8pm Ⓥ

★★ **Esplanade** Glan-y-Mor Pde, Promenade ☎ (0492) 74343 Telex no 61155 Plan **12** *C4*

Bedrooms with private bathrooms are offered by this Victorian, sea-front, family-holiday hotel, which is in the process of being upgraded.

55rm(44→11⋒)(16fb) CTV in all bedrooms ® **T** in 42 bedrooms S% sB&B→⋒£21.50—£28 dB&B→⋒£37—£50 **B**

Lift CTV 30P games room table tennis & pool table *xmas*

English & French **V** ♁ ☕ Lunch £4—£5 Tea 50p—£2.50 High Tea £4—£7 Dinner £7—£8.50 Wine £4.10 Last dinner 7.45pm

Credit cards [1] [2] [3]

See advertisement on page 422

L

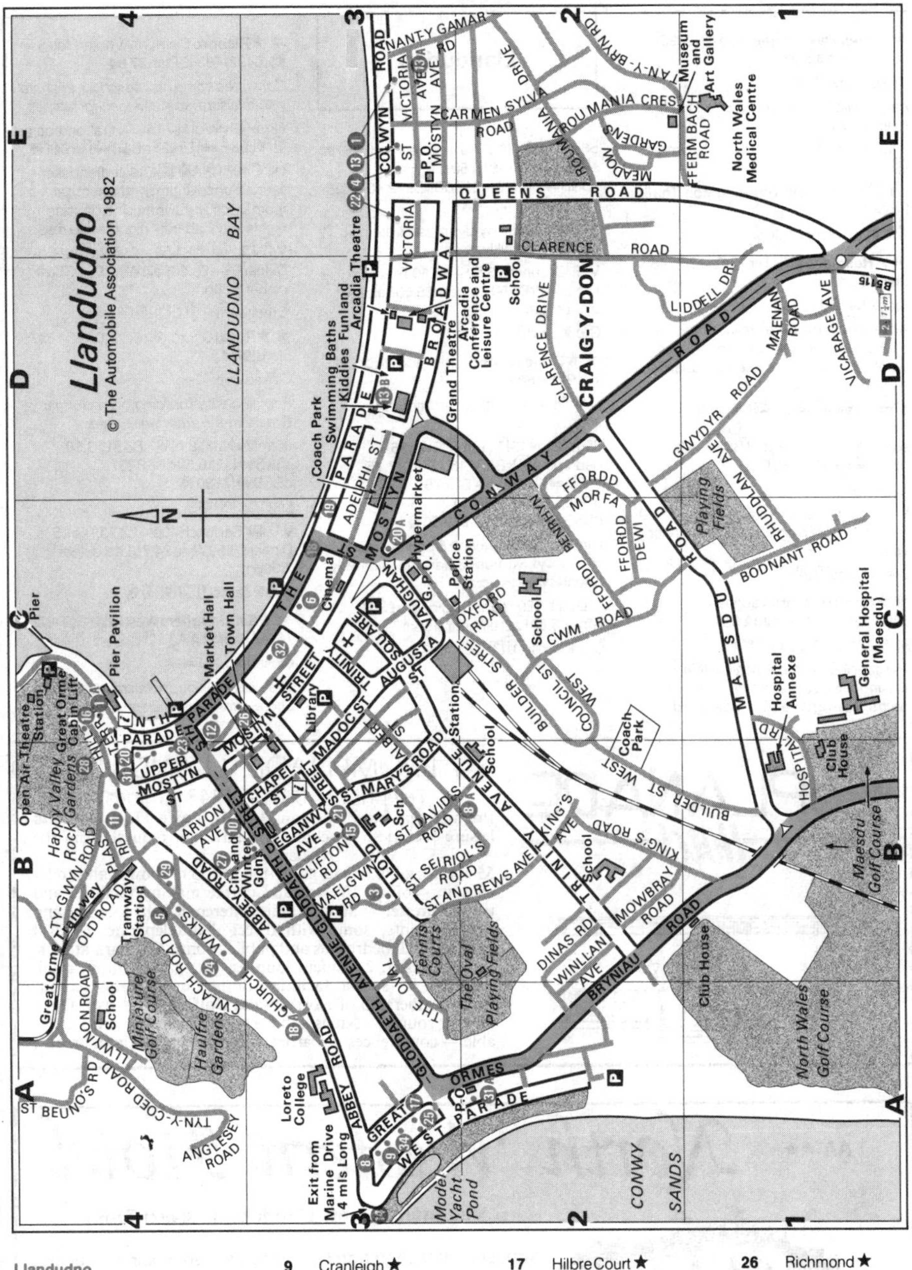

Llandudno

- 1 Bedford ★
- 1A Belle Vue ★★
- 2 Bodysgallen Hall ★★★
- 3 Branksome ★
- 4 Bromwell Court ★★
- 5 Bron Orme ★
- 6 Chatsworth House ★★
- 8 Clontarf ★
- 8A Cornerways ★
- 9 Cranleigh ★
- 10 Dunoon ★★
- 11 Empire ★★★
- 12 Esplanade ★★
- 13 Fairhaven ★
- 13A Floral ✕✕
- 13B Four Oaks ★★
- 14 Gogarth Abbey ★★★
- 15 Gwesty Leamore ★
- 16 Headlands ★★
- 17 Hilbre Court ★
- 18 Imperial ★★★
- 18A Lanterns ✕✕
- 19 Marine ★★★
- 20 Min-y-Don ★
- 20A North Western ★★
- 21 Oak Alyn ★
- 22 Ormescliffe ★★
- 24 Quinton ★
- 25 Ravenhurst ★
- 26 Richmond ★
- 27 Risboro ★★
- 28 Rothesay ★
- 29 Royal ★★
- 31 St Tudno ★★
- 31A Sandringham ★★
- 32 Somerset ★★
- 33 Sunnymede ★
- 34 Tan-Lan ★★

★★***Four Oaks*** Promenade ☎ (0492) 76506 Plan **13B** *D3*

Closed Nov—Feb

Large holiday hotel, family run and with modern facilities.

57rm(20🛁8🚿)(25fb) CTV in all bedrooms Ⓡ

Lift ☾ CTV Music & dancing Mon, Thu & Fri

V ☕ Last dinner 7.30pm

★★**Headlands** Hill Ter ☎ (0492) 77485 Plan **16** *C4*

Closed Jan & Feb

A relaxed atmosphere prevails in this personally-run hotel, a detached house situated on the Great Orme with superb sea and mountain views.

17rm(11🛁4🚿)(4fb) 3 CTV in all bedrooms Ⓡ sB&B£17—£18 sB&B🛁🚿£17—£18 dB&B£34—£36 dB&B🛁🚿£34—£36

10P *xmas*

V ☕ Bar lunch £1—£5 Tea 40p—£1.50 Dinner £9—£12&alc Wine £3 Last dinner 9pm

Credit cards [1] [3] Ⓥ

★★**North Western** Vaughan St ☎ (0492) 77694 Plan **20A** *C3*

RS 5—24 Dec & 2 Jan—1 Feb

This spacious Victorian hotel, within walking distance of sea and shopping centre, is being carefully modernised.

Llandudno

56rm(38🛁)(3fb) CTV in all bedrooms Ⓡ sB&B£12.70—£15.50 sB&B🛁£14.20—£17 dB&B£22.40—£28 dB&B🛁£25.40—£31

Lift 40P Disco wkly Live music & dancing wkly Cabaret wkly *xmas*

V ☕ Lunch £3.50—£5.50 Tea fr70p High Tea fr£3.50 Dinner fr£5.50&alc Last dinner 8pm

Credit card [1]

★★**Ormescliffe** Promenade ☎ (0492) 77191 Plan **22** *E3*

Holiday hotel located ½m from the shopping area.

65rm(23🛁13🚿)(15fb) CTV in 36 bedrooms Ⓡ sB&B£15.25—£17.75 sB&B🛁🚿£15.25—£19.75 dB&B£30.50—£35.50 dB&B🛁🚿£30.50—£39.50

Lift CTV 15P table tennis & pool table Disco twice wkly Live music & dancing twice wkly Cabaret wkly *xmas*

☕ Lunch fr£5 Tea fr75p Dinner fr£8.30 Wine £5.50 Last dinner 7.45pm

Credit cards [1] [3] Ⓥ

★★**Risboro** Clement Av (Inter Hotel) ☎ (0492) 76343 Plan **27** *B4*

Converted from a private school, this hotel with its leisure facilities is ideal for families.

68rm(48🛁20🚿)(7fb) CTV in all bedrooms Ⓡ **T** sB&B🛁🚿fr£24 dB&B🛁🚿fr£44

Lift ☾ 40P CFA (heated) snooker sauna bath solarium gymnasium games room Disco Thu Live music & dancing 4 nights wkly Cabaret 4 nights wkly *xmas*

V ☕ Lunch £3.50—£5&alc Tea 50p Dinner £8—£8.50&alc Wine £5.25 Last dinner 8.30pm

Credit cards [1] [2] [3] [5] Ⓥ

★★**Royal** Church Walk ☎ (0492) 76476 Plan **29** *B4*

Closed Dec—Feb

Pebble-dashed building located under Great Orme in a residential area.

35rm(7🛁3🚿)(6fb) Ⓡ sB&B£13.50 sB&B🛁🚿£16.50 dB&B£27 dB&B🛁🚿£30

Lift CTV 30P ♿

V ☕ Bar lunch 70p—£2.75 Tea fr55p Dinner £6.50 Wine £4.75 Last dinner 7.30pm

Credit cards [1] [2] [3] [5] Ⓥ

★★***Sandringham*** West Pde ☎ (0492) 76513 Plan **31A** *A2*

Closed Nov—Feb

The well-appointed hotel stands on West Shore, affording excellent views of

Snowdonia, Anglesey and the Conwy Estuary.
18rm(6🛁)(4fb) TV in all bedrooms ® ✈
CTV 10P
V ♀ ☕ Last dinner 7.30pm
See advertisement on page 424

★ ★**Somerset** Central Prom ☎ (0492) 76540 Plan **32** *C3*
Closed 15 Nov—Feb
Smartly fronted by patio and flower beds, this Victorian, sea-front, holiday hotel, long established and family-run, offers comfortable public rooms and bright bedrooms with private facilities.
37rm(29🛁8🚿)(4fb) CTV in all bedrooms sB&B🛁🚿£17—£23 dB&B🛁🚿£32—£43.70 B
Lift 20P
♀Lunch £5.25 Dinner £7.50 Wine £3.75 Last dinner 7.30pm
Credit cards 1 3 Ⓥ
See advertisement on page 424

★ ★**Tan-Lan** Great Orme's Rd West Shore ☎ (0492) 75981 Plan **34** *A3*
Closed Nov—mid Mar
This elegant family-run hotel provides comfortable bedrooms and warm hospitality.
18rm(8🛁10🚿)(5fb) CTV in all bedrooms ®sB&B🛁🚿£16—£17 dB&B🛁🚿£30—£32 B
10P
English, French & Italian ♀ ☕ Lunch £5—£6 Tea 75p—£1 Dinner £7.50—£8.50 Wine £3.90 Last dinner 8pm
See advertisement on page 424

★**Bedford** Promenade ☎ (0492) 76647 Plan **1** *E3*

Closed Oct–Mar

Detached Victorian building, ¾m from the main shopping area. Hotel undergoing major alterations during the currency of this guide.

31rm(3🛁2🚿)(9fb) sB&Bfr£17.50 sB&B🛁🚿fr£20 dB&Bfr£17.50 dB&B🛁🚿fr£20 **B**

☾ CTV 20P

🍴English, French & Italian **V** ♈ ☕ Lunch £6 Tea £1.50 High Tea £3–£5 Dinner fr£8&alc Wine £5.50 Last dinner 10.30pm

Credit cards 1 3

Llandudno

★***Branksome*** Lloyd St ☎ (0492) 75989 Plan **3** *B3*

Closed Jan–Mar

Holiday hotel situated in a quiet residential area, ½m from the beach and ¼m from the shops.

48rm(7🛁10🚿) Annexe: 5rm(10fb) **B**

CTV 12P sauna bath solarium gymnasium Disco wkly Live music & dancing wkly Cabaret 3 nights wkly *xmas*

🍴English, French & Italian **V** ♈ ☕ Last dinner 7pm

★**Bron Orme** Church Walks ☎ (0492) 76735 Plan **5** *B4*

Closed Oct–Mar

Located at the foot of Great Orme, only a short distance from beach and town centre.

9rm(4fb) ✗ S% * sB&B£8.50–£9 dB&B£16–£17

CTV **P** nc10yrs

🍴Continental ♈ ☕ ⁄ S% * Lunch £4.50 High Tea £3.50 Dinner £5.75 Wine £3.50 Last dinner 7pm

L

Llandudno

★Clontarf 1 Great Ormes Rd, West Shore ☎(0492) 77621 Plan **8** *A3*

RS Nov—Feb

Detached hotel situated in residential area, close to the West Shore.

10rm(1🛁3🚿)(2fb) ® 🐕 sB&B£10.50—£11.50 sB&B🛁🚿£12—£13 dB&B£20—£22 dB&B🛁🚿fr£25 B

CTV 10P ✽ nc7yrs

V Lunch £4.50&alc Tea 50p Dinner £7&alc Wine £3.50 Last dinner 7.30pm Ⓥ

★Cornerways 2 St Davids Pl ☎(0492) 77334 Plan **8A** *B3*

Closed mid Oct—mid Mar

This small, family-run, private hotel stands in a quiet residential area only a few minutes' walk from the town centre.

8rm(5🛁1🚿)(2fb) CTV in all bedrooms ® 🐕 S% *sB&Bfr£12 sB&B🛁🚿fr£14 dB&Bfr£24 dB&B🛁🚿fr£26

Unlicensed CTV 5P nc7yrs

British & Continental S% Lunch fr£5 Tea £1—£2 Dinner fr£7 Last dinner 7pm

Credit card 1 Ⓥ

★Cranleigh Great Orme's Rd, West Shore ☎(0492) 77688 Plan **9** *A3*

Closed Oct—Etr

Detached hotel in residential area, near West Shore.

13rm(4🚿)(4fb) TV available in bedrooms ® sB&B£10.50—£12.50 sB&B🚿£12—£14 dB&B£21—£25 dB&B🚿£24—£28

CTV 13P nc3yrs

S% Lunch fr£5 Tea fr75p Dinner fr£7 Wine £3.50 Last dinner 7.30pm

★*B* Fairhaven Promenade, Craigydon Pde (Guestaccom) ☎(0492) 76123 Plan **13** *E3*

Closed Nov—Feb

The bright, comfortable, sea-front holiday hotel offers bedrooms with facilities and well-kept public areas.

11rm(6🛁5🚿)(1fb) CTV in all bedrooms ® T S% sB&B🛁🚿£16—£18 dB&B🛁🚿£30—£34 B

CTV 5P

S% Lunch £3—£4.50 Dinner £7—£8.50 Wine £3.50 Last dinner 7pm

Credit cards 1 3 Ⓥ

★*H* Gwesty Leamore 40 Lloyd St ☎(0492) 75552 Plan **15** *B3*

Closed Dec

"Croeso" means "welcome", and this you will find at Leamore, a bright, clean hotel with well-equipped bedrooms and comfortable public areas, personally-run by the Welsh-speaking proprietors.

12rm(1🛁6🚿)(4fb) CTV in all bedrooms ® 🐕 S% sB&B£12—£14 sB&B🛁🚿£14—£16 dB&B£24—£27 dB&B🛁🚿£27—£29 B

CTV 4P

S% Bar lunch £2.50—£3.50 Dinner £6—£7.50 Wine £4.80 Last dinner 7.30pm Ⓥ

★Hilbre Court Great Ormes Rd, West Shore ☎(0492) 76632 Plan **17** *A3*

Closed Nov—Mar

Edwardian house in residential area, near West Shore.

10rm(3🛁2🚿)(1fb) CTV in all bedrooms sB&B£12.60—£14.50 dB&B£25.20—£30 dB&B🛁🚿£28.70—£33.20 B

CTV 5P nc3yrs

V Lunch £4.50 Tea £1 Dinner £8.70&alc Wine £4.60 Last dinner 7pm

Credit cards 1 3 Ⓥ

★*H* Min-y-Don North Pde ☎(0492) 76511 Plan **20** *B4*

Closed 21 Oct—Feb

Family-run holiday hotel on the sea-front, near the shops.

20rm(1🚿)(9fb) CTV in all bedrooms ® T 🐕 sB&B£13.23—£15.18 dB&B£26.46—£30.36 dB&B🚿£30.36—£33 B

→

CTV 5P xmas

V Lunch £3.95—£4.50 Tea £1.95 High Tea £2.95 Dinner £4.75—£5.75 Wine £3.99 Last dinner 7.30pm

Ⓥ

★**Oak Alyn** Deganwy Av ☎ (0492) 76497

Closed Dec (ex Xmas)
RS Jan—mid Feb

Three-storey Victorian house in a central position.

16rm (2⇌9ⓜ)(2fb) CTV in all bedrooms ® sB&B£10 sB&B⇌ⓜ£11.50 dB&B£20 dB&B⇌ⓜ£23 B

16P xmas

Lunch £2—£3 Tea £1 Dinner £5—£7&alc Wine £6 Last dinner 7.30pm

Credit cards 1 3

★**Quinton** 36 Church Walks ☎ (0492) 76879 Plan **24** *B4*

Closed Nov—Jan (except Xmas)

This family-run hotel stands in a quiet part of the town, both beaches being within walking distance.

15rm (4⇌3ⓜ)(8fb) CTV in all bedrooms ® **T** S% sB&B£10 sB&B⇌ⓜ£11—£12 dB&B£20 dB&B⇌ⓜ£22 B

CTV 20P xmas

Bar lunch £1.20—£1.95 Tea 40—65p Dinner £3.95 Wine £3.10 Last dinner 7.30pm

Ⓥ

★**Ravenhurst** West Pde ☎ (0492) 75525 Plan **25** *A3*

Closed 31 Dec—5 Jan

This hotel faces the West Shore, and has good views of the Snowdonia Range.

23rm (17⇌4ⓜ) Annexe: 1⇌ (4fb) CTV in all bedrooms ® sB&B£12.50—£13.50 sB&B⇌ⓜ£14.70—£15.70 dB&B£25—£27 dB&B⇌ⓜ£29.90—£31.40 B

14P games room ♿ xmas

V Lunch £3.50—£6&alc Tea £1.20—£1.40&alc Dinner £6.80—£10.50&alc Wine £4 Last dinner 7.45pm

Credit cards 1 3 5 Ⓥ

★**Richmond** St Georges Pl ☎ (0492) 76347 Plan **26** *C3*

Closed Nov—Feb

Large terraced hotel with a verandah.

26rm (23⇌3ⓜ)(8fb) CTV in all bedrooms ® sB&B⇌ⓜ£12—£13 dB&B⇌ⓜ£24—£26 B

Lift CTV

Bar lunch £2.45—£3.75 Tea 41—45p Dinner £6.50 Wine £4 Last dinner 7.30pm

★**Rothesay** 83 Church Walks ☎ (0492) 76844 Plan **28** *C4*

Closed mid Oct—Apr

Victorian terraced hotel just off North Parade.

22rm (1ⓜ)(3fb) *sB&B£10—£11 dB&B£20—£22 dB&Bⓜ£20—£22

CTV

*Bar lunch £1.50—£2.50 Tea 60p—£1 High Tea £1—£1.50 Dinner £4—£6 Wine £4 Last dinner 4pm

★*BL* **Sunnymede** West Pde ☎ (0492) 77130 Plan **33** *A2*

Closed 10 Nov—Feb

The caring, family-run hotel enjoys a good location, and very high standards of comfort prevail in bedrooms and public areas.

19rm (7⇌4ⓜ)(3fb) 2 CTV in all bedrooms ® sB&B£14—£16 sB&B⇌ⓜ£16—£18 dB&B£28—£32 dB&B⇌ⓜ£32—£36 B

CTV 19P

V Lunch £5—£6 Tea £1.50 Dinner £7—£8&alc Wine £4.50 Last dinner 7pm

Credit cards 1 3 Ⓥ

XX**Floral** Victoria St, Craig-y-don ☎ (0492) 75735 Plan **13A** *E3*

Closed Mon
Lunch not served Sat

V 60 seats *Lunch £6alc Dinner £14.50alc Wine £4.95 Last dinner 9.45pm nc 5yrs

Credit cards 1 3 5

XX**Lanterns** 7 Church Walks ☎ (0492) 77924 Plan **18A** *A3*

At this small, well-furnished and comfortable restaurant, the good atmosphere is enhanced by light, classical, background music. The menu, though short, offers a good range of imaginative dishes based on fresh ingredients, complemented by personal service.

Closed Mon & mid Feb—mid Mar
Lunch not served Tue—Sat Dinner not served Sun

English & French 30 seats *Sun Lunch £7.50 Dinner £12.50alc Wine £4.80 Last dinner 10.15pm

Credit cards 1 2 3 5 Ⓥ

LLANELLI
Dyfed
Map **2** SN50

£59.50 tw
£49.50 sng.

★★★***Diplomat*** Ael-y-Bryn ☎ (0554) 756156 Cor: 751649.

Family owned and managed, this quality hotel with commendable restaurant is popular with businessmen. Recent upgrading has provided comfortable bedrooms and a new leisure/function complex.

25rm (22⇌1ⓜ)(1fb) CTV in all bedrooms ® B

Lift 200P Disco & live music & dancing Sat Cabaret Sat

English, French & Italian **V** Last dinner 9.45pm

Credit cards 1 2 3 5

★★★**Stradey Park** Furnace (Trusthouse Forte) ☎ (0554) 758171 Telex no 48521

Conveniently positioned company-owned hotel with purpose-built accommodation designed for business clients.

80⇌(3fb) CTV in all bedrooms ® sB&B⇌£43.50 dB&B⇌£57.50 B

Lift ☾ 120P CFA xmas

Last dinner 9.30pm

Credit cards 1 2 3 4 5

LLANFAIRPWLLGWYNGYLL
Gwynedd
Map **6** SH57

★★★***Carreg Bran Country*** Church Ln (Minotel) ☎ Llanfairpwll (0248) 714224

Regency-style country house set below Britannia Bridge.

9⇌(4fb) CTV in all bedrooms ® T B

200P ✿ Live music Fri

V ♀ ☕ Last dinner 10pm

Credit cards 1 2 3 4 5

LLANFYLLIN
Powys
Map **6** SJ11

★★ *BL* **Bodfach Hall** ☎ (069184) 272

Closed Jan & Feb RS mid Nov—Xmas

A warm, relaxed atmosphere awaits the guest at this 17th-century country house. Ornate ceilings, wood-panelled walls and some original William Morris wallpaper in the lounge are noteworthy features.

9rm(7⇌2⫛)(2fb) CTV in all bedrooms ® sB&B⇌⫛fr£20 dB&B⇌⫛fr£40 B

20P ✿ ♪ *xmas*

V ♀ Lunch fr£6.50 Dinner fr£9.50 Wine £5.25 Last dinner 8.45pm

Credit cards 1 2 5

★★**Cain Valley** ☎ (069184) 366

A 15th-century country inn, with a Jacobean stairway and an oak-panelled lounge bar, set in the centre of the village.

14rm(8⇌6⫛)(3fb) CTV in 8 bedrooms TV in 6 bedrooms ® S% ✱sB&B⇌⫛£16.50 dB&B⇌⫛£33 B →

CTV 25P 2 xmas
English, French & German
*Lunch £5.50—£7 Tea 40p—£1 Dinner £8.25&alc Wine £4.50 Last dinner 9.30pm

LLANGAMMARCH WELLS
Powys
Map **3** SN94

★★★ *HL* **Lake** (05912) 202
The hotel is set in 50 acres and provides good sporting facilities, comfortably furnished accommodation and well-prepared food from a fixed-price menu.
25 4 CTV in all bedrooms ® **T**
sB&B £28.50—£36.50
dB&B £46.50—£65 B
70P 3 (hard) snooker
xmas
Welsh, English & French **V** Lunch £7.50&alc Tea 80p&alc High Tea £2.50&alc Dinner £14.50&alc Wine £6.50 Last dinner 6.30pm
Credit cards 1 2 3 V

LLANGOLLEN
Clwyd
Map **7** SJ24

★★★ **Bryn Howel** (2¾m E A539) (0978) 860331
Closed Xmas day
Mock Tudor house with modern extension. Fine views up the Dee Valley and good fishing facilities.
38 CTV in all bedrooms ® **T**
sB&B fr£32 dB&B fr£44
Lift CTV 200P sauna bath solarium
CFA
International **V** S% *Lunch fr£6&alc Tea fr75p High Tea fr£2.50 Dinner fr£9&alc Wine £5 Last dinner 10pm
Credit cards 1 2 3

★★★ **Hand** (Mount Charlotte) (0978) 860303 Telex no 61160
Modernised hotel with comfortable bedrooms, set beside River Dee.
59rm(50 9)(5fb) CTV in all bedrooms **T**
sB&B fr£28.80 dB&B fr£49.80 B
100P CFA

English & Continental **V** Lunch fr£5.70 Tea fr50p High Tea fr£4 Dinner fr£9&alc Wine £5.50 Last dinner 9pm
Credit cards 1 2 3 5 V

★★★ **Royal** Bridge St (Trusthouse Forte) (0978) 860202
Three-storey stone hotel, situated in the centre of town on the bank of the River Dee.
33 (3fb) CTV in all bedrooms ®
sB&B £43.50 dB&B £62.50 B
20P *xmas*
Last dinner 9pm
Credit cards 1 2 3 4 5

★★ *H* **Ty'n-y-Wern** (1m E on A5) (Guestaccom) (0978) 860252
Closed Xmas Day
This 18th century house enjoys an elevated position overlooking the Vale of Llangollen on the outskirts of the town. Personally run by the owners, it maintains traditional standards of hospitality and service and serves food prepared carefully and with flair.
12rm(7 2)(2fb) CTV in 4 bedrooms TV in 8 bedrooms ® S% sB&B £16—£18
sB&B £21—£23 dB&B £27—£30
dB&B £32—£37 B
CTV 80P
French **V** S% Lunch £8.50—£10.50&alc Tea 85p High Tea £5alc Dinner £8.50—£10.50&alc Wine £3.95 Last dinner 9.30pm
Credit cards 1 3

LLANGORSE
Powys
Map **3** SO12

★ **Red Lion** (087484) 238
Small character inn positioned close to The Brecon Beacons and Black Mountains.
10rm(5) CTV in all bedrooms ® **T**
sB&B £15—£18 dB&B £23—£26
dB&B £26—£30 B
30P 2 *xmas*

Mainly grills **V** Lunch £3.50—£5 Tea £1.50—£3 Dinner £5—£10.50&alc Wine £4.50 Last dinner 9.30pm
V

LLANGURIG
Powys
Map **6** SN98

★★ ***Glansevern Arms*** Pant Mawr (4m W on Aberystwyth Rd) (05515) 240
RS 1 wk Xmas
Small country-style inn, situated beside the road, with panoramic views from the rear.
7rm(5 2) CTV in all bedrooms B
25P
Last dinner 8pm

LLANGYNOG
Powys
Map **6** SJ02

★ *B* **New Inn** Pennant (069174) 229
Comfortable family-run inn set in mountain hamlet.
8rm(3)(2fb) ® available in bedrooms
sB&B £15—£17 dB&B £28—£32
dB&B £32—£40 B
CTV 30P pool table *xmas*
V *Lunch £6.55alc Tea 82palc High Tea £2.12alc Dinner £6.25&alc Wine £4.36 Last dinner 9.45pm
V

See advertisement under Bala

LLANGYBI
Gwent
Map **3** ST39

★★★★ *H* **Cwrt Bleddyn** (0633) 49521
The small, country house hotel provides good service and has recently been refurbished to a very high standard; an extension of 19 bedrooms is being added.
8 Annexe: 7 (4fb) 1 CTV in all bedrooms **T** *sB&B £45
dB&B £59 B
100P Live music Fri & Sat *xmas*
French *Tea £3.25 Wine £5.50 Last dinner 10pm
Credit cards 1 2 3 5

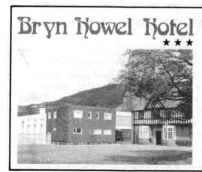

LLANIDLOES
Powys
Map **6** SN98

★***Red Lion*** Longbridge St ☎ (05512) 2270

Closed 25 Dec

Family run, market town inn, with friendly service.

6rm(2fb) ® ✂

CTV 8P

♕ Last dinner 9.30pm

LLANRHAEADR
Clywd
Map **6** SJ06

★★★**Bryn Morfydd** (Consort) ☎ Llanynys (074578) 280

Country mansion, ½m from the main road and set amongst green fields and trees.

18rm(17🛁1🚿)
Annexe: 12rm(5🛁2🚿)(2fb) CTV in all bedrooms ® **T** sB&B🛁🚿£25 dB&B£35 dB&B🛁🚿£35 **B**

CTV 100P ✿ ⛱ (heated) ⛳ 🎾(hard) shooting Disco wknds Live music & dancing wknds Cabaret wknds (in season) *xmas*

🍷Welsh, English & French **V** ♕ ☕ Lunch fr£2.50 Tea fr50p Dinner £8.50&alc Wine £4.25 Last dinner 9.30pm

Credit cards 1 2 3 5

LLANRWST
Gwynedd
Map **6** SH76

★★★**Maenan Abbey** Maenan ☎ Dolgarrog (049269) 247

19th century stone building with a galleried hall and the staircase as a feature. On the site of an old monastery, alongside A470.

12rm(9🛁3🚿)(2fb) CTV in all bedrooms ® sB&B🛁🚿£20—£24 dB&B🛁🚿£34—£40 **B**

☾ 60P ✿ 🎣 *xmas*

🍷English, French & Italian **V** ♕ ☕ Lunch £5.95—£8.95&alc Tea 95p—£2.50 Dinner £8.95—£9.95&alc Wine £4.95 Last dinner 9.45pm

Credit cards 1 2 3 5 Ⓥ

★★★🏠**Plas Maenan Country House** Maenan (3m N) ☎ Dolgarrog (049269) 232

Quiet secluded hotel in an elevated position, overlooking the Vale of Conwy and the river.

15🛁(3fb) 1⊠ CTV in all bedrooms ® sB&B🛁£20—£27 dB&B£36—£48 **B**

100P 2🚗 ✿ 🎣 👪 *xmas*

V ♕ ⚡ Lunch fr£5 Tea 75p Dinner fr£9&alc Wine £5 Last dinner 9.30pm

Credit cards 1 2 3 4 5 Ⓥ

★★**Eagles** ☎ (0492) 640454

Impressive stone hotel on the banks of the River Conwy.

12rm(10🛁1🚿)(6fb) CTV in all bedrooms ® ✱ sB&B£18.50—£20 sB&B🛁🚿£18.50—£20 dB&B£30—£40 dB&B🛁🚿£30—£40 **B**

CTV 60P 🎣 sauna bath solarium gymnasium pool table 👪

🍷Welsh, English & French **V** ♕ ☕ ✱ Lunch fr£5 Tea £1—£3 High Tea fr£3&alc Dinner fr£8.50&alc Wine £5.20 Last dinner 8.30pm

Credit cards 1 3 5

★★**Meadowsweet** Station Rd ☎ (0492) 640732

Small, intimate and friendly, the Victorian hotel is conveniently positioned for touring the Conwy Valley. Its attractive restaurant offers a high standard of food, the breakfast menu being particularly commendable, and the wine list is extensive.

10🚿(1fb) CTV in all bedrooms **T** sB&B🚿£21—£25 dB&B🚿£38—£45 **B**

10P *xmas*

🍷French ♕ ⚡ Lunch £6.50—£10 Dinner £14.50 Wine £4.95 Last dinner 9.30pm

Credit cards 1 2 3 Ⓥ

LLANSANTFFRAID-YM-MECHAIN
Powys
Map **7** SJ22

★**Lion** ☎ (069181) 207

Early 18th century former courthouse, now popular for good homemade fare.

6rm(2🛁2🚿)(1fb) CTV in all bedrooms ® S% sB&B£12.50 sB&B🛁🚿£15—£17 dB&B£25 dB&B🛁🚿£30—£32 **B**

40P

🍷English & Continental ♕ Bar lunch £5alc Dinner £7alc Wine £4.25 Last dinner 10pm

Credit card 1

LLANTWIT MAJOR
South Glamorgan
Map **3** SS96

★★***West House*** West St ☎ (04465) 2406

Pleasantly positioned in a quiet village setting, yet also convenient for businessmen, the attractive little country house hotel has a cosy bar and lounge plus an intimate dining room which maintains commendable standards of cooking.

19rm(14🛁)(2fb) CTV in 15 bedrooms TV in 4 bedrooms ® **B**

45P ⊭ *xmas*

🍷English & French ♕ ☕ Last dinner 9.30pm

Credit cards 1 2 3

See advertisement on page 430

✕✕✕**Colhugh Villa** Flanders Rd ☎ (04465) 2022

This pleasant restaurant of character stands at the heart of the village and offers honest, interesting food backed by friendly service.

Closed Mon Lunch not served Tue—Sat Dinner not served Sun

🍷English & French 60 seats Sun Lunch £7.50&alc Dinner fr£10.50&alc Wine £4.90 Last dinner 9.30pm 30P Live music Fri

Credit cards 1 2 3 5

LLANWNDA
Gwynedd
Map **6** SH45

★★★ *B* **Stables** (Inter Hotel) ☎ (0286) 830711

Modern bedrooms with excellent facilities plus good food in attractive restaurant are features of this rural hotel.

Annexe: 12→⋒(2fb) ⊬ in 4 bedrooms CTV in all bedrooms ® **T** ✱ sB&B→⋒£29 dB&B→⋒£46 B

40P ✲ ⌂ Live music & dancing Sat Apr—Oct ⛫ *xmas*

V ♉ ☕ ✱ Lunch £5.95 Tea 75p Dinner £10&alc Wine £4.85 Last dinner 9.45pm

Credit cards 1 2 3 Ⓥ

LLANYCHAER
Dyfed
Map **2** SM93

✕ **Penlan Oleu** ☎ Puncheston (034882) 314

This isolated, rustic restaurant, which also provides accommodation in some cosy bedrooms with en suite facilities, was converted from a Welsh farmhouse and is set high in the Preseli Mountains with magnificent views towards Ireland. Amenities and appointments have been kept simple, emphasis being placed on the presentation of quality fresh produce.

Closed Xmas Day & Boxing Day Lunch not served Sun

♉ English & French 20 seats Lunch £12.50alc Dinner £12.50alc Wine £4.20 Last dinner 9pm P ⊬ nc 7yrs

Credit cards 1 3

LLECHRYD
Dyfed
Map **2** SN24

★★★ ♣ **Castell Malgwyn** (½m S unclass towards Boncath) ☎ (023987) 382

Within the Teifi Valley, rich in Welsh history and culture, stands an elegant country mansion built in 1780. Now a personally-run hotel, it offers pleasant guest rooms, spacious lounges and commendable food standards. Its grounds, running beside the river, extend to 50 acres of garden, meadow and woodland.

24rm(20→2⋒)(4fb) CTV in all bedrooms ® **T** sB&B£25—£28 sB&B→⋒£25—£28 dB&B£48—£52 dB&B→⋒£48—£52 B

CTV 100P ✲ ⊡ & ⌂ (heated) ✎ ♪ U putting croquet *xmas*

V ♉ ☕ Lunch fr£5.75 Tea fr£1.20 Dinner fr£6.75&alc Wine £4.75 Last dinner 9pm

Credit cards 1 2 3 5 Ⓥ

LLYSWEN
Powys
Map **3** SO13

★ **Griffin Inn** ☎ (087485) 241

An ideal base for touring, beside the A470 south of Builth Wells, the small, personally-run inn has character bars and comfortable bedrooms.

6rm(4→2⋒) ®
sB&B→⋒£14.95—£16.95
dB&B→⋒£27.95—£32.50 B

CTV 14P ⛟ Live music & dancing mthly

V ♉ Lunch £7alc High Tea £5alc Dinner £10.50alc Wine £2.90 Last dinner 9.30pm

Credit cards 1 2 3 5 Ⓥ

LOCHAILORT
Highland *Inverness-shire*
Map **13** NM78

★ **Lochailort Inn** ☎ (06877) 208

A truly Highland welcome awaits you at this simple little roadside inn, and many a good fishing yarn is told beside the inviting, open log fires.

7rm(1fb) ✗ sB&B£13.50—£15.50 dB&B£27—£31

CTV 20P ⛟

V ♉ ☕ Lunch £4.50alc Tea 80palc High Tea £3.50alc Dinner £12alc Wine £3.50 Last dinner 9pm

Ⓥ

LOCHAWE
Strathclyde *Argyllshire*
Map **10** NN12

★★ **Carraig-Thura** ☎ Dalmally (08382) 210

Closed Jan—Etr RS Oct—Dec

Small, comfortable, family-run hotel with friendly and relaxed atmosphere.

12rm(8→4⋒) Annexe: 8rm(2→1⋒)(3fb) ⊬ in 2 bedrooms CTV available in 1 bedroom ® S% sB&B£18.50 sB&B→⋒£24—£34.50 dB&B£29 dB&B→⋒£40—£61

CTV 25P ⛟ ✲ ♪

♉ English & French ♉ ☕ ⊬ S% Bar lunch 90p—£4 Tea £1.80—£2 Dinner £12—£20 Wine £4.50 Last dinner 8pm

Credit cards 1 2 3 5

LOCHBOISDALE
Isle of South Uist, Western Isles
Inverness-shire
See **South Uist, Isle of**

LOCHCARRON
Highland *Ross & Cromarty*
Map **14** NG93

★ **Lochcarron** ☎ (05202) 226

Stone-built building on edge of village.

7rm(4→) CTV in all bedrooms ®
sB&B£14—£15 sB&B→£18—£20
dB&B£24—£28 dB&B→£30—£34

CTV 30P

♉ ☕ Lunch £2.50—£5&alc Tea £1—£1.25&alc High Tea £3.50—£4.50&alc Dinner £9—£10&alc Wine £3.95 Last dinner 8.30pm

Credit cards 1 3 Ⓥ

LOCHEARNHEAD
Central *Perthshire*
Map **11** NN52

★ *L* **Lochearnhead** Lochside ☎ (05673) 229

Closed Oct—Feb

Homely little hotel with lovely views.

14rm(1→3⋒) CTV in all bedrooms ®
sB&B£16.50—£21.60
sB&B→⋒£16.50—£21.60
dB&B£26.30—£33.50
dB&B→⋒£26.30—£33.50

CTV80P✿♩ squash

V Barlunch £1—£10 Dinner £8.50—£11alc Wine £4.20 Last dinner 9pm

Credit cards 1 2 3 5

★*HB* **Mansewood Country House** ☎(05673) 213 Telex no 29514 TXLING (Guestaccom)

RS Nov—Feb

The proprietor takes a pride in the food served at this comfortable and friendly small hotel.

6rm(2⇌1⋒) Ⓡ S% sB&B£12—£18 dB&B£25 dB&B⇌⋒£29 Ḃ

☾13P✿

Scottish & French ♔ ☕ ✂ *Lunch £2.20—£6.25&alc Tea 70p—£2.75 Dinner £8.50—£12 Wine £5.75 Last dinner 9pm Ⓥ

LOCHINVER
Highland *Sutherland*
Map **14** NC02

★★*HL* **Culag** (Best Western) ☎(05714) 209 Telex no 75206

Closed 15 Oct—1 May

Spacious traditional hotel beside the pier.

44rm(19⇌)(1fb) Ⓡ S% sB&B£27.50 sB&B⇌£35 dB&B£52.80 dB&B⇌£60.50

Lift ☾ CTV35P ♬ ✿♩♿

Lochearnhead — Lockerbie

International ♔ ☕ S% Lunch £7.50—£8 Tea £2—£3.50 Dinner £13.75—£14&alc Wine £5.50 Last dinner 8.45pm

Credit cards 1 2 3 5 Ⓥ

LOCHWINNOCH
Strathclyde *Renfrewshire*
Map **10** NS35

✕ **Gable End** 45 High St ☎(0505) 842775

This popular little restaurant at the heart of the village extends a warm welcome and offers an extended menu with an international flavour, dishes making good use of fresh produce and usually being cooked to order.

Closed Mon

Dinner not served Sun

International 30 seats *Dinner £9.25&alc Wine £5.20

LOCKERBIE
Dumfries & Galloway *Dumfriesshire*
Map **11** NY18

★★★ **Lockerbie House** (1m N off B723) (Consort) ☎(05762) 2610 Telex no 57515

Closed Xmas & New Year

The peaceful location of this large, family-run, country house hotel belies its proximity to the busy A74.

27rm(25⇌1⋒)(3fb) CTV in 26 bedrooms Ⓡ in 26 bedrooms sB&B⇌⋒fr£30 dB&B⇌⋒fr£46 Ḃ

CTV 100P✿ sauna bath solarium ⛳♿

British & French **V** ♔ Bar lunch £4 Dinner £13.50—£25 Wine £6.80 Last dinner 9pm

Credit cards 1 2 3 5 Ⓥ

★★**Dryfesdale** ☎(05762) 2427

Closed Xmas—New Year

Rural country mansion set in its own grounds but close to A74.

11rm(8⇌2⋒)(1fb) CTV in all bedrooms **T** sB&B£17 sB&B⇌⋒£25 dB&B£30 dB&B⇌⋒£40 Ḃ

CTV 50P 2🏠 ♬ ✿ *xmas*

British & French **V** ♔ ☕ Lunch £5.50—£8.80 Tea 80p—£1.70 Dinner £10.50alc Wine £4.60 Last dinner 9pm

Credit cards 1 2 3 5

★★***Somerton House*** Carlisle Rd ☎(05762) 2583

A robust Victorian house standing in its own grounds, with interesting architectural aspects especially the woodwork.

6rm(4⇌)(2fb) Ⓡ ✗ Ḃ

CTV 40P ♬ ✿ Live music & dancing wkly *xmas*

Mainly grills **V** ♔ ☕ Last dinner 9.30pm

Credit cards 1 3

★**Blue Bell** High St ☎ (05762) 2309
18th century town centre inn.
7rm(1fb) ®sB&B£10.50 dB&B£20
CTV 8P Live music wknds
Mainly grills Bar lunch £1.60—£6
Dinner fr£7.95 Wine £4.65 Last dinner 9pm

★***Townhead*** Townhead St ☎ (05762) 2298
Small three-storey hotel, with a modern extension, standing on the main road at the north end of the town.
8rm(2fb) TV in 2 bedrooms ®sB&B£9.50 dB&B£19
CTV 20P 2 *xmas*
Mainly grills **V** Last dinner 9.45pm

LODDISWELL
Devon
Map **3** SX74

XX**Lavinia's** ☎ Kingsbridge (0548) 550306
This charming, bright little restaurant stands behind farm buildings, in a rural location. The young proprietors produce an interesting table d'hôte selection of excellent dishes, all freshly prepared and well flavoured, including some very good desserts. A well-chosen wine list complements the food.
Closed Sun, Mon & Oct—Etr Lunch by reservation only
French 30 seats ✱Dinner £21 alc Wine £6.50 Last dinner 9.30pm 15P

London hotels and restaurants

London Hotels and Restaurants

Page		
452	X	Sagarmatha (NW1)
473	XX	Sailing Junk (W8)
467	★★★★	St George's (W1)
460	XX	St Quentin (SW3)
457	❀XX	Salloos (SW1)
463	X	Samratt (SW15)
452	XX	San Carlo (N6)
460	XX	San Frediano (SW3)
475	❀★★★★★	Savoy (WC2)
476	XXXXX	Savoy Hotel Grill (WC2)
471	X	Sav's (W1)
469	XX	Sawasdee (W1)
467	★★★★	Selfridge (W1)
462	XX	September (SW10)
450	XX	Shares (EC3)
477	X	Sheekey's (WC2)
456	★★★★★	Sheraton Park Tower (SW1)
454	X	Sheridan's (NW6)
474	X	Shireen (W12)
473	X	Siam (W8)
455	X	South of the Border (SE1)
455	XX	Spread Eagle (SE10)
456	★★★★	Stafford (SW1)
476	★★★	Strand Palace (WC2)
468	★★★	Stratford Court (W1)
460	X	Le Suquet (SW3)
453	★★★	Swiss Cottage (NW3)
460	XX	Tandoori (SW3)
468	XXX	Tandoori of Mayfair (W1)

Page		
459	❀❀XX	Tante Claire (SW3)
477	X	Taste of India (WC2)
457	XX	Tate Gallery (SW1)
458	X	Tent (SW1)
477	XX	Thomas de Quincey's (WC2)
450	X	Three Compasses (EC1)
460	XX	Tiger Lee (SW5)
477	❀XX	Tourment d'Amour (WC2)
450	★★★★	Tower Thistle (E1)
472	XX	Trat-West (W2)
454	★★	TraveLodge (NW7)
461	X	Trencherman (SW6)
458	X	Le Trou Normand (SW1)
462	X	Van B's (SW10)
472	X	Veronica's Chez Franco (W2)
452	XX	Viceroy of India (NW1)
454	X	Vijay (NW6)
454	X	Wakaba (NW3)
476	★★★★	Waldorf (WC2)
458	❀XXXX	Waltons (SW3)
467	★★★★	Westbury (W1)
471	★★★	White's (W2)
463	X	Wild Thyme (SW15)
475	XX	Winstons Eating House (WC1)
453	X	Yeti (NW2)
469	XX	Yumi (W1)
471	❀X	Yung's (W1)
459	XXX	Zen Chinese (SW3)
461	X	Zen Too (SW7)

London plans – key map

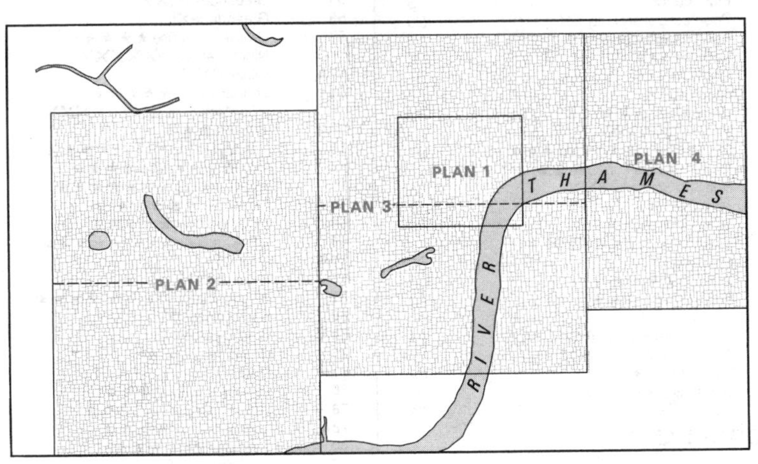

Keys to London town plans

To help you find details of establishments shown on this map first consult the Alphabetical List of London Hotels and Restaurants on pages 433-435.

LONDON PLAN 1

No.	Establishment	Grid
1	Alastair Little ✕	B4
1A	Ajimura Japanese ✕	D4
1B	Arirang(W1) ✕	A4
2	Au Jardin des Gourmets ❀✕✕	B4
3A	Bates English ✕	D3
4	Boulestin ❀✕✕✕	D3
5A	Berners ★★★	A5
6A	Le Cafe des Amis du Vin ✕	D4
6B	Cafe Pelican ✕	D3
7	Cafe Royal (Grill Room) ✕✕✕✕✕	A/B3
7A	Le Cafe du Jardin ✕	E4
7B	Le Caprice ✕✕	A1
8	Cavendish ★★★★	A2
11	Chesa (Swiss Centre) ✕✕	C3
12	Chez Solange ✕✕	C3
13A	La Corée Korean ✕	C5
14	La Cucaracha ✕✕	C4
15	Drury Lane Moat House ★★★	D5
16	Duke's ❀★★★★	A1
16A	Frith's ✕	B4
16B	Fuji Japanese ✕	B3
17	Gallery Rendezvous ✕✕	A3
18	Gay Hussar ❀✕✕	B4
20	Happy Wok ✕	D4
21	PS Hispaniola ✕✕✕	D1
23A	Il Passetto ✕	D5
24	Inigo Jones ❀❀✕✕✕✕	D3
25	Interlude de Tabaillau ✕✕	D4
28A	Last Days of the Raj ✕	D5
29	Lee Ho Fook ✕	B3
30	Little Akropolis ✕	B5
31	Marlborough Crest ★★★	C5
32	Mayflower ✕	B3
32A	Le Meridien ◯	A2
33	Neal Street ✕✕✕	D4
34	New World ✕	C3
35	L'Opera ✕✕✕	D5
37	Plummers ✕	D3
38	Poon's of Covent Gdn ❀✕✕	D3
39	Poon's (Leicester St) ❀✕	C3
40	La Provence ✕	D3
40A	Desaru ✕	B4
41A	Red Fort ✕✕	B3
42	Regent Palace ★★	B3
43	Regent Tandoori ✕	B3
44	Royal Horseguards Thistle ★★★	D1
44A	Royal Trafalgar Thistle ★★★	C2
44B	Rue St Jacques ❀❀✕✕	B5
45	Rules ✕✕✕	D3
46	Savoy ❀★★★★★	E3
	Savoy Hotel Grill ✕✕✕✕✕	
47	Sheekey's ✕	C3
50A	Stafford ★★★★	A1
52	Strand Palace ★★★	E3
52A	Taste of India ✕	E4
54	Thomas de Quincey's ✕✕	E3
55	Tourment d'Amour ❀✕✕	D3
57	Waldorf ★★★★	E4
60	Winstons Eating House ✕✕	C5
61	Yung's ❀✕	B3

LONDON PLAN 2

No.	Establishment	Grid
1	Al-Khayam Tandoori ✕	A6
2	L'Aquitaine ✕	A2
5	Ark ✕	A3
7	L'Artiste Affame ✕	A1
8	Athenaeum ★★★★	E4
9	Avoirdupois ✕✕	C1
10	Bali ✕✕	C6
12	Basil Street ★★★	D3
13	Berkeley ★★★★★	D4
14A	Bombay Brasserie ✕✕✕	B2
14B	Bombay Palace ✕✕✕	C6
15	Britannia ★★★★	E5
16	St Quentin ✕✕	C3
17	Bryanston Court ★★	D6
18	Capital ❀★★★★	D3
21	Central Park ★★★	A5
22	Chanterelle ✕	B2
24	Chesterfield ★★★	E5
25	Choys ✕	C1
26	Churchill ★★★★★	D6
26A	Ciboure ❀✕	E3
27	Claridge's ★★★★★	E6
28	Clifton-Ford ★★★	E6
30	Connaught ❀❀★★★★★	E5
32	La Croisette ✕	A1
33	Cumberland ★★★★	D6
33B	Dan's ❀✕	C1
34	Daphne's ✕✕	C2
37	Dorchester ❀★★★★★	E5
38	Dumpling House ✕	D3
39	Eatons ✕	E2
40	Ebury Court ★	E3
42	English Garden ❀✕✕	D2
43	English House ❀✕✕	D2
44	La Fantaisie Brasserie ✕	D3
45	Le Francais ✕✕	B1
48	Ganges ✕	B6
49A	Le Gavroche ❀❀❀✕✕✕✕	E5
49B	Gavvers ❀✕✕	E2
52	Gloucester ★★★★	A2
54	Good Earth (Kings Rd) ✕✕	D1
54A	Good Earth (Brompton Rd) ✕✕	C3
55	Greenhouse ✕✕✕	E5
56	Green Jade ✕	A6
57	Grosvenor House ★★★★★	E5
	Ninety Park Lane ✕✕✕✕✕	
57A	Hilaire ❀✕✕	B2
58	London Hilton ★★★★★	E4
	Hilton Hotel (Trader Vic's) ✕✕✕✕	
58A	Hogarth ★★	A2
59	Holiday Inn Marble Arch ★★★★	C6
60	Holiday Inn Chelsea ★★★★	D3
61	Hyatt Carlton Tower ★★★★★	D3
62	Hyde Park ★★★★★	D4
64	Inn on the Park ★★★★★	E4
65	Inter-Continental ❀❀★★★★★	E4
65A	Jakes ✕	A1
66	Kalamara's ✕	A5
67	Kensington Palace Thistle ★★★★	A3
68	Kerzenstuberl ✕	E6
74A	Le Poule au Pot ✕	E2
75	Hotel Lexham ★★	A2
75A	Library ✕✕	E5
76	London Embassy ★★★	A5
78	London International ★★★	A2
78A	London Marriot ★★★★	E6
80	Lowndes Thistle ★★★	D3
82	Ma Cuisine ❀✕	C2
83	Mandeville ★★★	E6
85	La Mange Tout ✕	C6
85A	Mario ✕✕	C2

LONDON

88	Masako✕✕✕	*E6*
88A	Menage a Trois✕✕	*D3*
88B	Meridiana✕✕	*C2*
88C	Mes Amis✕	*D3*
88D	Mijanou❀✕✕	*E2*
91	Mr Kai of Mayfair✕✕	*E5*
91A	Montcalm ★★★★	*D6*
91B	Montpeliano✕	*C3*
92	Mount Royal ★★★	*D6*
93	New Lotus Garden✕	*A1*
94	Nikita's✕✕	*A1*
95	L'Olivier✕✕	*A1*
98	Park Court ★★★	*A5*
99	Park Lane❀★★★★	*E4*
100	Poissonnerie✕	*C2*
101	Portman Inter-Continental ★★★★	*D6*
101A	Pontevecchio✕✕	*A1*
101B	Princess Garden of Mayfair✕✕✕	*E6*
102	Hospitality Inn ★★★	*A5*
102A	Read's❀✕	*A2*
102B	Relais des Amis✕	*E5*
102C	Rembrandt ★★★	*C3*
104	Royal Garden ★★★★★	*A4*
105	Royal Lancaster ★★★★	*B5*
106A	Salloos❀✕✕	*D3*
107	San Frediano✕✕	*C2*
107A	Savs✕	*A6*
108	Selfridge ★★★★	*E6*
109	Sheraton Park Tower ★★★★★	*D4*
111	Siam✕	*A3*
114	Stratford Court ★★★	*E6*
115	Le Suquet✕	*C2*
116	Tandoori✕✕	*C2*
117	Tandoori of Mayfair✕✕✕	*E5*
118	Tante Claire❀❀✕✕	*D1*
119	Tent✕	*E2*
121	Tiger Lee✕✕	*A1*
122	Trat-West✕✕	*C6*
123	Le Trou Normand✕	*D3*
123A	Van B's✕	*B1*
124	Waltons❀✕✕✕	*C2*
125	White's ★★★	*B5*
125A	Yumi✕✕	*D6*
126	Zen Chinese✕✕✕	*D1*
127	Zen Too✕	*B2*

LONDON PLAN 3

1	L'Amico✕✕	*C1*
1A	Auberge de Provence✕✕✕	*B2*
2	Aunties✕	*A6*
6	Brown's ★★★★	*A4*
7	Chambeli✕✕	*A5*
9	Gaylord✕	*A5*
12	Goring ★★★★	*A2*
13	Ho Ho Chinese✕	*A4*
15A	Ken Lo's Memories of China❀✕✕	*A1*
17	Lai Qila✕✕	*A6*
18	Langan's Brasserie✕✕	*A3*
18A	Les Halles✕	*D6*
20	May Fair Inter-Continental ★★★★★	*A4*
21	Mr Kai of Russell Square✕✕	*C6*
28	Ritz ★★★★★	*A3*
29	Royal Westminster Thistle ★★★★	*A1*
30	RSJ's✕	*E3*
30A	Rubens ★★★	*A2*
31	Hotel Russell ★★★★	*C6*
33	St George's ★★★★	*A5*
34	Sawasdee✕✕	*B6*
35	South of the Border✕	*E3*
36	Tate Gallery✕✕	*C1*
37	Three Compasses✕	*E6*
41	Westbury ★★★★	*A4*

LONDON PLAN 4

1	Baron of Beef✕✕✕	*A4*
2	La Bastille✕	*A4*
3	Le Gamin✕	*A4*
4	Ginnan✕	*A4*
5	Le Poulbot❀✕✕✕	*B4*
6	Shares✕✕	*C3*
7	Tower Thistle ★★★★	*C3*

London
Plan 1

To help you find details of establishments shown on this ma[p] consult the key listings on pages 436-7.

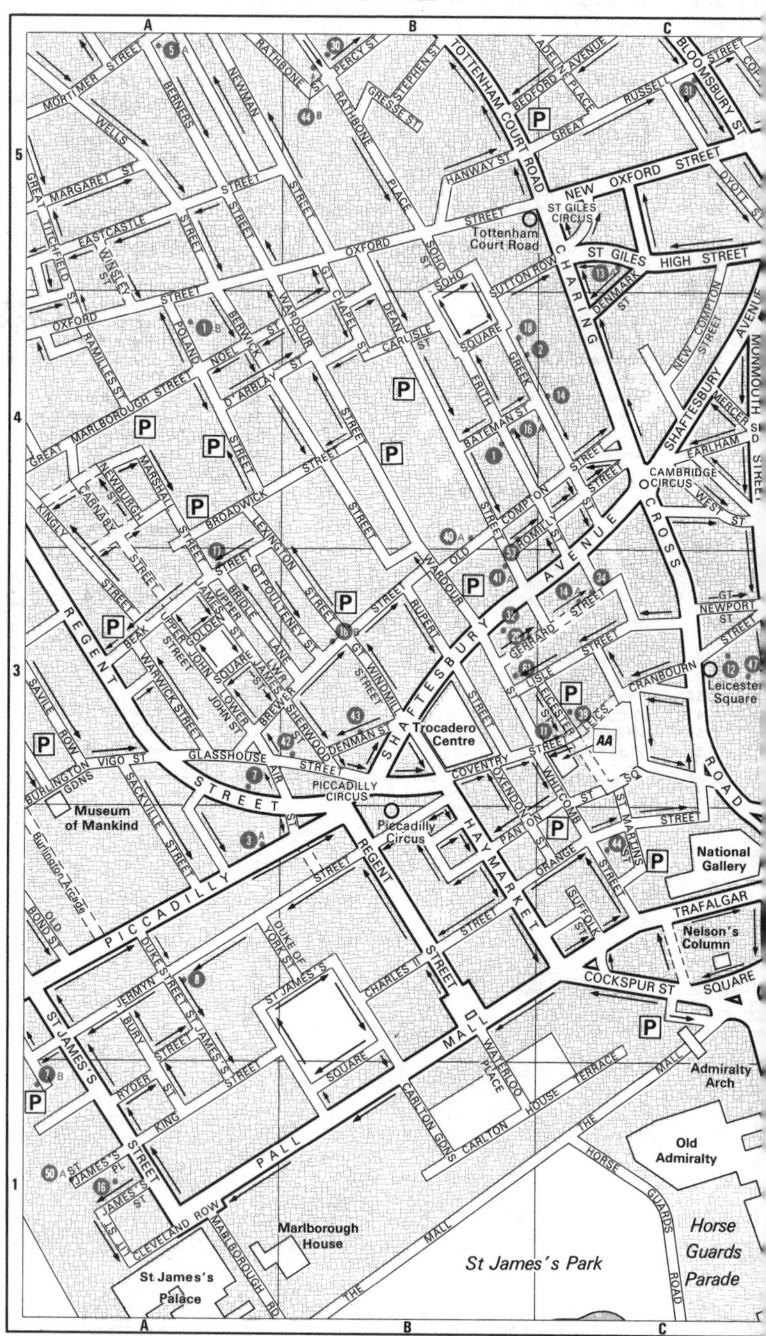

LONDON

London — Plan 1

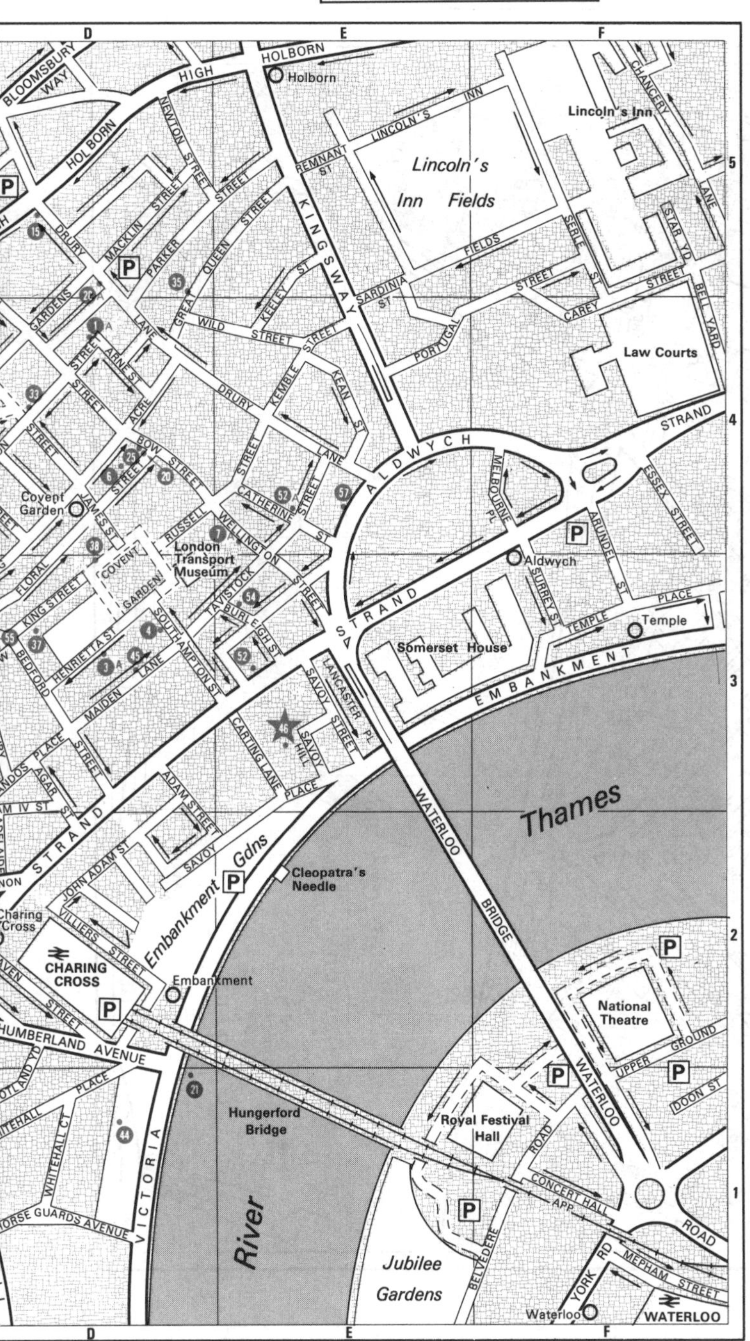

London — Plan 2

To help you find details of establishments shown on this map consult the Key listings on pages 436-7.

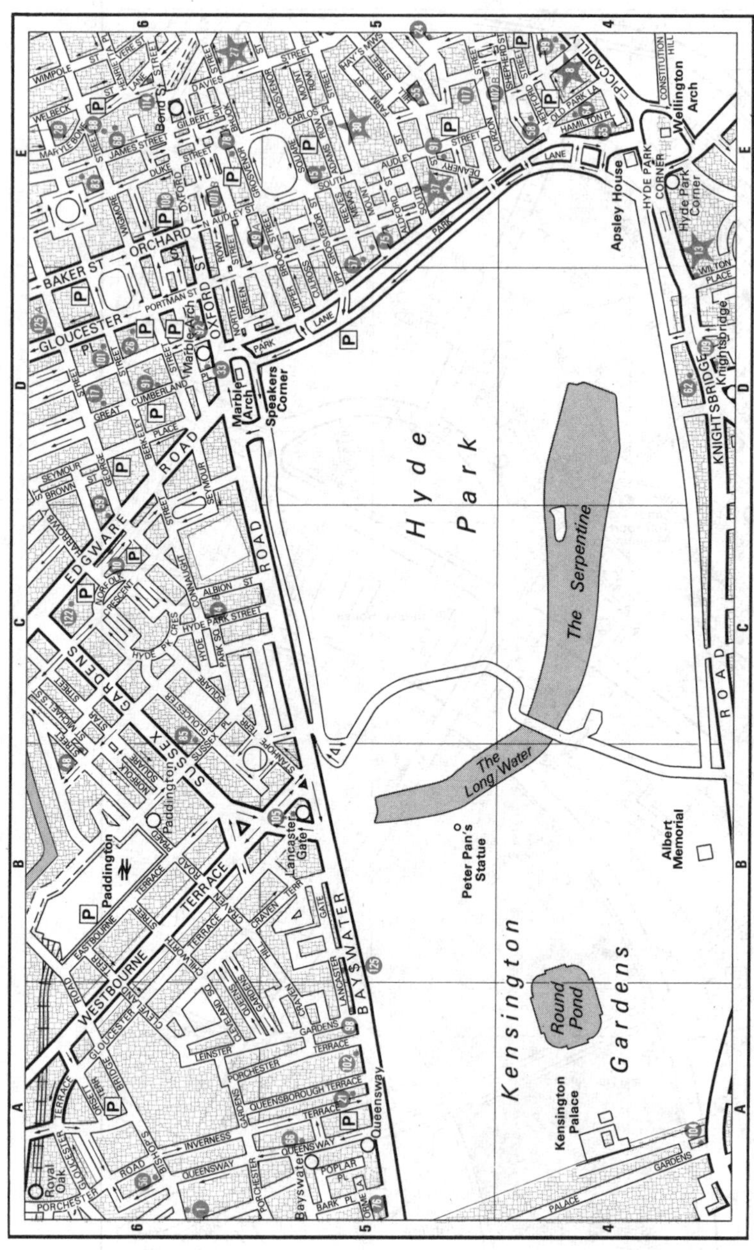

London
Plan 2

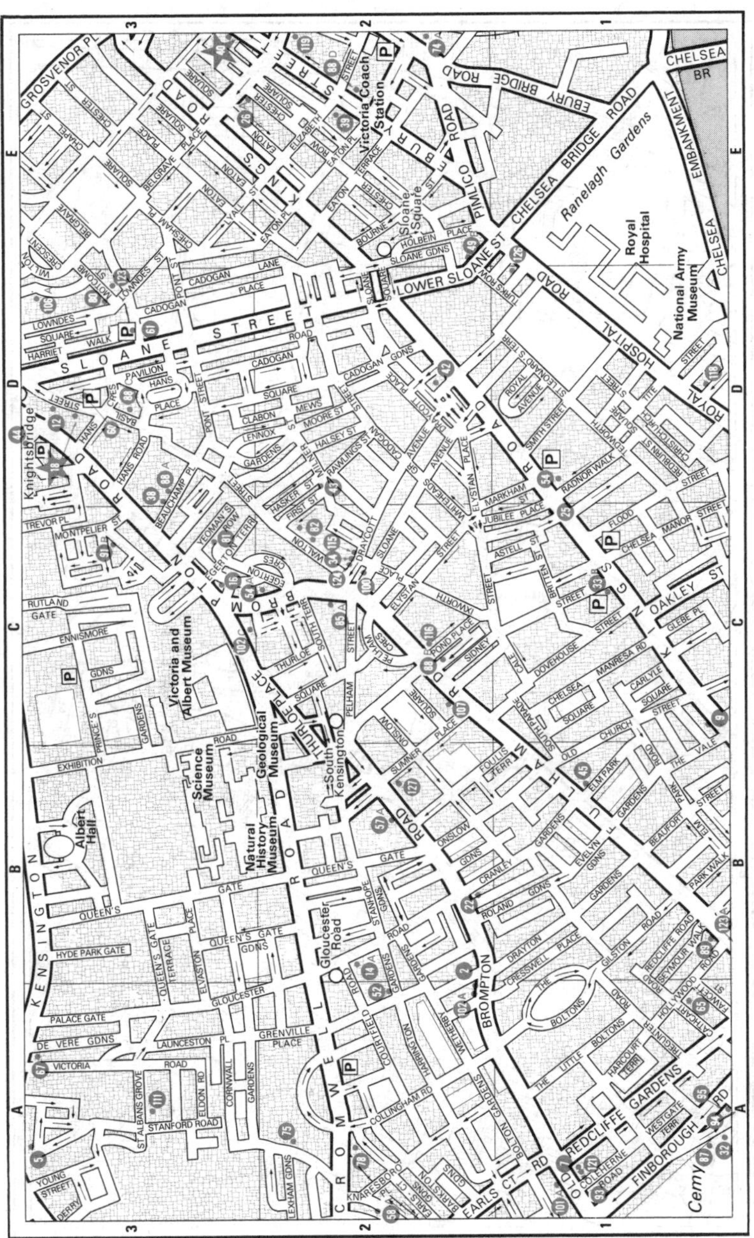

London — Plan 3

To help you find details of establishments shown on this map consult the Key listings on pages 436-7.

LONDON

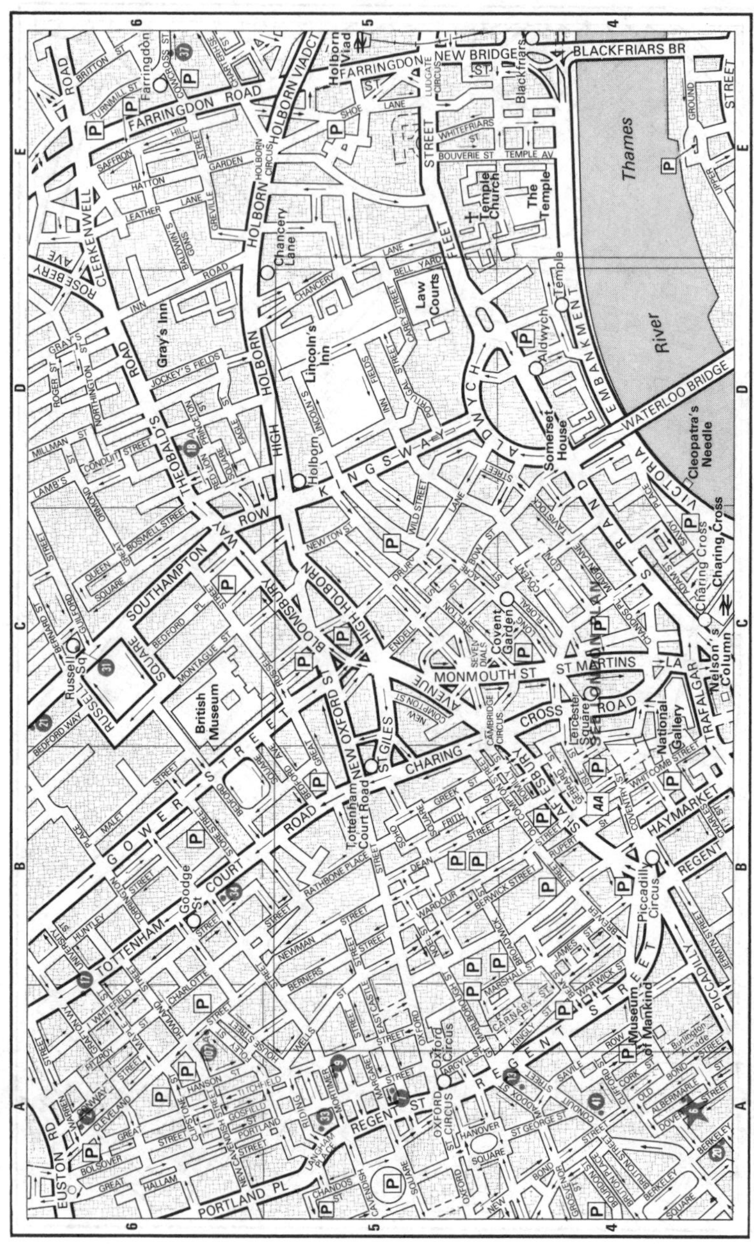

London

—

Plan 3

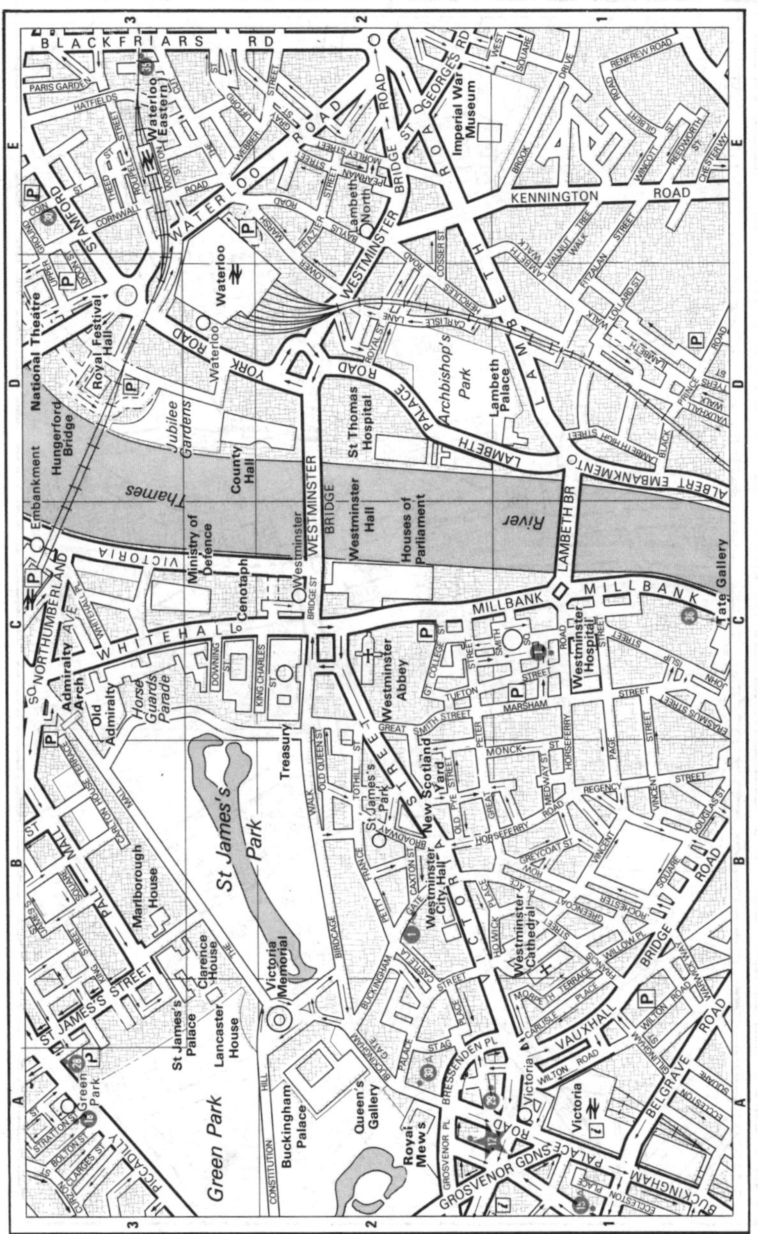

London
Plan 4

To help you find details of establishments shown on this map consult the Key listings on pages 436-7.

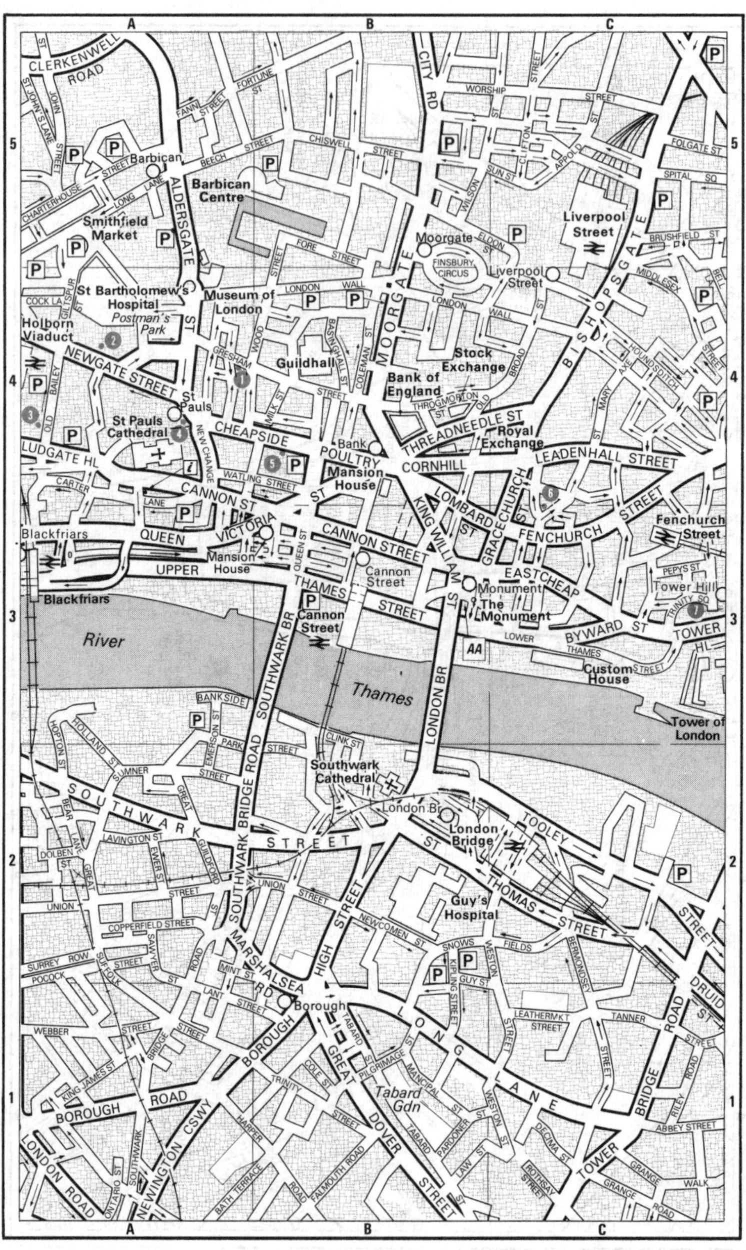

LONDON

London
Plan 5

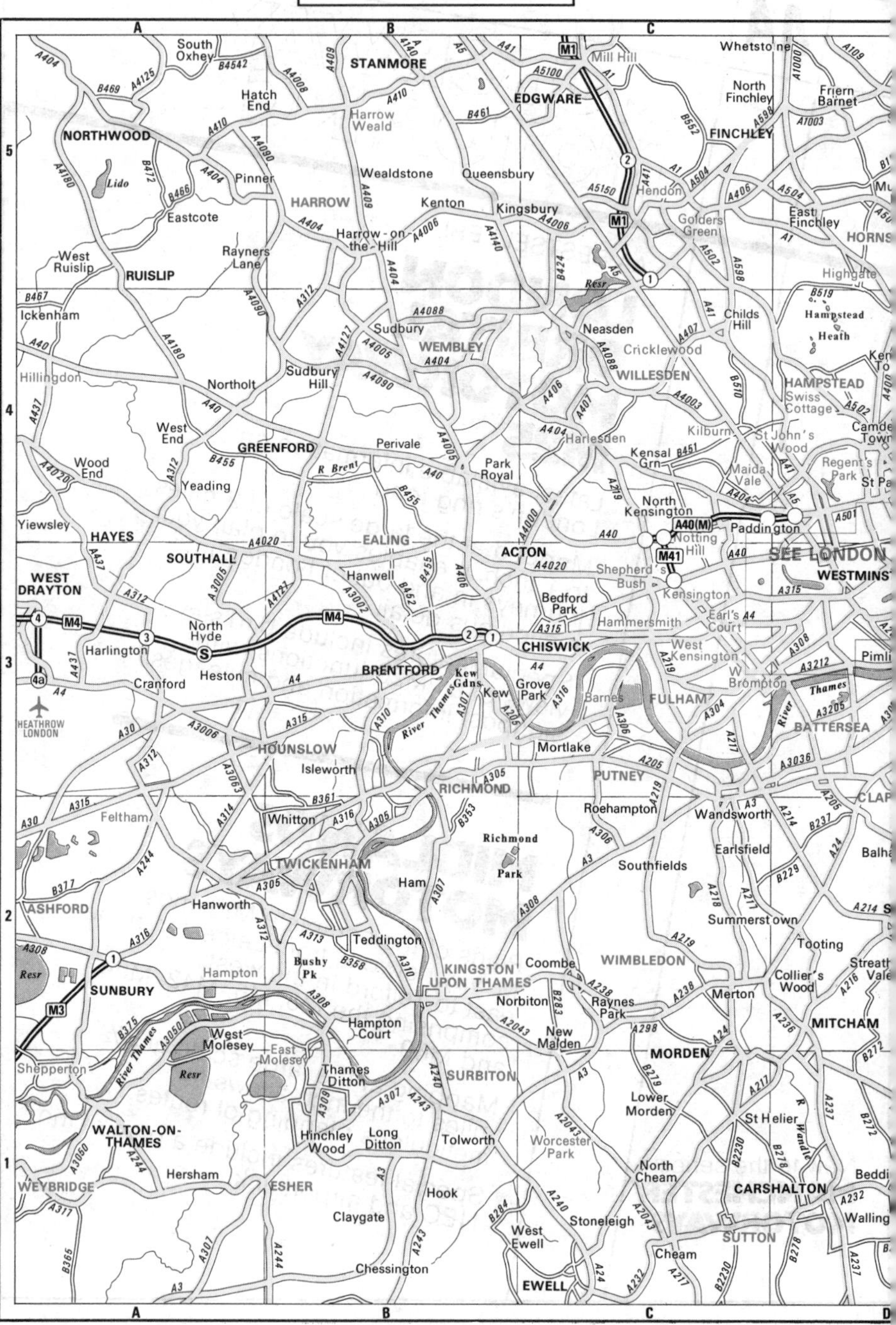

LONDON

London — Plan 5

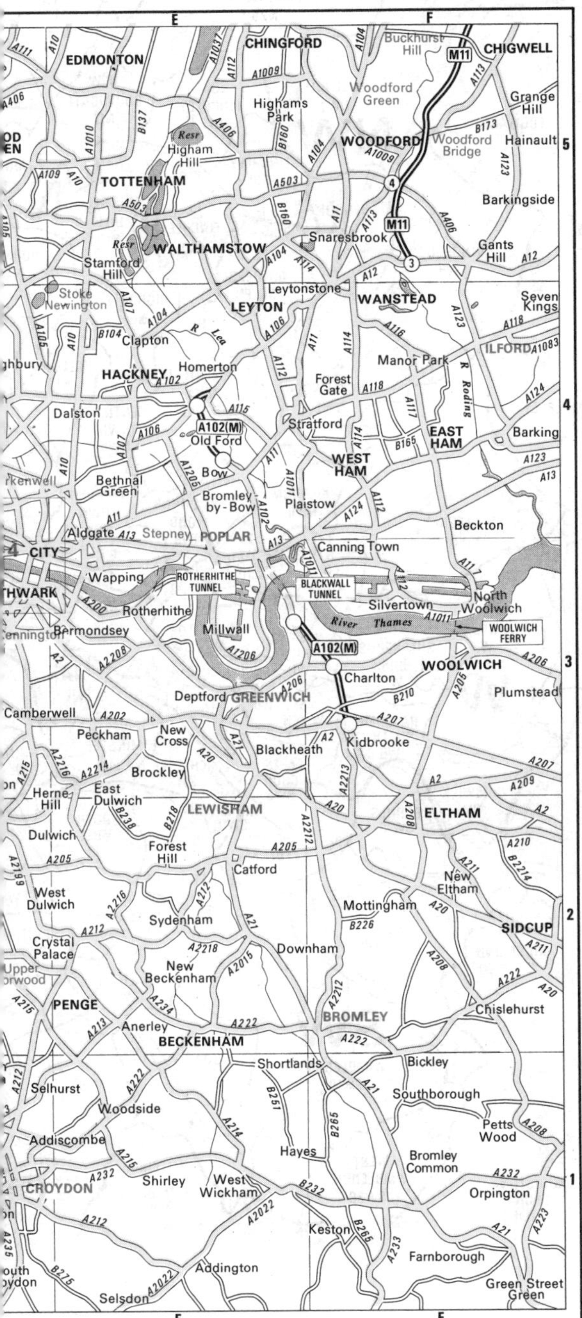

The place names shown in red are locations of AA Hotels and Restaurants outside the Central London plan area (*Plans 1-4*). Some of these fall within the London Postal District area and can therefore be found in the gazetteer under London, in postal district order (*see London Postal District map overleaf*). Others outside the London Postal District area can therefore be found under their respective place names in the main gazetteer.

London Postal Districts and ways in and out of London

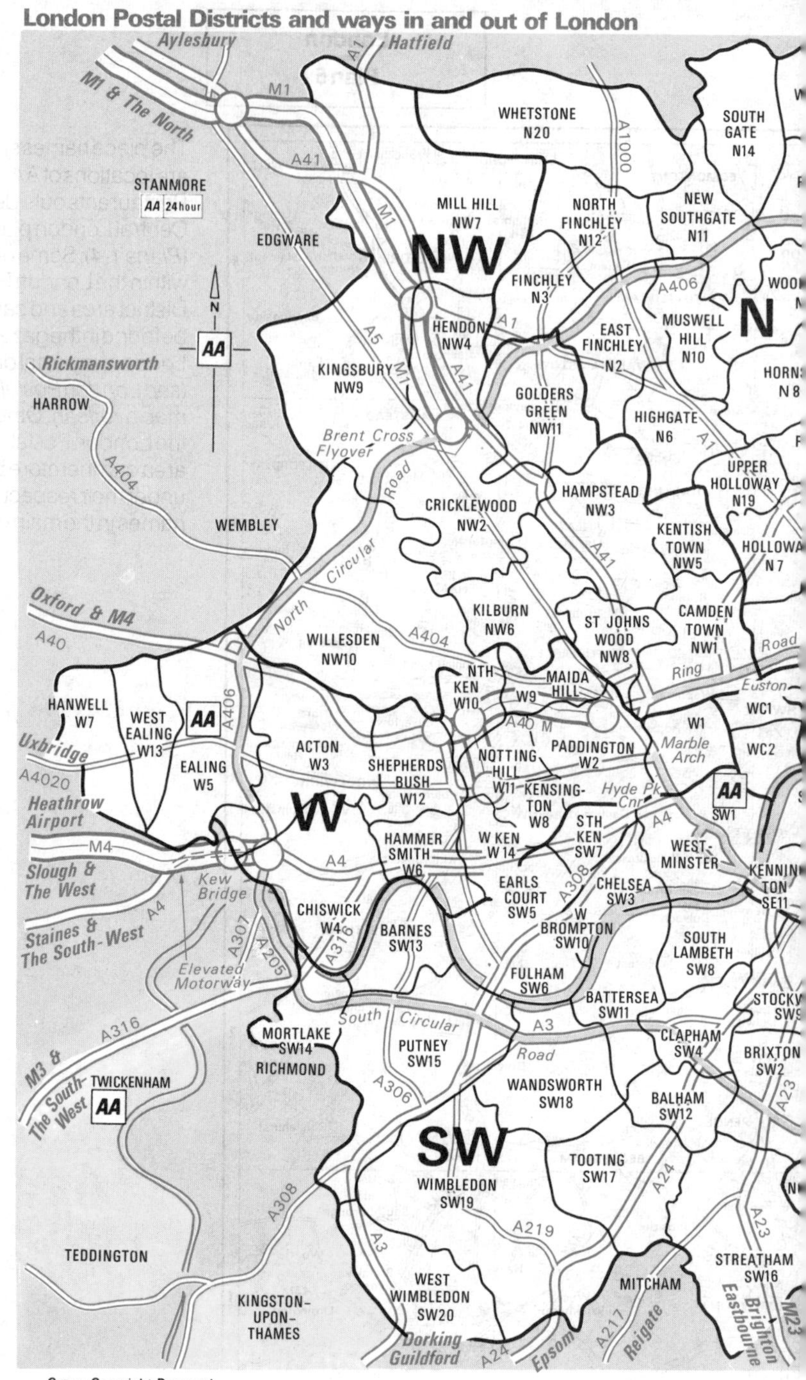

LONDON

London Postal Area Boundary
London Postal District Boundaries
Main Roads into and out of London
Signposted North and South Circular
Roads & Ring Road
Other Main Roads
Service Centre AA
Scale of Miles
0 1 2 3 4
LOWER EDMONTON N9
CHINGFORD E4
UPPER EDMONTON N18
Epping
WOODFORD E18
Chelmsford
Southend
GANTS HILL
Romford
WALTHAMSTOW E17
LEYTON E10
LEYTONSTONE E11
CLAPTON E5
FOREST GATE E7
MANOR PARK E12
ILFORD
HOMERTON E9
HACKNEY E8
E
BOW E3
STRATFORD E15
BARKING
Tilbury
BETHNAL GREEN E2
PLAISTOW E13
EAST HAM E6
R THAMES
STEPNEY E1
POPLAR E14
NORTH WOOLWICH E16
THAMESMEAD SE28
Free Ferry
ROTHERHITHE SE16
ABBEY WOOD SE2
DEPTFORD SE8
CHARLTON SE7
Erith
GREEN WICH SE10
NEW CROSS SE14
WOOLWICH SE18
SE
PECKHAM SE15
BLACKHEATH SE3
WELLING
BROCKLEY SE4
EAST DULWICH SE22
LEWISHAM SE13
FOREST HILL SE23
ELTHAM SE9
Rochester
Motorway
Dover
LEE SE12
CATFORD SE6
SYDENHAM SE26
SIDCUP
ANERLEY SE20
BROMLEY
Sevenoaks
Sevenoaks
Hastings
Maidstone
Folkestone
A10
A503
A104
A11
M11
A406
A12
A114
A106
A102 (M)
A117
A13
A202
A2
A102M
A205
A206
A207
A21
A20
A224
© The Automobile Association

LONDON

LONDON
Greater London, Plans **1—5,** pages 438—447 (Small scale maps 4—5 at back of book)

A map of the London postal area appears on pages 448—449

Places within the London postal area are listed below in postal district order, commencing East, then North, South and West, with a brief indication of the area covered. Detailed plans **1—4** show the locations of AA-appointed hotels and restaurants within the Central London postal districts which are indicated by a number, followed by a grid reference e.g. *A5* to help you find the location. Plan **5** shows the districts covered within the outer area keyed by a grid reference e.g. *A1*. **Other places within the county of London are listed under their respective place names and are also keyed to this plan or the main map section.**

If more detailed information is required the *AA Motorists Map of London*, on sale at AA offices, is in two parts: the 'West End and the City' shows one-way systems, banned turns, car parks, stations, hotels, places of interest, etc: 'Outer London' gives primary routes, car parks at surburban stations, etc. A theatre map of the West End is included.

For London Airports see under Gatwick & Heathrow.

E1 Stepney *and east of the Tower of London*
London plan **5** *E4*

★★★★**Tower Thistle** St Katherine's Way (Thistle) ☎01-488 4134 Telex no 885934 Plan 4: **7** *C3*

Located on the north bank of the Thames, overlooking the Tower of London and Tower Bridge, this large hotel offers comfortable accommodation to a large variety of clients.

826 (35fb) in 24 bedrooms CTV in all bedrooms **T** ✱sB £65—£85 dB £78—£99 (room only) **B**

Lift ☾ ## 120P 80 (charged) CFA

International ✱Lunch fr£14.95&alc Dinner fr£14.95&alc Wine £7 Last dinner 10pm

Credit cards 1 2 3 4 5 Ⓥ

✕***Blooms*** 90 Whitechapel High St ☎01-247 6001

Busy but friendly strictly Kosher restaurant with modestly priced menu.

Closed Sat Dinner not served Fri

Kosher 150 seats 80P

Credit cards 1 3

E14 Poplar
London plan **5** *E4*

✕**Good Friends** 139/141 Salmon Ln ☎01-987 5541

Simple restaurant specialising in nicely prepared Cantonese cuisine.

Closed 24—26 Dec

London E1 — London N1

Cantonese **V** 12 seats ✱Lunch £8—£12alc Dinner £8—£12alc Wine £4.50 Last dinner 11pm

Credit cards 1 2 3 5

EC1 City of London; *Barbican, Clerkenwell, Farringdon*
London plan **5** D4

✕**La Bastille** 116 Newgate St ☎01-600 1134 Plan 4: **2** *A4*

The small, intimate, city restaurant has some good wood carvings, and the portraits of Victorian judges on the walls set the atmosphere. A sound standard of French provincial cuisine is provided, the menu changing daily.

Closed 1 wk Aug & 2 wks Dec
Dinner not served

French 55 seats S% Lunch £15.50—£18 Wine £6.50

Credit cards 1 2 3 4 5

✕**Three Compasses** 66 Cowcross St ☎01-253 3368 Plan 3: **37** *E6*

There has been an inn on this site since the 18th century, and the present building, though modernised, retains some of its original character. The comfortably-appointed first-floor restaurant offers a short menu of interesting international dishes with friendly, informal service.

Closed 1 wk after Xmas & last 2wks Aug
Dinner not served

International **V** 40 seats ✱Lunch £5—£15&alc Wine £4.50 Last lunch 2.15pm

nc 8yrs Live music Sun

Credit cards 1 2 3

EC2 City of London; *Bank of England, Liverpool Street Station*

❀✕✕✕**Le Poulbot, London EC2**
45 Cheapside ☎01-236 4379 Telex no 8813079 Plan 4 **5** *B4*
(Rosette awarded for lunch only)

Very popular basement restaurant where an intimate, plush atmosphere prevails. There is a short fixed price menu, which changes daily, and the chef's individuality and flair is most evident, along with excellent presentation and good blending. Service is efficient and unobtrusive.

Closed Sat, Sun & Bank Hols
Dinner not served

French 45 seats S% ✱Lunch £24.50 Wine £9.80 Last lunch 3pm nc 4yrs

Credit cards 1 2 3 4 5

✕✕✕**Baron of Beef** Gutter Ln, Gresham St ☎01-606 9415 Plan 4: **1** *A4*

Spacious, panelled basement restaurant specialising in English cuisine.

Closed Sat & Sun

70 seats S% Lunch £25—£30alc Dinner £25—£30alc Wine £9.60 Last dinner 9pm

Credit cards 1 2 3 5

EC3 City of London; *Monument, Tower of London*

✕✕**Shares** 12—13 Lime St ☎01-623 1843 Plan 4: **6** *C3*

A modern, tastefully furnished, lunch-time restaurant with a small bar.

Closed Bank Hol's Dinner not served

International 74 seats S% ✱Lunch £22.50—£24.25 Wine £7.75

Credit cards 1 2 3 5

EC4 City of London; *Blackfriars, Cannon Street and Fleet Street*

✕**Le Gamin** 32 Old Bailey ☎01-236 7931 Telex no 8813079 Plan 4: **3** *A4*

Small tables and chairs in a large, airy basement create a French cafe style atmosphere. Half a bottle of wine is included in the fixed price of the short menu of carefully prepared dishes, representing good value and contributing to the restaurant's popularity.

Closed Sat, Sun & Banks Hol's
Dinner not served

French **V** 120 seats S% ✱Lunch £17.75 Wine £5.10 Last lunch 2.30pm

Credit cards 1 2 3 4 5

✕**Ginnan** 5 Cathedral Pl ☎01-236 4120 Plan 4: **4** *A4*

Simple modern Japanese restaurant with small party room.

Closed Sun & Bank Hols Dinner not served Sat

Japanese 60 seats ✱Lunch £4.80—£5.20 Dinner £16—£18 Wine £7 Last dinner 10pm

Credit cards 1 2 3 5

N1 Islington
London plan **5** *D4*

✕✕**Frederick's** Camden Passage ☎01-359 2888

Dating back to the 18th century, and originally called 'The Gun', this very popular and well-appointed restaurant was renamed in honour of Prince Augustus Frederick who died in 1813. The enterprising menu is changed fortnightly but always includes some delectable puddings, and the formal service is very efficient. →

To find any AA-appointed London hotel or restaurant see maps and index on pages 433—449

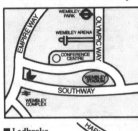

Closed Sun, Boxing Day, New Years Day Good Fri & Etr Mon

International **V** 150 seats S% Lunch £17—£18alc Dinner £17—£18alc Wine £4.65 Last dinner 11.30pm

Credit cards 1 2 3 4 5

Annas Place 90 Mildmay Park 01-249 9379

This small, bustling restaurant cum wine bar, simply furnished and prettily decorated, provides a blackboard menu of excellent Swedish fare at very reasonable cost. The informal atmosphere is enhanced by cheerful young staff, supervised by Anna herself.

Closed Sun, Mon, 2 wks Xmas, 2 wks Etr & Aug

Swedish & Continental 52 seats S% *Lunch £10—£14alc Dinner £12—£14alc Wine £4.95 Last dinner 10.15pm

X **Mr Bumbles** 23 Islington Grn 01-354 1952

Large brick fireplace and ceiling beams give the atmosphere of a country kitchen.

Closed Mon

Greek **V** 60 seats S% Lunch £6&alc Dinner £9alc Last dinner 11.30pm

Credit cards 1 2 3 5

X **M'sieur Frog** 31A Essex Rd 01-226 3495

Proprietor provides well prepared food in this friendly informal Bistro restaurant.

Closed 1 wk Xmas & 3 wks Aug Lunch not served Dinner not served Sun

French 63 seats S% Dinner fr £15.95alc Wine £4.95 Last dinner 11.15pm

Credit cards 1 3

X ***Portofino*** 39 Camden Passage 01-226 0884

Simple, Italian restaurant, where the walls are decorated with hanging bottles.

Closed Sun, Bank Hol's, Good Fri & Xmas

French & Italian **V** 65 seats Last dinner 11.30pm Live music Thu—Sat

Credit cards 1 2 3 5

N6 Highgate

London plan **5** *D5*

XX **Bayleaf Tandoori** 2 North Hill 01-340 1719

The smart, modern Italian restaurant has canopied windows and a walled frontage with attractive flower beds. The cuisine is that of North India, Tandoori dishes being the speciality.

Indian **V** 100 seats Lunch £7—£10alc Dinner £7—£10alc Wine £4.50 Last dinner 11.15pm

Ⓥ

London N1 — London NW2

XX **San Carlo** 2 High St, Highgate 01-340 5823

Good modern Italian restaurant with patio.

Closed Mon & Bank Hol's

Italian **V** 100 seats S% Lunch £15alc Dinner £20alc Wine £6.25 Last dinner 11.30pm 30P Live music nightly

Credit cards 1 2 3 4 5

X **China Garden** 12 Shepherds Hill 01-348 8606

Lunch not served

Pekinese & Szechuan **V** 70 seats S% *Dinner £10—£15&alc Wine £4.90 Last dinner 10.45pm

Credit cards 1 2 3

N8 Hornsey

X ***M'Sieur Frog*** 36 The High St 01-340 2116

An imaginative menu of well-prepared French provincial dishes is offered by this small, simple, French-style bistro.

Closed 1 wk Xmas & 3 wks Aug/Sep Lunch not served

French 44 seats Last dinner 11pm

Credit cards 1 3

N14 Southgate

X **L'Oiseau Noir** 163 Bramley Rd 01-367 1100

The restaurant combines simple elegance with a warm, friendly atmosphere and offers a regularly-changed and reasonably-priced menu of honest and well-prepared French dishes.

Closed Mon
Dinner not served Sun

French **V** 62 seats *Lunch £7.95—£15&alc Dinner fr £14&alc Wine £5.50 Last dinner 11pm

Credit cards 1 2 3 4 5

N16 Stoke Newington

London plan **5** *E4*

X **Eleganza** 70, High St 01-254 1950

A small, simple restaurant specialising in Pekinese cuisine of a good standard.

Lunch not served Sun

Pekinese **V** 55 seats Lunch £4—£10&alc Dinner £7—£10&alc Wine £5 Last dinner 11.30pm nc 4yrs

Credit cards 1 2 3 5

NW1 Regent's Park; *Baker Street, Euston and King's Cross stations*

London plan **5** *D4*

○ **Hotel Ibis Euston**

Cordington St 01-759 4888

300

Expected to open summer 1987

XX ***Viceroy of India*** 3—5 Glentworth St 01-486 3401

Modern, well-appointed North Indian restaurant with marble pillars, statues and well prepared authentic cooking.

Closed Xmas Day

North Indian **V** 125 seats Last dinner 11.30pm

Credit cards 1 2 3 4 5

X **Asuka** Berkeley Arcade, 209A Baker St 01-486 5026

The small, contemporary and very neat Japanese restaurant features a Suishi Bar and speciality dishes cooked at the table. Authentic fish cuisine figures prominently on the menu, quality materials are used throughout, and attentive, helpful staff will guide you in your choice of meal.

Closed Sun & 24 Dec—5 Jan
Lunch not served Sat

Japanese 62 seats S% *Lunch £5.50—£6.95&alc Dinner £18.90—£45&alc Wine £8 Last dinner 10.30pm

Credit cards 1 2 3 5

X **One Legged Goose** 17 Princess Rd, Regent's Pk 01-722 9665

Good Swedish food is a feature of this small friendly restaurant.

Closed 1st 3 wks Jan Lunch not served Sat Dinner not served Sun

V 50 seats Lunch £12alc Dinner £12alc Wine £5.25 Last dinner 11pm

Credit cards 1 3

X **Sagarmatha** 339 Euston Rd 01-387 6531

Posters and pictures of Nepal set the tone of this compact little restaurant which specialises in Nepalese cuisine. The atmosphere is friendly and informal, the manager is ready to help you in your choice.

Indian & Nepalese **V** 55 seats *Wine £3.95 Last dinner 11.45pm

Credit cards 1 2 3 5 Ⓥ

NW2 Cricklewood, Willesden

X **Quincy's 84** 675 Finchley Rd 01-794 8499

Flair and imagination are evident in the cooking at this restaurant, where dishes from a short but interesting menu are served in a friendly, informal atmosphere under the personal supervision of the owner.

Closed Mon & 1st 2 wks Jan
Lunch not served Sat

English & French **V** 30 seats *Lunch £8.50—£10.50 Dinner £13.75 Wine £6 Last dinner 10.30pm

Credit cards 1 3

LONDON

London NW2 — London NW3

LONDON

✕Yeti 68 Cricklewood Broadway ☏01-452 4789

This small, intimate restaurant specialises in North Indian and Nepalese cuisine, the quality of cooking owing much to the skilful blending of spices. Guests can relax in a friendly, informal atmosphere.

Indian & Nepalese **V** 50 seats S% Lunch £4—£10&alc Dinner £5—£10&alc Wine £4.80 Last dinner mdnt 20P

Credit cards 1 2 3 5

NW3 Hampstead *and Swiss Cottage*
London plan **5** *D4*

★★★★ *B* **Holiday Inn Swiss Cottage** King Henry's Rd, (Holiday Inns) ☏01-722 7711 Telex no 267396

A modern hotel with spacious comfortable bedrooms, large public lounge area and numerous sporting facilities.

291 (174fb) in 52 bedrooms CTV in all bedrooms **T** S% ✱sB&B £86.45—£91.05 dB&B £105.05—£114.25

Lift 50P 75 (heated) sauna bath solarium gymnasium table tennis pool table Live music nightly *xmas*

International **V** ✱Lunch fr£13.50 Dinner fr£15 Wine £8.26 Last dinner 10.30pm

Credit cards 1 2 3 4 5

★★★ **Charles Bernard** 5 Frognal ☏01-794 0101 Telex no 23560

Friendly and well managed modern hotel with pleasant bedrooms, public rooms and restricted lunch arrangements.

57 CTV in all bedrooms ® **T** S% ✱sB&B £43.70—£48.30 dB&B £57.50—£63.25

Lift CTV 20P

English & French S% ✱Bar lunch £6alc Tea £2 Dinner £8.50alc Wine £4.80 Last dinner 9.30pm

Credit cards 1 2 3 4 5 Ⓥ

★★★ **Post House** Haverstock Hill (Trusthouse Forte) ☏01-794 8121 Telex no 262494

Popular modern hotel with well-equipped bedrooms.

140 CTV in all bedrooms ® sB&B £57.50 dB&B £74.50

Lift 70P *xmas*

Last dinner 10.30pm

Credit cards 1 2 3 4 5

★★★ **Swiss Cottage** 4 Adamson Rd ☏01-722 2281 Telex no 297237

Elegantly furnished hotel with a spacious lounge and good quality antiques.

65rm(45 20)(4fb) CTV in all bedrooms **T** sB&B £36.50—£66 dB&B £55—£73 Continental breakfast

Lift 5P sauna bath

Continental Lunch £6&alc Tea £1.25 Dinner £10&alc Wine £5.50 Last dinner 9pm

Credit cards 1 2 3 4 5

✕✕ **Bunny's** 9 Pond St ☏01-435 1541

Basement restaurant serving Edwardian classic French dishes, and ground floor is a smart fish restaurant. Well prepared dishes are served with flair and imagination.

Closed Mon Lunch not served Mon—Sat

French 75 seats ✱Lunch £7.95 Dinner £10.50—£12.50&alc Wine £5.65 Last dinner 11.15pm Live music Sun lunch

Credit cards 1 2 3

✕✕ **Keats** 3 Downshire Hill ☏01-435 3544

(Rosette awarded for dinner only)

The intimate French restaurant cultivates a literary air, its lilac-painted walls decked with bookshelves and prints. Cuisine of a high standard is complemented by a very good wine list, and special gastronomique evenings are organised.

Closed Sun

French **V** 50 seats S% Lunch £9alc Dinner £20alc Wine £13 Last dinner 11pm nc 7yrs

Credit cards 1 2 3 5

To find any AA-appointed London hotel or restaurant see maps and index on pages 433—449

✕ ***Finches*** 250 Finchley Rd ☏01-435 8622

Good honest cooking and value for money can be found at this friendly, intimate little restaurant where the menu combines English and French cuisine.

English & French **V** 45 seats Last dinner 10.45pm

Credit cards 1 2 3 4 5

✕ ***Green Cottage II*** 122A Finchley Rd ☏01-794 3833

Offering over 40 dishes made completely from vegetables and vegetable substances, this claims to be the first vegetarian Chinese restaurant in Europe. Bright, air-conditioned surroundings, informal atmosphere and helpful staff all add to the guest's enjoyment of his meal.

Closed Tue & Xmas Day

Chinese **V** 80 seats Last dinner 11.15pm

Credit cards 1 2 5

✕ ***Hawelli Tandoori*** 102 Heath St ☏01-431 0172

A smart, modern Indian restaurant, tastefully decorated and furnished, specialises in North Indian cuisine of a high standard. Service is by willing, friendly staff and the atmosphere is relaxed and informal.

Closed Xmas Day

Tandoori **V** 75 seats Last dinner 11.15pm 1P

Credit cards 1 2 3 5

✕ **Peachey's** 205 Haverstock Hill ☏01-435 6744

There is a continental aura about this appealing and intimate little restaurant which offers an interesting French menu with daily "specials", backed by a comprehensive wine list. Visitors are assured of a warm welcome and helpful service. →

Closed Bank Hols, 10 days Xmas & 4 days Etr
Lunch not served Sat Dinner not served Sun
French V 38 seats S% Lunch fr£8.95&alc Dinner fr£8.95&alc Wine £5.45 Last dinner 11.30pm
Credit cards 2 3 5

X **_Wakaba_** 31 College Cres 01-586 7960
The small, two-section Japanese restaurant provides an informal, intimate atmosphere in which to enjoy a good variety of well-prepared and authentic dishes.
Closed Mon, 4 days Xmas, 4 days Etr & 1 wk Aug Lunch not served
Japanese V 38 seats Last dinner 11pm
Credit cards 1 2 3 5

NW4 Hendon
London plan **5** *C5*

★★★ **_Hendon Hall_** Ashley Ln (Kingsmead) 01-203 3341 Telex no 8956088
Georgian house (once the home of David Garrick) has been refurbished to provide comfortable modern accommodation.
52rm(49 3) CTV in all bedrooms ® B
Lift ☾ CTV 65P CFA Live music & dancing Sat *xmas*
English, American & French V Last dinner 10.15pm
Credit cards 1 2 3 5

NW6 Kilburn
London plan **5** *C4*

X **La Frimousse** 75 Fairfax Rd 01-624 3880
Situated close to Swiss Cottage, the smart, attractive restaurant produces original French cuisine from excellent raw materials.
Closed Sun
French 46 seats S% *Lunch fr£9.95 Dinner fr£21.50 Wine £6.75 Last dinner 11pm nc 6yrs
Credit cards 1 2 3 5

X **Peter's Bistro** 63 Fairfax Rd 01-624 5142
Green awning and fresh plants make the frontage of this restaurant very impressive. Inside, the relaxed and intimate atmosphere provides the ideal setting for a well-cooked meal chosen from the bistro-type menu.
Lunch not served Sat Dinner not served Sun
V 48 seats S% Lunch £20alc Dinner £22.50alc Wine £6.95 Last dinner 11.30pm nc 12yrs
Credit cards 1 2 3 5

To find any AA-appointed London hotel or restaurant see maps and index on pages 433—449

London NW3 — London NW11

X **Sheridan's** 351 West End Ln 01-794 3234
Closed Mon, 1—15 Jan & 18 Aug—2 Sep
Lunch not served Tue—Sat
English & French V 42 seats *Lunch £8.50 Dinner £13alc Wine £6 Last dinner 11pm
Credit cards 1 2 3 4 5 V

X **_Vijay_** 49 Willesden Ln 01-328 1087
Small Indian restaurant specialising in the vegetarian cuisine of southern India.
Closed Xmas
Southern Indian V 74 seats Last dinner 10.45pm
Credit cards 1 2 3 5

NW7 Mill Hill
London plan **5** *C5*

★★ **TraveLodge** M1 Scratchwood Service Area (Access from Motorway only) (Trusthouse Forte) 01-906 0611 Telex no 8814796
The restaurant facilities (mainly grills) are located in the adjacent service area.
100(12fb) CTV in all bedrooms ® sB&B £39.50 dB&B £51 B
☾ 120P CFA
Mainly grills
Credit cards 1 2 3 4 5

XX **Good Earth** 143—145 Broadway, Mill Hill 01-959 7011
Smart, modern restaurant specialising in very good Cantonese cuisine.
Chinese V 100 seats *Lunch £10—£16&alc Dinner £10—£16&alc Wine £5 Last dinner 11.30pm 10P

NW8 St John's Wood
London plan **5** *D4*

★★★★ **Ladbroke Westmoreland** (& Conference centre) 18 Lodge Rd (Ladbroke) 01-722 7722 Telex no 23101
Pleasant, modern hotel with well equipped bedrooms.
347(15fb) in 10 bedrooms CTV in all bedrooms ® T S% sB £69—£79 dB £85—£95 (room only) B
Lift ☾ ## 35P 45 (£1.50 per day) CFA Live music Mon—Fri *xmas*
V S% Lunch £5—£11&alc Tea fr£1.75 Dinner £11.50&alc Wine £8.95 Last dinner 9.45pm
Credit cards 1 2 3 4 5

XX **Lords Rendezvous** 24 Finchley Rd 01-722 4750
Modern, elegant Chinese restaurant with good food.
Closed Xmas Day & Boxing Day
Chinese V 100 seats *Lunch £13—£20&alc Dinner £13—£20&alc Wine £5.50 Last dinner 11.15pm
Credit cards 1 2 3 5 V

XX **_Oslo Court_** Prince Albert Rd 01-722 8795
A traditional, comfortable restaurant overlooking Regent's Park.
Dinner not served Sun
French V 55 seats Last dinner 11pm
Credit cards 1 2 3 4 5

X **_L'Aventure_** 3 Blenheim Ter 01-624 6232
Small, well-run French restaurant serving traditional dishes in intimate, friendly atmosphere.
Lunch not served Sat Dinner not served Sun
French 36 seats Last dinner 11pm
Credit card 2

X **_Fortuna Garden_** 128 Allitsen Rd, St John's Wood 01-586 2391
This friendly Chinese restaurant specialises in Peking cuisine but also serves other dishes designed to please the European palate. The food is authentic and well prepared, and the staff are cheerfully pleasant.
Pekinese V 80 seats Last dinner 11.30pm
Credit cards 1 2 3 5

NW10 Harlesden, Willesden
London plan **5** *C4*

X **_Khas Tandoori_** 39 Chamberlayne Rd 01-969 2537
Colourful and modern, the North Indian restaurant produces Tandoori dishes of a very high standard. Willing, friendly staff help to make eating there an enjoyable experience.
Closed Xmas Day
North Indian V 44 seats Last dinner mdnt
Credit cards 1 2 3 5

X **_Kuo Yuan_** 217 High Rd, Willesden 01-459 2297
Spacious restaurant offering well prepared Pekinese dishes in a relaxed friendly atmosphere.
Lunch not served Mon—Fri
Pekinese V 120 seats Last dinner 11pm

NW11 Golders Green
London plan **5** *C5*

XX **Luigi's** 1—4 Belmont Pde, Finchley Rd 01-455 0210
The proprietor's personal supervision and the good Italian cooking create a friendly atmosphere in this well-appointed restaurant.
Closed Mon Xmas Day & Good Fri
Italian V 80 seats *Lunch £5&alc Dinner £10—£15alc Wine £4.90 Last dinner 10.30pm
Credit cards 1 2 3 5

London SE1 — London SW1

SE1 Southwark, Waterloo
Plan **3**

✕**RSJ's** 13A Coin St ☎ 01-928 4554 Plan 3: **30** *E3*

Small, popular French restaurant offering well prepared dishes at reasonable price.

Closed Sun Lunch not served Sat

French 48 seats ✱Lunch £15alc Dinner £15alc Wine £5.95 Last dinner 11pm

✕**South of the Border** Joan St ☎ 01-928 6374 Plan 3: **35** *E3*

Very informal restaurant on two floors featuring some interesting South Pacific dishes on its international menu.

Lunch not served Sat

Australasian, Indonesian & South Pacific **V** 80 seats S% Lunch £18—£20alc Dinner £15—£16alc Wine £5 Last dinner 11.30pm

Credit cards 1 2 3 5

SE10 Greenwich
London plan **5** *E3*

✕✕**Mean Time** 47—49 Greenwich Church St ☎ 01-858 8705

Personally supervised restaurant with efficient and friendly service in a pleasant relaxed atmosphere.

Closed 25, 26 Dec & Good Fri
Lunch not served Sat

English & Continental **V** 100 seats Lunch £13.50alc Dinner £13.50alc Wine £5.50 Last dinner 11pm

Credit cards 1 2 3 5

✕✕**Spread Eagle** 2 Stockwell St ☎ 01-853 2333

A charming restaurant with great character has resulted from the conversion of an old coaching inn. Intimate alcoves are surrounded by authentic photographs and pictures, while the cheerful waiters who serve the food have a good knowledge of the French cuisine involved.

Closed Sun Lunch not served Sat

French **V** 60 seats S% Lunch £6—£9.75 Dinner £15alc Wine £7 Last dinner 10.45pm

Credit cards 1 2 3 5

✕**Le Papillon** 57 Greenwich Church St ☎ 01-858 2668

Well prepared French and English cuisine is available in this small, intimate oak panelled restaurant.

Lunch not served Sat Dinner not served Sun

French 36 seats Lunch fr£4.95&alc Dinner £12.50alc Wine £5.50 Last dinner 10.30pm

Credit cards 1 2 3 5

✕***Mr Chung*** 166 Trafalgar Rd ☎ 01-858 4245

Small, brightly decorated, modern restaurant with friendly and intimate atmosphere.

Pekinese 50 seats Last dinner 11.30pm

Credit cards 1 2 3 5

SE11 Kennington
London plan **5** *D3*

★★**London Park** Brook Dr, Elephant & Castle (Consort) ☎ 01-735 9191 Telex no 919161

Reasonably priced large hotel with small, adequately-appointed bedrooms.

364rm(34 258)(15fb) CTV in all bedrooms S% ✱sB&B£22.50 sB&B £27.50—£29.50 dB&B£37.50 dB&B £45

Lift ☾ 15P(charge) CFA *xmas*

English & French S% ✱Lunch £7alc Dinner £6.95&alc Wine £4.75 Last dinner 8.45pm

Credit cards 1 2 3 4 5 Ⓥ

SE13 Lewisham
London plan **5** *E2*

✕***Curry Centre*** 37 Lee High Rd ☎ 01-852 6544

Informal friendly service, and typical Indian decor are found at this simple restaurant.

Indian 60 seats Last dinner 11.45pm

Credit cards 1 2 3 5

SW1 Westminster; *St James's Park, Victoria Station, Knightsbridge, Lower Regent St*

★★★★★*L* **Hyatt Carlton Tower** Cadogan Pl ☎ 01-235 5411 Telex no 21944 Plan 2: **61** *D3*

Improvements continue at this luxurious modern hotel where bedrooms have recently been upgraded and where the refurbished lounge is proving an attraction, particularly when afternoon tea is served. For a more substantial meal, guests can choose between the fine roast beef of the Rib Room and the first-class, creative food served in the elegant Chelsea Room.

221 in 2 bedrooms CTV in all bedrooms **T** sB £140.15—£166.60 dB £176.80—£206.70 (room only)

Lift ☾ 40 (£6.50) CFA sauna bath solarium gymnasium

English & French Lunch fr£17.50 High Tea fr£6.75 Dinner fr£17.50 Wine £8.50 Last dinner 11pm

Credit cards 1 2 3 4 5

★★★★★*B* **Hyde Park** Knightsbridge (Trusthouse Forte) ☎ 01-235 2000 Telex no 262057 Plan 2: **62** *D4*

Traditional, elegant and very English in style, this hotel is small enough to permit personal and friendly service. Except for those on the top floor, the bedrooms are, arguably, the best of any London hotel.

180 1 CTV in all bedrooms **T** sB&B £144 dB&B £168

Lift ☾ CFA

Last dinner 10.30pm

Credit cards 1 2 3 4 5

★★★★★

★★★★★ BERKELEY HOTEL, LONDON SW1

Wilton Pl Knightsbridge ☎ 01-235 6000 Telex no 919252 Plan 2: **13** *D4*

In the 14 years since it was opened this hotel has become firmly established, having an international reputation and a clientele who return year after year to enjoy the superb service offered in this elegant and dignified hotel. Yet with most of the more mundane facilities discreetly out of sight and the absence of a bar, it retains an English atmosphere reminiscent of the Old Berkeley. However, with its chic, modern decor in the restaurant and Buttery, it has also kept pace with modern trends. Even so, with marbled floor and two luxurious sitting rooms, attractive decor that includes crystal chandeliers and gorgeous flower arrangements, it conveys an air of luxury reminiscent of past times. Air-conditioned bedrooms reach the same high standards. All the usual five-star facilities are provided and the room service can be particularly commended. Notable in London is the roof level swimming pool with a roof that can be opened in the Summer.

Chef Schmidl provides good French cooking in the main restaurant while in the Perroquet there is a hot/cold buffet at lunchtimes and a more formal menu at night.

160 CTV in all bedrooms **T** S% ✱sB £150 dB £185 (room only)

Lift ☾ 50 (charge) (heated) sauna bath solarium

French & Italian S% ✱Lunch £30alc Tea fr£2.50 Dinner £35alc Wine £7.50 Last dinner 10.45pm

Credit cards 1 2 3 5

LONDON

★★★★★ ***Sheraton Park Tower***
101 Knightsbridge ☎ 01-235 8050
Telex no 917222 Plan 2: **109** *D4*

Circular-shaped hotel with large, well-appointed bedrooms and friendly service.

295⛟ CTV in 265 bedrooms **T** ⛔ S%
✱sB⛟£127.65—£143.75
db⛟£144.90—£161 (room only) **B**
Lift ☾ # **P** ⛝ *xmas*
♅ ⊡ ✱Lunch £10.75 Tea £4.75 Dinner £16.75&alc Wine £8 Last dinner mdnt
Credit cards 1 2 3 4 5

★★★★ **Goring Hotel**
(see red star box opposite)

★★★★ **Cavendish** Jermyn St (Trusthouse Forte) ☎ 01-930 2111 Telex no 263187 Plan 1: **8** *A2*

Comfortable, modern hotel with efficient friendly service.

253⛟ CTV in all bedrooms **T** sB&B⛟£89
dB&B⛟£117 **B**
Lift ☾ 10P 80⌂ CFA *xmas*
♅ ⊡ Last dinner 11pm
Credit cards 1 2 3 4 5

❀★★★★ ***HB* Duke's** St James Pl (Prestige) ☎ 01-491 4840 Telex no 28283 Plan 1: **16** *A1*

This small hotel has been tastefully and elegantly refurbished to provide comfortable accommodation. The service is very professional, yet the hotel retains an informal, relaxing atmosphere. The cuisine is English and French and the cooking is of a very high standard.

52⛟(16fb) 1⊟ CTV in all bedrooms **T** ⛔ ✱sB⛟£110 dB⛟£145—£160 (room only)
Lift ☾ **P** ⛝
⊌English & French ♅ ⊡ ✱Lunch £16.50&alc Tea £2 Dinner £25alc Wine £7.50 Last dinner 10pm
Credit cards 1 2 3 4 5

★★★★ **Holiday Inn Chelsea** 17—25 Sloane St (Holiday Inns) ☎ 01-235 4377 Telex no 919111 Plan 2: **60** *D3*

Modern hotel with good leisure facilities and helpful staff.

198⛟⋒(22fb) CTV in all bedrooms **T** ⛔ S% ✱sB⛟⋒£93 dB⛟⋒£112 (room only) **B**
Lift ☾ # **P** ⛝ CFA ⊡(heated) *xmas*
V ♅ ⊡ S% ✱Wine £7.40 Last dinner 10.30pm
Credit cards 1 2 3 4 5

★★★★ **Royal Westminster Thistle**
49 Buckingham Palace Rd (Thistle) ☎ 01-834 1821 Telex no 916821 Plan 3: **29** *A1*

Extensive refurbishment of all bedrooms and public areas has now been completed, so that the hotel offers excellent accommodation with impressive lobby and lounge and a brasserie restaurant.

135⛟⋒(38fb) ⚟ in 30 bedrooms CTV in all bedrooms **T** ⛔ ✱sB⛟⋒fr£85
dB⛟⋒fr£105 (room only) **B**
Lift ☾ # **P** ⛝
⊌International ♅ ⊡ ✱Lunch fr£14.95&alc Dinner fr£21.95&alc Wine £7 Last dinner 11pm
Credit cards 1 2 3 4 5 Ⓥ

★★★★

★★★★ **GORING HOTEL, LONDON SW1**

Beeston Pl, Grosvenor Gdns ☎ 01-834 8211 Telex no 919166 Plan 3: **12** *A2*

Family owned since it opened in 1910, it is Mr George Goring who is now responsible for maintaining the unique atmosphere, which is special to those hotels where the proprietor personally runs it. From the moment you step inside you sense that you will be well cared for by the courteous and solicitous staff; everyone you meet, porters, receptionist, waiters or chambermaids, will greet you with a smile. Such a welcome change! The interior is smartly traditional with a black and white marble floor, plasterwork ceilings and crystal chandeliers, all beautifully maintained. The lounge is in two parts, the upper overlooking the pretty gardens and has a bar counter. A gas log fire burns, there are flowers and magazines as well as comfortable easy chairs to offer solid comfort in peaceful surroundings. Clean and comfortable bedrooms vary in size but are all one could wish for as is the prompt room service. In the elegant dining room, the staff serve you well from the good value fixed price or à la carte menus and the fairly traditional cooking is consistently well done.

90⛟⋒ CTV in all bedrooms **T** ⛔ S%
sB&B⛟⋒£82 dB&B⛟⋒£129
Lift ☾ 10P 4⌂(open £4.50 covered £6) ⛝
⊌English & French **V** ♅ ⊡ Lunch £12—£14.50&alc Tea £5 Dinner fr£16&alc Wine £7.50 Last dinner 10pm
Credit cards 1 2 3 5

★★★★ ***H* Stafford** 16—18 St James's Pl (Prestige) ☎ 01-493 0111 Telex no 28602 Plan 1: **50A** *A1*

Small comfortable, secluded hotel with elegant restaurant and lounges.

62⛟ 1⊟ CTV in all bedrooms **T** ⛔
Lift ☾ 6⌂ ⛝
⊌French **V** ♅ ⊡ S% ✱Lunch £16 Dinner £18 Wine £9 Last dinner 10pm
Credit cards 1 2 3 5

★★★ **Lowndes Thistle** 19 Lowndes St (Thistle) ☎ 01-235 6020 Telex no 919065 Plan 2: **80** *D3*

A modern and somewhat exclusive hotel in Belgravia with elegant Adam style sitting area and particularly attractive bedrooms.

80⛟⋒ ⚟ in 32 bedroom CTV in all bedrooms **T** ⛔ ✱sB⛟⋒£85—£105
dB⛟⋒£115—£135 (room only) **B**
Lift ☾ **P** ⛝
⊌International ♅ ⊡ ✱Lunch fr£13.75&alc Dinner fr£13.75&alc Wine £7 Last dinner 9.30pm
Credit cards 1 2 3 4 5 Ⓥ

★★★ ***L* Royal Horseguards Thistle**
Whitehall Court (Thistle) ☎ 01-839 3400 Telex no 917096 Plan 1: **44** *D1*

Modern very comfortable hotel with attractive restaurant.

284⛟⋒ ⚟ in 25 bedrooms CTV in all bedrooms Ⓡ **T** ⛔ ✱sB⛟⋒£70—£105
dB⛟⋒£85—£135 (room only) **B**
Lift ☾ **P** CFA ⛝
⊌International ♅ ⊡ ✱Lunch £12.50&alc Dinner £12.50&alc Wine £7.50 Last dinner 10pm
Credit cards 1 2 3 4 5 Ⓥ

★★★ ***L* Rubens** Buckingham Palace Rd ☎ 01-834 6600 Telex no 916577 Plan 3: **30A** *A2*

Modernised hotel with nicely-appointed rooms.

191rm(173⛟ 18⋒)(5fb) ⚟ in 11 bedrooms CTV in all bedrooms **T** ✱sB&B⛟⋒£63.75
dB&B⛟⋒£93.50 **B**
Lift ☾ # **P** *xmas*
⊌International **V** ♅ ⊡ ✱Lunch £10.50 Tea 85p—£3.45 Dinner £10.50&alc Wine £6.95 Last dinner 10pm
Credit cards 1 2 3 4 5

To find any AA-appointed London hotel or restaurant see maps and index on pages 433—449

★ EBURY COURT HOTEL, LONDON SW1

26 Ebury St ☎ 01-730 8147 Plan 2: **40** *E3*

This hotel occasionally attracts the odd criticism from people who think it a bit small and cramped, but these criticisms are insignificant among the whole hearted praise showered upon it. The Tophams, who have owned it since pre-war days have altered it and enlarged it over the years in an endearingly quaint way. Mrs Topham's influence is seen in the prettily decorated bedrooms which vary in size considerably but are well kept. Those in the front are double-glazed. There are two cosy little sitting rooms — one with television — and the club bar where guests can obtain temporary membership. In the basement is the restaurant which serves conventional style cooking of a good standard. Here, as in the rest of the hotel, you will be attended to by many long serving staff who do their best to make you feel at home. Altogether a charmingly old fashioned sort of hotel at sensible prices.

39rm(12) 4 * sB&B£34 dB&B£54 dB&B £64

Lift ☾ CTV P

English & French **V** Lunch £10.50alc Dinner £12alc Wine £4.55 Last dinner 9pm

Credit cards 1 3

XXX Auberge De Provence (St James Court Hotel) Buckingham Gate ☎ 01-834 6655 Telex no 919557 Plan 3: **1A** *B2*

A pleasantly cool restaurant with white walls, arches and hanging plants, which specialises in French regional cooking which is skilfully prepared under the direction of consultant/chef Jean André Charial. Service by young French staff is good.

French **V** 80 seats S% * Lunch fr£15 Dinner £25alc Wine £7.60 Last dinner 11pm P

Credit cards 1 2 3 5

XXX Dolphin Brasserie Rodney House, Dolphin Sq/Chichester St ☎ 01-828 3207

Following a change of management, the restaurant has been reopened with a new decor and a new chef. Set price and à la carte menus are offered, the standard of cuisine and accompanying wine list both being of a good standard and giving value for money. Management and service are friendly and willing.

British & French **V** 100 seats * Lunch £12&alc Dinner £14.50&alc Wine £6.20 Last dinner 10.45pm P Live music Mon—Sat

Credit cards 1 2 3 5

XX L'Amico 44 Horseferry Rd ☎ 01-222 4680 Plan 3: **1** *C1*

Extensive basement Italian restaurant with several separate rooms.

Closed Sat & Sun

Italian **V** 70 seats S% * Lunch £16alc Dinner £16alc Wine £5.50 Last dinner 10.30pm P nc 4yrs

Credit cards 1 2 3 5 Ⓥ

XX Le Caprice Arlington House, Arlington St ☎ 01-629 2239 Plan 1: **7B** *A1*

Modern, French restaurant, with large plants, and featuring photographs by David Bailey.

Lunch not served Sat

Dinner not served 24 Dec—2 Jan

French 70 seats Lunch £14alc Dinner £14alc Wine £5 Last dinner mdnt P nc 5yrs Live music nightly

Credit cards 1 2 3 5

❀XX Gavvers 61 Lower Sloane St ☎ 01-730 5983 Telex no 8813079 Plan 2: **49B** *E2*

(Rosette awarded for dinner only)

A Roux Brothers enterprise, the restaurant offers a very popular, value-for-money, fixed price menu, the charge covering not only half a bottle of wine but also service and VAT.

Closed Sun & Bank Hol's

Lunch not served

French 60 seats S% * Dinner £18.75 Last dinner 11pm P

Credit cards 2 5

❀XX Ken Lo's Memories of China 67 Ebury St ☎ 01-730 7734 Plan 3: **15A** *A1*

Kenneth Lo, acclaimed for his book on Chinese cooking, includes both classical and regional dishes on the menu of this elegant restaurant.

Closed Sun & Bank Hol

Chinese 80 seats Lunch fr£15.50 Dinner £19.50—£28 Wine £6 Last dinner 10.45pm P

Credit cards 1 2 3 5

❀XX Le Mazarin 30 Winchester St ☎ 01-828 3366

(Rosette awarded for dinner only)

Chef/patron Rene Bajard continues to impress guests with his "new classic cuisine", beautifully cooked and presented in cosy, candle-lit, basement surroundings. The fixed-price menu offers excellent value for money, there is an interesting wine list, and service is efficient, friendly and well-organised.

Closed Sun, Bank Hol's & 1 wk Xmas

Lunch not served

French **V** 55 seats S% Dinner £15.50—£22.50 Wine £7 Last dinner 11.30pm P

Credit cards 1 2 5

❀XX Mijanou 143 Ebury St ☎ 01-730 4099 Plan 2: **88D** *E2*

In a smart little restaurant fronted by her husband Neville, Sonia Blech continues to provide enjoyable dishes with a French influence.

Closed Sat, Sun, 1 wk Etr, 3wks Aug & 2wks Xmas

French 30 seats Lunch £10.75&alc Dinner £26.50&alc Wine £6.50 Last dinner 11pm P

Credit cards 1 2 5

XX Pomegranates 94 Grosvenor Rd ☎ 01-828 6560

Cuisine from at least 14 countries features in this basement restaurant.

Closed Sun & Bank Hols

Lunch not served Sat

International 50 seats * Lunch £12—£17.50 Dinner £12.50—£19.50 Wine £7.50 Last dinner 11.15pm P

Credit cards 1 2 3 4

❀XX Salloos 62—64 Kinnerton St ☎ 01-235 4444 Plan 2: **106A** *D3*

An amiable atmosphere prevails in the first-floor, family-run restaurant, tucked away in a quiet corner off Knightsbridge. Menus feature the subtler, Pakistani, style of dish, such as the seldom-encountered Indian Cheese Soufflé.

Closed Sun & Bank Hols

Pakistani **V** 70 seats Lunch £12—£20&alc Dinner £15—£20&alc Wine £6 Last dinner 11.15pm P

Credit cards 1 2 3 4 5

XX *Tate Gallery* Millbank Embankment ☎ 01-834 6754 Plan 3: **36** *C1*

Brightly decorated, popular restaurant with interesting menu featuring old English dishes, and excellent wine list.

Closed Sun, 24—26 Dec, New Year's Day, Good Fri & May Day Dinner not served

V 120 seats Last lunch 3pm P

Ciboure 21 Eccleston St ☎ 01-730 2505 Plan 2: **26A** *E3*

The bright, modern and well-appointed French restaurant offers a high standard of cooking, fish dishes being particularly impressive; service is professional but informal in style.

Closed Sun Lunch not served Sat

French 36 seats Lunch £14—£15 Dinner £18alc Wine £6.30 Last dinner 11.30pm nc 10yrs

Credit cards 1 2 3 5

Eatons 49 Elizabeth St ☎ 01-730 0074 Plan 2: **39** *E2*

Continental cuisine is featured in this small, friendly French-style restaurant.

Closed Sat, Sun & Bank Hol's

Continental 40 seats S% Lunch £15.50alc Dinner £15.50alc Wine £6.50 Last dinner 11.15pm

Credit cards 1 2 3 5

La Fantaisie Brasserie 14 Knightsbridge Gn ☎ 01-589 0509 Plan 2: **44** *D3*

Mirrored panels and soft pink walls give this popular "estamet" a serene and elegant atmosphere befitting the lightness and subtlety of the food. The thoughtfully-constructed menu features popular, modern dishes, prepared with attention to detail and excellently presented. Staff are smart, unobtrusively friendly and efficient.

Closed Sun, Xmas & New Year

French 54 seats * Lunch £14alc Dinner £15alc Wine £5.40 Last dinner 10.30pm

Credit cards 1 2 3 5

Le Poule au Pot 231 Ebury St ☎ 01-730 7763 Plan 2: **74A** *E2*

Friendly French restaurant featuring interesting authentic dishes.

Closed Sun Lunch not served Sat

French 50 seats Last dinner 11.15pm

Credit cards 1 2 3 4 5

Tent 15 Eccleston St ☎ 01-730 6922 Plan 2: **119** *E2*

The decor of this small French restaurant is in keeping with the name. The regular clientele is attracted by friendly service, an informal atmosphere and a good standard of cuisine, though the menu is not very extensive.

Closed Sat

French 45 seats S% * Lunch £12 Dinner £12 Wine £6.25 Last dinner 11.30pm

Credit cards 1 2 3

Le Trou Normand 27 Motcomb St ☎ 01-235 1668 Plan 2: **123** *D3*

This contemporary seafood restaurant is a little piece of Normandy set down in London. The Cuisine Normande, featuring Plats du Jour, fresh lobsters, traditional cheeses and desserts, is high in standard and reasonable in price, whilst a taste of luxury is offered by the Oyster and Champagne Bar in the basement.

Closed 23 Dec—3 Jan

French 36 seats * Lunch £16alc Dinner £22alc Wine £8 Last dinner 11.30pm

Credit cards 2 3 5

London SW1 — London SW3

★★★★

★★★★THE CAPITAL, LONDON SW3

Basil St, Knightsbridge ☎ 01-589 5171 Telex no 919042 Plan 2: **18** *D3*

"There are few hotels that can provide so much of one's ideal in a hotel" says one of our most experienced inspectors. And he is right! David Levin's gem of a hotel, a short distance from Harrods, provides formal yet friendly and welcoming service, good food and comfortable bedrooms, some of which are outstanding. The latter are individually decorated to a high standard and are beautifully done although compact in size. On the ground floor are the public rooms, recently refurbished by Nina Campbell (she also did Hambleton Hall). There is the cosy little lounge with its green colour scheme in which to relax, the lively bar and the stylishly elegant restaurant: very chic with its terracotta and cream festooned curtains and immaculate table appointments. Peter Schultz is the fine Restaurant Manager who will look after you here while you sample the delicious cooking from the hands of chef Brian Turner. He follows the modern French style, but he has not forgotten his roots and some of his dishes have an endearing earthy quality. One such, was a ragout of duck livers and giblets with a red wine sauce. Other dishes to gain acclaim were the perfectly cooked salad of sea food, terrine of rabbit, quenelles of smoked fish and the pigeon breasts with sauerkraut and red wine sauce. At the last moment, we have learned that Brian Turner is leaving to open his own restaurant.

60 CTV in all bedrooms **T** S% sB fr £100 dB £120—£140 (room only)

Lift ## 12 (£8 per day)

French **V** S% * Lunch £16.50—£19.50&alc Tea £4.50 Dinner £18.50&alc Wine £10.75 Last dinner 10.30pm

Credit cards 1 2 3 4 5

SW3 Chelsea, *Brompton*

★★★*HL* Basil Street Basil St, Knightsbridge SW3 ☎ 01-581 3311 Telex no 28379 Plan 2: **12** *D3*

Antique furniture and plenty of flowers create a country house atmosphere here.

95rm(69) CTV in all bedrooms **T** sB&B£39.80 sB&B £69 dB&B£64.50 dB&B £93.50 Continental breakfast

Lift CFA

International **V** Lunch £9.75—£10.75 Tea £3 High Tea £4.50 Wine £6.75 Last dinner 9.45pm

Credit cards 1 2 3 5

Waltons 121 Walton St ☎ 01-584 0204 Plan 2: **124** *C2*

Elegantly luxurious comfort is enhanced by discreet management supervision and professionally formal service here. Attention to detail is good, and standards of cuisine are reliable but never dull, for the chef's skill and artistry transform best-quality ingredients into some adventurous dishes. The beautifully flavoured sauces, often textured with cream, are particularly noteworthy.

Closed Bank Hol's

International 65 seats Lunch £11&alc Dinner £17.50&alc Wine £7.50 Last dinner 11.30pm nc2yrs

Credit cards 1 2 3 4 5

To find any AA-appointed London hotel or restaurant see maps and index on pages 433—449

LONDON

XXX ***Zen Chinese*** Chelsea Cloisters, Sloane Av ☎ 01-589 1781 Plan 2: **126** *D1*

The Chinese Zodiac is the background to an interesting menu including old Buddhist dishes and other delicacies.

Chinese 120 seats Last dinner 11.15pm

Credit cards 1 2 3 4 5

London SW3

❀❀❀XX TANTE CLAIRE, LONDON SW3

68 Royal Hospital Rd ☎ 01-352 6045 Plan 2: **118** *D1*

After a few teething troubles last autumn following the opening of the enlarged and refurbished premises, Pierre Koffman is back on form. The restaurant now has a sitting area, and the whole is very much improved with the fresh colour scheme in pastel shades. The Head Waiter, Jean-Pierre, with his young brigade, attends to you exceedingly well with interested and proficient service. The à la carte menu offers an interesting choice of delicious dishes while at luncheon there is still the fantastic value fixed price lunch and another short list of fish dishes of the day. Mr Koffman succeeds admirably with fish: delicate cooking, subtle flavours and exquisite sauces make them truly memorable. He cooks in the modern French style but without copying the French masters as so many do. His style is his own and despite the refined quality there is a subtle earthiness that probably comes from his background in south-west France. Dishes like his stuffed pigs trotter, made famous on TV, and his roast pigeon with a selection of cereals show this. Dishes that have particularly pleased our inspectors have included a brandade of salt cod with caviar accompanied by a lovely fresh tasting tomato sauce, and blinis (buckwheat yeast pancake) and the balotine of foie gras, full of wonderful flavour and with some poached leeks in a delicious mustardy vinaigrette. Fish dishes such as the fillet of bass with chopped black olives and salsify with a butter sauce was delightfully piquant. Meat dishes include the delicious roundels of spring lamb with the parsley charlotte and the garlic flavoured sauce, saddle of rabbit dressed on a cabbage leaf with julienne of cabbage and primeur carrots and again a subtly flavoured sauce. Vegetable can lack heat, perhaps the price of over presentation, but are always properly cooked. His desserts are ambrosian as evinced by his sandwich of caramel mousse with tuile-like pastry, garnished with pink grapefruit segments and with a grapefruit syrup; also by that old favourite, biscuit glacé flavoured with praline and with a zestful cullis of raspberries. Great attention is paid to detail — there is sometimes a hot beignet with the petits fours — Pierre Koffman can be one of the four best chefs in the country, but unfortunately the third rosette remains elusive. Never mind, on a good day you can eat as well here as anywhere in Britain.

Closed Sat, Sun, 2 wks Xmas/New Year, 2 wks Etr & 3 wks Aug/Sep

French 38 seats S% Lunch £19&alc Dinner £32alc Wine £7 Last dinner 11pm

Credit cards 2 5

XX ***Avoirdupois*** 334 Kings Rd ☎ 01-352 6151 Plan 2: **9** *C1*

Well prepared, varied and imaginative menu served in friendly atmosphere with soft live music.

English & French **V** 140 seats Last dinner 11.45pm Live music nightly

Credit cards 1 2 3 5

XX **Daphne's** 112 Draycott Av ☎ 01-589 4257 Plan 2: **34** *C2*

Warm cosy restaurant with fine French and English cooking.

Closed Sun & Bank Hol's Lunch not served Sat

English & French 96 seats ✱ Lunch £12alc Dinner £17alc Wine £6 Last dinner 11.30pm

Credit cards 1 2 3 5

❀XX **English Garden** 10 Lincoln St ☎ 01-584 7272 Plan 2: **42** *D2*

Well-researched Old English recipes, cooked with considerable skill, are featured in a fashionable conservatory, English-garden setting.

Closed 25 & 26 Dec

V 65 seats S% Lunch £20alc Dinner £27.50alc Wine £7.50 Last dinner 11.30pm

Credit cards 1 2 3 5

❀XX **English House** 3 Milner St ☎ 01-584 3002 Plan 2: **43** *D2*

This elegant, well-appointed restaurant serves thoroughly researched traditional English dishes; supervision and service are excellent.

Closed 25, 26 Dec & Good Fri

V 40 seats S% Lunch £10.50—£12.50&alc Dinner £17.50&alc Wine £7 Last dinner 11.30pm

Credit cards 1 2 3 5

XX **Le Français** 259 Fulham Rd ☎ 01-352 4748 Plan 2: **45** *B1*

The small, intimate restaurant features French regional menus (which are changed weekly) and classical dishes. Skilful and very enterprising cooking, coupled with friendly and efficient service, makes a meal here particularly good value for money.

Closed Sun

French 65 seats S% Lunch £11—£20 Dinner £20—£25 Wine £10.50 Last dinner 10.45pm

Credit cards 2 3

XX **Good Earth** 233 **Brompton Rd** ☎ 01-584 3658 Plan 2: **54A** *C3*

Modern Cantonese restaurant offering well prepared authentic dishes in a friendly informal atmosphere.

Closed 24—27 Dec

Chinese **V** 105 seats S% ✱ Lunch £5—£11&alc Dinner £7—£16&alc Wine £5 Last dinner 11.15pm

Credit cards 1 2 3 5

XX ***Good Earth*** 91 **King's Rd** ☎ 01-352 9321 Plan 2: **54** *D1*

Modern restaurant on two floors decorated with fine murals. Staff are helpful and friendly, serving some interesting set gourmet dishes.

Pekinese **V** 80 seats Last dinner 11.45pm

Credit cards 1 2 3 4 5

XX **Mario** 260—262A Brompton Rd ☎ 01-584 1724 Plan 2: **85A** *C2*

Well managed contemporary Italian restaurant with authentic cuisine and home-made pasta.

Closed Bank Hol's

Italian 80 seats ✱ Lunch fr£8.50&alc Dinner £12—£14alc Wine £6.25 Last dinner 11.30pm

Credit cards 1 2 3 5

XX **Ménage à Trois** 15 Beauchamp Pl ☎ 01-589 4252 Plan 2: **88A** *D3*

The basement restaurant is a "fun" place to dine in an intimate atmosphere with live piano music and open fires. The menu is restricted to starters and puddings — though no-one checks how many of these you have! — and the success of this original idea owes much to the innovative →

LONDON

preparation of quality ingredients. Service by a team of delightful young ladies adds another dimension to your enjoyment.

Closed Sun

V 70 seats Lunch £14—£17&alc Dinner £18—£25&alc Wine £5.95 Last dinner 11.30pm Live music wkly

Credit cards 1 2 3 5 V

XX**Meridiana** 169 Fulham Rd ☎01-589 8815 Plan 2: **88B** *C2*

Well managed and efficient contemporary Italian restaurant featuring open air balcony terrace, interesting authentic and home-made pasta.

Italian **V** 120 seats *Lunch £17.50alc Dinner £18.50alc Wine £5.50 Last dinner mdnt Live music nightly

Credit cards 1 2 3 5

XX**St Quentin** 243 Brompton Rd ☎01-589 8005 Plan 2: **16** *C3*

Stylish Brasserie serving adventurous tempting food.

Closed 1 wk Xmas

French 80 seats Lunch £9.50 Dinner £12.90 Wine £6.20 Last dinner mdnt

Credit cards 1 2 3 5

XX**San Frediano** 62 Fulham Rd ☎01-584 8375 Plan 2: **107** *C2*

This long-established and popular Italian restaurant provides an authentic atmosphere and traditional cuisine. Amenities are limited, though of an acceptable standard, and the value for money that the restaurant provides amply compensates for any short-fall.

Closed Sun

Italian **V** 85 seats Lunch £15alc Dinner £15alc Wine £4.70 Last dinner 11.15pm

Credit cards 1 2 3 5

XX**Tandoori** 153 Fulham Rd ☎01-589 7749 Plan 2: **116** *C2*

An intimate atmosphere is created by subdued lighting in this cosy basement restaurant. Pleasant waiters serve good quality curries and Tandoori dishes.

Closed 25 & 26 Dec

Indian **V** 65 seats Lunch £12alc Dinner £15alc Wine £5.20 Last dinner mdnt

Credit cards 1 2 3 4 5

X**Choy's** 172 Kings Rd ☎01-352 9085 Plan 2: **25** *C1*

Long established family Chinese restaurant with friendly atmosphere and particularly good vegetables.

Cantonese **V** 60 seats S% *Lunch £5—£15&alc Dinner £10—£15&alc Wine £5 Last dinner mdnt

Credit cards 1 2 3 5

To find any AA-appointed London hotel or restaurant see maps and index on pages 433—449

London SW3 — London SW5

X**Dans** 119 Sydney St ☎01-352 2718 Plan 2: **33B** *C1*

The busy restaurant, painted in delicate pastel shades, decked with hanging baskets and standing in a garden, offers simple dishes of outstanding quality; the atmosphere is cheerful and service unobtrusive but attentive.

Closed Sat, Sun & Bank Hol's

English & French **V** 50 seats Last dinner 11.15pm

Credit cards 2 3 5

X**Dumpling House** 9 Beauchamp Pl ☎01-589 8240 Plan 2: **38** *D3*

Peking and Szechuan dishes are the specialities of this popular restaurant. An extensive and authentic menu can be enjoyed in a casually friendly atmosphere, the special set dinners representing particularly good value for money.

Peking & Szechuan **V** 46 seats Lunch £8 Dinner £8 Wine £5.50 Last dinner 11.30pm

Credit cards 1 2 3 5

X**Ma Cuisine** 113 Walton St ☎01-584 7585 Plan 2: **82** *C2*

This small, well-appointed restaurant offers impeccably-cooked, inventive and imaginative dishes, efficiently served by friendly staff.

Closed Sat, Sun, Xmas, New Year, 1 wk Etr & 14 Jul—14 Aug

French 32 seats Wine £7.25 Last dinner 11pm nc 10yrs

Credit cards 2 5

X**Mes Amis** 31 Basil St ☎01-584 4484 Plan 2: **88C** *D3*

Popular restaurant featuring a good selection of traditional dishes.

International 90 seats Lunch £15alc Dinner £18alc Wine £6.95 Last dinner 11pm

Credit cards 1 2 3 4 5

X**Poissonnerie** 82 Sloane Av ☎01-589 2457 Plan 2: **100** *C2*

Popular and well appointed Oyster Bar and oak panelled fish restaurant, featuring high quality fresh seasonal dishes.

Closed Sun, 24 Dec—2 Jan & Bank Hol's

French **V** 100 seats Wine £6.50

Credit cards 1 2 3 5

X***Le Suquet*** 104 Draycott Av ☎01-581 1785 Plan 2: **115** *C2*

Very popular Sea Food French restaurant with formidable range of dishes.

French 50 seats Last dinner 11.30pm

Credit card 2

SW4 Clapham

London plan **5** D2/3

X**Maharani Indian** 117 Clapham High St ☎01-622 2530

Indian **V** 76 seats *Lunch £8alc Dinner £10alc Wine £3.50 Last dinner mdnt

Credit cards 1 2 3 5

SW5 Earl's Court

★★★***London International*** 147 Cromwell Rd, Kensington (Swallow) ☎01-370 4200 Telex no 27260 Plan 2: **78** *A2*

Large, friendly hotel with well-equipped bedrooms.

417(36fb) CTV in all bedrooms **T** S% sB&B£52—£57 dB&B£62—£68 Continental breakfast

Lift

English & French S% *Lunch £8alc Tea £1.05—£2.95 High Tea £3.50—£5.25&alc Dinner £10.95&alc Wine £6.50 Last dinner mdnt

Credit cards 1 2 3 5

★★***Hogarth*** Hogarth Rd (Inter Hotel) ☎01-370 6831 Telex no 8951994 Plan 2: **58A** *A2*

The modern hotel has well-equipped, attractive bedrooms and modest public areas. The standards of service are generally acceptable and plain food is available.

85rm(67 18)(10fb) CTV in all bedrooms ® **T** Continental breakfast

Lift 18

Mainly grills Last dinner 9.30pm

Credit cards 1 2 3 5

XX**Pontevecchio** 256 Old Brompton Rd ☎01-373 9082 Plan 2: **101A** *A1*

Reservations are advisable at this very lively and popular restaurant, where you can enjoy a range of authentic Italian dishes, including some home-made pasta, in a fashionable forecourt setting where the friendly and attentive service is personally superintended by the the patron.

Italian 100 seats *Lunch £15alc(incl wine) Dinner £15alc(incl wine) Wine £6.50 Last dinner 11.30pm

Credit cards 1 2 3 5

XX**Tiger Lee** 251 Old Brompton Rd ☎01-370 2323 Telex no 919660 Plan 2: **121** *A1*

The elegantly modern Chinese restaurant specialises in seafood and offers dishes with such evocative names as "Shadow of a Butterfly". The attentive and professional service is excellent and there are some fine French wines on the winelist.

Lunch not served

LONDON

🍲Cantonese 56 seats Dinner £22—£25&alc Wine £8.80 Last dinner 11pm P ⁄

Credit cards 1 2 3 5

X**L'Aquitaine** 158 Old Brompton Rd ☎01-373 9918 Plan 2: **2** *A2*

Closed Sun

🍲French 100 seats S% Lunch £11.50—£14.50 Dinner £18alc Wine £7.50 Last dinner 1.30am P

Cabaret Tue & Fri

Credit cards 1 2 3 5

X***L'Artiste Affamé*** 243 Old Brompton Rd ☎01-373 1659 Plan 2: **7** *A1*

French bistro-style restaurant.

Closed Sun, 24—26 Dec & Bank Hols

🍲French **V** 80 seats Last dinner 11.15pm

Credit cards 1 2 3 5

X***New Lotus Garden*** 257 Old Brompton Rd ☎01-370 4450 Plan 2: **93** *A1*

Popular Chinese restaurant with Colonial atmosphere, good service and authentic speciality cooking.

Closed Xmas

🍲Pekinese 55 seats Last dinner 12.30am

Credit cards 1 2 3 5

❀X**Read's** 152 Old Brompton Rd ☎01-373 2445 Plan 2: **102A** *A2*

Small well managed restaurant featuring skilful imaginative cooking complemented by subtlety and flair.

Closed 2 wks Xmas—New Year Dinner not served Sun

V 45 seats Last dinner 11pm

Credit cards 1 2 3 5

SW6 Fulham

London Plan **5** C3

❀XX**Gastronome One** 311—313 New Kings Rd ☎01-731 6381

Split level basement French restaurant featuring 'Nouvelle' dishes.

Closed Sun Lunch not served Sat

🍲French **V** 70 seats S% Lunch £12.50—£16.50 Dinner £16.50—£18.50 Wine £7 Last dinner 11.30pm P ⁄

Credit cards 1 2 3 5

❀X**L'Hippocampe** 131A Munster Rd ☎01-736 5588

Closed Sun, 24 Dec—31 Jan

Lunch not served Sat

🍲French 35 seats Lunch £4.50—£8.50&alc Dinner £20alc Wine £5.20 Last dinner 11pm P

Credit cards 1 2 3

London SW5 — London SW8

X**Mao Tai Szechuan** 58 New Kings Rd ☎01-731 2520

🍲Chinese & Szechuan **V** 90 seats S% *Lunch £12.50alc Dinner £12.50alc Wine £5.20 Last dinner 11.45pm P

Credit cards 1 2 3 5

❀X**Perfumed Conservatory** 182 Wandsworth Bridge Rd ☎01-731 0732

Fashionable restaurant and cocktail bar specialises in original and imaginative British cooking.

Closed Sun & Mon, Xmas Lunch not served Sat

40 seats *Lunch £15—£17.50 Wine £6 Last dinner 11.30pm P nc 10yrs

Credit cards 1 2 3

X***Trencherman*** 271 New Kings Rd ☎01-736 4988

This small cosy Bistro features authentic regional dishes.

🍲French 30 seats Last dinner 10.45pm P

Credit cards 2 3 4 5

SW7 South Kensington

★★★★**Gloucester** 4—18 Harrington Gdns (Rank) ☎01-373 5842 Telex no 917505 Plan 2: **52** *A2*

Modern, well managed hotel with good service and choice of restaurants.

531 ⇌ (2fb) ⁄ in 10 bedrooms CTV in all bedrooms ® in 473 bedrooms **T** S% *sB⇌fr£87 dB⇌fr£101 (room only) B

Lift ☾ ## 100 🚗 (£5.75 per day) CFA sauna bath solarium *xmas*

🍲English & Continental **V** ♁ ☕ ⁄ S% *Lunch £9.45&alc Tea £1.50—£2.50&alc High Tea £5&alc Dinner £10—£25&alc Wine £7.50 Last dinner 12.30am

Credit cards 1 2 3 4 5

★★★*L* ***Rembrandt*** Thurloe Pl ☎01-589 8100 Telex no 295828 Plan 2: **102C** *C3*

A professionally-managed hotel, with modern and well-equipped bedrooms.

200 ⇌ (25fb) CTV in all bedrooms **T** ✗ Continental breakfast B

Lift ☾ P sauna bath solarium gymnasium

♁ ☕ Last dinner 9.30pm

Credit cards 1 2 3 4 5

XXX**Bombay Brasserie** Courtfield Close, Gloucester Rd ☎01-370 4040 Plan 2: **14A** *B2 (classification for dinner only)*

This restaurant serves authentic regional dishes in an elegant colonial atmosphere.

🍲Indian **V** 175 seats Lunch fr£8.50 Dinner £18.50alc Wine £6.25 Last dinner mdnt P

Credit cards 1 2 3 5

❀XX**Hilaire** 68 Old Brompton Rd ☎01-584 8993 Plan 2: **57A** *B2 (Rosette awarded for dinner only)*

Fashionable, contemporary restaurant featuring imaginative fixed price menu.

Closed Sun & Public Hol's Lunch not served Sat

🍲French 50 seats Lunch £13.50—£14.50 Dinner £21—£23 Wine £7.50 Last dinner 11pm P nc 5yrs

Credit cards 1 2 3 5

X**Chanterelle** 119 Old Brompton Rd ☎01-373 5522 Plan 2: **22** *B2*

The attractive, pine-panelled restaurant features a fixed-price menu which represents particularly good value for money. Reliable standards of cooking are matched by attentive and friendly service.

Closed 4 days Xmas

🍲English & French 45 seats Lunch £7—£9.50 Dinner £11—£12 Wine £4.70 Last dinner 11.30pm P

Credit cards 1 2 3 5

X***Montpeliano*** 13 Montpelier St ☎01-589 0032 Plan 2: **91B** *C3*

Popular, fashionable Italian restaurant featuring authentic cuisine and efficient, friendly service.

Closed Sun, Xmas Day & Bank Hol's

🍲Italian **V** 80 seats Last dinner mdnt P ⁄

X***Zen Too*** 53 Old Brompton Rd ☎01-225 1609 Plan 2: **127** *B2*

Friendly and well-managed, this contemporary restaurant is attractively decorated and appointed in pink. The menu features a carefully-chosen selection of Chinese regional dishes.

🍲Chinese **V** 70 seats Last dinner 11.30pm

Credit cards 1 2 3 5

SW8 Battersea

London Plan **5** D3 (see also SW11)

❀❀❀XX**L'Arlequin**

(see rosette box overleaf)

❀XX**Chez Nico, London SW8** 129 Queenstown Rd ☎01-720 6960

This restaurant has been elegantly refurbished with attractive, pleasing decor, and the atmosphere is relaxing and informal. Although Nico Ladenis has moved to his new establishment, the same high standard of cooking that we have come to expect is maintained here.

Closed Sun, 1 wk Xmas, Bank Hols & 3 wks summer Lunch not served Sat & Mon

🍲French 45 seats S% *Lunch £14.50&alc Dinner £28alc Wine £8.95 Last dinner 10.45pm P nc 7yrs

Credit cards 1 3 5

❀❀✕✕L'ARLEQUIN, LONDON SW8

123 Queenstown Rd ☎01-622 0555

Christian Delteil's little restaurant continues to earn the plaudits of our members. He follows the modern fashion but refrains from the admixture of too many ingredients in a dish. They are always beautifully balanced and they always taste essentially 'clean'. His mousselines are as light as can be, yet flavoursome, while his fish cooking is perfect and his sauces just right to complement the dish without overpowering it. Among the reports we have had, persillée de ris de veau et homard, and confit de foie gras au poireaux with brioche, have been first courses to be enjoyed; raviolées de fenouil aux langoustines and a fricassée of scallops with ginger among the fish, while succulent Challand duck with its sapid sauce and meltingly tender foie gras dressed on a bed of darfin potatoes, garnished with apples and grapes with a port wine sauce have been highly lauded. Vegetables usually please but if there is a weak point it is the puddings. That is judging by the highest standards however; we are sure you will enjoy his sorbets which are among the best, but also marquise au chocolat and if you have room, the assiette gourmande — a selection. The wine list is well chosen. You will be well looked after by the smart young brigade. The room is quietly elegant but gleaming table appointments bright with flowers on crisp linen make for an appropriate setting in which to enjoy this delicious cooking. The fixed price luncheon is something of a bargain.

Closed Sat, Sun, 1 wk Xmas & 3 wks Aug

French 40 seats Lunch fr£12.50 Dinner £40alc Wine £9 Last dinner 11pm P

Credit cards 1 3 5

✕✕***Lampwicks*** 24 Queenstown Rd ☎01-622 7800

The tastefully-decorated, split-level restaurant features a fixed-price menu, the imaginative choice of dishes offering excellent value for money. Careful preparation and skilful cooking in the modern style are complemented by a choice from the Philippe Olivier cheese board.

Closed Sun, Mon, 2 wks Xmas & last 2 wks Aug

French **V** 30 seats Last dinner 10.30pm P

Credit cards 1 2 3 5

SW10 West Brompton

London plan **5** C3

✕✕**Brinkley's** 47 Hollywood Rd ☎01-351 1683

An imaginative menu is offered by this unusual and fashionable French restaurant where meals are served on a covered rear terrace by friendly young staff.

Closed Sun Lunch not served

English & French 60 seats Dinner £12.50—£14 Wine £6 Last dinner 11.30pm P

Credit cards 1 2 3 5

✕✕**Nikita's** 65 Ifield Rd ☎01-352 6326 Plan 2: **94** *A1*

Authentic Russian dishes served in friendly candle light atmosphere complemented by one of the best Vodka lists.

Closed Sun, Xmas Day, Bank Hol's Lunch not served

Russian 50 seats S% Dinner £20alc Wine £5.95 Last dinner 11.15pm P ✂

Credit cards 1 2 5

✕✕**L'Olivier** 116 Finborough Rd ☎01-370 4183 Plan 2: **95** *A1*

Fashionable basement restaurant with enterprising authentic cuisine at fixed price, and several imaginative à la carte dishes.

Closed Sun & 2 wks Xmas

French 50 seats Lunch fr£20&alc Dinner fr£20 Last dinner 11.45pm P

Credit cards 1 2 3 5

✕✕**September** 457 Fulham Rd ☎01-352 0206

Cooking is unpretentious and uncomplicated at this neatly compact restaurant and bar, a wide choice of dishes being accompanied by particularly good vegetables, though the range of desserts is limited. Service is friendly and reliable, and a meal here represents good value for money.

Closed Sun Lunch not served

International **V** 65 seats ✱Dinner £13.50alc Wine £6.25 Last dinner 11.30pm P

Credit cards 1 2 3 4 5

✕**Bagatelle** 5 Langton St ☎01-351 4185

Sophisticated and fashionable small French restaurant, featuring skilful imaginative cooking and friendly service, and a rear garden patio.

Closed Sun & Bank Hol's

French 60 seats ✱Lunch £12&alc Dinner £17alc Wine £6.20 Last dinner 11pm P

Credit cards 1 2 3 5

✕***Chelsea Wharf*** Lots Rd ☎01-351 0861

The popular, fashionable, riverside restaurant has extensive waterfront views. A menu which changes monthly offers a choice of fixed-price or à la carte meals, and service is friendly and helpful.

Closed Public Hols Lunch not served Mon

English & French **V** 90 seats Last dinner 11.30pm 6P

Credit cards 1 2 3 5

✕***La Croisette*** 168 Ifield Rd ☎01-373 3694 Plan 2: **32** *A1*

Popular small French restaurant specialising in shell fish. Good main basement ambience.

Closed Mon & 2 wks Xmas

French 55 seats Last dinner 11.30pm P

Credit card 2

✕**Jake's** 14 Hollywood Rd ☎01-352 8692 Plan 2: **65A** *A1*

This straightforward but stylish English restaurant has a lively and informal atmosphere which is complemented by thoroughly enjoyable food. Such dishes as breast of duck and home-made salmon fish-cakes are enhanced by herb-based and piquant sauces, whilst vegetables are fresh and simply-cooked. Service is unobtrusively friendly.

Dinner not served Sun

International **V** 60 seats ✱Lunch £8—£10alc Dinner £12—£14alc Wine £5.50 Last dinner 11.45pm P

Credit cards 1 2 3 4 5

✕**Van B's** 306B Fulham Rd ☎01-351 0863 Plan 2: **123A** *B1*

Unusually long and narrow, the first-floor dining room bears a remarkable resemblance to a carriage on the Orient Express, and a good standard of comfort is achieved by skilful lighting and tasteful furnishing. The fixed-price menu offers an enterprising selection of dishes, including home-made ice-cream and sorbet, which are very good value for money, and the standards of service are generally acceptable.

Lunch not served

French **V** 40 seats Dinner £12.50 Wine £6.85 Last dinner mdnt P

Credit cards 1 2 3

SW11 Battersea

London plan **5** D3 (see also SW8)

✕***Ormes*** 245 Lavender Hill ☎01-228 9824

Two-level restaurant featuring interesting imaginative fish dishes.

Closed Sun Lunch not served

68 seats Last dinner 11pm P

Credit cards 1 2 3 5

✕**Pollyanna's** 2 Battersea Rise ☎01-228 0316

Fashionable bistro-style decor is complemented by skilful and reliable cooking supervised by the proprietor.

Closed 24—27 Dec & 1 Jan Lunch not served Mon—Sat Dinner not served Sun

French **V** 70 seats Lunch £8.95 Dinner £10.95&alc Wine £5.50 Last dinner mdnt P

Credit cards 1 2 3

To find any AA-appointed London hotel or restaurant see maps and index on pages 433—449

SW13 Barnes
London plan **5** C3

X **Barnaby's** 39B High St, Barnes ☎ 01-878 4750

Small high street restaurant offering French specialities.

Closed Sun, Bank Hols, 3 wks Sep, 5 days Xmas & Etr Lunch not served Sat & Mon

French 24 seats S% Lunch £14alc Dinner £14alc Wine £5.95 Last dinner 10.15pm P

Credit cards 1 2 3 5

SW14 East Sheen
London plan **5** C3

X **Crowthers** 481 Upper Richmond Rd West, East Sheen ☎ 01-876 6372

Small family-run, tastefully decorated restaurant offering a fixed price menu.

Closed Sun, Mon, Xmas Day, New Year's Eve, 1 wk Feb & 2 wks Aug/Sep Lunch not served Sat

French **V** 30 seats Lunch £12 Dinner £17.50 Wine £6 Last dinner 11pm P nc 10yrs

Credit cards 1 2

X **Janine's** 505 Upper Richmond Rd West, East Sheen ☎ 01-876 5075

Small, intimate, candlelit Anglo-French restaurant.

Closed Mon 2 wks Feb/Mar, 2 wks Sep/Oct Lunch not served Tue—Sat Dinner not served Sun

English & French 34 seats * Lunch £9.50—£10.50 Dinner £9.95&alc Wine £4.50 Last dinner 11pm P

Credit cards 1 2 3 5

SW15 Putney
London plan **5** C3

XX ***Annia's*** 349 Upper Richmond Rd ☎ 01-876 4456

The unique restaurant, based on a Swedish country house design, is furnished with antiques. The menu features a good-value selection of authentic Swedish dishes, and Annia creates a relaxing atmosphere with natural, personal attention.

Closed Mon

French & Swedish 30 seats Last dinner 11.30pm Live music nightly

Credit cards 1 2 3 5

X **Berts** 34 Upper Richmond Rd ☎ 01-874 8839

A highly-original and eclectic cuisine is featured on the fixed-price menu of this small and very stylish restaurant. Wines are particularly good value for money, and service is very friendly and helpful.

Lunch not served except Sun & Xmas

English & French **V** 50 seats Lunch £7.45&alc Dinner £12.85&alc Wine £4.95 Last dinner 11pm P

Credit cards 1 3 V

X **Buzkash Afghan** 4 Chelverton Rd ☎ 01-788 0599

The atmosphere of this compact, authentic, Afghan restaurant is created largely by the traditional weaponry which decorates the walls, hanging alongside bright, woven carpets. Quietly attractive, friendly service makes guests feel comfortable and relaxed, whilst the food itself, with its aromas of exotic spices, is no disappointment.

Closed Sun, Xmas Day & Boxing Day

Afghan 48 seats S% * Lunch £12alc Dinner £12alc Wine £5.95 Last dinner 11pm P

Credit cards 1 2 3 5

X ***Samratt*** 18 Lacy Rd ☎ 01-788 9110

The individuality of this small, air-conditioned, Indian restaurant and take-away creates a relaxing atmosphere. Tandoori special dishes and curries to suit most tastes are available.

Closed Xmas

Indian **V** 46 seats Last dinner 11.50pm

Credit cards 1 2 3 5

X **Wild Thyme** 96 Felsham Rd ☎ 01-789 3323

An original, fixed-price menu which changes every six weeks is politely served in cheerful surroundings at this bright, conservatory restaurant.

Closed Sun

British & French 40 seats Lunch £11.50 Dinner £16 Wine £5.50 Last dinner 11pm P

Credit cards 1 2 3

SW16 Norbury
London plan **5** D2

X ***Malean*** 1585 London Rd, Norbury ☎ 01-764 2336

Small family-run Chinese restaurant.

Closed 25—27 Dec Lunch not served Sun

Pekinese & Szechuan **V** 38 seats Last dinner 11.45pm P

Credit cards 1 2 3 5

SW19 Wimbledon
London plan **5** C2

○ **Cannizaro House** West Side Common (Thistle) ☎ 01-937 8033

58

Due to have opened summer 1986

X **Les Amoureux** 156 Merton Hall Rd ☎ 01-543 0567

A converted Post Office with a candlelight atmosphere and eclectic cuisine.

Lunch not served

French **V** 50 seats S% Dinner £12.75alc Wine £6 Last dinner 10pm P

Credit cards 1 2

W1 West End
Piccadilly Circus, Soho, St Marylebone and Mayfair

★★★★★

★★★★★ CLARIDGE'S, LONDON W1

Brook St ☎ 01-629 8860 Telex no 21872 Plan 2: **27** *E6*

A bastion of tradition, this most elegant of hotels has been, traditionally, the second home of Royalty and other discriminating clients when visiting London. It is very much in the grand manner with marbled floors and its lofty lounge with marbled pillars where the Hungarian Quartet plays and where you will be attended to by waiters in knee breeches. An imposing and newly restored staircase leads to the upper floors, suites and bedrooms which are sumptuously done. The more mundane of the 5 Star facilities are discreetly hidden away and there is no bar so the atmosphere is something like that of a gracious and opulent private house. Mr Ron Jones, the fairly recently appointed General Manager, is making his mark here without making waves to disturb the even tenor; small improvements like the staircase and rearrangement of the Causerie are the sensible order of the day. More formal eating than in the Causerie takes place in the elegantly appointed restaurant decorated in the style of the inter-war years. Chef Mario Lesnik presents mostly classical dishes which are well cooked. Needless to say the attentive service matches the cooking; indeed the proficient service can provide practically any requirement you may need throughout the hotel. One of the things that lifts Claridges above most of its peers, is the real friendliness you can experience here; it is exceptional for this type of hotel.

189 CTV in all bedrooms **T** S% sB £105—£150 dB £160—£185 (room only)

Lift P Live music and dancing Lunch (Mon—Fri) Dinner (Sun—Thu)

British & French **V** S% * Lunch £31alc Tea £6alc Dinner £35alc Wine £5.30 Last dinner 11.30pm

Credit cards 1 2 3 5

★★★★★

★★★★★ THE CONNAUGHT, LONDON W1

Carlos Pl ☎ 01-499 7070 Plan 2: **30** *E5*

This hotel does not manifest the more obvious appurtenances of a 5 star hotel, but the moment you step through the front door you know that you are somewhere special, a feeling shared by an international clientele who return repeatedly to experience the discreet luxury of a stay here. It is very English in atmosphere, with two elegant sitting rooms, a mahogany staircase rising out of the hall, the club-like mahogany panelled restaurant and the simpler Grill room, there is also a smart cocktail bar. Bedrooms are individually decorated and well up to 5 star standard. Nice pieces of furniture, crystal chandeliers, pictures and lovely informal flower arrangements enhance the atmosphere. Catering is of the utmost importance and chef Michel Bourdin has shown that it is possible to produce epicurean cooking for large numbers. Mainly luxury hotel classical, he is able to offer something for everyone: simple grills, traditional British dishes to haute cuisine. Mousselines are light and flavoursome, full flavoured terrines, and sapid combinations of ingredients on melt-in-the-mouth pastry. His fish and meat dishes are always highly commended, also game with zestful sauces. Mouth watering puddings are served, but alas, the talented young patissiere does not have his predecessor's way with soufflés. Mr Chevalier will look after you in the restaurant with its 3 course menu priced according to the main course chosen, plus extras, while in the Grill Room where Mr Bovo is in charge, an à la carte menu is provided. In both cases, dishes in heavy print on the menu are the gastronomic delights, Mr Zago is the General Manager and he ensures that his friendly staff look after you proficiently: linkmen, reception staff, porters, waiters, valets and chambermaids will, without exception, provide smooth running service that cannot be beaten in London.

90 CTV in all bedrooms **T**

Lift

English & French Last dinner 10.30pm

S% Credit card 1

★★★★★ **The Dorchester**
(see red star box on page 465)

★★★★★ **Churchill** Portman Sq ☎ 01-486 5800 Telex no 264831 Plan 2: **26** *D6*

This modern hotel has become well established on the London scene over the years. It has luxurious décor with a Regency flavour.

489 CTV in all bedrooms **T** sB £130 dB £145 (room only)

Lift 75 (charge) CFA (hard)

International **V** S% Lunch £25alc Tea fr£7.50 Dinner £30alc Wine £8.40 Last dinner 11pm

Credit cards 1 2 3 4 5

See advertisement on page 466

★★★★★*L* **Grosvenor House** Park Ln (Trusthouse Forte) ☎ 01-499 6363 Telex no 24871 Plan 2: **57** *E5*

Significant improvements in both accommodation and standards of service are now taking place with the help of a committed and more permanent management team at this traditional hotel. The fine facilities available include ballroom, health club, swimming pool, three restaurants and a delightful lounge where traditional afternoon tea is served.

472 CTV in all bedrooms **T** sB&B £124.50 dB&B £159

Lift 20P 100 CFA (heated) sauna bath solarium gymnasium

Last dinner 11pm

Credit cards 1 2 3 4 5

★★★★★*BL* **Inn on the Park** Hamilton Pl, Park Ln (Prestige) ☎ 01-499 0888 Telex no 22771 Plan 2: **64** *E4*

Possibly the best modern hotel in London, it has splendid suites, excellent bathrooms and two restaurants.

228 in 24 bedrooms CTV in all bedrooms **T** S% sB £166.75 dB £189.75 (room only)

Lift 80 (£7 per night) *xmas*

International **V** S% Lunch £16.25—£19 Tea fr£8.50 Dinner fr£28 Wine £9.55 Last dinner mdnt

Credit cards 1 2 3 4 5

★★★★★ **Inter-Continental**
(see rosette box on page 465)

★★★★★ **London Hilton** 22 Park Ln ☎ 01-493 8000 Telex no 24873 Plan 2: **58** *E4*

This is one of the liveliest and most exciting hotels in London, and many of the bedrooms (especially those overlooking Hyde Park) have spectacular views. Extensive refurbishment continues, including upgrading of the bedrooms and the provision of a new first-floor restaurant and a popular lobby lounge. Other facilities include two further restaurants, a new shopping arcade, a disco and three bars.

501 in 23 bedrooms CTV in all bedrooms **T** *sB £126.50—£155.25 dB £147.20—£180.55 (room only)

Lift sauna bath solarium Disco 6 nights wkly Live music and dancing 6 nights wkly Cabaret 6 nights wkly *xmas*

International **V** Lunch £15—£20&alc Tea £4—£8&alc Dinner £17—£35&alc Wine £14 Last dinner 1am

Credit cards 1 2 3 4 5

★★★★★ **May Fair Inter-Continental** Stratton St ☎ 01-629 7777 Telex no 262526 Plan 3: **20** *A4*

Long established hotel, with friendly service. Facilities include a popular coffee house, elegant restaurant, small cinema and the Mayfair theatre.

322 (14fb) CTV in all bedrooms **T** sB £86—£120 dB £115—£145 (room only)

Lift *xmas*

English & French

Credit cards 1 2 3 4 5

★★★★★*L* **Ritz** Piccadilly (Prestige) ☎ 01-493 8181 Telex no 267200 Plan 3: **28** *A3*

The internationally-famous hotel, in the heart of London, is noted for its fine, ornate, public rooms and the elegant restaurant in the Louis XVI style where meals of a high standard are served. The Palm Court is a famous rendezvous for traditional English afternoon tea. Bedrooms are elegant and spacious, and about a third of them are being further upgraded this year.

128 CTV in all bedrooms **T** S% *sB £120—£130 dB £140—£190 (room only) **B**

Lift Live music and dancing Sat Cabaret Wed—Fri *xmas*

English & French S% *Lunch fr£18.75 Tea fr£8.50 Dinner fr£26.25 Wine £8.75

Credit cards 1 2 3 4 5

★★★★ **The Athenaeum**
(see red star box on page 466)

★★★★ **Brown's**
(see red star box on page 467)

To find any AA-appointed London hotel or restaurant see maps and index on pages 433—449

★★★★★

❀★★★★★THE DORCHESTER, LONDON W1

53 Park Ln ☎ 01-629 8888 Telex no 887704 Plan 2: **37** *E5*

(Rosette awarded only to Terrace Room)

Unashamedly catering for the rich and the glamorous, the Dorchester has a sumptuous decor in the public area; the promenade lounge with its pillars and gold leafed ceiling, the cocktail bar with a singer/pianist, the Spanish-style Grill room, and the charmingly elegant Terrace room with dancing. There is also the rarely met residents' library, provided not only with books and games, but also personal stereo. Another unusual feature since last year is the 24 hour television news service beamed direct from the USA. Bedrooms vary from the fantastic Oliver Messel suite to more moderately sized ones, and are air conditioned. Valet and room service is smoothly efficient as is the service throughout the hotel by courteous, dignified staff. Anton Mosimann is in charge of the catering and he produces excellent food. In the Grill Room, it is basically British in a modern interpretation, but in the Terrace Room he presents a more refined style of nouvelle cuisine with his own 'cuisine naturelle'. We have found this less successful

with meat than with fish, but such dishes without any fat or flour will find favour with the health conscious. Otherwise, oysters Moscovite, feuilleté of calves sweetbreads and crayfish, his version of roast duck with zestful sauce or the best end of lamb with shallots have been highly complimented as well as the now famous symphony of sea food.

280🛁 1▣ CTV in all bedrooms **T** ✗ S% ✱sB🛁£115—£145 dB🛁£165—£175(room only)

Lift ☾ 10P 50🚗(£12 per night) CFA ♫ Live music & dancing 6 nights wkly *xmas*

♕English & French **V** ♔ ☕ S% ✱Lunch £17 Tea £8 Dinner £17&alc Wine £10.70 Last dinner 10.30pm

Credit cards 1 2 3 4 5

❀❀★★★★★ INTER-CONTINENTAL, LONDON W1

1 Hamilton Pl, Hyde Park Corner ☎ 01-409 3131 Telex no 25853 Plan 2: **65** *E4*

(Rosettes awarded for Le Soufflé Restaurant)

In this American owned hotel is the art deco restaurant in red, black and silver, that is the scene for chef Peter Kromberg's talented cooking. Although he has been here for some time, it is only in the last couple of years that we have seen such a big improvement. This year was best of all and we think that the food is now worth a second rosette. The menu is marked by the use of expensive ingredients, but is none the worse for that provided you can afford to eat here. As its name suggests a range of soufflés are available among the first courses and puddings. But there are other good things, too: a recherché dish of ravioli stuffed with a mixture of pigeon puree and foie gras, cooked and served in a soup-like sauce from pigeon stock and morilles was much acclaimed. Fish dishes, like sole fillets with lobster and cucumber in butter sauce, are delicately cooked, while among the meat dishes duck breast stuffed with foie gras and baked in a pastry cage with its impeccable sauce, lamb fillet with blackcurrant sauce and a 'moneybag' filled with lambs sweetbreads have greatly impressed us. There is a tempting array of mouthwatering puddings. Service is first class under the able supervision of Josef Lanser, who is friendly, proficient and attentive, but they could do with a more knowledgable sommelier than our visits have experienced. For the rest, this modern hotel near Hyde Park Corner, provides good standards of public rooms and bedrooms. They have mini-bars, and in-house movies, and somewhat compact bathrooms.

491🛁🚿🚭 in 6 bedrooms CTV in all bedrooms **T** ✗ sB🛁🚿£163.30 dB🛁🚿£180.90 (room only)

Lift ☾ # 120🚗(charged) CFA sauna bath gymnasium Disco Mon—Sat *xmas*

♕International **V** ♔ ☕ 🚭 Lunch fr£15.60&alc Tea fr£4.80 High Tea fr£6.50 Dinner fr£15.60&alc Wine £9.50 Last dinner 1am

Credit cards 1 2 3 4 5

★★★★**Britannia** Grosvenor Sq ☎ 01-629 9400 Telex no 23941 Plan 2: **15** *E5*

This smart, comfortable hotel has bedrooms which are furnished to a high standard, and room service is efficient. The Carlton restaurant serves noteworthy meals in the modern French style.

356🛁🚭 in 48 bedrooms CTV in all bedrooms **T** S% ✱sB🛁fr£115 dB🛁fr£126.50 (room only) **B**

Lift ☾ # **P** CFA Live music & dancing nightly *xmas*

♕English, American & Japanese **V** ♔ ☕ 🚭 S% Lunch fr£14.95 Dinner £14.95—£24.40&alc Wine £9.50 Last dinner 12.30am

Credit cards 1 2 3 4 5

★★★★**Cumberland** Marble Arch (Trusthouse Forte) ☎ 01-262 1234 Telex no 22215 Plan 2: **33** *D6*

A commercial and tourist hotel with limited room service, but good coffee shop.

905🛁 CTV in all bedrooms **T** sB&B🛁£78.50 dB&B🛁£105 **B**

Lift ☾ **P** CFA ♫

♔ ☕ Last dinner 10.30pm

Credit cards 1 2 3 4 5

★★★★*B* **Holiday Inn—Marble Arch** 134 George St (Holiday Inns) ☎ 01-723 1277 Telex no 27983 Plan 2: **59** *C6*

Well appointed hotel with attractive garden-style coffee shop.

241🛁🚿(116fb) 🚭 in 36 bedrooms CTV in all bedrooms **T** ✗ S% sB🛁🚿fr£100.05 dB🛁🚿£106.95—£120.75 (room only) **B**

Lift ☾ # 100🚗 CFA ♫ ▭(heated) sauna bath solarium gymnasium ♿

♕Internationl ♔ ☕ S% Lunch £4.50—£12.75&alc Tea fr£1.20 Dinner £4.50—£13.50&alc Wine £8.75

Credit cards 1 2 3 4 5 Ⓥ

★★★★***London Marriot*** Grosvenor Sq ☎ 01-493 1232 Telex no 268101 Plan 2: **78A** *E6*

Modern tastefully furnished hotel with good restaurant. NCP car park under building.

229🛁(61fb) CTV in all bedrooms **T** ✗ Continental breakfast **B**

Lift ☾ # CFA *xmas*

♕French **V** ♔ ☕ Last dinner 11pm

Credit cards 1 2 3 4 5

★★★★**Montcalm** Great Cumberland Pl ☎ 01-402 4288 Telex no 28710 Plan 2: **91A** *D6*

The terraced, Georgian building has been completely modernised and offers formal service in a quiet atmosphere.

116🛁🚿(9fb) CTV in all bedrooms **T** S% ✱sB🛁🚿fr£115 dB🛁🚿£138 (room only)

Lift ☾ # **P** ♫

♕French ♔ ☕ S% ✱Lunch fr£7.50&alc Dinner fr£17.50&alc Wine £13 Last dinner 11pm

Credit cards 1 2 3 4 5

★★★★

★★★★THE ATHENAEUM, LONDON W1

Piccadilly (Rank) ☎ 01-499 3464 Telex no 261589 Plan 2: **8** *E4*

Continual upgrading of the bedrooms at this hotel ensure that they reach a very high standard. They are not a bad size for a modern hotel and the decoration and soft furnishings lend a warmth to the rooms. They have yew military-type pieces of furniture and are double glazed, very well-equipped and comfortable, with in-house movies available on the television. Room service, like that throughout the hotel, is smoothly proficient. On the ground floor public areas include the club-like panelled bar and a comfortable lounge where you can take your ease after a hard day's work. There is also the elegant restaurant which offers a good value, fixed price lunch including wine; additionally there is a pre-theatre dinner and a well chosen à la carte menu at night. Cooking is mostly French with a modern influence and is enjoyable. All staff are cheerful, friendly and enthusiastic so that you will enjoy that aspect of your stay. It has

a pleasing situation overlooking Green Park and is convenient for the West End of London.

112 in 54 bedrooms CTV in all bedrooms **T** (ex guide dogs) S%
sB £118—£130
dB £140—£160 (room only) **B**
Lift ☾ # CFA Live music 5 nights wkly *xmas*
International **V** S% Lunch £16.50—£17.50&alc Tea £4—£6 Dinner £13.50—£15.50&alc Wine £8.50 Last dinner 10.30pm
Credit cards 1 2 3 4 5

❀★★★★ *L* Park Lane Piccadilly

☎ 01-499 6321 Telex no 21533 Plan 2: **99** *E4*

(Rosette awarded for Bracewell's Restaurant)

The Palm Court lounge is very well appointed offering the elegance and atmosphere of the twenties. Bracewell's Restaurant is decorated with 16th century carved wood panelling and mirrored pillars, which create an elegant, formal atmosphere which is enhanced by attentive service. There is a choice of table d'hôte and à la carte menus, to which a Menu Gastronomique is added in the evening; mouth-watering desserts are much in evidence.

325 CTV in all bedrooms **T** S% ✱
sB £99.95—£119.95
dB £119.95—£129.95 (room only) **B**
Lift ☾ 180 (£9 per 24 hrs) CFA
International **V** S% ✱ Lunch fr£13.50 Tea £2.50—£6 Dinner £17.50—£19.50 Wine £8 Last dinner 12.30am
Credit cards 1 2 3 5

LONDON

★★★★

★★★★BROWN'S, LONDON W1

Dover St Albemarle St (Trusthouse Forte) ☎01-493 6020 Telex no 28686 Plan 3: **6** *A4*

A wealth of old, mellow panelling, pillars and chimney-pieces and moulded ceilings, all set off by lovely flower arrangements and cheerful chintz covers in the lounge, set the scene for this most English of hotels. Starting a long time ago as a building offering sets of chambers for the London "season", it has become a most distinguished hotel and one very popular with Americans. As an old building that has been extended and altered over the years, the bedrooms clearly vary a great deal in size and the corridors are narrow; nevertheless, they have been modernised to good effect, some with nice old pieces of furniture. The St George's bar is a popular rendezvous for drinks as is the lounge for coffee and particularly good afternoon teas. L'Aperitif restaurant serves fixed price and à la carte menus and the cooking is chiefly in the modern style. It is with regret that we learned that Barry Larvin, the

exceedingly able and pleasant restaurant manager left at the turn of the year. He will be sorely missed but we wish him well running his own restaurant. His manner was the epitome of the friendly, solicitous care that all staff here show towards their guests.

125➡ CTV in all bedrooms **T** sB&B➡£108.50 dB&B➡£148.50

Lift ☾ 𝐏 CFA ⛟ *xmas*

♱ ☕ Last dinner 10pm

Credit cards 1 2 3 4 5

★★★★Portman Inter-Continental 22 Portman Sq ☎01-486 5844 Telex no 261526 Plan 2: **101** *D6*

Well appointed modern hotel with efficient and friendly service.

278➡ ⚡ in 14 bedrooms CTV in all bedrooms **T** ✈ sB&B➡£113.60—£132 dB&B➡£137.50—£150.15 Continental breakfast

Lift ☾ ## CFA ◯ (hard) Live music & dancing Sun *xmas*

♱ ☕ ⚡ Lunch £14.80&alc Tea £1.20 High Tea £7.50 Dinner £24&alc Wine £7.50

Credit cards 1 2 3 4 5

★★★★St George's Langham Pl (Trusthouse Forte) ☎01-580 0111 Telex no 27274 Plan 3: **33** *A5*

Modern hotel whose top floor restaurant gives panoramic views across London.

85➡ CTV in all bedrooms Ⓡ **T** sB&B➡£88.50 dB&B➡£114.50 **B**

Lift ☾ ##

♱ ☕ Last dinner 10pm

Credit cards 1 2 3 4 5

★★★★ Selfridge Orchard St (Thistle) ☎01-408 2080 Telex no 22361 Plan 2: **108** *E6*

A modern hotel with small bedrooms and bathrooms, but comfortable and attractive public lounge and restaurant.

298➡ ⋒ ⚡ in 44 bedrooms CTV in all bedrooms **T** ✱ sB➡⋒£90—£105 dB➡⋒£125—£165 (room only) **B**

Lift ☾ ## 8 🏠 ⛟ *xmas*

♡ International ♱ ☕ ✱ Lunch fr£14.50&alc Dinner fr£14.50&alc Wine £7 Last dinner 10pm

Credit cards 1 2 3 4 5 Ⓥ

★★★★Westbury New Bond St (Trusthouse Forte) ☎01-629 7755 Telex no 24378 Plan 3: **41** *A4*

Comfortable commercial and tourist hotel with attractive wood-panelled lounges.

240➡ CTV in all bedrooms **T** sB&B➡£104 dB&B➡£127.50

Lift ☾ 𝐏 CFA ⛟

♱ ☕ Last dinner 11pm

Credit cards 1 2 3 4 5

★★★*B* Berners Berners St ☎01-636 1629 Telex no 25759 Plan 1: **5A** *A5*

Ideally situated in the heart of the West End, the hotel has been restored to retain the original beauty of the Edwardian era. Bedrooms are designed to a high standard and well-equipped, whilst both carvery restaurant and cocktail bar are air-conditioned.

232➡ ⋒ (10fb) ⚡ in 41 bedrooms CTV in all bedrooms **T** ✈ S% sB➡⋒£72—£81.50 dB➡⋒£99—£115 (room only)

Lift ☾ 𝐏 CFA ♿

V ♱ ☕ S% Lunch £10.75—£11.50&alc Tea £2.35—£2.50 Dinner £10.75—£11.50&alc Wine £6.50 Last dinner 10pm

Credit cards 1 2 3 5

★★★*L* Chesterfield 35 Charles St ☎01-491 2622 Telex no 269394 Plan 2: **24** *E5*

This traditional hotel in the centre of Mayfair now has the new Butlers restaurant, which offers an outstanding buffet lunch in addition to its à la carte menu. The colourful bedrooms are furnished to a high standard, and a warm atmosphere is created by flowers and antiques in the ground floor public rooms, which include a wood-panelled library.

113➡ ⋒ 1 ⊞ CTV in all bedrooms **T** ✈ ✱ sB➡⋒fr£95 dB➡⋒fr£110 (room only)

Lift ☾ 𝐏 ⛟

♡ International **V** ♱ ☕ ✱ Lunch fr£13.50&alc Tea fr£5.25 Dinner £19alc Wine £5.25 Last dinner mdnt

Credit cards 1 2 3 5

★★★*L* Clifton-Ford 47 Welbeck St ☎01-486 6600 Telex no 22569 Plan 2: **28** *E6*

Closed 24 Dec—1 Jan

This very good hotel offers considerable comfort and excellent service.

216➡ ⋒ CTV in all bedrooms **T** ✱ sB&B➡⋒£72.75 dB&B➡⋒£97.50 Continental breakfast **B**

Lift ☾ 20 🏠 (£8.50 per day) Live music nightly

♡ International **V** ♱ ☕ ✱ Lunch fr£10.50alc Tea fr£5.50 High Tea fr£9.20 Dinner fr£10.75&alc Wine £8 Last dinner 10.15pm

Credit cards 1 2 3 5 Ⓥ

★★★ Mandeville Mandeville Pl ☎01-935 5599 Telex no 269487 Plan 2: **83** *E6*

Possibly one of the best commercial and tourist hotels. Good room service and coffee shop. Sound French cuisine in the restaurant.

165➡ ⋒ CTV in all bedrooms **T** S% ✱ sB➡⋒£71.50 dB➡⋒£88 (room only) **B**

Lift ☾ 𝐏

♡ International ♱ ☕ S% ✱ Lunch £8—£15alc Tea £3.50alc Dinner £8—£15alc Wine £6 Last dinner 11.30pm

Credit cards 1 2 3 4 5

★★★Mount Royal Bryanston St, Marble Arch (Mount Charlotte) ☎01-629 8040 Telex no 23355 Plan 2: **92** *D6*

Set near Marble Arch, overlooking Hyde Park, the commercial and tourist hotel provides good coffee shop facilities.

701➡ ⋒ (31fb) CTV in all bedrooms Ⓡ **T** ✈ sB&B➡⋒fr£57.75 dB&B➡⋒fr£72.50 Continental breakfast **B**

Lift ☾ 𝐏 CFA *xmas*

♡ Mainly grills ♱ ☕ ✱ Lunch fr£9.95&alc Dinner fr£9.95&alc Wine £5.95 Last dinner 11pm

Credit cards 1 2 3 4 5 Ⓥ

To find any AA-appointed London hotel or restaurant see maps and index on pages 433—449

★★★**Stratford Court** 350 Oxford St ☎01-629 7474 Telex no 22270 Plan 2: **114** *E6*

Small, friendly central hotel.

140 (16fb) CTV in all bedrooms **T** S% sB&B £67—£70 dB&B £90—£95 Continental breakfast

Lift

S% Lunch £8.50—£10&alc Tea £3 Dinner £8.50—£10&alc Wine £6 Last dinner 9.30pm

Credit cards 1 2 3 4 5

★★**Bryanston Court** 56—60 Great Cumberland Pl ☎01-262 3141 Telex no 262076 Plan 2: **17** *D6*

Part of a terraced row of houses some 300 yards from Marble Arch, this cosy if somewhat cramped hotel offers compact bedrooms and showers, efficient service, dinners better than those in most London hotels and prices reasonable for the location.

56rm (10 46) CTV in all bedrooms **T** S% ✱sB&B £42 dB&B £54 Continental breakfast

Lift

S% ✱Lunch £14alc Tea 75p alc Dinner £14alc Wine £5.50 Last dinner 10pm

Credit cards 1 2 3 4 5

★★**Regent Palace** Glasshouse St Piccadilly (Trusthouse Forte) ☎01-734 7000 Telex no 23740 Plan 1: **42** *B3*

Good accommodation in this outstanding value for money hotel, adjacent to Piccadilly Circus.

999rm (34fb) CTV in all bedrooms ® sB&B £34 dB&B £48

Lift CFA *xmas*

Last dinner 9pm

Credit cards 1 2 3 4 5

○**Le Meridien** Piccadilly ☎01-734 8000 Plan 1: **32A** *A2*

284

Now open

This lavishly restored and elegant hotel has the outstanding feature of a splendid leisure club (available to residents as well as members). Boasting three restaurants, one in a glass conservatory, it is hard to believe one is so close to Piccadilly Circus. Service throughout is friendly and welcoming, although the bedrooms, smart though they are, are not quite as luxurious as the rest of the hotel.

XXXXX**Cafe Royal (Grill Room)** 68 Regent St ☎01-439 6320 Telex no 27234 Plan 1: **7** *A/B3*

The ornate decor of carved gilt mirrors, moulded ceilings and plush banquettes provides an effective backdrop to the traditionally formal service that complements sound French cuisine at this restaurant.

Closed Sun

Cosmopolitan **V** 65 seats S% Lunch £25alc Dinner £30alc Wine £9.10 Last dinner 10.30pm

Credit cards 1 2 3 4 5

XXXXX**'Ninety Park Ln'** 90 Park Ln ☎01-409 1290 Telex no 24871 Plan 2: **57** *E5*

Luxurious and elegant surroundings combine here with professional service.

Closed Sun Lunch not served Sat

French **V** 75 seats S% Lunch £17.50—£22.50&alc Dinner £29—£42.50&alc Wine £14 Last dinner 10.45pm nc 6yrs Live music Mon—Sat

Credit cards 1 2 3 4 5

XXXX **LE GAVROCHE, LONDON W1**

43 Upper Brook St ☎01-408 0881 Telex no 8813079 Plan 2: **49A** *E5*

Classically based, innovatively interpreted, Albert Roux and his brigade still provide the best food in the country, presented with real artistry. It is a joy in itself to see them presented for your delection, and this in itself stimulates your taste buds as much as an aperitif (at these prices that can be worthwhile!) Such standards of quality in ingredients, cooking and service do not come cheaply, but for those who appreciate them we think it provides value for money, particularly on some special occasion. From start to finish the attention to detail is awe-inspiring; even the canapes to start and the chocolates and petits fours to finish manifest the same supreme skill and dedication. Soups, particularly the sparklingly clear consommé, are superb, shellfish dishes with their sauces are too, while mousselines are beautifully light, yet definite in flavour. But the meat and game dishes are unsurpassed for strength of flavour. Roundels of spring lamb, cooked pink with a glazed sauce flavoured with mustard and basil; chicken of old fashioned flavour with mussels, shallots and chopped red capsicums in a saffron sauce are a miracle of composition, with all the individual flavours coming together beautifully, and where the total effect is greater than the sum of their parts. Vegetables and salads are equally good, particularly the beautiful, oily dressing with the latter. Desserts are a work of art in themselves and if you have room try assiette du chef, a selection of miniature delights. There is a Menu Exceptional of 6 courses and the à la carte menu, while at luncheon there is a good value fixed price menu. The wine list of about 500 is superb and features vintages back to 1918. Mr Silvano Geraldin and his brigade of immaculately attired young men will attend to you with unfailing attention and skill in a formal manner. The restaurant is appropriately furnished with a bar on the ground floor and the restaurant downstairs has an ante room convenient for smokers.

Closed Sat, Sun, Bank Hol's & 24 Dec—1 Jan Lunch not served 2 Jan

French 70 seats S% ✱Lunch £19.50—£35&alc Dinner £35&alc Wine £10.90 Last dinner 11pm nc 6yrs

Credit cards 1 2 3 4 5

XXXX**London Hilton Hotel (Trader Vic's)** Park Ln ☎01-493 7586 Telex no 24873 Plan 2: **58** *E4*

Lively Polynesian restaurant below Hilton Hotel.

Closed Xmas Day Lunch not served Sat

International 180 seats S% ✱Lunch £25—£30alc Dinner £35alc Wine £9 Last dinner 11.45pm

Credit cards 1 2 3 4 5

XXX**Greenhouse** 27A Hay's Mews ☎01-499 3331 Plan 2: **55** *E5*

Modern elegant dining room with formal but friendly service accompanying English and French cuisine.

Closed Sun, Bank Hol's & wk after Xmas Lunch not served Sat

English & French 85 seats Lunch £15.50alc Dinner £15.50alc Wine £5.55 Last dinner 11pm nc 5yrs

Credit cards 1 2 3 4 5

XXX***Masako*** 6—8 St Christopher Pl ☎01-935 1579 Plan 2: **88** *E6*

Authentic Japanese décor with armour, bamboo walls and waitresses in national costume.

Closed Sun, Xmas, 3 days New Year, Etr & Aug Bank Hol

Japanese 100 seats Last dinner 10pm

Credit cards 1 2 3 5

XXX**Princess Garden of Mayfair** 8—10 North Audley St ☎01-493 3223 Plan 2: **101B** *E6*

Closed Xmas & Etr

Peking **V** 150 seats Lunch £15—£20alc Dinner £25—£30 Wine £7.50 Last dinner 11.20pm nc 7yrs Live music Mon—Sat

Credit cards 1 2 3 5

XXX**Tandoori of Mayfair** 37A Curzon St ☎01-629 0600 Plan 2: **117** *E5*

Tropical plants complete the attractive decor of this elegant, modern, basement and ground-floor restaurant which offers

an interesting menu of Tandoori dishes and curries; smart staff provide friendly service.

Closed 25 & 26 Dec

Indian **V** 120 seats Lunch £13alc Dinner £13alc Wine £5.80 Last dinner mdnt

Credit cards 1 2 3 4 5

❀✕✕**Au Jardin Des Gourmets** 5 Greek St ☎01-437 1816 Plan 1: **2** *B4*

This long-established French restaurant at the heart of Soho continues to serve impressive meals, professional standards being maintained by the owner, Mr Berkmann, and his young English staff. The gourmet and prix fixée menus are augmented by an à la carte selection which offers such interesting dishes as noisettes d'agneau au vinaigre de framboises, and the extensive, reasonably-priced wine list includes some good vintages.

Closed Sun, Xmas & Etr Lunch not served Sat & Bank Hol's

French 85 seats ✱Lunch £12.50—£23.50&alc Dinner £12.50—£23.50&alc Wine £5.25 Last dinner 11.15pm

Credit cards 1 2 3 5

✕✕**Chambeli** 12 Great Castle St ☎01-636 0662 Telex no 261927 Plan 3: **7** *A5*

The elegantly modern air-conditioned restaurant with well-appointed tables serves curries and Tandoori dishes which are competently prepared from fresh, raw materials. The wine list, though small in size, is well-balanced and reasonably priced, whilst the well-supervised service is efficient.

Closed Sun

Indian **V** 70 seats S% Lunch £8.50&alc Dinner £8.50&alc Wine £4.95 Last dinner mdnt

Credit cards 1 2 3 5

✕✕**Chesa** (Swiss Centre) 10 Wardour St ☎01-734 1291 Plan 1: **11** *C3*

Swiss style restaurant offering authentic classical mostly French cuisine.

Closed 25 & 26 Dec

Swiss **V** 60 seats ✱Lunch £19.50&alc Dinner £19.50&alc Wine £6.40 Last dinner mdnt

Credit cards 1 2 3 4 5

✕✕***La Cucaracha*** 12 Greek St ☎01-734 2253 Plan 1: **14** *C4*

A maze of small white arched rooms that were once the cellars of an 18th-century monastery.

Closed Xmas

Mexican **V** 65 seats Last dinner 11.15pm Live music nightly

Credit cards 1 2 3 5

London W1

✕✕**Gallery Rendezvous** 53 Beak St ☎01-734 0445 Plan 1: **17** *A3*

Chinese paintings are permanently exhibited in the restaurant.

Closed Xmas & New Years Day

Pekinese **V** 130 seats Lunch £6&alc Dinner £6&alc Wine £5.50 Last dinner 11pm

Credit cards 1 2 3 5

❀✕✕**Gay Hussar** 2 Greek St ☎01-437 0973 Plan 1: **18** *B4*

A small, cosy and popular restaurant, the Gay Hussar has long been established as serving some of London's best, most authentic, Hungarian food. The lengthy menu provides a vast choice of dishes, and service is cheerful, if a little muddled at times.

Closed Sun

Hungarian 35 seats Last dinner 10.30pm

✕✕**Lai Qila** Tottenham Court Rd ☎01-387 4570 Plan 3: **17** *A6*

Good, modern, Indian restaurant.

Closed 25 & 26 Dec

Indian **V** 75 seats S% Lunch £8—£12 Dinner £10—£15 Wine £5.95 Last dinner 11.30pm

Credit cards 1 2 3 5

✕✕**Langan's Brasserie** Stratton St ☎01-491 8822 Plan 3: **18** *A3*

This popular, French-style brasserie features an extensive menu of well-prepared, authentic dishes at reasonable prices. It is well frequented by London society and by stars of television, stage and films.

Closed Sun & Public Hol's Lunch not served Sat

French 200 seats S% Lunch £16alc Dinner £16alc Wine £5.60 Last dinner 11.45pm Live music nightly

Credit cards 1 2 3 5

✕✕**Library** 115 Mount St ☎01-499 1745 Plan 2: **75A** *E5*

Small charming basement restaurant with a library atmosphere, and lady pianist.

Closed Sat, Sun, Xmas & New Year

30 seats ✱Lunch £15alc Dinner £15alc Wine £6.95 Last dinner 11pm nc 15yrs Live music nightly

Credit cards 1 2 3 5

✕✕**Mr Kai of Mayfair** 65 South Audley St ☎01-493 8988 Plan 2: **91** *E5*

Sophisticated, elegant restaurant serving both classical and regional Chinese dishes.

Closed Xmas & Bank Hols

Pekinese 120 seats ✱Lunch £15alc Dinner £15alc Wine £6.95 Last dinner 11.15pm nc 6yrs

Credit cards 1 3 5

❀✕✕**Odin's** 27 Devonshire St ☎01-935 7296

Masquerading as an art gallery, the comfortable English restaurant provides consistently good, interesting food; Mrs Langham's chocolate pudding is not to be missed!

Closed Sun & Public Hol's Lunch not served Sat

French 60 seats Last dinner 11.30pm

Credit card 2

✕✕**Red Fort** 77 Dean St ☎01-437 2525 Plan 1: **41A** *B3*

The exterior of this new Indian restaurant has the air of a pink palace. Inside, exquisite girls in red saris serve cocktails and such regional dishes as spiced and marinated quail baked in a charcoal fire.

Closed 25—27 Dec

Indian **V** 160 seats S% ✱Lunch £8—£15&alc Dinner £8—£15&alc Wine £5.95 Last dinner 11.15pm nc 5yrs

Credit cards 1 2 3 5

❀❀✕✕**Rue St Jacques**
(see rosette box on page 470)

✕✕**Sawasdee** 26—28 Whitfield St ☎01-631 0289 Plan 3: **34** *B6*

Closed Xmas day
Lunch not served Sat & Sun

Thai **V** 80 seats Last dinner 11.15pm

Credit cards 1 2 3 5

✕✕***Yumi*** 110 George St ☎01-935 8320 Plan 2: **125A** *D6*

Chinese restaurant offering consistently good and well presented food.

Closed Sun, Bank Hol's & 10 days Aug/Sep Lunch not served Sat

Japanese 70 seats Last dinner 10pm

Credit cards 1 2 3 5

✕**Alastair Little** 49 Frith St ☎01-734 5183 Plan 1: **1** *B4*

This little hotel is very popular with an avant garde clientele, providing a friendly and informal atmosphere, a daily menu of imaginative, eclectic dishes freshly cooked from quality ingredients (notably fresh fish), and carefully chosen and prepared vegetables. →

To find any AA-appointed London hotel or restaurant see maps and index on pages 433—449

XX Rue St Jacques 5 Charlotte St ☎ 01-637 0222 Plan 1: **44B** *B5*

It seems to us that Gunther Schlender, the chef, cooks far better here than he ever did at Carriers. He seems to have found his feet and is producing deliciously different dishes that absolutely bewitch the palate. He produces a well composed à la carte menu and a very good value fixed price luncheon menu. The maitre d'hotel Vincent Calcerono — has a well trained brigade who are solicitous for your well being and the hierarchy know their food and wine. The wine list of some 170 items is very good and particularly strong on classic Bordeaux and Burgundy. Dishes that have particularly pleased our inspectors were the warm terrine of sole with smoked and fresh salmon on a butter sauce, better than most even at this level; also his lobster and sweetbreads, melt-in-the-mouth puff pastry with a delicately flavoured armagnac sauce. Main dishes were a more earthy roast duck with red cabbage, sauerkraut and apple, but pride of place must go to the saddle of hare, superbly flavoured with a mound of pleurettes and morilles, and a game sauce made fruitily piquant with dried blackcurrants — 'perhaps the best sauce I have had this season' said one inspector. Vegetables are correctly cooked. A classic individual Charlotte Russe was near perfect, sorbets are refreshing and the soufflé of pear with bitter chocolate sauce was a great success. Finish with excellent coffee and petits fours. The restaurant — at ground floor and basement level — is well done so that you will enjoy the total experience.

Closed Sun, Bank Hol's & Xmas Lunch not served Sat

French **V** 70 seats ✱Lunch £15&alc Wine £9 Last dinner 11.15pm

Credit cards 1 2 3 5

Closed Sat, Sun 2 wks Xmas, last 3 wks Aug & Bank Hol's

French & Japanese 35 seats ✱Lunch £20alc Dinner £20alc Last dinner 11pm

Credit card 3

X *Arirang* 31—32 Poland St ☎ 01-437 6633 Plan 1: **1B** *A4*

There is an authentic atmosphere in this intimate little Korean restaurant, where the interesting menu of delicately prepared meals is served by friendly, young, national waitresses.

Closed Sun, Etr Mon & Xmas

Korean **V** 80 seats Last dinner 11pm

Credit cards 1 2 3 5

X Aunties 126 Cleveland St ☎ 01-387 1548 Plan 3: **2** *A6*

English restaurant specialising in home-made pies.

Closed Sun, 25 & 26 Dec, 1 Jan & Public Hols Lunch not served Sat

30 seats S% Lunch £11—£15 Dinner £15 Wine £6 Last dinner 11pm

Credit cards 1 2 3 5

X Desaru 60—62 Old Compton St ☎ 01-734 4379 Plan 1: **40A** *B4*

Modern Indian restaurant in heart of Soho. Window between restaurant and kitchen shows chefs at work.

Indonesian & Malaysian **V** 60 seats ✱Lunch £24 (2 persons) Dinner £24 (2 persons) Wine £5.50 Last dinner 11.45pm nc 12yrs

Credit cards 1 2 3 5

To find any AA-appointed London hotel or restaurant see maps and index on pages 433—449

X Frith's 14 Frith St ☎ 01-439 3370 Plan 1: **16A** *B4*

Tasteful design in modern style has created a bright and fresh atmosphere in this black-and-white Soho restaurant which features a table d'hôte lunchtime menu augmented by an à la carte selection in the evening. Wine by the glass is good, though the wine list itself is short, and service is friendly and polite.

Closed Sun
Lunch not served Sat & Bank Hol's

V 60 seats ✱Lunch £14—£16 Dinner £14—£16 Wine £6.50 Last dinner 11.30pm Live music Wed, Fri & Sat

Credit cards 1 2 3 5

X Fuji Japanese 36—40 Brewer St ☎ 01-734 0957 Plan 1: **16B** *B3*

Closed 2 wks Xmas
Lunch not served Sat & Sun

Japanese 54 seats S% ✱Lunch £14alc Dinner £25alc Wine £5.90 Last dinner 10:45pm

Credit cards 1 2 3 5

X Gaylord 79 Mortimer St ☎ 01-580 3615 Plan 3: **9** *A5*

Indian **V** 75 seats ✱Lunch £7.45—£8.50&alc Dinner £7.45—£8.50&alc Last dinner 11.30pm 25P

Credit cards 1 2 3 4 5 Ⓥ

X Ho Ho Chinese 29 Maddox St ☎ 01-493 1228 Plan 3: **13** *A4*

A red-painted, canopied front opens into a restaurant whose simple, modern decor is brightened by old Chinese photographs and prints. The cuisine is mainly Pekinese and Szechuan.

Closed Sun

Chinese **V** 80 seats ✱Lunch fr£8.50&alc Dinner £11—£14&alc Wine £5.50 Last dinner 10.45pm nc 6yrs

Credit cards 1 2 3 5

X Kerzenstuberl 9 St Christopher's Place ☎ 01-486 3196 Plan 2: **68** *E6*

Here you can relax in a typically Austrian atmosphere to enjoy authentic Austrian food and wine. Personal service is provided by the proprietors, and in the late evenings staff and guests sing along together to the strains of an accordion.

Closed Sun, Xmas, all Bank Hol's & 3 Aug—3 Sep Lunch not served Sat

Austrian **V** 50 seats Lunch £16alc Dinner £18—£20alc Wine £6.90 Last dinner 11pm Live music and dancing Mon—Sat

Credit cards 1 2 3 5 Ⓥ

X *Lee Ho Fook* 15 Gerrard St ☎ 01-734 9578 Plan 1: **29** *B3*

Authentic Chinatown atmosphere in this intimate restaurant.

Cantonese **V** 150 seats Last dinner 5am

Credit cards 1 2 3 5

X Little Akropolis 10 Charlotte St ☎ 01-636 8198 Plan 1: **30** *B5*

Small, intimate, candlelit, Greek restaurant.

Closed Sun & Public Hol's
Lunch not served Sat

Greek **V** 32 seats S% Lunch £9.50alc Dinner £9.50alc Wine £6.50 Last dinner 10.30pm

Credit cards 1 2 3 5

X *Mayflower* 66—70 Shaftesbury Av ☎ 01-734 9027 Plan 1: **32** *B3*

Small ground floor and basement restaurant with small alcoves and good food.

Cantonese 125 seats Last dinner 4am

Credit cards 1 2 3 5

X New World 1 Gerrard Pl ☎ 01-734 0677 Plan 1: **34** *C3*

This large ground-floor and basement restaurant has the authentic Chinatown ambience and atmosphere. Many of the dishes offered are well-flavoured provincial specialities, and service is courteously friendly.

Closed Xmas Day

Chinese **V** 530 seats S% ✱Lunch fr£4.35 Dinner fr£4.75 Wine £4.50 Last dinner 11.45pm

Credit cards 1 2 3 4 5

X *Regent Tandoori* 10 Denman St ☎ 01-434 1134 Plan 1: **43** *B3*

Located in the heart of the West End, this Indian restaurant has been thoughtfully designed to achieve a colourful ambience and an atmosphere of warmth. It tends to offer dishes from all round India, and the competent cuisine is matched by good service.

Tandoori **V** 44 seats Last dinner 11.30pm

✕**Relais des Amis** 17B Curzon St ☎01-499 7595 Plan 2: **102B** *E5*

Brick walls, tinted mirrors and fresh plants create a cool atmosphere.

International 100 seats Lunch £15alc Dinner £18alc Wine £5.95 Last dinner 11pm

Credit cards 1 2 3 5

✕**Sav's** 53 Cleveland St ☎01-580 7608 Plan 2: **107A** *A6*

This popular, family restaurant is unpretentious, the decor being plain though attractive. A range of Greek specialities is offered on the menu, which is accompanied by a wine list dominated by Greek and Cypriot wines, and service is friendly.

Closed Sat, Sun, Xmas Day, Boxing Day & Bank Hol's

English, Greek & Eastern Mediterranean 44 seats Lunch £2.35—£7.80&alc Dinner £2.35—£7.80&alc Wine £4.95 Last dinner 10.30pm

Credit cards 1 2 3 5

✕**Yung's** 23 Wardour St ☎01-437 4986 Plan 1: **61** *B3*

(Rosette awarded for dinner only)

This unusual restaurant, simply-appointed and situated on three floors, is open from afternoon until the early hours of the morning. Its speciality is Cantonese cuisine of a high standard, and the menu includes some interesting dishes.

Chinese **V** 100 seats Last dinner 4.30am

Credit cards 1 2 3 5

W2 Bayswater, Paddington

★★★★ *L* **Royal Lancaster** Lancaster Ter (Rank) ☎01-262 6737 Telex no 24822 Plan 2: **105** *B5*

A large, modern hotel provides friendly and efficient service. In an impressive situation, overlooking Hyde Park, it continues to improve its facilities and offers restaurants in contrasting styles — the elegant, formal La Rosette and a Mediterranean cafe.

London W1 — London W2

418 in 20 bedrooms CTV in all bedrooms **T** S% *sB&B £100.50—£120.50 dB&B £123—£143 Continental breakfast

Lift 100P (£7 per day) CFA *xmas*

International **V** *Lunch fr£10.50&alc Tea fr£5.50 Dinner fr£15.95&alc Wine £9.50 Last dinner 10.45pm

Credit cards 1 2 3 4 5

★★★**Central Park** Queensborough Ter ☎01-229 2424 Telex no 27342 Plan 2: **21** *A5*

Busy, modern, commercial hotel with an à la carte restaurant.

273rm (142 131)(15fb) CTV in all bedrooms **T** S% sB&B £45—£48 dB&B £60—£66 Continental breakfast

Lift 10P 20 (£1.50 per night) gymnasium Cabaret 6 nights wkly *xmas*

Mainly grills *Lunch £6—£8&alc Tea 75p—£1.25 Dinner £6—£8&alc Wine £5.50 Last dinner 10pm

Credit cards 1 2 3 4 5

★★★**Hospitality Inn** 104/105 Bayswater Rd (Mount Charlotte) ☎01-262 4461 Telex no 22667 Plan 2: **102** *A5*

This modern hotel provides smart, though small, public areas and well-equipped bedrooms; improvements and refurbishing continue. Breakfast and lunch are served buffet-style.

175 (12fb) CTV in all bedrooms ® **T** sB&B fr£55 dB&B fr£73

Lift 19P 55 CFA Live music Mon—Sat *xmas*

English & French Lunch fr£6.75&alc Tea £1alc Dinner fr£8.50&alc Wine £5.75 Last dinner 10.30pm

Credit cards 1 2 3 4 5 Ⓥ

★★★**London Embassy** 150 Bayswater Rd (Embassy) ☎01-229 2623 Telex no 27727 Plan 2: **76** *A5*

A busy commercial and tourist hotel with helpful staff, providing some lounge and room service.

193rm (184 8) CTV in all bedrooms ® **T** S% *sB&B £55—£66 dB&B £66—£77 Continental breakfast

Lift 40 (£2 per 24 hrs) CFA

Continental **V** S% *Lunch £8.95—£9.80&alc Tea 95p High Tea £2.50 Dinner £8.95—£9.80&alc Wine £5.20 Last dinner 10.15pm

Credit cards 1 2 3 4 5

★★★**Park Court** 75 Lancaster Gate (Mount Charlotte) ☎01-402 4272 Telex no 23922 Plan 2: **98** *A5*

The well-equipped bedrooms of this large, busy hotel include some executive rooms, and there is an informal, bistro-style restaurant.

412 (3fb) CTV in all bedrooms ® **T** *sB&B fr£49.75 dB&B fr£65.50

Lift CFA *xmas*

English & French **V** *Lunch £7.50&alc Tea £2 Dinner £8—£8.50&alc Wine £5.95 Last dinner 11pm

Credit cards 1 2 3 4 5 Ⓥ

★★★**White's** Lancaster Gate (Mount Charlotte) ☎01-262 2711 Telex no 4771 Plan 2: **125** *B5*

Friendly hotel overlooking Hyde Park.

55 1 CTV in all bedrooms **T** S% *sB fr£99.50 dB fr£120 (room only)

Lift 25P *xmas*

English & French **V** S% Lunch £25alc Tea £5.65alc Dinner £25alc Wine £6 Last dinner 10.30pm

Credit cards 1 2 3 4 5 Ⓥ

To find any AA-appointed London hotel or restaurant see maps and index on pages 433—449

LONDON

XXX ***Bombay Palace*** 2 Hyde Park Sq ☏01-723 8855 Plan 2: **14B** *C6*

In this comfortable, elegant restaurant, with its own bar, authentic and subtly-spiced Indian dishes are matched by impeccable service from friendly staff. At lunchtime, a popular self-service buffet has been introduced.

Indian 150 seats Last dinner 11.30pm

Credit cards 1 2 3 5

XX ***Bali*** 101 Edgware Rd ☏01-723 3303 Plan 2: **10** *C6*

Of the two restaurants here, the one on the ground floor is popular at lunchtime for cheaper, à la carte meals, whilst the smarter, more comfortable basement, which serves a set meal, thrives in the evening. Dishes from Indonesia, Malaysia and Java, ranging from mild and fragrant to fiery hot, are featured.

Indonesian & Malaysian 80 seats Last dinner 11pm

Credit cards 1 2 3 4 5

XX ***Trat-West*** 143 Edgware Rd ☏01-723 8203 Plan 2: **122** *C6*

Sound Italian food can be enjoyed at this bright, noisy restaurant with its bustling waiters.

Closed Etr Sun & Xmas

Italian 75 seats Last dinner 11.30pm

Credit cards 1 2 3 4 5

X **Ajimura Japanese** 51—53 Shelton St ☏01-240 0178 Plan 1: **1A** *D4*

Closed Bank Hols
Lunch not served Sat & Sun

Japanese **V** 50 seats S% ✱Lunch £5&alc Dinner £9—£19&alc Wine £4.80 Last dinner 11pm

Credit cards 1 2 3 5

X **Al-Khayam Tandoori** 27—29 Westbourne Gv ☏01-727 5154 Plan 2: **1** *A6*

The large, simply-furnished restaurant has subdued lighting and a good, bistro-style ambience. An interesting menu features curries, Tandoori dishes and house specialities, service by hustling waiters being prompt and friendly.

Indian **V** 70 seats ✱Lunch £10alc Dinner £15alc Wine £4 Last dinner 11.45pm

Credit cards 1 2 3 5

X **Ganges** 101 Praed St ☏01-723 4096 Plan 2: **48** *B6*

Modest restaurant in Bengal and Indian cuisine.

Closed Xmas & Boxing Day

Bengali & Indian **V** 28 seats ✱Lunch £5.50—£6.95&alc Dinner £5.50—£6.95&alc Wine £5.75 Last dinner 11.30pm

Credit cards 1 2 3 4 5

X ***Green Jade*** 29—31 Portchester Rd ☏01-229 7221 Plan 2: **56** *A6*

Staff warm to serious eaters in this busy yet cosy restaurant. The range of dishes on offer includes delicious, whole, steamed fish and Peking duck.

Lunch not served Sun

Chinese 50 seats Last dinner 11.15pm

Credit cards 1 2 3 5

X **Kalamara's** 76—78 Inverness Mews ☏01-727 9122 Plan 2: **66** *A5*

There are two Kalamara's restaurants in Inverness Mews — a smaller, unlicensed one, and this, which provides an all-Greek wine list to complement the authentic Greek cuisine.

Closed Sun & Bank Hol's Lunch not served

Greek **V** 86 seats Last dinner mdnt Live music nightly

Credit cards 1 2 3 5

X **Le Mange Tout** 34 Sussex Pl ☏01-723 1199 Plan 2: **85** *C6*

An inexpensive menu is offered by this small, cosy restaurant on the ground and lower floors.

Closed Xmas Day & some Public Hols
Lunch not served Sat

French **V** 35 seats Lunch £15—£20alc Dinner £15—£20alc Wine £5.50 Last dinner 11.30pm

Credit cards 1 2 3 5

X ***Veronica's Chez Franco*** 3 Hereford Rd ☏01-229 5079

A pretty restaurant with friendly service offering French and Italian dishes plus a British speciality menu.

Closed Sun & Bank Hol's Lunch not served Sat

International **V** 40 seats Last dinner mdnt

Credit cards 1 2 3 5

W5 Ealing

London plan **5** B4
See also **W13 Ealing (Northfields)**

★★★ **Carnarvon** Ealing Common (Consort) ☏01-992 5399 Telex no 935114

Modern purpose-built hotel, sited on the North Circular.

145 CTV in all bedrooms ® **T** S% sB&B £52.50 dB&B £62.50 Continental breakfast

Lift ☾ 150P CFA

European S% Lunch £13.50alc Dinner £13.50alc Wine £6.75 Last dinner 9.30pm

Credit cards 1 2 3 5

W6 Hammersmith

London plan **5** C3

★★★ **Novotel London** 1 Shortlands (Novotel) ☏01-741 1555 Telex no 934539

The modern hotel stands by the A4/44 which links Heathrow Airport with central London. It offers spacious public areas, a choice of two restaurants, bedrooms in process of upgrading and a typical English pub. A large range of facilities for meetings and exhibitions is available.

640 (640fb) in 20 bedrooms CTV in all bedrooms **T** S% sB fr£60.50 dB fr£74 (room only)

Lift 230 (charge) *xmas*

International S% ✱Lunch £7.25 Tea £3.50 High Tea 70p Dinner £2.50—£13 Wine £6.75 Last dinner mdnt

Credit cards 1 2 3 4 5

X ***Anarkali*** 303 King St ☏01-748 1760

Serves reasonably priced authentic Indian food.

Indian 82 seats Last dinner 11.30pm

Credit cards 1 2 3 5

X ***Aziz*** 116 King St ☏01-748 1826

A colour scheme of burgundy and imitation stone, enhanced by subdued lighting, creates a warm atmosphere for the enjoyment of a well-balanced menu of Tandoori dishes and traditional Indian curries. Service, under the supervision of the proprietor, is attentive.

Closed Sun & Xmas

Indian **V** 60 seats Last dinner 11.45pm

Credit cards 2 3 5

X **Light of Nepal** 268 King St ☏01-748 3586

This friendly, strikingly-decorated restaurant offers rather different Nepalese and Indian dishes.

Closed Xmas Day & Boxing Day

Indian & Nepalese **V** 100 seats Lunch £5—£8alc Dinner £6.50—£9alc Wine £5 Last dinner 11.45pm

Credit cards 1 2 3 4 5 Ⓥ

W8 Kensington

London plan **5** C3

★★★★★ **Royal Garden** Kensington High St (Rank) ☏01-937 8000 Telex no 263151 Plan 2: **104** *A4*

Considerable extension, refurbishment and upgrading have now taken place at this Kensington hotel which offers friendly, attentive service throughout and sound food in the Royal roof restaurant, where you can also dance to live music.

395 (63fb) CTV in all bedrooms **T** (ex guide dogs) S% ✱sB £89—£110 dB £120—£150 (room only)

Lift ☾ CFA 160 (£6.50 per 24 hrs)
Live music and dancing 6 nights wkly

International **V** Lunch £9.75—£17.50&alc Tea £3.50—£6.25 Dinner £22&alc Wine £9.80 Last dinner 11.30pm

Credit cards 1 2 3 4 5 Ⓥ

★★★★ **Kensington Palace Thistle** De Vere Gardens (Thistle) ☏01-937 8121 Telex no 262422 Plan 2: **67** *A3*

Large, busy hotel with formal restaurant and a coffee shop complemented by well furnished bedrooms.

298⇌♠(23fb)⅍in 32 bedrooms CTV in all bedrooms ®T ✈ *sB⇌♠£54—£85 dB⇌♠£71—£95 (room only) B

Lift ☾ CFA ♭ xmas

International ♈ ☐ *Lunch fr£14.75&alc Dinner fr£14.75&alc Wine £7 Last dinner 10pm

Credit cards 1 2 3 4 5 Ⓥ

★★★★**London Tara** Scarsdale Pl, off Wrights Ln (Best Western) ☎ 01-937 7211 Telex no 918834

The lively, modern hotel provides comfortable bedrooms, a formal restaurant plus brasserie and lounge service coffee shop, and a night spot.

831⇌ CTV in all bedrooms T ✈ (ex guide dogs) sB&B⇌♠£57.80—£69.80 dB&B⇌♠£69.80—£79.80 Continental breakfast B

Lift ☾ 30P 70🚗(charge) CFA Disco Mon—Sat ♿

French **V** ♈ ☐ Lunch fr£9&alc Dinner fr£9&alc Wine £7.50 Last dinner 11pm

Credit cards 1 2 3 4 5

★★★**Kensington Close** Wrights Ln (Trusthouse Forte) ☎ 01-937 8170 Telex no 23914

Large busy hotel with many modern facilities.

537⇌ CTV in all bedrooms ®T sB&B⇌£54.50 dB&B⇌£71.50 B

Lift ☾ 100🚗 CFA ⊡(heated) squash sauna bath solarium gymnasium *xmas*

Mainly grills ♈ ☐ Last dinner 11pm

Credit cards 1 2 3 4 5

★★**Hotel Lexham** 32—38 Lexham Gdns ☎ 01-373 6471 Plan 2: **75** *A2*

Closed 24 Dec—1 Jan

Quiet traditional family-type hotel.

63rm(23⇌7♠)(11fb) ✈ S% *sB&Bfr£20 sB&B⇌♠fr£24 dB&Bfr£29.50 dB&B⇌♠fr£36 B

Unlicensed Lift ☾ CTV ♭ ✿

English & Continental ♈ ☐ S% *Lunch fr£4&alc Tea fr90p Dinner fr£5.85 Last dinner 8pm

Credit cards 1 3 Ⓥ

✕✕✕**Belvedere** Holland House, Holland Park ☎ 01-602 1238

The elegantly-situated, aristocratic house retains its formal English flower garden and its peaceful, dignified atmosphere. The chef has a particularl flair with white fish, and many daily specialities appear among the reliable and enterprising dishes on the menu. Service is efficient and very attentive.

Closed Sun Lunch not served Sat

French 72 seats *Lunch £20—£25alc Dinner £20—£25 Wine £6.85 Last dinner 10.30pm 175P

Credit cards 1 2 3 5

London W8 — London W11

✕✕**Le Crocodile** 38C&D Kensington Church St ☎ 01-938 2501

This contemporary, Anglo-French restaurant is situated in an air-conditioned and well-furnished basement. Nouvelle cuisine specialities are enterprising and beautifully presented, the chef having a particular flair for classical desserts, and the menu is sensibly priced at two levels.

Closed Sun Lunch not served Sat

French 75 seats *Lunch £10.75&alc Dinner £16.75alc Last dinner 11pm ♭

Credit cards 1 2 3 5

✕✕***Kensington Tandoori*** 1 Abingdon Rd ☎ 01-937 6182

Small, engraved-glass screens afford privacy to diners at this, one of the best of London's Indian restaurants. Formal service and a good wine list complement a menu of North Indian and Persian dishes, all making good use of fresh food.

Indian 80 seats Last dinner mdnt

Credit cards 1 2 3 5

❀✕✕**La Ruelle** 14 Wrights Ln ☎ 01-937 8525

Set close to Kensington High Street, this elegant French restaurant features Cuisine Gourmande. Luxurious decor helps to create a romantic French atmosphere, service is attentive, and the chef, Mr D Omzet, provides an interesting choice of menus.

Closed Sat, Sun & Bank Hols

French **V** 70 seats Lunch £12.50—£21&alc Dinner £28alc Wine £10 Last dinner 11.30pm ♭ nc 12yrs

Credit cards 1 2 3 4 5

✕✕**Sailing Junk** 59 Melrose Rd ☎ 01-937 2589

A large mural dominates this basement Chinese restaurant.

Closed Xmas Day, Boxing Day & Good Fri Lunch not served

Chinese 50 seats S% Dinner £13.50 Wine £6 Last dinner 11.15pm ♭ nc 2yrs

Credit cards 1 2 3 5

✕**Ark** 35 Kensington High St ☎ 01-937 4294 Plan 2: **5** *A3*

Bustling French restaurant serving reasonably priced food.

Closed 4 days Xmas & 4 days Etr Lunch not served Sun

French **V** 95 seats S% Lunch £8—£10alc Dinner £8—£10alc Wine £4.45 Last dinner 11.30pm ♭

Credit cards 1 3 5

✕**Il Barbino** 32 Kensington Church St ☎ 01-937 8752

This tiny, crowded, Italian restaurant is not one for the claustrophobic! Meals are served on ground and first floor level, where an extensive à la carte menu is supplemented by a blackboard of daily specialities including several fresh fish dishes, many of which are temptingly displayed.

Closed Sun Lunch not served Sat

Italian 45 seats S% Lunch £10alc Dinner £10alc Wine £4.90 Last dinner 11.45pm ♭

Credit cards 1 2 3 4 5

✕***Maggie Jones*** 6 Old Court Pl, Church St ☎ 01-937 6462

Excellent English food is served at this busy, noisy restaurant, which is decorated on a farm house theme.

Lunch not served Sun

50 seats Last dinner 11.30pm

Credit cards 1 2 3 4 5

✕***Michel*** 343 Kensington High St ☎ 01-603 3613

French 40 seats Last dinner 10.45pm ♭

Credit cards 1 2 3 4 5

✕**Siam** 12 St Alban's Grove ☎ 01-937 8765 Plan 2: **111** *A3*

Small restaurant decorated in traditional style, featuring traditional Thai dance shows nightly.

Lunch not served Mon & Sat

Thai **V** 85 seats S% *Lunch £9alc Dinner £10.75&alc Wine £5.75 Last dinner 11.15pm ♭⅍ Cabaret nightly

Credit cards 1 2 3 4 5

W9 Maida Vale
London plan **5** C4

✕**Didier** 5 Warwick Pl ☎ 01-286 7484

The delightful, small restaurant is to be found in a quiet side street near to Little Venice. In unpretentious surroundings and a concerned atmosphere, you can choose your meal from a short English menu augmented with daily French specialities, everything being fresh and home-baked. Service, though simple in style, is sympathetic.

Closed Sat & Sun

French 35 seats *Lunch £13alc Dinner £13alc Wine £5.50 Last dinner 10.30pm ♭

Credit cards 1 2 3

W11 Holland Park, Notting Hill
London plan **5** C3

★★★**Hilton International Kensington** Holland Park Av ☎ 01-603 3355 Telex no 919763

Modern hotel with comfortable bedrooms and a Japanese restaurant. →

To find any AA-appointed London hotel or restaurant see maps and index on pages 433—449

LONDON

606 CTV in all bedrooms ® T sB £69—£90 dB £90—£110 (room only)
Lift ☾ # CFA 100 (charge)
International V Lunch £9.50—£15.50&alc Tea fr £5.25 Dinner £9.50—£15.50&alc Wine £7.90 Open 24 hours
Credit cards 1 2 3 4 5

XXX **Leith's** 92 Kensington Park Rd ☎ 01-229 4481
Popular, well established restaurant that continues to offer reliable and unusual food, particularly the varied starters. Good fixed price menu.
Closed Xmas Day & Boxing Day Lunch not served
International V 100 seats S% Dinner £20.50—£29.50 Wine £8.50 Last dinner 11.30pm
Credit cards 1 2 3 5

XX **Chez Moi** 1 Addison Av ☎ 01-603 8267
Tucked away off Holland Park Avenue, this well-established but unostentatious restaurant is patronised by the rich and famous. It offers a cosy, intimate atmosphere, quietly efficient service and a menu that is part traditional and part nouvelle in style.
Closed Sun, 2 wks Aug, 2 wks Xmas & Bank Hols Lunch not served
French 45 seats Dinner fr £16.50&alc Wine £6 Last dinner 11.30pm nc 10yrs
Credit cards 1 2 3 5

XX **La Pomme d'Amour** 128 Holland Park Av ☎ 01-229 8532
Smart French restaurant with attractive patio. Specialising in classical and provincial dishes.
Closed Sun Lunch not served Sat
French V 70 seats S% ✱ Lunch £9.75&alc Dinner £22alc Wine £5.90 Last dinner 10.45pm nc 10yrs
Credit cards 1 2 3 5

X **Cap's** 64 Pembridge Rd ☎ 01-229 5177 Telex no 298363
Small basement restaurant with country style decor providing sensibly priced French cuisine.

LONDON

London W11 — London WC1

Closed Sun & Bank Hols Lunch not served
English & French V 60 seats Dinner £10alc Wine £4.85 Last dinner 11.30pm 2P nc 4yrs
Credit cards 1 2 3 4 5

X **La Residence** 148 Holland Park Av ☎ 01-221 6090
Small pleasantly decorated restaurant with warm ground floor atmosphere and cool basement area. Friendly service.
Closed Mon & Bank Hols Lunch not served Sat
French 70 seats ✱ Lunch £8.60—£13.40 Dinner £10.90—£13.40 Wine £5.40 Last dinner 10.30pm nc 10yrs Live music Tue, Fri & Sun
Credit cards 1 2 3 5

X **Restaurant 192** 192 Kensington Park Rd ☎ 01-229 0482
The tiny restaurant-cum-wine-bar stands close to the Portobello Road on basement and ground levels. The decor may be simple but it contrasts with a bustling atmosphere as a short menu of interesting English dishes, simply made with quality goods, is served by the lively and cheerful staff.
Dinner not served Sun
English & French 32 seats ✱ Dinner £16alc Wine £5.50 Last dinner 11.30pm
Credit cards 1 2 3

W12 Shepherds Bush
London plan **5** C3

X **Shireen** 270 Uxbridge Rd ☎ 01-749 5927
This restaurant offers a short menu of less usual Northern Indian and Tandoori dishes.
Closed Xmas Day & Boxing Day
Indian V 40 seats Lunch £7—£12 Dinner £7—£12 Wine £4.70 Last dinner 11.30pm
Credit cards 1 2 3 5 Ⓥ

W13 Ealing (Northfields)
London plan **5** B4 **(see also W5)**

X ***Maxim Chinese*** 153—155 Northfield Av ☎ 01-567 1719
The enormous Chinese restaurant features an extensive menu which specialises in Peking dishes and includes some interesting set meals for those confused by the breadth of choice. Young, oriental staff willingly offer advice on dishes and provide cheerful service.
Lunch not served Sun
Pekinese V 100 seats Last dinner 12.30am
Credit cards 1 2 3 5

WC1 Bloomsbury, Holborn

★★★★ **Marlborough Crest** Bloomsbury St (Crest) ☎ 01-636 5601 Telex no 298274 Plan 1: **31** *C5*
169 (10fb) in 49 bedrooms CTV in all bedrooms ® T S% sB&B £85.25—£87.95 dB&B £102.50—£107.90
Lift ☾ *xmas*
French V ✱ Lunch £8.50—£10.50&alc Tea £3.25 Dinner £10.50&alc Wine £6.50 Last dinner 11.30pm
Credit cards 1 2 3 4 5

★★★★ **Hotel Russell** Russell Sq (Trusthouse Forte) ☎ 01-837 6470 Telex no 24615 Plan 3: **31** *C6*
Large hotel facing Russell Square with compact modern bedrooms.
318 CTV in all bedrooms T sB&B £63.50 dB&B £85
Lift ☾ CFA *xmas*
Last dinner 10.30pm
Credit cards 1 2 3 4 5

★★★ **Bloomsbury Crest** Coram St (Crest) ☎ 01-837 1200 Telex no 22113
Closed 23—26 Dec
Modern hotel with carvery restaurant.
239 (1fb) in 45 bedrooms CTV in all bedrooms ® T S% sB fr £61.65 dB fr £78.50 (room only)
Lift ☾

V 🏺 ☕ ✂ S% Lunch fr£10.95 Tea fr£1.25 High Tea fr£4 Dinner fr£10.95&alc Last dinner 10.45pm

Credit cards 1 2 3 4 5

★★★**London Ryan** Gwynne Pl, Kings Cross Rd (Mount Charlotte) ☎ 01-278 2480 Telex no 27728

Modern hotel with well-equipped bedrooms.

211 (19fb) CTV in all bedrooms ® T
*sB&B fr£47.25 dB&B fr£57.75 Continental breakfast

Lift ☾ 30P 10

English & French V 🏺 ☕ *Bar lunch £4—£7 Tea £1.50 Dinner £8.50&alc Wine £5.50 Last dinner 9.45pm

Credit cards 1 2 3 5 Ⓥ

✕✕**Mr Kai of Russell Square** 50 Woburn Pl ☎ 01-580 1188 Plan 3: **21** *C6*

A modern, well-run restaurant with friendly and attractive Mandarin waitresses.

Closed Xmas Day, Boxing Day, New Years Day & Bank Hols

Pekinese **V** 120 seats Lunch £8—£15&alc Dinner £20alc Wine £6.50 Last dinner 11.30pm

Credit cards 1 2 3 5

✕✕***Winstons Eating House*** 24 Coptic St ☎ 01-580 3422 Plan 1: **60** *C5*

The name of the restaurant relates to the Winston Churchill theme which runs through it. Tasteful decor and English cuisine attract a busy lunchtime trade.

Closed Xmas, New Year & Bank Hols Lunch not served Sat Dinner not served Sun

44 seats Last dinner 11.15pm Live music Mon—Sat

Credit cards 1 2 3 5

To find any AA-appointed London hotel or restaurant see maps and index on pages 433—449

London WC1 — London WC2

✕**Les Halles** 57 Theobalds Rd ☎ 01-242 6761 Plan 3: **18A** *D6*

A simple French brasserie with interesting food and wine.

Closed Sun & Bank Hols Lunch not served Sat

French **V** 100 seats S% Lunch £15—£20alc Dinner £20—£25alc Wine £6 Last dinner 11.30pm P

Credit cards 1 2 3 5

WC2 Covent Garden,
Leicester Square, Strand and Kingsway

★★★★★

❀★★★★★**SAVOY, LONDON WC2**

Strand ☎ 01-836 4343 Telex no 24234 Plan 1: **46** *E3*

(Rosette awarded for Savoy Restaurant)

For over a hundred years the Savoy has delighted its discerning clientele with high standards of food and service. There is the marble floored lobby to set the tone, leading to the comfortable and quiet reading room and on to the lofty and superb Thames Foyer with its central gazebo where there is live piano music. This is a popular rendezvous for refreshment and excellent afternoon teas. Beyond that is the famous, elegantly appointed River Room, where Anton Edelman, the maitre chef, provides fine food. There are fixed price menus at luncheon and dinner as well as the à la carte menu. There is dancing at night. The style is basically classical with modern lighter influences but the cooking of the best possible ingredients is delicious. This is the room to which we award the rosette, but the light panelled Grill Room also provides enjoyable food from the à la carte menu. As you would expect, the service is courteously dignified and attentive; indeed, so it is throughout the hotel, with good valet and room service. There is also the busy American Bar. The sumptuous suites have atmospheric views of the river, and the individually decorated bedrooms are of a standard that you would expect: huge bath sheets and real linen bed sheets — like all the Savoy Group hotels — and spacious bathrooms. The rooms are well equipped and include in-house movies and video channels. Under Willie Bauer, general manager, this grand hotel maintains the tradition of international hotellerie that so delights the contemporary discerning guest.

200 CTV in all bedrooms T
*sB £120 dB £145—£195 (room only)

Lift ☾ CFA 75 (£8.50 per day) Live music and dancing nightly *xmas*

English & French **V** 🏺 ☕ S%
*Lunch £16.50&alc Tea £7.50 Dinner £21—£25&alc Wine £6.50 Last dinner 10.30pm

Credit cards 1 2 3 5

LONDON

★★★★**Waldorf** Aldwych (Trusthouse Forte) ☎ 01-836 2400 Telex no 24574 Plan 1: **57** *E4*

Gracious, elegant hotel with good range of accommodation.

312 (13fb) CTV in all bedrooms **T** sB&B £80.50 dB&B £104.50

Lift (CFA *xmas*

Last dinner 10pm

Credit cards 1 2 3 4 5

★★★**Drury Lane Moat House** 10 Drury Ln (Queens Moat) ☎ 01-836 6666 Telex no 8811395 Plan 1: **15** *D5*

Hotel with comfortable bedrooms and Maudies Restaurant.

129 CTV in all bedrooms **T** S% sB fr£70 dB fr£92 (room only)

Lift (## 11P (£5 per day)

French S% Lunch £10—11&alc Dinner £16.50alc Wine £6.75 Last dinner 10pm

Credit cards 1 2 3 4 5

★★★**Royal Trafalgar Thistle** Whitcomb St (Thistle) ☎ 01-930 4477 Telex no 298564 Plan 1: **44A** *C2*

Modern but cosy, the comfortable hotel stands just off Trafalgar Square, offering compact but well-equipped bedrooms and friendly, helpful service. The new brasserie offers a French-style menu and mulled wine.

108 in 36 bedrooms CTV in all bedrooms ® **T** * sB £60—£85 dB £75—£95 (room only)

Lift (

International * Lunch fr£10.50alc Dinner fr£10.50alc Wine £7 Last dinner 11pm

Credit cards 1 2 3 4 5 Ⓥ

★★★**Strand Palace** Strand (Trusthouse Forte) ☎ 01-836 8080 Telex no 24208 Plan 1: **52** *E3*

Modernised compact Regency styled hotel.

775 CTV in all bedrooms ® **T** sB&B £59.50 dB&B £77.50

Lift (*xmas*

Last dinner 11.30pm

Credit cards 1 2 3 4 5

XXXXX **Savoy Hotel Grill** Embankment Gdns, Strand ☎ 01-836 4343 Telex no 24234 Plan 1: **46** *E3*

Here, creative dishes, based on ingredients of the highest quality and accompanied by well-made sauces and seasonally-selected vegetables, are complemented by impeccable service from an international team.

Closed Sun & Aug Lunch not served Sat

English & French **V** 85 seats S% Lunch £22.50alc Dinner £15—£25&alc Wine £8.50 Last dinner 11.30pm nc 10yrs Live music nightly

Credit cards 1 2 3 4 5

London WC2

XXXX INIGO JONES, LONDON WC2

14 Garrick St ☎ 01-836 6456 Plan 1: **24** *D3*

This Victorian building was once a stained glass workshop in which William Morris taught. Perhaps it is not stretching the imagination too much to draw a parallel between the style of Morris and Paul Gayler, the talented chef here. Both reacted against the tired old classic traditions and tried to break new ground with original ideas. Certainly Paul Gayler's cooking is individual, adventurous, often with a daring combination of ingredients that nearly always comes off, and is always attractively presented without looking too contrived. Despite the flair and skill evidenced here, one main course of duck breast disappointed: it was hard and of little flavour with a passion fruit sauce that tasted of overcooked caramel rather than anything else. But first courses of meuage du mareyeur, a mixture of various fish, including salmon and mussels in white wine and cream sauce, richly laced with mussel liquor was superb, as was the farandade of scallops wrapped in spinach, steamed, and served with strips of beetroot with a delicate Sauternes butter sauce. Delicious main courses tested were fillet of venison topped with a parsley mousse, wrapped in pastry and served with a sapid game sauce; and a tender, succulent fillet of flavoursome beef, enhanced with garlic and accompanied by a zesty shallot sauce. Vegetables are cooked 'al dente' and the puddings were highly praised: bourbon ice cream with cinnamon flavoured sabayoun, bavarois of lime and lemon with a tangy raspberry cullis and ginger sauce, as well as bavarois of bitter white chocolate with orange segments and armagnac sauce. Good coffee can complete your meal. The long wine list is strong on classics and there is a better than usual list of half bottles. The restaurant is stylish and so is the service, which is reserved but cheerful and friendly. The staff are anxious for you to enjoy yourself and they seem to anticipate your needs. Apart from the à la carte menu, there are fixed price luncheons and pre-theatre menus which are very good value indeed.

Closed Sun & Bank Hols Lunch not served Sat

French **V** 75 seats S% * Lunch £16.96&alc Dinner £16.96&alc Wine £10.55 Last dinner 11.30pm

Credit cards 1 2 3 5

XXX **Boulestin** 1A Henrietta St, ☎ 01-836 3819 Plan 1: **4** *D3*

Gracious and elegant, the Edwardian-style restaurant exudes comfort and affluence. Smartly dressed French staff provide professional and attentive service, whilst the menu offers a balanced and interesting selection of imaginative and attractively-presented classical dishes, well-geared to the seasonal availability of food. The extensive wine list is designed to appeal to a discerning clientèle.

Closed Sun, 1 wk Xmas, Bank Hols & last 3 wks Aug Lunch not served Sat

French **V** 70 seats * Lunch £16.57&alc Dinner £45alc Wine £10 Last dinner 11.15pm no babies

Credit cards 1 2 3 4 5

XXX **P S Hispaniola** Victoria Embankment, River Thames ☎ 01-839 3011 Plan 1: **21** *D1*

The restaurant is located on board a paddle steamer.

Closed 1 wk after Xmas Lunch not served Sat

French **V** 130 seats Lunch £11.50 Dinner £16.50—£18.50 Wine £7.50 Last dinner 11pm Live music nightly

Credit cards 1 3 4 5

XXX **Neal Street** 26 Neal St ☎ 01-836 8368 Plan 1: **33** *D4*

Modern restaurant with tasteful basement cocktail bar; serving very original cuisine.

Closed Sat & Sun, 1 wk Xmas & Bank Hols

International **V** 65 seats S% Lunch £27alc Dinner £27alc Wine £7.50 Last dinner 11pm

Credit cards 1 2 3 5

XXX **L'Opera** 32 Great Queen St ☎ 01-405 9020 Plan 1: **35** *D5*

Splendid, plush Edwardian restaurant in gilt and green occupying two floors in the centre of theatreland.

Closed Sun Lunch not served Sat

French **V** 100 seats Lunch £11.50—£17&alc Dinner £11.50—£17&alc Wine £5.95 Last dinner mdnt

Credit cards 1 2 3 5

XXX **Rules** 35 Maiden Ln, Strand ☎ 01-836 2559 Plan 1: **45** *D3*

Well established traditional restaurant with professional, efficient service.

Closed Sun, 24 Dec—2 Jan & Bank Hols

130 seats * Lunch £11&alc Dinner £11&alc Wine £5.85 Last dinner mdnt nc 6yrs

Credit cards 1 2 3 5

XX Chez Solange 35 Cranbourne St ☎ 01-836 0542 Plan 1: **12** *C3*

Good quality home cuisine in this elegant West End restaurant.

Closed Sun

French **V** 80 seats Lunch £12&alc Dinner £12&alc Wine £7.25 Last dinner 12.15am Live music nightly

Credit cards 1 2 3 4 5 V

XX *Interlude de Tabaillau* 7—8 Bow St ☎ 01-379 6473 Plan 1: **25** *D4*

Informal atmosphere, honest French cooking and good value for money.

Closed, Sun, Bank Hols, 2 wks Xmas, 10 days Etr, last 2 wks Aug & 1st wk Sep Lunch not served Sat

French 48 seats Last dinner 11.30pm

Credit cards 1 2 3 5

XX Poons of Covent Garden 41 King St ☎ 01-240 1743 Plan 1: **38** *D3*

Popular Chinese restaurant with extensive menu and rapid service.

Closed Sun & 24—27 Dec

Cantonese **V** 120 seats Last dinner 11.30pm

Credit cards 2 3 5

XX Thomas de Quincey's 36 Tavistock St ☎ 01-240 3972 Plan 1: **54** *E3*

Attractive hospitable restaurant serving original unusual dishes.

Closed Sun, Bank Hols & 3 wks Aug Lunch not served Sat

French 50 seats Lunch £25—£30alc Dinner £25—£30alc Wine £7 Last dinner 11.15pm

Credit cards 1 2 3 4 5

XX Tourment d'Amour 19 New Row ☎ 01-240 5348 Plan 1: **55** *D3*

Located in Covent Garden, at the heart of theatre-land, this small, intimate French restaurant offers a fixed price menu for two and three course meals, and helpful staff are delighted to describe any of the dishes to customers.

Closed Sun

Lunch not served Sat

French **V** 43 seats S% *Lunch £20.25 Dinner £20.25 Wine £9 Last dinner 11.30pm nc 10yrs

Credit cards 1 2 3 5

X *Bates English* 11 Henrietta St ☎ 01-240 7600 Telex no 922488 Plan 1: **3A** *D3*

The slick, 30's-style restaurant serves an inexpensive British menu to the accompaniment of live music, the quality of its cooking making it deservedly popular.

Continental 65 seats Last dinner 11.30pm

Credit cards 1 2 3 5

London WC2

X *Le Café des Amis du Vin* 11—14 Hanover Pl ☎ 01-379 3444 Plan 1: **6A** *D4*

Traditional French street cafe with imaginative menu.

Closed Sun & Xmas

French 120 seats Last dinner 11.30pm

Credit cards 1 2 3 4 5

X *Le Café du Jardin* 28 Wellington St ☎ 01-836 8769 Plan 1: **7A** *E4*

This lively French brasserie offers a limited selection of wholesome dishes, and food is served by aproned French waiters against the background of a suitably Gallic decor.

Closed Sun & Xmas Lunch not served Sat

French 116 seats Last dinner 11.30pm

Credit cards 1 2 3 4 5

X Cafe Pelican 45 St Martins Ln ☎ 01-379 0309 Plan 1: **6B** *D3*

A large and lively French cafe, the Pelican offers wholesome, provincial-style French dishes in an authentic atmosphere.

French **V** 200 seats *Lunch £12.95&alc Dinner £12.95&alc Wine £5.50 Last dinner 12.30am Live music nightly

Credit cards 1 2 3 5

X *La Corée Korean* 56 St Giles High St ☎ 01-836 7235 Plan 1: **13A** *C5*

This small and friendly restaurant offers an interesting gastronomic experience as competent and pleasant staff serve authentic and well-prepared Korean dishes.

Closed Sun, Bank Hols, 3 days Xmas & 2 days New Year

Korean **V** 60 seats Last dinner 11pm

Credit cards 1 2 3

X Happy Wok 52 Floral St ☎ 01-836 3696 Plan 1: **20** *D4*

The cosy, well-run Chinese restaurant stands at the heart of theatre land, offering a good range of well-prepared and authentic dishes served by charming staff.

Closed Sun, Xmas Day & Boxing Day

Chinese & Pekinese **V** 42 seats Lunch £12.50—£19 Dinner £12.50—£19 Wine £5 Last dinner 11.30pm

Credit cards 1 2 3 5

X Last Days of The Raj 22 Drury Ln ☎ 01-836 1628 Plan 1: **28A** *D5*

Bright, popular co-operative featuring authentic, honest and skilful Indian cuisine.

Indian **V** 44 seats S% Last dinner 11.30pm

Credit cards 1 2 3 4 5

X Il Passetto 230 Shaftesbury Av ☎ 01-836 9391 Plan 1: **23A** *D5*

Modern Italian restaurant with good home made food.

Closed Sun

Italian 42 seats Lunch £19alc Dinner £20alc Wine £4.75 Last dinner 11.30pm

Credit cards 1 2 3 5

X Plummers 33 King St ☎ 01-240 2534 Plan 1: **37** *D3*

Busy and lively, the simply-appointed restaurant offers good value for money in its selection of American and English food.

Closed Sun Lunch not served Sat

75 seats *Lunch £4—£14alc Dinner £4—£14alc Wine £4.95 Last dinner 11.30pm

Credit cards 1 2 3 5

X Poon's 4 Leicester St ☎ 01-437 1528 Plan 1: **39** *C3*

The restaurant is very popular, particularly with the Chinese, and its extensive menu includes a selection of dishes using wind-dried ingredients. Service is somewhat rushed, but food is consistently good, well-prepared and authentic, and glass panels between dining rooms and kitchen enable you to see it in course of preparation.

Closed Sun & Xmas

Cantonese **V** 100 seats S% *Lunch £6—£20&alc Dinner £6—£20&alc Wine £4.20 Last dinner 11.30pm

X *La Provence* 8 Mays Court ☎ 01-836 9180 Plan 1: **40** *D3*

Small, intimate, informal Italian restaurant.

French **V** 50 seats Last dinner 11pm

Credit cards 1 2 3 5

X Sheekey's 29—31 St Martin's Court ☎ 01-240 2565 Plan 1: **47** *C3*

One of the oldest fish restaurants in London, specialising in oysters.

Closed Sun Lunch not served Sat

50 seats Last dinner 11.15pm

Credit cards 1 2 3 5

X Taste of India 25 Catherine St ☎ 01-836 6591 Plan 1: **52A** *E4*

This small, elegant Indian restaurant features some very interesting specialities and authentic dishes, skilfully prepared with pungently-spiced sauces and formally served.

Indian **V** 140 seats S% Lunch £10—£12&alc Wine £5.50 Last dinner mdnt

Credit cards 1 2 3 4 5

To find any AA-appointed London hotel or restaurant see maps and index on pages 433—449

LONDON AIRPORTS
See under **Gatwick, Heathrow**

LONG EATON
Derbyshire
Map **8** SK43
See under Sandiacre

★★★**Novotel Nottingham Derby** Bostock Ln (S of M1 junc 25) ☎ (0602) 720106 Telex no 377585

Situated close to Junction 25 of the M1, this busy, large, modern hotel with well-equipped bedrooms is part of a French-owned company.

112 (112fb) CTV in all bedrooms **T** S% ✱sB £43 dB £54 (room only) **B**

Lift ☾ ## 180P CFA ✿ (heated) solarium petanque ♿

English & Continental S%
✱Lunch £6.50&alc Tea £1.75&alc High Tea £8.50alc Dinner fr£8.50&alc Wine £4.60 Last dinner 10.30pm

Credit cards [1] [2] [3] [5]

★★**Europa** 20 Derby Rd ☎ (0602) 728481 Telex no 377494

Closed 24 Dec—2 Jan

Three-storey Victorian building standing by the A6005 close to town centre.

21rm (6 3)(2fb) CTV in all bedrooms sB&B£20—£21 sB&B £27.50—£30 dB&B£34—£35 dB&B £42—£44 **B**

☾ CTV 25P ♿

V S% Lunch £5—£6 Tea £1—£1.50 High Tea £4—£5 Dinner fr£7.50&alc Wine £5.50 Last dinner 8.30pm

Credit cards [1] [2] [3] [5] Ⓥ

LONGFRAMLINGTON
Northumberland
Map **12** NU10

XX**Angler's Arms** Weldon Bridge (2m S off B6344) ☎ (066570) 655

Country inn and restaurant extending into converted railway carriages. Menu features classical as well as unusual dishes.

English, French & Portuguese 70 seats Lunch £7 Dinner £10alc Wine £5.75 Last dinner 9.30pm 50P

Credit cards [2] [3]

LONGHAM
Dorset
Map **4** SZ09

★★★**Bridge House** 2 Ringwood Rd ☎ Bournemouth (0202) 578828 Telex no 418484

Closed 25 & 26 Dec

25rm (21 4)3 CTV in all bedrooms ® **T** sB&B £28—£40 dB&B £50—£80 Continental breakfast

☾ 200P ✿ Live music and dancing Sat

English, French & Greek **V** (in season) Bar lunch £1—£5.75 Tea 90p—£2.10 Dinner £9.50&alc Wine £3.95 Last dinner 10pm

Credit cards [1] [2] [3] Ⓥ

LONGHORSLEY
Northumberland
Map **12** NZ19

★★★★*HBL* **Linden Hall** (Prestige) ☎ Morpeth (0670) 56611 Telex no 538224

An elegant Georgian style country house in 300 acres of parkland, it is impressively furnished with paintings and antiques, enlivened by fresh flowers. The lounges are peaceful and comfortable, while the bedrooms are very well equipped.

45 (10fb) 2 CTV in all bedrooms ® **T** S% sB&B £52.25 dB&B £62.50 **B**

Lift ☾ 180P CFA ✿ snooker putting croquet table tennis clay pigeon shooting sauna bath solarium Live music & dancing monthly ♿ *xmas*

V S% ✱Lunch fr£9.50&alc Tea fr80p High Tea fr£2.50 Dinner fr£12&alc Wine £5.55 Last dinner 10pm

Credit cards [1] [2] [3] [5] Ⓥ

LONG MELFORD
Suffolk
Map **5** TL84

★★★**Bull** (Trusthouse Forte) ☎ Sudbury (0787) 78494

The first recorded use of this building as an inn was in 1530, and 19th century brickwork has been removed to reveal the old plaster-and-timber frontage.

27 (4fb) CTV in all bedrooms ® sB&B £49.50 dB&B £67.50 **B**

40P *xmas*

Last dinner 10pm

Credit cards [1] [2] [3] [4] [5]

★**Crown Inn** Hall St ☎ Sudbury (0787) 77666

Situated in the main street of the village, the hotel has 15th-century walled gardens.

8rm (2) Annexe: 5rm (4 1)(2fb) 2 CTV in 9 bedrooms ® sB&B£20—£25 sB&B fr£25 dB&B fr£30 dB&B £35—£42 **B**

6P *xmas*

✱Lunch £4—£8 Dinner £5—£12 Wine £5.99 Last dinner 9.30pm

Credit cards [1] [2] [3] [5]

✿XX**Chimneys** Hall St ☎ Sudbury (0787) 79806

An attractive restaurant in the heart of the village, Chimneys is housed in a 16th-century, timber-framed building with a secluded rear garden. The English and Continental cuisine is in the light, modern style and based on quality ingredients. The menu, which will change each month, is accompanied by a wide-ranging wine list, and chef Roger Carter leads a keen young staff.

Closed Mon Dinner not served Sun

English & Continental **V** 55 seats Lunch £9.50&alc Dinner £15&alc Wine £5.50 Last dinner 9.30pm 16P

Credit cards [1] [3]

LONGNOR
Staffordshire
Map **7** SK06

XX ***Ye Old Cheshire Cheese*** High St ☎(029 883) 218

Charming old stone built inn set in small village within national park.

Closed Mon Dinner not served Sun

English & Continental **V** 70 seats Last dinner 9.45pm 100P

Credit cards 1 2 3 5

LONGRIDGE
Lancashire
Map **7** SD63

★★**Blackmoss Country House** Thornley (2m NE off Chipping rd) ☎(077478) 3148

Closed Xmas day

The personally-owned sandstone house, set in 3½ acres of grounds, offers bright, well-furnished bedrooms and good home cooking.

10rm(3→4⌂)(1fb) in 10 bedrooms ® sB&B£14—£19 sB&B→⌂£19—£24 dB&B£24 dB&B→⌂£29—£46

CTV 80P (heated) sauna bath solarium

V Dinner £6.50—£15&alc Wine £3.75 Last dinner 10.30pm

Credit cards 1 2 5 Ⓥ

X**Corporation Arms** Lower Rd ☎(077478) 2644

This attractive, personally-run, stone inn stands in rural surroundings. Comfortably furnished, it serves a grill-type menu supplemented by such 'specials' as chicken-in-the-pot and steak and kidney pie, all served by friendly staff and at good, honest prices.

Closed Xmas Day

V 55 seats S% *Lunch £7.50alc Dinner £8.50alc Wine £3.90 Last dinner 9.30pm 60P

Credit cards 1 2

LONGTOWN
Cumbria
Map **11** NY36

★★**Graham Arms** English St ☎(0228) 791213

Town centre hotel conveniently situated for fishing holidays.

15rm(3→2⌂)(4fb) CTV in 8 bedrooms TV in 2 bedrooms ® in 3 bedrooms sB&B£14.50 sB&B→⌂£19.50 dB&B£23 dB&B→⌂£28

CTV 10P 2

Lunch £6—£12&alc Tea £1.50—£2.20&alc High Tea £3—£6&alc Dinner £7—£14&alc Wine £4.90 Last dinner 8.30pm

Credit card 1

★ *H* **March Bank** Scotsdyke (3m N A7 Galashiels rd) ☎(0228) 791325

Closed Nov—Mar

(Rosette awarded for dinner only)

Patricia Grant uses the best of fresh ingredients to prepare an exceptional dinner at this small, friendly, family-run hotel on the English/Scottish border. Choice is limited, but specialities such as hake cooked in a white wine, cream and onion sauce can be recommended. The menu features home-made soup and sweets, together with locally-made Cumberland cheeses, and prices in the small wine bar are competitive.

6rm(3→)(1fb) S% sB&B£28—£32 dB&B£38—£40 dB&B→£42—£46

CTV 25P

International **V** S% Lunch £5—£8&alc Dinner £13—£15&alc Wine £6.90 Last dinner 8.30pm

Ⓥ

LOOE
Cornwall
Map **2** SX25

★★★**Hannafore Point** Marine Dr, Hannafore (Best Western) ☎(05036) 3273 Telex no 42513

Closed 27 Dec—1 Feb

This friendly, well-appointed hotel overlooks one of the most beautiful bays in Cornwall, and there are fine views from many bedroom balconies and from the floor-to-ceiling windows of the lounge.

40rm(39→1⌂)(10fb) CTV in all bedrooms ®**T** sB&B→⌂£26—£28.25 dB&B→⌂£43—£58

Lift 36P 6 (heated) *xmas*

English, French & Italian **V** Lunch £4.70—£6.20 Tea fr80p High Tea £1.70—£2.80 Dinner £10.50&alc Wine £5.45 Last dinner 9pm

Credit cards 1 2 3 5 Ⓥ

★★**Fieldhead** Portuan Rd, Hannafore ☎(05036) 2689

Closed Dec & Jan

Family-run hotel with relaxed, friendly atmosphere, overlooking Looe harbour and the coastline.

14rm(7→2⌂)(2fb) CTV in all bedrooms ® *sB&Bfr£15 sB&B→⌂£33—£35 dB&B£20 dB&B→⌂£38—£40

13P 2 (heated)

*Dinner fr£6.75&alc Last dinner 8.30pm

Credit cards 1 2 3 5

See advertisement on page 480

★**Commonwood** St Martin's Rd ☎(05036) 2929

Closed Nov—Feb

Once a privately-owned country house, Common Wood Manor is set dramatically on a wooded hillside and has superb views over the river. Family-run, it offers a comfortable standard of accommodation.

11rm(2→7⌂)(2fb) CTV in all bedrooms S% sB&B£24—£27 sB&B→⌂£27—£31 dB&B£31—£37 dB&B→⌂£37—£43

CTV 20P (heated)

S% Lunch £5.50alc Tea £1.20alc Dinner £7.50alc Wine £5 Last dinner 7.30pm

Credit cards 1 3

L

★Portbyhan West Looe Quay ☏(05036) 2071

Small friendly holiday hotel situated by West Looe harbour.

43rm(12⋔)(8fb) B

Lift CTV sauna bath solarium *xmas*

V

XX Trelaske County Hotel Polperro Rd, Trelaske (2m W on A387) ☏(05036) 2159

Family owned and run, the attractive, small, country house hotel stands in its own gardens. It offers good bedrooms, a well-appointed restaurant and a character bar.

Closed Mon & 5 Jan—5 Feb Lunch not served Tue—Sat Dinner not served Sun

English & French V 50 seats ✱Bar lunch £2.25—£4.50 Dinner £7.25—£8.95&alc Wine £5.25 Last dinner 9pm 30P

Credit cards 1 2 3 5

LORTON

Cumbria
Map **11** NY12

★Hollin House Church Ln ☏(090085) 656

Closed Nov—Feb

This charming, family-run hotel offers its guests spacious, comfortable bedrooms and good home cooking.

6rm(1→3⋔) 1 Ⓡ S% sB&B£17—£20 sB&B→⋔£19—£22 dB&B£24—£30 dB&B→⋔£28—£34

8P nc 16yrs

S% Tea £2.50 Dinner £8—£9 Wine £4.20 Last dinner 7.30pm

Credit cards 1 3

LOSTWITHIEL

Cornwall
Map **2** SX15

★★Carotel Motel Hillside Gdns ☏ Bodmin (0208) 872223

Small comfortable motel conveniently situated on the A390 in the ancient town of Lostwithiel.

20rm(13→7⋔) Annexe: 12→(3fb) CTV in all bedrooms ⓇT B

40P (heated) solarium Live music & dancing Sat *xmas*

V Last dinner 9.30pm

Credit cards 1 2 3 5

LOUGHBOROUGH

Leicestershire
Map **8** SK51

★★★Cedars Cedar Rd ☏(0509) 214459

Closed 26—28 Dec RS Sun evening

Situated off the A6, south of the town centre, the hotel provides well-equipped, comfortable accommodation. The building, which dates back to 1806, has recently undergone extensive modernisation.

37rm(23→14⋔)(4fb) CTV in all bedrooms ⓇT sB&B→⋔£17.50—£34 dB&B→⋔£28—£40 B

50P (heated) sauna bath solarium

V Lunch £3.95—£6.25&alc Tea 90p—£1.95 Dinner £8—£15&alc Wine £4.25 Last dinner 9pm

Credit cards 1 2 3 5 Ⓥ

★★★King's Head High St (Embassy) ☏(0509) 233222

Town centre inn with a large modern extension, standing on the A6.

86rm(69→9⋔)(4fb) CTV in all bedrooms ⓇT S% sBfr£28.50 sB→⋔fr£43 dBfr£42.50 dB→⋔fr£57(room only) B

Lift ☾ 80P CFA *xmas*

English & French V S% Lunch £5.95 Tea fr60p Dinner fr£7.95&alc Wine £4.45 Last dinner 9.15pm

Credit cards 1 2 3 4 5 Ⓥ

★★Great Central Great Central Rd (Minotel) ☏(0509) 263405 Telex no 946240

RS 24 Dec—1 Jan

Large Victorian hotel close to the old Great Central railway line.

21rm(8⇌8⋒)(1fb) CTV in all bedrooms ® T sB&B£15—£20 sB&B⇌⋒£17.50—£28 dB&B£20—£30 dB&B⇌⋒£26—£34 B

CTV 20P

V ♈ Lunch £2.95—£5.50 Dinner £6.50&alc Wine £4.20 Last dinner 9pm

Credit cards 1 2 3 5

LOUTH

Lincolnshire
Map **8** TF38

★★**Priory** Eastgate ☎ (0507) 602930

RS 24 Dec—1 Jan

Magnificent Gothic-style building set in its own impressive gardens, approximately ¼ mile from the town centre.

Loughborough — Lowestoft

12rm(6⇌2⋒)(2fb) CTV in all bedrooms ® ✗ sB&B£20—£25 sB&B⇌⋒£24—£30 dB&B£35—£40 dB&B⇌⋒£40—£45 B

CTV 25P ✿ (grass)

V Dinner £7.50&alc Wine £5.50 Last dinner 9pm

Credit cards 1 3 Ⓥ

LOWER BEEDING

West Sussex
Map **4** TQ22

★★★

❀★★★ SOUTH LODGE, LOWER BEEDING,

Brighton Rd ☎ (040376) 711

Opened only last summer, this hotel has quickly established a reputation under its manager, Richard Young. He has made an excellent job of choosing and training the right sort of staff. Built by Lord Godman in 1883 amidst 90 acres of natural woodland — it looks marvellous in late spring when the rhododendrons and azaleas are in flower. There is a lake stacked with trout and a fine rock garden. Tennis, croquet, clay pigeon shooting and riding are available. The many gabled rubble and ashlar building is in a much earlier style than Victorian, and has a fine staircase and oak panelling together with ornamental plasterwork ceilings. Chinese carpets, crystal chandeliers, flowers and antiques enhance the atmosphere. There is a drawing room and library as well as the elegant restaurant, beautifully appointed. Here you can enjoy set meals, including a vegetarian menu, or choose from the interesting à la carte. They make different claims for this cuisine but we think it is very much in the modern idiom. At any rate we

think the food is so good, under the chef James Haywood, that we awarded a rosette. Spacious bedrooms for your comfort complete the enjoyment of your stay in this luxuriously comfortable country house.

23⇌ CTV in all bedrooms **T** ✱sB&B⇌£57 dB&B⇌£80

☾ ## 25P 6 ✿ (hard) U *xmas*

English & French ♈ ✱ Lunch £11.50&alc Tea £4.50 Dinner £22&alc Wine £8 Last dinner 10.30pm

Credit cards 1 2 3 4 5

✗✗**Cisswood House** ☎ (040376) 216

Excellent cuisine is offered in this very elegant country restaurant.

Closed Sat before Xmas—10 Jan

Continental 80 seats ✱ Lunch £15alc Dinner £15alc Wine £7 Last dinner 9.30pm P

Credit cards 1 2 3 5

LOWER SLAUGHTER

Gloucestershire
Map **4** SP12

★★★ *B* **Manor**

☎ Cotswold (0451) 20456 Telex no 437287

Interesting 17th-century house with lovely garden. Service is friendly and good; bedrooms are particularly comfortable.

11⇌ Annexe: 10⇌(7fb) 2 CTV in all bedrooms ® **T** ✗ sB&B⇌£46—£50 dB&B⇌£60—£75 B

☾ 40P ✿ (heated) sauna bath solarium gymnasium croquet nc 8yrs *xmas*

English & French **V** ♈ Lunch £6.50—£8alc Dinner £12alc Wine £5.30 Last dinner 9.30pm

Credit cards 1 2 3 5

See advertisement on page 482

LOWESTOFT

Suffolk
Map **5** TM59

★★★**Victoria** Kirkley Cliff ☎ (0502) 4433

Modernised Victorian hotel situated on the clifftop at the southern end of the town.

45rm(27⇌5⋒)(5fb) in 36 bedrooms CTV in all bedrooms ® **T** S% sB&B£30—£35 sB&B⇌⋒fr£35 dB&Bfr£45 dB&B⇌⋒fr£48 B

Lift ☾ ## CTV 50P ✿ (heated) *xmas*

English & French **V** ♈ S% ✱ Lunch £2—£6 Tea 65p Dinner £8.95—£16.50 Wine £4.75 Last dinner 10pm

Credit cards 1 2 3 5

★★**Wherry** Bridge Rd, Oulton Broad ☎ (0502) 3521 Telex no 975621

25rm(20⇌5⋒)(2fb) CTV in all bedrooms ® **T** sB&B⇌⋒£33 dB&B⇌⋒£40 B

Lift ☾ 135P sauna bath solarium →

L

French Lunch £5—£6&alc Tea £1.50—£1.99 High Tea £2.50—£3.50 Dinner £8.75&alc Wine £4.50 Last dinner 10pm

Credit cards 1 2 3 5 V

★**Denes** Corton Rd (Toby) (0502) 64616

10 CTV in all bedrooms ® S% sB&B fr£20 dB&B fr£32

60P

Mainly grills V S% ✱Lunch fr£4.79 Dinner fr£4.79 Wine £4.99 Last dinner 10pm

Credit cards 1 2 3

LOWESWATER
Cumbria
Map **11** NY12

★★*L* **Scale Hill** Lorton (090085) 232

Closed 13 Jan—6 Mar

This comfortable and relaxing hotel, housed in a building which dates back to 1633, enjoys an idyllic situation. Good home cooking is its speciality.

15rm (11 1) Annexe: 2 (2fb) 1 S% sB&B£20—£25 sB&B £24—£29 dB&B£34—£44 dB&B £44—£54 B

25P ❀ *xmas*

S% Bar lunch fr80p Tea fr£1 Dinner £10 Wine £3.90 Last dinner 7.45pm

★**Grange Country House** Lamplugh (0946) 861211

Closed 20 Dec—4 Jan RS 1—19 Dec & 5 Jan—Mar

Comfortable, 17th-century country hotel situated in its own grounds at the head of Loweswater.

6rm (3) Annexe: 5rm (4) (1fb) 1 CTV in 7 bedrooms ® sB&B£16.50—£18 sB&B £18—£19.50 dB&B£33—£36 dB&B £36—£39 B

CTV 20P 2 (charge) ❀

V Lunch £4.50—£6.50 Tea £1—£3.50 High Tea £4.50—£6.50 Dinner £8—£10 Wine £4.60 Last dinner 8pm

LUDLOW
Shropshire
Map **7** SO57

★★★*HBL* **Feathers** Bull Ring (0584) 5261 Telex no 35637

One of England's finest and most well-known inns, it has been considerably refurbished inside to provide additional comfort while retaining the original character. The hospitality from Osmond Edwards, his manager, Peter Nash and the staff is warm and friendly, while the restaurant is gaining a reputation for good cooking.

37 (4fb) 7 CTV in all bedrooms ® T ✕ sB&B £42—£45 dB&B £57—£75 Continental breakfast B

Lift ☾ 38P CFA *xmas*

V Lunch £6—£8.50&alc Tea £2—£2.50 Dinner £12.50—£13.50&alc Wine £5.50 Last dinner 9pm

Credit cards 1 2 3 4 5 V

★★**Angel** Broad St (Consort) (0584) 2581

The hotel, which is reputed to be the oldest licensed premises in the town, retains its original, half-timbered frontage, though much of the rest of the building has been renewed. Lord Nelson made a speech from one of its balconies in 1803.

17 (1fb) 1 CTV in all bedrooms ® T ✕ sB&B £35—£37 dB&B £48—£60 B

34P 6 *xmas*

V Lunch £5—£6.50&alc Dinner £9—£10&alc Wine £5 Last dinner 9pm

Credit cards 1 2 3 5 V

★★**Overton Grange** (1½m S of Ludlow off B4361) (0584) 3500

Pleasantly situated in 2½ acres of gardens to the south of the town, this former Edwardian mansion provides comfortable accommodation and a relaxed atmosphere.

17rm (4 2) (2fb) CTV in all bedrooms ® T S% sB&B£16.50—£17.50 sB&B £25.50—£28.50 dB&B£36—£40 dB&B £45—£48 B

80P 3 ❀ croquet *xmas*

English & French V Lunch £9—£9.50 Tea 60—70p High Tea £3.50—£4.50 Dinner £9.50—£10&alc Wine £4.95 Last dinner 9.30pm

Credit cards 1 2 3 5

★**Cliffe** Dinham (0584) 2063

A Victorian building, formerly a private house, stands in pleasant gardens near the castle and offers simple but comfortable accommodation.

10rm (3 2) (1fb) CTV in 5 bedrooms ® ✕ S% sB&B£12.50 sB&B £18 dB&B£24 dB&B £29 B

CTV 50P ❀

V S% Bar lunch £1.50—£3.30 Dinner £7.50alc Wine £4.50 Last dinner 9.15pm

✕✕**Penny Anthony** 5 Church St (0584) 3282

Centrally situated near castle and Town Hall, this attractive small restaurant makes good use of local meat and vegetables in its carefully-prepared meals, providing a pleasant eating-place for visitors to the historic town.

Closed Sun, Dec & Jan

French V 50 seats ✱Lunch £3.95—£9&alc Dinner £6.75—£15&alc Wine £4.50 Last dinner 10pm

Credit cards 2 3 5 V

LUDWELL
Wiltshire
Map **3** SY92

★*L* ***Grove House*** Donhead (074788) 365

Closed Dec & Jan

A warm welcome is extended by this small, comfortable and personally-run hotel which provides good food and pleasant gardens for the enjoyment of its guests.

11rm(4⇌6🚿)(2fb) Ⓡ 🅱
⅟CTV 12P ⇌ ✽ nc 5yrs *xmas*
Last dinner 8.30pm
Credit cards [1] [3]

LULWORTH
Dorset
Map **3** SY88

★**Bishop's Cottage** ☎ West Lulworth (092941) 261
Closed end Oct—Feb
Three adjoining stone cottages converted to form this hotel which nestles in the hillside on the edge of Lulworth Cove.
11rm(4⇌) Annexe: 3rm(2⇌)(3fb) Ⓡ S%
sB&B£12.65—£13.75
dB&B£25.30—£27.50
dB&B⇌£29.70—£34.10 🅱
CTV 6P ⇌ ✽ ⇌ (heated)
English & French **V** S% Lunch £3—£8.50 Tea £1.50—£3 High Tea £2—£3.50 Dinner £6—£10 Last dinner 10pm
Credit cards [1] [3]

Ludwell — Luss

LUMBY
North Yorkshire
Map **8** SE43

★★★**Selby Fork** (southern junc A1/A63) (Anchor) ☎ South Milford (0977) 682711 Telex no 557074
Large, modern hotel on A1 with comfortable accommodation and good facilities.
109rm(59⇌50🚿)(20fb) ⅟ in 11 bedrooms CTV in all bedrooms Ⓡ **T** S%
sB&B⇌🚿£42.50—£46.50
dB&B⇌🚿£52.50—£56.50 🅱
300P 20 CFA ✽ (heated) (hard) sauna bath Disco Sat Apr—Oct *xmas*
V S% Lunch £9.25&alc Tea 60p High Tea £2.50—£5 Dinner £9.25&alc Wine £5.95 Last dinner 10pm
Credit cards [1] [2] [3] [4] [5] Ⓥ

LUNDIN LINKS
Fife
Map **12** NO40

★★★**Old Manor** Leven Rd ☎ (0333) 320368
Closed 1 & 2 Jan
Tasteful extension and conversion of the original mansion have produced this elegant hotel, looking across the golf course to the Firth of Forth.
19rm(15⇌)(2fb) CTV in all bedrooms Ⓡ **T**
sB&B£26.50—£36.50
sB&B⇌£34.50—£36.50
dB&B£36.50—£47 dB&B⇌£42.50—£47 🅱
60P ✽ *xmas*
V Lunch £6.85 Tea £1.20 Dinner £12&alc Wine £5.60 Last dinner 9.30pm
Credit cards [1] [2] [3] [5]

LUSS
Strathclyde *Dunbartonshire*
Map **10** NS39

★★***Colquhoun Arms*** ☎ (043686) 282 Telex no 727289
Village hotel by Loch Lomond.
23rm(5🚿)(3fb) CTV in all bedrooms 🅱
CTV 50P ✽ *xmas*
British & French **V** Last dinner 9.30pm
Credit cards [1] [2] [3] [4] [5]

★★**Inverbeg Inn** Inverbeg (3m N on A82) ☎ (043 686) 678 Telex no 777205
An attractive inn with modern, comfortable facilities, the Inverbeg stands close to the banks of Loch Lomond.
14rm(7⇌)(1fb) CTV in all bedrooms Ⓡ
sB&B£17.50—£22.50
sB&B⇌£20—£24.50 dB&B£27.50—£38
dB&B⇌£34—£45 🅱 →

80P

British & French V Lunch £7 Tea £1—£3.50 High Tea £3.75—£5.50 Dinner fr£9.50&alc Wine £2.45 Last dinner 11pm

Credit cards [1] [2] [3] [4] [5] [V]

LUTON
Bedfordshire
Map **4** TL02

★★★**Chiltern** Waller Av, Dunstable Rd (Crest) (0582) 575911 Telex no 825048

Comfortable hotel with friendly restaurant.

99 in 10 bedrooms CTV in all bedrooms ® T S% *sB £48.50 dB £57 (room only)

Lift 175P CFA

V *Lunch £9&alc Tea 75p Dinner £12.25&alc Wine £7.95 Last dinner 9.55pm

Credit cards [1] [2] [3] [4] [5]

★★★**Crest Hotel—Luton** Dunstable Rd (Crest) (0582) 575955 Telex no 826283

Closed 24 Dec—2 Jan

Modern hotel with well-equipped bedrooms.

133 in 10 bedrooms CTV in all bedrooms ® T S% sB fr£51.85 dB fr£65.70 (room only)

Lift 120P CFA

Mainly grills V S% Lunch £7.05—£9.55&alc Tea fr80p Dinner fr£10.95&alc Wine £5.80 Last dinner 9.45pm

Credit cards [1] [2] [3] [4] [5]

★★★**Strathmore Thistle** Arndale Centre (Thistle) (0582) 34199 Telex no 825763

Comfortable hotel with well appointed restaurant, pleasant coffee shop and friendly service.

151 (4fb) in 22 bedrooms CTV in all bedrooms ® T *sB £48—£70 dB £55—£78 (room only)

Lift 12P CFA

International *Lunch fr£11&alc Dinner fr£12.50&alc Wine £7 Last dinner 9.45pm

Credit cards [1] [2] [3] [4] [5] [V]

LUTTERWORTH
Leicestershire
Map **4** SP58

★★**Moorbarns** Watling St (2m W on A5) (04555) 2237

Closed 26—30 Dec

There is modern accommodation in the annexe of this large hotel on the A5.

Annexe: 11rm (6 5)(1fb) 2 CTV in all bedrooms ® *sB&B £32 dB&B £42

40P Live music and dancing Sat nc 5yrs

English, French & Italian *Lunch £6—£10 Dinner £8.50—£12

Credit cards [2] [3] [5]

LYDDINGTON
Leicestershire
Map **4** SP89

★★★**Marquess of Exeter** Main Rd Uppingham (0572) 822477

Charming 17th-century rural village inn with modern bedrooms in annexe.

Annexe: 15rm (11 4)(1fb) CTV in all bedrooms ® T S% sB&B £34—£39.50 dB&B £42—£53

40P Live music & dancing monthly xmas

International V S% *Lunch £5.50&alc Tea £1.20 Dinner £7.95&alc Wine £4.95 Last dinner 9.45pm

Credit cards [1] [2] [3] [5]

LYDFORD
Devon
Map **2** SX58

★★**Lydford House** (Guestaccom) (082282) 347

Closed Xmas Day & Boxing Day

Formerly the home of William Widgery, the Victorian artist, this hotel is set in three acres of grounds where the owners' daughter runs a riding school.

13rm (9 1)(3fb) CTV in all bedrooms ® sB&B £17 sB&B £18.50 dB&B £37

30P nc 5yrs

Lunch £7 Dinner £8&alc Wine £3.80 Last dinner 8.30pm

Credit cards [1] [2] [5] [V]

LYME REGIS
Dorset
Map **3** SY39
See also **Rousdon**

★★★**Alexandra** Pound St (02974) 2010

Closed 20 Dec—6 Feb

An 18th-century former residence of the Dowager Countess Poulett, with unrivalled views across the lawns to Lyme Bay.

26rm (18 2)(6fb) CTV in all bedrooms ® sB&B £21—£26 sB&B £23—£28 dB&B £40—£48 dB&B £40—£64

20P

English & French V Lunch £5.95—£6.25&alc Tea 60p—£1.75 High Tea £2.50 Dinner £10.50&alc Wine £4.75 Last dinner 8.30pm

Credit cards [1] [2] [3] [5]

★★★**Devon** Lyme Rd, Uplyme (02974) 3231 (Best Western)
(For full entry see Uplyme)

★★★*H* **Mariners** Silver St (02974) 2753 Telex no 46491

Closed Nov—Feb

17th-century coaching inn with pleasant atmosphere.

16rm (8 5)(1fb) CTV in all bedrooms ® available in bedrooms sB&B £23—£26 sB&B £26 dB&B £46 dB&B £46—£50

22P

English & Continental *Bar lunch £1.30—£2.60 Tea fr£2 Dinner £10.50 Wine £4.40 Last dinner 8.30pm

[V]

★★**Bay** Marine Pde (02974) 2059

Closed Dec—Feb

Gabled hotel with pleasant, attentive service and a sun terrace overlooking Lyme Bay and the Cobb.

21rm(9⇌3⋒)(3fb)®sB&B£17—£20 sB&B⇌⋒£19—£22 dB&B£34—£36 dB&B⇌⋒£38—£40 Ⓑ

##CTV 5P 20⛟

English & French V ♈ ☕ Lunch £4.50—£5.50 Tea 80p—£1.50 Dinner £8.50—£10 Wine £3.50 Last dinner 8.30pm

Credit card 3

★★**Buena Vista** Pound St (Inter Hotel) ☎(02974) 2494

Standing in an elevated position, the detached Regency house has some fine views of Lyme Bay and is within easy reach of the beach.

20rm(11⇌)(1fb) CTV in all bedrooms ®T sB&B£21—£29 sB&B⇌£21—£30 dB&B£40—£58 dB&B⇌£42—£60 Ⓑ

CTV 20P ❀ *xmas*

English & Continental V Wine £4.40 Last dinner 6pm

Credit cards 1 2 3 5 Ⓥ

Lyme Regis

★★**Dorset** Silver St ☎(02974) 2482

Closed Nov—Feb

Small, comfortable and friendly, the hotel provides good English food and extends a genuine welcome to guests.

12rm(1⇌7⋒)(2fb) CTV in all bedrooms ✱sB&B£11—£13.25 sB&B⇌⋒£12.30—£14.55 dB&B£22—£26.50 dB&B⇌⋒£24.60—£29.10 Ⓑ

13P

♈ ☕ ✱ Bar lunch £1—£3.50 Dinner £7.25 Wine £4.30 Last dinner 8pm

Credit cards 1 3

L

★★**Royal Lion** Broad St (ExecHotels) ☏(02974) 2768

Fine panelling and oak beams still exist in this 16th-century coaching inn.

22rm(14🛁8🚿)(4fb) 1⊟ CTV in all bedrooms ® *sB&B🛁🚿£19—£22 dB&B🛁🚿£38—£44 B

36P

V 🍷 Lunch £5alc Dinner £8.50&alc Wine £4 Last dinner 10pm

Credit cards 1 2 3 5 Ⓥ

Lyme Regis

★★**St Michael's** Pound St ☏(02974) 2503

A warm atmosphere and friendly service are features of this pleasant small hotel with comfortable lounges.

14rm(4🛁) ® *sB&B£16—£20 sB&B🛁£30—£38 dB&B£32—£40 dB&B🛁£35—£43 B

⊬ CTV 10P 🚗 *xmas*

🍷 ☕ *Bar lunch £1—£3 Tea 50p Dinner £6 Wine £4.50 Last dinner 7.30pm

Credit cards 1 3 5

★***Tudor House*** Church St ☏(02974) 2472

Closed mid Oct—mid Mar

Historic Elizabethan hotel with comfortable accommodation. Bar contains old water-well.

17rm(4🛁)(10fb)

CTV 12P 🏠

🍷 Last dinner 7.30pm

Credit card 3

L

✕✕***Drake's*** 14—15 Monmouth Rd ☎(02974) 2079

Food is not exclusively Italian at this town-centre ristorante, though the style of decor sets the Latin mood.

Closed Sun & Mon, & Oct—Thu before Etr Lunch not served

Italian 35 seats Last dinner 10pm

Credit cards [2] [3] [5]

LYMINGTON
Hampshire
Map **4** SZ39

★★★ *BL* **Passford House** Mount Pleasant (2m NW on Sway rd) ☎(0590) 682398 Telex no 47502

Colourful decor and cosy warmth bring to life this well-run hotel on the edge of the New Forest. Guests are accommodated in recently-refurbished, well-appointed bedrooms, and several recreational facilities are available.

54rm(34)(6fb) 1 CTV in all bedrooms ® **T** sB&B £40—£45 dB&B £66—£75

CTV 80P 4(charge) CFA & (heated) (hard) sauna bath solarium gymnasium croquet *xmas*

English & French Lunch fr£7.50&alc Tea £1.50—£3 Dinner fr£11.75&alc Wine £5.50 Last dinner 9pm

Credit cards [1] [2] [3] Ⓥ

Lyme Regis — Lympsham

★★★**Stanwell House** (Consort) ☎(0590) 77123 Telex no 477463

The cosy, attractive hotel provides well-appointed bedrooms and a good choice of honest, reliable cooking.

33rm(30)(4fb) 2 CTV in all bedrooms **T** sB&B £20—£23 sB&B £31—£39 dB&B £36—£38 dB&B £49—£58

English & French Lunch £7—£10 Tea 75p—£1 High Tea £5—£10 Dinner £10.75—£17 Wine £5.50 Last dinner 9.30pm

Credit cards [1] [2] [3] [5]

✕**Jarna Tandoori** 6 Queen St ☎(0590) 72603

Large picture tapestries hang on the walls of this small North Indian restaurant which specialises in Tandoori cuisine.

English & Indian **V** 50 seats S% ✱Lunch £4.25—£12.05&alc Dinner £4.25—£12.05 Wine £5.05 Last dinner mdnt

Credit cards [1] [2] [3] [5]

✕**Limpets** 9 Gosport St ☎(0590) 75595

Bistro style restaurant with pine decor.

Closed Sun & Mon (Oct—May) & Dec, Lunch not served

Continental 45 seats Dinner £14alc Wine £5.50 Last dinner 10.30pm

Credit cards [1] [2]

LYMM
Cheshire
Map **7** SJ68

★★★**Lymm** Whitbarrow Rd (De Vere) ☎(092575) 2233 Telex no 629455

Modern well furnished bedrooms are a feature of this hotel conveniently situated near the M6 and Manchester airport.

69 CTV in all bedrooms ® **T** S% sB&B £49.50—£52 dB&B £59—£64

☾ ### 160P CFA

French **V** S% Lunch £10.50—£11 Tea 68—85p Dinner £10.50—£11 Wine £6.50 Last dinner 10pm

Credit cards [1] [2] [3] [5]

LYMPSHAM
Avon
Map **3** ST35

★★ *HL* ***Batch Farm Country*** ☎ Edingworth (093472) 371

This small, peaceful, and personally-run hotel is also a working farm. Bedrooms, →

L

bar and lounge are comfortable, and the food is good.

10rm(3)(5fb)

CTV 50P billiards

V Last dinner 8pm

Credit cards 1 3

See advertisement under Weston-super-Mare

LYNDHURST
Hampshire
Map **4** SU30

★★★**Crown** High St (Best Western)
(042128) 2722

The elegant, Edwardian hotel, standing at the centre of the New Forest's principal village, offers modern comfort with traditional service.

43(4fb) 1 CTV in all bedrooms ® S% sB&B£37—£42.50 dB&B£56—£61

Lift (CTV 50P 9 pool table CFA *xmas*

English & French V S% *Lunch £9.25&alc Tea 70p alc Dinner fr£9.25&alc Wine £6.50 Last dinner 9.30pm

Credit cards 1 2 3 5 V

★★★**Lyndhurst Park** High St (Forest Dale) (042128) 2823 Telex no 477802

Georgian hotel with a modern extension and attractive garden.

L

Lympsham — Lyndhurst

59 in 2 bedrooms CTV in all bedrooms ® T sB&B£34—£40 dB&B£46—£48

Lift (100P CFA (heated) (hard) snooker Live music and dancing Sat *xmas*

V Bar lunch 95p—£2.50 Tea fr75p Dinner £10.45—£15.45 Wine £4.75 Last dinner 10pm

Credit cards 1 2 3 5

★★★ *L* **Parkhill** Beaulieu Rd
(042128) 2944

Closed 1st 2 wks Jan

Under the personal direction of Mr and Mrs Paul Ames, this elegant and finely-furnished Georgian mansion maintains an impressive standard of cuisine backed by agreeable service.

16rm(14 2) Annexe: 6(2fb) 1 CTV in all bedrooms ® T sB&B£32 dB&B£47—£65

50P (heated) *xmas*

French Lunch £8.75&alc Dinner £13.25&alc Wine £6.30 Last dinner 9pm

Credit cards 1 2 3 4 5 V

★★**Evergreens** Romsey Rd
(042 128) 2175

Small holiday hotel with attractive garden. Vegetable garden supplies kitchen.

20rm(3 10)(1fb) 1 ® TV available in bedrooms S% sB&B£18—£22 sB&B£22—£25 dB&Bfr£32 dB&B£40—£55

34P 3 (heated) Disco Sat in winter *xmas*

English & Continental V S% Lunch £2.50—£5.50 Tea £1.60—£2.50 Dinner fr£8.75&alc Wine £5.95 Last dinner 9pm

★★**Forest Point** Romsey Rd
(042128) 2420

This small, personally-managed hotel and restaurant offers warm hospitality, accommodation in tasteful, compact bedrooms, and good food.

9rm(4 3)(2fb) CTV in all bedrooms ® *sB&B£23 dB&B£37

CTV P *xmas*

English & French *Bar lunch £2 Tea £1.75 Dinner £7.50&alc Last dinner 9pm

Credit cards 1 2 3 4 5

★★ *L* ***Pikes Hill Forest Lodge*** Pikes Hill, Romsey Rd (042 128) 3677

Situated on the edge of the town, this hotel is one of the best in the area. Many bedrooms have now undergone refurbishment, and reception is enlarged.

The smart restaurant and comfortable lounges are in keeping with the rest of the establishment.

20rm(11➡4⛆)(2fb)1⊠CTV in all bedrooms ®Ƀ

CTV 45P ✿ ⛆ (heated) Live music & dancing Wed, Fri & Sat (in season) ♿ *xmas*

♔International **V** ♡ ☕ Last dinner 9.30pm

Credit cards [2] [3] [5]

Lyndhurst — Lynmouth

LYNMOUTH
Devon
Map **3** SS74
See also **Lynton**

★★★**Tors** ☎ Lynton (0598) 53236

Closed early Nov—Feb

Comfortable hotel in five acres of grounds, set on a hill above Lynmouth. There are fine views over the bay.

39rm(32➡)(1fb) CTV in 32 bedrooms ® **T** S% ✱sB&B£15.50—£16.50 sB&B➡£22—£26.50 dB&B£31—£33 dB&B➡£44—£53 Ƀ

Lift CTV 40P CFA ✿ ⛆ (heated) table tennis pool table

♡ ☕ S% ✱Lunch £16alc Tea 70p—£1.85 Dinner £10.25&alc Wine £5.20 Last dinner 9pm

Credit cards [1] [2] [3] [5]

★★**Bath** Sea Front (Exec Hotel) ☎ Lynton (0598) 52238

Closed Nov—Feb RS Mar

Traditional, family-run hotel situated in the centre of the village. →

24rm(12🛁1🚿)(8fb) CTV in 4 bedrooms ® S% sB&B£11.50—£18 sB&B🛁🚿£20 dB&B£23—£36 dB&B🛁🚿£40 B

CTV 13P 4🚗(75p per night)

English & French V 🍷 ☕ S% Lunch fr£5 Tea fr60p Dinner fr£9 Wine £4.50 Last dinner 8.30pm

Credit cards 1 2 3 5 Ⓥ

★★🌲**Beacon** Countisbury Hill ☎ Lynton (0598) 53268

Closed Nov—Feb

This small holiday hotel has magnificent views over Lynmouth.

7rm(2🛁3🚿) TV in all bedrooms ✈ ✱sB&B£14.25—£15.50 sB&B🛁🚿£14.75—£16 dB&B£24.50—£27 dB&B🛁🚿£27—£31 B

10P 🚫 ✿ nc 12yrs

English & Continental V 🍷 ☕ ✱Lunch £4.75 Tea 75p—£1.20 Dinner £6.75—£8.75 Wine £4.20 Last dinner 8pm

★*H* ***Bonnicott*** Watersmeet Rd ☎ (0598) 53346

Relaxed, comfortable Victorian rectory with friendly, attentive service and well cooked and presented food.

7rm(1🚿) B

CTV P 🚫 *xmas*

V 🍷 ☕ Last dinner 9.30pm

Credit cards 1 3

Lynmouth — Lynton

★**Rising Sun** The Harbour ☎ Lynton (0598) 53223

Closed 6 Dec—7 Feb

Stone built inn, set into the hill beside the harbour.

17rm(3🛁12🚿)(1fb) 1🛏 CTV in all bedrooms ® S% sB&B£17—£27 sB&B🛁🚿£21.50—£27 dB&B£34—£54 dB&B🛁🚿£43—£54 B

CTV P 🚫 ✿ 🐟 ♘

English & French V 🍷 Lunch £2.50—£5.50 Dinner £9.50&alc Wine £4.95 Last dinner 9pm

Credit cards 1 3

★**Rock House** ☎ Lynton (0598) 53508

A busy tea garden is one of the attractions of this delightful little Georgian hotel. Overlooking the harbour, it occupies a unique position beside the River Lyn, the fore-shore and the Manor Gardens.

7rm(1🛁2🚿)(1fb) 1🛏 CTV in 3 bedrooms ® sB&B£16 sB&B🛁🚿£18.50 dB&B£32 dB&B🛁🚿£37 B

CTV 7P 🚫 ✿ *xmas*

English & French V 🍷 ☕ Bar lunch £3.50—£5 Tea 55p Dinner £9&alc Wine £4.50 Last dinner 8.45pm

Credit cards 1 2 3 5 Ⓥ

★**Shelley's Cottage** Watersmeet Rd ☎ Lynton (0598) 53219

Closed Nov—Feb RS Mar

The origin of this hotel's name is that Shelley wrote part of 'Queen Mab' here in 1812.

13rm(3fb) ® in 10 bedrooms sB&B£11—£14 dB&B£22—£27 B

CTV P nc 4yrus

🍷 ☕ Bar lunch 70p—£2.75 Tea £1.25 Dinner £4.50&alc Wine £4.75 Last dinner 9pm

LYNTON

Devon

Map **3** SS74

See also **Lynmouth**

★★★*L* **Lynton Cottage** North Walk ☎ (0598) 52342

Closed Jan & Feb

The attractive, personally-run, holiday hotel occupies an elevated position commanding superb views and provides a warm, friendly atmosphere.

21rm(9🛁5🚿)(3fb) 1🛏 CTV in all bedrooms **T** sB&B£15—£18 sB&B🛁🚿£18—£22 dB&B£30—£36 dB&B🛁🚿£50—£60 B

CTV 26P 🚫 ✿ *xmas*

L

Cosmopolitan V Bar lunch £1.75—£7&alc Tea fr£1.50 Dinner fr£9.25&alc Wine £3.95 Last dinner 8.45pm

Credit cards 1 2 3 5 V

★★**Crown** Sinai Hill (Inter Hotel) ☎(0598) 52253

Closed Jan

A well-appointed inn, centrally situated and convenient for touring the Exmoor countryside and coastline.

16rm(15→1⋔)(5fb) 5 CTV in all bedrooms ® ✱ sB&B→⋔£20—£22.25 dB&B→⋔£36—£40.50 B

25P *xmas*

English & French V ✱ Bar lunch £1—£2.95 Dinner fr£8.95&alc Wine £6.45 Last dinner 8.30pm

Credit cards 1 2 3 5

★★**Hewitts** North Walk ☎(0598) 52293 Telex no 265871 (WQQ075)

Closed Jan

Twenty-seven acres of woodland surround this small Victorian mansion, with its splendid, galleried lounge and a restaurant offering imaginative menus.

12rm(9→1⋔)(2fb) 1 CTV in all bedrooms T S% ✱ sB&B£13—£19 sB&B→⋔£13—£19 dB&B£26—£39 dB&B→⋔£26—£39 B

CTV 10P *xmas*

Lynton

English & French V S% ✱ Bar lunch £1.50—£5.50 Tea £1.50—£2.50 Dinner £10—£14 Wine £4.50 Last dinner 9.30pm

Credit cards 1 2 3 5

★★***Rockvale*** Lee Rd ☎(0598) 52279

Closed Nov—Feb

Former Bristol merchant's holiday home, the hotel has been modernised and offers comfortable accommodation.

9rm(5→2⋔)(2fb) 1 CTV in all bedrooms ® B

CTV 10P

Last dinner 7.30pm

★★**Sandrock** Longmead ☎(0598) 53307

Closed Dec & Jan

Comfortable touring holiday hotel, close to the town centre.

10rm(4→2⋔)(3fb) CTV in all bedrooms ® sB&B£10.50—£12.50 sB&B→⋔£13.50—£16 dB&B£23—£27 dB&B→⋔£25—£30 B

CTV 9P

✱ Bar lunch fr£1.50 Dinner £7.50—£10.50 Wine £3 Last dinner 7.45pm

Credit cards 1 2 3 V

★**Castle Hill House Hotel & Restaurant** Castle Hill ☎(0598) 52291

Closed 2 Nov—28 Feb

Small, holiday hotel offering imaginatively cooked meals.

9rm(7→2⋔)(1fb) in 4 bedrooms CTV in all bedrooms ® T sB&B→⋔£14—£19 dB&B→⋔£28—£30 B

nc5yrs

V Lunch £7.50—£8.50&alc Tea fr£1 Dinner £7.50—£8.50&alc Wine £4.95 Last dinner 10pm

Credit cards 1 3 V

★*B* ***Chough's Nest*** North Walk ☎(0598) 53315

Closed mid Oct—Etr

Comfortable holiday hotel, situated high above the bay.

12rm(7→5⋔)(2fb) 2 B

CTV nc2yrs

V Last dinner 8.30pm

★**Combe Park** Hillsford Bridge ☎(0598) 52356

Closed Jan—mid Feb RS Nov & Dec mid Feb & Mar →

L

Former hunting lodge set in six acres of woodland.
9rm(6🛁2🚿)(3fb) ® *sB&B🛁🚿£18.50 dB&B🛁🚿£31 B
CTV 11P nc 12 yrs *xmas*
*Tea fr£1.40 Dinner fr£10.50 Wine £4.25 Last dinner 7.30pm

★**Fairholme** North Walk ☎(0598) 52263
Closed Oct—Mar
The small hotel stands in a breathtaking position overlooking the Bristol Channel.
12rm(6🛁1🚿)(1fb) CTV available in bedrooms sB&B£12 sB&B🛁🚿£13 dB&B£24 dB&B🛁🚿£26
CTV 12P (heated)
Bar lunch £1.30—£1.90 Tea 80p—£1.25 Dinner £6.50 Wine £4.75 Last dinner 7.30pm

★**Neubia House** Lydiate Ln (Guestaccom) ☎(0598) 52309
Closed 1 Dec—31 Jan
Small, quiet, friendly, well appointed hotel specialising in cordon-bleu food.
12rm(9🛁3🚿)(3fb) CTV in all bedrooms ® sB&B🛁🚿£15.25—£16.35 dB&B🛁🚿£30.50—£32.70 B
14P
V Bar lunch £2.50—£4.50 Dinner £8 Wine £4.50 Last dinner 7.30pm
Ⓥ

Lynton — Lytham St Annes

★***North Cliff*** North Walk ☎(0598) 52357
Closed Nov—Feb
Family run hotel with relaxed atmosphere and good views.
18rm(5🛁3🚿)(2fb) ®
CTV 13P
Last dinner 7.30pm

★*L* **Seawood** North Walk ☎(0598) 52272
Closed early Nov—end Mar
Overlooking the sea from its rising, wooded grounds, this pink-painted house offers quiet, comfortable accommodation, the bedrooms having good facilities.
12🛁🚿(1fb) 4 CTV in all bedrooms ® sB&B🛁🚿£12—£14.50 dB&B🛁🚿£24—£29 B
CTV 10P
English & Continental Bar lunch £2.50 Dinner £8.50 Wine £4.50 Last dinner 7.30pm
Ⓥ

LYTHAM ST ANNES
Lancashire
Map **7** SD32

★★★★**Clifton Arms** West Beach, Lytham (Whitbread) ☎(0253) 739898 Telex no 677463
Comfortable, old established hotel overlooking green and Ribble estuary.
45rm(41🛁4🚿) 1 CTV in all bedrooms ® **T** sB&B🛁🚿£45 dB&B🛁🚿£50—£70 B
Lift ☾ 50P CFA sauna bath solarium Live music & dancing nightly *xmas*
English & French Lunch £6.95—£8.50&alc Tea £1 Dinner £9.50—£10.50&alc Wine £4.95 Last dinner 10pm
Credit cards 1 2 3 5

★★★*B* **Grand** South Prom, St Annes ☎(0253) 721288
Grand Edwardian building now modernised throughout, situated on the sea front.
40🛁🚿(5fb) in 2 bedrooms CTV in all bedrooms ® **T** (ex guide dogs) *sB&B🛁🚿£40—£43 dB&B🛁🚿£50—£56 B
Lift ☾ 80P CFA *xmas*
International **V** *Lunch £5.75&alc Tea 85p High Tea £2.75 Dinner £9.25&alc Wine £4.45 Last dinner 10pm
Credit cards 1 2 3 5

★★**Chadwick** South Prom, St Annes ☎(0253) 720061

The large, family-run hotel with a sea-front location has a health complex with an Ancient Greek theme.

70rm(61⇌9⋔)(30fb) 2⊟ CTV in all bedrooms **T** ✗ sB&B⇌⋔£18—£20 dB&B⇌⋔£29—£32 **B**

Lift ☾ CTV 40P 1⌂ CFA ⊟ (heated) sauna bath solarium Disco Sat Live music and dancing Sat ♿ *xmas*

✈ ☕ ✂ Lunch £3.95—£4.20 Tea 60p—£2 Dinner £7.40—£7.90 Wine £4.40 Last dinner 8.15pm

Credit cards [1] [2] [3] [5] Ⓥ

★★**Fernlea** 15 South Prom, St Annes ☎(0253) 726726 Telex no 677150

Modern, sea-front hotel with extensive leisure facilities.

95⇌(35fb) CTV in all bedrooms **T** ✗ ✱sB&B⇌£22.75—£25 dB&B⇌£45 **B**

Lift ☾ CTV 50P CFA ⊟ (heated) squash snooker sauna bath solarium gymnasium *xmas*

English & French **V** ✈ ☕ ✱Lunch £6—£10 Tea 60p—£3.50 High Tea £1.25—£4.50 Dinner £9—£12.50 Wine £4.50 Last dinner 8pm

Credit cards [1] [2] [3] [5] Ⓥ

Lytham St Annes

★★***New Glendower*** North Prom, St Annes ☎(0253) 723241

Large, stone building overlooking the sea front.

68rm(65⇌)(6fb) CTV in 6 bedrooms **B**

☾ CTV 50P ⊟ (heated)

✈ ☕ Last dinner 8pm

Credit cards [1] [3]

★★**St Ives** 7—9 South Prom, St Annes ☎(0253) 720011

Modern, family hotel overlooking gardens, provides good leisure facilities.

73rm(65⇌2⋔)(44fb) CTV in all bedrooms **T** ✗ sB&B£19 sB&B⇌⋔£21 dB&B£32 dB&B⇌⋔£36 **B**

☾ # CTV 100P CFA ⊟ (heated) sauna bath solarium Live music & dancing 6 nights wkly (in summer) Cabaret wkly *xmas*

English & Continental **V** ✈ ☕ Lunch £3.75—£5 Tea 50p High Tea £5—£7.50 Dinner £7.50&alc Wine £4.75 Last dinner 9.30pm

Credit cards [1] [3]

See advertisement on page 494

★★**Savoy** 314 Clifton Drive North, St Annes ☎(0253) 728441

Modern, family-owned hotel with good furnishings throughout.

14⇌(6fb) 1⊟ CTV in all bedrooms ® ✱sB&B⇌£11.50—£14.50 dB&B⇌£23—£29 **B**

Lift CTV 14P solarium Disco wkly Live music & dancing wkly *xmas*

English & Continental **V** ✈ ☕ ✱Lunch £4&alc Tea £1.25 High Tea £3.50 Dinner £6.95&alc Wine £3.80 Last dinner 8pm

Credit cards [1] [2] [3] [5] Ⓥ

See advertisement on page 494

★**Carlton** 61 South Prom, St Annes ☎(0253) 721036

Closed Nov—Feb

Pleasant, family-run hotel overlooking the promenade gardens.

22rm(3⇌4⋔)(7fb) ® ✗ sB&B£13.80—£15 sB&B⇌⋔£15 dB&B£29—£30 dB&B⇌⋔£30 **B**

CTV 12P

English & Continental **V** ✂ Bar lunch 80p—£2 Dinner £7 Last dinner 7pm

Credit card [1]

★**Lindum** 63—67 South Prom, St Annes ☎(0253) 721534

Conveniently situated sea-front hotel. →

80rm(67⇝7⋒)(24fb) CTV in all bedrooms ®sB&B£15—£16 sB&B⇝⋒£16—£18 dB&B£26—£28 dB&B⇝⋒£28—£30 B

Lift ☾ CTV 20P CFA sauna bath solarium *xmas*

Bar lunch 75p—£2 Tea 60p Dinner £6.25—£6.95 Wine £5 Last dinner 7pm

Credit cards 1 2 3 V

MACCLESFIELD
Cheshire
Map **7** SJ97
See also **Bollington**

★**Ellesmere** Buxton Rd ☎ (0625) 23791

This very friendly and welcoming hotel is a traditional Cheshire half-timbered house standing in its own attractive grounds.

9rm(3⇝1⋒)(1fb) 1 CTV in 7 bedrooms TV in 2 bedrooms ®✱sB&B£18—£20 sB&B⇝⋒£25—£27.50 dB&B£27—£30 dB&B⇝⋒£33—£36 B

30P

International **V** ✱Lunch £3.25—£4.50 Tea 90p—£2.50 High Tea £2.50—£3.50 Dinner £7.25—£8.75 Wine £4.20 Last dinner 8.30pm

Credit cards 1 2 3 V

✕***Da Topo Gigio*** 15 Church St ☎ (0625) 22231

Friendly, informal restaurant with an emphasis on colourful and tasty Italian dishes.

Closed Sun, Mon & Aug

L

English, French & Italian **V** 59 seats Last dinner 10.30pm

Credit card 1

✕**Oliver's Bistro** 101 Chestergate ☎ (0625) 32003

The informal, bistro-style restaurant is set in a 400-year-old building at the centre of the town, its atmosphere enhanced by low beams, stone floors and rough-cast walls. A blackboard displays the menu of French cuisine, and food is well cooked, making good use of fresh raw ingredients. Service is informal and friendly.

French **V** 70 seats S% Lunch £2.25—£5.50&alc Dinner £2.75—£9&alc Wine £4.95 Last dinner 10pm

Credit cards 1 2 3

MACDUFF
Grampian *Banffshire*
Map **15** NJ76

★★**Deveron House** 25 Union Rd ☎ (0261) 32309

A compact and well modernised hotel situated by the harbour.

17rm(7⇝7⋒)(4fb) CTV in all bedrooms ® sB&B£16—£20 sB&B⇝⋒£18—£25 dB&B£26—£35 dB&B⇝⋒£30—£40 B

CTV 15P Disco Fri & Sat

V Lunch £4—£5&alc High Tea £3—£5.50 Dinner fr£8&alc Wine £5 Last dinner 9pm

Credit cards 1 2 3 5 V

★★**Fife Arms** Shore St (Inter Hotel/Exec Hotel) ☎ (0261) 32408

Situated in the town centre overlooking the harbour.

22rm(12⇝8⋒)(3fb) CTV in all bedrooms ®**T** S% sB&B£19 sB&B⇝⋒£21—£24.50 dB&B£28 dB&B⇝⋒£32—£39 B

☾ CTV P snooker sauna bath solarium gymnasium *xmas*

V Bar lunch £2.50—£5&alc Tea 50p—£1 High Tea £2.45—£4.95 Dinner £8.65&alc Wine £4.60 Last dinner 9pm

Credit cards 1 2 3 4 5 V

MACHYNLLETH
Powys
Map **6** SH70

★★*L* **Plas Dolguog** ☎ (0654) 2244

Set alongside the River Dulas, this 17th-century gentleman's residence has been carefully modernised to provide elegant and comfortable accommodation.

7rm(3⇝1⋒)(2fb) CTV available in bedrooms ®✱ sB&B£25 sB&B⇝⋒£30—£35 dB&B£35 dB&B⇝⋒£42—£48 B

20P ✿

V Tea fr£1.40 Dinner fr£7.90alc Wine £4.50 Last dinner 9pm

Credit cards 1 3 V

★★**Wynnstay** Maengwyn St (Trusthouse Forte) ☎ (0654) 2941

Former coaching inn situated in the centre of this market town.

26rm(20 1) CTV in all bedrooms ® sB&B£36.50 sB&B £44.50 dB&B£49.50 dB&B £57.50

42P

Last dinner 8.30pm

Credit cards 1 2 3 4 5

MADINGLEY
Cambridgeshire
Map **5** TL36

✕✕**Three Horseshoes** High St ☎ (0954) 210221

Though situated only a few miles from Cambridge, this is a picture-postcard, thatched, village inn, its setting park-like and its interior beamed and panelled. Food is mainly British, with a French country influence, and game figures prominently.

English & French **V** 32 seats Lunch £14alc Dinner £15.95alc Wine £5.95 Last dinner 10pm 70P

Credit cards 1 2 3 5

MAIDENCOMBE
Devon
See under **Torquay**

MAIDENHEAD
Berkshire
Map **4** SU88

★★★★**Fredrick's** Shoppenhangers Rd ☎ (0628) 35934 Telex no 849966

Herr Lösel continues to upgrade the hotel, offering beautifully-appointed bedrooms and willing service. His strong views on food are reflected in the consistently high standards of cuisine.

38rm(28 10)(5fb) CTV in all bedrooms **T**
*sB&B £54.50—£78 dB&B £78—£85

90P ✿

English & French **V** *Lunch fr£18.50&alc Tea £1.30 Dinner £25.50alc Wine £8.50 Last dinner 9.45pm

Credit cards 1 2 3 5

★★★**Thames Riviera** At the Bridge ☎ (0628) 74057

The riverside hotel has the distinctive Jerome's Restaurant on the ground floor, in addition to a cocktail bar and small, modern, coffee shop. Efficient and extensive services are provided, with professional standards of management.

35rm(29 6)(3fb) 1 CTV in all bedrooms ® **T** *sB £40—£45 dB £50—£55 (room only)

P *xmas*

English & French *Lunch £7.50&alc Tea £2.50 High Tea £4 Dinner £9.75&alc Wine £6 Last dinner 10pm

Credit cards 1 2 3 4 5

✕✕✕**Shoppenhangers Manor** Manor Ln ☎ (0628) 23444 Telex no 847502

Closed Sun & 26 Dec—3 Jan Lunch not served Sat

This elegantly-furnished, oak-panelled restaurant is situated in a 15th century manor house which has been internally restored to retain a warm atmosphere. Standing on the outskirts of the town, it provides an ideal venue for business or private parties. Cuisine is French (the à la carte menu being particularly enterprising), the wine list interesting, and service by continental staff attentive and courteous.

French 48 seats S% Lunch fr£18.95&alc Dinner fr£18.95&alc Wine £9.50 Last dinner 10.30pm 30P Live music Fri & Sat

Credit cards 1 2 3 4 5

MAIDSTONE
Kent
Map **5** TQ75

★★★**Larkfield** London Rd ☎ West Malling (0732) 846858

(For full entry see Larkfield)

★★**Boxley House** Boxley Rd, Boxley (3m N between A249 & A229) (Exec Hotel) ☎ (0622) 52226

Lovely 17th-century house in spacious parkland. Restaurant with minstrel's gallery features speciality evenings.

11rm(5 6) Annexe: 7rm(5 2)(3fb) 2 CTV in all bedrooms ® **T** S% *sB&B £29 dB&B £39

150P ✿ (heated) Disco Mon & Thu Live music and dancing Sat

English & French **V** *Lunch £6.50—£10.50 Tea fr£2.50 Dinner £9.50—£15.50 Wine £4.80 Last dinner 9pm

Credit cards 1 2 3 4 5

★★**Grange Moor** St Michael's Rd (off A26) ☎ (0622) 677623

Closed 26 & 27 Dec

Friendly family run hotel with tasteful, compact bedrooms and Tudor style restaurant. →

M

37rm(34🚿)(4fb)CTV in all bedrooms ® T sB&B£18—£24 sB&B🚿£26—£29 dB&B£28—£30 dB&B🚿£36—£40 B

50P

English & French V ☕ Lunch £6.50—£7&alc Tea 55—60p Dinner £6.50—£7&alc Wine £5.40 Last dinner 10pm

Credit cards [1] [3]

MALDON
Essex
Map **5** TL80

★★**Blue Boar** Silver St (Trusthouse Forte) ☎ (0621) 52681

An ancient inn, with pleasant well-equipped bedrooms and small public areas.

18🛁 Annexe: 5🛁 CTV in all bedrooms ® sB&B🛁£44.50 dB&B🛁£59.50 B

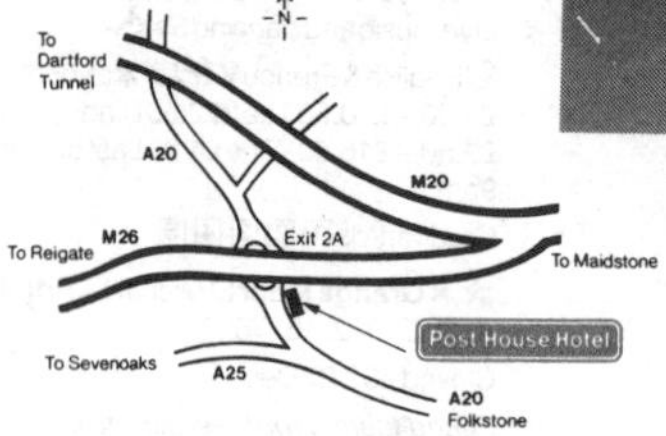

43P *xmas*

☕ Last dinner 9.30pm

Credit cards [1] [2] [3] [4] [5]

★**Benbridge** The Square, Heybridge ☎ (0621) 57666

Small proprietor run hotel offering modern accommodation and sound food.

12rm(6🚿)(2fb) CTV in all bedrooms ® sB&B£20—£23.50 sB&B🚿£20—£23.50 dB&B£29.50—£33 dB&B🚿£29.50—£33 B

40P

V ☕ ✻ Lunch £12.50alc Tea fr£2 Dinner £12.50alc Wine £4.50 Last dinner 9.30pm

Credit cards [1] [2] [3] [5] Ⓥ

M

✕Francine's 1A High St ☎ (0621) 56605

A short French menu of imaginative dishes is offered by this very small, quality restaurant, where fresh ingredients are used with skill to provide consistently good meals. The friendly young staff provide simple but efficient service and Francine's is very popular with local residents.

Closed Sun, Mon, 1 wk Xmas, 1 wk spring, 2 wks Aug Lunch by reservation only

French **V** 24 seats Dinner £14.50alc Wine £5.40 Last dinner 9.15pm 8P

Credit cards 1 3

MALHAM

North Yorkshire
Map **7** SD96

★Buck Inn ☎ Airton (07293) 317

Imposing stone inn in village centre.

10rm(1 3)(4fb) TV in 1 bedroom ® *sB&B£12.50—£16 sB&B £15.50—£19.50 dB&B£25—£32 dB&B £28—£35

CTV 50P *xmas*

V *Bar lunch £1.85—£2.50&alc Dinner £6.50 Wine £4.50 Last dinner 9.30pm

MALLAIG

Highland *Inverness-shire*
Map **13** NM69

★★Marine ☎ (0687) 2217

RS Nov—Mar

Close to the harbour and the railway station.

21rm(6)(2fb) ® sB&Bfr£13 sB&B fr£16 dB&Bfr£22 dB&B fr£26

CTV 6P

Bar lunch £3.95alc Tea 45palc Dinner £7.50alc Wine £3.50 Last dinner 8pm

Credit cards 2 3

★★West Highland ☎ (0687) 2210

Closed 10 Oct—20 Aprr

Large stone building overlooking the fishing port and the islands of Rhum, Eigg & Skye.

26rm(12)(6fb) ® sB&B£15—£18 dB&B£30—£34 dB&B £32—£38

CTV 30P

V Lunch £5.50 Tea £1.50 Dinner fr£9 Wine £2.50 Last dinner 8.30pm

Credit cards 1 2 3 4 5 Ⓥ

MALLWYD

Gwynedd
Map **6** SH81

★Brigand's Inn ☎ Dinas Mawddwy (06504) 208

Closed Jan

15th-century coaching inn with good atmosphere. A popular fishing hotel.

12rm(3)(1fb) ® *sB&B£14.95—£17.95 sB&B fr£17.95 dB&Bfr£29.90 dB&B fr£35.90

CTV 70P 2

V *Lunch fr£3.75 Tea fr£1.50 Dinner £6.50—£8.95&alc Wine £3.95 Last dinner 8.45pm

Credit cards 1 3 Ⓥ

MALMESBURY

Wiltshire
Map **3** ST98

★★★H Old Bell Abbey Row (Best Western/Exec Hotel) ☎ (06662) 2344 due to change to (0666) 822344

Comfortable relaxing hotel with well-appointed restaurant and attentive staff.

19rm(15 4)(2fb) 1 CTV in all bedrooms ® **T** sB&B £28.50—£43.50 dB&B £49.50—£57.50

25P 1 (£2 per night) table tennis Live music & dancing Sat monthly *xmas*

English & French **V** Lunch £7—£8.50&alc Tea £1—£2.50 Dinner £15&alc Wine £6.50 Last dinner 9.30pm

Credit cards 1 2 3 5 Ⓥ

★★★ BL Whatley Manor Easton Grey ☎ (06662) 2888 Telex no 449380

Finely restored country manor house with large comfortable rooms and charming courteous staff.

15 Annexe: 10(2fb) 1 CTV in all bedrooms ® in 10 bedrooms **T** *sB&B £44.50—£49.50 dB&B £62—£72

60P (heated) (hard) croquet *xmas*

English & Continental **V** *Lunch fr£8.50 Tea fr£2 Dinner fr£15 Wine £7.25 Last dinner 9pm

Credit cards 1 2 3 5

See advertisement on page 498

MALTON

North Yorkshire
Map **8** SE77

★★Green Man Market St ☎ (0653) 2662

Two ancient inns have been combined into this hotel, which stands at the centre of the market town. The beamed inglenook lounge retains its original character, whilst cosy, well-fitted bedrooms provide modern comforts. A good range of bar meals is always available, and simple, uncomplicated cooking is the norm in the restaurant.

25rm(3 12)(3fb) CTV in all bedrooms ® *sB&B£17—£19.50 sB&B £19.50 dB&B£28.50 dB&B £32

CTV 50P 6 (£1 per night)

V *Lunch £4.75—£5.95 Tea 60p—£2.75 High Tea £1.50—£7 Dinner £8.50 Wine £4.50 Last dinner 9.30pm

Credit cards 1 2 3

★★Talbot Yorkersgate (Trusthouse Forte) ☎ (0653) 4031

This impressive, Georgian, stone-built mansion stands on the eastern side of the town, overlooking the valley of the River Derwent. There is a magnificent staircase of the period, with a matching lounge of some elegance, although the bar is fairly mundane. Accommodation is spacious, the restaurant is attractive, and there are large gardens.

23rm(7)(1fb) CTV in all bedrooms ® sB&B£39.50 sB&B £47.50 dB&B£53.90 dB&B £61.50

CTV 20P *xmas*

Last dinner 9pm

Credit cards 1 2 3 4 5

★Wentworth Arms Town St, Old Malton ☎ (0653) 2618

Closed Xmas

Former 17th-century coaching inn.

7rm CTV in 2 bedrooms ® sB&B£13—£14 dB&B£26—£28

30P nc6yrs

Lunch £4alc Tea £2.50alc High Tea £5alc Dinner £7alc Wine £3.50 Last dinner 8.45pm

Credit card 3

MALVERN

Hereford & Worcester
Map **3** SO74

★★★Abbey Abbey Rd (De Vere) ☎ (06845) 3325 Telex no 335008

Imposing, creeper-clad, Gothic-style mansion with a modern wing, catering mainly for a commercial clientele.

105rm(84 21)(4fb) 1 CTV in all bedrooms ® **T** sB&B fr£42 dB&B fr£62

Lift ☾ 120P CFA

*Lunch fr£8&alc Tea fr£1 Dinner fr£9.50&alc Wine £5.75 Last dinner 8.30pm

Credit cards 1 2 3 5

★★★Colwall Park Colwall (3m SW B4218) (Inter Hotel) ☎ (0684) 40206 Telex no 335626

Charming hotel with pleasant gardens at foot of the Malvern Hills.

20rm(16 4)(2fb) CTV in all bedrooms ® **T** sB&B £28.50 dB&B £47.50

50P *xmas*

V Lunch £7.50 Tea £1.75—£2.75 Dinner £10.95—£13.50 Wine £4.75 Last dinner 9.30pm

Credit cards 1 2 3 Ⓥ

★★★ L Cottage in the Wood Holywell Rd, Malvern Wells (3m S A449) (Consort) ☎ (06845) 3487

Closed Xmas wk

Impressive, comfortable, country hotel nestling in the Malvern Hills. →

M

8 Annexe: 12 3 CTV in all bedrooms ® in 12 bedrooms T sB&B fr£42 dB&B £57.50—£82 Continental breakfast B

30P

V Lunch £7—£8.50 Tea 80p—£2.50 High Tea fr£2.50 Dinner £14.50—£25 Wine £5.50 Last dinner 9pm

Credit cards 1 3 V

★★★**Foley Arms** (Best Western) ☎ (06845) 3397 Telex no 437269

Popular, family run, town centre hotel with comfortable lounge overlooking River Severn.

Malvern

26rm(19 7)(1fb) 1 in 2 bedrooms CTV in all bedrooms ® T sB&B £33—£38.50 dB&B £52—£58.50 B

50P 4 CFA

English & French V S% Lunch £7.50—£9&alc Tea £1.20 Dinner £7.50—£9&alc Wine £3.95 Last dinner 9.15pm

Credit cards 1 2 3 4 5 V

★★**Broomhill** West Malvern Rd, West Malvern (2m W B4232) ☎ (06845) 64367

Closed Nov—Feb

Three-storey Victorian house with magnificent views.

10rm(2 2) CTV available in bedrooms ® *sB&B £15.50 dB&B £28 dB&B £32 B

CTV 10P nc5yrs

V *Bar lunch £2.50 Tea 45p Dinner £7 Wine £3.95 Last dinner 7pm

V

★★*H* **Cotford** 51 Graham Rd ☎ (06845) 2427

Closed 24 Dec—12 Jan

Comfortable, family-run hotel situated in a quiet road leading to the town centre.

14rm(7⇌)(2fb) CTV in all bedrooms ® S% sB&Bfr£16 sB&B⇌fr£21 dB&Bfr£33 dB&B⇌fr£37 B

10P ❁

V ♔ ☕ ⚡ Lunch fr£7.50 Tea fr£4 Dinner fr£9 Wine £5.50 Last dinner 9pm

Credit cards 1 3

★★**Essington** Holywell Rd, Malvern Wells (3m S A449) ☎ (06845) 61177

Small, family run hotel with 2 acres terraced gardens, offering personal service and home cooking.

10rm(8⇌2⋔)(2fb) 1⊟ CTV in all bedrooms ® sB&B⇌⋔£19—£22 dB&B⇌⋔£38—£44 B

30P ⇌ ❁ *xmas*

♔ Bar lunch £3.50alc Dinner £9.75—£11.75 Wine £5.50 Last dinner 8.15pm

Credit cards 1 3

★★ **Holdfast Cottage** Welland (4m SE) (Hotel situated on A4104 midway between Welland and Little Malvern) ☎ Hanley Swan (0684) 310288

The 17th century country house, providing accommodation in rooms decorated with floral wallpapers and matching materials and standing in a lovely, lawned garden, really does have the cottage atmosphere that its name suggests. Food is predominantly English, making good use of local produce and serving home-grown vegetables.

9rm(6⇌2⋔) CTV in all bedrooms ® ✱ sB&Bfr£18 sB&B⇌⋔fr£21 dB&B⇌⋔fr£40 B

16P ⇌ ❁ croquet *xmas*

V ♔ ☕ ✱ Tea 70palc High Tea £2.50alc Dinner fr£9.75&alc Wine £6.50 Last dinner 8.45pm

Ⓥ

Malvern

★★***Malvern Hills*** Malvern Wynds Point (4m S A449) ☎ Colwall (0684) 40237

Conveniently sited for guests who enjoy exploring the Malvern Hills, the hotel features a popular buffet-style lunch.

15rm(10⇌)(1fb) CTV in all bedrooms ® B

CTV 35P ❁ Live music & dancing 1st Thu of mth *xmas*

English & French V ♔ ☕ Last dinner 9.45pm

Credit cards 1 2 5

★★**Montrose** 23 Graham Rd ☎ (06845) 2335

Closed 22 Dec—6 Jan RS winter

A family-run hotel in a quiet road near the town centre.

14rm(2⇌6⋔)(1fb) CTV in 9 bedrooms ® ✗ S% sB&Bfr£18 sB&B⇌⋔£22—£34 dB&B£28—£30 dB&B⇌⋔£30—£34 B

CTV 16P ⇌

V ♔ ☕ S% Lunch £4—£7 High Tea £3 Dinner £6.50—£7.50 Wine £3.80 Last dinner 8pm

Credit cards 1 3 Ⓥ

★★**Mount Pleasant** Belle Vue Ter ☎ (06845) 61837

Closed Xmas

Elegant Georgian house in 1½ acres of terraced gardens.

14rm(11⇌3⋔) CTV in all bedrooms ® T ✗ sB&B⇌⋔£30—£34 dB&B⇌⋔£43—£48 B

20P ⇌ ❁ nc 8yrs

English & Spanish V ♔ ☕ Lunch £5.95—£7.50 Tea £1alc Dinner £6.95&alc Wine £4.95 Last dinner 9.30pm

Credit cards 1 2 3 5 Ⓥ

See advertisement on page 500

★★**Royal Malvern** Graham Rd ☎ (06845) 63411

14rm(11⇌) CTV in all bedrooms ® T sB&B£17—£30 sB&B⇌£19—£30 dB&B£28—£45 dB&B⇌£32—£45 B

8P ⇌ *xmas*

V ♔ ☕ ✱ Lunch £6alc Tea 75palc Dinner £7alc Wine £3.90 Last dinner 9.30pm

Credit cards 1 2 3 Ⓥ

★★**Thornbury** 16 Avenue Rd ☎ (06845) 2278

This quiet, well-run hotel stands in a large garden and is situated between the town and the railway station.

16rm(7⋔) Annexe: 3rm(2fb) CTV in all bedrooms ® ✗ sB&B£16—£19 sB&B⋔£19.50—£21 dB&B£29.50 dB&B⋔£34 B

10P ⇌ ❁

♔ ☕ Lunch £5.50—£6.50 Tea £1.25 High Tea £2 Dinner £8&alc Wine £6 Last dinner 8.15pm

Credit cards 1 3 Ⓥ

❀★★**Walmer Lodge** 49 Abbey Rd ☎ (06845) 4139

Closed Sun, Bank Hols, 2 wks Xmas & 2 wks summer

(Rosette awarded for dinner only)

Both local residents and visitors whose appetites have been sharpened by a walk on the nearby Malvern Hills choose to eat at this modest little hotel, the lively and humourous gourmet evenings being particularly popular. Food is rich, flavoursome and served in generous portions; dishes such as pâtés, terrines and chicken and ham kromeskies are often served with a delightful Cantonese sweet and sour relish. Daily 'specials' bring variety to the à la carte menu (which is charged fundamentally about every two months) and the wine list is well-balanced and reasonably priced.

8rm(5⇌3⋔) ✗ ✱ sB&B⇌⋔£16.10 dB&B⇌⋔£29.90

CTV 6P ⇌ nc 14yrs

English, French & Italian ✱ Dinner £11.96 Wine £4 Last dinner 9pm

M

❀✕✕**Croque-En-Bouche** 221 Wells Rd, Malvern Wells (3m S A449) ☏ (06845) 65612

Looking over the Severn Valley from the shadow of the Malvern Hills, this fine old stone house has become well known to gourmets from far and wide. A young husband and wife team serve meals in the French style, using only the best ingredients, brought in from France if necessary. Candle-lit and a warm atmosphere make for a leisurely and romantic meal — the mood enhanced, perhaps, by a wine list that includes some 400 of the finest vintages of this century! Booking (and punctuality) are essential.

Closed Sun, Mon, Tue & Xmas Lunch not served

French 24 seats S% Dinner £19.50 Wine £5.60 Last dinner 9.15pm

Credit cards 1 3

MAN, ISLE OF
Map **6**

ANDREAS
Map **6** SC49

✕✕***Grosvenor*** ☏ Kirk Andreas (062488) 576

Attractive restaurant with solid reputation for good-quality, well prepared food.

Closed Tues & Oct Dinner not served Sun

International 50 seats Last dinner 9pm 50P

Credit cards 1 3

BALLASALLA
Map **6** SC27

✕**La Rosette** ☏ (0624) 822940

It is advisable to book well in advance at this charming little French restaurant, for it is equally popular with local people and tourists. Cosy and well-furnished, it offers an array of attractive, good-value dishes coupled with friendly service.

French **V** 45 seats ✱Lunch £5—£10alc Dinner £11—£17alc Wine £7.50 Last dinner 10.30pm P nc 4yrs

CASTLETOWN
Map **6** SC26

★★★**Golf Links** Fort Island ☏ (0624) 822201 Telex no 627636

At southerly extreme of island, surrounded by golf course.

72rm (24 18)(14fb) CTV in all bedrooms **T** sB&B £28.50—£42.25 dB&B £56—£64 **B**

60P CFA (heated) 18 (hard) *xmas*

Lunch £6.50 Tea £2.50 Dinner £7.50 Last dinner 9pm

Credit cards 1 2 3 5

DOUGLAS
Map **6** SC37

★**Woodbourne** Alexander Dr ☏ (0624) 21766

Closed Oct-20 May

Friendly, comfortable public house in residential area.

10rm sB&B £14.50

CTV P nc 15yrs

Lunch £2.50—£3.50 Wine £3.50 Last dinner 9pm

Credit card 3 Ⓥ

✕✕✕**Boncompte's** King Edward Rd, Onchan ☏ (0624) 75626

Set in a fine position overlooking Douglas Bay, this popular and friendly restaurant appeals to both tourists and locals. It offers an attractive menu of well-prepared food accompanied by a good wine list.

Closed Sun Lunch not served Sat

Continental **V** 90 seats ✱Lunch fr£6.50&alc Dinner £12—£15alc Wine £5.90 Last dinner 10pm 10P nc 5yrs

Credit cards 1 3 5 Ⓥ

✕La Cucina 52 Bucks Rd ☎ (0624) 23959

This pleasant and friendly little Italian restaurant where the owner enthusiastically recreates the dishes of his native land.

Closed Mon
Lunch not served Sat
Dinner not served Sun

Italian **V** 30 seats Lunch £3.75—£3.95&alc Dinner £10alc Wine £5 Last dinner 9.30pm

Credit card [1]

PORT ERIN
Map **6** SC16

✕Molyneux's Seaford ☎ (0624) 833633

Pleasant, family run restaurant overlooking the bay, and serving well prepared fish.

Lunch not served

V 45 seats S% ✱Dinner £12.50—£14.50 Wine £6 Last dinner 10pm 30P

Credit card [3]

MANCHESTER
Greater Manchester
Map **7** SJ89
See plan page 502/503 See also **Salford**

★★★★Grand Aytoun St (Trusthouse Forte) ☎ 061-236 9559 Telex no 667580 Plan **5** *E4*

Large six-storey Victorian building in the city centre.

140rm(123➡13⋒) CTV in all bedrooms ® sB&B➡⋒£57 dB&B➡⋒£67.50 **B**

Lift ☾ CFA

Last dinner 10pm

Credit cards [1] [2] [3] [4] [5]

★★★★Hotel Piccadilly Piccadilly (Embassy) ☎ 061-236 8414 Telex no 668765 Plan **10** *E4*

Extensive services are provided at this hotel, which has recently been enhanced by total refurbishment of the bedrooms.

255➡ 3 in 34 bedrooms CTV in all bedrooms ® **T** S% sB➡£63.50—£81 dB➡⋒£86—£98 (room only) **B**

Lift ☾ 80P CFA Live music and dancing Sat *xmas*

Man, Isle of — Manchester

International **V** S% Lunch £11.50—£13&alc Tea £1.50—£2 Dinner £11.50—£13&alc Wine £7 Last dinner 10.30pm

Credit cards [1] [2] [3] [5]

★★★★Portland Thistle 3—5 Portland St, Piccadilly (Thistle) ☎ 061-228 3567 Telex no 669157 Plan **11** *E5*

Modern hotel behind a restored 19th-century warehouse façade.

219➡⋒(4fb) 1 in 51 bedrooms CTV in all bedrooms ® **T** ✱sB➡⋒£60—£75 dB➡⋒£79—£95 (room only) **B**

Lift ☾ ## 80P 40 (heated) sauna bath solarium gymnasium

International ✱Lunch fr£8.50 Dinner fr£11.95 Wine £7 Last dinner 10pm

Credit cards [1] [2] [3] [4] [5] Ⓥ

★★★Post House Palatine Rd, Northenden (Trusthouse Forte) ☎ 061-998 7090 Telex no 669248 Plan **12** *D1*

Modern building, 7m south of the city centre at the junction of the B5167/A5103. It is close to motorways M56 and M63 and convenient for the airport.

200➡ CTV in all bedrooms ® sB&B➡£55.50 dB&B➡£69.50 **B**

Lift ☾ 123P 120 CFA ♿

Last dinner 10.30pm

Credit cards [1] [2] [3] [4] [5]

★★★Willow Bank 340—342 Wilmslow Rd, Fallowfield ☎ 061-224 0461 Telex no 668222 Plan **20** *E1*

Large Victorian house with modern extensions, 2 miles from the city centre.

123rm(104➡16⋒)(2fb) CTV in 122 bedrooms **T** S% sB£27.50 sB➡⋒£33.50—£37.50 dB➡⋒£48 (room only) **B**

☾ CTV 70P 30 (charge) Live music & dancing Sat *xmas*

European **V** S% ✱Lunch fr£4.50&alc Tea fr£2.50 High Tea fr£2.50 Dinner fr£7.50&alc Wine £4.50 Last dinner 10.15pm

Credit cards [1] [2] [3] [5]

○Ramada Renaissance Market Place West, Blackfriars St ☎ 01-235 5264

205➡⋒ Expected to open summer 1987

✕✕✕*Terrazza* 14 Nicholas St ☎ 061-236 4033 Plan **18** *D4*

Spacious, well appointed restaurant with attractive decor and extensive menu.

Closed Sun

International **V** 110 seats Lunch £5.95&alc Dinner £7.50—£9.50&alc Wine £5.10 Last dinner 11.30pm

Credit cards [1] [2] [3] [4] [5] Ⓥ

✕✕*Le Bijou* Clarence St ☎ 061-236 6657 Plan **13** *D4*

The French atmosphere of this basement bistro is accentuated by murals and scenes of Paris. An extensive menu, accompanied by an adequate wine list, is served by a smart, efficient, and friendly young staff.

Closed Sun Lunch not served Sat

French **V** 46 seats Last dinner 11pm Live music Thu & Sat

Credit cards [1] [2] [3] [5]

✕✕Casa España 100 Wilmslow Rd, Rusholme ☎ 061-224 6826 Plan **2** *E1*

Located just south of the city centre, the typically Spanish restaurant features archways and roughcast walls with tiles and plates as a setting for its pine furnishings. Smart and efficient staff offer an extensive menu of Iberian dishes and an ample wine list which includes jugs of fruity Sangria. A separate coffee/bar lounge is provided.

Spanish **V** 40 seats S% Lunch fr£3.75&alc Dinner £12alc Wine £3.95 Last dinner 11pm 15P

Credit cards [1] [2] [3] [5] Ⓥ

✕✕*Connaught* 58-60 George St ☎ 061-236 0191 Plan **3** *D4*

This fashionable, modern Cantonese-style restaurant is situated on the first floor of a new building at the heart of city-centre Chinatown. Whilst enjoying the Oriental →

M

Manchester

1	Armenian Taverna ✕
2	Casa Espana ✕✕
3	Connaught ✕✕
4	Gaylord ✕✕
5	Grand ★★★★
6	Isola Bella ✕✕
9	Market ✕
10	Hotel Piccadilly ★★★★
11	Portland Thistle ★★★★
12	Post House ★★★
13	Le Bijou ✕✕
13A	Mina-Japan ✕
14	Rajdoot ✕✕
15	Sam's Chop House ✕
16	Simpsons ★★
17	Steak & Kebab ✕
17A	39 Steps ✕
18	Terrazza ✕✕✕
19	Truffles ✕✕
20	Willow Bank ★★★
21	Woo Sang ✕✕
22	Yang Sing ❁✕✕

decor and comfortable furnishings, guests can choose from an extensive and reasonably-priced menu, service being provided by friendly and helpful staff.

Closed Xmas Day & Boxing Day

Cantonese **V** 150 seats Last dinner 11.45pm

Credit cards 1 2 3 5

✕✕ ***Gaylord*** Amethyst House, Marriot's Court, Spring Gardens ☎ 061-832 6037 Plan **4** *D5*

This city-centre Indian restaurant is one of a famous chain with branches in New Delhi, Bombay and Hong Kong. The pungence and warmth of fragrant spices is expertly utilised to create exotic dishes which are served by a pleasant and helpful staff against an authentic Indian background.

Closed 25 Dec & 1 Jan

Indian **V** 102 seats Lunch £3.95&alc Dinner £5.95–£7.95&alc Wine £4.95 Last dinner 11.30pm

Credit cards 1 2 3 5 V

✕✕ **Isola Bella** Booth St ☎ 061-236 6417 Plan **6** *D4*

Situated in a basement close to the Town Hall, this popular Italian restaurant is decorated in true Terrazza style and offers a good selection of typical dishes, all cooked by competent chefs. An attractive display of salads and other foods helps to create a Mediterranean atmosphere, and a skilled team of waiters give fast yet attractive service.

Closed Sun & Bank Hols

Italian **V** 70 seats S% Lunch £17alc Dinner £17alc Wine £6 Last dinner 10.45pm

Credit cards 1 3 5

✕✕ **Rajdoot** St James House, South King's St ☎ 061-834 2176 Plan **14** *C5*

The spacious, city-centre, Indian restaurant is comfortably furnished and decorated within Indian figures and →

M

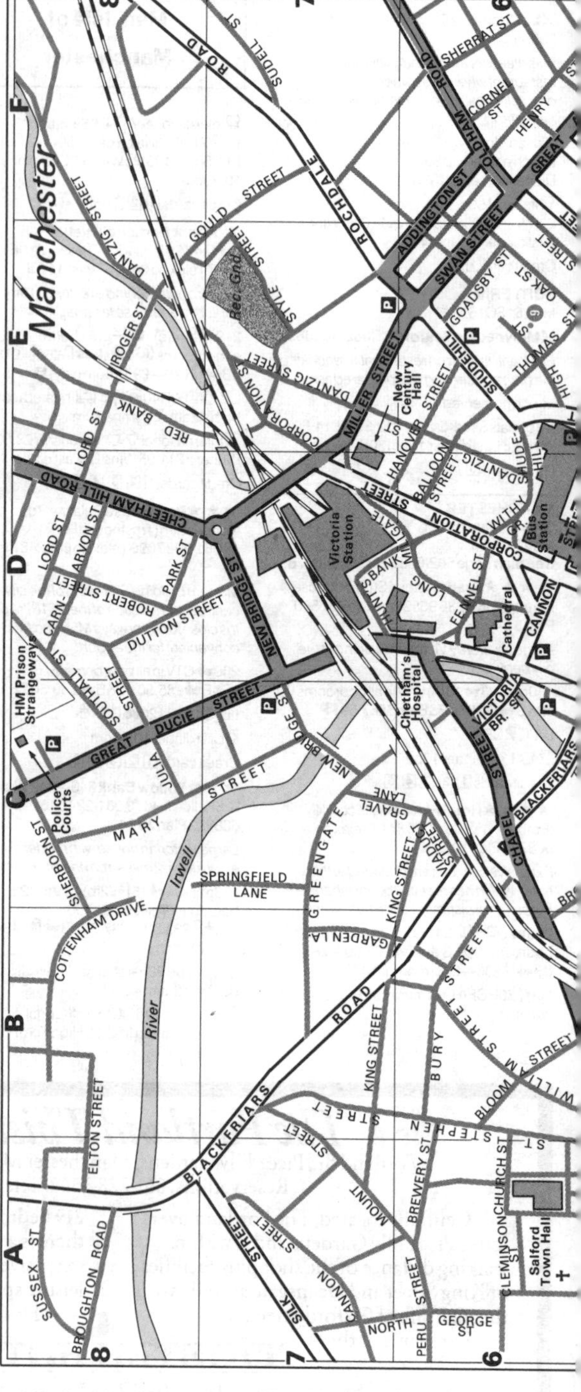

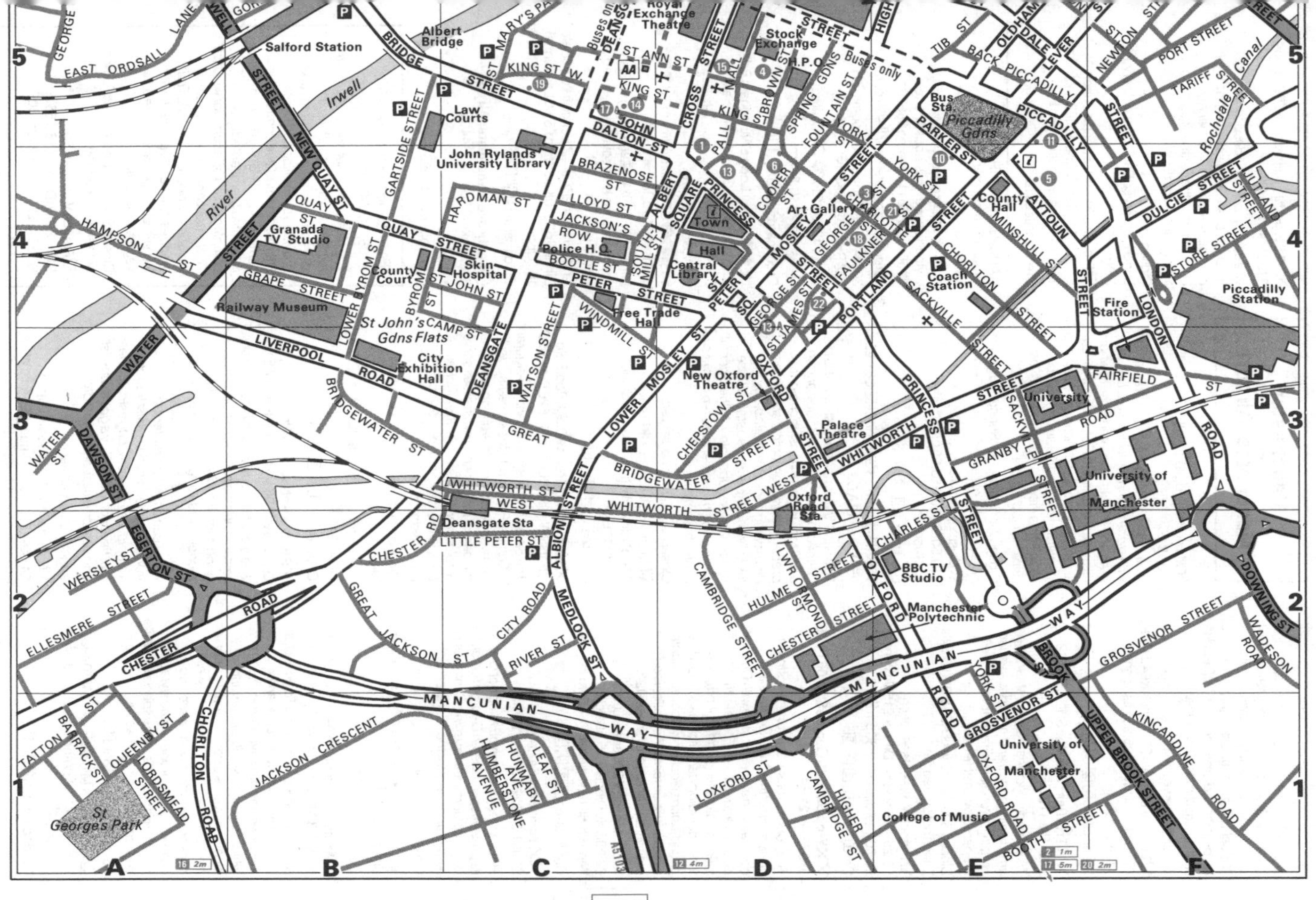
M
Salford Station
Albert Bridge
Royal Exchange Theatre
Stock Exchange
H.P.O.
Buses only
Bridge Street
Law Courts
John Rylands University Library
John Dalton St
Cross Street
King St
St Ann St
Spring Gdns
Fountain St
Bus Sta.
Piccadilly Gdns
Piccadilly
Back Piccadilly
Parker St
Oldham
Dale
Lever
Tib St
Newton St
Port Street
Tariff Street
Rochdale Canal
Dulcie Street
Jutland Street
Store Street
Piccadilly Station
Fire Station
London Road
Fairfield St
Irwell
River
New Quay St
Quay Street
Granada TV Studio
Railway Museum
Grape Street
Lower Byrom St
County Court
Skin Hospital
St John St
St John's Gdns Flats
Camp St
City Exhibition Hall
Liverpool Road
Water Street
Dawson St
Egerton St
Hampson St
East Ordsall Lane
George
Gartside Street
Hardman St
Brazenose St
Lloyd St
Jackson's Row
Police H.Q.
Bootle St
South Mill St
Albert Square
Princess
Town Hall
Central Library
Peter Street
Windmill St
Free Trade Hall
Watson Street
Deansgate
Great Bridgewater Street
Lower Mosley St
New Oxford Theatre
Chepstow St
Oxford Street
Palace Theatre
Whitworth Street
Mosley Street
Art Gallery
Charlotte St
George St
Faulkner St
St James St
Portland Street
County Hall
Aytoun
Minshull St
Chorlton Street
Coach Station
Sackville Street
Princess Street
University
Granby Row
University of Manchester
Whitworth St West
Deansgate Sta
Little Peter St
Chester Rd
Oxford Road Sta.
Charles St
BBC TV Studio
Manchester Polytechnic
Lwr Ormond St
Hulme Street
Chester Street
Cambridge Street
Albion Street
Medlock St
City Road
River St
Great Jackson St
Mancunian Way
Downing St
Wadeson Road
Grosvenor Street
Brook St
York St
Upper Brook Street
Kincardine Road
Grosvenor St
Oxford Road
College of Music
Booth Street
Higher Cambridge St
Loxford St
Leaf St
Hunmaby Ave
Humberstone Avenue
Jackson Crescent
Chorlton Road
Chester Road
Wersley St
Ellesmere Street
Tatton St
Barrack St
Queenby St
Lordsmead Street
St George's Park
A5103

statues. Its speciality is charcoal cooking, and good food is authentically flavoured with traditional blends of fragrant spices. The set-price menus are highly recommended, and service is by friendly staff dressed in local costume.

Lunch not served Sun

Indian **V** 87 seats S% Lunch fr£4.50&alc Dinner £10alc Wine £5.85 Last dinner 11.30pm

Credit cards 1 2 3 5

XXTruffles 63 Bridge St 061-832 9393 Plan **19** *C5*

This friendly, Victorian-style restaurant has an upstairs lounge and provides a varied range of interesting French dishes, well-prepared by an able chef.

Closed Sun, Mon 2 wks Aug & Bank Hol's Lunch not served Sat

French **V** 32 seats *Lunch £5.25—£9.95&alc Dinner £15alc Wine £5.50 Last dinner 10.30pm

Credit cards 1 2 3 5

XXWoo Sang 19 George St 061-236 3697 Plan **21** *E4*

The popular, busy, Cantonese restaurant at the heart of the Chinatown area is decorated in authentic style with Oriental pictures and statues. There is an extensive menu of interesting and well-prepared food, including daily 'specials' and a low-priced lunch selection which represents excellent value for money, all served by a friendly and efficient Chinese staff.

M

Cantonese **V** 200 seats Lunch £2.60&alc Dinner £15.50alc(2 persons) Wine £5.50 Last dinner 11.45pm

Credit cards 1 2 3 5

XXYang Sing 34 Princess St 061-236 2200 Plan **22** *D4*

Housed in a Victorian building not far from its previous premises in George Street, this large, colourful and bustling Cantonese restaurant caters for the connoisseur.

Closed Xmas day

Cantonese **V** 140 seats Wine £5.25 Last dinner 11pm

Credit cards 1 2

XArmenian Taverna 3—5 Princess St 061-834 9025 Plan **1** *D4*

Set on Albert Square, by the Town Hall, this basement restaurant is pleasantly furnished and displays a large, lively mural which, together with its arches and alcoves, creates a convincingly Armenian atmosphere. The food, which is well cooked and attractively presented, authentically reproduces the style of the region, with kebabs as the speciality, whilst service is friendly and casual.

Lunch not served Sat & Sun

Armenian & Middle Eastern **V** 70 seats Bar lunch £10alc Wine £5.20 Last dinner 11.30pm

Credit cards 1 2 3 5

Manchester — Manchester Airport

XMarket 30 Edge St 061-834 3743 Plan **9** *E6*

A friendly and simply-furnished restaurant with stone flooring and assorted bric-a-brac, the Market is situated close to where the old market stood. Refreshingly different and freshly prepared food shows flair and inventiveness, and the air of the place is casual and friendly. As space is limited, booking is advisable.

Closed, Sun, Mon, 1wk Spring, Aug & 1wk Xmas Lunch not served

Cosmopolitan 30 seats Dinner £10.50alc Wine £3.65 Last dinner 10.30pm

Credit cards 1 2 Ⓥ

XMina-Japan 63 George St 061-228 2598 Plan **13A** *D3*

This is the first Japanese restaurant to be opened in this country outside London, and it features an extensive choice of well prepared and presented dishes, many of them being cooked at the table by the friendly and experienced staff, whose national dress adds colour to the Oriental setting which has been created from a city-centre basement.

Closed Mon Lunch not served

Japanese **V** 65 seats *Dinner £7—£16&alc Wine £5.80 Last dinner 11.30pm 15P

Credit cards 1 2 3 5

XSam's Chop House Black Pool Fold, Chapel Walks 061-834 1526 Plan **15** *D5*

The Sam of the busy, city-centre restaurant is Samuel Pepys, and the stone-flagged and wooded floors of the dining rooms set the period well. Friendly waitresses serve wholesome English food, the lunches being extremely popular with local businessmen.

Closed wknds & Bank Hols Dinner not served

119 seats Lunch fr£7.50&alc Wine £5 Last lunch 3pm

Credit cards 1 2 3 5

XSteak & Kabab 846 Wilmslow Rd, Didsbury 061-445 2552 Plan **17** *E1*

The blackboard menu of this cottage-style restaurant in the southern suburbs offers a good choice and represents value for money. In a setting of low beams and rough-cast walls, the more adventurous visitor can enjoy some interesting dishes from à la carte selection whilst the less intrepid may choose a huge steak. The food is accompanied by a good wine list and service is casual and friendly.

Lunch not served Sat

International **V** 120 seats Lunch £4.50—£5.50&alc Dinner fr£5&alc Wine £4 Last dinner 11.30pm

X39 Steps 39 South King St 061-834 9155 Plan **17A** *C5*

The cheery, colourful decor of this small, modern, basement restaurant in the city centre is matched by the friendly enthusiasm of the girls serving good French and Italian food.

Closed Sun

Lunch not served Sat Dinner not served Mon

French & Italian **V** 55 seats Lunch £1.95—£15&alc Dinner £3.95—£15&alc Wine £4.25 Last dinner 11pm

Credit cards 1 3

MANCHESTER AIRPORT

Greater Manchester

Map **7** SJ78

★★★★**Excelsior** Ringway Rd, Wythenshawe (Trusthouse Forte) 061-437 5811 Telex no 668721

Large modern hotel near the airport.

308 (3fb) CTV in all bedrooms ®**T** sB&B £62 dB&B £78

Lift (## 350P CFA (heated)

Last dinner 10.30pm

Credit cards 1 2 3 4 5

★★★**Valley Lodge** Altrincham Rd Wilmslow (0625) 529201 Telex no 666401

Tyrolean style hotel.

105 2 CTV in all bedrooms ®**T** S% sB&B £43 dB&B £55

Lift (400P CFA (heated) squash snooker sauna bath solarium gymnasium Disco Tue & Thu—Sat

International **V** Lunch fr£6.85&alc Dinner fr£7.50&alc Wine £5.60 Last dinner 10.30pm

Credit cards 1 2 3 5

○**Ladbroke Manchester Airport** (Ladbroke) 061-436 4404

168

Due to open end 1986.

XXMoss Nook Ringway Rd 061-437 4778

The restaurant is set near the end of the airport runway, but nothing can detract from the fine food and wine provided by Pauline and Derek Harrison in smart and comfortable surroundings. Modern French cuisine is beautifully presented and complemented by a superior wine list. The tantalising choice of dishes includes, at one extreme, Les Trois Viandes du Chef (three meats with individual sauces) and, at the other, vegetarian meals.

Closed Sun, & 25 Dec for 2wks Lunch not served Sat & Mon

French **V** 50 seats S% Lunch £18.15&alc Dinner £18.15&alc Wine £6.95 Last dinner 9.30pm 30P nc12yrs

Credit cards 1 2 3 5

MANORBIER
Dyfed
Map **2** SS09
★★ ***H*** **Castle Mead** ☎ (083 482) 358
Closed Nov—Etr
Small, secluded, country house style hotel with cosy, comfortable bedrooms and intimate bar and lounges. Attractive garden leads to beach.
8rm(6🛁) Annexe: 3🛁(2fb) ®
sB&B£15.50—£17.50
sB&B🛁£15.50—£17.50 dB&B£31—£35
dB&B🛁£31—£35
CTV 20P ✿

🍷☕ Bar lunch fr£1.25 Tea fr£1.20 Dinner fr£7.50 Wine £2.80 Last dinner 8pm
Credit card 2

MANSFIELD
Nottinghamshire
Map **8** SK56
★★ **Midland** Midland Pl (Home Brewery)
☎ (0623) 24668

This former private house, standing close to the town centre, was built in 1704 and converted into a hotel by the Midland Railway Company in 1874; today it offers comfortable and well-equipped accommodation.
27rm(16🛁4🚿)(2fb) CTV in all bedrooms
® T ✈ sB&B£25—£34.50
sB&B🛁🚿£27—£31.50 dB&B£36—£40
dB&B🛁🚿fr£40 B
CTV 20P
V 🍷 Lunch fr£4.25 Tea £1alc Dinner £4.95—£6.50 Wine £4.10 Last dinner 9.30pm
Credit cards 1 2 3

M

MARAZION
Cornwall
Map **2** SW53

★★**Mount Haven** Turnpike Rd ☎(0736) 710249
Closed Xmas
Personally run in a friendly atmosphere this one time coaching inn has fascinating galleried restaurant comfortable bedrooms and excellent parking.
17⇌(4fb) CTV in all bedrooms ®T ✗ sB&B⇌£17.50—£18.50 dB&B⇌£35—£37 B
40P
V ♡ ☕ Bar lunch £4—£6 Tea 75p Dinner £10&alc Wine £5 Last dinner 8.30pm
Credit cards 1 3 V

★**Cutty Sark** The Square ☎Penzance (0736) 710334
A comfortable inn with convivial atmosphere in the heart of the town.
13rm(4⇌2⋒)(3fb) CTV in 12 bedrooms sB&B£9—£11 dB&B£18—£25 dB&B⇌⋒£22—£25 B
CTV 25P pool table
Mainly grills V ♡ ☕ Lunch £5alc Dinner £6.50alc Wine £4.75 Last dinner 9.30pm

MARCH
Cambridgeshire
Map **5** TL49

★**Olde Griffin** High St ☎(0354) 52517
The 17th-century posting inn is popular with local townsfolk for small functions.
15rm(8⇌3⋒)(1fb) 1 CTV in all bedrooms ® ✗ S% *sB&Bfr£16 sB&B⇌⋒fr£19.50 dB&Bfr£28 dB&B⇌⋒£33.50—£42.50 B
CTV 50P Disco Thu, Fri & Sun Live music & dancing mthly *xmas*
V ♡ S% *Lunch fr£3.25&alc Dinner £5.25&alc Wine £5.25 Last dinner 9.30pm
Credit cards 1 3 V

MARFORD
Clwyd
Map **7** SJ35

★**Trevor Arms** Springfield Ln ☎Chester (0244) 570436
10⋒ 1 CTV in all bedrooms ® ✗ S% sB&B⋒£25—£27 dB&B⋒£32—£34
Continental breakfast B
70P
V ♡ ☕ S% *Lunch £4—£9&alc Tea 80p High Tea £4—£9&alc Dinner £4—£9&alc Wine £3.50 Last dinner 10pm
Credit cards 1 3 V

MARGATE
Kent
Map **5** TR37

★★**Walpole Bay** Fifth Av, Cliftonville (1m E) ☎Thanet (0843) 221703
Closed Oct—May
Friendly, old fashioned hotel with good accommodation.
44rm(22⇌)(10fb) CTV in 5 bedrooms sB&B£19—£25 sB&B⇌£25—£35 dB&B£35—£40 dB&B⇌£40—£50 B
Lift ☾ CTV 1 (£3 per night) ♿
V ♡ ☕ *Lunch £6 Tea £1 Dinner £8 Wine £3.25 Last dinner 8pm
Credit cards 1 2 3 5 V

MARKET DRAYTON
Shropshire
Map **7** SJ63

★★**Corbet Arms** High St ☎(0630) 2037
Ancient inn with a Georgian façade and a pillared entrance.
12rm(10⇌2⋒)(2fb) CTV in all bedrooms ®T sB&B⇌⋒£20—£24 dB&B⇌⋒£32—£35 B
CTV 45P 2 bowls
Mainly grills V ♡ ☕ Lunch £4.95—£6.50 Tea £1.30—£2.50 Dinner £6.50—£8.50&alc Wine £4 Last dinner 9pm
Credit cards 1 2 3 5 V

★★***Tern Hill Hall*** (on A53) ☎Tern Hill (063 083) 310
Large, detached hotel in spacious grounds.
10rm(7⇌) CTV in all bedrooms ® ✗
90P 6
♡ Last dinner 9pm
Credit cards 1 2 3

MARKET HARBOROUGH
Leicestershire
Map **4** SP78

★★★**Three Swans** High St ☎(0858) 66644
This historic inn, dating from the 15th century, stands on the A6 in the town centre.
18rm(11⇌7⋒)(3fb) 2 CTV in all bedrooms ®
50P 8
English & French V ♡ ☕ Lunch £6.50—£7 Tea fr£1.50 High Tea fr£4.50 Dinner £11—£13 Wine £5.10 Last dinner 9.45pm
Credit cards 1 2 3 4 5

MARKET RASEN
Lincolnshire
Map **8** TF18

★★★*H* **Limes** Gainsborough Rd ☎(0673) 842357
Comfortable former country house in 3½ acres of grounds with a warm friendly atmosphere.
13rm(10⇌3⋒) Annexe: 4⇌(4fb) 1 CTV in all bedrooms ®T sB&B⇌⋒£32—£35 dB&B⇌⋒£40—£45 B
50P squash ♿
English & French V ♡ ☕ Lunch £5.60—£6.50&alc Tea £3.50—£4 High Tea £4.50—£5 Dinner £6.50—£7.50&alc Wine £4.75 Last dinner 9.30pm
Credit cards 1 3 5 V

MARKET WEIGHTON
Humberside
Map **8** SE84

★★**Londesborough Arms** 44 High St ☎(0696) 72219

A three-storey Georgian building with porticoed entrance, the hotel has been enhanced by recent upgrading.

14rm(9→5⋒)(1fb) 1⊞ CTV in all bedrooms ®**T**✗ sB&B→⋒£20 dB&B→⋒£32—£36 **B**

50P 1🚗

V ♡ ☕ Lunch £4 Tea 50p—£1.10 Dinner £3.80—£5.85&alc Wine £3.65 Last dinner 9.30pm

Credit cards 1 2 3 5

MARKINGTON
North Yorkshire
Map **8** SE26

★★★*BL* **Hob Green**
☎ Harrogate (0423) 770031 Telex no 57780

Closed Feb

Delightful country house lovingly restored to give a relaxing elegant atmosphere, with beautiful lounges and very well equipped bedrooms. Fresh produce from the garden is used in delectable French cuisine.

12→ 2⊞ CTV in all bedrooms ®**T**✗ sB&B→£42—£46 dB&B→£57.50—£65 **B**

50P ✿ *xmas*

Market Weighton — Marlborough

English & French ♡ ☕ ✱ Lunch £5.95—£8.95 Tea fr£3.50 Dinner fr£12.50 Wine £6.75 Last dinner 9.30pm

Credit cards 1 2 3 5

MARKS TEY
Essex
Map **5** TL92

★★★**Marks Tey** London Rd (Paten)
☎ Colchester (0206) 210001

The purpose-built hotel stands close to the A12 and offers modern bedroom facilities; friendly staff provide a good range of services.

108→(11fb) CTV in all bedrooms ®**T** S% sB&B→£39 dB&B→£49 **B**

☾ CTV 160P ⚲(hard) CFA gymnasium *xmas*

English & French **V** ♡ ☕ S% Lunch £8.45&alc Tea 80p Dinner £8.45&alc Wine £5.25 Last dinner 10pm

Credit cards 1 2 3 5 Ⓥ

MARLBOROUGH
Wiltshire
Map **4** SU16

★★★*H* **Ivy House** High St ☎(0672) 53188

The attractive, ivy-clad house, with its own car park and rear garden, stands in the town centre. Recently modernised and personally-run, it offers both comfort and friendly service; food is sound and the wine list excellent.

16→⋒ Annexe: 1→ CTV in 16 bedrooms ®**T**✗ ✱ sB&B→⋒£38—£45 dB&B→⋒£40—£50 **B**

14P 2🚗 ✿ nc 8yrs

English & French ♡ ☕ ✱ Tea £1.75 Dinner £9 Wine £7 Last dinner 9pm

Credit cards 1 3

★★**Castle & Ball** High St (Trusthouse Forte) ☎(0672) 55201

A 17th-century inn with a tile-hung Georgian façade. The interior has been completely modernised yet retains its charm and character.

38rm(7→) CTV in all bedrooms ® sB&B£40.50 sB&B→£48.50 dB&B£54.50 dB&B→£62.50 **B**

CTV 50P *xmas*

♡ ☕ Last dinner 9pm

Credit cards 1 2 3 4 5

M

★★*H* **Merlin** 36—39 High St ☎ (0672) 52151

An end-of-terrace hotel with an attractive frontage onto the High Street, the Merlin has a well-maintained interior and offers rooms that are comfortable, though small, together with friendly and attentive service.

9rm(2🛁3🚿) Annexe: 1🛁(1fb) CTV in all bedrooms ✱sB&B£25 sB&B🛁🚿£30 dB&B£30 dB&B🛁🚿£40 B

P 🏠 *xmas* ✱Lunch £6.50 Dinner £7.95&alc Wine £4.50 Last dinner 9.30pm

Credit cards 1 2 3 5

MARLOW

Buckinghamshire
Map **4** SU88

★★★★**Compleat Angler** Marlow Br (Trusthouse Forte) ☎ (06284) 4444 Telex no 848644

A gem of a place in luxuriant fragrant gardens with uninterrupted river views. The house has fine period furniture and tapestries.

46🛁 CTV in all bedrooms sB&B🛁£83 dB&B🛁£106

☾90P CFA ✿ 🎾(hard) *xmas*

🍷 ☕ Last dinner 10pm

Credit cards 1 2 3 4 5

Greater Manchester
Map **7** SJ98

★*B* **Springfield** Station Rd ☎ 061-449 0721

Personally owned and run, the small, delightfully furnished, Victorian style hotel provides good home cooking.

7rm(5🛁2🚿)(2fb) CTV in all bedrooms ® T ✱sB&B🛁🚿£25 dB&B🛁🚿£35 B

8P 🏠

✱Dinner £7.25 Wine £4.25 Last dinner 7.45pm

Credit cards 1 3

MARSH BENHAM

Berkshire
Map **4** SU46

✕**Red House** ☎ Newbury (0635) 41637

Set in peaceful rural surroundings just off the A4, the attractive, thatched, country inn is personally supervised by the proprietor and extends a warm welcome. Its speciality is good, wholesome English food which represents excellent value.

Dinner not served Sun

V 55 seats Lunch fr£7.95&alc Dinner £10.95—£13.95&alc Wine £5.25 Last dinner 9.45pm 60P

Credit cards 1 2 3 5 ⓥ

MARSTON TRUSSELL

Northamptonshire
Map **4** SP68

★★**Sun Inn** ☎ Market Harborough (0858) 65531

Modern accommodation is provided in the extension of this traditional, rural, village inn.

10rm(9🛁) CTV in all bedrooms ® T sB&B£30—£35 sB&B🛁£30—£35 dB&B🛁£40—£45 B

35P

🍽 English & French **V** 🍷 ☕ Lunch £6.75—£7.50&alc Tea 75p—£1 Dinner £10.75—£15&alc Wine £6.50 Last dinner 9.30pm

Credit cards 1 2 3 5 ⓥ

MARTINHOE

Devon
Map **3** SS64

★👥*HBL* **Old Rectory** ☎ Parracombe (05983) 368

Closed mid Oct—Etr

A sympathetically restored and well maintained former Georgian rectory in 3 acres of natural grounds and old English gardens, 950 feet above sea level. Tony and Elizabeth Pring run it as their home and offer comfortable individually decorated bedrooms and quiet, beautifully furnished lounges. The vinery at the back of the house is very pleasant.

10rm(7🛁2🚿) CTV in 5 bedrooms dB&B£32—£36 dB&B🛁🚿£40—£44

14P 🚫 ✿ putting nc 10yrs ♿

V 🚭 Dinner £10.50—£11.50 Wine £5 Last dinner 7.30pm

ⓥ

See advertisement under Lynton

MARTOCK

Somerset
Map **3** ST41

★**White Hart** East St ☎ (0935) 822005

Friendly inn situated in the town centre opposite the Corn Exchange.

10rm(2fb) CTV in 3 bedrooms TV in 7 bedrooms ® sB&B£17.95—£19.10 dB&B£31.30—£35.90

CTV 15P 2🚗 🚫 skittle alley

🍷 Lunch £4.25—£9.75&alc Dinner £4.25—£9.75&alc Wine £3.25 Last dinner 9.30pm

Credit cards 1 3

✕✕***Hollies*** Bower Hinton ☎ (0935) 822232

Housed in an attractive building of Ham stone and standing in a pleasant garden with good car parking, the restaurant offers a sensible menu choice of well prepared and presented dishes together with a warm welcome and friendly service; some bedroom accommodation is also available.

Closed Mon Dinner not served Sun

V 65 seats Last dinner 9.45pm 40P

Credit cards 1 2 3 5

MARYPORT

Cumbria
Map **11** NY03

★★**Ellenbank** Birkby (2m NE A596) ☎ (0900) 815233

14rm(11🛁2🚿) CTV in all bedrooms ® ✱sB&B🛁🚿£19.50 dB&B🛁🚿£29.50—£33

40P ✿ *xmas*

✱Bar lunch fr£2.50 Tea £1.50 Dinner fr£9.50 Wine fr£3.50 Last dinner 9.30pm

★***Waverley*** Curzon St ☎ (0900) 812115

Situated on the edge of the town, this hotel is close to the sea, lakes and fells.

20rm(1🛁4🚿)(2fb) CTV in 5 bedrooms ® in 5 bedrooms B

CTV

V 🍷 ☕ Last dinner 7.45pm

Credit cards 1 3

✕✕**Retreat** Birkby (1½m NE A596) ☎ (0900) 814056

Closed Mon

🍽 Continental **V** 36 seats ✱Lunch £8.15alc Dinner £10&alc Wine £5.20 Last dinner 9pm 19P 🚭

Credit cards 1 3

MARY TAVY

Devon
Map **2** SX57

★★👥***Moorland Hall*** ☎ (082281) 466

RS 2 Nov—21 Mar

Converted from a farmhouse in 1877 the hotel stands gracefully in four acres of private gardens, offering attractive and comfortable accommodation in peaceful surroundings.

10rm(4🛁2🚿) ® sB&B£18 sB&B🛁🚿£22 dB&B£29 dB&B🛁🚿£33 B

☾CTV 20P 🚫 ✿ nc 13yrs

☕ Bar lunch £3.15alc Tea £1.65 Dinner £9.50 Wine £5.90 Last dinner 7.30pm

Credit cards 1 3

See advertisement under Tavistock

MASHAM

North Yorkshire
Map **8** SE28

★★👥*H* **Jervaulx Hall** ☎ Bedale (0677) 60235

Closed Dec—Feb

Early 19th-century country house adjoining Jervaulx Abbey, with its own lawn and gardens.

8🛁 ® sB&B🛁£29—£31 dB&B🛁£56—£60

CTV 20P 🚫 ✿ croquet ♿

🍷 ☕ ✱Tea £2.50 Dinner £13 Wine £4.90 Last dinner 8pm

ⓥ

★**Riseber Lodge** Leyburn Rd ☎ Ripon (0765) 89307

Bedrooms are simple but neat and the lounge comfortable in this cosy, family-run hotel.

M

9rm(5🛁)CTV in all bedrooms Ⓡ 🐕 *sB&Bfr£14 sB&B🛁fr£16 dB&Bfr£28 dB&B🛁fr£32 B

20P 🚗 ✿ *xmas*

🍷 ☕ *Dinner £6.95 Wine £3.95 Last dinner 7.30pm

MATLOCK
Derbyshire
Map **8** SK36

★★★**New Bath** New Bath Rd (2m S A6) (Trusthouse Forte) ☎ (0629) 3275

Large, much extended, Georgian-style building high above the A6.

56🛁(3fb) CTV in all bedrooms Ⓡ sB&B🛁£47.50 dB&B🛁£65.50 B

☾ 250P CFA ✿ (heated) & (heated) 🎾(hard) sauna bath solarium gymnasium *xmas*

🍷 ☕ Last dinner 10pm

Credit cards 1 2 3 4 5

★★★ **B Riber Hall** Riber (Pride of Britain) ☎ (0629) 2795

The Elizabethan manor house enjoys a peaceful location next to Riber Castle, three miles from Matlock.

Annexe: 11🛁(2fb) 9 CTV in all bedrooms Ⓡ **T** 🐕 *sB&B🛁£45—£55 dB&B🛁£59—£90 Continental breakfast B

50P 🚗 ✿ 🎾 nc10yrs

English & French **V** 🍷 ☕ *Lunch £10&alc Tea £3.50 Dinner £20alc Wine £6.75 Last dinner 9.30pm

Credit cards 1 2 3 4 5 Ⓥ

★★**Red House** Old Rd, Darley Dale (2½m N A6) ☎ (0629) 734854

7rm(2🛁2🚿)(1fb) CTV in all bedrooms Ⓡ *sB&Bfr£18 sB&B🛁🚿fr£25 dB&Bfr£34 dB&B🛁🚿fr£38 B

16P ✿

V 🍷 ☕ *Lunch £4.50—£8 Tea 60p—£1.50 High Tea fr£2.25 Dinner fr£4.50&alc Wine £4.50 Last dinner 11.30pm

Credit cards 1 2 3 5 Ⓥ

★★***Temple*** Temple Walk ☎ (0629) 3911

Here, simple accommodation is offered in what is reputed to be the oldest building in the area, standing in an elevated position above the A6.

13rm(1🛁2🚿)(3fb) 1 CTV in all bedrooms Ⓡ B

CTV 30P *xmas*

V 🍷 ☕ Last dinner 9.30pm

Credit cards 1 2 3 5

★**Greyhound** Market Pl, Cromford (2½m S on A5012 at junc with A6) ☎ Wirksworth (062982) 2551

Closed Xmas

Large 3-storey Georgian inn in centre of old town.

7rm(4fb) sB&B£12—£14 dB&B£24—£28 B

CTV 70P pool table Live music & dancing Sat

V 🍷 ☕ *Lunch £3—£5 Tea fr50p Dinner £6.50—£8.50 Wine £3.50 Last dinner 8.30pm

MAUCHLINE
Strathclyde *Ayrshire*
Map **11** NS42

✕**La Candela** 5 Kilmarnock Rd ☎ (0290) 51015

Small village restaurant with dark wood frontage and a red canopy.

French & Italian 45 seats S% Lunch £2—£12 Dinner £2.50—£18&alc Wine £3.50 Last dinner 10.30pm Live music Fri—Sun

Credit cards 1 2 Ⓥ

See advertisement on page 510

MAWGAN PORTH
Cornwall
Map **2** SW86

★★*H* **Tredragon** ☎ St Mawgan (0637) 860213
Closed Nov—Etr (except Xmas)
Comfortable, family holiday hotel, with fine views of the beach and direct access to it.
30rm (13 11)(11fb) ✱sB&B£12—£16 sB&B £18—£24 dB&B£24—£32 dB&B £30—£40
CTV 28P (heated) sauna bath solarium Live music & dancing wkly *xmas*
English & French ✱Bar lunch £1.30—£3.50 Tea 60p Dinner £6.75 Wine £3.75 Last dinner 8pm
Credit cards 1 3

MAWNAN SMITH
Cornwall
Map **2** SW72

★★★**Budock Vean** ☎ (0326) 250288
Closed Jan & Feb
This very professionally run hotel stands in its own golf course which runs down to Helford River.
53 (3fb) 1 CTV in all bedrooms T ✱sB&B fr£35.75 (incl dinner) dB&B fr£71.50 (incl dinner)
Lift 100P (heated) (hard) billiards Live music & dancing Sat in season *xmas*
French ✱Tea fr75p Dinner £12&alc Wine fr£4.75 Last dinner 9pm
Credit cards 1 2 3 5
See advertisement under Falmouth

★★★ *HL* **Meudon** (Inter Hotel)
☎ Falmouth (0326) 250541 Telex no 45478
Closed Dec & Jan
Friendly, relaxing manor house where comfortable lounges overlook superb sub-tropical gardens.
30 (1fb) CTV in all bedrooms T ✱sB&B £30—£38 dB&B £60—£68
50P 2 CFA

English & French V ✱Lunch £8—£12&alc Tea £1.20 High Tea £4—£6 Dinner £15&alc Wine £4.50 Last dinner 8.45pm
Credit cards 1 2 3 5

★★★**Trelawne** ☎ Falmouth (0326) 250226
Closed 19 Dec—Feb
Small, family-run, holiday hotel on the coast with two acres of grounds and gardens.
16rm (11 2)(2fb) CTV in all bedrooms ® T ✱sB&B£22—£27 sB&B £25—£30 dB&B£44—£54 dB&B £50—£60
20P (heated)
✱Lunch £3.60alc Tea 95p Dinner £7.90—£10.90 Wine £3.90 Last dinner 8.30pm
Credit cards 1 2 3 5 V
See advertisement under Falmouth

X **Dionysus** ☎ Falmouth (0326) 250714
Small, modern restaurant situated in the heart of the village.
Lunch not served
English & Greek V 36 seats Dinner £9.50alc Wine £4.75 Last dinner 10.30pm
P
Credit card 3 V

MAYFIELD
East Sussex
Map **5** TQ52

X **Old Brew House** High St ☎ (0435) 872342
A cottage-style, timber-framed building dating from the 16th century houses this small restaurant where guests can enjoy the personal attention of the proprietors in an intimate, candle-lit atmosphere. The fixed-price menu offers very good value, its interesting range of dishes usually based on local or regional ingredients. Cooking is honest and reliable, the home-made ice-cream and sorbet being particularly noteworthy.

Closed Sun, Mon, 2 wks early summer/late autumn & 24 Dec—2 Jan
Lunch not served Tue—Fri
French 22 seats Lunch £5.95—£6.50 Dinner £9—£15 Wine £5.95 Last dinner 9pm
Credit cards 2 3 5

MAYPOOL (near Churston)
Devon
Map **3** SX85

★★**Lost & Found Inn** ☎ (0803) 842442
A journey through country lanes will bring you to this stone-faced restaurant which looks out over the Dartmouth Estuary from its elevated and peaceful setting. The extensively renovated interior includes a large lounge bar and several dining rooms where an imaginative chalk-up menu offers a good range of well-prepared foods, freshly cooked to order and served in an informal atmosphere.
16rm (8 8) 1 CTV in all bedrooms ® T sB&B £28.50—£35 dB&B £57—£70
30P nc14yrs *xmas*
Lunch £5—£7&alc Dinner £8.75—£12.75&alc Wine £4.85 Last dinner 9.30pm
Credit cards 1 2 3 4 5
See advertisement under Dartmouth

MEALSGATE
Cumbria
Map **11** NY24

★★**Pink House** ☎ Low Ireby (09657) 229
Closed 25—26 Dec & 1 Jan
Detached rural hotel in ½ acre of gardens.
6rm (3 3)(2fb) in 1 bedroom CTV in 1 bedroom TV in 1 bedroom sB&B£15 sB&B £17.50 dB&B£30 dB&B £35
CTV 15P
V Lunch £4.25—£8.20 Dinner £4.75—£8.50&alc Wine £3.95 Last dinner 9pm
Credit card 1

MEASHAM
Leicestershire
Map **8** SK31

★★***Measham Inn*** Tamworth Rd (ExecHotel) ☎(0530) 70095 Telex no 34610

Low-rise modern hotel on A453.

31⇌ CTV in all bedrooms ®T ℞

100P CFA sauna bath Disco Fri

Mainly grills **V** Last dinner 9.30pm

Credit cards 1 2 3 5

MEIGLE
Tayside *Perthshire*
Map **11** NO24

★★ *H* **Kings of Kinloch** ☎(08284) 273

Closed Jan

An 18th-century mansion set in its own grounds, off the A94 1½m west of Meigle.

7rm(1⇌1⋒)(2fb) TV available in bedrooms ✱sB&B£24 sB&B⇌⋒£30 dB&B£42 dB&B⇌⋒£45

45P 2 putting clay pigeon shooting

Cosmopolitan **V** ✱Lunch £6.50—£12.80 Tea 70p—£1 High Tea £4—£8 Dinner £8.50—£15 Wine £5.10 Last dinner 8.45pm

Credit card 1

MELBOURN
Cambridgeshire
Map **5** TL34

✕**Pink Geranium** ☎ Royston (0763) 60215

The charming thatched cottage stands at the centre of the village, the pink colour wash of the exterior walls echoed in the interior decor, and even in the bill! Comfortable, well-used settees and armchairs, old beams and an abundance of flowers make for a relaxed, warmly inviting atmosphere, whilst competent cooking brings a French influence to many English favourites and makes good use of fine, fresh produce.

Closed Sun & Mon Lunch not served Sat

English & French 45 seats S% ✱Lunch £7.25&alc Dinner £12.50—£15alc Wine £5.50 Last dinner 9.30pm 20P

Credit cards 1 2 3

MELKSHAM
Wiltshire
Map **3** ST96

★★★ *BL* **Beechfield House** Beanacre (1m N A350) (Prestige) ☎(0225) 703700 Telex no 444969

This attractive Victorian house stands in extensive grounds on the edge of the town. With fine, quality appointments throughout, it offers comfortable bedrooms, including some in a converted coach house and excellent food.

8⇌ Annexe: 8⇌ 1 CTV in all bedrooms **T** sB&B⇌£40—£75 dB&B⇌£60—£85 ℞

40P (heated) (grass) croquet xmas

English & French **V** Lunch fr£9.50&alc Tea £1.25—£2 High Tea £2—£4 Dinner £18.50alc Wine £5.95 Last dinner 6.30pm

Credit cards 1 2 3 5

★★ *H* **Conigre Farm** Semington Rd ☎(0225) 702229

The 17th-century farmhouse offers a warm, friendly atmosphere and comfortable bedrooms in a variety of sizes, some of them in a converted stable block. Rooms are all named after Dickens characters, and Mr Bumble's Restaurant offers a good selection of well-prepared dishes.

4rm(1⇌) Annexe: 5rm(2⇌3⋒) 1 CTV in all bedrooms ®T ✱sB&B£16 sB&B⇌⋒£25—£30 dB&B£28 dB&B⇌⋒£35 ℞

16P 1

V ✱Lunch £5.95—£9.85&alc Dinner £9.85&alc Wine £5.66 Last dinner 10.30pm

Credit cards 1 2 3

★★ *HB* **Kings Arms** Market Pl ☎(0225) 707272

This attractive, fully-licensed hotel in the town centre provides attentive, very friendly service. Well maintained and comfortable bedrooms are equipped with a good range of facilities.

14rm(9⇌1⋒) CTV in all bedrooms ®T sB&B£19.50 sB&B⇌⋒£27 dB&B⇌⋒£36 ℞

40P xmas

V Lunch £6.50—£7&alc Tea fr50p Dinner £7&alc Wine £4.50 Last dinner 9pm

Credit cards 1 2 3 5 Ⓥ

See advertisement on page 512

MELLING
Lancashire
Map **7** SD57

★★**Melling Hall** (Exec Hotel) ☎ Hornby (0468) 21298

A converted 17th-century manor house, set in open country on the edge of the village.

13rm(6⇌2⋒)(1fb) CTV in all bedrooms ® ✱sB&Bfr£16 sB&B⇌⋒fr£21 dB&Bfr£25 dB&B⇌⋒fr£30 ℞

CTV 45P xmas

English & Continental **V** ✱Bar lunch £2.50alc Tea 50palc Dinner fr£9.50&alc Wine £4.80 Last dinner 9.45pm

Credit cards 1 2 3 Ⓥ

MELROSE
Borders *Roxburghshire*
Map **12** NT53

★★**Burt's** The Square ☎(089682) 2285

Dating from 1722, this converted town house is of architectural interest.

21rm(13⇌5⋒)(1fb) CTV in all bedrooms ®T sB&B£20—£24 sB&B⇌⋒£20—£24 dB&B£36—£40 dB&B⇌⋒£40—£44 ℞

CTV 36P snooker

English & French Lunch £7.25—£8.25 Dinner £9.50alc Wine £5 Last dinner 9.30pm

Credit cards 1 2 3 5

M

★★*George & Abbotsford* (Consort) ☎(089682) 2308
Three-storey, stone, coaching inn standing on the main road in the centre of this Border town.
31rm(20⛟11⛆)(3fb) ® T ⛿
#CTV 150P 4🚗
European ⛉ ☕ Last dinner 9.15pm
Credit cards 1 2 3 4 5

★*Bon-Accord* The Square ☎(089682) 2645
Small family-run country town hotel.
7rm(2fb) ® CTV
V ⛉ ☕ Last dinner 8pm
Credit cards 1 3 5

MELTHAM
West Yorkshire
Map **7** SE01

★★★**Durker Roods** Bishops Way ☎ Huddersfield (0484) 851413 Telex no 51324
Closed Xmas Day
Converted mill owner's mansion.
32rm(25⛟⛆)(3fb) CTV in all bedrooms ® T ✱sB&B⛟⛆£25—£35 dB&B⛟⛆£30—£40 ⛿
☾ 100P ✿

Melrose — Melton Mowbray

V ⛉ ☕ ✱Lunch £6&alc Tea 60p Dinner £8—£10&alc Wine £4.50 Last dinner 9.30pm
Credit cards 1 2 3 5

MELTON MOWBRAY
Leicestershire
Map **8** SK71

★★★**Harboro'** Burton St (Anchor) ☎(0664) 60121 Telex no 341713
Commercial hotel, which was a former coaching inn, situated on the A606.
28rm(24⛟4⛆)(1fb) ⚟ in 5 bedrooms CTV in all bedrooms ® T
✱sB&B⛟⛆£26—£39
dB&B⛟⛆£36—£49 ⛿
☾ 40P
V ⛉ ☕ ✱Lunch £9.50&alc Tea 60p—£3.95 High Tea £4.20—£7.40 Dinner £9.50&alc Wine £5.95 Last dinner 10pm
Credit cards 1 2 3 5 Ⓥ

★★★*George* High St (Inter Hotel) ☎(0664) 62112
A town-centre coaching inn dating from the 17th century, the George provides comfortable accommodation; a good range of bar snacks is available in the cosy atmosphere of its three bars.
19rm(17⛟2⛆)(1fb) 4⛶ CTV in all bedrooms ® ⛿
15P 2🚗 *xmas*
English & French ⛉ ☕ Last dinner 10pm
Credit cards 1 2 3 4

★★**Kings Head** Nottingham St (Home Brewery) ☎(0664) 62110
Central hotel with modern accommodation.
15rm(4⛟8⛆)(1fb) CTV in all bedrooms ® sB&Bfr£28 sB&B⛟⛆fr£32.50 dB&Bfr£35 dB&B⛟⛆fr£39.50 ⛿
CTV 100P 20🚗
⛉Lunch £4.95alc Dinner £4.95alc Wine £4.10 Last dinner 9pm
Credit cards 1 2 3

★★**Sysonby Knoll** Asfordby Rd ☎(0664) 63563
Closed Xmas
This comfortable little hotel stands in its own grounds on the outskirts of the market town, having pleasant views over the River Eye and surrounding countryside.
21rm(13⛟3⛆)(1fb) 1⛶ CTV in all bedrooms ® T ✱sB&B£20 sB&B⛟⛆£26—£29 dB&B£28 dB&B⛟⛆£32—£34 ⛿
CTV 20P ✿ ⛾

M

V ♕ ☕ S% Lunch £6alc Dinner £5.50—£6.50&alc Wine £4.30 Last dinner 9pm
Credit cards 1 3 V

MELVICH
Highland *Caithness*
Map **14** NC86
★★ **B Melvich** ☎ (06413) 206
This friendly roadside hotel has stunning sea views.
14rm(8⌂) CTV in all bedrooms ® *sB&B£15 sB&B⌂£18.50 dB&B£28 dB&B⌂£35
CTV 10P ✿
V ♕ ☕ *Bar lunch fr£2.50 Tea fr£1 High Tea fr£4 Dinner fr£8.50 Wine £3.40

MEMBURY
Devon
Map **3** SY29
★★ ***Lea Hill Farm*** ☎ Stockland (040488) 388
Closed Jan RS Feb (wknds)
Converted farmhouse with attractive dining room.
6rm(5⌂1⌂)(4fb) CTV in 3 bedrooms ® B
CTV 30P ✿ *xmas*
English & French Last dinner 8.30pm
Credit card 1

Melton Mowbray — Mere

MENAI BRIDGE
Gwynedd
Map **6** SH57
★★ **Anglesey Arms** ☎ (0248) 712305
Standing at the end of the Menai Suspension Bridge, at the gateway to Anglesey, this hotel provides comfortable, modern accommodation.
17rm(12⌂4⌂) CTV available in bedrooms ® sB&B fr£21 sB&B⌂ fr£23 dB&B⌂ fr£46 B
CTV 35P ✿
V ♕ ☕ Lunch fr£5 Dinner fr£7&alc Wine £4 Last dinner 9pm
Credit cards 1 3

★★ **Gazelle** Glyn Garth (2m NE A545) ☎ (0248) 713364
Former Posting Inn beside Menai Straits, this hotel provides good well cooked food.
9rm(4⌂1⌂) Annexe: 2rm(1⌂)(1fb) CTV in 10 bedrooms TV in 1 bedroom ® *sB&B£18 sB&B⌂£20 dB&B£29 dB&B⌂£36 B
50P

V ♕ ☕ Lunch £6alc Tea £1alc Dinner fr£7.55&alc Wine £4.50 Last dinner 9.15pm
Credit cards 1 3

MENDHAM
Suffolk
Map **5** TM28
★ ***Sir Alfred Munnings Country*** Studio Corner ☎ Harleston (0379) 852358
The inn, set in quiet countryside, offers informal service and a good range of private facilities.
14rm(1⌂6⌂) ® B
CTV 40P (heated)
English & French ♕ ☕ Last dinner 9.30pm
Credit cards 1 2 3 5

MERE
Wiltshire
Map **3** ST83
★★ **Old Ship** Castle St (Inter Hotel) ☎ (0747) 860258
16th-century building of architectural interest with comfortable bedrooms and modern annexe, with good range of meals served in restaurant.
14rm(6⌂) Annexe: 10rm(8⌂2⌂)(3fb) 2 CTV in all bedrooms ® T sB&B£25 sB&B⌂£27 dB&B£35 dB&B⌂£40 B
50P →

M

Lunch £9alc Tea 60p High Tea £3.50 Dinner £9alc Wine £4.80 Last dinner 9.30pm

Credit cards 1 3 V

MERE BROW
Lancashire
Map **7** SD41

✕**Crab & Lobster** ☎ Hesketh Bank (077473) 2734.

The restaurant is housed in an old cottage, which was converted in 1962, and has been recently extended.

Closed Sun, Mon & Xmas—30 Jan Lunch not served

50 seats S% ✱Dinner £14alc Wine £5.50 Last dinner 9.30pm P

MERIDEN
West Midlands
Map **4** SP28

★★★**Manor** (De Vere) ☎ (0676) 22735 Telex no 311011

A popular restaurant overlooking the swimming pool and separate large banqueting facilities are features of this Georgian-style hotel.

32 CTV in all bedrooms ® T S% sB&B £47 dB&B £58 B

☾ 270P CFA (heated) Live music & dancing Sat Cabaret Sat *xmas*

English & French V S% Lunch £8.50&alc Tea 95p Dinner £9.75&alc Wine £5.75 Last dinner 10pm

Credit cards 1 2 3 5

M

MERTHYR TYDFIL
Mid Glamorgan
Map **3** SO00

★★**Tregenna** Park Ter ☎ (0685) 3627

The modernised hotel stands in a side road near the town centre. Public rooms have good facilities and there are well-constructed chalet bedrooms to the rear; bedrooms in the main building are in process of upgrading.

12rm (8 4) Annexe: (7) (6fb) CTV in all bedrooms ® T sB&B fr£25 dB&B fr£34

☾ CTV 20P *xmas*

Mere — Middleham

English, French & Italian V Lunch £5.75—£6&alc Tea £1—£1.25 Dinner £8—£9 Wine £6 Last dinner 10pm

Credit cards 1 3 V

MEVAGISSEY
Cornwall
Map **2** SX04

★★***Spa*** Polkirt Hill ☎ (0726) 842244

Peaceful, comfortable, family run hotel with good gardens and pleasant bedrooms, most with sea views.

10rm (5) (1fb) CTV in all bedrooms ® B

CTV 20P 2 (hard) nc5yrs

Last dinner 6pm

Credit cards 1 2 3 5

★★**Tremarne** Polkirt Hill ☎ (0726) 842213

Closed Nov—Mar

Comfortable, friendly family holiday hotel with good food, pleasant garden and fine views.

14rm (4 10) (2fb) CTV in all bedrooms ® sB&B £16—£18.50 dB&B £26—£34 B

14P (heated) games room nc 5yrs

Bar lunch fr80p Tea fr£1.25 Dinner £8.75—£9.50 Wine £4.95 Last dinner 8.30pm

Credit cards 1 3 V

★★**Trevalsa Court** Polstreath ☎ (0726) 842468

Closed mid Dec—mid Jan

Country house of character in a peaceful situation overlooking the sea.

10rm (5 2) CTV in all bedrooms ® sB&B £14.50 sB&B £14.50 dB&B £29—£31 dB&B £40—£50 B

45P

English, French & Italian ✱Bar lunch £2.50alc Dinner £7.50alc Last dinner 6pm

Credit cards 1 2 3 5

★**Sharksfin** The Quay ☎ (072684) 3241

Closed Dec & Jan

Set near the harbour, this restaurant was once a sardine warehouse and cannery; now it offers extensive menus and pleasant service by local staff.

11rm (4fb) CTV in all bedrooms ✱sB&B £13.25—£15.25 dB&B £20.50—£24.50

P

✱Dinner £4.50&alc Wine fr£4.60 Last dinner 8.30pm

Credit cards 1 2 3 5

MICKLETON
Gloucestershire
Map **4** SP14

★★★**Three Ways** (Inter Hotel) ☎ (038677) 231 Telex no 337497

A modern bedroom wing, attractive restaurant and conference room are features of this convenient touring hotel.

37rm (34 3) (5fb) CTV in all bedrooms ® T ✱sB&B £28.33 dB&B £46—£52 B

Lift ☾ 30P (charge) CFA Cabaret Sat *xmas*

V Lunch £6.50—£8 Tea 60p—£1.65 High Tea £2.50—£3.50 Dinner £10—£12 Wine £5.60 Last dinner 9pm

Credit cards 1 2 3 5 V

MIDDLEHAM
North Yorkshire
Map **7** SE18

★★**Millers House** Market Pl ☎ Wensleydale (0969) 22630

Closed Dec & Jan

An 18th-century former merchant's house, in the corner of the Market Place.

6rm (5 1) CTV in all bedrooms ® sB&B £20 dB&B £38 B

8P nc 11yrs

English & French Dinner £10 Wine £4.95 Last dinner 5.30pm

Credit card 1 V

MIDDLESBROUGH
Cleveland
Map **8** NZ42

★★★**Blue Bell** Acklam (Swallow) ☎ (0642) 593939 Telex no 53168

A two-storey hotel with a modern wing, standing by a busy roundabout.

60🛁🚿⅍ in 10 bedrooms CTV in all bedrooms Ⓡ **T** S% ✱sB&B🛁🚿£29—£39 dB&B🛁🚿£39—£46 B

Lift ☾ CTV 200P CFA Disco Thu *xmas*

Mainly grills **V** S% ✱Bar lunch £1.50—£2.50 Dinner £9&alc Wine £6.50 Last dinner 9.45pm

Credit cards 1 2 3 4 5

★★★**Ladbroke Dragonara** (& Conferencentre) Fry St (Ladbroke) ☎ (0642) 248133 Telex no 58266

Multi-storey modern hotel near the town centre.

140rm(126🛁14🚿)(11fb) CTV in all bedrooms Ⓡ **T** S% ✱sB&B🛁🚿£35—£52 dB&B🛁🚿£62—£68 B

Lift ☾ 60 CFA ♿

International **V** S% ✱Lunch £7—£7.50 Dinner £9.75—£10.50&alc Wine £5.99 Last dinner 10pm

Credit cards 1 2 3 5 Ⓥ

★★★***Marton Hotel & Country Club*** Stokesley Rd, Marton (3m S of A172) ☎ (0642) 317141

A modern functionally built three storey hotel at the junction of the A172 and A174. Spacious public areas and conference banqueting facilities. Bright and cheerful bedrooms, warm and comfortable facilities.

52🛁(2fb) CTV in all bedrooms B

☾ # CTV 300P CFA billiards Live music & dancing wkly Cabaret wkly

English, French & Italian **V** Last dinner 10pm

Credit cards 1 2 3 5

★★★***Marton Way*** Marton Rd ☎ (0642) 817651 Telex no 587783

This comfortable, modern hotel surrounds a courtyard car park; both lunch and dinner are available from the popular, good-value carvery.

Annexe: 52🛁🚿(4fb) CTV in all bedrooms Ⓡ B

☾ 200P CFA

English & French Last dinner 10pm

Credit cards 1 2 3 5

MIDDLETON-IN-TEESDALE
Co Durham
Map **12** NY92

★★*HB* ***Teesdale*** Market Pl ☎ Teesdale (0833) 40264

The friendly, family-run hotel offers very comfortable accommodation and good home cooking.

14rm(7🛁)(1fb) B

CTV P *xmas*

English, French, German & Italian **V** Last dinner 8.30pm

Credit card 3

MIDDLETON STONEY
Oxfordshire
Map **4** SP52

★★**Jersey Arms** ☎ (086989) 234

Charming Cotswold stone inn, with comfortable bedrooms, some suites and friendly staff.

6🛁 Annexe: 8🛁(1fb) 1 CTV in all bedrooms **T** sB&B🛁£32 dB&B🛁£42 B

55P

English & French Lunch £11alc Dinner £11alc Wine £6.50 Last dinner 9.30pm

Credit cards 1 2 3 5

See advertisement under Oxford

MIDDLE WALLOP
Hampshire
Map **4** SU23

★★**Fifehead Manor** ☎ Andover (0264) 781565

Closed 1 wk Xmas

A small manor house on the fringe of the village has been tastefully restored to provide comfortable accommodation in both the main building and annexe. In the restaurant a sophisticated à la carte menu of French cuisine is served by a willing young staff.

11🛁🚿 CTV in all bedrooms **T** S% sB&B🛁🚿£36—£42 dB&B🛁🚿£50—£65 B

50P 1 croquet ♿

English & French S% Lunch £16&alc Tea £1.75 Dinner £16&alc Wine £3.50 Last dinner 9.30pm

Credit cards 1 2 3 4 5

✕**Old Drapery Stores** ☎ Andover (0264) 781301

This delightful, late Georgian building, known to generations of villagers as 'Southwells: Drapers and Hatters', has been tastefully restored, retaining some of the original counters in the bar. The dishes on the fixed-price menu are freshly cooked, and overnight accommodation is available.

Closed Sun Lunch not served Sat

Continental 42 seats ✱Lunch £10.50—£12.75&alc Dinner £10.50—£12.75 Wine £5.50 Last dinner 9.45pm 14P

Credit cards 2 3 5

MIDHURST
West Sussex
Map **4** SU82

★★★**Spread Eagle** South St (Best Western) ☎ (073081) 2211 Telex no 86853

The unique and famous coaching inn, dating from 1430, features an outstanding lounge bar and restaurant. Bedrooms are individually furnished with antiques, and the 24-hour service is both friendly and efficient. →

37🛁 CTV in all bedrooms **T** S% sB&B£35 sB&B🛁£44—£56 dB&B£45 dB&B🛁£55—£125 **B**

☾80P CFA ✿ *xmas*

🍷English & French 🍵 ☕ S% Lunch fr£10.50&alc Tea fr£1.25 Dinner fr£14.50&alc Wine £6.75 Last dinner 9.15pm

Credit cards 1 2 3 5 Ⓥ

★★**Angel** North St ☎ (073081) 2421

This country-town, commercial hotel, recently refurbished to provide comfortable accommodation, has character and a friendly, informal atmosphere.

17rm(12🛁4🚿) CTV in all bedrooms **T** ✱sB&B🛁🚿£30 dB&B🛁🚿£44

P *xmas*

🍵 ☕ ✱Tea 60p Last dinner 9.30pm

Credit cards 1 2 3 4 5

✕✕**Olde Manor House** Church Hill ☎ (073081) 2990

Located in a sleepy market town, the restaurant offers exposed beams, a log fire and an enthusiastic welcome. The varied continental menu shows Spanish influence and is complemented by a comprehensive wine list.

Closed Mon
Dinner not served Sun

🍷English & Spanish 50 seats Lunch £7&alc Wine £4.95 Last dinner 10.30pm ₱

Credit cards 1 2 3 5

MILDENHALL
Suffolk
Map **5** TL77

★★**Bell** High St (Best Western) ☎ (0638) 717272

Parts of this former coaching inn date from 1600.

18rm(12🛁2🚿)(3fb) CTV in all bedrooms Ⓡ**T** sB&Bfr£24 sB&B🛁🚿fr£27.50 dB&Bfr£36 dB&B🛁🚿fr£39 **B**

25P *xmas*

V 🍵 ☕ Lunch £5.95—£10 Tea 60p High Tea £3 Dinner £7—£12&alc Wine £4.25 Last dinner 9pm

Credit cards 1 2 3 5 Ⓥ

M

Midhurst — Milngavie

★★**Riverside** Mill St ☎ (0638) 717274

Popular with families from the nearby Air Force Base, the listed, red brick house stands at the end of the town's main road, its rear lawns stretching down to the River Lark.

19rm(9🛁6🚿)(4fb) CTV in all bedrooms Ⓡ **T** ✱sB&B£22 sB&B🛁🚿£25 dB&B£32 dB&B🛁🚿£35 **B**

Lift 25P ✿ ♪

🍷International **V** 🍵 ☕ ✱Lunch £5.15—£9&alc Tea 60p alc Dinner £5.15—£9&alc Wine £4.75 Last dinner 9pm

Credit cards 1 2 3 5 Ⓥ

MILFORD HAVEN
Dyfed
Map **2** SM90

★★**Lord Nelson** Hamilton Ter ☎ (06462) 5341 Telex no 48622

RS Xmas Day

Comfortable, modern hotel.

29rm(21🛁6🚿)(3fb) 🚭 in 3 bedrooms CTV in all bedrooms Ⓡ**T** ✱sB&B£25 sB&B🛁🚿£25 dB&B£37 dB&B🛁🚿£37 **B**

☾CTV 23P Disco 5 nights wkly Cabaret mthly

🍷English & French 🍵 ☕ ✱Bar lunch 80p—£4.95 High Tea fr85p Dinner fr£7.95 Wine £4.75 Last dinner 9pm

Credit cards 1 2 3 5 Ⓥ

★★***Sir Benfro*** Herbrandston (3m W on unclass rd) ☎ (06462) 4242

Small friendly hotel.

12🛁(1fb) CTV in all bedrooms Ⓡ**T** **B**

50P ✿ ⛵ ⛳ *xmas*

🍷English & French 🍵 ☕ Last dinner 9.45pm

Credit cards 1 2 3 4 5

MILFORD-ON-SEA
Hampshire
Map **4** SZ29

★★★**Westover Hall** Park Ln ☎ Lymington (0590) 43044

This late Victorian house boasts fine, wood-panelled walls, well-appointed bedrooms and fine sea views across to the Isle of Wight. Service is warmly informal, and you are assured of the personal attention of the proprietors.

11rm(9🛁2🚿) CTV in all bedrooms Ⓡ**T** sB&B£16—£26 sB&B🛁🚿£18—£26 dB&B£32—£48 dB&B🛁🚿£36—£60 **B**

40P 🚫 ✿ Live music & dancing Sat mthly *xmas*

🍷English & French **V** 🍵 ☕ Lunch £5.75—£8&alc Tea £1.50—£2.50 Dinner £8.75—£12&alc Wine £4.75 Last dinner 9.30pm

Credit cards 1 2 3 5 Ⓥ

✕**Mill House** 1 High St ☎ Lymington (0590) 42611

Small personally run village restaurant with baked prawns a delicious speciality.

Closed Mon & 20 Oct—3 Nov Dinner not served Sun

🍷English & French **V** 50 seats Lunch £4.60—£5.20&alc Dinner £7.95&alc Wine £4.65 Last dinner 9.30pm ₱

Credit cards 1 2 3 5 Ⓥ

MILNGAVIE
Strathclyde *Dunbartonshire*
Map **11** NS57

★★★**Black Bull Thistle** Main St (Thistle) ☎ 041-956 2291 Telex no 778323

A former coaching inn has been tastefully restored to retain the character of its historic past. Quality and tradition are reflected in the beamed ceilings, polished oak and tapestries of the public rooms, whilst bedrooms offer all modern facilties.

27rm(22🛁)(3fb) CTV in all bedrooms Ⓡ**T** ✱sB🛁£42—£49 dB🛁£47—£55 (room only) **B**

☾120P

🍷International 🍵 ☕ ✱Lunch fr£4.50&alc Dinner fr£11&alc Wine £7 Last dinner 9pm

Credit cards 1 2 3 4 5 Ⓥ

MILTON
Dyfed
Map **2** SN00

★★**Milton Manor** ☏ Carew (06467) 398

This personally-run Georgian manor house stands in 7 acres of secluded grounds.

26rm(14→13⋒)(1fb) CTV in 14 bedrooms ® S% sB&B£16.15—£17.75 sB&B→⋒£17.75—£21.20 dB&B£28—£30.70 dB&B→⋒£30.70—£36.70 B

CTV 40P ✿ U solarium putting games room 🏠 *xmas*

International V ♁ ☕ S% Bar lunch £2.50—£4.25&alc Tea fr60p High Tea £2.50—£4.25 Dinner fr£6.85&alc Wine £3.90 Last dinner 9.30pm

Credit card 1 Ⓥ

MILTON ABBAS
Dorset
Map **3** ST80

★★♣**Milton Manor** ☏ (0258) 880254

Closed Nov—Etr

Tudor-style hotel in its own grounds.

12rm(5→3⋒)(2fb) ✗ sB&B£23 sB&B→⋒£25 dB&B£35 dB&B→⋒£39

CTV 20P ✿ putting croquet nc12yrs

Lunch £5—£7 Dinner £8.50—£10 Wine £3.85 Last dinner 7.30pm

Credit cards 1 3 Ⓥ

MILTON COMMON
Oxfordshire
Map **2** SP60

★★**Belfry** Brimpton Grange (Inter Hotel) ☏ Great Milton (08446) 381 Telex no 837968

Closed 25 Dec—30 Dec

Large, half-timbered, country house in extensive grounds.

60rm(52→8⋒) CTV in all bedrooms ® ✱ sB&B→⋒£36—£40 dB&B→⋒£44—£60 Continental breakfast B

☾ 200P ✿ CFA ⛆ Disco Sat 🏠

English & Continental ♁ ☕ ✱ Lunch £8.50 Tea 65p Dinner £10.50—£11.50 Wine £5.75 Last dinner 9.30pm

Credit cards 1 2 3 5 Ⓥ

See advertisement under Oxford

★★★

❀❀❀★★★♣**LE MANOIR AUX QUAT' SAISONS, MILTON, GREAT**

(9m SE of Oxford, follow signs to Wallingford from junction A40/A329 (M40 junction 7) then second turning right) (Prestige) ☏ (08446) 8881 Telex no 837552

Closed 25 Dec—21 Jan

The great news this year is the unanimous recommendation from our inspectors to award three rosettes. We have watched Raymond Blanc develop from the start of his career to reach a pinnacle of near perfection. He cooks in the modern style but gains an eclectic inspiration from classic, French provincial and even oriental sources, the latter particularly influencing the artistic presentation of dishes; and, of course, you may be sure that he is always seeking out the best quality produce. At lunch there is a good value fixed price menu as well as the 6 course Menu Gourmand and à la carte which features a page of seasonal specialities. Reports of many memorable dishes have been ecstatic, but we think items like the mousse of asparagus encased in leeks and served with a chervil juice demonstrates his delicacy of touch, while roast teal with a garnish of braised chicory and St Emilion sauce shows his gastronomic taste, and the apparent simplicity that takes such unremitting attention to detail to achieve. His puddings and chocolates come up to the same standards. Like all the best cooks his sense of balance in the composition of dishes is such that you can always taste the constituent parts, but the total effect is complete. The wine list of nearly 300 is outstanding, but like all the costs here, it is expensive; nevertheless they represent good

value. As always you will be beautifully served by the immaculately turned out, courteous young staff, well trained by the urbane restaurant manager, Alain Desenclos perhaps, the best outside London. All this takes place in a lovely Cotswold stone manor in 27 acres of grounds which, as you would expect, includes a kitchen plot to produce vegetables and herbs for the kitchen. The bedrooms are luxuriously decorated and furnished and superbly equipped. The public areas, particularly the lounge, are all most attractive and flowers abound. The atmosphere is that of a restaurant with rooms and so is the operation: continental breakfast is served in your bedroom, the restaurant is shut Sunday night and all day Monday; however, on those occasions, residents can be served something to eat in their room.

10→(2fb) 2⊟ CTV in all bedrooms T ✗ S% dB&B→£95—£220 Continental breakfast B

☾ 50P ✿ ⛆(heated) ℘(hard) U

French V ♁ ⚡ S% Lunch £19.50—£24&alc Dinner £36&alc Last dinner 10.30pm

Credit cards 1 2 3 4 5

MILTON, GREAT
Oxfordshire
Map **4** SP60

MILTON KEYNES
Buckinghamshire
Map **4** SP83

See **Newport Pagnell, Wicken & Woburn**

○**Post House** 500 Saxon Gate West (Trusthouse Forte) ☏ (0908) 667722

163→⋒

Due to have opened September 1986.

MINCHINHAMPTON
Gloucestershire

See **Amberley**

MINEHEAD
Somerset
Map **3** SS94

★★★**Beach** The Avenue (Trusthouse Forte) ☏ (0643) 2193

Built in 1874 of local brick and now fully modernised, the hotel is close to the Explanade and the beach.

34rm(32→2⋒)(3fb) CTV in all bedrooms ® sB&B→⋒£41.50 dB&B→⋒£56.50 B

40P ⛆(heated) 🏠 *xmas*

♁ Last dinner 8.45pm

Credit cards 1 2 3 4 5

★★★**Benares** Northfield Rd (Consort) ☎(0643) 2340
Closed Nov—Feb (except Xmas)
Friendly holiday and business hotel, with good restaurant and fine garden.
21rm(16⇌1⋔)(2fb) CTV in all bedrooms Ⓡ sB&B£19 sB&B⇌⋔£23 dB&B£38 dB&B⇌⋔£44 B
20P 2🚗(£1.25 per night) ✿ *xmas*
English, French & Italian V Bar lunch £3.50—£7 Tea 60p Dinner £9.75&alc Wine £5.15 Last dinner 8.30pm
Credit cards 1 2 3 5 Ⓥ

★★★*HL* **Northfield** Northfield Rd (Best Western) ☎(0643) 5155 Telex no 42513
This superior holiday hotel has increased facilities for every guest. Proprietors and staff provide an excellent choice of food, an individual friendly welcome and good service, whilst the gardens are a must for real garden lovers.
27rm(25⇌2⋔)(6fb) CTV in all bedrooms Ⓡ T ✱ sB&B⇌⋔£30.25—£37.75 dB&B⇌⋔£54.50—£75.50 B
Lift 24P ✿ (heated) sauna bath gymnasium putting ♿ *xmas*
V ✱ Lunch £2—£6.25 Tea £1.50 Dinner £9.95—£14.45 Wine £4 Last dinner 8.15pm
Credit cards 1 2 3 5

Minehead

★★**Beaconwood** Church Rd, North Hill ☎(0643) 2032
Closed Dec—Feb RS Nov
Peaceful, family-run hotel outside the town centre.
16rm(7⇌4⋔)(3fb) CTV in all bedrooms Ⓡ sB&B£14.80—£16.30 sB&B⇌⋔£18.80—£20.30 dB&B£29.60 dB&B⇌⋔£37.60 B
CTV 25P ✿ (heated) *xmas*
V Lunch £4.50alc Dinner £8.20&alc Wine £4 Last dinner 7.30pm
Credit cards 1 3 Ⓥ

★★**Merton** Western Ln, The Parks (Guestaccom/Exec Hotel) ☎(0643) 2375
Closed Nov—Etr
Small, holiday and business hotel, that is comfortable and personally run.
12rm(3⇌3⋔)(3fb) S% sB&B£11—£13.50 dB&B£22—£27 dB&B⇌⋔£25.20—£30.20
CTV 14P ✿ ♿
S% Dinner £8—£8.50 Last dinner 8pm
Credit cards 1 3

★★**Winsor** The Avenue ☎(0643) 2171
Closed mid Oct—Apr
Large, seasonal, holiday hotel run by the owners.
33rm(10⇌1⋔)(3fb) CTV in 10 bedrooms Ⓡ sB&B£12.50 sB&B⇌⋔£14.50 dB&B£25 dB&B⇌⋔£29 B
CTV 26P
V Lunch £3.25 Dinner £6 Wine £3.75 Last dinner 8pm
Credit cards 1 2 3 5 Ⓥ

★★**York** The Avenue (Best Western) ☎(0643) 5151
The detached, stone-built, gabled hotel stands on the main road from the town centre to the beach. The large bar offers a good range of bar foods, and facilities are sound throughout.
23rm(5⇌4⋔)(2fb) CTV in 8 bedrooms Ⓡ T S% ✱ sB&Bfr£12 sB&B⇌⋔fr£15 dB&Bfr£24 dB&B⇌⋔fr£30
CTV 10P nc5yrs
S% ✱ Bar lunch £1.65—£5.75 Dinner £6.50—£8&alc Wine £4.50 Last dinner 9pm
Credit cards 1 2 3 5

★*H* **Kingsway** Ponsford Rd ☎(0643) 2313
Comfortable, privately-owned and run holiday hotel.

M

10rm(2⥊)(2fb) CTV in all bedrooms sB&B£12—£15 dB&B£24—£28 dB&B⥊£28—£32

CTV 10P nc3yrs *xmas*

V Lunch fr£6 Tea fr£1 Dinner fr£7.50&alc Wine £3.60 Last dinner 7pm

Credit cards 1 3 V

★Mentone The Parks ☎ (0643) 5229

Closed Nov—Mar

The small, privately owned and personally run hotel offers thoughtfully prepared, imaginative menus and provides an ideal centre for touring.

9rm(4⥊2⥊) CTV in all bedrooms ® ✱sB&B£10—£15.50 dB&B£20—£31 dB&B⥊£20—£31

5P 2 nc10yrs

English, Asian & Continental ✱Tea fr30p Dinner £5.50 Wine £3.50 Last dinner 7.15pm

V

MINSTEAD
Hampshire
Map **4** SU21

✕Honeysuckle Cottage
☎ Southampton (0703) 813122

Closed Sun, Mon, Tue & Xmas wk Lunch not served

Set in a delightful, beamed cottage in a quiet village location, this family-run restaurant provides cheerful service and honest, predominantly English, food.

46 seats Dinner £16 Wine £5.80 Last dinner 9.30pm 21P

Credit card 1 V

MINSTER LOVELL
Oxfordshire
Map **4** SP31

★★*B* Old Swan ☎ Witney (0993) 75614

A small, Cotswold-stone hotel of considerable charm and quality, the Old Swan complements comfortable bedrooms and lounges with a popular restaurant and friendly service.

10⥊⥊1 CTV in all bedrooms ®T sB&B⥊⥊fr£33 dB&B⥊⥊£49—£55 B

50P *xmas*

V Lunch £7.50&alc Dinner £11alc Wine £5.50 Last dinner 9.30pm

Credit cards 1 2 3

MOCHRUM
Dumfries & Galloway *Wigtownshire*
Map **10** NX34

★Greenmantle ☎ Port William (09887) 357

Converted from a 17th century manse, this hotel stands in its own grounds in the centre of this small country village.

7rm(6⥊)(1fb) sB&B£11.50—£15.50 sB&B⥊£11.50—£15.50 dB&B⥊£23—£31 B

CTV 20P

Lunch £5.50 Tea £1 Dinner £7—£8&alc Wine £4.25 Last dinner 9.30pm

MODBURY
Devon
Map **3** SX65

★Modbury Inn Brownston St ☎ (0548) 830275

This popular, cosy hostelry has delightful public rooms with exposed beams and brasses, whilst bedrooms are modern and fitted. Good food is accompanied by a range of ales.

6rm(1⥊) CTV in all bedrooms ® ✱sB&B£12.65 dB&B£25.30 dB&B⥊£27.30

CTV 6P nc8yrs

✱Lunch £3—£4 Dinner £4alc Wine £4.25 Last dinner 9.30pm

V

M

✕**Modbury Pippin** 35 Church St ☎ (0548) 830765

A terraced shop has been converted to provide this village-centre restaurant, where economical lunches and more sophisticated evening meals can be obtained.

Closed Sun, Mon (ex Jun—Sep); Tue & Wed Nov—Dec & Feb-Mar; & Jan

European **V** 28 seats Lunch £5.90alc Dinner £7.50&alc Wine £4 Last dinner 9.30pm nc 5yrs

Credit cards 1 2 3 5 V

MOELFRE

Gwynedd

Map **6** SH58

✕✕**Old Ship's Bell** ☎ (024888) 693

An attractive cottage-style restaurant stands on a hill overlooking the village and small bay. The well-chosen menu offers a good selection of fish, poultry and meat dishes, and diners can enjoy panoramic sea views through the picture windows of the well-equipped dining room.

Closed Mon (except Jul & Aug) & Jan Lunch not served (except Sun) Bar lunches available Jul & Aug Dinner not served Sun (except Bank Hol's)

English & French 50 seats Lunch (Sun) £5.95 Dinner £13.50 Wine £3.95 Last dinner 9.30pm 4P

Credit cards 1 3

MOFFAT

Dumfries & Galloway *Dumfriesshire*

Map **11** NT00

★★★**Ladbroke** Ladyknowe (Ladbroke) ☎ (0683) 20464

Closed 1 wk Xmas

A modern, two-storey building at the foot of the main square.

51rm(44 4)(2fb) in 1 bedroom CTV in all bedrooms ® S%

*sB&B £19.50—£37.50 dB&B £39—£59

70P pool Live music & dancing Thu & Sun in season *xmas*

V * Bar lunch 85p—£4.65 Tea 50p High Tea £3.50—£4.50 Dinner £9.50&alc Wine £5.95 Last dinner 9pm

Credit cards 1 2 3 4 5 V

★★**Annandale** High St ☎ (0683) 20013

Closed Dec—Mar

A modernised and extended coaching inn dating from 1780.

19rm Annexe: 5 (4fb) CTV in all bedrooms ® sB&B £16—£17 sB&B £20—£21 dB&B £30—£32 dB&B £34—£36

50P

V Bar lunch £3.95alc Dinner £6.75—£7 Wine £4.35 Last dinner 8.15pm

Credit cards 1 2 3 5 V

★★*B* **Beechwood Country House** ☎ (0683) 20210

Closed Jan

Located on the outskirts of the town, the charming, welcoming hotel is operated in the country-house style and is renowned for its good home cooking.

8rm(5 3) ® **T** sB&B £20—£24 dB&B £40—£44

CTV 25P croquet *xmas*

Bar lunch £4.85—£6 Tea £2.50—£4 Dinner £12.75—£15 Wine £3.99 Last dinner 9pm

Credit cards 1 2 3 4 5

★★**Moffat House** High St (Exec Hotel) ☎ (0683) 20039

RS Nov—Mar except Xmas & New Year

Fine 18th century Adam mansion with wide country views at rear. Nicely decorated rooms and attentive service.

14rm(6 8)(4fb) ® sB&B £25—£27 dB&B £39—£42

CTV 40P 6

Scottish & French **V** Bar lunch £5alc High Tea £5.50alc Dinner £10alc Wine £5.50 Last dinner 8.45pm

Credit cards 1 2 3 5

★**Balmoral** High St ☎ (0683) 20288
Two-storey hotel with characteristic shutters.
15rm(2⇌)(1fb) CTV in 2 bedrooms ®
✱sB&Bfr£15 dB&Bfr£24 dB&B⇌fr£30 B
CTV 12P Disco Sat *xmas*
☥ ☕ ✱Lunch £4.20alc Tea 55p—£2 High Tea fr£3.80 Dinner fr£8.80&alc Wine £3.50 Last dinner 8.30pm
Credit cards 1 2 3 5

MOLD
Clwyd
Map **7** SJ26
See **Northop Hall**

Moffat — Monk Fryston

MONIAIVE
Dumfries & Galloway *Dumfriesshire*
Map **11** NX79
★★**Woodlea** ☎ (08482) 209
Closed Nov—Mar
A family hotel with many recreational facilities, set in five acres of grounds.
14rm(7⇌)(8fb) CTV in all bedrooms ®
sB&B£17.50—£18 dB&B£35—£38
dB&B⇌£45—£48 B
CTV 20P ✽ (heated) (hard)
sauna bath solarium gymnasium putting croquet clay pigeon shooting
☥ ☕ Bar lunch fr80p Tea £1.75—£1.80 Dinner £7.50—£8 Wine £4.60 Last dinner 8.30pm

MONK FRYSTON
North Yorkshire
Map **8** SE52
★★★**Monk Fryston Hall** ☎ South Milford (0977) 682369 Telex no 556634
A medieval country mansion, standing in its own grounds and ornamental gardens, popular with businessmen. →

M

24rm(21➡3⋒)(2fb) CTV in all bedrooms ® T S% sB&B➡⋒£37—£40 dB&B➡⋒£51—£55 ₿

☾60P 2🚗(charge) ⇌ ❁ ♿ *xmas*

🍷 ☕ S% Lunch £7.20—£7.80&alc Tea £1.35—£1.50 Dinner £10.60—£11.50&alc Wine £7.20 Last dinner 9.30pm

Credit cards 1 2 3

MONKLEIGH

Devon
Map **2** SS42

★★***Beaconside*** ☎ Bideford (02372) 77205

Comfortable, small, secluded hotel with good food and atmosphere.

9rm(4➡2⋒)(2fb) CTV in all bedrooms 🐕 ₿

⚡CTV 16P ❁ ⛆(heated) 🎾(grass)

V 🍷 ☕ Last dinner 8pm

Credit cards 1 5

See advertisement under Torrington, Great

MONMOUTH

Gwent
Map **3** SO51

★★★**Kings Head** Agincourt Sq (Inter Hotel) ☎ (0600) 2177 Telex no 497294

Comfortable, traditional hotel with Charles I associations.

28rm(20➡8⋒) Annexe: 3➡(2fb) 1⊞ CTV in all bedrooms **T** sB&B➡⋒£46 dB&B➡⋒£64 ₿

☾20P CFA *xmas*

🍽 Welsh, English & French **V** 🍷 Lunch £9&alc Dinner £13.50&alc Last dinner 9pm

Credit cards 1 2 3 5

★**Talocher Farmhouse** Wonastow Rd ☎ Dingestow (060083) 236

Small, character, rural hotel.

10rm(1➡)(2fb) S% sB&B£15 dB&B£25 dB&B➡£25 ₿

CTV 20P 2🚗 ❁ ⛆ 🎣 sauna bath solarium

V ✱Lunch £5—£8&alc Dinner £6—£8&alc Wine £3.75 Last dinner 9pm

Ⓥ

MONTACUTE

Somerset
Map **3** ST41

★★*B* **Kings Arms Inn** Bishopston ☎ Martock (0935) 822513

Dating back to the 16th century, this attractive, Ham stone inn stands at the centre of the village. It offers a pleasant lounge and bars, an attractive restaurant and good bedrooms.

11➡(1fb) 1⊞ CTV in all bedrooms ® **T** ✱sB&B➡£33—£40 dB&B➡£45—£55 ₿

12P ⇌

🍷 ☕ ⚡ ✱Bar lunch £3.45—£3.95 Dinner £11.50alc Wine £4.80 Last dinner 9pm

Credit cards 1 2 3 5

Monk Fryston — Moreton

MONTROSE

Tayside *Angus*
Map **15** NO75

★★★**Links** Mid Links (Best Western) ☎ (0674) 72288

Businessman's hotel with its own popular disco.

20rm(18➡2⋒)(4fb) CTV in all bedrooms ® **T** sB&B£23—£25 sB&B➡⋒£28—£33 dB&B£30—£35 dB&B➡⋒£40—£45 ₿

☾CTV 45P Disco nightly ♿

V 🍷 ☕ ✱Lunch £4.75—£5.50&alc Tea £1—£1.30 Dinner £5.50—£6.50&alc Wine £5.50 Last dinner 10pm

Credit cards 1 2 3 5

★★★**Park** John St ☎ (0674) 73415 Telex no 76367

Friendly, efficient hotel of a good modern standard.

59rm(43➡6⋒)(4fb) CTV in all bedrooms ® S% sB&B£18—£25 sB&B➡⋒£20—£35 dB&B➡⋒£30—£48 ₿

☾CTV 100P CFA ❁ 👪

V 🍷 ☕ Lunch £4.75—£5.50 Tea £1—£2.50 Dinner £6.20—£7.25&alc Wine £4.85 Last dinner 9.30pm

Credit cards 1 2 3 5 Ⓥ

MORAR

Highland *Inverness-shire*
Map **13** NM69

★★***Morar*** ☎ Mallaig (0687) 2346

Closed Nov—Mar

Family run hotel above the white sands of Morar.

28rm(18➡)(4fb) ® ₿

CTV 50P ❁ 🎣 👪

V 🍷 Last dinner 8.30pm

MORECAMBE

Lancashire
Map **7** SD46

★★★**Elms** Bare ☎ (0524) 411501

Pleasant, comfortable hotel serving home grown English food.

39rm(29➡3⋒)(3fb) 1⊞ CTV in all bedrooms 🐕 sB&Bfr£20 sB&B➡⋒fr£21.50 dB&Bfr£38 dB&B➡⋒fr£42 ₿

Lift ☾CTV 80P 12🚗(charge) CFA ❁ putting Live music and dancing nightly 👪 *xmas*

V 🍷 ☕ S% Lunch fr£5&alc Dinner fr£8.50&alc Wine £5 Last dinner 9pm

Credit cards 1 2 3 4 5 Ⓥ

★★★**Headway** Marine Rd East ☎ (0524) 412525

Closed 18 Dec — 4 Jan RS Nov — 17 Dec & 5 Jan — Mar

This modern, well furnished, family-owned hotel looks across the Bay towards Lakeland.

54➡(4fb) CTV in all bedrooms ® **T** 🐕 sB&B➡£27 dB&B➡£45.50

Lift ☾20P

🍷 ☕ Lunch £8.50&alc Tea fr£1.90 High Tea fr£5 Dinner £7.35&alc Wine £4.80 Last dinner 8.30pm

Credit cards 1 2 3 5 Ⓥ

★★★**Strathmore** Marine Rd East (Consort) ☎ (0524) 421234 Telex no 57515

Closed Xmas

Friendly traditional hotel with resident proprietors.

56rm(31➡10⋒)(2fb) CTV in all bedrooms ® **T** 🐕 sB&B£16—£18 sB&B➡⋒£28—£33 dB&B£32—£35 dB&B➡⋒£40—£47 ₿

Lift ☾30P 12🚗 games room

🍽 English & French **V** 🍷 ☕ Lunch fr£5.25 Tea fr75p Dinner fr£6.25 Wine £5.50 Last dinner 9.30pm

Credit cards 1 2 3 5 Ⓥ

★★**Clarendon** Promenade, West End ☎ (0524) 410180

Closed Xmas wk

Tall, sea-front hotel overlooking the bay.

33rm(20➡7⋒)(4fb) CTV in all bedrooms ® **T** S% sB&Bfr£15.50 sB&B➡⋒fr£19.50 dB&Bfr£30 dB&B➡⋒fr£36 ₿

Lift ☾ # CTV P 2🚗

S% Lunch fr£4 High Tea £3.50—£7 Dinner £4.50—£7.50&alc Wine £3.60 Last dinner 9pm

Credit cards 1 2 3 4 5

MORETON

Merseyside
Map **7** SJ28

★★★**Leasowe Castle** Leasowe (1m N of Moreton off A551) (Exec Hotel) ☎ 051-606 9191 Telex no 627189

The castle dates back four hundred years and the Star Chamber has a ceiling taken from the Palace of Westminster; bedrooms, however, are modern.

46rm(26➡20⋒)(3fb) 3⊞ CTV in all bedrooms ® **T** 🐕 sB&B➡⋒£24.12—£36.80 dB&B➡⋒£33.35—£48.27 ₿

☾CTV 100P ❁ sauna bath solarium gymnasium pool table 👪 *xmas*

V 🍷 ☕ Lunch £6.95 Tea £2.58 High Tea £6.56 Dinner £8.04&alc Wine £5.11 Last dinner 10.30pm

Credit cards 1 2 3 5 Ⓥ

MORETONHAMPSTEAD
Devon
Map **3** SX78

★★ **Glebe House** North Bovey (1½m SW) ☎ (0647) 40544
Closed 20 Dec—Feb
Welcoming former Victorian vicarage offering well-prepared food.
9rm(5 4)(1fb)
sB&B £13.50—£15.50
dB&B £27—31 B
CTV 40P
International **V** Tea £1.50—£2 High Tea £4.50—£5.50 Dinner £10.50—£12.50&alc Last dinner 9.30pm
Credit cards 1 3 V

★★ *B* **White Hart** The Square ☎ (0647) 40406
Built 1637, this traditional inn has been modernised but retains its original character.
18 CTV in all bedrooms ®
sB&B £22.50 dB&B £38 B
10P snooker nc10yrs *xmas*
English & French **V** Bar lunch £1.10—£3.50 Tea 50p&alc Dinner £7.75&alc Wine £4.45 Last dinner 8.30pm
Credit cards 1 2 3 5 V

MORETON-IN-MARSH
Gloucestershire
Map **4** SP23

★★★ *L* **Manor House** High St ☎ (0608) 50501 Telex no 837151
Fine Cotswold hotel, with very comfortable well furnished rooms and candlelit restaurant.
38rm(34 2)(1fb) 4 CTV in all bedrooms **T** * sB&B £22.50—£24 sB&B £35—£37 dB&B £47—£49 dB&B £52.50—£62 B
Lift 20P 4 (charge) (heated) (hard) sauna bath putting nc12yrs *xmas*
* Lunch £6—£7.50 Tea £1—£2 Dinner £13 Wine £6 Last dinner 9pm
Credit cards 1 2 3 5 V

★★ **Redesdale Arms** High St ☎ (0608) 50308 Telex no 837928
Comfortable well run hotel with good restaurant.
9rm(3) Annexe: 8rm(5 3)(3fb) 1 CTV in all bedrooms ® **T** sB&B fr £23.75 sB&B fr £31 dB&B fr £38 dB&B £42—£49.50 B
30P *xmas*
English & French **V** Lunch £6.25 Dinner £8.95&alc Wine £5.35 Last dinner 9.30pm
Credit cards 1 2 V

★★ **White Hart Royal** High St (Trusthouse Forte) ☎ (0608) 50731
A company-owned hotel with a cobbled hallway and a character lounge bar.
21rm(5) Annexe: 6rm(1) CTV in all bedrooms ® sB&B £37.50 sB&B £45.50 dB&B £53.50 dB&B £61.50 B
CTV 10P *xmas*
Last dinner 9.30pm
Credit cards 1 2 3 4 5

MORFA NEFYN
Gwynedd
Map **6** SH24

★★ **Bryn Noddfa** ☎ Nefyn (0758) 720843
Closed 24 Dec—Feb RS 1—23 Dec
Family run holiday hotel in quiet situation.
9rm(1 5)(2fb) CTV in all bedrooms ®
sB&B £12.75 sB&B £13.50
dB&B £25.50 dB&B £27 B
16P
Bar lunch £1.30—£3.70 Tea 75p Dinner £4.75&alc Wine £4.25 Last dinner 9pm
Credit card 3 V

M

★★**Links Way** ☎ Nefyn (0758) 720258

Ideally located for golfing and beaches, this comfortable, modernised hotel maintains good standards in accommodation and food, backing these with friendly service.

26rm(11→10⋒)(1fb) ® S% *sB&B£14.90—£16.05 sB&B→⋒£17.80—£18.95 dB&B£29.80—£32.10 dB&B→⋒£35.60—£37.90 B

CTV 60P 2⌂ Live music & dancing Sat

English & Italian V ✂ S% *Lunch £4.25alc Dinner £6.95—£8.50&alc Wine £4.25 Last dinner 9pm

Ⓥ

MORTEHOE

Devon

Map **2** SS44

★**Glenhaven** Chapel Hill ☎ Woolacombe (0271) 870376

Closed Jan

Small, holiday hotel with a friendly atmosphere, in a peaceful location.

11rm(1→6⋒)(4fb) 3 S% sB&B£8.95—£11.50 sB&B→⋒£10.15—£12.70 dB&B£17.90—£23 dB&B→⋒£20.30—£25.40 B

CTV 12P ✽

S% Bar lunch 50p—£1.50 Tea 50p Dinner £6.50 Wine £3.10 Last dinner 6.30pm

M

MOTHERWELL

Strathclyde *Lanarkshire*

Map **11** NS75

★★★***Garrion*** Merry St ☎ (0698) 64561

Large commercial hotel in the town centre.

52rm(28→8⋒) CTV in all bedrooms ® T B

Lift ☾ 100P CFA billiards sauna bath gymnasium

English & French V Last dinner 9.30pm

Credit cards 1 2 3 5

MOTTRAM ST ANDREW

Cheshire

Map **7** SJ87

★★★**Mottram Hall** Prestbury (DeVere) ☎ Prestbury (0625) 828135 Telex no 668181

Georgian mansion built in 1721, standing in formal gardens surrounded by 120 acres of parkland.

71→⋒(4fb) 6 CTV in all bedrooms ® T S% sB&B→⋒fr£55 dB&B→⋒fr£70 B

☾ 150P CFA ✽ (grass) snooker Live music & dancing Sat Sep—May

International V S% Lunch £9&alc Tea £1.25 Dinner £15&alc Wine £7 Last dinner 10pm

Credit cards 1 2 3 5

Morfa Nefyn — Much Wenlock

MOULSFORD-ON-THAMES

Oxfordshire

Map **4** SU58

★★**Beetle & Wedge** Ferry Lane ☎ Cholsey (0491) 651381

This pretty, rose-brick hotel, its garden bordering the Thames, provides neat, attractive bedrooms. Restaurant and bars are popular.

10rm(9→1⋒) Annexe: 5rm(1→)(2fb) 1 CTV in all bedrooms ® T *sB&B→⋒£34 dB&B→⋒£48 B

54P ✽

V *Lunch £7.50—£9.95&alc Tea 65p—£1 Dinner £9.95&alc Wine £5.50 Last dinner 9.45pm

Credit cards 1 2 3 5 Ⓥ

MOULTON

North Yorkshire

Map **8** NZ20

✕✕**Black Bull Inn** ☎ Barton (032577) 289

You can dine in a converted railway carriage at this charming village inn. Unpretentious menus offer a good selection of freshly cooked dishes at reasonable prices, and the friendly service is in keeping with the character of the establishment.

Closed Sun & 23—31 Dec

100 seats *Lunch £7&alc Dinner £15alc Wine £4.75 Last dinner 10.15pm 80P nc7yrs

Credit cards 1 2 3

MOUNT HAWKE

Cornwall

Map **2** SW74

★***HBL*** **Tregarthen Country Cottage** Banns Rd ☎ Porthtowan (0209) 890399

An intimate and cosy hotel run by Mr and Mrs Clive Hutton who, with their staff look after the guest's every need. The rooms are comfortable, and the bedrooms attractively decorated, while the food is carefully cooked using good, local produce.

6rm(4→2⋒) *sB&B→⋒£14 dB&B→⋒£28

CTV 15P ✽ *xmas*

*Dinner £7 Wine £5.50 Last dinner 8pm

Credit card 1 Ⓥ

MOUSEHOLE

Cornwall

Map **2** SW42

★★**Carn Du** Raginnis Hill ☎ (0736) 731233

Closed 2nd wk Jan—mid Mar

The small, personally-run hotel serves home-cooked food with an emphasis on fresh local fish and vegetables. Its windows offer panoramic views across Mount's Bay.

7rm(1→5⋒) CTV in 3 bedrooms ® *sB&B→⋒fr£18 dB&B→⋒fr£28

CTV 12P *xmas*

*Dinner £8 Wine fr£4.60 Last dinner 8pm

Credit cards 1 2 3

★★***L Lobster Pot*** ☎ Penzance (0736) 731251

Closed 4 Jan—mid Mar

Well-appointed character hotel and restaurant overhanging the small village harbour.

14rm(11→3⋒) Annexe: 12rm(8→1⋒)(5fb) CTV in all bedrooms ® T B

xmas

Last dinner 9.45pm

Credit cards 1 2 3

MUCH BIRCH

Hereford & Worcester

Map **3** SO53

★★★**Pilgrim** (Inter Hotel) ☎ Golden Valley (0981) 540742

Closed 29 Dec—6 Jan

With splendid views of the countryside from most of its rooms, this hotel offers comfort and relaxation for the traveller.

19rm(1→2⋒) CTV in all bedrooms ® T sB&B£37.50—£38.50 sB&B→⋒£37.50—£38.50 dB&B£55 dB&B→⋒fr£55 B

60P ✽ croquet putting *xmas*

English & Continental V Lunch £10.50—£12 Tea £1—£3 High Tea £5—£7.50 Dinner £10.50—£12&alc Wine £6.50 Last dinner 9.45pm

Credit cards 1 2 3 4 5 Ⓥ

See advertisement under Hereford

MUCH WENLOCK

Shropshire

Map **7** SO69

★**Gaskell Arms** Bourton Rd ☎ (0952) 727212

This pleasant and comfortable hotel, originally a seventeenth-century coaching inn, has been tastefully modernised and stands conveniently close to the town centre.

11rm(3→)(2fb) CTV in 3 bedrooms TV in 8 bedrooms ® sB&B£16—£18 sB&B→£25—£28 dB&B£28—£30 dB&B→£38—£40 B

30P 1⌂ ✽

V S% Lunch £4—£8 Dinner £7—£9 Wine £4.50 Last dinner 9.30pm

Credit cards 1 3 5 Ⓥ

MUDEFORD
Dorset see **Christchurch**

MUIRHEAD
Strathclyde *Lanarkshire*
Map **11** NS66

✕✕**La Campágnola** 112 Cumbernauld Rd ☎ 041-779 3405

Smart little Italian restaurant with good atmosphere.

Closed Sun

Italian 80 seats S% ✱Lunch fr£4.45&alc Dinner £12alc Wine £5.45 Last dinner 10.30pm P Live music & dancing Thu—Sat

Credit cards 1 2 3 5

MUIR OF ORD
Highland *Ross & Cromarty*
Map **14** NH55

★★**Ord Arms** Great North Road ☎ (0463) 870286

Attractive, sandstone building set back from the main road on the northern outskirts of town.

12rm(3 3)(2fb) CTV in all bedrooms ® sB&B£15.18—£16.75 sB&B £20.24—£22.24 dB&B£25.30—£27.30 dB&B £30.36—£32.36

100P 3 *xmas*

V Lunch £6.25—£7.25 Tea £1.50—£2.50 High Tea £4.25—£4.75 Dinner £8.50—£10.50&alc Wine £4.25 Last dinner 10pm

Credit card 1 Ⓥ

★★ *L* **Ord House** ☎ (0463) 870492

Closed Nov—Mar

A 17th century listed building retaining a traditional country house character.

13rm(9)(1fb) sB&B£18 sB&B £20 dB&B£36 dB&B £40

CTV 50P

Scottish, French, Italian & Portuguese V Bar lunch £1—£5&alc Tea £2&alc Dinner £10&alc Wine £5.50 Last dinner 8.30pm

MULL, ISLAND OF
Strathclyde, *Argyllshire* Map **10**

CRAIGNURE
Map **10** NM73

★★★**Isle of Mull** (Scottish Highland) ☎ (06802) 351 Telex no 778215

Closed Nov—Mar

Comfortable, friendly tourist hotel with panoramic views from all rooms.

60 (8fb) CTV in all bedrooms ®

☾ 50P Cabaret Wed & Sat

Scottish & French V Bar lunch £3.50 Tea £1 Dinner £10 Wine £6 Last dinner 8.30pm

Credit cards 1 2 3 5

SALEN
Map **10** NM54

✕**Puffer Aground** Main Road ☎ Aros (06803) 389

Old roadside cottages have been converted to make this restaurant which has an adjoining craft shop.

Closed Sun & Mon (early & late season) mid Oct—Apr

30 seats Lunch £6alc Dinner fr£7&alc Last dinner 8.30pm 24P

TOBERMORY
Map **13** NM55

★***Mishnish*** Main St ☎ (0688) 2009

Small, traditional, Highland hotel overlooking the picturesque Tobermory Bay.

12rm(7 3)®

CTV Live music nightly

Last dinner 9pm

★ *L* **Tobermory** 53 Main St ☎ (0688) 2091

Closed late Oct—mid Mar

A friendly and comfortable little tourist hotel overlooking Tobermory Bay.

15rm(2 2)(2fb) ®✱sB&B£13.50 dB&B£27 dB&B £30

CTV

✱Bar lunch fr£3.75 Dinner fr£7 Wine £4.25 Last dinner 7.30pm

★ ***HB*** **Ulva House** ☎ (0688) 2044

Closed Nov—Feb

On the hillside with views of the bay, this small friendly, family-run hotel has pretty, compact bedrooms, and an excellent local reputation for their home cooking.

6rm(3fb) in 6 bedrooms ® sB&B£15.70 dB&B£31.40

8P

International V Lunch £11.50&alc Dinner £11.50&alc Wine £4.45 Last dinner 8pm

MULLION
Cornwall
Map **2** SW61

★★★**Polurrian** ☎ (0326) 240421 Telex no 265871 (WJJ114)

Closed Nov—Etr

Family holiday hotel superbly situated in 12 acres of terraced grounds overlooking Polurrian Cove with its fine surfing beach.

42rm(39)(5fb) 5 CTV in all bedrooms T S% ✱sB&B£20.50—£35 sB&B £22.50—£37 dB&B£41—£70 dB&B £45—£74

☾ CTV 80P 3 (£2.50 per night) CFA & (heated) (hard) squash snooker sauna bath solarium gymnasium badminton putting table tennis pool table croquet Disco wkly Live music and dancing wkly

V S% ✱Lunch £4—£7.50&alc Tea £1—£2.85&alc High Tea £3.50 Dinner £10.50&alc Wine £4.25 Last dinner 9.30pm

Credit cards 1 3 5 Ⓥ

★★**Mullion Cove** ☎ (0326) 240328

Closed Dec—Feb except xmas

The hotel offers a relaxed, friendly atmosphere and panoramic views over Mount's Bay. →

38rm(17🛁1🚿)(1fb)CTV in 26 bedrooms ®✱sB&B£13.90 sB&B🛁🚿£16.50 dB&B£27.80 dB&B🛁🚿£33 B

CTV 60P 10🚗 ✿ ≈ (heated) 🎾(hard) sauna bath solarium *xmas*

☕ ✱Dinner £9.50&alc Wine fr£4 Last dinner 9pm

Credit cards 1 3

MUMBLES (near Swansea)
West Glamorgan
Map **2** SS68
See also **Langland Bay** and **Swansea**

★**St Annes** Western Ln ☎ Swansea (0792) 69147

Closed Xmas

Small, quiet, modern hotel overlooking Swansea Bay.

23rm(15🛁1🚿)(1fb) CTV in all bedrooms ✗ S% sB&B£15.53 sB&B🛁🚿£19.55 dB&B£23 dB&B🛁🚿£27.60

CTV 45P

☕ S% Bar lunch fr£1.20 Tea fr80p Dinner £5.75—£6.75 Wine £4.90 Last dinner 7pm

Mullion — Nairn

MUNDESLEY-ON-SEA
Norfolk
Map **9** TG33

★★**Manor** ☎ (0263) 720309

Closed 2—11 Jan

26rm(9🛁13🚿)(3fb) sB&B£20—£22 sB&B🛁🚿£22—£24 dB&B£26 dB&B🛁🚿£28 B

CTV 40P ✿ ≈ (heated) Live music and dancing Sat *xmas*

V ☕ S% Lunch £4.50&alc Tea 40p Dinner £5.50—£7.50&alc Wine £3.75 Last dinner 9pm

★**Ingleside** Cromer Rd ☎ (0263) 720530

11rm(5🛁4🚿)(3fb) CTV in all bedrooms sB&B £10—£18 sB&B🛁🚿£11.50—£19.50 dB&B£20—£36 dB&B🛁🚿£23—£39 B

70P ✿ pool table Disco Thu Live music & dancing Tue, Fri & Sat Cabaret Sat *xmas*

☕ Lunch £2.50—£4 Tea £1 High Tea £2.50 Dinner £3.50—£7.50&alc Wine £4.50 Last dinner 10pm

Credit cards 1 2 3

MUNGRISDALE
Cumbria
Map **11** NY33

★*H* **The Mill** ☎ Threlkeld (059683) 659

Charming country hotel, providing hospital, comfort and good home cooking.

8rm(2🛁)(1fb) CTV in 2 bedrooms ® sB&B£18—£18.75 sB&B🛁£22.50—£23.25 dB&B£28—£29.50 dB&B🛁£37—£38.50

CTV 12P ✿ badminton games room *xmas*

English & French V ☕ Tea £2—£2.50 Dinner £9.50 Wine £3.95 Last dinner 8pm

NAIRN
Highland *Nairnshire*
Map **14** NH85

★★★★**Golf View** Seabank Rd (Norscot/Clan)
☎ (0667) 52301 Telex no 75134

Well situated hotel overlooking Moray Firth, and offering fine, mainly nouvelle cuisine.

55rm(46🛁9🚿)(4fb) 1 CTV in all bedrooms T sB&B🛁🚿£34—£39 dB&B🛁🚿£56—£70 B

Lift ☾ 30P CFA ✿ ≈ (heated) 🎾(hard) sauna bath Live music & dancing 1—2 nights wkly *xmas*

☕ Lunch £5—£6.50 Tea £3 Dinner £15—£17.50&alc Wine £5.25 Last dinner 9.30pm

Credit cards 1 2 3 4 5 Ⓥ

M

★★★★ **Newton** Inverness Rd (Consort) ☎ (0667) 53144

Imposing combination of Georgian and Scottish Baronial architecture with fine views over Moray Firth to the Ross-shire Hills.

30 Annexe: 14 (7fb) CTV in all bedrooms ® in 14 bedrooms **T** sB&B £24—£36 dB&B £39—£64

Lift CTV 40P (hard) sauna bath solarium *xmas*

V Lunch £5.25—£6.50 Tea fr £1.85 High Tea fr £4 Dinner £11.50&alc Wine £5.40 Last dinner 9.30pm

Credit cards 1 2 3 5 V

★★★ **Royal Marine** Marine Rd (Exec Hotel) ☎ (0667) 53381

Standing near the beach, this resort hotel has a strong coach tour trade in the summer; in winter it draws its clientele primarily from business people.

43rm(33 4)(7fb) CTV in 20 bedrooms sB&B £20—£22 sB&B £21—£23 dB&B £42—£46 dB&B £42—£46

Lift CTV 40P

V Lunch £3.50—£4.50 Tea £1.25—£1.85 High Tea £4—£4.25 Dinner £10—£11.75 Wine £4.25 Last dinner 8.30pm

Credit cards 1 2 3 5

★★★ **Windsor** Albert St ☎ (0667) 53108

Extended and renovated family hotel in residential area.

60rm(30 24)(7fb) CTV in all bedrooms ® **T** sB&B £22—£25 sB&B £25—£27 dB&B £36—£38 dB&B £40—£45

Lift CTV 40P CFA bowling Live music and dancing Wed & Sat Cabaret Sat *xmas*

Scottish & French **V** Lunch £3.50—£4.50&alc Tea £1.50—£2.50 High Tea £3.95—£5.95 Dinner £9.50—£10.50&alc Wine £4.50 Last dinner 9.30pm

Credit cards 1 2 3 5 V

★★ ***Alton Burn*** Alton Burn Rd ☎ (0667) 52051

Only the golf course stands between the Moray Firth and this family-run hotel which offers good food, friendly service and some nice family bedrooms.

19rm(7 3)(7fb)

CTV 30P (heated)

English, French & Italian **V**

Credit cards 1 3

❀★★ ***HBL*** **Clifton** ☎ (0667) 53119

Closed Dec—Feb

(*Rosette awarded for dinner only*)

This Victorian style, ivy covered hotel, owned by Mr and Mrs MacIntyne is extremely well furnished and decorated in authentic manner. The bedrooms are all individually designed and the food and wine are both very good.

16rm(15 1)(2fb) 2 sB&B £34—£39 dB&B £62—£69

CTV 12P

V Lunch £10—£12alc Tea £2alc Dinner £12—£15alc Wine £6 Last dinner 9.30pm

Credit cards 1 2 3 5

★ **Washington** 8 Viewfield St ☎ (0667) 53351

Traditional family hotel in a detached mansion, set in a residential area.

20rm(6)(8fb) ® sB&B £12.50—£13.50 sB&B £12.50—£13.50 dB&B £25—£27 dB&B £28—£30

CTV 20P Live music & dancing Sat Cabaret Wed

Bar lunch £2.50alc Dinner £6—£8&alc Wine £4.20 Last dinner 10pm

NANT-DDU (near Merthyr Tydfil)
Powys
Map **3** SO01

★★ **Nant-ddu Lodge** Cwm Taf (5m N of Merthyr Tydfil on A470 towards Brecon) ☎ Merthyr Tydfil (0685) 79111

A former hunting lodge of Lord Tredegar, situated in spectacular scenery of the Brecon Beacons.

10rm(7 3)(1fb) Annexe: 1 1 CTV in all bedrooms ® **T** sB&B £26—£30 dB&B £30—£40

60P *xmas*

English & French **V** Lunch £6.50—£12.50 Tea 75p—£3 High Tea £2—£5&alc Dinner £8.50—£12.50&alc Wine £5.25 Last dinner 9.15pm

Credit cards 1 2 3 V

NANTWICH
Cheshire
Map **7** SJ65

❀★★★ **Rookery Hall**
(see red star box on next page)

★★ ***Alvaston Hall*** Middlewich Rd (Best Western) ☎ (0270) 624341 Telex no 36311

Large 19th-century building with a modern extension in an attractive rural setting.

39rm(26 13) Annexe: 33rm(21 12)(12fb) 1 CTV in all bedrooms ® **T**

250P CFA (heated) (hard) squash sauna bath solarium Disco Sat *xmas*

English & Italian **V** Last dinner 10pm

Credit cards 1 2 3 5

★★ **Lamb** Hospital St ☎ (0270) 625286

A 200-year-old coaching inn in the centre of town.

16rm(6 2)(2fb) CTV in 8 bedrooms ® sB&B fr £18.50 sB&B fr £25 dB&B fr £30 dB&B fr £37

CTV 15P 10

V Lunch fr £5.50 High Tea fr £5.50 Dinner fr £9.50&alc Wine £5 Last dinner 9.30pm

Credit cards 1 3 V

N

★★★

❀★★★ ♣ROOKERY HALL, NANTWICH

Worleston (2m N B5074) (Pride of Britain) ☎ (0270) 626866 Telex no 367169

Closed 19 Jan—11 Feb

This was one of our previous Red Star hotels, until it changed hands. However, the new owners, Peter and Audrey Marks, have now proved themselves so that we are delighted to award Red Stars again. They ensure that the needs of their guests come first and have imbued their young, well turned out staff with the right attitude to achieve it; they seem to sense you need something before you get round to asking for it. It is a splendid building in its own grounds with a small lake and fountain set amongst the verdant Cheshire pasture land. Although about 200 years old, it was largely changed to a French Chateau-like building in the last century. The public rooms are impressive with some splendid panelling, crystal chandeliers and ornamental plasterwork. There is no bar but the salon and morning room more than make up for it; pictures, looking glasses and ornaments abound while your comfort is pandered to by the sumptuous seating. Bedrooms are individually decorated and furnished to the same high standard as well as being provided with so many things

for your convenience; you are even welcomed with a quarter bottle of Tattinger champagne. In the beautifully appointed candlelit dining rooms a splendid six course dinner is served, cooked by the chef Clive Howe in the modern style and thoroughly deserving our rosette.

9 Annexe: 2 1 CTV in all bedrooms T
sB&B £57.50—£72.50
dB&B £85—£125 B
CTV 50P (hard) clay pigeon shooting nc 10yrs *xmas*
Lunch £12.95—£16.95&alc Tea £2.50—£5 Dinner £22.50—£26.50&alc Wine £9.50 Last dinner 9.15pm
Credit cards 1 2 3 4 5

N

✕✕**Churche's Mansion** Hospital St ☎ (0270) 625933

The restaurant is set in a comfortable, half-timbered building which is one of Cheshire's most famous houses. Open brick fireplaces and oak panelling create an appropriate atmosphere in which to enjoy traditional English fayre, where jugged hare or rabbit pie can be followed by a pudding prepared from a recipe of yesteryear. The house itself is open for viewing between April and October.

Closed Xmas
Dinner not served Sun

70 seats *Lunch £5.50—£6.50 Dinner fr£13.50 Wine £4.50 Last dinner 9.30pm 35P
Credit cards 1 3 5

NARBERTH
Dyfed
Map **2** SN11

★★**Plas-Hyfryd** Morfield Rd (Guestaccom) ☎ (0834) 860653

A family-run hotel in an 18th-century mansion, which was formerly the rectory.

12rm (9 3)(1fb) CTV in all bedrooms ®
*sB&B £21.50 dB&B £34.50 B
CTV 30P (heated) *xmas*
Lunch £9.50alc Tea £1 Dinner £7.25&alc Wine £4.20 Last dinner 9.30pm
Credit cards 1 3 V

NARBOROUGH
Leicestershire
Map **4** SP59

★★**Charnwood** 48 Leicester Rd (off A46 2m S of M1, junc 21) ☎ Leicester (0533) 862218

Closed 1 wk fr 25 Dec

Converted Victorian house in a Leicester suburb, conveniently near the M1.

20rm (5 15) CTV in all bedrooms ® T
*sB&B £21—£25.50
dB&B £27—£33 B
40P
English & French V *Lunch £4.25—£5.20&alc Tea 60p—£2 Dinner £6.90—£7.50&alc Wine £4.75 Last dinner 9.30pm
Credit cards 1 2 3 V

NEASHAM
Co Durham
Map **8** NZ31

★★★**Newbus Arms Hotel & Restaurant** Hurworth Rd (Best Western) ☎ (0325) 721071 Telex no 58664

Elegant period house in its own gardens, with impressive public and conference areas.

15 3 CTV in all bedrooms ® T S%
sB&B £45 dB&B £55 B
100P squash *xmas*
English & French V *Lunch £9.50—£20 Tea £1.75—£5.25 Dinner £12.50—£25&alc Wine £6.75 Last dinner 10pm
Credit cards 1 2 3 5 V

NEATH
West Glamorgan
Map **3** SS79

★★**Glyn Clydach House** Longford Rd, Neath Abbey ☎ Skewen (0792) 813701

Closed 26—30 Dec RS Sun

Small country house in rural location with golf and other sporting facilities.

8rm(1➡4⋔) Annexe: 1➡(1fb) 1⊟ CTV in all bedrooms ®T sB&Bfr£22 sB&B➡⋔£27.50—£32.50 dB&Bfr£35 dB&B➡⋔£35—£40 B

40P ✽ (heated) ⚑ ℚ(hard) ⌡ snooker gymnasium

English & French V ♆ ☕ ✻Bar lunch £1.60—£4&alc Tea fr£1&alc Dinner £9alc Wine £4.90 Last dinner 10pm

Credit cards 1 2 3 5

NEEDHAM MARKET

Suffolk
Map **5** TM05

★★**Limes** ☎(0449) 720305

Closed Xmas

Originally built in 1485 Boule House, a Georgian front was added in 1751.

11➡(4fb) CTV in all bedrooms ®T sB&B➡fr£33 dB&B➡fr£50 B

60P

English & French ♆ ☕ Lunch £8.50&alc Tea 60p High Tea 85p—£7 Dinner £9&alc Wine £5.20 Last dinner 9.30pm

Credit cards 1 2 3 5

NEFYN

Gwynedd
Map **6** SH34

★**Caeau Capel** Rhodfar Mor ☎(0758) 720240

Closed Nov—Etr

Detached holiday hotel set in its own grounds in a quiet cul-de-sac.

23rm(6➡)(6fb) ✻sB&B£12.65—£13.80 sB&B➡£17.25—£18.40 dB&B£25.30—£27.60 dB&B➡£34.50—£36.80 B

CTV 30P ✽ ℚ(grass) putting

V ♆ ☕ ✻Bar lunch £2alc Tea 50p alc Dinner £7.50—£7.95 Wine £4.35 Last dinner 8.30pm

Credit cards 1 3 Ⓥ

NELSON

Lancashire
Map **7** SD83

★★**Great Marsden** Barkerhouse Rd ☎(0282) 64749

Victorian building in its own grounds.

12rm(3➡3⋔)(2fb) CTV in 4 bedrooms TV in 8 bedrooms ® S% ✻sB&B£20 sB&B➡⋔£20 dB&B£30 dB&B➡⋔£30

Lift CTV 100P ✽

V ♆ ☕ S% ✻Lunch £5.70&alc Tea £4&alc High Tea £6.50—£8.50&alc Dinner £6.50—£8.50&alc Wine £3.75 Last dinner 8.30pm

Credit card 4

NESSCLIFF

Shropshire
Map **7** SJ31

✕***Old Three Pigeons*** ☎(074381) 279

Pork dishes are a speciality in this old village inn.

English & French **V** 60 seats Last dinner 10.30pm 150P

Credit cards 1 2 3 4 5

NETHERLEY

Kincardineshire *Grampian*
Map **15** NO89

✕✕**Lairhillock Inn** ☎ Newtonhill (0569) 30001

(*Classification awarded for dinner only*)

The country pub has a separate, Victorian-style restaurant with raftered ceiling; the balconied lounge is an attractive feature, and a pianist provides discreet music most nights. The emphasis is on quality country cooking, and the dishes on the short menu are based, whenever possible, on fresh ingredients and local produce. The restaurant is not open at lunchtime, but food can be obtained at the bar.

Closed Xmas day, Boxing day evening 1 & 2 Jan

V 70 seats Lunch £8.75 Dinner £14.50 Wine £5.95 Last dinner 9.30pm 125P nc5yrs Live music 5 nights wkly

Credit cards 1 2 3

NETHY BRIDGE

Highland *Inverness-shire*
Map **14** NJ02

★★★**Nethybridge** (Best Western) ☎(047982) 203

Large, traditional Highland hotel offering friendly service, comfortable lounges and spacious bedrooms.

63rm(62➡1⋔)(3fb) CTV in 16 bedrooms sB&B➡⋔fr£23 dB&B➡⋔fr£45 B

Lift ☾ CTV 100P 6 CFA ✽ snooker Live music & dancing wknds *xmas*

V ♆ ☕ Lunch £4—£7 Tea £1—£2.50 Dinner fr£9.50 Wine £4.50 Last dinner 9.30pm

Credit cards 1 2 3 5 Ⓥ

NEW ABBEY

Dumfries & Galloway *Kirkcudbrightshire*
Map **11** NX96

★***Abbey Arms*** 1 The Square ☎(038785) 215

Modestly appointed family run village inn, home cooking and friendly service.

6rm (3fb) ®

CTV 6P

♆ ☕ Last dinner 6.15pm

NEWARK-ON-TRENT

Nottinghamshire
Map **8** SK75

★★**Grange** London Rd/Charles Street Corner ☎(0636) 703399

Closed 23 Dec—3 Jan

Comfortable and modern accommodation in a large converted former mid-Victorian private house standing on A6065, ¼ mile SE of town centre.

9rm(4➡) CTV in all bedrooms ® ✻sB&B£17.50 sB&B➡£24.95 dB&B£27.95 dB&B➡£33.50 B

CTV 9P nc 12yrs

♆ ✻Dinner £7—£8alc Wine £4.95 Last dinner 9.30pm

Credit cards 1 3 Ⓥ

★★**Midland** Muskham Rd ☎(0636) 73788

Small inn with modest accommodation.

10rm(2➡)(2fb) CTV in 2 bedrooms ® S% sB&Bfr£15.50 sB&B➡fr£25 dB&Bfr£25.80 dB&B➡fr£32 B

CTV 20P

V ♆ Lunch fr£3.95 Dinner £5.35—£6.45 Wine £2.20 Last dinner 8.30pm

Credit cards 2 5 Ⓥ

★★**Robin Hood** Lombard St (Anchor) ☎(0636) 703858 Telex no 858875

Large coaching inn offering modern accommodation.

20➡⋔(4fb) in 4 bedrooms CTV in all bedrooms ®T S% sB&B➡⋔£35—£40 dB&B➡⋔£45—£52 B

☾ 50P CFA

V ♆ ☕ S% Lunch £9.25—£13.95 Tea 60—80p Dinner £9.25—£13.95 Wine £5.95 Last dinner 10pm

Credit cards 1 2 3 5 Ⓥ

★**Ram** (Home Brewery) ☎(0636) 702255

This coaching inn stands near the castle in town centre.

15rm(11➡1⋔)(1fb) CTV in all bedrooms ®T sB&Bfr£23 sB&B➡⋔fr£25 dB&Bfr£35 dB&B➡⋔fr£40 B

CTV 10

V ♆ Lunch fr£4.50&alc Tea fr55p Dinner fr£6&alc Wine £4.95 Last dinner 8.45pm

Credit cards 1 2 3

○**Little Chef Lodge** A1 Southbound Carriageway North Muskham (3m N) ☎(0636) 703635

30➡⋔

Due to have opened September 1986

NEWBRIDGE

Cornwall
Map **2** SW43

✕✕**Enzo of Newbridge** ☎ Penzance (0736) 63777

Midway between Penzance and St Just, the restaurant is housed in a Cornish stone cottage with conservatory-style extension. The authentic Italian menu features →

local fish as available, and the à la carte selection offers wide scope, pasta being served as starter or main course.

Closed Sun Lunch not served

Italian **V** 70 seats ✱Dinner £9.50alc Wine £5.50 Last dinner 9.30pm 26P

Credit cards 1 2 5

See advertisement under Penzance

NEWBRIDGE-ON-WYE
Powys
Map **3** SO05

★***New Inn*** ☎ (059789) 211

A 16th-century village inn with a modern restaurant.

10rm(2➡1⋒)(3fb) ®

CTV 100P billiards

English & French **V** Last dinner 9pm

Credit card 1

NEWBRIGHTON
Merseyside
See **Wallasey**

NEWBURGH
Grampian *Aberdeenshire*
Map **15** NJ92

★★**Udny Arms** Main St ☎ (03586) 444 Telex no 265871

Small Victorian hotel overlooking estuary.

26rm(17➡9⋒) CTV in all bedrooms ®T ✱sB&B➡⋒£32—£34 dB&B➡⋒£44—£48

50P CFA

British & French **V** S% ✱Lunch £7alc Tea £2alc Dinner fr£15.25&alc Wine £5.35 Last dinner 9.30pm

Credit cards 1 2 3

N

NEWBURY
Berkshire
Map **4** SU46
See also **Elcot**

★★★**Chequers** Oxford St (Trusthouse Forte) ☎ (0635) 38000 Telex no 849205

Bedrooms vary in style and standard, but improvements are continuing steadily at this coaching inn. Public areas are pleasant and comfortable, whilst service throughout is helpful and friendly.

Newbridge — Newcastle-under-Lyme

62rm(54➡6⋒)(3fb) CTV in all bedrooms ®T sB&B➡⋒£50.50 dB&B➡⋒£68.50

60P CFA *xmas*

Last dinner 9.30pm

Credit cards 1 2 3 4 5

○**Granada Lodge** Oxford Rd, Chieveley, M4/A34 Service Area. ☎ (0635) 248024 59➡
Due to open Summer 1987

NEWBY BRIDGE
Cumbria
Map **7** SD38

★★★**Swan** (Exec Hotel/Inter Hotel) ☎ (0448) 31681 Telex no 65108

Closed 3—13 Jan

Delightfully situated by River Leven, this 17th-century coaching inn is now a comfortable hotel.

36➡(11fb) CTV in all bedrooms ®T S% sB&B➡£32.50—£40 dB&B➡£54—£64

CTV 100P 4 *xmas*

English & Continental **V** S% Lunch £7—£7.50 Tea 85p—£2.50 Dinner £10—£12&alc Wine £6.95 Last dinner 9.30pm

Credit cards 1 2 3 5

★★★*B* **Whitewater** The Lakeland Village ☎ (0448) 31133

Set on the banks of the River Leven, an impressive building of stone and slate has been converted with enthusiasm and flair to provide a sumptuous hotel, with extensive leisure facilities.

35➡(10fb) 1 CTV in all bedrooms ®T ✱sB&B➡£44 dB&B➡£55

Lift 100P (heated) sauna bath solarium gymnasium *xmas*

✱Bar lunch £2.50—£4.50 Tea £1.60 Dinner £9.95&alc Last dinner 8.30pm

Credit cards 1 2 3 5

NEWCASTLETON
Borders *Roxburghshire*
Map **12** NY48

✕**Copshaw Kitchen** ☎ Liddesdale (054121) 250

This attractive restaurant was once a grocer's shop; today, a thriving antique business has developed in parallel with the restaurant trade, and many of the delightful articles that surround you as you eat are actually for sale. It is for its interesting and varied menu and the standard of its cuisine, however, that the Copshaw Kitchen is particularly noteworthy.

Closed Tue Dinner not served Sun & Mon

V 36 seats ✱Lunch £3.50—£5.50&alc Dinner £7—£9.50&alc Wine £4.75 Last dinner 9pm 12P

NEWCASTLE-UNDER-LYME
Staffordshire
Map **7** SJ84

★★★***Clayton Lodge*** Clayton Rd, Clayton (A519) (Embassy) ☎ (0782) 613093

Large private house extended to form a modern comfortable hotel.

50➡ CTV in all bedrooms ®T

400P CFA

English & French **V** Last dinner 10pm

Credit cards 1 2 3 4 5

★★★**Post House** Clayton Rd (Trusthouse Forte) ☎ (0782) 625151 Telex no 36531

This long, purpose-built hotel provides extensive parking space within easy reach of busy public rooms and bedrooms. It is conveniently situated adjacent to Junction 15 of the M6, and many of its rooms have views across the motorway to wooded hills.

125➡(47fb) CTV in all bedrooms ®T sB&B➡£52.50 dB&B➡£68.50

128P

Last dinner 10.30pm

Credit cards 1 2 3 4 5

★★★**Thomas Forshaw** Liverpool Rd (Consort) ☏ (0782) 612431 due to change to 717000 Telex no 36681

Modern hotel with good size bedrooms in main block and separate annexe.

43 Annexe: 32 (8fb) in 8 bedrooms CTV in all bedrooms ® T S% sB&B £39.50 dB&B £49.50 B

(150P CFA Live music & dancing Wed & Sat *xmas*

European V S% Lunch £3.50—£5.50 Tea fr70p High Tea fr£4.95&alc Dinner fr£9.50 Wine £4.75 Last dinner 10pm

Credit cards 1 2 3 5 V

See advertisement under Stoke on Trent

★★**Borough Arms** King St (Best Western) ☏ (0782) 629421

Located north east of the town centre, this comfortable hotel was built as a pottery factory, being converted to an inn in 1853.

24rm(12 12) Annexe: 15 (1fb) in 7 bedrooms CTV in all bedrooms ® T sB&B £25 sB&B £34 dB&B £37.50 dB&B £47.50 B

40P

V Lunch fr£6.50 Tea fr85p Dinner fr£9&alc Wine £6.15 Last dinner 10.30pm

Credit cards 1 2 3 5

★*H* **Deansfield** 98 Lancaster Rd ☏ (0782) 619040

Large Victorian house in tree lined residential area.

8rm(6) Annexe: 3 (2fb) CTV in all bedrooms **T**

(CTV 20P 2 badminton *xmas*

English & French V S% Lunch £3.50alc Tea £1.20alc Dinner £7alc Wine £3.50 Last dinner 8pm

Credit cards 1 2 3 5

Newcastle-under-Lyme — Newcastle upon Tyne

NEWCASTLE UPON TYNE

Tyne & Wear
Map **12** NZ26
See plan on page 532/533

★★★★*B* **Gosforth Park Thistle** High Gosforth Park, Gosforth (Thistle) ☏ 091-236 4111 Telex no 53655 Plan **5** *D8*

Large modern hotel set in 167 acres of woodland overlooking Newcastle racecourse.

178 (21fb) 1 in 30 bedrooms CTV in all bedrooms ® T ✱sB £58—£70 dB £70—£90 (room only) B

Lift (## 300P CFA (heated) squash sauna bath solarium gymnasium Live music & dancing Fri & Sat *xmas*

International ✱Lunch £20alc Dinner fr£13.50&alc Wine £7 Last dinner 11pm

Credit cards 1 2 3 4 5 V

★★★★ **Holiday Inn** Great North Rd ☏ (0632) 365432 Plan **5A** *D8*
(For full entry see Seaton Burn)

★★★**County Thistle** Neville St (Thistle) ☏ 091-232 2471 Telex no 537873 Plan **2** *C4*

A traditional town centre hotel offering comfortable accommodation, situated opposite the main railway station.

115 (8fb) in 20 bedrooms CTV in all bedrooms ® T ✱sB £39—£50 dB £45—£57 (room only) B

Lift (CFA

International ✱Lunch fr£10&alc Dinner £10&alc Wine £7 Last dinner 9.30pm

Credit cards 1 2 3 4 5 V

★★★**Hospitality Inn** 64 Osborne Rd, Jesmond (Mount Charlotte) ☏ 091-281 7881 Telex no 53636 Plan **1** *E8*

This executive hotel was converted from a terraced private residence.

88rm(85 3)(6fb) 1 CTV in all bedrooms ® T S% ✱sB&B fr£41.50 dB&B fr£49.85 B

Lift (45P 8 (charge) *xmas*

English & French V S% ✱Lunch £5.50&alc Tea £1—£2.50 High Tea £5alc Dinner £7.50—£8&alc Last dinner 10.45pm

Credit cards 1 2 3 4 5 V

★★★**Imperial** Jesmond Rd (Swallow) ☏ 091-281 5511 Telex no 537972 Plan **6** *F8*

The functional, modern hotel offers comfortable bedroom accommodation and good leisure facilities.

130 CTV in all bedrooms ® T S% sB&B fr£42.50 dB&B fr£56 B

Lift (120P CFA (heated) sauna bath solarium gymnasium Disco Sat *xmas*

French S% Lunch fr£6&alc Dinner fr£9.50&alc Wine £5.75 Last dinner 10pm

Credit cards 1 2 3 4 5

★★★**Newcastle Crest** New Bridge St (Crest) ☏ 091-232 6191 Telex no 53467 Plan **3** *E5*

Functional accommodation and a choice of restaurants are offered by this modern, city centre hotel.

178 in 46 bedrooms CTV in all bedrooms ® T S% ✱sB £52.85 dB £68.20 (room only) B

Lift (## CFA sauna bath solarium

V ✱Lunch £7.35&alc Tea £2.50 Dinner £11.50&alc Wine £7.98 Last dinner 10pm

Credit cards 1 2 3 4 5

★★★**Newcastle Moat House** Coast Rd ☏ (0632) 628989 Not on plan
(For full entry see Wallsend)

★★★**Northumbria** Osborne Rd, Jesmond (Mount Charlotte) ☏ 091-281 4961 Telex no 53636 Plan **9** *E8*

An unpretentious, traditional hotel, the Northumbria is favoured mainly by a business clientele.

71rm(23 33)(2fb) CTV in all bedrooms ® T S% ✱sB&B fr£35.50 dB&B fr£43.75 B

Lift (45P sauna bath Live music & dancing 4 nights wkly *xmas* →

N

Newcastle upon Tyne

1	Avon ★★★
1A	Cairn ★★
2	County Thistle ★★★
3	Newcastle Crest ★★★
4	Fishermans Lodge ✕✕✕
5	Gosforth Park Thistle ★★★★
5A	Holiday Inn ★★★★ *(See under Seaton Burn)*
6	Imperial ★★★
6A	Jade Garden ✕
7	Mandarin ✕✕
8	Michelangelo ✕✕✕
8A	Morrach ★★
9	Northumbria ★★★
10	Osborne ★
11	Ristorante Roma ✕
12	Swallow ★★★
13	Whites ★★

English & French V S% ✱Lunch £5.50&alc Dinner £7.50—£8&alc Wine £5.25 Last dinner 9.45pm

Credit cards 1 2 3 4 5 V

★★★**Swallow** Newgate Arcade (Swallow) ☎ 091-232 5025 Telex no 538230 Plan **12** *C5*

Modern purpose-built hotel with roof top restaurant, situated in the city centre precinct.

94 (5fb) in 7 bedrooms CTV in all bedrooms ® T S% ✱sB&B fr£46.50 dB&B fr£60 B

Lift 125P CFA Live music & dancing Sat

V S% ✱Lunch £4—£6&alc Tea 70p Dinner £8.25—£10&alc Wine £4.90 Last dinner 9.30pm

Credit cards 1 2 3 5

N

★★**Cairn** 97 Osborne Rd ☎ 091-281 1358 Plan **1A** *E8*

The family-run, commercial hotel stands close to the town centre.

50rm(25 7)(2fb) CTV in all bedrooms ® T ✱sB&B £15.80 sB&B £23.90 dB&B £25.90 dB&B £29.90 B

25P

✱Lunch 4.95&alc Wine £4.50 Last dinner 9.30pm

Credit cards 1 2 3 4 5

★★**Morrach** 82-86 Osborne Rd, Jesmond ☎ 091-281 3361 Plan **8A** *E8*

Modest but clean accommodation is available at this family-run hotel. Dinners represent good value, and there is also a small coffee shop which remains open throughout the day and evening.

34rm(7 5)(1fb) 1 CTV in all bedrooms ® sB&B £18.40—£24.15 sB&B £24.15—£29.90 dB&B £27.60—£34.50 dB&B £33.35—£40.25

CTV 24P 3 snooker

V Lunch £3.40—£5 Tea 50p—£2.50 Dinner fr£6&alc Wine £4.50 Last dinner 9.30pm

Credit cards 1 2 3 V

★★*Whites* 38—40 Osborne Rd Jesmond ☎ 091-281 5126 Plan **13** *E8*

Modern, comfortable hotel behind impressive Victorian façade, where friendly proprietors create a welcoming atmosphere.

24rm(8 8)(1fb) CTV in all bedrooms ® B

CTV 24P *xmas*

English & Continental V Last dinner 9.45pm

Credit cards 1 2 3 4 5

★**Osborne** Osborne Rd, Jesmond ☎ 091-281 3385 Plan **10** *E8*

Comfortable hospital hotel in residential area.

25rm(1 9) CTV in all bedrooms ® T sB&B £12—£20 sB&B £17—£26 dB&B £24—£30 dB&B £30—£38 B

6P

V Lunch fr£5 Tea fr50p High Tea fr£4 Dinner fr£6 Wine £3.50 Last dinner 8.30pm

Credit cards 1 3

✕✕✕**Fishermans Lodge** Jesmond Dene, Jesmond ☎ 091-281 3281 Plan **4** *F8*

An excellent seafood restaurant situated alongside Ouse Burn in attractive Jesmond Dene. The dining rooms are very tastefully decorated and there are also two comfortable lounges. An appetising variety of fish dishes is available, such as the lavish sea food platter. Some meat and poultry dishes are also available and the sweets are delectable.

Closed Sun Bank Hols & 25 Dec—2 Jan Lunch not served Sat

French 65 seats Lunch £8.90—£10&alc Dinner £16alc Wine £7.50 Last dinner 11pm 45P nc 3yrs

Credit cards 1 2 3 5

✕✕✕**Michelangelo** 25 King St Quayside ☎ (0632) 614415 Plan **8** *E4*

An interesting range of French and Italian dishes is featured in this smart and popular restaurant on the quayside. Flambé specialities are popular, and a very

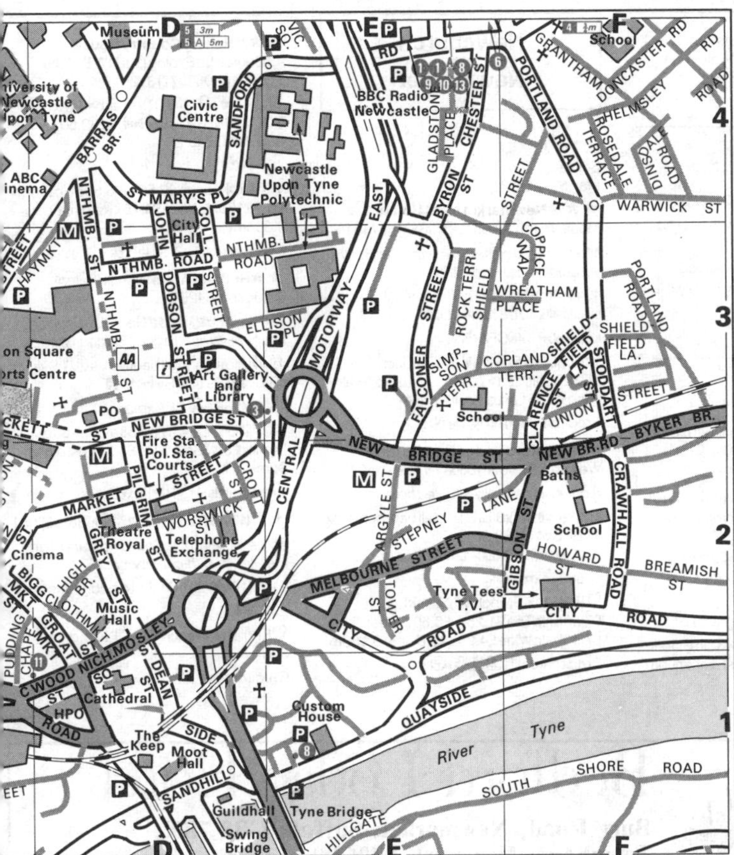

reasonably priced businessman's lunch is served on weekdays.

Closed Sun Lunch not served Sat

French & Italian **V** 80 seats Lunch £5.95 Wine £6.35 Last dinner 11pm

Credit cards 1 2 3 5

✕✕Mandarin 14—16 Stowell St ☎ 091-261 7960 Plan **7** *C5*

Situated in an historically interesting part of the city centre, this comfortably spacious Cantonese restaurant is decorated in the traditional manner. The menu offers a good choice of Chinese soups as well as an interesting selection of Dim Sum and your main course selection is from a vast range of traditional Cantonese dishes.

Cantonese **V** 98 seats S% ✱Lunch fr£3.20&alc Dinner fr£9&alc Wine £5.50 Last dinner 11pm nc 6yrs

Credit cards 1 2 3 5

✕Jade Garden 53 Stowell St ☎ 091-261 5889 Plan **6A** *C5*

This popular restaurant, standing in the older part of the town, offers an extensive Cantonese menu and a wine list that includes some Chinese wines; service is pleasant, though extremely informal.

Cantonese **V** 100 seats ✱Lunch £3—£8.50&alc Dinner £3.20—£8.50&alc Wine £6 Last dinner 11pm

Credit cards 1 2 3 5

✕Ristorante Roma 22 Collingwood St ☎ 091-232 0612 Plan **11** *D4*

The intimate, city-centre trattoria is staffed by attentive Italian waiters who are pleased to offer advice on the interesting menu, which includes a number of house specialities as well as traditional Italian dishes. Pasta can be recommended particularly, being made on the premises. The wine list that accompanies your meal predictably has a strong Italian influence.

Closed Xmas day & New Year's day Lunch not served Sun

English & Italian **V** 70 seats ✱Lunch £2.95—£10&alc Dinner £8—£12alc Wine £4.65 Last dinner 11.30pm Live music mthly

Credit cards 1 2 3

NEWCASTLE UPON TYNE AIRPORT

Tyne & Wear
Map **12** NZ17

★★★ ***Stakis Airport*** Woolsington (Stakis) ☎ Ponteland (0661) 24911 Telex no 537121

A modern purpose-built hotel within the airport complex.

100 (2fb) CTV in all bedrooms ® **T**

Lift 120P CFA *xmas*

V Last dinner 10pm

Credit cards 1 2 3 5

NEWCHURCH

Kent
Map **5** TR05

✕Newchurch House ☎ Dymchurch (0303) 872553

Once a shop, the ground floor of this house has now been converted into a licensed country restaurant where a young English couple offer good standards of cuisine and service to a mainly local clientele.

Closed Mon →

N

English & French **V** 30 seats Lunch £5—£10alc Dinner £7—£10&alc Wine £4.25 Last dinner 10pm 15P

Credit cards 1 3 V

NEWENT
Gloucestershire
Map **3** SO72

✕**Soutters** Culver St ☎ (0531) 820896

Small, personally run bistro with relaxed atmosphere. Must book.

Closed Sun & Mon Lunch not served

French **V** 18 seats Dinner £14alc Wine £5 Last dinner 9.30pm nc

Credit cards 2 3 5

NEWGATE STREET
Hertfordshire
Map **4** TL30

★★★**Ponsbourne** ☎ Cuffley (0707) 875221

RS Bank Hol & Sun (pm)

Peaceful 18th century country house with well appointed restaurant, comfortable rooms and leisure facilities.

26rm Annexe:6 (1fb) 1 CTV in all bedrooms **T** sB&B £35—£50 dB&B £50—£60

150P 1 (grass)

French **V** Lunch £12—£14&alc Dinner fr£16.50&alc Wine £7.50 Last dinner 9pm

Credit cards 1 2 3 5

Newchurch — Newmarket

NEWMARKET
Suffolk
Map **5** TL66

★★★**Newmarket Moat House** Moulton Rd (Queens) ☎ (0638) 667171

Modern hotel close by Newmarket Heath yet adjoining town centre.

49 (2fb) CTV in all bedrooms ® sB&B £40 dB&B £50

Lift 60P 5 CFA

English & French **V** Lunch fr£9.25&alc Tea fr70p Dinner fr£9.25&alc Wine £5.55 Last dinner 9.45pm

Credit cards 1 2 3 5 V

★★**Bedford Lodge** Bury Rd (Best Western) ☎ (0638) 663175 Telex no 97267

A quiet but centrally-situated hotel.

12rm(6 6)(3fb) CTV in all bedrooms ® **T** sB&B £38.50 dB&B £49.50—£66

50P *xmas*

English & French **V** *Lunch £7.50&alc Tea £1.25—£3.50 Dinner £7.50&alc Wine £4.90 Last dinner 9.15pm

Credit cards 1 2 3 5 V

★★*H* **Rosery Country House** 15 Church St, Exning (2m NW B1103) ☎ Exning (063877) 312

11rm(7 1) 1 CTV in all bedrooms ® **T** *sB&B £22 sB&B £32.50 dB&B £43.25

25P

V *Lunch £2.50—£6.50&alc Dinner £8—£18&alc Wine £4.75 Last dinner 9.30pm

Credit cards 1 2 3 5 V

★★**Rutland Arms** High St (Paten) ☎ (0638) 664251

The main building is a Georgian coaching house built round a cobbled courtyard.

45 (2fb) CTV in all bedrooms ® **T** S% sB&B £39 dB&B £49

CTV 26P 8 CFA *xmas*

V S% Lunch £8.45&alc Tea 50p Dinner £8.45&alc Wine £5.25 Last dinner 9pm

Credit cards 1 2 3 5 V

★★***White Hart*** High St ☎ (0638) 663051

Three-storey gabled building standing on the site of a 17th-century inn.

21rm(10)(2fb) CTV in all bedrooms ®

25P 2

English & French **V** Last dinner 9pm

Credit cards 1 3

NEW MILTON
Hampshire
Map **4** SZ29

★★★★

★★★★ CHEWTON GLEN, NEW MILTON

Christchurch Rd (Relais et Châteaux/ Prestige) ☎ Highcliffe (04252) 5341 Telex no 41456

One of the most popular of our Red Star hotels for those who can afford it, although praise has been less fulsome over the last year or so. Their own high standards of hospitality are difficult to maintain, but under the able manager, Mr Brockett levels of service will not be allowed to deteriorate. The new drive and landscaping has made the approach through the 30 acres of grounds and gardens very attractive. The interior has been beautifully done with Persian rugs over the wood floor and some nice pieces of furniture in the hall; everywhere, vibrant colour schemes and flowers lend their charm, as they do in the delightful fresh bedrooms and suites, immaculately kept and provided with all for your comfort. The public areas consist of the bar, drawing room and the two other sitting areas, beside the elegant restaurant. Here is provided a good value table d'hôte lunch and dinner; there is an à la carte menu and a Menu Gourmand. Pierre Chevillard is the chef and an exceptional one at that. He cooks in the modern French style and uses the best possible ingredients. He has harmonious gastronmic taste, his seasonings are exact and his cooking refined, as was demonstrated by a test meal of a

mousse of wild mushroom and chicken with a truffled cream sauce, turbot wrapped in cabbage with a touch of chopped tomato in a butter sauce with dill, breast of Challons duck with red wine sauce and beautifully cooked vegetables and finally, a crême brulée with blackcurrants. This is a heavenly place in the summer when one can enjoy the garden, just lazing, or swim, play tennis, croquet or putt.

44 1 CTV in all bedrooms **T** S% sB&B £60—£105 dB&B £152—£248 Continental breakfast

CTV 100P CFA (heated) (hard) snooker nc 7yrs *xmas*

French **V** S% Lunch fr£14&alc Tea £5 Dinner £35alc Wine £6.50 Last dinner 9.30pm

Credit cards 1 2 3 4 5

NEWPORT
Gwent
Map **3** ST38

★★★★ Celtic Manor The Coldra ☎ Llanwern (0633) 413000

The 19th century manor, once used as a maternity home, is situated close to the motorway. It offers well-appointed bedrooms, elegant public rooms, two good restaurants and a cellar bar.

17 2 CTV in all bedrooms **T** sB&B £59.50 dB&B £76.70

CTV 150P

French **V** *Lunch £10—£12alc Tea £3alc Dinner £15&alc Wine £5.50 Last dinner 10.30pm

Credit cards 1 2 3 5 V

★★★ *H* Kings High St ☎ (0633) 842020

The hotel enjoys a central location, close to castle ruins and shopping area. It retains its original façade, although the interior has recently been gutted and refitted in a tasteful, modern style.

47 (2fb) CTV in all bedrooms ®**T** *sB&B £39 dB&B £49 Continental breakfast

Lift in bedrooms 10P 20 *xmas*

International *Tea £1.95 Wine fr£6 Last dinner 9.30pm

Credit cards 1 2 3 4 5

See advertisement on page 536

★★★ Ladbroke (& Conferencentre) The Coldra (Ladbroke) ☎ (0633) 412777 Telex no 497205

Modern well-equipped hotel with comfortable bedrooms.

119 (5fb) in 11 bedrooms CTV in all bedrooms ®**T** S% sB&B £47.50 dB&B £63

200P games room Live music & dancing Sat *xmas*

International S% *Lunch £4.75—£8.50 Tea 50p Dinner £10.25&alc Wine £5.99 Last dinner 10pm

Credit cards 1 2 3 5

See advertisement on page 536

★★★ Ladbroke Wentloog Castle ☎ (0633) 680591
(For full entry see Castleton)

★★ New Inn Motel ☎ (0633) 412426
(For full entry see Langstone)

★★ *Priory* High St, Caerleon (3m NE B4236) (Golden Oak Inns) ☎ Caerleon (0633) 421241

Character hotel in village. Comfortable bedrooms and popular restaurant.

16rm (16) Annexe: 5rm (5)(1fb) CTV in all bedrooms ®**T** →

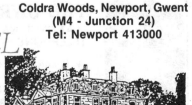

70P xmas

English & French V Last dinner 9.45pm

Credit cards 1 2 3

★★**Queens** 19 Bridge St (Anchor) (0633) 62992 Telex no 858875

A town centre hotel.

43rm(20 9)(2fb) CTV in all bedrooms ®T sB&B£22—£26 sB&B £30—£38.50 dB&B£36—£40 dB&B £38—£48 B

CTV snooker *xmas*

Newport

V ✱Dinner £4.05—£10.55 Tea 75—95p High Tea £1.50—£2.75 Dinner £8.75—£12.65&alc Wine £5.95 Last dinner 10pm

Credit cards 1 2 3 5 V

★★**Westgate** Commercial St (Exec Hotel) (0633) 66244 Telex no 498173

A traditional hotel in the town centre.

72rm(29 22)(7fb) CTV in all bedrooms ®T S% sB&Bfr£28.50 sB&B fr£38.50 dB&Bfr£39 dB&B fr£49 B

Lift 35P 3 CFA Disco Fri

English & Continental V S% ✱Lunch £5.75—£6.95&alc Tea £2 High Tea £4.50 Dinner £6.95&alc Wine £4.75 Last dinner 10.30pm

Credit cards 1 2 3 5 V

N

NEWPORT
Isle of Wight
See **Wight, Isle of**

NEWPORT
Shropshire
Map **7** SJ71

★★**Royal Victoria** St Mary's Street (Wolverhampton & Dudley) ☎ (0952) 810831

Simple but comfortable accommodation is available at this 18th-century town centre hotel.

21rm(10➡5⋒)(2fb) CTV in all bedrooms ®✱sB&B£20—£25 sB&B➡⋒£23—£29 dB&B£29—£36 dB&B➡⋒£32—£34 B

CTV 100P

English & French ✱Lunch fr£7.95&alc Dinner £7.95&alc Wine £4.30 Last dinner 9.30pm

Credit cards 1 2 3 5

NEWPORT PAGNELL
Buckinghamshire
Map **4** SP84

★★**Swan Revived** High St ☎ (0908) 610565 Telex no 826801

15th-century coaching inn with a friendly, welcoming atmosphere.

31rm(12➡19⋒) CTV in all bedrooms ®T S% sB&B➡⋒£20—£36 dB&B➡⋒£28—£40 B

Lift ☾ 15P 3⌂ Disco Sun

Mainly grills V ✱Lunch £6.50—£11.25&alc Tea fr£1 Dinner £6.50—£11.25&alc Wine £5.10 Last dinner 9.45pm

Credit cards 1 2 3 5

✕✕**Glovers** 18—20 St John Street ☎ (0908) 616398

Dark beams and bare stone walls create a relaxed atmosphere in the small, split-level restaurant. A separate bar is available for cocktails, and a fixed-price menu is professionally served by friendly staff.

Closed Sun, Mon, 25 Dec—4 Jan Lunch not served Sat

French V 36 seats Lunch £13alc Dinner £15alc Wine £5 Last dinner 10pm 6P

Credit cards 1 2 3 5

NEWQUAY
Cornwall
Map **2** SW86 **See plan**

★★★***Atlantic*** Dane Rd ☎ (0637) 872244 Plan **1** *B3*

Closed Oct—mid May (except Etr & 1 wk Oct)

Spacious family hotel in large grounds.

80rm(62➡) CTV in 62 bedrooms B

Lift ☾ CTV 100P 6⌂ CFA ✿ & (heated) squash billiards sauna bath solarium gymnasium Disco twice wkly Live music & dancing twice wkly ♿

V Last dinner 8.45pm

Credit cards 1 2 3 5

★★★***Barrowfield*** Hillgrove Rd ☎ (0637) 872560 Plan **2** *D2*

Modern family hotel near beach.

76rm(72➡4⋒)(16fb) 20 CTV in all bedrooms ® B

Lift ☾ CTV 58P 18⌂ CFA & (heated) sauna bath solarium gymnasium Disco twice wkly Live music & dancing 3 nights wkly Cabaret twice wkly *xmas*

English & French Last dinner 8.30pm

Credit cards 1 3

See advertisement on page 538

★★★*HL* **Hotel Bristol** Narrowcliff ☎ (0637) 875181 Plan **5** *D2*

In an ideal position directly overlooking Tolcarne beach, this hotel has been under the same ownership since 1927.

95rm(66➡)(2fb) CTV in 66 bedrooms S% sB&B£22.50—£23.50 sB&B➡£27.50—£28.50 dB&B£42.50—£44.50 dB&B➡£52.50—£54.50 B

Lift ☾ CTV 100P 5⌂(£2.50 per night) CFA (heated) snooker sauna bath solarium Disco wkly Live music and dancing twice wkly Cabaret twice wkly *xmas*

V S% Lunch £7&alc Tea £2 Dinner £10.50&alc Wine £4.50 Last dinner 8.30pm

Credit cards 1 2 3 5

★★★**Edgcumbe** Narrowcliff ☎ (0637) 872061 Plan **9** *E3*

Closed Dec—Feb

Family holiday-hotel with traditional services and good facilities.

86rm(61➡25⋒)(42fb) CTV in all bedrooms ®sB&B➡⋒£16—£30.50 dB&B➡⋒£32—£61 B

Lift ☾ CTV 70P & (heated) snooker sauna bath solarium Disco wkly Live music and dancing 3 nights wkly Cabaret twice wkly

V Lunch £6.50&alc Tea 65p—£3.75&alc Dinner £9.25&alc Wine £4.75 Last dinner 8.30pm

Credit cards 1 3

See advertisement on page 539

★★★*HL* ***Glendorgal*** Lusty Glaze Rd ☎ (0637) 874937 Plan **10** *E3*

Friendly, personally-run, secluded hotel in 15 acres of grounds and headland.

27➡ Annexe: 49rm(47➡) CTV in all bedrooms ® B

☾ 40P ✿ (heated) (hard) sauna bath solarium Disco twice wkly Live music & dancing 4 nights wkly *xmas*

English & Continental V Last dinner 8.30pm

See advertisement on page 539

★★★**Kilbirnie** Narrowcliff ☎ (0637) 875155 Plan **12** *E3*

Closed 22—28 Dec

Family holiday-hotel ¾m from town centre. Comfortably appointed with fine coastal views.

69rm(65➡)(8fb) CTV in all bedrooms sB&B➡£17—£27.50 dB&B➡£34—£55 B

☾ CTV 60P 6⌂ (heated) snooker sauna bath solarium Disco wkly (in season) Live music and dancing 4 nights wkly (in season)

Bar lunch £2.50—£4.60 Tea fr40p Dinner fr£9 Wine £4.50 Last dinner 8.30pm

Credit cards 1 3

★★★***Hotel Mordros*** 4 Pentire Av ☎ (0637) 876700 Plan **16** *A2*

This modern, family, holiday hotel offers good bedrooms, a non-smokers' lounge and a well-equipped gymnasium. It is personally run by the owners, and the atmosphere is friendly and informal.

30➡⋒(10fb) CTV in all bedrooms ®

Lift CTV 18P (heated) sauna bath solarium gymnasium Disco 3 nights Live music & dancing twice wkly Cabaret 4 nights wkly *xmas*

English & Continental V Last dinner 8.30pm

★★★**Hotel Riviera** Lusty Glaze Rd (Best Western) ☎ (0637) 874251 Telex no 42513 Plan **19** *E3*

Good interesting food is a feature of this comfortable, proprietor-run clifftop hotel.

50rm(31➡11⋒)(9fb) CTV in all bedrooms sB&B£25.50—£30.50 sB&B➡⋒£26.50—£31.50 dB&B£51—£61 dB&B➡⋒£53—£63 B

Lift ☾ CTV 60P CFA ✿ (heated) squash snooker sauna bath games room table tennis Disco Sat & 6 nights wkly (in summer) *xmas*

English & Continental V Lunch £3.75—£7&alc Tea 40—50p Dinner £8.50—£9.50alc Wine £5.75 Last dinner 8.30pm

Credit cards 1 2 3

★★★**St Rumons** Esplanade Rd, Fistral Bay ☎ (0637) 872978 Plan **20** *A2*

Closed Nov—Apr (except Xmas & Etr)

Modern family hotel overlooking Fistral Bay.

78rm(73➡3⋒)(39fb) CTV in all bedrooms ®✱sB&B£19.05—£25.05 (incl dinner) sB&B➡⋒£20.80—£28.05 (incl dinner) dB&B£38.10—£50.10 (incl dinner) dB&B➡⋒£41.60—£56.10 (incl dinner) B

Lift ☾ 55P & (heated) sauna bath solarium gymnasium games room Disco 6 nights wkly Live music & dancing 6 nights wkly *xmas*

English & Continental V ✱Lunch £5.50 Tea 50p—£1.40 Dinner £9.75—£11.75&alc Wine £4.40 Last dinner 8.30pm

Credit cards 2 3 5 V

N

N

★★★*L* **Trebarwith** Island Estate
☎(0637) 872288 Plan **22** *C2*

Closed 5 Oct—Mar

Family owned and run hotel, with a garden having its own steps to the beach.

43rm(32⇌6⋒)(6fb) 5⊟ CTV in all bedrooms **T** ✱ ✻ sB&B£18—£28.50 dB&B£24—£44.30 dB&B⇌⋒£36—£57

☾ 40P ⇌ ✿ ⊟(heated) ♪ snooker sauna bath solarium Disco wkly Live music & dancing 3 nights wkly Cabaret twice wkly ⌂

♡ ⊐ ✻ Bar lunch £2alc Tea 75palc Dinner £9.50&alc Wine £5.50 Last dinner 8.30pm

Credit cards 1 3 Ⓥ

Newquay

★★★*L* **Windsor** Mount Wise
☎(0637) 875188 Plan **26** *B1*

Closed Nov—Etr

Large well-appointed family hotel close to the town centre and the beaches.

42rm(35⇌1⋒)(13fb) 1⊟ CTV in all bedrooms ® ✱ sB&B£16—£24 sB&B⇌⋒£18—£26 dB&B£32—£48 dB&B⇌⋒£36—£52 **B**

50P ⇌ ✿ ⊟ & ⌒ (heated) squash sauna bath solarium gymnasium putting Disco twice wkly Live music & dancing 3 nights wkly Cabaret twice wkly ⌂

V ♡ ⊐ Bar lunch £1—£4 Tea 65p Dinner £10.50&alc Wine £4.95 Last dinner 8.30pm

Credit cards 1 3 4 5 Ⓥ

See advertisement on page 540

★★**Beachcroft** Cliff Rd ☎(0637) 873022 Plan **3** *D2*

Closed Nov—mid Apr

Large family hotel in its own gardens, close to the town centre and beach. →

N

Newquay

1 Atlantic ★★★
2 Barrowfield ★★★
3 Beachcroft ★★
4 Bewdley ★★
5 Hotel Bristol ★★★
6 Cedars ★★
7 Corisande Manor ★★
8 Cross Mount ★★
9 Edgcumbe ★★★
10 Glendorgal ★★★
11 Great Western ★★
12 Kilbirnie ★★★
13 Hotel Kontiki ★★
15 Minto House ★★
16 Hotel Mordros ★★★
16A Philema ★★
17 Pine Lodge ★★
18 Porth Veor Manor House ★★
19 Hotel Riviera ★★★
20 St Rumons ★★★
21 Sandy Lodge ★★
22 Trebarwith ★★★
23 Trevone ★
24 Water's Edge ★★
25 Whipsiddery ★★
26 Windsor ★★★

59rm(19⇌25⋔)(10fb) CTV in all bedrooms sB&B£11.50—£15.50 sB&B⇌⋔£11.50—£15.50 dB&B£22—£29 dB&B⇌⋔£24—£36

Lift ☾ CTV 80P ✿ ▭ & ⩪ (heated) sauna bath solarium games room Disco wkly Live music & dancing twice wkly

V ♱ ☕ ✱ Bar lunch 50p—£1.50 Tea 50p—£1.50 Dinner £4.50—£6.50 Last dinner 8pm

Credit card [1] Ⓥ

N

★★**Bewdley** Pentire Rd ☎ (0637) 872883 Plan **4** *B2*

Closed Nov—Feb

On the outskirts of town overlooking Fistral Beach and the Gannel Estuary.

31rm(4⇌17⋔)(7fb) CTV in 20 bedrooms Ⓡ S% sB&B£13.50—£22 sB&B⇌⋔£14.50—£23 dB&B£25—£42 dB&B⇌⋔£27—£44

CTV 35P ⩪ (heated) *xmas*

English & Italian **V** ♱ ☕ S% ✱ Lunch £3.50—£6.50 Tea £1—£1.75 High Tea fr£1.90 Dinner £5.50—£6.50 Wine £4.05 Last dinner 7.30pm

Credit cards [1] [3]

★★**Cedars** Mount Wise ☎ (0637) 874225 Plan **6** *B1*

Closed Dec—Mar except Xmas

Small friendly country-house style hotel.

36rm(13⇌17⋔)(8fb) CTV in all bedrooms Ⓡ S% ✱ sB&B£11.50—£21.85 sB&B⇌⋔£13.80—£24.15 dB&B£23—£43.70 dB&B⇌⋔£27.60—£52.90 B

CTV 32P ⩪ (heated) sauna bath solarium gymnasium Disco twice wkly Live music & dancing 3 nights wkly Cabaret wkly *xmas*

♱ ☕ ⚡ S% ✱ Bar lunch 75p—£3 Tea 50p—£1.25 Dinner £4—£6.75 Last dinner 7.30pm

See advertisement on page 542

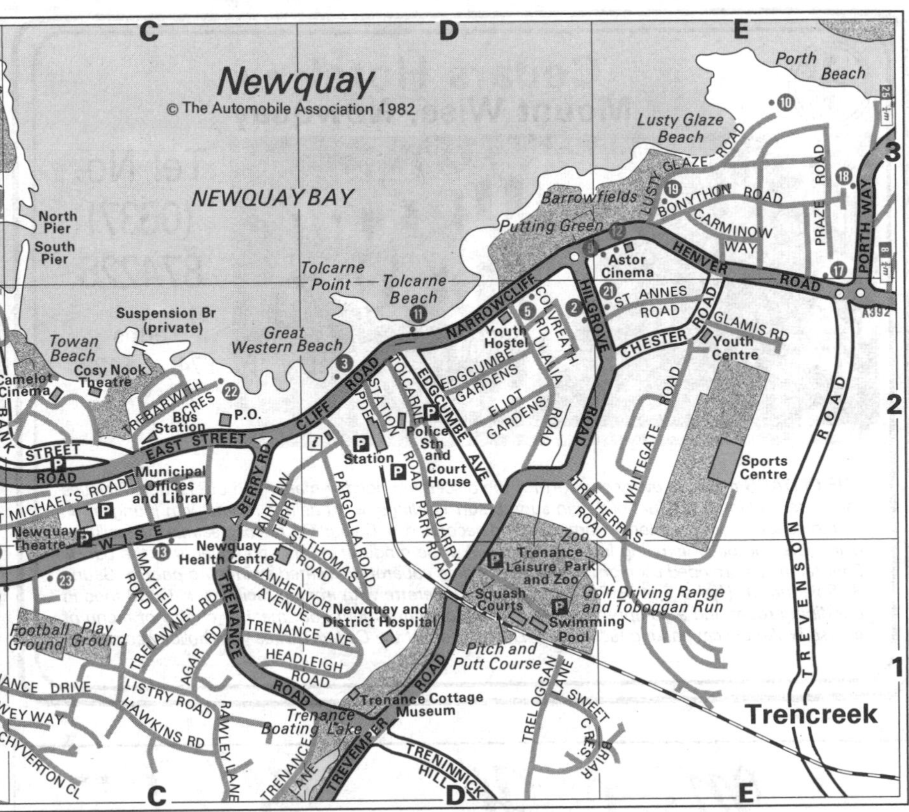

N

★★**Corisande Manor** Riverside Av, Pentire (Exec Hotel) ☎ (0637) 872042 Plan **7** *A2*

Closed 12 Oct–8 May

Character hotel with pleasant views.

19rm(4🛁8🚿)(3fb) sB&B£12–£16.50 sB&B🛁🚿£13.50–£17 dB&B£24–£33 dB&B🛁🚿£27–£34 B

CTV 19P ✻ solarium croquet putting nc 3yrs

English, French & Italian Bar lunch £2.50–£4 Tea 60p–£1.60 Dinner £6–£7.50 Wine £4 Last dinner 7.30pm

★★**Cross Mount** Church St, St Columb Minor ☎ (0637) 872669 Plan **8** *E3*

Closed Nov & Xmas

Dating from the 17th century, the small hotel retains old stone walls and beams.

12rm(4🛁2🚿)(2fb) Ⓡ ✻sB&B£11.50–£13 sB&B🛁🚿£13–£14.50 dB&B£23–£26 dB&B🛁🚿£26–£29 B

CTV 10P

✻Lunch £1.10–£7.50 Tea fr60p High Tea £1.50 Dinner fr£7&alc Wine £3.50 Last dinner 9.45pm

Credit cards [1] [3] Ⓥ

★★**Great Western** Cliff Rd ☎ (0637) 872010 Plan **11** *D2*

Close to the beaches, this hotel is situated in the centre of town and has good views.

45rm(26🛁19🚿)(10fb) CTV in all bedrooms Ⓡ S% sB&B🛁🚿£15–£20 dB&B🛁🚿£30–£40

Lift CTV 30P 10 CFA Disco wkly Live music and dancing wkly Cabaret wkly ♿

V S% Lunch £3.50–£6 Tea 75p–£2 High Tea £4–£6 Dinner £6–£8 Wine £3.50 Last dinner 7.45pm

Credit cards [1] [2] [3] [4] [5]

★★***Hotel Kontiki*** Mount Wise (cars use Brecken Terrace) ☎ (0637) 871137 Plan **13** *C2*

Large, family hotel, close to the town centre and beaches.

58🛁 Annexe: 12🛁(18fb) 2 CTV in all bedrooms Ⓡ B

Lift ☾ # CTV 50P 5 (heated) sauna bath solarium Live music & dancing nightly Cabaret twice wkly *xmas*

English & French **V** Last dinner 8.30pm

Credit cards [1] [2] [3] [5]

★★**Minto House** 38 Pentire Cres, Pentire ☎ (0637) 873227 Plan **15** *A2*

Closed Nov–Apr

Family hotel situated on the banks of the Gannel Estuary.

25rm(14🛁11🚿) Annexe: 3🛁(7fb) CTV in all bedrooms Ⓡ sB&B🛁🚿£13–£17 dB&B🛁🚿£26–£34

16P ✻ sauna bath solarium Disco wkly (in season) Live music & dancing wkly (in season) Cabaret wkly (in season) ♿

English & Continental Bar lunch £1–£3.75p Tea 85p Dinner £10.50 Wine £3.75 Last dinner 8pm

Credit cards [1] [2] [3] [5]

See advertisement on page 542

★★**Philema** 1 Esplanade Rd, Pentire ☎ (0637) 872571 Plan **16A** *A2*

RS Dec–Feb

Comfortable, friendly hotel with convivial atmosphere, overlooking golf course.

31rm(15🛁11🚿)(20fb) 1 CTV in all bedrooms Ⓡ sB&B£14–£17 sB&B🛁🚿£15–£18 dB&B£28–£34 dB&B🛁🚿£29–£35

CTV 31P (heated) sauna bath solarium games room table tennis pool table *xmas* →

Bar lunch £1.50—£3 Dinner £4.60—£7 Wine £3.40 Last dinner 7.30pm
Credit cards 1 3 Ⓥ

★★***Pine Lodge*** 91 Henver Rd ☎(0637) 872549 Plan **17** *E3*
Small friendly family-run hotel close to the town centre and beaches.
11rm(2⇌1⫿)Annexe:5rm(1⇌4⫿)(2fb) CTV in all bedrooms ®B
⅟ 20P ⇌ (heated)
Last dinner 8pm
Credit cards 1 3

★★**Porth Veor Manor House** Porthway ☎(0637) 873274 Plan **18** *E3*
Closed mid Nov—mid Jan
The personally-run hotel provides peace and comfort, with a good choice of well-cooked meals.
16rm(13⇌3⫿)(3fb) CTV in all bedrooms ®sB&B⇌⫿£20.50—£26 (incl dinner) dB&B⇌⫿£39—£50 (incl dinner) B
48P (grass) putting
English & Continental V Lunch £5—£7&alc Tea 45—80p High Tea £1.50 Dinner £5—£11.50&alc Wine £4.40 Last dinner 9pm
Credit cards 1 2 3 Ⓥ

Newquay

★★**Sandy Lodge** Hillgrove Rd ☎(0637) 872851 Plan **21** *E2*
Closed Nov—17 Apr
Small family hotel situated close to Barrowfield.
46rm(10⇌28⫿)(12fb) CTV in all bedrooms sB&B£9—£18.50 sB&B⇌⫿£9.50—£19.50 dB&B£16—£35 dB&B⇌⫿£17—£37 B
CTV 40P & (heated) sauna bath solarium gymnasium Disco 3 nights wkly Live music & dancing wkly Cabaret twice wkly *xmas*
English, French & Italian V Lunch £2.50—£3.60 Tea 60—85p High Tea £1.75—£2.50 Dinner £7.50—£8.50 Wine £4.25 Last dinner 8pm
Ⓥ

★★**Water's Edge** Esplanade Rd, Fistral Bay ☎(0637) 872048 Plan **24** *A2*
Closed Nov—Apr
Small family-owned hotel near Fistral Bay.
20rm(12⇌4⫿)(5fb) 1 CTV in all bedrooms ® *sB&B£13.80—£22.43 (incl dinner) dB&B£27.60—£44.85 (incl dinner) dB&B⇌⫿£31.05—£48.30 (incl dinner) B

CTV 18P 1 (£2 per day) solarium
English & French V *Bar lunch £1.45—£2.40 Tea 50p—£1.45 Dinner £9.50 Wine £3.95 Last dinner 8.15pm
Ⓥ

★★*HL* **Whipsiderry** Trevelgue Rd, Porth ☎(0637) 874777 Plan **25** *E3*
Closed mid Oct—Etr
Friendly hotel offering good restaurant, comfort and excellent value.
20rm(3⇌17⫿)(5fb) CTV in 18 bedrooms ®sB&B£16—£23 sB&B⇌⫿£17.50—£25.50 dB&B£32—£46 dB&B⇌⫿£35—£51
CTV 32P (heated) putting pool table Disco twice wkly Live music & dancing wkly Cabaret twice wkly
English & Continental V Bar lunch £1.70—£3.40 Tea 85p—£1.20 Dinner £6.25—£10.50 Wine £3.95 Last dinner 8pm
Ⓥ

See advertisement on page 544

★**Trevone** Mount Wise ☎(0637) 873039 Plan **23** *C1*
Closed mid Nov—Mar
Small family hotel situated close to town centre and beaches.
34rm(5⇌19⫿)(4fb) sB&B£6.50—£10.50 sB&B⇌⫿£7.50—£11.50 dB&B£13—£21 dB&B⇌⫿£15—£23 →

N

CTV 25P table tennis pool table Disco twice wkly Cabaret in summer 4 nights wkly in summer 3 nights wkly in winter

English, French, Italian & Indian Bar lunch 70p—£2.50 Tea 35p Dinner £6.50—£7.50 Wine £4.50 Last dinner 7.30pm

NEW QUAY
Dyfed
Map **2** SN35

★★**Black Lion** ☎ (0545) 560209

Built at the same time (1830) and of the same stone as the harbour at New Quay, this small character hotel offers comfortable accommodation, commendable food standards and friendly local service. Overlooking the bay from its elevated position, it is a firm favourite with locals and tourists alike.

7rm(4 2)(2fb) CTV in all bedrooms ® sB&B £24—£28 dB&B £34—£42

CTV 50P

British, French & Italian V ✱Bar lunch £4.75alc Tea 95p—£2.95 Dinner £9.50alc Wine £5.50 Last dinner 9.30pm

Credit cards 1 2 3 5 Ⓥ

★**New Quay** ☎ (0545) 560282

Directly overlooking seafront and harbour, the convivial little hotel has some recently modernised bedrooms and popular bars, including an attractive wine bar.

11rm(2fb) in 11 bedrooms ® sB&B£10—£14 dB&B£19.50—£25

CTV Disco 6 nights wkly in summer

Bar lunch £2.50—£5.50 Dinner £5.50&alc Wine £3.75 Last dinner 9.30pm

Credit cards 1 3 Ⓥ

NEWTON ABBOT
Devon
Map **3** SX87

★★★***Globe*** Courtenay St ☎ (0626) 54106

Principal town centre hotel.

18rm(6 9)(1fb) CTV in all bedrooms ® T

xmas

English & French V Last dinner 10pm

Credit cards 1 2 3 4 5

★★***Queens*** Queens St ☎ (0626) 63133

Commercial corner-sited town hotel, with good service and attentive staff.

26rm(16)(6fb) CTV in all bedrooms ®

8P *xmas*

V Last dinner 9.30pm

Credit cards 1 3 5

★***H*** **Hazelwood House** 33A Torquay Rd ☎ (0626) 66130

A warm welcome is extended by this small hotel, which stands only five minutes' walk from the town centre. In a well-appointed dining room which features ecclesiastical panelling, guests can enjoy some tasty and original dishes, all prepared to order, accompanied by selected French wines.

6rm(1 3)(1fb) CTV in all bedrooms ® ✱sB&B£15—£17.50 sB&B £17.50—£19 dB&Bfr£24 dB&B fr£28

6P

English & French V ✱Lunch fr£5.95&alc Dinner fr£5.95&alc Wine £5.65 Last dinner 9.30pm

Credit cards 1 3 Ⓥ

NEWTON FERRERS
Devon
Map **2** SX54

★★ **Court House** ☎ Plymouth (0752) 872324

Creeper-clad manor set in spacious terraced lawns and gardens.

10rm(7)(3fb) in 1 bedroom CTV in all bedrooms ® S% ✱sB&B£15—£28 sB&B £18—£30 dB&B£18—£30 dB&B £18—£32

CTV 12P 3 (heated) croquet
xmas

N

International **V** ⛾ ☕ Lunch £4.50—£10&alc Tea 50-75p High Tea 50p—£2.50 Dinner £9—£12.50&alc Wine £4.60 Last dinner 9.15pm

Credit cards 1 3 Ⓥ

See advertisement under Plymouth

★★**River Yealm** Yealm Rd ☎ Plymouth (0752) 872419

Gabled building in its own grounds with river frontage and jetty.

19rm(4🛁) Annexe: 4🛁(1fb) Ⓡ sB&B£17 sB&B🛁£18 dB&B£34 dB&B🛁£36 Ⓑ

CTV 60P 1🚗 ✿

V ⛾ ☕ Bar lunch fr£2 Tea fr40p Dinner fr£8.50 Wine £3.60 Last dinner 9pm

NEWTON MEARNS

Strathclyde *Renfrewshire*
Map **11** NS55

✕**La Vecchia Romagna** 108 Ayr Rd ☎ 041-639 1162

Tucked in among a small group of shops just south of Mearns Cross, the smart, basement, Italian restaurant provides good value for money, offering a reasonable choice of authentic Italian dishes with a number of house specialities.

Closed Sun

Italian **V** 48 seats ✱Lunch £3.75&alc Dinner £5.50—£12.50&alc Wine £4.90 Last dinner 11pm 60P

Credit cards 1 2 3 5

NEWTONMORE

Highland *Inverness-shire*
Map **14** NN79

★★**Glen** Main St ☎ (05403) 203

Small, comfortable family hotel of traditional Scottish design.

8rm(3🛁2🚿)(2fb) Ⓡ **T** S% sB&B£15.50 sB&B🛁🚿£17 dB&B£27 dB&B🛁🚿£30 Ⓑ

CTV 30P ✿ Disco Fri

V ⛾ ☕ Bar lunch £2—£9 Tea £1 Dinner £9 Wine £3.50 Last dinner 9pm

Credit cards 1 3 5

❀★*H* **Ard-Na-Collie** Kingsussie Rd ☎ (05403) 214

Closed Nov—Mar

(Rosette awarded for dinner only.)

This former shooting lodge has been converted to a homely and very relaxing hotel of great character. The food is of a most commendable character — dinner consists of a set main course augmented by a choice of starters and puddings, all prepared to Cordon Bleu standards.

10rm(1🛁3🚿)(1fb) S% sB&B£17—£20 dB&B£25—£35 dB&B🛁🚿£35—£45

CTV 12P 2🚗 ✿

English & French S% Dinner £11 Wine £4.50 Last dinner 8pm

NEWTON POPPLEFORD

Devon
Map **3** SY08

✕**Bridge End House** Harpford (½m E A3052) ☎ Colaton Raleigh (0395) 68411

The restaurant, a thatched, colour-washed cottage, stands on the outskirts of the village beside the River Otter. Its interior maintains the cottage theme, with tapestry seating in the aperitif bar, which displays facsimiles of bills dated at the beginning of the last century, and lace napkins and flowers in the pleasant, beamed dining room. The home-cooked food is generally traditional, though there is a selection of dishes to tempt the more adventurous.

Closed Mon Dinner not served Sun

English & French **V** 42 seats ✱Lunch £7.60—£13.10 Dinner £7.60—£13.10 Wine £4.90 Last dinner 10pm 24P

Credit cards 1 3

NEWTON SOLNEY

Derbyshire
Map **8** SK22

★★★**Newton Park** (Embassy) ☎ Burton-on-Trent (0283) 703568

Large Georgian-style building on the B5008.

27rm(26🛁1🚿) CTV in all bedrooms Ⓡ **T** ✱sB🛁🚿fr£39 dB🛁🚿fr£50 (room only) Ⓑ

☾ ## 200P ✿

V ⛾ ☕ ✱Lunch £5.65—£6.65 Tea fr65p Dinner £9.65—£10.65 Wine £5.65 Last dinner 9.30pm

Credit cards 1 2 3 4 5

See advertisement under Burton-on-Trent

NEWTON STEWART

Dumfries & Galloway *Wigtownshire*
Map **10** NX46

★★★**Bruce** Queen St ☎ (0671) 2294 Telex no 295141

Closed Dec & Jan

Modern family run hotel with attractive restaurant.

18🛁🚿(2fb) CTV in all bedrooms Ⓡ **T** S% ✱sB&B🛁🚿£24.50 dB&B🛁🚿£41 Ⓑ

CTV 20P 2🚗 solarium gymnasium

English & French **V** ⛾ S% ✱Lunch £3alc Dinner £11—£12.20 Wine £4.95 Last dinner 8.30pm

Credit cards 1 2 3 5

See advertisement on page 546

❀★★★ *HBL* **Kirroughtree** (see red rosette box on next page)

★★*H* **Creebridge House** ☎ (0671) 2121

RS 20 Dec—5 Jan

A very pleasant country house style hotel set in secluded grounds on the town outskirts.

17rm(12🛁1🚿)(1fb) CTV in 14 bedrooms TV in 3 bedrooms Ⓡ **T** S% sB&B£19—£22 sB&B🛁🚿£21—£27 dB&B£38—£42 dB&B🛁🚿£42—£54 Ⓑ

40P 1🚗 ✿

Scottish & French **V** ☕ S% Bar lunch £6alc Tea £1.50alc Dinner £11.50—£13 Wine £6 Last dinner 9pm

Credit cards 1 3

N

★★★ **HBL Kiroughtree** Minnigaff ☎(0671) 2141

Closed 8 Nov—5 Mar

(Rosette awarded for dinner only.)

A turretted Georgian mansion in splendid landscaped grounds, this is a relaxing and comfortable hotel. The public areas are richly decorated and the bedrooms are most comfortable. Chef Macphee's straight forward cooking continues to satisfy visitors.

20 Annexe: 2 (4fb) 4 CTV in all bedrooms T sB&B £32—£36 dB&B £64—£68

40P putting croquet bowling nc10yrs

British & French V Lunch £12alc Tea £1.20alc Dinner £21alc Wine £6.25 Last dinner 9.30pm

★★**Crown** 101 Queen St ☎(0671) 2727

This modestly appointed but pleasant former coaching inn stands adjacent to the town's market.

10rm(4 1)(1fb) CTV in 5 bedrooms ® sB&B fr£13.50 sB&B fr£19.50 dB&B fr£27 dB&B fr£31

CTV 30P pool Live music and dancing Sat (mthly)

Newton Stewart — Newtown

V Bar lunch £2.20—£8.40 Tea fr70p High Tea £3.25—£4.50 Dinner fr£9&alc Wine £5.30 Last dinner 8.30pm

Credit cards 1 3 V

★★**Galloway Arms** Victoria St (Consort) ☎(0671) 2282

A wide range of meals is offered by this friendly town-centre hotel, a former 18th century coaching inn.

23rm(14 2)(2fb) in 2 bedrooms CTV in all bedrooms ®

*sB&B £22.50—£26 dB&B £39

8P 12 shooting Disco 3 nights weekly *xmas*

V Bar lunch £2.95—£7 Tea £2.10 High Tea £4—£8 Dinner £11.50 Last dinner 10pm

Credit cards 1 3

NEWTOWN
Powys
Map **6** SO19

★★★**Bear** Broad St (Consort) ☎(0686) 26964 Telex no 35205

Coaching inn dating from Tudor times, situated in the town centre, with a modern extension at the rear.

34rm(24 5)(5fb) CTV in all bedrooms ® T sB&B £25—£30 dB&B £37—£45

50P *xmas*

V Lunch £6—£7&alc Tea 50p Dinner £8.75—£9.25&alc Wine £4.75 Last dinner 9.30pm

Credit cards 1 2 3 5 V

★★**Elephant & Castle** Broad St ☎(0686) 26271

RS 24&25 Dec

Now completely modernised, the hotel dates from the early nineteenth century and is the birthplace of Robert Owen, the famous Welsh pioneer. It enjoys a pleasant setting beside the River Severn.

21rm(19 2)(3fb) CTV in all bedrooms ® T S% sB&B fr£18 dB&B fr£28

CTV 35P

V S% Lunch fr£6 Tea fr50p High Tea fr£4 Dinner fr£9&alc Wine £4 Last dinner 9.30pm

Credit cards 1 2 3 5 V

N

NEWTOWN LINFORD
Leicestershire
Map **4** SK50

★★**Johnscliffe** 73 Main St (Exec Hotel)
☎ Markfield (0530) 242228

Closed 24 Dec—4 Jan

Fine rural views are available from this converted Edwardian house with its extensive grounds.

8rm(2🛁3🚿)(1fb) 2📺 CTV in 5 bedrooms Ⓡ sB&B£19.50
sB&B🛁🚿£22.50—£28.50
dB&B🛁🚿£37.50—£47.50 B
CTV 40P ❀ *xmas*

🍷English & French **V** ☕ S% Lunch £5.95—£6.75 Tea 50—75p High Tea £2—£3 Dinner £8.45—£9.95 Wine £6.50 Last dinner 10pm
Credit cards [1] [2] [3] [5]

NOLTON HAVEN
Dyfed
Map **2** SM81

★★**Mariners Inn** ☎ Camrose (0437) 710469

The small, family-run inn stands near to the sea and within the Pembrokeshire National Park. It provides modern bedrooms which are cosy and compact, character bars and a new restaurant complex which serves a good standard of food.

11rm(4🛁7🚿)(3fb) CTV in all bedrooms Ⓡ S% sB&B🛁🚿£18.40—£20.70
dB&B🛁🚿£32.20—£39.10 B
20P Disco Wed 🕺 *xmas*

🍷Welsh, English & French **V** ☕ S% Lunch £7&alc Tea £2 Dinner £7&alc Wine £4.85 Last dinner 10pm
Credit cards [1] [2] [3] Ⓥ

Norman Cross — North Ballachulish

NORMAN CROSS
Cambridgeshire
Map **4** TL19

★★★**Crest** Great North Rd (Crest) ☎ Peterborough (0733) 240209 Telex no 32576

Large modern hotel, convenient for A1.

99rm(79🛁20🚿)(28fb)⍻ in 10 bedrooms CTV in all bedrooms S% ✱sB&B🛁🚿£49.35—£59.35 dB&B🛁🚿£65.20 Ᏼ

☾⌗130P CFA sauna bath solarium gymnasium games room ♿

V ♉ ☕ ⍻ S% ✱Lunch £8.35 Tea £1 Dinner £11.50&alc Wine £5.80 Last dinner 10pm

Credit cards [1] [2] [3] [4] [5]

NORTHALLERTON
North Yorkshire
Map **8** SE39

★★★ ♣L ***Solberge Hall*** Newby Wiske (3¼m S off A167) (Best Western) ☎ (0609) 779191

This gracious, porticoed, country house dates from the Victorian era and stands in twelve acres of grounds. Carefully chosen furnishings enhance its character, the comfortable bedrooms offer many extra facilities, and service is friendly.

15rm(13🛁) 2⊞ CTV in all bedrooms **T** Ᏼ

50P ✻ billiards

♔French ♉ ☕ Last dinner 9.30pm

Credit cards [1] [2] [3] [5]

★★**Golden Lion** Market Pl (Trusthouse Forte) ☎ (0609) 2404

Sympathetically modernised inn with Georgian façade offering comfortable old world atmosphere and stylish dining room.

29rm(11🛁) CTV in all bedrooms Ⓡ sB&B£41 sB&B🛁£44 dB&B£53.50 dB&B🛁£61.50 Ᏼ

CTV 60P *xmas*

♉ Last dinner 9.30pm

Credit cards [1] [2] [3] [4] [5]

NORTHAMPTON
Northamptonshire
Map **4** SP76

★★★**Grand** Gold St ☎ (0604) 250511 Telex no 311198

68rm🛁🚿(2fb) CTV in all bedrooms Ⓡ**T** S% ✱sB&Bfr£26 sB&B🛁🚿fr£36 dB&B🛁🚿fr£48 Ᏼ

Lift ☾70P CFA

♉ ☕ ✱Lunch £6.50 Tea 55p—£2 Dinner fr£6.50 Wine £4.25 Last dinner 10pm

Credit cards [1] [2] [3] [4] [5]

★★★**Northampton Moat House** Silver St, Town Centre (Queens) ☎ (0604) 22441 Telex no 311142

137🛁🚿(4fb)⍻ in 21 bedrooms CTV in all bedrooms Ⓡ**T** S% sB&B🛁🚿£51.25 dB&B🛁🚿£66.50 Ᏼ

Lift ☾150P CFA sauna bath solarium gymnasium Live music and dancing Sat (Sep—May)

♔English & French **V** ♉ ☕ S% ✱Lunch £7.75&alc Dinner £8.75&alc Wine £5.95 Last dinner 10.30pm

Credit cards [1] [2] [3] [5]

★★★**Westone Moat House** Ashley Way, Weston Favell (3m E off A45) (Queens) ☎ (0604) 406262 Telex no 312587

Closed 25 Dec—1 Jan

30🛁 Annexe: 34🛁(4fb) CTV in all bedrooms Ⓡ**T** S% ✱sB&B🛁£40 dB&B🛁£50 Ᏼ

Lift ☾ CTV 100P 2⌂(charge) ✻ sauna bath solarium gymnasium croquet putting Live music and dancing Sat mthly ♘ *xmas*

♔International **V** ♉ ☕ S% ✱Lunch fr£7&alc Tea fr75p Dinner fr£8&alc Wine £6 Last dinner 9.45pm

Credit cards [1] [2] [3] [5] Ⓥ

★★**Thorplands Toby Motel** Talavera Way, Round Spinney (Toby) ☎ (0604) 494241

Annexe: 31🛁(8fb)⍻ in 7 bedrooms CTV in all bedrooms Ⓡ**T** ⛌ (except guide dogs) ✱sB&B🛁£35—£40 dB&B🛁£45—£50 Ᏼ

☾⌗31P ✻

V ✱Lunch £7.20alc Dinner £7.20alc Wine £3.65 Last dinner 10.30pm

Credit cards [1] [2] [3] [5]

★***Lime Trees*** 8 Langham Pl, Barrack Rd (from city centre follow signs A508 Leicester) ☎ (0604) 32188

Closed Xmas—New Year

Family run hotel featuring picture exhibition in attractive restaurant.

12rm(2🛁2🚿) Annexe: 10rm(3🛁2🚿) (2fb) CTV in all bedrooms Ⓡ**T** Ᏼ

CTV 2P

V ♉ ☕ Last dinner 9pm

Credit cards [1] [3]

○**Swallow** Eagle Drive (Swallow) Access from junction 15, M1 Motorway ☎ (0604) 68700

122🛁🚿

Due to have opened September 1986

✕**Napoleon's Bistro** 9—11 Welford Rd ☎ (0604) 713899

Closed Sun Lunch not served Sat

♔French **V** 44 seats ✱Lunch fr£5.70&alc Dinner £10.60alc Wine £5.70 Last dinner 10pm Ᵽ

Credit cards [1] [2] [3] [5]

✕**Vineyard** 7 Derngate ☎ (0604) 33978

Closed Sun

♔French **V** 30 seats Lunch £13alc Dinner £15alc Wine £6 Last dinner 10.10pm Ᵽ⍻

Credit cards [1] [2] [3] [5]

NORTH BALLACHULISH
Highland *Inverness-shire*
Map **14** NN06

★***Loch Leven*** ☎ Onich (08553) 236

Now overshadowed by the bridge this family run hotel is set beside the old ferry landing, overlooking Loch Leven.

10rm(1fb) Ᏼ

N

CTV 100P Live music & dancing wkly

Scottish & Continental V Last dinner 8.30pm

Credit cards 1 3

NORTH BERWICK
Lothian *East Lothian*
Map **12** NT58

★★★**Marine** Cromwell Rd (Trusthouse Forte) (0620) 2406 Telex no 727363

Built in the grand resort style, this hotel has excellent views across the Firth of Forth.

86rm(78 8)(9fb) CTV in all bedrooms Ⓡ sB&B £43.50 dB&B £67.50

Lift CTV 200P CFA (heated) (hard) squash billiards sauna bath solarium *xmas*

Last dinner 9.30pm

Credit cards 1 2 3 4 5

★★**Blenheim House** Westgate (0620) 2385

Standing close to the beach, with a fine view across West Bay, this attractively decorated tourist hotel has a pleasant lounge.

11rm(5 1)(2fb) CTV in all bedrooms Ⓡ sB&B fr£20 sB&B fr£22 dB&B fr£40 dB&B fr£44

30P

V Lunch £5—£6.50 Dinner £9—£11&alc Wine £5.30 Last dinner 9pm

★★***Nether Abbey*** Dirleton Av (0620) 2802

Closed Nov—Mar

The privately owned and managed resort hotel is situated at the western end of the town.

16rm(4 6)(2fb) Ⓡ

CTV 60P

V Last dinner 8.30pm

Credit cards 1 3

★★**Point Garry** West Bay Rd (0620) 2380

Closed Nov—Mar

Family run hotel with pleasant garden.

15rm(2 6)(4fb) Ⓡ S% sB&B £19.80 sB&B £22 dB&B £36 dB&B £40

CTV 10P snooker

English & French V S% ✱Lunch £5—£7.50 Tea 50p Dinner £8.80&alc Wine £4.75 Last dinner 9pm

Ⓥ

✕**Al Vagabondo** 35 High St (0620) 3434

The simply-decorated but friendly little restaurant creates an authentic trattoria atmosphere, and the proprietors are always on hand to ensure that you enjoy their freshly prepared fare.

Closed Mon (in winter) Lunch not served Sun

Continental 56 seats ✱Lunch fr£3&alc Dinner £10alc Wine £5.50 Last dinner 10pm Live music & dancing mthly

Credit cards 1 2 3 5

North Ballachulish — North Stoke

NORTH CAVE
Humberside
Map **8** SE83

✕**Sundial** 18 Westgate (04302) 2537

Closed 1 wk Feb, 2 wks Jul/Aug

Lunch not served V 45 seats Dinner £10—£11alc Wine £5 Last dinner 9.30pm 20P

Credit cards 1 2 3 Ⓥ

NORTH FERRIBY
Humberside
Map **8** SE92

★★★**Crest Hotel—Humber Bridge** Ferriby High Rd (Crest) Hull (0482) 645212 Telex no 592558

RS 25, 26 Dec & 1 Jan

A multi-storey, modern hotel with views of the Humber Bridge.

102 in 10 bedrooms CTV in all bedrooms T S% ✱sB £50.50—£52.50 dB £66—£68 (room only)

75P CFA

International V S% ✱Lunch £8&alc Tea £1.50—£1.90 Dinner £11.95—£14.95&alc Wine £6.50 Last dinner 9.45pm

Credit cards 1 2 3 4 5

NORTHIAM
East Sussex
Map **5** TQ82

★★**Hayes Arms** Village Gn (Exec Hotel) (07974) 3142

Closed 16 Jan—9 Feb

This fifteenth-century farmhouse, extended in Georgian times, offers bedrooms individually furnished with antiques, and there are two inglenook fireplaces. Good English cooking is backed by personal and attentive service.

7(1fb) 1 CTV in all bedrooms Ⓡ sB&B £25—£31 dB&B £46—£54

40P *xmas*

Bar lunch £5.50alc Tea fr60p Dinner £10.50—£11 Wine £5.50 Last dinner 9pm

Credit cards 1 2 3 5

NORTHLEACH
Gloucestershire
Map **4** SP11

★**Wheatsheaf** Cotswold (0451) 60244

Good food, friendly service and warm bedrooms are provided by this small, personally-run inn.

9rm(1 4)(2fb) CTV in all bedrooms Ⓡ T ✱sB&B fr£18 sB&B fr£20 dB&B fr£28 dB&B fr£35

20P 3

V Lunch £6.50—£10 Tea 60p—£1.50 Dinner £10alc Wine £4.25 Last dinner 9.30pm

Credit cards 1 2 3 5

NORTHOP HALL
Clwyd
Map **7** SJ26

★★★**Chequers** (Inter Hotel) Deeside (0244) 816181 Telex no 617112

Old manor house in wooded parkland has well equipped bedrooms, and some Welsh dishes on an extensive menu.

29rm(27 2)(3fb) in 1 bedroom CTV in all bedrooms Ⓡ T S% sB&B £30—£33 dB&B £49—£55

150P 1 *xmas*

V Lunch £4.50—£7&alc Tea 50p Dinner £8.75—£9.75&alc Wine £4.50 Last dinner 9.45pm

Credit cards 1 2 3 5 Ⓥ

See advertisement under Mold

NORTHREPPS
Norfolk
Map **9** TG23

✕✕**Northrepps Cottage** Overstrand (026378) 202

Closed Mon, Tue (Sep—May) & 2 wks Oct

English & French 32 seats ✱Lunch fr£5.50&alc Dinner £10.75alc Wine £5.25 Last dinner 9.15pm 200P Live music Sun Live music and dancing Sat

Credit cards 1 3

NORTH STIFFORD
Essex
Map **5** TQ68

995126 £52 Sing £66 Twin Bed & Bkfst

★★★**Stifford Moat House** (Queens Moat) Grays Thurrock (0375) 371451

Quiet hotel with modern, well-equipped bedrooms and friendly well-run restaurant.

64 CTV in all bedrooms Ⓡ T S% sB&B £26.95—£47.30 dB&B £35.75—£60.50

100P CFA (hard) croquet petanque Live music and dancing Sat Cabaret Sat

English & French V ✱Lunch £11&alc Dinner £11&alc Wine £5.95 Last dinner 9.40pm

Credit cards 1 2 3 4 5

0375-371451 390909

NORTH STOKE
Oxfordshire
Map **4** SU68

★★★*B* **Springs** Wallingford Rd Wallingford (0491) 36687 Telex no 849794

A country house has been enlarged and refurbished in the last few years to provide individually styled and furnished bedrooms and a restaurant with a superb view across the lake, which is floodlit at night. A tennis court, attractive lawns and a guitar-shaped swimming pool are further attractions.

34rm(33 1)(7fb) 2 CTV in all bedrooms T sB&B £57.50—£65 dB&B £86—£100

80P (heated) (hard) sauna bath solarium gymnasium croquet pitch & putt *xmas* →

N

🍷French V ♡ ☕ Lunch fr£11.50&alc Tea fr£4 Dinner £16.50—£18.50&alc Wine £8 Last dinner 10.15pm
Credit cards 1 2 3 4 5 V

NORTHWICH
Cheshire
Map **7** SJ67

★★★**Hartford Hall** School Ln, Hartford (2m SW off bypass A556) (Consort) ☎(0606) 75711
Gabled 16th-century house in its own grounds.
21🛁🚿(3fb) CTV in all bedrooms ®T S% *sB&B🛁🚿£27.50—£37.50 dB&B🛁🚿£39.50—£55 B

North Stoke
—
Norwich

☾CTV 50P✿
🍷English & French V ♡ ☕ S% *Lunch £4.95—£10&alc Dinner £10.75&alc Last dinner 10pm
Credit cards 1 2 3 5 V

★★**Woodpecker** London Rd (GW Hotels) ☎(0606) 45524
Closed 25 Dec(pm)
This well-furnished hotel, situated just off the bypass road, has bedrooms in a modern extension block.
34rm(28🛁1🚿)(3fb) CTV in all bedrooms ®T sB&B🛁🚿£38 dB&B🛁🚿£48 B
☾CTV 100P✿
🍷English & French V ♡ ☕ Lunch £6—£7 Tea 70p High Tea £2.50 Dinner £7.50—£10 Wine £5 Last dinner 9.30pm
Credit cards 1 2 3 5

NORWICH
Norfolk
Map **5** TG20

★★★**Arlington** 10 Arlington Ln, Newmarket Rd (Best Western) ☎(0603) 617841 Telex no 975392

N

41rm(31🛁4🚿)(3fb) CTV in all bedrooms Ⓡ T sB&B£30 sB&B🛁🚿£38—£42 dB&B🛁🚿£52 B

☾ 60P ⌗ 1 🚗 *xmas*

English & French V ♁ ☕ ⚡ Lunch £6.95—£10.95 Tea £3.50 High Tea £6.95—£10.95 Dinner £6.95—£15.95&alc Wine £3.95 Last dinner 10.30pm

Credit cards 1 2 3 5 Ⓥ

★★★**Lansdowne** 116 Thorpe Rd (Embassy) ☎ (0603) 620302

38rm(28🛁10🚿)(1fb) CTV in all bedrooms Ⓡ T S% ✱sB£31 sB🛁🚿£41 dB🛁🚿£55 (room only) B

Lift ☾ CTV 60P CFA

♁ S% Lunch fr£8&alc Dinner fr£8&alc Wine £5 Last dinner 9.15pm

Credit cards 1 2 3 4 5 Ⓥ

★★★**Maids Head** Tombland (Queens Moat) ☎ (0603) 628821 Telex no 975080

Part of the hotel is more than 700 years old, showing the original fireplace and kingpin pillars.

80rm(69🛁11🚿)(1fb) 1⊟ CTV in all bedrooms Ⓡ **T** ✱sB&B🛁🚿£34.50—£40.50 dB&B🛁🚿£53—£63 B

Lift ☾ 55P 45🚗 CFA *xmas*

English & French V ♁ ☕ ⚡ ✱Lunch £3.75—£7 Tea £1.95—£2.50 Dinner £8.75—£9.50&alc Wine £5 Last dinner 9.45pm

Credit cards 1 2 3 5

★★★**Hotel Nelson** Prince of Wales Rd ☎ (0603) 628612 Telex no 975203

The hotel stands on the banks of the River Wensum close to the city centre.

122🛁⚡ in 6 bedrooms CTV in all bedrooms Ⓡ **T** ✗ S% sB&B🛁fr£45.50 dB&B🛁fr£55.50 B

Lift ☾ 119P 30🚗 sauna bath *xmas*

V ♁ ⚡ S% Lunch fr£8.95&alc Dinner fr£8.95&alc Wine £5.40 Last dinner 9.45pm

Credit cards 1 2 3 4 5 Ⓥ

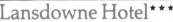

Norwich — Nottingham

★★★**Hotel Norwich** 121—131 Boundary Rd (Best Western) ☎ (0603) 410431 Telex no 975337

102🛁🚿(16fb) ⚡ in 6 bedrooms CTV in all bedrooms Ⓡ **T** ✗ S% sB&B🛁🚿£39—£43 dB&B🛁🚿£49—£53 B

☾ 225P CFA *xmas*

V ♁ ☕ S% Lunch fr£8.95&alc Dinner fr£8.95&alc Wine £5.40 Last dinner 10pm

Credit cards 1 2 3 5 Ⓥ

★★★**Post House** Ipswich Rd (Trusthouse Forte) ☎ (0603) 56431 Telex no 975106

Commercial hotel on outskirts with consistently satisfactory standards.

120🛁 CTV in all bedrooms Ⓡ sB&B🛁£49.50 dB&B🛁£64.50 B

☾ 200P CFA ✿ ⊟ & ⌒ (heated) sauna bath solarium gymnasium *xmas*

♁ Last dinner 9.45pm

Credit cards 1 2 3 4 5

★★★**Sprowston Hall** Wroxham Rd, Sprowston (2m NE A1151) ☎ (0603) 410871 Telex no 975356

Imposing building up a long driveway, offering a pleasant, relaxing stay.

26rm(18🛁8🚿) Annexe: 14rm(12🛁2🚿)(4fb) 4⊟ CTV in all bedrooms Ⓡ **T** S% sB&B🛁🚿£37.50 dB&B🛁🚿£47.50 B

☾ 200P CFA ✿ putting croquet Live music and dancing Sat mthly ⌂ *xmas*

English & Continental V ♁ ☕ S% Lunch fr£7.50 Dinner fr£8.50 Wine £6.50 Last dinner 9.30pm

Credit cards 1 2 3 4 5 Ⓥ

★★**Castle** Castle Meadow ☎ (0603) 611511 Telex no 975582

78rm(28🛁)(4fb) CTV in all bedrooms Ⓡ S% sB&B£25.95—£26.95 sB&B🛁£36.95—£37.95 dB&B£37.90—£39.90 dB&B🛁£47.90—£49.90 B

Lift ☾ P CFA *xmas*

English & French V ♁ ☕ ⚡ S% Lunch £3.50—£8&alc Tea 70p—£2.50 High Tea £2.50—£4.50 Dinner £8&alc Wine £5 Last dinner 9.30pm

Credit cards 1 2 3 4 5 Ⓥ

★★**Oaklands** 89 Yarmouth Rd, Thorpe St Andrew (Best Western) ☎ (0603) 34471 Telex no 975392

42rm(23🛁3🚿)(4fb) CTV in all bedrooms Ⓡ T sB&B£25—£28 sB&B🛁🚿£30—£34 dB&B£40 dB&B🛁🚿£45 B

☾ CTV 60P ✿ snooker ⌂ *xmas*

V ♁ ☕ ⚡ Lunch £5.95—£7.95&alc Tea £2.25—£3.25 High Tea £7.95—£9.95 Dinner £7.95—£9.95&alc Wine £3.95 Last dinner 10pm

Credit cards 1 2 3 5

★★**Station** 5-7 Riverside Rd ☎ (0603) 611064

20rm(5🛁5🚿) CTV in all bedrooms Ⓡ sB&B£20 sB&B🛁🚿£24 dB&B£32 dB&B🛁🚿£34 B

CTV 3P V ♁ ☕ Lunch £4.95&alc Tea 60p High Tea £3.50 Dinner £4.95&alc Wine £5 Last dinner 9.30pm

Credit cards 1 3 Ⓥ

✕✕**Marco's** 17 Potter Gate ☎ (0603) 624044

Warm, friendly restaurant offering good portions and very good value for money.

Closed Sun, Mon & Aug

Italian V 40 seats S% Lunch £15—£18&alc Dinner £25alc Wine £6.50 Last dinner 10pm P

Credit cards 1 2 3 4 5

NOTTINGHAM
Nottinghamshire
Map **8** SK54
See plan on page 552/553

★★★★**Albany** St James's St (Trusthouse Forte) ☎ (0602) 470131 Telex no 37211 Plan **1** *C4*

Located beside the inner ring road, the modern, city-centre hotel is adjacent to a multi-storey car park. Many of the recently refurbished rooms have fine views over the city or castle, and conferences and functions are well catered for. →

N

Nottingham

1	Albany ★★★★
1A	Les Artistes Gourmands ✕ *(See under Beeston)*
2	Bestwood Lodge ★★★
2A	Cambridge ★★
3	Edwalton Hall ★★
4	Flying Horse ★★
5	La Grenouille ✕
8	Rhinegold ✕✕
9	Royal ★★★★
9A	Rufford ★★
10	Savoy ★★★
11	Something Special ✕✕✕
12	Strathdon Thistle ★★★
13	Trattoria Conti ✕✕
14	Stakis Victoria ★★★
15	Waltons ★★★

152 CTV in all bedrooms ®**T** sB&B £53 dB&B £72 **B**

Lift ☾ ## CFA

Last dinner 11pm

Credit cards 1 2 3 4 5

★★★★**Royal** Wollaton St (Queens Moat) ☎ (0602) 414444 Telex no 37101 Plan **9** *B5*

Closed xmas day

This modern, purpose-built, city-centre hotel rises to nine storeys and features a first-floor arcade with a transparent roof over its brick-built archways, wrought iron fencing and a profusion of potted plants, trees and shrubbery. Most of the hotel's public areas, including bars and four restaurants, are situated off the arcade. Two squash courts, a small gymnasium, sun beds and jacuzzi are available for the use of guests, and there are also extensive conference and function facilities.

201 in 66 bedrooms CTV in all bedrooms ®**T** sB £30.75—£50 dB £53.50—£68 (room only) **B**

Lift ☾ ## 720 squash solarium gymnasium

English, French & Italian **V** Lunch £3.50—£8.50 Tea £1—£1.20 High Tea £2.50—£3 Dinner £6—£11&alc Wine £4.50 Last dinner 1.30am

Credit cards 1 2 3 5

★★★**Bestwood Lodge** Bestwood Country Park, Arnold (3m N off A60) (Consort/Exec Hotels) ☎ (0602) 203011 Telex no 575151 Plan **2** *C8*

A former hunting lodge, built in 1865, set in 70 acres of parkland and woods.

35rm (16 19)(4fb) 2 CTV in all bedrooms ®**T** ✻ sB&B £27.50 dB&B £35 **B**

150P Disco wkly

French **V** ✻ Lunch £5.50&alc Tea 65p High Tea £5 Dinner £8—£10alc Wine £5.95 Last dinner 10.30pm

Credit cards 1 2 3 5 Ⓥ

See advertisement on page 554

N

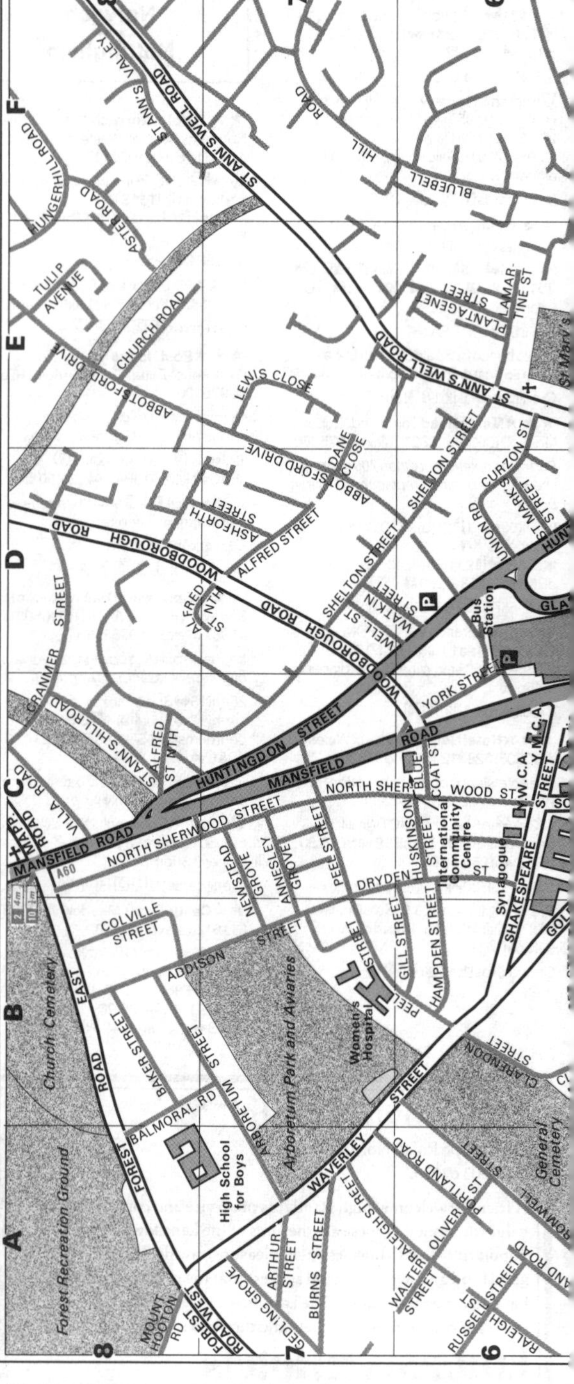

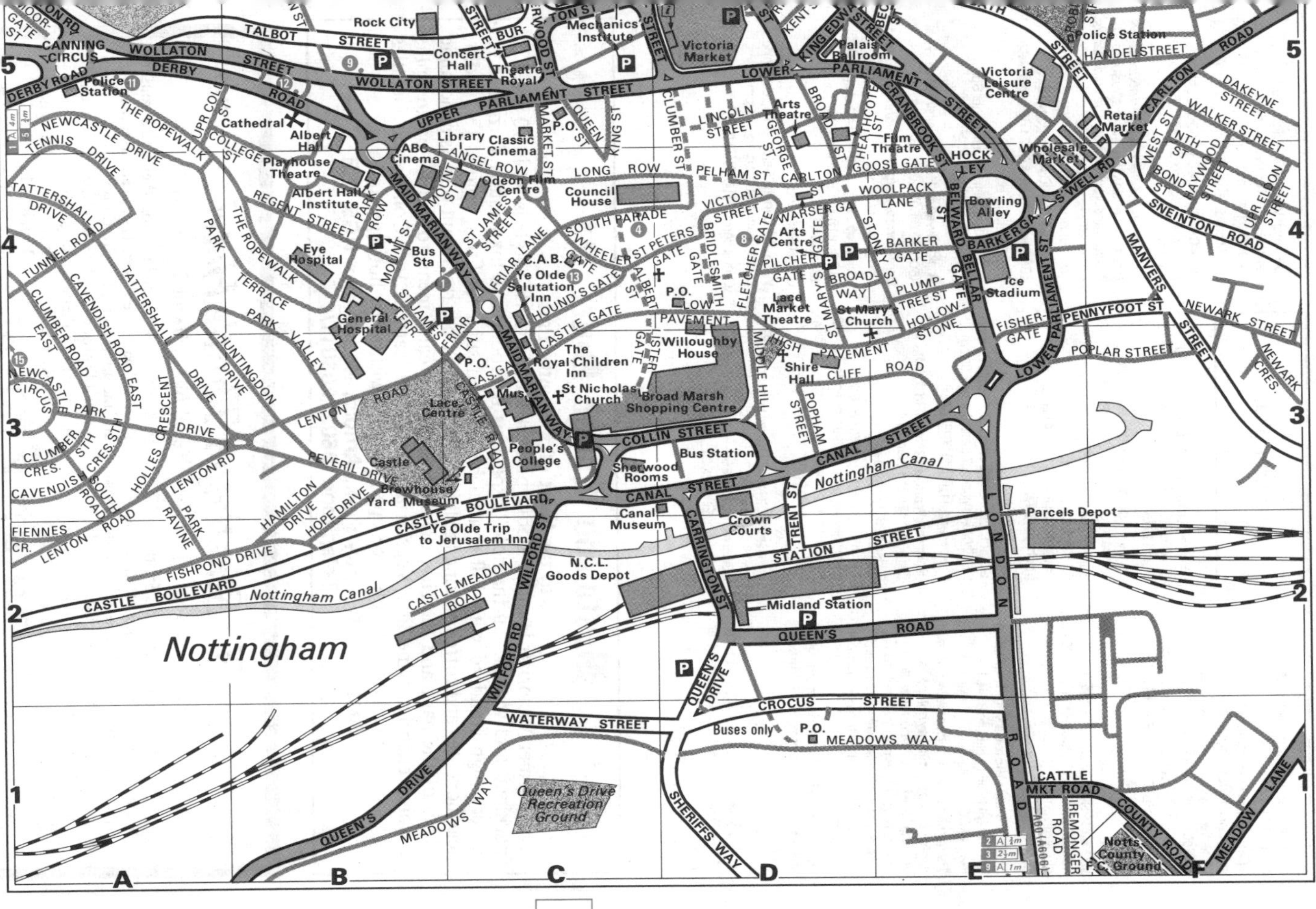
Nottingham
Rock City
Mechanics' Institute
Victoria Market
Palais Ballroom
Police Station
HANDEL STREET
Victoria Leisure Centre
Retail Market
Wholesale Market
Concert Hall
Theatre Royal
Police Station
Cathedral
Albert Hall
Playhouse Theatre
Albert Hall Institute
Library
Classic Cinema
ABC Cinema
Odeon Film Centre
Council House
Arts Theatre
Film Theatre
Bowling Alley
Ice Stadium
Arts Centre
Lace Market Theatre
St Mary's Church
Shire Hall
Eye Hospital
Bus Sta
General Hospital
C.A.B.
Ye Olde Salutation Inn
The Royal Children Inn
St Nicholas' Church
Broad Marsh Shopping Centre
Willoughby House
Lace Centre
Castle
Brewhouse Yard Museum
People's College
Bus Station
Sherwood Rooms
Canal Museum
Crown Courts
Ye Olde Trip to Jerusalem Inn
N.C.L. Goods Depot
Midland Station
Parcels Depot
Notts County F.C. Ground
Queen's Drive Recreation Ground
Buses only
P.O.
Nottingham Canal
CANNING CIRCUS
DERBY ROAD
WOLLATON STREET
TALBOT STREET
UPPER PARLIAMENT STREET
LOWER PARLIAMENT STREET
KING EDWARD STREET
CRANBROOK STREET
HOCKLEY
CARLTON ROAD
MANVERS STREET
SNEINTON ROAD
MAID MARIAN WAY
LONG ROW
PELHAM ST
GOOSE GATE
WOOLPACK LANE
BELWARD ST
BELLAR GATE
BARKER GATE
STONEY ST
FLETCHER GATE
BRIDLESMITH GATE
VICTORIA STREET
SOUTH PARADE
WHEELER GATE
ST PETERS GATE
ALBERT ST
LISTER GATE
MIDDLE HILL
HIGH PAVEMENT
LOW PAVEMENT
CASTLE GATE
HOUND'S GATE
FRIAR LANE
ST JAMES'S STREET
MOUNT ST
THE ROPEWALK
PARK TERRACE
PARK VALLEY
HUNTINGDON DRIVE
LENTON ROAD
PEVERIL DRIVE
HOPE DRIVE
HAMILTON DRIVE
CASTLE ROAD
COLLIN STREET
CANAL STREET
CARRINGTON ST
STATION STREET
TRENT ST
QUEEN'S ROAD
LONDON ROAD
CASTLE BOULEVARD
FISHPOND DRIVE
CASTLE MEADOW ROAD
WILFORD RD
WILFORD ST
WATERWAY STREET
CROCUS STREET
MEADOWS WAY
QUEEN'S DRIVE
SHERIFFS WAY
CATTLE MKT ROAD
IREMONGER ROAD
COUNTY ROAD
MEADOW LANE
A60 (A606)
NEWCASTLE DRIVE
TENNIS DRIVE
TATTERSHALL DRIVE
TUNNEL ROAD
CAVENDISH ROAD EAST
CLUMBER ROAD EAST
NEWCASTLE CIRCUS
HOLLES CRESCENT
LENTON RD
PARK RAVINE
FIENNES CR.
PENNYFOOT ST
POPLAR STREET
NEWARK STREET
NEWARK CRES.
POPHAM STREET
CLIFF ROAD
N

★★★*H* **Savoy** Mansfield Rd ☎ (0602) 602621 Telex no 377429 Plan **10** C8

The three popular restaurants included in this modern hotel's public areas enjoy a deserved reputation for good value food and attentive, friendly service.

182⇌(3fb) in 66 bedrooms CTV in all bedrooms ®T S% sB&B⇌£38 dB&B⇌£46 B

Lift ☾ CTV 260P 60

V S% Lunch £5.25&alc Tea 60p&alc Dinner £7.25&alc Wine £3.60 Last dinner 11pm

Credit cards 1 2 3 5

★★★**Stakis Victoria** Milton St (Stakis) ☎ (0602) 419561 Telex no 37401 Plan **14** *D5*

This attractive, red-brick building in the city centre, formerly a railway hotel, has undergone extensive modernisation. There are spacious public areas and extensive function facilities, as well as a choice of different styles of well equipped bedrooms.

167⇌(5fb) 1 CTV in all bedrooms ®S% *sB⇌£38—£43 dB⇌£45—£50 (room only) B

Lift ☾ 20P *xmas*

V *Lunch £6 Tea fr40p High Tea fr£4.50 Dinner £9 Wine £5.95 Last dinner 9.45pm

Credit cards 1 2 3 5

Nottingham

★★★**Strathdon Thistle** Derby Rd (Thistle) ☎ (0602) 418501 Telex no 377185 Plan **12** *B5*

Large modern hotel with well equipped bedrooms.

69rm(42⇌27)(4fb) in 6 bedrooms CTV in all bedrooms ®T *sB⇌£42—£50 dB⇌£50—£65 (room only) B

Lift ☾ 4P CFA

International *Lunch £7.50&alc Dinner £10.20&alc Wine £7 Last dinner 9.30pm

Credit cards 1 2 3 4 5 V

★★★*L* **Waltons** 2 North Rd, The Park ☎ (0602) 475215 Plan **15** *A3*

Closed 26 Dec & 1 Jan

Just west of the city centre, a large Georgian house stands adjacent to the A52 and offers accommodation in comfortable, well-equipped bedrooms complemented by elegant public areas.

9rm(3⇌6)(1fb) CTV in all bedrooms ®T S% *sB&B⇌£24.50—£29.50 dB&B⇌£40—£50

CTV 10P 9 sauna bath solarium

French V *Lunch fr£6.50&alc Tea fr£3 High Tea fr£5 Dinner £10alc Wine £4.95 Last dinner 10pm

Credit cards 1 2 3

★★**Cambridge** 63—65 Loughborough Rd, West Bridgford ☎ (0602) 81145 Plan **2A** *E1*

A pair of large, semi-detached houses have been converted to provide well-equipped, modern accommodation. The hotel stands on the A60, south of the city centre and near Trent Bridge cricket ground.

19rm(1⇌7) ® *sB&B£14 sB&B⇌£16 dB&B£24 dB&B⇌£26

CTV 35P billiards

*Dinner fr£6 Last dinner 8pm

Credit cards 1 3

★★**Edwalton Hall** Edwalton (3½m S A606) ☎ (0602) 231116 Plan **3** *E1*

Large former Victorian private house in its own grounds.

10rm(3⇌)(1fb) CTV in all bedrooms ®T sB&B fr£18.50 sB&B⇌fr£33 dB&B⇌fr£48

CTV 60P putting

V *Lunch £5alc Tea 75palc Dinner £10alc Wine £5 Last dinner 10pm

Credit cards 1 2 3 5

N

★ ★**Flying Horse** Poultry (Berni)
☎ (0602) 502831 Plan **4** *C4*
Closed Xmas
Over 500 years old, this large hotel has extensive restaurant and bar facilities.
58rm(27🛁) CTV in all bedrooms ® ✗
sB£17—£22.50 sB🛁fr£19.50
dB🛁£29.50—£35 (room only)
☾36P
🍷✗✱Lunch £7.50alc Dinner £7.50alc Wine £4.50 Last dinner 10.30pm
Credit cards 1 2 3 5

★ ★**Rufford** 53 Melton Rd, West Bridgford ☎ (0602) 814202 Plan **9A** *E1*
Closed Xmas RS wknds
This popular commercial hotel, situated in a suburb of Nottingham, has well-equipped bedrooms and a basement games room.
31🚿 CTV in all bedrooms ® **T** ✗
sB&B🚿£23—£25
dB&B🚿£34.50—£36.50 **B**
☾36P pool table
🍷 ☕ Tea £1.80—£2.80 Dinner £8.05—£9.05 Wine £5.50 Last dinner 8pm
Credit cards 1 2 3 5

✕✕✕**Something Special** 103 Derby Rd, Canning Circus ☎ (0602) 412139 Plan **11** *A5*
Natural caves form the background to the bar in this ambitious restaurant, which also has a small private functions suite on the first floor. The extensive à la carte menu is complemented by a comprehensive wine list that offers choices from most European countries.
Lunch not served Sat
Continental **V** 45 seats ✱Lunch £4.95—£6&alc Dinner fr£8.95&alc Wine £4.95 Last dinner 11pm 15P
Credit cards 1 2 3 5 Ⓥ

✕✕**Rhinegold** King John Chambers, Fletcher Gate ☎ (0602) 501294 Plan **8** *D4*
Compact city centre restaurant, tucked away off a small courtyard.
Closed all Bank Hol's
English & French **V** 46 seats Lunch £7.76&alc Dinner £10alc Wine £4.75 Last dinner 10.30pm **P**
Credit cards 1 2 3

✕✕**Trattoria Conti** 14—16 Wheeler Gate ☎ (0602) 474056 Plan **13** *C4*
Light and airy Italian city centre restaurant.
Closed Sun, last wk Jul—1st wk Aug
English & Italian 70 seats ✱Lunch £4.35&alc Dinner £8—£12alc Wine £4.65 Last dinner 11.15pm 10P
Credit cards 1 2 3 5

✕**La Grenouille** 32 Lenton Boulevard
☎ (0602) 411088 Plan **5** *A5*
Simple French restaurant in a Victorian terrace.
Closed Sun, Bank Hols, 2 wks summer & 24 Dec—2 Jan Lunch not served
French **V** 38 seats ✱Dinner fr£6.90&alc wine £5.80 Last dinner 9.30pm **P**

NUNEATON
Warwickshire
Map **4** SP39

★ ★***Chase*** Higham Ln (Golden Oak Inns)
☎ (0203) 383406
Modernised hotel, popular with business clientele.
28🛁 CTV in all bedrooms ® ✗ **B**
CTV 350P ✿
🍷Last dinner 10pm
Credit cards 1 2 3

★ ★**Longshoot Motel** Watling St (Toby)
☎ (0203) 329711 Telex no 311100
Closed 2 wks Xmas
Set at the A5/A47 junction, the busy motel has dining facilities in the main house and bedrooms in a separate unit at the rear.
Annexe: 47🛁🚿 CTV in all bedrooms ® **T** ✗ (ex guide dogs)
✱sB&B🛁🚿£19.50—£29.50
dB&B🛁🚿£29.50—£40.50
☾115P
Credit cards 1 2 3 5

Nunnington — Oban

NUNNINGTON
North Yorkshire
Map **8** SE67

❀✕✕**Ryedale Lodge** ☎(04395) 246
(Rosette awarded for dinner only)
Set between the Howardian Hills and the North York Moors is this comfortable and stylish restaurant, tastefully converted from a former railway station. The cooking is personally handled by the proprietress, Mrs Laird, and the menu reflects her interest in English and European food. Fresh food and game in season is prepared with flair and style, and there is also a good wine list. There are also five bedrooms, all with private facilities.
Lunch not served
V 30 seats Dinner £14.95 Wine £5.50 Last dinner 9pm 30P
Credit cards 1 3

OAKFORD
Devon
Map **3** SS92

✕**Higher Western** (2m W on A361) ☎ Anstey Mill (03984) 210
Built of white-painted stone with a slate roof, the restaurant stands in an elevated and exposed postition between Hampton and South Morton. Lunch can be chosen from the 3-course menu or from an à la carte selection, the freshly-prepared dishes including fish, poultry and regular traditional roasts, together with a good range of starters and sweets, served by friendly staff.
Lunch not served Mon Dinner not served Sun
English & Continental 22 seats ✱Lunch £3.50&alc Dinner £7&alc Wine £4.25 Last dinner 10pm 15P
Credit cards 1 3 V

OAKHAM
Leicestershire
Map **4** SK80

★★★

❀❀★★★**HAMBLETON HALL, OAKHAM**
Hambleton (3m E off A606) (Relais et Chateâux) ☎(0572) 56991 Telex no 342888
On the edge of Rutland Water in its own grounds stands this luxurious Victorian country house. Tim and Stefa Hart, the owners, opened the hotel in 1980 after employing Nina Campbell to design the interior which is charming. There is seating around the fire place in the hall, a smart yet cosy bar, and an elegant drawing room overlooking the garden. Comfortable seating, attractive soft furnishings, antiques, pictures and flowers all help to create a delightful atmosphere. The bedrooms are individually decorated and furnished to a high standard, complete with mineral water, shortbread, flowers and superior toiletries. But nice as the hotel is, the food is even better. Nicholas Gill, the talented Chef, is a superb cook and produces most enjoyable meals. Ingredients are of the best and the finished dishes seem to reflect the enthusiastic influence of Mr Gill — no slave to modern fashion but with unerring flair that produces sapid items and presented with real artistry. Perhaps some of his sauces could be more refined but they are

mostly 'gutsy'. In the well appointed dining rooms, as throughout the hotel, you will be attended to by a team of young people who offer the best of friendly hospitality. This is an all round favourite with so many of our members.
15fl(1fb) 1 CTV in all bedrooms **T** S% sB&Bfl£66—£72.50 dB&Bfl£85—£125 Continental breakfast
Lift 60P 1 (hard) nc 9yrs *xmas*
English & French **V** S% Lunch £23.50&alc Tea £1.95 Dinner £28—£30.50&alc Wine £9.50 Last dinner 9.30pm
Credit cards 1 2 3 4 5

★★★**Crown** High St ☎(0572) 3631
Former coaching inn, situated in the town centre, catering for both the commercial and tourist trade.
25rm(23)(2fb) 1 CTV in all bedrooms ®S% ✱sB&B£34 sB&B£34 dB&B£42 dB&B£42
(24P
V ✱Lunch £12.50alc Tea 50p—£2 Dinner £12.50alc Wine £5.95 Last dinner 10pm
Credit cards 1 2 3 5

★★**George** Market Pl ☎(0572) 56971
Former coaching inn in the town centre, catering mainly for commercial trade.
19rm(8)(2fb) CTV in all bedrooms ® **T** sB&B£25—£26.50 sB&B£34.50—£36.50 dB&B£30—£34 dB&B£39.50—£42
CTV 10P 1 Live music & dancing Mon *xmas*
English & French **V** Lunch £2.50—£5 Dinner £8—£11 Wine £5.25 Last dinner 10pm
Credit cards 1 2 3 4 5 V

★***Rutland Angler*** Mill St ☎(0572) 55839
This 18th century house which was a former nursing home, is situated just off the A606 near the town centre.
9rm(1)(1fb) TV in all bedrooms ®
TV 40P Cabaret wkly
V Last dinner 2pm
Credit card 2

✕✕**Noel Arms** Bridge St, Langham (2m NW A606) ☎(0572) 2931
Large old inn with considerable character, in Langham.
English, French & Italian **V** 100 seats S% Lunch £6.25&alc Dinner £6.25&alc Wine £4.95 Last dinner 9.30pm 25P
Credit cards 1 2 3 5 V

OBAN
Strathclyde *Argyllshire*
Map **10** NM83
See plan

★★★**Alexandra** Corran Esp (Scottish Highland) ☎(0631) 62381 Telex no 778215 Plan **1** *A5*
Closed Nov—Mar
The hotel occupies a quiet position towards the northern end of the Promenade, most of its public rooms enjoying fine views of the bustling harbour and bay.
56rm(47 2fl)(2fb) CTV in all bedrooms ®sB&Bfr£31 sB&Bflfr£34 dB&Bfr£52 dB&Bflfr£58
Lift (40P pool table Live music and dancing Mon Cabaret Fri
Scottish, French & Italian **V** Lunch £4.95 Tea £1.65 High Tea £4.50 Dinner £9.50 Wine £5.95 Last dinner 9pm
Credit cards 1 2 3 5

N

★★★**Caledonian** Station Sq ☎ (0631) 63133 Telex no 777210 Plan **2** *B2*

Closed Jan & Feb

Set in the town centre close to the railway and bus stations, this five-storey Victorian building overlooks the bay and harbour.

69⇌(9fb) ® CTV in all bedrooms S% sB&B⇌£26.50—£29.50 dB&B⇌£42—£49 ℞

Lift ☾ 6P

Scottish & French ♀ ☕ S% ✱ Lunch £3.25—£6 Tea 75p—£1.50 High Tea

Oban

£3.25—£4.75 Dinner £6.40—£9.75 Wine £4.30 Last dinner 8.45pm

Credit cards 1 2 3 5 Ⓥ

★★★**Great Western** Esplanade (Scottish Highland) ☎ (0631) 63101 Telex 778215 Plan **4** *B4*

Closed Dec—Feb

Large hotel in commanding seafront location with superb views of the bay from the ornate lounge and cocktail bar.

74rm(65⇌6⋔)(2fb) 1⊟ CTV in all bedrooms ® sB&B£31 sB&B⇌⋔£34 dB&B£52 dB&B⇌⋔£58 ℞

Lift ☾ 25P Disco Sat Cabaret Mon, Thu & Sun

V ♀ ☕ Bar lunch £1.75—£3 Tea 70p Dinner £10&alc Wine £5.80 Last dinner 9pm

Credit cards 1 2 3 5

O

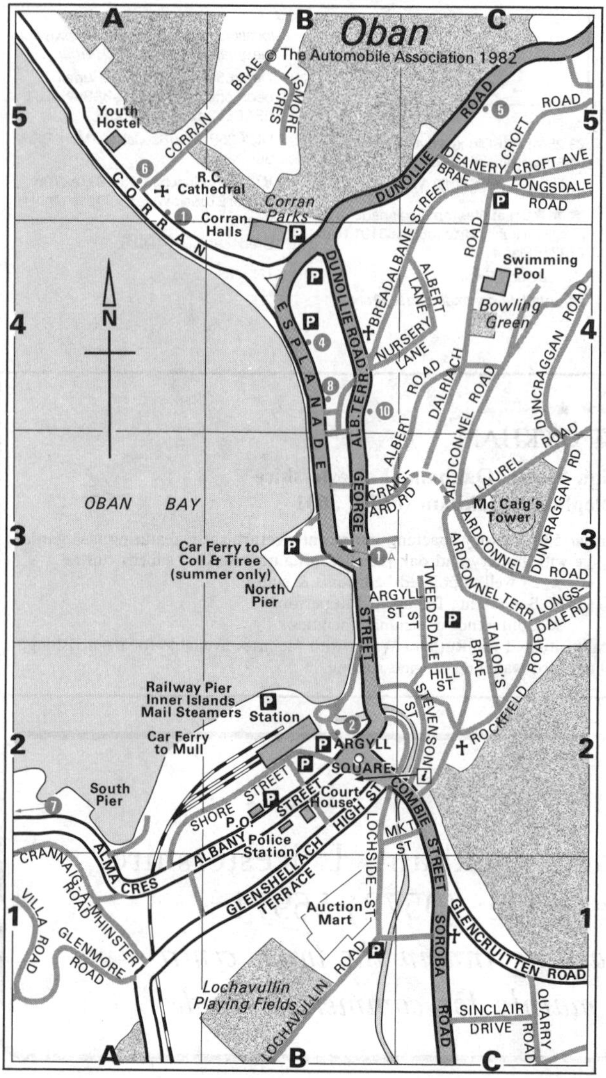

Oban

© The Automobile Association 1982

A B C
5 4 3 2 1

Youth Hostel
Corran Brae
Lismore Cres
Dunollie Road
Road
Croft
Deanery Brae
Croft Ave
Longsdale Road
Corran
R.C. Cathedral
Corran Halls
Corran Parks
Corran Esplanade
Breadalbane Street
Albert Lane
Road
Swimming Pool
Bowling Green
Duncraggan Road
Nursery Lane
Dunollie Road
Alb. Terr
Esplanade
Albert Road
Dalriach Road
Ardconnel Road
Laurel Road
Duncraggan Rd
N
Oban Bay
Craig-Ard Rd
George Street
Mc Caig's Tower
Ardconnel Terr
Car Ferry to Coll & Tiree (summer only)
North Pier
Argyll St
Tweedsdale St
Longsdale Rd
Tailor's Brae
Hill St
Road
Railway Pier Inner Islands Mail Steamers
Station
Stevenson St
Rockfield Road
Car Ferry to Mull
Argyll Square
South Pier
Shore Street
Court House
Stafford Street
P.O.
Police Station
Combie Street
Alma Cres
Albany
Glenshellach Terrace
High St
Lochside St
Mkt St
Crannaig-a-Mhinster Road
Villa Road
Glenmore Road
Auction Mart
Soroba Road
Glencruitten Road
Lochavullin Playing Fields
Lochavullin Road
Sinclair Drive
Quarry Road

Oban

1	Alexandra ★★★
1A	Argyll ★★
2	Caledonian ★★★
4	Great Western ★★★
5	King's Knoll ★
6	Lancaster ★★
7	Manor House ★★
8	Park ★★

★★***Argyll*** Corran Esp ☎ (0631) 62353 Plan **1A** *B3*

Situated on the front, near the north pier, the hotel has good views of the bay. The comfortable accommodation has recently been modernised, and a friendly atmosphere prevails.

29rm(7⋔)(4fb) ₿

☾ CTV 4P Live music & dancing 4 nights wkly *xmas*

Mainly grills V Last dinner 9pm

Credit cards 1 3

★★**Lancaster** Corran Esp ☎ (0631) 62587 Plan **6** *A5*

Closed Xmas day & New Year's Day RS 26 Dec—2 Jan

Seafront hotel popular with tourist and business trade alike.

28rm(3⇌14⋔)(3fb) CTV in all bedrooms ® sB&B£18—£20 sB&B⇌⋔£20—£23 dB&B£36—£40 dB&B⇌⋔£40—£46

CTV 20P (heated) sauna bath solarium

V Lunch £4.50—£5&alc Tea fr50p Dinner £7—£8&alc Wine £4.80 Last dinner 8pm

★★***Manor House*** Gallanach Rd ☎ (0631) 62087 Plan **7** *A2*

RS 24—25 Dec & 1—2 Jan

Comfortable small hotel with relaxed atmosphere and good food.

11rm(7⇌4⋔) ®

CTV 20P

French V Last dinner 8.30pm

Credit cards 1 3 5

★★**Park** Esplanade (Norscot/Clan) ☎ (0631) 63621 Telex no 779713 Plan **8** *B4*

Large painted stone hotel overlooking Oban Bay.

82rm(39⇌33⌂)CTV in all bedrooms ® sB&B£22—£24 sB&B⇌⌂£25—£29 dB&B£36—£40 dB&B⇌⌂£40—£46 B

Lift ☾ CTV 20P *xmas*

Lunch fr£3.50 Dinner £10—£12 Wine £5.25 Last dinner 8.30pm

Credit cards 1 2 3 4 5 V

★King's Knoll Dunollie Rd ☎(0631) 62536 Plan **5** *C5*

Good-value accommodation is provided by this small, family-owned hotel which stands on a hillside overlooking the bay.

18rm(1⇌)(3fb) ® available in bedrooms S% sB&B£11—£13 dB&B£22—£26 dB&B⇌£28—£30 B

CTV 9P ✽

S% Lunch £3.50 Tea £1 Dinner £6 Wine £4 Last dinner 7.30pm

Credit card 1 V

OLDBURY
West Midlands
Map **7** SO98

✕✕Jonathan's
16 Wolverhampton Rd, Quinton
☎021-429 3757

The Victorian and Edwardian periods are evoked in this popular restaurant, where wood panelling and rich drapery provide an intimate atmosphere. It is also possible to eat in the cloistered garden. British cooking of the highest quality is based on recipes researched from Victorian and Edwardian times and provides exciting and unusual dishes. A good range of wines is available including some interesting, little-known ones.

Lunch not served Sat

V 130 seats Lunch £15alc Dinner £15alc Wine £5.50 Last dinner 10.30pm 9P

Credit cards 1 2 3 5

OLDHAM
Greater Manchester
Map **7** SD90

★★★Bower Hollinwood Av, Chadderton (2¼m SW A6104) (De Vere) ☎061-682 7254 Telex no 666883

RS 25—31 Dec

A well-furnished, modern hotel with new bedroom extensions, the Bower stands in its own grounds.

66rm(42⇌24⌂)(1fb) 1 CTV in all bedrooms ® T S% sB&B⇌⌂£20—£55 dB&B⇌⌂£40—£75 B

☾ 140P CFA ✽ Live music and dancing Fri, Sat & Sun lunch *xmas*

Continental **V** S% Lunch £7—£13.50&alc Tea 60p—£1.60 Dinner £7—£13.50&alc Wine £5.25 Last dinner 9.15pm

Credit cards 1 2 3 5

OLD RAYNE
Grampian *Aberdeenshire*
Map **15** NJ62

★*H* Lodge ☎(04645) 205

Friendly, homely small hotel, just off A96. The attractive annexe comprises modern, timber clad chalet style bedrooms.

2rm Annexe: 4⇌⌂(1fb) CTV in 5 bedrooms ® in 5 bedrooms ✱sB&B£10 sB&B⇌⌂£15 dB&B£18 dB&B⇌⌂£22.50

CTV 50P

Bar lunch £3.85alc High Tea £3.25alc Dinner £8.50alc Wine £4 Last dinner 8pm

OLD SODBURY
Avon
Map **3** ST78

★★Cross Hands ☎ Chipping Sodbury (0454) 313000

RS Xmas night

Mellow Cotswold stone building in a rural setting alongside the main A46 Bath/Stroud road.

24rm(3⇌17⌂) 1 CTV in all bedrooms ® T ✱sB&B£20.50—£27.95 sB&B⇌⌂£25.95—£30.95 dB&B£35.95 dB&B⇌⌂£43.95—£49.95 Continental breakfast B

☾ 200P ✽ *xmas*

Mainly grills **V** Lunch £3.95—£8.50&alc Tea 75p Dinner £3.95—£8.50&alc Wine £5.15 Last dinner 10.30pm

Credit cards 1 2 3 5

See advertisement under Bristol

OLLERTON
Nottinghamshire
Map **8** SK66

★Hop Pole ☎ Mansfield (0623) 822573

Ivy-covered coaching inn.

12rm(1⇌5⌂)(2fb) CTV in 2 bedrooms ® sB&B£17.50—£26 sB&B⇌⌂£21—£28 dB&B£27.50—£30 dB&B⇌⌂£34—£40

CTV 45P ✽ sauna bath solarium gymnasium

V Lunch £5.50—£6.20&alc Tea 80p—£1.50&alc Dinner £5.80—£6.70&alc Wine £4 Last dinner 10pm

Credit cards 1 2 3 V

ONICH
Highland *Inverness-shire*
Map **14** NN06

★★Allt-Nan-Ros ☎(08553) 210

Closed Nov—Mar

The friendly, roadside hotel offers good food and views of the loch.

20rm(16⇌4⌂)(1fb) 1 CTV in all bedrooms ® T ✱sB&B⇌⌂£24—£27.50 dB&B⇌⌂£44—£51 B

☾ CTV 50P ✽ Live music & dancing Sat

Scottish & French Lunch £6.50—£10 Tea £2.50 Dinner £12—£16 Wine £4.50 Last dinner 9pm

Credit cards 1 2 3 5 V

O

★★*HL* **Lodge on the Loch** Creag Dhu (Inter Hotel) ☎ (08553) 237

Closed Nov—Mar

Hospitable, inviting hotel in superb lochside and mountain setting, facing south with panoramic views.

20rm(12🛁5🚿)(2fb) CTV in all bedrooms ®T S% sB&B£16—£22 sB&B🛁🚿£20.50—£30.50 dB&B£32—£44 dB&B🛁🚿£41—£61 B

☾ CTV 50P ✿ Live music & dancing wkly

European V ☕ S% Lunch £1.50—£4.50&alc Tea £1&alc High Tea £2.50—£3.50&alc Dinner £12&alc Wine £5 Last dinner 10pm

Credit cards 1 2 3 5 Ⓥ

See advertisement under Fort William

★★*B* **Onich** (Consort) ☎ (08553) 214

RS Nov—Mar

Recently refurbished, the hotel provides comfortable accommodation, and its nicely laid out garden runs down to the lochside.

27rm(25🛁2🚿)(6fb) CTV in all bedrooms ®T sB&B🛁🚿£23.50—£25 dB&B🛁🚿£42—£45 B

55P ✿ solarium gymnasium putting

☕ Bar lunch £5alc Tea £2.75 High Tea £5—£6&alc Dinner £9—£10 Wine £4.95 Last dinner 9pm

Credit cards 1 2 3 5

ORFORD (near Woodbridge) Suffolk

Map **5** TM44

★★***Crown & Castle*** (Trusthouse Forte) ☎ (0394) 450205

An 18th-century posting house associated with smugglers.

9rm(1🛁) Annexe: 10🛁 2 CTV in all bedrooms ® sB&B£33.50 sB&B🛁£41.50 dB&B£50 dB&B🛁£58 B

20P ✿ *xmas*

☕ Last dinner 9pm

Credit cards 1 2 3 4 5

✕✕ **Kings Head Inn** ☎ (0394) 450271

Remarkable, two-storey, medieval inn, in the shadow of St Bartholomew's Church.

Closed Mon & Jan Dinner not served Sun

V 32 seats Lunch £13alc Dinner £13alc Last dinner 9pm 100P

Credit card 5 Ⓥ

✕ ***Butley Oysterage*** Market Hill ☎ (0394) 450277

Closed Jan & Feb

48 seats Last dinner 8.15pm

ORKNEY

Map **16**

KIRKWALL

Map **16** HY41

★★**Ayre** Ayre Rd ☎ (0856) 2197

Closed 1—3 Jan

Family run hotel overlooking harbour.

31rm(3🛁6🚿)(1fb) CTV in 3 bedrooms ® T sB&B£17.90—£22.30 sB&B🛁🚿£24.40—£25.80 dB&B£32.30—£40.60 dB&B🛁🚿£40.30—£43.10

CTV 25P sauna bath

International V ☕ ✱ Lunch fr£2 Dinner £8alc Wine £4.50 Last dinner 8.30pm

Credit cards 1 3

STROMNESS

Map **16** HY21

★★***Stromness*** Victoria St ☎ (0856) 850298

RS 1—4 Jan

Friendly, family run hotel with modernised bar overlooking harbour.

40rm(12🛁2🚿)(4fb) ® B

Lift CTV 5P ✿ billiards Live music & dancing wkly

V ☕ Last dinner 9pm

Credit cards 1 3

⚘✕✕**Hamnavoe** 35 Graham Pl ☎ (0856) 850606
(Rosette awarded for dinner only)
No visit to Orkney should be complete without a visit to this charming restaurant in a quiet street of the historic town. Local produce is featured strongly on the menu, and the cooking reflects the unique talent of chef/partner Denis Moylan. Service is caring and attentive.
Closed Tue
V 36 seats ✱Lunch £10—£14.50 Dinner £10—£14.50 Wine £6.25 Last dinner 10pm ₱ nc 10yrs
Credit cards 1 3

ORTON
Cumbria
Map **12** NY60

✕**Gilded Apple** ☎ (05874) 345
The compact, first-floor restaurant has heavy stone walls, soft lighting and, on chilly evenings, a crackling log fire. An imaginative menu features freshly-cooked dishes, even the rolls being baked daily, and pleasant friendly service is provided by the young and enthusiastic proprietors.
Closed Mon Lunch not served Tue—Sat
25 seats ✱Lunch fr£5.50 Dinner £10.50alc Wine £5.95 Last dinner 9.30pm 2P nc 10yrs
Credit cards 1 3

OSTERLEY
Greater London
London plan **5** *B3* (page 446)

★★**Osterley** 764 Great West Rd ☎ 01-568 9981
Friendly hotel where improvements are producing an increasing number of good, comfortable bedrooms.
60rm(52🛁4🚿) Annexe: 4rm(16fb) CTV in all bedrooms ®**T** ✱sB&B£29 sB&B🛁🚿£38 dB&B£35 dB&B🛁🚿£45 Continental breakfast **B**
P Live music & dancing Sat *xmas*
English & French ✱Lunch £7.95&alc Tea 95p Dinner £7.95&alc Wine £4.95 Last dinner 10pm
Credit cards 1 2 3 5

OSWESTRY
Shropshire
Map **7** SJ22

★★★**Wynnstay** Church St (Trusthouse Forte) ☎ (0691) 655261
A Georgian coaching inn close to the town centre offers well-equipped, modern accommodation with pleasantly period-style public areas.
26rm(24🛁2🚿)(1fb) 1 CTV in all bedrooms ®sB&B£37 sB&B🛁🚿£45 dB&B£52 dB&B🛁🚿£60 **B**
70P ✿
Last dinner 9.30pm
Credit cards 1 2 3 4 5

★★ *L* **Sweeney Hall** Morda (1m S on A483) ☎ (0691) 652450
This hotel is made from two large country houses standing in very spacious grounds.
7rm(5🛁) ®sB&B£21.50 sB&B🛁£25.50 dB&B£34 dB&B🛁🚿£40.50—£45
CTV 80P 1 ✿
English, French & Italian **V** Lunch £9&alc Dinner £9&alc Wine £4.80 Last dinner 9.30pm
Credit cards 1 3 V

OTHERY
Somerset
Map **3** ST33

★***Rhynelander*** Glastonbury Rd (Guestaccom) ☎ Burrowbridge (082369) 382
RS Jan
Small, friendly, country hotel, personally-run by the owners.
6rm(4🚿)(1fb) CTV in all bedrooms ®**B**
CTV 10P ✿ *xmas*
Last dinner 9pm
Credit cards 1 3

OTLEY
West Yorkshire
Map **8** SE24

★★★***Chevin Lodge*** Yorkgate ☎ (0943) 467818 Telex no 51538
Constructed of pine in Scandinavian style, the hotel stands in 50 acres of birchwood. Attractively appointed bedrooms and public areas, maintaining the pinewood theme throughout, offer modern comforts and facilities, whilst the restaurant's three menus provide a choice between local and international dishes, supported by a good wine list.
18🛁🚿(2fb) CTV in all bedrooms ®**T B**
☾ ## 50P ✿ *xmas*
English & French **V** Last dinner 9.30pm
Credit cards 1 2 3
See advertisement under Leeds

OTTERBURN
Northumberland
Map **12** NY89

★★★**Percy Arms** (Consort) ☎ (0830) 20261
RS Jan & Feb
This former posting house has been carefully modernised to form a warm, comfortable hotel.
30rm(26🛁4🚿)(1fb) 1 in 1 bedroom CTV in 28 bedrooms ®**T** sB&B🛁🚿£26—£30 dB&B🛁🚿£46—£56 **B**
CTV 40P 10 ✿ Live music & dancing Sat *xmas*
Lunch £6—£7 Tea £1.40—£3 Wine £3.50 Last dinner 8.45pm
Credit cards 1 2 3 5

★★**Otterburn Tower** ☎ (0830) 20620
Turreted manor house dating from 1245 and sensitively modernised, with grand public rooms.
12rm(4🛁1🚿)(3fb) 2 CTV in 1 bedroom TV in 4 bedrooms ®sB&B£20 sB&B🛁🚿£22.50—£27.50 dB&B£32.50 dB&B🛁🚿£37.50—£42.50 **B**
CTV 50P 1 ✿ CFA *xmas*
V Lunch £7.50—£8.50&alc Tea £1—£2.50 Dinner £8.50—£10&alc Wine £4.50 Last dinner 9.30pm
Credit cards 1 2 3 5 V

OTTERY ST MARY
Devon
Map **3** SY19

★★★**Salston** (Best Western) ☎ (040481) 2310 Telex no 42551
This converted, red-brick, country house, set in its own grounds, has pleasant views of the countryside. Good recreational facilities are provided, and an attractive small, cellar restaurant (open Tue—Sat) serves à la carte meals.
30🛁(14fb) 1 in 10 bedrooms CTV in all bedrooms ®**T** sB&B🛁£25—£40 dB&B🛁£38—£60 **B**
100P CFA ✿ (heated) squash sauna bath solarium gymnasium *xmas*
English & French **V** Lunch £3.50—£10 Tea £1.05—£1.20 Dinner £10.50—£11.50 Wine £5.50 Last dinner 9.45pm
Credit cards 1 2 3 4 5
See advertisement on page 562

⚘✕✕**Lodge** 17 Silver St ☎ (040481) 2356
(Rosette awarded for dinner only)
This delightful, well-appointed little restaurant, situated in a side road near Ottery St Mary Church, offers an interesting dinner (giving a choice in all courses and including coffee) for £16.50. Service is cheerfully friendly, dishes are full of flavour, freshly cooked from good ingredients, and the home-made puddings can certainly be recommended. Lunches are available only if a prior reservation has been made.
Closed Mon Dinner not served Sun
International **V** 25 seats Lunch £18.50 Dinner £18.50 Wine £5.75 Last dinner 9.30pm ₱
Credit cards 2 3 5

OULTON
West Yorkshire
Map **8** SE32

★★★**Crest** The Grove (Crest) ☎ Leeds (0532) 826201 Telex no 557646

Conveniently located at the junction of the A639 and A642, the up-to-date hotel offers motel-style accommodation in a wing separated from the public areas by spacious car parks. Guests can relax in good lounge bars and an attractive, well-appointed restaurant.

40 in 4 bedrooms CTV in all bedrooms ®S% sB £45.50—£49.50 dB £56.50—£60.50 (room only) B

200P pool table *xmas*

French **V** Lunch £7.95—£8.50&alc Tea 75p—£1 Dinner £11.50—£13&alc Wine £6.25 Last dinner 9.45pm

Credit cards 1 2 3 4 5

OUNDLE
Northamptonshire
Map **4** TL08

★★★**Talbot** New St (Anchor) ☎ (0832) 73621 Telex no 32364

Period stone and slate building with the original coaching entrance.

39 (2fb) in 6 bedrooms CTV in all bedrooms ®**T** S% *sB&B £20—£41 dB&B £40—£52 B

60P CFA *xmas*

Oulton — Oxford

English & French **V** *Lunch £7.50 Tea 50p High Tea £1.75 Dinner £9.95&alc Wine £5.95 Last dinner 9.30pm

Credit cards 1 2 3 4 5 V

OVINGTON
Northumberland
Map **12** NZ06

★★**Highlander Inn** ☎ Prudhoe (0661) 32016

This stone-built village inn features a restaurant which offers good-value French cuisine under the personal supervision of the French proprietor.

3rm(1) Annexe: 12rm(11)(1fb) CTV in all bedrooms ® sB&B £17.50 sB&B £17.50 dB&B £27.50 dB&B £27.50

CTV 20P

French **V** Lunch £5.50&alc Dinner £8.75—£10.75alc Wine £4.95 Last dinner 9.30pm

Credit cards 2 5

OXFORD
Oxfordshire
Map **4** SP50
See plan page 564/565

★★★★**Randolph** Beaumont St (Trusthouse Forte) ☎ (0865) 247481 Telex no 83446 Plan **12** *C3*

A large, Gothic-style, city-centre hotel of the mid-Victorian period provides accommodation in some fine rooms and suites, though top-floor bedrooms tend to be small.

109 (5fb) CTV in all bedrooms ®**T** sB&B £59 dB&B £75.50 B

Lift 60 CFA *xmas*

Last dinner 10.15pm

Credit cards 1 2 3 4 5

★★★**Eastgate** The High, Merton St (Anchor) ☎ (0865) 248244 Telex no 83302 Plan **3** *E2*

Standing at the heart of the city, the hotel has recently been remodelled to include elegantly furnished public rooms with a smart carvery restaurant and busy student bar. Bedrooms range from the sumptuous to the more modest, but cheerful service is provided throughout.

42 1 in 3 bedrooms CTV in all bedrooms ®**T** *sB&B £52 dB&B £62 B

Lift 35P CFA

O

V ✱Lunch £6.25—£9.75&alc Dinner £6.25—£9.75&alc Wine £5.95 Last dinner 9.30pm

Credit cards 1 2 3 5 V

★★★**Ladbroke Linton Lodge** Linton Rd, Park Town (Ladbroke) ☎ (0865) 53461 Telex no 837093 Plan **6** *C5*

Hotel offers a blend of modern and more traditional accommodation.

71rm(70 1)(1fb) 1 in 5 bedrooms CTV in all bedrooms ® T S% sB £47—£57 dB £60—£70 (room only) B

Lift ☾ 40P CFA ❀ pool table & table tennis *xmas*

Oxford

V Lunch £7—£8.50&alc Tea fr £1 Dinner fr £9.75&alc Wine £5.99 Last dinner 9.30pm

Credit cards 1 2 3 5 V

❀❀❀★★★ **Le Manoir Aux Quat' Saisons** ☎ Great Milton (08446) 8881

(For full entry see under Milton Gt)

★★★**Oxford Moat House** Godstow Rd, Wolvercote Roundabout (Queens Moat)
☎ (0865) 59933 Telex no 837926 Plan **9** *B5*

The large, modern hotel caters mainly for conferences, providing well-equipped bedrooms for delegates.

155 CTV in all bedrooms ® T S% ✱sB&B fr £48 dB&B fr £58 B

☾ CTV 250P ❀ *xmas*

V ✱Lunch fr £5.95 Tea fr 75p Dinner fr £8.25 Wine £5.95 Last dinner 9.30pm

Credit cards 1 2 3 4 5

★★*Cotswold Lodge* 66A Banbury Rd ☎(0865) 512121 Plan **1** *C5*

Closed Xmas Day evening—New Year's Eve

A hotel with many modern bedrooms, where the Greek proprietors give the food a Mediterranean flavour.

52🛁 CTV in all bedrooms **T** ✈ **B**

☾60P

English & French **V** Last dinner 10.30pm

Credit cards 1 2 3 5

See advertisement on page 566

★★Royal Oxford Park End St (Embassy) ☎(0865) 248432 Plan **14** *B2*

Closed 24—28 Dec

Traditional hotel with modern bedroom facilities.

25rm(12🛁)(2fb) CTV in all bedrooms ⓡ **T** S% ✱sB&B fr£30 sB&B🛁 fr£41 dB&B fr£46 dB&B🛁 fr£56 **B**

☾12P

English & French S% ✱Bar lunch £1.50—£2.50 Tea fr55p Dinner fr£6.50&alc Wine £4.45 Last dinner 9.30pm

Credit cards 1 2 3 4 5

★★TraveLodge Peartree Roundabout (junc A34/A43) (Trusthouse Forte) ☎(0865) 54301 Telex no 83202 Plan **18** *B5*

Modern hotel with a grill and carvery restaurant.

100🛁(42fb) CTV in all bedrooms ⓡ sB&B🛁 £41 dB&B🛁 £52 **B**

☾120P CFA ✽ (heated)

Mainly grills

Credit cards 1 2 3 4 5

O

★★Victoria 180 Abingdon Rd ☎(0865) 724536 Plan **19** *D1*

Small, family run hotel, carefully renovated to provide homely accommodation.

15rm(5🚿)(2fb) CTV in all bedrooms ⓡ sB&B £22.50—£24.50 sB&B🚿 £29.50—£32.50 dB&B £32.50—£35.50 dB&B🚿 £38.50—£42.50 **B**

CTV P (heated)

V S% Lunch fr£4.50 Tea fr£1.15 Dinner fr£9.50 Last dinner 9.30pm

Credit card 1

See advertisement on page 566

★River 17 Botley Rd ☎(0865) 243475 Plan **13** *A2*

Closed Xmas & New Year RS Winter wknds

Small, friendly, family-run hotel overlooking the River Thames offering moderately priced accommodation.

16rm(6🛁5🚿)(5fb) CTV in all bedrooms ⓡ sB&B £20 sB&B🛁🚿 £26.50 dB&B £35 dB&B🛁🚿 £40

25P ✽

V Lunch fr£5 Tea fr75p Dinner fr£7.50 Wine £5 Last dinner 8pm

Credit card 3

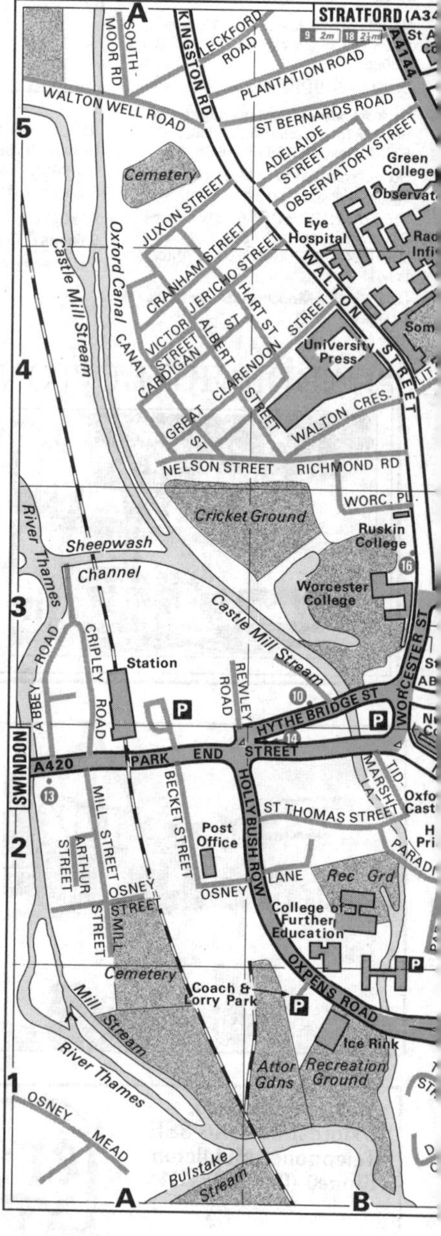

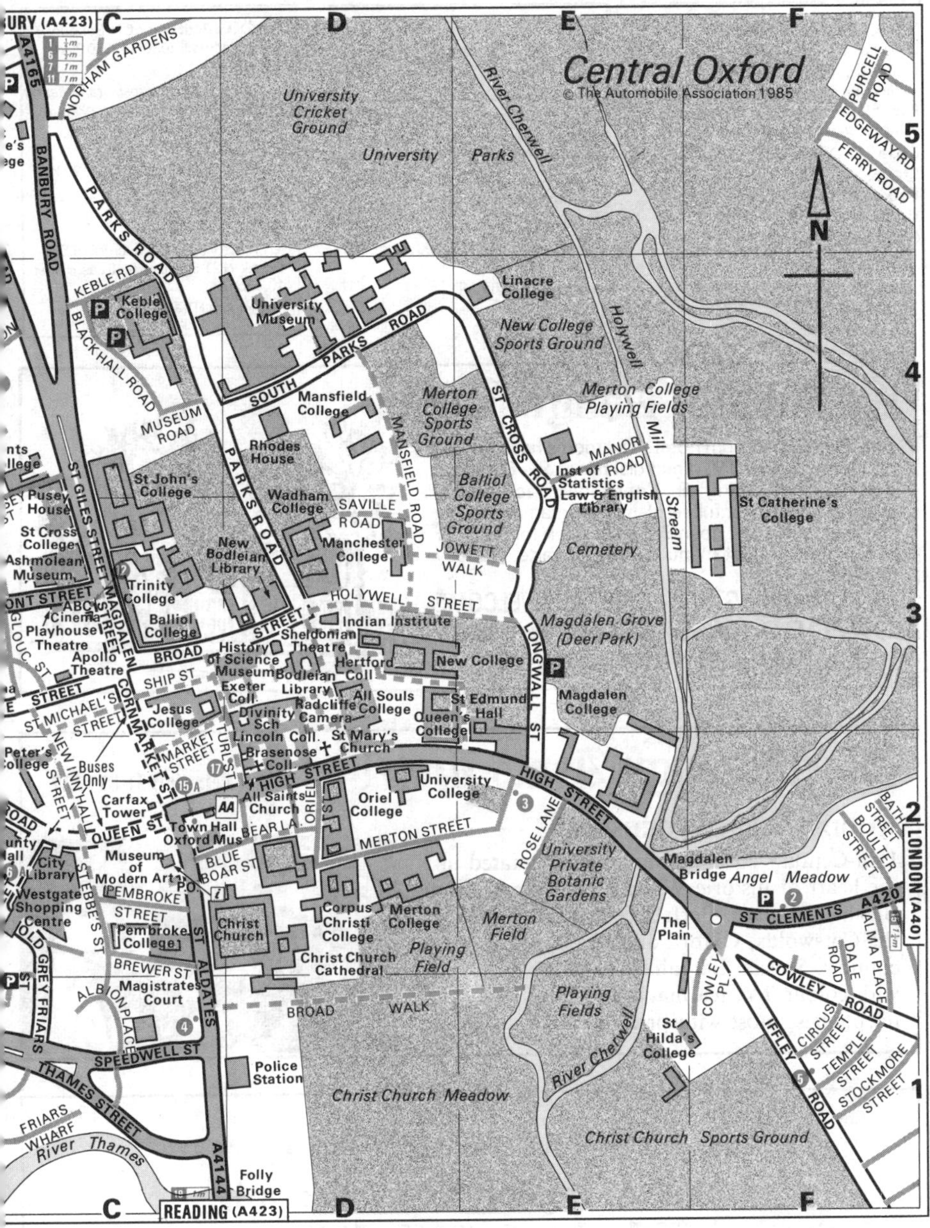

Central Oxford

Oxford

1	Cotswold Lodge ★★	**9**	Oxford Moat House ★★★	**15A**	La Sorbonne ✕✕
3	Eastgate ★★★	**10**	Paddyfield ✕✕	**16**	Standard Indian ✕
4	Restaurant Elizabeth ✕✕✕	**11**	Le Petit Blanc ❀✕✕	**17**	Taj Mahal ✕
5	Isis ★★	**12**	Randolph ★★★★	**18**	TraveLodge ★★
6	Ladbroke Linton Lodge ★★★	**13**	River ★	**19**	Victoria ★★
6A	Liaison ✕	**14**	Royal Oxford ★★		
7	Lotus House ✕				
8	Michel's Brasserie ✕				

XXX**Restaurant Elizabeth** 84 St Aldates ☏ (0865) 242230 Plan **4** *C1*

In an early 17th century building this restaurant run by Signor Lopez offers, French, Spanish and Greek dishes complemented by an extensive wine list.

Closed Mon, Xmas—31 Dec & Good Fri

French, Greek & Spanish 45 seats **V**
*Lunch fr£11&alc Dinner £18.20alc Wine £6.95 Last dinner 10.45pm

Credit cards 1 2 3 5

Oxford

XX***Paddyfield*** 39/40 Hythe Bridge St ☏ (0865) 248835 Plan **10** *B3*

Smart city centre restaurant providing good Cantonese food.

Closed 25—27 Dec

Cantonese & Pekinese **V** 90 seats Last dinner 11.45pm 20P

Credit cards 1 2 3 5

XX**Le Petit Blanc** 61A Banbury Rd, Summertown ☏ (0865) 53540 Plan **11** *C5*

Delightful, bistro style restaurant offering exquisitely cooked French cooking in classical and modern style, with charming service.

Closed Wed, 1st 2 wks Jan, end 2 wks Aug—1st wk Sep
Lunch not served Thur
Dinner not served Tue

French **V** 65 seats Lunch fr£15.50 Dinner fr£21.50 Wine £6.40 Last dinner 10.15pm

Credit cards 1 3

O

XXLa Sorbonne 130A High St ☎(0865) 241320 Plan **15A** *C2*

French **V** 60 seats S% Lunch £10—£22&alc Dinner £10—£12&alc Wine £5.85 Last dinner 11pm nc

Credit cards 1 2 3 5 V

XLiaison 29 Castle St ☎(0865) 242944 Plan **6A** *C2*

Closed 25 & 26 Dec Lunch not served Sun

Cantonese & Szechuan **V** 50 seats Lunch £3.50 Dinner £7—£20&alc Wine £5.10 Last dinner 11.20pm

Credit cards 1 2 3

XLotus House 197 Banbury Rd, Summertown ☎(0865) 54239 Plan **7** *C5*

At this simple, informal, two-roomed restaurant in Summertown, an extensive menu features some unusual Cantonese, Pekinese and Szechuan dishes. Set meals are available, but staff are happy to help you with choices.

Closed Xmas Day & Boxing Day

Pekinese **V** 70 seats Lunch £3.25&alc Dinner £6&alc Wine £5.25 Last dinner 11.45pm 3P

Credit cards 1 2 3 5

XMichel's Brasserie 10 Little Cladendon St ☎(0865) 52142 Plan **8** *B4*

The atmosphere here is of a typical brasserie, and the dishes on the fixed price menu, as well as the chef's specialities are well presented and accompanied by fresh vegetables. The service is attentive and friendly.

Closed Boxing Day & New Year's Day

French **V** 50 seats Lunch fr£6.45&alc Dinner fr£11.95&alc Wine £4.80 Last dinner 11pm

Credit cards 1 2 3

XStandard Indian 117 Walton St ☎(0865) 53557 Plan **16** *B3*

Families are welcome at this restaurant, which offers sound Indian cuisine at fair prices.

Indian 44 seats Last dinner 11.30pm

Credit cards 1 2 3 5

XTaj Mahal Turl St ☎(0865) 243783 Plan **17** *D2*

First floor restaurant decorated with Indian carvings and paintings.

Indian **V** 52 seats Last dinner 11pm

Credit cards 1 2 3 5

OXTED
Surrey
Map **5** TQ35

★★Hoskins Station Road West (Inter-Hotels) ☎(08833) 2338 Gatwick plan **15**

Modern circular hotel with well-equipped bedrooms.

10 CTV in all bedrooms **T** S% sB&B £36 dB&B £47.50

Lift CTV 30P Live music & dancing Wed & Thu

Mainly grills ✱ Lunch £4—£8.50&alc Dinner £4—£8.50&alc Wine £5 Last dinner 10pm

Credit cards 1 2 3 5

PADSTOW
Cornwall
Map **2** SW97

★★★Metropole Station Rd (Trusthouse Forte) ☎(0841) 532486

Large detached traditional hotel in an elevated position overlooking the river estuary.

43 CTV in all bedrooms ® sB&B £43.50 dB&B £66.50

Lift CTV 40P (heated)

Last dinner 8.30pm

Credit cards 1 2 3 4 5

★★Old Custom House Inn South Quay ☎(0841) 532359

Closed Jan—Feb

Pleasant personally-run inn by harbours edge and once the old custom house.

25 (2fb) CTV in all bedrooms ® **T** sB&B £30—£35 dB&B £40—£44

French **V** Bar lunch £2—£3.30&alc Tea £1.75—£3 Dinner £8.50—£11.25&alc Wine £3.50 Last dinner 9.30pm

Credit cards 1 2 3 5 V

See advertisement on page 568

XXSeafood ☎(0841) 532485

This specialist fish restaurant is run by the owners with considerable flair. The friendly and efficient staff serve dishes that are carefully prepared from local fish, shellfish and vegetables, and the extensive wine list contains some good house wines.

Closed Sun & 21 Dec—18 Mar Lunch not served

English & French 75 seats Dinner £12.95&alc Wine £6.50 Last dinner 9.30pm

Credit cards 1 2 3 5

PAIGNTON
Devon
Map **3** SX86

★★★Palace Esplanade Rd (Trusthouse Forte) ☎(0803) 555121

The impressive sea-front hotel has views of sea and beach. Bedrooms are well-equipped, public rooms comfortable and spacious, and there is a sports/leisure centre on site. Staff are attentive and pleasant.

54 CTV in all bedrooms sB&B £45.50 dB&B £67.50

Lift 60P CFA (heated) (hard) sauna bath solarium gymnasium *xmas*

Last dinner 9pm

Credit cards 1 2 3 4 5

★★★Redcliffe Marine Dr ☎(0803) 526397

Unusual mid-Victorian building with a central tower, pinnacles and battlements, overlooking the sea.

63rm (56 7)(8fb) CTV in all bedrooms **T** sB&B £23—£30 dB&B £46—£60

Lift CTV 80P CFA (heated) Live music & dancing 4 nights wkly *xmas* →

O

🍽English & French V 🍷 ☕ Lunch £6.25—£6.75 Tea 80p—£1 Dinner £8.50—£9.50&alc Wine £5.60 Last dinner 8.30pm

Credit cards 1 2 3 Ⓥ

★★ ***Alta Vista*** Alta Vista Rd, Roundham (from A379 follow signs Roundham) ☎(0803) 551496

Closed 15 Oct—25 Mar

Hotel overlooks Goodrington Sands

28rm(15🛁⫛)(5fb) CTV in all bedrooms ® ✗ B

CTV 30P ✿ 🏠

Paignton

🍽British, French & Italian 🍷 ☕ Last dinner 7.30pm

Credit cards 1 3

★★ **Dainton** 95 Dartmouth Rd, Three Beaches, Goodrington ☎(0803) 550067

RS winter wknds

Of modern construction, but Tudor in style, the hotel stands on a corner site, with a side road leading to the beach. Public rooms are in character with the Tudor exterior, whilst bedrooms are modern and comfortable.

10rm(6⫛)(3fb) CTV available in bedrooms ® ✱ sB&B£13—£14 sB&B⫛£14.50—£17 dB&B£26—£31 dB&B⫛£31 B

CTV 17P 🚌

V 🍷 ☕ ✱ Lunch £3.50—£8.50&alc Dinner £6.35—£10&alc Wine £4.25 Last dinner 9pm

Credit cards 1 3 Ⓥ

★★**Lyndhurst** Lower Polsham Rd
☎(0803) 551140

Closed Nov—Mar (ex Xmas)

Standing on a corner and overlooking seafront lawns, this family-owned hotel is ideally situated for holidays. It offers a relaxed, informal atmosphere where children are welcome.

30rm(5⇌16fh)(2fb) CTV in all bedrooms ®sB&B£10.50—£15.75 sB&B⇌fh£11.50—£17.50 dB&B£21—£31.50 dB&B⇌fh£23—£35

Lift CTV 12P Live music & dancing twice wkly *xmas*

V ☕ ⊐ ⚟ Bar lunch £1.75—£2.50 Tea 50p High Tea 95p—£1.95 Dinner £6 Wine £4.50 Last dinner 8pm

Credit cards 1 3 Ⓥ

★★***St Ann's*** Alta Vista Rd, Goodrington (from A379 follow signs Roundham)
☎(0803) 557360

Closed Dec—Mar

Hotel overlooks Goodrington Sands.

28rm(25⇌3fh)(6fb) CTV in 12 bedrooms ® B

CTV 30P ✿ ⇀ (heated) sauna bath solarium Disco Thu Live music & dancing Tue

English & French ☕ ⊐ Last dinner 7.30pm

Credit card 1

★★**Seaford** 2—4 Stafford Rd (off Sands Rd) ☎(0803) 557341

Detached gabled villa with newly extended frontage.

24rm(12⇌12fh)(9fb) CTV in all bedrooms ®sB&B⇌fh£13—£15 dB&B⇌fh£26—£30 B

Lift 10P Live music and dancing wkly Cabaret twice wkly (Apr-Nov) *xmas*

English & French V ⚟ *Lunch £2—£3 Dinner £4—£6&alc Wine £3 Last dinner 7.45pm

★**Oldway Links** 21 Southfield Rd
☎(0803) 559332

Large hilltop Georgian building comfortably modernised with attractive lounge bar.

Paignton — Pangbourne

20rm(1⇌)(2fb) CTV in 10 bedrooms ® *sB&B£10—£15 sB&B⇌£10—£15 dB&B£20—£30 dB&B⇌£20—£30 B

CTV 20P ⇎ ✿ ♗ *xmas*

English & French V ☕ ⊐ *Bar lunch £1—£5 Tea £2 High Tea £2.50 Dinner £10alc Wine £4.95 Last dinner 9pm

Ⓥ

★**Torbay Holiday Motel** Totnes Rd
☎(0803) 558226

Hotel complex with a pleasant restaurant catering for the tourist and commercial clientele.

66fh CTV in all bedrooms ® sB&Bfh£15.41—£16.56 dB&Bfh£26.22—£28.52 B

CTV 150P ✿ ⇀ (heated) Live music & dancing wkly ♗

English & French V ☕ Bar lunch £3.50alc Dinner £4.90&alc Wine £3.85 Last dinner 9pm

Credit cards 1 3

✕**Luigis** 59 Torquay Rd ☎(0803) 556185

A Latin warmth and friendliness are captured in this intimate Italian restaurant. The aperitif area is very interesting and there is a good selection of pasta available, together with a variable choice of meat and fish dishes. The wine list is extensive and service is unfailingly attentive.

Lunch not served Sun & Mon

Italian V 40 seats Lunch £3.75&alc Dinner £10.50 Wine £6.95 Last dinner 11pm P

Credit card 3

PAINSWICK
Gloucestershire
Map **3** SO80

★★★*BL* **Painswick** Kemps Ln
☎(0452) 812160 Telex no 43605

RS Sun night

This delightful, Georgian house was originally a vicarage and enjoys a quiet setting behind the parish church with views across the valley. The interior is most ornate, and there is a comfortable, lightwood-panelled aperitif lounge and a separate lounge for non-smokers, whilst the well-appointed dining room, with darkwood panelling and crystal chandeliers, offers well-prepared food coupled with attentive service.

15⇌fh(2fb) CTV in all bedrooms **T** sB&B⇌fh£42—£47.50 dB&B⇌fh£59—£70 B

25P ⇎ ✿ croquet *xmas*

English & French ☕ ⊐ Bar lunch fr£5 Tea fr80p Dinner fr£14.50 Wine £6.50 Last dinner 9.30pm

Credit cards 1 2 3 5

See advertisement under Gloucester

PAISLEY
Strathclyde *Renfrewshire*
Map **11** NS46

Hotels and restaurants are listed under Glasgow Airport

PANGBOURNE
Berkshire
Map **4** SU67

★★★**Copper Inn** (Best Western)
☎(07357) 2244 Telex no 849041

Comfortable, well managed hotel with well-equipped bedrooms and honest, enjoyable food.

21⇌fh(1fb) 1⊟ CTV in all bedrooms ®**T** ✗ S% *sB&B⇌fh£45.75—£49.25 dB&B⇌fh£58.50—£63.50 B

30P ⇎ ✿ ♗

English & French V ☕ *Lunch £8.95—£9.75&alc Tea fr80p Dinner £15alc Wine £6.75 Last dinner 9.30pm

Credit cards 1 2 3 4 5

See advertisement under Reading

P

PARBOLD
Lancashire
Map **7** SD41

★★**Lindley** Lancaster Ln (Whitbread) ☎ (02576) 2804

Closed 24, 25 & 31 Dec & 1 Jan

This well-equipped hotel is located in a quiet suburb.

9rm(2🛁7🚿)(1fb) CTV in all bedrooms Ⓡ S% ✱sB&B🛁🚿£28.60 dB&B🛁🚿£33 **B**

60P

English & French ✱Lunch £5.95alc Dinner £9.50alc Wine £5 Last dinner 10pm

Credit cards 1 2 3

✕**Prescotts Farm** Lees Ln, Dalton (1m S on unclass rd off A5209) ☎ (02576) 4137

A converted brick-built cottage, at least 100 years old, stands in pleasant rural surroundings. Its rough-cast walls and low, oak-beamed ceilings add a farmhouse atmosphere to the restaurant where a well-produced array of Italian dishes is complemented by polished service and an adequate wine list.

Closed Mon & 13—27 Jul Lunch not served Sat

English, French & Italian **V** 40 seats Lunch £10alc Dinner £10alc Wine £5.20 Last dinner 10pm 40P

Credit card 1

PARKEND
Gloucestershire
Map **3** SO60

★★**Parkend House** ☎ Dean (0594) 563666

The personally-run country house hotel stands in an elevated position overlooking the village. It offers well-equipped bedrooms, comfortable bar and lounge and a restaurant where good food is enjoyed in a pleasant atmosphere.

6🛁(1fb) CTV in all bedrooms Ⓡ ✱sB&B🛁£17.50 dB&B🛁£29 **B**

15P (heated) sauna bath *xmas*

English & French ✱Lunch fr£1 Tea fr£1.30 High Tea fr£1 Dinner fr£7.50&alc Wine £4.80 Last dinner 9pm

Credit cards 1 3

PARKGATE
Cheshire
Map **7** SJ27

★★★**Ship** The Parade (Anchor) ☎ 051-336 3931 Telex no 858875

Attractive stone-fronted inn with modern bedrooms overlooking the Dee Estuary.

26🛁🚿 2 in 3 bedrooms CTV in all bedrooms Ⓡ**T** ✱sB&B🛁🚿fr£38 dB&B🛁🚿fr£48 **B**

100P *xmas*

English & French ✱Lunch £2.90—£5.95&alc Dinner £2.90—£10,50&alc Wine £5.95 Last dinner 9.30pm

Credit cards 1 2 3 5 Ⓥ

★★**Parkgate** Boathouse Ln (Whitbread) ☎ 051-336 5001 Telex no 629469

The fine period house is set in its own grounds close to the Dee marshes and provides well-furnished and comfortable accommodation.

30rm(17🛁13🚿)(3fb) 1 CTV in all bedrooms Ⓡ**T** sB&B🛁🚿£24—£40 dB&B🛁🚿£47—£57 **B**

140P

French **V** Lunch £5—£9.95 Dinner £9.95—£10.50&alc Wine £5.10 Last dinner 9.45pm

Credit cards 1 2 3 5

✕✕**Le Bistrot** The Parade ☎ 051-336 4187

This black and white building, looking across the Dee estuary towards Wales, has recently been skilfully converted into a typically French bistro. The well-prepared food is competitively priced, and a short à la carte menu is supplemented by daily blackboard specials; service is pleasantly attentive.

International **V** 65 seats Lunch £9alc Dinner £9alc Wine £4.25 Last dinner 11pm 60P

Credit cards 1 2 3 5

✕✕**Mr Chows** The Parade ☎ 051-336 2385

A rickshaw stands outside the mock Tudor building, attractively decked with window boxes and fixed canopies, where dining rooms on two floors overlook the Dee estuary. Inside, the atmosphere is congenial, an oriental mood being created by revolving parasols, gently moving fans, pampas grass and red dragon motifs.

Closed Xmas Day
Lunch not served

Chinese **V** 125 seats ✱Dinner £8.50—£14&alc Wine £5.25 Last dinner 11.30pm

Credit cards 1 2 3 5

PARKHAM
Devon
Map **2** SS32

★★★**Penhaven Country House** ☎ Horns Cross (02375) 388

This Victorian rectory on the edge of the village has been lovingly restored to create a hotel with a friendly, relaxed atmosphere.

12rm(9🛁) CTV in all bedrooms Ⓡ**T** sB&B£17—£19 sB&B🛁£24—£28 dB&B£34—£38 dB&B🛁£48—£56 **B**

30P *xmas*

V Lunch £7.50—£8.50 Tea fr£1.35 High Tea fr£1.50 Dinner £8.50—£10&alc Wine £5.95 Last dinner 9.30pm

Credit cards 1 2 3 5 Ⓥ

PATTERDALE
Cumbria
Map **11** NY31

★★**Patterdale** (Consort) ☎ Glenridding (08532) 231

Closed end Oct—Etr

This hotel lies at the foot of the Kirkstone Pass facing Ullswater.

53rm(12🛁20🚿) Annexe: 6rm(2fb) Ⓡ sB&B£16.50 sB&B🛁🚿£18.50 dB&B£33 dB&B🛁🚿£37 **B**

CTV 50P 1

Bar lunch 80p—£2.70 Tea 65p alc Dinner fr£8 Wine £4.20 Last dinner 8pm

Credit cards 1 2

PATTINGHAM
Staffordshire
Map **7** SO89

★★★**Patshull Park** Patshull (1½m W of Pattingham) (Best Western) ☎ (0902) 700100 Telex no 334849

The modern hotel unit stands in a 280-acre park which has been developed for leisure, incorporating a golf course and well-stocked lakes.

28🛁 CTV in all bedrooms Ⓡ**T** ✱sB&B🛁£34.75 dB&B🛁£49.50 **B**

200P 18

English & French ✱Lunch fr£5.25 Tea fr75p Dinner fr£7.95 Wine £4.95 Last dinner 9.30pm

Credit cards 1 2 3 5

See advertisement under Wolverhampton

PEASMARSH
East Sussex
Map **5** TQ82

★★**Flackley Ash** (Best Western) ☎ (079721) 651

Peaceful, hospitable Georgian manor house with modern bedrooms.

20rm(17🛁3🚿)(7fb) 3 CTV in all bedrooms Ⓡ**T** S% sB&B🛁🚿£35—£40 dB&B🛁🚿£50—£55 **B**

40P croquet *xmas*

English & French Lunch £3—£8 Tea £1 High Tea £2.50 Dinner £9.25—£10.50&alc Wine £5.50 Last dinner 10pm

Credit cards 1 2 3 5 Ⓥ

PEAT INN
Fife
Map **12** NO40

✽XX Peat Inn ☎(033484) 206

This popular country inn provides very high standards of elegance and comfort, as well as a most imaginative cuisine in the modern style. Seafood from local fishing villages is of top quality and freshness, earning the chef/patron justifiable acclaim. In addition the wine list is one of the most comprehensive in Scotland.

Closed Sun, Mon, 2 wks Jan, 1 wk Apr & 1 wk Oct

French 48 seats S% Lunch £11 Dinner £23&alc Wine £6.50 Last dinner 9.30pm 24P

Credit cards [2] [3] [5]

PEEBLES
Borders *Peeblesshire*
Map **11** NT24

★★★ **Park** Innerleithen Rd (Swallow) ☎(0721) 20451 Telex no 53168

Traditional Scottish building with a modern extension, overlooking the River Tweed and the Border hills.

26→(3fb) 1 CTV in all bedrooms Ⓡ S% sB&B→fr£38 dB&B→fr£52.50

☾60P ✽ putting Live music & dancing Sat (Nov—Apr) *xmas*

Scottish & French **V** S% Lunch £6.95&alc Tea £1.20alc High Tea £5alc Dinner £10.95&alc Wine £4.90 Last dinner 10pm

Credit cards [1] [2] [3] [5]

★★★ *H* **Peebles Hydro** (Consort) ☎(0721) 20602 Telex no 72568

Overlooking the Tweed Valley, this large conference and family hotel stands in its own grounds above the town.

139rm(131→8⋒)(26fb) CTV in all bedrooms Ⓡ **T** S% sB&B→⋒£36.55—£41.20 dB&B→⋒£40.20—£69.90

Lift ☾200P CFA ✽ (heated) (hard) squash snooker sauna bath solarium gymnasium Live music and dancing twice wkly *xmas*

V S% Lunch fr£7 Tea fr80p Dinner fr£12 Wine £6.60 Last dinner 9pm

Credit cards [1] [2] [3] [5] Ⓥ

★★★ **Tontine** High St (Trusthouse Forte) ☎(0721) 20892

Traditional hotel with attractive Adam dining room.

37rm(36→1⋒)(3fb) CTV in all bedrooms Ⓡ sB&B→⋒£43.50 dB&B→£59.50

☾CTV 30P CFA *xmas*

Last dinner 9.30pm

Credit cards [1] [2] [3] [4] [5]

★★

★★ CRINGLETIE HOUSE, PEEBLES

☎Eddleston (07213) 233

Closed Jan & Feb

In 28 acres of grounds a few miles north of Peebles is this hotel built of red sandstone in Scots baronial style in 1666. In the grounds is a walled kitchen plot, as well as a tennis court, putting green and croquet lawn. It was once the home of Colonel Murray who accepted the surrender of Quebec, and it is now owned by Mr and Mrs Maguire. He mostly looks after the front of the house and supervises the dining room, while Mrs Maguire supervises the kitchen to good effect in either of two first floor dining rooms. The style is homely but the food provided for the four course dinner is tasty. Also on the first floor is the elegant panelled drawing room with painted ceiling where you can take after dinner coffee or just relax at any time. It is a nicely decorated room with comfortable seating. On the ground floor is the hall and cosy bar, the latter very much a rendezvous to chat about the day's activities. There is a TV room as well. Open fires burn when

necessary and there are always flower arrangements to lend their fresh charm. Bedrooms vary in size and are homely but prettily done. Staff are well trained and polite.

16rm(8→1⋒)(2fb) sB&B£22 sB&B→⋒£24 dB&B£44 dB&B→⋒£50

Lift CTV 40P ✽ (hard) croquet putting

International Lunch £4—£10.50 Tea £1.25—£3 Dinner £15.50 Wine £3.95 Last dinner 8.30pm

★★ **Dilkusha** Chambers Ter ☎(0721) 20590

Quiet hotel with panelled dining room and cocktail bar.

5rm(3→2⋒)(3fb) CTV in all bedrooms Ⓡ *sB&B→⋒£22 dB&B→⋒£35

15P

V *Lunch fr£7 Tea £2.50 High Tea £4.50—£7 Dinner £10alc Wine £3.60 Last dinner 9pm

Credit cards [2] [3]

★★ **Kingsmuir** Springhill Rd ☎(0721) 20151

Tasteful bedrooms are offered by this family-run hotel.

9→(2fb) CTV in all bedrooms Ⓡ *sB&B→£20 dB&B→£32

P ✽

*Lunch £5.70&alc Dinner £8.80 Wine £3.90 Last dinner 8.30pm

Credit cards [1] [2] [3]

★★ **Venlaw Castle** Edinburgh Rd ☎(0721) 20384

Closed Nov—Mar

This baronial-style mansion on a wooded hillside has a cocktail bar that was originally a library.

12rm(5→4⋒)(2fb) Ⓡ sB&B£18—£19 sB&B→⋒£20—£21 dB&B£34—£38 dB&B→⋒£36—£40

CTV 20P ✽

English & French Bar lunch £2.50—£5 Dinner £9.50 Wine £4.25 Last dinner 8.30pm

Credit cards [1] [2] [5]

See advertisement on page 572

★ **County** 35 High St ☎(0721) 20595

The small, homely and personally-run hotel, parts of which date back to the early 18th century, stands on the town's main street.

11rm(1fb) CTV in all bedrooms Ⓡ sB&B£13 dB&B£26

☾CTV 5P

Mainly grills **V** Lunch fr£2.95&alc Tea 50p—£1.65 High Tea £3.25—£6.50 Dinner fr£6.50&alc Wine £4.95 Last dinner 10pm

Ⓥ

PELYNT
Cornwall
Map **2** SX25

★★ **Jubilee Inn** ☎ Lanreath (0503) 20312

A charming inn that has been completely modernised.

10rm(5→1⋒)(1fb) CTV in 8 bedrooms *sB&B£11.50—£14.50 sB&B→⋒£14.50—£17.50 dB&B£23—£27 dB&B→⋒£29—£32

CTV 80P 6 ✽ *xmas*

English & Continental **V** *Lunch £5.90—£7.50&alc Dinner £8.50alc Wine £4.15 Last dinner 10pm

Credit cards [1] [3] Ⓥ

P

PEMBROKE
Dyfed
Map **2** SM90
See also **Lamphey**

★★**Coach House Inn** 116 Main St (ExecHotels) ☎ (0646) 684602 Telex no 48407

An attractive internal courtyard lounge complements the original coach house building in this proprietor-run hotel. Comfortable, purpose-built bedrooms are fitted with pine furnishings.

14rm(13⇌1⋒)(3fb) CTV in all bedrooms ® T ✗ (ex guide) sB&B⇌⋒£25.50—£26 dB&B⇌⋒£36—£38 B

8P ❀ solarium ♨ *xmas*

♡ English & French V ♡ ☕ Lunch £5.90—£6&alc Tea fr£1.50 Dinner £5.90—£6&alc Wine £4 Last dinner 10pm

Credit cards [1] [2] [3] [5] Ⓥ

★★**Holyland** Holyland Rd
☎ (0646) 681444

Originally a fine Georgian mansion, this comfortable hotel stands within its own grounds in the Pembrokeshire National Park and has recently been totally refurbished. Comfortable, modern bedrooms and attractive public rooms are complemented by friendly service from proprietors and staff.

10rm(3⇌7⋒)(2fb) CTV in all bedrooms ® sB&B⇌⋒£19.50—£21.20 dB&B⇌⋒£32—£36 B

Pembroke — Pembroke Dock

50P ✈ ❀ *xmas*

♡ English, French & Italian V ♡ ☕ ✱ Bar lunch 88p—£3 Tea 60p Dinner £7.20&alc Wine £5 Last dinner 9.30pm

Credit cards [1] [3]

★★**Old Kings Arms** Main St
☎ (0646) 683611

Closed Xmas Day, Boxing Day & New Years Day

The character small hotel offers friendly, personal service and promotes commendable cooking standards; bedrooms are modern and compact, while the restaurant, with its flagged floor, is charmingly reminiscent of bygone days.

21⇌ CTV in all bedrooms ® sB&B⇌£21.50—£24 dB&B⇌£30—£34 B

21P

V ♡ Lunch fr£7.50&alc Dinner fr£8.50&alc Last dinner 10pm

Credit cards [1] [2] [3]

★★**Underdown Country House** Grove Hill ☎ (0646) 683350

This delightful little country house hotel promotes a personal, homely style. It is splendidly furnished with the owners' own antiques and offers fine home cooking in the warmth and charm of an attractive restaurant; bedrooms combine character with modern facilities.

6rm(4⇌2⋒)(2fb) 1 ☐ CTV in all bedrooms ® sB&B⇌⋒£27.50—£32.50 dB&B⇌⋒£35—£42.50

☾ CTV 40P 2 ⌂ ❀

♡ English & French ♡ ☕ S% Lunch £9.95alc Tea £1.50alc Dinner £9.95alc Wine £4.20 Last dinner 9.30pm

Credit cards [1] [3]

PEMBROKE DOCK
Dyfed
Map **2** SM90

★★★**Cleddau Bridge** The Avenue
☎ (0646) 685961

The modern and well-appointed hotel provides comfortable bedrooms and is popular with tourists and businessmen alike. A good centre for touring Pembrokeshire, it commands fine views of Milford Haven.

24⇌(3fb) CTV in all bedrooms ® T S% sB&B⇌£37.50 dB&B⇌£49 B

☾ CTV 200P ❀ ⛆ (heated) ♨ ♿

♡ English & French V ♡ ☕ Lunch £9alc Tea £1.50alc Dinner £11—£12alc Wine £4.80 Last dinner 9.30pm

Credit cards [1] [2] [3] [5] Ⓥ

P

PENARTH
South Glamorgan
Map **3** ST17

★★***Glendale*** 8—10 Plymouth Rd
☎ (0222) 706701

Closed 25 Dec

A small, well-kept, friendly hotel.

18rm(8🛁3⋔)(3fb) CTV in all bedrooms ® ⚡ CTV 🚸

English & Italian V 🍷 ☕ Last dinner 9.30pm

Credit cards 1 2 3

Penarth

★**Walton House** 37 Victoria Rd
☎ (0222) 707782

Closed Xmas Day

Pleasant small hotel near town centre.

12rm(4🛁1⋔)(1fb) CTV in all bedrooms sB&B£16.50 sB&B🛁⋔£19.50 dB&B£30 dB&B🛁⋔£34

CTV 16P 🎵

English, French & Italian 🍷 Lunch fr£6 High Tea fr£5 Dinner fr£8 Wine £4.50 Last dinner 7.30pm

Credit cards 1 3 5

✕✕✕**Caprice** The Esplanade
☎ (0222) 702424

Comfortably appointed, and promoting professional standards of personal service, this well-established and agreeable first-floor restaurant stands within easy reach of Cardiff city centre, commanding extensive views over the Bristol Channel.

Closed Sun →

P

English & Continental V 80 seats S% Lunch £8.95&alc Dinner £12.95&alc Wine £4.75 Last dinner 11pm

Credit cards 1 2 3 5

XII Piccolino The Esplanade Cardiff (0222) 703428

This tiny restaurant, looking across the Bristol Channel from its position near the yacht club, offers a mainly Italian menu which includes a few simple English dishes.

English, French & Italian V 40 seats Last dinner 11.30pm

Credit cards 1 2 3

PENCRAIG

Hereford & Worcester
Map **3** SO52

★★ **Pencraig Court** Ross-On-Wye (0989) 84306

Closed Xmas & New Year

Peaceful small country hotel set in gardens and woodland.

11rm(8)(2fb) 1 CTV available in bedrooms S% *sB&B£18—£23 sB&B£24—£29 dB&B£26—£36 dB&B£30—£40

CTV 25P

English & French V S% *Bar lunch £2.75 Tea fr80p Dinner £11.50 Wine £4.50 Last dinner 9.30pm

Credit cards 1 2 3 V

See advertisement under Ross-on-Wye

PENDOGGETT

Cornwall
Map **2** SX07

★★H ***Cornish Arms*** Bodmin (0208) 880263

Closed Xmas Day & Boxing Day

Delightful, small hotel in a 17th-century former ale house, with beamed ceilings.

7rm(5)

CTV 40P nc 14yrs

Last dinner 8.45pm

Credit cards 1 2 3 5

PENNAL

Gwynedd
Map **6** SH60

★★★B **Talgarth Hall** Plas Talgarth Estate (065475) 631

Classical Georgian manor house in beautiful Snowdonia.

10(3fb) CTV in all bedrooms ® T *sB&B£30 dB&B£60

50P & (heated) (hard) squash sauna bath solarium gymnasium Live music & dancing Tue & Thu *xmas*

English & French V Lunch £1—£5 Dinner £5—£7.50&alc Wine £3.75 Last dinner 9.30pm

Credit cards 1 2 3 5

★★ **Llugwy Hall Country House** (1m E on A483) (065475) 228

Closed Feb RS Jan

Gracious Elizabethan country house in wooded surroundings by the River Dovey.

11rm(9)(2fb) CTV in all bedrooms ® sB&B£33—£37 sB&B£33—£37 dB&B£40—£43 dB&B£40—£43

40P shooting *xmas*

English & French V Lunch £4.95—£6 Tea £1.20—£1.50 Dinner £7—£10&alc Wine £5.45 Last dinner 9pm

Credit cards 1 2 3 5 V

★ **Riverside** (065475) 285

Roadside village inn catering for local and tourist clientele.

7rm(1fb) sB&B£15.50—£16.50 dB&B£31—£33

CTV 60P 4

Bar lunch £1.50—£3.75 Dinner £6.50—£8 Wine £4.95 Last dinner 8.45pm

PENN STREET

Buckinghamshire
Map **4** SU99

XX **Hit or Miss** High Wycombe (0494) 713109

Old coaching inn providing tasty well-cooked food.

Closed Mon & last wk Jul—1st wk Aug Dinner not served Sun

French 36 seats *Lunch £7.20&alc Dinner £14.50alc Wine £4.20 Last dinner 9.30pm 100P nc9yrs

Credit cards 1 2 5

PENRITH

Cumbria
Map **12** NY53

See also **Edenhall & Shap**

★★★B **North Lakes Gateway** Ullswater Rd (Consort) (0768) 68111 Telex no 64257

The hotel is modern, but retains such character features as the 200-year-old beams in the restaurant and foyer. Its excellent facilities include a leisure club and conference facilities. Traditional English food is complemented by friendly and efficient service.

57(8fb) 2 in 6 bedrooms CTV in all bedrooms ® T S% sB&B£47—£59 dB&B£68—£80

Lift # CTV 120P (heated) squash sauna bath solarium gymnasium *xmas*

V S% Lunch £8—£10&alc Tea 95p—£1.20 Dinner £12—£14&alc Wine £6.50 Last dinner 9.45pm

Credit cards 1 2 3 5 V

★★ **Abbotsford** Wordsworth St (0768) 63940

The hotel is situated beneath the wooded Penrith Beacon.

11rm(92)(3fb) 1 CTV in all bedrooms ® S% sB&B£18.50—£20 dB&B£33—£37

CTV 20P

V S% Lunch £4—£5 Tea fr80p High Tea fr£4 Dinner fr£8.50 Wine £3.95 Last dinner 10pm

Credit cards 1 2 3 5 V

P

★★**Clifton Hill** Clifton (2¾m S A6)
☎(0768) 62717

Large Edwardian house with several later additions.

57rm(55🛁2🚿)(2fb) CTV in all bedrooms S% sB&B🛁🚿£21.50 dB&B🛁🚿£30 B

CTV 200P 25🚗✿ *xmas*

V🍷☕⚡S% Lunch fr£4.25 Tea fr£2.75 High Tea fr£3.50 Dinner fr£7.50 Wine £3.75 Last dinner 8.30pm

★★**George** Devonshire St ☎(0768) 62696

Closed 25—26 Dec & 1 Jan

Former coaching inn, offering courteous and personal service.

31rm(11🛁20🚿)(1fb) CTV in all bedrooms ®T sB&B🛁🚿£25—£27 dB&B🛁🚿£36—£38 B

☾30P

🍽English & French 🍷☕ Lunch £3.45—£5.50 Tea £2 Dinner £7.95—£9.25 Wine £4.50 Last dinner 8.30pm

Credit card 1

★**Glen Cottage** Corney Sq ☎(0768) 62221

Closed Xmas Day, Boxing Day & New Years Day

White stucco-faced cottage of charm and character, built in 1756.

7rm(4🛁)(3fb) CTV in all bedrooms sB&B£13 sB&B🛁£16—£18 dB&B£23—£25 dB&B🛁£26—£28

3🚗(50p per day)

🍷⚡Lunch £2.95—£5 Dinner £3.95—£6 Wine £4.25 Last dinner 9.15pm

Credit cards 1 2 3 4 5

★**Station** Castlegate ☎(0768) 62072

Pleasant rather old fashioned hotel with friendly hospitality.

22rm (4fb) ®✱sB&B£11.50 dB&B£23 B

CTV 12P 4🚗 snooker *xmas*

V🍷☕⚡✱Lunch £3.50&alc Tea £1&alc High Tea £2&alc Dinner £3.50&alc Wine £2 Last dinner 10pm

PENSHURST

Kent
Map **5** TQ54

★★***Leicester Arms*** (Whitbread)
☎(0892) 870551

This picturesque, seventeenth-century inn offers helpful and friendly management, good standards of service and cooking, and accommodation in modern, well-equipped bedrooms.

7rm(6🛁1🚿)2⊞ CTV in all bedrooms ®T B

36P

🍽European V🍷 Last dinner 9.30pm

Credit cards 1 2 3 5

PENYBONT

Powys
Map **3** SO16

★★***Severn Arms*** ☎(059787) 224

Closed Xmas wk

Standing beside the A44, the small, character, inn-style hostelry is brightly decorated and offers modern facilities including popular bars and cosy cottage bedrooms.

10🛁(6fb) CTV in 7 bedrooms ®B

CTV 20P ✿🐟

V🍷 Last dinner 9pm

PENZANCE

Cornwall
Map **2** SW43

★★★🏠*L* **Higher Faugan** Newlyn (off B3315) ☎(0736) 62076

Closed Nov—Feb

Holiday hotel in secluded surroundings, set in 10 acres of ground.

11rm(10🛁1🚿) 1⊞ CTV in all bedrooms ® T✗✱sB&B🛁🚿£20.50—£28 dB&B🛁🚿£41—£56 B

15P 2🚗⊞✿ ⛆(heated) 🎾(hard) snooker putting

🍽International 🍷☕✱Bar lunch £1.50—£4.50 Dinner £10.35 Wine £4 Last dinner 8.30pm

Credit cards 1 2 5 Ⓥ

★★★**Mount Prospect** Britons Hill (Exec Hotel) ☎(0736) 63117 Telex no 45143

Well-appointed hotel in gardens overlooking Mounts Bay and Penzance harbour.

26rm(23🛁3🚿)(2fb) CTV in all bedrooms ®T sB&B🛁🚿fr£31 dB&B🛁🚿fr£50 B

☾CTV 14P ✿ ⛆(heated)

🍷☕ Lunch fr£5.75&alc Tea fr£1 Dinner fr£10.35&alc Wine £4.50 Last dinner 9pm

Credit cards 1 2 3 5 Ⓥ

★★★***Queen's*** The Promenade ☎(0736) 62371

Large, traditional hotel on the sea front with exceptional views over Mount's Bay.

71rm(47🛁24🚿)(9fb) CTV in all bedrooms ®B

Lift ☾150P sauna bath gymnasium *xmas*

🍽British & French V🍷☕ Last dinner 8.45pm

Credit cards 1 2 3 5

★★**Sea & Horses** 6 Alexandra Ter ☎(0736) 61961

Closed Xmas

Friendly, personally run small hotel with comfortable bedrooms and good food.

11rm(2🛁6🚿)(4fb) CTV available in all bedrooms ®✗ sB&B£12.50—£13.50 sB&B🛁🚿£13.50—£14.50 dB&B£24—£26 dB&B🛁🚿£26—£28 B

10P 1🚗

V🍷S% Bar lunch 75p—£3.50 Dinner £6.95 Wine £4 Last dinner 6pm

Credit cards 1 3 Ⓥ

★**Alexandra** Alexandra Ter, Seafront ☎(0736) 62644

Closed Xmas

This personally-run holiday hotel offers good facilities and has glorious views over Mount's Bay.

23rm(13⇌10⋒)(7fb) CTV in all bedrooms ®T✱sB&B£12—£14.50 sB&B⇌⋒£14.50—£17 dB&B£24—£29 dB&B⇌⋒£29—£34 B

14P3 ⌂ ⚘

English & French V ♆ ☕ Wine £3.50 Last dinner 7.30pm

Credit cards 1 2 3 Ⓥ

★H **Estoril** 46 Morrab Rd ☎(0736) 62468

Closed Dec & Jan

Comfortable, private hotel with very warm welcome. Bedrooms have good facilities and food is also good.

10rm(5⇌5⋒)(1fb) CTV in all bedrooms ® T sB&B⇌⋒£15.50—£16.50 dB&B⇌⋒£30—£32 B

☾ 4P ⇌ nc7yrs

Wine £4 Last dinner 7.30pm

Credit cards 1 3 Ⓥ

★**Minalto** Alexandra Rd ☎(0736) 62923

Closed Mid Oct—Mid Nov RS Mid Nov—Mar

Small family hotel in quiet location close to the beach and the town centre.

Penzance — Perranporth

10rm(3fb) CTV in 1 bedroom TV in 1 bedroom ® ✗ sB&B£11—£12 dB&B£22—£24 B

CTV 10P

♆ ☕ Lunch £5—£6&alc Tea 60—80p Dinner £5—£6&alc Wine £3 Last dinner 8pm

Ⓥ

★**Southern Comfort** Alexandra Ter, Seafront ☎(0736) 66333

Quiet, comfortable hotel, personally run with good food and atmosphere.

12rm(6⋒)(4fb) CTV in all bedrooms ® ✗ sB&B£11—£13 sB&B⋒£14—£16 dB&B£22—£26 dB&B⋒£28—£32 B

CTV 8P 2 ⌂ ⇌

♆ ☕ Bar lunch £2—£5.50 Tea £1 High Tea £2—£5.50 Dinner £7—£8&alc Wine £4 Last dinner 7.30pm

Ⓥ

★HL **Tarbert** 11—12 Clarence St (Minotel) ☎(0736) 63758

Closed Xmas

Small comfortable hotel in central situation. Good food and bedrooms, friendly atmosphere.

13rm(9⋒)(3fb) CTV in all bedrooms ®

sB&B£13—£15 sB&B⋒£15—£17 dB&B£26—£30 dB&B⋒£30—£34 B

5P ⇌ ⚘

English & French Bar lunch £5&alc High Tea £3.50 Dinner £7 Wine £4.85 Last dinner 7.30pm

Credit cards 1 2 3 5 Ⓥ

PERRANPORTH

Cornwall
Map **2** SW75

★★***Promenade*** ☎(087257) 3118

Closed Oct—Apr

Family holiday hotel near to and overlooking the beach.

35rm(15⇌)(6fb) ✗

☾ CTV 27P Disco 3 nights wkly Live music & dancing 3 nights wkly

V ♆ Last dinner 7.30pm

★H **Beach Dunes** Ramoth Way, Reen Sands ☎ Truro (0872) 572263

Closed Nov—Feb RS Mar

Peaceful, friendly hotel, with good facilities, and overlooking the sea.

7rm(2⇌1⋒) Annexe: 3⇌(2fb) CTV in all bedrooms ® ✗ sB&B£13.50—£18.50 sB&B⇌⋒£15.50—£21 dB&B£27—£37 dB&B⇌⋒£31—£42 B

18P ⇌ ✿ ▭(heated) squash nc3yrs

V ♆ ☕ ✗ Bar lunch £2.50—£5.50 Tea £1.50 Dinner £8.50 Wine £3.75 Last dinner 6.30pm

Credit cards 1 2 3 4 Ⓥ

P

Rosemary, Brenda & John invite you to

SOUTHERN COMFORT HOTEL

AA ★

- Licensed Bar
- En-suite rooms
- Colour TV and tea making all rooms
- Private car park

Alexandra Terrace, Sea Front, Penzance (0736) 66333

Enjoy the friendly relaxed atmosphere, traditional cuisine and personal attention at Southern Comfort Hotel. Superb sea views over Mounts Bay & St. Michael's Mount.

Tarbert Hotel ★ HL

11 CLARENCE STREET, PENZANCE, CORNWALL, TR18 2NU

Family-run Georgian hotel, full of character. The warm, friendly atmosphere encourages guests to return to the Tarbert from all over the world. The charming lounge bar features exposed granite walls and open fires.

*AA Merit Award for Hospitality and Public Rooms
*Special diets catered for *Private car park
*En suite rooms *Children welcome
*On parle Français *Man spricht Deutsch

Tel: John & Del James (0736) 63758

Enzo

LICENSED ITALIAN RESTAURANT, NEWBRIDGE

●

Dine in comfort, Italian style, amid orange, lemon and grapefruit trees. Choose from the original menu or watch Enzo as he cooks the steak or fresh fish of your choice on the charcoal grill.

●

Situated in Newbridge within easy reach of Penzance. On the main Penzance to St Just road A3071.

For reservations telephone: Penzance 3777

P

★

Ramoth Way, Reen Sands, Perranporth Tel: Truro (0872) 572263
Resident Proprietors: Margaret & Keith Wooldridge

A small family hotel, situated in the sand dunes overlooking Perran Bay. The hotel is unique in Perranporth, in that it is able to offer facilities not normally found in a small hotel. Facilities at a glance: ★Direct access to the beach ★40ft × 16ft heated indoor pool ★Squash court ★Radio/intercom in all bedrooms ★Ample parking ★Colour TV in all bedrooms ★Most bedrooms with bathroom en suite ★Tea/coffee making facilities in all bedrooms ★Full central heating ★Well-stocked bar with residential licence ★High standard of food and drink ★Full fire certificate.

The hotel adjoins Perranporth golf course — 18 holes-discount rates.

PERRANUTHNOE
Cornwall
Map **2** SW52

★*HL* **Ednovean House** Ednovean Ln (on A394 5m E of Penzance) ☎ Penzance (0736) 711071

This comfortable hotel with well-appointed public rooms stands in a quiet location with views over the bay. Food is good, making provision for vegetarian and other diets.

9rm(6🚿) sB&B£13.15—£14.70 sB&B🚿£15.75—£17.50 dB&B£26—£28.50 dB&B🚿£30—£34

CTV 12P ✿ putting, croquet nc 7yrs

V Dinner £7.50&alc Wine £4.75 Last dinner 7pm

Ⓥ

PERSHORE
Hereford & Worcester
Map **3** SO94

★★★**Angel Inn** ☎ (0386) 552046

The old, family-run hotel offers hospitality, a relaxing atmosphere, freshly-prepared food and comfortable rooms. Riverside gardens add to its charm.

16🛁 2🛗 CTV in all bedrooms ® **T** *sB&B🛁£34 dB&B🛁£50 **B**

50P ✿

V *Lunch £3.50—£14 Tea 65p—£1.25 Dinner £9.50—£14&alc Wine £5.25 Last dinner 9.30pm

Credit cards 1 2 3 5

See advertisement under Worcester

★★*L* ***Avonside*** Main Rd, Wyre Piddle (2m NE on B4084) ☎ (0386) 552654

Closed Dec—Feb

Guests enjoy the relaxing atmosphere at this hotel set beside the river in the village of Wyre Piddle.

7rm(6🛁1🚿)(1fb) CTV in all bedrooms **B**

7P ✿ (heated) nc 7yrs

V Last dinner 8.30pm

P

★**Manor House** Bridge St ☎ (0386) 552713

Closed Xmas day

The small hotel at the end of the town, personally run by the proprietor, offers guests value-for-money accommodation.

8rm(1fb) sB&B£13.90 dB&B£26.50

CTV 50P

V Lunch £5.50—£6 Dinner £7.95—£8.50&alc Wine £4.95 Last dinner 9.30pm

Credit cards 1 2 3 4 5 Ⓥ

★**Star** Bridge St ☎ (0386) 552704

Town centre inn with a small garden, bordering the banks of the River Avon.

9rm CTV in all bedrooms ® sB&B£20—£25 dB&B£26.50—£35

50P

*Lunch £5alc Dinner £8alc Wine £4 Last dinner 9.30pm

Credit cards 1 3

✕**Zhivago's** 22 Bridge St ☎ (0386) 553828

There is a slight emphasis on Italian cuisine at this small continental restaurant in the main street, and a complete Italian meal at a realistic price appears among the variety of dishes on the menu. The half-timbered dining room on the ground floor has seating for about forty people, and there is a cocktail lounge on the first floor.

Closed Mon & 3—24 Aug Dinner not served Sun

English, French, Italian & Russian **V** 60 seats Lunch £4.50—£7.50&alc Dinner £15alc Wine £6 Last dinner 10.45pm

Credit cards 1 2 3 5

PERTH
Tayside *Perthshire*
Map **11** NO12
See plan

★★★

❀★★★ **BALCRAIG HOUSE, PERTH**

Scone (2½m NE off A94 towards New Scone) (Prestige) ☎ (0738) 51123
Plan **1** *D4*

(Rosette awarded for dinner only).

This Victorian mansion is not untypical of hotels among our Red Star list, but it is rare to find it run by the owners, Michael and Kitty Pearl, in such an unusual way. Not only is it a sympathetically run country house, but they also have 130 acres of farm and a market garden, run chiefly to supply tip top quality ingredients for the hotel kitchen — not just common or garden things but rare breeds of animals and poultry together with a vast array of vegetables. As the farming is adventurous so is the cooking for the five course dinners. The wine list is something of a hobby of Michael Pearl and it features about 300 items including some very old vintages. The stylish bedrooms are all you would expect and the bathrooms positively sybaritic as well as having murals by Sally Anderson.

10🛁(3fb) 1🛗 CTV in all bedrooms S% sB&B🛁£47.50—£55 dB&B🛁£75—£85 **B**

20P ✿ ⛳18 (hard) croquet shooting *xmas*

S% Tea 80p—£3.75&alc Dinner £21&alc Wine £4.50 Last dinner 10pm

Credit cards 1 2 3 5 Ⓥ

★★★***Huntingtower*** Crieff Rd, Almondbank (3m W off A85) ☎ Almondbank (073883) 771 Telex no 76204
Plan **3** *A4*

This comfortable hotel, standing in its own extensive grounds, offers well-equipped and tastefully refurbished bedrooms; in the beautifully panelled restaurant, interesting and well-cooked food is served.

15rm(13🛁2🚿)(2fb) **T** CTV in all bedrooms ®

☾ 100P ✿

International Last dinner 9.30pm

Credit cards 1 2 3 5

See advertisement on page 582

★★★**Isle of Skye** Queen's Bridge, Dundee Rd (Toby) ☎ (0738) 24471 Plan **4** *D2*

Recently refurbished traditional hotel standing on the north bank of the river.

23rm(12🛁11🚿)(2fb) 1🛗 CTV in all bedrooms ® **T** sB&B🛁🚿£32 dB&B🛁🚿£48 **B**

☾ # 60P CFA Disco nightly *xmas*

Scottish & French **V** Lunch £6.35—£6.95&alc Tea 90p—£1.60 High Tea £3.50—£7 Dinner £6.35—£7.50&alc Wine £4.40 Last dinner 9.45pm

Credit cards 1 2 3 5

★★★*L* ***Royal George*** Tay St (Trusthouse Forte) ☎ (0738) 24455 Plan **9** *C3*

Spacious Georgian/Victorian hotel overlooking River Tay, with modern bedrooms, comfortable lounges and elegant restaurant.

43🛁(2fb) CTV in all bedrooms ® sB&B🛁£43.50 dB&B🛁£65.50 **B**

☾ 20P 12 ✿ *xmas*

Last dinner 10pm

Credit cards 1 2 3 4 5

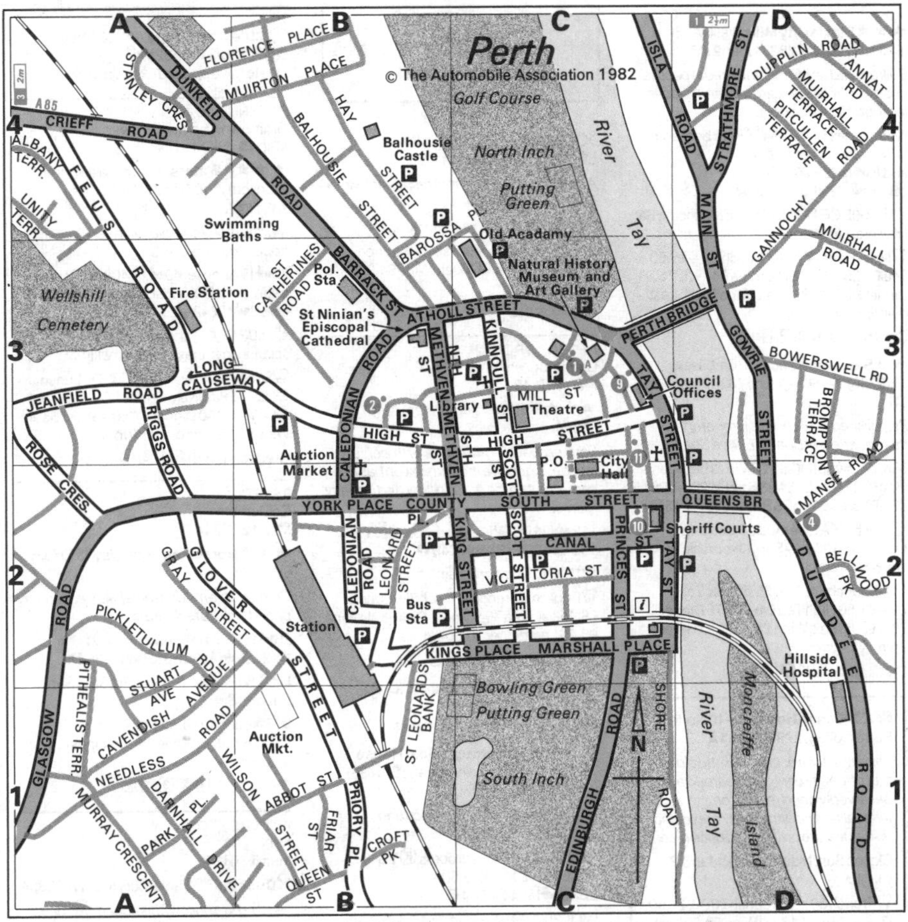

Perth

Perth

1	Balcraig House ✿★★★♣♣		3	Huntingtower ★★★		10	Salutation ★★
1A	Coach House ✿✕✕		4	Isle of Skye ★★★		11	Timothy's ✕✕
2	Stakis City Mills ★★★		9	Royal George ★★★			

P

★★★**Stakis City Mills** West Mill St (Stakis) ☎ (0738) 28281 Plan **2** *B3*

Built around an old mill, the stream passes under the hotel and can be seen in places through the glass floors.

78rm(77⇌⌂)(1fb) 2⊠⊬ in 12 bedrooms CTV in all bedrooms ®**T** sB&B⇌⌂£39.90—£44.90 dB&B⇌⌂£59.80—£60 **B**

☾ ## 100P CFA ✿ Live music & dancing Sat (in winter) *xmas*

♡ Mainly grills **V** ♡ ⊒ Lunch £4—£5.50 Tea £1.25—£2.75 High Tea £4—£6.75 Dinner £7.50—£13&alc Wine £5.20 Last dinner 10pm

Credit cards 1 2 3 4 5

★★**Salutation** South St (Embassy) ☎ (0738) 22166 Telex no 76357 Plan **10** *C5*

Established in 1699, was temporary headquarters of Bonnie Prince Charlie.

68rm(22⇌38⌂)(2fb) CTV in all bedrooms ® sB&B£20—£25 sB&B⇌⌂£20—£25 dB&B£38—£45 dB&B⇌⌂£38—£45 **B**

☾ CTV ⁋ CFA Live music & dancing Mon—Wed (May—Sep) Live music Wed, Thu & Fri *xmas*

♡ ⊒ Lunch £4.75—£5.50&alc Tea £1—£1.50 High Tea £4—£4.75 Dinner £8—£9.50&alc Wine £4.45 Last dinner 9pm

Credit cards 1 2 3 4 5

✿✕✕**Coach House** 8—10 North Port ☎ (0738) 27950 Plan **1A** *C3*

This attractive restaurant in the older part of the city centre has earned a deservedly good reputation. Interesting and attractively presented dishes feature on the fixed price menu.

Closed Sun, Mon, 1st 2 wks Jan & 2 wks Jul

♡ French 36 seats Lunch £8—£11.50 Dinner £16—£17.50 Wine £5.50 Last dinner 10pm ⁋

Credit cards 1 3

P

Perth — Pett Bottom

✕✕**Timothy's** 24 St John Street ☎ (0738) 26641 Plan **11** *C3*

A cosy, cheerful, informal restaurant with a bustling atmosphere.

Closed Sun, Mon, 1 wk after Xmas

♡ English & Danish 48 seats ✱ Lunch £3.50alc Dinner £5.50alc Wine £4.20 Last dinner 10.15pm

Credit card 1

PETERBOROUGH

Cambridgeshire
Map **4** TL19

★★★**Bull** Westgate (Paten) ☎ (0733) 61364

Former coaching inn with a 17th-century façade. Extensive modernisation has been carried out on the ground floor and in many rooms.

112⇌(3fb) CTV in all bedrooms ®**T** S% sB&B⇌£39 dB&B⇌£49 **B**

☾ 100P CFA gymnasium

♡ English & French **V** ♡ ⊒ S% Lunch £8.45&alc Tea 70p Dinner £8.45&alc Wine £5.25 Last dinner 10.30pm

Credit cards 1 2 3 5 Ⓥ

★★★**Crest** Great North Rd (Crest) ☎ (0733) 240209

(For full entry see Norman Cross)

★★★**Peterborough Moat House** Thorpe Wood (Queens Moat) ☎ (0733) 260000 Telex no 32708

Modern hotel with conference and banqueting facilities.

98⇌⌂ CTV in all bedrooms ®**T** S% sB&B⇌⌂£34—£49.50 dB&B⇌⌂£44—£64 **B**

Lift ☾ 200P ✿ CFA Live music & dancing Sat ♿

♡ International **V** ♡ ⊒ S% Lunch £8.25&alc Tea fr 70p Dinner £9.50&alc Wine £5.95 Last dinner 10pm

Credit cards 1 2 3 5 Ⓥ

◯**Little Chef Lodge** A1 Southbound ☎ (0733) 231109 32⇌⌂

Due to have opened October 1986

PETERHEAD

Grampian *Aberdeenshire*
Map **15** NK14

★★★*B* **Waterside Inn** Fraserburgh Rd (Consort) ☎ (0779) 71121 Telex no 739413

Modern hotel complex with very well appointed bedrooms.

70⇌⌂ Annexe: 40⇌⌂(40fb) CTV in all bedrooms ®**T** S% sB&B⇌⌂£34—£42 dB&B⇌⌂£42—£50 **B**

☾ 250P CFA ✿ snooker sauna bath solarium gymnasium Disco wkly ♔

♡ Scottish & French **V** ♡ ⊒ S% Lunch £3.25—£8.50&alc Tea fr £1.50 High Tea £3.25—£7.50 Dinner £7.50—£12.75&alc Wine £5.95 Last dinner 10pm

Credit cards 1 2 3 5 Ⓥ

PETERLEE

Co Durham
Map **12** NZ44

★★★**Norseman** Bede Way ☎ (0783) 862161

Comfortable modern hotel with reasonably priced feature restaurant.

26⇌⌂ CTV in all bedrooms ®**T** S% ✱ sB&B⇌⌂£28 dB&B⇌⌂£38 **B**

Lift ☾ 50P snooker Disco Fri, Sat & Sun Cabaret Sat

V ♡ ✱ Lunch fr £4.50&alc Dinner £5—£6.50&alc Wine £5 Last dinner 9.30pm

Credit cards 1 2 3 5 Ⓥ

PETT BOTTOM

Kent
Map **5** TR15

✕**Duck Inn** ☎ Canterbury (0227) 830354

Nestling in a hollow, this country inn has a cosy dining room and wood fires. Waitress service and quiet, beautiful gardens are features of this country inn.

Closed Mon, Xmas day & Boxing day
Lunch not served Sun

🍴English & French **V** 30 seats ✱Lunch £12alc Dinner £12alc Wine £5.25 Last dinner 9.30pm 50P

Credit cards [1] [2]

PETTY FRANCE
Avon
Map **3** ST78

★★★**Petty France** (on A46 S of junct with A433) ☎ Didmarton (045423) 361

Charming, family run coaching inn with ambitious menu of well prepared food.

8rm(7🛁1🚿) Annexe: 12rm(11🛁1🚿)(1fb) 1⊞ CTV in all bedrooms ® **T** S% sB&B🛁🚿£27.50—£35 dB&B🛁🚿£43.50—£50 Continental breakfast **B**

50P ✿ ⌂ *xmas*

🍴English & French **V** ♔ ☕ Lunch £11.50&alc Tea £1—£2 Dinner £11.50&alc Wine £7 Last dinner 9.30pm

Credit cards [1] [2] [3] [4] [5] Ⓥ

✕✕**The Restaurant at Bodkin House** Badminton (on A46 S of jct with A433) ☎ Didmarton (045423) 310

This charming, small restaurant in rural setting was once a coaching inn. Its panelled bar still has an open fireplace and flagstone floor, the dining rooms are comfortable and there is a small lounge. Attractively-presented English dishes, well-prepared from good seasonal and raw materials, are complemented by a selective wine list and quietly courteous service. Booking is essential and half-an-hour is required for meal preparation.

Closed Mon (winter) Dinner not served Sun

🍴English & French **V** 45 seats Lunch £7—£8.95&alc Dinner £15alc Wine £5.50 Last dinner 9.30pm 25P ⚡

Credit cards [1] [2] [3] [5] Ⓥ

PEVENSEY
East Sussex
Map **5** TQ60

★★**Priory Court** Pevensey Castle ☎ (0323) 763150

Dating from 15th century, this agreeable, family run hotel has some attractive, well-furnished bedrooms, cosy public rooms, reliable cooking standards and offers good value for money.

9rm(5🛁1🚿)(1fb) 1⊞ CTV in 2 bedrooms ® ✗ S% sB&B£19—£23 sB&B🛁🚿£28 dB&B£27—£35 dB&B🛁🚿£45—£48 **B**

CTV 30P ✿ *xmas*

V ♔ ☕ S% Lunch £10alc Tea 50palc Dinner £10alc Wine £5.50 Last dinner 11pm

Credit cards [1] [2] [3] Ⓥ

PICKERING
North Yorkshire
Map **8** SE78

★★**Forest & Vale** 2 Hungate, Malton Rd (Consort) ☎ (0751) 72722 Telex no 57515

Comfortable country hotel with well kept garden. Large restaurant serving mainly English food.

17rm(7🛁5🚿) Annexe: 6rm(5🛁1🚿)(3fb) CTV in all bedrooms ® sB&B🛁🚿£26—£28 dB&B£35 dB&B🛁🚿£38—£44 **B**

CTV 70P 1🏠 ✿ ⌂

🍴English & French **V** ♔ ☕ Lunch £5.75&alc Tea £2 Dinner £9.25&alc Wine £5.50 Last dinner 9.30pm

Credit cards [1] [2] [3] [5] Ⓥ

★★ *B* **White Swan** Market Pl ☎ (0751) 72288

Parts of this tastefully modernised coaching inn date back to the 16th century, and it retains much of its original character and charm. Under the personal supervision of the proprietors it offers a hospitable and friendly atmosphere, fine cuisine with the emphasis on fresh produce, and competitive prices.

13🛁(1fb) CTV in all bedrooms ® sB&B🛁fr£26.50 dB&B🛁£42—£57 **B**

30P ⇶ *xmas*

🍴English & French ♔ Lunch fr£6.50 Dinner fr£10 Wine £5.55 Last dinner 9pm

Credit cards [1] [3]

✕**Blacksmiths Arms** Aislaby (2m NW on A170) ☎ (0751) 72182

A congenial atmosphere pervades this 18th-century stone inn where French and British dishes can be enjoyed.

Closed Mon Tue & Jan Dinner not served Sun

40 seats ✱ Dinner £10.50alc Wine £4.60 Last dinner 9.15pm 20P

Credit card [1]

PIDDLETRENTHIDE
Dorset
Map **3** SY79

★★**Old Bakehouse** ☎ (03004) 305

Closed Jan

The cottage-style hotel stands at the centre of the village, providing friendly attention from owners and staff. Good menus feature well-prepared food, and the simple bedroom accommodation is largely contained in an annexe.

3🛁 Annexe: 7rm(6🛁1🚿) 3⊞ CTV in all bedrooms ® sB&B🛁🚿£19.25 dB&B🛁🚿£32.50—£37.50 **B**

16P ⇶ ✿ ⛆ (heated) nc 12yrs

🍴English & Continental **V** Lunch £6alc Dinner fr£8.75&alc Wine £4.50 Last dinner 9pm

Credit cards [1] [3]

See advertisement on page 584

PITLOCHRY
Tayside *Perthshire*
Map **14** NN95
See plan

★★★ *L* **Atholl Palace** (Trusthouse Forte) ☎ (0796) 2400 Telex no 76406 Plan **3** *D2*

Large imposing hotel with superb views and very good leisure facilities.

84🛁(5fb) CTV in all bedrooms ® sB&B🛁£43.50 dB&B🛁£69.50 **B**

Lift ☾ CTV 150P CFA ✿ ⛆ (heated) 🎾(hard) snooker sauna bath solarium gymnasium ⌂ *xmas*

♔ ☕ Last dinner 9pm

Credit cards [1] [2] [3] [4] [5]

★★★**Fisher's** Atholl Rd ☎ (0796) 2000 Plan **12** *B3*

Well-established, four storey building in the town centre, backed by fine gardens.

75rm(49🛁5🚿)(9fb) CTV in 25 bedrooms ✱sB&B£19.50—£24 sB&B🛁🚿£19.50—£26.50 dB&B£35—£46 dB&B🛁🚿£35—£50 🅱

Lift ☾ CTV 50P 13 (charge) ✿

✱Lunch £4.50—£10 Tea fr55p Dinner £9—£15 Wine £4 Last dinner 8.30pm

Credit cards [1] [2] [3] [5]

★★★**Green Park** Clunie Bridge Rd ☎ (0796) 3248 Plan **13** *A4*

Closed Nov—Mar

Extended country house hotel standing on the banks of Loch Faskally and backed by woodland.

39rm(30🛁5🚿)(10fb) CTV in 35 bedrooms Ⓡ**T** in 16 bedrooms sB&Bfr£20 sB&B🛁🚿fr£23 dB&Bfr£40 dB&B🛁🚿fr£46 🅱

CTV 50P 4 (£1 per night) CFA ✿ table tennis putting Live music & dancing Sat (Apr—12 May)

Scottish & French Lunch fr£4.75 Tea fr80p Dinner fr£10.50 Wine £4 Last dinner 8pm

★★★**Pitlochry Hydro** (Scottish Highland) ☎ (0796) 2666 Telex no 778215 Plan **16** *C4*

Set in its own grounds, the hotel offers commanding views over the south west of the town across the valley.

64🛁(4fb) CTV in all bedrooms Ⓡ sB&B🛁£34 dB&B🛁£58 🅱

Lift ☾ CTV 100P ✿ (hard) Live music & dancing Wed & Thu

V ✱Bar lunch £1.75—£3.25 Tea 75p Dinner £8.50 Wine £5.90 Last dinner 8.30pm

Credit cards [1] [2] [3] [5]

★★★**Scotland's** 40 Bonnethill Rd (Best Western) ☎ (0796) 2292 Plan **17** *C3*

Popular tourist hotel, close to town centre and curling rink.

57rm(21🛁36🚿)(11fb) CTV in all bedrooms Ⓡ**T** S% sB&B£20.20—£28.50 sB&B🛁🚿£22.20—£30.50 dB&B£34.40—£51 dB&B🛁🚿£38.40—£55 🅱

Lift ☾ CTV 60P CFA ✿ pool table *xmas*

V Lunch £7.50 Tea 50p&alc High Tea £4.50—£5.50&alc Dinner £10 Wine £5.20 Last dinner 8.30pm

Credit cards [1] [2] [3] [4] [5] Ⓥ

★★**Acarsaid** 8 Atholl Rd ☎ (0796) 2389 Plan **1** *D2*

Closed 25 Oct—15 Apr

Personally-run modern hotel at the southern entrance to the town.

18rm(15🛁3🚿)(1fb) CTV in 5 bedrooms Ⓡ sB&B🛁🚿£16—£17.50 dB&B🛁🚿£32—£35

CTV 20P ✿

Lunch £5.50—£7 Tea £1.50—£1.75 High Tea £4.50—£6 Dinner £9—£9.50&alc Wine £4.50 Last dinner 8pm

Credit cards [1] [3] Ⓥ

★★**Airdaniar** 160 Atholl Rd (Guestaccom) ☎ (0796) 2266 Plan **2** *B3*

Closed Nov—Mar

Detached stone house at northern end of the town.

10rm(2🛁4🚿)(1fb) CTV in all bedrooms Ⓡ sB&B£14.85—£16.85 dB&B£29.30—£33.60 dB&B🛁🚿£35.70—£37.70 🅱

18P ✿

V Bar lunch £4.10alc Dinner £8.75 Wine £3.75 Last dinner 8pm

Credit cards [1] [3]

★★*H* **Birchwood** 2 East Moulin Rd (Inter Hotel) ☎ (0796) 2477 Plan **4** *D2*

Closed Xmas, New Year & Jan

Secluded, well-appointed hotel with high quality annexe bedrooms.

11rm(6🛁2🚿) Annexe: 5🚿(4fb) CTV in all bedrooms Ⓡ sB&B£18.50—£21.50 sB&B🛁🚿£20—£23.50 dB&B£31—£37 dB&B🛁🚿£34—£41 🅱

25P ✿

V Lunch £5alc Tea £3 Dinner £9.75&alc Wine £4.95 Last dinner 8.30pm

Credit cards [1] [3] Ⓥ

★★*HL* **Burnside** 19 West Moulin Rd (Inter Hotel) ☎ (0796) 2203 Plan **5** *C3*

Closed Nov—Mar

Comfortable hotel, personally-run by the proprietors, with attractive floral arrangements throughout.

17🛁🚿 Annexe: 6rm(2🛁1🚿)(6fb) CTV in all bedrooms Ⓡ sB&Bfr£19.90 sB&B🛁🚿fr£23 dB&Bfr£34.80 dB&B🛁🚿fr£41 🅱

30P ✿

Scottish & Continental **V** Lunch fr£5 Tea fr£1.90 Dinner fr£9.25&alc Wine £5.25 Last dinner 8.30pm

Credit cards [2] [3] [5] Ⓥ

See advertisement on page 586

★★***Castlebeigh*** 10 Knockard Rd ☎ (0796) 2925 Plan **6** *C3*

Closed Nov—Mar

Nicely appointed privately owned hotel with fine views.

18🛁 Ⓡ 🅱

CTV 36P ✿ nc 14yrs

V Last dinner 7.50pm

★★**Claymore** 162 Atholl Rd ☎ (0796) 2888 Plan **7** *B3*

Closed 25 Oct—Etr

Privately owned hotel with warm, welcoming public rooms.

7rm(4🛁1🚿)(1fb) CTV in all bedrooms Ⓡ sB&Bfr£17 dB&Bfr£33.50 dB&B🛁🚿fr£38.50 🅱

25P ✿ Live music & dancing Wed

Bar lunch fr£4.60 Dinner fr£9.50 Wine £4.75 Last dinner 8.30pm

Credit cards [1] [3]

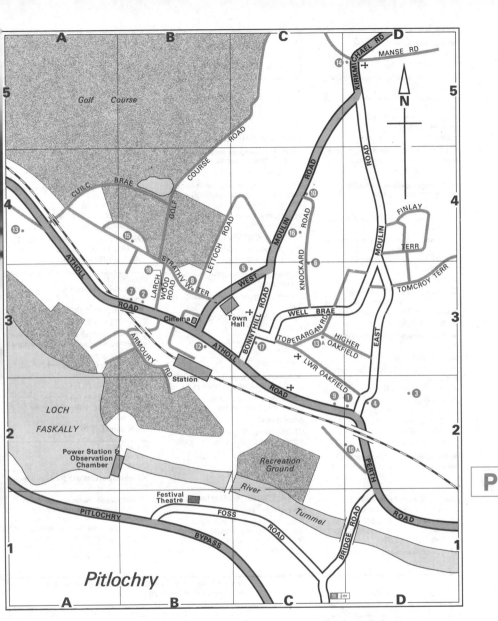

Pitlochry

1	Acarsaid ★★	8	Craigard ★★	13A	Knockendarroch House ★
2	Airdaniar ★★	9	Craig Urrard ★	14	Moulin Inn ★★
3	Atholl Palace ★★★	10	Craigvrack ★★	15	Pine Trees ★★
4	Birchwood ★★	10A	Dundarach ★★	16	Pitlochry Hydro ★★★
5	Burnside ★★	11	Dunfallandy House ★	17	Scotland's ★★★
6	Castlebeigh ★★	12	Fisher's ★★★	18	Tigh-na-Cloich ★
7	Claymore ★★	13	Green Park ★★★		

★★*H* **Craigard** Strathview Ter ☎(0796) 2592 Plan **8** *B3*

Closed 25 Oct–16 Apr

Family run hotel with good reputation for home made food.

10rm(3⇌3⋒)(1fb) CTV in all bedrooms ® sB&B£15.50–£18.50 sB&B⇌⋒£17.50–£21 dB&B£29–£35 dB&B⇌⋒£33–£40

10P

Lunch £5alc Tea £1.85 Dinner £10 Wine £4.40 Last dinner 7.30pm

Credit card 3 Ⓥ

★★**Craigvrack** West Moulin Rd (Minotel) ☎(0796) 2399 Plan **10** *C4*

Closed Nov–Mar

Friendly, modern, privately owned hotel on Braemar road.

18rm(8⇌5⋒)(2fb) CTV in all bedrooms ® sB&B£12.50–£15 sB&B⇌⋒£14.50–£17 dB&B£25–£30 dB&B⇌⋒£29–£34 B

20P putting games room

English & French **V** Bar lunch £2.50–£4.50 Tea 75p Dinner £8.75 Wine £4 Last dinner 9pm

Credit cards 1 3

★★**Dundarach** Perth Rd ☎(0796) 2862 Plan **10A** *D2*

Closed 14 Nov–Jan

24rm(18⇌6⋒)(2fb) CTV in 5 bedrooms ® *sB&B⇌⋒£18–£20 dB&B⇌⋒£30–£36 B

CTV 30P

Lunch £4–£4.50 Tea 80p High Tea £3.75–£4 Dinner £7–£7.50 Wine £5.70 Last dinner 8.30pm

Credit cards 1 3

★★**Moulin Inn** 11–13 Kirkmichael Rd, Moulin (Consort) ☎(0796) 2196 Plan **14** *D5*

Closed Jan & Feb

Charming little hotel on the hillside above the town. Its history dates back to 1700.

18rm(11⇌1⋒)(3fb) ® sB&B£15–£18.50 sB&B⇌⋒£20–£23.50 dB&B£26–£33 dB&B⇌⋒£34–£39 B

CTV 40P Live music & dancing Sat

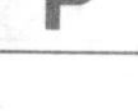

Scottish, English & Continental **V** Lunch £4–£7 Tea fr£2 High Tea £4–£6 Dinner £9.50–£9.75 Wine £4.75 Last dinner 8.45pm

Credit cards 1 2 4 5

★★ *Pine Trees* Strathview Ter ☎(0796) 2121 Plan **15** *B4*

Closed early Jan–late Mar

Fine 19th-century mansion set in the secluded grounds sheltered by pine trees, and near town centre.

26rm(15⇌2⋒) Annexe: 2⇌(3fb) CTV in all bedrooms ® B

CTV 30P 10 *xmas*

V Last dinner 8.30pm

Credit cards 1 2 3 5

★***Craig Urrard*** 10 Atholl Rd ☎(0796) 2346 Plan **9** *C2*

Small friendly hotel with smart new lounge bar.

10rm(4⋒) Annexe: 2⋒(5fb) CTV in all bedrooms ®

CTV 12P

Last dinner 7.30pm

Credit cards 1 2 3

★***Dunfallandy House*** Logierait Rd (2m S unclass rd) ☎(0796) 2251 Plan **11** *C1*

Converted 18th-century house overlooking River Tummel.

8rm(4fb) ® B

CTV 20P 3 Disco wkly Live music & dancing twice wkly Cabaret twice wkly *xmas*

V Last dinner 9pm

Credit cards 1 2 3 5

★**Knockendarroch House** Higher Oakfield ☎(0796) 3473 Plan **13A** *C3*

Closed Dec–Feb

This small, family-run hotel enjoys a splendid setting in oak-shaded grounds. The bedrooms are spacious, the public rooms relaxing and the views wonderful.

6rm(1⇌5⋒)(2fb) ® sB&B⇌⋒£15–£44 dB&B⇌⋒£30–£44 B

CTV 10P

Scottish & French **V** Dinner £8.50–£12.50 Wine £4.10 Last dinner 7.30pm

Credit cards 2 3 Ⓥ

★**Tigh-na-Cloich** Larchwood Rd ☎(0796) 2216

Closed Nov–Feb
RS Mar

This hotel built on the site of the old Sentinel Stone, is compact and comfortable.

14rm(2⇌4⋒)(1fb) CTV in 6 bedrooms ® sB&B£12.50–£13.75 dB&B£25–£27.50 dB&B⇌⋒£29–£31.50 B

CTV 13P 1

British & French Tea £1 Dinner £8–£9&alc Wine £4 Last dinner 7.30pm

Credit cards 1 2 3 4 5

PLOCKTON

Highland *Ross & Cromarty*
Map **14** NG83

★★*HL* **Haven** ☎(059984) 223

Closed 21 Dec–10 Feb

Comfortable and attractive family-run hotel in one of Scotland's most beautiful villages.

13⇌ CTV in all bedrooms ® sB&B⇌£18–£19.50 dB&B⇌£34–£37 B

8P nc 7yrs

V Lunch £5 Tea 70p Dinner £9.50–£10.50&alc Wine £4.20 Last dinner 8.30pm

Credit cards 1 3 Ⓥ

PLUMTREE

Nottinghamshire
Map **8** SK63

✕**Perkins Bar Bistro** Old Railway Station ☎(06077) 3695

Tony and Wendy Perkins have tastefully converted the 19th-century Plumtree station into a cosy restaurant which retains the character of the Victorian buildings. The small but appetising selection of dishes available shows a French influence and an emphasis on fresh food.

Closed Sun & Mon
English & French 65 seats Lunch £9.50alc Dinner £10.75alc Wine £4.10 Last dinner 10pm 50P
Credit cards 1 2

PLYMOUTH
Devon
Map **2** SX45
See plan on page 588/589
See also **Down Thomas**

★★★★**Holiday Inn** Armada Way (Holiday Inns) ☎ (0752) 662866 Telex no 45637 Plan **9** *C3*

Purpose-built modern hotel with well-appointed spacious rooms, adjacent to the Hoe.

217➡⋒(121fb)⁄ in 14 bedrooms CTV in all bedrooms **T** S% ✱sB➡⋒£46—£51 dB➡⋒£56—£61 (room only) **B**

Lift ☾ ## 25P 105 CFA (heated) sauna bath solarium gymnasium games room ♿ *xmas*

V ⁄✱Lunch £1.75—£9.95 Tea £1 High Tea £1.95 Dinner £1.75—£8.95 Wine £6.50 Last dinner 10.30pm

Credit cards 1 2 3 4 5

★★★**Astor** Elliot St, The Hoe (Mount Charlotte) ☎ (0752) 225511 Telex no 45652 Plan **1** *C2*

Dating from the 1800s, the hotel has been modernised with well-appointed rooms.

Plumtree — Plymouth

56rm(49➡4⋒)(3fb) CTV in all bedrooms **T** ✱sB&B➡⋒fr£35.50 dB&B➡⋒fr£51 Continental breakfast **B**

Lift ☾ CFA *xmas*

English & French **V** Lunch £5.75—£6&alc Dinner £8—£8.50&alc Wine £5 Last dinner 9.30pm

Credit cards 1 2 3 5 Ⓥ

★★★**Duke of Cornwall** Millbay Rd (Best Western) ☎ (0752) 266256 Telex no 45424 Plan **4** *B3*

Closed 25, 26 & 31 Dec

A splendid example of Victorian Gothic architecture, the hotel is built in heavy grey stone with turrets, gables and wrought-iron balconies.

67rm(50➡17⋒)(4fb) CTV in all bedrooms ® S% sB&B➡⋒£32—£34 dB&B➡⋒£44—£48 **B**

Lift ☾ ## 100P

English & French **V** Lunch £6—£7 Tea £1.03—£1.50 Dinner £8—£10&alc Wine £5.75 Last dinner 10pm

Credit cards 1 2 3 5

See advertisement on page 590

★★★**Mayflower Post House** Cliff Rd, The Hoe (Trusthouse Forte) ☎ (0752) 662828 Telex no 45442 Plan **11** *B2*

Situated at the end of Plymouth Hoe, the attractive restaurant and coffee shop of this purpose-built hotel command fine views over Plymouth Sound. Executive bedrooms and private suites are comfortable and well-appointed.

106➡(69fb) CTV in all bedrooms ® sB&B➡£54 dB&B➡£70 **B**

Lift ☾ 149P CFA ✿ (heated) *xmas*

Last dinner 10.30pm

Credit cards 1 2 3 4 5

★★★***New Continental*** Millbay Rd ☎ (0752) 220782 Plan **2B** *B3*

Listed building, totally refurbished, and featuring executive restaurant and coffee shop.

76rm(63➡13⋒)(8fb) 2 CTV in all bedrooms ®**T B**

Lift ☾ ## 80P

Last dinner 10pm

Credit cards 1 2 3 5

★★★**Novotel Plymouth** Marsh Mills Roundabout, 270 Plymouth Rd (Novotel) ☎ (0752) 221422 Telex no 45711 Plan **14** *F4*

Modern hotel with pleasant atmosphere and a French theme in the restaurant. →

P

Plymouth

1	Astor ★★★
1A	Camelot ★★
2	Chez Nous ✿✕
2A	Clouds ✕
2B	Continental ★★★
3	Drake ★
4	Duke of Cornwall ★★★
7	Grosvenor ★★
8	Highlands ★★
9	Holiday Inn ★★★★
9A	Imperial ★
10	Invicta ★★
11	Mayflower Post House ★★★
12	Merchantman ★
13	Merlin ★
14	Novotel Plymouth ★★★
15	Strathmore ★★

100🛁(100fb) CTV in all bedrooms **T** S% ✱sB🛁£38.50 dB🛁£45 (room only) **B**

Lift ☾ 160P CFA ✿ ♨ (heated) billiards, petanque

Continental **V** ♀ ☕ ⚡ S% Lunch £5–£6.95&alc Tea 80–90p Dinner £8.95–£14&alc Wine £5.75 Last dinner 11.30pm

Credit cards 1 2 3 4 5 Ⓥ

★★**Camelot** 5 Elliot St, The Hoe ☎(0752) 221255 Plan **1A** *C2*

Set in a Georgian terrace, the city-centre hotel has recently been refurbished.

18🛁(4fb) CTV in all bedrooms Ⓡ **T** ✈ S% sB&B£21–£25 sB&B🛁£21–£25 dB&B£32–£40 dB&B🛁£32–£40 **B**

☾ CTV *xmas*

English & Continental **V** ♀ ☕ S% Lunch £3.75–£6.50 Tea 1.50 Dinner £5.50–£7.75&alc Wine £4.25 Last dinner 9.30pm

Credit cards 1 2 3 5 Ⓥ

★★**Grosvenor** 9 Elliot St, The Hoe ☎(0752) 260411

This busy commercial hotel, converted from a Georgian-style house, features a lower-ground restaurant whose wall murals depict various ghouls.

14rm(8🛁6🚿) CTV in all bedrooms Ⓡ **T** ✈ sB&B🛁🚿£17.50–£23 dB&B🛁🚿£27.50–£35 **B**

CTV **P** *xmas*

Continental **V** ♀ ☕ ✱ Lunch £5.50alc High Tea £1.75alc Dinner £8.50&alc Wine £5.50 Last dinner 10.30pm

Credit cards 1 3 4

★★***Highlands*** Dean Cross Rd, Plymstock (3m SE off A379) ☎(0752) 43643 Plan **8** *F4*

Family-run hotel with good food and pleasant staff. 3 miles from Plymouth.

9rm(4🛁2🚿)(1fb) TV in all bedrooms Ⓡ 24P 🚗 ♨

English & French **V** ♀ Last dinner 9.30pm

P

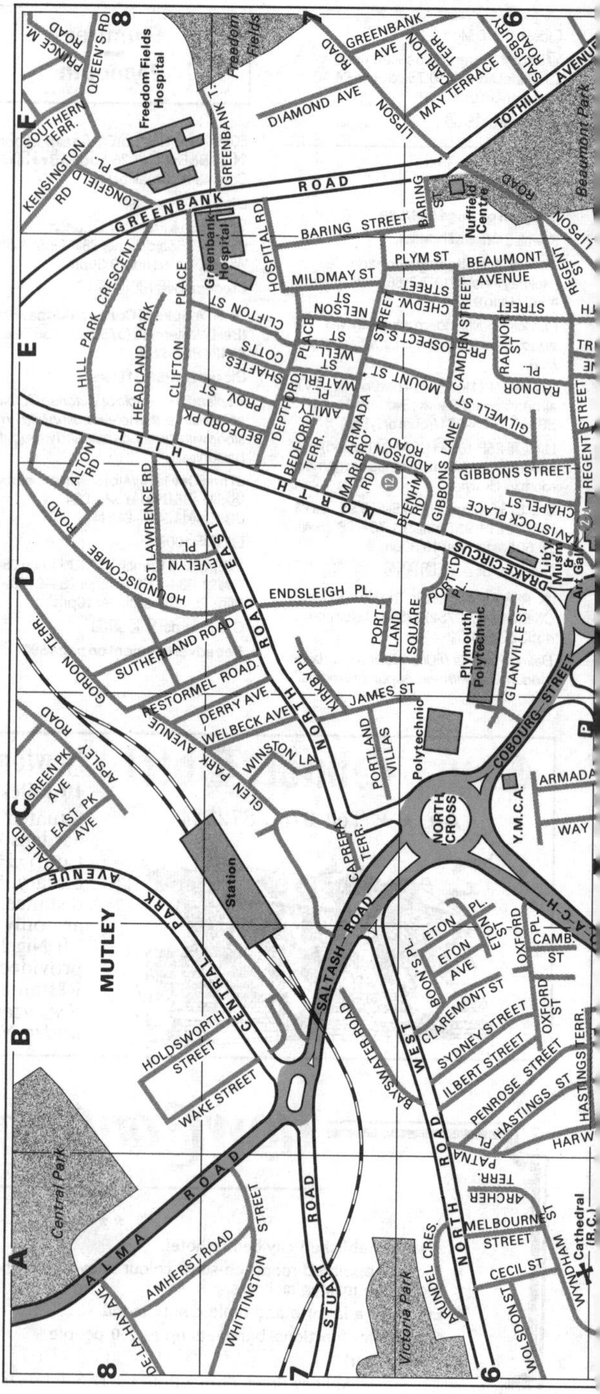

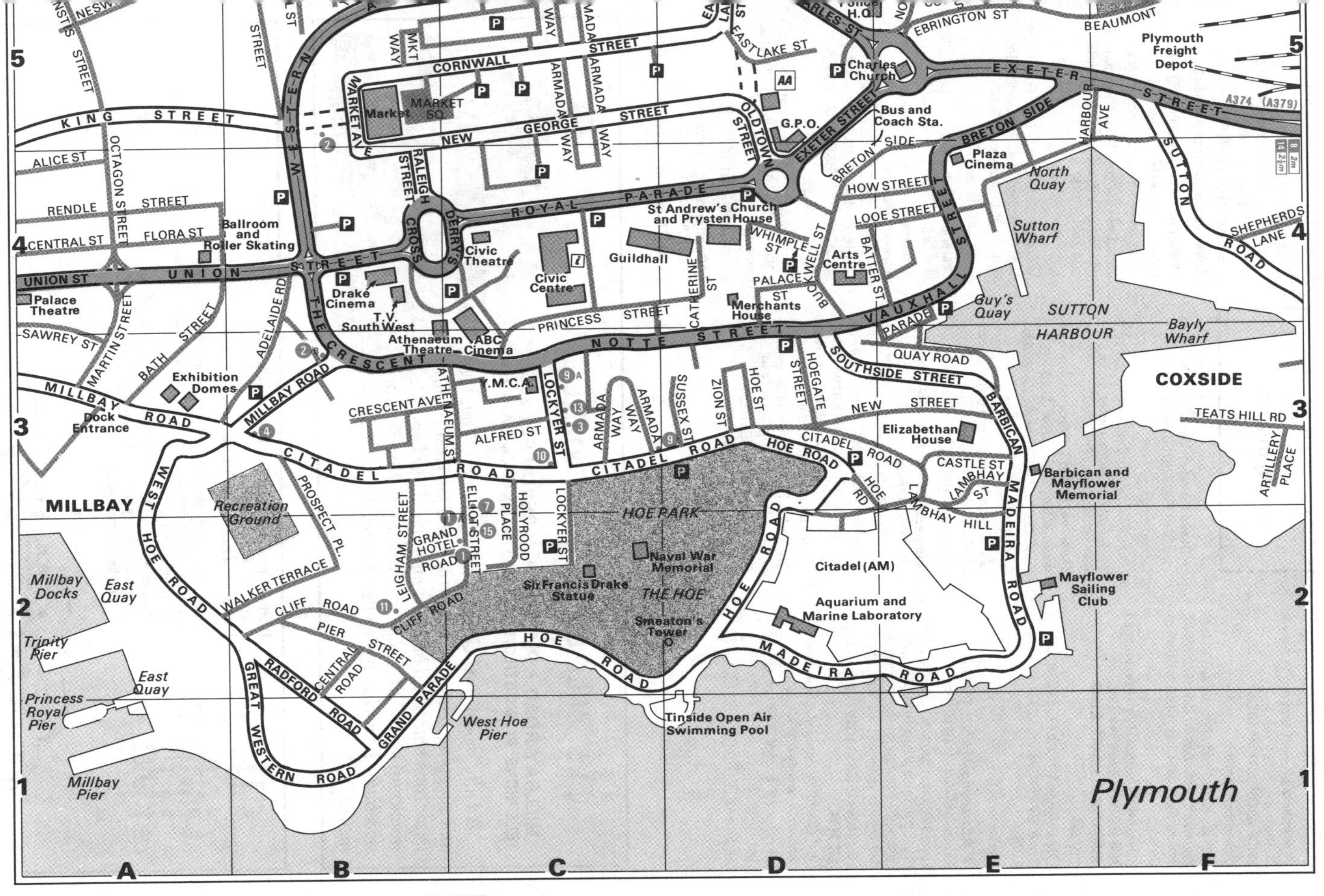
Plymouth
P
COXSIDE
SUTTON HARBOUR
MILLBAY
HOE PARK
THE HOE
Plymouth Freight Depot
Bayly Wharf
North Quay
Sutton Wharf
Guy's Quay
Barbican and Mayflower Memorial
Mayflower Sailing Club
Plaza Cinema
Bus and Coach Sta.
Charles Church
G.P.O.
Arts Centre
St Andrew's Church and Prysten House
Merchants House
Elizabethan House
Guildhall
Civic Centre
Civic Theatre
ABC Cinema
Athenaeum Theatre
T.V. South West
Drake Cinema
Y.M.C.A.
Citadel (AM)
Aquarium and Marine Laboratory
Naval War Memorial
Smeaton's Tower
Sir Francis Drake Statue
Tinside Open Air Swimming Pool
West Hoe Pier
Recreation Ground
Exhibition Domes
Ballroom and Roller Skating
Palace Theatre
Dock Entrance
East Quay
Millbay Docks
Trinity Pier
Princess Royal Pier
Millbay Pier
Market
MARKET SQ.
GRAND HOTEL
EXETER STREET
SUTTON ROAD
SHEPHERDS LANE
TEATS HILL RD
ARTILLERY PLACE
HARBOUR AVE
BRETON SIDE
EBRINGTON ST
BEAUMONT
VAUXHALL STREET
QUAY ROAD
PARADE
SOUTHSIDE STREET
BARBICAN
MADEIRA ROAD
NEW STREET
CASTLE ST
LAMBHAY ST
LAMBHAY HILL
CITADEL ROAD
HOE ROAD
HOE RD
HOEGATE STREET
BATTER ST
HOW STREET
LOOE STREET
BUCKWELL ST
WHIMPLE ST
PALACE ST
OLDTOWN STREET
EAST LAKE ST
ROYAL PARADE
CATHERINE ST
NOTTE STREET
HOE ST
ZION ST
SUSSEX ST
ARMADA WAY
PRINCESS STREET
LOCKYER ST
ALFRED ST
HOLYROOD PLACE
ELLIOT STREET
ATHENAEUM ST
CRESCENT AVE
LEIGHAM STREET
CLIFF ROAD
PIER STREET
CENTRAL ROAD
GRAND PARADE
RADFORD ROAD
GREAT WESTERN ROAD
WEST HOE ROAD
WALKER TERRACE
PROSPECT PL.
MILLBAY ROAD
ADELAIDE RD
THE CRESCENT
DERRY'S CROSS
RALEIGH STREET
NEW GEORGE STREET
CORNWALL STREET
MKT WAY
MARKET AVE
WESTERN APPROACH
UNION STREET
UNION ST
KING STREET
OCTAGON STREET
FLORA ST
RENDLE STREET
CENTRAL ST
ALICE ST
SAWREY ST
MARTIN STREET
BATH STREET
A374
(A379)
A B C D E F
1 2 3 4 5

★ ★**Invicta** 11–12 Osborne Pl, Lockyer St, The Hoe
☎(0752) 664997 Plan **10** *C5*
Closed 2 wks Xmas
Well-appointed bedrooms are available at this recently-refurbished, city-centre hotel, those at the front facing "Drake's Bowling Green".
23rm(6🛁13🚿)(5fb) CTV in all bedrooms **T** ✗ ✱sB&Bfr£19 sB&B🛁🚿fr£25 dB&Bfr£28 dB&B🛁🚿fr£35 **B**
CTV 4🚗
🍷Mainly grills **V** ☕ 🍵 Tea £1–£1.50 Dinner £6–£10 Wine £5.25 Last dinner 9.30pm
Credit cards 1 3

★ ★***Strathmore*** Elliot St, The Hoe (Consort) ☎(0752) 662101 Plan **15** *C2*
Linked Victorian houses located near the Hoe incorporate attractive public rooms, canopied restaurant and basement disco; the hotel is popular with business people.
55rm(40🛁15🚿)(3fb) CTV in all bedrooms ®**T** ✗ **B**
Lift ☾ CTV 6P Disco nightly Live music & dancing twice wkly *xmas*
🍷English & French **V** ☕ 🍵 Last dinner 10pm
Credit cards 1 2 3 5

Plymouth

★**Drake** 1 Windsor Villas, Lockyer St, The Hoe ☎(0752) 229730 Plan **3** *C3*
Closed Xmas
Soundly-appointed hotel offering personal service by the resident owner, within walking distance of The Hoe.
14rm(1🛁2🚿)(4fb) CTV in all bedrooms ✱sB&B£16–£18 sB&B🛁🚿£20–£25 dB&B£27–£29 dB&B🛁🚿£30–£35 **B**
CTV 10P 🚌
🍷Mainly grills ☕ ✱Lunch £6.70alc Dinner £6.70alc Wine £4.50 Last dinner 8.30pm
Credit cards 1 2 3

★**Imperial** Lockyer St, The Hoe ☎(0752) 227311 Plan **9A** *C3*
Closed 25–31 Dec
This detached Victorian hotel near the Hoe has pleasant public rooms where a log fire burns in winter. Friendly, attentive service is given by proprietors and staff.
22rm(2🛁14🚿)(5fb) CTV in all bedrooms ® in 2 bedrooms ✗ sB&B£18–£19 sB&B🛁🚿£24–£25 dB&B£34 dB&B🛁🚿£38–£39 **B**
CTV 15P 1🚗 🚌 👪

☕ 🍵 Bar lunch £2–£3 Tea 60p–£1 Dinner £8.50–£8.95 Wine £4.75 Last dinner 8.15pm
Credit cards 1 2 3 5 Ⓥ
See advertisement on page 592

★**Merchantman** Addison Rd ☎(0752) 669870 Plan **12** *D7*
Quiet, small friendly hotel in city centre.
29rm(6🛁4🚿)(3fb) CTV in all bedrooms ® sB&B£15–£18 sB&B🛁🚿£24 dB&B£30 dB&B🛁🚿£35 **B**
☾ CTV 5P
🍷English & French **V** ☕ 🍵 🚭 Lunch £2alc Tea 50palc High Tea £2alc Dinner £8alc Wine £4.35 Last dinner 9.15pm
Credit cards 1 2 3 Ⓥ

★**Merlin** 2 Windsor Villas, Lockyer St, The Hoe ☎(0752) 228133 Plan **13** *C3*
A commercial and tourist hotel close to the Hoe and city centre.
24rm(11🚿)(5fb) CTV in all bedrooms sB&B£16–£16.50 sB&B🚿£22–£22.50 dB&B£32–£33 dB&B🚿£32–£33
CTV 15P 3🚗 🚌
🍷English & French **V** ☕ Lunch £7alc Tea £2 Dinner £6–£6.50&alc Wine £4.95 Last dinner 9pm
Credit cards 1 2 3 5

○**Copthorne** Armada Way
☎(0752) 224161
135🛁🚿 Expected to open January 1987

P

Invicta Hotel ★★

11/12 OSBORNE PLACE,
LOCKYER STREET
THE HOE
PLYMOUTH PL1 2PU
Tel: (0752) 664997

This modernised, licenced, family-run hotel and conference suite, is directly opposite the gateway to the world famous Plymouth Hoe and is also in direct line of a minutes walk from the City Centre and historical Barbican. The Hotel is also ideally suited to travellers using Brittany Ferries.

- ★ 23 bedrooms, 19 with private facilities, Colour TV, telephone. C/Heating in all rooms.
- ★ Excellent restaurant food.
- ★ Licensed Bar & Lounge.
- ★ Private conference or party suite with bar for 10 - 100 Persons.
- ★ Garage Parking.

For full Colour Brochure & Tariff — Telephone (0752) 664997 or write to 'Invicta Hotel'.

Strathmore Hotel

★★★

- ★ Located on the Historic Plymouth Hoe.
- ★ 59 bedrooms all with bath/shower en-suite.
- ★ All rooms have colour television, telephone, radio and intercom.
- ★ Jesters Restaurant is renowned for the quality of the food and high standard of service.
- ★ Celebration Suite excellent conference and banqueting facilities for up to 100 persons.

Elliott Street, The Hoe, Plymouth PL1 2PP Tel: (0752) 662101

P

★

Small comfortable hotel run by resident proprietors. Ideally situated on Plymouth Hoe within easy walking distance of theatre, cinemas, main shopping centre and sea front. Restaurant and bar open every evening.

Private car park

Weekend bargain breaks Oct-May

Lockyer Street, The Hoe, Plymouth
Telephone: Plymouth (0752) 229730

❀ ✕ **Chez Nous** 13 Frankfort Gate ☎ (0752) 266793 Plan **2** *B5*

Small, typically French style restaurant in the modern part of the city. The interesting, freshly prepared dishes are listed daily on a blackboard and are carefully explained by the owner. The menu price is fixed and offers very good value for money.

Closed Sun, Mon, 10 days Feb, 10 days Sep & Bank Hols

French 28 seats ✱ Lunch fr£15&alc Dinner fr£15&alc Wine £6.50 Last dinner 10.30pm

Credit cards 1 2 3 5

✕ **Clouds** 102 Tavistock Pl ☎ (0752) 262567 Plan **2A** *D6*

A small basement restaurant with a relaxed and comfortable atmosphere where guests can make their selection from the carefully cooked dishes on a short but imaginative à la carte menu. Friendly service and good value help to make the restaurant very popular locally.

Closed Sun & Mon Lunch not served Sat

English & French **V** 35 seats ✱ Lunch £4.50alc Dinner £12alc Wine £5.50 Last dinner 10pm

Credit cards 1 2 3 5

POCKLINGTON
Humberside
Map **8** SE84

★★ **Feathers** Market Sq ☎ (07592) 3155 Due to change to (0759) 303155

Traditional three-storey coaching inn in the market town.

6rm(5 1) Annexe: 6 (1fb) 1 CTV in all bedrooms Ⓡ ✱ sB&B£23—£25 sB&B £23—£25 dB&B £36—£38

CTV 60P 6 xmas

✱ Lunch fr£4.75&alc Dinner fr£5.95&alc Wine £3.95 Last dinner 9.30pm

Credit cards 1 2 3 5 Ⓥ

POLKERRIS
Cornwall
Map **2** SX05

✕ ***Rashleigh Inn*** (Rashleigh Room) ☎ Par (072681) 3991

Well-appointed dining room of the 'Inn on the Beach'.

Closed Sun—Thu (end Oct—Etr) Lunch not served (buffet only)

V 24 seats Last dinner 9pm 160P Live music Sat

POLMONT
Central *Stirlingshire*
Map **11** NS97

★★★ **Inchyra Grange** Grange Rd (InterHotel) ☎ (0324) 711911 Telex no 777693

Closed 1—4 Jan

A converted mansion with a modern bedroom wing is situated north of the M9 between Junctions 4 and 5.

30 CTV in all bedrooms Ⓡ **T** sB&B £39.50—£45 dB&B £55—£61

☾ 150P ✿ Live music & dancing Sat (except Jun—Aug) Cabaret Sat (except Jun—Aug)

Scottish & French **V** Lunch £7&alc Tea 75p High Tea £5.50alc Dinner £9.50&alc Wine £5.25 Last dinner 9.15pm

Credit cards 1 2 3 5 Ⓥ

POLPERRO
Cornwall
Map **2** SX25

★ **Claremont** ☎ (0503) 72241

Closed mid Nov—Etr

Small personal hotel in an elevated position, overlooking the picturesque village of Polperro.

10rm(4) sB&B£14.50 dB&Bfr£26 dB&B fr£31

P

CTV 16P(charge) nc 4yrs

Lunch fr£4 Dinner fr£7 Last dinner 7pm

✕Kitchen at Polperro Fish Na Bridge ☎(0503) 72780

An intimate, cottage style restaurant, personally run and offering good food.

Closed Mon, Sun—Thu (Winter) & Sun (Spring & Autumn) Lunch not served

English & French **V** 22 seats Dinner £7.25—£10.50 Wine £5.95 Last dinner 9.30pm

Credit cards 1 2 3 5

POLZEATH
Cornwall
Map **2** SW97

★★Pentire Rocks ☎ Trebetherick (020886) 2213

The chalet-style hotel has a bedroom extension and busy bistro restaurant.

16rm(1 12)(3fb) TV in 3 bedrooms CTV in 10 bedrooms ® sB&B£13—£15 sB&B £13—£15 dB&B£24—£28 dB&B £24—£28

CTV 30P pool *xmas*

V Lunch £4.50 Tea £1.25—£1.50 Dinner £8.50—£9&alc Wine £3 Last dinner 9.30pm

Credit cards 1 2 3 Ⓥ

Polperro — Poole

PONTERWYD
Dyfed
Map **6** SN78

★★Dyffryn Castell ☎(097085) 237

Set on the A44, this historic coaching inn promotes a cosy, friendly atmosphere and commendably high food standards. In an elevated position amid beautiful scenery, it is within easy reach of the famous Devil's Bridge Falls and the Vale of Rheidol Narrow Gauge Railway.

7rm(2 1)(5fb) CTV in 4 bedrooms ® S% sB&B£15.95 sB&B £16.95 dB&B£23.90 dB&B £25.90

CTV 60P games room *xmas*

French **V** S% Lunch £4.50—£7.95&alc Tea 75p—£1.50 High Tea £2.95—£7.95 Dinner £2.95—£7.95&alc Wine £4.95 Last dinner 10pm

Credit cards 1 3 Ⓥ

POOLE
Dorset
Map **4** SZ09
For hotel locations and additional hotels see **Bournemouth**

★★★★Hospitality Inn The Quay (Mount Charlotte) ☎(0202) 671200 Telex no 418374

The modern-style hotel on the quayside affords pleasant views over Poole Harbour and is popular with business clients.

68rm(65 3)CTV in all bedrooms ® **T** sB&B fr£47.25 dB&B fr£57.75

Lift 150P CFA *xmas*

Lunch fr£10 Tea fr£2.50 Dinner fr£12 Last dinner 9.30pm

Credit cards 1 2 3 4 5 Ⓥ

★★★Antelope High St (Whitbread) ☎(0202) 672029

An original coaching inn stands at the centre of the town yet only a few hundred yards from the quay. Though it dates back to the 15th century, its interior has been carefully updated and refurbished so that it provides very comfortable, well-appointed bedrooms and a restaurant which offers a good menu choice. Service throughout the hotel is by friendly, attentive staff.

21rm(19 2)(1fb) 1 in 3 bedrooms CTV in all bedrooms ® **T** sB&B fr£35 dB&B fr£45

CTV 10P *xmas* →

V Lunch £6—£9.50&alc Tea 75p High Tea £2 Dinner £9.50&alc Wine £5.10 Last dinner 10pm

Credit cards 1 2 3 5

★★★**Dolphin** High St ☎ (0202) 673612 Telex no 417205

Located in the new shopping complex, within walking distance of the quay and the harbour.

68rm(54→13⋒) 1 CTV in all bedrooms ®T sB&B£19—£25 sB&B→⋒£19—£36 dB&B→⋒£33—£48 B

Lift ☾ 50P Disco nightly

V Lunch £4.25—£6.25 Tea 65p—£2.50 Dinner £8.50—£11.25 Wine £4.50 Last dinner 9.30pm

Credit cards 1 2 3 4 5

★★★***Harbour Heights*** 73 Haven Rd, Sandbanks ☎ (0202) 707272

A large modern hotel with harbour views.

49rm(34→13⋒)(1fb) CTV in all bedrooms ®T B

Lift ☾ 84P Live music & dancing 4 nights wkly *xmas*

English & French V Last dinner 9.30pm

Credit cards 1 2 3 5

★★★***Salterns*** 38 Salterns Way, Lilliput ☎ (0202) 707321 Telex no 41259

This unusual hotel, set beside the Marina, houses the yacht club bar. Very comfortable bedrooms are complemented by a small, first-floor lounge with views over the harbour and a compact, intimate restaurant.

10→ CTV in all bedrooms ®T

☾ 15P squash snooker *xmas*

English & French Last dinner 10pm

Credit cards 1 2 3 5

P

★★★**Mansion House Hotel**
(see red star box top of next column)

★★★**Sandbanks** Banks Rd, Sandbanks ☎ (0202) 707377

Closed Jan—Feb

Family holiday hotel on the Sandbanks peninsula, with sea views to one side, and Poole harbour on the other.

115rm(83→10⋒) CTV in all bedrooms ® T sB&B→⋒£24—£31 dB&B→⋒£48—£62 B

Lift ☾ CTV 200P CFA (heated) sauna bath solarium gymnasium Disco twice wkly (in summer) *xmas*

English & French V S% Lunch £7 Tea £1 Dinner £8 Wine £4.25 Last dinner 8.30pm

Credit cards 1 2 3 5

See advertisement under Bournemouth

★★**Seawitch** 47 Haven Rd, Canford Cliffs ☎ (0202) 707697 Westbourne & Branksome plan **73** *A1*

RS 25 Dec—5 Jan

The pleasant hotel stands close to Sandbanks, between Bournemouth and Poole. Its attractive restaurant offers a good range of well-prepared dishes, and service is pleasant.

9rm(7→2⋒)(2fb) CTV in all bedrooms ®T S% sB&B→⋒£22.45—£30.25 dB&B→⋒£32.75—£44 B

35P

International V S% Lunch £5.45—£7.95&alc Dinner £12alc Wine £5.45 Last dinner 9.45pm

Credit cards 1 2 3

★★★

★★★MANSION HOUSE HOTEL, POOLE

Thames St ☎ (0202) 685666 Telex no 41495

Closed 24 Dec—10 Jan

Quietly situated off Poole's busy quay near St James' Church, this house was built about 200 years ago. It has a classical facade behind which lies the fine hotel which has been created by the Leonard family. An elegant sweeping staircase leads to the entrance hall. On this floor is the Benjamin Lester room for breakfast and the charming drawing room, decorated with panache. Individually decorated bedrooms are well and attractively done, comfortable as well as being equipped with all those things our members have come to expect in Red Star hotels and which include a glass of sherry, fruit, flowers and books to name just a few. On the lower ground floor are the other public areas; reception, a bar in more rustic style, and another smarter panelled one as an ante-room to the restaurant. In this well appointed room are several fixed price and à la carte menus. Good raw materials are soundly cooked and full use is made of the locally caught shellfish. Non residents are charged an extra £3 for meals, and we have received some complaints about this. While we cannot dictate to hotel keepers about how they manage their hotels, we do deprecate this irritating habit. However, that aside, the enthusiastic owners have improved the whole hotel immeasurably and imbued their staff with the will to give polite and friendly service.

19→⋒ CTV in all bedrooms T S% sB&B→⋒£49—£53.50 dB&B→⋒£67—£71 B

70P Live music & dancing mthly nc 12yrs

English & French S% Lunch £9.75—£10.35&alc Tea £1—£3 Dinner £14.75&alc Wine £6.50 Last dinner 10pm

Credit cards 1 2 3 5

See advertisement under Bournemouth

★**Fairlight** 1 Golf Links Rd, Broadstone (3m NW B3074) ☎ (0202) 694316

Closed 22 Dec—4 Jan

Quietly situated, this small, comfortable and friendly hotel offers a set dinner menu of quality.

10rm(6→1⋒) ✱sB&B£18 sB&B→⋒£20 dB&B£28 dB&B→⋒£32 B

CTV 10P

✱Bar lunch £1—£3 Dinner £8.50 Wine £4.95 Last dinner 7.30pm

Credit cards 1 3

✕✕**Le Chateau** 13 Haven Rd, Canford Cliffs ☎ (0202) 707400 Westbourne & Branksome plan **69** *A1*

An attractive small restaurant in Canford Cliffs, Le Chateau has delightful interior decor and furnishings. A warm welcome from the proprietor promises a good meal, and there is an interesting selection of dishes on the menu. Fresh ingredients are used, including vegetables in season, and the homemade patés and soups are good. The sauces are very fine and the desserts are excellent.

Closed Sun & Mon

French V 35 seats S% ✱Lunch £8.50—£9.50&alc Dinner £15alc Wine £5.50 Last dinner 10pm

Credit cards 1 2 3 5

✕✕**Warehouse** The Quay ☎ (0202) 677238

This first-floor restaurant stands on the quay, offering fine views of the harbour. Attentive and pleasant service enhances your comfort, while the extensive menu provides a fine selection of food with the emphasis on fresh fish dishes.

Closed Sun & 2 wks after Xmas Lunch not served Sat

French V 80 seats S% Lunch £7.95&alc Dinner £13.50alc Wine £5.50 Last dinner 10pm

Credit cards 1 2 3 5

✗**Gulliver's** 292 Sandbanks Rd, Lilliput ☎(0202) 708810

The restaurant is housed in a terraced, double-fronted property in a pleasant shopping area between Poole and Sandbanks. A short but interesting menu offers a good choice of dishes, well prepared from fresh ingredients; service is friendly and attentive, the atmosphere relaxed.

Closed Mon & 26 Dec Dinner not served Sun

French 36 seats Lunch fr£4.95&alc Dinner £12alc Wine £5.80 Last dinner 11pm

Credit cards [1] [3]

✗**Isabel's** 32 Station Rd, Lower Parkstone ☎(0202) 747885

On a corner site in a shopping centre between Bournemouth and Poole this double-fronted restaurant has a cosy, if somewhat dark, interior and mainly booth-style seating. A good range of well-prepared food can be enjoyed in a pleasant atmosphere.

Closed 25—26 Dec Lunch not served

English & French **V** 46 seats ✱Dinner £15alc Wine £5 Last dinner 10.30pm

Credit cards [1] [2] [3] [5]

✗**Rajpoot Tandoori** 69 High St ☎(0202) 676330

The terraced restaurant in the town centre has an attractive brick exterior with arched windows. Staff in authentic Indian dress offer attentive service, and the menu covers a wide range of well-known Indian dishes; some English food is available for the less adventurous.

English & Indian **V** 86 seats Lunch £3.75—£7.50 Dinner £5—£10 Wine £4.75 Last dinner 11.30pm

Credit cards [1] [2] [3] [5]

POOLEWE

Highland *Ross & Cromarty*
Map **14** NG88

★★**Pool House** ☎(044586) 272

Closed 15 Oct—Etr

Small friendly, family run tourist hotel.

13rm(5🛁1🚿) CTV in all bedrooms ® ✱sB&B£12.50—£15 dB&B£25—£30 dB&B🛁🚿£31—£36

20P

✱Lunch £3.50alc Tea fr60p High Tea £4.50alc Dinner £8—£9 Wine £3.85 Last dinner 8.30pm

Credit card [3]

★**Poolewe** ☎(044586) 241

This modest but friendly, family-run, Highland hostelry provides reasonably-priced food at all times.

5rm(1fb) CTV in all bedrooms ® ✱sB&B£12.50—£15 dB&B£25—£30

CTV P

✱Lunch £4alc Tea £1.50 High Tea £3—£4.50 Dinner £8alc Wine £4.35 Last dinner 9pm

Credit cards [1] [3]

POOLEY BRIDGE

Cumbria
Map **12** NY42

★★★

★★★ SHARROW BAY, POOLEY BRIDGE

Sharrow Bay (1¾m S unclass rd) (Relais et Châteaux) ☎(08536) 301

Closed early Dec—early Mar

Situated in its own delightful gardens on Ullswater, with spectacular views across the lake, this greystone house, in a style reminiscent of the Italian Lakes, offers the ultimate in gracious living. Francis Coulson and Brian Sacks have owned the hotel for 37 years and they have had time to perfect their operation. Richly furnished with sumptuous seating and damask drapes, adorned with antiques and porcelain, it is bright with flowers, and provided with plenty of books and magazines. The bedrooms, whether in the main building, Bankhouse with its own breakfast and sitting room or the other annexes, are all up to the same luxurious standards, although many of the single rooms are small. But as much as anything it is the food that people enjoy here most, the hearty breakfasts and afternoon teas as well as the more ambitious luncheons and dinners. The cooking shows some modern influences but it is substantially classically based with some British dishes included on the menus, culminating in the six course dinner offering plenty of choice. The best of produce is used and it shows in the appetising dishes produced under the supervision of Brian Sacks. The avuncular Francis Coulson looks after the meals and all his staff provide courteous, formal service.

12rm(8🛁) Annexe: 18rm(16🛁2🚿) CTV in all bedrooms ® in 6 bedrooms
T S% sB&B£59(incl dinner)
sB&B🛁🚿£60—£75(incl dinner)
dB&B£110—£118(incl dinner)
dB&B🛁🚿£130—£170(incl dinner)

25P 2 nc13yrs

V S% Lunch £17.50—£19.50 Tea £5 Dinner £27.50 Wine £4.75 Last dinner 8.45pm

★ ★**Swiss Chalet Inn** ☎(08536) 215

Closed Sun & Mon (Nov—Mar)

An inn full of Swiss charm and character offers comfortable and well-appointed bedrooms and serves excellent Continental and English food.

6rm(2⇌4⋒) 1⊟ CTV in all bedrooms ® ✱sB&B⇌⋒£22 dB&B⇌⋒£40 B

55P ✿ Live music twice wkly in summer *xmas*

Continental ⊕ ☕ ✱Tea £1.80—£2.65 High Tea £2.50—£6.50 Wine £5.80 Last dinner 10pm

Credit cards 1 3

POOL-IN-WHARFEDALE
West Yorkshire
Map **8** SE24

✿✿×××**POOL COURT, POOL-IN-WHARFEDALE**

Pool Bank ☎ Arthington (0532) 842288

(Rosettes awarded for dinner only)

Michael and Hanni Gill's chic restaurant is looking up! There cannot be a more enthusiastic restaurateur in the country, always researching here and abroad looking for ideas to incorporate on his enterprising menu of four courses priced according to the main course chosen. It is stylishly decorated, particularly the bar and lounge, in attractive pastel shades, and now it has four luxurious bedrooms. Mr Gill and his team of young people look after you very well; they have succeeded in combining formal service with a warm and cheerful friendliness. Take an aperitif with appetising little savouries while you choose your meal and then proceed to the elegantly appointed dining rooms to eat. From home-made rolls to the petits fours served with the coffee, you will see the excellence of his ingredients cooked with panache by Chef Melvin Jordan and his enthusiastic brigade. We would like to see more flavour in his mousselines and a depth of character in the sauces, but overall we think the improvement in the standards justify two rosettes. Dishes like the scallops in limpid lobster jelly showed a delicacy of touch that is unusual. Other dishes to please were a daily fish dish of mousse of lobster, salmon and lemon sole in a delicious sauce, a timbale of veal with kidneys, and a fillet of tender beef with a charlotte of thinly sliced carrots and courgettes filled with zestful durelles and accompanied with a refined red wine sauce. Puddings have always been a delight, whether the treacle tart enlivened with tangy orange and lemon juice, the parfaits, or the famous amaretti schokoladentorte. With a list of 200 wines you will easily find something to complement your meal.

Closed Sun & Mon, 2 wks July/Aug & 2 wks Xmas Lunch not served

V 65 seats Dinner £10&alc Wine £6.95 Last dinner 9.30pm 65P

Credit cards 1 2 3 5

Pooley Bridge — Porlock Weir

PORLOCK
Somerset
Map **3** SS84

★ ★ *H* **Oaks** Doverhay ☎ (0643) 862265

There are fine views of the Bristol Channel from this hotel, standing in its own grounds and offering accommodation in peaceful comfort. An imaginative range of freshly prepared food is available.

11rm(3⇌8⋒)(2fb) CTV in all bedrooms S% ✱sB&B⇌⋒fr£23 dB&B⇌⋒fr£36 B

12P ⇌ ✿ *xmas*

British & French ⊕ ☕ S% ✱Lunch fr£5.95 Tea fr70p Dinner fr£8.75 Wine £4.25 Last dinner 8.45pm

Credit cards 2 5 Ⓥ

★***Ship Inn*** High St ☎ (0643) 862507

RS Nov—Feb

Attractive, friendly, well-appointed, 13th century inn, and good food.

11rm(5⇌1⋒)(3fb) CTV in all bedrooms ® B

20P 2🚗 ✿

V ⊕ Last dinner 9pm

PORLOCK WEIR
Somerset
Map **3** SS84

★ ★**Anchor Hotel & Ship Inn**
☎ Porlock (0643) 862753

RS Nov—Feb

Ten yards from the picturesque harbour stands an attractive and comfortable hotel, part 15th century and thatched.

24rm(19⇌1⋒)(1fb) 1⊟ CTV in all bedrooms ® **T** S% sB&B£25—£30 sB&B⇌⋒£30—£36 dB&B£40—£46 dB&B⇌⋒£48—£56 B

25P ✿ *xmas*

French ⊕ ☕ S% Lunch £5.50—£7.95&alc Tea £1.50 High Tea £5—£7 Dinner £9.75&alc Wine £5.75 Last dinner 9.15pm

Credit cards 1 2 3

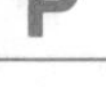

PORT APPIN
Strathclyde *Argyllshire*
Map **14** NM94

❀★★ AIRDS, PORT APPIN

☎ Appin (063173) 236
Closed Dec—Feb
(Rosette awarded for dinner only)

This tranquil haven, an early 18th century ferry inn, has views to match over the beautiful Lyne of Lorne, towards the Morven Hills, an aspect that can be enjoyed from the dining room and two sitting rooms. It is smoothly and proficiently run by the owners, Mr and Mrs Allen. He is mostly about the hotel to look after you with his team of charming, smiling girls in their plaid skirts, for whom nothing seems too much trouble. Apart from the comfortable sitting rooms there is a small bar and a larger public one where you can meet the locals. Bedrooms are not large but they are modern, spotlessly clean and comfortable. Mrs Allen supervises the kitchen with great skill and full use is made of the best quality local produce on the four course menu. It is a welcome change to sample adept cooking without the excesses met with in more pretentious establishments.

The long wine list is outstanding. In keeping with the peaceful environment there is no television. This hotel is a great favourite with our members.

15rm(8🛁3🚿)(1fb) sB&B£43(incl dinner) dB&B£86(incl dinner) dB&B🛁🚿£90(incl dinner)
30P ✿ nc5yrs
Bar lunch fr£2 Tea £2 Dinner £17 Wine £7 Last dinner 8pm
S%

PORT ASKAIG
Isle of Islay, Strathclyde *Argyllshire*
See **Islay, Isle of**

PORT DINORWIC
Gwynedd
Map **6** SH56

✕Sea Horse 20 Snowdon St ☎ (0248) 670546
The small, popular restaurant has a warmly informal atmosphere. Interesting and well-prepared dishes can be chosen from a sensible, short menu — but booking is essential.
Closed Sun, 1 wk Feb, 2 wks Oct, Xmas Day, Boxing Day & New Years Day Lunch not served
French 45 seats Dinner £11.20alc Wine £5.35 Last dinner 9.30pm nc6yrs
Credit cards 1 3

PORT ELLEN
Isle of Islay Strathclyde *Argyllshire*
See **Islay, Isle of**

PORT ERIN
Isle of Man
See **Man, Isle of**

PORT GAVERNE
Cornwall
Map **2** SX08

★★Headlands ☎ Bodmin (0208) 880260
Closed Nov
Spectacularly positioned over a rock inlet, the hotel offers comfortable, recently refurbished bedrooms; meals may be taken in the dining room or in Slatters Bistro.
11rm(7🛁4🚿)(1fb) CTV in all bedrooms S% ✻sB&B🛁🚿£22.50—£25 dB&B🛁🚿£45—£50 B
35P ✿ sauna bath *xmas*
English & French **V** S% ✻Lunch fr95p&alc Tea fr70p High Tea fr95p Dinner fr£7.50&alc Wine £4.95 Last dinner 10pm
Credit cards 1 2 3 4
See advertisement on page 598

★★H Port Gaverne ☎ Bodmin (0208) 880244
Closed 11 Jan—27 Feb
Well appointed, friendly hotel nestled in a valley and next to the beach.
16🛁 Annexe:3🛁 CTV in 2 bedrooms ® in 2 bedrooms **T** S% sB&B🛁£21.50—£27.50 dB&B🛁£43—£55 B
☾ CTV 25P 2 (£1 per night) *xmas*
English & French **V** S% Lunch £1.25—£3&alc Tea 50p Dinner £9.50&alc Wine £3.95 Last dinner 9.30pm
Credit cards 1 2 3 5 Ⓥ
See advertisement on page 598

PORTHCAWL
Mid Glamorgan
Map **3** SS87

★★★Seabank The Promenade (Whitbread) ☎ (065671) 2261
This company-owned, character hotel occupies a commanding position overlooking the Bristol Channel. A recent major refurbishment has created comfortable modern bedrooms, spacious public rooms and a small leisure complex.
64rm(42🛁)(6fb) CTV in all bedrooms ® **T** sB&B£30 sB&B🛁£40—£45 dB&B£38 dB&B🛁£48—£53 B →

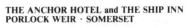

Lift ☾ 150P ✿ sauna bath solarium gymnasium *xmas*

English & French V ♈ ☕ Lunch £6.50&alc Tea 85p—£2.50 High Tea £4.50—£6 Dinner £8.75&alc Wine £5.25 Last dinner 10pm

Credit cards 1 2 3 5

★★**Glenaub** 50 Mary St ☎ (065671) 8242

Small personally managed hotel with comfortable bedrooms and commendable food standards.

15 ➡ CTV in all bedrooms T ✈

Porthcawl

CTV 10P ⛟ *xmas*

V ♈ ☕ Last dinner 9.30pm

Credit cards 1 2 5

★★B **Maid of Sker** West Rd (towards Kenfig), Nottage (2m NW off A4106) ☎ (065671) 2172

Small modern hotel located conveniently for the M4 in village of Nottage.

10 ➡ (10fb) CTV in all bedrooms ® ✈ B

100P ✿ Disco Sat

V ♈ Last dinner 9.45pm

Credit cards 1 2 3

★B **Brentwood** 37—41 Mary St ☎ (065671) 2725

Small personally run friendly hotel, with comfortable modern bedrooms.

25rm (17 ➡ 2 ⋔) (4fb) CTV in 17 bedrooms ® B

⅟ CTV 15P *xmas*

Last dinner 10.30pm

Credit cards 1 2 3

P

★Rose & Crown Nottage (2m N B4283) (Berni) ☎ (065671) 4850

This small, friendly, character inn is very popular, being conveniently positioned between beach and M4 link road. The stone-flagged floors of the bars form an effective contrast to the modern comforts provided by the bedrooms.

7🛁 CTV in all bedrooms Ⓡ ✱sB&B🛁£23 dB&B🛁£35 B

80P

✱Lunch £9.10alc Dinner £6.50—£7.50 Wine £4.60

Credit cards [1] [2] [3] [5] Ⓥ

★Seaways 26—30 Mary St ☎ (065671) 3510

Small, comfortable, commercial style hotel, family owned and managed.

16rm(2🛁4🚿)(1fb) CTV in 12 bedrooms Ⓡ T sB&B£15—£23 sB&B🛁🚿£23 dB&B£27—£35 dB&B🛁🚿£35 B

CTV pool table nc 5yrs

Lunch £2.20—£3.20&alc Dinner £5.75—£9.50&alc Wine £4.80 Last dinner 9pm

Credit cards [1] [2] [3] [5] Ⓥ

Porthcawl — Port Isaac

PORTHLEVEN
Cornwall
Map **2** SW62

★Torre Vean Manor ☎ Helston (0326) 562412

Secluded small hotel offering friendly atmosphere and good, interesting food.

6rm(2fb) sB&B£12—£15 dB&B£24—£30

CTV 8P

English & French **V** Lunch £2.50—£4 Dinner £5.75&alc Wine £4.40 Last dinner 8.30pm

Credit cards [1] [3]

PORTHMADOG
Gwynedd
Map **6** SH53

★★Royal Sportsman High St (Trusthouse Forte) ☎ (0766) 2015

Centrally situated two-storey hotel.

16rm(15🛁)(4fb) CTV in all bedrooms Ⓡ sB&B🛁£42.50 dB&B£48 dB&B🛁£56 B

28P

Last dinner 9pm

Credit cards [1] [2] [3] [4] [5]

★★Tyddyn Llwyn Black Rock Rd ☎ (0766) 2205

Modern hotel in rural setting.

9rm(8🛁1🚿)(1fb) Ⓡ S% sB&B🛁🚿fr£16.50 dB&B🛁🚿fr£33

CTV 30P

Lunch £4—£5 Tea £2.50—£3 High Tea £2.50—£3 Dinner £4—£7&alc Wine £4.55 Last dinner 9.30pm

Credit cards [1] [3]

PORT ISAAC
Cornwall
Map **2** SW98

See also **Port Gaverne** and **Trelights**

★★Castle Rock ☎ Bodmin (0208) 880300

Closed Nov—Etr

Set in an elevated position with commanding sea views, this hotel is close to the beach and the town centre.

19rm(11🛁3🚿)(3fb) CTV in 7 bedrooms Ⓡ sB&B£14.50—£17.30 sB&B🛁🚿£15.50—£21 dB&B£29—£34.60 dB&B🛁🚿£31—£42 B

CTV 20P

V Bar lunch £3.20—£4.70 Tea 60p Dinner £9.50 Wine £4.25 Last dinner 8.30pm

Credit cards [1] [5] Ⓥ

See advertisement on page 600

P

★★**Slipway** The Harbour Front (Guestaccom/Exec Hotel) ☎ (0208) 880264

Closed Nov—mid Mar

11rm(5⋔)(1fb) sB&B£16—£21 dB&B£32—£36 dB&B⋔£35—£42 B

CTV 5P 6

English & French Bar lunch £4.90alc Dinner £8.95&alc Wine £4.25 Last dinner 9.30pm

Credit cards 2 5 V

Port Isaac — Portland

PORTLAND
Dorset
Map **3** SY67

★★★**Portland Heights** Yeates Corner (Best Western) ☎ (0305) 821361 Telex no 418493

Modern style hotel with good amenities overlooking Chesil Beach.

67rm(66⋔1⋔) CTV in all bedrooms ® T sB&B⋔£40—£45 dB&B⋔£52.50—£65 B

160P CFA (heated) squash sauna bath solarium gymnasium hairdressing salon

English & French V Lunch £11alc Tea £1.25—£3 Dinner £10.25—£11&alc Wine £4.95 Last dinner 9.30pm

Credit cards 1 2 3 5 V

★★***Pennsylvania Castle*** Pennsylvania Rd ☎ (0305) 820561

An 18th century mock castle standing in grounds overlooking the sea.

P

12rm(5➡5⋒)CTV in all bedrooms ®ℝ
30P ⛟ ✿ *xmas*
🍷International **V** ♡ ☕ Last dinner 10pm
Credit cards 1 2 3 5

PORTLOE
Cornwall
Map **2** SW93

★★*HB* **Lugger** (Inter Hotel) ☎ Truro (0872) 501322
Closed mid Nov—early Mar
This charming old inn on the harbour edge has delightful small bedrooms (some of them in an annexe) refurbished in a Victorian "olde worlde" style.
20rm(14➡5⋒)CTV in all bedrooms ®✈
sB&B➡⋒£31—£39.50
dB&B➡⋒£62—£79 ℝ
20P ⛟ sauna bath solarium nc 12yrs
🍷English & Continental **V** ♡ ☕ Bar lunch £5.25alc Tea £1.75—£2.50 Dinner £10.95—£12.50 Wine £4.40 Last dinner 9pm
Credit cards 1 2 3 5 Ⓥ
See advertisement under St Mawes

PORTPATRICK
Dumfries & Galloway *Wigtownshire*
Map **10** NX05

★★★**Fernhill** (Exec Hotel) ☎ (077681) 220
Detached mansion with extensions, set in elevated position overlooking village and harbour.
11rm(9➡) Annexe: 4rm(1➡3⋒)(1fb) CTV in all bedrooms ®S% sB&Bfr£20
sB&B➡⋒fr£23 dB&Bfr£37
dB&B➡⋒fr£40 ℝ
45P ✿ ⌂ *xmas*
🍷Scottish & French **V** ♡ Bar lunch fr£2&alc Tea 75p Dinner fr£11&alc Wine £4 Last dinner 10pm
Credit cards 1 2 3 5 Ⓥ

✿★★♣ *HBL* **Knockinaam Lodge** (2m S on unclass road) (Pride of Britain) ☎ (077681) 471
Closed 9 Jan—14 Mar
Delightful country lodge whose lawns stretch down to a secluded sandy cove. The new owners, M and Mme Frichor offer a relaxed peaceful atmosphere with pretty bedrooms, while Chef Galmiche, with his modern style of French cuisine, maintains the hotel's reputation for fine food.
10➡(2fb) CTV in all bedrooms **T**
sB&B➡£42—£80
dB&B➡£64—£120
25P ⛟ ✿ croquet ⌂
🍷French ☕ Lunch £1.50—£6.50&alc Tea £1.50 High Tea £6 Dinner £13—£21&alc Wine £6.40 Last dinner 9.30pm
Credit cards 1 2 3 5

★★**Portpatrick** (Mount Charlotte) ☎ (077681) 333
RS Nov—Etr
Large clifftop resort hotel with good amenities for families with children.
60rm(31➡1⋒)(5fb) CTV in all bedrooms
sB&B➡⋒fr£30 dB&B➡⋒fr£49.75
Lift ☾ 50P CFA ✿ ⛆(heated) ⛳ 🎾(grass) snooker ⌂ ♿ *xmas*
🍷English & French **V** ♡ ☕ Lunch £4.50—£5 Tea £1—£2.25 Dinner £9.25—£9.50 Wine £5.50 Last dinner 9.30pm
Credit cards 1 2 3 5 Ⓥ

★*H* **Mount Stewart** South Cres ☎ (077681) 291
Two-storey stone house set on a hillside overlooking the harbour.
8rm(5fb) ® sB&B£12.75—£16
dB&B£25.50—£32
CTV 25P ⛟
♡ Lunch £1.95—£3 Dinner fr£6.75&alc Wine £4.50 Last dinner 9pm

PORT QUIN
Cornwall
Map **2** SW98

★***Trevose House*** ☎ Bodmin (0208) 880593
Closed last 2 wks Nov & last 2 wks Jan
Completely renovated Victorian house specialising in fresh local food.
6rm(2⋒)(2fb) ℝ
CTV 15P ⛟ ✿ nc 10yrs *xmas*
🍷International **V** ♡ Last dinner 8.45pm

PORTREE
Isle of Skye, Highland *Inverness-shire*
See **Skye, Isle of**

PORTSCATHO
Cornwall
Map **2** SW83

★★★**Rosevine** Porthcurnick Beach ☎ (087258) 206
Closed Nov—Etr
Comfortably appointed country hotel in secluded setting with good sea views.
16rm(10➡1⋒)(1fb) CTV available in bedrooms **T** S% *sB&B£19.50—£21.45
dB&B£39—£42.90
dB&B➡⋒£39—£42.90 ℝ
CTV 40P ⛟ ✿ ⌂
🍷English, French & Italian **V** ♡ ☕ S% *Bar lunch 85p—£3.40 Tea 65p Dinner £11.55 Wine £4.05 Last dinner 8.45pm
Credit cards 1 2 3 5 Ⓥ
See advertisement under Truro

★★*H* **Gerrans Bay** Gerrans ☎ (087258) 338
Closed Nov—Etr (except Xmas)
Small hotel in the heart of the Roseland Peninsula with rural coastal views.
15rm(11➡)(2fb) ®S%
sB&B£14.50—£17.50
sB&B➡£16.50—£19.50 dB&B£29—£35
dB&B➡£33—£39
CTV 16P ⛟ *xmas* →

P

☕ Bar lunch 70p—£3.50 Tea 70p—£1.50 Dinner £9.50—£11 Wine £4.60 Last dinner 8pm

Credit cards 1 2 3 V

★★ H ***Roseland House*** Rosevine ☎ (087258) 644

Closed Jan

Small, comfortable, friendly hotel in a commanding position with unrestricted views, standing in six acres with private beach.

19rm(8→1⫛)(4fb) 2 [four-poster] [dogs] B [no smoking] CTV 25P 3 [garage] [tennis] [garden] [fishing] nc5yrs *xmas*

V ☕ Last dinner 7.30pm

PORTSMOUTH & SOUTHSEA
Hampshire
Map **4** SZ69

★★★★ B **Holiday Inn** North Harbour (Holiday Inns) ☎ (0705) 383151 Telex no 86611

Very comfortable hotel with excellent leisure facilities.

170→⫛(76fb) CTV in all bedrooms **T** sB&B→⫛£60.55—£64.78 dB&B→⫛£78.55—£83.13 B

Lift ☾ ## 200P CFA [indoor pool](heated) squash snooker sauna bath solarium gymnasium Disco Mon, Wed, Fri & Sat [disabled] *xmas*

[restaurant] English & French **V** ☕ [no smoking] Lunch £11.95(incl wine)&alc Dinner £11.95&alc

Credit cards 1 2 3 4 5

★★★ **Crest** Pembroke Rd, Southsea (Crest) ☎ (0705) 827651 Telex no 83697

This functional modern hotel offers a choice of restaurants, smart, well-equipped bedrooms, compact bathrooms with showers, and some good sea views.

165→⫛(12fb) [no smoking] in 27 bedrooms CTV in all bedrooms ® **T** S% sB&B→⫛£59.50—£61.50 dB&B→⫛£75.50—£78.50 B

Lift ☾ ## 80P CFA

[restaurant] International **V** ☕ [no smoking] Lunch £9.25—£9.50&alc Dinner £12.75—£13.25&alc Wine £7 Last dinner 10pm

Credit cards 1 2 3 4 5

P

Portscatho — Portsmouth & Southsea

★★★ **Hospitality Inn** South Pde, Southsea (Mount Charlotte) ☎ (0705) 731281 Telex no 86719

The large sea-front hotel has spacious public rooms and some very well-appointed bedrooms.

115→⫛(8fb) CTV in all bedrooms ® **T** *sB&B→⫛fr£44.50 dB&B→⫛fr£57.75 B

Lift 50P *xmas*

[restaurant] English & French ☕ *Lunch fr£6.50&alc Tea fr75p High Tea £4 Dinner £7.75&alc Wine £5.50 Last dinner 9.45pm

Credit cards 1 2 3 5 V

★★★ **Pendragon** Clarence Pde, Southsea (Trusthouse Forte) ☎ (0705) 823201 Telex no 86376

Overlooking Southsea Common, this hotel has many modern facilities.

58rm(40→)(1fb) CTV in all bedrooms ® **T** sB&B£39.50 sB&B→£47.50 dB&B£57 dB&B→£65 B

Lift ☾ 4P 6 [garage] CFA [garden] *xmas*

☕ Last dinner 9pm

Credit cards 1 2 3 4 5

★★ B **Keppels Head** The Hard (Anchor) ☎ (0705) 833231 Telex no 858875

Well established modernised hotel with very limited lounge facilities. Some bedrooms enjoy views across the Solent. Close to Royal dockyard, I.O.W. ferry and Nelson's Victory.

25rm(16→9⫛)(4fb) [no smoking] in 5 bedrooms CTV in all bedrooms ® S% sB&B→⫛£43—£47 dB&B→⫛£53—£58 B

Lift ☾ 18P *xmas*

V ☕ Lunch £3.50—£8 Tea 60p—£1 Dinner £10alc Wine £5.75 Last dinner 9.30pm

Credit cards 1 2 3 4 5 V

★★ **Ocean** St Helen's Pde, Southsea ☎ (0705) 734233

Closed 24—31 Dec

Standing on the sea-front, with good views of the Solent, this comfortable, family-run hotel offers breakfasts which are served only in the bedrooms and good indoor leisure facilities.

48rm(16→)(4fb) CTV in all bedrooms ® **T** S% sB&B£25.50 sB&B→£29.50 dB&B£42.50 dB&B→£46.50

Lift CTV 30P [tennis] squash snooker sauna bath gymnasium

[restaurant] Mainly grills ☕ S% Bar lunch £2—£4 Dinner £7.50&alc Wine £3.75 Last dinner 10pm

Credit cards 1 3 V

✕ **Bistro Montparnasse** 103, Palmerston Rd, Southsea ☎ (0705) 816754

A small bistro brightly decorated and with a friendly informal atmosphere. Cooking is of a very good standard with a few specialities.

Closed Sun, 1st wk Jan & Bank Hols Lunch not served

[restaurant] English & French 40 seats Dinner £11.40alc Wine £5.80 Last dinner 11pm [parking]

Credit cards 1 2 3 5

✕ **Le Talisman** 123 High St ☎ (0705) 811303

Closed Sun & Mon Lunch not served Sat

[restaurant] French **V** 36 seats Lunch £15—£20alc Dinner £15—£20alc Wine £4.45 Last dinner 9.30pm [parking]

Credit cards 1 3 5

PORTSONACHAN
Strathclyde *Argyllshire*
Map **10** NN01

❀★★*H* **Portsonachan**
☎ Kilchrenan (08663) 224
Closed Dec—Feb except Xmas & New Year
(*Rosette awarded for dinner only*)
On the banks of the picturesque Loch Awe, the hotel is popular for fishing, providing simple but comfortable accommodation. It is noted for its outstanding hospitality and imaginative cooking.
18rm(6)(1fb) ® B
CTV P 2 ❀ *xmas*
Last dinner 9pm
Credit cards 1 3

PORT TALBOT
West Glamorgan
Map **3** SS79

★★★**Aberafan** Aberavon Seafront (Consort) ☎ (0639) 884949 Telex no 48222
Comfortable modern hotel overlooking the beach.
64(9fb) CTV in all bedrooms ®**T** S%
sB&B£33—£43 dB&B£51—£61 B
Lift ☾ CTV 150P CFA Live music & dancing Fri & Sat *xmas* ♿
Welsh, English & French **V** S%
Lunch £6.75 Tea 50—60p Dinner fr£8.85&alc Wine £4.80 Last dinner 10.30pm
Credit cards 1 2 3 5 Ⓥ

★★★**Ladbroke Twelve Knights**
Margam Rd, Margam (2m SE A48) (Ladbroke) ☎ (0639) 882381
Sited conveniently close to the M4 motorway, the hotel provides compact, well-equipped bedrooms, a comfortable new bar complex and a popular restaurant.
11(1fb) CTV in all bedrooms ®**T**
sB&B£35—£42 dB&B£44—£50 B
120P
Mainly grills **V** Lunch £4.15—£12&alc Tea fr75p Dinner £4.15—£12&alc Wine £4.50 Last dinner 10.30pm
Credit cards 1 2 3 5 Ⓥ

PORT WILLIAM
Dumfries & Galloway *Wigtownshire*
Map **10** NX34

★★★ **Corsemalzie House**
(Inter Hotel) ☎ Mochrum (098 886) 254
Closed 21 Jan—6 Mar
Country house hotel in extensive grounds.
15rm(10 5)(1fb) CTV in all bedrooms ®✱sB&B£25—£31 dB&B£40—£51 B
30P ❀ putting croquet
Scottish & French ✱Lunch £6.40—£8 Tea 60p—£2.50 Dinner £10.75—£12.75&alc Wine £4.50 Last dinner 9.15pm
Credit cards 1 2 3 5 Ⓥ

★★**Monrieth Arms** ☎ (09887) 232
Traditional homely family-run hotel.
12rm(2)(2fb) S% sB&Bfr£12.75 sB&Bfr£14.25 dB&Bfr£25.50 dB&Bfr£27
CTV 8P
S% Lunch fr£4.50 Tea fr£1.50 Dinner fr£7 Wine £4 Last dinner 8pm
Credit card 3 Ⓥ

PORTWRINKLE
Cornwall
Map **2** SX35

★**Whitsand Bay** Portwrinkle
☎ St Germans (0503) 30276
RS Dec—Feb
Holiday and golfing hotel overlooking sea, run with real warmth by owners.
27rm(24)(12fb) ® S%
*sB&B£12—£15 sB&B£17 dB&B£30 dB&B£34 B
CTV 50P (heated) sauna bath solarium gymnasium hairdressing salon Disco wkly in school hols *xmas*
English & French **V** S%
*Lunch £3.50 Tea £2 Dinner £7.50 Wine £3.10 Last dinner 8.15pm
Ⓥ

POTARCH
Grampian *Aberdeenshire*
Map **15** NO69

★**Potarch** ☎ Kincardine O'Neil (033 984) 339
Small and friendly hotel set close to River Dee in beautiful Dee Valley.
6rm(2)(1fb) CTV in all bedrooms ®
sB&B£16 dB&B£26 dB&B£30
CTV 30P nc 3yrs
English & French Bar lunch £4—£9 Dinner £11 Wine £4.30 Last dinner 8.30pm

POTTO
North Yorkshire
Map **8** NZ40

★★★**Potto Hall** ☎ Stokesley (0642) 700186 Telex no 587121
This Victorian country house in its own grounds features an impressive array of Victorian pictures and original features; it also incorporates a night club.
14rm(11 3)CTV in all bedrooms ® **T**
S% sB&B£32 dB&B£43
CTV 400P
English & Continental **V** Lunch £4.95alc Tea £1.20 Dinner £10.95alc Wine £3.95 Last dinner 9.30pm
Credit cards 1 2 3

POUNDISFORD
Somerset
Map **3** ST22

XX**Well House** ☎ Blagdon Hill (082342) 566
The restaurant forms part of an original Tudor manor house, set in acres of open countryside, and is reached via the cobbled courtyard containing the old well. Meals are traditionally English, eaten in the Baronial Hall, where a log fire burns in the huge stone fireplace during the winter.
Closed Mon Dinner not served Sun
V 45 seats Lunch £5.75—£6.25 Dinner £9.50—£10.50 Wine £4.75 Last dinner 10pm 43P
Credit cards 1 2 3 5

POWBURN
Northumberland
Map **12** NU01

★★

★★**BREAMISH HOUSE, POWBURN**
☎ (066578) 266
Closed Jan
(Rosette awarded for dinner only)
In five acres of woodland gardens with a burn running through it, is this nicely proportioned Georgian house. The interior is not one of the grand sort but more homelike, particularly with the well furnished drawing room, and its marble fireplace, bookshelves, ornaments, and comfortable seating. There are flowers and posies in the well appointed dining room (the solid elbow chairs come from the old Empress of Burmuda). It is candle lit and makes a suitable setting for the enjoyable cooking. The style is fairly simple, eschewing the modern fashion, but allowing the good ingredients to speak for themselves. The dishes are skilfully cooked and cleanly presented and the five course dinner represents good value. Bedrooms are very good, some being spacious and well above the standard expected from a two star hotel. They are comfortable, and equipped with television, radio, telephone, hairdryer as well as things like fruit, flowers and sweets. All is very pleasing and much to the liking of our members who staunchly support the rosette and Red Stars we award. Graham Taylor, the Managing Director, is to be congratulated for achieving such high standards and choosing such good natured staff to provide a friendly service.

10rm(7 2)CTV in all bedrooms ®
sB&B£25—£30
dB&B£45—£50 B
30P nc 12yrs
Lunch £8—£9 Tea 80p—£1 Dinner £13—£15 Wine £3.85 Last dinner 9pm

POWFOOT
Dumfries & Galloway *Dumfriesshire*
Map **11** NY16

★★**Golf** Links Av ☎ Cummertrees (04617) 254
Traditional hotel with modern extensions on estuary and next to golf course in small village.
21rm(7 7)(2fb) CTV in all bedrooms ®
S% sB&B£16—£18
sB&B£23.30—£25
dB&B£30.40—£34
dB&B£38—£40.60
CTV 100P 10 Live music mthly *xmas*
V Lunch £4—£7 Tea £1—£2.50 Dinner £8.50—£10 Wine £4 Last dinner 8.15pm

PRAA SANDS
Cornwall
Map **2** SW52

★★**Prah Sands** ☎ Penzance (0736) 762438
Closed mid Dec—mid Jan
Family hotel positioned at the water's edge.
22rm(12)(6fb) CTV in all bedrooms ®
sB&B£13—£18 sB&B£15—£21
dB&B£26—£36 dB&B£30—£42 B
CTV 40P (heated) (hard)
English, French & Italian *Lunch £5—£6.50 Tea 95p—£2 High Tea £3—£5.50 Dinner £7.75—£8.75&alc Last dinner 9pm
Credit cards 1 3
See advertisement under Penzance

PRESTBURY
Cheshire
Map **7** SJ97

XXX**Bridge** ☎ (0625) 829326
The restaurant is picturesquely situtated at the heart of the village, and the interior is most attractive. Dating back to the 17th century, it still retains features of the group of cottages that it was then. The cuisine is French, and, in addition to the extensive à la carte menu, good-value three-course lunch and dinner menus are available, plus a number of seasonal speciality dishes.
Dinner not served Sun
English & French 90 seats Lunch £6.50—£6.90&alc Dinner £10—£11&alc Wine £6.50 Last dinner 9.45pm 40P Live music Tue—Sat
Credit cards 1 2 3 5

✕✕✕**Legh Arms** ☎(0625) 829130

This smart and attractive restaurant, set in a picturesque village, dates back to the 15th century and has associations with Bonnie Prince Charlie. The à la carte menu is essentially French, with a varied and interesting choice of dishes; a competitively-priced three-course lunch menu is also available.

International **V** 80 seats Last dinner 10pm 40P

Credit cards 1 2 3 5

✕✕**White House** ☎(0625) 829376

Originally a farmhouse and subsequently put to many other uses, this building at the centre of the attractive village is now a popular restaurant offering a good choice of mainly English dishes, with a blackboard selection to supplement the à la carte menu. Its low beams and roughcast walls help to create a pleasant and relaxed atmosphere.

Closed Mon

V 70 seats Lunch £6.50&alc Dinner £10.50&alc Wine £5.20 Last dinner 10pm 25P

Credit cards 1 2 5

PRESTEIGNE

Powys
Map **3** SO36

★★*BL* **Radnorshire Arms** High St (Trusthouse Forte) ☎(0544) 267406

Attractive coaching inn with charming bedrooms and lounges. Tasteful modern accommodation is available in the Garden Rooms.

6 Annexe: 10 CTV in all bedrooms ® sB&B £45.50 dB&B £60.50 **B**

CTV 20P 6 *xmas*

Last dinner 9pm

Credit cards 1 2 3 4 5

Prestbury — Preston

PRESTON

Lancashire
Map **7** SD52
See also Bartle and Barton

★★★**Broughton Park** Garstang Rd Broughton (3m N on A6) ☎Broughton (0772) 864087 Telex no 67180

Elegant Edwardian country house with most bedrooms in modern extension. Also extensive leisure complex.

98(12fb) 4 CTV in all bedrooms ®**T** sB&B fr£45 dB&B fr£55 **B**

Lift ☾ 286P (heated) sauna bath solarium gymnasium hairdressing *xmas*

English & French **V** ✱Lunch fr£5.95 Tea fr60p High Tea fr£1.95 Dinner fr£10.25&alc Wine £5 Last dinner 10.30pm

Credit cards 1 2 3 5

★★★**Crest** The Ringway (Crest) ☎(0772) 59411 Telex no 677147

Modern, comfortable, well furnished, central hotel.

126(11fb) in 23 bedrooms CTV in all bedrooms ®**T** S% sB £52—£62 dB £72—£92 (room only) **B**

Lift ☾ 25P CFA *xmas*

International **V** Lunch £6.95—£8&alc Tea 70—90p Dinner £11.50—£12&alc Wine £6.95 Last dinner 9.45pm

Credit cards 1 2 3 5

★★★**Ladbroke** (& Conference centre), Leyland Way ☎Leyland (07744) 22922 (For full entry see Leyland)

★★★**Novotel Preston** Reedfield Pl, Walton Summit (Located at M6 junc 29/A6) (Novotel) ☎(0772) 313331 Telex no 677164

100(100fb) CTV in all bedrooms **T** S% ✱sB £40.50 dB £47 (room only) **B**

Lift ☾ 120P (heated) pool

Continental **V** S% ✱Lunch £4.95—£8.50&alc Tea 70p alc High Tea £2.50alc Dinner £8.50&alc Last dinner mdnt

Credit cards 1 2 3 5 Ⓥ

★★★**Swallow Hotel — Preston** Preston New Rd, Samlesbury (junc A59/A677) (Swallow) ☎Samlesbury (077477) 351 Telex no 677362

Modern hotel and conference centre, situated at the junction of the A59 and the A677, 1m from junction 31 of the M6.

80rm(54 26)(54fb) in 10 bedrooms CTV in all bedrooms ®**T** S% sB £32—£47 dB £42—£60 (room only) **B**

Lift ☾ 250P CFA (heated) squash solarium

International **V** Lunch £6—£10 Tea 70p—£1 Dinner £6.50—£12.50 Wine £6 Last dinner 10.30pm

Credit cards 1 2 3 5

★★★**Tickled Trout** Preston New Rd, Samlesbury (junc 31 M6/A59) ☎Samlesbury (077477) 671 Telex no 677625

Large modern hotel on the banks of the River Ribble at the junction of the M6 and the A59.

66(53fb) 1 in 10 bedrooms CTV in all bedrooms ®**T** sB&B £28—£42 dB&B £40—£50 **B**

☾ 150P 10 CFA Live music & dancing Sat *xmas*

English & French **V** Lunch £6.50 Tea £1 Dinner £15alc Wine £5.95 Last dinner 10.15pm

Credit cards 1 2 3 5

★★**Vineyard** Cinnamon Hill, Chorley Rd, Walton-Le-Dale (2m S A49) (Consort) ☎(0772) 54646

Closed Xmas Day night

This popular hotel has a cosmopolitan restaurant and a Manhattan-style cocktail bar. Bedrooms are modern and well-furnished.

14(1fb) CTV in all bedrooms ®**T** sB&B £35 dB&B £48 **B** →

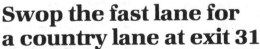

☾200P Live music & dancing Fri & Sat Cabaret Fri

French V Lunch £2.50—£4.95&alc Tea £1.50 Dinner £3.95—£11 Wine £4.55 Last dinner 10.15pm

Credit cards 1 2 3 5 V

PRESTWICK
Strathclyde *Ayrshire*
Map **10** NS32

★★★**Carlton** (Consort/Toby) ☎ (0292) 76811

Modern low-rise hotel in its own grounds, standing on the main road.

37➡(2fb) CTV in all bedrooms ® T sB&B➡£33 dB&B➡£48 B

☾CTV 200P ✽ Live music & dancing 4 nights wkly *xmas*

French V Lunch £4.75—£5.25 Tea £1.50 Dinner £9.50—£9.75&alc Wine £5 Last dinner 11pm

Credit cards 1 2 3 5

★★***Parkstone*** Esplanade ☎ (0292) 77286

Detached building situated on the Esplanade, looking out to the Isle of Arran.

28rm(6➡9⋒)(2fb) CTV in all bedrooms ® ✖ B

CTV 60P 4🚗

V Last dinner 8.30pm

Credit card 1

★★**St Nicholas** 41 Ayr Rd ☎ (0292) 79568

A cosy family run hotel on the main road with a good reputation for their high teas.

16rm(7⋒)(3fb) CTV in 5 bedrooms TV in 11 bedrooms ® ✖ S% sB&B£16—£18 sB&B⋒£18—£20 dB&B£27—£29 dB&B⋒£29—£31

CTV 50P ✽ Live music & dancing Sun

V S% Lunch £3—£5&alc High Tea £5—£8&alc Dinner £6—£10&alc Wine £3.75 Last dinner 8.30pm

Credit cards 1 2 3 5

★★**Towans** Prestwick Airport ☎ (0292) 77831

Standing right beside the airport, the hotel caters mainly for transit guests and local functions.

30rm(8➡4⋒)(7fb) CTV in 6 bedrooms ® T S% sBfr£18.50 sB➡⋒fr£21.50 dBfr£28 dB➡⋒fr£31 (room only)

☾CTV 140P ✽ Live music & dancing Sat *xmas*

V S% Lunch fr£5 Tea fr£1.10 Dinner fr£10.50 Wine £4.50 Last dinner 8.30pm

Credit cards 1 2 3 4 5

★**Auchencoyle** 13 Links Rd ☎ (0292) 78316

Small, family run hotel facing golf course. Popular for high teas.

6rm(3⋒)(3fb) TV in 1 bedroom ® ✖ S% sB&B£11.50 dB&B£25 dB&B⋒£29

CTV 20P pool table Live music & dancing Fri & Tue Cabaret Fri & Tue

S% Lunch £2.75—£3.25 Tea 75p—£1.50 High Tea £2.50—£6 Dinner £5—£8 Wine £4 Last dinner 9.30pm

PRINCETHORPE
Warwickshire
Map **4** SP37

★★**Woodhouse** Leamington Rd ☎ Marton (0926) 632303

Closed 25 & 26 Dec

Converted country house in quiet setting offering a variety of sporting facilities.

8rm(4➡1⋒) Annexe: 14rm(10⋒)(3fb) CTV in all bedrooms ® T ✱sB&B£22—£25.50 sB&B➡⋒£31.50—£32.50 dB&B£34—£38 dB&B➡⋒£46—£49

100P ✽ (heated) (hard) Disco Sat

English & French V ✱ Lunch £7.75—£10.25&alc Tea 50p High Tea £3.75 Dinner £10.25&alc Wine £5.95 Last dinner 10.30pm

Credit cards 1 2 3 5 V

PRIORS HARDWICK
Warwickshire
Map **4** SP45

✕✕***Butchers Arms*** ☎ Byfield (0327) 60504

The stone-built inn enjoys a country setting on the outskirts of the village and offers a varied choice of continental meals.

Lunch not served Sat Dinner not served Sun

English, French & Portuguese V 100 seats Last dinner 9.30pm 80P

PUDDINGTON
Cheshire
Map **7** SJ37

✕✕✕**Craxton Wood** Parkgate Rd (on A540 junc A550) ☎ 051-339 4717

Charming country house with elegant attractive restaurant.

Closed Sun, last 2 wks Aug, Bank Hol's & 1 wk Xmas

French 80 seats S% ✱ Lunch £10.95&alc Dinner £16.75alc Wine £5.70 Last dinner 10pm 40P

Credit cards 1 2 3 5

PUDSEY
West Yorkshire
Map **8** SE23

✕**Tiberio** 68 Galloway Ln ☎ Bradford (0274) 665895

This small, sophisticated, Italian restaurant is conveniently placed near the Leeds/Bradford ring road. Skilfully produced, classic, Italian dishes from the à la carte menu are complemented by an international wine list and a high standard of service.

Closed Mon, 1st 2 wks Jan & 2 wks Jul Lunch not served Sat

English & Italian V 66 seats Lunch £6.50 Dinner £13alc Wine £5.25 Last dinner 11pm 30P

Credit cards 1 2 3

PULBOROUGH
West Sussex
Map **4** TQ01

★*BL* **Chequers** Church Place (Minotel) ☎ (07982) 2486

A delightful, family, country hotel provides warm and friendly hospitality and serves good home cooking.

9rm(7➡2⋒)(1fb) CTV in all bedrooms sB&B➡⋒£22.50—£30 dB&B➡⋒£36—£39 B

14P ✽

Lunch fr£4.50 Tea 80p—£2.50 Dinner £7.95—£8.50 Wine £4.50 Last dinner 8pm

Credit cards 1 2 3 5

❀✕**Stane Street Hollow** Codmore Hill ☎ (07982) 2819

A charming, cosy restaurant run by a Swiss chef and his wife, who extend a warm welcome into their home. The menu changes monthly, allowing the most to be made of seasonal foods. The dishes hav a Swiss influence and are well prepared. The wine list also includes some Swiss wines.

Closed Sun, Mon, 2 wks May, 3 wks Oct & 24 Dec—6 Jan Lunch not served Tue & Sat

French & Swiss 35 seats ✱ Lunch £6.80—£7.25&alc Dinner £14.50alc Wine £6.65 Last dinner 9.15pm 15P

PUTSBOROUGH
Devon
Map **2** SS44

★★★***Putsborough Sands*** ☎ Croyde (0271) 890555

Closed Oct—Etr

Purpose-built comfortable holiday hotel, family-owned and run, in a fine coastal situation.

54rm(30➡2⋒)(16fb) ✖ B

☾CTV 40P (heated) squash sauna bath solarium Disco twice wkly Live music & dancing wkly *xmas*

International Last dinner 8.30pm

Credit cards 1 2 3

P

QUEENSFERRY
Clwyd
Map **7** SJ36

XX **Amantola Tandoori** Welsh Rd, Sealand ☎ Chester (0244) 811383

Situated outside the town, in the suburb of Sealand, the restaurant offers an interesting selection of dishes, including several curries and a few European dishes. The food is authentic, well-cooked and attractively presented, served by friendly and attentive waiters in a comfortable dining area with some individual alcoves.

English & Indian **V** 250 seats *Lunch £10—£12 Wine £4.50 Last dinner mdnt 200P

Credit cards 1 2 3 5

QUEENSFERRY (SOUTH)
Lothian *West Lothian*
Map **11** NT17

★★★ **Forth Bridges Moat House** Forth Bridge (Queens Moat) ☎ 031-331 1199 Telex no 727430

Situated close to the southern approach to the Forth Road Bridge, the hotel has splendid views over the Firth of Forth.

108 (6fb) CTV in all bedrooms ® **T** sB £50—£55 dB £65.25—£70.25 (room only)

200P (heated) squash snooker sauna bath solarium gymnasium Disco Thu *xmas*

Scottish & French Lunch £7.25—£7.50 Tea fr65p Dinner £8.50—£10&alc Wine £4.85 Last dinner 9.45pm

Credit cards 1 2 3 5

XX **Hawes Inn** ☎ 031-331 1990

Historic inn overlooking the Firth of Forth where Robert Louis Stevenson is said to have started 'Kidnapped'.

Lunch not served Sat
Dinner not served Sun in Winter

Scottish & French **V** 60 seats S% Lunch fr£5.95&alc Wine £5.40 Last dinner 10pm 60P 5 bedrooms available Live music Sat

Credit cards 1 2 3 5

QUORN
Leicestershire
Map **8** SK50

★★★★ *HB* **Quorn Country**
Charnwood House, Leicester Rd (on A6 in village centre) ☎ (0509) 415050

RS Boxing Day & New Years Day

Standing in spacious grounds alongside the River Soar. Constructed of natural stone and brick the hotel provides well equipped and quite luxurious accommodation, catering mainly for businessmen.

19 (1fb) 1 CTV in all bedrooms ® **T** sB&B £50 dB&B £65

100P *xmas*

English & French **V** Lunch £8.25&alc Tea 65p Dinner £10.95&alc Wine £6.50 Last dinner 10pm

Credit cards 1 2 3 5

RAASAY, ISLE OF
Highland *Inverness-shire*
Map **13** NG53

★★ **Isle of Raasay** ☎ (047862) 222

Closed Oct—Mar

Modern comforts, fine home cooking and good hospitality, make up the appeal of this extended island hotel.

12 CTV in all bedrooms ® sB&B £18 dB&B £36

CTV 12P

Bar lunch fr£1.75 Tea fr£1 Dinner fr£12.50 Wine £5 Last dinner 8pm

RAGLAN
Gwent
Map **3** SO40

★★ **Beaufort Arms** ☎ (0291) 690412

Set at the centre of Raglan, overlooking the church, the comfortable and tastefully-appointed hotel has recently been fully renovated. Bedrooms are well-fitted whilst public rooms present an old world character.

10 CTV in all bedrooms ® **T** *sB&B £22 dB&B £36

60P *xmas*

English & Continental *Lunch £1—£7 Dinner £5—£20 Wine £3 Last dinner 10pm

Credit cards 1 2 3 4 5

RAINHILL
Merseyside
Map **7** SJ49

★ **Rockland** View Rd ☎ 051-426 4603

Large Georgian house with a modern extension set in its own pleasant gardens.

12rm(2) Annexe: 10rm(4 6)(5fb) TV in 14 bedrooms ® sB&B £20—£22 sB&B £23—£25 dB&B £34—£38 dB&B £38—£41

CTV 30P

Lunch £4.50&alc Tea 60p High Tea £2.50 Dinner £7.50&alc Wine £4 Last dinner 8.15pm

Ⓥ

RAMPSIDE (near Barrow-in-Furness)
Cumbria
Map **7** SD26

★★ ***Clarkes Arms*** (Whitbread) ☎ Barrow-in-Furness (0229) 20303

Small country hotel set in its own grounds, overlooking Morecambe Bay.

10rm(9)(2fb) CTV in all bedrooms ®

CTV 100P

English, Chinese, French & Italian **V** Last dinner 9.30pm

Credit cards 1 2 3

RAMSBOTTOM
Greater Manchester
Map **7** SD71

★★ **Old Mill** Springwood ☎ (070682) 2991

The waterwheel is intact in this black and white building which has modern style bedrooms.

17 1 CTV in all bedrooms ® **T** sB&B £35 dB&B £46—£49.50

CTV 100P

French **V** S% Lunch £4.95&alc Dinner £10—£15alc Wine £4.65

Credit cards 1 2 3 5

RAMSBURY
Wiltshire
Map **4** SU27

XX **Bell** The Square ☎ Marlborough (0672) 20230

This restaurant, standing in the town square, offers a wide choice of varied and well-prepared dishes, generously served in attractive surroundings by an attentive young staff; the sweet trolley is noteworthy.

English, French & Italian **V** 54 seats *Lunch £12.50 Dinner £12.50 Wine £4.50 Last dinner 9.30pm 40P

Credit cards 1 2 3 5 Ⓥ

RAMSGATE
Kent
Map **5** TR36

★★ **San Clu** Victoria Pde ☎ Thanet (0843) 592345

Old fashioned family-run hotel with reasonable accommodation.

54rm(22)(7fb) CTV in all bedrooms **T** S% sB&B £17—£21 sB&B £23—£25 dB&B £28—£36 dB&B £40—£44 Continental breakfast

Lift 12P CFA Live music & dancing Thu (Jul—Aug) Cabaret Xmas & New Year *xmas*

English & French **V** S% Lunch £8.50&alc Tea £2 High Tea £4 Dinner £9&alc Wine £5 Last dinner 9pm

Credit cards 1 2 3

★★ **Savoy** Grange Rd ☎ Thanet (0843) 592637

The friendly, family-run hotel has modern, comfortable bedrooms and a restaurant that is popular with a local clientele.

12rm(1 6) Annexe: 11rm(2 9)(3fb) CTV in all bedrooms ® **T** S% sB&B £15 sB&B £20—£23 dB&B £22—£26 dB&B £26.50—£31

CTV 20P

French S% Lunch £5&alc Tea £2.50 Dinner £12alc Wine £4 Last dinner 10pm

Credit cards 1 2 3 5

R

RANGEMORE
Staffordshire
Map **7** SK12

★★ **HL *Needwood Manor*** ☎ Burton-on-Trent (0283) 712932

A 19th century, red-brick house stands in a park setting just three miles west of the southern end of the Burton upon Trent bypass. Notable features of the hotel are its fine pitch pine staircase and gallery.

Closed Xmas wk

11rm(1🛁1🚿)(3fb) CTV in 1 bedroom 🐕 30P ✻

Last dinner 9pm

Credit cards [1] [3]

RANGEWORTHY
Avon
Map **3** ST68

★ **Rangeworthy Court** Wooton Rd ☎ (045422) 347

Closed 23 Dec–2 Jan

This fine example of a Cotswold-stone manorial house stands in well-tended gardens. Attractively furnished with antiques, it offers a good standard of comfort and hospitality.

14rm(1🛁6🚿)(1fb) 1 sB&B£21.50 sB&B🛁🚿£28.50 dB&B£30 dB&B🛁🚿£34–£38

CTV 60P ✻

English & Continental ✻Lunch £10 Tea £1.50 Dinner £7.75–£9.50&alc Wine £4.65 Last dinner 8.30pm

Credit card [3] Ⓥ

RANTON
Staffordshire
Map **7** SJ82

✕✕✕ ***Yew Tree*** ☎ Seighford (078575) 278

Despite considered extension, the farmhouse still retains its cottage appearance and stands in attractive old gardens. Inside, heavy beams, dark reproduction furniture and subdued colours create a warm, country atmosphere. A young, well-trained staff serve a menu of popular French dishes with some interesting and unusual additions, and there is a reasonably-priced wine list.

Closed Mon Lunch served Sun only

French **V** 90 seats Last dinner 9.30pm 50P

Credit cards [1] [2] [3] [5]

RATHO
Lothian *Midlothian*
Map **11** NT17

✕ **Bridge Inn** ☎ 031-333 1320

The compact inn sits beside Union Canal, which supplies the decorative theme of the restaurant. There are many historically interesting prints and pictures as well as an impressive array of old bottles. Service is friendly and attentive, though informal, and the menu features a good selection of Taste of Scotland dishes.

Closed New Years Day

Scottish & French **V** 70 seats S%

✻Lunch £2.85–£6&alc Dinner £11alc Wine £5.75 Last dinner 10pm 50P

Credit cards [1] [2] [3] [5]

RAVENGLASS
Cumbria
Map **6** SD09

★ **Pennington Arms** ☎ (06577) 222

A country inn in a quiet village on the estuary of the River Esk, Mite and Irt.

18rm(5🛁) Annexe: 12rm(2🛁1🚿)(7fb) sB&B£10–£16 sB&B🛁🚿£15–£19 dB&B£20–£28 dB&B🛁🚿£26–£30

CTV 50P 3 ✻ pool ♿

V Lunch £4.75–£6&alc Tea 65p–£3&alc High Tea £3–£6.50&alc Dinner £5.50–£9&alc Wine £4 Last dinner 10pm

Ⓥ

RAVENSCAR (near Scarborough)
North Yorkshire
Map **8** NZ90

★★ **Raven Hall** ☎ (0723) 870353

Closed Jan–Feb

A cliff-side mansion overlooking the sea, on the site of a Roman signal station.

57rm(37🛁)(20fb) CTV in all bedrooms Ⓡ **T** ✻sB&B£22–£25.50 sB&B🛁£28–£35 dB&B£44–£51 dB&B🛁£56–£70

☾ CTV 200P 2 ✻ (hard) snooker solarium bowling putting table tennis Disco Wed (May–Oct) Live music & dancing Sat (Mar–Jan) *xmas*

V ✻Lunch £2.50–£5.50 Tea 80p–£2 High Tea £3.50–£4.50 Dinner £9.25–£10 Wine £4.50 Last dinner 8.30pm

Credit cards [1] [2] [3] [5] Ⓥ

RAVENSTONEDALE
Cumbria
Map **12** NY70

★★ **H Black Swan** ☎ Newbiggin-on-Lune (05873) 204

Closed Jan & Feb

This very pleasant and friendly family-run inn provides pretty bedrooms and good food.

6rm(3🛁)(1fb) sB&B£22 sB&B🛁£27 dB&B£34 dB&B🛁£39

CTV 20P 2 ✻ *xmas*

Lunch £7 Tea £1.85 Dinner £12&alc Wine £5.35 Last dinner 8.45pm

Credit cards [1] [2] [3] Ⓥ

READ
Lancashire
Map **7** SD73

✕✕ **Belvedere Hotel** ☎ Padiham (0282) 72250

The large, detached house stands on a hillside overlooking the valley and has been owned and run for many years by a charming Italian. In the attractively decorated and comfortable restaurant, typically Italian food is served; you can also take your ease in a pleasant bar/sun lounge.

Closed Mon Lunch not served Sat & Sun

English & Italian 100 seats Lunch £14alc Dinner £14alc Wine £4.95 Last dinner 9.30pm 40P

Credit card [3]

READING
Berkshire
Map **4** SU77

★★★★ **Ramada** Oxford Rd ☎ (0734) 598753 Telex no 847785

A modern purpose built hotel situated in centre of town.

200🛁🚿(126fb) in 14 bedrooms CTV in all bedrooms Ⓡ **T** sB🛁🚿£64–£71 dB🛁🚿£72–£82 (room only)

Lift ☾ # 75 (heated) sauna bath solarium gymnasium hairdressing salon Live music & dancing Fri ♿ *xmas*

French **V** Lunch £11.50 Tea £2.75 Dinner £18alc Wine £6.50 Last dinner 11.30pm

Credit cards [1] [2] [3] [4] [5]

★★★ **Post House** Basingstoke Rd (Trusthouse Forte) ☎ (0734) 875485 Telex no 849160

Comfortably appointed commercial hotel with well appointed restaurant and good food.

143🛁(51fb) CTV in all bedrooms Ⓡ **T** sB&B🛁£60.50 dB&B🛁£75

☾ 240P CFA ✻ & (heated) sauna bath solarium gymnasium

Last dinner 10.30pm

Credit cards [1] [2] [3] [4] [5]

✕ ***Hong Kong*** 14 West St ☎ (0734) 585372

There is a friendly welcome for everyone at this small, popular and family-run Chinese restaurant. Oriental murals and prints brighten the room and create an appropriate atmosphere in which to enjoy a meal from the comprehensive selection of mainly Pekinese dishes. Cuisine is of a high standard, and there is a range of set dinners for those unfamiliar with Chinese food.

Cantonese, Pekinese & Szechuan **V** 100 seats Last dinner 11.20pm

Credit cards [1] [2] [3] [5]

R

Redbourn — Redruth

REDBOURN
Hertfordshire
Map **4** TL11

★★★**Aubrey Park** Hemel Hempstead Rd ☎ (058285) 2105 Telex no 82195

Busy hotel in quiet setting with modern bedrooms and two restaurants.

81 ⇌ ⋒ (3fb) CTV in all bedrooms ® **T** S% sB ⇌ ⋒ £49—£55 dB ⇌ ⋒ £72—£78 (room only) **B**

☾ 100P ✽ ⛆ (heated) games room ♣ ♿

English & French **V** ♁ ☕ ✱ Lunch £6.50&alc Tea 80p Dinner £8—£11&alc Wine £5.75 Last dinner 10pm

Credit cards 1 2 3 4 5

REDBROOK
Clwyd
Map **7** SJ54

★★**Redbrook Hunting Lodge** Wrexham Rd ☎ Redbrook Maelor (094873) 204

On a prominent corner site in a rural position on the A495/A525, 1m from Whitchurch, the hotel has pleasant gardens.

11rm (8 ⇌ 2 ⋒) (1fb) 1 ⊞ CTV in all bedrooms ® **T** sB&B fr £22.75 sB&B ⇌ ⋒ fr £25 dB&B ⇌ ⋒ £33 **B**

CTV 100P ✽

V ♁ ☕ ✱ Lunch fr £7&alc Tea 50p—£2 Dinner £7&alc Wine £3.70 Last dinner 9pm

Credit cards 1 2 3 5 Ⓥ

REDCAR
Cleveland
Map **8** NZ62

★★★**Hotel Royal York** Coatham Rd ☎ (0642) 486221

51rm (50 ⇌ 1 ⋒) (3fb) CTV in all bedrooms **T** ✱ sB&B ⇌ ⋒ £15.50—£21.50 dB&B ⇌ ⋒ £22.50—£29.50 **B**

Lift ☾ 300P Disco Thu, Fri & Sat *xmas*

English, French, Italian & Spanish **V** ♁ ☕ Lunch £2.25—£4.25&alc Tea 45p—£1.25 Dinner £2.25—£4.25&alc Wine £4.10 Last dinner 10pm

Credit cards 1 2 3 5 Ⓥ

REDDITCH
Hereford & Worcester
Map **7** SP06

★★★**Southcrest** Pool Bank (Best Western) ☎ (0527) 41511 Telex no 338455

Closed 25 Dec—1 Jan RS Sun

Busy hotel in 7 acres of grounds, popular for lunch and dinner.

60rm (55 ⇌ 5 ⋒) (1fb) CTV in all bedrooms ® **T** sB&B ⇌ ⋒ fr £38 dB&B ⇌ ⋒ fr £46 **B**

☾ 100P ⛟ ✽ ♿

English & French **V** ♁ Lunch fr £7.50&alc Dinner fr £8.50&alc Wine £5.20 Last dinner 9.15pm

Credit cards 1 2 3 5

REDLYNCH
Wiltshire
Map **4** SU22

✕✕**Langley Wood** ☎ Romsey (0794) 390348

An attractive, creeper-clad house of red brick stands in very pleasant grounds among dense woodland on the edge of Redlynch. Guests enjoy imaginative and freshly prepared dishes chosen from a good menu — but booking is essential if you are not to risk disappointment.

Lunch not served wkdays Dinner not served Sun

English & French **V** 30 seats Lunch £10alc Dinner £13.50alc Wine £4.50 Last dinner 11pm 30P

Credit cards 1 2 3 5 Ⓥ

REDRUTH
Cornwall
Map **2** SW64

★★★***Penventon*** (Consort) ☎ (0209) 214141

Family owned and run Georgian Manor with modern bedrooms and leisure facilities. Set in 4½ acres. →

R

55rm(35➡10⋒)(3fb) 1🛗CTV in all bedrooms ®T ⊞

☾300P✽⊡(heated) billiards sauna bath solarium gymnasium Disco Wed—Sun ⌂ xmas

♡English, French & Italian V ♧ ☕ Last dinner 9.30pm

Credit cards 1 2 3

See advertisement under Truro

★★***Crossroads Motel*** Scorrier (2m E off A30) (Best Western) ☎ (0209) 820551

Modern, friendly hotel with good restaurant and character bars.

30rm(25➡5⋒)(2fb) CTV in all bedrooms ®T ⊞

145P♿

V ♧ ☕ Last dinner 10pm

Credit cards 1 2 3 5

RED WHARF BAY

Gwynedd
Map **6** SH58

★★**Bryn Tirion** Tynygongl ☎ (0248) 852366

Closed Nov—Apr

This family-run holiday hotel is comfortably appointed and lies within easy reach of the sea.

20➡(3fb) CTV in all bedrooms ®✖ S% sB&B➡fr£20 dB&B➡fr£34 ⊞

65P✽

♧ ☕ Lunch fr£4.50 Tea fr£2 Dinner £7.50alc Wine £4 Last dinner 9pm

Credit cards 1 3 Ⓥ

★**Min-y-Don** ☎ Tynygongl (0248) 852596

RS Nov—Feb

Comfortably appointed family run hotel, only a few minutes from the sea.

19rm(2➡)(1fb) ®S% ✱sB&B£14 sB&B➡£19 dB&B£26 dB&B➡£34—£38 ⊞

CTV 100P Disco Sat Cabaret Sun

♧ ☕ ✱Bar lunch 95p—£3.25 Tea fr£1 Dinner fr£6.95&alc Wine £4.95 Last dinner 8.45pm

Credit cards 1 3 Ⓥ

REEPHAM

Norfolk
Map **9** TG12

★★***Old Brewery House*** Market Sq (Consort) ☎ Norwich (0603) 870881

Georgian fronted hotel, concealing an impressive sporting complex.

28rm(19➡)(4fb) 1🛗CTV in 24 bedrooms TV in 4 bedrooms ®T ⊞

⚡CTV 120P✽⊡(heated) squash sauna bath solarium gymnasium Disco mthly ⌂ ♿

♡English & Continental V ♧ ☕ Last dinner 9pm

Credit cards 1 2 3

REIGATE

Surrey
Map **4** TQ25

★★**Bridge House** Reigate Hill ☎ (07372) 44821 Telex no 268810 Gatwick plan **1A**

Modern building set into hillside with nicely appointed bedrooms, large restaurant and lively atmosphere.

30rm(28➡2⋒)(3fb) CTV in all bedrooms ®T✖ sB&B➡⋒£33.50—£43 dB&B➡⋒£47—£56 ⊞

☾CTV 100P

♡English & Continental V Lunch £8.75—£9.75&alc Dinner £12.50—£15.50&alc Wine £6.25 Last dinner 10.30pm

Credit cards 1 2 3 5

★★**Reigate Manor** Reigate Hill (Best Western) ☎ (07372) 40125 Gatwick plan **19**

Georgian manor house with some well equipped bedrooms and imaginative good cooking.

15rm(2➡13⋒)
Annexe: 12rm(11➡1⋒)(1fb) CTV in all bedrooms ®T✖ S% sB➡⋒£32.75—£36 dB➡⋒£42.50—£46.75 (room only) ⊞

100P Disco Sat

♡English & French ♧ ☕ S% Lunch £9.50alc Tea 75p alc Dinner £9.50—£10.50&alc Wine £5.65 Last dinner 10pm

Credit cards 1 2 3 5 Ⓥ

RENFREW

Strathclyde *Renfrewshire*
Map **11** NS56

For hotels and restaurants see Glasgow Airport

RENISHAW

Derbyshire
Map **8** SK47

★★★***Sitwell*** (Inter Hotel) ☎ Eckington (0246) 435226 Telex no 547303

Closed Xmas Day night RS Sat

Converted 18th-century coaching inn with good quality, spacious, modern accommodation and imaginative food.

31rm(23➡8⋒) CTV in all bedrooms ®T ⊞

☾120P Disco twice wkly

♡English & Continental V ♧ ☕ Last dinner 9.30pm

Credit cards 1 2 3 5

RETFORD (EAST)

Nottinghamshire
Map **8** SK78

★★★*L* **West Retford** North Rd ☎ (0777) 706333 Telex no 56143

Situated on the A620, this large Georgian country house offers very attractive public areas and two annexes of well-equipped, comfortable, modern bedrooms.

Annexe: 31➡⋒(15fb) CTV in all bedrooms ®T S% sB➡⋒£39.50 dB➡⋒£46 (room only) ⊞

☾CTV 100P✽ Disco Sat CFA

♡French V ♧ ☕ S% Lunch £6.75—£7&alc Tea 95p Dinner £10—£10.50 Wine £5.25 Last dinner 10.30pm

Credit cards 1 2 3 5 Ⓥ

RHAYADER
Powys
Map **6** SN96

★★**Elan Valley** Elan Valley (2½m SW B4518) ☎ (0597) 810448

Closed Xmas

Detached hotel in rural surroundings between the town and the Elan Lakes.

11rm(1⛼2⋒)(1fb) sB&B£19.50 sB&B⛼⋒£21 dB&B£32 dB&B⛼⋒£35 B

CTV 50P 6⌂ ✿ ⛹

V ♈ ☕ Lunch £6.50 Tea 75p—£1.50 Dinner £7.50 Wine £4 Last dinner 8pm

Credit card 2 Ⓥ

Rhayader — Rhossili

★*Elan* West St ☎ (0597) 810373

A 16th-century cottage-style hotel near the centre of the town.

15rm(1⛼)(2fb) B

CTV 12P

♈ ☕ Last dinner 8pm

RHOSSILI
West Glamorgan
Map **2** SS48

★★**Worms Head** ☎ Gower (0792) 390512

Closed 24 & 25 Dec

Bright cliff-top hotel with magnificent views of the sea and the bay.

21rm(2⛼3⋒)(2fb) Ⓡ ✖ sB&B£14.50 dB&B£29 dB&B⛼⋒£31 B

CTV 20P

V ♈ Lunch £3.50—£5.50 Dinner £6.50 Last dinner 8pm

R

RHU
Strathclyde *Dunbartonshire*
Map **10** NS28

★★★*L* **Rosslea Hall** (Best Western) ☎(0436) 820684

The family-owned hotel stands in landscaped gardens and has splendid views of Gareloch from many bedrooms and the restaurant.

31rm(27⇌4⋒)(1fb) CTV in all bedrooms ®T sB&B⇌⋒£37—£38.50 dB&B⇌⋒£52.50—£55 B

☾50P ❁ Live music Fri & Sat

Lunch £6.50 Tea £2.25 Dinner £11—£13&alc Wine £7 Last dinner 10.30pm

Credit cards 1 2 3 5 V

★**Ardencaple** (Alloa Brewery) ☎(0436) 820200

Closed New Years Day

Attractive inn with interior theme linked to Clyde steamers.

13rm(4⇌5⋒)(2fb)2 CTV in all bedrooms ®sB&B£21.45 sB&B⇌⋒fr£25.58 dB&Bfr£33.83 dB&B⇌⋒fr£39.30

TV 50P

European * Lunch 85p—£4.50 Tea 65p High Tea £2.85—£5.50 Dinner £7.50alc Wine £3.50 Last dinner 9.15pm

Credit cards 1 2 3 5

RHYDWYN
Gwynedd
Map **6** SH38

✕ **Lobster Pot** Church Bay ☎(0407) 730241

This cottage-style restaurant stands at Church Bay, almost at the end of the road. Beneath the old beams of the dining room, predictably, guests choose from a menu specialising in lobster and other fish dishes, although a wider range is available.

Closed Sun—Fri (Sep—Etr) Bar lunches only

64 seats Bar lunch £1.60—£3.80 Dinner £10.80alc Wine £4.40 Last dinner 9.45pm P

Credit cards 1 3 5

R

Rhu — Richmond upon Thames

RICHMOND
North Yorkshire
Map **7** NZ10

★★**Frenchgate** 59—61 Frenchgate ☎(0748) 2087

Closed mid Dec—mid Feb

Stone-built, Georgian, gentleman's town house, enclosing a 16th-century cottage.

12rm(3⇌3⋒) CTV in all bedrooms ®T sB&B£19.50 sB&B⇌⋒£22.50—£26.50 dB&B£34.50 dB&B⇌⋒£36.50 B

6P nc7yrs

English & French Lunch £6.50alc Dinner £8.50&alc Wine £4.20 Last dinner 8.30pm

Credit cards 1 2 3 5 V

★★**King's Head** Market Sq (Consort) ☎(0748) 2311 Telex no 57515

Fine Georgian coaching Inn, with comfortable accommodation, attractive restaurant and coffee shop.

29rm(20⇌1⋒) 1 CTV in all bedrooms ® T sB&B£25—£30 sB&B⇌⋒£30—£35 dB&B£38 dB&B⇌⋒£42—£45 B

30P *xmas*

English & French V Lunch fr£5.95 Tea 95palc Dinner £9.75 Wine £5.95 Last dinner 9pm

Credit cards 1 3 V

★★***Terrace House*** Maison Dieu ☎(0748) 2342

The tastefully furnished manor house offers comfortable accommodation and warm hospitality.

8⇌⋒(2fb) CTV in all bedrooms ®B

CTV 50P 3 ❁ *xmas*

Last dinner 10pm

Credit cards 1 2 3

RICHMOND UPON THAMES
Greater London
London Plan **5** *B3* (page 446)

★★★**Petersham** Nightingale Ln, Richmond Hill ☎01-940 7471 Telex no 928556

Victorian hotel overlooking the Thames. Richmond Gate hotel nearby, under the same ownership, is used as an annexe.

56⇌(3fb)3 CTV in all bedrooms T sB&B⇌£55—£60 dB&B⇌£65—£70 B

Lift ☾60P 2 (charge £3.50) ❁ Live music & dancing Fri & Sat

English & French V Lunch £12&alc Tea £1.75 Dinner £15&alc Wine £7.50 Last dinner 9.15pm

Credit cards 1 2 3 4 5 V

★★★***Richmond Hill*** 146—150 Richmond Hill (Best Western) ☎01-940 2247 Telex no 21844

Situated close to the park, the welcoming and informal hotel offers bedrooms which are, for the most part, modernised and upgraded.

125rm(110⇌4⋒)(11fb) CTV in all bedrooms ®T B

Lift ☾150P CFA squash Live music & dancing Sat *xmas*

English & French V Last dinner 9pm

Credit cards 1 2 3 5

✕✕**Kew Rendezvous** 110 Kew Rd ☎01-948 4343

This very popular and contemporary Chinese restaurant on two floors features authentic Pekinese dishes, freshly cooked from quality materials. Some kitchen delay inevitably occurs occasionally, but the results are usually worth waiting for.

Closed 25 & 26 Dec

Chinese & Pekinese V 75 seats Lunch £10alc Dinner £12alc Wine £6 Last dinner 11.45pm P

Credit cards 1 2 3 5

❀✕✕ **Lichfields** Lichfield Ter, Sheen Rd ☎01-940 5236

This popular, friendly and well-appointed restaurant provides skilful French cooking of many imaginative dishes such as mille feuille of crab served with cardamom orange in white wine sauce or breast and ballotine of wild duck with juniper and mare de bourgogne, accompanied by well presented, tasty, fresh vegetables. The wine list is extensive and reasonably priced, while the service is friendly and well supervised.

Closed Sun Mon, 24 Dec—2 Jan & 1st 2 wks Sep Lunch not served Sat

English & French 36 seats S% Lunch £15—£27 Dinner £15—£27 Wine £7 Last dinner 10.30pm

Credit cards 1 2

✕ **Red Lion Chinese** 18 Red Lion St ☎01-940 2371

Small modern Pekinese restaurant with attractive decor.

Closed 25—27 Dec

Pekinese 88 seats ✱Lunch £5—£12&alc Dinner £5—£12&alc Wine £4.50 Last dinner 11.15pm

Credit cards 1 2 3 5

RINGWOOD
Hampshire
Map **4** SU10

★★**Struan** Horton Rd ☎Ringwood (04254) 3553

(For full details see Ashley Heath)

RIPON
North Yorkshire
Map **8** SE37

★★★**Ripon Spa** Park St (Best Western) ☎(0765) 2172 Telex no 57780

An Edwardian hotel near the town centre stands in seven acres of lawns and landscaped gardens; it features spacious public lounges, a conservatory with facilities for conferences and a well-appointed restaurant.

41rm(35⇌6⋒) 1⊟ CTV in all bedrooms Ⓡ T ₿

Lift ☾ 100P CFA ✿ Live music & dancing mthly *xmas*

Wine £4.25 Last dinner 9pm

Credit cards 1 2 3 5 Ⓥ

★★*HB* **Bridge** 16—18 Magdalen Rd ☎(0765) 3687

This bay-windowed Victorian house, overlooking the River Ure, offers charming bedrooms and well-restored public rooms.

11⇌⋒(2fb) 1⊟ in 3 bedrooms CTV in all bedrooms ⓇT sB&B⇌⋒£27.50—£44 dB&B⇌⋒£39—£58 ₿

14P ✿ *xmas*

English, French & Italian **V** Lunch £4.50—£15&alc Tea £1.50—£4.50 Dinner £9alc Wine £4.90 Last dinner 8.30pm

Credit cards 1 2 3 5

★★**Unicorn** Market Place (Consort) ☎(0765) 2202 Telex no 57515

This hotel has stood in the medieval market place since its days as a post-house. It provides well-fitted bedrooms, a comfortable first-floor lounge, and bars and a restaurant retaining some original features on the ground floor.

27rm(14⇌13⋒)(2fb) CTV in all bedrooms ⓇT✱sB&B⇌⋒£28—£32 dB&B⇌⋒£44—£50 ₿

15P 4

English & French **V** ✱Lunch £5—£6.50 Tea £1.50 Dinner £9—£12.50 Wine £5 Last dinner 10pm

Credit cards 1 2 3 5 Ⓥ

✕ **New Hornblower** Duck Hill ☎(0765) 4841

A small and fashionable restaurant near the town centre, the New Hornblower was converted from Victorian cottages. The menu features good English and international cuisine, and the well-cooked food is served in an informal and friendly atmosphere.

Closed Mon & Feb Lunch not served

International 24 seats Dinner £9.50alc Wine £5.10 Last dinner 10pm

Credit cards 1 3

RIPPONDEN
West Yorkshire
Map **7** SE01

✕✕ **Over the Bridge** Millfold ☎Halifax (0422) 823722

Over the old packhorse bridge and beside a stream, converted millworkers' cottages make a smart and comfortable restaurant. The restoration, whilst providing modern facilities, has retained old features and made good use of natural materials. Cuisine is international, with a French bias, and there is a very good wine list.

Closed Sun Lunch not served

English & French **V** 48 seats S% ✱Dinner £14.50 Wine £6 Last dinner 9.30pm 50P nc 10yrs

Credit cards 2 3

ROADE
Northamptonshire
Map **4** SP75

❀✕ **Roadhouse** 16—18 High St ☎(0604) 863372

This former village inn has been transformed into a good restaurant by Susan and Christopher Kewley. Concentrating on local produce, the cooking is best described as French country style. A relaxed and friendly atmosphere prevails, and with three simple bedrooms also available, it is possible to combine an inexpensive stay with a true British breakfast.

Closed Sun & Mon Lunch not served Sat

French 32 seats S% Lunch £8—£9&alc Dinner £27&alc (2 persons incl wine) Wine £5.50 Last dinner 10pm 15P

Credit cards 1 2 3

ROBERTSBRIDGE
East Sussex
Map **5** TQ72

XXBough House 43 High St ☎ (0580) 880440

The name of this charming, 14th-century, oak-beamed restaurant stems from the fact that in medieval times it was apparently the custom to hang a bough beside the door to indicate that the premises were licensed. Today, reliable cooking is complemented by garden-fresh vegetables, but service can be complicated by delay. Incidentally, beware of the dog!

Closed Sun, Mon, 1—14 Mar & 1—14 Oct Lunch not served

V 24 seats S% Dinner £11—£14 Last dinner 10pm

Credit cards 1 2 3 5

XXTrompe L'Oeil 13 High St ☎ (0580) 880362

Cosy, charmingly decorated restaurant, where several fixed price menus and an à la carte are available. The French proprietress, Nancy Pidgeon oversees the preparation of delicately flavoured, innovative dishes.

Closed Sun & Mon
Lunch not served Sat

French **V** 32 seats Lunch fr£8.95&alc Dinner fr£8.95&alc Wine £6.50 Last dinner 10.30pm 6P

Credit cards 1 2 3 5

ROBIN HOOD'S BAY
North Yorkshire
Map **8** NZ90

★***Grosvenor*** Station Rd ☎ Whitby (0947) 880320

This small, friendly hotel is managed by the resident proprietors and offers good-value meals at lunch and dinner, snacks also being available throughout the day.

13rm(2fb)

CTV *xmas*

Last dinner 9pm

Credit cards 1 3

ROCHDALE
Greater Manchester
Map **7** SD91

★★★**Norton Grange** Manchester Rd, Castleton ☎ (0706) 30788

17rm(15 2)(1fb) CTV in all bedrooms ®T S% sB&B£35 sB&B £35 dB&B£46 dB&B £46—£51

98P Live music & dancing Fri & Sat

French **V** S% Lunch £7&alc Dinner £11&alc Wine £4.75 Last dinner 10pm

Credit cards 1 2 3 5 Ⓥ

★★**Midway** Manchester Rd, Castleton ☎ (0706) 32881

Extensively modernised hotel with wine bar and two restaurants.

29rm(2 19)(1fb) 1 CTV in all bedrooms ®T sB&B£19.20—£24 sB&B £23.20—£29 dB&B £32—£40

100P

V Lunch £7alc Tea fr65p Dinner £7alc Wine £4.95 Last dinner 11pm

Credit cards 1 2 3

XXX **Moorcock** Huddersfield Rd, Milnrow (3m SE on A640) ☎ Saddleworth (04577) 2659

The stone building stands in open, hilly moorland, its impressive table including a good display of fresh market produce and some particularly good home-made soups. Servic is both pleasant and skilful.

Closed Mon Dinner not served Sun

International **V** 70 seats Lunch £6.50—£8.75&alc Dinner £8.75&alc Wine £5.75 Last dinner 10pm 100P

Credit cards 1 2 3 5

ROCHESTER
Kent
Map **5** TQ76

★★★**Crest** Maidstone Rd (on A229 1m N of M2 jct 3) (Crest) ☎ Medway (0634) 687111 Telex no 965933

RS Xmas

Ideally located for Rochester Airport, a modern professional hotel with good size well-appointed bedrooms.

105 in 14 bedrooms CTV in all bedrooms ®T *sB fr£47 dB fr£57 (room only)

Lift 120P Live music Sun *xmas*

V *Lunch £6.95—£9&alc Tea £1.20 High Tea £1.20 Dinner £11.50&alc Wine £6.25 Last dinner 10pm

Credit cards 1 2 3 4 5

ROCHESTER
Northumberland
Map **12** NY89

★**Redesdale Arms** ☎ Otterburn (0830) 20668

Small, friendly inn with good range of interesting food in bar and dining room.

11rm(1fb) 3 CTV in all bedrooms ® sB&Bfr£12.50 dB&Bfr£25

30P

S% Bar lunch £2—£6 Tea £1—£4 Dinner £3.50—£9.50 Wine £3.50 Last dinner 10pm

Ⓥ

ROCHFORD
Essex
Map **5** TQ89

XX **Renoufs** 1 South St ☎ Southend-on-Sea (0702) 544393

Well-managed restaurant with attentive service.

Closed Sun, Mon, 1st 3 wks Jan, last 2 wks June 1st 3 wks Aug Lunch not served Sat

English & French **V** 70 seats Lunch £9—£17&alc Dinner £9—£17&alc Wine £4.50 Last dinner 10pm

Credit cards 1 2 3 5

ROCK (near St Minver)
Cornwall
Map **2** SW97

★★**St Enodoc** ☎ Trebetherick (020886) 3394

This elevated hotel has unrestricted views of the Camel Estuary and offers comfortable accommodation in a friendly, relaxed atmosphere; menus are carefully prepared and a new leisure complex is available.

13rm(5 2)(2fb) CTV in all bedrooms **T** S% sB&B£20—£23.50 sB&B £21.50—£25 dB&B£40—£47 dB&B £43—£50

CTV 33P squash snooker sauna bath solarium gymnasium games room *xmas*

English & French S% Bar lunch £2.50—£7.50 Tea 90p Dinner £7.95—8.55&alc Wine £4.90 Last dinner 9.30pm

Credit cards 1 2 3

ROCKCLIFFE
Dumfries & Galloway *Kirkcudbrightshire*
Map **11** NX85

★★★ *L* **Baron's Craig** ☎ (055 663) 225

Closed 12 Oct—8 Apr

Elegant hotel offering modern and traditional accommodation, set in secluded wooded grounds in picturesque village on Solway coast.

25rm(20)(2fb) CTV in all bedrooms *sB&B£24—£27 sB&B £33—£37 dB&B£44—£50 dB&B £56—£68

CTV 50P putting

*Lunch fr£6.50 Tea fr80p Dinner fr£12.50 Wine £4.95 Last dinner 9pm

Credit cards 1 3

ROMALDKIRK
Co Durham
Map **12** NY92

★★*B* **Rose & Crown** (Best Western) ☎ Teesdale (0833) 50213

Charming old village inn with wide ranging inexpensive bar meals.

8rm(5 3) Annexe: 5rm(4 1)(3fb) 1 CTV in all bedrooms ®T *sB&B £29—£35 dB&B £40—£45

60P *xmas*

English & French **V** *Lunch £2.95—£6.50 Tea £1—£2.95 High Tea £2.95—£4.50 Dinner £11.50&alc Wine £5.90 Last dinner 9.30pm

Credit cards 1 2 3 5

R

ROMILEY
Greater Manchester
Map **7** SJ99

✕ **Waterside** 166 Stockport Rd
☎ 061-430 4302

Stone and brick built cottage, about 200 years old, beside the Peak Forest Canal.

Closed Mon Dinner not served Sun

English & French 36 seats ✱Lunch £5.95&alc Dinner £10.50alc Wine £4.75 Last dinner 10pm 12P

Credit cards 1 3 V

ROMSEY
Hampshire
Map **4** SU32

★★★ **Potters Heron** ☎ Chandlers Ford (04215) 66611
(For full entry see Ampfield)

★★★ **White Horse** Market Pl (Trusthouse Forte) ☎ (0794) 512431

Comfortable lounges and helpful staff make this hotel popular with business people and tourists alike.

33(7fb) CTV in all bedrooms ® sB&B£50.50 dB&B£66.50 B

60P CFA *xmas*

Last dinner 10pm

Credit cards 1 2 3 4 5

✕✕ **Old Manor House** 21 Palmerston St
☎ (0794) 517353

The interesting and historic manor, dating back to the 16th century, is well maintained and offers a comfortable restaurant, separate bar and small patio. Italian chef/patron Brijoli produces meals that are enterprising and beautifully presented, using only the best ingredients and always including a good selection of fresh sea-food. Acceptable standards of supervision and service are complemented by a very good wine list.

Closed Mon & 24—30 Dec Dinner not served Sun

French 52 seats S% ✱Lunch £6.95 Dinner £18—£22 Wine £5.50 Last dinner 9.30pm 12P

Credit cards 1 2 3 5

ROSEBANK
Strathclyde *Lanarkshire*
Map **11** NS84

★★★ **Popinjay** Consort ☎ Crossford (055 586) 441 Telex no 776496

Tudor style hotel with grounds extending to River Clyde.

37rm(29 8)(1fb) 2 CTV in all bedrooms ® T sB&B£29—£40 dB&B£38—£50 B

100P *xmas*

International V Lunch £5—£5.50&alc Tea £1.50—£2.50 Dinner fr£8&alc Wine £4.50 Last dinner 10pm

Credit cards 1 2 3 5 V

ROSEDALE ABBEY
North Yorkshire
Map **8** SE79

★★ **Milburn Arms** (Guestaccom)
☎ Lastingham (07515) 312

This charming country inn, managed by the friendly resident proprietors, provides comfort, hospitality and good food.

7rm(3 2) 1 CTV in all bedrooms ® sB&B£17.50—£22 sB&B£19.50—£26.50 dB&B£28—£34 dB&B£34—£39 B

CTV 35P pool Live music & dancing Fri mthly *xmas*

Lunch £5—£10 Dinner £5—£10&alc Wine £4.95 Last dinner 9pm

Credit cards 1 3 V

★★**White Horse Farm** (ExecHotel/Minotel)
☎ Lastingham (07515) 239
Closed Xmas Day
Converted 17th-century farmhouse overlooking unspoilt Rosedale.
15rm(7🛁8🚿)(3fb) CTV in all bedrooms Ⓡ sB&B🛁🚿£21—£28 dB&B🛁🚿£42 B
50P 🚗 ✿ stabling *xmas*
English & Continental **V** Lunch £6.50—£7.50 Tea £2.60—£3 Dinner £12.50—£13.50&alc Wine £6 Last dinner 9pm
Credit cards 2 5 Ⓥ

ROSEHALL
Highland *Sutherland*
Map **14** NC40

★★**Achness** ☎ (054984) 239
Closed Oct—Feb
Friendly and comfortable Highland Hotel.
5rm Annexe: 7🛁 TV in 6 bedrooms Ⓡ S% *sB&B£22.50 sB&B🛁£24.50 dB&B£45 dB&B🛁£49
CTV 40P 🚗 ✿ clay pigeon shooting
S% *Bar Lunch £3.50 Tea 80p Dinner fr£10 Wine £3.50 Last dinner 8pm
Credit cards 1 3

Rosedale Abbey — Ross-on-Wye

ROSLIN
Lothian *Midlothian*
Map **11** NT26

✕ **Ye Olde Original Rosslyne** Main St
☎ 031-440 2384
The friendly restaurant has a Victorian theme and offers a modest à la carte menu of competently-prepared dishes, many of them from the grill. Home-baked puddings are particularly good.
Mainly grills 60 seats *Lunch fr£5.50&alc Dinner £10—£13&alc Wine £4.25 Last dinner 9pm 24P nc
Credit cards 1 2 3

ROSSINGTON
South Yorkshire
Map **8** SK69

★★**Mount Pleasant** (On A638 Great North Rd 1½m E of village) ☎ Doncaster (0302) 868696
Closed Xmas Day
Converted 18th-century estate house with 80 acres of woodland and farmland.
20rm(7🛁8🚿) Annexe: 8rm(2🛁) 1 CTV in all bedrooms **T** sB&B£14.50—£20.50 sB&B🛁🚿£20.50—£28 dB&B£26—£29 dB&B🛁🚿£32—£42.
100P 2 (charge) 🚗 ✿
V Lunch £3.95—£9&alc Tea £1.75—£2.50 High Tea £4—£6.75 Dinner £5.95—£8.95&alc Wine £3.60 Last dinner 9.30pm
Credit card 1
See advertisement under Doncaster

ROSS-ON-WYE
Hereford & Worcester
Map **3** SO62
See also **Kerne Bridge, Pencraig** and **Symonds Yat**

★★★*H* **Chase** Gloucester Rd (Consort/Queens Moat) ☎ (0989) 63161
Georgian style hotel set in gardens, close to Ross town centre.
40🛁(2fb) 2 CTV in all bedrooms **T** S% sB&B🛁£48.50 dB&B🛁£66 B
☾ 200P CFA ✿ *xmas*
English & French **V** Lunch fr£11 Tea £1.40—£3.60 Dinner £12.50—£25 Wine £6.50 Last dinner 9.45pm
Credit cards 1 2 3 5 Ⓥ

★★★*HB* **Pengethley Manor** (4m N on A49 Hereford rd) (Best Western)
☎ Harewood End (098987) 211
Telex no 35332
Fully modernised Georgian house, set in peaceful surroundings.

10rm(9➡1⋒) Annexe: 10➡(3fb) 1▣✂ in bedrooms CTV in all bedrooms **T** S% ✱sB&B➡⋒£55—£80 dB&B➡⋒£80—£150 **B**

85P 3🚗✿ ≈(heated) ♪ billiards Live music & dancing Fri 👪 *xmas*

V ♁ ☕ S% ✱Lunch £15alc Dinner £22alc Wine £7.25 Last dinner 9.30pm

Credit cards 1 2 3 5

★★★**Royal** Palace Pound (Trusthouse Forte) ☎ (0989) 65105

A warm welcome and friendly service await tourist and businessman alike at this hotel in a prominent position overlooking the Horseshoe bend of the River Wye.

Ross-on-Wye

30➡(3fb) CTV in all bedrooms ® sB&B➡£50.50 dB&B➡£68.50 **B**

20P✿ *xmas*

♁ ☕ Last dinner 9.30pm

Credit cards 1 2 3 4 5

★★★**Walford House** Walford Rd (2m S B4228) ☎ (0989) 63829

9rm(8➡1⋒) Annexe: 1➡(2fb) 1▣ CTV in all bedrooms ® **T** ✱dB&B➡⋒£40—£50 **B**

100P ⊞ ✿ 👪 *xmas*

♡French **V** ♁ Lunch £17.50alc Dinner £15&alc Wine £6.30 Last dinner 9.30pm

Credit cards 1 2 3 5

★★**Chasedale** Walford Rd ☎ (0989) 62423

Quiet family-run hotel on the edge of Ross-on-Wye. →

12rm(8⇔)(3fb) CTV in 8 bedrooms S% sB&B£18—£19 sB&B⇔£22—£24 dB&B£28—£30 dB&B⇔£36—£38 ℞

CTV 14P ✽ *xmas*

English & French V Lunch £5.50—£7 Tea £1 Dinner £7.75—£12.50 Wine £5 Last dinner 9pm

Credit cards 1 3 V

★★**Hunsdon Manor** Weston-under-Penyard (2m E A40) ☎ (0989) 62748

A 16th-century manor house with later additions, standing in 2½ acres of lawns and gardens.

Ross-on-Wye

12rm(2⇔4⋒)(2fb) CTV in all bedrooms ® S% sB&B£20 sB&B⇔⋒£22—£25 dB&B£25—£27 dB&B⇔⋒£30—£32 ℞

CTV 50P ✽ *xmas*

International V Lunch fr£5.50&alc Tea 75p—£1.45 Dinner £7.50—£8.50&alc Wine £3.95 Last dinner 9.30pm

Credit cards 1 2 3 5 V

★★**King's Head** 8 High St ☎ (0989) 63174

RS Xmas

14th century coaching inn with popular dining room and rear annexe.

13rm(12⇔1⋒) Annexe: 9⇔(3fb) CTV in all bedrooms ® sB&B⇔⋒£25 dB&B⇔⋒£40 ℞

20P

V Lunch £2.50—£3.50 Tea £1 High Tea £1.50 Dinner £11 alc Wine £5 Last dinner 9pm

V

★**Orles Barn** Wilton ☎ (0989) 62155

Closed Nov

Small family-run hotel in well kept gardens, close to the junction of the A40 and the A49.

10rm(5⇌3⋒)(2fb) CTV in 5 bedrooms ® ✱sB&B£14—£18 sB&B⇌⋒£17—£20 dB&B£26—£30 dB&B⇌⋒£32—£36 B CTV 20P ✿ ⇝ ♪ ⛹

♉English, French & Spanish V ♡ ☕ ✱Lunch £5.75—£7&alc Tea 75p—£2.50 Dinner £6.75—£7.50&alc Wine £4.50 Last dinner 9.30pm

Credit cards 1 2 3 5 Ⓥ

Ross-on-Wye — Rosthwaite

★**Rosswyn** 17 High St ☎ (0989) 62733

Small 15th-century town centre inn serving good selection of real ales.

9rm(4⇌2⋒) 3▭ CTV in all bedrooms ® S% sB&Bfr£14 sB&B⇌⋒fr£16 dB&Bfr£26 dB&B⇌⋒fr£32 B CTV Ᵽ ▭ ✿

♉International V ♡ S% ✱Bar lunch £1.20—£3.50 Dinner £9.95—£12 Wine £4.50 Last dinner 9.30pm

Credit cards 1 3

ROSTHWAITE
Cumbria
Map **11** NY21
See also **Borrowdale** and **Grange-in-Borrowdale**

★★★**Scafell** ☎ Borrowdale (059684) 208

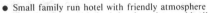

Closed Jan—mid Feb

A traditional-style hotel stands in a delightfully peaceful setting at the head of Borrowdale Valley. →

R

21rm(20➡1⋒)(3fb) CTV available in bedrooms ®
*sB&B➡⋒£17.95—£19.95
dB&B➡⋒£35.90—£39.90 B
50P ✿ xmas
International ♔ ⊐ *Bar lunch £4.70alc Tea 65p—£1.25 Dinner fr£10.25&alc Wine £4.05 Last dinner 8.15pm

ROTHBURY
Northumberland
Map **12** NU00

★★***Coquet Vale*** Station Rd ☎ (0669) 20305

Large, detached grey-stone building in an elevated position overlooking the valley.

9rm(5⋒)(2fb) CTV in all bedrooms ® B
CTV 30P
V ♔ Last dinner 8.30pm
Credit cards 1 3

ROTHERHAM
South Yorkshire
Map **8** SK49

★★★**Rotherham Moat House** (Queens Moat) Moorgate Rd ☎ (0709) 364902 Telex no 547810

A modern luxury hotel offering comprehensive facilities, particularly for the business executive.

64➡⋒(3fb) CTV in all bedrooms ® **T** S%
*sB➡⋒£20—£38 dB➡⋒£23.50—£44 (room only) B
Lift ☾ CTV 90P CFA sauna bath solarium gymnasium Live music & dancing Fri & Sat
English & French **V** ♔ ⊐ *Lunch £5.95&alc Tea 65p Dinner £9—£10.75&alc Wine £5.25 Last dinner 9.45pm
Credit cards 1 2 3 5 Ⓥ

★★**Brentwood** Moorgate Rd ☎ (0709) 382772 Telex no 547291

Closed 26 & 27 Dec

A stone-built Victorian residence in its own grounds with a modern extension.

13rm(3➡6⋒) Annexe: 20rm(17➡3⋒) 1 CTV in all bedrooms ® **T** S%
*sB&B£15—£21 sB&B➡⋒£15—£29
dB&B➡⋒£20—£35 B
50P ✿
English & French **V** ♔ *Lunch £3.95—£7&alc Dinner £9.50 Wine £4.65 Last dinner 9pm
Credit cards 1 2 3 4 5 Ⓥ

★**Elton** Main St, Bramley (3m E A631) ☎ (0709) 545681

A two-storey stone building, which was originally a farmhouse.

15rm(2➡3⋒)(1fb) CTV in all bedrooms ® in 9 bedrooms **T** sB&B£18—£25.50 sB&B➡⋒£25—£29.50 dB&B£32 dB&B➡⋒£34 B
☾ 20P
English & French **V** ♔ ⊐ Lunch £6.25—£8.65&alc Tea fr75p Dinner fr£8.65&alc Wine £5.35 Last dinner 9.45pm
Credit cards 1 2 3 Ⓥ

R

ROTHERWICK
Hampshire
Map **4** SU75

★★★★ *HBL* **Tylney Hall** (Prestige) ☎ Hook (025672) 4881 Telex no 859864

An elegant country house in 66 acres of parkland recently converted to a very comfortable hotel. The restaurant is oak panelled and the lounges are ornately decorated. The bedrooms are very well furnished and appointed and the staff are hospitable and friendly.

37➡⋒3 CTV in all bedrooms **T**
S% sB&B➡⋒£58.85—£90.95
dB&B➡⋒£69.55—£214 B
Lift ☾ 120P ✿ (heated) (hard) snooker croquet *xmas*
English & French **V** ♔ ⊐ S%
Lunch fr£13 Tea fr£4.50 Dinner fr£19 Wine £9.20 Last dinner 9.30pm
Credit cards 1 2 3 5

See advertising under Basingstoke

ROTHES
Grampian *Morayshire*
Map **15** NJ24

★★★ *L* **Rothes Glen** ☎ (03403) 254

Closed Jan

This superbly-furnished, castle-style mansion has peacocks and Highland cattle in the grounds; well-equipped bedrooms are tastefully decorated.

16rm(2➡)(5fb) CTV in all bedrooms **T**
sB&B£35 sB&B➡£40 dB&B£52.75
dB&B➡£57.75 B
CTV 40P ✿
♔ Lunch £8.58 Dinner £17.60&alc Wine £5.15 Last dinner 9pm
Credit cards 1 2 3 5 Ⓥ

ROTHESAY
Isle of Bute Strathclyde *Buteshire*
See **Bute, Isle of**

ROTHLEY
Leicestershire
Map **8** SK51

★★★ *L* **Rothley Court** Westfield Ln (Best Western) ☎ Leicester (0533) 374141 Telex no 341995

The splendid manor house's long and colourful history is evinced by a chapel built in the 13th century by the Knights Templar. The hotel's public rooms and main bedrooms have rich wood panelling and comfortable furnishings, and there is also a more modern annexe of rooms. The ever-increasing popularity of the restaurant is due to the light, modern French cooking of chef Bruce Sangster.

15rm(13➡2⋒) Annexe: 20rm(17➡1⋒) CTV in all bedrooms ® in 20 bedrooms **T**
*sB&B£42 sB&B➡⋒£47.50—£55
dB&B£50 dB&B➡⋒£58.50—£68.50 B
☾ 100P CFA ✿ *xmas*
French ♔ ⊐ *Lunch £11.50&alc Tea £1.50 Dinner £15.75—£16.50&alc Wine £5.50 Last dinner 10pm
Credit cards 1 2 3 5 Ⓥ

XX ***Red Lion Inn*** ☎ Leicester (0533) 302488

The restaurant is in a single-storey building to the rear of this large inn at the junction of the A6 and the B5328.

Lunch not served Sat Dinner not served Sun
English & French **V** 60 seats Last dinner 10pm 100P
Credit cards 1 2 3 4 5

ROUSDON
Devon
Map **3** SY29

★★**Orchard Country** ☎ Lyme Regis (02974) 2972

Located in a quiet country setting between Lyme Regis and Seaton, this comfortable family hotel has a good reputation for its freshly-prepared foods and varied choice.

Closed Nov—15 Apr except Xmas week
14rm(7➡4⋒) CTV in 6 bedrooms ®
sB&B➡⋒£21—£23 dB&B➡⋒£40—£44 B
CTV 20P ✿ nc 8yrs *xmas*
♔ ⊐ *Tea fr75p Dinner fr£8.50 Wine £4.50 Last dinner 8.15pm
Credit cards 1 3 Ⓥ

ROWARDENNAN
Central *Stirlingshire*
Map **10** NS39

★**Rowardennan** ☎ Balmaha (036087) 273

Closed Nov RS Dec—Mar

Personally run historic inn on Loch Lomondside.

11rm(1➡)(3fb) ® in 6 bedrooms
sB&B£16—£18 sB&B➡£18—£20
dB&B£26—£28 dB&B➡£32—£34
CTV 50P
V ♔ ⊐ Bar lunch £3—£6 Tea fr£2.50 High Tea £3—£5 Dinner £8.50—£10 Wine £4 Last dinner 8.45pm

ROWEN
Gwynedd
Map **6** SH77

★ **Tir-y-Coed Country House** ☎ Tynygroes (049267) 219 Due to change to (0492) 650219

Closed Xmas RS Nov—Feb

Detached, Edwardian house situated in a small peaceful village.

7rm(5➡1⋒) Annexe: (1⋒)(1fb) CTV in 7 bedrooms ® sB&B➡⋒£15—£17.50
dB&B➡⋒£27.75—£32.75 B
8P ✿

 Bar lunch £1.50—£3 Tea 75p—£1.50 Dinner £7 Wine £5 Last dinner 7.30pm

Ⓥ

ROWSLEY
Derbyshire
Map **8** SK26

★★★*BL* **Peacock** (Embassy) Matlock (0629) 733518

Former Dower house built in 1652, on the A6, 2m south of Bakewell.

14rm(10 4) Annexe: 6rm(1)(5fb) 1 CTV in all bedrooms Ⓡ **T** S% sB&B£31.50—£36.50 sB&B£43.50—£48.50 dB&B£49 dB&B£72

45P 5(50p per night) *xmas*

V S% Lunch £8.25 Tea £1.40—£4.25 Dinner £14.75 Wine £5.10 Last dinner 9pm

Credit cards 1 2 3 5 Ⓥ

See advertisement under Matlock

ROY BRIDGE
Highland *Inverness-shire*
Map **14** NN28

★★**Glenspean Lodge** (039781) 224

This hotel set in its own grounds overlooks Monessie Gorge.

13rm(2 1)(3fb) sB&B£16—£18 dB&B£28—£32 dB&B£32—£36

TV 30P 2

Bar lunch £3.60—£5.50 Tea £1 Dinner £8 Last dinner 8pm

Ⓥ

ROZEL BAY
Jersey
See **Channel Islands**

RUABON
Clwyd
Map **7** SJ34

★★**Wynnstay Arms** High St (0978) 822187

Originally a coaching inn dating back to the 19th century, the village-centre hotel offers traditional hospitality. The old stable block was the headquarters or Mr Watkin-Wynn's private army, which fought in the Crimean Wars.

9rm(2)(1fb) CTV in all bedrooms Ⓡ S% sB&B£21.50—£23.50 sB&B£23.50 dB&B£32—£35 dB&B£37

80P 2

English & French **V** S% Lunch fr£5.50 Dinner fr£8.50&alc Wine £4.75 Last dinner 9.45pm

Credit cards 1 2 3 4 5 Ⓥ

RUAN HIGH LANES
Cornwall
Map **2** SW93

★★*L* **Hundred House** Truro (0872) 501336

Closed Dec—Feb

Small, family-run hotel, set in three acres of gardens and grounds.

10rm(6 4) CTV in all bedrooms Ⓡ sB&B£16—£24 dB&B£32—£48

25P nc 9yrs *xmas*

English & Continental Bar lunch £4—£5alc Tea fr60p Dinner fr£10.50 Wine £3.95 Last dinner 9pm

Credit cards 1 2 3

★★ **Poisue Manor** Truro (0872) 501270

RS Nov—Feb

Charming 18th-century manor in secluded setting and with a relaxed atmosphere.

13rm(10)(4fb) CTV in 11 bedrooms Ⓡ **T** sB&B£17—£18.50 sB&B£19—£20.50 dB&B£34—£37 dB&B£38—£41

CTV 20P *xmas*

Lunch £2.50—£6 Tea 45p—£1.75 High Tea £3.60 Dinner £7.50—£9.50&alc Wine £4.50 Last dinner 8.15pm

Credit cards 1 3

★***Pendower Beach House*** Truro (0872) 501241

Closed Jan

The superbly-positioned beach hotel provides a friendly, relaxed atmosphere.

12rm(1 1) Annexe: 1(3fb)

CTV 50P (hard)

V Last dinner 8pm

Credit cards 1 3

RUGBY
Warwickshire
Map **4** SP57

★★★**Brownsover Hall** Brownsover Ln, Old Brownsover (1½m N A426) (0788) 73131

A mock-Gothic Hall on the outskirts of the town, set in seven acres of woodland, caters for small conferences and wedding parties, their numbers easily absorbed in the rambling house.

31rm(21 10)(3fb) 1 CTV in all bedrooms Ⓡ **T** S% *sB£23—£42.25 dB£30—£52.50 (room only)

CTV 80P

French **V** *Lunch fr£6.80&alc Tea fr50p Dinner fr£9&alc Wine £4.50 Last dinner 9.30pm

Credit cards 1 2 3 5 Ⓥ

★★★**Clifton Court** Lilbourne Rd, Clifton-upon-Dunsmore (0788) 65033

Popular business hotel in peaceful surroundings.

14rm(10 4) CTV in all bedrooms Ⓡ *sB&B£43.50—£45 dB&B£56—£59

CTV 120P *xmas*

English, French & Italian **V** *Lunch £4.50—£6.50&alc Tea fr60p Dinner fr£8.50&alc Wine £5.45 Last dinner 10pm

Credit cards 1 3 Ⓥ

★★★**Post House** Crick (0788) 822101
(For full entry see Crick)

R

★★*H* **Dun Cow** The Square, Dunchurch (3m S A426) ☎ (0788) 810233 Telex no 312242

16th century coaching inn, well furnished with antiques.

23➡ Annexe: 5rm (2fb) 3⊟ CTV in all bedrooms **T** S% ✱sB&B➡£28—£45 dB&B➡£38—£60 **B**

☾ CTV 120P 6🏠 🏠 *xmas*

English & French **V** ♡ ☕ S% ✱Lunch £7.95—£9.95&alc Tea 95p—£3.50 High Tea £2.95—£4.95 Dinner £8.95—£10.95&alc Wine £4.50 Last dinner 10.30pm

Credit cards 1 2 3 4 5

★★ **Hillmorton Manor** Hill St, Hillmorton (2m SE off A428) ☎ (0788) 65533

Located in the centre of a village on the south-east of Rugby, this extended house is ideal for small parties and for gatherings of business people.

12(1➡10⋒)(1fb) CTV in all bedrooms ® S% ✱sB&B➡⋒fr£28 dB&B➡⋒fr£40

CTV 45P ⊞ *xmas*

English & French **V** ♡ ☕ ✱Lunch fr£6 Tea fr£1.50 Dinner fr£8&alc Wine £4.70 Last dinner 10pm

Credit cards 1 2 3 Ⓥ

✕ **Andalucia** 10 Henry St ☎ (0788) 76404

Dim lighting creates an intimate atmosphere in this modest restaurant where the unique flavours of original Spanish dishes may bring memories of a bygone holiday flooding back!

Dinner not served Sun

English & Continental **V** 54 seats Lunch fr£6.50&alc Dinner £7.50—£9.95&alc Wine £5.75 Last dinner 10.30pm ₱

Credit cards 1 2 3 5

RUGELEY
Staffordshire
Map **7** SK01

★★ ***Cedar Tree*** Main Rd, Brereton ☎ (08894) 4241

A three-storey white-painted 18th-century building located between Lichfield and Rugeley.

16rm (7➡)(1fb) CTV in 11 bedrooms ® ✈ **B**

CTV 200P ✿ squash

V ♡ Last dinner 10pm

Credit cards 1 2 3 5

★ **Eaton Lodge** Wolseley Rd (Wolverhampton & Dudley) ☎ (08894) 3454

Large Gothic style building with recent extension.

12rm (1➡6⋒) CTV in all bedrooms ® ✱sB&B£16.50—£18 sB&B➡⋒£19 dB&B£22 dB&B➡⋒£26 **B**

200P ✿ *xmas*

♡ ☕ ✱Lunch £3.75 Tea 40—50p Dinner £9.50alc Wine £4.30 Last dinner 9.15pm

Credit cards 1 2 3 Ⓥ

Rugby — Rushlake Green

RUNCORN
Cheshire
Map **7** SJ58

★★★ **Crest** Wood Ln, Beechwood (Crest) ☎ (0928) 714000 Telex no 627426

The large, modern hotel is well furnished; it stands conveniently close to the M56, yet in rural surroundings.

128➡⋒(4fb) ⊬ in 21 bedrooms CTV in all bedrooms ® **T** S% ✱sB&B➡⋒£52.35 dB&B➡⋒£68.20 **B**

Lift ☾ CFA ✿ Live music & dancing Sat ♿ 🏠

V ♡ ☕ ⊬ ✱Lunch £5.60—£8.95 Tea 70p Dinner £11.50—£12.50&alc Last dinner 10pm

Credit cards 1 2 3 4 5

0928 714000

RUSHLAKE GREEN
East Sussex
Map **5** TQ61

★★★ **PRIORY COUNTRY HOUSE, RUSHLAKE GREEN**

☎ (0435) 830553 Telex no 957210

Closed Xmas eve—mid Jan

Originally a monastery from the 15th century with a collection of farm buildings around it, this well restored hotel has retained much of the original character. Located amongst 1,000 acres in the peaceful and appealing farmlands of East Sussex, it has become a country retreat with a most relaxing atmosphere. The owners, Mr and Mrs Dunn, have a team of pleasant, warm staff who are ever willing to please and who anticipate their guest's needs. Although there is no bar, drinks are served in the log-fired sitting rooms which have comfortable sofas and chairs as well as fresh flowers and magazines. The dining room evokes country pursuits with its display of guns, its stone floor and exposed beams, and they keep a good table. Waitresses wear long, floral skirts which add to the country atmosphere. The bedrooms are rather cottage-like in appearance but equipped with many extras including fruit, and magazines which all add to one's convenience. The hotel also has

accommodation in its annexe as well as rooms in the nearby village; these latter are most luxurious and have their own sitting room and breakfast room. Peter and Jane Dunn are the owners who run the hotel and they ensure high standards of hospitality. Incidentally, it is handy for Glyndebourne.

6➡ Annexe: 9➡ 2⊟ CTV in all bedrooms **T** sB&B➡£39 dB&B➡£58—£100

P ⊞ ✿ ♪ pheasant & clay pigeon shooting nc 9yrs

English & French ♡ ☕ Lunch £12.75 Dinner £19.50 Wine £6.75 Last dinner 9pm

RUSHDEN
Northampton
Map **4** SP96

★ **Westward** Shirley Rd ☎ (0933) 312376

Closed 23 Dec—3 Jan

16rm (1⋒) Annexe: 10rm (3fb) CTV in 19 bedrooms TV in 7 bedrooms ® ✈ sB&B£16.50—£26.50 sB&B⋒£26.50 dB&B£30—£34 dB&B⋒£34

CTV 16P ⊞ ⛱ (heated)

Dinner £5—£7.50&alc Wine £4.75 Last dinner 8pm Ⓥ

RUSHYFORD
Co Durham
Map **8** NZ22

★★★ **Eden Arms** (Swallow) ☎ Bishop Auckland (0388) 720541 Telex no 53168

Comfortably modernised, the hotel offers well appointed bedrooms and attractive lounges.

51rm (50➡1⋒)(2fb) 1⊟ CTV in all bedrooms ® **T** S% sB&B➡⋒£30—£39.50 dB&B➡⋒£40—£50 **B**

☾ 200P ✿ ⛱ (heated) pool table Live music & dancing Sat (Sep—Jun) ♿ *xmas*

English & French **V** ♡ ☕ S% Lunch fr£6&alc Tea 75p—£1.95 High Tea £3.85—£4.50 Dinner fr£8.95&alc Wine £5.50 Last dinner 9.30pm

Credit cards 1 2 3 4 5 Ⓥ

R

RUSPER
West Sussex
Map **4** TQ23

★★★*B* **Ghyll Manor** ☏ (029384) 571
Telex no 877557

The 14th-century Tudor manor house stands in magnificent grounds and offers some spacious, airy bedrooms that have been tastefully appointed with the accent on comfort. The atmosphere is warm and friendly, the menu imaginative and the cooking good.

8rm(7➡1⋒) Annexe: 14➡5⋒ CTV in all bedrooms ® T S% sB&B➡⋒£50—£90 dB&B➡⋒£56—£120 Continental breakfast ⋒

☾60P ✿ (heated) (hard) xmas

S% Lunch fr£9&alc Tea £1.50 High Tea £3.50 Dinner £12.50&alc Wine £6.85 Last dinner 10pm

Credit cards 1 2 3 4 5 Ⓥ

RUTHIN
Clwyd
Map **6** SJ15

★★★ **Ruthin Castle** (Best Western) ☏ (08242) 2664 Telex no 61169

Impressive 15th-century stone castle situated in its own well-kept grounds.

58rm(56➡2⋒)(4fb) 1⊟ sB&B➡⋒fr£30.50 dB&B➡⋒£49—£68 ⋒

Lift ☾ CTV 200P CFA ✿ snooker *xmas*

Continental V Lunch fr£6.25 Tea 75p—£1.90 Dinner fr£8.95&alc Wine £4.95 Last dinner 9.30pm

Credit cards 1 2 3 5 Ⓥ

RUTHWELL
Dumfries & Galloway *Dumfriesshire*
Map **11** NY16

★ *BL* ***Kirklands*** (1m E of Clarencefield off B724) ☏ Clarencefield (038787) 284

Tastefully decorated hotel offering high standard of accommodation.

5⋒(1fb) 1⊟ CTV in all bedrooms ® ⋒

CTV 15P ✿

V Last dinner 8.45pm

Credit cards 1 3

RYDE
Isle of Wight
See **Wight, Isle of**

RYE
East Sussex
Map **5** TQ92

★★ **Mermaid Inn** Mermaid St ☏ (0797) 223065

Rebuilt in 1410, the Mermaid is famous for its beams, panelling and wall frescoes. Rooms are small, but charmingly furnished with antiques, the restaurant specialises in fresh fish and roasts, and the staff are friendly and cheerful.

29rm(20➡6⋒) S% sB&Bfr£31 sB&B➡⋒fr£34 dB&Bfr£42 dB&B➡⋒fr£48

CTV P nc8yrs *xmas*

Lunch £8&alc Dinner £10&alc Last dinner 9.30pm

Credit cards 1 2 3 5

★★ **George** High St (Trusthouse Forte) ☏ (0797) 222114

Historic coaching inn with many original features, well-appointed bedrooms and country kitchen style restaurant.

17rm(12➡5⋒) CTV in all bedrooms ® sB&B➡⋒£48.50 dB&B➡⋒£66.50 ⋒

CTV 9P 8 *xmas*

Last dinner 9pm

Credit cards 1 2 3 4 5

★★ **Hope Anchor** Watchbell St ☏ (0797) 222216

Great character and charm combine with a warm, family atmosphere in this comfortable, 17th-century free-house which has extensive, open views of the countryside west of the town.

15rm(6➡)(1fb) ® sB&B£23 sB&B➡£27.50 dB&B£36 dB&B➡£43

CTV 12P →

English & French Bar lunch £1.10—£7 Tea £1 High Tea £3.50 Dinner £8.10&alc Wine £5 Last dinner 9pm

Credit cards 1 2 3 4 5 V

★★***Saltings*** Hilders Cliff, High St (0797) 223838

Family-run hotel with nautical decor.

15rm(2 6)(2fb) CTV available in bedrooms ®

CTV 30P *xmas*

V Last dinner 9.45pm

Credit cards 1 3

✕✕**Simmons** 68 The Mint (0797) 222026

Well appointed family run 15th-century cottage restaurant featuring individual and enterprising style of cooking.

Closed Mon, Boxing Day, New Years Day, 1st Tue, Wed & Thu Oct & 3 wks Feb Lunch not served Tue—Sat Dinner not served Sun

French 24 seats S% Lunch £8.75 Dinner £11&alc Wine £5.95 Last dinner 10pm

Credit cards 1 2 3 5

✕**Flushing Inn** Market St (0797) 223292

The cosy, historic restaurant, run by the same family for twenty years, boasts a sixteenth-century wall fresco. The simple, excellent-quality fish and seafood on the menu is popular with visitors and locals alike.

Closed Tue & 3 wks Jan Dinner not served Mon

V 36 seats Lunch £7.80—£10.50&alc Dinner £11—£15&alc Wine £6.90 Last dinner 9.15pm

Credit cards 1 2 3 5

✕**Monastery** 6 High St (0797) 223272

Housed in a 17th-century building the restaurant overlooks a secluded walled garden flanked by remains of the Augustinian chapel.

Closed Tue Lunch not served Mon—Sat

V 54 seats S% Lunch fr£6&alc Dinner £15&alc Wine £4.25 Last dinner 9pm Live music wknds

SAFFRON WALDEN
Essex
Map **5** TL53

★★**Saffron** 10—18 High St (0799) 22676 Telex no 81653

Closed 25—30 Dec RS Sun

A 16th-century hotel combining old world charm with modern comforts and providing high standards of cuisine.

21rm(5 6)(2fb) 1 CTV in all bedrooms ® in 6 bedrooms **T** sB&B£18.50—£31.50 sB&B £31.50 dB&B£28—£45 dB&B £45 Continental breakfast

12P

International Lunch £12.50&alc Tea £1 Dinner £12.50&alc Wine £5.25 Last dinner 9.30pm

Credit cards 1 3 V

Rye — St Andrews

✕**Old Hoops** 15 King St (0799) 22813

The first-floor restaurant, located in a bustling market town, maintains a friendly, rustic atmosphere. The two patrons mingle with their guests to supervise the serving of an interesting French menu supported by a complementary wine list.

Closed 26—30 Dec & Good Fri Dinner not served Sun

International **V** 42 seats ✱Lunch 95p—£4.75&alc Dinner 95p—£6.80&alc Wine £4.70 P

Credit cards 1 2 3 5 V

ST AGNES
Cornwall
Map **2** SW75

★★**Rose in Vale Country House** Rose in Vale, Mithian (087255) 2202

Attractive Georgian house with modern extension, set in peaceful valley.

15rm(8 4)(3fb) ® sB&B£12.55—£15.80 sB&B £13.55—£16.80 dB&B£25.10—£31.60 dB&B £27.10—£33.60

CTV 40P (heated) solarium croquet badminton

English & Continental **V** Bar lunch £1.10—£3.95 Tea 45p—£1.75 Dinner £6.95&alc Wine £4.20 Last dinner 8pm

Credit cards 1 3 V

★★***Rosemundy House*** (087255) 2101

Closed 20 Oct—29 Mar

Country-house style hotel in four acres of private, wooded gardens. Close to village centre with many rooms of character, some parts of the house date from 1780.

42rm(25 10)(10fb) CTV in 14 bedrooms TV in 1 bedroom ®

CTV 50P (heated)

Last dinner 8pm

★**Lamorna House** Chapel Porth Rd, Goonvrea (087255) 2670

Closed mid Oct—Etr

Small hotel in a quiet location.

10rm(1fb) ® sB&B£8.95—£12.35 dB&B£17.90—£24.70

CTV 12P

Bar lunch 65p—£3.25 Tea 40p Dinner £7 Wine £5.50 Last dinner 7.30pm

★*H* **Sunholme** Goonvrea Rd (087255) 2318

Closed Nov—Mar

Small family hotel in a rural location.

11rm(4)(3fb) TV in all bedrooms sB&B£11—£13.50 sB&B £13.50—£16 dB&B£22—£27 dB&B £27—£32

CTV 20P

Bar lunch £1.50—£3.50 Tea 75p—£1.50 Dinner fr£7.50 Wine £3.95 Last dinner 7.30pm

Credit cards 1 3 V

ST ALBANS
Hertfordshire
Map **4** TL10

★★★*BL* **Noke Thistle** Watford Rd (2¾m Sat junc A405/B4630) (Thistle) (0727) 54252 Telex no 893834

Convenient, comfortable hotel.

57 in 5 bedrooms. CTV in all bedrooms ® **T** ✱sB £56—£62 dB £64—£72 (room only)

150P CFA

International ✱Lunch fr£10.25&alc Dinner fr£14.25&alc Wine £7 Last dinner 9.30pm

Credit cards 1 2 3 4 5 V

★★★**St Michael's Manor** Fishpool St (0727) 64444

Gracious, 16th-century manor in delightful grounds with well-equipped bedrooms and friendly service.

26rm(9) 4 CTV in all bedrooms **T** S% sB&B£45.50 sB&B £45.50 dB&B£58 dB&B £58

70P nc5yrs

English & French **V** Lunch £8.50&alc Tea 55p Dinner £11.50&alc Wine £5.45 Last dinner 9.30pm

Credit cards 1 2 3 5 V

★★★***Sopwell House*** Cottonmill Ln (0727) 64477

An 18th-century mansion, surrounded by three acres of gardens, and reputed to have once had royal connections.

27rm(25 1)(1fb) CTV in all bedrooms **T**

100P CFA

French **V** Last dinner 9.30pm

Credit cards 1 2 3 5

ST ANDREWS
Fife
Map **12** NO51

★★★★**Old Course Golf & Country Club** Old Station Rd (0334) 74371 Telex no 76280

Closed 25—28 Dec RS Nov—Apr

Occupying a unique position, almost on the famous St Andrews links, the hotel has been tastefully refurbished to meet the demands of the international golfer.

146 (19fb) CTV in all bedrooms ® **T** sB&B £44—£72 dB&B £74—£115

Lift 150P (heated) sauna bath solarium gymnasium Live music nightly

International **V** Lunch £9.50&alc Tea £1.25&alc Dinner £16.50&alc Wine £7 Last dinner 10pm

Credit cards 1 2 3 4 5

★★★★*L* **Rusacks Marine** Pilmour Links (Trusthouse Forte) (0334) 74321

Victorian hotel overlooking golf course and beach.

50🛁🚿🚭in 10 bedrooms CTV in all bedrooms ®T S% *sB🛁🚿£55—£63 dB🛁🚿£85—£111 (room only) 🅱
Lift ☾ 30P *xmas*
🍷International V 🍵 ☕ 🚭 S% *Lunch £8.50&alc Tea £1.50—£4.75 Dinner £15&alc Wine £5.90 Last dinner 10pm
Credit cards 1 2 3 5

★★★*HBL* **Rufflets Country House** ☎ (0334) 72594
Closed mid Jan—mid Feb
Set in beautifully landscaped gardens, this hospitable hotel has been in the same family for 35 years. The food, featuring many Scottish recipes, is most innovative, while the bedrooms, several being re-decorated, are very sympathetically done. Additional accommodation is available in a charming cottage by the hotel entrance.
18rm(16🛁2🚿) Annexe:3🛁(2fb) CTV in all bedrooms ® 🐕 *sB&B🛁🚿£36 dB&B🛁🚿£60—£64 🅱
100P 6🚗(£2 per night) ✿ putting 🏠 *xmas*
🍷Scottish & French V 🍵 ☕ *Lunch £6—£7&alc Tea £2alc Dinner £14—£16&alc Wine £7 Last dinner 9.30pm
Credit cards 1 2 3 4 5

St Andrews

★★★*B* **St Andrews Golf** 40 The Scores (Inter-Hotel) ☎ (0334) 72611 Telex no 946240
This comfortable hotel continues to improve under the personal supervision of the proprietor.
23rm(20🛁3🚿)(10fb) CTV in all bedrooms ®T sB&B🛁🚿£40—£42 dB&B🛁🚿£60—£64 🅱
Lift ☾ 🅿 CFA sauna bath solarium Live music & dancing Sat (in Winter) *xmas*
🍵 ☕ Lunch fr£7 Tea fr£2.75 High Tea fr£6 Dinner fr£13.25&alc Wine £6.75 Last dinner 9.30pm
Credit cards 1 2 3 4 5 Ⓥ

★★★**Scores** 76 The Scores (Best Western) ☎ (0334) 72451 Telex no 946240
Located only a 'short iron' (or 150 yards) from the first tee of the famous golf course, the hotel has a commanding view over the extensive West Sands and St Andrews links.
30🛁🚿(1fb) 1🛏 CTV in all bedrooms ® sB&B🛁🚿£25—£45 dB&B🛁🚿£42—£75 🅱
Lift ☾ 🅿 ✿ *xmas*
🍵 ☕ Bar lunch £2—£8 Tea £1.50 Dinner £5—£8.50&alc Wine £5 Last dinner 10pm
Credit cards 1 2 3 5 Ⓥ

★★***Ardgowan*** 2 Playfair Ter ☎ (0334) 72970
Closed Dec—Mar RS mid Mar & Apr
Family run hotel offering personal attention and friendly service.
15rm(1🛁8🚿) CTV in all bedrooms ® 🐕 CTV 🅿
🍷Scottish & French V Last dinner 9pm
Credit cards 1 3

★★**Russell** 26 The Scores ☎ (0334) 73447
Closed Xmas & New Year
Small family-run hotel with views of the sea.
7rm(1🛁6🚿)(1fb) CTV in all bedrooms ® 🐕 dB&B🛁🚿£40—£44
🅿 🚐
🍷Scottish & French V Lunch fr£7.50 Dinner £12.50alc Wine £5.95 Last dinner 9.30pm
Credit cards 1 2 3 5

✕✕***Grange Inn*** Grange ☎ (0334) 72670
Fine views, natural stonework and Victoriana are features of this attractive, cottage-style restaurant, which lies a mile south of the town. The menu specialises in local meat, game and seafood, making →

S

good use of fresh produce, and the quaint bar is popular for its own fine food.

Scottish & French 36 seats Last dinner 9.30pm 30P

ST ANNES
Lancashire
See **Lytham St Annes**

ST ASAPH
Clwyd
Map **6** SJ07

★★★**Oriel House** Upper Denbigh Rd (0745) 582716

Closed Xmas Day & Boxing Day

St Andrews — St Austell

Modernised hotel set in picturesque area alongside private stretch of river.

19rm(12 7)(2fb) 1 in 2 bedrooms CTV in all bedrooms ® T
*sB&B £24 dB&B £39 B
CTV 100P 2 Disco Sat
English & French Wine £4.50
Last dinner 9.15pm
Credit cards 1 2 3 5 V

ST AUBIN
Jersey
See **Channel Islands**

ST AUSTELL
Cornwall
Map **2** SX05

★★★★*H* **Carlyon Bay** Sea Rd, Carlyon Bay (Brend) Par (072681) 2304
Telex no 42551

The comfortable hotel, standing in its own grounds in a clifftop position, offers good sporting facilities and a private beach.

74rm(69)(4fb) CTV in all bedrooms
sB&B £35.08—£41.98
dB&B £63.25—£88.55 B

Lift ℂ CTV 100P 2 (£1.73 per day) ✽ (heated) & (heated) 18 (hard) snooker sauna bath solarium gymnasium table tennis putting Live music and dancing 3 nights wkly xmas

English & French V Lunch fr£7.76 Tea fr75p Dinner fr£10.63&alc Wine £5.25 Last dinner 9pm

Credit cards 1 2 3 5

★★★**Porth Avallen** Sea Rd, Carlyon Bay ☎ Par (072681) 2802

Closed 23—31 Dec

Comfortable hotel in secluded position.

25rm(19 2)(1fb) 2 CTV in 23 bedrooms ® T S% sB&B£23—£29.50 sB&B £29.50—£37 dB&Bfr£33.50 dB&B £45.50—£49.50 B

ℂ CTV 50P ✽

V Lunch £5—£7.50 Tea 45p—£1.50 High Tea £1—£2.50 Dinner £8.25—£11.25&alc Wine £3.75 Last dinner 8.30pm

Credit cards 1 2 3 5

★★ *L* **Boscundle Manor** Tregrehan (2m E off A390) ☎ Par (072681) 3557

Closed mid Dec—mid Jan

RS mid Jan—mid Feb

A lovely, eighteenth-century manor house, set in secluded grounds and furnished with many fine antiques, features a well-appointed restaurant with a high standard of cuisine.

9rm(4 4)CTV in all bedrooms T S% sB&B£33—£40 sB&B £33—£40 dB&B £50—£60

12P ✽ (heated) gymnasium croquet

International S% Dinner £16 Wine £5.50 Last dinner 9.30pm

Credit cards 1 2 3 Ⓥ

★★**Clifden** 36—39 Aylmer Sq ☎ (0726) 73691

Closed 24 Dec—1 Jan

Family run town centre hotel with first floor restaurant.

15rm(3 1)CTV in all bedrooms ® T S% sB&B£17.50—£18.50 sB&B £22—£25 dB&B£30—£32 dB&B £34—£36

St Austell — St Columb Major

CTV

V Lunch £3.50—£4&alc Tea fr45p High Tea £1.10—£3.50 Dinner £5—£7.50&alc Wine £3.75 Last dinner 9pm

Credit cards 1 2 3 5 Ⓥ

★★**Cliff Head** Sea Rd, Carylon Bay (2m E off A390) ☎ Par (072681) 2125

Large family hotel in its own grounds and gardens overlooking Carlyon Bay.

48rm(30 3)(4fb) in 2 bedrooms CTV in 20 bedrooms ® sB&B£16.53—£21.81 SB&B £19.84—£24.72 dB&B£31.74—£40.73 dB&B £37.03—£46.55 B

CTV 60P 8 ✽ & (heated) pool table Live music & dancing Thu & Sat Cabaret Tue *xmas*

V Lunch £4.50—£5.50 Tea 85p—£1.50 High Tea £1.50—£2.35 Dinner £6.15—£7.95 Wine £4.25 Last dinner 9.15pm

Credit cards 1 2 3 5 Ⓥ

★★***Pier House*** Harbour Front, Charlestown ☎ (0726) 75272

Small harbour-side character hotel in unspoilt village.

12rm(4)(3fb)

CTV 10

French V Last dinner 10pm

★★**White Hart** Church St ☎ (0726) 72100

Closed Xmas Day & Boxing Day

Well appointed, busy inn, centrally located.

20rm(6)(2fb) CTV in all bedrooms ® S% *sB&B£18—£19.50 sB&B £19.50—£22.50 dB&B£27.50—£29 dB&B £29—£30.50 B

V S% Lunch £4—£5 Tea 75p—£1 Dinner £6.75—£7.75 Wine £2.50 Last dinner 8.30pm

Credit cards 1 2 3 5 Ⓥ

ST BOSWELLS

Borders *Roxburghshire*
Map **12** NT63

★★★ *L* **Dryburgh Abbey** Newton St Boswells ☎ (0835) 22261 (For full entry see Dryburgh)

★★ *L* **Buccleuch Arms** The Green ☎ (0835) 22243

Standing on the edge of an appealing village, the attractive hotel has some very comfortable bedrooms and a tastefully-appointed lounge.

17rm(10)(2fb) CTV in all bedrooms ® T sB&B£20—£23 sB&B £20—£23 B

60P 4 ✽ *xmas*

International V

Credit cards 1 2 3 5

ST BRELADE

Jersey
See **Channel Islands**

ST CLEARS

Dyfed
Map **2** SN21

★★ *B* **Forge Restaurant & Motel** ☎ (0994) 230300

Closed Xmas

This small, personally-run motel provides comfortable bedrooms within a small complex well distanced from the A40, together with bars and a separate grill restaurant.

Annexe: 10(2fb) CTV in all bedrooms ® T S% sB&B £21.50 dB&B £32

80P ✽ (heated)

Mainly grills *Lunch £7.50alc Tea 50palc High Tea £7.50alc Dinner £7.50alc Wine £3.75 Last dinner 9.30pm

Credit cards 1 2 3 Ⓥ

ST CLEMENTS BAY

Jersey
See **Channel Islands**

ST COLUMB MAJOR

Cornwall
Map **2** SW96

XX ***Old Rectory Hotel & Country Club*** Bridge Hill ☎ (0637) 880656

Charming, moated, old rectory with a high, panelled, first-floor restaurant and →

S

gallery, where a warm welcome is given, in a stone-walled bar with flagged floor and large, open, log fire. Good cooking (fish and the wide choice of vegetables being particularly noteworthy) combined with friendly service and a pleasant atmosphere will make your meal an enjoyable experience.

English & French **V** Last dinner 10pm
40P

Credit cards 1 2 3 5

See advertisement under Newquay

ST COMBS
Grampian *Aberdeenshire*
Map **15** NK06

★★**Tufted Duck** ☎ Inverallochy (03465) 2481

Modern hotel overlooking bay.

18rm(11➡7⋒)(2fb) CTV in all bedrooms ®T S% sB&B➡⋒£22—£26.50 dB&B➡⋒£36.70 B

CTV 50P ✿ Disco Fri (mthly)

Scottish, French & Italian **V** S% Lunch £5.50—£10 Tea 75p High Tea £1.75—£5 Dinner £5.50—£14&alc Wine £5.65 Last dinner 9.30pm

Credit cards 1 2 3 5 Ⓥ

St Columb Major — St David's

ST DAVID'S
Dyfed
Map **2** SM72

★★★**Warpool Court** (Inter Hotel) ☎ (0437) 720300

Closed early Jan—mid Feb

Originally built as St David's Cathedral Choir School in the 1860's, and enjoying spectacular scenery, this country house hotel looks out over St Bride's Bay from seven acres of Italian gardens. Under new ownership, it offers stylish bedrooms, some containing unique, ornamental Victorian tiles, comfortable public rooms and promising food standards.

25rm(16➡9⋒)(3fb) CTV in all bedrooms ®T sB&B➡⋒£27—£36 dB&B➡⋒£44—£62 B

100P ✿ (heated) (hard) croquet pool table Live music and dancing Fri *xmas*

V Lunch £7.50—£10.50 Tea £1.50—£2 High Tea £2—£4 Dinner £12.50—£18&alc Wine £4.95 Last dinner 9.15pm

Credit cards 1 2 3 4 5

★★***Grove*** High St ☎ (0437) 720341

RS Jan & Feb

This small, cosy, Regency property is personally managed and offers friendly service. With its attractive, enclosed grounds and gardens, it provides a peaceful holiday or an ideal touring base.

10rm(7➡2⋒)(2fb) 1 CTV in all bedrooms ® B

65P ✿ billiards

Last dinner 8.30pm

Credit cards 1 3

★★**Old Cross** Cross Sq ☎ (0437) 720387

Closed Nov—Feb

An 18th century house, recently extended, facing the market cross in the square.

17➡(4fb) CTV in all bedrooms ® sB&B➡£14.50—£21.50 dB&B➡£29—£43 B

20P

V Bar lunch 90p—£4 Tea £1.20—£1.80 Dinner fr£8.50&alc Wine £3.95 Last dinner 8.30pm

★★**St Non's** ☎ (0437) 720239

RS Jan—Feb

Comfortable hotel near cathedral.

20➡(5fb) CTV in all bedrooms ®T sB&B➡£17—£29 dB&B➡£34—£45 B

50P Live music and dancing Sat *xmas*

S

International Bar lunch 75p—£4.75 Tea 75p—£2 Dinner £10.50&alc Wine £4.90 Last dinner 9pm

Credit cards 1 2 3 5

ST FILLANS
Tayside *Perthshire*
Map **11** NN62

★★★**Four Seasons** (076485) 333

Closed end Oct—Etr

A bright and airy hotel with a continental atmosphere.

12 (6fb) TV in all bedrooms ® in 6 bedrooms **T** S% sB&B £26—£36 dB&B £45—£65

50P 3

British, French & Italian S% Lunch £8.50&alc High Tea £3.50—£5.50 Dinner £13.50&alc Wine £4.50 Last dinner 9.45pm

Credit cards 1 2

★★**Drummond Arms** (Inter Hotel) (076485) 212

Closed mid Oct—Etr

Four-storey, roadside hotel in an attractive position overlooking the wooded shore of Loch Earn.

33rm(19 4)(3fb) ® in 26 bedrooms S% sB&B £15—£22 sB&B £18—£25 dB&B £30—£38 dB&B £36—£44

CTV 40P

S% Bar lunch £2—£5 Tea £2.75 High Tea £3.95—£5 Dinner £9.50—£10.50&alc Wine £4.95 Last dinner 9.30pm

Credit cards 1 2 3 5 Ⓥ

ST HELENS
Isle of Wight
See **Wight, Isle of**

ST HELENS
Merseyside
Map **7** SJ59

★★★**Post House** Lodge Ln Wigan (0942) 717878
(For full entry see Haydock)

St David's — St Ives

ST HELIER
Jersey
See **Channel Islands**

ST IVES
Cambridgeshire
Map **4** TL37

★★★**Dolphin** Bridge Foot, London Rd (0480) 66966

The modern town-centre, purpose-built hotel gives views of the adjacent river and countryside.

10 Annexe: 12 (2fb) CTV in all bedrooms ® **T** * sB&B £36 dB&B £47—£65

50P

* Lunch £6.25 Tea 45p Dinner £8.95&alc Last dinner 10pm

Credit cards 1 2 3 4 5

★★★**Slepe Hall** Ramsey Rd (0480) 63122 Telex no 32339

Closed 25 & 26 Dec

Small, comfortable hotel set back from main road.

14rm(10)(2fb) 2 CTV in all bedrooms **T** sB&B £27.50—£30 sB&B £40—£45 dB&B £39.50—£45 dB&B £51—£57

120P

V Lunch £9.50£10.50&alc Tea 75p—£1 High Tea £5alc Dinner £9.50—£10.50&alc Wine £5.45 Last dinner 10pm

Credit cards 1 2 3 4 5

★★**Golden Lion** Market Hill (0480) 63159

Modernised 16th century inn situated in the town centre, popular with both business and tourist clientele.

21rm(17 1)(3fb) CTV in 17 bedrooms ® sB&B £17 sB&B £25—£28.50 dB&B £38—£45

CTV

V Lunch £5.95 Dinner £6.75&alc Wine £3.95 Last dinner 10pm

Credit cards 1 3 5 Ⓥ

★★**St Ives Motel** London Rd (0480) 63857

RS 25—26 Dec

Privately owned small hotel with modern accommodation.

16 (2fb) CTV in all bedrooms ® sB&B £20.50—£26 dB&B £31.25—£37 Continental breakfast

80P

English & French **V** Lunch £11.50alc Tea 70palc Dinner £11.50alc Wine £4.98 Last dinner 9.30pm

Credit cards 1 2 3 5 Ⓥ

★***Pike & Eel*** Overcote Ln, Needingworth (3m E off A1123) (0480) 63336

Closed Xmas night

Dating from the 16th century, this popular inn enjoys a very pleasant location beside the Great Ouse.

9rm(2 2)(3fb) CTV in all bedrooms

CTV 200P Live music Sat

French **V** Last dinner 10pm

Credit cards 1 2 3 5

See advertisement on page 630

ST IVES
Cornwall
Map 2 SW54
See plan on page 631

★★★***Carbis Bay*** Carbis Bay Penzance (0736) 795311 Plan **2** *B2*

Closed Nov—Etr

Large, detached property close to its own beach with fine views across St Ives Bay.

28rm(18 1)(7fb) CTV in all bedrooms ®

CTV 80P (heated)

International Last dinner 8.30pm

Credit cards 1 2 3 5

See advertisement on page 630

★★★**Chy-an-Drea** The Terrace (Consort) Penzance (0736) 795076 Plan **5** *B4*

Closed mid Nov—Feb

Hotel situated in a commanding position overlooking the sea. →

S

33rm(22⇌11⋒)CTV in all bedrooms ®T sB&B⇌⋒£19—£24 dB&B⇌⋒£38—£48 B

5P 20⌂ sauna bath solarium gymnasium nc4yrs

♔Lunch fr£3 Dinner fr£9 Wine £4.75 Last dinner 8.30pm

Credit cards 1 2 3 5 V

★★★H **Garrack** Higher Ayr ☎ Penzance (0736) 796199 Plan **9** *A5*

The secluded hotel, enjoying panoramic views of St Ives Bay and in its own grounds, has a country house atmosphere and now incorporates a small indoor pool and leisure complex.

St Ives

19rm(13⇌2⋒) Annexe: 2rm(3fb) CTV available in bedrooms T sB&B£15—£22 dB&B£30—£44 dB&B⇌⋒£39—£51 B

CTV 30P ✿ (heated) sauna bath solarium *xmas*

English & French ♔ Lunch £10alc Dinner £9.50&alc Wine £4.95 Last dinner 8.30pm

Credit cards 1 2 3 5 V

See advertisement on page 632

★★★**Porthminster** The Terrace (Best Western) ☎ Penzance (0736) 795221 Plan **14** *B4*

Traditional hotel in a commanding position overlooking St Ives Bay.

50rm(25⇌25⋒)(10fb) CTV in all bedrooms ®sB&B⇌⋒£23.50—£27.50 dB&B⇌⋒£47—£55 B

Lift ☾ 32P 10⌂✿ (heated) sauna bath solarium Disco wkly *xmas*

♔ Lunch £8.60alc Tea 60p Dinner £9.50&alc Wine £4.50 Last dinner 8.30pm

Credit cards 1 2 3 4 5 V

See advertisement on page 632

S

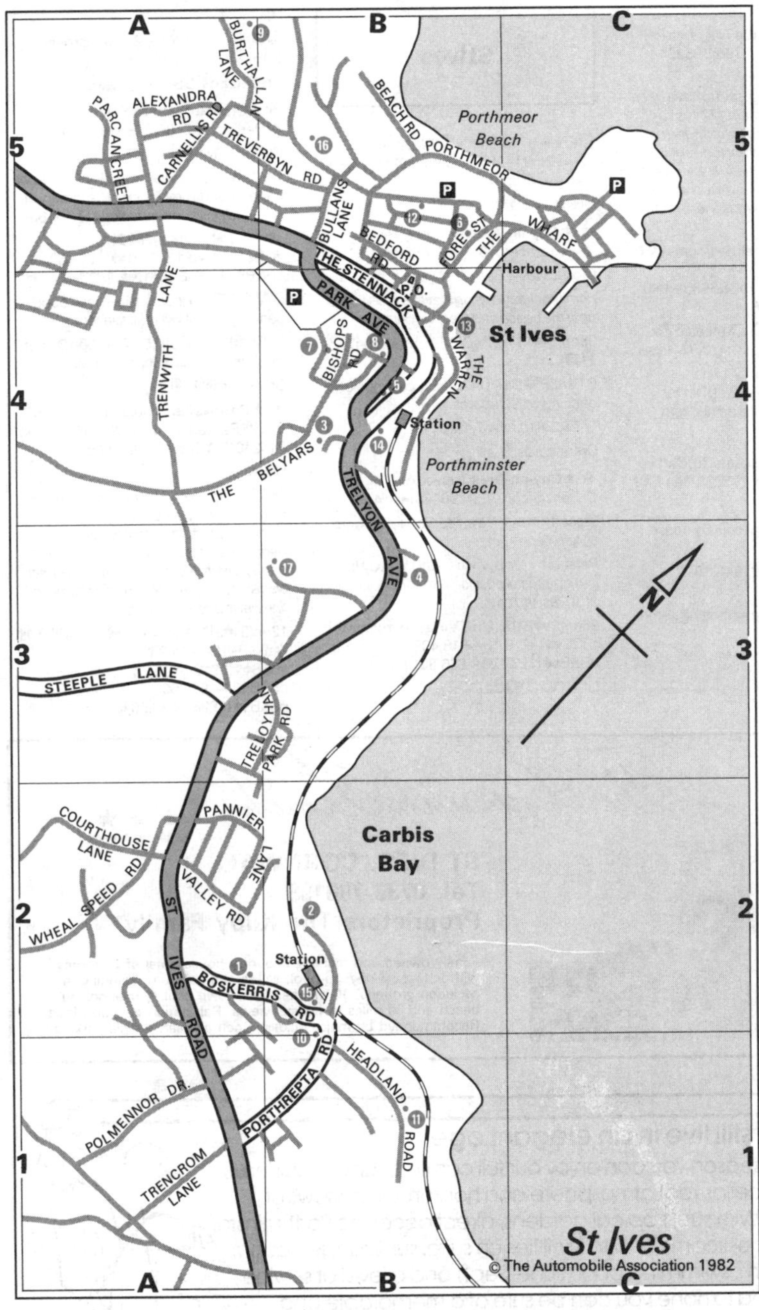

St Ives

1 Boskerris ★★
2 Carbis Bay ★★★
3 Chy-an-Albany ★★
4 Chy-an-Dour ★★
5 Chy-an-Drea ★★★
6 Chy-an-Fore ★
7 Chy-Morvah ★★
8 Dunmar ★
9 Garrack ★★★
10 Hendra's ★★
11 Cornwallis ★★
12 Ocean Breezes ★
13 Pedn-Olva ★★
14 Porthminster ★★★
15 St Uny ★★
16 Trecarrell ★
17 Tregenna Castle ★★★

S

★★★**Tregenna Castle** Tregenna Park, St Ives Rd ☎ Penzance (0736) 795254 Telex no 45128 Plan **17** *B3*

This castle-type building, said to have been erected as a private home in 1774, is situated high on a hill and surrounded by extensive grounds which include an 18-hole golf course and have fine views of St Ives Bay. The hotel retains much of the original character and atmosphere of the building.

83rm(68)(5fb) CTV in all bedrooms ® T sB&B£18.50—£45 sB&B £32—£36.50 dB&B£35—£40 dB&B £59—£78 B

Lift ☾ 100P 16 CFA (heated) (hard/grass) squash putting *xmas*

English & French V Lunch £1.50—£10 Tea £1.20—£2.20 Dinner fr£12&alc Wine £5.75 Last dinner 9pm

Credit cards 1 2 3 5

★★*HL* **Boskerris** Boskerris Rd, Carbis Bay ☎ Penzance (0736) 795295 Plan **1** *A2*

Closed mid Oct—Etr

Well-appointed hotel with country house atmosphere.

20rm(15)(4fb) sB&B£16—£18 dB&B £34—£42 B

CTV 20P (heated) putting games room

St Ives

English & French V Bar lunch £2—£3.50 Tea £1.20 Dinner £11 Wine £4 Last dinner 8pm

Credit card 5

★★***Chy-an-Albany*** Albany Ter ☎ Penzance (0736) 796759 Plan **3** *B4*

Closed Nov—Feb

Family holiday hotel in elevated position near the beach and the town centre.

35rm(3 9)(8fb) CTV in all bedrooms ® B

CTV 45P Disco twice wkly Live music & dancing wkly Cabaret wkly

Last dinner 7.45pm

Credit cards 1 3

★★**Chy-an-Dour** Trelyon Av ☎ Penzance (0736) 796436 Plan **4** *B3*

Closed Xmas—New Year RS Nov—Xmas & New Year—Feb

Personally run by owners this holiday hotel is in a peaceful position with superb views of St Ives and bay.

26rm(2 24)(2fb) TV in all bedrooms ® sB&B £16.10—£18.40 dB&B £32.20—£36.80

Lift CTV 22P

Dinner £8.05 Wine £3.90 Last dinner 8.15pm

Credit cards 1 3

★★**Chy-Morvah** The Belyars ☎ Penzance (0736) 796314 Plan **7** *B4*

Closed Nov—Mar

The family-type hotel, with swimming pool, gardens and entertainment, stands in an elevated position overlooking St Ives Bay.

40rm(11 4)(8fb) 2 *sB&B£12—£19 sB&B £13.50—£21 dB&B£24—£38 dB&B £27—£42 B

CTV 15P (heated) Live music and dancing 6 nights wkly (in season)

*Bar lunch fr75p Tea fr50p Dinner fr£7 Wine £3 Last dinner 7.30pm

Credit cards 1 3

★★**Cornwallis** Headland Rd, Carbis Bay ☎ Penzance (0736) 795294 Telex no 946240 (CWEASY G) Plan **11** *B1*

Closed Jan

This friendly, personally-managed hotel caters for family holidays, having a commendable annexe of comfortable bedrooms incorporated within a small, quality leisure/sports complex. The hotel also enjoys a commanding position with fine views over Carbis Bay.

12rm(5 3) Annexe: 10(13fb) ® T *sB&B£12—£14.25 sB&B £13—£15.25 dB&B£24—£28.50 dB&B £26—£30.50 B

S

CTV 29P (heated) sauna bath solarium gymnasium Disco twice wkly Live music wkly (in season) *xmas*

V Lunch £4.95 Tea 50p Dinner £11alc Wine £4.95 Last dinner 10pm

Credit cards 1 2 3 5 Ⓥ

★★***Hendra's*** Carbis Bay ☎ Penzance (0736) 795030 Plan **10** *B1*

Closed end Sep—mid May

Character holiday hotel built of Cornish granite, overlooking the bay.

38rm(13 2)(12fb)

CTV 16P 14 Live music & dancing wkly

V Last dinner 8pm

★★***Pedn-Olva*** The Warren ☎ Penzance (0736) 796222 Plan **13** *B4*

RS Oct—Mar

The beautifully situated, owner-managed hotel offers an outdoor pool, sunbathing terraces, and bedrooms with uninterrupted sea or harbour views.

33rm(14 17)(6fb)

CTV (heated) Disco wkly

English & French

★★**St Uny** Carbis Bay ☎ Penzance (0736) 795011 Plan **15** *B2*

Closed early Oct—Etr

Castle-style, comfortable family hotel, set in its own grounds and gardens close to the beach.

32rm(14 2)(4fb) 1 sB&B£17—£20 (incl dinner) sB&B £21—£25 (incl dinner) dB&B£34—£40 (incl dinner) dB&B £42—£50 (incl dinner)

CTV 26P 4 nc5yrs

V Lunch £4.75 Tea 40p—£1.50 Dinner £7.50—£10 Wine £4.80 Last dinner 7.45pm

Credit cards 1 3

★**Chy-an-Fore** 28 Fore St ☎ Penzance (0736) 794155 Plan **6** *B5*

Small, terraced family hotel set in the heart of the town and close to the beach.

11rm(3fb) ® sB&B£9.75—£13 dB&B£19.50—£26

CTV 5P 1 (£4 per week) *xmas*

St Ives — St Mary's Bay

Dinner £5.25—£5.75 Wine £4 Last dinner 7pm

Credit card 1

★**Dunmar** Pednolver Ter ☎ Penzance (0736) 796117 Plan **8** *B4*

Closed end Sep—Etr

Small, family hotel overlooking the town and the bay.

18rm(4 7)(8fb) CTV in 15 bedrooms ✱sB&B£9.35—£13.95 sB&B £11.35—£15.95 dB&B£18.70—£27.90 dB&B £22.70—£31.90

CTV 20P

✱Lunch £2.50—£4 Tea £1 Dinner £5—£7 Wine £4.25 Last dinner 6.30pm

★*H* **Ocean Breezes** Clodgy View, Barnoon ☎ Penzance (0736) 795587 Plan **12** *B5*

Closed Nov & RS Jan—Feb

Informal hotel close to the old town.

21rm(5)(3fb) in 4 bedrooms CTV available in bedrooms sB&B£12—£14.50 dB&B£24—£29 dB&B £27—£30

CTV 7P solarium pool room *xmas*

V Bar lunch £1—£3.50 Tea £1.50 Dinner £7.50—£8.50 Wine £3.75 Last dinner 7pm

Credit cards 1 2 3 5

★**Trecarrell** Carthew Ter ☎ Penzance (0736) 795707

Closed Jan & Feb RS Mar

Personally managed small hotel in a quiet position above the town.

16rm(2 7)(2fb) CTV available in bedrooms ® in 6 bedrooms S% sB&B£11.50—£14.50 sB&B £13.50—£16.50 dB&B£22—£28 dB&B £27—£32

CTV 15P 1 Cabaret wkly *xmas*

V ✱Lunch £3—£5 Tea £1.25 Dinner £6.50—£8.50&alc Wine £3 Last dinner 7.15pm

Credit cards 1 3 Ⓥ

ST LAWRENCE
Jersey
See **Channel Islands**

ST LAWRENCE
Isle of Wight
See **Wight, Isle of**

ST LEONARDS-ON-SEA
East Sussex
Map **5** TQ80
See **Hastings & St Leonards**

ST MARTIN
Guernsey
See **Channel Islands**

ST MARY CHURCH
Devon
Map **3** SX96
See **Torquay**

ST MARY'S BAY
Kent
Map **5** TR02

★★**Pirate Springs Country Club** Coast Dr ☎ New Romney (0679) 64930

This modern, family-run sea front hotel has an attractive lounge and dining room and offers comfortable accommodation within its well-frequented sports and leisure complex.

11rm CTV in all bedrooms ® S% sB&B£12.50—£15 dB&B£25—£30

CTV 50P (heated) (hard) squash snooker sauna bath solarium nc 12yrs *xmas*

French Lunch £5.50—£6.50 Tea 40—50p Dinner £10.75—£11.75 Wine £4.10 Last dinner 9.30pm

Credit card 1 Ⓥ

S

ST MARY'S LOCH
Borders *Selkirkshire*
Map **11** NT22

★***Rodono*** ☎ Cappercleuch (0750) 42232

Sandstone shooting lodge set in hillside overlooking Loch and Border hill country.

11rm(2fb) ® Ɓ
CTV 15P ✿ ♪
♈ ☕ Last dinner 7.30pm

ST MAWES
Cornwall
Map **2** SW83

★★★*L* **Idle Rocks** (Inter Hotel) ☎ (0326) 270771

Closed Nov—Mar

Family owned hotel situated on the harbour-side with pleasant views from the public rooms.

15rm(13🛁2🚿) Annexe: 9🛁(5fb) CTV in all bedrooms ® sB&B🛁🚿£31—£39.50 dB&B🛁🚿£62—£79 Ɓ
Ᵽ 🚗 nc 6yrs
🍷 English & Continental **V** ♈ ☕ ⁄ Lunch fr£6.50 (Sun only) Tea £1.75—£2.50 Dinner £10.95—£12.50 Wine £4.50 Last dinner 9.30pm
Credit cards 1 2 3 5 Ⓥ

★★**Green Lantern** Marine Pde ☎ (0326) 270502

Closed mid Dec—mid Jan

The hotel is in a central position on the sea front with views of the harbour.

10rm(3🛁4🚿)(1fb) CTV in 4 bedrooms ® ✗ sB&B£10.50—£17.50 sB&B🛁🚿£15—£17.50 dB&B£27—£35 dB&B🛁🚿£27—£35
CTV Ᵽ 🚗 nc 10yrs
🍷 English & Continental **V** Lunch £7.50 Dinner £12.50—£17.50 Wine £4.50 Last dinner 9.30pm
Credit cards 1 2 3

★★**Rising Sun** ☎ (0326) 270233

Small character inn at the harbour's edge.

13rm(7🛁) 1 ⁄ in all bedrooms CTV in 1 bedroom TV in 1 bedroom ®
*sB&B£21.28—£23 sB&B🛁🚿£23—£34.50 dB&B£46—£51.25 dB&B🛁🚿£51.75—£69
CTV Ᵽ 🚗
V ♈ ☕ * Bar lunch 75p—£2.75 Tea £1.50—£2.50 Dinner fr£11.50 Last dinner 8.45pm
Credit cards 1 2 3 5

★★**St Mawes** The Seafront ☎ (0326) 270266 Telex no 45117

Closed mid Nov—mid Feb

Comfortable, small village hotel on seafront.

7rm(2🛁) CTV in all bedrooms ® S% sB&B£17 sB&B🛁£19.50 dB&B£34 dB&B🛁£39
Ᵽ 🚗 nc 5yrs
🍷 English & French **V** ♈ S% Lunch £7—£10 Dinner £9.50&alc Wine £4 Last dinner 8.15pm
Credit cards 1 3 Ⓥ

ST MAWGAN
Cornwall
Map **2** SW86

★**Dalswinton Country House** ☎ (0637) 860385

Closed Xmas

Small hotel in a secluded position with pleasant rural views.

10rm(3🛁2🚿)(3fb) S% sB&B£11.50—£14.38 sB&B🛁🚿£16.10—£18.40 dB&B£23—£28.75 dB&B🛁🚿£27.03—£32.78 Ɓ
15P 🚗 ✿ ⛆ (heated) table tennis
♈ ☕ S% Lunch £2.50—£5 Tea £1—£2 Dinner fr£6.30 Wine £4.50 Last dinner 7.30pm
Credit cards 1 3 Ⓥ

S

★Pen-y-Morfa-Country ☏ (0637) 860363

Small modern hotel in the heart of the village.

11rm(4fb) CTV in 6 bedrooms

CTV 45P (heated) sauna bath solarium *xmas*

Last dinner 7.45pm

Credit card 3

ST MELLION
Cornwall
Map **2** SX36

★★★St Mellion ☏ Liskeard (0579) 50101

Closed Xmas

This friendly, modern hotel, set in its own grounds and offering excellent sporting facilities, provides accommodation in a separate bedroom block and meals in restaurant, grill room or coffee shop.

Annexe: 24 CTV in all bedrooms ®T dB&B £74—£80

CTV 500P (heated) (hard) squash snooker sauna bath solarium archery badminton table tennis

English & Continental **V** ✱Lunch £6—£9.25 Tea 45p—£1.25 High Tea £1.25—£2.50 Dinner £7.50—£11&alc Wine £5.40 Last dinner 9.15pm

Credit cards 1 2 3 5

ST PETER PORT
Guernsey
See **Channel Islands**

ST SAVIOUR
Guernsey
See **Channel Islands**

ST SAVIOUR
Jersey
See **Channel Islands**

ST WENN
Cornwall
Map **2** SW69

★ Wenn Manor ☏ St Austell (0726) 890240

A friendly atmosphere and home cooking can be enjoyed in this proprietor run hotel with 4 acres of grounds.

9rm(6 1)(4fb) ® available in bedrooms sB&B £13.50—£15 sB&B £14.50—£16 dB&B £27—£30 dB&B £29—£32

CTV 20P 1 (heated) croquet putting *xmas*

Bar lunch £3.50alc Tea 55palc Dinner £6.50 Wine £3.50 Last dinner 8pm

Credit cards 1 3 Ⓥ

SALCOMBE
Devon
Map **3** SX73

★★★*H* Bolt Head (Best Western) ☏ (054884) 3751

Closed 16 Nov—2 Apr

Swiss chalet-style hotel, standing 140 feet above sea level, overlooking the sea and estuary.

28rm(26 2)(6fb) CTV in all bedrooms ®T sB&B £29—£46 dB&B £58—£92

30P (heated)

English & French **V** Lunch £8 Tea £1.25—£2.50 Dinner £16 Wine £6.50 Last dinner 9pm

Credit cards 1 2 3 5 Ⓥ

★★★St Elmo Sandhills Rd, North Sands (Inter Hotel) ☏ (054884) 2233

Closed Nov—Etr

Overlooking countryside and estuary from its quiet location in sub-tropical grounds, the hotel offers well-fitted bedrooms and comfortable, tastefully-appointed public rooms.

23rm(20 3)(4fb) CTV in all bedrooms ®✱sB&B £21.50—£34 sB&B £25—£37 dB&B £43—£68

30P (heated) solarium

English & French **V** S% ✱Bar lunch £1.15—£7.50 Tea fr85p Dinner →

£11.50—£15.50 Wine £4.65 Last dinner 8.30pm

Credit cards [1] [3] Ⓥ

★★★*H* **Soar Mill Cove** Soar Mill Cove, Malborough (3m W of town off A381 at Malborough) ☎ Kingsbridge (0548) 561566

Closed Dec—Feb

A single-level building provides attractive bedrooms with private terraces, a comfortable lounge, friendly personal service and well-prepared fresh food.

14(3fb) CTV in all bedrooms ®
✻sB&B£30—£40 dB&B£58—£80 B

30P (heated) (grass) games room putting *xmas*

International ✻Lunch £7—£15&alc Tea £1—£4&alc High Tea £3—£8&alc Dinner £16—£18&alc Wine £4.50 Last dinner 9pm

Credit cards [1] [3]

★★★**South Sands** ☎ (054884) 3741

Tourist and commercial hotel situated on South Sands with direct access to the beach.

25(6fb) CTV in all bedrooms ® T
sB&B£25—£30 dB&B£50—£60

45P (heated) sauna bath solarium gymnasium *xmas*

Lunch £6.95 Tea 65p Dinner £14.50—£16.50 Wine £4.20 Last dinner 9.30pm

Credit cards [1] [2] [3] [5]

Salcombe

★★★*HBL* **Tides Reach** South Sands ☎ (054884) 3466

Closed Dec—Feb

Set right at the waters' edge, this secluded and comfortable hotel has been in the ownership of the Edwards family for some time. The bedrooms are charmingly decorated and many overlook the estuary, as does the attractive cool dining room where fine food is served, with the emphasis on locally caught fresh fish. There are very good sports facilities.

42rm(39 3)(3fb) CTV in all bedrooms T
sB&B£31.50—£52(incl dinner)
dB&B£62—£102(incl dinner) B

Lift ☾ 100P (heated) squash billiards sauna bath solarium gymnasium nc 8yrs

English & Continental V Bar lunch £2.25—£6.75 Tea £1.35—£1.55 Dinner £13.25&alc Wine £6.40 Last dinner 10pm

Credit cards [1] [2] [3] [5]

★★*H* **Castle Point** Sandhills Rd ☎ (054884) 2167

Closed mid Oct—Etr

Friendly hotel offering attentive service and good cooking. It stands in secluded grounds and overlooks the estuary.

20rm(7 4) CTV in 12 bedrooms ®
✻sB&B£15—£23 sB&B£20—£30 dB&B£20—£35 dB&B£30—£50 B

CTV 40P 3(£1 per night) nc 6yrs

English & French ✻Bar lunch £1—£4 Tea £1.20—£1.70 Dinner fr£9.95&alc Wine £4.35 Last dinner 9pm

Credit cards [1] [3] [5] Ⓥ

★★*H* **Grafton Towers** Moult Rd, South Sands (Exec Hotel) ☎ (054884) 2882

Closed 8 Oct—Mar

This creeper-clad Victorian villa now offers accommodation in a new wing extension. Standing in a secluded, elevated position, the hotel enjoys panoramic views, and the intimate bar sports an interesting collection of headgear from around the world.

15rm(7 2)(1fb) CTV in 10 bedrooms TV in 2 bedrooms ®sB&B£15—£20.50 sB&B£18.50—£24.50 dB&B£30—£41 dB&B£37—£49 B

12P

English & Continental Tea 50—75p Dinner £9—£10 Wine £4.50 Last dinner 8.30pm

Credit cards [1] [3] Ⓥ

★**Knowle** Onslow Rd ☎ (054884) 2846
Closed Oct—Feb
Hotel overlooks estuary.
9rm(1🛁5🚿) Annexe: 6rm(1🛁1🚿)(4fb) CTV in 7 bedrooms TV in 2 bedrooms ® sB&B£14—£19 sB&B🛁🚿£14—£19 dB&B£28—£38 dB&B🛁🚿£28—£38 B
CTV 40P ✿
English & Continental V ✱Bar lunch £2 Tea £1—£2 Dinner £9.50 Wine £4.10 Last dinner 7.45pm
Credit cards 1 3 V

Salcombe

★**Melbury** Devon Rd ☎ (054884) 2883
Closed end Sep—mid May RS Etr
Friendly, welcoming hotel with new dining room wing overlooking estuary.
14rm(4🛁5🚿)(2fb) ® sB&B£14—£17 sB&B🛁🚿£15.50—£18.50 dB&B£28—£34 dB&B🛁🚿£31—£37
CTV 18P ✿ nc5yrs

Bar lunch £1.50—£4.50 Dinner fr£7.50 Wine £3 Last dinner 7.30pm

★**Sunny Cliff** Cliff Rd ☎ (054884) 2207
Closed 13 Oct—Mar
Small, friendly holiday hotel on a clifftop location, and sloping down to the water's edge. There are fine estuary views.
12rm(2🛁)(2fb) S% sB&B£16—£17.25 sB&B🛁£18—£19.25 dB&B£32—£34.50 dB&B🛁£36—£38.50 B
CTV 14P 1 ✿ (heated) snooker
English & French S% Bar lunch £1—£2.75 Tea 60p Dinner £8.50 Wine £5.65 Last dinner 8pm
Credit cards 1 3 V

S

✕✕Galley Fore St ☎ (054884) 2828
Well established restaurant with good views of estuary serving mainly English food but with some French influence.
Closed Mon—Thu (in winter)
65 seats Lunch £3.95—£5.95&alc Dinner £6—£8&alc Wine £5.95 Last dinner 10pm
₱
Credit cards [2] [3]

SALEN
Island of Mull, Strathclyde *Argyllshire*
See **Mull, Isle of**

SALFORD
Greater Manchester
Map **7** SJ89
See also **Manchester**

★Beaucliffe 254 Eccles Old Rd, Pendleton ☎ 061-789 5092
RS 24 Dec—1 Jan
Pleasantly furnished hotel with resident proprietor.
21rm(2→15⋒)(5fb) Ⓡ in 17 bedrooms sB&B£18—£20 sB&B→⋒£20—£28 dB&B£25—£32 dB&B£32—£44 ₿
CTV 25P 1🚗
International **V** ♨ ☕ Lunch £5.50alc Tea £2alc High £4alc Dinner £6.50—£11&alc Wine £4.25 Last dinner 8pm
Credit cards [1] [2] [3] [5] Ⓥ

SALISBURY
Wiltshire
Map **4** SU12

★★★Red Lion Milford St (Best Western) ☎ (0722) 23334
Former coaching inn dating from 1320 containing many items of historic interest.
60rm(58→2⋒)(4fb) 3▭ CTV in all bedrooms Ⓡ ✕ sB&B→⋒£35—£40 dB&B→⋒£55—£60 ₿
Lift ☾ 8P 10🚗 CFA Disco Tue & Sat *xmas*
V ♨ ☕ Lunch fr£5 Tea fr£1 Dinner fr£9.50 Wine £5 Last dinner 9.30pm
Credit cards [1] [2] [3] [5] Ⓥ

★★★*Rose & Crown* Harnham Rd, Harnham (Queens Moat) ☎ (0722) 27908 Telex no 47224
A 13th-century building with new wing, comfortable bedrooms and good food.
28→⋒ 4▭ CTV in all bedrooms Ⓡ **T** ₿
☾ 43P CFA ✿ *xmas* ♿
🍽 English & French **V** ♨ ☕ Last dinner 9.30pm
Credit cards [1] [2] [3] [4] [5]

★★★White Hart St John Street (Trusthouse Forte) ☎ (0722) 27476
City Centre hotel with variety of bedroom styles and pleasant open plan lounge.
69rm(57→) CTV in all bedrooms Ⓡ sB&B£42.50 sB&B→£50.50 dB&B£61 dB&B→£69 ₿
☾ 85P *xmas*
♨ ☕ Last dinner 9.45pm
Credit cards [1] [2] [3] [4] [5]

★★Cathedral Milford St ☎ (0722) 20144
Terraced hotel in the middle of town amidst shops and many other attractions.
36rm(15→3⋒)(3fb) CTV in all bedrooms Ⓡ **T** ✕ sB&B£24.50—£28.50 sB&B→£29.50—£36.50 dB&B£30.50—£36.50 dB&B→£41.50—£48.50 ₿
Lift ☾ ₱
🍽 Mainly grills **V** ♨ Bar lunch £1.50—£4.50alc Dinner fr£8alc Wine £4.50 Last dinner 9pm
Credit cards [1] [3] Ⓥ

✕✕Dutch Mill 58A Fisherton St ☎ (0722) 23447
Tucked away in a side street near the market square, the first-floor restaurant provides a pleasant atmosphere, friendly, attentive service and an à la carte menu featuring a limited but well-selected range

S

of fresh food which includes particularly well-prepared vegetables.

Lunch not served Nov—May

French **V** 24 seats S% Lunch £9.50alc Dinner £11.50alc Wine £5 Last dinner 11pm

Credit cards 1 2 3 V

XX**Harpers** Market Sq (0722) 333118

In the centre of the city, looking down on the market place, a warm, attractive, first-floor restaurant with pleasantly relaxing decor offers daily specials in addition to its extensive à la carte and table d'hôte menus; a lunchtime shoppers' menu offers particularly good value.

Closed Sun (Nov—Apr) & Xmas Day & Boxing Day
Lunch not served Sun & Bank Hols

English & Continental **V** 60 seats Lunch £4.50—£8.95&alc Dinner £6.95—£8.95&alc Wine £4.75 Last dinner 10.30pm

Credit cards 1 2 3 5 V

SALTASH

Cornwall
Map **2** SX45

★***Holland Inn*** (07555) 3635

Closed Xmas

Situated three miles west of Saltash, on the A388, this busy inn provides accommodation in separate chalet bedrooms.

Annexe: 30 CTV in all bedrooms ®
30P

Last dinner 9.30pm

Credit cards 1 3

SAMPFORD PEVERELL

Devon
Map **3** ST01

★***Green Headland*** Tiverton (0884) 820255

Closed Dec—early Jan

Small, comfortable privately-run hotel, popular with tourists and businessmen.

6rm (3fb) ®

CTV 100P Disco wknds

V Last dinner 8.30pm

Credit card 1

○**Little Chef Lodge** Adjacent M5 jct 27 (Trusthouse Forte) 01-567 3444

40
Due to have opened Oct/Nov 1986

SANDBACH

Cheshire
Map **7** SJ76

★★★*B* **Chimney House** Congleton Rd (Whitbread) (0270) 764141 Telex no 367323

Large country house in Tudor style.

52 (3fb) CTV in all bedrooms ® **T**
sB&B £45 dB&B £55

110P sauna bath solarium *xmas*

English & French **V** Lunch fr £8 Tea fr 90p Dinner fr £11&alc Last dinner 10pm

Credit cards 1 2 3 5

★★★**Saxon Cross** Holmes Chapel Rd (M6 junc 17) Crewe (0270) 763281 Telex no 367169

Closed 26 Dec RS 24 & 25 Dec

In a rural setting, yet conveniently placed for access to the M6 motorway, the modern, single-storey motel offers well-equipped bedrooms.

52 (13fb) CTV in all bedrooms ® **T** S%
sB&B £28.50—£37.50
dB&B £35—£45.50

200P CFA

English & French **V** Lunch fr £6.75&alc Dinner fr £9 Wine £5.50 Last dinner 9.30pm

Credit cards 1 2 3 5 V

S

SANDBANKS
Dorset
See **Poole**

SANDERSTEAD
Greater London
Map **4** TQ36

★★★★**Selsdon Park** (Best Western) ☎ 01-657 8811 Telex no 945003

Large mansion in 200 acre grounds. Popular with conferences and has excellent leisure facilities.

150 (5fb) 1 CTV in all bedrooms **T** S% sB&B £58—£78 dB&B £80—£100

Lift ☾ 200P 15 (£1.50 per night) CFA ✽ & (heated) (hard & grass) squash snooker sauna bath solarium gymnasium croquet Live music & dancing Sat *xmas*

International **V** S% Lunch £12.25—£13.25&alc Dinner £13.75—£18&alc Wine £7.50 Last dinner 9.30pm

Credit cards 1 2 3 5

See advertisement under Croydon

SANDIACRE
Derbyshire
Map **8** SK43
See also **Long Eaton**

★★★**Post House** Bostocks Ln (N of M1 junc 25) (Trusthouse Forte) ☎ Nottingham (0602) 397800 Telex no 377378

Large modern hotel with well equipped bedrooms.

107 (14fb) CTV in all bedrooms ® sB&B £53.50 dB&B £67.50

☾ 180P ✽ CFA *xmas*

Last dinner 10pm

Credit cards 1 2 3 4 5

SANDOWN
Isle of Wight
See **Wight, Isle of**

SANQUHAR
Dumfries & Galloway *Dumfriesshire*
Map **11** NS70

★★**Mennockfoot Lodge** Mennock ☎ (06592) 382

An unusual hotel in a secluded riverside setting. It is modestly appointed but provides a friendly atmosphere.

1 Annexe: 8rm(2)(1fb) sB&B £14 sB&B £15 dB&B £22 dB&B £24

CTV 26P ✽

English & Continental **V** Lunch £5alc Dinner £10alc Wine £3.80 Last dinner 8.30pm

★**Nithsdale** 1—7 High St ☎ (06592) 506

Homely, friendly hotel in main street of small town. Limited lounge facilities.

6rm(1)(2fb) TV in all bedrooms ® sB&B fr £12 sB&B fr £12 dB&B fr £24 dB&B fr £24

CTV ✽ *xmas*

Mainly grills S% Bar lunch £1.70—£5.50 Tea fr 50p High Tea £4—£7 Dinner £10alc Wine £3.75 Last dinner 10pm

Ⓥ

SARK
Channel Islands
See **Channel Islands**

SAUNDERSFOOT
Dyfed
Map **2** SN10

★★★**St Brides** St Brides Hill (Inter Hotel) ☎ (0834) 812304 Telex no 48350

Closed 1—10 Jan

Comfortable clifftop hotel with good sea views.

48rm(33 15)(4fb) CTV in all bedrooms ® **T** sB&B £32—£34 dB&B £50—£58

☾ 70P CFA ✽ (heated) Live music & dancing Sat *xmas*

English & French **V** Lunch £6.25—£6.50&alc Tea 75p—£2.95 Dinner £9.95—£12.95&alc Wine £5.95 Last dinner 9.15pm

Credit cards 1 2 3 5 Ⓥ

★★**Glen Beach** Swallow Tree Woods ☎ (0834) 813430

RS Nov—Jan (except Xmas)

Small, personally run family hotel, set in woodlands with access to beach.

13rm(3 7)(3fb) CTV in all bedrooms ® sB&B £20—£25 dB&B £40—£50

35P ✽ Disco, Live music & dancing & Cabaret Mon & Thu Jul & Aug *xmas*

English & French **V** Lunch £6.50 Dinner £9&alc Wine £5.80 Last dinner 9.30pm

Credit cards 1 2 3 Ⓥ

SAUNDERTON
Buckinghamshire
Map **4** SP70

★★**Rose & Crown** Wycombe Rd (Exec Hotel) ☎ Princes Risborough (08444) 5299

Closed 25—31 Dec

The small, friendly, proprietor-run hotel offers wholesome food in a cosy restaurant, a good bar atmosphere and bedrooms which, though small, are clean and comfortable.

15rm(5 7) CTV in all bedrooms ® **T** S% sB&B £21.50—£32.50 sB&B £29.50—£40 dB&B £38.75—£52

CTV 60P ✽

V Lunch £9.50—£11.75&alc Dinner £9.75—£12.50&alc Wine £5.50 Last dinner 9.30pm

Credit cards 1 2 3 5

SAUNTON
Devon
Map **2** SS43

★★★★**Saunton Sands** (Brend) ☎ Croyde (0271) 890212 Telex no 42551

Flanked by dunes and overlooking a wide, sandy beach, the purpose-built hotel provides many amenities. Public areas are

bright and well-appointed, whilst nothing seems too much trouble for the attentive staff. Self-catering facilities are also available.

102⇌(12fb) CTV in all bedrooms ✈ sB&B⇌£32.48—£40.83 dB&B⇌£58.65—£81.65 B

Lift ☾ CTV 140P 2🚗 CFA ✿ ▭(heated) ⚲(hard) squash snooker sauna bath solarium putting Live music & dancing wkly ⚘ *xmas*

English & French ♁ ☕ Lunch fr£7.48&alc Tea fr80p Dinner fr£11.78&alc Wine £4.75 Last dinner 9.30pm

Credit cards 1 2 3 5

Saunton — Scarborough

SAVERNAKE
Wiltshire
See **Burbage**

See advertisement under Marlborough

SCALASAIG
Isle of Colonsay, Strathclyde *Argyllshire*
See **Colonsay, Isle of**

SCARBOROUGH
North Yorkshire
Map **8** TA08
See plan

★★★★**Crown** Esplanade (Quality) ☏ (0723) 373491 Telex no 52277 Plan **3** *C3*

Regency period hotel overlooking the bay from South Cliffs.

83⇌(8fb) ⚟ in 10 bedrooms CTV in all bedrooms ® **T** sB&B⇌£28—£40 dB&B⇌£48—£70 B

Lift ☾ CTV 16P 15🚗(£1.15 per night) CFA snooker solarium gymnasium table tennis pool table hairdressers *xmas* →

S

V ☕ Lunch £5.75—£7&alc Tea £1.25—£3.50 Dinner £9.25—£10.50&alc Wine £4.50 Last dinner 9.30pm

Credit cards 1 2 3 5 Ⓥ

★★★★**Holbeck Hall** Seacliffe Rd (Consort) ☎ (0723) 374374 Plan **6** *D1*

Closed Jan & Feb

A former Victorian residence in 3 acres of gardens and grounds offering panoramic views over Scarborough.

30 🛁 🚿 (2fb) CTV in all bedrooms **T** sB&B 🛁 🚿 £28.75—£34.50 dB&B 🛁 🚿 £57.50—£69 **B**

☾ 50P ✿ *xmas*

French **V** ☕ Lunch fr£6.75 Tea fr£1 Dinner fr£11.75 Wine £7.40 Last dinner 9.30pm

Credit cards 1 2 3 5

★★★★**Royal** St Nicholas Street ☎ (0723) 364333 Telex no 52472 Plan **10** *C3*

Elegant Regency building by town centre with very comfortable, modern bedrooms.

137rm(102 🛁 30 🚿)(19fb) in 10 bedrooms CTV in all bedrooms Ⓡ **T** S% sB&B 🛁 🚿 £35—£40 dB&B 🛁 🚿 £60—£65 **B**

Lift ☾ CTV CFA (heated) billiards sauna bath solarium gymnasium Disco wkly Live music & dancing twice wkly Cabaret wkly (summer only) *xmas*

Scarborough

British & Continental **V** ☕ S% Lunch fr£6 Tea fr£1.20 High Tea fr£4.50 Dinner fr£12 Wine £5.50 Last dinner 11.30pm

Credit cards 1 2 3 5 Ⓥ

★★★**Clifton** Queens Pde ☎ (0723) 375691 Telex no 527667 Plan **2A** *B4*

Victorian in origin, but modern and well-furnished, the hotel overlooks the magnificant North Bay.

70rm(30 🛁 34 🚿) 1 CTV in all bedrooms **T** **B**

Lift ☾ CTV 30P

Last dinner 8.30pm

Credit cards 1 2 3

See advertisement on page 644

★★★**Hotel St Nicholas** St Nicholas Cliff ☎ (0723) 364101 Telex no 52351

Newly refurbished Victorian hotel which is situated near to the beach and town centre.

150rm(111 🛁)(14fb) 4 CTV in all bedrooms Ⓡ **T** sB&B£24 sB&B 🛁 £30 dB&B£40 dB&B 🛁 £52 **B**

Lift ☾ 40 (charge £2) (heated) sauna bath solarium disco nightly Cabaret Xmas & New Year *xmas*

English & Continental ☕ Lunch £1.20—£4 Tea 50p High Tea £3 Dinner £10 Wine £5.45 Last dinner 9pm

Credit cards 1 2 3 5

★★**Brooklands** Esplanade Gdns, South Cliff ☎ (0723) 376576 Plan **1** *C1*

RS Dec—Mar

A friendly atmosphere prevails in this comfortable, unpretentious hotel, which enjoys the personal supervision of the resident proprietor.

53rm(41 🛁)(4fb) CTV in all bedrooms Ⓡ **T** sB&B£17—£22 sB&B 🛁 £17—£22 dB&B£30—£32 dB&B 🛁 £32—£34

Lift CFA

☕ Lunch £4—£5 Dinner £8—£10 Wine £6.30 Last dinner 6.30pm

Credit cards 1 3 Ⓥ

See advertisement on page 644

★★**Central** 1-3 The Crescent ☎ (0723) 365766 Plan **2** *C3*

The family-run hotel, overlooking the bay, offers a wide choice of menus, the dinner-time a la carte and table d'hote selections being supplemented by an extensive bar-meal menu at lunchtime.

40rm(9 🛁)(5fb) CTV in all bedrooms Ⓡ *sB&B£14 sB&B 🛁 £16.50 dB&B£28 dB&B 🛁 £33 **B**

Lift ☾ 15P *xmas*

*Dinner £5.50&alc Wine £4 Last dinner 10.30pm

Credit cards 1 2 3 4 5

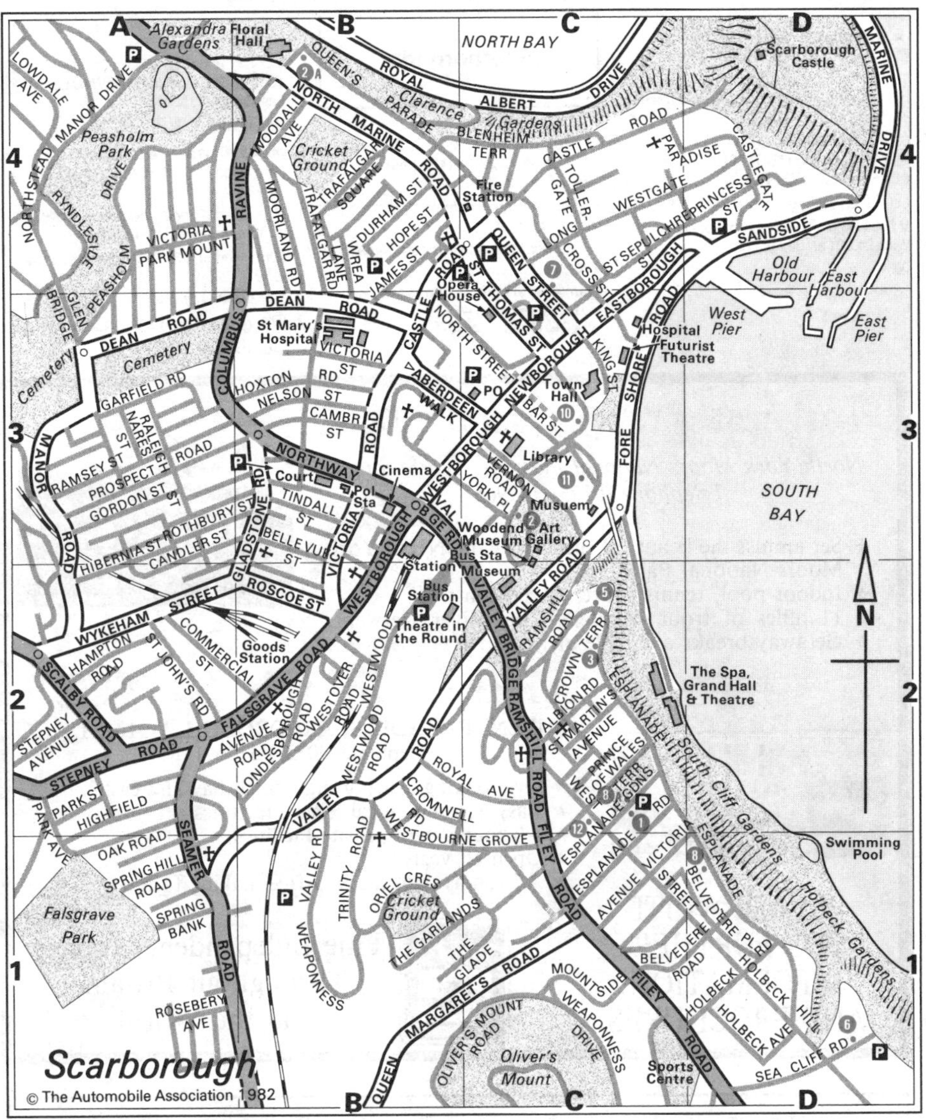

★★**Esplanade** Belmont Rd ☎ (0723) 360382 Plan **5** *C2*

Closed Dec—Feb (except Xmas & New Year)

Large seaside hotel overlooking South Cliffs and the sea.

81rm(61⇌12⋒)(5fb) CTV in 73 bedrooms ®T S% sB&B£20—£21 sB&B⇌⋒£23—£24 dB&B⇌⋒£42—£44 B

Lift ☾ CTV 24P CFA ✿ Live music & dancing Tue Cabaret Sun *xmas*

♁ ☕ S% Lunch £4.50 Tea fr60p Dinner £7.50 Wine £5.60 Last dinner 8.30pm

Credit cards 1 2 3 5

★★**Mayfair** 42 The Esplanade ☎ (0723) 360053 Plan **8** *D1*

Regency style with bright cheerful bedrooms and comfortable lounges.

18rm(11⇌1⋒)(4fb) TV available in bedrooms ® * sB&B£14—£16 sB&B⇌⋒£14—£16 dB&B⇌⋒£28—£32

Lift CTV P 🚌

♁ ☕ * Bar lunch £1.30alc Tea 55palc Dinner £6alc Wine £3.80 Last dinner 4.30pm

Credit cards 1 3

Scarborough

1	Brooklands ★★
2	Central ★★
2A	Clifton ★★★
3	Crown ★★★★
5	Esplanade ★★
6	Holbeck Hall ★★★★
7	Lanterna Ristorante ✕✕
8	Mayfair ★★
8A	Red Lea ★★
10	Royal ★★★★
11	St Nicholas ★★★
12	Southlands ★★

★★**Red Lea** Prince of Wales Ter ☎(0723) 362431 Plan **8A** *C2*

This comfortable, traditional hotel is managed by the friendly family which owns it.

67rm(48→19⋒)(8fb) CTV in all bedrooms ®T✲ ✱sB&B→⋒£17–£19 dB&B→⋒£34–£38 ®

Lift ☾ ♨ CTV games room *xmas*

V ⌂ ☕ ✱Lunch £5 Tea 70p Dinner £7 Wine £4.30 Last dinner 8pm

Ⓥ

Scarborough

★★**Southlands** 15 West St, Southcliff (Consort) ☎(0723) 361461 Telex no 57515 Plan **12** *C2*

Friendly, family run hotel with spacious modern bedrooms.

Closed mid Nov–Mar except Xmas & New Year

58rm(45→9⋒)(8fb) CTV in all bedrooms ®T sB&B→⋒£25–£27 dB&B→⋒£43–£45 ®

Lift ☾ CTV 40P CFA *xmas*

V ⌂ ☕ Lunch fr£5.95&alc Tea fr65p High Tea fr£3.95 Dinner fr£9&alc Wine £3.95 Last dinner 8.30pm

Credit cards [1] [2] [3] [5] Ⓥ

★★✚*L* ***Wrea Head Country*** Scalby (3m NW off A171) ☎(0723) 378211 Plan **13** *A2*

Converted Victorian residence standing in 14 acres of landscaped gardens.

20rm(15→5⋒)(3fb) CTV in all bedrooms ® ®

50P 3⌂✲⊂ *xmas*

English & French V ⌂ ☕ Last dinner 9pm

Credit cards [1] [2] [3] [5]

S

XX**Lanterna Restaurante** 33 Queen St ☏(0723) 363616 Plan **7** *C4*

A good range of international cuisine, together with courteous service, is offered by this comfortable, intimate restaurant.

Lunch not served

Italian & Continental **V** 36 seats Dinner £9alc Wine £5.50 Last dinner 9.30pm nc2yrs

Credit card [3]

SCARISTA

Western Isles *Inverness-shire*

See **Harris, Isle of**

SCILLY, ISLES OF

No map

ST MARY'S
Hugh Town

★★**Bell Rock** Church St ☏ Scillonia (0720) 22575

Closed Nov—Jan RS Feb

Holiday hotel with pleasant service, good food and a swimming pool in the walled garden.

19rm(14 3)(3fb) CTV in all bedrooms ® T sB&B £18—£23.50 dB&B£32—£43 dB&B £36—£47

(heated) games room

International * Bar lunch 70p—£2.95 Dinner £8.95 Wine £4.25 Last dinner 8pm

Credit cards [1] [3]

Scarborough — Scilly, Isles of

★★**Godolphin** Church St ☏ Scillonia (0720) 22316

Closed mid Oct—mid Mar

This granite hotel, located near the town centre, caters for tourists, offering good food and featuring attractive lounges and an unusual bar with sea-shell decoration.

31rm(25 2)(3fb) CTV in all bedrooms ® sB&B£13—£19 sB&B £15—£21 dB&B£26—£38 dB&B £30—£42

sauna bath

Bar lunch fr90p Tea fr£1 Dinner fr£10 Wine £4 Last dinner 8pm

Credit cards [1] [3]

★★**Tregarthens** Hughtown (Best Western) ☏ Scillonia (0720) 22540

Closed Nov—mid Mar

There are views of harbour and coastline from the public rooms of this pleasant hotel, set in small, terraced gardens. Good food is served by pleasant and courteous staff.

32rm(24)(5fb) CTV in all bedrooms ® sB&B£30—£33.50 (incl. dinner) sB&B £32—£37.50 (incl. dinner) dB&B£50—£60 (incl. dinner) dB&B £61—£70 (incl. dinner)

English & French **V** Bar lunch £1.25—£3.50 Tea 75p—£1 Dinner £9.75—£10.95 Wine £4.50 Last dinner 8pm

Credit cards [1] [2] [3] [5] Ⓥ

TRESCO
New Grimsby

★★**New Inn** Scillonia ☏ (0720) 22844

Closed Nov—Feb

Standing on a small harbour, close to the sea, the centuries-old inn offers accommodation in modern, cosy bedrooms, many of which have fine views.

12rm(10)(3fb) ® sB&B£25—£34.06 (incl. dinner) dB&B £50—£68.12 (incl. dinner)

CTV (heated)

Cosmopolitan **V** Bar lunch £4.50—£12 Dinner £11—£14 Wine £4.40 Last dinner 8.30pm

TRESCO
Old Grimsby

❀★★★*H* **Island** Scillonia
☎(0720) 22883
Closed mid Oct—mid Mar
In a lovely setting right on the rocky coastline this relaxing hotel provides comfortable public rooms and nicely furnished, modernised bedrooms. The restaurant has a comprehensive menu of interesting dishes, including good fish and local produce where possible. The extensive cold buffet on Sunday evenings can be recommended. The managers and courteous friendly staff offer fine hospitality.
32rm(27→) CTV in 24 bedrooms ® in 5 bedrooms **T** S% sB&B£39—£45 (incl. dinner) sB&B→£55—£63 (incl. dinner) dB&B£43—£48 (incl. dinner) dB&B→£50—£80 (incl. dinner)
CTV (heated) bowls, croquet
English & Continental S% Lunch £10alc Tea fr70p Dinner £17 Wine £6.50 Last dinner 8.15pm

SCOLE
Norfolk
Map **5** TM17
★★**Scole Inn** (Best Western) ☎ Diss (0379) 740481
11→⋔ Annexe: 12→⋔(2fb) 3 CTV in all bedrooms ® **T** sB&B→⋔£33—£40 dB&B→⋔£48—£60 B
CTV 60P *xmas*
V Lunch £8.50&alc Tea 80p Dinner £8.50&alc Wine £4.25 Last dinner 10pm
Credit cards 1 2 3 5 V

SCOTCH CORNER (near Richmond)
North Yorkshire
Map **8** NZ20
★★★**Scotch Corner** Great North Rd (Scottish Highland) ☎ Richmond (0748) 2943 Telex no 778215
Established hotel in its own grounds and gardens situated at the junction of the A1 and the A66.
42→(4fb) 1 CTV in all bedrooms ® **T** S% sB&B→£34 dB&B→£58 B
Lift ☾ 250P 6 CFA
English & French **V** S% Lunch £6.95&alc Tea 95p Dinner £6.95&alc Wine £4.95 Last dinner 10pm
Credit cards 1 2 3 5

○**Little Chef Lodge**
A1 North bound ☎ Richmond (0748) 3768
40→⋔
Due to open November 1986

SCOURIE
Highland *Sutherland*
Map **14** NC14
★★**Eddrachilles** Badcall Bay ☎ (0971) 2080
Closed Nov—Feb
Magnificently situated at the head of Badcall Bay this hotel offers modern, comfortable accommodation combined with a historic dining room.
11rm(3→8⋔)(1fb) CTV available in bedrooms ® sB&B→⋔£21.45—£30.40 dB&B→⋔£35—£43 B
20P nc3yrs
Bar lunch £1.50—£3.50 Dinner £6.85&alc Wine £3.80 Last dinner 8.30pm

★★*HL* **Scourie** (Exec Hotel) ☎ (0971) 2396
Closed 28 Oct—13 Mar
A shingle-clad building and part of a 17th century tower house, make up this hotel.
18rm(16→) sB&B£17—£20 sB&B→£22.50—£24 dB&B£34—£38 dB&B→£42.85—£45 B
CTV 30P
British & French Lunch £6—£6.25 Tea £1.20—£1.30 Dinner £8—£8.50 Wine £3.50 Last dinner 8.30pm
Credit cards 1 3 5

SCRATCHWOOD
(M1 Motorway Service Area)
Access only from Motorway
Greater London Map **4** TQ19
★★**TraveLodge** See under **London NW7**

SCUNTHORPE
Humberside
Map **8** SE81
★★★**Royal** Doncaster Rd (Anchor) ☎ (0724) 868181 Telex no 527479
RS Public Hols
Popular, comfortable villa-style hotel with relaxing atmosphere.
33rm(32→1⋔)(1fb) in 6 bedrooms CTV in all bedrooms ® **T** sB&B→⋔£30—£39.50 dB&B→⋔£35—£47.50 B
☾ 33P CFA *xmas*
V Lunch £9.90alc Tea 75palc Dinner £9.90alc Wine £5.95 Last dinner 10pm
Credit cards 1 2 3 5 V

★★★**Wortley House** Rowland Rd (Consort) ☎ (0724) 842223
The large house, suitably converted and extended, stands near the town centre; spacious public areas of comfort and style are complemented by up-to-date bedrooms.
32rm(27→5⋔)(2fb) 3 CTV in all bedrooms ® **T** S% sB&B→⋔£25—£39.50 dB&B→⋔£30—£46 B
☾ 150P *xmas*
English & Continental **V** S% Lunch fr£6.50&alc Tea fr£1.50 High Tea fr£1.50 Dinner fr£7.50&alc Wine £6.50 Last dinner 9.30pm
Credit cards 1 2 3 4 5 V

★***Bridge House*** Station Rd ☎ (0724) 847590
This town-centre hotel near the railway station offers spacious, well-equipped accommodation with an attractive restaurant and bar.
19rm CTV in all bedrooms ® B
☾ 50P
Mainly grills Last dinner 10pm
Credit cards 1 2 3 5

SEAFORD
East Sussex
Map **5** TV49

✕✕**Bentley's** 30A High St ☎ (0323) 892220

Once the home of William Pitt, the 300-year-old house has been converted into an attractive small restaurant. Co-ordinated decor and soft furnishings create a pleasant setting in which to enjoy cuisine nouvelle of a reliable standard, followed by home-made sorbet and other delicious desserts.

Closed Mon, Tue, 2 wks Nov & 2 wks Feb Lunch not served Wed—Sat Dinner not served Sun

🍷French 22 seats Dinner £10.25 Wine £4.95 Last dinner 9.30pm ℙ

SEAHOUSES
Northumberland
Map **12** NU23

★★*H* **Beach House** Sea Front ☎ (0665) 720337

Closed mid Nov—mid Mar

A warm welcome is extended by the owners of this very pleasant and well-furnished hotel, and bedrooms have good views towards the Farne Islands.

14rm(7🛁7🚿)(3fb) 1⊟ CTV in all bedrooms ®sB&B🛁🚿£18.50—£24 dB&B🛁🚿£37—£59.40 Ɓ

CTV 16P 🚌 ✿

🍷English & Continental ♈ ⚟ Lunch £4—£5 Tea £1—£2 Dinner £8—£9.50 Wine £4.30 Last dinner 8pm

Credit cards 1 3 Ⓥ

★★**Olde Ship** ☎ (0665) 720200

Closed end Oct—Etr

In an elevated situation, overlooking the harbour, the hotel features public areas with a maritime theme. The friendly proprietors, aided by local staff, offer very pleasant service.

10rm(2🛁5🚿)(1fb) CTV in all bedrooms ® ✗ sB&B£13.50—£14.50 sB&B🛁🚿£15—£17 dB&B£27—£29 dB&B🛁🚿£30—£34

CTV 10P 2🚗 🚌 ⚝

V ♈ ☕ Bar lunch £1—£2 Tea 60p Dinner £6.50 Wine £2.50 Last dinner 7.45pm

★★**St Aidans** ☎ (0665) 720355

Closed 16 Nov—14 Feb

Seafront hotel with a cosy bar and a comfortable restaurant.

8rm(1🛁3🚿)(3fb) CTV in all bedrooms ® sB&B£12—£17 sB&B🛁🚿£14.50—£19.50 dB&B£24—£34 dB&B🛁🚿£29—£39 Ɓ

10P 🚌 ✿

🍷English & Continental **V** Dinner £8.50&alc Wine £4.50 Last dinner 8pm

Credit cards 1 3

★**White Swan** North Sunderland (1½m SE) (Minotel) ☎ (0665) 720211

A modest country inn with neat bright bedrooms, 1m from the village and the sea.

18rm(3🛁4🚿)(5fb) CTV available in bedrooms ®sB&B£15—£18 sB&B🚿£17—£20 dB&B£30—£34 dB&B🚿£34—£36 Ɓ

CTV 40P

V ♈ Lunch £3.50—£6 High Tea £1.50—£6 Dinner £8.50—£10&alc Wine £4 Last dinner 10pm

Credit cards 1 3 Ⓥ

SEALE
Surrey
Map **4** SU84

★★★**Hog's Back** Hog's Back (on A31) (Embassy) ☎ Runfold (02518) 2345 Telex no 859352

A friendly hotel with spectacular views from the rear gardens.

50🛁🚿(6fb) CTV in all bedrooms ®**T** S% sB🛁🚿£55 dB🛁🚿£65(room only) Ɓ

☾ 130P ✿ games room ♿ ⚝ xmas

V ♈ S% Lunch £6.75—£9.50&alc Dinner £6.75—£9.50&alc Wine £5.10 Last dinner 9.30pm

Credit cards 1 2 3 4 5 Ⓥ

SEAMILL
Strathclyde *Ayrshire*
Map **10** NS24

★**Inverclyde** Ardrossan Rd ☎ West Kilbride (0294) 823124

The small, family-run hotel stands in the centre of the village.

7rm ®sB&B£12.50 dB&B£25

CTV 🚌 *xmas*

V ♈ ☕ S% Lunch £4alc Tea fr75p High Tea £3.25—£6.95 Dinner £6.50alc Wine £4 Last dinner 8pm

Credit cards 1 3

SEASCALE
Cumbria
Map **6** NY00

★**Wansfell** Drigg Rd ☎ (0940) 28301

This hotel offers views of the Isle of Man.

15rm(2fb) CTV in all bedrooms ® ✻sB&B£18 dB&B£28 Ɓ

50P Disco Fri & Sat

🍷English & French **V** ♈ ✻Lunch £6alc Dinner £8.50alc Wine £4.50 Last dinner 9pm

Credit card 1 Ⓥ

SEATON
Devon
Map **3** SY29

★★**Bay** East Walk ☎ (0297) 20073

Closed Nov—Mar

A large holiday hotel situated on the promenade with good sea views.

33rm(11🛁)(3fb) CTV in all bedrooms ® ✻sB&B£15.55—£17.50 sB&B🛁£17.50—£21.50 dB&B£31.10—£35 dB&B🛁£35—£43 Ɓ

70P Live music & dancing wkly *xmas*

🍷English & French **V** ♈ ☕ ✻Bar lunch 80p—£3 Tea 80p—£2 Dinner fr£5.50&alc Wine £4 Last dinner 9pm

Credit cards 1 3 Ⓥ

SEATON BURN
Tyne & Wear
Map **12** NZ27

★★★★**Holiday Inn** Great North Rd (Holiday Inns) ☎ 091-236 5432 Telex no 53271 Newcastle-upon-Tyne Plan **5A** *D8*

Modern two storey purpose built hotel, situated six miles north of Newcastle, east of the A1/A108 junction.

150🛁🚿(150fb) CTV in all bedrooms **T** S% ✻sB&B🛁🚿fr£64.18 dB&B🛁🚿fr£75.95 Ɓ

☾ ⊞ 200P CFA ✿ ⊡(heated) sauna bath solarium gymnasium Live music 4 nights wkly ♿ *xmas*

🍷International ♈ ☕ ⚟

Credit cards 1 2 3 4 5

SEAVIEW
Isle of Wight
See **Wight, Isle of**

SEAVINGTON ST MARY
Somerset
Map **3** ST41

✕✕**Pheasant** ☎ South Petherton (0460) 40502

Set in the village, this charming, owner-run hotel has a particularly well-appointed restaurant. Standards of cuisine are high, and an interesting and unusual range of dishes is available on the ambitious a la carte and good-value table d'hote menus. Well-balanced wine list, caring service and relaxing, unhurried atmosphere all add to your enjoyment.

Closed Sun & 26 Dec—3 Jan Lunch not served

🍷English, French & Italian **V** 52 seats Dinner fr£9.50&alc Wine £5.90 Last dinner 9.30pm 60P 10 bedrooms available

Credit cards 1 2 3 4 5 Ⓥ

SEDGEFIELD
Co Durham
Map **8** NZ32

★★★**Hardwick Hall** ☎ (0740) 20253 Telex no 537681

Comfortable hotel within country park with attractive bars and splendid fireplaces.

17🛁(1fb) CTV in all bedrooms **T** ✗ sB&B🛁fr£36 dB&B🛁fr£48 Ɓ

200P ✿ Disco twice wkly Live music and dancing wkly ⚝

🍷English & French **V** ♈ ☕ Lunch £6.50—£8 Dinner £10.25—£12.50 Wine £6 Last dinner 9.30pm

Credit cards 1 2 3 5

★**Crosshill** 1 The Square ☎ (0740) 20153

Small, friendly hotel, supervised by proprietors.

8rm(5→3⋒)(2fb) CTV in all bedrooms ® **T** S% sB&B→⋒£25—£30 dB&B→⋒£37.50—£40 **B**

CTV 7P *xmas*

V ♡ ☕ S% Lunch £3.50—£6 Tea £1.75—£4 High Tea £4—£5 Dinner £6.50—£10 Wine £5 Last dinner 9.30pm

Credit cards 1 3 Ⓥ

SEDLESCOMBE

East Sussex
Map **5** TQ71

★★**Brickwall** The Green ☎ (042487) 253

Friendly family-run hotel with country house atmosphere.

25rm(18→6⋒)(4fb) 2 CTV in all bedrooms ® **T** ✱ sB&B→⋒fr£28 dB&B→⋒fr£40 **B**

25P 2 ✿ (heated) putting croquet *xmas*

English & French ♡ ☕ ✱ Lunch £6—£8 Dinner fr£9 Wine £5.50 Last dinner 8.45pm

Credit cards 1 2 3 5

✗✗**Holmes House** ☎ (042487) 450

Chef Patron provides very good food in this converted 17th century cottage fitted with paintings and antiques.

Closed Mon Lunch not served Sat Dinner not served Sun

International **V** 45 seats S% Lunch fr£8&alc Dinner fr£9&alc Wine £4.75 Last dinner 9pm

Credit cards 1 2 3 5 Ⓥ

✗**Tithe Barn** Lower Green ☎ (042487) 393

Small, intimate, family-run restaurant with welcoming, open log fires.

Lunch not served Mon & Tue Dinner not served Sun

English & French **V** 50 seats Lunch £3.50—£8&alc Dinner £8.75&alc Wine £5 Last dinner 10pm 40P

Credit cards 1 2 3 4 5

SEIGHFORD

Staffordshire
Map **7** SJ82

✗**Hollybush Inn** ☎ (078575) 280

Set in a village three miles from Junction 14 of the M6, the older parts of this attractively-proportioned inn, dating from 1675, feature open fires and heavy beams; lounge and restaurant are housed in a modern extension. Dishes from the popular a la carte or more unusual fixed-price menus are served by pleasant, friendly staff.

Dinner not served Sun

V 25 seats ✱ Lunch £7.50&alc Dinner £7.50&alc Wine £3.95 Last dinner 9.30pm 100P

Credit cards 1 3 Ⓥ

Sedgefield — Shaftesbury

SELKIRK

Borders *Selkirkshire*
Map **12** NT42

★**Heatherlie House** Heatherlie Park ☎ (0750) 21200

Detached Victorian house just off town centre, a small family run hotel.

7rm(1→)(3fb) CTV in 5 bedrooms TV in 1 bedroom ® sB&B£14.50—£16 dB&B£29—£32 dB&B→£34—£37 **B**

CTV 15P CFA ✿ *xmas*

British & French **V** ♡ ☕ Lunch £3.50—£6.50 Tea 80p—£1.20 High Tea £3.95—£5 Dinner £7—£9 Wine £5 Last dinner 8.30pm

Credit cards 1 2 3 5 Ⓥ

SENNEN

Cornwall
Map **2** SW32

★★*L* **Tregiffian** ☎ (073687) 408

Closed Nov—Feb

A converted Cornish granite farmhouse set amidst moorland with a view of Sennen Cove.

8rm(4→4⋒) Annexe: 4⋒(1fb) CTV in 4 bedrooms ® sB&B→⋒£15.50—£20 dB&B→⋒£31—£40 **B**

CTV 20P ✿

International **V** ♡ ☕ Bar lunch £1—£3 Tea fr80p High Tea fr£2 Dinner fr£8.30&alc Wine £4.75 Last dinner 8.30pm

Credit cards 1 3 5 Ⓥ

SETTLE

North Yorkshire
Map **7** SD86

★★★**Falcon Manor** Skipton Rd (Consort) ☎ (07292) 3814

Set in its own grounds amid pleasant countryside on the edge of the town, an impressive stone-built hotel provides well-furnished bedrooms and good food served in an attractive restaurant.

16rm(14→2⋒)(4fb) 2 CTV in all bedrooms ® **T** sB&B→⋒£30—£32 dB&B→⋒£47—£59 **B**

80P ✿ solarium bowling green *xmas*

English & Continental **V** ♡ ☕ Lunch £4.35—£4.75 Tea 70p—£2.10 High Tea £3.50—£5.50 Dinner £10&alc Wine £4.95 Last dinner 9.30pm

Credit cards 1 3 5 Ⓥ

★★*B* **Royal Oak** Market Pl ☎ (07292) 2561

Closed xmas day evening

This owner-run, town-centre pub, originally built in 1684, offers good bedrooms and an attractive restaurant serving good food.

6rm(5→1⋒) CTV in all bedrooms ® **T** ✱ sB&B→⋒£22.95—£24.50 dB&B→⋒£39.90—£44

20P 2

V ♡ ☕ ✱ Lunch £5.50 Tea £2.95 High Tea £3.90 Dinner £8.50alc Wine £4.25 Last dinner 10pm

SEVENOAKS

Kent
Map **5** TQ55

★★**Royal Oak** Upper High St ☎ (0732) 451109

21rm(18→3⋒)(1fb) CTV in all bedrooms ® **T** S% ✱ sB&B→⋒£35 dB&B→⋒£40

☾ 20P

♡ ✱ Lunch £8.50 Dinner £11—£15 Wine £4.60 Last dinner 9.30pm

Credit cards 1 3 5

★★*L* **Sevenoaks Park** Seal Hollow Rd ☎ (0732) 454245

The efficient, family-run hotel provides above-average public areas, friendly service and good standards of cooking.

16rm(3→3⋒)(4fb) CTV in all bedrooms **T** S% sB&B£22.10 sB&B→⋒£30.80 dB&B£27.50 dB&B→⋒£35.20—£49.50

CTV 23P 2 ✿ (heated)

English & French S% ✱ Lunch £7.65 Tea fr£3.50 High Tea fr£3.50 Dinner fr£7.65&alc Wine £4.80 Last dinner 9.30pm

Credit cards 1 2 3 4 5

SHAFTESBURY

Dorset
Map **3** ST82

★★★**Grosvenor** The Commons (Trusthouse Forte) ☎ (0747) 2282

Modernised, former coaching inn whose central arch leads to inner courtyard.

47rm(41→1⋒)(4fb) 1 CTV in all bedrooms ® sB&B→⋒£43 dB&B£53 dB&B→£61 **B**

xmas

♡ ☕ Last dinner 9pm

Credit cards 1 2 3 4 5

★★★**Royal Chase** Royal Chase Roundabout (Best Western) ☎ (0747) 3355

A former monastery, the hotel also has Georgian and some Victorian parts. It offers modern comforts without losing its original character.

32rm(27→3⋒)(15fb) 1 CTV in all bedrooms ® **T** S% sB&B→⋒£33—£38 dB&B→⋒£51—£58 **B**

CTV 50P ✿ (heated) sauna bath solarium pool table putting croquet *xmas*

♡ ☕ S% Lunch £6alc Tea fr£1.50 High Tea £3alc Dinner £8.50&alc Wine £5.50 Last dinner 9.30pm

Credit cards 1 2 3 5 Ⓥ

S

Shaldon — Sheffield

SHALDON
Devon
see **Teignmouth**

SHANKLIN
Isle of Wight
See **Wight, Isle of**

SHAP
Cumbria
Map **12** NY51

★ ★ **Shap Wells** (situated 3m SW of Shap Village off A6) ☎ (09316) 628

Closed Jan & 1st 2 wks Feb

Set in its own extensive grounds in a quiet location, the large hotel stands close to the M6 and provides a convenient base from which to explore many interesting areas, notably the Lake District.

94rm(69🛁3🚿)(11fb) sB&B£15—£16 sB&B🛁🚿£21—£24 dB&B£27—£29 dB&B🛁🚿£36—£39 B

CTV 200P ✽ 🎾 🎣 snooker ♿

English & French **V** Lunch £4.50 Dinner £8.50—£9.75 Wine £5 Last dinner 8.30pm

Credit cards 1 2 3 5 Ⓥ

See advertisement under Kendal

SHAPWICK
Somerset
Map **3** ST43

★ ★ ***Shapwick House*** Monks Dr (Best Western) ☎ Ashcott (0458) 210321

This large, historic house, surrounded by pleasant gardens in a rural setting near the Polden Hills, dates from the 16th century, whilst the hexagonal dovehouse in the grounds is 300 years older.

12rm(5🛁6🚿)(3fb) CTV in all bedrooms ® B

100P 2🚗 ✽ *xmas*

English & Japanese Last dinner 9.30pm

Credit cards 1 2 3 5

SHAWBOST
Isle of Lewis, Western Isles *Ross & Cromarty*
See **Lewis, Isle of**

SHEFFIELD
South Yorkshire
Map **8** SK38

★ ★ ★ ★ **Grosvenor House** Charter Sq (Trusthouse Forte) ☎ (0742) 20041 Telex no 54312

Modern, fourteen storey hotel in the town centre.

103🛁 CTV in all bedrooms ® **T** sB&B🛁£54 dB&B🛁£68 B

Lift ☾ 82🚗 CFA

Last dinner 9.45pm

Credit cards 1 2 3 4 5

★ ★ ★ ★ **Hallam Tower Post House** Manchester Rd, Broomhill (Trusthouse Forte) ☎ (0742) 686031 Due to change to 670067 Telex no 547293

Twelve-storey, modern tower block hotel, overlooking the city.

136🛁 CTV in all bedrooms ® sB&B🛁£53.50 dB&B🛁£67.50 B

Lift ☾ 120P CFA ✽ *xmas*

Last dinner 10.15pm

Credit cards 1 2 3 4 5

★ ★ ★ **Charnwood** 10 Sharrow Ln ☎ (0742) 589411

Originally built as a country house, this hotel is now restored, well-fitted and thoughtfully-equipped, it appeals to both businessmen and tourists, providing stylish bedrooms and smart, tasteful, public areas with conference facilities.

21🛁 CTV in all bedrooms ® **T** S% ✱sB&B🛁£33—£43 dB🛁£47.50—£57.50 B

☾ 23P

English & French **V** ✱Lunch fr£7.25&alc Tea fr95p High Tea £3—£4.50 Dinner fr£8.95&alc Wine £6 Last dinner 10pm

Credit cards 1 2 3 5 Ⓥ

★ ★ ★ *HL* **Hotel St George** Kenwood Rd (Swallow) ☎ (0742) 583811 Telex no 547030

Modern hotel situated in own grounds and gardens, close to city centre. Recently updated public rooms offer comfort and relaxation in pleasant surroundings.

116rm(108🛁8🚿) CTV in all bedrooms ® **T** S% sB&B🛁🚿£36—£48 dB&B🛁🚿£48—£62 B

Lift ☾ 160P CFA ✽ (heated) 🎣 solarium gymnasium *xmas*

English & French **V** S% Lunch fr£7.50 Tea £1.50alc Dinner fr£9 Wine £5.50 Last dinner 10pm

Credit cards 1 2 3 5

★ ★ ★ **Mosborough Hall** High St, Mosborough (7m SE A616) ☎ (0742) 484353

Closed 26 Dec & Bank Hols

A period manor house with Elizabethan elements, in a village setting.

12rm(7🛁3🚿)(2fb) 6 CTV in all bedrooms **T** ✱sB&B£20—£37 sB&B🛁🚿£20—£37 dB&B£32—£48 dB&B🛁🚿£32—£48 B

☾ CTV 100P ✽

French **V** ✱Lunch fr£6.75&alc Tea fr65p Dinner £9—£10&alc Wine £5.90 Last dinner 9.30pm

Credit cards 1 2 3

★ ★ ★ **Royal Victoria** Victoria Station Rd ☎ (0742) 768822

Large four-storey Victorian hotel near the former railway station in the town centre.

72rm(48🛁🚿) CTV in all bedrooms ® **T** ✱sB&B fr£24.50 sB&B🛁🚿fr£37 dB&B fr£40 dB&B🛁🚿fr£47

Lift ☾ 250P CFA

English & French **V** S% ✱Lunch £7 Tea 65p Dinner £8.50 Wine £4.75 Last dinner 10pm

Credit cards 1 2 3 5 Ⓥ

★ ★ ★ **Staindrop Lodge** Lane End ☎ (0742) 864727
(For full entry see Chapeltown)

S

★★**Roslyn Court** 178—180 Psalter Ln, Brincliffe ☎ (0742) 666188

Three-storey building in a residential area.

31rm(21➡10⋒)(2fb) CTV in all bedrooms ®T ✱sB&B➡⋒£21—£26 dB&B➡⋒£33—£41 B

☾CTV 25P

V ♔ ☕ ✱Bar lunch £1.80—£4 Tea 50p Dinner £5.50 Wine £4.20 Last dinner 9pm

Credit cards 1 2 3 5 Ⓥ

★★**Rutland** 452 Glossop Rd, Broomhill (Inter Hotel/Exec Hotel) ☎ (0742) 664411 Telex no 547500

RS Xmas Day—28 Dec

Seven detached stone houses, interconnected by walkways, form a modern hotel which is popular with businessmen. Public rooms include a spacious reception lounge with separate public lounge, writing room and small, intimate restaurant with adjoining cocktail bar and an extremely good bedroom annexe stands close by.

73rm(68➡1⋒) Annexe: 17rm(15➡2⋒) (9fb) CTV in all bedrooms ®T ✱sB&B£19—£23 sB&B➡⋒£24—£32.50 dB&B➡⋒£34—£40 B

Lift ☾80P CFA

V ♔ ☕ ✱Lunch £4.25—£4.75&alc Dinner £7.25&alc Wine £4.85 Last dinner 9.30pm

Credit cards 1 2 3 5 Ⓥ

★★**St Andrews** 46—48 Kenwood Rd (Swallow) ☎ (0742) 550309 Telex no 547030

Two detached houses joined by glass corridor at first floor level. Situated in residential area.

41rm(9➡21⋒)(2fb) CTV in 24 bedrooms ®sB&Bfr£24 sB&B➡⋒£25—£34 dB&Bfr£34 dB&B➡⋒£35—£44 B

CTV 100P ✿

V ♔ ☕ Lunch £5.50 Tea 75p Dinner £6.50&alc Wine £5.50 Last dinner 8.45pm

Credit cards 1 2 3

✕✕**Mogul Room** 36—42 Church Ln, Dore (5m SW of A621) ☎ (0742) 365948

Four terrace cottages have been converted to form this restaurant which provides Indian food of some style in attractive surroundings.

Lunch not served Mon

♁Asiatic & Indian V 70 seats Lunch £3.50—£6.50&alc Dinner £5.50—£7&alc Wine £4.50 Last dinner 11.45pm 20P

Credit cards 1 2 3 5

S

SHEPPERTON

Surrey London plan **5** *A1* (page 446)

★★★**Shepperton Moat House** Felix Ln (Queens Moat) ☎ Walton-on-Thames (0932) 241404 Telex no 928170

Closed 26—30 Dec

Quietly situated in 11 acres of grounds next to River Thames, this busy modern conference and commercial hotel has well equipped bedrooms, compact bathrooms and some leisure activities.

160➡⋒CTV in all bedrooms ®T ✗ S% sB&B➡⋒£45—£48 dB&B➡⋒£57—£63 B

Lift ☾225P CFA ✿ golf sauna bath snooker solarium gymnasium *xmas*

♁English & French V ♔ ☕ Lunch £9—£10.50&alc Tea 60—£80p Dinner £9.50—£10.50&alc Wine £5.25 Last dinner 10pm

Credit cards 1 2 3 5 Ⓥ

See advertisement under Walton-on-Thames

SHEPTON MALLET

Somerset
Map **3** ST64

★★**Shrubbery** Commercial Rd ☎ (0749) 2555

RS Sun evenings

Owner-managed, small tourist hotel, with a cellar restaurant, in the centre of the town.

7rm(5➡1⋒)(1fb) CTV in all bedrooms ® sB&B£20 sB&B➡⋒£22 dB&B➡⋒£38 B

12P 🚫 ✿ croquet

♁English & French V ♔ ☕ Bar lunch £4.50 Tea £1 Dinner £6.50&alc Wine £4.50 Last dinner 9pm

Credit cards 1 2 3 5 Ⓥ

✕✕**Bowlish House** Coombe Ln, Bowlish (on the Wells road A371) ☎ (0749) 2022

The attractive Georgian restaurant on the outskirts of the town offers a country house atmosphere, gracious dining room and four bedrooms. Menus are simple, fixed-price and sound, whilst the wine list covers all countries and over 400 wines, many of which are also on the off sale list.

Closed 24—28 Dec Lunch not served

♁International 26 seats ✱Dinner £12 Wine £4 Last dinner 10pm 10P ⚡

S%

✕✕**Thatched Cottage** Frome Rd ☎ (0749) 2058

This unspoiled cottage restaurant stands in an attractive garden just out of town. Family-run, it provides friendly, efficient service and offers a good table d'hôte menu at lunchtime, supplemented by a wide à la carte choice in the evening.

Closed Mon Lunch not served Sat Dinner not served Sun

♁English & French 35 seats Lunch £7.75—£8.75&alc Dinner £15alc Wine £6.65 Last dinner 9pm 40P

Credit cards 1 2 3 5 Ⓥ

✕**Blostin's** 29 Waterloo Rd ☎ (0749) 3648

The popular, proprietor-run bistro is simply-appointed but pleasant, with a cordially informal atmosphere and cheerful, prompt service. Menus, which include some unusual dishes, display good use of seasonal raw materials, while standards of cooking and presentation are high. Some fine wines and a very dependable house wine are available.

Closed Sun, 1—14 Jan & 1—7 Jun
Lunch not served

♁French V 30 seats Lunch £5.95 Dinner £8.95—£12.50 Wine £4.95 Last dinner 9.30pm

Credit cards 1 3 4 5 Ⓥ

SHERBORNE

Dorset
Map **3** ST61

★★★**Post House** Horsecastles Ln (Trusthouse Forte) ☎ (0935) 813191 Telex no 46522

Modern hotel complex with pleasant, good size rooms.

60➡(12fb) CTV in all bedrooms ®T sB&B➡£47.50 dB&B➡£63.50 B

☾100P CFA ✿ putting green *xmas*

♔ ☕ Last dinner 10pm

Credit cards 1 2 3 4 5

★★*B* **Half Moon** Half Moon St (Toby) ☎ (0935) 812017

15➡⋒(2fb) CTV in all bedrooms ®T (guide dogs only) sB&B£23.50—£31 dB&B£33.50—£41 B

70P

V ♔ Lunch £6.80—£7.80&alc Dinner £6.80—£7.80&alc Wine £4.35 Last dinner 10pm

Credit cards 1 2 3 5

✕✕**Grange Hotel** Oborne (1½m NE off A30) ☎ (0935) 813463

This attractive, country house restaurant in the hamlet of Oborne offers relaxed surroundings, pleasant appointments and service by attentive staff. The extensive menu includes a selection of fresh vegetables and the sweet trolley offers a good choice of freshly-made desserts.

Closed Mon, 1st wk Jan, last wk Aug & 1st 2 wks Sept Lunch not served Tue—Sat Dinner not served Sun

♁English & Continental V 50 seats Lunch £6.90 Dinner £11.30alc Wine £4.90 Last dinner 10.15pm 20P

Credit cards 1 3

✕**Pheasant's** 24 Greenhill ☎ (0935) 815252

Standing at the head of the town's High Street, the restaurant is housed in an attractive period property with stone walls and stone-tiled roof. The very pleasant interior promotes a relaxing atmosphere, and service is attentive. A sound menu of well-prepared dishes is augmented by daily specials.

Closed Sun
Lunch by reservation only

♁English & French V Lunch £6—£8&alc Dinner £6—£8&alc Wine £4.95 Last dinner 10.30pm 10P

Credit cards 1 2 3 5 Ⓥ

SHERBURN IN ELMET
North Yorkshire
Map **8** SE43

✕***Bon Viveur*** 19 Low St ☎ South Milford (0977) 682146

A cosy lounge bar with open fires and low beams takes up the ground floor of this old village building, whilst the restaurant, serving French and international dishes which are prepared and cooked on the premises, is on the first floor. Smart staff give expertly professional service and the wine list is good.

Closed Sun, Mon, 1st 2 wks Jan & all Aug
Lunch not served

French 45 seats 10P

SHERINGHAM
Norfolk
Map **9** TG14

★★**Beaumaris** South St ☎ (0263) 822370

Closed Xmas wk

25rm(18 3)(5fb) CTV in all bedrooms ® sB&B£16.50—£20.50 sB&B £17.50—£21.50 dB&B£32—£40 dB&B £35—£43

CTV 25P

✱Lunch £5.75—£7.50&alc Tea 80p Dinner fr£8.50&alc Wine £5.50 Last dinner 8.30pm

Credit cards 1 2 3 Ⓥ

★★**Southlands** South St ☎ (0263) 822679

Closed mid Oct—Etr

18rm(13 1)(2fb) CTV in all bedrooms ® ✱sB&B£17.50—£22 sB&B £20—£22 dB&B£35—£44 dB&B £40—£44

22P

V ✱Bar lunch £1.50—£6 Tea 50p Dinner £9—£10.50 Wine £3.80 Last dinner 7.45pm

★***Two Lifeboats*** Promenade ☎ (0263) 822401

Established in 1720, this hotel was once used by smugglers.

8rm(2fb) ®

CTV

Last dinner 9pm

SHETLAND
Map **16**

LERWICK
Map 16 HU44

★★★**Kveldsro House** ☎ (0595) 2195

Closed Xmas & New Year

Stone building in an elevated position overlooking the bay.

14rm(9) CTV in all bedrooms ® T sB&B£29.90 sB&B £40.25 dB&B £43.70

28P

V Lunch £5.50 Tea £1 Dinner £9.50&alc Wine £4.30 Last dinner 9pm

★★★**Lerwick Thistle** South Rd (Thistle) ☎ (0595) 2166 Telex no 75128

Modern hotel overlooking bay.

60 (1fb) in 6 bedrooms CTV in all bedrooms ® ✱sB £35—£42 dB £42—£52 (room only)

60P sauna bath solarium gymnasium Live music & dancing Tue & Thu

International ✱Bar lunch £2.90 Dinner fr£9&alc Wine £7 Last dinner 8.30pm

Credit cards 1 2 3 4 5 Ⓥ

★★★**Shetland** Holmsgarth Rd ☎ (0595) 5515 Telex no 75432

Overlooking the harbour, this modern, purpose-built hotel has well equipped bedrooms, attractive public areas and good function and leisure facilities.

66 (4fb) CTV in all bedrooms ® T sB&B £45 dB&B £52

Lift 150P (heated) sauna bath solarium gymnasium Live music & dancing Tue

International V ✱Lunch £3—£5&alc Tea 75p High Tea £2.65 Dinner £9.50alc Wine £5.80 Last dinner 9.30pm

Credit cards 1 2 3 4 5

VIRKIE
Map **16** HU31

★***Meadowvale*** ☎ Sumburgh (0950) 60240

Modern timber-clad, two-storey building, near the sea and overlooking Sumburgh Airport.

11rm(3)(1fb) T

CTV 20P billiards

V

WHITENESS
Map **16** HU44

★***Westing's*** Wormadale ☎ Gott (059584) 242

Closed Jan RS Feb—Apr

This small, privately-owned hotel offers comfortable and well-equipped bedrooms and attractive public areas.

9rm() CTV in all bedrooms ®

CTV 15P

V Last dinner 9pm

Credit cards 1 2 5

SHIELDAIG
Highland *Ross & Cromarty*
Map **14** NG85

★***Tigh an Eilean*** ☎ (05205) 251

Closed Nov—Mar

A small family-run hotel, beautifully situated on the shores of Loch Torridon.

13rm(4)(2fb) ®

CTV 20P

V Last dinner 8pm

SHIFNAL
Shropshire
Map **7** SJ70

★★★*H* **Park House** Park St ☎ Telford (0952) 460128

RS 24—28 Dec

Georgian style hotel in spacious grounds with good, friendly service and comfortable, well equipped accommodation.

37rm(35⇌2⋒)(1fb) CTV in all bedrooms **T** sB&B⇌⋒£40—£60 dB&B⇌⋒£50—£80 **B**

Lift ☾ 130P ✿ ▭(heated) sauna bath solarium

French Lunch £8.50&alc Tea £1.50 Dinner £17&alc Wine £6.50 Last dinner 10.30pm

Credit cards 1 2 3 5 Ⓥ

SHINFIELD
Berkshire
Map **4** SU76

✿✿ XXX **Chez Nico** The Old Vicarage, Church Ln ☎ Reading (0734) 883783

As we suggested, the transition of Nico Ladenis from Battersea to Shinfield has done no harm; on the contrary, all our reports suggest that he is cooking better than ever. The old house in attractive gardens has been refurbished with an attractive salmon pink colour scheme, and the conservatory extension is charming in the summer. Crisp linen, sparkling cutlery and crystal and decorative porcelain are appropriately fine table appointments. As before, Mrs Ladenis looks after the restaurant with intelligence and skill, well supported by her brigade of smart young staff. The menu is arranged so that a starter and main course are priced together according to the main course selected, the other courses are à la carte; at lunch there is a fixed price meal that represents terrific value. The wine list of some 100 items is well chosen so that you will easily find something appropriate to drink. But to the food! Mr Ladenis's style has not changed but his enthusiasm, skill and innovation leads him to ever better results. Perhaps some items in a dish are not always necessary but they never conflict; generally his well balanced dishes are exactly seasoned and show the best sort of gastronomic skill. He cooks in the modern French style but does his own thing and achieves a clean effect in his cooking that is uncompromising in allowing the real taste of the best quality produce to come through. Mousseline of sole and crab with a shellfish sauce was perfect. He has a delicate touch with fish, as demonstrated by his lightly cooked scallops with ginger in a shellfish sauce. His terrines are full of flavour as are the accompanying Sauternes aspic. Well hung beef and tender ducks are full of flavour. And the sauces — what sauces indeed! Magnificent: limpid and of intense flavour that does not overpower the meats they are perhaps his strongest point according to many. Vegetables are delicious as are the mouth watering desserts; tangy sorbets, rich chocolate pavés and crisp pastry for the fruit tarts. One criticism perhaps, is the preponderence of iced puddings. However, you will enjoy your meal here and congratulate Mr Ladenis on what he has achieved, wish him well and hope he will earn three rosettes next year.

Closed Mon & Xmas
Lunch not served Tue
Dinner not served Sun

French 48 seats ✱ Lunch fr£17.50&alc Dinner £30alc Wine £11.50 Last dinner 10pm 30P nc10yrs

Credit cards 1 2 3 4 5

CHANGED HANDS

SHIPDHAM
Norfolk
Map **5** TF90

★★ *HBL* **Shipdham Place** Church Cl ☎ Dereham (0362) 820303

Closed 1 wk Xmas RS Jan, Feb 2 wks Mar

A most relaxing hotel where one feels more like a guest in a private house. The original 17th century building has been extended during the centuries, and offers a variety of different styles of most comfortable bedrooms. The five course dinner uses produce from the kitchen garden as well as the London and Paris markets.

9⇌ **T** S% sB&B⇌£38.50—£55 dB&B⇌£49.50—£66

CTV 24P ✿ croquet

English & French S% Dinner £20.35 Wine £8 Last dinner 9pm

SHIPHAM
Somerset
Map **3** ST45

★★ *H* **Daneswood House** Cuck Hill (Guestaccom) ☎ Winscombe (093484) 3145

RS 24 Dec—Jan

This proprietor-run, country-house hotel in village setting offers a relaxed, informal atmosphere. Bedrooms and public rooms are comfortable, with tastefully co-ordinated decor and fabrics, whilst the restaurant offers a range of interesting, good-quality dishes, prepared with enthusiasm.

10rm(1⇌4⋒) 1 CTV in all bedrooms Ⓡ sB&Bfr£25 sB&B⇌⋒£27.50—£32.50 dB&B£30—£32 dB&B⇌⋒£32—£55 **B**

CTV 25P 2 ✿

English & Continental **V** Lunch £6.95—£7.95&alc Dinner £10.95—£11.95&alc Wine £5.50 Last dinner 9pm

Credit cards 1 2 3 4 5

Shipham — Shiptonthorpe

★**Penscot Farmhouse** The Square (Minotel) ☎ Winscombe (093484) 2659

RS Dec & Jan except Xmas

Attractive, personally-run, cottage hotel, with a separate restaurant serving good food.

18rm(12⋒)(2fb) 1⊞ ®sB&B£12.50—£16 sB&B⋒£15.50—£19 dB&Bfr£25 dB&B⋒fr£31 B

CTV 40P ✿ ⌁ *xmas*

V ♡ ☕ Lunch £4.50—£6.50&alc Tea 50p—£1.50 Dinner £4.50—£6.50&alc Wine £4 Last dinner 9pm

Credit cards 1 2 3 5 V

SHIPLEY
Shropshire
Map **7** SO89

✕✕**Thornescroft** Bridgnorth Rd ☎ Pattingham (0902) 700253

Georgian farmhouse with a matching extension.

Closed Sun, Mon, 2 wks mid Aug & 1 wk Xmas—New Year

♡English & Continental **V** 50 seats S% Lunch £4.75—£5&alc Dinner £7.50—£8&alc Wine £5.05 Last dinner 9pm P

Credit cards 1 2 3 5

SHIPLEY
West Yorkshire
Map **7** SE13

✕**Aagrah** 27 Westgate ☎ Bradford (0274) 594660

Converted from small, residential premises in the town centre the two-level restaurant is decorated and embellished in typically Indian style. Guests are warmly welcomed, and courteous service complements the Indian, Kashmiri and Persian food, authentically flavoured with herbs and spices.

Closed Xmas evening & 23 Jul

Lunch not served (except for parties)

♡Asian & Kashmiri **V** 40 seats ✱Dinner £5.25—£9&alc Wine £3.80 Last dinner 12.45am 10P nc

Credit cards 1 2 3 5 V

SHIPSTON-ON-STOUR
Warwickshire
Map **4** SP24

✕✕**Old Mill** ☎ (0608) 61880

Just out of the town centre, a stone-built former mill stands on the banks of the River Stour. The restaurant is run by two young couples whose courtesy and friendliness ensures a warm welcome. Food is in the country style, well-presented in a modern, light manner, with particularly good vegetables. Accommodation is available in five good bedrooms.

Dinner not served Sun

♡European 50 seats Lunch £10—£17.50 Dinner £14.50—£17.50 Wine £7.50 Last dinner 9.15pm 12P

Credit cards 1 2 3 5

SHIPTONTHORPE
Humberside
Map **8** SE84

✕✕**Paul's Place** York Rd ☎ Market Weighton (0696) 73351

About three miles west of Market Weighton, on the A1079, the restaurant offers an imaginative range of Chinese dishes, cooked with skill and experience and served by helpful staff. The wine list is better than average, and there is a good lounge bar.

Closed Mon Lunch not served Sat

♡Pekinese & Cantonese **V** 85 seats ✱Lunch £7alc Dinner £7alc Wine £5.50 Last dinner 10.30pm 50P nc 12yrs

Credit cards 1 2 3 V

SHIPTON-UNDER-WYCHWOOD
Oxfordshire
Map **4** SP21

★★**Shaven Crown** ☎ (0993) 830330

Parts of this unusual, small hotel, which is both smart and comfortable, date from the 15th century; two Cotswold-stone houses have been joined together with two bars and a good restaurant, all run with care and charm by the owners.

8rm(4🛁1🚿)(1fb) CTV in all bedrooms Ⓡ ✈ sB&B£20 dB&B£40 dB&B🛁🚿£48 B

20P 🚌 ✿ *xmas*

English & French 🍷 ☕ Bar lunch £3.50alc Tea £1.50alc Dinner £10alc Wine £4.85 Last dinner 9.30pm

Credit cards 1 3 Ⓥ

✕**Lamb Inn** High St ☎ (0993) 830465

The small, Cotswold-stone, village inn has a popular bar and provides some bedroom accommodation. Its well-polished restaurant offers a short, fixed-price menu of British fare, prepared from fresh, good-quality ingredients and complemented by kindly, informal service.

Lunch not served Mon—Sat Dinner not served Sun

V 30 seats Sun lunch fr£7.50 Bar lunch fr£1 Dinner fr£11.50 Wine £5 Last dinner 9pm 20P nc 14yrs

Credit cards 1 2 3 5

SHIRLEY
West Midlands
Map **7** SP17

✕**Chez Julien Brasserie** 1036 Stratford Rd, Monkspath ☎ 021-744 7232

This extremely popular little French restaurant with an authentic brasserie style is situated on the busy Stratford Road. The use of good ingredients, sympathetically cooked, then served by polite staff, makes for an enjoyable and memorable meal.

Closed Sun
Lunch not served Sat

French 80 seats S% Lunch fr£6.20&alc Dinner fr£10&alc Wine £5.80 Last dinner 10.30pm 30P

Credit cards 1 2 3 5

SHORNE
Kent
Map **5** TQ67

★★★**Inn on the Lake** Watling St (A2) ☎ (047482) 3333 Telex no 966356

Hotel has spacious modern bedrooms, some overlooking lake.

78🛁(2fb) CTV in all bedrooms Ⓡ ✈ sB&B🛁£44—£50 dB&B🛁£50—£60

☾ 250P CFA ✿ ♪ Live music & dancing Sat

English & French 🍷 ☕ Lunch £9 Tea £1.10 Dinner £12alc Last dinner 9.45pm

Credit cards 1 2 3 5

SHRAWLEY
Hereford & Worcestershire
Map **7** SO86

★★★**Lenchford** ☎ Worcester (0905) 620229

A late Georgian house on the banks of the River Severn has been modernised to a high standard to create this hotel.

12rm🛁🚿(1fb) CTV in all bedrooms Ⓡ **T** ✈ ✱sB&B£24.50 sB&B🛁🚿£29.50 dB&B🛁🚿 B

100P ✿ ⛵ (heated) ♪ 🏠

🍷 ☕ ✱Lunch £8.50&alc Dinner £9.50&alc Wine £4.70 Last dinner 9.30pm

Credit cards 1 2 3

SHREWSBURY
Shropshire
Map **7** SJ41

★★★***Ainsworth's Radbrook Hall*** Radbrook Rd ☎ (0743) 4861

This hotel with its extensive leisure facilities, was originally the house of the Head of the Clan McPherson

43rm(35🛁8🚿) Annexe: 5🚿 CTV in all bedrooms Ⓡ **T** B

SEE OUR ENTRIES ON PAGES 757 AND 570

☾CTV 250P CFA ✿ squash sauna bath solarium Disco Sat Live music & dancing Sat *xmas*

V ♔ Last dinner 10.30pm

Credit cards 1 2 3 5

★★★**Lion** Wyle Cop (Trusthouse Forte) ☎ (0743) 53107

Large Georgian Inn with Dickensian associations and modern well equipped accommodation.

59⇌(3fb) 1⊟ CTV in all bedrooms ® sB&B⇌£45 dB&B⇌£64 ₿

Lift ☾72P CFA *xmas*

♔ Last dinner 10pm

Credit cards 1 2 3 4 5

★★★**Lord Hill** Abbey Foregate (De Vere) ☎ (0743) 52601 Telex no 35104

Large Georgian-style building with later additions including a modern annexe.

22rm(8⇌14⋔) Annexe: 24⇌(2fb) CTV in all bedrooms ®T S% sB&B⇌⋔£29—£42 dB&B⇌⋔£44—£55 ₿

☾150P CFA

English & French V ♔ ☕ S% Lunch £3.50—£4.50 Tea 70p High Tea £4—£5 Dinner £9.95&alc Wine £7.95 Last dinner 9.30pm

Credit cards 1 2 3 5

Shrewsbury

★★★**Prince Rupert** Butcher Row (Consort) ☎ (0743) 52461 Telex no 35100

Dating back to the 15th-century, the hotel is named after James I's grandson and was Prince Rupert's Civil War headquarters. It is privately owned and managed.

70⇌(4fb) 2⊟ CTV in all bedrooms ®T ✈ ✱ sB&B⇌£40 dB&B⇌£55 ₿

Lift ☾ CTV 60P games room CFA

English, French & Italian V ♔ ☕ ✱ Lunch £7&alc Tea £1—£5 High Tea £4—£8 Dinner £10&alc Wine £5 Last dinner 10.45pm

Credit cards 1 2 3 4 5 Ⓥ

★★**Lion & Pheasant** 49—50 Wyle Cop ☎ (0743) 248288

Closed Xmas

This historic building, parts of which date from the 16th century, is situated just east of the town centre. Having recently undergone extensive renovation, it provides comfortable and well-equipped accommodation.

19rm(4⇌8⋔)(1fb) CTV in all bedrooms ® T S% ✱ sB&B£18—£19.50 sB&B⇌⋔£25—£26 dB&B£30—£32 dB&B⇌⋔£39.50—£42 ₿

30P

V ♔ ☕ S% ✱ Lunch £4.75—£6.25 Tea 50p—£1.75 High Tea £2.75—£4.50 Dinner £7.75&alc Wine £4.90 Last dinner 9.15pm

Credit cards 1 2 3 5 Ⓥ

★★**Shelton Hall** Shelton (2m NW A5) ☎ (0743) 3982

The family-run hotel, housed in an 18th century buliding, stands on high ground just outside the town centre; huge cedar and copper beech trees are a feature of the mature gardens which surround it.

11rm(1⇌5⋔)(2fb) CTV in all bedrooms ® sB&B£20—£26 sB&B⇌⋔£34 dB&B£32 dB&B⇌⋔£38

CTV 50P ✿

V ♔ Lunch £7 Dinner £9&alc Wine £5.25 Last dinner 9pm

Credit cards 1 3

See advertisement on page 656

✕✕***Albright Hussey*** Albright Hussey (3m N off A528) ☎ Bomere Heath (0939) 290523

The battle of Shrewsbury (1406) was fought on the site of this restaurant.

Closed Mon, Aug & Bank Hols Dinner not served Sun

English & French V 50 seats Last dinner 10pm 50P

Credit cards 1 2 3 5

S

XX**Old Police House** Castle Ct, off Castle St ☎ (0743) 60668

The comfortable little restaurant is tucked away in a narrow alley. Its interior has been attractively restored and the menu reflects a Victorian/Edwardian theme. It makes good use of local produce and your meal is complemented by a good selection of wines and by informally friendly service.

Closed Sun

English & French **V** 30 seats Lunch £4.75—£6.75 Dinner £10.95—£11.95 Wine £4.95 Last dinner 9.45pm 2P

Credit cards 1 2 3

SIDCOT

Avon

Map **3** ST45

★★ **Sidcot** ☎ Winscombe (093484) 2271

Small, personally-run, holiday hotel set in 4 acres of grounds with access to A38.

9 (3fb) CTV in 6 bedrooms TV in 1 bedroom

CTV 65P

English & French **V** Last dinner 9.30pm

Credit cards 1 2 3

SIDMOUTH

Devon

Map **3** SY18

★★★★ *H* **Victoria** Esplanade (Brend) ☎ (03955) 2651 Telex no 42551

Large hotel in its own grounds, set in an elevated position overlooking the sea.

61 (10fb) CTV in all bedrooms **T**

sB&B £39.10—£44.85

dB&B £59.80—£96.60

S

Lift ☾ CTV 100P 4 (£2.30 per day) CFA ✻ & (heated) (hard) snooker sauna bath solarium putting Live music wkly xmas

English & French **V** Lunch fr£7.76 Tea fr86p Dinner £12.65&alc Wine £5.46 Last dinner 9pm

Credit cards 1 2 3 5

★★★**Bedford** Esplanade ☎ (03955) 3047

Closed end Oct—mid Mar

Large traditional hotel on a corner of the promenade. There are fine sea views.

41rm(20 5)(8fb) CTV in all bedrooms ® S% ✻ sB&B£15—£18 sB&B £16—£20 dB&B£30—£36 dB&B £44—£56 B

Lift ☾ TV

V S% Lunch £4—£6 Tea £1—£1.50 Dinner £8 Last dinner 8.15pm

Credit cards 2 3 5

★★★**Belmont** Sea Front ☎ (03955) 2555

Jan—15 Feb

Large hotel overlooking well tended gardens and with good sea views. It is personally run with caring services.

50 CTV in all bedrooms ® **T** S% sB&B £30—£34 dB&B £60—£68 B

Lift ☾ 32P ✻ nc 2yrs *xmas*

Sidmouth

S% Lunch fr£8.50&alc Tea fr£2.50 Dinner fr£9.50&alc Wine £6.50 Last dinner 8.30pm

★★★***Byes Links*** Sid Rd ☎ (03955) 3129

Closed Nov—14 Mar

Adjacent to The Byes, an extensive sylvan glade beside the River Sid, and a few minutes' walk from the shops, this family-run hotel is comfortable, with modern fittings.

18rm(8 8)(3fb) CTV in all bedrooms ® B

☾ CTV 40P ✻ Live music & dancing twice wkly *xmas*

V Last dinner 8.30pm

Credit card 3

★★★**Fortfield** Station Rd ☎ (03955) 2403

Country house style hotel set within 3 acres of grounds and overlooking the sea.

52rm(37 5)(7fb) CTV in all bedrooms ® **T** sB&B£22—£32 sB&B £24—£37 dB&B£44—£64 dB&B £48—£74 B

Lift ☾ CTV 60P CFA ✻ (heated) sauna bath solarium games room putting *xmas*

Bar lunch £2.50—£5.50 Tea 65p Dinner £9—£10&alc Wine £4.10 Last dinner 8.30pm

Credit cards 1 3 5 Ⓥ

See advertisement on page 658

★★★*HL* **Riviera** The Esplanade ☎ (03955) 5201 Telex no 42551

Attractive hotel in a fine position on the sea front, with its own sun patio.

34rm(25 4) CTV in all bedrooms **T** sB&B £26.50—£39 dB&B £53—£78 B

Lift ☾ 12P 9 (charged) *xmas*

English & French **V** Lunch £8&alc Tea 80p Dinner £11.50&alc Wine £4.50 Last dinner 9pm

Credit cards 2 5 Ⓥ

See advertisement on page 658

★★★**Royal Glen** Glen Rd ☎ (03955) 3221

During the last century, members of the Royal Family (including Princess Victoria, later to become Queen Empress) visited this country house hotel with its old world charm.

37rm(18 10)(5fb) CTV in 25 bedrooms TV in 12 bedrooms **T** sB&B£13.74—£14.63 sB&B £16.10—£24.90 dB&B£27.48—£29.26 dB&B £32.20—£49.80 B →

The Fortfield Hotel AA ★★★

SIDMOUTH

Sidmouth (03955) 2403

A large country house style hotel in its own grounds overlooking the sea, privately owned and managed by the Doddrell family. The feeling of warm courteous hospitality greets you at the entrance and your eye is immediately caught by the tasteful decor.

Our new leisure centre with its indoor swimming pool, sauna and games room augments the existing luxury and comfort for which the Fortfield is renowned. Solarium, 55 bedrooms with colour television, radio and intercom, many with private bathrooms, balconies, plenty of free parking in our grounds, sun terraces, lift, licensed bar, two lounges, TV room, beautiful dining room seating 120, night porter.

S

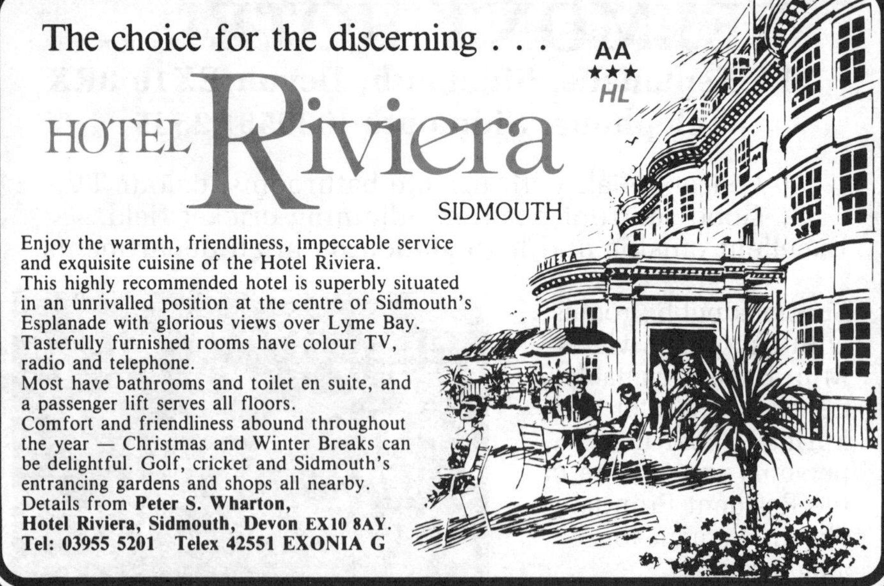

##CTV 16P 8🚗(60p per day) ⛟ ▭(heated) nc8yrs

♆ ☕ Lunch £5 Tea £1 Dinner £6 Last dinner 7.30pm

Credit cards [2] [3]

★★★**Salcombe Hill House** Beatland Rd ☎ (03955) 4697

Closed Nov—Feb

Standing in own grounds, hotel is short distance from sea front.

33rm(23→5⋔)(5fb) CTV in all bedrooms Ⓡ sB&B£17—£24 sB&B→⋔£18—£28.50 dB&B£34—£48 dB&B→⋔£38—£57 B

Lift ☾ 35P 5🚗(charge) ⛟ ✽ ⏦(heated) 🎾(grass) games room putting nc3yrs

V ♆ ☕ ⚡ Lunch £5—£7 Tea £1.25—£1.50 Dinner £7—£9 Wine £4.20 Last dinner 8pm

Credit cards [1] [3] [5] Ⓥ

★★★*H* **Westcliff** Manor Rd ☎ (03955) 3252

Closed Nov & Jan
RS Dec & Feb

Comfortable hotel with spacious grounds, close to the beach

38rm(32→3⋔)(12fb) CTV in all bedrooms ✈ sB&B£17.50—£26.75 sB&B→⋔£21.50—£29.75 dB&B£35—£53.50 dB&B→⋔£43—£59.50 B

Lift 45P ⛟ ✽ ⏦(heated) gymnasium putting croquet table tennis pool

Live music & dancing Sat

♛ English & Continental ♆ ☕ Lunch £6.25 Tea 85p Dinner £10.50 Wine £3.95 Last dinner 8.30pm

Credit cards [1] [3]

Sidmouth

★★**Abbeydale** Manor Rd ☎ (03955) 2060

Closed Nov—Feb

Comfortable friendly holiday hotel offering good service and cuisine.

17rm(16→1⋔) CTV in all bedrooms Ⓡ ✈ *sB&B→⋔£18—£22 dB&B→⋔£36—£44

Lift 24P ⛟ nc4yrs

♆ ☕ ⚡ *Bar lunch £3.15—£3.75 Tea fr60p&alc Dinner fr£7.50 Wine £3.50 Last dinner 8pm

Ⓥ

★★**Applegarth** Church St, Sidford (2m N B3175) ☎ (03955) 3174

About a mile from the sea, this attractive 16th century hotel, standing in an attractive garden, offers neat bedrooms, the personal attention of the owners, and a menu of well prepared and presented food.

7rm(3→1⋔) CTV in all bedrooms Ⓡ *sB&B£19 sB&B→⋔£22 dB&B£40 dB&B→⋔£40 B

CTV 20P ⛟ ✽ *xmas*

♛ English & French *Lunch £1.95—£5.50 Dinner £7.95&alc Wine £6.35 Last dinner 9pm

Credit cards [1] [2] [3] Ⓥ

★★⛰ ***Brownlands*** Sid Rd ☎ (03955) 3053

Closed Oct—Etr (except Xmas)

Standing in 5 acres of grounds with panoramic views towards the sea, within one mile from the town.

17rm(4→5⋔)(3fb) CTV in 11 bedrooms B ⚡ CTV 40P 3🚗 ✽ ⛪ *xmas*

V ♆ ☕ Wine £3.50 Last dinner 8pm

See advertisement on page 660

★★**Littlecourt** Seafield Rd ☎ (03955) 5279

Closed 6 Nov—21 Mar
RS Xmas

Regency house with its own garden, in a quiet position only a short distance from the shops and the sea. →

21rm(12➡5⌒)(3fb) CTV in all bedrooms ®sB&B£18—£26(incl dinner) sB&B➡⌒£19.50—£28(incl dinner) dB&B£36—£55(incl dinner) dB&B➡⌒£39—£59(incl dinner) B

CTV 14P ✽ (heated) *xmas*

V Lunch £5.80—£6.20 Tea fr50p Dinner £7.50—£8 Wine £4.40 Last dinner 8pm

Credit cards 1 3

★★**Royal York & Faulkner** Esplanade ☎(03955) 3043

Regency-style building, personally-run, on the sea front close to shopping facilities.

Sidmouth

71rm(22➡6⌒)(8fb) CTV in all bedrooms ®S% sB&B£16.60—£20 sB&B➡⌒£19—£24.50 dB&B£33.20—£40 dB&B➡⌒£41.70—£49 B

Lift 5P solarium gymnasium

English & French V Lunch £4.50—£6.50&alc Tea £1—£2&alc Dinner £7.50—£8.50 Wine £3.75 Last dinner 8pm

Credit cards 1 2 3

★★**Westbourne** Manor Rd ☎(03955) 3774

Closed Nov—Feb

This Victorian house in its own grounds, with award winning garden, has an intimate bar and a gracious dining room.

14rm(8➡1⌒)(2fb) CTV in all bedrooms ® sB&B£17.50—£19.50 sB&B➡⌒£20.50—£21.50 dB&B£35—£39 dB&B➡⌒£41—£43 B

14P ✽

V Bar lunch £1—£3.50 Tea 45—75p Dinner £7.50 Last dinner 7.30pm

Ⓥ

★★**Woodlands** Station Rd ☎ (03955) 3120

A converted period house on the approach road to the sea front, offering a quiet atmosphere.

30rm(14 4)(1fb) Ⓡ sB&B£12.20—£17.60 sB&B £14.40—£19 dB&B£24.40—£35.20 dB&B £28.80—£38

CTV 25P nc 3yrs *xmas*

V Lunch fr£3.25—£4.25 Dinner £4.50 Wine £3.95 Last dinner 8pm

SILLOTH
Cumbria
Map **11** NY15

★★**Golf** Criffel St ☎ (0965) 31438

Closed Xmas Day

This seaside hotel, overlooking the Solway Firth, caters equally for family holidays and for the businessman.

23rm(15 8)(4fb) CTV in all bedrooms Ⓡ**T** ✱sB&B fr£24 dB&B fr£34

✱Lunch fr£5.78 Tea fr60p Dinner fr£8.50 Wine £4.30 Last dinner 9.30pm

Credit cards 1 2 5 Ⓥ

★★**Queen's** Park Ter, Criffel St (Exec Hotel) ☎ (0965) 31373

Situated on the sea front with excellent views.

22rm(11) CTV in 18 bedrooms Ⓡ in 6 bedrooms ✱sB&B fr£17.50 sB&B fr£22 dB&B fr£28 dB&B fr£33

CTV 12 18 sauna bath

✱Lunch £5.30—£6.30 Dinner £8.50 Wine £4.70 Last dinner 8.30pm

Credit cards 1 3

SILVERDALE
Lancashire
Map **7** SD47

★**Silverdale** Shore Rd ☎ (0254) 701206

Closed Xmas Day

Pleasant, small, family run hotel with attractive walled garden, near shore.

9rm(2)(1fb) sB&B fr£15 sB&B fr£16.50 dB&B fr£25 dB&B fr£28

CTV 25P Disco Sat

Bar lunch 85p—£2.40 Dinner £4—£7.50 Wine £4.60 Last dinner 9pm

Credit card 1

SIMONSBATH
Somerset
Map **3** SS73

★★ *HBL* **Simonsbath House**
☎ Exford (064 383) 259
Closed 21 Dec—14 Jan

Overlooking the beautiful valley of the River Barle this small hotel was the first house to be built on Exmoor in 1654. It has well appointed public rooms and comfortable bedrooms, and offers a peaceful, quiet holiday.

8 2 CTV in all bedrooms S% sB&B £29—£34 dB&B £54—£64

30P 2 (£1 per night) squash nc 10yrs

S% Dinner £15alc Wine £5.25 Last dinner 8.30pm

Credit cards 1 2 3 5 Ⓥ

SIX MILE BOTTOM
Cambridgeshire
Map **5** TL55

★★★ *B* **Swynford Paddocks** (Best Western) ☎ (063870) 234 Telex no 817438

Closed 1 & 2 Jan

Peaceful country house with spacious, elegant rooms.

15 2 CTV in all bedrooms Ⓡ**T** →

S

✻sB&B🛁£44—£52.50 dB&B🛁£60—£70 B

30P ✿ ⚲(hard) croquet pitch & putt *xmas*

English & French V ✻Lunch £7.95—£9.95&alc Tea £1.50 Dinner £15alc Wine £5.95 Last dinner 9.30pm

Credit cards 1 2 3 5

SKEABOST BRIDGE

Isle of Skye, Highland *Inverness-shire*

See **Skye, Isle of**

SKEGNESS

Lincolnshire

Map **9** TF56

★★**County** North Parade ☎(0754) 2461

Large, four-storey sea front hotel to the north of the town centre.

44rm(33🛁11🚿)(2fb) CTV in all bedrooms ®T ✻sB&B🛁🚿£28 dB&B🛁🚿£44 B

Lift CTV 40P 4 sauna bath *xmas*

✻Lunch fr£7&alc Tea fr£1 Dinner fr£7&alc Wine £3.50 Last dinner 9.30pm

Credit cards 1 2 3 5

★★**Links** Drummond Rd, Seacroft ☎(0754) 3605

A large gabled building, ¼ mile from the town centre and close to the sea front.

Six Mile Bottom — Skipton

21rm(2🛁3🚿)(2fb) CTV in 5 bedrooms ® sB&B£15—£17 sB&B🛁🚿£20 dB&B£30—£34 dB&B🛁🚿£34 B

CTV 30P Live music & dancing Sat (Etr—New Year) *xmas*

V Lunch £3.45—£5.95 Tea £1—£1.50 High Tea £1.65—£2.95 Dinner £6.50—£7.95&alc Wine £3.45 Last dinner 9pm

Credit cards 1 3 Ⓥ

★★**Vine** Vine Rd, Seacroft (Exec Hotel) ☎(0754) 3018

Closed 25 & 26 Dec

Tennyson reputedly wrote 'Come Into the Garden, Maud' at this hotel, which dates back to 1660. Standing in pleasant grounds, half a mile south of the town centre, it provides comfortable accommodation.

20rm(17🛁)(4fb) CTV in all bedrooms ✻sB&B£21—£23 sB&B🛁£22—£24 dB&B£36—£42 dB&B🛁£38—£44 B

CTV 120P 2 ✿ U

V ✻Lunch £5—£6&alc Tea fr70p High Tea fr£1.80 Wine £4.75 Last dinner 9.15pm

Credit cards 1 2 3 5 Ⓥ

SKELMORLIE

Strathclyde *Ayrshire*

Map **10** NS16

★★★ *BL* **Manor Park** ☎Wemyss Bay (0475) 520832

Closed 4 Jan—2 Mar

Imposing mansion set in its own magnificent grounds, 2m south of Skelmorlie.

7rm(5🛁1🚿) ®T sB&B fr£27.50 sB&B🛁🚿fr£32.50 dB&B🛁🚿£55—£65 B

150P ✿ *xmas*

Scottish & Continental V S% Lunch fr£7&alc Tea fr£2.50 Dinner fr£12.50&alc Wine £5.25 Last dinner 9.30pm

SKIPTON

North Yorkshire

Map **7** SD95

★**Midland** Broughton Rd ☎(0756) 2781

The stone-built pub, situated opposite the station, offers adequate facilities.

9rm(2fb) ® sB&B£13 dB&B£25

CTV 30P 2 Live music Thu & Sat

V S% ✻Lunch £1.60—£8.10 Dinner £1.80—£9.50 Wine £4.30 Last dinner 8pm

Credit cards 2 3

XXX **Oats** Chapel Hill ☎ (0756) 68118

The à la carte and fixed-price menus of this small, luxurious hotel restaurant offer a delectable range of French dishes, prepared with meticulous care. A comfortable lounge bar adjoining the restaurant features antiques and objets d'art.

Closed Xmas

French **V** 50 seats Lunch £7.75—£10.75&alc Dinner £15.50—£18&alc Wine £5.25 Last dinner 10pm 30P
5 bedrooms available

Credit cards 1 2 3 4 5

X ***Le Caveau*** 86 High St ☎ (0756) 4274

Situated in the centre of the town, below street level, this unusual little restaurant is a conversion of one-time dungeons. The lunchtime menu provides an attractive choice of dishes, and a more adventurous selection supplements this in the evening; service is pleasant and friendly.

Closed Sun Dinner not served Mon

French **V** 30 seats Last dinner 9.30pm

Credit card 3

SKYE, ISLE OF

Highland *Inverness-shire*
Map **13**

ARDVARSAR

Map **13** NG62

★★**Ardvasar** ☎ (04714) 233

Closed Jan & Feb

Modernised 18th century coaching inn with fine views, specialising in Scottish cuisine using local produce.

12rm(4)(1fb) TV available on request Ⓡ ✱sB&B£15—£17 sB&B£17 dB&B£25—£30 dB&B£30—£35

CTV 30P

Scottish & French **V** ✱Lunch £1—£6&alc Tea 60p&alc Dinner £11—£14&alc Wine £5 Last dinner 9.30pm

Credit card 3

Skipton — Skye, Isle of

BROADFORD

Map **13** NG62

★★***Broadford*** ☎ (04712) 204

Closed mid Oct—Mar

Modernised, extended coaching inn catering for tour parties.

20rm(3 6) Annexe: 9rm(2 7)(1fb) Ⓡ

CTV 20P

Last dinner 9pm

Credit cards 1 3

COLBOST

Map 13 NG24

X **Three Chimney's** ☎ Glendale (047081) 258

Small charming croft house restaurant offering good home cooked Scottish fare. Dinner reservations advised.

Closed Nov—Mar Lunch not served Sun

35 seats Lunch £5.25alc Dinner £12alc Wine £4.95 Last dinner 9pm P

Credit cards 1 3

DUNVEGAN

Map **13** NG24

★***Dunvegan*** ☎ (047022) 202

Small, friendly, family-run Highland hotel.

6rm(2fb) CTV in all bedrooms Ⓡ

CTV 60P Cabaret nightly in season

Last dinner 9pm

HARLOSH

Map **13** NG24

★ *H* **Harlosh** ☎ Dunvegan (047022) 367

Closed Nov—Mar

(Rosette awarded for dinner only)

This small, isolated, family-run hotel is superbly situated in the sheltered coastal bay of Loch Bracadale. Modest but comfortable accommodation is enhanced by the warm hospitality extended by the owners, Mr and Mrs Banks, and their friendly staff. The dining room offers a range of enjoyable dishes, many of them based on the abundant, locally-caught seafood.

7rm(2)(3fb) sB&B£12.50—£14 dB&B£25—£28 sB&B£28—£31

TV 20P P

V Tea 70palc Dinner £8—£9&alc Wine £4.50 Last dinner 9pm

Ⓥ

ISLE ORNSAY

Map **13** NG61

★★**Duisdale** ☎ (04713) 202

RS Nov—Mar

An attractive, stone-built house in well-tended and extensive gardens, the hotel has an open outlook across the South of Sleat.

24rms(5)(2fb) Ⓡ S% sB&B£17.50 dB&B£35 dB&B£41

CTV 20P solarium croquet putting

V S% Bar lunch £4.50alc Tea 50p&alc High Tea £6 Dinner £11.50 Wine £3.50 Last dinner 8.30pm

Credit cards 1 3 Ⓥ

❀★★♣*HL* **Kinloch Lodge**
☎(04713) 214
Closed Xmas & 11 Jan—Feb
(*Rosette awarded for dinner only*)
A sea journey to Skye to stay as guests of Lord and Lady McDonald has the ring of a tourist's dream. Nevertheless, the reality will not be a disappointment, for Kinloch Lodge offers a personal welcome, simple but prettily decorated bedrooms and food fit to grace the table of a Lord. Homely lounges have log fires and splendid views.
10rm(8⇌) ®sB&B£25—£45 sB&B⇌£25—£45 dB&B£40—£90 dB&B⇌£40—£90 B
CTV 20P ✽ games room
Tea £2 Dinner £19.50 Wine £4.20 Last dinner 8pm
Credit cards 1 3

★***Hotel Eilean Iarmain*** Campus Croise, Sleat ☎(04713) 332 Telex no 75252
Gaelic-speaking staff extend a friendly welcome at this characterful hotel close to the quiet harbour.
7rm Annexe: 4rm(1fb) 1 B
10P ✽ Live music & dancing Fri *xmas*
Last dinner 8.15pm
Credit cards 1 3

KNOCK
Map **13** NG60
★★*H* **Toravaig House** Knock Bay (Inter Hotel) ☎ Isle Ornsay (04713) 231
Closed Nov—Feb
Large comfortable friendly house, in secluded remote location.
10rm(5⇌2⫿) ® sB&B£20—£22 dB&B£40 dB&B⇌⫿£44 B
CTV 20P ✽
V Lunch £5—£6 Tea £2—£2.50 Dinner £10—£11 Last dinner 8pm
Credit cards 2 3 5 V

Skye, Isle of

PORTREE
Map **13** NG44
★★★**Coolin Hills** ☎(0478) 2003
Closed Xmas & New Years Day
Converted shooting lodge with fine views over Portree Bay, this is a friendly and comfortable hotel.
16rm(12⇌4⫿) Annexe: 9rm(5⇌4⫿)(5fb) CTV in all bedrooms ® sB&B⇌⫿£20—£25 dB&B⇌⫿£40—£46 B
CTV 50P ✽
V Lunch £4—£5 Tea fr 70p High Tea £2.50—£4 Dinner fr £8.50 Wine £3.75 Last dinner 8.30pm
Credit cards 1 3 V

★★**Rosedale** ☎(0478) 2531
Closed Oct—mid May
Delightful, modernised harbour hotel with lots of atmosphere.
19rm(9⇌7⫿) Annexe: 3⇌(2fb) ® sB&B£17—£20 sB&B⇌⫿£22—£26 dB&B£34—£38 dB&B⇌⫿£38—£48 B
CTV 18P
Dinner £10—£10.50 Wine £4.50 Last dinner 8pm V

★★**Royal** ☎(0478) 2525
A well-appointed hotel in a central location overlooking the harbour.
28rm(19⇌⫿)(3fb) CTV in 12 bedrooms sB&B£18—£20 dB&B£36—£49 dB&B⇌⫿£39—£52
☾CTV 20P Live music twice wkly
V Lunch fr £5.60 Tea fr 75p Dinner fr £9.50 Wine £4.50 Last dinner 8.30pm V

★**Isles** Somerled Sq ☎(0478) 2129
Closed Nov—Mar
A well-appointed, small, family run hotel in central location near shops.
10rm(5⫿) CTV in all bedrooms ® sB&B fr £16 dB&B fr £32 dB&B⫿ fr £37
CTV ✽

Lunch fr £5 Dinner fr £10 Wine £4.30 Last dinner 8.30pm

★**King's Haven** Bosville Ter ☎(0478) 2290
Closed Nov—Mar
Comfortable, small hotel with friendly hospitality, an attractive dining room with log burning stove and good food.
7rm(1⇌4⫿)(1fb) CTV in all bedrooms ® sB&B£16.50—£18.50 dB&B£33—£35 dB&B⇌⫿£35—£37
✽
V Dinner £10.50—£12.50 Wine £5.20 Last dinner 7.30pm

SKEABOST BRIDGE
Map **13** NG44
★★★♣*L* **Skeabost House**
☎(047032) 202
Closed mid Oct—mid Apr
Fine, family-run Scottish mansion at the head of a loch.
21rm(14⇌1⫿(3fb) ® sB&B£20—£22 sB&B⇌⫿£26 dB&B£38—£44 dB&B⇌⫿£48—£52
☾CTV 40P ✽ snooker putting
Lunch £2.35—£6 Tea £1—£2.20 Dinner £10.80 Wine £6 Last dinner 8.30pm

SLIGACHAN
Map **13** NG42
★★**Sligachan** ☎(047852) 204
This stone building replaces the original 18th-century coaching inn which stood nearby.
23rm(8⇌)(1fb) S% ✱sB&B£20—£25 sB&B⇌£25—£30 dB&B£40—£50 dB&B⇌£50—£60 B
CTV 30P 5 ✽
V S% ✱Bar lunch £3.50—£7.50 Tea 75p—£1.95 Dinner fr £10.50 Wine £4.50 Last dinner 9pm
Credit cards 1 3 V

UIG
Map **13** NG36
★★*B* **Uig** ☎(047042) 205
Closed Oct—mid Apr
Well appointed family run hotel overlooking Uig Bay.

S

12rm(6→6⋒) Annexe: 13rm(7→6⋒)(2fb) ®sB&B→⋒£24 dB&B→⋒£48 B
20P ✽ U nc12yrs ♿
♁ ☕ Lunch £2—£5 Tea £1—£2.50 High Tea £3.50—£5 Dinner £9—£11 Wine £3.50 Last dinner 8.15pm
Credit cards 1 2 3 5 Ⓥ

★**Ferry Inn** ☎ (047042) 242
Closed Xmas Day, 1 & 2 Jan
RS Nov—Mar
Stone house set back from the road with views over the bay and the harbour.
6rm(1→)(2fb) ®sB&B£16—£25 sB&B→£30 dB&B£fr£25 dB&B→fr£30
12P ⛟
V ♁ ☕ Bar lunch £5alc Tea 80palc High Tea £7alc Dinner £8alc Wine £4.80 Last dinner 8.30pm

---

SLEAFORD
Lincolnshire
Map **8** TF04

★★**Carre Arms** Mareham Ln ☎ (0529) 303156
Predominantly commercial public house hotel next to the railway and close to the town centre.
14rm(3→) CTV in all bedrooms ®
✱sB&B£18.75—£22.75 sB&B→£24.75 dB&B£29.75 dB&B→£34.75—£37.75
50P
♁ ☕ ✱Lunch £3.50—£5.50 Tea £1 Dinner £5.50—£10&alc Wine £3.50 Last dinner 9.30pm
Credit cards 1 3 5 Ⓥ

★***Lion*** Northgate ☎ (0529) 302127
Small coaching inn with original entrance and courtyard.
10rm(2fb) CTV in all bedrooms ®
CTV
♁

SLIGACHAN
Isle of Skye, Highland, *Inverness-shire*
See **Skye, Isle of**

SLOUGH
Berkshire
Map **4** SU97

★★★★**Holiday Inn** Ditton Rd, Langley (Holiday Inns) ☎ (0753) 44244 Telex no 848646
Modern hotel with extensive leisure facilities.
305→(134fb) ⚟ in 30 bedrooms CTV in all bedrooms **T** S% ✱sB→fr£60.95 dB→fr£66.70 (room only) B
Lift ☾ ## 350P ✽ CFA ▭(heated) ᑫ(hard) sauna bath solarium gymnasium ♿ *xmas*
French **V** ♁ ☕ ⚟ S% ✱Lunch £11.25 High Tea £3.25 Dinner £11.25&alc Wine £6.50 Last dinner 10.30pm
Credit cards 1 2 3 4 5

SMALLWAYS
North Yorkshire
Map **12** NZ11

★**A66 Motel** ☎ Teesdale (0833) 27334
A single-storey extension to an inn, with a motel unit.
6rm(1→) CTV in all bedrooms S% sB&B£15 dB&Bfr£22 dB&B→fr£28
30P ✽ ♔
V ♁ ☕ Lunch £4—£9 Tea £1.20—£1.60 High Tea £3.50—£4 Dinner £6—£12&alc Wine £6.25 Last dinner 11pm
Credit cards 1 3 5

SNAINTON
North Yorkshire
Map **8** SE98

★★**Coachman Inn** ☎ Scarborough (0723) 85231
An 18th-century, stone-built coaching inn close to the North Yorkshire moors.
10rm(5→3⋒) Annexe: 2⋒(3fb) CTV in 7 bedrooms ®✱sB&B→⋒fr£22 dB&B→⋒fr£36 B
CTV 50P ✽ ♔
♁ ✱Bar lunch £5.50alc Dinner £10.50alc Wine £5.50 Last dinner 9pm
Credit cards 1 2 3 5

SOLIHULL
West Midlands
Map **7** SP17

★★★**George** High St ☎ 021-704 1241
RS Xmas
An old coaching inn with modern extensions overlooking a medieval bowling green.
46rm(41→) CTV in all bedrooms ® **T** S% ✱sB£31 sB→£45 dB£44 dB→£57.50 (room only) B
☾ 130P *xmas*
French **V** ♁ ☕ S% ✱Lunch £8—£8.75&alc Tea 85p Dinner £9.20—£9.95&alc Wine £5.55 Last dinner 9pm
Credit cards 1 2 3 5 Ⓥ
See advertisement under Birmingham

★★★**St John's Swallow** 651 Warwick Rd (Swallow) ☎ ~~021-705 6777~~ Telex no 339352
Set in a leafy residential area at the edge of the town centre, within easy reach of the major business and tourist areas, the large, modern hotel offers specialist conference facilities.
215rm(200→⋒)(15fb) CTV in all bedrooms ® in 200 bedrooms **T** S% sB&B£20—£27 sB&B→⋒£27.50—£44 dB&B£27—£35 dB&B→⋒£35—£55 B
Lift ☾ CTV 400P CFA Live music and dancing Sat ♿ *xmas*

V ♁ ☕ S% Lunch £8.25&alc Tea 65p Dinner £10.75&alc Wine £5.50 Last dinner 9.45pm
Credit cards 1 2 3 4 5

★★**Flemings** 141 Warwick Rd, Olton ☎ 021-706 0371 Birmingham district plan **23**
Closed Xmas wk
This vastly extended hotel, midway between Birmingham and the NEC, has conference facilties and a games room.
85rm(29→56⋒)(3fb) CTV in all bedrooms ® S% sB&B→⋒£18—£26 dB&B£28—£36 dB&B→⋒£28.50—£36 B
☾ CTV 85P ✽ snooker
V ♁ ☕ S% Lunch £6—£10 Tea 60p Dinner £8.40—£12 Wine £4.30 Last dinner 9.30pm
Credit cards 1 3 Ⓥ

★★*B* **Saracens Head** Stratford Rd, Shirley (Golden Oak Inns) ☎ 021-744 1016 Birmingham District plan **31A**
A tastefully-styled modern hotel in a busy shopping area provides well-equipped bedrooms and is conveniently located for the NEC and Airport; it also makes an ideal base for touring.
34rm(1→33⋒) CTV in all bedrooms ® **T** ✗
90P
Continental ♁ ☕ Last dinner 9.30pm
Credit cards 1 2 3

✕✕**Liaison French Cuisine** 761 Old Lode Ln ☎ 021-743 3993
The green awnings of this small, stylish, suburban restaurant reflect the colour scheme within. Cuisine is in the modern idiom, decoratively presented.
Closed 1 wk Xmas & Aug Lunch not served
French **V** 32 seats Dinner £15alc Wine £6.25 Last dinner 10pm
Credit cards 1 2 3 5

SOMERTON
Somerset
Map **3** ST42

★★★*HBL* **Lynch Country House** Behind Berry ☎ (0458) 72316
Set in a delightful garden, this comfortable hotel has the atmosphere of a country house. The bedrooms are comfortable and well appointed and guests are made to feel very welcome. The food is good and well presented, prepared by the chef/proprietor.
6rm(5→1⋒) CTV in all bedrooms **T** ✱sB&B→⋒£35 dB&B→⋒£50
P ⛟ ✽ ⛱ ♔ *xmas*
✱Lunch £6&alc Dinner £12—£14alc Last dinner 9.30pm
Credit cards 1 2 3

0217113000

SONNING
Berkshire
Map **4** SU77

★★★**White Hart** ☎ Reading (0734) 692277 Telex no 849031

This hotel dates back to pre-Elizabethan times and the annexe is converted from a row of 13th-century cottages set in lovely gardens leading down to the Thames.

12 Annexe 13rm(12 1)(2fb) 6 CTV in all bedrooms ® **T** S% sB&B fr£49 dB&B fr£64 dB&B fr£64 B

80P Live music & dancing wkly *xmas*

English & French Lunch £10.95—£18 Tea 75p High Tea £3.50 Dinner £16.50&alc Wine £7.50 Last dinner 9.45pm

Credit cards 1 2 3 5 V

SOUTHAMPTON
Hampshire
Map **4** SU41 **See plan**

★★★★**Polygon** Cumberland Pl (Trusthouse Forte) ☎ (0703) 226401 Telex no 47175 Plan **8** *B3*

Town centre hotel with spacious public areas.

119 (1fb) CTV in all bedrooms ® sB&B £57 dB&B £71.50 B

Lift 120P 4 CFA *xmas*

Last dinner 10pm

Credit cards 1 2 3 4 5

★★★**Dolphin** High St (Trusthouse Forte) ☎ (0703) 226178 Telex no 477735 Plan **3** *C1*

Traditional hotel with spacious public rooms and modest bedrooms.

73rm(68 5) CTV in all bedrooms ® sB&B £47.50 dB&B £61.50 B

Lift 70P CFA *xmas*

Last dinner 9.45pm

Credit cards 1 2 3 4 5

★★★**Post House** Herbert Walker Av (Trusthouse Forte) ☎ (0703) 228081 Telex no 477368 Plan **9** *B1*

This modern hotel is conveniently located, having some spectacular dockland views. Bedrooms are spacious whilst the restaurant features imaginative and well-cooked food.

132 CTV in all bedrooms ® sB&B £53 dB&B £69 B

Lift 250P CFA (heated)

Last dinner 10pm

Credit cards 1 2 3 4 5

★★★**Southampton Moat House** 119 Highfield Ln, Portswood (Queens Moat) ☎ (0703) 559555 Telex no 47186 Plan **10** *C5*

RS 26 Dec—2 Jan

The well-managed hotel has comfortable, well-equipped bedrooms, compact public areas, and a friendly atmosphere throughout.

74rm(60 6)(9fb) CTV in 66 bedrooms ® in 66 bedrooms **T** sB&B £35—£40.25 dB&B £47—£50 B

120P CFA

French **V** Lunch £9alc Tea 70palc High Tea £3.95alc Dinner £11.50alc Wine £4.90 Last dinner 9.45pm

Credit cards 1 2 3 4 5

★★★*L* **Southampton Park** Cumberland Pl (Forest Dale) ☎ (0703) 223467 Telex no 47439

Closed Xmas night

Formerly The Royal, and now completely refurbished, the hotel offers modern bedrooms and a choice of contemporary restaurants. Standards of service are friendly.

75 in 2 bedrooms CTV in all bedrooms ® **T** sB&B £36.50—£42 dB&B £46.50—£52 B

Lift 9P CFA

V Lunch £1.95—£7.50 Tea fr50p Dinner £8.95—£12.95 Wine £4.75 Last dinner 9.30pm

Credit cards 1 2 3 5

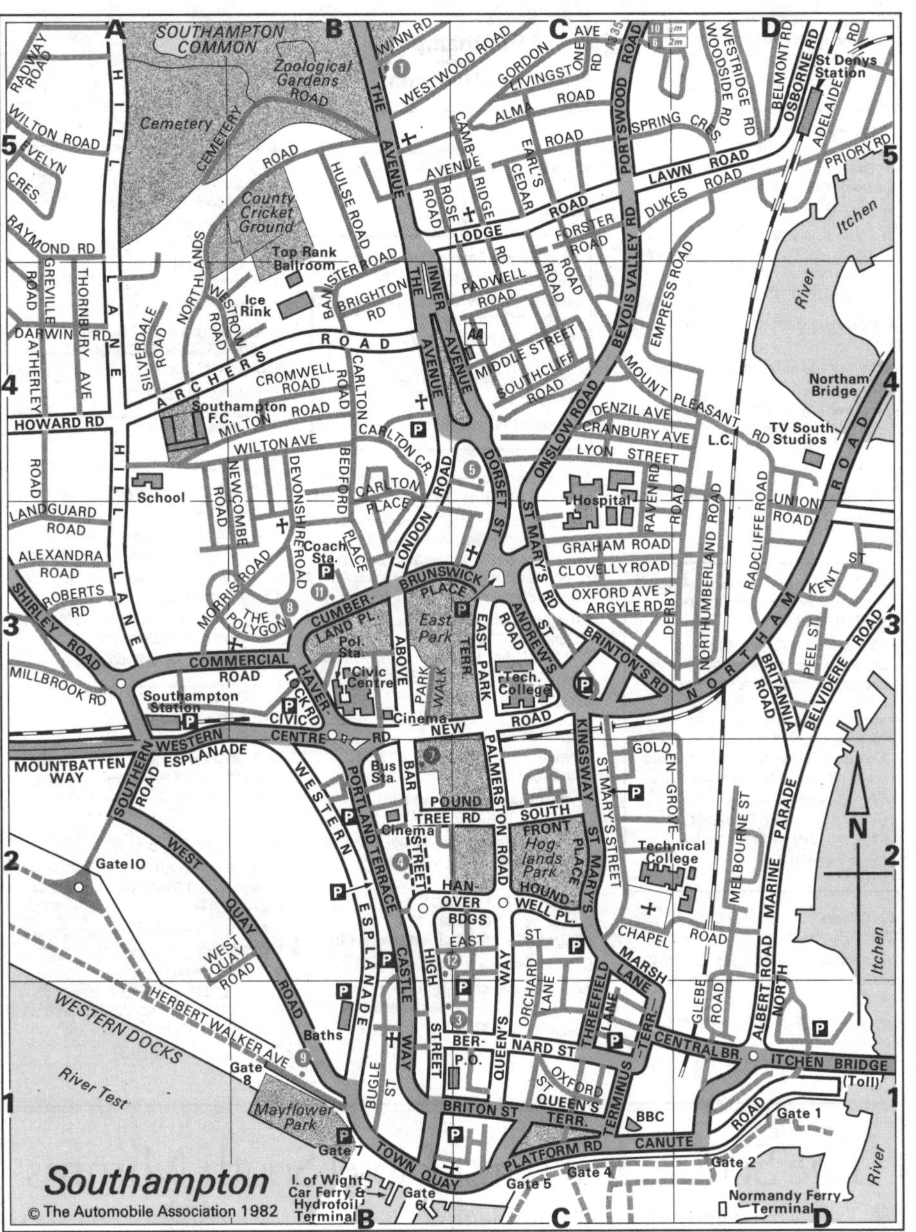

Southampton

1	Albany ★★	6	Kohinoor Tandoori ❀✕✕	10	Southampton Moat House ★★★
3	Dolphin ★★★	7	Pearl Harbour ✕	11	Southampton Park ★★★
4	Golden Palace ❀✕	8	Polygon ★★★★	12	Star ★★
5	Olivers ✕ ✕	9	Post House ★★★		

S

★★**Albany** Winn Rd, The Avenue ☎(0703) 554553 Plan **1** *B5*

RS 4 days Xmas & Bank Hol's

Small friendly hotel in quiet area.

32rm(12⇌20⋒) Annexe: 2m(1⇌1⋒)(6fb) CTV in all bedrooms ® sB&B⇌⋒£33.50—£36.50 dB&B⇌⋒£43—£46 B

Lift ☾ 50P ✿

English & Italian **V** S% Lunch £6.50&alc Tea 50p Dinner £6.50&alc Wine £4.60 Last dinner 9.15pm

Credit cards 1 2 3 5

★★**Star** High St ☎(0703) 30426 Plan **12** *B2*

Family run hotel with good home made food.

33rm(14⇌8⋒)(1fb) CTV in all bedrooms ® sB&B£28 sB&B⇌⋒£36—£39 dB&B⇌⋒£46—£49 B

Lift ☾ 30P

✱Lunch £1—£5.65 Dinner £7&alc Wine £4.95 Last dinner 8.45pm

Credit cards 1 2 3 5

❀ ✕✕**Kohinoor Tandoori** 2 The Broadway, Portswood ☎(0703) 582770 Plan **6** *C5*

The cosiness of this intimate restaurant is emphasised by the high-backed seats that enclose the tables, and the cheerfully informal atmosphere is enhanced by the native costumes of the staff. Outstandingly fresh and well-flavoured food includes some interesting Tandoori dishes.

Indian **V** 40 seats Lunch £10alc Dinner £10alc Wine £4.50 Last dinner 11.30pm 10P Live music mthly

Credit cards 1 2 3

✕✕**Olivers** Ordnance Rd ☎(0703) 224789 Plan **5** *C4*

Charming wood panelled restaurant, with candlelit tables offering homemade French cuisine.

Closed Sun & 24—31 Dec Lunch not served Sat

English & French **V** 85 seats Lunch £6.25 Dinner £6.35—£9.50 Wine £5.45 Last dinner 9.30pm 12P

Credit cards 1 2 3 5

❀ ✕**Golden Palace** 17A Above Bar St ☎(0703) 226636 Plan **4** *B2*

Modern Chinese restaurant with excellent Cantonese cuisine.

English & Cantonese **V** 85 seats ✱Lunch £2.50—£7&alc Dinner £5—£8&alc Wine £4.70 Last dinner 11.40pm P

Credit cards 1 2 3 5 Ⓥ

✕**Pearl Harbour** 86A—88A Above Bar St ☎(0703) 39833 Plan **7** *B2*

This large, modern and well-appointed restaurant offers an extensive selection of well-prepared Cantonese and Pekinese dishes, reasonably priced and served by friendly, cheerful staff.

English, Cantonese, Pekinese Szechuan **V** 125 seats Lunch £2.50—£15&alc Dinner £7.50—£18&alc Wine £4.80 Last dinner 11.30pm P

Credit cards 1 2 3 5

SOUTH BRENT

Devon
Map **3** SX66

★★**Glazebrook House** ☎(03647) 3322

Substantial Victorian house with good food, imaginative decor and friendly owners.

12rm(8⇌1⋒)(2fb) 1 CTV in all bedrooms ® S% ✱sB&B£25 sB&B⇌⋒£30 dB&B£35 dB&B⇌⋒£40

CTV 75P ✿ snooker *xmas*

English, French & Italian **V** Lunch £7.50 Dinner £9—£15&alc Wine £4.50

Credit cards 1 2 3

SOUTHEND-ON-SEA

Essex
Map **5** TQ88

★**Balmoral** 34 Valkyrie Rd, Westcliff-on-Sea ☎(0702) 342947

Located in a residential area, the efficiently run, friendly hotel provides small, well-equipped bedrooms and compact public areas. Food is home-cooked and the atmosphere warm.

19rm(14⇌5⋒)(3fb) CTV in all bedrooms ® **T** sB&B⇌⋒£24—£27 dB&B⇌⋒£37.50—£39.50 B

CTV 16P

English & French Bar lunch £1.50—£3.50 Tea £1 Dinner £6.50&alc Last dinner 7.30pm

Credit cards 1 3

SOUTH GODSTONE

Surrey
Map **5** TQ34

✕✕**La Bonne Auberge** Tilburstow Hill ☎(0342) 892318 Gatwick Plan **1**

Edwardian country house in large grounds, offering sound French cuisine.

Closed Mon, Dinner not served Sun

French **V** 80 seats S% Lunch £14—£18.50 Dinner £19.50—£24 Wine £5.95 Last dinner 10pm 60P

Credit cards 1 2 3 5 Ⓥ

SOUTH MIMMS

Hertfordshire
Map **4** TL20

★★★**Crest** Bignells Corner (junc A1/A6) (Crest) ☎ Potters Bar (0707) 43311 Telex no 299162

RS Xmas

Modern, commercial hotel.

115⇌(6fb) in 20 bedrooms CTV in all bedrooms ® **T** S% sB⇌£54 dB⇌£64 (room only) B

☾ CTV 150P CFA ✿ (heated) sauna bath solarium gymnasium

V S% ✱Lunch £9.80—£10.20&alc Tea £2.75—£2.85 Dinner £11.50—£11.95&alc Wine £6.25 Last dinner 9.45pm

Credit cards 1 2 3 4 5

S

SOUTH MOLTON
Devon
Map **3** SS72

★★ **Marsh Hall Country House** ☎ (07695) 2666

Closed 23—25 Dec

Elegant Victorian house set in peaceful grounds with terraced lawns. The well appointed bedrooms have magnificent views and the menus are carefully prepared.

8rm(5 3)(2fb) 1 CTV in all bedrooms ® T ∗ sB&B £26.95—£28.90 dB&B £47.20—£51.40

20P clay pigeon shooting croquet

International Lunch £2.50—£8.75&alc Tea £1.70—£2 High Tea £2.75—£5&alc Dinner £11.95—£15 Wine £5

Credit cards 1 2 3 5 V

✕ ***Stumbles*** 134 East St ☎ (07695) 3683

Situated in South Molton's main shopping street, the modern, elegantly-furnished restaurant has an attached wine bar and a courtyard at the rear. The à la carte menu offers a short but varied choice, and cuisine is based on good, local, raw materials.

Closed Sun & Xmas Day

French **V** 50 seats Last dinner 9.30pm

30P Dancing Mon—Sat

Credit cards 1 2 3 5

SOUTH NORMANTON
Derbyshire
Map **8** SK45

★★★★ **Swallow** Carter Ln East (junc 28 M1 Motorway) (Swallow) ☎ Ripley (0773) 812000 Telex no 377264

Large, modern hotel, conveniently situated next to the M1.

123 (30fb) CTV in all bedrooms ® T S% sB&B £53.50 dB&B £66

200P CFA (heated) sauna bath solarium gymnasium xmas

International **V** S% ∗ Lunch £6—£7.75&alc Tea 80p—£2 High Tea £7.75 Dinner £7.75—£10.50&alc Wine £5.85 Last dinner 10.30pm

Credit cards 1 2 3 5

SOUTHPORT
Merseyside
Map **7** SD31

★★★★ ***Prince of Wales*** Lord St (Quality) ☎ (0704) 36688 Telex no 67415

Ideal for business or pleasure this leading hotel has banqueting and conference facilities.

101rm(82 18)(6fb) CTV in all bedrooms ® T

Lift 95P CFA sauna bath solarium gymnasium Disco 4 nights wkly *xmas*

English & French **V** Last dinner 10pm

Credit cards 1 2 3 5

★★★ **Royal Clifton** Promenade ☎ (0704) 33771 Telex no 677191

Large seaside hotel overlooking promenade and gardens.

115rm(104 2)(29fb) 5 CTV in all bedrooms ® ∗ sB&B £20—£30 sB&B £32—£40 dB&B £40—£50 dB&B £48—£60

Lift CTV 120P (heated) sauna bath solarium gymnasium CFA Live music & dancing three nights wkly *xmas*

English & French Bar lunch £1.75—£5 Tea 95p—£1.75 Dinner £8.50&alc Wine £4.95 Last dinner 11pm

Credit cards 1 2 3 5 V

★★★ **Scarisbrick** Lord St (Consort) ☎ (0704) 43000 Telex no 67107

Large hotel, recently refurbished, now offering good all round facilities.

60rm(56 4)(5fb) 6 CTV in all bedrooms ® T ∗ sB&B £29—£40 dB&B £44—£60

Lift CTV 36P 12 pool table games complex Live music & dancing nightly *xmas*

V ∗ Lunch £3.55—£4.60 Tea fr65p High Tea £3.15—£4.60 Dinner fr£9&alc Wine £4.50 Last dinner 9pm

Credit cards 1 2 3 4 5

★★ **Balmoral Lodge** 41 Queens Rd ☎ (0704) 44298

Closed Xmas Day & Boxing Day

Friendly hotel with well equipped bedrooms. Home cooking.

12rm(7 5)(1fb) 1 CTV in all bedrooms ® T sB&B £17—£26 dB&B £30—£32

CTV 10P

Lunch £5 Dinner £7&alc Wine £4.50 Last dinner 8.30pm

Credit cards 1 2 3 5 V

See advertisement on page 670

★★ **Bold** Lord St ☎ (0704) 32578

Former coaching house at the northern end of this fashionable street.

24rm(14 5)(2fb) CTV in all bedrooms ® T sB&B £22—£25 sB&B £29—£32 dB&B £33 dB&B £39—£50

CTV 12P(charge) *xmas*

English, French, Greek, Italian & Spanish **V** ∗ Lunch £4.90—£5.90&alc Tea 60p—£1 Dinner £7.20&alc Wine £4.90 Last dinner 10pm

Credit cards 1 2 3 5 V

See advertisement on page 670

★★ **Carlton** 86—88 Lord St (Exec Hotel) ☎ (0704) 35111

Pleasantly furnished friendly hotel in the elegant main boulevard.

25rm(13 6)(4fb) CTV in all bedrooms ® T sB&B £20—£21 sB&B £25—£26 dB&B £28—£30 dB&B £42—£44

Lift 17P Disco Thu *xmas*

English & French **V** Lunch £6alc Tea 75p—£2 High Tea £3—£6 Dinner £7.50&alc Wine £5.50 Last dinner 9.45pm

Credit cards 1 2 3 V

★★ **Lockerbie House** 11 Trafalgar Rd, Birkdale ☎ (0704) 65298

Detached house in a residential area close to Birkdale Station and the famous golf course.

14rm(4 6)(3fb) TV in 11 bedrooms CTV in 3 bedrooms ® sB&B £16.50—£18.50 sB&B £18.50 dB&B £34—£36

CTV 14P 2 snooker →

S

♡ ☕ Bar lunch £2.50—£4.50 Tea £1.50—£2.75 Dinner £6.50 Wine £5.50 Last dinner 8pm

Credit cards 1 2 3 V

★**Metropole** Portland St ☎ (0704) 36836

Pleasant, family-run hotel.

27rm(8 bath 8 shower)(1fb) CTV in 14 bedrooms S% sB&B£17 sB&B bath shower £19.75—£20.50 dB&B£30 dB&B bath shower £36—£38 B

CTV 12P *xmas*

♡ ☕ S% Lunch £3.25—£4 Tea fr75p Dinner £6.50—£7.50 Wine £3.75 Last dinner 8.30pm

Credit cards 1 2 3

XX**Squires** 78—80 King St ☎ (0704) 30046

Attractive and charmingly furnished restaurant with extensive, mainly French, menu. The food is expertly cooked and well presented with efficient service.

Closed Bank Hols Lunch not served

French 42 seats S% *Dinner £15alc Wine £5.95 Last dinner 10.30pm

Credit cards 1 2 3 5

SOUTHSEA
Hampshire
Map **4** SZ69
See **Portsmouth** and **Southsea**

Southport — Southwell

SOUTH SHIELDS
Tyne & Wear
Map **12** NZ36

★★★**Sea** Sea Front ☎ 091-456 6227 Telex no 537406

RS 24—26 Dec

Comfortable hotel with well appointed accommodation and good value dinner.

30rm(27 bath 3 shower)(2fb) CTV in all bedrooms ® T sB&B bath shower £31.50 dB&B bath shower £43.50 B

40P 6 garages (charge) Disco fortnightly

English & French ♡ Lunch £4—£4.50&alc Dinner £6.60&alc Wine £5.25 Last dinner 9.30pm

Credit cards 1 2 3 5 V

★★**New Crown** Mowbray Rd ☎ 091-455 3472

Large pub with comfortable bars, attractive dining rooms and modest bedrooms.

11rm(3 bath 2 shower)(2fb) CTV in all bedrooms ® T *sB&B fr£19 sB&B bath shower fr£22 dB&B fr£30 dB&B bath shower fr£34

40P Live music & dancing wkly

V *Lunch £4.95—£8&alc Dinner £5—£8&alc Wine £3.95 Last dinner 9.30pm

Credit cards 1 2 3 5

SOUTH UIST, ISLE OF
Western Isles, *Inverness-shire*
Map **13** NF71

LOCHBOISDALE
Map **13** NF71

★★**Lochboisdale** ☎ (08784) 332

Traditional tourist/fishing hotel close to pier. Free golf to residents.

20rm(8 bath)(2fb) ® in 15 bedrooms S% *sB&B£18.95 sB&B bath £23.95 dB&B£35.90 dB&B bath £41.90

CTV 100P

♡ ☕ *Lunch fr£6 Tea fr£1.50 Dinner fr£9&alc Wine £4 Last dinner 9pm

Credit cards 1 3

SOUTHWELL
Nottinghamshire
Map **8** SK75

★★★**Saracen's Head** Market Pl (Anchor) ☎ (0636) 812701 Telex no 377201

Ancient coaching inn where many English monarchs have stayed.

27rm(12 bath 15 shower) 1 in 6 bedrooms CTV in all bedrooms ® *sB&B bath shower £39.50 dB&B bath shower £49.50 B

80P 2 garages CFA

English & French ✱Lunch £6.95&alc Dinner £9.95&alc Wine £5.95 Last dinner 10pm

Credit cards 1 2 3 4 5 V

SOUTHWOLD
Suffolk
Map **5** TM57

★★★ ***Swan*** Market Pl ☎(0502) 722186 Telex no 97223

An 18th-century former coaching inn with the original Georgian fireplace and door frames; as well as many fine paintings.

34rm(9 10) Annexe: 18 (5fb) CTV in all bedrooms

Lift ☾ CTV 50P *xmas*

English & French **V** Last dinner 8.30pm

Credit cards 1 2 3 5

★★**Crown** High St ☎(0502) 722275 Telex no 97223

The hotel dates from the early Georgian period when it was a coaching inn. It is also the headquarters of Adnam's wine merchants, and an extensive list of good quality wines is available.

12rm(10 1)(1fb) CTV in all bedrooms **T** S% sB&B£16—£20 SB&B £16—£20 dB&B £32 Continental breakfast

8P 9 *xmas*

English & French **V** Lunch £8—£10 Tea fr £1.50 Dinner £10—£12 Wine £4.25 Last dinner 10pm

Credit cards 1 2 3

★★***Pier Avenue*** Pier Avenue ☎(0502) 722632

13rm(5 3)(1fb) CTV in all bedrooms ®

CTV 10P

Last dinner 9.30pm

Credit cards 1 2 3

★★***Randolph*** 41 Wangford Rd, Reydon ☎(0502) 723603

Small, friendly, family run hotel in quiet area.

12rm(2)(3fb)

CTV 25P 3 *xmas*

V Last dinner 8pm

Southwell — Spean Bridge

XX**Dutch Barn** Ferry Rd ☎(0502) 723172

Opposite the sand dunes, where the harbour road nears the beach, an old barn built to store fishing equipment has been converted into an attractive cottage restaurant. The short, fixed-price menu is supplemented by a blackboard listing daily specials in which local produce, particularly locally-caught sole, features prominently.

Closed Mon Dinner not served Sun

English & French **V** 50 seats Lunch £2.25—£6.95 Dinner £6.95&alc Wine £3.95 Last dinner 9.45pm 12P Live music & dancing Sat

Credit cards 1 2 3 V

SOUTH WOODHAM FERRERS
Essex
Map **5** TQ89

XX***Ruchita Tandoori*** Unit 1B, Town Sq ☎ Chelmsford (0245) 321306

A short, a la carte menu including Tandoori specialities is offered at this first-floor restaurant in the town's modern shopping complex, where spacious, comfortable surroundings are complemented by courteous service from young staff.

Indian **V** 52 seats Last dinner mdnt 100P

Credit cards 1 2 3 5

SOUTH ZEAL
Devon
Map **3** SX69

★★**Oxenham Arms** ☎ Okehampton (0837) 840244

RS Xmas Day night

A 12th century inn of great character located in the village centre.

8rm(6) CTV in all bedrooms ® **T** sB&B£22—£28 sB&B £28 dB&B£32 dB&B £40

CTV 8P *xmas*

V Lunch £4.50—£8.50 Tea 55p Dinner £10—£12.50 Wine £3.95 Last dinner 9pm

Credit cards 1 2 3 5 V

SPALDING
Lincolnshire
Map **8** TF22

★★**Dembleby** Broad St ☎(0775) 67060

Situated close to the town centre, the hotel features a large walled garden, part of which stands on the site of an old abbey.

8rm(6) CTV in all bedrooms sB&B£18.40 sB&B £23 dB&B £36.80

20P

✱Lunch £5.50&alc Dinner £8alc Wine £4.50 Last dinner 9.30pm

Credit cards 1 2 3 5 V

★★**Red Lion** Market Pl ☎(0775) 2869

Former coaching inn.

25rm(8 1) Annexe: 6rm (2fb) TV in all bedrooms ✱sB&B£18.97 sB&B £24.15 dB&B£28.75 dB&B £31.05

CTV 25P 3

English French & Italian **V** Lunch £3.50—£6.50 Dinner £3.50—£6.50&alc Wine £3.95 Last dinner 9pm

Credit cards 1 2 3 5

★★**Woodlands** 80 Pinchbeck Rd ☎(0775) 69933

Standing just north of the town centre, an Edwardian house has been tastefully converted to provide modern, well-equipped accommodation.

6rm(1 5)(1fb) CTV in all bedrooms ® S% ✱sB fr£31.50 dB fr£41.50 (room only)

40P

English & French **V** ✱Lunch £7.25&alc Tea 90p—£1.95 High Tea £4.50 Dinner £8.50&alc Wine £5.25 Last dinner 10pm

Credit cards 1 2 3 4 5 V

SPEAN BRIDGE
Highland *Inverness-shire*
Map **14** NN28
See also **Letterfinlay** and **Roy Bridge**

★★**Spean Bridge** ☎(039781) 250 →

S

Originally a coaching inn, log fires still provide a welcome.

7🛁🚿 Annexe: 19rm(17🛁3🚿)(2fb) ®S% sB&B£13.50—£15.50 sB&B🛁🚿£14.50—£16.50 dB&B£38 dB&B🛁🚿£36—£38 B

CTV 50P ⛳9 ♪

V ☕ ☐ S% Bar lunch 50p—£2.75 Tea 60—70p Dinner £8—£9.50 Last dinner 9pm

Credit cards [1] [2] [3] [5] (V)

SPELDHURST
Kent
Map **5** TQ54

XX George & Dragon Inn ☎ Langton (089286) 3125

Historic oak beamed village pub. The restaurant on the first floor features enterprising skilful cuisine with outstanding wine list.

Lunch not served Sat Dinner not served Sun

🍷 English & French 50 seats Lunch £8—£9&alc Dinner £16.50&alc Wine £5.50 Last dinner 10pm 50P

Credit cards [1] [2] [3] [5]

SPEY BAY
Grampian *Morayshire*
Map **15** NJ36

★★**Spey Bay** ☎ Fochabers (0343) 820424

A friendly, seafront hotel next to the golf course.

10rm(6🛁4🚿)(2fb) CTV in 3 bedrooms ® ✗ sB&B🛁🚿£18 dB&B🛁🚿£32—£34 B

CTV 20P ⛳18 🎾(hard) ♪ Live music and dancing Sat

V ☕ ☐ Bar lunch 60p—£4 Tea fr80p High Tea fr£4 Dinner fr£7.50 Wine £3.90 Last dinner 8.30pm

Credit cards [1] [3] [5]

Spean Bridge — Stafford

STADDLE BRIDGE
North Yorkshire
Map **8** SE49

❀ **XX McCoys (Tontine Inn)**
☎ East Harsley (060982) 671

(Rosette awarded for dinner only). At first sight, this restaurant may appear rather strange, with its huge parasols, massive pot plants and rather ordinary seating in the lounge, but individual cooking is complemented by a well-chosen wine list and a warm and friendly atmosphere — a combination that will soon allay your doubts.

Closed Sun, Xmas & Public Hols

🍷 International 60 seats Last dinner 11pm 80P

Credit card [3]

STAFFORD
Staffordshire
Map **7** SJ92

★★★**Tillington Hall** Eccleshall Rd (DeVere) ☎ (0785) 53531 Telex no 36566

In recent years, this Victorian country house has been considerably extended and transformed into a large, modern hotel with good conference and function facilities. It is conveniently sited on the northern outskirts of the town, only half a mile from Junction 14 of the M6.

93rm(90🛁3🚿)(4fb) CTV in all bedrooms ® T S% sB&B🛁🚿£27—£47 dB&B🛁🚿£42—£53 B

Lift ☾ 200P CFA 🎾(hard) table tennis pool table *xmas*

🍷 French V ☕ ☐ S% Lunch £7.50&alc Tea £3 Dinner £7.50&alc Wine £5.25 Last dinner 9.45pm

Credit cards [1] [2] [3] [4] [5]

★★**Abbey** 65—68 Lichfield Rd ☎ (0785) 58531

Closed Xmas & New Year

A row of terraced houses has been converted to offer comfortable accommodation at a very reasonable price.

21rm(1🛁6🚿)(1fb) CTV in all bedrooms ® ✗ sB&B£18.50 sB&B🛁🚿£21 dB&B£28 dB&B🛁🚿£34 B

CTV 21P 7🚗(charge) ✗

V ⚡ Bar lunch £3—£4 Dinner £4.50—£5&alc Wine £4 Last dinner 8pm

Credit cards [1] [3]

★★**Albridge** 73 Wolverhampton Rd ☎ (0785) 54100

Closed 25 & 26 Dec

Small, friendly, family run hotel.

11rm(1🛁9🚿) Annexe: 8rm(2fb) CTV in 11 bedrooms ®S% *sB&B£17.95—£19.95 sB&B🛁🚿£21.95—£23.95 dB&B£23.95—£26.95 dB&B🛁🚿£34.95—£38.95 B

CTV 20P

V ☕ ☐ *Bar lunch £1.95alc Dinner £5—£5.85&alc Wine £4.85 Last dinner 9.45pm

Credit cards [1] [2] [3] [5]

★★**Garth** Wolverhampton Rd, Moss Pit (Wolverhampton & Dudley) ☎ (0785) 56124

The hotel, a considerably extended and well-modernised house set in its own grounds on the southern edge of the town, is conveniently close to Junction 13 of the M6. Its bars and restaurant are popular with local residents.

32rm(24🛁)(2fb) CTV in all bedrooms ® *sB&B£21—£23 sB&B🛁£21—£31.50 dB&B£28—£30 dB&B🛁£28—£39.50 B

☾ 150P ❀

V ☕ ☐ *Lunch £2.50&alc Dinner £11alc Wine £4.30 Last dinner 9.30pm

Credit cards [1] [2] [3] (V)

S

★★**Swan** Greengate St (Berni) ☎ (0785) 58142

Closed Xmas

Sixteenth century inn with grill restaurant and extensive menu.

32rm(30⇌2⋒)(5fb) 1⊟ CTV in all bedrooms ® ✗ sB⇌⋒£27.50 dB⇌⋒£47 (room only)

☾ 50P CFA ✿

Mainly grills ♀ ☕ ✗ ✱ Lunch £7.50alc Dinner £7.50alc Wine £4.50 Last dinner 10.30pm

Credit cards 1 2 3 5

★**Vine** Salter St (Wolverhampton & Dudley) ☎ (0785) 51071

400 year old inn, said to be the oldest licensed house in Stafford.

27rm(9⇌18⋒)(5fb) CTV in all bedrooms ® T ✱ sB&B⇌⋒£21—£28 dB&B⇌⋒£30—£35 B

☾ 24P

♀ ☕ ✱ Lunch £1.50—£2.75 Tea £1 Dinner £6alc Wine £4.70 Last dinner 9.30pm

Credit cards 1 2 3 V

See advertisement on page 674

STAINES
Surrey
Map **4** TQ07

★★*B* **Thames Lodge** Thames St (Anchor) ☎ (0784) 64433 Telex no 8812552 Heathrow plan **8** *B1*

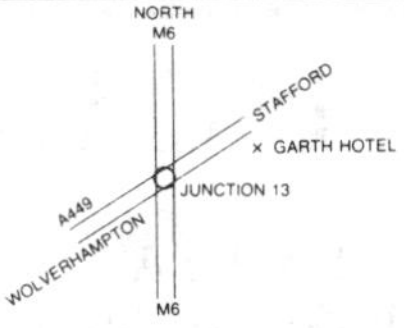

Large Victorian building with a riverside patio, boat moorings and wide windowed dining room overlooking the Thames. →

S

47🛁🚿⊁in 5 bedrooms CTV in all bedrooms ®T ✱sB&B🛁🚿£28—£48 dB&B🛁🚿£39—£58 B

☾32P

V ♀ ✱Lunch £9.75—£15 Dinner £9.75—£15 Wine £5.45 Last dinner 10pm

Credit cards 1 2 3 4 5 Ⓥ

STAMFORD
Lincolnshire
Map **4** TF00

★★★*HB* **George of Stamford** St Martins ☎(0780) 55171 Telex no 32578

This large, historic coaching house, just south of the town centre, has a wealth of character and offers modern, well-equipped bedrooms complemented by friendly service.

48rm(46🛁2🚿)(3fb) 4⊞ CTV in all bedrooms T S% sB&B🛁🚿£45—£49 dB&B🛁🚿£64—£90 B

☾100P CFA ✿ *xmas*

♀English French & Italian V ♀ ☕ Lunch £17alc Tea 95palc Dinner £17alc Wine £6 Last dinner 10.30pm

Credit cards 1 2 3 4 5

★★***Crown*** ☎(0780) 63136

Closed Xmas Day Night

An old two-storey, stone-built hotel in the town centre, catering for a predominantly commercial clientele.

18rm(5🛁8🚿)(1fb) 1⊞ CTV in all bedrooms ®T B

40P

♀Continental V ♀ ☕ Last dinner 10.30pm

Credit cards 1 2 3 4 5

★★**Garden House** St Martins ☎(0780) 63359

A charming, eighteenth-century house, little changed externally, has been sympathetically improved to provide modern comforts. The hanging baskets and trailing greenery of the conservatory lounge make an effective link with the secluded, walled gardens and lawns behind.

S

Staines — Staverton

21rm(11🛁)(2fb) CTV in all bedrooms **T** sB&Bfr£22.50 sB&B🛁fr£33.50 dB&Bfr£39.50 dB&B🛁fr£49.50 B

26P 4🚗 ✿ ♿

♀English & French V ♀ ☕ Bar lunch £6alc Tea £2.75alc Dinner £12.50 Wine £5.25 Last dinner 9.30pm

Credit cards 1 3 Ⓥ

★★**Lady Anne's** 37—38 High St, St Martins ☎(0780) 53175 Telex no 32376

An 18th century stone built house in 3½ acres of ground on the B1081.

26rm(13🛁7🚿)(6fb) 2⊞ CTV in all bedrooms ® available in bedrooms **T** sB&B£15—£28 sB&B🛁🚿£25—£33 dB&B£30—£35 dB&B🛁🚿£35—£55 B

CTV 150P ✿ ♿ *xmas*

V ♀ ☕ Lunch £6.50 Tea £1—£3.50 Dinner £7.50—£9.50&alc Wine £6 Last dinner 9.45pm

Credit cards 1 2 3 5

STANDISH
Greater Manchester
Map **7** SD51

★★**Cassinellis Almond Brook Motor Inn** Almond Brook Rd ☎(0257) 425588 Telex no 677662

RS Xmas Day & New Year Day

Conveniently-sited for access to the M6 motorway, this modern motel, featuring an Italian theme, offers accommodation in good, modern bedrooms.

43🛁🚿 Annexe: 20rm(15fb) CTV in all bedrooms ®T ✗ S% sB&B£29—£34.95 sB&B🛁🚿£29—£34.95 dB&B£28—£39 dB&B🛁🚿£39 B

☾P CFA Disco 3 nights wkly Cabaret Sat *xmas*

♀English & Italian V ♀ S% Lunch £2.95—£3.50&alc Dinner £8alc Wine £4.95 Last dinner 10.30pm

Credit cards 1 2 3 5

✕✕**Beeches** School Ln ☎(0257) 426432

The delightfully-furnished restaurant maintains a high standard of cooking and an extensive menu, using fresh produce. Service is friendly yet professional, and some bedrooms are available.

V 65 seats Lunch £5.50—£7&alc Dinner £5.50—£7&alc Wine £5.20 Last dinner 9.45pm 70P

Credit cards 1 2 3 5 Ⓥ

STANHOPE BRETBY
Derbyshire
Map **8** SK22

✕✕**Stanhope Arms** Ashby Rd East (on A50) ☎ Burton-on-Trent (0283) 217954

Large roadside inn with extensive catering and function trade. Friendly service and value for money.

♀English & French V 120 seats Lunch £5.50—£7.75&alc Dinner £8.50alc Wine £5.75 Last dinner 10pm 150P 18 bedrooms available

Credit cards 1 2 3 5 Ⓥ

STAPLETON
North Yorkshire
Map **8** NZ21

✕**Bridge Inn** ☎ Darlington (0325) 50106

Village public house features Victorian style restaurant offering delicious food and good wine list.

Closed Mon Lunch not served Sat Dinner not served Sun

♀Cosmopolitan V 32 seats Lunch £6.50—£10.50 Dinner £12—£15&alc Wine £5.50 Last dinner 9.30pm P

Credit cards 1 2 3 5 Ⓥ

STAVERTON
Devon
Map **3** SX76

★***Sea Trout Inn*** ☎(080426) 274

A comfortable village inn in a peaceful situation offering attentive service from the resident owners.

6rm ®B

CTV 70P *xmas*

V ♀ Last dinner 9.30pm

Credit cards 1 2 3 5

STEEPLE ASTON
Oxfordshire
Map **4** SP42

★★**Hopcrofts Holt** ☎(0869) 40259
Telex no 837488

This 15th-century, character, highwayman's inn has been comfortably appointed to provide modern accommodation. The dining room offers a carvery selection at lunchtime and an à la carte menu in the evening.

36rm(24🛁12🚿)(3fb) CTV in all bedrooms ®T ✱sB&B🛁🚿£32 dB&B🛁🚿£40 B

☾P✿

English & French ☕ ✱Lunch £8.25&alc Tea fr75p Dinner £14.50alc Wine £5.75 Last dinner 9.30pm

Credit cards 1 2 3 5

STEPPINGLEY
Bedfordshire
Map **4** TL03

✕**French Horn** ☎Flitwick (0525) 712051

Beamed 16th century pub, offering sound, mainly French food.

Closed Mon

English & French 50 seats ✱Lunch £12—£15alc Dinner £12—£15alc Wine £6 Last dinner 10pm 30P

Credit cards 1 2 3 5 Ⓥ

STEPPS
Strathclyde *Lanarkshire*
Map **11** NS66

★★**Garfield House** Cumbernauld Rd ☎041-779 2111

Closed New Years Day

The Victorian, sandstone house, extended and converted, has tastefully modernised public rooms and caters mainly for a business clientele.

27🛁🚿(2fb) CTV in all bedrooms ®T ✱sB&B🛁🚿£26—£36 dB&B🛁🚿£36—£46 B

☾70P✿ *xmas*

V ☕ ✱Lunch £4.95—£10&alc Dinner £9.50alc Wine £5.25 Last dinner 9.30pm

Credit cards 1 2 3 5 Ⓥ

STEVENAGE
Hertfordshire
Map **4** TL22

★★★**Blakemore** Little Wymondley (2m NW A602) ☎(0438) 355821
(For full entry see Hitchin)

★★★**Roebuck** Old London Rd, Broadwater (Trusthouse Forte) ☎(0438) 365444 Telex no 825505

Charming 15th century inn with modern bedrooms.

54🛁(1fb) CTV in all bedrooms ® sB&B🛁£50.50 dB&B🛁£63.50 B

☾80P CFA✿ *xmas*

☕ Last dinner 9.45pm

Credit cards 1 2 3 4 5

★★★**Stevenage Moat House** High St, Old Town (Queens Moat) ☎(0438) 359111 Telex no 8950511 (QMH STEV)

Historically interesting old world hotel with modern, well-equipped bedrooms.

61rm(60🛁1🚿)(5fb) CTV in all bedrooms ®S% sB&B🛁🚿£37.50—£40.50 dB&B🛁🚿£46—£48 B

☾100P✿ pool table

International V ☕ S% Lunch £7.95—£8.25&alc Tea 75p Dinner £7.95—£8.25&alc Wine £5.95 Last dinner 9.45pm

Credit cards 1 2 3 4 5

STEWARTON
Strathclyde *Ayrshire*
Map **10** NS44

★★★

★★★ CHAPELTOUN HOUSE, STEWARTON

(Pride of Britain) ☎(0560) 82696
Closed Xmas & Boxing Day & 1st 2 wks Jan

Without question, this is one of Scotland's most popular hotels with our members. Built in baronial style at the turn of the century, it is set in 20 acres and was converted into a hotel by Alan and Elizabeth Russell. With great individual flair they have selected and trained a team of girls who provide cheerful and friendly service that is hard to beat. You sense this the moment you step into the handsome panelled hall with open fires and oak staircase leading off it. The large bedrooms are furnished with Victorian and Edwardian period furniture and are comfortable beyond the ordinary, as well as containing so many extras including flowers, fruit and a glass of sherry. There is a smart bar and a comfortable drawing room overlooks the garden. Take an aperitif in either while you choose your meal. The Chef provides a modest fixed price menu and à la carte at lunch, while dinner is a four course affair.

Most enjoyable dishes are provided and feature both Scottish and Continental items. Puddings are Elizabeth Russell's own creations and are deliciously homely, laid out on a buffet for self help. The owners are to be congratulated on the standards achieved here.

6rm(4🛁2🚿) CTV in all bedrooms sB&B🛁🚿£60 dB&B🛁🚿£80

50P 4✿ nc12yrs

V ☕ Lunch fr£10.50&alc Dinner £19.50 Wine £6.50 Last dinner 9pm

Credit cards 1 2 3

S

STIRLING
Central *Stirlingshire*
Map **11** NS79

★★**King Robert** Glasgow Rd, Bannockburn ☎ Bannockburn (0786) 811666
Modern hotel featuring attractive split level cocktail bar and restaurant.
21⇌(1fb) CTV in all bedrooms **T** ✈ S% ✱sB&B⇌£26 dB&B⇌£36
CTV 100P ✿
V ♈ S% ✱ Bar lunch £3.50—£8 Dinner £9.50&alc Wine £4.35 Last dinner 9pm
Credit cards 1 2 3 5

★★**Terraces** 4 Melville Ter (Consort) ☎ (0786) 72268
A small, Georgian town house, set in an elevated terrace close to the shopping centre, has been converted to create a hotel which is popular with businessmen.
14rm(8⇌4⫫)(2fb) CTV in all bedrooms ® **T** ✱sB&B£19.95 sB&B⇌⫫£23.50—£25.50 dB&B£29.95 dB&B⇌⫫£37 **B**
☾25P
♉ International **V** ♈ ☕ ✱ Lunch £5.25&alc Tea 65p High Tea £2.95—£3.95 Dinner £7.75&alc Wine £4.75 Last dinner 9pm
Credit cards 1 2 3 5 Ⓥ

Stirling — Stockbridge

★***Kings Gate*** 5 King St ☎ (0786) 73944
A 19th century hotel in the shopping area.
15rm(5⇌)(2fb) ®
CTV 4P
V ♈ ☕ Last dinner 9pm
Credit cards 1 2 3

○**Granada Lodge** Granada Motorway Service Area Pirnhall Roundabout Junction 9, M9 with M80 (3m S of town centre) ☎ Toddington (05255) 3881
36rms
Newly completed, and offering a high standard of reasonably-priced accommodation, the hotel utilises the services and dining facilities of the neighbouring service area.

✕✕**Heritage** 16 Allan Park ☎ (0786) 73660
An 18th century, painted, stone building of architectural interest situated at the foot of Castle Rock.
Closed Xmas & New Year
♉ International **V** 40 seats Lunch £7.82&alc Dinner £14.38 Wine £4.60 Last dinner 9.30pm 20P ⚡
Credit cards 1 3 5 Ⓥ

STOCKBRIDGE
Hampshire
Map **4** SU33

★★**Grosvenor** High St (Whitbread) ☎ Andover (0264) 810606
Popular fishing inn with spacious bedrooms and cosy public rooms.
25⇌ 1⊟ CTV in all bedrooms ® **T** ✈ sB&B⫫fr£41 dB&B⫫fr£52 **B**
45P ⊞ ✿ sauna bath
♉ English & French **V** ♈ ☕ Lunch £7.50—£8.50&alc Tea £1.50—£3 Dinner £11.50—£12&alc Wine £5.50 Last dinner 10pm
Credit cards 1 2 3 5 Ⓥ

✕✕**Game Larder** New St ☎ Andover (0264) 810414
Skilfully converted from an 18th-century malthouse and brewery, the restaurant features log fires and attractive flower displays. The short, menu lists inventive and skilfully prepared dishes making good use of local game and fresh fish enhanced by imaginative sauces. Service, though a little unreliable, is friendly.
Closed Sun & Mon
♉ English & French **V** 60 seats S% Lunch £8alc Dinner £15.50alc Wine £5.80 Last dinner 9.30pm 6P
Credit cards 1 2 3 5 Ⓥ

STOCKPORT
Gt Manchester
Map **7** SJ88

★★★**Alma Lodge** 149 Buxton Rd (Embassy) ☏ 061-483 4431

Closed Xmas Day night RS Boxing Day night

A converted Victorian house with a modern extension, standing on the A6 1½m SE of the town.

65rm(53⇌)(1fb) CTV in all bedrooms ®T S% ✱sB£26.50 sB⇌£37–£43 dB⇌£47.50–£54 (room only) B

☾200P CFA Live music & dancing wkly

English & French V ♡ ☕ S% ✱Lunch fr£7.50&alc Tea fr55p Dinner fr£7.95&alc Wine £5.50 Last dinner 9.30pm

Credit cards 1 2 3 4 5 V

★★★**Belgrade** Dialston Ln (Consort) ☏ 061-483 3851 Telex no 667217

This large, busy, commercial hotel, set in a residential area convenient for the airport, offers a choice of two restaurants.

160⇌(10fb) CTV in all bedrooms ®T ✗ S% ✱sB&B⇌£37 dB&B⇌£38

Lift ☾200P *xmas*

English & French ♡ ☕ ✱Lunch fr£5.75&alc Tea fr75p Dinner fr£10.25&alc Wine £5.95 Last dinner 11pm

Credit cards 1 2 3 5 V

★★★**Bramhall Moat House** Bramhall Lane South ☏ 061-439 8116
(For full entry see Bramhall)

★★**Rudyard** 271 Wellington Road North Heaton Chapel (1½m N off A6) (Toby) ☏ 061-432 2753

The theme is colonial, with veranda, louvre windows, ceiling fans, appropriate plants and photographs of Kipling's India. Bedrooms, however, are modern and well-appointed.

21⇌(2fb) CTV in all bedrooms ®T ✗ (except guide dogs) ✱sB&B⇌£32.50–£38 dB&B⇌£44–£47 B

☾80P

♡ ☕ ✱Lunch £5.25&alc Tea 65p Dinner £5.25&alc Wine £4.35 Last dinner 10pm

Credit cards 1 2 3 5

Stockport — Stockton-on-Tees

★★**Wycliffe Villa** 74 Edgeley Rd, Edgeley ☏ 061-477 5395

Closed Bank Hols RS Sun

This pleasant and well-furnished hotel displays an Italian influence in the restaurant.

12rm(2⇌10⫛) CTV in all bedrooms ®T ✗ sB&B⇌⫛£26–£27 dB&B⇌⫛£35–£36

CTV 18P ⛟ nc5yrs

French & Italian Lunch £3.85–£4&alc Dinner £8.75alc Wine £5.25 Last dinner 9.30pm

Credit cards 1 2 3 5

★**Acton Court** Buxton Rd ☏ 061-483 6172

Closed Boxing Day & New Years Day RS Bank Hols

The busy, commercial hotel, situated on the A6 east of the town, has a popular restaurant.

25rm(9⇌1⫛) CTV in 23 bedrooms ®T ✱sB&B£16.50–£18.50 sB&B⇌⫛£26 dB&B£30 dB&B⇌⫛£37.50 B

CTV 200P ⛟ ✿ Disco Tue & Fri Live music & dancing Sat & Sun

French V ✱Lunch £4&alc Dinner £8.50–£11.50&alc Wine £4.95 Last dinner 10.15pm

Credit cards 1 2 3 5

STOCKTON-ON-TEES
Cleveland
Map **8** NZ41

★★★★**Swallow** 10 John Walker Sq (Swallow) ☏ (0642) 679721 Telex no 587895

Modern multi-story town centre hotel.

127⇌⫛(8fb) ⚟ in 40 bedrooms CTV in all bedrooms ®T S% ✱sB&B⇌⫛£46 dB&B⇌⫛£60 B

Lift ☾ ## 400 ⌂ CFA *xmas*

English & French V ♡ ☕ ⚟ S% ✱Lunch £7&alc Tea 70p Dinner £10.50&alc Wine £4.95 Last dinner 10pm

Credit cards 1 2 3 4 5

★★★**Billingham Arms** The Causeway, Billingham (3m NE A19) ☏ (0642) 553661 Telex no 587746

Modern brick building close to the shopping area.

64rm(43⇌12⫛)(1fb) ⚟ in 4 bedrooms CTV in all bedrooms ®T S% sB&B£18 sB&B⇌⫛£31–£41 dB&B£26 dB&B⇌⫛£41–£49 B

Lift ☾ CTV 50P CFA solarium Disco Thu Fri & Sat Live music & dancing Sat

English & French V ♡ ☕ Lunch £7.50&alc Tea £2.95 Dinner £10.75&alc Wine £5.95 Last dinner 10pm

Credit cards 1 2 3 4 5 V

See advertisement on page 678

★★★**Golden Eagle** Trenchard Av, Thornaby-on-Tees (1m E A174) ☏ (0642) 766511 Telex no 587565

Large, modern hotel in a residential and shopping area.

57⇌⫛ ⚟ in 5 bedrooms CTV in all bedrooms ® S% ✱sB⇌⫛£21–£28 dB⇌⫛£38 (room only) B

Lift ☾80P CFA solarium

V ♡ S% ✱Lunch £5alc Dinner £9alc Wine £4.50 Last dinner 9.30pm

Credit cards 1 3

★★★**Post House** Low Ln, Thornaby-on-Tees (Trusthouse Forte) ☏ (0642) 591213 Telex no 58426

Situated on the A1044 close to the interchange with the A174 towards Yarm.

136⇌(23fb) CTV in all bedrooms ® sB&B⇌£46.50 dB&B⇌£62.50 B

☾250P CFA ✿

♡ ☕ Last dinner 10.15pm

Credit cards 1 2 3 4 5

★★**Parkmore** 636 Yarm Rd, Eaglescliffe (3m S A19) (Best Western) ☏ (0642) 786815

Comfortable hotel whose well appointed bedrooms have good facilities. →

S

55rm(47⇨8⋔)4⊡CTV in all bedrooms ® T sB&B⇨⋔£27—£29.50 dB&B⇨⋔£35—£38 ₿

☾CTV 140P ✽ ⊡(heated) snooker sauna bath solarium gymnasium

English & French V Lunch £6—£7 Tea £2—£3 High Tea £4—£5 Dinner £9—£10&alc Wine £5.50 Last dinner 9.30pm

Credit cards 1 2 3 5

★**Claireville** 519 Yarm Rd, Eaglescliffe (3m S A135) ☎(0642) 780378

RS Xmas Day & New Years Day

This modestly-furnished, family-run hotel is set in an acre of gardens.

21rm(1fb) CTV in 16 bedrooms ® sB&B£15.50—£17.50 dB&Bfr£28 ₿

CTV 20P ✽

Bar lunch £3.50alc Dinner £6.25&alc Wine £4.30 Last dinner 7.15pm

Credit cards 1 3 5 Ⓥ

★***Stonyroyd*** 187 Oxbridge Ln ☎(0642) 607734

A sedate old house, with comfortable, spacious lounges and cosy bedrooms, is managed by the friendly proprietors.

13rm(2⋔)(1fb) CTV in all bedrooms ® T ₿

CTV 6P solarium

Last dinner 7.30pm

Stockton-on-Tees — Stoke-on-Trent

STOKE GABRIEL
Devon
Map **3** SX85

★★★ *H* **Gabriel Court** ☎(080428) 206

Closed Feb

Charming Manor house with tranquil Elizabethan garden and cosy lounges.

22rm(15⇨5⋔)(4fb) sB&B£22—£24 sB&B⇨⋔£24—£30 dB&B⇨⋔£44—£48

CTV 15P 7 ✽ (heated) (grass) xmas

V Lunch fr£6 (Sunday only) Tea fr£1.20 Dinner fr£12 Wine £6 Last dinner 8.30pm

Credit cards 1 2 3 5

STOKE-ON-TRENT
Staffordshire
Map **7** SJ84
See also **Newcastle-under-Lyme**

★★★★**North Stafford** Station Rd (Trusthouse Forte) ☎(0782) 48501 Telex no 36287

Located opposite the railway station entrance, the attractive, ornamented, brick-faced hotel offers comfortable accommodation and friendly service. The work of local potters is on display.

64rm(48⇨21⋔)(1fb) CTV in all bedrooms ® T sB&B⇨⋔£55 dB&B⇨⋔£72 ₿

Lift ☾ 120P CFA

Last dinner 10pm

Credit cards 1 2 3 4 5

★★★**Clayton Lodge** See Newcastle-under-Lyme

★★★***Haydon House*** 1—13 Haydon St, Basford ☎(0782) 629311

Extended and modernised Victorian house which has retained character. Quietly located yet close to A53/A500 junction.

17rm(9⇨8⋔) CTV in all bedrooms ® in 8 bedrooms T ₿

50P

V Last dinner 10.30pm

Credit cards 1 2 3 5

★★★**Stakis Grand** 66 Trinity St, Hanley (Stakis) ☎(0782) 22361

The hotel, a prominent Victorian building on the main road close to the city centre, offers some rooms with good views. Friendly service makes it popular with both businessmen and tourists.

93⇨⋔(8fb) in 10 bedrooms CTV in all bedrooms ® S% sB⇨⋔£44—£46 dB⇨⋔£55—£57 (room only) ₿

Lift ☾ 130P *xmas*

V ♁ ☕ S% Lunch £5.50&alc Tea £3 Dinner £8.95&alc Wine £5.65 Last dinner 10pm

Credit cards 1 2 3 5

★★**Central** 86—96 Wellesley St Shelton ☎ (0782) 272380

Closed xmas eve—2 Jan

38rm(33⇌5⋒)(8fb) CTV in all bedrooms Ⓡ ✗ ✱ sB&B⇌⋒£18 dB&B⇌⋒£32

☾ CTV ♿

♁ ☕ ✱ Lunch £4.75 Dinner £4.75 Wine £5 Last dinner 7.30pm

Credit cards 1 3

★★**George** Swan Sq, Burslem ☎ (0782) 84021

Situated in Burslem town centre, the busy, predominantly commercial hotel offers comfortable, well-equipped bedrooms.

38rm(19⇌1⋒)(4fb) CTV in all bedrooms Ⓡ T ✱ sB&B£23 sB&B⇌⋒£31 dB&B£35 dB&B⇌⋒£42 B

Lift 15P sauna bath solarium gymnasium Live music & dancing Thu Cabaret Fri

♉ International ♁ ☕ ✱ Lunch £5.95&alc Dinner £6.95&alc wine fr£5.95 Last dinner 10.30pm

Credit cards 1 2 3 5

STOKESLEY

North Yorkshire
Map **8** NZ50

✕ ***Golden Lion*** High St ☎ (0642) 710265

The small, country-town inn overlooks the main square.

♉ French **V** 80 seats Last dinner 9.30pm 4P

Credit cards 1 2 3 5

STONE

Staffordshire
Map **7** SJ93

★★★**Crown** High St (Toby) ☎ (0785) 813535

Built in 1779, the hotel's attractive, brick, bow front is a feature of the High Street. Traditional English and regional dishes are served in the oak-panelled restaurant, and bedrooms (many of them in a modern extension to the rear) are well-equipped.

13⇌ Annexe: 16⋒(4fb) CTV in all bedrooms Ⓡ sB&B⇌⋒£26.50 dB&B⇌⋒£31 B

☾ 200P bowling green *xmas*

♉ French **V** ♁ Lunch £8&alc Dinner £8&alc Wine £6.95 Last dinner 10pm

Credit cards 1 2 3

★★★**Stone House** ☎ (0785) 815531

This Edwardian country house stands in extensive and very pleasant grounds off the A34 about a mile south of the town and six miles north of Junction 14 of the M6 motorway.

22rm(13⇌9⋒)(2fb) CTV in all bedrooms **T** sB&B⇌⋒fr£26.50 dB&B⇌⋒fr£38.95 B

100P ❁ ♿

♉ International **V** ♁ ☕ ✱ Lunch fr£5.95&alc Tea fr75p Dinner fr£9.25&alc Wine £4.75 Last dinner 9.30pm

Credit cards 1 2 3 5 Ⓥ

★★**Mill** Mill St ☎ (0785) 818456

At the end of a narrow little lane off the High Street stands a brown brick mill built in 1795. It has now been converted into a popular bar and restaurant, bedrooms and public rooms being contained in the Mill House opposite. Here, in 1835, was born the originator of Hovis bread.

9rm(1⇌4⋒)(1fb) CTV in all bedrooms Ⓡ ✗ sB&B£15—£21 sB&B⇌⋒£19—£25 dB&B£25—£30 dB&B⇌⋒£30—£36 B

100P 8🚗 ❁ ♿

♉ English & French **V** ♁ ☕ ⚟ Lunch £8&alc Tea £1 Dinner £8&alc Wine £6 Last dinner 10pm

Credit cards 1 3 5 Ⓥ

S

✕La Casserole 6 Oulton Rd ☎ (0785) 814232

In the tiny bar of this restaurant, a converted shop to the north of the town centre, a fixed-price menu and wide range of daily specials is displayed. Cuisine is French, featuring some adventurous combinations of flavour, and generous portions are served.

Closed Sun & 23—29 Dec Lunch not served

French 50 seats Last dinner 11pm

STON EASTON
Somerset
Map **3** ST65

★★★

★★★ STON EASTON PARK, STON EASTON

(Pride of Britain) ☎ Chewton Mendip (076121) 631 Telex no 444738

The owners, Peter and Christine Smedley, have certainly created one of the loveliest of hotels and, with their own brand of hospitality, it is now probably the best hotel in the West Country. They were able to start with the splendid Palladian house in its flat, but interesting grounds laid out by Humphrey Repton which contain a castle folly, icehouse and the cascading River Somer. The interior also has some superb decorative features, particularly in the very grand drawing room. The Smedleys consulted Jean Munro to design the interior, and this she did with outstanding eclat. Pleasing colour schemes, delightful furnishings, antique furniture, and some very fine pictures, all add up to an embarrassment of riches. Some of these attributes are carried through to the spacious bedrooms which are beautifully done. Take a drink in the drawing room or elegant library with its mahogany shelves while you wait for a delicious dinner to be served in either of the two elegant dining rooms. There is a fixed price lunch but at dinner Mark Harrington, promoted from second

chef, provides and interesting à la carte menu. He seems to follow no particular manner although he is influenced by the modern lighter style. At any rate, his cooking is very enjoyable according to all the reports we have received so far. As you might expect the wine list is also excellent.

20rm(19)(1fb) 6 CTV in all bedrooms **T** ✱sB&B£60 dB&B£80—£165 Continental breakfast

CTV 40P 2 snooker croquet nc12yrs *xmas*

English & French **V** ✱Lunch £14 Tea £2.50 High Tea £5 Dinner £25alc Wine £7 Last dinner 9.30pm

Credit cards 1 2 3 5

STONE CROSS
East Sussex
Map **5** TQ60

★★★ Glyndley Manor Hailsham Rd (2m NW of B2104) ☎ Eastbourne (0323) 843737 Telex no 877440

Charming, family run country house with well appointed lounge.

20rm(17 3)(5fb) CTV in all bedrooms **T** S% ✱sB&B£39.60 dB&B£63.80 B

60P (hard) *xmas*

English & French **V** S% ✱Lunch £9.35&alc Tea £1 Dinner £11&alc Wine £5.50 Last dinner 9pm

Credit cards 1 2 3 4 5

See advertisement under Eastbourne

Stone — Storrington

STONEHAVEN
Grampian *Kincardineshire*
Map **15** NO88

★★★ Commodore Cowie Park ☎ (0569) 62936 Telex no 739111

Friendly, modern commercial hotel.

40 CTV in all bedrooms ® sB&B£38 dB&B£48 B

CTV 250P

International **V** Lunch £5.50—£7.50 Tea 75p—£1.20 High Tea £4.25—£6.50 Dinner £10.50—£12.50&alc Wine £6 Last dinner 9.45pm

Credit cards 1 2 3 4 5 V

★★County Arduthie Rd ☎ (0569) 64386

Closed 1 Jan

Friendly commercial hotel in northeast coastal town.

14(4fb) CTV in all bedrooms ® **T** S% ✱sB&Bfr£20 dB&Bfr£34 B

CTV 130P squash snooker sauna bath solarium gymnasium petanque

V ✱Lunch £2—£7 Tea £2 High Tea £3.50—£7.50 Dinner £7.95&alc Wine £4.50 Last dinner 10pm

Credit card 3

★★St Leonards Bath St ☎ (0569) 62044

Closed 1—3 Jan

Comfortable business hotel set in residential area.

14rm(10 1)(2fb) CTV in all bedrooms ® **T** S% sB&B£27—£32 sB&B£32—£35 dB&B£35—£40 dB&B£40—£45

CTV 40P

English & French **V** Lunch fr£5.50&alc Dinner fr£9.50&alc Wine £6 Last dinner 9pm

Credit card 3

STONEHOUSE
Gloucestershire
Map **3** SO80

★★★ Stonehouse Court Bristol Rd ☎ (045382) 5155

Closed 25 Dec—14 Jan

The 17th-century manor court, conveniently located within a mile of Junction 13 of the M5, offers comfortable bedrooms and attractive public rooms. A new bedroom wing and conference centre are due for completion in 1986, but the rest of the building retains its original charm.

23rm(22 1)(4fb) CTV in all bedrooms **T** sB&B£38—£42 dB&B£55—£65 B

100P sauna bath solarium gymnasium putting & croquet nc11yrs

English & Continental **V** Lunch £4.50—£9&alc Tea fr£1 Dinner £16alc Wine £6 Last dinner 10pm

Credit cards 1 2 3 5 V

See advertisement under Gloucester

STORNOWAY
Isle of Lewis, Western Isles *Ross & Cromarty*
See **Lewis, Isle of**

STORRINGTON
West Sussex
Map **4** TQ01

✕✕✕Manleys Manleys Hill ☎ (09066) 2331

In this most attractive and comfortable beamed restaurant, chef/patron Karl Löderer continues consistently to provide fine food. The cuisine is mainly French, though some Austro/German variations add both richness and flair.

Closed Mon, 1st wk Jan, last 2 wks Aug & 1st wk Sep Dinner not served Sun

Austrian & French **V** 36 seats S% Lunch £25.30alc Dinner £25.30alc Wine £6.80 Last dinner 9.30pm 18P

Credit cards 1 2 3 4 5

S

✕**Cottage Tandoori** 25 West St ☎(09066) 3605

This very popular Indian restaurant features an extensive choice of authentic dishes, including well-prepared Tandoori specialities. The cottage-style setting is enhanced by cheerful and attentive service.

Indian 72 seats S% ✱Lunch £10alc Dinner £15alc Wine £4.50 Last dinner 10pm 12P

Credit cards 1 2 3 5 Ⓥ

STOURBRIDGE
West Midlands
Map **7** SO88

★★**Talbot** High St (Wolverhampton & Dudley) ☎(0384) 394350

The busy, town-centre hotel, said to be over 500 years old, is a popular meeting place for shoppers and business people.

25rm(23➡2⋔)(3fb) 2⊟ CTV in all bedrooms ®T ✱sB&B➡⋔£28—£38 dB&B➡⋔£38—£48 B

☾ P

V ♅ ☕ ✱Lunch £4 Tea 50p Dinner £5.35&alc Wine £4.30 Last dinner 9.15pm

Credit cards 1 2 3 Ⓥ

STOURPORT-ON-SEVERN
Hereford & Worcester
Map **7** SO87

★★★**Stourport Moat House** 35 Hartlebury Rd (Queens Moat) ☎(02993) 77333

Modernised hotel with sports and conference facilities.

69➡ 2⊟ CTV in all bedrooms ®T S% sB&B➡£33.50—£36 dB&B➡£44.50—£48 B

☾ 400P CFA ✿ ⛆ ♔(hard) squash golf range Disco 4 nights wkly *xmas*

English & French **V** ♅ ☕ S% Lunch £6.50—£7.50&alc Tea 60—70p Dinner £7.50—£8.50&alc Wine £5.75 Last dinner 10pm

Credit cards 1 2 3 4 5 Ⓥ

★★***Swan*** High St (Golden Oak Inns) ☎(02993) 2050

This town-centre hotel has comfortable, refurbished bedrooms and a popular, value-for-money restaurant.

35rm(8➡27⋔) CTV in all bedrooms ® ✗ B

CTV 80P

♅ Last dinner 10pm

Credit cards 1 2 3

STOW CUM QUY
Cambridgeshire
Map **7** TL56

★**Quy Mill** Newmarket Rd ☎Teversham (02205) 4114

Small family run hotel offering comfortable, if modest, accommodation.

8rm(1➡)(1fb) CTV in all bedrooms

30P

♅ ☕ Last dinner 9.15pm

Credit cards 1 3

STOWMARKET
Suffolk
Map **5** TM05

★★**Cedars** Needham Rd ☎(0449) 612668

Closed 25—31 Dec

Situated on the outskirts of the town, the family-managed hotel has some fine examples of open timbers and exposed studwork in the 16th-century main building.

20rm(10➡5⋔)(1fb) CTV in all bedrooms ®T sB&B£22 sB&B➡⋔£28 dB&B£30 dB&B➡⋔£38 B

50P ✿

Mainly grills ♅ ☕ Lunch £8alc Tea £2alc Dinner £8alc Wine £4.95 Last dinner 9pm

Credit cards 1 2 3 Ⓥ

STOW-ON-THE-WOLD
Gloucestershire
Map **4** SP12

★★★ ♔ ***BL* Wyck Hill House** Burford Rd ☎(0451) 31936

This Cotswold-stone manor house dates from the early 1700s and has panoramic views across beautiful countryside from its landscaped, hillside gardens. The interior is magnificently furnished, and spacious bedrooms have modern comforts.

16➡⋔(4fb) 1⊟ CTV in all bedrooms **T** ✱sB&B➡⋔£65 dB&B➡⋔£70 Continental breakfast B

Lift ☾ 90P ✿ nc6yrs *xmas*

International ♅ ☕ ✱Lunch £6.95alc Tea £3.50 Dinner £14.50alc Last dinner 9.30pm

Credit cards 1 2 3

★★**Fosse Manor** ☎(0451) 30354

Closed 1 wk Xmas

Comfortable, well equipped, proprietor supervised hotel with friendly informal atmosphere. Restaurant provides consistently good cooking.

15rm(8➡4⋔) Annexe: 6rm(2➡)(7fb) 1⊟ CTV in all bedrooms ® S% sB&B£21—£24.50 sB&B➡⋔£24.50 dB&B£42—£49 dB&B➡⋔£49—£60 B

CTV 100P ✿

English & Continental **V** ♅ ☕ Lunch fr£8.50 Tea fr65p High Tea fr£2.50 Dinner £9.50—£15 Wine £4.60 Last dinner 9.30pm

Credit cards 1 2 3 5

See advertisement on page 682

★★**Grapevine** Sheep St ☎(0451) 30344

Closed 25 Dec—12 Jan

Small, attractive terrace town house with well appointed character bedrooms and pleasant public rooms.

14rm(12➡2⋔)(2fb) CTV in all bedrooms ®T ✗ sB&B➡⋔£24—£29 dB&B➡⋔£48—£58 B

14P ⊞ →

S

English & Continental Lunch £5—£10alc Tea fr£1.50 Dinner fr£8.95&alc Wine £4.25 Last dinner 9.30pm

Credit cards [1] [3] Ⓥ

★★B **Old Farmhouse** Lower Swell (1m W B4068) ☎(0451) 30232

Closed 21 Dec—28 Jan

Small, attractive, personally run hotel with some of the bedrooms in the Old Stable House, a converted part 16th-century barn.

7 Annexe:6 (1fb) 2 CTV in all bedrooms ®sB&B£19—£23 sB&B £25—£28.50 dB&B£29—£33.50 dB&B £35—£44 B

25P

V Bar lunch £4.75alc Dinner £8.90—£9.30&alc Wine £5.15 Last dinner 9pm

Credit cards [1] [3] Ⓥ

Stow-on-the-Wold

★★**Old Stocks** The Square ☎(0451) 30666

Closed 25—30 Dec

Hospitable small hotel with well appointed bedrooms.

19rm(16 3)(7fb) CTV available in bedrooms ®sB&B £19 dB&B £38 B

CTV 2

V Bar lunch 90p—£4 Tea 55p—£1 Dinner £5.95—£7.95 Wine £5 Last dinner 9.30pm

Credit cards [1] [2] [3] [5]

S

★ ★**Royalist** Digbeth St ☏(0451) 30670

A proprietor supervised hotel. The building retains some of the features of its historic past.

9rm(5➡) Annexe: 2rm(1➡3⋒)(2fb) 1⊞ ⚟ in all bedrooms CTV in all bedrooms ® sB&B£17.50 sB&B➡⋒£26.50 dB&B➡⋒£38.50 B

12P nc5yrs

♕ Bar lunch fr£3 Dinner fr£8.75&alc Wine £6.25 Last dinner 9.30pm

Credit cards 1 2 3 5 Ⓥ

★ ★**Stow Lodge** The Square ☏(0451) 30485

Closed 22 Dec—Mid Jan

Comfortable, privately owned hotel in its own grounds, set back from the Market Square.

11rm(10➡) Annexe: 10➡(2fb) 1⊞ ⚟ in 1 bedroom CTV in all bedrooms ® ✈ ✱sB&B➡£26—£34 dB&B£40—£47 dB&B➡£42—£50 B

☾30P ⊞ ✿ nc5yrs

♕ ⚟ ✱Bar lunch £5.90—£9.70 Dinner £8—£8.50&alc Wine £5.50 Last dinner 9.30pm

Credit cards 2 5

★ ★ *B* **Unicorn Crest** Sheep St (Crest) ☏(0451) 30257 Telex no 437186

Former 16th century coaching inn with recently refurbished bedrooms.

20rm(17➡3⋒)(1fb) ⚟ in 2 bedrooms CTV in all bedrooms ® sB➡⋒£44.85—£45.90 dB➡⋒£60.70—£62.80 (room only) B

CTV *xmas*

♕ ☕ S% ✱Tea 60p Dinner £10.55 Last dinner 9.30pm

Credit cards 1 2 3 4 5

STRACHUR

Strathclyde *Argyllshire*
Map **10** NN00

★ ★ ★**Creggans Inn** ☏(036986) 279 Telex no 727396

A 17th century inn, extensively and tastefully modernised, with compact bedrooms.

Stow-on-the-Wold — Stratford-upon-Avon

22rm(15➡2⋒) CTV available in bedrooms sB&B£30—£36 sB&B➡⋒£35—£41 dB&B£50—£56 dB&B➡⋒£60—£66 B

CTV 80P ✿ ♩ ⌂ ♿ *xmas*

☺Scottish & French **V** ♕ ☕ Lunch £8alc Tea £1.90alc Dinner £15alc Wine £5.80 Last dinner 9.30pm

Credit cards 1 2 3 5

STRANRAER

Dumfries & Galloway *Wigtownshire*
Map **10** NX06

★ ★ ★ *L* **North West Castle** (ExecHotel) ☏(0776) 4413 Telex no 777088

Tasteful combination of old and new buildings with good leisure facilities. Bedrooms are thoughtfully equipped and new bedrooms are spacious and attractive.

74➡⋒ Annexe: 4➡⋒(12fb) 1⊞ CTV in all bedrooms ®**T** ✱sB&B➡⋒£25—£28 dB&B➡⋒£39.50—£45.50 B

Lift ☾ 100P CFA ⊞ ⊡(heated) snooker sauna bath solarium pool table bowling table tennis Live music and dancing Sat ⌂ *xmas*

V ♕ ☕ Lunch £5&alc Tea £2.25 Dinner £9—£10&alc Last dinner 9.30pm

STRATFORD-UPON-AVON

Warwickshire
Map **4** SP25 **See plan page 685**

★ ★ ★ ★**Moat House International** Bridgefoot (Queens Moat) ☏(0789) 67511 Telex no 311127 Plan **11** *C2*

Very busy, large modern hotel on banks of River Avon.

249➡⋒ CTV in all bedrooms **T** ✱sB➡⋒£45—£48 dB➡⋒£60—£62.50 (room only) B

Lift ☾ ## 350P ✿ ♩ Disco 6 nights wkly Live music & dancing 3 nights wkly ⌂ *xmas*

V ♕ ☕ ⚟ ✱Lunch fr£7.90 Tea fr£1.95 High Tea £1.20—£5 Dinner fr£9.50&alc Wine £8.50 Last dinner 11.30pm

Credit cards 1 2 3 4 5

★ ★ ★ ★**Shakespeare** Chapel St (Trusthouse Forte) ☏(0789) 294771 Telex no 311181 Plan **13** *B2*

Famous black and white timbered 16th century building whose bedrooms are named after Shakespearian characters.

66➡ 1⊞ CTV in all bedrooms ® sB&B➡£55 dB&B➡£81 B

Lift ☾ CTV 45P CFA *xmas*

♕ ☕ Last dinner 9.30pm

Credit cards 1 2 3 4 5

★ ★ ★ ★ *HL* **Welcombe** Warwick Rd ☏(0789) 295252 Telex no 31347 Plan **15** *C3*

Closed 28 Dec—3 Jan

The hotel combines the English charm, atmosphere and hospitality that the overseas visitor to Stratford will expect, yet modern facilities are provided in both manor house and garden wing.

82➡(6fb) CTV in all bedrooms ®**T** S% ✱sB&B➡£49—£62 dB&B➡£72—£130 B

☾ 100P CFA ✿ ⛳18 ♩ snooker croquet putting ⌂ *xmas*

☺English & French **V** ♕ ☕ S% Lunch £11—£13&alc Tea £2—£4.50 Dinner £16.50—£18.50&alc Wine £9.75 Last dinner 9.30pm

Credit cards 1 2 3 5

See advertisement on page 684

★ ★ ★**Alveston Manor** Clopton Bridge (Trusthouse Forte) ☏(0789) 204581 Telex no 31324 Plan **1** *C1*

Popular tourist hotel, said to have Shakespearian connections.

110➡ CTV in all bedrooms ®**T** sB&B➡£52.50 dB&B➡£73 B

☾ 200P CFA ✿ *xmas*

Last dinner 9.30pm

Credit cards 1 2 3 4 5

★ ★ ★**Arden** Waterside (Mount Charlotte) ☏(0789) 294949 Telex no 311726 Plan **2** *B2*

The building dates from the Regency period and is situated opposite the Royal Shakespere Theatre. →

S

57➡⋒(7fb)CTV in all bedrooms ®T
✱sB&B➡⋒fr£37.25 dB&B➡⋒fr£55.50
B

☾60P✿♿

V♔☕✱Lunch £4.65—£7.95 Tea fr75p High Tea £4.75—£6 Dinner fr£8.55 Wine £5.65 Last dinner 9pm

Credit cards 1 2 3 4 5 Ⓥ

★★★**Charlecote Pheasant Country**
☎(0789) 840649
(For full entry see Charlecote)

★★★**Falcon** Chapel St (Queens Moat)
☎(0789) 205777 Telex no 312522 Plan **6** *B2*

A modernised hotel in the town centre.

Stratford-upon-Avon

Origins date from the 15th century.

73➡(13fb) 1⊟CTV in all bedrooms ®T
S% sB&B➡£29—£44 dB&B➡£44—£75
B

Lift ☾100P 24🚗CFA✿*xmas*

♔English & Continental V♔☕Lunch £7.25—£8.50&alc Tea £1.75—£2.75 High Tea £4.50—£6.50 Dinner £9—£10&alc Wine £5.20 Last dinner 9pm

Credit cards 1 2 3 4 5 Ⓥ

★★★**Grosvenor House** Warwick Rd (Best Western) ☎(0789) 69213 Telex no 311699 Plan **8** *C3*

Closed 24—27 Dec

This family-run hotel is particularly hospitable, and a friendly atmosphere prevails; the well-equipped health centre is now an added attraction.

57rm(24➡30⋒)(11fb) 2⊟CTV in all bedrooms ✗ S% sB&B£24.20—£25.50 sB&B➡⋒£32.20—£44.70 dB&B£36.50—£39.50 dB&B➡⋒£46.50—£55.50 B

☾CTV 50P CFA sauna bath solarium gymnasium

S

English & Continental Lunch £7.50—£9&alc Tea 80p—£1 High Tea £4—£5 Dinner £9.50—£12.50&alc Wine £4.50 Last dinner 8.45pm

Credit cards 1 2 3 5 V

See advertisement on page 686

★★★**Swan's Nest** Bridgefoot (Trusthouse Forte) ☎ (0789) 66761 Plan **14** *C1*

Standing beside the River Avon, the hotel is conveniently placed for both town and theatre. It offers guests comfortable bedrooms and a choice of menus.

60⇌(1fb) CTV in all bedrooms ® T sB&B⇌⋒£50.50 dB&B⇌⋒£69.50 B

☾ 100P CFA ✲ *xmas*

Last dinner 10.15pm

Credit cards 1 2 3 4 5

Stratford-upon-Avon

★★★**White Swan** Rother St (Trusthouse Forte) ☎ (0789) 297022 Plan **16** *A3*

Traditional 15th-century inn situated in the town centre.

35⇌(4fb) 1⊟ CTV in all bedrooms ® sB&B⇌⋒£48.50 dB&B⇌⋒£66.50 B

P ☾ CFA *xmas*

Last dinner 9pm

Credit cards 1 2 3 4 5

★★***Haytor*** Avenue Rd ☎ (0789) 297799 Plan **9** *C4*

RS Jan

Friendly quiet hotel with secluded walled garden.

18rm(5⇌11⋒)(2fb) 3⊟ CTV in all bedrooms

CTV 20P ✲ *xmas*

V Last dinner 8pm

See advertisement on page 686

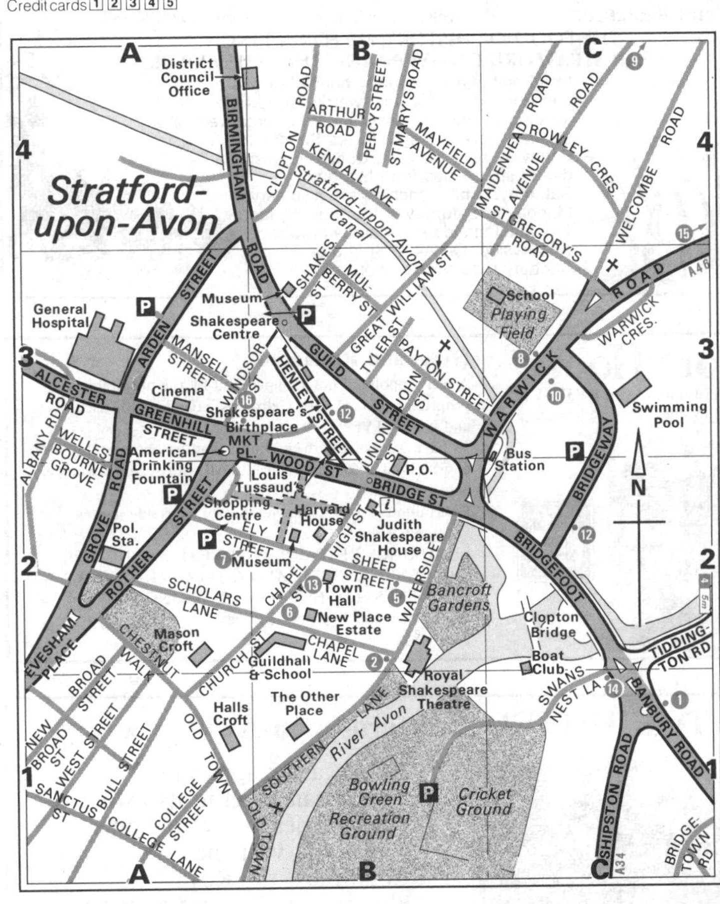

Stratford-upon-Avon

1 Alveston Manor ★★★
2 Arden ★★★
4 Charlecote Pheasant ★★★ *(Listed under Charlecote)*
5 Christophi's ✕✕
6 Falcon ★★★
7 Giovanni ✕
8 Grosvenor House ★★★
9 Haytor ★★
10 Hylands ★★
11 Moat House International ★★★★
12 Rumours ✕✕
13 Shakespeare ★★★★
14 Swans Nest ★★★
15 Welcombe ★★★★
16 White Swan ★★★

S

★★**Hylands** Warwick Rd ☎ (0789) 297962 Plan **10** *C3*

Closed 24–26 Dec

This small, privately-run hotel near the town centre has an attractive rear garden and a relaxed atmosphere.

16➡(1fb) CTV in all bedrooms ® ✗ S% *sB&B➡£20–£32 dB&B➡£37–£47 ⊟ 17P ⊞

S% Lunch £4.50–£6 Tea £1 Dinner £8.50–£11.50&alc Last dinner 7.30pm

Credit cards 1 3 Ⓥ

Stratford-upon-Avon

XX***Christophi's*** 21–23 Sheep St ☎ (0789) 69196 Plan **5** *B2*

Hand clapping, plate throwing and all the fun and games of a Greek taverna can be seen in this well-appointed dining room. Genuine Greek food and wine make it a popular venue for tourists and local residents in search of a lively evening meal.

Closed Sun Lunch not served

International 150 seats Last dinner mdnt Live music & dancing nightly Cabaret Fri & Sat

Credit cards 1 2 3 5

XX**Rumours** 10 Henley St ☎ (0789) 204297 Plan **12** *C3*

Close to Shakespeare's birthplace, a pretty little English restaurant with pastel décor specialises in cuisine of the light, nouvelle style, though satisfying portions are served. The à la carte menu features interesting dishes although those with simpler tastes, including vegetarians, are not forgotten.

Closed 1st 2 wks Jan

S

V 24 seats ✱Lunch £4.50—£5.50 Dinner £10.50—£11.95&alc Wine £6 Last dinner 10.30pm

nc8yrs

Credit cards 1 2 3 5

✕**Giovanni** 8 Ely St ☎ (0789) 297999 Plan **7** *B2*

The small, neat, Italian restaurant stands in a quiet road just off the busy town centre; booking is necessary, as it has a regular clientele.

Closed Sun

Italian & Continental 50 seats Wine £5.90 Last dinner 11.30pm

Credit cards 1 2 3

Stratford-upon-Avon — Strathblane

STRATHBLANE
Central *Stirlingshire*
Map **11** NS57

★★★*B* **Country Club** Milngavie Rd (Inter Hotel) ☎ Blanefield (0360) 70491

Converted country manor mansion with popular restaurant.

10rm(7 3)(3fb) CTV in all bedrooms ® **T** S% sB&B £35 dB&B £45

100P

Scottish, English, French & Italian **V** S% Lunch £7—£18&alc Dinner £13.50—£18&alc Wine £6 Last dinner 10pm

Credit cards 1 2 3 5

★★**Kirkhouse Inn** ☎ Blanefield (0360) 70621

Closed 1 Jan

Hotel with good standards throughout, situated in a lovely village.

18rm(10) CTV in all bedrooms **T** sB&B£26 sB&B £35 dB&B£39 dB&B £46

350P snooker Live music & dancing Fri & Sat *xmas*

→

S

French **V** Lunch fr£6.95 Tea fr60p High Tea fr£4.95 Dinner fr£12.95&alc Wine £5.90 Last dinner 10pm

Credit cards 1 2 3 5 V

STRATHCARRON

Highland *Ross & Cromarty*
Map **14** NG94

✕**Carron** Cam Allt ☎ Lochcarron (05202) 488

This small roadside restaurant offers good food and friendly service in comfortable surroundings.

Closed Sun & mid Oct—Etr

V 42 seats Lunch £5.25alc Dinner £12alc Wine £3.95 Last dinner 9.15pm 50P

Credit cards 1 3

STRATHMIGLO

Fife
Map **11** NO21

✕✕***Strathmiglo Inn*** ☎ (03376) 252

This charming little restaurant is set in a village inn which has a right of way running straight through it.

Dinner not served Sun

Scottish, French & Italian **V** 30 seats Last dinner 9.45pm 6P

Credit cards 1 2 3 5

STRATHPEFFER

Highland *Ross & Cromarty*
Map **14** NH45

★**Brunstane Lodge** ☎ (0997) 21261

Closed 1&2 Jan

The small, friendly, family-run hotel caters mainly for tourists.

6rm(1→1⋒)(1fb) ® in 4 bedrooms sB&B£14—£16 dB&B£30—£32 dB&B→⋒£34—£38 B

CTV 12P ✿ Live music & dancing Sat

V Bar lunch £2—£4.50 Dinner £6.50—£8.50&alc Wine £4 Last dinner 8.30pm

✿★*HL* **Holly Lodge** ☎ (0997) 21254

Oct—Apr

(Rosette awarded for dinner only.)

Decorative standards are high and the atmosphere relaxed and informal in this charming, small hotel, which stands in a quiet, elevated position above the Victorian spa resort. Cuisine is of award-winning excellence, and though the main-course choice is rather limited during the week, the substantial, home-cooked dishes are preceded by delicate starters and followed by wickedly delicious desserts. The wine list is short but keenly priced.

7rm(2→3⋒) CTV in all bedrooms ® sB&B£17—£20 dB&B→⋒£36—£44

12P ✿

*Dinner £8—£12 Wine £4.50 Last dinner 8pm

STRATHTUMMEL

Tayside *Perthshire*
Map **14** NN86

★★*HB* **Port-an-Eilean** ☎ Tummel Bridge (08824) 233

Mid Oct—Apr

Comfortable hotel in a splendid location by the Loch side, personally supervised by the proprietors.

10rm(8→)(1fb) ® sB&B£16.50 sB&B→£20 dB&B£33 dB&B→£38

20P 2 ✿

Bar lunch £5alc Tea 70p Dinner £9 Wine £4.30 Last dinner 8.45pm

STRATHYRE

Central *Perthshire*
Map **11** NN51

★**The Inn** Main St ☎ (08774) 224

Attractively modernised roadside inn.

7rm(4→) ® S% dB&B£20—£25 dB&B→£20—£25

CTV 30P

Mainly grills **V** S% Lunch £4alc Tea 75palc High tea £4alc Dinner £8.50alc Wine £3.75 Last dinner 9pm

STRATTON

Cornwall
Map **2** SS20

★**Stamford Hill** ☎ Bude (0288) 2709

Closed Oct—Etr

Small, family hotel in an elevated position with good rural views. It is a Georgian manor house built on the site of the Battle of Stamford Hill (1643).

17rm(5→4⋒)(10fb) 1 ® S% sB&B£9—£12.50 sB&B→⋒£11—£13.50 dB&B£18—£25 dB&B→⋒£22—£27 B

CTV 17P ✿ badminton putting games room

S% Bar lunch £1.25—£1.50 Dinner £4.50—£5 Wine £4.50 Last dinner 7pm

Credit cards 1 3

STRATTON ON THE FOSSE

Somerset
Map **3** ST65

✕**Fosse House Hotel** South St ☎ (0761) 233154

The pleasant little hotel and restaurant are personally run by friendly young proprietors. A well-prepared though limited menu of mainly Austrian dishes, complemented by a suitable wine list, represents good value for money.

Lunch not served Tue—Sat

Austrian & French 24 seats *Lunch fr£8.50 Dinner fr£10 Wine £5.20 Last dinner 9.30pm 6P

Credit card 3

STREATLEY

Berkshire
Map **4** SU58

★★★*L* **Swan** (Consort) ☎ Goring-on-Thames (0491) 873737

Tastefully renovated and well appointed hotel with superb riverside setting and a bar in an Oxford barge.

S

25➡CTV in all bedrooms ®T
sB&B➡£49.50—£52.25
dB&B➡£74.50—£88 B

☾CTV 120P❁pool table ⌂ *xmas*

V ⚘ ☕ Lunch £10—£12.50&alc Tea £2.75 Dinner £15.95—£22.50&alc Wine £6.95 Last dinner 9.30pm

Credit cards 1 2 3 4 5

STREET
Somerset
Map **3** ST43

★★★**Bear** 53 High St ☎ (0458) 42021

Recently refurbished hotel in town centre. Hotel bedrooms are particularly

Streatley — Street

comfortable, while annexe is simpler in style.

10rm(8➡2⋔) Annexe: 5➡(3fb) CTV in all bedrooms ®T sB&B➡⋔£29—£33
dB&B➡⋔£41—£45 B

16P❁

V ⚘ ☕ Lunch £6.75—£7.25 Tea 50—55p Dinner £9.35—£10&alc Wine £4.75 Last dinner 10pm

Credit cards 1 2 3 5 Ⓥ

★★★**Wessex** (Consort) ☎ (0458) 43383 Telex no 57515 (Attn 75)

Useful modern hotel near town centre.

50➡⋔(4fb) CTV in all bedrooms ®T
sB&B➡⋔£22.50—£33
dB&B➡⋔£33.50—£44.50 B

Lift ☾60P 30⌂ CFA Live music and dancing Sat ♿ *xmas*

V ⚘ ☕ Lunch £1.50—£3.50 Tea 40p—£1.25 Dinner £7.50&alc Wine £4.25 Last dinner 9.30pm

Credit cards 1 2 3 5

S

STREETLY
West Midlands
Map **7** SP09

★★***Parson & Clerk Motel*** Chester Rd (junc A452/B4138) (Golden Oak Inns) ☎ 021-353 1747

Bedrooms, breakfast and light meals are provided in a modern block some seventy-five yards from the main hotel building, whilst more substantial, grill-type meals are available in the main restaurant.

Annexe: 30🚿 CTV in all bedrooms ® 🐕 B

CTV 200P 🚗

🍷 Last dinner 10pm

Credit cards [1] [2] [3]

STRETE
Devon
Map **3** SX84

✕✕**Laughing Monk** ☎ Stoke Fleming (0803) 770639

The candle-lit restaurant occupies a former Victorian schoolhouse next to the church in the centre of this coastal village.

Closed Sun & Mon (in winter) Lunch not served

V 74 seats S% Dinner £14alc Wine £5.10 Last dinner 9.30pm 20P nc10yrs

Credit cards [1] [2] [3] [5] Ⓥ

STROMNESS
See **Orkney**

STRONTIAN
Highland *Argyllshire*
Map **14** NM86

★★**Kilcamb Lodge** ☎ (0967) 2257

Closed Jan—Mar

Situated on the outskirts of the village with grounds stretching down to Loch Sunart.

10rm (3🛁7🚿) (2fb) ® sB&B🛁🚿£21.50 dB&B🛁🚿£43

CTV 50P 🚗 ✿ clay pigeon shooting

V 🍷 ☕ Bar lunch £1.90—£10 Last dinner 7.30pm

Ⓥ

★★**Loch Sunart** ☎ (0967) 2471

Closed Nov—Mar

Small, family run Highland hotel.

10rm (5🛁) (1fb) sB&B fr£15 sB&B🛁 fr£16.50 dB&B fr£30 dB&B🛁 fr£33

CTV 30P 🚗 ✿

V 🍷 ☕ Bar lunch 65p—£5.75 Tea fr70p High Tea fr£2.75 Dinner fr£9.75 Wine £3.95 Last dinner 7.30pm

STROUD
Gloucestershire
Map **3** SO80
See also **Amberley** and **Painswick**

★★★**Bear of Rodborough** Rodborough Common (½m SW) (Anchor) ☎ Amberley (045 387) 3522 Telex no 437130

Character Cotswold stone hotel giving fine views over its extensive grounds and 900 acres of adjoining National Trust land.

47rm (46🛁1🚿) (2fb) 1⊟ ⁄ in 7 bedrooms CTV in all bedrooms ® T *sB&B🛁🚿£39.50—£46.50 dB&B🛁🚿£52.50—£67.50 B

☾ 200P 🏠 *xmas*

V 🍷 ⁄ *Lunch £11.50&alc Dinner £11.50&alc Wine £5.75 Last dinner 9.45pm

Credit cards [1] [2] [3] [5] Ⓥ

★★★ ***H* Burleigh Court** Brimscombe (2½m SE off A419) ☎ (0453) 883804

Closed 24—30 Dec RS Sun

Hospitable country house hotel with comfortable bedrooms.

11rm (8🛁3🚿) Annexe: 5🛁 (3fb) CTV in all bedrooms **T** 🐕 sB&B🛁🚿£37 dB&B🛁🚿£47 B

40P 2🚘 (£2 per night) 🚗 ✿ ⛱ (heated) putting 🏠

🍽 International **V** 🍷 ☕ Lunch £7.95—£9.95&alc Tea £1&alc High Tea £3.95—£6.95&alc Dinner £11—£14.95&alc Wine £4.45 Last dinner 8.30pm

Credit cards [1] [2] [3]

★★**London** 30—31 London Rd ☎ (04536) 79992

RS Public Hols & Sun

Town centre hotel with attractive restaurant.

10rm (2🛁6🚿) CTV in all bedrooms 🐕 sB&B fr£20 sB&B🛁🚿£25—£35 dB&B fr£30 dB&B🛁🚿£35—£48 B

10P 🚗 nc6yrs

🍽 English & Continental **V** 🍷 *Lunch fr£6 Dinner fr£10.50&alc Wine £4.50 Last dinner 9.30pm

Credit cards [1] [3] [5] Ⓥ

★**Alpine Lodge** Stratford Rd ☎ (04536) 4949

A privately-owned hotel with popular bars.

10rm (8🛁) (4fb) CTV in all bedrooms ® **T** sB&B🛁£18—£22 dB&B🛁£30—£32 B

CTV 50P 🏠

🍽 Mainly grills 🍷 ☕ *Lunch £2.50—£4&alc Tea 60p Dinner £6&alc Wine £4 Last dinner 9pm

Credit cards [1] [3] Ⓥ

★**Imperial** Station Rd (Berni) ☎ (04536) 4077

Closed Xmas

Town centre hotel with popular grill restaurant and bars.

17rm (1🚿) CTV in all bedrooms ® 🐕 sB🚿£16.50 dB🚿£33 (room only)

20P

🍽 Mainly grills 🍷 ⁄ *Lunch £7.50alc Dinner £7.50alc Wine £4.50 Last dinner 10pm

Credit cards [1] [2] [3] [5]

STRUY
Highland *Inverness-shire*
Map **14** NH43

★★**Cnoc** Erchless Castle Estate ☎ (046376) 264

This friendly little hotel, ideal for anglers, offers good, home-made cooking.

7rm (2🛁2🚿) (2fb) ® sB&B £14.50 sB&B🛁🚿£14.50—£16.50 dB&B £23 dB&B🛁🚿£23—£27

CTV 40P 🚗 ✿ 🏠

V Bar lunch £3.20alc Tea 75p&alc Dinner £9.50&alc Wine £3.95 Last dinner 9pm

Credit cards 1 3 V

STUDLAND
Dorset
Map **4** SZ08

★★★*L* **Knoll House** Ferry Rd (092944) 251

Closed mid Oct—end Mar

A rambling building amid pine trees with lawns and gardens extending down to the beach. Hotel situated in National Trust land.

57rm(42) Annexe: 21rm(14)(30fb) S% sB&B£31—£42(incl dinner) sB&B£38—£48(incl dinner) dB&B£62—£84(incl dinner) dB&B£70—£96(incl dinner)

CTV 100P (heated) 9 (hard) sauna solarium gymnasium Disco wkly in season

Lunch £8 Tea £1—£1.80 Dinner £8.50 Wine £4.50 Last dinner 8.30pm

★★ **Manor House** (092944) 288

Closed Nov—Mar

Gothic-style manor house with secluded gardens and grounds overlooking the sea and cliffs.

20rm(13 7)(9fb) 4 CTV in all bedrooms ® dB&B£35—£53 B

40P (hard) nc 5yrs

English & French V S% Bar lunch £1.50—£5 Tea 70p High Tea £2—£6 Dinner £10—£12 Wine £4.75 Last dinner 8.30pm

Credit card 1

Struy — Sunderland

STURMINSTER NEWTON
Dorset
Map **3** ST71

XX **Plumber Manor** (2m SW on Hazelbury Brian rd) (Pride of Britain) (0258) 72507

(Rosette awarded for dinner only)

A comfortable and good restaurat has been provided in this family home since the 17th century. The chef is Brian Prideaux-Brune, who produces good Anglo-French dishes and sauces, with seasonal variations, from fresh ingredients. A comprehensive French and German wine list ranges from a sound house wine to some good vintages. Good bedrooms are available.

Closed Mon (Nov—Mar), last 2 wks Jan & Feb Lunch not served

English & French 60 seats Dinner £14.50—£16.50 Wine £6 Last dinner 9.30pm

20P

Credit card 1

SULGRAVE
Northamptonshire
Map **4** SP54

X **Thatched House Hotel** (029576) 232

A 17th-century Cotswold stone restaurant in a quiet country village.

English & French V 50 seats Lunch £4.75—£8.50 Dinner £6.50—£11 Wine £4.05 Last dinner 9.15pm 16P

Credit cards 1 2 3 5 V

SUNDERLAND
Tyne & Wear
Map **12** NZ35

★★★ **Seaburn** Queens Pde, Seaburn (Swallow) (0783) 292041 Telex no 53168

The modernised, sea-front hotel offers well-appointed bedrooms and lofty, spacious public rooms.

82rm(79 3)(4fb) CTV in all bedrooms ® T S% sB&B£41 dB&B£53 B

Lift CTV 110P CFA Live music and dancing Sat *xmas*

English & French V S% Lunch £4.50—£7.50&alc Tea 60p—£2.50 Dinner £7.25—£8.95&alc Wine £5.25 Last dinner 9.35pm

Credit cards 1 2 3 5

★★ **Mowbray Park** Toward Rd (0783) 78221 Telex no 587746

This town-centre, commercial hotel provides a range of bars and good-value menus.

58rm(33 2)(2fb) CTV in all bedrooms ® T S% ✱ sB&B£19—£23 sB&B£24—£30.50 dB&B£35—£43 B

Lift ## 20 (charge) *xmas*

English & French V S% ✱ Lunch fr£5.50 Dinner £7.95 Wine £5 Last dinner 9.30pm

Credit cards 1 2 3 4 5 V

★ **Gelt House** 23 St Bedes Ter (0783) 672990

A small, friendly hotel is situated in a tree-lined private road close to the town centre and offers simple, clean and comfortable accommodation.

15rm(3 3) Annexe: 8(2fb) CTV in all bedrooms ® T ✱ sB&Bfr£18 sB&Bfr£24 dB&Bfr£28 dB&Bfr£34 B

CTV 14P sauna bath

✱ Dinner £6.50—£7.50 Wine £4.20 Last dinner 8.30pm

Credit cards 1 3

S

✕✕**Maltings** Bonner's Field Complex, Bonner's Field Wharf, Monkwearmouth ☎(0783) 654862

A turn-of-the-century brewery has been tastefully converted to form this charming, riverside restaurant which boasts the largest collection of 'Mousey Thompson' oak furniture in daily use.

Closed Mon Dinner not served Sun

English & Continental **V** 120 seats ✱Lunch £6.50 Dinner £7.50 Wine £4.25 Last dinner 10.30pm

180P Disco Thu, Fri & Sat

Credit cards 1 2 3 5

SURBITON
Greater London
London plan **5** *B1* (page 446)

❀✕✕**Chez Max** 85 Maple Rd ☎01-399 2365

Chef/patron Max Markaman has replaced his previous à la carte selection with a fixed-price, two-course menu which includes coffee but allows each guest to make his own decision about a dessert. Cuisine is individualistic, making good use of sauces, the wine list remains well balanced, and service is well supervised by the chef's charming English wife.

Closed Sun, Mon, 25—26 Dec, 1—14 Jan & 1wk Jul Lunch not served Sat

French 30 seats Lunch fr£15.50 Dinner £20 Wine £7.50 Last dinner 10.30pm nc6yrs

Credit cards 1 2 3 5

✕**Surbiton Rendezvous** 110 Ewell Rd ☎01-399 6713

This small, tastefully-appointed Chinese restaurant specialises in Peking cuisine. Food is authentic and reasonably priced, friendly service by pleasant Chinese waiters being supervised by the proprietor.

Closed Xmas Day & Boxing Day

Pekinese **V** 60 seats ✱Lunch fr£3.30&alc Dinner £10—£12&alc Wine £5.50 Last dinner 11.30pm

Credit cards 1 2 3 5 V

S

Sunderland — Sutton Coldfield

SUTTON
Greater London
London Plan **5** *C1* (page 446)

❀✕**Partners 23** 23 Stonecot Hill ☎01-644 7743

Andy Thomason and his partner Tim McEntire achieved their ambition in opening this charming little restaurant. It continues to serve a very good four-course meal each evening using such first-rate materials as pheasant and English lamb in season. The well-balanced wine list is reasonably priced and the service remains friendly and warm.

Closed Sun, Mon & 25 Dec—3 Jan Lunch not served Sat

English & French 34 seats Lunch £9.25—£14.75 Dinner £16.50 Wine £5.95 Last dinner 9.30pm

Credit cards 1 2 3 5 V

SUTTON BENGER
Wiltshire
Map **3** ST97

★★★**Bell House** (Berni) ☎Seagry (0249) 720401

RS Xmas night

Comfortable village hotel with good bedrooms and attractive restaurant.

14 1 CTV in all bedrooms ®**T** ✱sB&B£26.95—£35.95 dB&B£44.95—£54.95 Continental breakfast

50P *xmas*

International **V** Lunch £4—£6.95&alc Tea 75p Dinner £11alc Wine £5.15 Last dinner 10.30pm

Credit cards 1 2 3 5

See advertisement under Chippenham

SUTTON COLDFIELD
West Midlands
Map **7** SP19

★★★★**Penns Hall** Penns Ln, Walmley (Embassy) ☎021-351 3111 Telex no 335789

Considerably extended mansion with grounds and a lake.

115 CTV in all bedrooms ®**T** sBfr£50 dBfr£60 (room only)

Lift 500P CFA Live music and dancing Sat (Oct—May) *xmas*

English, French & Italian ✱Lunch £12alc Tea 80palc Dinner £12alc Wine £5.20 Last dinner 9.45pm

Credit cards 1 2 3 4 5 V

★★★**Moor Hall** Moor Hall Drive, Four Oaks (Best Western) ☎021-308 3751 Telex no 335127

Popular hotel in quiet residential area.

50(1fb) CTV in all bedrooms ®**T** sB&B£42—£46 dB&B£50—£55

180P CFA 18 sauna bath solarium gymnasium *xmas*

International **V** Lunch £6.50—£9.50 Tea £1.25—£2.50 Dinner £10.95—£15.50 Wine £5.95 Last dinner 10.30pm

Credit cards 1 2 3 4 5 V

★★**Cloverley** 17 Anchorage Rd ☎021-354 5181

Situated close to the railway station, the friendly hotel has comfortable, well-equipped bedrooms and provides warm, informal service; it is particularly popular with commercial guests.

26rm(620)(3fb) 2 CTV in all bedrooms ®**T** S% ✱sB&B£24—£38 dB&B£40.50—£44.25

CTV 35P Live music & dancing Fri & Sat *xmas*

English & French **V** Lunch £4.85—£6.85 Tea £1.20—£2 High Tea £3.20—£5 Dinner £7—£12.50&alc Wine £4.75 Last dinner 10pm

Credit cards 1 2 3 V

Sutton Coldfield — Swanage

★★**Sutton Court** 66 Lichfield Rd ☏021-355 6071 Telex no 335518

Extensively refurbished Victorian building on main crossroads offering good accommodation and having a well known restaurant.

34rm(23⇌11⋒)(11fb) 1⊟ ⊬ in 4 bedrooms CTV in all bedrooms ® T S% sB&B⇌⋒£29.15—£39.75 dB&B⇌⋒£39.25—£47.50 B

☾CTV 70P 9⌂

♁English & French V ♔ ⊒ S% Lunch £4.95—£14.95 Tea £2.50—£4.95 Dinner £12.50—£14.95 Wine £5.95 Last dinner 9.30pm

Credit cards 1 2 3 4 5 Ⓥ

See advertisement under Birmingham National Exhibition Centre

○**New Hall** Walmley Rd (Thistle) ☏021-378 2200

68⇌⋒

Due to have opened September 1986

XX**Le Bon Viveur** 65 Birmingham Rd ☏021-355 5836

The bustle of the main road is shut out from the relaxed atmosphere and comfortable surroundings of this restaurant by a discreetly-curtained shop front. The established popularity of the Italian owner and the staff is a tribute not only to their skill but also to the willing attention that they give to customers. Predominantly French food, using good, fresh ingredients represents excellent value for money.

Closed Sun, Mon & 3 wks Aug Lunch not served Sat

♁French V 44 seats Lunch £5.95—£6.50&alc Dinner £15alc Wine £5.95 Last dinner 10.30pm 8P ⊬ nc5yrs

Credit cards 1 2 3 5

SUTTON-ON-SEA
Lincolnshire
Map **9** TF58

★★**Bacchus** High St (Home Brewery) ☏(0521) 41204

A predominantly holiday hotel with large grounds, close to the sea front.

22rm(6⇌)(1fb) CTV available in 6 bedrooms ® S% sB&B£15.70 sB&B⇌£16.91 dB&B£26.57 dB&B⇌£31.40 B

CTV 60P 10⌂ ✿ putting bowls *xmas*

V ♔ ⊒ ✱Lunch £3.50&alc Dinner £6.90&alc Wine £3.80 Last dinner 8pm

Credit cards 1 2 3

★★**Grange & Links** Sea Ln, Sandilands ☏(0521) 41334

16rm(11⇌3⋒)(1fb) 1⊟ CTV in all bedrooms ® ✱sB&B£23 sB&B⇌⋒£32.20 dB&B⇌⋒£43.70 B

CTV 60P ⊭ ✿ ♧(hard) snooker Disco Sat Live music and dancing Wed Cabaret Sat (summer season) ♗ *xmas*

♁English & French V ♔ ✱Lunch £7alc Dinner £8.50&alc Wine £3.95 Last dinner 8.30pm

Credit cards 1 2 3 5

SUTTON SCOTNEY
Hampshire
Map **4** SU43

○**Little Chef Lodge** A34 Southbound (Trusthouse Forte) ☏01-567 3444

40⇌⋒

Due to have opened September 1986.

SUTTON UPON DERWENT
Humberside
Map **8** SE74

★★**Old Rectory** ☏Elvington (090485) 548

A converted and restored Georgian vicarage stands in nearly two acres of grounds and gardens. The hotel offers spacious and comfortable bedrooms, a lounge with separate bar and elegant dining room where good food is served.

6rm(2⋒)(2fb) CTV in all bedrooms ® sB&B£20 dB&B£32 dB&B⋒£36

50P ⊭ ✿

♔Dinner £10.50 Wine £5 Last dinner 7pm

Credit card 1

SWAFFHAM
Norfolk
Map **5** TF80

★★**George** Station Rd (Consort) ☏(0760) 21238

Closed Xmas

Large, country hotel situated on main crossroads of this market town.

31rm(17⇌) CTV in all bedrooms ® S% ✱sB&B£28 sB&B⇌£36 dB&B£36 dB&B⇌£44.50 B

☾100P CFA

V ♔ ⊒ S% ✱Lunch £6&alc Tea 85p—£1.65 Dinner £8.50&alc Wine £5.95 Last dinner 9pm

Credit cards 1 2 3 4 5 Ⓥ

SWALLOWFIELD
Berkshire
Map **4** SU76

★★*B* **The Mill House** (Exec Hotel) ☏Reading (0734) 883124 Telex no 847423

Tasteful conversion of an early 18th century house has provided comfortable, relaxing hotel accommodation. Bedrooms are well-equipped whilst the personal supervision of the owners ensures a warm, informal atmosphere.

10rm(5⇌5⋒)(2fb) 1⊟ CTV in all bedrooms ® T ✱sB&B⇌⋒£24—£47.75 dB&B⇌⋒£48—£59.50 B

40P ✿ ♪ ♗

♁English & French V ♔ ⊒ S% ✱Lunch £9.20—£11.65&alc Tea fr£2.50 Dinner £14&alc Wine £5.95 Last dinner 10pm

Credit cards 1 2 3 5 Ⓥ

SWANAGE
Dorset
Map **4** SZ07

★★★*HL* **Grand** Burlington Rd ☏(0929) 423353

Standing in a cliff-top position with fine views of Swanage Bay, the hotel has been refurbished to provide a high standard of comfort and service. A good range of dishes is available in the fine restaurant, there are good leisure facilities, and the hotel has its own private beach. →

S

30rm(22 8)(5fb) 1 CTV in all bedrooms ® T sB&B £22—£26 dB&B £44—£52 B

Lift 15P (heated) sauna bath solarium gymnasium pool table *xmas*

English & French Lunch £10&alc Tea £1.50alc Dinner £10&alc Wine £4.50 Last dinner 10pm

Credit cards 1 2 3 5 V

★★★*H* **Pines** Burlington Rd (0929) 425211 Telex no 418297

Well-appointed, modern cliff-top hotel with good food and attentive staff.

Swanage

51rm(46 3)(26fb) CTV in all bedrooms T sB&B £23.50—£25.50 sB&B £23.50—£27.30 dB&B £47—£55 B

Lift 60P CFA Live music and dancing wkly (in season) *xmas*

English & Continental V Lunch £6.50—£7.50 Tea 85p—£1 High Tea £4.50 Dinner £9.50—£16 Wine £2.55 Last dinner 9pm

Credit cards 1 3 V

★★**Sefton** Gilbert Rd (0929) 423469

Closed Jan—Early Mar & 2 Nov—Dec

Quiet, pleasantly furnished hotel, with personal attention by resident owners.

15rm(6)(2fb) ® sB&B £18.50—£21 sB&B £19—£22 dB&B £34—£40 dB&B £40—£45 B

CTV 10P nc 7yrs

International Bar lunch £1—£5 Tea 45p—55p Dinner £8—£11 Wine £4.90 Last dinner 7.30pm

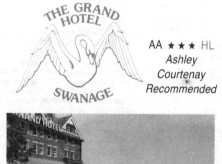

Credit card 1

S

★***Suncliffe*** Burlington Rd (0929) 423299
Closed Oct—Etr
Detached, brick gabled hotel in a quiet residential area.
14rm(17)(5fb)
CTV 14P 4
Last dinner 7.30pm

★**York** Cauldon Av (0929) 422704
Closed Mid Oct—Etr
Detached colour-washed hotel with a mansard roof, in a quiet location within walking distance of the sea front and facing tennis courts.
22rm(4)(3fb) S%
*sB&B£12.10—£14.20 dB&B£24.20—£28.40 dB&B£28.70—£32.90
Lift CTV 15P 4(75p per night)
V S% *Tea 55p—£1.50 High Tea £3—£4 Dinner £7 Wine £3.70 Last dinner 8pm

SWANSEA
West Glamorgan
Map **3** SS69
See also **Langland Bay** and **Mumbles**

★★★★**Dragon** Kingsway Circle (Trusthouse Forte) (0792) 51074 Telex no 48309
The modern, city-centre hotel offers comfortable bedrooms, dining room, coffee shop and bar; service is generally attentive and friendly.
118 CTV in all bedrooms ®T
sB&B£52 dB&B£68
Lift CTV 40P CFA *xmas*
Last dinner 10pm
Credit cards 1 2 3 4 5

★★★**Dolphin** Whitewalls (Inter Hotel) (0792) 50011 Telex no 48128
This popular, businessman's hotel in the centre of Swansea features recently upgraded bedrooms and a new coffee shop on the ground floor.
65(6fb) CTV in all bedrooms ®T S%
*sB&B£35 dB&B£46.50
Lift *xmas*
International V S% *Lunch £3.50—£5 Tea £1.75—£3 Dinner £7.50 Wine £5 Last dinner 9.30pm
Credit cards 1 2 3 5 V

★★★**Fforest Motel** Pontardulais Rd, Fforestfach (on A483 1½m S of M4 junc 47) (Whitbread) (0792) 588711
The modern motel is conveniently located close to the M4 and has comfortable, well-equipped bedrooms, a grill restaurant and spacious, modern bars. It is popular with businessmen.
18 CTV in all bedrooms ®
sB&B£42 dB&B£50
CTV 250P
Mainly grills V Lunch £4.50—£4.75&alc Tea 80p—£1 Dinner £6.50alc Wine £5.10 Last dinner 9.45pm
Credit cards 1 2 3

★★★*H* **Ladbroke** Phoenix Way, Swansea Enterprise Park (1m S M4, between jct 44 & 45, SW of Llansamlet) (Ladbroke) (0792) ~~790190~~ Telex no ~~48589~~ [handwritten: 310330]
114(18fb) in 8 bedrooms CTV in all bedrooms ®T S% *sBfr£46.50 dBfr£55 (room only)
200P (heated) sauna bath gymnasium Live music & dancing Sat *xmas*
English, French & Italian V *Lunch £6.50—£7.50 Tea £1.20 High Tea £5.50 Dinner £9.75&alc Wine £5.99 Last dinner 9.45pm
Credit cards 1 2 3 5 V
See advertisement on page 696

★★*H* **Beaumont** 72 Walter Rd (0792) 43956
This small, personally owned and managed hotel has undergone commendable upgrading recently. It offers →

S

comfortable bedrooms, quality, character lounges and hospitable service from proprietors and staff.

16rm(2⇌13ⓜ) 1⊟ CTV in all bedrooms ® T sB&B⇌ⓜfr£30 dB&B⇌ⓜfr£45 ⓑ

CTV 10P ⊞ sauna bath

☉Welsh, English & French V ☉ ☐ *Lunch fr£7.50 Tea fr75p Dinner fr£12.50 Wine £4.95 Last dinner 9pm

Credit cards 1 2 3 5 Ⓥ

★*HBL* **Windsor Lodge** Mount Pleasant ☎ (0792) 42158

Closed 25 & 26 Dec

In a quiet residential area not far from the city centre, this Georgian house has been beautifully refurbished. The bedrooms, though compact, are most comfortably appointed. The food is well cooked and the staff are friendly and attentive.

18rm(8⇌3ⓜ) CTV in all bedrooms ® *sB&B£23.75 sB&B⇌ⓜ£28.75 dB&B£35.50 dB&B⇌ⓜ£39.50 ⓑ

25P ⊞ sauna bath

☉English & French ☉ ☐ *Lunch £6—£12 Tea 50p—£2.50 High Tea £1—£3.50 Dinner £9.50—£13.50 Wine £4.80 Last dinner 9pm

Credit cards 1 2 3 5 Ⓥ

Swansea — Swindon

SWAY
Hampshire
Map **4** SZ29

★★**White Rose** Station Rd (Exec Hotel) ☎ Lymington (0590) 682754

In this small, old-fashioned, family-run hotel the guest will find friendly, helpful service and particularly good standards of cooking.

13rm(9⇌)(2fb) CTV in all bedrooms ® S% *sB&B£17—£21 sB&B⇌£22—£28 dB&B£34—£38 dB&B⇌£39—£46 ⓑ

Lift 50P ⊞ ✿ ⌂ *xmas*

V ☉ ☐ *Lunch £5.50—£10.50&alc Tea fr75p Dinner £7.50—£10.50&alc Wine £4.20 Last dinner 9pm

Credit cards 1 3 Ⓥ

SWINDON
Wiltshire
Map **4** SU18

★★★★**Blunsdon House** Blunsdon (3m N off A419) (Best Western) ☎ (0793) 721701 Telex no 444491

Friendly family-run hotel, with well-appointed restaurant and separate carvery.

91rm(89⇌2ⓜ)(16fb) 5⊟ CTV in all bedrooms ® T ⊠ sB&B⇌ⓜ£52.50—£60 dB&B⇌ⓜ£60—£67.50 ⓑ

Lift ☾ 250P CFA ✿ ⊡(heated) squash snooker sauna bath solarium gymnasium ⚘ *xmas*

☉English & French V ☉ ☐ Lunch fr£7.50&alc Dinner fr£7.50&alc Wine £5.75 Last dinner 10pm

Credit cards 1 2 3 4 5 Ⓥ

★★★**Crest** Oxford Rd, Stratton St Margaret (3m NE A420) (Crest) ☎ (0793) 822921 Telex no 444456

RS Xmas

A purpose built hotel with useful access to Swindon's business areas and through-routes.

95⇌ⓜ(7fb) ⊬ in 12 bedrooms CTV in all bedrooms ® T S% *sB⇌fr£45.50 dB⇌fr£55.50 (room only) ⓑ

☾ 170P ♿ ⚘

V ☉ ☐ *Lunch fr£9.50 Tea fr65p Dinner fr£11.50 Wine £5.80 Last dinner 9.45pm

Credit cards 1 2 3 4 5

★★★**Goddard Arms** High St, Old Town (Anchor) ☎ (0793) 692313 Telex no 444764

Grey-tiled and creeper-clad inn in one of the old parts of town, with a modern motel in the grounds.

S

 0792- 310330

18rm(14→4⌂) Annexe: 47→⊁in 6 bedrooms CTV in all bedrooms ® ✱sB&B→⌂£49.50 dB&B→⌂£59.50 B ☾120P CFA & *xmas*
V ✱Lunch £8alc Dinner £10alc Wine £5.95 Last dinner 9.30pm
Credit cards 1 2 3 4 5 V

★★★**Post House** Marlborough Rd (Trusthouse Forte) ☎ (0793) 24601 Telex no 444464
The comfortable, modern hotel attracts tourist and business trade; it is situated away from the town centre, north of the M4's Junction 15.

Swindon

104→(29fb) CTV in all bedrooms ® T sB&B→£54.50 dB&B→£70.50 B
☾200P CFA ✲ ⊡ & ⌒ (heated) sauna bath solarium gymnasium
Last dinner 10pm
Credit cards 1 2 3 4 5

★★★***Wiltshire*** Fleming Way (Kingsmead) ☎ (0793) 28282 Telex no 444250
The modern, purpose-built hotel is situated close to the main shopping area; guests are entitled to complimentary parking in the adjacent, multi-storey car-park.
85→⌂ CTV in all bedrooms ® T B
Lift ☾600⌂ CFA Live music & dancing Sat *xmas*
English & French V Last dinner 10.30pm
Credit cards 1 2 3 4 5

S

SYMONDS YAT (EAST)
Hereford & Worcester
Map **3** SO51

★★**Royal** ☎ (0600) 890238

Up narrow road, the grounds of this hotel reach down to River Wye.

19rm(6 3)(2fb) 1 Ⓡ
sB&B£19.50—£21.50
sB&B £21.50—£23.50
dB&B£40—£44 dB&B £43—£53
80P sauna bath nc5yrs *xmas*

English & French **V** Lunch £10alc Tea £1.50alc Dinner £12.50alc Wine £4.50 Last dinner 10pm

Credit cards 1 3

SYMONDS YAT (WEST)
(near Ross-on-Wye)
Hereford & Worcester
Map **3** SO51

★★**Paddocks** ☎ (0600) 890246

Closed Nov—Feb except Xmas wk

In a picturesque setting in the Wye Valley this hotel provides modest, comfortable accommodation and friendly informal service.

25rm(12 3)(4fb) CTV available in bedrooms Ⓡ S% *sB&B£16
sB&B £18 dB&B£32 dB&B £36
CTV 150P (hard) Live music & dancing Wed Fri & Sat *xmas*

English & French **V** *Lunch £6 Tea fr60p High Tea £2—£6 Dinner £10&alc Wine £5 Last dinner 8.30pm

Credit card 3 Ⓥ

★★**Wye Rapids** ☎ (0600) 890366

Secluded and relaxing hotel standing high above the Wye Rapids.

17rm(4 4)(2fb) sB&B£19.50
sB&B £28.50 dB&B£31—£35
dB&B £41.50—£45
CTV 15P 6 *xmas*

English & French **V** Lunch £5.95&alc Tea £1.20—£1.50 Dinner £8.95&alc Wine £4 Last dinner 8.30pm

Credit cards 1 2 3 5

TADDINGTON
Derbyshire
Map **7** SK17

XX**Waterloo** ☎ (029885) 230

A roadside inn on the A6, 5m east of Buxton.

Dinner not served Sun & Mon

English & French 200 seats Lunch £5.95—£9.80&alc Dinner £5.95—£9.80&alc Wine £5.95 Last dinner 8.30pm 150P

Credit cards 1 2 3 5 Ⓥ

TAIN
Highland *Ross & Cromarty*
Map **14** NH68

★★★**Royal** High St ☎ (0862) 2013

Nicely appointed and comfortable hotel catering for business people and holidaymakers.

25rm(15 7) CTV in all bedrooms Ⓡ **T**
S% sB&B£19.50—£22 sB&B £27
dB&B£37—£39 dB&B £37—£39
10P 6 (charge £1.50 per night) *xmas*

V S% Lunch £11.50alc Dinner £10.50&alc Wine £4 Last dinner 9.30pm

Credit cards 1 2 3 5 Ⓥ

★★**Mansfield** Scotsburn Rd ☎ (0862) 2052

Imposing mansion with some recently built modern rooms. Located on the western fringe of town.

18rm(14 4)(2fb) CTV in all bedrooms
Ⓡ **T** sB&B £23—£27 dB&B fr£36
CTV P

V Bar lunch £5alc Tea £1alc High Tea £4alc Dinner £13alc Wine £4

Credit cards 1 3

TALLADALE
Highland *Ross & Cromarty*
Map **14** NG97

★*H* **Loch Maree** Loch Maree
☎ Lochmaree (044589) 200

Closed end Oct—Mar
RS April

A traditional Highland and fishing hotel with a reputation for hospitality and good home cooking.

15rm sB&B£21—£23 dB&B£42—£46
12P 4

Lunch £5—£6 Tea £1—£4 Dinner £10—£11 Wine £3.95

TALLAND BAY
Cornwall
Map **2** SX25

★★★ *BL* ***Talland Bay*** (Inter Hotel)
☎ Polperro (0503) 72667

Closed 13 Dec—13 Feb

Well-appointed hotel in a secluded position with good views and access to beach.

19rm(17) Annexe: 4 (3fb) 1 CTV in all bedrooms Ⓡ in 1 bedroom
20P (heated) solarium nc 5yrs

English & French **V** Last dinner 9pm

Credit cards 1 2 3 5

TALSARNAU
Gwynedd
Map **6** SH63

★★ *L* **Maes y Neuadd** (2m SE on unclass rd off B4573) ☎ Harlech (0766) 780200

Closed 12 Jan—5 Feb

An attractive, Welsh, granite and slate country house has been sympathetically modernised to offer comfortable bedrooms, lounge and dining room; sound food can be enjoyed from a set-price menu.

14rm(11 1) CTV in all bedrooms **T**
sB&B£26 sB&B £28—£31
dB&B £56—£62
50P nc 7yrs *xmas*

International **V** Tea £1.20 Dinner £13.75—£15.75 Wine £5.50 Last dinner 9pm

Credit cards 1 3

TAL-Y-BONT (near Conway)
Gwynedd
Map **6** SH76

★★**Lodge** ☎ Dolgarrog (049269) 766

Single-storey accommodation is available behind the main hotel facilities, in this quiet Conwy valley village.

Annexe: 10⇌fi CTV in all bedrooms ®T sB&B⇌fi £25—£30 dB&B⇌fi £36—£40 B

30P ✿

British & French V Lunch £5.25—£8&alc Tea 50p Dinner £7—£11.50&alc Wine £4.50 Last dinner 9.30pm

Credit cards 1 2 3 5 Ⓥ

TAL-Y-LLYN
Gwynedd
Map **6** SH70

★★**Tyn-y-Cornel** ☎ Abergynolwyn (065477) 282

Closed Jan RS Dec

Delightful lakeside hotel where most rooms have beautiful views.

4rm(2⇌) Annexe: 12rm 11⇌1fi(4fb) CTV in all bedrooms ®T sB&B£20—£25 sB&B⇌fi £22—£26 dB&B£40—£48 dB&B⇌fi £44—£50 B

60P ✿ (heated) sauna bath solarium

English & Continental Lunch £4.75—£5.50 Tea 80p—£1 Dinner £9.50—£10&alc Wine £4.25 Last dinner 9.30pm

Credit cards 1 2 3 5 Ⓥ

★ **Minffordd**
(see red star box next column)

TAMWORTH
Staffordshire
Map **4** SK20

★★***Castle*** Ladybank ☎ (0827) 57181

Modern accommodation is offered in this hotel next to the historic castle.

25rm(7⇌18fi)(3fb) CTV in all bedrooms ®T B

CFA Disco 3 nights wkly

V Last dinner 10pm

Credit cards 1 2 3

TANGUSDALE
Isle of Barra, Western Isles *Inverness-shire*
See **Barra, Isle of**

★

★MINFFORDD, TAL-Y-LLYN

☎ Corris (065473) 665

Closed Jan & Feb RS Nov—Dec & Mar

At the foot of Cader Idris, this modest little stone building has a pleasing garden and a paddock. It is a cosy, comfortable little hotel that owes much of its welcome character to the good natured friendliness of the owners, Mr and Mrs Pickles, who often introduce their guests to one another so that a house party atmosphere can be achieved. There is no television, another aspect that adds to the general atmosphere of sociability. There are two sitting rooms and a sun lounge as well as the dining room. Jonathon Pickles, the son, cooks fresh and local food to produce enjoyable meals for the sensibly short menu, which changes daily. Bedrooms are comfortable and attractively decorated, and provided with radio, telephone and tea making facilities. Everything is spotlessly clean and highly polished. There are superb views and the hotel provides a haven for a relaxed stay or a centre for walking or sightseeing.

7rm(3⇌2fi)(1fb) ®T sB&B£26 dB&B£42 dB&B⇌fi £52 B

12P ✿ nc 3yrs *xmas*

Dinner £10.95alc Wine £5 Last dinner 8.30pm

Credit cards 1 3 5

TANGMERE
West Sussex
Map **4** SU90

✕**Old Timbers** Arundel Rd ☎ Chichester (0243) 773294

Wholesome, spicy simple fare is offered at this 18th-century timbered cottage restaurant, which has been extensively refurbished to provide an elegant atmosphere.

Closed Sun

English & Continental V 64 seats Lunch £5.75&alc Dinner £10.50&alc Wine £5.25 Last dinner 9.45pm 50P

Credit cards 1 3 5 Ⓥ

TAPLOW
Buckinghamshire
Map **4** SU98

★★**Taplow House**

Berry Hill ☎ Maidenhead (0628) 70056
Telex no 848522

Closed 24 Dec—1 Jan

27rm(12⇌15fi)(2fb) 1 CTV in all bedrooms ®T sB&B⇌fi £34—£43.50 dB&B⇌fi £44—£52.75 B

100P ✿ croquet archery

English & French V Lunch £6alc Tea £1.50alc High Tea £1.50alc Dinner £6alc Wine £4.75 Last dinner 9.45pm

Credit cards 1 2 3 5

○**Cliveden**
(see red star box overleaf)

T

○CLIVEDEN, TAPLOW

☏ Burnham (06286) 5069

21 bath

Now open

This hotel opened too late for us to properly inspect it before we went to print. However we have had a look at it and found it to be very special indeed. Now belonging to the National Trust, the house has been the centre of Britain's political and social life for 300 years. It is probably the grandest country house it is possible for the ordinary guest to stay at. In more than 400 acres of grounds bordered by the River Thames it is in the Georgian style and rebuilt by John Barry after a fire in 1850. The formal gardens with the notable parterre make the whole thing stunning. The interior is equally stunning. The panelled Great Hall with massive carved stone chimney piece and with elaborately carved staircase leads to the first floor bedrooms with handsome, arched doorcases. The elegant and ornate French dining room is in green and gilt with painted freeze, and the long dining room is beautifully proportioned and with elegant table appointments. There is a library and the boudoir, once that of Nancy Astor, is now a very pretty sitting room in the Wedgewood style. All, including the spacious bedrooms, have valuable antiques, suits of armour, portraits, photographs and other memorebilia as well as attractive flower arrangements and rich damask hangings and tapestries. Recreational facilities abound in or outside the hotel. Although very expensive, this hotel is a must for the collector of country houses. John Sinclair has come to run it after five years at the Lancaster in Paris and we know that he intends to achieve the highest standards; time will tell. He has gone some way to achieving this by engaging John Webber, ex Gidleigh Park, as chef and we know he cooks well. If you come down to breakfast rather than have it in your room, be prepared to eat it at a communal table in private house style.

TARPORLEY

Cheshire
Map **7** SJ56

★★ **B Willington Hall** Willington (3m NW off unclass rd linking A51 & A54 1m S of Kelsall) ☏ Kelsall (0829) 52321

Closed Xmas Day

This mock Elizabethan house, built in 1825, is set in parkland with excellent views. Comfortably furnished, it offers good home cooking.

10 bath (1fb) CTV in all bedrooms Ⓡ **T** sB&B bath £30.50 dB&B bath £48

60P 1 garage (hard) nc 5yrs

V Lunch £10alc Dinner £10alc Wine £3.90 Last dinner 9.30pm

Credit cards 1 2 3 5 Ⓥ

★***Swan*** 50 High St ☏ (08293) 2411

Closed Xmas

A friendly, unpretentious former Georgian coaching house.

9rm(1fb) TV in all bedrooms Ⓡ

CTV 35P

V Last dinner 9.15pm

Credit cards 1 2 3 5

TARBERT

Western Isles *Inverness-shire*
See **Harris, Isle of**

TARBERT Loch Fyne

Strathclyde *Argyllshire*
Map **10** NR86

★★★ *H* **Stonefield Castle** (Norscot/Clan) ☏ (08802) 836 Telex 776321

Closed Nov—Mar

In a quiet, secluded position, surrounded by fifty acres of beautiful grounds, the hotel combines the charm and character of a previous age with modern comforts.

33rm(28 bath 4 shower) CTV in all bedrooms Ⓡ **T** sB&B bath shower £27—£45 dB&B bath shower £44—£80 **B**

50P (heated) (hard) sauna bath solarium

Lunch fr £5 Dinner £15—£18 Wine £5.25 Last dinner 9pm

Credit cards 1 2 3 4 5 Ⓥ

❀★**West Loch** ☏ (08802) 283

Closed Nov

(Rosette awarded for dinner only.)

The small, roadside, family-run hotel has a reputation for producing fine, imaginative food. The style of cooking is international and the intentionally limited dinner menu, which is changed daily, features fresh local sea-food and game in season.

6rm(2fb) sB&B £20 dB&B £31 **B**

CTV 20P

European Bar lunch £9alc Tea £2.50alc Dinner £14.50 Wine £6 Last dinner 8.30pm

Credit card 1

TAUNTON

Somerset
Map **3** ST22

★★★★

❀★★★★CASTLE, TAUNTON

Castle Gn (Prestige) ☏ (0823) 72671 Telex no 46488

Last year we were hoping to see the award of a second rosette here but, alas, the chef, Christopher Oakes, left at the end of May to open his own restaurant. We wish him well. Otherwise the hotel is popular with our members for its friendly service and good food. The Chapman family continue to upgrade the bedrooms and the newest ones are very luxurious, comfortable and well equipped, with extras that include a miniature of sherry, flowers and magazines as well as good quality toiletries. Room service is proficient and smartly done. On the gound floor is the Rose Room which has a counter to serve as bar during opening hours; and there are other sitting areas for those who want to be quiet. There are some antiques, pictures and fresh flowers. Although the hotel is in the centre of a busy town, the entrance to the bow bar is from the street only, so the traffic does not impinge on the rest of the hotel. Once part of the Norman

Taunton Castle, archaeological ruins remain in the garden. Mr Prior is the Manager and he runs the hotel with quiet efficiency and makes sure his friendly staff do all they can to meet your needs.

35 bath shower (1fb) 5 CTV in all bedrooms **T** sB bath shower £48.50—£60.95 dB bath shower £81—£148.90 (room only) **B**

Lift 30P 10 garage (£3.50 per day) CFA Live music & dancing wknds *xmas*

English & French Lunch £8.50—£9.95&alc Tea £2alc Dinner £18.50&alc Wine £5 Last dinner 9pm

Credit cards 1 2 3 5

★★★**County** East St (Trusthouse Forte) ☏ (0823) 87651 Telex no 46484

Popular town centre hotel with well equipped bedrooms, extensive conference and banqueting facilities.

68rm(60 bath) CTV in all bedrooms Ⓡ sB&B £39.50 sB&B bath £47.50 dB&B £55.50 dB&B bath £63.50 **B**

Lift CTV 100P CFA *xmas*

Last dinner 9.30pm

Credit cards 1 2 3 4 5

★ ★ **Corner House** Park St ☎ (0823) 84683

Privately owned and run holiday hotel in a central situation.

30rm(20⋒)(5fb) CTV in all bedrooms ® ✗ sB&Bfr£25 sB&B⇌fr£30.70 dB&Bfr£45 dB&B⇌fr£45

CTV 38P ⇌

English & French **V** ☕ ⚡ Lunch £9alc Dinner £9alc Wine £3.50 Last dinner 9pm

Credit cards 1 2 3

Taunton

★ ★ *HB* **Falcon** Henlade (3m E A358) (ExecHotel) ☎ (0823) 442502

Closed 22 Dec—14 Jan

Small, informal hotel with comfortable, well appointed bedrooms with easy access to the motorway.

11rm(9⇌2⋒) 1 ⚡ in 3 bedrooms CTV in all bedrooms ® **T** ✗ S% sB&B⇌⋒£31—£35 dB&B⇌⋒£45—£49 B

25P ⇌ ✿ nc5yrs

☕ ⚡ S% Tea 50p Dinner £8.75alc Wine £4.25 Last dinner 8.30pm

Credit cards 1 3 V

★ ★ **St Quintin** Bridgwater Rd, Bathpool ☎ (0823) 59171

Small, comfortable and friendly, the family owned and run hotel has easy access to Junction 25 of the M5.

6rm(3⇌) Annexe: 4rm(3fb) CTV in all bedrooms ® **T** ✗ sB&B£15—£22 sB&B⇌£21.50—£27 dB&B£26—£38 dB&B⇌£31—£42 B

CTV 30P ⇌ ✿ →

T

🍷☕ Bar lunch £3.50alc Tea £1.50alc Dinner £3.50—£6.50&alc Wine £4 Last dinner 9pm

Credit cards 1 2 3 5 Ⓥ

✕✕Rajpoot Tandoori Corporation St ☎ (0823) 79300

The well-appointed and comfortable Indian restaurant features a good menu with curry and vegetarian dishes, all well cooked and presented. Friendly service is provided by waiters smartly clad in green Indian dress waistcoats.

Closed 25 Dec

🍽 Indian **V** 100 seats Lunch £10alc Dinner £10alc Wine £4.45 Last dinner mdnt 🅿 🚭

Credit cards 1 2 3

TAVISTOCK

Devon

Map **2** SX47

★★★Bedford Plymouth Rd (Trusthouse Forte) ☎ (0822) 3221

Built on the site of Tavistock Abbey, this hotel in traditional style has been upgraded over recent years to provide comfortable accommodation and attractive public rooms.

32rm(30🛁) CTV in all bedrooms Ⓡ sB&B🛁£45.50 dB&B🛁£63.50 Ⓑ

12P ✿ *xmas*

🍷☕ Last dinner 9pm

Credit cards 1 2 3 4 5

✕Hidden Table 67 West St ☎ (0822) 66520

Small intimate restaurant converted from terraced house with short choice of courses.

Lunch not served

🍽 Continental 30 seats ✱Dinner £13.50—£14.50 Wine £6 Last dinner 9.30pm 🅿 nc10yrs Live music Sat

Credit cards 1 2 3 5 Ⓥ

TAYNUILT

Strathclyde *Argyllshire*

Map **10** NN03

★★Brander Lodge Bridge of Awe (Consort) ☎ (08662) 243

Closed Jan—Feb

Small, comfortable family run Highland hotel with relaxing, friendly atmosphere.

20🛁(2fb) CTV in all bedrooms Ⓡ ✱ ✱sB&B🛁£21.50—£23.70 dB&B🛁£52—£57.20 Ⓑ

100P ✿ ♪ Live music & dancing Tue & Fri ♨ *xmas*

🍽 Scottish English & French **V** 🍷☕ 🚭 ✱Bar lunch £2.60—£4.50 Tea £1.95alc High Tea ££3.50alc Dinner £7.50—£9.50&alc Wine £3.82 Last dinner 9pm

Credit cards 1 3 4 Ⓥ

★★Polfearn (Consort) ☎ (08662) 251

RS Nov—Feb

Family-run, small granite hotel with gardens and a grazing field at the front.

16rm(2🛁12🚿)(2fb) Ⓡ sB&B£16—£18 sB&B🛁🚿£18—£20 dB&B£30—£34 dB&B🛁🚿£32—£36

CTV 30P 🚌 ✿ nc3yrs

V 🍷☕ Bar lunch £4—£8alc Tea £2.50alc High Tea £5alc Dinner £10alc Wine £4 Last dinner 9pm

TEBAY (WEST) SERVICE AREA

(M6 Motorway) Cumbria

Map **12** NY60

★★Tebay Mountain Lodge (Exec Hotel) ☎ Orton (05874) 351

There are lovely views of the Cumbrian mountains from this hotel, which lies between the Lake District and the Yorkshire Dales.

30🛁🚿(5fb) CTV in all bedrooms Ⓡ **T** S% sB&B🛁🚿£31—£35 dB&B🛁🚿£42—£48 Ⓑ

☾ # CTV 40P ✿

Continental V Lunch £4—£7 Tea £2 High Tea £3.75 Dinner £4.50—£6.50 Wine £2.75 Last dinner 9.30pm
Credit cards 1 2 3 5 V

TEDBURN ST MARY
Devon
Map **3** SX89

★★**King's Arms Inn** (06476) 224
Pleasant village-centre inn with a congenial atmosphere and a popular bar. It is conveniently located for the A30.
7rm(1)(1fb) CTV in all bedrooms ® sB&B£15.50 sB&B£17.50 dB&B£25 dB&B£29
CTV 52P
Lunch £4.85alc Dinner £5.65—£10.20 Wine £4.12 Last dinner 9.15pm
Credit cards 1 2 3 5

TEE-SIDE AIRPORT
Co Durham
Map **8** NZ31

★★★**St George** Middleton St George (Mount Charlotte) Darlington (0325) 332631 Telex no 58664
Modern hotel within airport complex.
59 CTV in all bedrooms ®
*sB&B fr£36.75 dB&B fr£47.25 B
150P 8 (£2 per night) CFA squash sauna bath solarium games room *xmas*
English & French V *Lunch fr£5.50&alc Tea fr75p High Tea fr£5.50 Dinner fr£8.50&alc Wine £5.35 Last dinner 10.15pm
Credit cards 1 2 3 5 V

TEIGNMOUTH
Devon
Map **3** SX97

★★★**London** Bank St (Exec Hotel) (06267) 6336
A town-centre inn has been modernised to offer popular bars, some leisure facilities and an open, roof-top swimming pool.
26rm(21 5)(12fb) 1 CTV in all bedrooms ® T sB&B £22—£28 dB&B £38—£45 B
Lift 8P CFA (heated) sauna bath solarium Disco twice wkly in season *xmas*
English & French Lunch £4.75—£6&alc Tea 60p—£3 High Tea £3.50—£5.50 Dinner £7.75—£8.75&alc Wine £4.40 Last dinner 10.30pm
Credit cards 1 2 3 5 V

★★*H* **Glendaragh** Barn Park Rd (06267) 2881
Closed 17 Oct—27 Mar
Originally the manor house, the hotel has tasteful, comfortable bedrooms and friendly, personal service.
16rm(13 1)(2fb) CTV in all bedrooms ® sB&B£17.50—£20 sB&B £17.50—£20 dB&B £35—£40 B
15P 1 games room
Bar lunch £1—£2.50 Dinner £8.50 Last dinner 8pm
Credit cards 1 3 V

★★**Venn Farm Country House** Higher Exeter Rd (Best Western) (06267) 2196 Telex no 42513
Peaceful countryside surrounds this Devon farmhouse.
10rm(8 2)(2fb) CTV in all bedrooms ® sB&B £27—£30 dB&B £42—£54 B
50P
English & Continental V Bar lunch £3—£8 Tea £2—£5 Dinner £9.50—£10.50&alc Wine £6 Last dinner 9pm
Credit cards 1 2 3 5 V

★**Bay** 15 Powderham Ter Sea Front (06267) 4123
Closed Dec—Mar
Hotel features comfortable lounge bar overlooking seafront lawns and tennis courts.
20rm(4 6)(5fb) CTV in all bedrooms ® S% sB&B£12—£13 sB&B £15—£17 dB&B£24—£26 dB&B £30—£34 B
CTV 16P *xmas*
V S% Lunch £4.50alc Tea 50palc High Tea 50palc Dinner £4.50alc Wine £4.15 Last dinner 7.30pm
Credit cards 2 3 5

★**Belvedere** Barnpark Rd (06267) 4561
Four-storey, detached building, dating from 1850, set in a quiet position.
13rm(1 4)(4fb) ® sB&B£10.50—£12.50 dB&B£21—£25 dB&B £24—£28 B
CTV 10P 1 *xmas*
V Lunch £4.50—£5.50 Tea £1.25—£1.50 High Tea £4.50—£6 Dinner £7.25 Wine £4.75 Last dinner 7.30pm
Credit card 1 V

★**Coombe Bank** Landscore Rd (06267) 2369
Central holiday hotel with warm welcome from young owners.
11rm(3)(2fb) ® *sB&B£10—£11.50 sB&B £11.50—£13 dB&B£20—£23 dB&B £21.50—£24.50 B
CTV 12P *xmas*
English & French *Bar lunch 50p—£1.80 Tea fr35p Dinner fr£6 Wine £3.80 Last dinner 7.30pm
Credit cards 1 3 V

★*B* **Drakes** 33 Northumberland Pl (06267) 2777
RS Nov
The running of this small, tastefully-appointed and comfortable hotel is personally supervised by the resident owners. An interesting choice of well-cooked food is available throughout the day in the Bistro Coffee Shop, and candlelit suppers are served in the exquisite restaurant.
6rm(1 2)(1fb) CTV in all bedrooms ® S% sB&B£11—£15 sB&B £13—£17 dB&B£21.20—£28 dB&B £25.20—£32 B
xmas
English & Continental V S% Lunch £3.55—£6.65&alc Tea 75—95p Dinner £4.60—£7.50&alc Wine £3.50 Last dinner 10pm
Credit cards 1 2 3

T

★**Glenside** Ringmoor Rd, Shaldon (1m S off A379) (Guest accom) ☎ Shaldon (0626) 872448

On the south bank of the Teign Estuary stands a cottage-style hotel which was built as a private residence in about 1820. Tastefully appointed in keeping with its style and character, it offers a warm welcome and provides a high standard of home cooking.

10rm(2➡7⋒)(3fb) 1⊟ CTV in all bedrooms Ⓡ✱sB&B£9—£12 dB&B£18—£24 dB&B➡⋒£21—£27 B

10P ✿ *xmas*

✱Bar lunch £4—£6&alc Tea fr40p Dinner £6.50—£7&alc Wine £4.75 Last dinner 7.30pm

Credit cards 1 3

✕✕**Minadab** 60 Dawlish Rd ☎ (06267) 2044

Small, friendly restaurant in a thatched cottage serving interesting dishes with a continental influence and using good raw ingredients.

Closed Sun & Mon (in winter) Lunch not served

French & Italian **V** 30 seats ✱Dinner £10.50&alc Wine £4.75 Last dinner 10pm 7P

Credit cards 1 2 3 5

TELFORD

Shropshire
Map **7** SJ60

★★★**Buckatree Hall** Ercall Ln, Wellington (Best Western) ☎ (0952) 51821 Telex no 35701

Closed 26—27 Dec

Large, secluded house standing in attractive and well-tended grounds at the foot of the Wrekin.

37➡(1fb) CTV in all bedrooms Ⓡ**T** sB&B➡fr£39.50 dB&B➡fr£48 B

☾120P ✿

English & French Lunch fr£7.50&alc Tea fr75p Dinner fr£7.50&alc Wine £4.95 Last dinner 10pm

Credit cards 1 2 3 5 Ⓥ

★★★**Telford Hotel Golf & Country Club** Great Hay, Sutton Hill (Queens Moat) ☎ (0952) 585642 Telex no 35481

Former home of Abraham Darby III, with many rooms looking down Ironbridge Gorge, hotel also has modern leisure complex.

58➡⋒(4fb) CTV in all bedrooms Ⓡ**T** S% ✱sB&B➡⋒£46—£53 dB&B➡⋒£56—£63 B

☾200P ✿ (heated) 18 squash snooker sauna bath *xmas*

V ✱Lunch fr£6.75&alc Tea fr£1.20 Dinner fr£8.50&alc Wine £5.95 Last dinner 10pm

Credit cards 1 2 3 5

★★**Charlton Arms** Wellington (GW Hotel) ☎ (0952) 51351 Telex no 629462

Old coaching inn with Georgian frontage.

27rm(21➡1⋒)(2fb) CTV in all bedrooms Ⓡ**T** S% sB&B£30—£32 sB&B➡⋒£33—£36 dB&B£40—£45 dB&B➡⋒£45—£48 B

☾75P

V S% Lunch £5.50—£13.50 Tea 50p Dinner £8—£13.50 Wine £5.75 Last dinner 9.30pm

Credit cards 1 2 3 5

★★**Falcon** Holyhead Rd, Wellington ☎ (0952) 55011

Closed Xmas

13rm(2➡3⋒)(1fb) sB&Bfr£21 sB&B➡⋒fr£24.50 dB&Bfr£26.50 dB&B➡⋒fr£32.50 B

CTV 30P nc 2yrs

V Bar lunch 70p—£5 Dinner £6.50—£11.50 Wine £4.85 Last dinner 9pm

Credit cards 1 3

★**White House** Wellington Rd, Donnington (off A518) ☎ (0952) 604276

25rm(10➡10⋒)(5fb) CTV in all bedrooms Ⓡ✱sB&B£18.50 sB&B➡⋒£28.50 dB&B£28.50 dB&B➡⋒£38.50 B

CTV 100P ✿

English & French **V** ✱Lunch £6.50&alc Tea 90p Dinner £9.50&alc Wine £4.50 Last dinner 9.30pm

Credit cards 1 3 Ⓥ

◯**Telford Moat House** Foregate, Telford Centre (Queens Moat) ☎ (0952) 506007

100➡⋒ Due to have opened July 1986

TEMPLE SOWERBY

Cumbria
Map **12** NY62

★★*HBL* **Temple Sowerby House** ☎ Kirkby Thore (07683) 61578

Closed 23 Dec—4 Jan & 1st 2 wks Feb

A charming and tastefully decorated Georgian house, retaining many original features in its elegant and comfortable rooms. The bedrooms are stylishly decorated and the finely furnished house is fresh with flowers.

8➡ Annexe: 4➡ 2⊟ CTV in all bedrooms Ⓡ**T** sB&B➡£30—£35 dB&B➡£44—£50 B

30P 1 ✿

Tea £1.50 Dinner £12—£13.50 Wine £5.50 Last dinner 9pm

Credit cards 1 2 3 Ⓥ

TENBY

Dyfed
Map **2** SN10

★★★**Imperial** The Paragon (Best Western) ☎ (0834) 3737

Traditional seaside hotel with historic perimeter walls.

46rm(36➡10⋒)(18fb) CTV in all bedrooms **T** sB&B➡⋒£25—£40 dB&B➡⋒£50—£80 B

Lift ☾ 16P 16 CFA games room Live music & dancing 4 nights wkly (in season) twice wkly (out of season) *xmas*

British, French & Italian **V** Lunch £6.25—£7.50 Tea 65p—£2.50 Dinner £11—£12.95&alc Wine £5.25 Last dinner 9.30pm

Credit cards 1 2 3 4 5 Ⓥ

★★*L* ***Atlantic*** The Esplanade ☎ (0834) 2881

The comfortable, traditional-style hotel commands fine views across the South Beach. Personally owned and managed, it promotes a high standard of hospitable service and good food; two character lounges offer a pleasant and relaxed atmosphere.

33rm(20➡4⋒)(7fb) CTV in all bedrooms Ⓡ**T** B

CTV 28P ✿ CFA *xmas*

Last dinner 8.30pm

Credit cards 1 3

★★**Fourcroft** The Croft ☎ (0834) 2886

Closed Nov—Etr

A hand-painted Roman scene is an interesting feature of the new, attractive, outdoor swimming pool of this newly-equipped hotel overlooking the harbour. Friendly service and a relaxed atmosphere will make your stay here a pleasant one.

38rm(36➡2⋒)(8fb) CTV in all bedrooms Ⓡ**T** sB&B➡⋒£19—£23 dB&B➡⋒£34—£42 B

Lift ✿ (heated)

British, French & Italian **V** Bar lunch 80p—£4 Tea 50p—£1.50 Dinner £9—£12&alc Wine £3.50 Last dinner 8pm

Credit cards 1 3 Ⓥ

★★***Royal Lion*** ☎ (0834) 2127

Closed mid Nov—mid Feb

There is now a sea-food bistro on the lower ground floor of this friendly, resort hotel overlooking the harbour.

36rm(14➡1⋒)(6fb) CTV in all bedrooms Ⓡ B

Lift

V Last dinner 10.30pm

Credit cards 1 3

★**Buckingham** The Esplanade (Minotel) ☎ (0834) 2622

Closed Dec—Feb

Friendly holiday hotel overlooking the beach and Caldey Island.

21rm(15➡2⌐)(4fb)CTV in all bedrooms ®sB&B➡⌐fr£18 dB&B➡⌐fr£36 B
P ⇆
British & Continental V Bar lunch fr£2.50 Dinner fr£7 Wine £4.25 Last dinner 8pm
Credit cards 1 2 3 5

★Croft ☎ (0834) 2576
Closed Nov—Mar
Traditional, informal, personally run, holiday hotel overlooking the harbour.
20rm(11➡)(3fb) ®S% sB&B£15—£16 sB&B➡£17—£18 dB&B£30—£32 dB&B➡£38—£40 B

Tenby

CTV 5P 2🚗(charge £1)
V S% Lunch £4alc Tea 50palc High Tea £2alc Dinner £7alc Wine £5 Last dinner 7.30pm
Credit cards 1 2 3 V

★ H Harbour Heights 11 The Croft
☎ (0834) 2132
Small comfortable hotel overlooking Carmarthen Bay and Tenby Harbour, offering commendable food standards.
9➡⌐(4fb) CTV in all bedrooms ® S% sB&B➡⌐£15—£20 dB&B➡⌐£30—£35 B
P ⇆ nc 8yrs *xmas*
English & French V S% Lunch £2.50—£5 Dinner £6.50—£7.50 Wine £3.50 Last dinner 7.15pm
Credit cards 1 2 3 5

T

TENTERDEN
Kent
Map **5** TQ83

★ ★ **White Lion** High St (Inter Hotel) ☎ (05806) 2921 Telex no 8950511

Comfortable hotel with modern bedrooms and popular bar and restaurant.

12rm(8)(2fb) 3 CTV in all bedrooms ® sB&B£26—£28.50 sB&B£30—£33.50 dB&B£36—£40 dB&B£42—£45 B

CTV 65P Live music & dancing Thu

English & French **V** Lunch £4.95—£8.95&alc Tea £1.75—£2.25 Dinner £8.50—£10.95&alc Wine £5.25 Last dinner 9.30pm

Credit cards 1 2 3 5 V

Tenterden — Tetbury

TETBURY
Gloucestershire
Map **3** ST89

★★★

★★★ **CALCOT MANOR, TETBURY**

Calcot (3m W at jct A4135/A46) (Pride of Britain) ☎ Leighterton (066689) 227

Closed 1st wk Jan

Barbara and Brian Ball's newish hotel has quickly made its mark with our members. They, their son and friendly staff create one of the most pleasant of atmospheres, friendly and considerate without being intrusive. The hotel is set in pleasant rolling countryside a few miles from Tetbury — still a good place for country furniture and clocks — and set in a quadrangle made up of the house and old farm buildings. There is a 14th century Tithe Barn built in Cotswold stone, but the house is 15th century. The Balls have converted it beautifully with attractive colour schemes. The reception rooms offer plenty of space and comfort in which to relax and are refreshingly light, with some nice pieces of furniture, pictures, flowers, games and magazines. The restaurant is in salmon pink and green overlooking the garden. It has good table appointments and elbow chairs, and is candle lit. It is a delightful room in which to partake of the enjoyable cooking of a four course, fixed price meal. Good ingredients are used and

the standard of cooking is near rosette. Bedrooms are individually decorated, some are very stylish, and are very comfortable. Several have antiques, and all have flowers, mineral water and superior quality toiletries.

7 Annexe: 3 1 CTV in all bedrooms **T** S% sB&B£45—£65 dB&B£65—£110 B

50P 6 CFA (heated) croquet nc 12yrs *xmas*

English & French S% *Lunch £8.50—£12.50 Tea £1—£2.50 Dinner £15.50—£18.50 Wine £5.50 Last dinner 9.30pm

Credit cards 1 2 3 5

★ ★ ★ **Hare & Hounds** (Best Western) ☎ Westonbirt (066688) 233

A traditional country hotel in 9 acres of grounds close to the magnificent Westonbirt Aboretum.

23rm(19)(2fb) CTV in all bedrooms ® **T** S% sB&B£34—£42 dB&B£48—£56 B

50P 4(£1 per night) (hard) squash *xmas*

English & Continental S% Lunch £7&alc Tea 75p&alc Dinner £11—£12&alc Wine £4.50 Last dinner 9pm

Credit cards 1 2 3 V

★ ★ ★ *HBL* **Snooty Fox** Market Pl (Best Western) ☎ (0666) 52436 Telex no 449848

Honey coloured Cotswold stone building facing the old Market Hall, this popular hotel has been ambitiously refurbished to a high standard. The bedrooms are individually designed while the oak panelled restaurant provides a delightful setting for the excellent food.

12rm(11 1) 1 CTV in all bedrooms ® **T** sB&B£42.50—£48.50 dB&B£57.50—£80 Continental breakfast B

P *xmas*

Lunch £9.50—£11.50&alc Tea £1—£3 Dinner £11.50&alc Wine £5.75 Last dinner 9.30pm

Credit cards 1 2 3 5

★ ★ **Close** 8 Long St ☎ (0666) 52272 Telex no 43232

A 16th-century wool merchant's house with a walled garden, offering comfortable bedrooms and good service.

12rm(10 2)(2fb) 1 CTV in all bedrooms ® **T** S% *sB&B£32—£45 dB&B£48—£74 Continental breakfast B

12P *xmas*

T

Ⓖ International V ⓥ ☕ ✱ Lunch fr£7.85&alc Tea £2alc Dinner fr£14.75&alc Wine £5.40 Last dinner 9.45pm

Credit cards 1 2 3 5

✕ **Hubbits** 7 New Church St ☎ (0666) 53306

A terraced cottage of Cotswold stone has been converted to create a cosy, friendly and homely restaurant with a small aperitif bar at the rear. Good quality, fresh produce is used to create sound English meals.

Closed Mon & 2 wks Jan Dinner not served Sun

V 30 seats Lunch £3.75—£7&alc Dinner £9.75&alc Wine £4.75 Last dinner 9.30pm ℙ

Credit cards 1 2 3

TETFORD

Lincolnshire
Map **8** TF37

★ **White Hart** ☎ (065883) 255

Closed Xmas

Cosy 16th-century inn associated with Tennyson, in peaceful village.

6rm ® ✈ sB&B£16 dB&B£24 Ɓ

CTV 30P

Ⓖ English & French **V** Bar lunch £3.60alc Dinner £8alc Wine £3.25 Last dinner 9.30pm

Credit cards 1 3

Tetbury — Tewkesbury

TEWKESBURY

Gloucestershire
Map **3** SO83

★★★ **Bell** Church St (Best Western) ☎ (0684) 293293 Telex no 43535

Comfortable, traditional hotel dating from Elizabethan times with well appointed bedrooms and attractive new restaurant.

25rm(23⇌2⋒) 2⊟ CTV in all bedrooms ® ✱ sB&B⇌⋒£43—£46 dB&B⇌⋒£59.50—£63 Ɓ

☾ CTV 50P CFA *xmas*

Ⓖ English & French **V** ⓥ ☕ ✱ Bar lunch £1.95—£6 Tea 75p—£3.50 High Tea £3.50—£6 Dinner £11.50—£14.50&alc Wine £7 Last dinner 9.15pm

Credit cards 1 2 3

★★★ **Royal Hop Pole Crest** Church St (Crest) ☎ (0684) 293236 Telex no 437176

Attractive hotel with comfortable bedrooms and courtyard garden.

29rm(27⇌2⋒)(2fb) 1⊟ ⁄ in 3 bedrooms CTV in all bedrooms ® **T** S% ✱ sB&B⇌⋒£50.85—£60.85 dB&B⇌⋒£68.70—£78.70 Ɓ

☾ 40P CFA *xmas*

V ⓥ ☕ ⁄ ✱ Lunch £7.90&alc Tea £1.50 Dinner £11.50&alc Wine £6.25 Last dinner 9.30pm

Credit cards 1 2 3 4 5

★★★ **Tewkesbury Park Golf & Country Club** Lincoln Green Ln (Whitbread) ☎ (0684) 295405 Telex no 43563

Modern comfortable hotel with extensive leisure facilities.

82⇌ CTV in all bedrooms ® **T** sB&B⇌£49—£52 dB&B⇌£57—£68 Ɓ

☾ CTV 180P CFA ✿ (heated) 18 squash snooker sauna bath solarium gymnasium Disco Thu (Sep—Mar) *xmas*

Ⓖ English & French **V** ⓥ ☕ Lunch £7.50—£8.50&alc Tea £1.50—£2 High Tea £2—£2.50 Dinner £11—£15&alc Wine £6.95 Last dinner 9.30pm

Credit cards 1 2 3 5 Ⓥ

★★ *B* **Tudor House** High St ☎ (0684) 297755

Character hotel of historic interest sensitively upgraded to offer modern facilities.

16rm(8⇌4⋒)(1fb) 1⊟ CTV in all bedrooms ® **T** ✈ ✱ sB&B£24 sB&B⇌⋒£30—£33 dB&B£34 dB&B⇌⋒£44—£60 Ɓ

CTV 22P ✿ →

V ♡ ☕ ✱ Lunch £8.25—£8.95 Tea 75p Dinner £8.25—£8.95&alc Wine £3.80 Last dinner 9pm

Credit cards 1 2 3 5

✕ **Telfords** 61 High St ☎ (0684) 292225

A welcoming restaurant in a colourful Georgian building in the High Street. There is a comfortable lounge and a pretty dining room, where imaginative dishes are cooked to order from fresh produce.

Closed Sun, 26 Dec, 1 Jan & mid wk Feb & Nov Lunch not served Mon & Sat (except by prior arrangement)

English & French V 30 seats ✱ Lunch £6.95&alc Dinner £11.50alc Wine £4.45 Last dinner 11pm

Credit cards 1 2 3 V

THAKEHAM (near Storrington)
West Sussex
Map **4** TQ11

★★★ ***H* Abingworth Hall** Storrington Rd ☎ West Chiltington (07983) 3636 Telex no 877835

This charming country hotel, situated on the Sussex Downs, is surrounded by well-kept gardens which include a natural lake. It provides comfortable bedrooms complemented by elegant public rooms, and service is warm and hospitable. The food shows a French influence and is particularly honest and full of flavour, though comparatively plain.

23rm(22 1) CTV in all bedrooms T sB&B £42—£70 dB&B £55—£78 B

35P 1 (charge) (heated) (hard) croquet pitch & putt boule nc 10yrs *xmas*

English & French ♡ ☕ Lunch £10—£11.50&alc Tea £2.50 Dinner £16.50&alc Wine £6 Last dinner 9.30pm

Credit cards 1 2 3 4 5 V

Tewkesbury — Thirsk

THAME
Oxfordshire
Map **4** SP70

★★★ ***H* Spread Eagle** Cornmarket ☎ (084 421) 3661

Closed 29 & 30 Dec

A very special hotel with warm hospitality and modern bedrooms.

26 (1fb) CTV in all bedrooms T S% sB&B £39.75—£42 dB&B £51—£53 Continental breakfast B

100P CFA *xmas*

English & French V ♡ ☕ S% Lunch £9.40—£10.75&alc Tea £1.20—£1.50 High Tea £5.50—£7.50 Dinner fr£10.70&alc Wine £5.15 Last dinner 9.30pm

Credit cards 1 2 3 5

THETFORD
Norfolk
Map **5** TL88

★★★ **Bell** King St (Trusthouse Forte) ☎ (0842) 4455 Telex no 818868

This 15th century coaching house has been carefully converted to an elegant, comfortable hotel.

46 (1fb) 1 CTV in all bedrooms ® sB&B £47.50 dB&B £65.50 B

65P *xmas*

♡ ☕ Last dinner 10pm

Credit cards 1 2 3 4 5

★★ **Historical Thomas Paine** White Hart St (Best Western) ☎ (0842) 5631

Partly Georgian hotel, reputed to be the birthplace of Thomas Paine, a famous son of Thetford.

14rm(7 7)(1fb) 1 CTV in all bedrooms ® T sB&B £28.50—£32.50 dB&B £37.50—£41.50 B

30P

V ♡ ☕ Lunch £5.60—£6.60&alc Tea 80p—£1 Dinner £8.75—£9.75&alc Wine £6 Last dinner 9.30pm

Credit cards 1 2 3 5 V

THIRLSPOT
Cumbria
Map **11** NY31

★★ ***Kings Head*** ☎ Keswick (0596) 72393

RS Nov—Mar

Attractively situated at the foot of Helvellyn, on the A591, the 17th century coaching inn retains many of its former charactéristics, despite modernisation.

13rm(6)(3fb) CTV in all bedrooms ® B

60P

♡ Last dinner 9pm

THIRSK
North Yorkshire
Map **8** SE48

★★ **Golden Fleece** Market Pl (Trusthouse Forte) ☎ (0845) 23108

Historic, ivy-clad coaching inn in the market square.

22rm(6) CTV in all bedrooms ® sB&B £39.50 sB&B £47.50 dB&B £55.50 dB&B £63.50 B

50P *xmas*

♡ ☕ Last dinner 9pm

Credit cards 1 2 3 4 5

★★ **Three Tuns** Market Pl ☎ (0845) 23124

A three-storey coaching inn situated in the market square.

13rm(6 1)(2fb) CTV in all bedrooms ® S% ✱ sB&B £25—£27.50 sB&B £32 dB&B £36 dB&B £36—£41 B

20P 3 (£1 per night) *xmas*

♡ Lunch £5.25 Dinner £8.50alc Wine £4.50 Last dinner 9.30pm

Credit cards 1 2 3 5 V

★ ***H* Sheppard's** Church Farm, Front St, Sowerby ☎ (0845) 23655

A charming conversion of old farm buildings has formed a hotel set round a cobbled courtyard in a quiet village; thoughtfully managed by the proprietor, it serves a particularly good dinner.

3 Annexe: 3rm(2fb) CTV in 3 bedrooms Ⓡ ✱sB&B£15 sB&B £25 dB&B£20 dB&B £32

35P ❁ *xmas*

✱Dinner £6.25—£8.75&alc Wine £4.95 Last dinner 10pm

Credit cards 1 2 3

THORNBURY
Avon
Map **3** ST69

❀★★★ **Thornbury Castle**
(see red star box)

See advertisement on page 710

THORNE
South Yorkshire
Map **8** SE61

★★**Belmont** Horsefair Gn ☎ (0405) 812320

Conversion of a detached house near the centre of this quiet market town, and close to the M18 motorway.

22rm(8 4)(2fb) CTV in 12 bedrooms TV in 1 bedroom Ⓡ in 12 bedrooms **T** sB&Bfr£17 sB&B fr£27 dB&Bfr£29 dB&B fr£38

CTV 20P ♿

English & French **V** Lunch fr£5.50&alc Tea fr75p Dinner fr£5.50&alc Wine £4 Last dinner 9pm

Credit cards 1 3 Ⓥ

See advertisement on page 710

★★★

❀★★★ THORNBURY CASTLE, THORNBURY

(Prestige) ☎ (0454) 418511
Telex no 449986

Closed 5 days Xmas

Pass through the meticulously cared for vineyard to this part-ruined but romantic castle dating from the 15th century. It was owned by Henry VIII who stayed there with Anne Boleyn and Mary Tudor also lived there for some years. As we go to press, we learn that the hotel has been sold. We hope, however, that standards will be maintained. Stone mullion windows with some bays, flagstone floors, panelling, beams, carved chimney pieces, heraldic shields and open fireplaces all contribute to the baronial atmosphere. Paintings, antiques and flowers abound, the decor is attractive and the seating comfortable. The upper floors contain the sensitively converted bedrooms which vary in size but nevertheless have most attractive soft furnishings, are comfortable and well equipped. Colin Hingston is the chef who produces the excellent dishes for the sensibly sized menu, using fresh raw materials of fine quality. With the outstanding, long wine list featuring items at not unreasonable cost you will be able to choose something to complement your meal. The staff, some of long service, are proficient and provide friendly and attentive service.

12 3 CTV in all bedrooms **T** S% sB&B £50.50—£57.75 dB&B £74—£170 Continental breakfast

40P ❁ nc12yrs

English & French S% Lunch fr£13.50 Dinner £22.50alc Wine £5.25 Last dinner 9.30pm

Credit cards 1 2 3 4 5

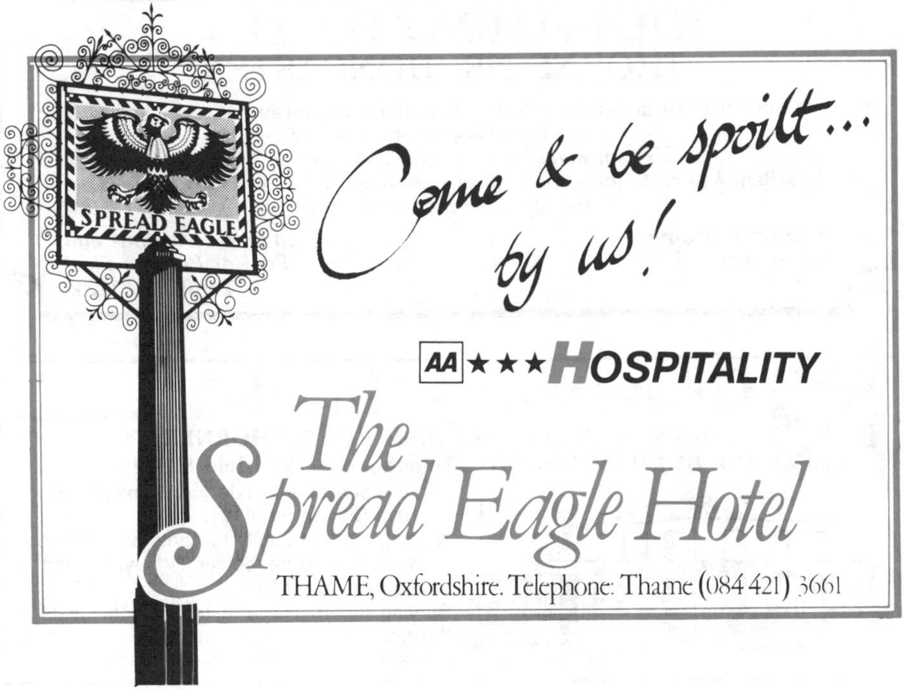

T

THORNHILL
Dumfries & Galloway *Dumfriesshire*
Map **11** NX89

★★**Buccleuch & Queensberry**
☎(0848) 30215

Traditional country town hotel in central position.

11rm(4🛁1🚿)(2fb) ®S% sB&Bfr£17.50 sB&B🛁🚿fr£22 dB&Bfr£32 dB&B🛁🚿fr£38

CTV 25P 4🚗(£1)

♉ ☕ Bar lunch £3.50alc Tea fr55p High Tea £4.75alc Dinner fr£9&alc Wine £4 Last dinner 8pm

Credit cards 1 3

Thornhill — Thornley

★★**Trigony House** Closeburn (2m S off A76) ☎ Closeburn (08484) 211

Attractive and pleasantly appointed country mansion close to, but screened by trees from A76.

6rm(1🛁2🚿) Annexe: 3rm(1fb) ® sB&B£14—£17.50 sB&B🛁🚿£20.50—£24 dB&B£21—£26 dB&B🛁🚿£29.50—£34 ℗

CTV 40P 2🚗✿🐎

V ♉ ☕ Bar lunch £3.25alc Tea £1.20alc High Tea £3.75alc Dinner £7.50&alc Wine £4.50 Last dinner 8.45pm

Ⓥ

THORNLEY
Co Durham
Map **8** NZ33

★★**Crossways** Dunelm Rd (5m SE of Durham City) ☎ Wellfield (0429) 821248

Modern proprietor-run hotel just outside the village, with good restaurant offering value for money.

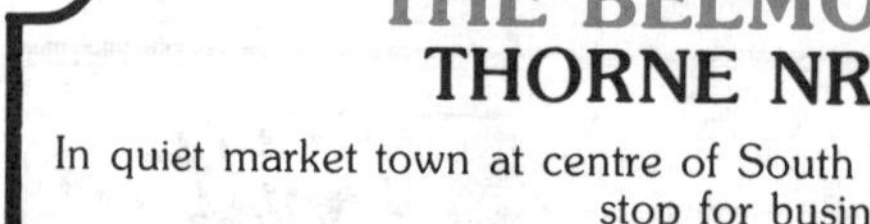

12rm(4🛁8🚿) CTV in all bedrooms ®✈ sB&B🛁🚿£22—£27 dB&B🛁🚿£31—£38 ℗

200P ✿ Disco Fri Live music & dancing Sat
English & French V Lunch £7.50&alc Tea £3.50 High Tea £6.50 Dinner £7.50&alc Wine £5.50 Last dinner 9.45pm
Credit cards 1 2 3 5 V

THORNTHWAITE
Cumbria
Map **11** NY22

★★**Swan** ☎ Braithwaite (059682) 256
Closed Nov—Etr
A 17th-century inn amid fine mountain scenery overlooking Lake Bassenthwaite with Skiddaw in the background.
14rm(3 5) CTV in 8 bedrooms S% sB&B£11.10—£13 sB&B £14.25—£16.35 dB&B£22.20—£26 dB&B £28.50—£32.70 B
CTV 60P 3 (£1.50 per night) ✿
Bar lunch 80p—£5.25 Tea 55p—£1.20 Dinner £9 Wine £4.20 Last dinner 8.30pm
Credit cards 1 3 V

★★**Thwaite Howe** ☎ Braithwaite (059682) 281
Closed 6 Nov—14 Mar
Victorian villas on the edge of a forest built for the owners of the local lead mines.
8 TV in all bedrooms R sB&B £26 dB&B £42
10P ✿ nc 12yrs
English & Continental Lunch £6 Tea 75p Dinner £8.50 Wine £4.50 Last dinner 7.30pm

THORNTON
Fife
Map **11** NT29

★**Crown** 7 Main St ☎ Glenrothes (0592) 774416
The informal, friendly, commercial hotel has a restaurant which lies separate from, and behind, the main building.
11rm(3) CTV in all bedrooms R sB&B£17 sB&B £19 dB&B£29 dB&B £32 B
CTV 150P *xmas*
V ✻Lunch £2.60—£4&alc Tea 85p High Tea £4—£7&alc Dinner £6—£9&alc Wine £3.95 Last dinner 7pm
V

THORNTON
West Yorkshire
Map **7** SE03

XX**Cottage** 869 Thornton Rd ☎ Bradford (0274) 832752
A large, half-timbered roadside building offers good car parking, and a spacious restaurant where heavy beams and low lighting create an old world atmosphere. Extensive international à la carte and table d'hôte menus feature local game and fresh fish, and service is courteous, both here and in the well-appointed cocktail lounge.
Closed Sun Lunch not served Sat
French 80 seats ✻Lunch £11.50alc Dinner £11.50&alc Last dinner 10.15pm
60P
Credit cards 1 2 3 5 V

THORNTON CLEVELEYS
Lancashire
Map **7** SD34

XX***Victorian House*** Trunnah Rd ☎ Blackpool (0253) 860619
The owner of this excellent restaurant on the Fylde is fascinated by the Victorian era, and guests enjoy a traditional welcome and good food in a setting like something from a Dickens novel. Well-prepared dishes, based on the best produce available, are served by young girls in Victorian dresses.
Closed Sun Lunch not served except by prior arrangement.
40 seats Last dinner 9pm 20P

X**River House** Skippool Creek, Thornton-Le-Fylde (2m E A585) ☎ Blackpool (0253) 883497
Elegantly furnished, friendly restaurant beside River Wyre, renowned for high standard of cooking. All meals cooked individually and must be ordered in advance.
International V 40 seats ✻Lunch £16—£20alc Dinner £16—£20&alc Wine £4.50 Last dinner 9.30pm 20P
Credit cards 1 2 V

THORNTON DALE
North Yorkshire
Map **8** SE88

★***New Inn*** Pickering Rd ☎ Pickering (0751) 74226
Closed Nov—Feb
The New Inn stands at the centre of the village. It is dated at around 1600. Although small it offers homely comforts.
6rm(1fb) R
CTV 7P
Last dinner 9pm

THORNTON HOUGH
Merseyside
Map **7** SJ38

★★★***Thornton Hall*** Neston Rd ☎ 051-336 3938
There are some attractive bedrooms in the main building of this hotel, originally a private residence, whilst others are contained in a modern annexe set in a pleasant garden.
38 CTV in all bedrooms R T B
200P CFA ✿ Live music & dancing Fri
French V
Credit cards 1 2 3 4 5

THORNTON WATLASS
North Yorkshire
Map **8** SE28

★***Buck Inn*** ☎ Bedale (0677) 22461
Village inn overlooking the cricket ground on the green.
6rm R
CTV P Live music & dancing Sat nc5yrs
V Last dinner 9.45pm

THORPE (DOVEDALE)
Derbyshire
Map **7** SK15

★★★***Izaak Walton*** (1m W on Ilam rd) ☎ Thorpe Cloud (033529) 261
A much extended 18th-century farmhouse enjoying excellent views of Dovedale.
33(3fb) 2 CTV in all bedrooms T B
100P ✿ Live music & dancing Sat *xmas*
English & French V Last dinner 9.15pm
Credit cards 1 2 3 5

★★★**Peveril of the Peak** (Trusthouse Forte) ☎ Thorpe Cloud (033529) 333
Much extended and modernised old house with splendid views.
41(7fb) CTV in all bedrooms R sB&B £48 dB&B £65.50 B
100P CFA ✿ (hard) *xmas*
Last dinner 9.15pm
Credit cards 1 2 3 4 5

THORPE BAY
Essex
See **Southend-on-Sea**

THORPE-LE-SOKEN
Essex
Map **5** TM12

XX**Henry House** High St ☎ Clacton-on-Sea (0255) 861616
In this pleasantly decorated restaurant with old beams, the menu includes interesting fish dishes, attractively presented and using good, fresh ingredients.
Closed Mon Lunch not served Tue—Sat Dinner not served Sun
V 40 seats Bar lunch £5alc Dinner £13alc Wine £4.75 Last dinner 9.30pm 25P
Credit cards 1 3

XX**Thorpe Lodge** Landermere Rd ☎ Clacton-on-Sea (0255) 861509
A converted farmhouse in rural surroundings provides some bedroom accommodation and two homely dining rooms. It is a family concern, where the accent is on home cooking using fresh, local produce; service is caring and the atmosphere relaxing.
V 56 seats Lunch £8.50—£12.50&alc Dinner £8.50—£12.50&alc Wine £5.10 Last dinner 9.15pm 25P
Credit cards 1 3 5 V

T

THORPE MARKET
Norfolk
Map **9** TG23

★★ ***Elderton Lodge*** ☎ Southrepps (026379) 547

Friendly, comfortable hotel standing in 6 acres of peaceful grounds.

7rm(3)(4fb) CTV in all bedrooms ®
30P 2 *xmas*

English & Continental **V** Last dinner 9.30pm

Credit cards 1 3

THORVERTON
Devon
Map **3** SS90

★ **Berribridge House** ☎ Exeter (0392) 860259

Small cottage hotel, run by the owners, with a warm, friendly atmosphere and an attractive restaurant.

6rm(4) CTV in all bedrooms
sB&B£20—£25 sB&B£24—£29
dB&B£54—£60 dB&B£68—£75

12P

English & French **V** Tea £1.50—£2.50 Dinner £10&alc Wine £5 Last dinner 9pm

Credit cards 1 3

THREE COCKS
Powys
Map **3** SO13

★ *L* **Three Cocks** ☎ Glasbury (04974) 215

Closed Jan

(*Rosette awarded for dinner only*)

The attractive, stone-built hotel stands near the smal village of Three Cocks, providing a good standard of cuisine and courteous, friendly service by the proprietor and his wife. Food is imaginatively prepared, using fresh ingrediets wherever possible; vegetables are particularly good, being fresh and attractively presented. Your meal may be chosen from the fixed-price, four-course menu, or from an à la carte selection which changes monthly to include seasonal produce where possible.

7rm(1fb) sB&B£18 dB&B£36
CTV 40P *xmas*

Belgian Lunch £15 Dinner £15 Wine £4.60 Last dinner 9pm

Credit cards 1 3 V

THRESHFIELD
North Yorkshire
Map **7** SD96

★★★ **Wilson Arms** (Consort)
☎ Grassington (0756) 752666 Telex no 57515

Closed Jan RS Feb

Large hotel in its own grounds on the edge of the village.

28(3fb) CTV in all bedrooms ® **T**
sB&B£32—£40 dB&B£46—£56
Lift CTV 50P 3(charge) *xmas*

V Lunch £6.50—£7.50&alc Tea £1—£2&alc High Tea £5alc Dinner £10.95&alc Wine £5.95 Last dinner 9.30pm

Credit cards 1 2 3 5 V

THURLESTONE
Devon
Map **3** SX64

★★★★ **Thurlestone**
☎ Kingsbridge (0548) 560382

Spacious hotel, built, owned and managed by the Grose family for 90 years, which has fine country and sea views.

68rm(653)(13fb) CTV in all bedrooms **T** sB&B£30—£60
dB&B£60—£120
Lift 100P 30 CFA
(heated)& (hard) squash snooker sauna bath solarium gymnasium badminton Disco Sat, Cabaret twice wkly (in season) *xmas*

T

🍷French **V** ☕ 🍽 Lunch £6&alc Tea 70p—£2.50 Dinner £15&alc Wine £6.50 Last dinner 9pm

Credit cards 1 2 3 5

★ ★ *H* **Furzey Close** ☎ Kingsbridge (0548) 560333

Closed Nov—Etr

The well-furnished hotel has a relaxing, country house atmosphere. Offering friendly service and commendable food standards, it provides cosy bedrooms, comfortable lounges and dining room, and a fine sheltered garden.

10rm(5🛁2🚿)(2fb) CTV in all bedrooms Ⓡ ✱sB&B£12—£17.50 dB&B£13—£19.50 dB&B🛁🚿£15.50—£21.50 B

14P 🚫 ✿ nc 8yrs *xmas*

S% ☕ 🍽 Tea fr £1 Dinner fr £8.50&alc Wine £4.95 Last dinner 8.30pm

Ⓥ

THURSO

Highland *Caithness*
Map **15** ND16

★ ★ **Pentland** Princes St ☎ (0847) 63202

Popular commercial and tourist hotel near town centre.

57rm(17🛁9🚿)(3fb) **T** in 9 bedrooms sB&B£13.50—£20 sB&B🛁🚿£18.50—£30 dB&B£27—£30 dB&B🛁🚿£34—£39

☾ CTV P

Thurlestone — Tintagel

V ☕ 🍽 Lunch £3.50alc Tea £1alc High Tea £5alc Dinner £6.50alc Wine £4.10 Last dinner 8.30pm

★ ***St Clair*** Sinclair St ☎ (0847) 63730

Friendly, comfortable town centre hotel.

27rm(2🛁4🚿)(3fb) CTV in all bedrooms **T**
☾ CTV 6🚗 Disco Fri Live music & dancing Sat *xmas*

V ☕ 🍽 Last dinner 9pm

TIDEFORD

Cornwall
Map **2** SX35

✕✕ **Heskyn Mill** ☎ Landrake (075538) 481

This picturesque restaurant is housed in a converted cornmill which retains all the original machinery and stands in its own grounds by the river. Personally-run, it offers a warm and friendly atmosphere, and the staff's attractive uniforms are matched by the table linen. The dining room is situated on the first floor and provides an ideal setting for an intimate dinner; the short menu of freshly-prepared dishes makes effective use of local and seasonal produce.

Closed Sun & Mon

🍷English & French **V** 50 seats ✱Lunch £17alc Dinner £17alc Wine £4.95 Last dinner 9.45pm 25P

Credit cards 2 3

TINTAGEL

Cornwall
Map **2** SX08

★ ★ *H* **Atlantic View** Treknow
☎ Camelford (0840) 770221

Closed Oct—Mar

Small, comfortable, family hotel in a prominent position with good sea views.

10rm(8🛁2🚿)(3fb) 3🛏 Ⓡ S% sB&B🛁🚿£19.65—£26.65 dB&B🛁🚿£29.30—£36 B

CTV 16P 🚫 ✿ ▭(heated) solarium nc6yrs

🍷English & French ☕ 🍽 S% Bar lunch £2—£2.80 Tea £1.50—£2 Dinner £8.50—£9.50 Wine £5.70 Last dinner 8pm

Credit cards 1 2 3 5

★ ★ **Bossiney House** ☎ Camelford (0840) 770240

Closed 4 Oct—Etr

Modern holiday hotel in its own grounds, with sea views.

20rm(11🛁6🚿)(1fb) Ⓡ sB&B£20—£24 sB&B🛁🚿£21.50—£25.50 dB&B£31—£35 dB&B🛁🚿£34—£38 B

→

CTV 30P ⛟ ✽ ▭(heated) sauna bath solarium putting

♡ ☕ Bar lunch £2—£3.50 Tea 60p Dinner £8.50 Wine £4.50 Last dinner 8pm

Credit cards 2 5

TINTERN
Gwent
Map **3** SO50

★★**Beaufort** (Embassy) ☎ (02918) 777

Small hotel overlooking Tintern Abbey.

24rm(17➡7⋔)(2fb) CTV in all bedrooms ®**T** S% ✻sB&B➡⋔fr£35 dB&B➡⋔fr£50 **B**

100P ✽ ♪ games room *xmas*

♛English & French **V** ♡ ☕ S% ✻Bar lunch 95p—£7.50 Tea 80p—£1.50 Dinner £9.50—£18 Wine £4.45 Last dinner 9pm

Credit cards 1 2 3 4 5 Ⓥ

★★**Royal George** ☎ (02918) 205

Traditional hotel a few minutes' walk from the river.

5rm(1➡) Annexe: 14➡⋔(13fb) CTV in all bedrooms ®**T** sB&B£25—£27.50 sB&B➡⋔£27.50—£29.50 dB&B➡⋔£40—£45 **B**

30P ⛟ ✽ Live music & dancing Fri mthly *xmas*

♛English & French **V** ♡ ☕ Lunch £6.50—£7.50 Tea £1.60—£2 Dinner £9.75—£10.50&alc Wine £3.75 Last dinner 9.30pm

Credit cards 1 2 3 Ⓥ

TISBURY
Wiltshire
Map **3** ST92

✕**Garden Room** 2—3 High St ☎ (0747) 870907

A friendly restaurant with effectively simple decor serving excellent food, prepared with skill and care by the chef. There is also a well chosen wine list.

Closed Mon & 2 wks Feb
Lunch not served Sat
Dinner not served Sun

♛English & Continental 30 seats Lunch ££7.50 Dinner £14.50 Wine £6 Last dinner 10pm **P**

Credit cards 1 3 Ⓥ

TITCHWELL
Norfolk
Map **9** TF74

★★**Manor** (Best Western)
☎ Brancaster (0485) 210221

Comfortable and friendly family hotel facing the bird watching area of the salt marshes.

7rm(4➡1⋔) Annexe: 3➡(2fb) CTV available in bedrooms ® sB&B£22—£26.50 sB&B➡⋔£25—£28.50 dB&B£41—£47 dB&B➡⋔£44—£50

CTV 50P ⛟ ✽ Live music & dancing mthly *xmas*

V ♡ ☕ Lunch £6.10 Tea 70p—£1.05 Dinner £10.35&alc Wine £5.40 Last dinner 9.30pm

Credit cards 1 2 3 5

TIVERTON
Devon
Map **3** SS91

★★★**Tiverton** Blundells Rd ☎ (0884) 256120 Telex no 42551

Modern, privately-owned and run, purpose-built hotel, ideal for tourists and business people.

29➡⋔(29fb) CTV in all bedrooms ®**T** sB&B➡⋔£23—£27 dB&B➡⋔£36—£42

☾ 100P CFA *xmas*

♛English & French **V** ♡ ☕ Lunch £6.50alc Tea 60palc Dinner £8.95alc Wine £5.25 Last dinner 9.15pm

Credit cards 1 2 3 5 Ⓥ

★★**Hartnoll Country House** Bolham (1½m N on A396) ☎ (0884) 252777

Georgian house in its own grounds, with busy bars and varied styles of bedrooms.

10rm(8➡)(3fb) 1▣ CTV in all bedrooms ® S% sB&B£15—£20 sB&B➡£20—£25 dB&B£25—£30 dB&B➡£35—£40

☾ 100P ✽ Live music & dancing Sat ♘ *xmas*

V ♡ ☕ ✻Lunch £3.50—£8.50&alc Tea fr55p High Tea fr£1.50 Dinner fr£3.50&alc Wine £4 Last dinner 10pm

Credit cards 1 2 3 5

✕✕**Henderson's** 18 Newport St
☎ (0884) 254256

An attractive, double-fronted restaurant near the market features a welcoming, low-seated area. The table d'hôte dinner menu represents good value, a short à la carte selection offers fish, when available, and the wine list is extensive.

Closed Sun, Mon, 1 wk Xmas & 3 wks Aug

♛English, French & Italian **V** 50 seats ✻Lunch £5—£8alc Dinner fr£10.50&alc Wine £4 Last dinner 9.30pm **P**

Credit cards 1 2 3 5

TOBERMORY
Island of Mull, Strathclyde, *Argyllshire*
See **Mull, Isle of**

TODMORDEN
West Yorkshire
Map **7** SD92

★★**Queen** Rise Ln ☎ (070681) 2961

The Victorian railway hotel stands opposite the station, to which it was originally joined by an overhead walkway; it provides well-equipped bedrooms and a smart restaurant.

6rm(4⋔) 1▣ CTV in all bedrooms ® ✈ sB&B fr£16 sB&B⋔£20—£24 dB&B fr£30 dB&B⋔£38—£45 **B**

CTV 10P 2⌂ Live music & dancing Sun

♛English & American **V** ♡ Bar lunch £3.55—£4.45 Dinner £8.50alc Wine £4.60 Last dinner 10.30pm

Credit cards 1 2 3 5 Ⓥ

TOMINTOUL
Grampian *Banffshire*
Map **15** NJ11

★★**Richmond Arms** ☎ (08074) 209

This old-fashioned, friendly, fishing hotel offers a limited dinner menu of honest, home-cooked dishes.

27rm(9➡)(7fb) ® ✻sB&B fr£11.50 sB&B➡fr£13 dB&B fr£23 dB&B➡fr£26 **B**

CTV 18P 2⌂ ✽ ♪ Live music & dancing Sat

V 🏆 ☕ ✱Lunch fr£4 Tea fr£1.10 High Tea fr£3.90 Dinner fr£8.50 Wine £2.95 Last dinner 9pm

★**Gordon Arms** The Square ☎ (08074) 206

Situated in the village square with views of the surrounding hills.

35rm(5🛁2🚿)(5fb) ® sB&B£14.50—£15.75 dB&B£29—£31 dB&B🛁🚿£33—£35.50

CTV P ♪ *xmas*

V 🏆 ☕ Lunch £5—£6 Tea 75—85p High Tea £4—£4.75 Dinner £8.50—£9.50 Wine £4.20 Last dinner 8pm

Credit cards 1 3 Ⓥ

TONBRIDGE
Kent
Map **5** TQ54

★ ★**Rose & Crown** High St (Trusthouse Forte) ☎ (0732) 357966

An historic posting & coaching house, with modern well equipped bedrooms particularly in the original building.

52🛁(1fb) 1 CTV in all bedrooms ® sB&B🛁£48.50 dB&B🛁£66.50 B

☾ 62P CFA ✿ *xmas*

🏆 ☕ Last dinner 10pm

Credit cards 1 2 3 4 5

TONGUE
Highland *Sutherland*
Map **14** NC55

★ ★**Tongue** (Inter Hotel) ☎ (084755) 206 Telex no 837495

Closed Nov—24 Mar RS 25 Mar—Apr & 27 Sep—Oct

The friendly, family-run hotel provides specific facilities for fishing and offers a good selection of well-prepared local products in its comfortable dining room.

20rm(14🛁)(1fb) in 6 bedrooms CTV in all bedrooms ® T ✱sB&B£21.45 sB&B🛁🚿£26.45 dB&B£32.90 dB&B🛁🚿£42.90 B

CTV 36P ✿ ♪ Live music & dancing Fri mthly

International V 🏆 ☕ ✱Lunch £2—£4.25 Tea 70p Dinner £8.95&alc Wine £5.25 Last dinner 8.30pm

Credit cards 1 2 3 5 Ⓥ

Tomintoul — Torquay

★**Ben Loyal** ☎ (084755) 216

RS Nov—Mar

Small, friendly family run tourist hotel.

13rm(6🛁6🚿) Annexe: 6rm sB&B£14.50 sB&B🛁🚿£19.50 dB&B£28.40 dB&B🛁🚿£39 B

CTV 18P

V 🏆 ☕ Bar lunch £3.25alc Tea 90palc Dinner £9 Wine £3.50 Last dinner 7.45pm

Credit cards 2 3

TORBAY
Devon
See under **Brixham**, **Paignton** and **Torquay**

TORCROSS
Devon
Map **3** SX84

★**Grey Homes** ☎ Kingsbridge (0548) 580220

Closed Nov—Mar

Modestly-appointed, family-run hotel occupying a superb position looking down on beach.

6rm(3🛁)(1fb) ® ✱sB&B£14—£15 sB&B🛁£16—£17 dB&B£28—£30 dB&B🛁£32—£34

CTV 15P 3🚗(charged) ✿

🏆 ☕ ✱Tea fr£1 Dinner fr£7 Wine £3.70 Last dinner 7.30pm

TORMARTON
Avon
Map **3** ST77

★ ★**Compass Inn** (Inter Hotel) ☎ Badminton (045421) 242

Closed 24—26 Dec

Old, family-run inn offering modern facilities.

19rm(14🛁1🚿)(6fb) CTV in all bedrooms ® T sB&Bfr£27.95 sB&B🛁🚿fr£34.95 dB&Bfr£39.95 dB&B🛁🚿fr£49.95 B

160P 1🚗 ✿

V 🏆 Bar lunch fr£5 Dinner £12alc Wine £5.60 Last dinner 9.30pm

Credit cards 1 2 3 5

TORPHINS
Grampian *Kincardineshire*
Map **15** NJ60

★ ★**Learney Arms** ☎ (033982) 202

A friendly, family-run hotel offers spacious bedrooms, comprehensive bar meals and a small, attractive, à la carte restaurant.

10rm(2🛁2🚿)(1fb) TV in 4 bedrooms ® ✱sB&B£14 sB&B🛁🚿£19 dB&B£28 dB&B🛁🚿£33 B

CTV P ✿ shooting

🏆 ☕ ✱Lunch £5alc Dinner £7.50 Wine £4.25 Last dinner 9.30pm

Credit cards 1 2 3

TORQUAY
Devon
Map **3** SX96
See Central & District plans

★ ★ ★ ★ ★**Imperial** Park Hill Rd (Trusthouse Forte) ☎ (0803) 24301 Telex no 42849 Central plan **18** *F1*

The spacious hotel, overlooking the town from its elevated position, provides a well-appointed restaurant and public rooms, together with an excellent new health and beauty centre. Most of the bedrooms have been refurbished to a very high standard, and service is pleasant and courteous.

167🛁(7fb) CTV in all bedrooms T sB&B🛁£72 dB&B🛁£124 B

Lift ☾ CTV 200P 60🚗 CFA ✿ (heated) & (heated) (hard) squash sauna bath solarium gymnasium *xmas*

🏆 ☕ Last dinner 9.30pm

Credit cards 1 2 3 4 5

See advertisement on page 718

T

T

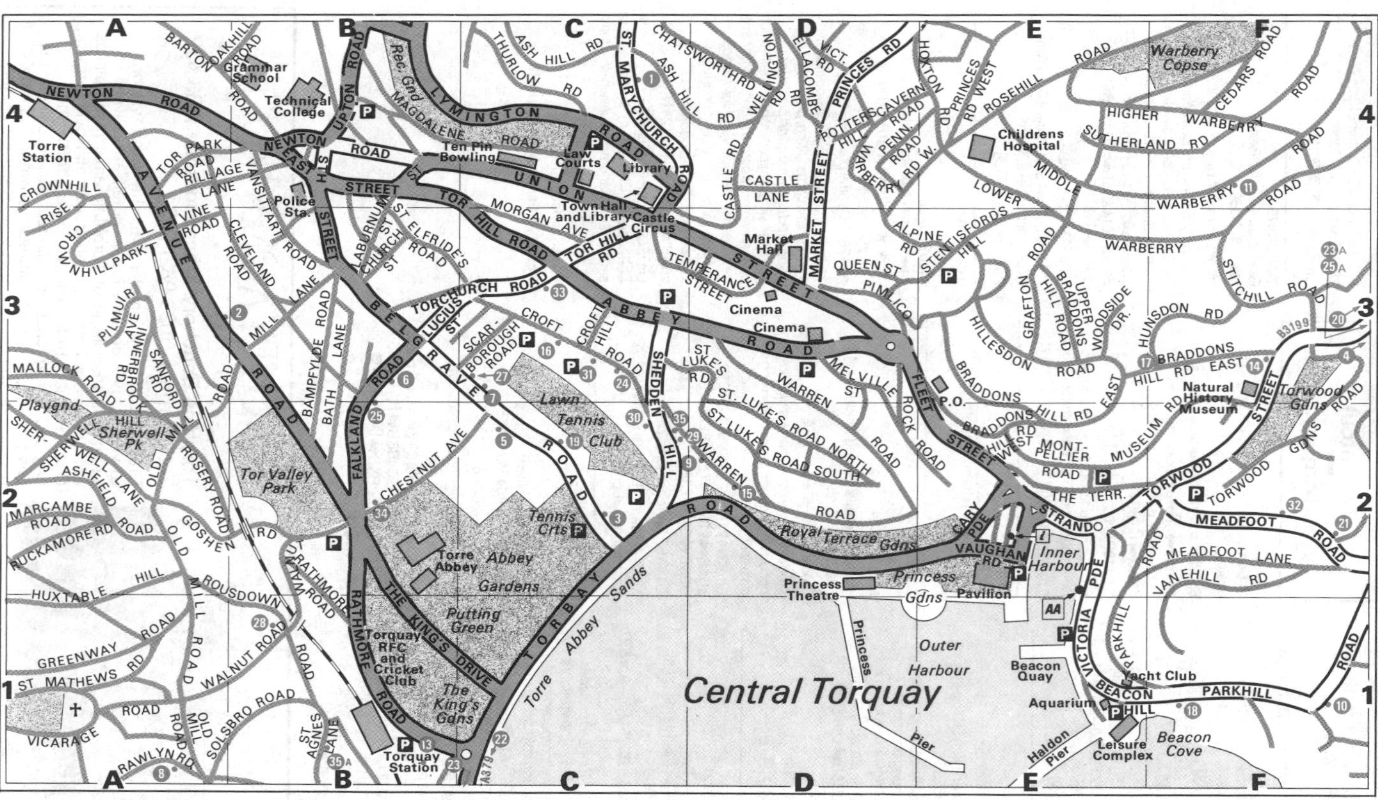
Central Torquay
Outer Harbour
Inner Harbour
Beacon Quay
Beacon Cove
Haldon Pier
Princess Pier
Princess Theatre
Princess Gdns
Pavilion
Aquarium
Leisure Complex
Yacht Club
Royal Terrace Gdns
Torre Abbey Sands
Torre Abbey
Torre Abbey Gardens
Putting Green
Tennis Crts
Lawn Tennis Club
The King's Gdns
Torquay RFC and Cricket Club
Torquay Station
Torre Station
Tor Valley Park
Sherwell Hill Pk
Playgnd
Rec. Gnd
Ten Pin Bowling
Law Courts
Library
Town Hall and Library
Castle Circus
Market Hall
Cinema
P.O.
Police Sta.
Technical College
Grammar School
Childrens Hospital
Warberry Copse
Natural History Museum
Torwood Gdns
Vicarage
NEWTON ROAD
AVENUE ROAD
TORBAY ROAD
ABBEY ROAD
FLEET STREET
UNION STREET
TOR HILL ROAD
BELGRAVE ROAD
FALKLAND ROAD
RATHMORE ROAD
THE KING'S DRIVE
SHEDDEN HILL
ST. MARYCHURCH ROAD
LYMINGTON ROAD
MAGDALENE ROAD
MARKET STREET
TORWOOD STREET
VICTORIA PDE
MEADFOOT ROAD
PARKHILL ROAD
CARY PDE
VAUGHAN RD
STRAND
THE TERR.
MONT-PELLIER ROAD
MUSEUM RD
BRADDONS HILL RD EAST
BRADDONS HILL RD WEST
HUNSDON RD
STITCHILL ROAD
WARBERRY ROAD
LOWER WARBERRY ROAD
MIDDLE WARBERRY ROAD
HIGHER WARBERRY ROAD
CEDARS ROAD
ROSEHILL ROAD
PRINCES RD
ELLACOMBE RD
WELLINGTON RD
CASTLE RD
CASTLE LANE
ASH HILL RD
THURLOW RD
CHATSWORTH RD
HOXTON RD
PIMLICO
QUEEN ST
ALPINE RD
STENTIFORDS HILL
GRAFTON ROAD
HILLESDON ROAD
UPPER BRADDONS HILL ROAD
WOODSIDE DR.
ROCK ROAD
MELVILLE ST
WARREN ROAD
ST. LUKE'S ROAD NORTH
ST. LUKE'S ROAD SOUTH
TEMPERANCE STREET
CROFT ROAD
CROFT HILL
SCARBOROUGH ROAD
LUCIUS ST
TORCHURCH ROAD
ST ELFRIDE'S ROAD
CHESTNUT AVE
BATH LANE
BAMPFYLDE ROAD
MILL LANE
CLEVELAND ROAD
VANSITTART ROAD
EAST STREET
UPTON ROAD
BARTON ROAD
OAKHILL ROAD
TOR PARK ROAD
VINE ROAD
HILLPARK
CROWNHILL RISE
PILMUIR AVE
INNERBROOK RD
SANFORD RD
ROSERY ROAD
OLD MILL ROAD
GOSHEN RD
ROUSDOWN ROAD
WALNUT ROAD
SOLSBRO ROAD
ST AGNES LANE
RAWLYN RD
ST MATHEWS RD
GREENWAY ROAD
HUXTABLE HILL
RUCKAMORE RD
MARCAMBE ROAD
ASHFIELD ROAD
SHERWELL LANE
MALLOCK ROAD
MEADFOOT LANE
VANEHILL RD
BEACON HILL
A379
B3199

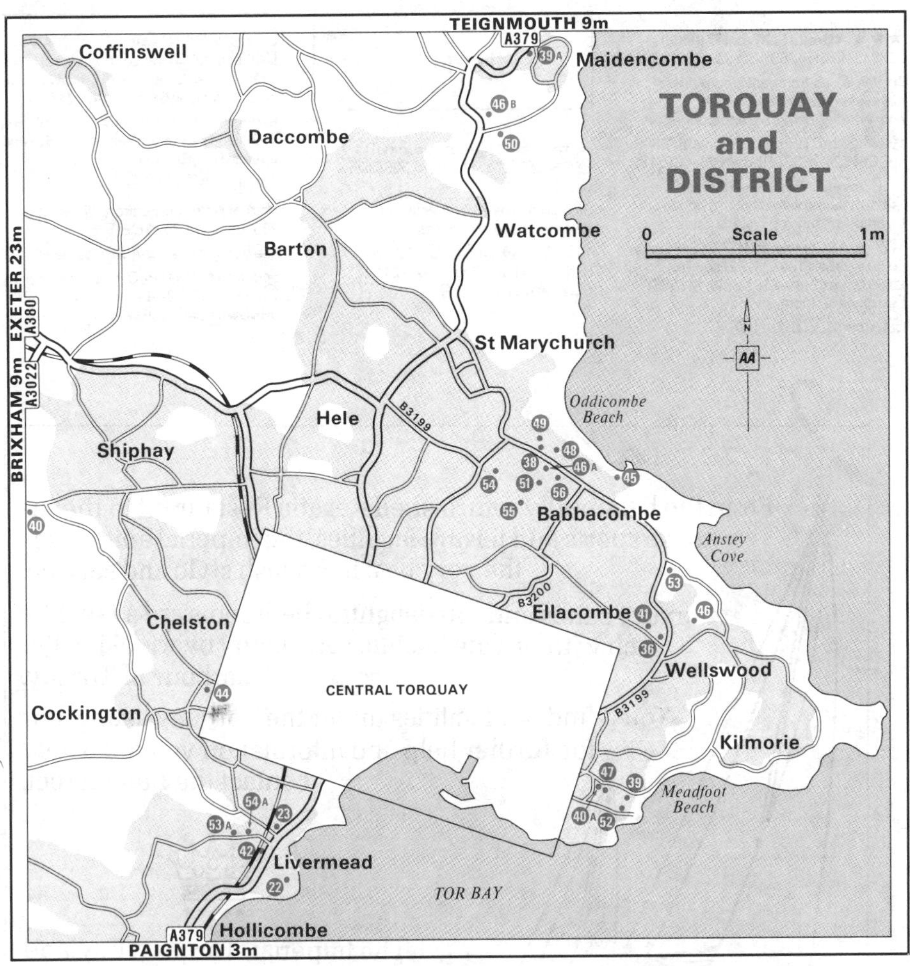

Torquay District

36	Ansteys Lea ★★
38	Ashley Rise ★
39	Hotel Balmoral ★★
39A	Bowden Close ★★
40	Brigantine Manor ★★
40A	Clevedon ★★
41	Coppice ★★
42	Corbyn Head ★★★
44	Fairmount House ★
45	Glen ★★
46	Gleneagles ★★★
46A	Green Mantle ✕✕
46B	Maidencombe House ★★★
47	Meadfoot Bay ★★
48	Morningside ★
49	Norcliffe ★★
50	Orestone House ★★
51	Oswald's ★★★
52	Overmead ★★★
53	Palace ★★★★
53A	Panorama ★
54	Penrhyn ★★
54A	Sunleigh ★
55	Sunray ★★
56	Viscount ★★

Torquay Central

1	Albaston ★★
2	Bancourt ★★
3	Belgrave ★★★
4	Burlington ★★
5	Bute Court ★★
6	Carlton ★
7	Cavendish ★★
8	Chelston Towers ★★
9	Conway Court ★★
10	Devonshire ★★★
11	Fonthill ★★
13	Grand ★★★★
14	Gresham Court ★★
15	Homers ★★★
16	Howden Court ★★
17	Hunsdon Lea ★★
18	Imperial ★★★★★
19	Kistor ★★★
20	Lansdowne ★★
21	Lincombe Hall ★★★
22	Livermead Cliff ★★★
23	Livermead House ★★★
23A	Lisburne ✕
24	Hotel Nepaul ★★★
25	Nethway ★★
25A	Old Vienna ✕
27	Rainbow House ★★★
28	Red House ★★
29	Roseland ★★
30	Shedden Hall ★★
31	Shelley Court ★
32	Sydore ★★
33	Templestowe ★★
34	Toorak ★★★
35	Vernon Court ★★
35A	Windsurfer ★

T

★★★★**Grand** Sea Front ☎ (0803) 25234 Telex no 42891 Central plan **13** *B1*

This large, sea-front, family hotel offers friendly service and features the comfortable Boaters bar and lounges.

109🛁(20fb) CTV in all bedrooms Ⓡ **T** S% sB&B🛁£24—£52 dB&B🛁£48—£104 **B**

Lift ☾ 35⌂ CFA ✽ ▭ & ≈ (heated) ✂(hard) sauna bath solarium gymnasium Live music & dancing Wkly ☃ *xmas*

♁English & Continental **V** ♁ ☕ S% Lunch £6.50—£9&alc Tea £1—£2 High Tea £3.50 Dinner £11—£12&alc Wine £5.50 Last dinner 9.30pm

Credit cards 1 2 3 5 Ⓥ

Torquay

★★★★**Palace** Babbacombe Rd ☎ (0803) 22271 Telex no 42606 District plan **53**

Standing in some 20 acres, this hotel offers extensive sporting facilities.

141rm(112🛁29🚿)(10fb) CTV in all bedrooms **T** sB&B🛁🚿£37—£41 dB&B🛁🚿£74—£82 **B**

Lift ☾ CTV 100P 40⌂(charged) CFA ✽ ▭(heated) & ≈ (heated) ⛳ ✂(hard) squash billiards sauna bath Disco wkly Live music & dancing 5 nights wkly ☃ *xmas*

♁English & French **V** ♁ ☕ Lunch fr£7 Tea fr£2 High Tea fr£4.50 Dinner fr£12.50 Wine £6 Last dinner 9.15pm

Credit cards 1 2 3 5

★★★**Belgrave** Seafront ☎ (0803) 28566 Central plan **3** *C2*

Sea front hotel next to Abbey gardens.

54rm(50🛁4🚿)(12fb) CTV in all bedrooms Ⓡ sB&B🛁🚿£22—£28 dB&B🛁🚿£44—£56 **B** →

T

T

Lift ☾ 80P 6🚗(50p per day) CFA ⇶ ✽ ⛵ (heated) Live music & dancing twice wkly (Jun—Sep) *xmas*

🍽 English & French 🍷 ☕ Bar lunch £2—£6 Tea fr60p Dinner £7—£8 Wine £5.10 Last dinner 8.30pm

Credit cards [1] [2] [3] [5]

★★★**Corbyn Head** Torquay Rd, Sea Front, Livermead ☎ (0803) 213611 District plan **42**

Large, modernised hotel with an attractive exterior.

50rm(47🛁3🚿)(4fb) 6⇶ CTV in all bedrooms ® sB&B🛁🚿£26—£36 dB&B🛁🚿£52—£72 **B**

☾ 50P CFA ⇶ ⛵ (heated) *xmas*

🍽 English & French **V** 🍷 ☕ Bar lunch £3.50—£10 Tea £3.50—£4.50 Dinner £10.50—£13&alc Wine £7.50 Last dinner 9pm

Credit cards [1] [2] [3] [5] Ⓥ

Torquay

★★★***Devonshire*** Parkhill Rd ☎ (0803) 24850 Telex no 42712 Central Plan **10** *F1*

Large detached hotel with pleasant garden, set in a quiet position.

54rm(27🛁6🚿) Annexe: 12rm(10🛁2🚿) (9fb) CTV in all bedrooms **B**

☾ CTV 50P 3🚗 CFA ✽ ⛵ (heated) 🎾(hard) Cabaret wkly 👶 *xmas*

🍽 English, French, German & Italian **V** 🍷 ☕ Last dinner 8.45pm

Credit cards [1] [2] [3] [5]

★★★**Gleneagles** Asheldon Rd, Wellswood ☎ (0803) 23637 District plan **46**

Closed Nov—Etr

All rooms have balconies in this attractive, modern-style hotel which stands in a quiet location with magnificent wooded views towards Ansteys Cove. The tastefully-appointed interior offers a high degree of comfort.

41rm(38⇥3⋒)(6fb) CTV in all bedrooms sB&B⇥⋒£18—£26 dB&B⇥⋒£34—£50 Ᵽ

CTV 30P ✽ ⛵ (heated) solarium Live music & dancing Mon & Fri (in season) ♔

⊖French **V** ♕ ☕ Lunch £6—£7.50 Tea 65—75p High Tea £4—£5 Dinner £8.50—£9.50 Wine £4.80 Last dinner 8pm

Credit cards 2 3 5 Ⓥ

Torquay

★★★*HBL* **Homers** Warren Rd ☎ (0803) 213456 Central plan **15** *D2*

Closed Jan—9 Feb

Delightful hotel above Tor Bay, with panoramic views, Andre and Helen Bissonette provide it with a gracious country house atmosphere. The tastefully furnished lounges overlook the terraced gardens, and the bedrooms are individually decorated and very well equipped. The very attractive restaurant provides imaginative dishes combined with a very good wine list.

15rm(13⇥2⋒)(2fb) 1⊟ CTV in all bedrooms **T** ✱sB&B⇥⋒£30—£38 dB&B⇥⋒£56—£80 Ᵽ

5P ⊞ ✽ nc 9yrs *xmas*

⊖English & French ♕ ☕ ⚡ ✱Lunch fr£8.95 Tea fr£1.50 Dinner £9.95—£13.50&alc Wine £5.95 Last dinner 8.30pm

Credit cards 1 2 3 5 Ⓥ

★★★*HL* **Kistor** Belgrave Rd (Inter Hotel) ☎ (0803) 212632 Central plan **19** *C2*

Commercial and tourist hotel close to the beach, affording personal attention.

52rm(51⇥1⋒)(14fb) CTV in all bedrooms **T** S% sB&B⇥⋒£20—£35 dB&B⇥⋒£36—£54 Ᵽ

Lift CTV 40P CFA ✽ ⊡ (heated) sauna bath solarium gymnasium Disco wkly Live music & dancing wkly *xmas*

⊖English & Continental **V** ♕ ☕ S% Lunch £4.30—£6.45 Tea 75p High Tea £1.50—£3.50 Dinner £8—£9 Wine £4.30 Last dinner 8.30pm

Credit cards 1 2 3 5 Ⓥ

See advertisement on page 722

★★★**Lincombe Hall** Meadfoot Rd ☎ (0803) 213361 Central plan **21** *F2*

Large detached Victorian-style building, ¼m from the beach and the town centre.

44rm(28⇥3⋒)(6fb) 1⊟ CTV in 43 bedrooms Ⓡ in 43 bedrooms **T** ✱sB&B⇥⋒£22.50—£24.50 dB&B⇥⋒£45—£49

☾ CTV 50P CFA ✽ ⛵ (heated) ⚲(hard) sauna bath solarium croquet putting Disco wkly in season Live music & dancing wkly in season Cabaret wkly in season ♔ *xmas*

V ♕ ☕ ⚡ ✱Lunch fr£4.95 Tea fr£1.50 Dinner fr£8.50 Wine £4.50 Last dinner 8.30pm

Credit cards 1 2 3 5 Ⓥ

T

Torquay

★★★*HL* **Livermead Cliff** Torbay Rd (Best Western) ☎(0803) 22881 Telex no 42918 Central & District plan **22**

Castlellated three-storey red stone building whose grounds are enclosed by a sea wall. (Sports facilities at nearby hotel 'Livermead House' available to guests).

64rm(54⇌10⋒)(21fb) CTV in all bedrooms ®**T** S%
sB&B⇌⋒£23—£32.50
dB&B⇌⋒£45—£63 **B**

Lift ☾ CTV 60P 12⌂ CFA ✿ ⩯(heated) ⌡ solarium Live music & dancing twice wkly in summer Cabaret Xmas ⌂ *xmas*

☕English & Continental **V** ♀ ☕ S% Lunch £5.25—£6.50&alc Tea £1 Dinner £8.75—£9&alc Wine £5.20 Last dinner 8.30pm

Credit cards 1 2 3 5 Ⓥ

★★★*H* **Livermead House** Torbay Rd (Best Western) ☎(0803) 24361 Telex no 42918 Central & District plan **23**

Attractive hotel facing the sea with bright public rooms, good sporting facilities and friendly staff.

67rm(56⇌11⋒)
Annexe: 2rm(1⇌1⋒)(10fb) CTV in all bedrooms ®**T** S%
sB&B⇌⋒£23—£31.50
dB&B⇌⋒£45—£61 **B**

Lift ☾ CTV 120P 5⌂ ✿ ⩯(heated) ♤(hard) ⌡ squash snooker sauna bath solarium gymnasium hairdressing salon

T

Live music & dancing twice wkly in summer, Etr & Xmas Cabaret Xmas ♿ *xmas*

English & Continental **V** S% Lunch £5.25—£6.50&alc Tea £1 Dinner £8.75—£9&alc Wine £5.20 Last dinner 8.30pm

Credit cards 1 2 3 5 V

★★★***Maidencombe House*** Teignmouth Rd, Maidencombe ☎ (0803) 36611 District plan **46B**

RS Xmas

Spacious hotel with well equipped bedrooms and modern open-plan lounge.

21rm(14 bath)(5fb) CTV in all bedrooms ® **B**

☾ CTV 100P ❋ (heated) billiards Live music & dancing Sat

English & French

Credit cards 1 3

★★★*HL* **Hotel Nepaul** Croft Rd ☎ (0803) 28457

Soundly-appointed hotel in a good position with fine views.

39rm(34 bath 5 shower)(6fb) 2 CTV in all bedrooms ® **T** sB&B £18.50—£26 dB&B £37—£52 **B**

Lift ☾ CTV 22P 5 ❋ (heated) (hard/grass) snooker Live music & dancing 2 nights wkly *xmas*

Torquay

English & French **V** Lunch fr£5.25 Tea fr£1.25 Dinner fr£9.50&alc Wine £4.50 Last dinner 9pm

Credit cards 1 2 3 5

★★★**Oswald's** Palermo Rd, Babbacombe ☎ (0803) 39292 District plan **51**

The many spacious rooms of this hotel and its proximity to the downs and beaches make it ideal for family holidays.

52rm(23 bath 21 shower)(3fb) CTV in all bedrooms ® ✱ sB&B £11.03—£16.07 sB&B £12.88—£17.92 dB&B £22.06—£32.14 dB&B £25.76—£35.84

Lift ☾ CTV 30P ❋ *xmas*

✱ Lunch fr£3.95 Tea fr35p Dinner fr£6.45 Last dinner 8.30pm

Credit cards 1 3 V

See advertisement on page 724

★★★***Overmead*** Daddyhole Rd (Consort) ☎ (0803) 27633 District plan **52**

Closed Dec—Feb except Xmas

Stone-built, split level hotel with a modern wing extension set in a quiet position.

62rm(39 bath 9 shower)(10fb) CTV in 10 bedrooms ® **B**

Lift ☾ CTV 6P 20 ❋ (heated) billiards Live music & dancing 3 nights wkly *xmas*

Last dinner 8.30pm

Credit cards 1 2 3 5

★★★**Rainbow House** Belgrave Rd ☎ (0803) 213232 Central plan **27** *C3*

Modern soundly appointed hotel near the sea front.

100rm(92 bath 8 shower)(15fb) CTV in all bedrooms ® **T** S% ✱ sB&B £25—£29 dB&B £44—£52

Lift ☾ CTV 100P CFA ❋ & (heated) (hard) squash snooker sauna bath solarium gymnasium Live music & dancing nightly Cabaret Fri & Sat *xmas*

International S% Lunch £4.50—£6 Dinner £8.50—£10.50&alc Wine £4.95 Last dinner 8.45pm

Credit cards 1 2 3 5

See advertisement on page 725

★★★*L* **Toorak** Chestnut Av ☎ (0803) 211866 Central plan **34** *B4*

Well run, quiet hotel with lounges and recreational facilities.

31rm(28 bath) Annexe: 10rm(9 bath)(19fb) CTV in all bedrooms **T** S% sB&B £21.50—£38 dB&B £43—£76 **B** →

T

☾CTV 60P CFA ✽ ⛆ (heated) ⚲(hard) snooker Disco wkly in season Live music & dancing wkly in season ⌂ *xmas*

♉English & French **V** ♆ ⛾ S% Lunch fr£5.50 Tea fr£1.50 Dinner fr£9.75&alc Wine £4.25 Last dinner 9.30pm

Credit cards 1 3

★★**Albaston** 27 St Marychurch Rd ☏(0803) 26758 Central plan **1** *C4*

Closed Dec

Small family-run hotel, occupying a main road position, ½m from the town centre.

12rm(1🛁5⋔)(4fb) TV available in bedrooms ®S% ✱sB&B£9—£11

sB&B🛁⋔£11—£13 dB&B£18—£22 dB&B🛁⋔£22—£26 B

CTV 12P ⇄ ⌂

♉English & French **V** ♆ ⛾ S% Lunch £1.75—£8&alc Tea 70p—£1.50 High Tea £1—£1.50 Dinner £6.50—£10&alc Wine £4.75 Last dinner 10pm

Credit cards 1 3 Ⓥ

Torquay

★★**Ansteys Lea** Wellswood ☏(0803) 24843 District plan **36**

Relaxed informal restaurant with French cuisine and good wine.

26rm(4🛁4⋔)(8fb) CTV in 8 bedrooms ® S% sB&B£11—£14.50 sB&B🛁⋔£13—£17.25 dB&B£20—£27 dB&B🛁⋔£24—£32.50 B

CTV 18P ✽ ⛆ (heated) solarium games room Disco Fri Live music & dancing Tue ⌂ *xmas*

♉English & French **V** ♆ ⛾ S% Lunch £3.75—£4.95 Tea 60—75p High Tea £1.50—£1.85 Dinner £5.70—£6.85&alc Wine £3.75 Last dinner 7.30pm

Ⓥ

T

T

★★*L* **Hotel Balmoral** Meadfoot Sea Rd ☎ (0803) 23381 District plan **39**

Closed Nov

A comfortable family-run hotel in a quiet position, with views over Meadfoot beach.

23rm(7⋔)(7fb) CTV in all bedrooms
*sB&B£11.50—£15
sB&B⋔£13.50—£16.50 dB&B£23—£30
dB&B⋔£27—£33 B

18P pool room Cabaret twice wkly
xmas

English & French **V** *Lunch fr£4.50 Tea fr65p Dinner fr£6.50 Wine £4.25 Last dinner 8.30pm

Credit cards 1 2 3 Ⓥ

★★***Bancourt*** Avenue Rd ☎ (0803) 25077 Central plan **2** *A3*

Modern hotel complex a short distance from the shops and sea front.

52rm(20⇌)(11fb) CTV in all bedrooms Ⓡ B

CTV 30P (heated) Disco wkly Live music & dancing twice wkly Cabaret wkly *xmas*

International **V** Last dinner 8pm

Credit cards 1 3

Torquay

★★**Bowden Close** Teignmouth Rd, Maidencombe ☎ (0803) 38029 Not on plan

Closed Nov—Etr

Personally run hotel with well appointed rooms, offering a warm welcome.

19rm(4⇌13⋔)(4fb) CTV in all bedrooms Ⓡ sB&B£14—£18
sB&B⇌⋔£14—£18 dB&B£28—£36
dB&B⇌⋔£28—£36

30P games room

Lunch £6 Tea 50p Dinner £7 Wine £4.25 Last dinner 8.30pm

★★**Brigantine Motor** 56 Marldon Rd, Shiphay ☎ (0803) 63162 District plan **40**

An extended private house, now a family run tourist/commercial hotel, situated in a residential position.

14rm(6⇌2⋔)(3fb) CTV in all bedrooms Ⓡ
*sB&B£16 sB&B⇌⋔£19 dB&B£26
dB&B⇌⋔£29 B

CTV 30P *xmas*

Bar lunch £1—£3.50 Tea £1.20—£2 High Tea £1.50—£2.50 Dinner £5—£6 Wine £4 Last dinner 7.30pm

Credit cards 1 3 Ⓥ

★★**Burlington** 462—466 Babbacombe Rd ☎ (0803) 24374 Central plan **4** *F3*

Closed Nov—Mar

A tourist hotel situated on a main road about ¼ mile from beach and town centre.

43rm(7⇌12⋔)(9fb) Ⓡ sB&B£10.50—£15
sB&B⇌⋔£12.75—£17.75
dB&B£21—£30 dB&B⇌⋔£24.50—£34

CTV 30P putting pool table *xmas*

Bar lunch £2—£5&alc Tea 60p Dinner £6.50—£7.50 Wine £5 Last dinner 8pm

Credit cards 1 3 Ⓥ

★★**Bute Court** Belgrave Rd ☎ (0803) 23771 Central plan **5** *C2*

White-painted Victorian building whose spacious and modernised rooms have good sea views.

46rm(34⇌8⋔)(11fb) CTV in all bedrooms Ⓡ T sB&B£16—£20.50
sB&B⇌⋔£18—£24.50 dB&B£28—£41
dB&B⇌⋔£32—£45 B

Lift CTV 36P 4 (heated) snooker Disco Thu (summer) Live music & dancing Mon, Wed, Fri Cabaret Sun *xmas*

International Lunch £3—£4.50 Tea £1—£1.50 High Tea £3—£4 Dinner £5.50—£7 Wine £3.95 Last dinner 5.30pm

Credit cards 1 2 3 5 Ⓥ

T

Torquay

★ ★**Cavendish** Belgrave Rd ☎ (0803) 23682 Central plan **7** *C3*

Closed Nov—Mar except Xmas

Imposing villa with extension, near shops and sea front.

58rm(18⇌18ʃ)(7fb) CTV in 36 bedrooms ®sB&B£16—£21.50 sB&B⇌ʃ£19—£24.50 dB&B£28—£39 dB&B⇌ʃ£34—£50 B

Lift ☾ CTV 24P & ⩫ (heated) sauna bath solarium gymnasium Live music & dancing twice wkly (in season) Cabaret wkly (in season) *xmas*

English & Continental ⊽ Bar lunch £1.25—£3 Tea fr £1.25 Dinner fr £7.50&alc Wine £4.50 Last dinner 8pm

Credit cards 1 2 3 5

★ ★**Chelston Tower** Rawlyn Rd ☎ (0803) 607351 Central plan **8** *A1*

Closed Jan

Well proportioned villa with central tower, this friendly hotel offers good food and service. It is set in well kept gardens with good sea views.

22rm(7⇌2ʃ)(11fb) sB&B£13—£18 sB&B⇌ʃ£15—£20 dB&B£26—£36 dB&B⇌ʃ£30—£40 B

CTV 40P ✿ ⩫ (heated)

⊽ Dinner £7—£7.50 Wine £3.90 Last dinner 7.30pm

Ⓥ

★ ★**Clevedon** Meadfoot Sea Rd ☎ (0803) 24260 District plan **40A**

Closed Oct—Mar

Friendly hotel with spacious sun lounge and good home cooking.

14rm(3⇌6ʃ)(4fb) CTV in all bedrooms ® sB&B£11.45—£14.45 sB&B⇌ʃ£13.45—£16.45 dB&B£22.90—£28.90 dB&B⇌ʃ£26.90—£36.90

CTV 8P ✿ table tennis nc 3yrs

English & Continental ⊽ Bar lunch £1.60—£2.80 Dinner £5.50 Wine £4.80 Last dinner 7.15pm

Credit card 3

★ ★***Conway Court*** Warren Rd ☎ (0803) 25363 Central plan **9** *D2*

Closed Nov—Mar

Friendly, holiday hotel with spectacular views across Tor Bay.

40rm(14⇌17ʃ)(4fb) 4 ® B

☾ CTV P ✿ Live music & dancing twice wkly Cabaret wkly *xmas*

English & French **V** ⊽ Last dinner 8pm

Credit cards 2 3 5

★ ★**Coppice** Barrington Rd ☎ (0803) 27786 District plan **41**

Closed Nov—Mar

The pleasant, family, holiday hotel, under personal supervision, is out of the town centre yet conveniently near to amenities. It is attractively set amid sub-tropical gardens, complete with pool.

26rm(16⇌2ʃ)(10fb) CTV available in bedrooms ®sB&B£10.50—£13.50 sB&B⇌ʃ£12.50—£15.50 dB&B£21—£27 dB&B⇌ʃ£25—£31 B

CTV 26P ✿ ⩫ (heated) Disco wkly Cabaret wkly

⊽✱ Bar lunch £2.50—£5&alc Dinner £7&alc Last dinner 8pm

★ ★**Fonthill** Lower Warberry Rd ☎ (0803) 23894 Central plan **11** *F4*

Closed Oct—Apr

Modern hotel with many balconied rooms overlooking pool.

32⇌(9fb) CTV in 10 bedrooms ®in 10 bedrooms sB&B⇌£11.50—£15.50 dB&B⇌£23—£31

CTV 26P ✿ ⩫ (heated) Disco Thu

⊽ Bar lunch £1—£3 Tea £1 Dinner £4.90 Wine £3.50 Last dinner 8pm

Credit cards 1 3

T

Torquay

★★**Glen** Beach Rd, Babbacombe
☎ (0803) 38340 District plan **45**

Overlooking the sea from its secluded setting on a wooded cliffside, the comfortably-appointed hotel maintains an old world charm and a friendly atmosphere under the personal direction of its resident proprietor.

18rm(5⫪)(3fb) Ⓡ sB&B£11.50—£14 sB&B⫪£13—£15.50 dB&B£23—£28 dB&B⫪£26—£31 B

CTV 18P ✿ *xmas*

Bar lunch 70p—£2.75 High Tea 55p—£1.50 Dinner £7—£8.50 Wine £4.50 Last dinner 8pm

Credit cards 1 3 5 Ⓥ

★★**Gresham Court** Babbacombe Rd
☎ (0803) 23007 Central plan **14** *F3*

Closed Nov—Mar

Sited on a corner, and within easy walking distance of harbour and town centre, this family-operated hotel continues to be popular for its friendly, informal, atmosphere.

34rm(8⫪6⫪)(4fb) Ⓡ sB&B£10—£14.50 sB&B⫪£12—£16.50 dB&B£20—£29 dB&B⫪£24—£33 B

Lift CTV 4P Disco wkly Live music & dancing twice wkly Cabaret wkly

Bar lunch £1.50—£3.50 Dinner £4 Wine £4.25 Last dinner 8pm

Credit cards 1 3

★★**Howden Court** 23 Croft Rd ☎ (0803) 24844 Central plan **16** *C3*

Large villa in its own grounds.

32rm(12⫪20⫪)(11fb) CTV in 10 bedrooms S% sB&B⫪£17.85—£20.50 dB&B⫪£28.70—£35.14

CTV 25P ✿ games room Disco Mon (Mar—Nov) Live music & dancing Thu (Mar—Nov) *xmas*

V S% Bar lunch 80p—£2.75 Tea fr80p Dinner fr£6.50 Wine £4.75 Last dinner 8pm

★★**Hunsdon Lea** Hunsdon Rd
☎ (0803) 26538 Central plan **17** *F3*

Closed Nov—Mar except Xmas

This friendly, family, holiday hotel enjoys the personal attention of its proprietors and a quiet setting which is nevertheless conveniently close to central shopping area, harbour and amenities.

17rm(8⫪3⫪)(5fb) CTV in all bedrooms sB&B£11.50—£15.50 sB&B⫪£13.50—£17.50 dB&B⫪£27—£41

CTV 12P ✿ (heated) solarium table tennis pool table *xmas*

Bar lunch £2.50 Dinner fr£6.95&alc Wine £4.30 Last dinner 7.30pm

★★**Lansdowne** Babbacombe Rd
☎ (0803) 22822 Central plan **20** *F3*

Closed Nov—Mar except Xmas

Hotel with a modern exterior in a quiet position, ¼m from the town centre.

30rm(24⫪2⫪)(10fb) CTV in all bedrooms Ⓡ sB&B£13.50—£16.50 sB&B⫪£13.50—£16.50 dB&B⫪£27—£33 B

CTV 30P (heated) table tennis pool table *xmas*

English, French & Italian Bar lunch £1—£4&alc Tea fr45p Dinner £6—£7&alc Wine £4.20 Last dinner 8.30pm

Credit cards 1 3 Ⓥ

★★**Meadfoot Bay** Meadfoot Sea Rd
☎ (0803) 24722 District plan **47**

Closed Oct—Apr except Xmas

Double-fronted villa standing in its own grounds in the Meadfoot Bay area.

26rm(11⫪4⫪)(5fb) CTV in 15 bedrooms TV in 11 bedrooms Ⓡ sB&B£11.50—£19 sB&B⫪£14.50—£22 dB&B£18—£33 dB&B⫪£24—£39 B

CTV 20P ✿ games room *xmas*

Bar lunch £2.95alc Dinner £7.95alc Wine £5.50 Last dinner 8pm

Credit cards 1 2 Ⓥ

★★*Morningside* Sea Front, Babbacombe Downs ☎ (0803) 37025 District plan **48**

Closed Oct—Etr

On Babbacombe Downs with panoramic views towards Lyme Bay.

16rm(8⇌2⋒)(3fb) CTV in 12 bedrooms Ⓡ **T** ✗

CTV 16P ⊭ nc 10yrs

V ♁ ☕ Last dinner 7.45pm

Credit card [3]

★★Nethway Falkland Rd ☎ (0803) 27630 Central plan **25** *B5*

RS Nov—Dec

Hotel is in elevated position near Abbey gardens.

27rm(12⇌12⋒)(4fb) sB&B£14—£18 sB&B⇌⋒£18—£22 dB&B⇌⋒£29—£37 **B**

☾ CTV 26P ✿ ⛆ (heated) snooker table tennis badminton Live music & dancing twice wkly Cabaret wkly in summer nc 5yrs ♿ *xmas*

V ♁ ☕ ✱ Bar lunch 80p—£2 Tea fr55p Dinner fr£6.25&alc Wine £3.95 Last dinner 7.30pm

Credit card [3] Ⓥ

★★Norcliffe Babbacombe Downs Rd, Babbacombe ☎ (0803) 38456 District plan **49**

Closed Nov—Etr

Imposing villa on Babbacombe sea front, offering fine views and near to the shops.

20rm(9⇌1⋒)(2fb) CTV in all bedrooms Ⓡ sB&B£9—£18 dB&B£18—£36 dB&B⇌⋒£28—£56

16P ⊭

♁ ☕ Bar lunch fr£1.20 Tea fr£1.40 Dinner fr£6.50 Wine £3.50 Last dinner 7.30pm

★★ ♣ *HB* **Orestone House** Rockhouse Lane, Maidencombe (Inter Hotel & ExecHotel) ☎ (0803) 38098 District plan **50**

Closed Jan & Feb

Peacefully set in a quiet valley with good sea views, the pretty Georgian house offers hospitable service from owners and staff. Its charm and character are complemented by the more tangible advantages of modern, cosy bedrooms and commendable food standards.

Torquay

20rm(11⇌7⋒)(4fb) CTV in all bedrooms Ⓡ **T** sB&B£19—£24 sB&B⇌⋒£22—£28 dB&B⇌⋒£44—£56 **B**

CTV 30P ✿ ⛆ (heated) games room putting green ⌂ *xmas*

☋ English & French **V** ♁ ☕ Bar lunch £5alc Tea £1.50—£2.50 Dinner fr£9.75 Wine £4.75 Last dinner 9pm

Credit cards [1] [2] [3] [5] Ⓥ

★★*Penrhyn* Cary Park, Babbacombe ☎ (0803) 37385 District plan **54**

Closed Nov—Feb

Two adjoining villas have been linked by a new reception area in this hotel which overlooks the Park gardens.

20rm(6⇌10⋒)(5fb) Ⓡ **B**

CTV 19P ⊭ ✿

V ♁ ☕ Last dinner 8pm

★★Red House Rousdon Rd, Chelston ☎ (0803) 607811 Central plan **28** *B1*

A red stone house in a quiet residential area has been tastefully modernised and equipped with good leisure and health facilities. Compact bedrooms are furnished in the modern style, whilst comprehensive catering facilities are amalgamated with a pleasant bar area.

10rm(9⇌1⋒)(3fb) CTV in all bedrooms S% sB&B⇌⋒£13—£21 dB&B⇌⋒£22—£38 **B**

10P ⊭ ✿ ▣ & ⛆ (heated) sauna bath solarium gymnasium table tennis pool table *xmas*

♁ ☕ S% Lunch £3.15 Tea 52p—£1.35 High Tea £1—£2 Dinner £6.50&alc Wine £4.50 Last dinner 7.30pm

★★Roseland Warren Rd ☎ (0803) 213829 Central plan **29** *C2*

New owners have completely redecorated and refurbished the hotel, which has a tasteful, pleasing atmosphere enhanced by friendly staff. In its elevated position overlooking Torbay it is central to the town and convenient for the beach.

34rm(18⇌16⋒)(5fb) 3▤ CTV in all bedrooms Ⓡ **T** ✗ sB&B⇌⋒£15—£21 dB&B⇌⋒£28—£40

Lift ☾ ⚑ games room Live music & dancing Mon & Sat Cabaret Tue & Thu *xmas*

V ♁ ☕ ⚟ Lunch fr£1.50&alc Dinner £6.50&alc Wine £4.95 Last dinner 10pm

Credit cards [1] [3]

★★Shedden Hall ☎ (0803) 22964 Central plan **30** *C2*

Closed Jan—Feb

Family-run holiday hotel with a pleasant garden, and overlooking Torbay.

27⇌⋒(5fb) 1▤ CTV in 23 bedrooms Ⓡ sB&B£13—£17 dB&B£22—£30 dB&B⇌⋒£26—£38

CTV 27P ✿ ⛆ (heated) solarium pool table

♁ ☕ Bar lunch 65p—£2.50 Tea fr50p Dinner fr£7&alc Wine £4.70

Credit cards [1] [2] [3] [5]

★★Sunray Aveland Rd, Babbacombe ☎ (0803) 38285 District plan **55**

RS Dec—Mar

This modern, friendly hotel, under family ownership, is efficiently run by experienced staff. Conveniently situated a short distance from Cary Park, it is also within easy reach of the Downs.

23rm(11⇌9⋒)(3fb) CTV in 14 bedrooms Ⓡ sB&B£13 sB&B⇌⋒£16 dB&B£26 dB&B⇌⋒£32 **B**

♯ CTV 15P 1⌂ *xmas*

☋ English & French ♁ ☕ ⚟ S% Dinner £6.50 Wine £4.50 Last dinner 8pm

Credit cards [1] [3]

★★*Sydore* Meadfoot Rd ☎ (0803) 24758 Central plan **32** *F2*

This villa in its own grounds is near town centre and harbour.

13rm(4⇌2⋒)(5fb) CTV in 7 bedrooms TV in 6 bedrooms **B**

CTV 20P ⊭ ✿ ⌂ *xmas*

V ♁ ☕ Last dinner 8.30pm

T

★★**Templestowe** Tor Chruch Rd ☎(0803) 25145 Central plan **33** *C3*

Holiday hotel personally supervised by the resident owners, close to the beach and the town centre.

90rm(45🛁5🚿)(24fb) CTV in all bedrooms ®✱sB&B£12—£20 sB&B🛁🚿£14—£22 dB&B£24—£40 dB&B🛁🚿£28—£44 **B**

Lift ☾ CTV 60P ✿ ≈(heated) Q(hard) solarium Disco wkly Live music & dancing twice wkly Cabaret wkly xmas

English & French **V** ☕ ✱Lunch £4—£4.50 Tea 40p Dinner £6—£6.50 Wine £3.50 Last dinner 8pm

Credit cards 1 3 5

★★***Vernon Court*** Warren Rd ☎(0803) 22676 Central plan **35** *C2*

Closed Nov—Mar

In superb, commanding position offering panoramic views over Torbay and the sea.

19rm(12🛁2🚿)(4fb) CTV in all bedrooms ® **B**

CTV 9P ✿ nc 3yrs *xmas*

Last dinner 8pm

Credit cards 1 3

★★***Viscount*** St Albans Rd, Babbacombe ☎(0803) 37444 District plan **56**

Closed Nov—Mar

Friendly holiday hotel with pleasant sun terrace.

20rm(7🛁🚿)(3fb) TV in all bedrooms ® **B**

CTV 20P ≈(heated)

V ☕ Last dinner 8pm

★**Ashley Rise** 18 Babbacombe Rd, Babbacombe ☎(0803) 37282 District plan **38**

Closed Nov—Feb except Xmas

Detached modern hotel on the main Babbacombe road into Torquay, near the sea front and the shops.

29rm(2🛁5🚿)(5fb) ® ✱sB&B£10.75—£13.75 dB&B£19.50—£23.50 dB&B🛁🚿£23.50—£27.50 **B**

Torquay

CTV 14P 3 Live music & dancing 3 nights wkly *xmas*

✱Tea fr 50p Dinner fr £5.50 Wine £4.20 Last dinner 7pm

Ⓥ

★**Carlton** Falkland Rd ☎(0803) 27666 Central plan **6** *B3*

Closed 28 Dec—15 Feb

A popular, family, hotel offers friendly service under the personal direction of the proprietor. A range of lounges and facilities has much to offer to all age groups.

34rm(23🛁1🚿)(17fb) CTV in 6 bedrooms ✱sB&B£10.25—£13.75 sB&B🛁🚿£11.75—£15.25 dB&B£20.50—£27.50 dB&B🛁🚿£23.50—£30.50 **B**

Lift CTV 26P ✿ ≈(heated) Disco wkly (in season) Live music & dancing twice wkly Cabaret wkly *xmas*

V ☕ Lunch fr £4 Tea fr 55p High Tea fr £2.50 Dinner fr £5.50 Wine £3.50 Last dinner 7.30pm

Credit cards 1 3 Ⓥ

★**Fairmount House** Herbert Rd, Chelston (Guestaccom) ☎(0803) 605446 District plan **44**

RS Nov—Feb

Quiet well-appointed hotel with personal service.

7rm(2🛁3🚿)(3fb) ®sB&B£12—£14 sB&B🛁🚿£14—£16 dB&B£24—£28 dB&B🛁🚿£28—£32 **B**

CTV 8P ✿ *xmas*

English & Continental ☕ Bar lunch £2.50—£5 Tea 60p Dinner £7 Wine £3.95 Last dinner 7.30pm

Credit cards 2 3 Ⓥ

★***Panorama*** Livermead Hill ☎(0803) 605249 District plan **53A**

Located just off the sea-front and Livermead Sands, the hotel offers comfortable, modern bedrooms, and an interesting lounge.

15rm(11🛁)(2fb) CTV available in bedrooms ®

☾ CTV 15P *xmas*

☕ Last dinner 7pm

Credit cards 1 5

★***Shelley Court*** Croft Rd ☎(0803) 25642 Central plan **31** *C3*

Attractive villa-style hotel with a new extension, set in its own grounds, overlooking Abbey Sands.

29rm(2🛁14🚿)(1fb)

CTV 18P ✿ solarium Disco twice wkly Cabaret twice wkly *xmas*

V ☕ Last dinner 7.30pm

★**Sunleigh** Livermead Hill ☎(0803) 607137 District plan **54A**

Closed Nov—Dec RS Jan—Etr

Set in its own grounds only a few hundred yards from Livermead beach, the hotel has sea views from its slightly elevated position. Bedrooms have recently been refurbished, the lounge bar has modern fittings, and the comfortably equipped lounge is furnished with delightful antiques.

23rm(21🚿)(3fb) CTV in all bedrooms ® S% sB&B🚿£12.50—£14.25 dB&B🚿£25—£28.50

CTV 18P ✿ Live music & dancing Wed & Fri *xmas*

V S% Bar lunch £3alc Dinner £4.80alc Wine £4.20 Last dinner 7pm

★ *B* **Windsurfer** St Agnes Ln ☎(0803) 606550 Central plan **35A** *B1*

Closed Dec—9 Jan

The semi-detached villa stands in a quiet location near Abbey lawns and Torbay station. Bedrooms are well-equipped and public rooms tastefully and comfortably appointed.

10rm(5🛁5🚿)(7fb) CTV in all bedrooms ® sB&B🛁🚿£14.10—£17 dB&B🛁🚿£28.20—£34

12P

☕ Bar lunch £3—£4 Dinner £7 Wine £5 Last dinner 7.30pm

Credit card 2

XX**Green Mantle** 135 Babbacombe Rd ☎ (0803) 34292 District plan **46A**

Surroundings in this restaurant are elegant and there is a relaxed atmosphere where carefully-prepared, attentively-served food makes your meal a memorable one.

Closed Sun, 1st 2 wks Nov Lunch not served

French 20 seats Dinner £10.50—£13 Wine £5 Last dinner 10pm

Credit cards 2 3 5

X**Lisburne** 7 Lisburne Sq ☎ (0803) 26968 Central plan **23A** *F3*

Regency style restaurant offering wide range of good, freshly prepared food.

Lunch not served Tue & Sat

French **V** 24 seats ✱Lunch £2.50—£7&alc Dinner £10—£16 Wine £5.50 Last dinner 10pm

Credit cards 1 2 3 5

X**Old Vienna** 6 Lisburne Sq ☎ (0803) 25861 Central plan **25A** *F3*

The continental training and experience of the Austrian proprietor of this restaurant result in some interesting dishes and rich, beautifully decorated sweets. The small, intimate dining room is located on the ground floor of a Georgian terraced building.

Closed 1 wk summer & 1 wk Oct Lunch by reservation only

Austrian **V** 40 seats ✱Lunch £12alc Dinner £12—£15alc Wine £6.25 Last dinner 10pm

Credit cards 1 2 3 V

TORRIDON
Highland *Ross & Cromarty*
Map **14** NG85

★★**Loch Torridon** ☎ (044587) 242

Closed Nov—Feb

On the southern shores of Loch Torridon, looking across to Torridon village.

24rm(11)(3fb) S% sB&B£16—£19.75 sB&B£20—£23 dB&B£31—£36.70 dB&B£32—£47.30

CTV 40P Disco wknds

Scottish & French S% Bar lunch £2.20—£5.50 Tea £1.30 Dinner £11.75 Wine £5.60 Last dinner 8.45pm

Credit cards 1 2 3 4 5 V

TORRINGTON, GREAT
Devon
Map **2** SS41

★★***Castle Hill*** South St ☎ (0805) 22339

Commercial and holiday hotel in a quiet situation on the edge of the town.

6rm(5) CTV in all bedrooms

CTV 35P

V Last dinner 1.45pm

Credit cards 1 2 3 5

X**Rebecca's** 8 Potacre St ☎ (0805) 22113

This cosy restaurant provides many old English dishes such as Elizabethan Pork Stew and Devilled Spatchcock, most of which are home-made; a Tiffin menu is served all day until 7pm.

Closed Sun, 25—27 Dec

V 42 seats Lunch £5—£6alc Dinner £10—£12.50&alc Wine £4.85 Last dinner 10pm

Credit cards 1 2 3 V

TOTLAND BAY
Isle of Wight
See **Wight, Isle of**

TOTNES
Devon
Map **3** SX86

★★**Bourton Hall** Newton Rd ☎ (0803) 862608

RS Sun

(Rosette awarded for dinner only)

Built in the 19th century, in the style of a French chateau, the hotel offers elegance and grace with a superb painted ceiling and some fine carved fireplaces. The food is most imaginative and uses good quality materials. There is also a well balanced wine list.

20rm(5 15) Annexe: 2rms CTV in all bedrooms ® sB&B£28 dB&B£40

CTV 60P (heated) nc 7yrs *xmas*

English & French **V** Lunch £7.50&alc Tea £1 Dinner £15alc Wine £5.75 Last dinner 9pm

Credit cards 1 3 V

See advertisement on page 732

★★**Royal Seven Stars** ☎ (0803) 862125

This town-centre hotel, originally a coaching inn dating back to 1660, offers character bars and public rooms. Bedrooms, though modest, have modern facilities and the small, covered courtyard is both interesting and attractive.

18rm(10)(5fb) CTV in all bedrooms ® ✱sB&B£22.50—£24 sB&B£29.50—£32 dB&B£32—£34 dB&B£39.50—£42

CTV 25P *xmas*

Lunch £6—£6.50&alc Dinner £8.50—£9.50&alc Wine £5.25 Last dinner 9.30pm

Credit cards 1 3 5

See advertisement on page 732

XX**Elbow Room** ☎ (0803) 863480

A delightful 400-year-old terraced cottage features a cosy lounge and an intimate, bar. The exposed stone walls and beamed →

T

ceiling of the dining room, where the tables are decorated with fresh flowers and candles, are a fine setting for the enjoyment of fresh, home-cooked food (of which sweets are a speciality).

Closed Sun & Mon

International 34 seats Lunch £2.95&alc Dinner £5.50—£7.30&alc Wine £4.65 Last dinner 10pm

Credit cards 1 2 3 V

TOTON
Nottinghamshire
Map **8** SK53

XX **Grange Farm** Nottingham (0602) 729426

Conversion of a farmhouse and outbuildings has created extensive lounges and a dining room with exposed brickwork and beams; a cosy atmosphere prevails, and there are some interesting displays of porcelain and antiques. Good service is given by friendly, efficient staff under the supervision of the owners, and the well-cooked, tasty and imaginative dishes, predominantly British in style, represent excellent value for money.

Closed Sun, Bank Hol Mons, 24—26 Dec & New Years Day Lunch not served Mon

V 180 seats Lunch £6.90 Dinner fr£9.10 Wine £4.50 Last dinner 9pm 130P Live music & dancing & Disco Sat

Credit cards 1 3

Totnes — Trebarwith

TREARDDUR BAY
Gwynedd
Map **6** SH27

★★★ **Beach** (Best Western) (0407) 860332 Telex no 61529

Closed 25—27 Dec

Prominent hotel with extensive facilities including a special health clinic, set back from the beach.

26rm(22 4)(3fb) CTV in all bedrooms ® **T** sB&B £25 dB&B £38 Continental breakfast

CTV 150P squash snooker sauna bath solarium Disco three nights wkly Live music & dancing mthly

V Lunch £3.75—£6.50 Tea £1—£2.25 High Tea £1.80—£2.95 Dinner £5.50—£8&alc Wine £3.50 Last dinner 10.30pm

Credit cards 1 2 3 5 V

★★★ **Trearddur Bay** (0407) 860301 Telex no 61609

Impressive, three-storey hotel with its own helipad, close to the beach.

28rm(19) CTV in 6 bedrooms TV in 22 bedrooms ® **T** * sB&B £16.75—£20.75 sB&B £21.75—£22.75 dB&B £30.50—£36.50 dB&B £37.50—£50.50

CTV 200P (heated) xmas

V * Lunch £6—£8.50 Tea £2 High Tea £3.50—£5.50 Dinner £10&alc Wine £5.75 Last dinner 9.30pm

Credit cards 1 2 3 5

★★ ***Seacroft*** Ravenspoint Rd (0407) 860348

Two-storey hotel near the beach.

6rm(1 2)(3fb) ®

CTV 30P

French **V** Last dinner 9pm

TREBARWITH
Cornwall
Map **2** SX08

X **Mill House Inn** Camelford (0840) 770200

Attractively converted corn mill (AA Inn of the Year, 1985) with charming restaurant serving well cooked food.

Closed 24—27 Dec Lunch not served

French 26 seats * Bar lunch fr£1.50 Dinner £9alc Wine £4.90 Last dinner 9pm 40P nc 10yrs

Credit cards 1 3

T

TREBETHERICK
Cornwall
Map **2** SW97
★★**St Moritz** (Inter Hotel) ☎ (020886) 2242
Closed Jan
Comfortable family hotel near beach.
50⇌ (4fb) CTV in all bedrooms ® T S% *sB&B⇌£21—£28 dB&B⇌£36—£52
CTV 200P ✿ solarium Disco wkly Cabaret wkly *xmas*
V ☕ *Lunch £5—£6 Dinner £9.50—£10.50 Wine £5.50 Last dinner 8.30pm
Credit cards 1 2 5 Ⓥ

TREFRIW
Gwynedd
Map **6** SH76
★**Hafod House** ☎ Llanrwst (0492) 640029
8rm (2fb) 1⊟ CTV in all bedrooms ® *sB&B£11—£13.50 dB&B£22—£27 B
30P
English & French V ☕ *Lunch £6.25&alc Tea £1.35 Dinner £6.50&alc Wine £4.25 Last dinner 9.30pm
Credit cards 1 3

TREGARON
Dyfed
Map **3** SN65
★***Talbot*** The Square ☎ (09744) 208
The small, character, market town hostelry features popular bars and friendly, personal service. The grill-style menu, though limited, makes good use of quality produce.
14rm (4⇌) (2fb) CTV in 6 bedrooms ® B
CTV 20P
Mainly grills ☕ Last dinner 8.30pm

TRELIGHTS
Cornwall
Map **2** SW97
★★***Long Cross*** ☎ Bodmin (0208) 880243
Closed Oct—Etr
Fine Victorian house standing in 3 acres of gardens, with panoramic views of the North Cornwall coast.
14rm (4⇌4⋒) (9fb) 1⊟
CTV 20P ✿
☕ Last dinner 8pm

TREMADOG
Gwynedd
Map **6** SH54
★★**Madoc** ☎ Porthmadog (0766) 2021
Early 19th-century inn with oak beams and a granite fireplace.
21rm (1⇌3⋒) (3fb) ® in 6 bedrooms sB&B£16.50 dB&B£33 dB&B⇌⋒£38.50 B
CTV 14P 4🚗 *xmas*
V ☕ Lunch £4.50—£5.50 Tea £1—£1.25 High Tea £1.50—£2 Dinner £4.50—£7.50&alc Wine £3.50
Credit cards 1 3

TREYARNON BAY
Cornwall
Map **2** SW87
★★**Waterbeach** St Merryn ☎ Padstow (0841) 520292
Closed Dec & Jan
Comfortable, personally run, family holiday hotel in a peaceful setting, 200 yards from the beach.
16rm (7⇌2⋒) (2fb) ® sB&B£16—£21 dB&B£32—£42 dB&B⇌⋒£36—£46
CTV 20P 3🚗 (£1 per night) ✿ (hard) putting table tennis
V ☕ *Lunch £2.50alc Tea 35palc Dinner £7.50 Wine £3.65 Last dinner 8.15pm
Credit cards 1 2 3

TRING
Hertfordshire
Map **4** SP91
★★**Rose & Crown** High St (Whitbread) ☎ (044282) 4071
Though some of the hotel's quality bedrooms are small, all have been recently renovated to a high standard with many extras. There is a grill-type restaurant.
28rm (26⇌2⋒) (1fb) 2⊟ CTV in all bedrooms ® T *sB&B⇌⋒£40 dB&B⇌⋒£48 B
☾ CTV 70P 4🚗 ✿ *xmas*
Mainly grills ☕ *Wine £4.90 Last dinner 9.30pm
Credit cards 1 2 3 4 5

✕**Kanak Bahar Tandoori** 75 High St ☎ (044282) 7788
Located in the High Street, this authentic Indian restaurant offers a good range of Tandoori dishes. Décor and atmosphere enhance the typically eastern style of courteous service.
Closed Xmas Day & Boxing Day
Indian V 56 seats *Lunch £6—£10&alc Wine £4.90 Last dinner 11.30pm
Credit cards 1 2 3 5 Ⓥ

TROON
Strathclyde *Ayrshire*
Map **10** NS33
★★★★**Marine** Crosbie Rd (Scottish Highland) ☎ (0292) 314444 Telex no 777595
Victorian, red sandstone, traditional golfing hotel overlooking two golf courses and offering a choice of three restaurants.
69⇌ (5fb) 1⊟ CTV in all bedrooms ® T sB&B⇌£36—£50 dB&B⇌£72 B
Lift ☾ CTV 100P CFA ✿ *xmas*
Scottish & French ☕ Lunch £9.95&alc Tea £3.50 High Tea £6.50 Dinner £14.95&alc Wine £5.95 Last dinner 10pm
Credit cards 1 2 3 5

T

★★★**Sun Court** Crosbie Rd ☎ (0292) 312727

Spacious former home of a wealthy industrialist, overlooking the sea; facilities incorporate a Real Tennis Court and squash courts.

20rm(18⇌)(1fb) CTV in all bedrooms **T** S% ✱sB&B£31 sB&B⇌£34 dB&B£50 dB&B⇌£55 **B**

CTV 70P ✿ (hard) squash real tennis

Scottish, French & Italian S% ✱Lunch £7.50&alc Dinner £11.50&alc Wine £4.80 Last dinner 9.30pm

Credit cards 1 2 5

★★**Ardneil** 51 St Meddans Street ☎ (0292) 311611

This family-run hotel near the station has several popular bars and a busy food trade.

8rm(3⇌)(2fb) CTV in all bedrooms ® sB&B£15 sB&B⇌£18 dB&B£27 dB&B⇌£32

CTV 20P ✿ pool room

V Bar lunch £4.50alc Tea £1.25alc High Tea £4.75alc Dinner £8alc Wine £5.75 Last dinner 9pm

Credit cards 1 2 3

★★**Craiglea** South Beach ☎ (0292) 311366

Family run resort hotel on seafront.

21rm(11⇌1⋔)(2fb) CTV in 20 bedrooms ® in 12 bedrooms **T** sB&B£22—£25 sB&B⇌⋔£24—£28 dB&B£35—£38 dB&B⇌⋔£38—£42 **B**

CTV 14P Live music & dancing Sat (winter) *xmas*

V Lunch £5—£6.85&alc Tea £1.75 Dinner £8—£9.90&alc Wine £4.50 Last dinner 8.45pm

Credit cards 1 2 3 5 Ⓥ

★★*L* **Piersland House** Craigend Rd (InterHotel) ☎ (0292) 314747

A listed historic building in Tudor style with open fires, wood panelling and carvings.

13rm(8⇌5⋔)(2fb) 1 CTV in all bedrooms ® **T** sB&B⇌⋔£35—£42 dB&B⇌⋔£50—£65 **B**

150P ✿ croquet *xmas*

Troon — Trowbridge

Scottish, English & Continental **V** Bar lunch £1.95—£9.50&alc Tea £1.25—£3.50 High Tea £4—£6 Dinner £13.50&alc Wine £7 Last dinner 9.30pm

Credit cards 1 2 3 5

★★***South Beach*** South Beach Rd (Minotel) ☎ (0292) 312033

RS Oct—Mar

Large, white-painted hotel, close to the seafront and offering good value accommodation and food.

29rm(7⇌9⋔)(4fb) CTV in 16 bedrooms ® in 16 bedrooms **B**

CTV 40P billiards

Last dinner 9pm

Credit cards 1 2 3

✿✕**Campbell's Kitchen** 3 South Beach ☎ (0292) 314421

(Rosette awarded for dinner only).

This popular little bistro restaurant enjoys a good local reputation. The cosy interior is delightfully simple, with subdued lighting and a friendly, relaxed atmosphere. The short, imaginative menu reflects a French influence, and service is unobtrusively efficient.

Closed Mon, 25—26 Dec, 1&2 Jan Dinner not served Sun

French **V** 36 seats Lunch £3—£9.50 Dinner £14&alc Wine £4.55 Last dinner 9.30pm **P**

Credit card 1

TROTTON
West Sussex
Map **4** SU82

★★**Southdowns** (ExecHotel) ☎ Rogate (073080) 521

Quietly situated in a picturesque area four miles south-west of the town, the family-run country restaurant features English-style cooking and well-equipped bedrooms with all modern facilities.

16⇌(2fb) 1 CTV in all bedrooms ® **T** sB&B⇌£25—£30 dB&B⇌£35—£45 **B**

CTV 70P ✿ (heated) solarium *xmas*

V Lunch £6.50—£12.50&alc Dinner £6.50—12.50&alc Wine £4.95 Last dinner 10pm

Credit cards 1 2 3 4 5 Ⓥ

TROUTBECK (near Windermere)
Cumbria
Map **11** NY32

★★**Mortal Man** (2½m N off A592) ☎ Ambleside (0966) 33193 Plan **20** *B5*

Closed mid Nov—mid Feb

Old lakeland inn, built in 1689, originally known as the White House.

13rm(7⇌1⋔) ® S% sB&B£30—£32(incl dinner) sB&B⇌⋔£32.50—£34.50(incl dinner) dB&B£60—£64(incl dinner) dB&B⇌⋔£65—£69(incl dinner) **B**

CTV 20P ✿ nc5yrs

S% Bar lunch 80p—£3.50 Dinner £12 Wine £6 Last dinner 8pm

Ⓥ

TROWBRIDGE
Wiltshire
Map **3** ST85

★*B* ***Hilbury Court*** Hilperton Rd ☎ (02214) 2949

Closed 24 Dec—1 Jan

Attractive, peaceful late Georgian house with comfortable, well appointed bedrooms.

12rm(3⇌)(2fb) CTV in all bedrooms ®

CTV 20P ✿

Last dinner 7.30pm

Credit cards 1 3

★**Polebarn House** Polebarn Rd ☎ (02214) 65624

Clean simply furnished hotel in grade II listed building.

11rm(4)(2fb) CTV in all bedrooms ® S% sB&B£15—£19.50 sB&B£17.50—£23.50 dB&B£21—£27.50 dB&B£25—£32.50 B

10P Disco Fri & Sat

International S% Bar lunch £2.75—£4.25&alc Dinner £6.50—£7.50&alc Wine £3.95 Last dinner 9pm

Credit cards [1] [2] [3] Ⓥ

TRURO
Cornwall
Map **2** SW84

★★★**Brookdale** Tregolls Rd ☎ (0872) 73513

Closed Xmas

Small, professional hotel convenient for the city and touring in the area.

21rm(17 4) CTV in all bedrooms ® T S% sB&B£21.50 sB&B£30.50 dB&B£36.60 dB&B£44 B

50P 10

English, French & Italian S% Bar lunch 95p—£7 Tea fr80p High Tea fr£2.50 Dinner £9.50—£10.75 Wine £4.50 Last dinner 8.45pm

Credit cards [1] [2] [3] [5] Ⓥ

★★★**Royal** Lemon St ☎ (0872) 70345

RS Xmas

Commercial and tourist hotel in central situation with modern bedrooms. →

T

34 (4fb) CTV in all bedrooms ® T S%
sB&B £23.75—£29.75
dB&B £39.50—£43 B
☾ CTV 18P 18 CFA
S% Lunch £5—£6.50&alc Tea £1.25—£1.75 Dinner £5—£6.50&alc Wine £4.50 Last dinner 9.30pm
Credit cards 1 3

★ ★**Carlton** Falmouth Rd (0872) 72450
Closed 20 Dec—6 Jan

Detached Victorian mansion with extension. Family run by Chef proprietor. Quiet situation but close to city centre.

24rm(4 16)(3fb) CTV in all bedrooms ® T *sB&B £19.50—£22.50
sB&B £22.50 dB&B £28
dB&B £35.50 B
30P
*Dinner fr£5.75&alc Wine £3.65 Last dinner 8pm
Credit cards 1 3 V

✕ ***Withies Country*** Penmount Farm, Newquay Rd (0872) 70007

Converted from former farm buildings, this is a small, country restaurant. The dining room, offers a warm atmosphere that is complemented by friendly, informal service. The menu restricts itself to traditional country fare, providing a light lunch (with bar snacks offered as an alternative) and an extensive dinner selection.

Closed Sun, Bank Hols & 2 wks Oct
V 36 seats Last dinner 9pm 30P
Credit cards 1 2 3 5

TUNBRIDGE WELLS (ROYAL)
Kent
Map **5** TQ53

★ ★ ★ *L* **Spa** Mount Ephraim (0892) 20331 Telex no 957188

Well-run hotel with good compact bedrooms and skilful cooking.

75rm(73 2)(4fb) CTV in all bedrooms ® T S% sB&B £47—£52
dB&B £66—£76 Continental breakfast B
Lift ☾ 130P CFA (heated) (hard) sauna bath solarium gymnasium croquet putting *xmas*
English & French **V** Lunch fr£9.50&alc Tea £1.50—£5 Dinner £14alc Wine £6 Last dinner 9.30pm
Credit cards 1 2 3 4 5 V

★ ★**Calverley** Crescent Rd (0892) 26455 Telex no 957565

The good, well-run, old-fashioned hotel provides spacious bedrooms and friendly service.

43rm(21 2)(2fb) 1 CTV in all bedrooms ® *sB&B fr£22
sB&B fr£26 dB&B fr£40
dB&B fr£42
Lift ☾ CTV 34P
V *Lunch fr£5.50&alc Tea fr£1.50 Dinner fr£6.50&alc Wine £5 Last dinner 8.30pm
Credit cards 1 2 3 5

★ ★**Hand & Sceptre** 21 London Rd, Southborough (2m N A26) (0892) 37055

Friendly hotel with well equipped compact bedrooms.

25rm(23 2)(2fb) CTV in all bedrooms ® T S% sB&B £25.75—£28.50
dB&B £36—£40 B
40P Live music & dancing Fri & Sat
English & French **V** *S% Bar lunch £2—£2.50 Tea 60p Dinner £7.95&alc Wine £4.75 Last dinner 8.30pm
Credit cards 1 2 3 5 V

★★**Royal Wells Inn** Mount Ephraim ☎(0892) 23414

Closed Bank Hol Mon's, Good Fri & 25—26 Dec

Comfortable, old fashioned hotel with high standard of cooking.

15🛁 ⌂ 2📺 CTV in all bedrooms **T** S% sB&B🛁 ⌂ £31 dB&B🛁 ⌂ £43 **B**

CTV 25P 🚌

🍷English & French **V** 🏆 ☕ S% ✱ Lunch £8.25&alc Dinner £8.75—£12.50&alc Wine £4.95 Last dinner 10pm

Credit cards 1 2 3 5 Ⓥ

Tunbridge Wells (Royal)

★★*HB* **Russell** 80 London Rd (Inter-Hotel) ☎(0892) 44833 Telex no 95177

Comfortable, well-appointed bedrooms are complemented by a warm, friendly atmosphere in this small, family-run hotel.

21rm(12🛁 9⌂)(3fb) CTV in all bedrooms ®**T** ✗ sB&B🛁 ⌂ fr£38 dB&B🛁 ⌂ fr£50 **B**

20P 🚌

🍷English & French **V** 🏆 ☕ Bar lunch fr£2 Tea fr80p Dinner fr£10.50&alc Wine £5 Last dinner 9.30pm

Credit cards 1 2 3 5 Ⓥ

★★**Wellington** Mount Ephraim (Exec Hotel) ☎(0892) 42911 Telex no 23152

The Victorian atmosphere here is combined with friendly service.

61rm(37🛁 8⌂)(3fb) 5📺 CTV in 16 bedrooms S% sB&B£19 sB&B🛁 ⌂ £26—£30 dB&B£36 dB&B🛁 ⌂ £38—£45 **B** →

T

Lift ☾CTV 35P CFA ✿ sauna bath solarium gymnasium pool table *xmas*

English & French V Lunch £3.25alc Tea 80p Dinner £8 Wine £4.50 Last dinner 9pm

Credit cards 1 2 3 5 V

XX **Thackeray's House** 85 London Rd (0892) 37558

A charming town house, once the home of the Victorian novelist, William Makepeace Thackeray, has been converted into a restaurant which offers a good standard of French cuisine, providing a four-course meal at a reasonable, all-inclusive price.

Closed Sun, Mon, 1 wk Xmas & 2 wks Jul

English & French 35 seats S% Lunch £9—£12&alc Dinner £18—£25&alc Wine £6.85 Last dinner 9.30pm

Credit cards 1 3

TURNBERRY
Strathclyde *Ayrshire*
Map **10** NS20

★★★★ *HL* **Turnberry** (06553) 202 Due to change to (0655) 31000 Telex no 777779

Closed Jan—25 Feb

Imposingly situated on a hillside overlooking the championship golf courses, this old hotel is being restored to its former grandeur. It has beautifully appointed rooms and a high standard of food.

Tunbridge Wells (Royal) — Tuxford

130 CTV in all bedrooms T S% sB&B £110 dB&B £150

Lift ☾CTV 200P CFA ✿ (heated) 18 (hard) snooker sauna bath solarium gymnasium Live music nightly

Scottish & French V S% Lunch £12.50&alc Tea £2.50—£5.50 Dinner £23.50&alc Wine £11.25 Last Dinner 9.30pm

Credit cards 1 2 3 4 5

TURVEY
Bedfordshire
Map **4** SP95

★★ **Laws** (023064) 213 Telex no 825711

The nicely-appointed hotel, now under new ownership, is scheduled for major conversion and refurbishment.

10 (1fb) 1 CTV in all bedrooms ® sB&B £35—£55 dB&B £45—£65

60P ✿

English & French V Lunch £13alc Tea £1.25 Dinner £13alc Wine £5.50 Last dinner 9.15pm

Credit cards 1 3 V

TUTBURY
Staffordshire
Map **8** SK22

★★★ **Ye Olde Dog and Partridge** High St (Best Western) Burton-on-Trent (0283) 813030

Closed 25—26 Dec & 1 Jan

Remarkable 15th-century timbered inn with elegant period décor.

4rm(1) Annexe: 14rm (12 2)(1fb) 3 CTV in all bedrooms ® T sB&B £40—£46 dB&B £50—£60

☾100P ✿ Live music nightly nc 10yrs

English & French V Lunch £7.50&alc Dinner £7—£8.50&alc Wine £5 Last dinner 10pm

Credit cards 1 2 3 5 V

TUXFORD
Nottinghamshire
Map **8** SK77

★★ ***Newcastle Arms*** (0777) 870208

Large 18th century inn modernised with comfortable accommodation.

12rm(7)(1fb) 1 CTV in all bedrooms ® T

50 2

V Last dinner 9.30pm

Credit cards 1 2 3 5

T

TWEEDSMUIR
Borders *Peeblesshire*
Map **11** NT12

★★**Crook Inn** ☏ (08997) 272

Set in the upper Tweed Valley and dating from the 17th century, the inn provides both character and warmth in comfortable bedrooms, relaxing lounges and a restaurant serving Scottish fare.

Closed Xmas

8rm(5 1) ®

CTV 60P 3

Last dinner 8.45pm

TWICKENHAM
Greater London
London plan **5** *B2* (page 446)

✕**Cezanne** 68 Richmond Rd ☏ 01-892 3526

This smart, spacious restaurant offers an English menu of inexpensive dishes served in a friendly and informal atmosphere.

Closed Sun & Bank Hols Lunch not served Sat

French 38 seats Lunch £11.40alc Dinner £11.40alc Wine £4.50 Last dinner 10.30pm

Credit cards 1 2 3 V

✕**Quincey's** 34 Church St ☏ 01-892 6366

Friendly, intimate, small restaurant.

Closed Sun Lunch not served Sat

French 33 seats ✻Lunch £7.95—£13.95 Dinner £7.95—£13.95 Wine £5.10 Last dinner 11pm

Credit cards 1 2 3 5

TWO BRIDGES
Devon
Map **2** SX67

★★**Two Bridges** ☏ Princetown (082289) 206

Closed Jan—Feb

A coaching inn which dates from the 18th century is centrally situated on Dartmoor, with the West Dart River running through the grounds. Here may be seen llamas and other rare breeds of animal!

22rm(1 6) 1 CTV in 10 bedrooms **T**
sB&B£12—£18 sB&B £16—£24
dB&Bfr£24 dB&B £34—£40

CTV 150P 1 snooker

V Lunch £1.50—£5 Dinner £5.60—£10 Wine £3.95 Last dinner 9pm

Credit cards 1 3

See advertisement under Tavistock

TYNEMOUTH
Tyne & Wear
Map **12** NZ36

★★★**Grand** Grand Pde (Consort) ☏ 091-257 2106

Predominantly a commercial hotel in pleasant sea front location.

39rm(34)(3fb) CTV in all bedrooms ®
✻sB&B£20—£27.50
sB&B £24—£31.50 dB&B£33—£42
dB&B £36—£48

Lift Disco Thu, Fri & Sat *xmas*

International **V** ✻Lunch fr£4.95&alc Tea 60p Dinner £7.50—£8.50&alc Wine £6 Last dinner 9.30pm

Credit cards 1 2 3 5 V

★★★**Park** Grand Pde ☏ 091—257 1406

RS Xmas & New Year

A modern functional hotel situated in a prominent position on sea front.

31rm(20 2)(4fb) CTV in all bedrooms
®sB&B£25.30
sB&B £30.80—£40.15
dB&B£36—£47.85
dB&B £36—£47.85

400P Live music and dancing Wed

V Lunch £5.30—£8.25&alc Dinner £6.90—£10&alc Wine £5.30 Last dinner 9.30pm

Credit cards 1 2 3 5

TYNET
Grampian *Banffshire*
Map **15** NJ36

★★**Mill Motel** ☏ Clochan (05427) 233

Closed 1 & 2 Jan

Converted mill whose modern facilities blend well with the original features.

15rm(12 3)(1fb) CTV in all bedrooms
®sB&B fr£19 dB&B fr£34

100P Live music and dancing Wed & Sat

V Lunch £4 Tea fr£1.50 High Tea £2.40—£6.50 Dinner £8.50—£9.75 Last dinner 8.45pm

Credit cards 1 2 3 5

TYWYN
Gwynedd
Map **6** SH50

★★**Corbett Arms** Corbett Sq (Consort) ☏ (0654) 710264

Family run hotel with relaxing atmosphere near Sea and Cader Idris Range.

25rm(12 11)(2fb) CTV in 14 bedrooms
®S% ✻sB&Bfr£17.25 sB&B fr£20
dB&B fr£40

CTV 35P 8 *xmas*

British & French **V** ✻Lunch fr£4.50 Tea fr£2.25 Dinner fr£8.25&alc Wine £3.75 Last dinner 8.30pm

Credit cards 1 2 3 5 V

★**Greenfield** High St ☏ (0654) 710354

Closed Dec RS Jan & Feb

Small family-run hotel with separate restaurant serving good, inexpensive meals.

14rm(3fb) sB&B£10.75—£11.25
dB&B£21.50—£22.50

CTV

Lunch £3.50 Dinner £4.25&alc Wine £4.25 Last dinner 8.30pm

UCKFIELD
East Sussex
Map **5** TQ42

◯**Horsted Place** Little Horsted (2m S A26) (Pride of Britain) ☎ (0825) 75315
18 Now Open.

✕**Percy's** 119 High St ☎ (0825) 61366
(Classification awarded for dinner only.)
Restaurant features daily specialities of different nationalities; also tastefully decorated, entertaining wine bar.
Closed Sun, Mon & Bank Hols
English, French & Italian **V** 40 seats S% Lunch £10alc Dinner £11.50&alc Wine £4.75 Last dinner 10pm 10P Live music Thu, Fri & Sat
Credit cards 1 3

UDDINGSTON
Strathclyde *Lanarkshire*
Map **11** NS66

★★**Redstones** 8—10 Glasgow Rd ☎ (0698) 813774
Closed 1&2 Jan RS 31 Dec
14rm(12 2) CTV in all bedrooms ® T sB&B £31.50 dB&B £42
33P
V Lunch £4.50—£5.50&alc Tea £1 High Tea £4.50—£5.50 Dinner £8.50&alc Wine £4.25 Last dinner 9.30pm
Credit cards 1 2 3 5 Ⓥ

✕***Il Buongustaio*** 84 Main St ☎ (0698) 816000
This homely little Italian restaurant, with character wooden floor, real looms and Victoriana, offers warm, friendly service and a standard a la carte menu supplemented by seasonal specialities.
Continental 45 seats Last dinner 10pm
Credit cards 1 2 3 5

UIG
Isle of Skye, Highland *Inverness-shire*
See **Skye, Isle of**

UIST (SOUTH), ISLE OF
Western Isles *Inverness-shire*
See **South Uist, Isle of**

ULLAPOOL
Highland *Ross & Cromarty*
Map **14** NH19
See also **Leckmelm**

★★★**Ladbroke** North Rd (on A835) (Ladbroke) ☎ (0854) 2314
Closed mid Oct—mid Apr
Modern, low-rise complex standing on the main north road.
60 (21fb) CTV in all bedrooms ® *sB £39 dB £58.50 (room only)
#80P sauna bath
V *Bar lunch £1.50—£4.50 Tea £1 High Tea £3—£5 Dinner £9.75&alc Wine £5.99 Last dinner 9pm
Credit cards 1 2 3 5

★★*BL* **Ceilidh Place** West Argyle St ☎ (0854) 2103
Closed Nov—Feb
A friendly and informal hotel specialises in vegetarian cuisine and features contemporary Scottish music.
26rm(8)(7fb) S% sB&B £13.50—£22 sB&B £26 dB&B £28—£42 dB&B £50
30P
V S% *Lunch £4.95alc Tea £1—£2 High Tea £4.95 Dinner £9.50&alc Wine £4.50 Last dinner 9pm
Credit cards 1 2 3 5 Ⓥ

★★**Four Seasons** Garve Rd ☎ (0854) 2905
The modern, purpose-built hotel has split-level, semi open-plan public areas.
16(3fb) CTV in all bedrooms ® in 6 bedrooms S% sB&B £17.50—£20 dB&B £32—£36
50P water skiing
English & French **V** S% Lunch £8&alc Tea £2.50 Dinner £8&alc Wine £3.50 Last dinner 8.30pm
Credit cards 1 2 3 Ⓥ

★★*L* **Harbour Lights** Garve Rd ☎ (0854) 2222
Closed Nov—Mar
Bright, comfortable modern hotel with elegant harbour lounge and chandelier dining room.
22rm(9 6)(4fb) in all bedrooms CTV in 6 bedrooms ® in 18 bedrooms S% sB&B £15—£18 sB&B £16—£19 dB&B £28—£30 dB&B £32—£40
CTV 32P
Mainly grills **V** S% Lunch 95p—£2.95 Tea £1.20—£1.40 Dinner £3.95—£7.75 Wine £4.50 Last dinner 9pm
Credit cards 1 3 4 5

★***Ferry Boat Inn*** Shore St ☎ (0854) 2366
Closed 23 Dec—2 Jan
A small, friendly, family run hotel in pleasant shore location.
12rm(1fb)
TV
V Last dinner 9pm
Credit cards 1 5

ULLSWATER
Cumbria
See **Glenridding, Patterdale, Pooley Bridge** & **Watermillock**

ULVERSTON
Cumbria
Map **7** SD27

★★**Lonsdale House** Daltongate ☎ (0229) 52598
Closed 1 wk after Xmas
Originally built as an 18th-century town house, it has now been converted into a family-run hotel.
23rm(20) 1 CTV in all bedrooms ® T *sB&B £19.55 sB&B £25.30 dB&B £27.60—£29.90 dB&B £27.60—£39.10
CTV
V *Dinner £6.50—£8.50&alc Wine £4.50 Last dinner 9pm
Credit cards 1 2 3 5 Ⓥ

★★**Sefton House** Queen St ☎ (0229) 52190

Situated near the centre of the town, this very pleasant commercial hotel offers good accommodation and a warm, friendly welcome.

11rm(2⇌5⋒) CTV in all bedrooms ® T ✱ ✻sB&B£19—£23 sB&B⇌⋒£23—£29 dB&B£30—£36 dB&B⇌⋒£38—£45 B

CTV 6P 2🚗 ⇌

V ♁ ☕ Lunch £5alc Tea 50palc Dinner £8.90alc Wine £4.95 Last dinner 8.30pm

Credit cards 1 3

★★**Virginia House** Queen St ☎ (0229) 54844

The newly-furnished hotel provides good all-round facilities; set in a delightful Georgian house, family owned and run, it offers good meals in a pleasant restaurant.

7⋒(1fb) CTV in all bedrooms ® ✱ S% sB&B⋒£25 dB&B⋒£39 B P ⇌ ✿

V ♁ ☕ ⚟ S% ✻Lunch £3—£7.50&alc Dinner £6.50—£12.50&alc Wine £4.50 Last dinner 9pm

Credit cards 2 3 Ⓥ

★**Railway** Princes St ☎ (0229) 52208

Closed Xmas Day

A small hotel near the sea and the 2,000 acres of Birkrigg Common.

8rm(2fb) CTV in all bedrooms ® S% ✻sB&B£15—£17 dB&B£23—£26 B

40P 2🚗 ⇌

♁ ✻Lunch £4alc Dinner £6alc Wine £3.50 Last dinner 9pm

Ⓥ

✕***Mandalay Malaysian*** 5 Fountain St ☎ (0229) 55047

This very good little restaurant stands near the centre of the town and is run by a Malaysian lady helped by various members of her family, who are happy to explain their interesting menu and its daily 'specials'.

Closed Sun

Lunch not served

Malaysian V 40 seats Last dinner 10pm

P

Credit cards 1 3

Ulverston — Uplyme

UMBERLEIGH
Devon
Map **2** SS62

★★**Rising Sun Inn** (Berni) ☎ High Bickington (0769) 60447

Closed Oct—Feb

This very friendly 17th-century village inn has character bars, cosy bedrooms and its own fishing.

6rm(4⇌) Annexe: 2rm ® sB&B£26 sB&B⇌£26 dB&B£56 dB&B⇌£56

CTV 15P ⇌ ⚲ nc14yrs

V ♁ Bar lunch 70p—£1.50 Dinner £8—£9 Wine £4.50 Last dinner 8pm

Credit cards 1 3

UNDERBARROW
Cumbria
Map **7** SD49

★★**Greenriggs Country House** ☎ Crosthwaite (04488) 387

Closed Jan—Feb RS Nov—Dec & Mar (Fri, Sat & Sun only)

An 18th-century house has been tastefully converted into an hotel of charm and character which offers a warm welcome and a comfortable stay.

12rm(6⇌2⋒)(4fb) ® sB&B£16—£21 sB&B⇌⋒£20—£25 dB&B£40 dB&B⇌⋒£63 B

CTV 30P ⇌ ✿ croquet xmas

♁ ☕ ⚟ Bar lunch £2—£4 Tea £1—£1.50 Dinner £12.50 Wine £4 Last dinner 8pm

Ⓥ

UPHALL
Lothian *West Lothian*
Map **11** NT07

★★★ *B* **Houstoun House** ☎ Broxburn (0506) 853831 Telex no 727148

Closed 1—3 Jan

The historic, baronial hotel features a fine restaurant and a superb cellar; character period bedrooms are supplemented by a modern but tasteful extension.

30rm(29⇌1⋒) 10 CTV in all bedrooms T S% ✻sB&B⇌⋒£48.50—£60 dB&B⇌⋒£66.50—£85 Continental breakfast B

(100P ✿

V ♁ S% ✻Lunch £11.50 Dinner £17 Wine £3.80 Last dinner 9.30pm

Credit cards 1 2 3 5

UPHOLLAND
Lancashire
Map **7** SD50

★★***Holland Hall*** 6 Lafford Ln ☎ (0695) 624426

Overlooking the golf course, this well-furnished and comfortable hotel is popular for its delightful restaurant.

11rm(4⇌7⋒)(1fb) CTV in all bedrooms ® ✱ B

(200P ✿ ⛳18 Disco Fri Sat & Sun *xmas*

English & French V ♁ ☕ Last dinner 11pm

Credit cards 1 2 3 5

UPLYME
Devon
Map **3** SY39

See **Lyme Regis** for details of other hotels

★★★**Devon** Lyme Rd (Best Western) ☎ Lyme Regis (02974) 3231 Telex no 42513

Closed Nov—26 Mar

Former 16th-century monastery which has been converted into a relaxing hotel.

21rm(18⇌3⋒)(4fb) CTV in all bedrooms ® sB&B⇌⋒£26.50—£31.50 dB&B⇌⋒£53—£63 B

30P ⇌ ✿ ⛱ (heated) *xmas*

English & French ♁ ☕ Bar lunch £1.50—£5 Tea £1 Dinner £10.25 Wine £6 Last dinner 8.15pm

Credit cards 1 2 3 5

CWRTDLEN Langwing

UPPER SLAUGHTER
Gloucestershire
Map **4** SP12

★★★ **Lords of the Manor** (Consort) ☎ Cotswold (0451) 20243 Telex no 83147

Closed 4—18 Jan

Comfortable 17th-century manor house hotel in 7½ acres of grounds.

15rm(14 1) 2 ® T S% *sB&B fr£40 dB&B £50—£90 Continental breakfast

CTV 20P 3 nc 2yrs *xmas*

V S% Lunch fr£7.50 Tea fr£1.25 Dinner fr£12.50 Wine £5.95 Last dinner 9.30pm

Credit cards 1 2 3 5 V

UPPINGHAM
Leicestershire
Map **4** SP89

★★★ **Falcon** High St (Inter Hotel) ☎ (0572) 823535

Former coaching inn situated in the centre of the attractive old town.

25rm(19 6)(1fb) 1 CTV in all bedrooms T *sB&B £38.50 dB&B £52.50

18P

English & French V Lunch £12.50alc Tea £1.50 High Tea £1.10—£6 Dinner £12.50alc Wine £6.50 Last dinner 9.45pm

Credit cards 1 2 3 5 V

★*H* **Garden House** 16 High St West ☎ (0572) 822352

Very friendly family run hotel with cosy, attractively decorated bedrooms, many of them overlooking the walled garden.

12rm(4)(1fb) CTV in all bedrooms ® sB&B£17 sB&B £21 dB&B£26 dB&B £30

CTV

Lunch £6.50alc Tea £1.50alc High Tea £2.50alc Dinner £8.25alc Wine £4.25 Last dinner 9pm

Credit cards 1 3

★*B* **Lake Isle** High Street East ☎ (0572) 822951

RS 2 wks end Feb & 2 wks Sep/Oct

Though there is no lake near this town-centre hotel, the recent addition of a tiny walled garden has helped to create an oasis of tranquility. Well known for its attractive accommodation, the hotel is now becoming still more popular for exceptionally fine food, as David and Clare Whitfield, ably assisted by a young team, create excellent French dishes from mainly local fresh produce and serve them in a farmhouse kitchen style dining room. A superb selection of wines is available, and the proprietor is happy to show his cellar to guests if time allows.

5rm(2 3)(1fb) CTV in all bedrooms ® S% sB&B £22—£26 dB&B £30—£34

3P 1

English & French V *Lunch £6.75—£8 Dinner £11.75—£14.50 Wine £4.50 Last dinner 10pm

Credit cards 1 2 3 5 V

UPTON UPON SEVERN
Heretord & Worcester
Map **3** SO84

★★ **White Lion** High St ☎ (06846) 2551

Closed Xmas Day

Town-centre hotel with a Georgian façade which is popular with tourists.

10rm(8 2) 1 CTV in all bedrooms ® T sB&B £32.50 dB&B £44.50—£47.50

14P 1

English & French V Lunch £9.80&alc Tea 75p Dinner fr£9.80&alc Wine £4.70 Last dinner 9.15pm

Credit cards 1 2 3 4 5 V

USK
Gwent
Map **3** SO30

★★*L* **Glen-yr-Afon** Pontypool Rd ☎ (02913) 2302

Elegant country house style hotel with attractive library. Good home cooked food.

15rm(1 11)(2fb) CTV in 14 bedrooms sB&B£22—£35 sB&B £25—£35 dB&B£33—£55 dB&B £35—£55

CTV 30P croquet *xmas*

V Lunch £7—£9&alc Tea £1.50—£3.50 High Tea £2.50—£5.50 Dinner £7—£11&alc Wine £5.50 Last dinner 8.30pm

V

★★ **Three Salmons** Bridge St ☎ (02913) 2133

RS 24—26 Dec

A one-time coaching inn, The Three Salmons is well-known as a retreat for anglers, having assumed the role of character hotel and restaurant.

10rm(9 2) Annexe: 18rm(16 1)(1fb) 2 CTV in all bedrooms ® T *sB&B £25—£28 dB&B £35—£40

39P

V *Lunch fr£7.50&alc Dinner £13—£14alc Wine £4.95 Last dinner 9.30pm

Credit cards 1 2 3

X **Il Giardino** Bridge St ☎ (02913) 2459

Attractive cottage-style restaurant.

Continental V 25 seats S% Lunch £15alc Dinner £15alc Wine £6.75 Last dinner 9.30pm

Credit cards 2 3 V

U

UXBRIDGE
Greater London
Map **4** TQ08

★★★**Master Brewer Motel** Western Av ☏(0895) 51199
(For full entry see Hillingdon)

✕✕✕**Giovanni's** Denham Lodge, Oxford Rd ☏(0895) 31568

Attractively situated restaurant surrounded by landscaped gardens.

Closed Sun Lunch not served Sat

Italian **V** 80 seats S% *Lunch £17alc Dinner £17alc Wine £5.90 Last dinner 10.30pm 30P Live music Thu, Fri & Sat

Credit cards 1 2 3 4 5

VENTNOR
Isle of Wight
See **Wight, Isle of**

VERYAN
Cornwall
Map **2** SW93

★★★*L* **Nare** ☏Truro (0872) 501279

Attractive hotel, personally run, in magnificent situation commanding extensive views. Fine gardens and good amenities.

34rm(19⇌9⌂) Annexe: 3⇌(7fb) TV available in bedrooms Ⓡ
*sB&B£18—£29.75 sB&B⇌⌂£18—£31.50 dB&B£36—£59.50 dB&B⇌⌂£36—£63

CTV 120P ✿ (heated) (hard) snooker sauna bath solarium gymnasium table tennis *xmas*

English & Continental **V** *Bar lunch £4.50alc Tea 70palc Dinner £11.50 Wine £4.40 Last dinner 9.15pm

Credit cards 1 2 3 5 Ⓥ

★★**Elerkey House** ☏Truro (0872) 501261

Closed Nov—Mar

Small country hotel in this picturesque old Cornish village. Peaceful atmosphere and pleasant garden.

8rm(4⇌1⌂) CTV in 3 bedrooms
sB&B£15—£17.50
sB&B⇌⌂£16.50—£19 dB&B£28—£33
dB&B⇌⌂£31—£36 B

CTV 12P ✿ nc 8yrs

Tea £1—£1.50 Dinner £9 Wine £4.70 Last dinner 8.30pm

Credit cards 1 3

✕**Treverbyn House** Pendower Rd ☏Truro (0872) 501201

A tiny, personally-run restaurant, in a picturesque setting, and offering good home cooking.

Closed Nov—Feb RS Oct & Mar Lunch not served

French 20 seats S% Dinner £10.50—£11 Wine £3.80 Last dinner 8.30pm 9P nc 7yrs

VIRKIE
Shetland
See **Shetland Isles**

WADEBRIDGE
Cornwall
Map **2** SW97

★★**Molesworth Arms** Molesworth St (Best Western)
☏(020881) 2055

RS Xmas Day

Original 16th-century inn, comfortably furnished and offering a relaxed atmosphere.

16rm(9⇌)(2fb) CTV in all bedrooms Ⓡ
sB&B£17.83 sB&B⇌£17.83
dB&B£32.20 dB&B⇌£32.20

CTV 50P 4

V Lunch £3.80alc Dinner £8alc Wine £4.48 Last dinner 9.30pm

Credit cards 1 3

U

WADHURST
East Sussex
Map **5** TQ63

❀★★**Spindlewood** Wallcrouch (2¼m SE of Wadhurst on B2099) ☎ Ticehurst (0580) 200430

Closed 24–26 Dec RS Bank Hols

The small, relaxing, family-run hotel is peacefully situated and furnished with antiques. Imaginative country cooking is complemented by good, personal service and attention to detail.

9rm(8➡1⋔) CTV in all bedrooms ®**T** ✗ sB&B➡⋔£30–£35 dB&B➡⋔£62–£70 ₿

80P ✱ ⚲(hard)

English & French **V** Lunch £10.50–£17.50&alc Tea fr£1 Dinner fr£17.50 Wine £5.70 Last dinner 9pm

Credit cards 1 3

WAKEFIELD
West Yorkshire
Map **8** SE32

★★★**Cedar Court** Denby Dale Rd, Calder Grove ☎ (0924) 276310 Telex no 557647

RS Xmas Day & Boxing Day

Strategically placed close to Junction 39 of the M1 motorway, the hotel has a large, landscaped car park. The bedrooms are well-equipped and smartly-furnished with all amenities, public areas have style, and the restaurant serves haute cuisine meals. There is a separate carvery.

100➡(2fb) in 24 bedrooms CTV in all bedrooms ®**T** sB&B➡£55 dB&B➡£65 ₿

Lift ☾ ## 240P ✱

English & French **V** Lunch £8.50&alc Tea 95p High Tea £4 Dinner £9.50&alc Wine £5.95 Last dinner 10pm

Credit cards 1 2 3 5

★★★**Post House** Queen's Dr, Ossett (Trusthouse Forte) ☎ (0924) 276388 Telex no 55407

Well designed modern hotel with coffee shop and restaurant.

96rm CTV in all bedrooms ® sB&B➡£53.50 dB&B➡£68.50 ₿

Lift ☾ CTV 140P CFA ✱

Last dinner 10.15pm

Credit cards 1 2 3 4 5

★★★**Stoneleigh** Doncaster Rd (Inter Hotel) ☎ (0924) 369461 Telex no 51458

A row of Victorian houses has been stylishly converted into a well-equipped hotel which offers attractive cocktail and lounge bars, a very good restaurant and services of a high standard.

36rm(27➡9⋔)(2fb) CTV in all bedrooms ®**T** ✗ sB&B➡⋔£40.50–£42.50 dB&B➡⋔£45.50–£47.50 ₿

Lift ☾ 80P

English & Italian **V** Lunch fr£7.95 Tea fr90p High Tea fr90p Dinner fr£9.95 Wine £5 Last dinner 10pm

Credit cards 1 3 4 5

★★★**Swallow** Queen St (Swallow) ☎ (0924) 372111 Telex no 557464

Modern, tower block in the town centre.

64rm(60➡4⋔)(4fb) CTV in all bedrooms ®**T** S% sB&B➡⋔fr£45 dB&B➡⋔fr£55 ₿

Lift ☾ 60P CFA *xmas*

English & French **V** S% Lunch fr£6.25&alc Tea fr80p Dinner fr£10&alc Wine £5.50 Last dinner 9.15pm

Credit cards 1 2 3 5

★★★**Waterton Park** Walton Hall, The Balk, Walton (3m SE off B6378) ☎ (0924) 257911

A Georgian mansion, set on the island of a picturesque lake, provides an attractive setting for this up-to-date hotel with good conference and leisure facilities. Bedrooms, like public rooms, are fitted and furnished to a high standard, whilst the cuisine is designed to please perceptive palates.

26rm(25➡1⋔)(2fb) 1 CTV in all bedrooms ®**T** ✗ *sB&B➡⋔fr£45 dB&B➡⋔£52–£65 Continental breakfast ₿

☾ 100P ✱ (heated) squash snooker sauna bath solarium gymnasium Live music & dancing Sat

V *Lunch £5.50–£7.95 Tea 75p Dinner £9.95&alc Wine £4.95 Last dinner 10pm

Credit cards 1 2 3 5 Ⓥ

WALBERSWICK
Suffolk
Map **5** TM47

★★**Anchor** ☎ Southwold (0502) 722112 Telex no 97223

The gabled, mock-Tudor exterior of this hotel gives way to the Scandinavian-style lounge and dining room while there are also chalets in a garden setting.

6rm(2➡) Annexe: 8➡(2fb) CTV in all bedrooms ® *sB&B£14–£19 sB&B➡£16.50–£21.50 dB&B£28–£34 dB&B➡£30.50–£36.50 ₿

CTV 25P ✱ *xmas*

*Lunch fr£5.75 Tea fr60p Dinner fr£7.50 Wine £4 Last dinner 8.30pm

Credit cards 1 2 3 5

WALKERBURN
Borders *Peeblesshire*
Map **11** NT33

★★**Tweed Valley** Galashiels Rd (Inter Hotel) ☎ (089687) 220 Telex no 946240 Ref 190 14620

The privately owned and managed hotel, which has an attractive, wood-panelled dining room, was recently refurbished.

16rm(12➡4⋔)(2fb) 1 CTV in all bedrooms ®**T** sB&B➡⋔£27–£32 dB&B➡⋔£37–£54 ₿

35P ✱ sauna bath solarium gymnasium

V S% Lunch £4.50–£8&alc Tea 70p–£1 High Tea £4.75–£8&alc Dinner £10.50–£15&alc Wine £4.95 Last dinner 9.30pm

Credit cards 1 2 3 5 Ⓥ

WALL
Northumberland
Map **12** NY96

★★***Hadrian*** ☎ Humshaugh (043481) 232

Creeper clad inn richly furnished with antiques; bedrooms simple and clean.

8rm(2➡5⋔) CTV in 2 bedrooms ® ₿

CTV 50P 4 ✱ nc 12yrs

English & French **V** Last dinner 9.30pm

WALLASEY
Merseyside
Map **7** SJ29

★★**Belvidere** Seabank Rd, New Brighton ☎ 051-639 8145

Family owned and run, the pleasant, commercial-style hotel is located in a residential area.

24rm(10➡)(2fb) CTV in all bedrooms sB&B£17 sB&B➡£19.50 dB&B£27 dB&B➡£34

☾ CTV 40P 3 (£2 per night)

French **V** Lunch £3.95–£6.50 Tea £1–£2.50 Dinner £6.50–£12.50 Wine £3.25 Last dinner 9.30pm

Credit cards 1 3

★**Grove House** Grove Rd ☎ 051-630 4558

This pleasantly furnished hotel with good restaurant stands in a residential area.

14rm(1fb) CTV in all bedrooms ®**T** ✗ *sB&B£23.50 dB&B£36 ₿

16P ✱

English & French **V** *Lunch fr£5.75 Dinner £6.85–£7.50&alc Wine £5.11 Last dinner 9pm

Credit cards 1 3 5

WALLINGFORD
Oxfordshire
Map **4** SU68

★★★**Shillingford Bridge** Shillingford (2m N A329) ☎ Warborough (086732) 8567

Closed Xmas Day

Hotel with spacious rooms and formal restaurant overlooking the Thames.

27rm(20 7)(2fb) 2 CTV in all bedrooms ® T sB&B £35—£40 dB&B £45—£55
120P (heated) squash Live music & dancing Sat
V Lunch £8.50—£10&alc Dinner £8.50—£10&alc Wine £5.50 Last dinner 10pm
Credit cards 1 2 3 5

★ ★ ***George*** High St (Kingsmead) ☎ (0491) 36665
Timbered Tudor inn with small, well-equipped bedrooms.
18rm(7 2)(1fb) CTV in all bedrooms ® T
80P squash *xmas*
English & French V Last dinner 10.30pm
Credit cards 1 2 3 5

X **Brown & Boswell** 28 High St ☎ (0491) 34078
The relaxing décor of this quality, proprietor-run restaurant features unusual pickled-pine panelling. The daily fixed-price menu includes wine, and the full menu provides some attractive dishes for vegetarians and whole-food devotees, all meals being home-cooked from sound, fresh ingredients and complemented by a well-researched wine list.

Closed Mon, last 2 wks March & 2nd wk Oct Lunch not served Tue Dinner not served Sun
International V 35 seats Lunch £3.50—£4.50&alc Dinner £15&alc Wine £4.75 Last dinner 10pm
Credit cards 1 2 3 5

WALLSEND
Tyne & Wear
Map **12** NZ26

★ ★ ★ **Newcastle Moat House** Coast Rd (Queens Moat) ☎ 091-262 8989 Telex no 53583
Spacious modern hotel with comfortable bedrooms.
162 (15fb) CTV in all bedrooms ® T S% sB&B £44 dB&B £50
Lift 500P Disco Wed
English & French V S% Lunch £9&alc Tea £1.50 High Tea £5—£8 Dinner £9—£11&alc Wine £5 Last dinner 10pm
Credit cards 1 2 3 5 V

WALSALL
West Midlands
Map **7** SP09
See also **Barr, Great**

★ ★ ★ *B* **Barons Court** Walsall Rd, Walsall Wood (3m NE A461) (Best Western) ☎ Brownhills (0543) 376543 Telex no 333061
Just outside the town, this large, mock Tudor building has some elaborate bedrooms and a popular leisure complex.
76 (5fb) 21 CTV in all bedrooms ® T S% sB&B £37—£45 dB&B £45—53
Lift 180P CFA (heated) sauna bath solarium gymnasium Live music & dancing Sat *xmas*
English & French V S% Lunch £6—£10&alc Tea 90p—£1 Dinner £10—£12&alc Wine £5.75 Last dinner 9.45pm
Credit cards 1 2 3 4 5 V

★ ★ ★ **Crest Hotel—Birmingham/Walsall** Birmingham Rd (Crest) ☎ (0922) 33555 Telex no 335479
RS Xmas
The modern hotel offers well-appointed bedrooms, a choice of three bars and the popular Orangery Restaurant.
101 in 10 bedrooms CTV in all bedrooms ® T S% sB £54.65 dB £70.80 (room only)
→

Lift ☾ # CTV 220P CFA games room Live music & dancing 6 nights wkly

♀ French V ♀ ☕ ⅄ Lunch £7.65&alc Tea 80p—£1 Dinner £11.95&alc Wine £6 Last dinner 10pm

Credit cards 1 2 3 4 5

★★★ **Fairlawns** 178 Little Aston Rd, Aldridge (3m NE off A454) (Consort) ☎ Aldridge (0922) 55122 Telex no 339873

RS 25 Dec—1 Jan

On the A454, between Aldridge and the A452 Chester Road, stands a modern, comfortable hotel where the owners take an active role in providing service to guests.

30rm (21 ⛀ 9 ⋒) (2fb) CTV in all bedrooms ® T S% sB&B ⛀ ⋒ £37.50 dB&B ⛀ ⋒ £45 B

☾ CTV 65P 2 ⌂ (£5 per night) ✿ Live music & dancing Fri

♀ English & French V ♀ ☕ S% Lunch £1.15—£8.50&alc Tea £1—£2.50 Dinner £11.25&alc Wine £6 Last dinner 10pm

Credit cards 1 2 3 4 5 Ⓥ

★★ **Beverley** 58 Lichfield Rd ☎ (0922) 614967

A converted house on the outskirts of the town offers facilities for small conferences and private functions.

23rm (1 ⛀ 4 ⋒) Annexe: 4rm (1 ⛀ 2 ⋒) (2fb) ® T * sB&B £17 sB&B ⛀ ⋒ £25 dB&B £30 dB&B ⛀ ⋒ £33

CTV 40P

♀ ☕ * Lunch £3.95 Dinner £5.95&alc Wine £4.95 Last dinner 8.30pm

Credit cards 1 3

★★ **County** Birmingham Rd (Queens Moat) ☎ (0922) 32323

RS 24—27 Dec

Extended and modernised house with a Tudor façade, now a commercial businessman's hotel.

47rm (11 ⛀ 18 ⋒) (1fb) CTV in all bedrooms ® T sB&B £26 sB&B ⛀ ⋒ £33 dB&B £36 dB&B ⛀ ⋒ £40 B

☾ 120P

♀ English & French V ♀ ☕ Lunch £6.75—£7&alc Tea 80p Dinner £7.75&alc Wine £4.50 Last dinner 9.45pm

Credit cards 1 2 3 5 Ⓥ

★ **Abberley** Bescot Rd ☎ (0922) 27413

Set on a busy road, the small, town hotel provides value-for-money accommodation and food; it is popular with businessmen.

14rm (1 ⋒) ⅄ in 4 bedrooms CTV in all bedrooms ® ✗ S% sB&B £17.25 sB&B ⋒ fr £25.30 dB&B fr £28.75 dB&B ⋒ fr £38.10

CTV 16P ✿ *xmas*

V ♀ ☕ S% Lunch £5&alc Tea £3 High Tea £3 Dinner £5.75&alc Last dinner 8pm

Ⓥ

✕ **L'Auchel** 196c Walsall Wood Rd, Lazy Hill, Aldridge (4m NE) ☎ (0922) 57322

Pleasant, French family style restaurant, offering interesting food.

Closed Sun Lunct not served Mon & Sat

♀ French 44 seats Lunch fr £5.75&alc Dinner £9.45—£12.70&alc Wine £5.20 Last dinner 10pm P

Credit cards 1 2 5 Ⓥ

WALSHFORD

North Yorkshire
Map **8** SE45

✕✕✕ ***Bridge Inn*** (Byron Room) Great North Road ☎ Wetherby (0937) 62345

The Byron Room at the Bridge Inn is among the most beautiful in Britain, having an eighteenth-century Italian ceiling and fine plasterwork. This is matched by the cuisine, with its English and French menu of uncomplicated style, the pleasing variety of dishes receiving every care and attention.

Closed Mon Dinner not served Sun

♀ English & French 70 seats Last dinner 9pm 100P

Credit cards 1 2 3 5

WALTHAM, GREAT

Essex
Map **5** TL61

✕✕ **Windmill** ☎ Chelmsford (0245) 360292

The small country pub features a restaurant decorated in Victorian style where good, traditional English fare is served at reasonable cost in a warm, cheerful atmosphere.

Closed Sun & Bank Hols Lunch not served Sat

♀ English & French **V** 36 seats S% Lunch £15alc Dinner £15alc Wine £5.70 Last dinner 9.30pm 50P

Credit cards 1 3

WALTON ON THE HILL

Surrey
Map **4** TQ25

✕✕ **Ebenezer Cottage** 36 Walton St ☎ Tadworth (073781) 3166

Early 16th-century cottage restaurant offering traditional English food in a number of period styled dining rooms.

Closed Mon & 26 Dec—2 Jan Dinner not served Sun

68 seats * Lunch £10.50—£11.25&alc Dinner fr £14.50&alc Wine £5.95 Last dinner 9.30pm 20P ⅄

Credit cards 1 2 3 5 Ⓥ

WALTON UPON THAMES

Surrey
See **Shepperton** and **Weybridge**

WAMPHRAY

Dumfries & Galloway *Dumfriesshire*
Map **11** NY19

★ *H* **Red House** ☎ Johnstone Bridge (05764) 214

Closed 16 Nov—Etr

Small, comfortable hotel set in its own grounds, in a pleasant rural setting, with friendly owner and staff.

6rm (1fb) ® S% * sB&B £14.75 dB&B £29.50 B

CTV 20P 1 ⌂ ✿

♀ ☕ ⅄ * Lunch £5 Tea £2 High Tea £5 Dinner £7.50 Wine £5.45 Last dinner 8pm

Credit card 5 Ⓥ

W

WANSFORD
Cambridgeshire
Map **4** TL09

★★**Haycock** ☎ Stamford (0780) 782223 Telex no 32710

Situated in the centre of the quiet village, a 17th-century, stone-built coaching inn on the banks of the River Nene features a very popular restaurant and an award-winning garden.

20rm(19)(4fb)3 CTV in all bedrooms **T** S% sB&B fr£33 sB&B £48—£58 dB&B £64—£80 **B**

☾300P outdoor chess, petanque *xmas*

V S% Lunch £18alc Tea 95p&alc High tea £2.50—£3alc Dinner £18alc Wine £6.50 Last dinner 10.30pm

Credit cards 1 2 3 4 5

WANTAGE
Oxfordshire
Map **4** SU48

★★**Bear** Market Pl (Consort) ☎ (02357) 66366 Telex no 41363

Comfortable hotel with well-equipped bedrooms and beautifully appointed restaurant.

34rm(31 3)(2fb) CTV in all bedrooms Ⓡ **T** ✱ sB&B £35—£39.50 dB&B £54.50 **B**

Lift *xmas*

French **V** ✱ Lunch £6.85&alc Dinner £9.95&alc Wine £5.15 Last dinner 9.45pm

Credit cards 1 2 3 5

See advertisement under Oxford

WARE
Hertfordshire
Map **5** TL31

★★★**Ware Moat House** Baldock St (Queens Moat) ☎ (0920) 5011

Modern, two-storey brick hotel with good car parking.

50rm(44 6) in 6 bedrooms CTV in all bedrooms Ⓡ **T** ✱ sB&B fr£43 dB&B fr£54 **B**

Lift ☾100P

Wansford — Wareham

English & French **V** Lunch fr£8.50&alc Tea fr75p Dinner £9&alc Wine £5 Last dinner 9.30pm

Credit cards 1 2 3 5

✕**Ben's Brasserie** 14 High St ☎ (0920) 68383

A very popular, modern town centre Brasserie with good home cooking and friendly service.

Closed Sun & Bank Hols

French **V** 45 seats Lunch £11—£15alc Dinner £11—£15alc Wine £4.50 Last dinner 9.45pm

Ⓥ

WAREHAM
Dorset
Map **3** SY98

★★★*BL* ***Priory*** Church Green ☎ (09295) 2772

In a tranquil setting next to the church, with two acres of garden running down to the river, the converted 16th century priory features gracious drawing rooms, furnished with antiques. Breakfast and lunch are taken in the nicely-appointed Greenwood Room, but dinner is served in the more unusual cellar restaurant with its stone walls and flagged floor. Bedrooms are well-equipped, subtly decorated and provided with private facilities.

15rm(9 4) 2 CTV in all bedrooms **T** **B**

20P 2 Live music Sat *xmas*

French **V** Last dinner 9.45pm

Credit cards 1 2 3 5

★★★**Springfield Country** Grange Rd, Stoborough (1½m S off A351) ☎ (09295) 2177

The pleasant, family owned and run hotel stands in quiet surroundings, offering comfortable bedrooms, relaxing lounges and friendly service.

32(7fb) CTV in all bedrooms Ⓡ **T** sB&B £37—£42 dB&B £53.50—£63.50 **B**

Lift ☾100P (heated) (hard) snooker solarium table tennis nc2yrs

English & French **V** Bar lunch £4.50alc Tea 75palc High Tea £6alc Dinner fr£9alc Wine £5.40 Last dinner 9pm

Credit cards 1 2 3 5

★★*L* **Kemps Country House** East Stoke ☎ Bindon Abbey (0929) 462563

Closed 25 Dec—5 Jan

Guests are offered friendly attention at this pleasant hotel with its comfortable lounges and attractive, well-appointed restaurant where an extensive menu of well-prepared food is served.

5rm(1 3) Annexe: 4(4fb) CTV in all bedrooms Ⓡ sB&B £30—£35 sB&B £30—£35 dB&B £50 dB&B £50—£60 **B**

20P

French Lunch £5—£6&alc Dinner £11—£13&alc Wine £5 Last dinner 9.30pm

Credit cards 1 2 3 5 Ⓥ

See advertisement on page 748

★★**Worgret Manor** ☎ (09295) 2957

Closed 25—27 Dec

Quiet Georgian hotel with modern extension.

9rm(5)(3fb) CTV in all bedrooms Ⓡ sB&B £22 sB&B £25 dB&B £36 dB&B £40 **B**

CTV 40P

English & French **V** Lunch £5.25&alc Tea 75p Dinner £8&alc Wine £4.50 Last dinner 9.15pm

Credit cards 1 2 3 5

See advertisement on page 748

★**Black Bear** 14 South St ☎ (09295) 3280

An 18th century coaching inn with simple bedrooms situated in the town centre.

14rm(1)(3fb) TV in all bedrooms Ⓡ sB&B £16.75 dB&B £33 dB&B £35 **B**

CTV Live music & dancing mthly

English & French **V** Lunch £3.75—£8 Dinner £3.75—£8&alc Wine £4.35 Last dinner 9.15pm

Credit cards 1 2 3 Ⓥ

0929-552177

W

✕**Old Granary** The Quay ☏ (09295) 2010

The attractive restaurant, converted from a granary, enjoys a very pleasant position on the banks of the River Frome. Light lunches are served from the à la carte menu, which is supplemented by table d'hôte meals at dinner — either choice representing good value for money.

V 75 seats ✱Lunch £4.95&alc Dinner £9.75&alc Wine £4.85 Last dinner 9pm

Credit cards 1 2 3 5

WARK
Northumberland
Map **12** NY87

★***Battlesteads*** ☏ Bellingham (0660) 30209

A pleasant village inn with charm and character conveyed by the proprietors.

7rm(2fb)

CTV 50P

Mainly grills **V** Last dinner 9.30pm

WARMINSTER
Wiltshire
Map **3** ST84

★★★★ **Bishopstrow House**
(see red star box next column)

★★★★

★★★★ **BISHOPSTROW HOUSE, WARMINSTER**

Boreham Rd (2m SE A36) (Relais et Châteaux) ☏ (0985) 212312 Telex no 444829

What changes have taken place here since last year! The owners have set their sights high and they have hit the target. Already one of our most elegant and beautifully furnished country hotels, it has now gained more bedrooms through the conversion of the coach house. Actually most of them are duplex suites, furnished with most attractive soft furnishings. Eight of the bedrooms also have jacuzzis. The restaurant has been enlarged and there is a terrace for al fresco eating in good weather, while a pianist plays at weekends. Recreational facilities have not been forgotten and in addition to the existing ones, an indoor tennis court and super swimming pool were created over the winter. To match all this they have opted to provide more services so that they now qualify for four stars without losing their Red Star qualities. Indeed, under John Coe — formerly at the British Embassy in Paris and now the manager here — the hospitable attitude of the staff is as good as ever. There are ample delightful public rooms (but no bar) where open fires burn when necessary. Simon Colloms is the chef and he cooks the best of ingredients in the modern French manner to most enjoyable effect. This opulent Georgian country house is set in twenty seven acres of grounds which stretch under the main road to the river beyond.

26(2fb) 1 CTV in all bedrooms **T**
sB&B £53—£65
dB&B £78—£128 Continental breakfast

35P & (heated) (hard)
squash sauna bath solarium nc3yrs
xmas

English & French Lunch £8.50—£15.50 Tea £1.75—£4.50 Dinner £16.50—£21.50 Wine £8.50 Last dinner 9.30pm

Credit cards 1 2 3 5

★ ★**Old Bell** Market Pl ☏ (0985) 216611

Contrasting colour-washed brick building in the centre of Warminster with a colonnaded arcade front, and double doors leading to an inner courtyard.

16rm(9➡1⋔)(2fb) CTV in all bedrooms Ⓡ ✱sB&B£23—£27 sB&B➡⋔fr£27 dB&B£29—£35 dB&B➡⋔fr£35 B

20P

✱Lunch £6.50alc Dinner £6.50alc Wine £4.50 Last dinner 10.30pm

Credit cards 1 2 3 5 Ⓥ

WARREN ROW
Berkshire
Map **4** SU88

✕✕***Warrener*** ☏ Littlewick Green (062882) 2803

This beautifully decorated and well run country restaurant features Swedish and French dishes, imaginatively cooked, well presented and complemented by excellent personal service from the patron.

Closed Sun, Mon Lunch not served Sat

French 40 seats Last dinner 9.30pm 20P

Credit cards 1 2 3 5

WARRINGTON
Cheshire
Map **7** SJ68

★ ★ ★**Fir Grove** Knutsford Old Rd ☏ (0925) 67471 Telex no 628117

A well-furnished hotel offers good bedrooms and a pleasant restaurant serving quality food.

38rm(18➡20⋔) CTV in all bedrooms Ⓡ**T** S% sB&B➡⋔fr£32 dB&B➡⋔fr£43 B

200P

English & French **V** S% ✱Lunch fr£8.50&alc Dinner fr£8.50&alc Wine £4 Last dinner 10pm

Credit cards 1 2 3 5

★ ★**Paddington House** 514 Old Manchester Rd ☏ (0925) 816767

35rm(17➡20⋔)(1fb) CTV in 25 bedrooms TV in 12 bedrooms Ⓡ**T** S% sB&B➡⋔£32.82 dB&B➡⋔£37.95—£45.54 B

Lift 100P 1

English & French **V** S% Lunch £12&alc Tea £1—£3.50 High Tea £5.75—£12&alc Dinner £12&alc Wine £4.50 Last dinner 9.30pm

Credit cards 1 2 3 Ⓥ

★ ★**Patten Arms** Parker St (GW Hotels) ☏ (0925) 36602

Closed 24—26 Dec RS Sun

Tall brick-built hotel with a modern extension, close to the railway station and the town centre.

43rm(29➡14⋔)(1fb) CTV in all bedrooms Ⓡ**T** S% sB&B➡⋔£15—£35 dB&B➡⋔£30—£45 B

25P Live music & dancing Fri

S% Lunch £5—£5.50&alc Tea 50p—75p Dinner £6—£6.50&alc Wine £5 Last dinner 9.30pm

Credit cards 1 2 3 5

★**Ribblesdale** Balmoral Rd, Grappenhall ☏ (0925) 601197

Small, quiet, friendly hotel supervised by resident owners.

15rm(7➡)(1fb) CTV in all bedrooms Ⓡ in 10 bedrooms S% sB&B£19—£22 sB&B➡£24—£27 dB&B£29—£32 dB&B➡£35—£40

CTV 25P

V S% Lunch £4—£7&alc Tea £2—£4&alc High Tea £2—£4&alc Dinner £7.75—£10&alc Wine £4.50 Last dinner 9pm

Credit cards 1 2 3 Ⓥ

★**Rockfield** Alexandra Rd, Grappenhall (1¾m SE off A50) ☏ (0925) 62898

Closed Xmas—New Year

A detached Edwardian house set in a quiet residential area of Warrington.

7rm(3➡) Annexe: 8rm(2➡) CTV in all bedrooms Ⓡ sB&B£20—£22 sB&B➡£25—£28 dB&B£30—£35 dB&B➡£36—£40 B

CTV 20P Disco Fri & Sat

V Bar lunch £1.50—£6.50 Tea 75p Dinner £7—£8&alc Last dinner 9pm

Credit cards 1 3 Ⓥ

WARSASH
Hampshire
Map **4** SU40

✕***Chon-Chola Tandoori*** 25 Shore Rd ☏ Locks Heath (04895) 3110

The simple North Indian restaurant is not decorated in the traditional style but has a nautical theme in keeping with the area. Cooking is of a high standard, the atmosphere informal and relaxing with service by willing, friendly staff.

Indian **V** 34 seats Last dinner 11.30pm 30P

Credit cards 1 2 3 5

WARWICK
Warwickshire
Map **4** SP26
See also **Barford** and **Leamington Spa**

★ ★ ★**Ladbroke** Longbridge Rbt (junc A41/A46/A429) (Ladbroke) ☏ (0926) 499555 Telex no 312468

A modern hotel on the outskirts of Warwick on the A46.

150rm(149➡1⋔)(3fb) in 3 bedrooms CTV in all bedrooms Ⓡ**T** ✱sB&B➡⋔fr£52 dB&B➡⋔fr£78 B

Lift 220P (heated) table tennis pool table *xmas*

✱Lunch fr£8.50&alc Tea fr£1.50 Dinner fr£10.95&alc Wine £5.99 Last dinner 10pm

Credit cards 1 2 3 5 Ⓥ

★ ★**Lord Leycester** Jury St (Consort) ☏ (0926) 491481 Telex no 41363

Central hotel near Warwick Castle on a busy road through Warwick.

50rm(36➡14⋔)(2fb) 1 CTV in all bedrooms **T** sB&B➡⋔£32 dB&B➡⋔£42—£46 B

40P pool table *xmas*

English & French **V** Lunch £8.50alc Tea 60palc High tea £3 alc Dinner £9.50alc Wine £4.40 Last dinner 8.30pm

Credit cards 1 2 3 5 Ⓥ

See advertisement on page 750

W

★★**Warwick Arms** High St ☎ (0926) 492759

Closed 25 Dec—1 Jan

A busy hotel dating back to 1591, in the centre of Warwick.

29rm(11⇌18⋔)(4fb) CTV in all bedrooms ®T sB&B⇌⋔£28—£30 dB&B⇌⋔£44—£46 Ⓑ

20P

English & French ⚲ ☕ Lunch £5.25—£5.75 Tea 75p—£1.35 High Tea £4—£5 Dinner £8.50—£9.50&alc Wine £6.95 Last dinner 9.30pm

Credit cards 1 2 3 5 Ⓥ

★★**Woolpack** Market Pl (Toby) ☎ (0926) 496191

Closed Xmas Day & New Years Day

Following extensive alterations in 1984, this hotel now offers comfortable bedrooms, carvery restaurant, coffee shop and a choice of two bars.

30rm(9⇌7⋔)(2fb) CTV in all bedrooms ® T ✱ sB&Bfr£19.50 sB&B⇌⋔fr£26.50 dB&Bfr£29.50 dB&B⇌⋔fr£38 Ⓑ

☾ ℙ

V ⚲ ☕ S% Lunch £6.45—£7 Tea fr50p High Tea fr£2 Dinner £6.45—£7 Wine £4.30 Last dinner 10pm

Credit cards 1 2 3 5

Warwick — Wasdale Head

✕✕✕**Westgate Arms** Bowling Green St ☎ (0926) 492362

The restaurant is modern in style, but it retains traces of the old Bowling Green Inn which stood here from the time of Elizabeth I. The interesting menus, fresh produce and value for money represented by the cuisine have brought the place an enviable reputation.

Closed Sun, Bank Hol Mons & Xmas

English & French **V** 80 seats Last dinner 10.35pm 48P Live music Fri wkly and Sat mthly

Credit cards 1 2 3 5

✿✕✕**Randolph's** Coten End ☎ (0926) 491292

In the early 1980s, the Randolph family transformed a row of tiny, timbered, sixteenth-century cottages at the edge of the town into this low-beamed, warm restaurant. The food is predominantly French, and the proprietor searches the markets to offer exciting and unusual dishes. The delicate presentation of the food is delightful — but portions are generously robust! Well-made sauces are a notable feature of the cuisine.

Closed Sun & 1 wk Xmas Lunch not served

French 30 seats Dinner £17.50alc Wine £5.70 Last dinner 10pm ℙ

Credit cards 1 3 4 Ⓥ

WASDALE HEAD
Cumbria
Map **11** NY10

★★**Wasdale Head Inn** ☎ Wasdale (09406) 229

Closed mid Nov—27 Dec

Situated at the head of the spectacular Wasdale Valley, the hotel is the perfect centre for those who simply want a peaceful holiday in lovely surroundings. Both accommodation and food are very

good, and a warm welcome is extended by the staff.

10rm(8⇌2ⓜ)(2fb) ®T
sB&B⇌ⓜ£32.50—£35.50(Incl dinner)
dB&B⇌ⓜ£63—£66(Incl dinner) B

50P ✽

V Bar lunch £4.50alc Tea 65palc High Tea £4.50alc Dinner £9.45—£11 Wine £5 Last dinner 7.30pm

Credit cards 1 3

WASHINGBOROUGH
Lincolnshire
Map **8** TF07

★★ **Washingborough Hall** Church Hill (Minotel) ☎ Lincoln (0522) 790340

Beautifully preserved and tastefully modernised, this 200-year-old, stone-built, former manor house stands in three acres of attractive gardens and grounds at the centre of the peaceful village approximately 2½ miles east of Lincoln.

12rm(9⇌3ⓜ) 1 in 2 bedrooms CTV in all bedrooms ®T sB&B⇌ⓜ£25—£33 dB&B⇌ⓜ£35—£45 B

50P ✽

International V Lunch £7.50alc Tea £1.50alc Dinner £9.50alc Wine £4.50 Last dinner 9.30pm

Credit cards 1 2 3 5 Ⓥ

WASHINGTON
Tyne & Wear
Map **12** NZ35

★★★ **George Washington** Stone Cellar Rd, District 12 (Consort) ☎ 091-417 2626 Telex no 537143

A modern hotel with extensive leisure facilities offers comfortable and very well appointed bedrooms which are equally suitable for family use or for business.

70rm(68⇌2ⓜ)(39fb) CTV in all bedrooms ®T S% sB&B⇌ⓜfr£46.75 dB&B⇌ⓜfr£54.45 B

CTV 200P CFA ✽ (heated) 9&18 squash snooker sauna bath solarium gymnasium hairdressing salon

V S% Lunch 95p—£8.50 Tea fr85p High Tea fr£6.40 Dinner fr£12.50&alc Wine £5.95 Last dinner 9.30pm

Credit cards 1 2 3 5 Ⓥ

Wasdale Head — Waterhouses

★★★ **Post House** Emerson District 5 (Trusthouse Forte) ☎ 091-416 2264 Telex no 537574

Conveniently situated post house close to A1(M) with spacious bedrooms and recently updated public rooms.

138⇌(52fb) CTV in all bedrooms ®
sB&B⇌£48.50 dB&B⇌£64.50 B

Lift 198P CFA ✽

Last dinner 10pm

Credit cards 1 2 3 4 5

WATCHET
Somerset
Map **3** ST04

★★ *L* **Downfield** 16 St Decuman's Rd ☎ (0984) 31267

A pleasant, detached Victorian house in well-tended gardens overlooking the harbour.

6rm(2⇌4ⓜ)(2fb) CTV in all bedrooms ®
sB&B⇌ⓜ£20—£25
dB&B⇌ⓜ£24.30—£30

22P ✽ *xmas*

English, French & German V Lunch £5.50alc Tea £1.20alc Dinner £7alc Wine £3.85 Last dinner 9.30pm

Credit cards 1 2 3 5 Ⓥ

See advertisement under Minehead

WATERGATE BAY
Cornwall
Map **2** SW86

★★ **Tregurrian** St Mawgan ☎ (0637) 860280

Closed Oct—Apr

A family-run hotel, close to the beach.

28rm(20ⓜ)(8fb) ®sB&B£11—£17.50
sB&Bⓜ£14.50—£21 dB&B£22—£35
dB&Bⓜ£26—£39 B

CTV 22P ✽ (heated) solarium pool table nc2yrs

Bar lunch £1.50alc Tea 55palc Dinner £5.50alc Wine £3.70 Last dinner 7.30pm

Ⓥ

★ ***Cleavelands*** ☎ St Mawgan (0637) 860273

Closed end Sep—Etr

Family holiday hotel near the beach.

22rm(7⇌2ⓜ)(8fb) B

CTV 38P

English & Continental V Last dinner 7.45pm

WATERHOUSES
Staffordshire
Map **7** SK05

✕✕ **Olde Beams** Leek Rd ☎ (05386) 254

Built in 1746, this lovely old stone cottage, with attractive lawned gardens to the rear, stands at the centre of the village. Once an inn, the restaurant retains an unsophisticated atmosphere, with oak beams, open fire, Windsor chairs, chintz and crisp linen. Chef Nigel Wallis makes excellent use of fresh produce in his French country style of cooking, and both à la carte and table d'hote selections represent very good value for money — the lunchtime menu being particularly popular with regular customers.

Closed Sun, Mon & 1st 2 wks Jan

French 50 seats Lunch £8.75&alc Dinner £16.50alc Wine £7 Last dinner 10pm 21P nc4yrs

Credit cards 2 3 5

W

WATERMILLOCK
Cumbria
Map **12** NY42

★★★ HBL Leeming House Ullswater (Prestige) ☏ Pooley Bridge (08536) 622 Telex no 64111

Closed Dec—mid Mar

Luxurious Georgian style house in large landscaped grounds and woodland with views over Ullswater. The lounges are lavishly furnished and decorated, and traditional English food is served in the lovely Regency dining room.

18rm(14⇌2⋒) T ✈ sB&B⇌⋒£36.50—£40 dB&B⇌⋒£70—£86 Continental breakfast B

CTV 35P ✿ ⅃ nc 8yrs

English & French Lunch £10alc Tea £1—£4 Dinner £22.50 Wine £3.50 Last dinner 8.45pm

Credit cards 1 2 3 5 V

★★ Ramsbeck Hotel-on-Ullswater ☏ Pooley Bridge (08536) 442

Closed early Jan—mid Feb

(Rosette awarded for dinner only).

The spacious and comfortable hotel stands in fourteen acres of grounds on the shores of Ullswater. In a restaurant overlooking the lake, guests can select an excellent meal from à la carte or table d'hôte menus or French classical cuisine. The meal is completed by a range of delicious desserts and accompanied by a good wine list.

13rm(7⇌2⋒)(2fb) CTV in 11 bedrooms TV in 1 bedroom *sB&Bfr£17 sB&B⇌⋒fr£25 dB&Bfr£34 dB&B⇌⋒£40—£45 B

CTV 30P ✿ ⅃ sailing school

French *Lunch £6.95—£7.95 Tea £1.25—£4.25 Dinner £10.95—£17.95&alc Wine £5.75 Last dinner 9pm

Credit cards 1 3 V

★

★ OLD CHURCH, WATERMILLOCK

☏ Pooley Bridge (08536) 204

Closed Nov—2 Apr

Many people think this is one of our nicest one star hotels and awarding it a Red Star has been very popular. It certainly offers some of the best hospitality you could wish for. Mrs Whitemore looks after the front of the house with the aid of naturally friendly local girls; between them they offer charmingly good natured service. The 18th century stone house is set on the edge of Ullswater in four acres of informal grounds and enjoys breathtaking views. As you enter the hall there is a splendid carved wooden chimney piece where a fire burns in season. There is a comfortable sitting room in which to relax among the pleasant decor, lots of flowers, pictures and prints, as well as a bar & TV room. The dining room is nicely appointed with polished tables and is the scene for Kevin Whitemore's cooking. He provides a five course dinner of limited choice but you will

enjoy the hearty, honest to goodness cooking. Bedrooms are comfortable and are provided with flowering plants and good quality toiletries. Rowing boats and sailboards are available. With its sensible prices, this is just the place for a Lakeland break.

11rm(7⇌)(1fb) sB&B£22 sB&B⇌fr£27 dB&Bfr£44 dB&B⇌fr£54

CTV 30P ✿ ⅃

Tea fr£3 Dinner fr£14.50 Wine £6.50 Last dinner 8.15pm

WATFORD
Hertfordshire
Map **4** TQ19

★★★ Ladbroke (& Conference centre) Elton Way, Watford by-pass ☏ (0923) 35881

(For full entry see Bushey)

✕ *Flower Drum* 16 Market St ☏ (0923) 26711

A well-appointed pleasant restaurant with extensive menus.

Closed Xmas

Pekinese & Szechuan **V** 70 seats Last dinner 11.30pm

Credit cards 1 2 3 5

WATTON
Norfolk
Map **5** TF90

★★ H Clarence House 78 High St ☏ (0953) 884252

The small, family-managed hotel provides value-for-money accommodation in comfortable surroundings and a friendly atmosphere.

6rm(1⇌5⋒) CTV in all bedrooms Ⓡ ✈ S% sB&B⇌⋒£24 dB&B⇌⋒£38 B

CTV 6P nc 12yrs

English & French Lunch £6.50 Dinner £11.50 Wine £4.95 Last dinner 9pm

Credit cards 1 2 3 5 V

W

WEEDON
Northamptonshire
Map**4** SP65

★★★**Crossroads** (Best Western) (0327) 40354 Telex no 312311

Closed 25—26 Dec RS 24 Dec

This busy, fully modernised and extended hotel stands at the junction of the A5 and A45. Originally a toll house, it still maintains the working clock tower.

10 Annexe: 40 (3fb) 1 CTV in all bedrooms ®**T** sB&B fr£40 dB&B fr£50

100P

V Lunch £12alc Tea 75palc High Tea £5alc Dinner £12alc Wine £5.95 Last dinner 10.15pm

Credit cards 1 2 3 5 Ⓥ

WELLINGBOROUGH
Northamptonshire
Map**4** SP86

★★★**Hind** Sheep St (Queens Moat) (0933) 222827

32 (1fb) 1 CTV in all bedrooms ®S% sB&B fr£40.25 dB&B fr£50.60

13P 3 CFA

English & French **V** S% Lunch fr£6.35&alc Tea fr70p Dinner fr£8.45 Wine £5.25 Last dinner 9.30pm

Credit cards 1 2 3 4 5 Ⓥ

★★**High View** 156 Midland Rd (0933) 78733

Friendly, main commercial, family-run hotel close to the town centre.

15 (1fb) CTV in all bedrooms ®**T** sB&Bfr£17.50 sB&B fr£23.50 dB&Bfr£26 dB&B fr£31

8P 1 games room

V Lunch £5.70—£7.10&alc Dinner £5.70—£7.10&alc Wine £4.80 Last dinner 8.30pm

Credit cards 1 2 3 5

★***Columbia*** 19 Northampton Rd (0933) 222094

31rm (18 6) CTV in all bedrooms ®

CTV 20P

Mainly grills **V** Last dinner 9pm

WELLINGTON
Shropshire
Map**7** SJ61
See **Telford**

WELLINGTON
Somerset
Map**3** ST12

★★**Beam Bridge** Sampford Arundel (2½m SW A38) Greenham (0823) 672223

Small hotel on Devon/Somerset border; a good touring centre.

7rm (2) (1fb) CTV in all bedrooms ® sBfr£16 sB fr£19 dBfr£28 dB fr£33 (room only)

CTV 100P gymnasium

English & French **V** Bar lunch £1.75—£5 Tea fr75p Dinner £10alc Wine £4.50 Last dinner 9.30pm

Credit cards 1 2 3

WELLS
Somerset
Map**3** ST54

★★★B **Swan** Sadler St (Best Western) (0749) 78877 Telex no 449658

Part 16th century and part Victorian building which overlooks the West Front of the Cathedral.

32rm (27 5) (1fb) 8 CTV in all bedrooms **T** sB&B fr£35 dB&B fr£55

35P CFA *xmas*

V Lunch £7.95&alc Dinner fr£10.95 Wine £5.50 Last dinner 9.30pm

Credit cards 1 2 3 5 Ⓥ

See advertisement on page 754

W

★★*H* **Crown** Market Pl (Exec Hotel) ☎(0749) 73457

Charming proprietor supervised Market Square hotel near cathedral, providing very sound food.

18rm(11→7⋒)(1fb) 4⊞ CTV in all bedrooms ® T sB&B→⋒£24—£29 dB&B→⋒£34—£47.50 B

13P squash *xmas*

V ♁ ⊐ Lunch £7.25—£8.25&alc Tea £1.85—£2.25 High Tea £2.50—£6.50 Dinner £11.95—£12.95&alc Wine £5.25 Last dinner 10pm

Credit cards 1 2 3 4 5 Ⓥ

Wells

★★**White Hart** Sadler St ☎(0749) 72056

A central, business and touring hotel with busy bars and a first floor lounge.

10rm(1→5⋒) Annexe: 5→(2fb) ® sB&B£19.50—£21.50 sB&B→⋒£24.50—£26.50 dB&B£31.50—£33.50 dB&B→⋒£35.50—£37.50 B

CTV 12P 3⌂ *xmas*

♁English & French V ♁ Lunch £5.25—£6.10&alc High tea £2.50—£5.50 Dinner £7.75—£8.25&alc Wine £4.80 Last dinner 9.30pm

Credit cards 1 2 3 5

★**Ancient Gate House** Sadler St ☎(0749) 72029

Enthusiastically run hotel of great character backing on to Cathedral green.

10rm(1→2⋒)(1fb) 6⊞ CTV in all bedrooms sB&B£19—£20 sB&B→⋒£25.50—£26.50 dB&B£31.50—£32.50 dB&B→⋒£35.50—£36.50 B

16P

W

English & Italian V S% Lunch £3.75—£5.95&alc High tea £2.50—£4.50 Dinner £7.95—£8.95&alc Wine £4.90 Last dinner 10.30pm

Credit cards 1 2 3 5

WELLS-NEXT-THE-SEA
Norfolk
Map **9** TF94

★**Crown** The Buttlands (Minotel) Fakenham (0328) 710209

Part 16th century, but with a Georgian façade, the friendly, popular coaching inn faces a quiet, tree-lined green at the rear of this coastal town.

14rm(3 1)(3fb) CTV in all bedrooms ® sB&B£21.50—£22.50 sB&B£33—£35 dB&B£33—£35 dB&B£38—£40

10P *xmas*

English & Continental V Lunch fr£7.50&alc Tea fr£1.50 Dinner £9.50—£10.50&alc Wine £5.50 Last dinner 9.30pm

Credit cards 1 2 3 5

WELSH HOOK
Dyfed
Map **2** SM92

XX**Stone Hall** Letterston (0348) 840212

Stone Hall stands near the hamlet of Welsh Nook between Haverfordwest and Fishguard. The charming restaurant in the 600-year-old part of the house serves imaginative food prepared by a talented young chef whose experience was gained in Nice and Britanny.

Dinner not served Sun

French V 32 seats Lunch £7.50—£9&alc Dinner £7.50—£9&alc Wine £4.90 Last dinner 9.30pm 50P 5 bedrooms available

Credit cards 1 3 Ⓥ

WELSHPOOL
Powys
Map **7** SJ20

★★**Royal Oak** (0938) 2217

Situated in the heart of the small market town, this hotel has comfortable bedrooms and an attractive, part-timbered dining room.

25rm(14 5)(1fb) 1 CTV in 19 bedrooms ® S% sB&B£16.50—£18.50 sB&B£19.50—£21.50 dB&B£33—£35 dB&B£37—£39

CTV 80P *xmas*

English & French S% Lunch £5.75—£7&alc Tea £2—£3.50 High tea £3.50—£5 Dinner £7—£9&alc Wine £4.75 Last dinner 9pm

Credit cards 1 2 3

★**Garth Derwen** Buttington (2½m NE A458) Trewern (093874) 238

Closed mid Dec—mid Jan

Small, personally run, comfortable hotel with good home cooking.

8rm(5)(4fb) 1 sB&B£16 sB&B£18—£23 dB&B£25—£26 dB&B£30—£36

CTV 20P

V Lunch £3.60—£5.95&alc Tea £1.55 High Tea £3.95 Dinner £6.25—£6.95&alc Wine £4.90 Last dinner 7.30pm

Credit cards 1 3 Ⓥ

WELWYN
Hertfordshire
Map **4** TL21

★★**Clock Motel** (043871) 6911 Telex no 825626

Closed Xmas night

This hotel has some newly built, well equipped bedrooms.

£48.50 or B/fast.

72rm(68 4)(3fb) CTV in all bedrooms ® T sB&B£20—£32.95 dB&B£32.95—£39.95 →

W

250P Live music and dancing Sat Cabaret Sat

V ☕ S% *Lunch £6.10—£10.50&alc Tea 60p—£2.25 Dinner £6.10—£10.50&alc Wine £5.77 Last dinner 9.45pm

Credit cards 1 2 3 5

WELWYN GARDEN CITY
Hertfordshire
Map **4** TL21

★★★**Crest** Homestead Ln (Crest)
☎ (0707) 324336 Telex no 261523

The small, purpose-built hotel, run by friendly staff, is located in a residential area. It caters for a busy commercial trade.

58rm (51 7) in 6 bedrooms CTV in all bedrooms ® S%
sB&B £55.25—£57.25
dB&B £71—£73 B

Lift ☾ 80P CFA ✽

English & Continental **V** S% Lunch £8—£9 Tea 80p—£1.20 High tea £1.60—£2.50 Dinner £11.95—£13&alc Wine £6.25 Last dinner 9.30pm

Credit cards 1 2 3 4 5

WEMBLEY
Greater London
London plan **5** *B4* (page 446)

XX**Moghul Brasserie** 525 High Rd
☎ 01-903-6967

Closed Xmas

Indian **V** 50 seats S% *Lunch £7.50alc Dinner £7.50alc Wine £4.95 Last dinner 11.15pm 20P

Credit cards 1 2 3 5

X**Woodlands** 402A High Rd ☎ 01-902 9869

A friendly, intimate atmosphere prevails in this South Indian vegetarian restaurant.

Closed Xmas Day

South Indian **V** 50 seats Lunch £4&alc Dinner £4&alc Wine £5 Last dinner 10.30pm 2P

Credit cards 1 2 3 5 Ⓥ

WENTBRIDGE (near Pontefract)
West Yorkshire
Map **8** SE41

★★★ *H* **Wentbridge House**
☎ Pontefract (0977) 620444 Telex no 946240

RS 24 & 25 Dec

This converted country mansion with pleasant, well-kept grounds provides well-furnished bedrooms and consistently good food.

17rm (10 7) Annexe: 3rm 1 CTV in all bedrooms **T** S% sB&Bfr£24.75
sB&B £34—£55 dB&Bfr£29.75
dB&B £47.50—£64.75 Continental breakfast B

120P 3 ✽

English & French S% *Lunch £9&alc Dinner £14alc Wine £6.50 Last dinner 9.30pm

Credit cards 1 2 3 5

WEOBLEY
Hereford & Worcester
Map **3** SO45

★★**Red Lion** ☎ (0544) 318220

A 14th century timbered inn situated in the village centre.

7rm (2 5) CTV in all bedrooms ® **T**
sB&B fr£29.50 dB&B fr£39.50 B

50P *xmas*

English & French **V** Bar lunch fr£3.75&alc Tea fr£1 Dinner £13alc Wine £6 Last dinner 9.30pm

Credit cards 1 2 3 5

WEST BAY
Dorset
see **Bridport**

WEST BEXINGTON
Dorset
Map **3** SY58

★★**Manor** Beach Rd
☎ Burton Bradstock (0308) 897616

Comfortable stone manor house in pleasant gardens with well decorated bedrooms and good quality food.

10rm (6 4) (1fb) CTV in all bedrooms ®
sB&B £19—£21
dB&B £34.50—£38 B

25P ✽

English & French **V** Lunch £8.95—£9.95 Tea £1.65—£1.95 High tea £2.05—£2.35 Dinner £11.25—£11.75 Wine £4.95 Last dinner 9.30pm

Credit cards 1 2 3 Ⓥ

See advertisement under Bridport

WEST BROMWICH
West Midlands
Map **7** SP09
See also **Barr, Great**

★★★**West Bromwich Moat House**
Birmingham Rd (Queens Moat)
☎ 021-553 6111 Telex no 336232
Birmingham district plan **34**

RS Bank Hols

A modern, purpose-built hotel by junction 1 of the M5.

181 CTV in all bedrooms ® **T**
sB&B £47—£51.50
dB&B £61—£67.50 B

Lift ☾ 240P CFA

International **V** Lunch fr£8.65&alc Tea fr£1.20 Dinner fr£8.90&alc Wine £5.95 Last dinner 9.45pm

Credit cards 1 2 3 5 Ⓥ

WEST CHILTINGTON
West Sussex
Map **4** TQ01

★★**Roundabout** Monkmead Ln (1¾m S) (Best Western) ☎ (07983) 3838 Telex no 946240

Quiet Tudor style hotel with compact well furnished bedrooms.

21rm (18 3) (4fb) 4 CTV in all bedrooms ® **T** S%
sB&B £34.75—£38.75
dB&B £51.75—£55.75 B

W

45p ✿ nc3yrs *xmas*
🍷English & French **V** ♔ ☕ S% Lunch £8.95—£10.95&alc Tea £1—£1.75 Dinner £11—£13&alc Wine £7.50 Last dinner 9pm
Credit cards 1 2 3 4 5

WESTCLIFF-ON-SEA
Essex
See **Southend-on-Sea**

WESTERHAM
Kent
Map **5** TQ45
★★★ *B* **Kings Arms** Market Sq
☎ (0959) 62990
RS Xmas eve
This family-owned hotel, a 200-year-old building has been attractively decorated and tastefully furnished. It provides spacious bedrooms, a comfortable bar lounge and a charming restaurant offering à la carte and, during the week, carvery menus.
14 (2fb) 1 CTV in all bedrooms ® **T** sB&B £42—£44 dB&B £55—£68
40P
🍷International ♔ Lunch £10—£12 Tea £1—£1.25 Dinner £10—£12&alc Wine £6.50 Last dinner 10pm
Credit cards 1 2 3 5 Ⓥ

WESTGATE-ON-SEA
Kent
Map **5** TR37
★★ ***Ivyside*** 25 Sea Rd ☎ Thanet (0843) 31082
Generally acceptable bedrooms, mainly designed and furnished for families with children.
51rm (24 25) (44fb) CTV in all bedrooms ®
CTV 30P CFA ✿ & (heated) squash billiards sauna bath solarium Disco twice wkly Live music & dancing wkly *xmas*
🍷English & Continental **V** ♔ ☕ Last dinner 8.30pm
Credit cards 1 3

West Chiltington — Weston-super-Mare

WESTHILL
Grampian *Aberdeenshire*
Map **15** NJ80
★★★ ***Westhill Inn*** ☎ Aberdeen (0224) 740388 Telex no 739925
Modern, custom-built hotel, just off the A944, within a developing area 6m west of Aberdeen.
38 Annexe: 14rm (6 8) CTV in all bedrooms ®
Lift 350P CFA sauna bath solarium gymnasium Live music & dancing Fri & Sat
V ♔ ☕ Last dinner 9.45pm
Credit cards 1 2 3 5

WEST LULWORTH
Dorset
See **Lulworth**

WEST MERSEA
Essex
Map **5** TM01
✕ **Le Champenois** (Blackwater Hotel) 20—22 Church Rd ☎ (0206) 383338
Traditional French hospitality is combined with a homely atmosphere and personal service.
Closed 5—21 Jan Lunch not served Tue Dinner not served Sun
🍷English & French **V** 42 seats Lunch £7.70—£8.80&alc Dinner £14.50alc Wine £5.70 Last dinner 9.45pm 15P
Credit cards 1 2 Ⓥ

WESTON
Shropshire
Map **7** SJ52
★★★ ***Hawkstone Park*** (Best Western) ☎ Lee Brockhurst (093924) 611
Much extended and modernised former country house with excellent golfing facilities.
43 Annexe: 16 (6fb) CTV in all bedrooms ®
CTV 300P CFA ✿ (grass) billiards sauna bath solarium gymnasium *xmas*
♔ ☕ Last dinner 9.30pm
Credit cards 1 2 3 5
See advertisement under Shrewsbury

WESTON-ON-THE-GREEN
Oxfordshire
Map **4** SP51
★★★ ***Weston Manor*** (Best Western) ☎ Bletchington (0869) 50621 Telex no 83409
Efficiently run 14th century manor house set in 11 acres, featuring a unique oak panelled restaurant with a minstrels gallery.
17 Annexe: 6 1 (1fb) 2 CTV in all bedrooms ® **T**
CTV 50P ✿ (heated) squash *xmas*
🍷English & French **V** ♔ ☕ Last dinner 9.45pm
Credit cards 1 2 3 5

WESTON-SUPER-MARE
Avon
Map **3** ST36
★★★ **Berni Royal** South Pde (Berni) ☎ (0934) 23601
Closed Xmas
The detached, Georgian-style building stands in its own gardens, a short distance from the beach and within easy reach of the shops. Recently refurbished, it now offers comfortable bedrooms and public areas.
37 (6fb) 2 CTV in all bedrooms ® S% *sB £26 dB £45 (room only)
Lift 90P ✿
🍷Mainly grills ♔ ☕ *Lunch £7.50alc Dinner £7.50alc Wine £4.50 Last dinner 10.15pm
Credit cards 1 2 3 5
★★★ *L* **Grand Atlantic** Beach Rd (Trusthouse Forte) ☎ (0934) 26543
Well appointed comfortable hotel with attractive garden.
79 (2fb) CTV in all bedrooms ® sB&B £44.50 dB&B £67.50 →

Lift ☾CTV 150P CFA ❀ ⛱ (heated) 🎾(hard) 🎪 *xmas*

🍷 ☕ Last dinner 9.30pm

Credit cards [1] [2] [3] [4] [5]

★★★**H Royal Pier** Birnbeck Rd
☎ (0934) 26644

Comfortable hotel with good sized lounges, looking across Weston Bay.

40rm(33 🛁 3 🚿)(4fb) CTV in all bedrooms **T**
✂ sB&B£24.30—£28.50
sB&B🛁🚿£26.55—£31
dB&B£47.25—£53.50
dB&B🛁🚿£49.50—£56 **B**

Lift ☾CTV 100P 🚗 pool table table tennis Live music Fri & Sat *xmas*

Weston-super-Mare

🍷 European **V** 🍷 ☕ Lunch £6—£7&alc Tea £1.25—£2.50 Dinner £8.50—£10&alc Wine £5 Last dinner 9.30pm

Credit cards [1] [2] [3] [5]

★★***Rozel*** Madeira Cove ☎ (0934) 415268

Large, traditional family-owned and run holiday and business hotel on the sea front.

56rm(28 🛁 5 🚿)(20fb) CTV in all bedrooms ®**T B**

Lift ☾50P 50🚗 CFA ⛱ (heated) sauna bath solarium 🎪 *xmas*

🍷 English & French **V** 🍷 ☕ Last dinner 8pm

Credit cards [1] [2] [3]

★**Beachlands** 17 Uphill Road North
☎ (0934) 21401

A small, warm, personally-run hotel stands close to the coast, offering good-value accommodation with sound home cooking and useful parking facilities.

18rm(9➡6⋔)(4fb)®
sB&B£13.50—£14.75
sB&B➡⋔£16—£17.25
dB&B£27—£29.50
dB&B➡⋔£32—£34.50 B

CTV 14P *xmas*

V ☕ Bar lunch 80p—£4.50 Tea 70p—£1.50 High Tea £2.50—£3.50 Dinner £6.95 Wine £4.70 Last dinner 7.30pm

Credit cards 1 2 3 5

WEST RUNTON
Norfolk
Map **9** TG14

★★★**Links Country Park Hotel & Golf Club** ☎ (026375) 691

A popular golfing and tourist hotel in open country above the village.

22rm(20➡2⋔)(5fb) CTV in all bedrooms ® **T** sB&B➡⋔£20—£35 dB&B➡⋔£35—£65

Lift ☾ 100P CFA ✿ ⛳9 *xmas*

English & French **V** ☕ Lunch £6.95—£7.50&alc Tea £1—£2.50 High Tea £2—£3.50 Dinner £9.95—£12.25&alc Wine £6.75 Last dinner 9.30pm

Credit cards 1 2 3

XX**Mirabelle** Station Rd ☎ (026375) 396

Closed Mon & 1st 2 wks Nov Dinner not served Sun (Nov—May)

Continental **V** 50 seats Lunch £6.50—£8.30&alc Dinner £11.25—£14&alc Wine £5.25 Last dinner 9pm 20P

Credit cards 1 2 3 5

WESTWARD HO!
Devon
Map **2** SS42

★★***Buckleigh Grange*** Buckleigh Rd ☎ Bideford (02372) 74468

Closed Nov—Apr

Comfortable family-run holiday hotel in a quiet situation.

11rm(2⋔)(2fb)®

CTV 20P ✿ (grass)

V ☕ Last dinner 7pm

★★**Culloden House** Fosketh Hill ☎ Bideford (02372) 79421

Closed Nov—Feb

The friendly, relaxed hotel specialises in cricket and golfing holidays.

9rm(2➡5⋔)(3fb) CTV in all bedrooms S%
*sB&B£25—26.25
sB&B➡⋔£28—£29.40
dB&B£37.50—£40
dB&B➡⋔£44—£46.25 B

CTV 9P

V ☕ S% *Lunch £5.50—£6.50 Tea £1.25—£1.50 High Tea £2.50—£3 Dinner £8.50—£9.50 Wine £4.95 Last dinner 9pm

Credit cards 1 2 3 5 Ⓥ

WEST WITTON
North Yorkshire
Map **7** SE08

★★**Wensleydale Heifer Inn** (Consort) ☎ Wensleydale (0969) 22322 Telex no 57515

A 17th-century village inn on the main road through this Dales village.

10rm(6➡4⋔) Annexe: 10rm(5➡5⋔)(1fb) 2 CTV in all bedrooms ® sB&B➡⋔£28 dB&B➡⋔£40—£50 B

30P *xmas*

British & Continental **V** ☕ Lunch £6.95 Dinner £11.95 Wine £5.95 Last dinner 9pm

Credit cards 1 2 3 Ⓥ

WEST WOODBURN
Northumberland
Map **12** NY88

★***Fox & Hounds*** ☎ Bellingham (0660) 60210

Closed Xmas Day and Boxing Day

An 18th-century roadside inn with a modern dining room where home cooking is provided.

10rm (2fb)

CTV 30P

Last dinner 8.30pm

WETHERAL
Cumbria
Map **12** NY45

★★★*B* **Crown** (Consort) ☎ (0228) 61888 Telex no 64175

Charming, character hotel which started life as a farmhouse in the 18th century, was extended in the 19th century and recently has been completely modernised.

51rm (49 2) (6fb) 1 CTV in all bedrooms ® **T** S% sB&B £47—£57 dB&B £59—£69

CTV 80P CFA squash snooker sauna bath

English & French **V** S% Lunch £6—£8&alc Tea 60P—£2.50 Dinner £8.95—£11&alc Wine £6.95 Last dinner 9.30pm

Credit cards 1 2 3 5 Ⓥ

★**Killoran Country House** The Green ☎ (0228) 60200

Built in the late 1800's as a country residence, this hotel retains much of its original atmosphere.

10rm (1fb) 1 TV in all bedrooms ® *sB&B £19.50 dB&B £35

CTV 60P 1 Live music and dancing Sat

V Lunch £6.50—£9&alc Dinner £6.50—£9&alc Wine £3.95 Last dinner 9.15pm

Credit cards 1 3 5

X**Fantails** ☎ (0228) 60239

Set in a building which dates back to the 17th century, the charming restaurant features oak beams, leaded windows and open fires. Food, chosen from a short but interesting à la carte menu is of a very high standard.

Closed Sun, Mon & Feb

English & Continental **V** 50 seats Lunch £9.90alc Dinner £12alc Wine £5.50 Last dinner 9.30pm 25P

Credit cards 1 2 3 5

WETHERBY
West Yorkshire
Map **8** SE44

★★★**Ladbroke Wetherby** Leeds Rd (junc A1/A58) (Ladbroke) ☎ (0937) 63881 Telex no 556428

Modern hotel with good facilities, bars and restaurants.

72 (2fb) CTV in all bedrooms ® **T** sB £35.50—£49.50 dB £48—£66 (room only)

125P *xmas*

French **V** Lunch £6.50—£7.50 Dinner £9.75&alc Wine £5.99 Last dinner 9.45pm

Credit cards 1 2 3 5 Ⓥ

XXX**L'Escale** 16 Bank St ☎ (0937) 63613

Attractive and smart, this little French restaurant is built of local stone with bay windows. Helpful and attentive waiters provide polished, professional service in keeping with the high standard of French cuisine featured. The room doubles as a gallery, for the tasteful paintings that line the walls are for sale.

Closed Mon Lunch not served Tue—Sat Dinner not served Sun

French **V** 65 seats *Lunch £6.95 Dinner £10&alc Wine £5.40 Last dinner 10.30pm 10P nc (dinner)

Credit cards 1 2 3 5

XXX**Linton Spring** Sicklinghall Rd ☎ (0937) 65353

Set in an elegant country mansion with its own grounds, the restaurant offers an imaginative, international menu of varied and interesting dishes, with a high percentage of home-made items, expertly prepared and served in comfortable, smart surroundings; there is a particularly good wine list.

Closed Mon & 1st wk Jan Lunch not served Sat Dinner not served Sun

English & Continental **V** 80 seats Lunch £8.25—£8.95 Dinner £18alc Wine £6.25 Last dinner 10pm 50P Disco nightly

Credit cards 1 2 3 4 5 Ⓥ

WETHERSFIELD
Essex
Map **5** TL73

X**Rudi's** Village Green ☎ Great Dunmow (0371) 850723

Beamed, galleried and spotlessly kept, the restaurant offers a French menu with some Austrian specialities.

Closed Mon Dinner not served Sun

Austrian & French **V** 56 seats S% Lunch £6.60—£7&alc Dinner fr£8.50&alc Wine £4.80 Last dinner 9.30pm 10P Live music last Fri in mth

Credit cards 2 3

WEYBOURNE
Norfolk
Map **9** TG14

★★*L* **Maltings** (Consort) ☎ (026370) 731 Telex no 57515

Formerly a manor, malting house and dairy, this original Norfolk flintstone house dates from the 16th century.

11rm (7) Annexe: 11rm (7 2) (2fb) 1 CTV in all bedrooms **T** S% *sB&B £25—£30 sB&B £30—£32 dB&B £38—£40 dB&B £42—£45

150P *xmas*

International **V** S% Lunch £5—£7.50 Tea 65p alc Dinner £12—£12.50&alc Wine £5 Last dinner 9pm

Credit cards 1 2 3 5

W

XX**Gasche's Swiss** ☎ (026370) 220

Friendly, family atmosphere in village cottage restaurant.

Closed Mon Dinner not served Sun

English & Continental **V** 65 seats Lunch £7.45&alc Dinner £13.90&alc Wine £4.55 Last dinner 9pm 35P

Credit cards 1 2 3 5

WEYBRIDGE
Surrey
London plan **5** *A1* (page 446)

★★★*B* **Ship Thistle** Monument Green (Thistle) ☎ (0932) 848364 Telex no 894271

Comfortable, friendly hotel with helpful service. Rooms are tastefully furnished and Wooster's restaurant specialises in English food.

39🛁🚿(8fb) in 6 bedrooms CTV in all bedrooms ®**T** ✱sB🛁🚿£59—£69 dB&B🛁🚿£69—£79 (room only) **B**

☾50P 16 ✿ *xmas*

International ✱Lunch fr£10.50&alc Dinner fr£10.50&alc Wine £7 Last dinner 9pm

Credit cards 1 2 3 4 5 Ⓥ

XX**Colony Chinese** 3 Balfour Rd ☎ (0932) 42766

This contemporary Chinese restaurant features authentic regional cuisine and iron plate sizzling dishes. Friendly, helpful service is provided by young, attentive staff, and good standards of cooking are enhanced by honest, well-made, traditional sauces; good use is also made of sea-food, lobster and fresh vegetables.

Closed Xmas

Pekinese 80 seats ✱Lunch £10—£15alc Dinner £12—£20alc Wine £5.50 Last dinner 11pm

Credit cards 1 2 3 5

Weybourne — Weymouth

WEYMOUTH
Dorset
Map **3** SY67

★★**Crown** 51—52 St Thomas Street ☎ (0305) 785695

Closed Xmas day and Boxing day

An imposing brick hotel with ornamental stone embellishments, close to the harbour and shops.

79rm(39🛁5🚿)(12fb) ® sB&B£16.10—£17.10 sB&B🛁🚿£18.40—£19.40 dB&B£27.60—£30.60 dB&B🛁🚿£32.20—£35 **B**

Lift ☾CTV 8 (£1 per night in season) CFA Live music & dancing 6 nights wkly (in season)

Lunch £3.50—£8 Dinner fr£5.25 Wine £4.35 Last dinner 8pm

Credit cards 1 3 Ⓥ

★★*B* **Glenburn** 42 Preston Rd, Preston (3m NE A353) ☎ Preston (0305) 832353

Closed 26—30 Dec

Pleasant, well-furnished, private hotel.

13rm(5🛁8🚿)(1fb) CTV in all bedrooms ® sB&B🛁🚿fr£21 dB&B🛁🚿fr£40 **B**

25P ✿ nc3yrs

V Lunch £1—£6 Tea fr£1 High Tea fr£1 Dinner fr£8&alc Wine £4.50 Last dinner 9.30pm

Credit cards 1 3 Ⓥ

★★**Old York** 55 The Esplanade ☎ (0305) 786558

Closed Xmas Day and Boxing Day

A sea front hotel in a Georgian style terraced development.

12🚿(1fb) CTV in all bedrooms ® sB&B🚿£20—£23 dB&B🚿£34—£42 **B**

CTV

English & French **V** Dinner £8alc Last dinner 10.30pm

Credit cards 1 3 Ⓥ

★★**Hotel Prince Regent** 139 The Esplanade (Consort) ☎ (0305) 771313 Telex no 946240

Closed 24—28 Dec

Victorian hotel on seafront opposite pier.

50rm(25🛁8🚿)(25fb) CTV in all bedrooms **T** ✱sB&Bfr£21.75 sB&B🛁🚿fr£28.50 dB&Bfr£37.50 dB&B🛁🚿fr£43 **B**

Lift ☾ CFA Live music & dancing twice wkly (in season)

English & French **V** ✱Lunch fr£6.50&alc Tea fr60p Dinner fr£6—£7.50&alc Wine £3.85 Last dinner 8.30pm

Credit cards 1 2 3 5

★★**Rembrandt** 12 Dorchester Rd ☎ (0305) 780384

A brick building with a modern extension and good restaurant.

42rm(21🛁10🚿) CTV in all bedrooms ®**T** ✱sB&B£16.10—£18.40 sB&B🛁🚿£25.30 dB&B£32.20—£34.50 dB&B🛁🚿£41.40 **B**

☾CTV 100P 3 (heated) Disco wkly Live music & dancing wkly *xmas*

English & French **V** ✱Lunch fr£4.60&alc Tea 70p—£2 Dinner fr£6.90&alc Wine £5.27 Last dinner 10pm

Credit cards 1 2 3 4 5

See advertisement on page 762

★★**Hotel Rex** 29 The Esplanade ☎ (0305) 773485

Closed 25—27 Dec

The hotel has a terraced Georgian façade and offers views across Weymouth Bay.

21rm(14🛁7🚿)(4fb) CTV in all bedrooms ®**T** sB&B🛁🚿£20—£23.50 dB&B🛁🚿£35—£46 **B**

Lift ☾CTV 8 (£1 per night)

International Tea fr£1 Dinner £5—£6&alc Wine £4.35 Last dinner 10.30pm

Credit cards 1 3 Ⓥ

★★**Streamside** 29 Preston Rd ☎ Preston (0305) 833121

The pleasant, attractive mock Tudor hotel on the edge of the town centre offers neat, clean, small bedrooms, with well- →

W

appointed bars, lounge and restaurant. Well-prepared food, chosen from an extensive menu, is served by attentive, friendly staff.

15rm(10⇌4⋒)(4fb) CTV in all bedrooms S% sB&B£20—£22 sB&B⇌⋒£23—£25 dB&B£34—£36 dB&B⇌⋒£39 B
CTV 40P ✱ pool table *xmas*

English & French **V** Lunch £5—£8.50 Tea 80p—£1.25 High Tea £1.25—£2.50 Dinner £6.50—£8.50&alc Wine £4.80 Last dinner 9.30pm

Credit cards 1 2 3 5

Weymouth

✕**Sea Cow Bistro** Custom House Quay ☎(0305) 783524

Predictably, fish figures prominently on the dinner menu of this bright, comfortable quayside restaurant, and lobster is featured as a speciality. Service is efficient and friendly. A good range of dishes is available at lunchtime, also, but this meal is on a self-service basis.

Closed Xmas Day, Boxing Day & New Years Day Dinner not served Sun (Oct—Jun)

Cosmopolitan **V** 120 seats Lunch fr£5.95 Dinner £11.50alc Wine £5.20 Last dinner 10.15pm

Credit cards 1 3

✕**Turks Head Inn** (3m NW B3157) 6 East St ☎(0305) 783093
(For full entry see Chickerell)

W

WHEDDON CROSS
Somerset
Map **3** SS93

★★ **Raleigh Manor Country House** ☎ Timberscombe (064 384) 484

Closed mid Nov—mid Mar

The hotel, a late Victorian manor with splendid views over the moor, features Exmoor Explorer holidays.

7rm(2→1⋔) ® ✱sB&B£15.50 dB&B£31 dB&B→⋔£34—£42 B

CTV 12P nc 12yrs

✱Dinner fr£7 Wine £4.50 Last dinner 7pm

WHIMPLE
Devon
Map **3** SY09

★★

★★ **WOODHAYES, WHIMPLE**
☎ (0404) 822237

Given Red Stars for the first time last year, the award has proved most popular with our members. John Allen's little Georgian house is set in 3 acres of charming gardens on the outskirts of this village whose main industry is cider making. The interior, with its gothic mouldings, bold patterned wallpaper and period furniture is Victorian in style but none the worse for that. The hall with some seating and the two sitting rooms, bright with flowers and with open fires in season, are comfortably furnished and supplied with lots of books and magazines. The candlelit dining room is small but not cramped, and the mahogany tables with elegant settings help to make it a charming room in which to enjoy your meal. The fixed price menu offers a sensible choice and the reasonable wine list complements the menu. The lofty bedrooms are spacious, comfortable and well furnished with period pieces and reproduction Victorian chairs. Good quality toiletries, flowers, and books are thoughtful touches that add

their attraction. But most of all this hotel is very civilised: Mr Allen and his small staff are friendly and obliging and create an aura of unaffected hospitality which should be the aim of every hotelkeeper.

7→ CTV in all bedrooms **T** S% sB&B→£45—£50 dB&B→£65—£70 B

20P 4⌂ croquet nc 12yrs *xmas*

English & French S% Lunch £14.50 Dinner £21.50 Wine £7.95 Last dinner 8pm

Credit cards 1 2 3 5 V

WHIPPINGHAM
Isle of Wight
See **Wight, Isle of**

WHITBY
North Yorkshire
Map **8** NZ81

★★ **Royal** West Cliff (Consort) ☎ (0947) 602234

An imposing building, overlooking the harbour and the Abbey.

134rm(23→44⋔)(20fb) CTV in 4 bedrooms ® ✱sB&B£15—£18.50 sB&B→⋔£17—£20.50 dB&B£30—£37 dB&B→⋔£34—£41 B

Lift ☾ CTV P *xmas*

English & Continental ✱Lunch £6&alc Dinner £6.50&alc Wine £5 Last dinner 8.45pm

Credit cards 1 2 3 5 V

★★ **Saxonville** Ladysmith Av (off Argyle Rd) ☎ (0947) 602631

Closed mid Oct—mid May (except Etr)

Tastefully converted from a row of town houses, this family run hotel has spacious public rooms and bright, cheerful bedrooms.

22rm(5→9⋔)(4fb) ® CTV in all bedrooms S% sB&B£15.50—£18 sB&B→⋔£18 dB&B£31—£36 dB&B→⋔£36

20P

S% Lunch £3.50—£6 Dinner £8—£8.50&alc Wine £4.20 Last dinner 8pm

Credit cards 1 2 3 V

★★ **Sneaton Hall** Sneaton (3m S B1416) ☎ (0947) 605929

Closed Nov—Etr

There are excellent views of sea or countryside from most of the bedroom windows at the hotel, a Georgian house just a short distance from the town. Family-owned, it provides an ideal base for anyone touring the North Yorkshire Moors.

9rm(4→3⋔)(1fb) CTV in all bedrooms ® sB&Bfr£16.50 sB&B→⋔fr£17.50 dB&Bfr£33 dB&B→⋔fr£35

14P

V Dinner £10 Wine £5 Last dinner 8pm

Credit card 5

★ **White House** Upgang Ln, West Cliff ☎ (0947) 602098

This Victorian farmhouse was converted into the present hotel in the 1920's.

12rm(5→)(3fb) CTV in all bedrooms ® sB&B£11—£14 sB&B→£12—£15 dB&B£24—£26 dB&B→£26—£28 B

CTV 50P 2⌂ *xmas*

English & French **V** Lunch £5.25 High Tea £2.25—£4.75 Dinner £6—£7.75&alc Wine £3.75 Last dinner 10pm

Credit card 3

WHITCHURCH
Hereford & Worcester
Map **3** SO51

✕✕ **Gallery** Wayside ☎ Symonds Yat (0600) 890408

This small but comfortable restaurant is aptly named on two scores: a wealth of paintings is displayed round the room, and there is also a gallery overlooking the diners. On a fine day, guests can sit in the garden and order their meal from a choice of 25 items of traditional English and French cuisine.

Closed Sun & 1st 2 wks Nov

English & French **V** 40 seats S% Lunch £16alc Dinner £16alc Wine £5.50 Last dinner 9.30pm 12P

Credit cards 1 2 3

WHITCHURCH
Shropshire
Map **7** SJ54

★★★ **Dodington Lodge** Dodington ☎ (0948) 2539

Standing a quarter of a mile south of the town centre, close to the A41, the hotel has recently been modernised to provide comfortable, well-equipped accommodation..

9rm(5→2⋔) CTV in all bedrooms ® **T** ✱sB&B£22 sB&B→⋔£25 dB&B£28 dB&B→⋔£32

200P *xmas*

International Wine fr£4.80 Last dinner 9.30pm

Credit cards 1 3 5

★★★ **Terrick Hall Country** Hill Valley (off A49 NE of town centre) (Minotel) ☎ (0948) 3031

Closed 26—31 Dec

Busy hotel close to a golf course and sporting facilities.

10→(7fb) CTV in all bedrooms ® **T** sB&B→£22.50—£26.50 dB&B→£33—£39 B

30P 18 (hard) squash snooker sauna bath →

W

International V Lunch fr£5.95&alc Tea fr50p High Tea fr£2.75 Dinner fr£7.95&alc Wine £5.50 Last dinner 9.15pm

Credit cards 1 2 3 5

★★**Hollies Motel** Chester Rd ☎ (0948) 2184

Situated on the main road just north of the town centre, this late Victorian property has attractive public areas and comfortable, well-equipped bedrooms, most of the latter in a purpose-built annexe.

4rm(2) Annexe: 10(1fb) CTV in 12 bedrooms ® sB&B £20—£25 dB&B £25—£30

30P *xmas*

English, Italian & Polish V Lunch £1.40—£3.60&alc Tea 65p—£1 Dinner £4.40—£4.95&alc Wine £2.75 Last dinner 10.30pm

Credit cards 1 2 3 5 Ⓥ

★★**Redbrook Hunting Lodge** Wrexham Rd ☎ Redbrook Maelor (094873) 204 (For full entry see Redbrook, Clwyd)

WHITEBRIDGE

Highland *Inverness-shire*
Map **14** NH41

★★*HBL* **Knockie Lodge**
☎ Gorthleck (04563) 276

Closed end Oct—Apr

(Rosette awarded for dinner only).

This remote and attractive white painted country house is set in 10 acres of grounds overlooking Loch Ness. The rooms are elegant and comfortable and the welcome is sincere. Fresh local produce is cooked with enthusiasm by the young staff to provide excellent meals.

10 sB&B fr£30 dB&B £50—£70

30P nc10yrs

Bar lunch £2.50—£7.50 Dinner £15 Wine £5 Last dinner 8.45pm

Credit cards 1 2 3 Ⓥ

★★**Whitebridge** (Exec Hotel)
☎ Gorthleck (04563) 226

Closed Dec—Mar RS Nov

A family run traditional Highland hotel.

12rm(3 5)(1fb) CTV in all bedrooms ® sB&B fr£14.25 sB&B fr£16.75 dB&B fr£28.50 dB&B fr£33.50

30P 2(50p per night)

V Lunch £7—£8 Tea 75p—£1.50 Dinner £8.50—£9&alc Wine £5 Last dinner 8pm

Credit cards 1 2 3 5

WHITEBROOK

Gwent
Map **3** SO50

★★*H* **Crown at Whitebrook** (Exec Hotel) ☎ Monmouth (0600) 860254 Telex no 498280

Closed Xmas Day & Boxing Day

Peacefully situated in the steeply wooded Wye Valley, 2½ miles from the A466, an ancient Welsh inn has been combined with a French restaurant and cosy modern bedrooms under the management of two brothers, John and David Jackson, both experienced hoteliers. The standard of cuisine is very commendable, being based on quality fresh produce from their own gardens or local farms; delicious Wye salmon is also offered during the season. The Crown also boasts a collection of fine and rare French wines, and regular wine-tastings are arranged during the winter.

12 1 T S% sB&B fr£27 dB&B fr£43

40P

French S% Lunch £8.75—£12&alc Tea 75p Dinner fr£12&alc Wine £5 Last dinner 10pm

Credit cards 1 2 3 5 Ⓥ

WHITEHAVEN

Cumbria
Map **11** NX91

★★**Roseneath Country House** Low Moresby (3m NE off A595) ☎ (0946) 61572

Closed Xmas RS Jan

Georgian country house occupying an elevated position with views towards the Solway Coast.

10rm(4 6)(1fb) CTV in all bedrooms ® in 4 bedrooms T sB&B £23.50 dB&B £37.50

20P nc 12yrs

English & Continental V Tea £1.75 Dinner £9.50—£10.50&alc Wine £4.25 Last dinner 9pm

Credit cards 1 3 Ⓥ

WHITENESS

Shetland
See **Shetland Isles**

WHITING BAY

Isle of Arran, Strathclyde *Bute*
See **Arran, Isle of**

WHITLAND

Dyfed
Map **2** SN21

★*HB* **Waungron Farm** Waungron Isaf (1m SW off B4328) ☎ (0994) 240682

Secluded farm hotel with cosy, well-appointed bedrooms and good food in the attractively converted restaurant.

Annexe: 14rm(8 6)(3fb) 1 CTV in all bedrooms ® S% sB&B fr£22.50 dB&B fr£35

100P *xmas*

S% Lunch fr£6.50 Dinner fr£7.50&alc Wine £3.95 Last dinner 9pm

Credit cards 1 3 Ⓥ

WHITLEY BAY

Tyne & Wear
Map **12** NZ37

★★**Ambassador** South Pde ☎ 091-253 1218

Closed Xmas Day

Neat, clean bedroom accommodation is provided by this comforting hotel.

28rm(14⇌)(5fb) CTV in all bedrooms ® T sB&Bfr£18 sB&B⇌£22—£33 dB&B£28—£30 dB&B⇌£33—£38 B

☾CTV P

English & French V Lunch £4.50—£5.50&alc Tea 85p Dinner £8.50&alc Wine £4.50 Last dinner 9.30pm

Credit cards 1 3 5

★★**Holmedale** 106 Park Av ☎ 091-251 3903

Friendly, unpretentious hotel, managed by resident proprietors.

20rm(5⇌2fh)(3fb) CTV in all bedrooms ® T ✱sB&Bfr£14.95 sB&B⇌fhfr£21 dB&Bfr£23 dB&B⇌fhfr£28.75 B

CTV 10P

English & Continental ✱Dinner fr£6.50&alc Wine £4.60 Last dinner 9pm

Credit cards 1 2 3 5

★★**Windsor** South Pde ☎ 091-252 3317

Closed 25 & 26 Dec

Friendly, informal hotel with modern, well appointed bedrooms.

46rm(21⇌1fh) CTV in all bedrooms ® T S% sB&Bfr£19 sB&B⇌fh£21—£30 dB&Bfr£22 dB&B⇌fh£25—£35 B

☾CTV 16P 2

English & French V Lunch fr£5.50 Tea fr£1 Dinner £6—£10 Wine £4.50 Last dinner 9.30pm

Credit cards 1 2 3 5

★**Cavendish** (formerly Manuels) 51—52 Esplanade ☎ 091-253 3010

Simple seaside hotel managed by proprietor and his family.

11rm(5⇌2fh)(2fb) CTV in 8 bedrooms ® in 1 bedroom T ✱sB&B£10—£12 sB&B⇌fh£15 dB&B£22.50 dB&B⇌fh£22.50 B

CTV 20P

V ✱Lunch £2.20—£3.75 Tea £1 Dinner £6&alc Wine £4.50 Last dinner 9.30pm

Credit cards 1 3

★**Downton** South Pde ☎ 091-252 5941

A small, family-run hotel, offering comfortable accommodation and friendly service, caters for both the businessman and the family on holiday.

22rm(7fh)(5fb) CTV in all bedrooms ® S% ✱sB&Bfr£14.95 sB&Bfhfr£18.45 dB&Bfr£23 dB&Bfhfr£26.45 B

CTV Live music & dancing Fri & Sat

V S% ✱Lunch fr£2 Tea fr£1.50 Dinner fr£6 Wine £3.50 Last dinner 8pm

Credit cards 1 3 V

★***Newquay*** 50—54 South Pde ☎ 091-253 2211

Small, friendly hotel with comfortable accommodation.

34rm(15⇌)(2fb) CTV in all bedrooms ® B

☾CTV 27P Disco 3 nights wkly *xmas*

Last dinner 8.30pm

Credit cards 1 3 5

WHITSTABLE

Kent

Map **5** TR16

★★**Marine** Marine Pde, Tankerton (1m E) ☎ (0227) 272672

A comfortable, traditional, well-run hotel, facing the sea.

17rm(4⇌10fh) CTV in 14 bedrooms sB&B£27—£30 sB&B⇌fh£32—£35 dB&B⇌fh£49—£55 B

CTV 17P 3(70p per night) snooker

English & French Lunch £6—£6.50alc Tea 80p Dinner £8—£8.50&alc Wine £4.90 Last dinner 8.15pm

Credit cards 1 3 V

X***Rajpoot Tandoori*** Harbour St ☎ (0227) 264700

Well-presented Rajpoot specialities, with good, delicate sauces, are offered in the authentic atmosphere of this pleasant Indian restaurant.

Indian 34 seats Last dinner mdnt

WHITTINGTON

Shropshire

Map **7** SJ33

★**Ye Olde Boot Inn** (Frederic Robinson) ☎ Oswestry (0691) 662250

A modernised old inn set in rural surroundings.

8rm(2fb) CTV in all bedrooms sB&B£11.50 dB&B£23 B

100P

✱Lunch £3—£5.50&alc Dinner £3.50—£6.50&alc Wine £3.20 Last dinner 10pm

WHITTLESLEY

Cambridgeshire

Map **4** TL29

XX**Falcon Hotel** Paradise Ln ☎ Peterborough (0733) 203247

English & French V 36 seats ✱Lunch £10.50alc Dinner £10.50alc Wine £4.95 Last dinner 10pm 40P

Credit cards 1 2 3 5 V

WHITWELL-ON-THE-HILL

North Yorkshire

Map **8** SE76

★★★ *L* **Whitwell Hall Country House** ☎ (065381) 551 Telex no 57697

Magnificent country house built in 1835 in Tudor Gothic style. Situated in 18 acres of garden and woodland with splendid views.

11rm(8⇌3fh) Annexe: 9rm(6⇌3fh) 1 CTV in all bedrooms ® T sB&B⇌fh£31—£36 dB&B⇌fh£47—£69 B

40P 4(charge) (heated) (hard) sauna bath croquet putting nc 13yrs *xmas*

V Lunch £4—£8&alc Tea £1&alc Dinner £15&alc Wine £6 Last dinner 8pm

Credit cards 1 2 3

WICK

Highland *Caithness*

Map **15** ND35

★★★**Ladbroke** Riverside (Ladbroke) ☎ (0955) 3344

A modern purpose built hotel in central location near river. →

W

48🛁(6fb) CTV in all bedrooms ⊗ **T** ✱sB🛁£11.50—£32 dB🛁£23—£44

☾22P snooker Live music & dancing Wed (Jun—Sep)

British & French **V** ✱Lunch £9.25&alc Tea 50palc Dinner £9.25&alc Wine £5.99 Last dinner 9pm

Credit cards [1] [2] [3] [4] [5] Ⓥ

★★**Mackay's** Union St ☎(0955) 2323

Housed in a Victorian building, the friendly commercial and tourist hotel stands by the River Wick in the town centre. Owners of many years' standing have modernised the interior of the premises to provide up-to-date facilities.

27rm(15🛁)(5fb) CTV in 20 bedrooms ✱sB&B£17 sB&B🛁£21.50 dB&B£30 dB&B🛁£35

Lift CTV

✱Lunch £4.50&alc Tea 30p&alc High Tea £4.50&alc Dinner £8&alc Wine £4.15 Last dinner 8.30pm

Credit cards [1] [3]

★★**Station** Bridge St (Consort) ☎(0955) 4545

Closed 31 Nov—4 Jan

A town centre Victorian hotel, standing on the banks of the River Wick.

33rm(3🛁18🚿) in 6 bedrooms CTV in 23 bedrooms ⊗ **T** sB&B£19—£25 sB&B🛁🚿£22—£30 dB&B£26—£32 dB&B🛁🚿£28—£40

Lift ☾CTV

Scottish & French **V** Lunch £4.90 Tea £1.70 High Tea £4.90alc Dinner £10 Last dinner 9pm

Credit cards [1] [2] [3] [4] [5]

WICKEN (Milton Keynes, Bucks)
Northamptonshire
Map **4** SP73

★★**Wicken Country** Cross Tree Rd ☎(090857) 239

Closed 25 Dec—1 Jan

16rm(4🛁6🚿) CTV in all bedrooms **T** ✱sB&B£26.50 sB&B🛁🚿£29.50 dB&B£38 dB&B🛁🚿£44

40P 2 (heated) (hard)

English & Continental **V** ✱Lunch £12.50alc Tea £2alc High Tea £7.50alc Dinner £12.50alc Wine £5.75 Last dinner 9.30pm

Credit cards [1] [2] [3] [5]

WICKHAM
Hampshire
Map **4** SU51

★★*B* **Old House** ☎(0329) 833049

Closed 12 days Xmas, 2 wks Etr & 2 wks Jul/Aug

RS Sat & Sun

Elegant and charming Georgian house with tastefully furnished bedrooms and fine restaurant where excellent French provincial cooking is available.

10rm(8🛁)(1fb) CTV in all bedrooms **T** S% sB&B🛁🚿£45—£52 dB&B🛁🚿£60—£70

12P

French S% Lunch fr£18alc Dinner fr£18alc Wine £7.50 Last dinner 9.30pm

Credit cards [1] [2] [3] [5]

WIDEMOUTH BAY
Cornwall
Map **2** SS20

★★**Trelawny** Marine Dr ☎(028885) 328

Closed Oct—Whit RS Etr

A small, friendly hotel overlooking Widemouth Bay.

10rm(2🚿)(3fb) S% sB&B£11.50—£12.65 sB&B🚿£13.23—£13.80 dB&B£23—£25.30 dB&B🚿£26.45—£31.05

CTV 40P

S% Lunch 65p—£3.95 Tea 50p—£1.20 Dinner £4.95 Wine £2.60 Last dinner 7.30pm

Credit cards [1] [2] [3]

WIDNES AUG → ✱
Cheshire
Map **7** SJ58

★★**Hillcrest** 75 Cronton Ln ☎051-424 1616 Telex no 627098

Family hotel with modern extension, attractive bar, lounge and restaurant.

46rm(28🛁18🚿)(4fb) CTV in 40 bedrooms TV in 6 bedrooms ⊗ **T** S% sB&B🛁🚿£27.50 dB&B🛁🚿£38.50

☾150P *xmas*

English & French **V** ✱Lunch £8—£12&alc Tea £1.95 Dinner £5.15&alc Wine £5.25 Last dinner 10pm

Credit cards [1] [2] [3] [5] Ⓥ

WIGAN
Greater Manchester
Map **7** SD50

★★★**Brocket Arms** Mesnes Rd ☎(0942) 46283

A large hotel, close to the town centre.

27rm(25🛁2🚿) CTV in all bedrooms ⊗ S% sB&B🛁🚿£20—£25 dB&B🛁🚿£31—£36

☾60P

V S% Lunch £7.50&alc Tea 60p Dinner £7.50&alc Last dinner 9.30pm

Credit cards [1] [2] [3] [5] Ⓥ

★★**Bel-Air** 236 Wigan Ln ☎(0942) 41410

11rm(8🛁2🚿)(1fb) 1 CTV in all bedrooms ⊗ ✱sB&B🛁🚿£22 dB&B🛁🚿£27

CTV 8P

International ✱Lunch £4.95&alc Dinner £6.95&alc Wine £4.95 Last dinner 9pm

Credit cards [1] [2] [3] [4] [5]

★★**Bellingham** 149 Wigan Ln ☎(0942) 43893

A commercial hotel, off the A49 on the north side of town.

18rm(4🛁10🚿)(2fb) CTV in all bedrooms ⊗ sB&Bfr£22 sB&B🛁🚿fr£25 dB&Bfr£31 dB&B🛁🚿fr£35

☾CTV 25P

Dinner £7&alc Wine £4.95 Last dinner 9pm

Credit cards [1] [2] [3] [5]

★★**Cassinellis Almond Brook Motor Inn** Almond Brook Rd ☎(0257) 425588

(For full entry see Standish)

WIGHT, ISLE OF
Map **4**

BEMBRIDGE
Map **4** SZ68

★★**Birdham** 1 Steyne Rd ☎(0983) 872875

Small comfortable inn with good cuisine.

14rm(11🚿)(5fb) in 2 bedrooms CTV in all bedrooms ⊗ S% sB&B🚿£16.50 dB&B£27.80 dB&B🚿£33

☾CTV 100P pool table

Continental **V** Lunch £5—£7&alc Dinner £6—£10&alc Wine £4.65 Last dinner 9.15pm

Credit card [2]

★★ *BL* **Elms Country** ☎(0983) 872248

RS 21 Oct—Feb

Quiet family house with attractive garden and friendly atmosphere.

12rm(10🛁2🚿)(4fb) CTV in all bedrooms ⊗ **T** ✱sB&B🛁🚿fr£24 dB&B🛁🚿fr£38

60P

Cosmopolitan **V** ✱Lunch £6 Tea £1.60 High Tea £4 Dinner £8.50&alc Wine £3.80 Last dinner 9.30pm

★★*BL* **Highbury** Lane End ☎(0983) 872838

Closed 24—27 Dec

Small, family run hotel where the hospitality is warm and natural, the cooking very reliable and the bedrooms prettily decorated.

W ✱

051, 424 9118
HILLCREST
>27/8/87

9rm(6→2⋔)(9fb) 1 TV in all bedrooms sB&B£18.50—£27 sB&B→⋔£28—£29 dB&B→⋔£40.50—42.50 B

9P (heated) sauna bath solarium croquet lawn

English & French V ✱Lunch £5—£6&alc Tea £1.35—£1.55 Dinner £9.50—£10&alc Wine £5.50 Last dinner 10pm

Credit cards 1 2 3 5

CHALE
Map **4** SZ47

★Clarendon Hotel & Wight Mouse Inn ☎ Niton (0983) 730431

The hotel, with its separate inn, has bright, attractive bedrooms and an attractively appointed restaurant; a warm welcome is assured at all times.

13rm(2→7⋔)(9fb) CTV in all bedrooms ® sB&B£14.95 sB&B→⋔£17.25 dB&B£29.90 dB&B→⋔£34.50 B

CTV 100P boule Live music & dancing nightly *xmas*

V Lunch £3—£6&alc Dinner £3—£8&alc Wine £3.95 Last dinner 10pm

Ⓥ

COWES
Map **4** SZ49
See also Whippingham

★★★Holmwood Egypt Point ☎ (0983) 292508

Closed mid Nov—Jan

20→⋔ CTV in all bedrooms ® T sB&B→⋔£31 dB&B→⋔£42 B

English & French V Bar lunch £2—£3 Tea 50p—£1 Dinner £6.50—£7.50&alc Wine £5.10 Last dinner 9pm

Credit cards 1 2 3 4 5 Ⓥ

Wight, Isle of

Superbly situated hotel, overlooking the Solent.

19rm(7→7⋔) CTV in 11 bedrooms ® T sB&Bfr£20 sB&B→⋔fr£27.50 dB&Bfr£40 dB&B→⋔fr£48 B

CTV 12P

French V Lunch fr£9&alc Tea fr80p Dinner fr£9&alc Wine £4.50 Last dinner 9.30pm

Credit cards 1 2 3 5

★★Cowes 260 Arctic Rd, West Cowes ☎ (0983) 291541

Modernised former public house with comfortably appointed bedrooms and friendly atmosphere.

15rm(14→1⋔)(4fb) CTV in all bedrooms T sB&B→⋔fr£26.38 dB&B→⋔fr£36.75 B

☾25P sauna bath

V Lunch £9.16 Dinner £9.16 Wine £4.48 Last dinner 10pm

Credit cards 1 2 3 5 Ⓥ

See advertisement on page 768

★★Fountain High St (Whitbread) ☎ (0983) 292397

The popular coaching inn, has smart, modernised bedrooms. Friendly informal staff help to create a relaxing atmosphere.

✕G's Restaurant 10 Bath Rd ☎ (0983) 297021

Attractively decorated, this small cottage restaurant offers a warm welcome and a friendly, informal atmosphere in which to enjoy a well-cooked meal from a short but interesting menu of French-style dishes.

Closed Sun (except Bank Hols) & Feb Lunch by reservation only

English & French 32 seats Lunch £14—£16alc Dinner £14—16alc Wine £5.90 Last dinner 9.30pm

Credit cards 1 2 3 5

FRESHWATER
Map **4** SZ38

★★★Albion ☎ (0983) 753631

Closed Nov—Mar

Ideally situated on the sea front, the well-run, thoughtfully-appointed hotel offers good lounge facilities and a friendly, relaxing atmosphere.

43rm(37→)(20fb) CTV in all bedrooms ® S% sB&B£16—£21 sB&B→£19.50—£21 dB&B£32—£36.50 dB&B→£39.75—£42

CTV 75P →

W

S% Lunch £6 Tea 75p Dinner £10&alc Wine £4 Last dinner 8.30pm

Credit cards [1] [2] [3] Ⓥ

NEWPORT
Map **4** SZ48

✕**Lugley's** 42 Lugley St ☎ (0983) 521062

Cooking is good and imaginative at this small, intimate restaurant where the cook/proprietress varies an already interesting menu by the inclusion of her own specialities.

Closed Sun, 2 wks Oct & 2 wks Feb Lunch by reservation only

Wight, Isle of

International **V** 16 seats Lunch £8 Dinner £11.75alc Wine £5.25 Last dinner 9.30 nc 12yrs

Ⓥ

✕**Valentino's** 93 High St, Carisbrooke (1m W B3401) ☎ (0983) 522458

An intimate little Italian restaurant stands just outside the town; good Italian cooking is produced by an English chef.

French & Italian **V** 85 seats S% ✱Lunch £1.95—£8&alc Dinner fr £8&alc Wine £4.90 Last dinner 10.30pm

Credit cards [1] [3] Ⓥ

RYDE
Map **4** SZ59

★★★**Hotel Ryde Castle** Esplanade ☎ (0983) 63755

17rm (10 7) 6 CTV in all bedrooms Ⓡ **T** sB&B fr £22 dB&B fr £44

90P Live music & dancing Sat nc 8yrs

V Lunch £5.50&alc Dinner £8.50&alc Wine £4.50 Last dinner 9.45pm

Credit cards [1] [3] Ⓥ

★★ *B* **Biskra House Beach Hotel** 17 St Thomas's Street ☎ (0983) 67931

The small, privately-owned hotel has a friendly, informal atmosphere and provides accommodation in some excellently-appointed bedrooms. An international menu is available in the more formal, ground floor, restaurant, whereas that in the basement offers Italian fondues, but cooking is of a high standard throughout.

9rm(4→5⋔) CTV in all bedrooms **T** ✗ *sB&B→⋔£20—£28 dB&B→⋔£40—£56

14P

French & Italian **V** Lunch £1.95—£4.95&alc Dinner £4.50—£10.95&alc Wine £4.95 Last dinner 10.30pm

Credit cards 1 3

★★ **Yelf's** Union St (Trusthouse Forte) ☎ (0983) 64062

Informal hotel with warm, friendly atmosphere.

21→ CTV in all bedrooms ® sB&B→£44.50 dB&B→£61.50 B

P *xmas*

Last dinner 9pm

Credit cards 1 2 3 4 5

ST HELENS

Map **4** SZ68

✗ ***Hay Loft*** Upper Green ☎ (0983) 872014

Small, simple bistro with lively atmosphere.

Closed Oct—wk before Etr & Sun Lunch not served

International 56 seats Last dinner 10pm

P

ST LAWRENCE

Map **4** SZ57

★★ ***H Rocklands*** ☎ (0983) 852964

Closed 30 Sep—25 May

A very friendly family hotel with many facilities for children.

16rm(9→2⋔) Annexe: 4rm(17fb) 1 CTV in all bedrooms ✗

Wight, Isle of

CTV 18P (heated) billiards sauna bath solarium

English & Continental **V** Last dinner 8pm

SANDOWN

Map **4** SZ58

★★★ **Broadway Park** Melville St ☎ (0983) 402007 due to change to 405214

Closed Oct—Dec & Jan—Apr RS Apr—24 May & 6—30 Sep

Country house in landscaped gardens with good recreational facilities.

52rm(42→1⋔)(5fb) CTV in all bedrooms ® **T** ✗ sB&B→⋔£22—£30 dB&B→⋔£44—£56 B

Lift ☾ 100P (heated) (grass) snooker putting games room Disco twice wkly Live music & dancing twice wkly

English & French Bar lunch fr£2.50 Tea fr80p Dinner fr£8 Last dinner 8.30pm

Credit cards 1 2 3 Ⓥ

★★★ **Melville Hall** Melville St ☎ (0983) 406526

Large house in quiet area with attractive gardens.

36rm(23→5⋔)(7fb) CTV in all bedrooms ® **T** ✗ sB&B£14—£23 sB&B→⋔£17—£26 dB&B£22—£40 dB&B→⋔£28—£46

☾ 26P (heated) games room Live music & dancing 4 nights wkly Cabaret Sat

English & Continental Bar lunch £1.50—£4 Tea 52p Dinner £7.95&alc Wine £4.20 Last dinner 8.30pm

Credit cards 1 3 Ⓥ

★ **Rose Bank** High St ☎ (0983) 403854

Closed Xmas wk

Small, friendly family hotel overlooking the sea.

9rm(3⋔)(2fb) sB&B£11—£13 dB&B£22—£26

CTV P nc6yrs

Lunch £4—£4.75 Tea fr75p Dinner fr£7 Wine £3.75 Last dinner 7pm

See advertisement on page 770

SEAVIEW

Map **4** SZ69

★★ **Seaview** High St ☎ (098371) 2711

A smart, compact restaurant offers first-class, French-inspired food, and there are two attractive and popular bars. The small, charming hotel is very tastefully furnished.

15rm(11→)(1fb) CTV in all bedrooms *sB&Bfr£18 sB&B→fr£24 dB&Bfr£31 dB&B→fr£38 B

12P

English & French **V** *Lunch £6.95&alc Tea fr70p Dinner £8.30—£8.80&alc Wine £4.75 Last dinner 9.30pm

Credit cards 1 2 3

SHANKLIN

Map **4** SZ58

★★★ ***Cliff Tops*** Park Rd ☎ (0983) 863262

Closed 25 Dec—6 Jan

Hotel has good Channel views and large well-kept gardens.

102rm(80→3⋔)(15fb) CTV in all bedrooms **T** B

Lift ☾ 40P CFA (heated) sauna bath Disco wkly Live music & dancing 5 nights wkly

English & French Last dinner 9pm

Credit cards 1 2 3 5

See advertisement on page 770

★★ *B* **Belmont** Queens Rd ☎ (0983) 862864

Closed Xmas & New Year

A Victorian house has been tastefully furnished and decorated to create a pleasant hotel with particularly good bedrooms. Personally supervised by the owners, it offers a warm welcome to guests. →

W

16rm(9➡5⫛)(3fb) 2⊟ CTV in all bedrooms ® T sB&B£13—£20 sB&B➡⫛£15—£22 dB&B£26—£40 dB&B➡⫛£30—£44 B

12P ⇌ ≏ (heated) solarium

V ♱ ☐ Lunch £4.95—£5.95 Tea 75p—£1.50 Dinner £7.95—£10.95&alc Wine £3.80 Last dinner 9.45pm

Credit cards [1] [3] Ⓥ

★★**Fernbank** Highfield Rd ☎ (0983) 862790

Closed 25 Dec—9 Jan

Small, privately run hotel with nicely appointed accommodation and good recreation facilities.

Wight, Isle of

20rm(8➡8⫛)(5fb) CTV in all bedrooms ® T sB&B£13—£13.50 sB&B➡⫛£14.35—£15 dB&B£26—£27 dB&B➡⫛£28.70—£30

CTV 18P ⇌ ✽ ⊟ (heated) sauna bath solarium pool table nc 7yrs

♱ ☐ ✗ Lunch £1—£4 Tea 50p Dinner £6.50 Wine £4 Last dinner 8pm

Credit cards [1] [3]

★★**Luccombe Hall** Luccombe Rd (Exec Hotels) ☎ (0983) 862719

Closed 2—30 Jan

Well-appointed comfortable hotel with good leisure facilities.

31rm(27➡3⫛)(15fb) CTV in all bedrooms ® sB&B➡⫛£20.50—£28 dB&B➡⫛£35—£50 B

CTV 30P ✽ ⊟ & ≏ (heated) ⚲ (grass) squash sauna bath solarium games room ♿ ⌂ *xmas*

♉ English & Continental V ♱ ☐ Lunch £5.50—£7.50 Tea 75p—£1 Dinner £10.75—£11.50&alc Wine £4.35 Last dinner 8.30pm

Credit cards [1] [3] Ⓥ

★★**Melbourne Ardenlea** Queen's Rd ☎(0983) 862283
Closed Dec—Feb
Family-run hotel, set in well tended gardens.
55rm(32(bath)5(shower))(8fb) CTV in 31 bedrooms ®sB&B£12—£18 sB&B(bath)(shower)£14—£20 dB&B£24—£36 dB&B(bath)(shower)£28—£40 B
CTV 25P ✿ (heated) sauna bath solarium Live music & dancing 3 nights wkly
Lunch £4.50—£5.50 Dinner £6.50—£7.50&alc Wine £4.20 Last dinner 8pm
Credit card [3] Ⓥ

Wight, Isle of

✕***Punch's Bistro*** Chine Hill, 1—3 Esplanade ☎(0983) 864454
Small, attractively decorated restaurant serving short menu of French dishes.
Closed Mon Lunch not served
French 36 seats Last dinner 10pm
Credit cards [1] [2] [3] [5]

TOTLAND BAY
Map **4** SZ38
★★**Country Garden** Church Hill ☎(0983) 754521
The small, privately-owned and personally supervised hotel stands in a peaceful, rural setting. It has an informally friendly atmosphere and offers comfortable accommodation in spacious, well-appointed bedrooms.
16(bath) CTV in all bedrooms ®**T** sB&B(bath)£22—£25 dB&B(bath)£44—£50
☾32P ✿ nc 14yrs *xmas* →

English & French V S% Lunch £4.95—£6.50 Dinner £8.50—£9.95&alc Wine £5.20 Last dinner 9.30pm

Credit cards 1 2 3 5 V

★★**Sentry Mead** Madeira Rd
Freshwater (0983) 753212

Small, cosy, family-run hotel.

13rm(5)(2fb) CTV available in bedrooms S% *sB&B£12—£15 sB&B£14—£17 dB&B£24—£30 dB&B£28—£34

CTV 10P putting

European V S% *Bar lunch £2.50—£4.75&alc Tea 45—75p Dinner £6.50—£8.50&alc Wine £3.50 Last dinner 8pm

Credit card 2 V

VENTNOR
Map **4** SZ57

★★★**Royal** Belgrave Rd (Trusthouse Forte) (0983) 852186

Well-appointed hotel overlooking the sea, with many other facilities.

54(2fb) CTV in all bedrooms ® sB&B£41.50 dB&B£61.50 B

Lift 56P CFA (heated)

Last dinner 9pm

Credit cards 1 2 3 4 5

Wight, Isle of

★★★**Ventnor Towers** Madeira Rd (Consort) (0983) 852277 Telex no 951182

Clifftop hotel, with comfortable lounges, set in grounds accommodating many outdoor sports.

30rm(17 5)(4fb) CTV in all bedrooms T S% sB&B£17.50—£19.50 sB&B£21.50—£23 dB&B£35—£39 dB&B£43—£46 B

40P 1 (heated) (hard) snooker *xmas*

English, French & Italian V S% Lunch £6.25—£6.75 Tea 75p—£1 High Tea £2—£2.95 Dinner £8—£9.95 Wine £4.50 Last dinner 8.30pm

Credit cards 1 2 3 4 5 V

★★*HBL* **Bonchurch Manor**
Bonchurch (1m E) (0983) 852868

Closed Jan—Feb

Charming Victorian house, thoughtfully modernised to provide a high standard of comfortable accommodation. The bedrooms are particularly well equipped and the cooking is creative and well prepared. Service is warm and friendly.

12rm(8 3)(4fb) CTV in all bedrooms ® sB&B£23 sB&B£23 dB&B£46 B

10P (heated) nc7yrs *xmas*

English & French Lunch £5.95 Tea 70p Dinner £10 Wine £5 Last dinner 8pm

Credit card 3

★★*B* **Highfield** Leeson Rd, Bonchurch
(0983) 852800

This charming Victorian house has a warm, friendly atmosphere and an attractive garden. Tastefully decorated and furnished, it provides good, comfortable accommodation and offers an interesting menu of good, honest cooking.

12 2 CTV in all bedrooms T *sB&B£19.60—£24 dB&B£39—£48

P

W

♔ ☕ Last dinner 8.30pm

Credit cards 1 3

★★**Metropole** The Esplanade ☎ (0983) 852181

Closed Nov—Feb

Seafront resort hotel with friendly informal atmosphere.

35rm(10→1⋔)(12fb) CTV in all bedrooms ®✱sB&B£12—£18 sB&B→⋔£14—£20 dB&B£24—£36 dB&B→⋔£28—£40

Lift 20P

V ♔ ☕ ✱Bar lunch £1.50—£3 Tea 60—75p Dinner £6.50 Wine £3.90 Last dinner 8pm

Credit cards 1 3

★**LMadeira Hall** Trinity Rd ☎ (0983) 852624

Closed Nov—Feb

Beautifully situated hotel with Dickens associations. Good leisure facilities.

12rm(6→2⋔)(4fb) CTV in all bedrooms ® S% sB&B£16—£17 sB&B→⋔£17—£18 dB&B£32—£34 dB&B→⋔£34—£36 B

CTV 12P ✿ (heated) putting

♔S% Lunch £4—£4.50 Dinner £5—£6 Wine £3.50

Credit cards 1 2 3 Ⓥ

WHIPPINGHAM
Map **4** SZ59

★★**Padmore House** Beatrice Av ☎ (0983) 293210

Friendly, well-appointed, Queen Anne style hotel set in Medina Valley.

11rm(6→1⋔)(1fb) CTV in all bedrooms ® sB&B£21 sB&B→⋔£23—£32.50 dB&B→⋔£49—£54 B

20P ✿ (heated)

French V ♔ ☕ S% Lunch £6.95—£7.95 Tea fr75p Dinner £8.50—£10 Wine £5.50 Last dinner 9.30pm

Credit cards 1 2 3 5 Ⓥ

See advertisement on page 768

YARMOUTH
Map **4** SZ38

★★***Bugle*** The Square ☎ (0983) 760272

RS Nov—Etr

Small, friendly inn with pleasant modern rooms and comfortable bedrooms.

10rm(2→2⋔)(2fb) B

CTV 12P

V ♔ ☕ Last dinner 9pm

Credit cards 1 2 3 5

★★**George** Quay St ☎ (0983) 760331

RS Nov—Etr

Small hotel near Yarmouth Pier, dating from Charles II's time.

20rm(7→)(2fb) CTV in all bedrooms sB&B£15—£20 dB&B£30—£40 dB&B→£40—£50

3P 4 ✿ *xmas*

♔ ☕ Lunch £5.25—£5.50 Tea 85p—£1.50 Dinner £8.25—£9.25&alc Wine £3.75 Last dinner 9pm

Credit cards 1 2 3 4 5 Ⓥ

WIGTON
Cumbria
Map **11** NY24

★★***Greenhill Lodge*** Red Dial (2m S off A595) ☎ (0965) 43304

A converted 17th-century, manor house, standing off the A595, serves extensive, good-quality, home-made bar meals and dinners.

8rm(3→)(2fb) 2 CTV in 3 bedrooms TV in 5 bedrooms ® T B

120P ✿

English & French V ♔ ☕ Last dinner 9.15pm

Credit cards 1 2 3 5

★★**Wheyrigg Hall** (4m NW on B5302) ☎ Abbeytown (09656) 242

Conveniently situated on B5302 between Silloth and Wigton, the family-run hotel is a converted farmhouse. In addition to its very busy and popular restaurant, it offers six comfortable and well-appointed bedrooms.

6rm(2→)(2fb) CTV in all bedrooms ® ✱sB&Bfr£16 sB&B→fr£19 dB&Bfr£26 dB&B→fr£28 B

60P ✿ *xmas*

V ♔ ☕ ✱Lunch £5—£5.25 Tea fr£2 High Tea £3—£6 Dinner £8.50 Wine £3.60

Credit cards 1 2 3 5

WILLERBY
Humberside
Map **8** TA03

★★★**Willerby Manor** Well Ln ☎ Hull (0482) 652616 Telex no 592629

Closed Xmas Day & Boxing Day

A converted and extended private residence, standing in its own well-kept gardens, provides functional, well-equipped bedrooms which are popular with business people and an attractive restaurant, lounge bar and cellar bar.

41rm(28→13⋔) CTV in all bedrooms ® T ✱sB→⋔£36.25—£48.25 dB→⋔£53.40—£59.50 (room only) B

☾ 250P CFA ✿

French ♔ ✱Lunch £7&alc Dinner £7.50—£8.50&alc Wine £5.50 Last dinner 9.45pm

Credit cards 1 3 Ⓥ

WILLITON
Somerset
Map **3** ST04

❀★★**White House** Long St
☎(0984) 32306
Closed Nov—mid May
(Rosette awarded for dinner only). Personally-run by the proprietors, Dick and Kay Smith, this white-painted, Georgian house offers comfortable accommodation and a popular restaurant. Dinner, served in a pleasant, beamed dining room, features an uncomplicated menu with a choice of interesting dishes prepared to a high standard from good, fresh ingredients and complemented by a comprehensive wine list.
8rm(3🛁) Annexe: 5rm(4🛁)(2fb) CTV in all bedrooms sB&B£22 sB&B🛁£24—£25 dB&B£39 dB&B🛁£43—£45 B
12P
French Dinner £17 Wine £6 Last dinner 8.30pm
Ⓥ

WILMCOTE
Warwickshire
Map **4** SP15
★★**Swan House** The Green
☎Stratford-upon-Avon (0789) 67030
Closed 24—28 Dec
Quiet village inn opposite Mary Arden's House.
8rm(5🛁3🚿)(2fb) CTV in all bedrooms Ⓡ sB&B🛁🚿£28—£32 dB&B🛁🚿£35 B
38P
English & French **V** Bar lunch £1—£5 Tea 60p Dinner £12alc Wine £4 Last dinner 9.30pm
Credit cards 1 2 3 Ⓥ
See advertisement under Stratford-upon-Avon

WILMINGTON
Devon
Map **3** SY29
★★*H* **Home Farm** ☎(040483) 278
RS Jan—Feb
Delightful, cottage style hotel, with good food served in pleasant restaurant.
8rm(4🛁) Annexe: 5rm(2🛁)(2fb) CTV in 6 bedrooms ⓇS% sB&B£23.50—£29 sB&B🛁£29—£35 dB&B£37—£53 dB&B🛁£43—£59 B
CTV 20P
V Lunch £7—£8.50 Tea 75p—£1.25 Dinner £10—£12.50 Wine £4.75 Last dinner 8.30pm
Credit cards 1 2 3 5 Ⓥ

WILMSLOW
Cheshire
Map **7** SJ88
See also **Manchester Airport**

❀★★★*H* **Stanneylands**
Stanneylands Rd ☎(0625) 525225
Telex no 666358
RS 26 Dec—1 Jan
Standing in its own grounds, which contain many varieties of trees and shrubs from all over the world, the family owned and run hotel provides food and service of the highest standard.
33🛁(2fb) 1 CTV in all bedrooms **T** sB&B🛁£30—£49 dB&B🛁£40—£65 B
☾80P
English & French **V** Lunch £6.50—£7.50&alc Tea £1 Dinner £16&alc Wine £5.50 Last dinner 10pm
Credit cards 1 2 3 4 5

✕✕**Mandarin** Parsonage Green
☎(0625) 524096
Popular friendly Chinese restaurant with good range of oriental dishes and 7-course banquet dinner.
Cantonese **V** 80 seats Lunch £2.50—£3&alc Dinner £9—£12&alc Wine £5.20 Last dinner 11.30pm 35P
Credit card 3 Ⓥ

✕✕**Yang Sing Bistro** 70—72 Grove St
☎(0625) 528799
This most interesting first-floor restaurant is decorated in the fresh bistro style. Though the menu is quite short, it offers a good choice of authentic Chinese dishes, the seafood being particularly recommended; booking is advisable.
Closed Mon
Lunch not served Tue—Sat
Cantonese **V** 100 seats S% Dinner £10alc Wine £4.50 Last dinner 11.15pm
Live music 4 nights wkly Ⓥ

WIMBORNE MINSTER
Dorset
Map **4** SZ09
★★★**King's Head** The Square (Trusthouse Forte) ☎(0202) 880101
Comfortable, attractive town centre hotel.
28rm(17🛁)(3fb) CTV in all bedrooms Ⓡ sB&B£40.50 sB&B🛁£48.50 dB&B£58.50 dB&B🛁£66.50 B
Lift CTV 25P *xmas*
Last dinner 9.30pm
Credit cards 1 2 3 4 5

★★**Coach House Motel** Tricketts Cross
☎(0202) 871222
(For full entry see Ferndown)

✕✕**Old Town House** 9 Church St
☎(0202) 888227
This attractive, terraced restaurant in the town centre offers a neat, cosy interior and the attentive service of the chef/patron. The menu features a good selection of dishes with the emphasis on fresh ingredients, and there is a small bar area.
Closed Sun, Mon, 26 Dec—6 Jan, 2 wks Etr & 2 wks Jul Lunch not served
Continental 54 seats ✱Dinner £10alc Wine £4.75 Last dinner 10pm
Credit card 3

WINCANTON
Somerset
Map **3** ST72
★★**Dolphin** High St ☎(0963) 32215
The main building of this old, family-run coaching inn contains pleasant bedrooms and a first-floor lounge, whilst the restaurant is across the yard.
10rm(4🛁2🚿) CTV in all bedrooms Ⓡ sB&B£18.50—£21.50 sB&B🛁🚿£21.50 dB&B£32.50 dB&B🛁🚿£36.50
20P
Bar lunch 90p—£2.50 Dinner £8.95—£9.50 Wine £4.95 Last dinner 8.30pm
Credit cards 1 2 3

★★**Holbrook House** Castle Cary Rd, Holbrook ☎(0963) 32377
Closed New Year's Eve
Quietly situated country house hotel where proprietors offer a charming welcome. Comfortable throughout.
20rm(8🛁6🚿)(4fb) Ⓡ sB&B£19—£20.50 sB&B🛁🚿£22.50—£27 dB&B£38—£41 dB&B🛁🚿£45—£50 B
CTV 40P 2🚗(£1 per night)
(heated) (hard & grass) squash croquet table tennis *xmas*
V Lunch £6—£7&alc Tea £1.50 High Tea £4—£5 Dinner £8.50—£10&alc Wine £5 Last dinner 8.30pm
Credit cards 1 2 3 Ⓥ

✕**Paupers Bistro** 6 South St ☎(0963) 32752
This simply-appointed, bistro-style, little restaurant in the town centre has a very informal and relaxing atmosphere. The à la carte blackboard menu varies from day to day, making good use of fresh, raw materials to provide seasonal dishes in both traditional and modern style. Service is genuinely helpful, and there is a sound wine list.
Closed Sun & 25—30 Dec Lunch not served Sat
20 seats Lunch £12.50alc Dinner £12.50alc Wine £4.80 Last dinner 10pm
Credit cards 2 3 5

WINCHELSEA
East Sussex
Map**5** TQ91

✕Manna Plat Mill Rd ☎ Rye (0797) 226317

A small, proprietor-run restaurant, hidden away among Winchelsea's historic lanes, is set in a slate-tiled house with 13th-century vaulted cellars. In the smalll bar and dining room, made attractive by pink napery and the pictures of local artists, short, fixed-priced menus make good use of fresh local ingredients to provide a varied range of British dishes.

Closed Mon (except Bank Hol's)
Lunch not served Sat
Dinner not served Sun

English & French 26 seats ✻Lunch £4.75alc Dinner £7.50alc Wine £4.50 Last dinner 9pm P

Credit card 1 Ⓥ

Winchelsea — Winchester

WINCHESTER
Hampshire
Map**4** SU42

★★★★**Wessex** Paternoster Row (Trusthouse Forte) ☎ (0962) 61611 Telex no 47419

Modern two-storey brick building in the Cathedral precincts.

94rm(92➡2⋔) CTV in all bedrooms ®T sB&B➡⋔£58.50 dB&B➡£75.50 B

Lift ☾ CTV 40 CFA *xmas*

Last dinner 10pm

Credit cards 1 2 3 4 5

W

Winchester

★★★ *BL* **Lainston House** Sparsholt (3m NW off A272) (Prestige) ☎ (0962) 63588 Telex no 477375

Two miles from Winchester, and surrounded by peaceful parkland, this pleasing Georgian house provides a warm welcome. The elegant public rooms include a splendid, panelled bar and comfortable drawing room, whilst bedrooms vary from luxury suites to more functional rooms, though all are attractively decorated and very well kept.

32rm(30⇌1 fi)(1fb) CTV in all bedrooms **T** ✱sB⇌fi£54 dB⇌fi£80—£112(room only) B

☾150P ✿ (hard) Live music Fri & Sat xmas

English & French **V** ✱Lunch £12.50alc Tea £2alc High Tea £3.75alc Dinner £19alc Wine £7.50 Last dinner 10.15pm

Credit cards 1 2 3 4 5

★★★ **Royal** St Peter Street (Best Western) ☎ (0962) 53468 Telex no 477071

Formerly an historic Bishop's house, the centrally-situated, well-managed hotel has been skilfully modernised and offers good standards of comfort, especially in the new wing bedrooms.

59rm(58⇌1 fi)(4fb) CTV in all bedrooms ® **T** ✱sB⇌fi fr£47.35 dB⇌fi fr£62 (room only) B

☾70P ✿

English & French ✱Lunch £6.50—£7.50&alc Tea 80p—£3.50 Dinner £11.50&alc Wine £6.50 Last dinner 9.30pm

Credit cards 1 2 3 4 5

W

XX**Cellar Peking** 32/33 Jewry St ☎(0962) 64178

A smart, modern basement restaurant tastefully decorated and not in the usual Chinese style. A pleasant, friendly and informal atmosphere is created by the very attentive staff. Food is of high standard.

Closed 24—26 Dec

Pekinese & Szechuan **V** 90 seats *Lunch £7.50 Dinner £9.75—£15&alc Wine £4.75 Last dinner 10.30pm nc 5yrs

Credit cards 1 2 3 5 V

XX**Old Chesil Rectory** 1 Chesil St ☎(0962) 53177

An historic 15th-century building with low oak beams and sloping floors houses a restaurant where meals with a French influence are served in a candlelit atmosphere. The regularly-changed, competitively-priced menu, which includes particularly good vegetables and some spectacular puddings, is complemented by an adequate wine list and attentive, genial service.

Closed Mon Lunch not served Sat Dinner not served Sun

V 60 seats Lunch fr£6.75&alc Dinner fr£6.75&alc Wine £5.50 Last dinner 10pm

Credit cards 1 2 3 5

Winchester — Windermere

WINDERMERE
Cumbria
Map **7** SD49 **See plan on page 778**

★★★★**Old England** Bowness (Trusthouse Forte) ☎(09662) 2444 Telex no 65194 Plan **21** *A2*

Large, rambling four-storey hotel by the waterside, with fine views of the lake and the fells.

82(8fb) CTV in all bedrooms ® sB&B£49.50 dB&B£76.50

Lift 60P CFA (heated)

Last dinner 9.15pm

Credit cards 1 2 3 4 5

★★★**Beech Hill** Newby Bridge Rd (Quality) ☎(09662) 2137 Telex no 65156 Plan **2** *B1*

Leisure facilities are a feature of this hotel.

47rm(37 10)(4fb) in 11 bedrooms CTV in all bedrooms ® *sB&B£41 dB&B£58

50P CFA (heated) sauna bath solarium gymnasium Disco Sat *xmas*

British & French **V** *Bar lunch £1.95—£6.50 Tea 75p—£1 Dinner £8.95 Wine £4.95 Last dinner 9pm

Credit cards 1 2 3 5

★★★**Belsfield** Bowness (Trusthouse Forte) ☎(09662) 2448 Telex no 65238 Plan **3** *B2*

Well appointed bedrooms and lounges.

66rm(38 21)(2fb) CTV in all bedrooms ® sB&B£40 sB&B£48 dB&B£62.50 dB&B£70.50

Lift 80P CFA (heated) *xmas*

Last dinner 9.30pm

Credit cards 1 2 3 4 5

★★★**Burn How Motel** Back Belsfield Rd, Bowness ☎(09662) 6226 Plan **5** *B1*

Closed Jan

Spacious chalet-style accommodation.

18(10fb) 4 CTV in all bedrooms ® S% sB&B£25—£28 dB&B£38—£48 Continental breakfast

30P sauna bath solarium gymnasium *xmas*

English & French **V** S% Bar lunch £1.50—£6&alc Tea 75p Dinner £10.50&alc Wine £6 Last dinner 9.15pm

Credit cards 1 2 3 5 V

W

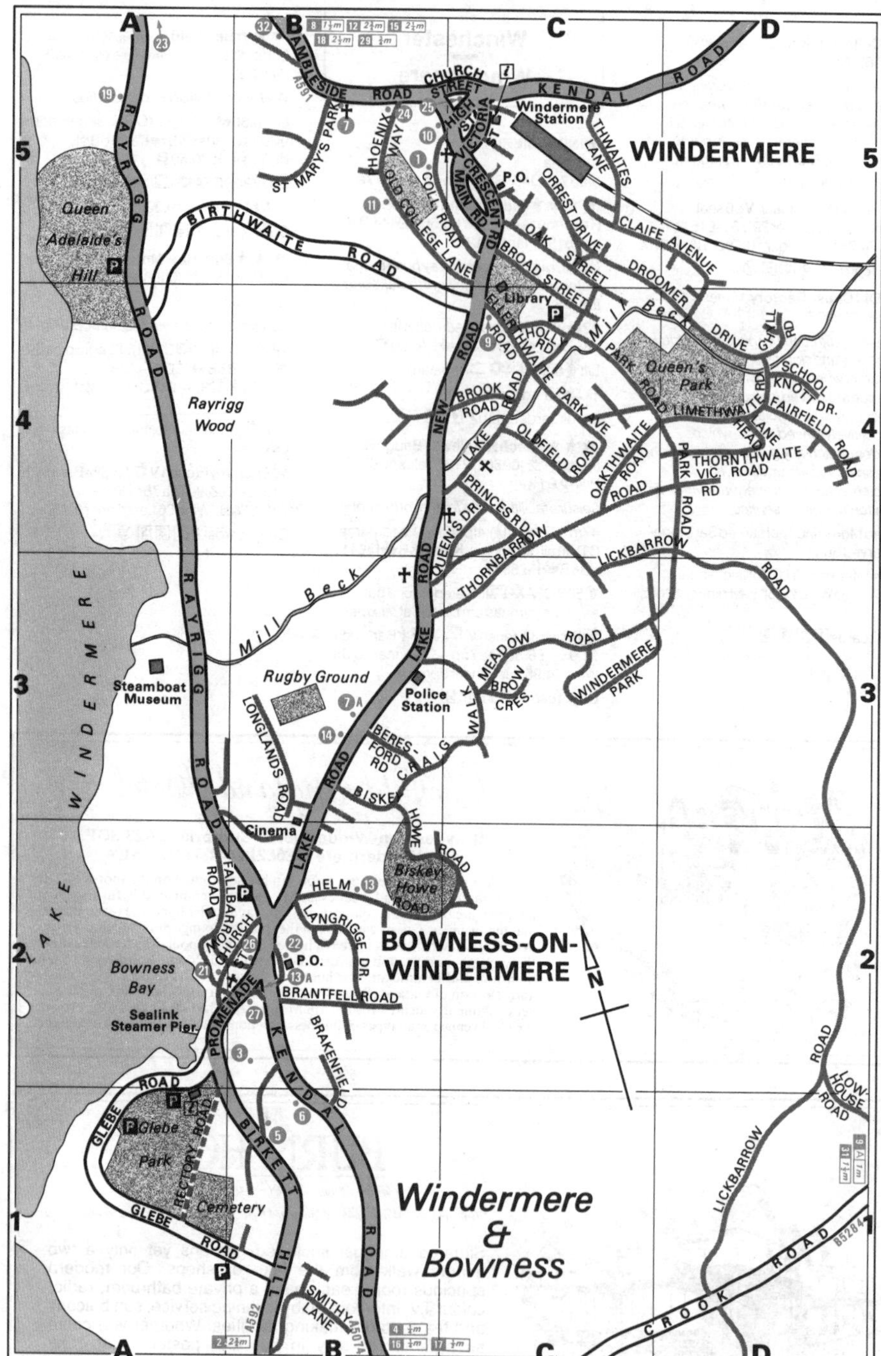
Windermere & Bowness
WINDERMERE
BOWNESS-ON-WINDERMERE
LAKE WINDERMERE
Queen Adelaide's Hill
Rayrigg Wood
Steamboat Museum
Rugby Ground
Police Station
Cinema
Biskey Howe
Bowness Bay
Sealink Steamer Pier
Glebe Park
Cemetery
Windermere Station
Library
Queen's Park
P.O.
Mill Beck
AMBLESIDE ROAD
CHURCH STREET
KENDAL ROAD
THWAITES LANE
ST MARY'S PARK
PHOENIX WAY
OLD COLLEGE LANE
COLLEGE ROAD
HIGH STREET
VICTORIA STREET
CRESCENT RD
MAIN RD
ORREST DRIVE
CLAIFE AVENUE
DROOMER DRIVE
OAK STREET
BROAD STREET
BIRTHWAITE ROAD
RAYRIGG ROAD
NEW ROAD
ELLERTHWAITE ROAD
HOLLY RD
PARK ROAD
GHYLL RD
SCHOOL KNOTT DR.
FAIRFIELD ROAD
LIMETHWAITE RD
HEAD LANE
THORNTHWAITE ROAD
BROOK ROAD
LAKE ROAD
OLDFIELD ROAD
PARK AVE
OAKTHWAITE ROAD
VIC. RD
PRINCES RD
QUEEN'S DR.
THORNBARROW ROAD
LICKBARROW ROAD
MEADOW ROAD
WINDERMERE PARK
BROW CRES.
CRAIG WALK
BERESFORD RD
LONGLANDS ROAD
BISKEY HOWE ROAD
HELM ROAD
LANGRIGGE DR.
FALLBARROW ROAD
CHURCH ST
PROMENADE
BRANTFELL ROAD
BRAKENFIELD
KENDAL ROAD
BIRKETT HILL
RECTORY ROAD
GLEBE ROAD
SMITHY LANE
LOW HOUSE ROAD
LICKBARROW ROAD
CROOK ROAD
A591
A592
A5074
B5284
N
W

Windermere

1 Applegarth ★★
2 Beech Hill ★★★
3 Belsfield ★★★
4 Bordriggs Country House ★★
5 Burn How Motel ★★★
6 Burnside ★★★
7 Cedar Manor ★
7A Craig Foot Country House ★★
8 Quarry Garth Country House ★
9 Ellerthwaite Lodge ★★
9A Gilpin Lodge Country House XX
10 Grey Walls ★★
11 Hideaway ★★
12 Holbeck Ghyll ★★
13 Hydro ★★★
13A Jacksons Bistro X
14 Knoll ★
15 Langdale Chase ★★★
16 Lindeth Fell ★★
17 Linithwaite ★★
18 Low Wood ★★★
19 Miller Howe ★★
21 Old England ★★★★
22 Porthole Eating House X
23 Priory Country House ★★★
24 Ravensworth ★
25 Roger's X
26 Royal ★★
27 St Martins ★★
29 Sun ★★
31 Wild Boar ★★★
32 Willowsmere ★

Windermere

★★★**Burnside** Kendal Rd, Bowness ☏ (09662) 2211 Telex no 65430 Plan **6** *B1*

45rm(32 13)(10fb) 3 CTV in all bedrooms ®T sB&B £29—£35 dB&B £38—£52

Lift 60P Live music & dancing Sat (winter) *xmas*

V Lunch £5.50 Tea £1.95 High Tea £3.50 Dinner £8.50—£11.50&alc Wine £4.95 Last dinner 9pm

Credit cards 1 2 3 5 V

★★★**Damson Dene Cottage Hotel & Country Club** Lythe Valley (4m S A5074) ☏ Crosthwaite (04488) 227

(For full entry see Crosthwaite)

★★★**Hydro** Helm Rd, Bowness (Mount Charlotte) ☏ (09662) 4455 Telex no 65196 Plan **13** *B2*

Modernised Victorian hotel overlooking Lake Windermere, with views of the Langdale Pikes.

97rm(90 7)(13fb) CTV in all bedrooms ®* sB&B fr£36.75 dB&B fr£55

Lift 100P CFA *xmas*

* Wine £5.75 Last dinner 8.30pm

Credit cards 1 2 3 5 V

★★★ **HL Langdale Chase** ☏ Ambleside (0966) 32201 Plan **15** *B5*

Large Victorian building in extensive grounds which descend to the lake shore.

28rm(18 6)(3fb) 1 CTV in all bedrooms ®T S% sB&B £30 sB&B £38 dB&B £58 dB&B £66

CTV 36P grass croquet *xmas*

English & French V S% Lunch £8.25 Tea £3.75 Dinner £15 Wine £4.50 Last dinner 8.45pm

Credit cards 1 2 3 5

★★★**Low Wood** (3m N A591) ☏ Ambleside (0966) 33338 Telex no 65273 Plan **18** *B5*

Standing on the northern bank of Lake Windermere, this original coaching inn has spacious garden and lawns.

82rm(64 18)(10fb) CTV in all bedrooms ®T S% sB&B £26.50—£36 dB&B £55—£66

CTV 200P CFA putting *xmas*

English & French V S% Lunch £2.95—£8.50 Tea 90p—£2 High Tea £2.15—£4.20 Dinner £10.50—£11&alc Wine £5.50 Last dinner 10pm

Credit cards 1 2 3 5 V

★★★**Priory Country House** Rayrigg Rd, Bowness ☏ (09662) 4377 Plan **23** *A5*

Closed Jan →

The grounds of this hotel include a lakeside frontage with a jetty for the hotels power-boat.

15rm(13⇌2⋒)(2fb) CTV in all bedrooms ®T ✗ *sB&B⇌⋒£30—£40 dB&B⇌⋒£60—£80 Ɓ

40P ⇌ ✿ snooker nc 12yrs *xmas*

English & French V ♀ ☕ *Bar lunch £2.20—£5 Tea £1.75—£3.50 Dinner £12.50 Wine £5.25 Last dinner 9.30pm

Credit cards 1 2 3 5

★★★ *HL* **Wild Boar** Crook (2½m S of Windermere on B5284 Crook road) (Best Western) ☎ (09662) 5225 Telex no 65273 Plan **31** *D1*

A converted 18th century house, situated 2m from Bowness in a setting of woodlands and fell slopes.

38rm(33⇌5⋒)(2fb) 2⊟ CTV in all bedrooms ®T S% sB&B⇌⋒£26.50—£36 dB&B⇌⋒£55—£66 Ɓ

60P CFA ⇌ Live music & dancing Sat (Oct—Apr) *xmas*

English & French V ♀ ☕ S% Lunch £3.50—£5.95&alc Tea 75p Dinner £14.25&alc Wine £5.15 Last dinner 8.45pm

Credit cards 1 2 3 4 5 Ⓥ

Windermere

★★**Applegarth** College Rd ☎ (09662) 3206 Plan **1** *B5*

Closed Jan—Feb

An elegant and individual mansion, built in 1890 and quietly situated within easy reach of all amenities.

15rm(1⇌14⋒)(5fb) 2⊟ CTV in all bedrooms ®T S% sB&B⇌⋒£18—£25 dB&B⇌⋒£36—£50 Ɓ

CTV 20P ✿ *xmas*

V ♀ ☕ S% Bar lunch £1—£4 Tea £1—£2 Dinner £8alc Wine £4.50 Last dinner 9pm

Credit cards 1 2 3 Ⓥ

★★**Bordriggs Country House** Longtail Hill, Bowness ☎ (09662) 3567 Plan **4** *B1*

A peaceful and relaxing hotel with attractive gardens, and having a gracious, comfortable lounge.

10⇌ Annexe: 2⇌(3fb) CTV in all bedrooms *sB&B⇌£17.50 dB&B⇌£35 Ɓ

14P ⇌ ✿ ⛆(heated) nc10yrs

International ♀ ☕ *Dinner fr£9.50&alc Wine fr£4.40 Last dinner 8.30pm

Credit cards 1 3

★★

✿✿★★MILLER HOWE, WINDERMERE

Rayrigg Rd ☎ (09662) 2536 Plan **19** *A5*

Closed 7 Dec—18 Mar

(*Rosette awarded for dinner only*)

For the few who are unaware of the background of this hotel, it should be explained that it is the internationally acclaimed brain-child of that dedicated hotel-keeper, John Tovey. He is a person who has contributed a great deal to the ideals of good hotel-keeping, but his equal, if not greater, claim to fame is for his cooking; individual, innovative and daring, his 5 course dinners are something our readers rave about. They are an unashamedly theatrical event: you assemble for aperitifs and to choose your wine from the above average wine list; at the given time you will be called to the restaurant when the lights will be dimmed at 8.30pm and dinner commences. Each table is served banquette style and there is no choice of dishes until the puddings but you are sure to enjoy a memorable occasion. You will also enjoy the hearty breakfasts, packed picnic lunches and afternoon teas. Everything is fresh and home made — a rare event these days. The hotel is set in 4 acres of grounds which, like a number of rooms in the hotel, enjoy breath-taking views over the lake and fells. There are a number of comfortable sitting rooms where you

can take your ease, equally comfortable bedrooms with delightful soft furnishings and many thoughtful extras which include hair dryers, cassette players and even binoculars in rooms with a view. All over the hotel there are fresh flowers which do much to enhance the stylish interiors. Needless to say, Mr Tovey has imbued his staff with his own helpful and hospitable attitude so that you will be well looked after by the friendly staff. Certainly this is an exceptional hotel in every way.

13rm(11⇌2⋒) 1⊟ CTV available in bedrooms sB&B⇌⋒fr£75(incl dinner) dB&B⇌⋒£104—£160(incl. dinner) Ɓ

60P ⇌ ✿ nc 12yrs

V ♀ ☕ ⚡ *Tea fr£3 Dinner fr£20 Wine £6.75 Last dinner 8.30pm

Credit cards 1 2 5

★★**Craig Foot Country House** Lake Rd, Bowness ☎ (09662) 3902 Plan **7A** *B3*

Closed Jan & Feb

The elegant and very comfortable house has magnificent lake views and a lovely restaurant serving good food.

9rm(1⇌6⋒) Annexe: 1⇌(1fb) CTV in all bedrooms ® *sB&B£17.50—£19.70 dB&B⇌⋒£35—£39.40 Ɓ

CTV 20P ✿ *xmas*

☕ ⚡ Dinner £9.95 Wine £4.75 Last dinner 8pm

★★***Ellerthwaite Lodge*** New Rd ☎ (09662) 5115 Plan **9** *C4*

Closed Dec—Feb

This charming, detached house in the centre of Windermere features an attractive new coffee shop in its basement.

10rm(7⇌2⋒) CTV in all bedrooms ®T Ɓ

20P ✿ ⌂

Last dinner 8.30pm

Credit cards 1 2 3 5

★★**Grey Walls** Elleray Rd ☎ (09662) 3741 Plan **10** *B5*

Comfortable hotel with modernised bedrooms, personally supervised.

17rm(3⇌11⋒)(2fb) 1⊟ CTV in all bedrooms ®S% *sB&B⇌⋒£18—£18.50 dB&B£29—£32 dB&B⇌⋒£32—£36 Ɓ

CTV 20P ⇌

English & French ♀ ☕ ⚡ *Lunch fr£5 Tea 50p—£2.50 Dinner fr£8.50 Wine £4.30 Last dinner 8pm

Credit cards 1 2 3 Ⓥ

★★**Hideaway** Phoenix Way ☎ (09662) 3070 Plan **11** *B5*

Comfortable, secluded family hotel.

12rm(6⇌6⋒)(2fb) 6⊟ CTV in all bedrooms ®sB&B⇌⋒£20—£25 dB&B⇌⋒£40—£50 Ɓ

16P ⇌ ✿ *xmas*

English & Continental V ♀ ☕ ⚡ Tea £2alc Dinner £10alc Wine £6 Last dinner 7.30pm

★★♣ *BL* **Holbeck Ghyll** Holbeck Ln ☎ Ambleside (0966) 32375 Plan **12** *B5*

Closed Dec—Feb RS Nov & Mar

Standing in its own attractive grounds, the hotel has spacious, comfortable lounges and a beautiful, oak-panelled hall with inglenook fireplace.

14rm(11⇌2⋒)(3fb) 1⊟ CTV in all bedrooms ®sB&Bfr£20 dB&Bfr£36 dB&B⇌⋒£37—£48 Ɓ

12P ⇌ ✿ putting

♀ ☕ ⚡ Tea 75p—£1 Dinner fr£9 Last dinner 8pm

Credit card 1

★★♣ *HB* **Lindeth Fell** Upper Storrs Park Rd, Bowness ☎ (09662) 3286 Plan **16** *B1*

Closed Nov—19 Mar

A comfortable country house, set in its own grounds in an elevated position, overlooks Lake Windermere. The resident proprietors pride themselves on producing English food of a very high quality.

15rm(8 7)(4fb) CTV in all bedrooms ® sB&B fr£25 dB&B £50—£55

20P (grass) croquet putting nc5yrs

Bar lunch £2.50—£4 Tea £1.50—£3 Dinner fr£12.50 Wine £3.10 Last dinner 8.15pm

Credit cards 1 2 3 5

★★ *HBL* Linthwaite Bowness (09662) 3688 Plan **17** *B1*

Closed Nov—Etr

A charming house in extensive, attractive gardens, it is a warm and friendly hotel that is beautifully cared for. Mr Liddel is always around to look after guests while Mrs Liddel prepares very good five course dinners using fresh produce.

11 (1fb) CTV in all bedrooms **T** S% sB&B £34 (incl dinner) dB&B £31—£35.50 (incl dinner)

20P putting nc8yrs

English & French S% Tea £1.40 Dinner £11 Wine £2 Last dinner 8pm

See advertisement on page 782

Windermere

★★ *H* Royal Bowness (Best Western) (09662) 3045 Telex no 65273 Plan **26** *B2*

A 17th century hotel, once known as the White Lion, but renamed the Royal after a visit by Queen Adelaide in 1840. There is a secluded garden.

29rm(25 4)(5fb) 1 CTV in all bedrooms ® **T** S% sB&B £23.65—£30.50 dB&B £47.30—£61

16P 5 (£1 per day) *xmas*

English & French **V** S% Lunch £6.50alc Tea 75palc High tea £3.50alc Dinner £10.50&alc Wine £5 Last dinner 10pm

Credit cards 1 2 3 4 5 Ⓥ

★★ *St Martin's* Lake Rd, Bowness (09662) 3731 Plan **27** *B2*

Closed Jan RS Dec

A small, friendly hotel with a very good restaurant.

17rm(3 5)(1fb)

CTV 10P

English, French & Italian Last dinner 9pm

Credit cards 1 2 3 5

★★ Sun Troutbeck Bridge (3m N) (09662) 3274 Plan **29** *B5*

A roadside inn by the A591, on the outskirts of Windermere.

10rm(2 2)(2fb) CTV in all bedrooms S% sB&B£15—£16 sB&B £16—£16.50 dB&B£26—£27 dB&B £30—£32

CTV 10P

V S% Lunch £3.90alc High tea £4.95alc Dinner £6.50alc Wine £6 Last dinner 8.30pm

Credit cards 1 2 3 4 5

★ Cedar Manor Ambleside Rd (09662) 3192 Plan **7** *B5*

Closed Jan

Standing in an attractive garden, the comfortably furnished old vicarage offers a particularly good dinner.

6rm(3 2)(2fb) 1 CTV in all bedrooms ® sB&B fr£20 dB&B fr£38 dB&B fr£40

12P *xmas*

English & French **V** Lunch fr£4.50 Tea fr£1.20 Dinner fr£9.50 Wine £4.20 Last dinner 8.30pm

Credit cards 1 3 Ⓥ

See advertisement on page 782

W

Windermere

★**Knoll** Bowness ☎ (09662) 3756 Plan **14** *B3*

Closed Nov—Feb

The friendly, informal hotel, set in its own secluded grounds, has fine views of Lake Windermere.

12rm(4🛁3🚿)(4fb) CTV in all bedrooms Ⓡ ✈ S% sB&B£15—£17 dB&B£30—£34 dB&B🛁🚿£32—£36

CTV 20P 🚗 ✿ nc3yrs

⚡S% Dinner fr£8 Wine £4.25 Last dinner 7pm

Ⓥ

★🌲 ***Quarry Garth Country House*** Troutbeck ☎ (09662) 3761 Plan **6** *B3*

Small family run hotel in spacious grounds, serving good home cooking and having attractive bedrooms.

7🛁(2fb) CTV in all bedrooms Ⓡ **B**

CTV 30P 3🏠 🚗 ✿ ♩ *xmas*

🍷English & French **V** ♕ ☕ Last dinner 9.15pm

★**Ravensworth** Ambleside Rd ☎ (09662) 3747 Plan **24** *B5*

Small, comfortably furnished hotel near village centre. Warm, friendly atmosphere.

13rm(10🛁3🚿)(2fb) CTV in all bedrooms Ⓡ sB&B🛁🚿£15.50—£20 dB&B🛁🚿£31—£40 **B**

14P 🚗 *xmas*

🍷English & Austrian ⚡ Dinner £8—£9 Wine £6 Last dinner 7pm

★*H* **Willowsmere** Ambleside Rd ☎ (09662) 3575 Plan **32** *B5*

Closed Nov—Etr

A small, friendly hotel, managed by the proprietor and his family.

13rm(11🛁2🚿) Annexe: 1🚿(7fb) Ⓡ ✱sB&B🛁🚿£14.50 dB&B🛁🚿£29

CTV 20P 🚗 ✿

🍷English & Austrian ⚡ ✱ Wine £3.22 Last dinner 7pm

Credit cards 1 2 3 5

✕✕**Gilpin Lodge Country House** Crook Rd, (2m S of Windermere on B5284) ☎ (09662) 2295 Plan **9A** *D1*

Two miles from Bowness, on the B5284, stands a charming country house restaurant with rooms. All the food on the interesting table d'hôte menu is of a very high standard, freshly prepared from good raw ingredients. Booking is essential.

Closed 3/4 wks Jan

🍷French 35 seats ✱ Lunch £9.75&alc Dinner £14.75&alc Wine £6 Last dinner 9pm 15P 6 bedrooms available nc12yrs

Credit cards 1 2 3 5

✕**Jackson's Bistro** West End, Bowness ☎ (09662) 6264 Plan **13A** *B2*

Kindly staff and a warm style of décor help to create a pleasant atmosphere in this attractive, lively little bistro in the centre of Bowness, where the short menu offers an interesting choice of reasonably priced dishes.

Closed Mon & last 2 wks Jan

🍷European 48 seats Dinner £9alc Wine £4.10 Last dinner 10pm ₽

Credit cards 1 2 3

❀✕**Porthole Eating House** 3 Ash St, Bowness ☎ (09662) 2793 Plan **22** *B2*

(Rosette awarded for dinner only). This delightful restaurant is one of the oldest eating-houses in Lakeland. It offers a cosy, welcoming atmosphere, with roaring log fires and a very pleasant staff, whilst the menu includes an interesting mixture of English and Italian dishes, all very well prepared and accompanied by an excellent wine list.

Closed Tue, Dec, Jan & part Feb Lunch not served

🍷French & Italian **V** 36 seats Last dinner 11pm ₽

Credit cards 1 2 3 5

✕**Rogers** 4 High St ☎ (09662) 4954 Plan **25** *C5*

The warm atmosphere, attractive decor and quality napery of this delightful little restaurant on the edge of town help to make it the ideal setting in which to enjoy a very good meal. The menu offers a range of French and English dishes, all based on fresh produce, and features speciality set meals in winter. Reservations are necessary.

Closed Sun (except Bank Hol's) Lunch not served Mon & Sat

English & French 24 seats Lunch £10alc Dinner £15alc Wine £5.50 Last dinner 9.30pm P

Credit cards 1 2 3 5

WINDSOR

Berkshire
Map **4** SU97
See also **Datchet**

★★★★ *BL* **Oakley Court** Windsor Rd, Water Oakley (2m W A308) (Prestige) ☎ Maidenhead (0628) 74141 Telex no 849958

This Victorian gothic castellated building is a very well-appointed country hotel. Its peaceful grounds run down to the River Thames, and the hotel enjoys a friendly, informal atmosphere, with spacious public rooms and comfortable well-equipped bedrooms.

63🛁 Annexe: 27🛁 (4fb) 6 CTV in all bedrooms **T** S% sB&B🛁 £68—£125 dB&B🛁 £82—£145 **B**

☾ 120P squash snooker croquet Live music 4 nights wkly *xmas*

French **V** S% Lunch £14&alc Tea £3.50—£6.50 Dinner £19&alc Wine £9.50 Last dinner 10pm

Credit cards 1 2 3 4 5

★★★ **Castle** High St (Trusthouse Forte) ☎ (0753) 851011 Telex no 849220

Modernised Georgian style hotel with large bedrooms, comfortable bar and restaurant.

85🛁 CTV in all bedrooms ® sB&B🛁 £62.50 dB&B🛁 £83 **B**

Lift ☾ 90P CFA *xmas*

Last dinner 9.45pm

Credit cards 1 2 3 4 5

★★ **Aurora Garden** Bolton Av ☎ (0753) 868686 Telex no 849462

A large Victorian house in a residential area has been converted and modernised to provide a cosy, friendly hotel with an adjoining conference wing. Bedrooms vary in size but have good facilities, and there is a comfortable lounge area, though dining room and bar are small.

14rm (3🛁 11🚿) (1fb) CTV in all bedrooms **T** ✱sB&B🛁🚿 £42 dB&B🛁🚿 £52

25P *xmas*

✱Lunch £8.50&alc Tea £3.50 Dinner £9.50&alc Wine £5.25 Last dinner 9pm

Credit cards 1 2 3 4 5

★★ **Royal Adelaide** 46 Kings Rd ☎ (0753) 863916

This sympathetically modernised Victorian building, offering sound accommodation and pleasing service, has a bar and beer garden which are popular with local clientele.

39rm (12🛁 23🚿) (1fb) CTV in all bedrooms ® **T** S% sB&Bfr £25.75 sB&B🛁🚿 £35.50 dB&Bfr £33.75 dB&B🛁🚿 £46.50 **B**

20P *xmas*

French S% Lunch £6.50 Tea 80p High tea £3 Dinner £9.25&alc Last dinner 9pm

Credit cards 1 2 3 5

See advertisement on page 784

★★ **Ye Harte & Garter** High St (Berni) ☎ (0753) 863426

Closed Xmas

Very conveniently situated hotel, opposite Windsor Castle →

50rm(34➡9⋒)(6fb) CTV in all bedrooms ®✈ sB£29—£34 dB➡£49 (room only)

Lift ☾ ℙ

Mainly grills ✿ ⅟ ✱ Lunch £7.50alc Dinner £7.50alc Wine £4.50 Last dinner 10pm

Credit cards 1 2 3 4 5

✕ **La Taverna** 2 River St ☎ (0753) 863020

Closed Sun, 25&26 Dec

English & Italian **V** 56 seats ✱ Lunch £15alc Last dinner 11pm ℙ

Credit cards 1 2 3 5

WINSFORD

Somerset
Map **3** SS93

★★**Royal Oak Inn** ☎ (064385) 232

Thatched inn of immense character, with comfortable bedrooms and versatile restaurant.

6➡ CTV in all bedrooms **T** sB&B➡fr£42.75 dB&B➡fr£64

CTV 20P 2 ♪ *xmas*

V ✿ Lunch fr£5.95 Tea fr£1.20 Dinner fr£12.50 Wine £5.75 Last dinner 9.30pm

Credit cards 1 2 3 5

WINSLOW

Buckinghamshire
Map **4** SP72

★★**Bell** Market Sq ☎ (029671) 2741

The historic coaching inn, now restored to provide plain, comfortable accommodation, retains several lovely inglenook fireplaces. A warm, welcoming atmosphere is enhanced by courteous, friendly service.

15rm(6➡6⋒)(2fb) CTV in all bedrooms ® **T** ✱ sB&B➡⋒£30—£35 dB&B➡⋒£35—£42 B

CTV 65P

✿ ⅟ ✱ Lunch £7.50 Dinner £7.50&alc Wine £5.25 Last dinner 9.15pm

Credit cards 1 3 Ⓥ

Windsor — Wishaw

WINTERBOURNE

Avon
Map **3** ST68

★★★ *B* **Grange** Northwoods (2m NW of village B4427) ☎ (0454) 777333 Telex no 449205

Tranquil country house style hotel with very comfortable new bedrooms and fine restaurant serving high quality food.

32➡(4fb) CTV in all bedrooms ® **T** sB➡⋒£43—£46 dB➡⋒£55—£60 (room only) B

☾ 60P ✿ U

French **V** ✿ Lunch £11—£13 Tea £1—£1.50 Dinner £14—£16&alc Wine £5.95 Last dinner 11pm

Credit cards 1 2 3 5 Ⓥ

See advertisement under Bristol

WINTERBOURNE ABBAS

Dorset
Map **3** SY69

★★ *HL* **Whitefriars** Coryhold Ln ☎ Martinstown (030588) 206

An attractive small hotel with well-appointed bedrooms and serving interesting, very well cooked food.

7rm(6➡1⋒) ⅟ CTV in all bedrooms ® ✱ sB&B➡⋒£25 dB&B➡⋒£35—£40 B

16P ✿ nc12yrs *xmas*

✿ Lunch £6&alc Tea 75p Dinner £8&alc Wine £6 Last dinner 9pm

Credit cards 1 3

WISBECH

Cambridgeshire
Map **5** TF40

★★**Queens** South Brink ☎ (0945) 583933

Situated close to the centre of the market town, this family-managed hotel offers a welcome to tourists and commercial guests alike.

16➡⋒ Annexe: 5rm (2fb) CTV in all bedrooms ® **T** S% sB&B➡⋒fr£25 dB&B➡⋒fr£35 B

30P

S% Lunch fr£7.25&alc Dinner fr£7.25&alc Last dinner 10pm

Credit cards 1 2 3 4 5

★★**Rose & Crown** Market Pl (Best Western) ☎ (0945) 583187 Telex no 32817

Old coaching inn set in the market square.

23rm(19➡)(2fb) 2 CTV in all bedrooms ® **T** sB&B£21.75—£23.95 sB&B➡⋒£30.50—£33.50 dB&B£32.50—£35.50 dB&B➡⋒£38.50—£42 B

CTV 10P *xmas*

✿ Lunch £7—£10alc Dinner £8—£14alc Wine £5 Last dinner 9.15pm

Credit cards 1 2 3 5

★★**White Lion** South Brink ☎ (0945) 584813

Once a coaching inn, this modernised hotel is centrally situated and overlooks the River Nene.

18rm(8➡4⋒)(1fb) CTV in all bedrooms ® **T** S% ✱ sB&Bfr£24 sB&B➡⋒fr£30 dB&Bfr£36 dB&B➡⋒fr£42.50 B

25P

English, French, Chinese & Indian **V** ✿ ✱ Lunch fr£8&alc Tea fr75p Dinner fr£8&alc Wine £5.75 Last dinner 9.30pm

Credit cards 1 2 3 5 Ⓥ

WISHAW

Warwickshire
Map **7** SP19

★★★★**Belfry** Lichfield Rd (A446) (DeVere) ☎ Curdworth (0675) 70301 Telex no 338848

A busy hotel with fine leisure facilities, linked with national golf centre.

168rm(162➡6⋒)(5fb) 4 CTV in all bedrooms ® **T** S% ✱ sB&B➡⋒£54.50—£64.50 dB&B➡⋒£64—£85 B

Lift ☾ 500P CFA (heated) 18 (hard) squash snooker sauna bath solarium gymnasium driving range putting Disco Mon—Sat

W

English & French V S% Lunch £10.50—£18.50 Tea 50p High Tea £4—£6 Dinner fr£10.50&alc Wine £7 Last dinner 10.30pm

Credit cards 1 2 3 5 V

★★★ **Moxhull Hall** Holly Ln (ExecHotel) 021-329 2056

The fine, red-brick house, standing in eight acres of garden and woodland just off the A446, is popular with local families for its leisurely atmosphere and French-style bistro.

11rm(6 5)(1fb) CTV in all bedrooms ® T sB&B £32.50 dB&B £39.50 B

60P

English & French V Lunch £7.95&alc Dinner £7.95&alc Wine £4.95 Last dinner 10pm

Credit cards 1 2 3 5 V

See advertisement under Sutton Coldfield

WITCHINGHAM, GREAT (Lenwade)
Norfolk
Map **9** TG01

★★ L **Lenwade House** Norwich (0603) 872288

13rm(9 4)(2fb) CTV in all bedrooms ® T sB fr£29.50 dB fr£44.50 (room only) B

CTV 40P (heated) (grass) squash solarium croquet putting nc5yrs *xmas*

English & French Lunch fr£5.95&alc Dinner fr£8.95&alc Wine £4.95 Last dinner 9pm

Credit cards 1 2 3 5 V

WITHAM
Essex
Map **5** TL81

★★ **Rivenhall Motor Inn** Rivenhall End (0376) 516969 Telex no 99414

Closed 26—30 Dec RS Sat & Sun

Attractive bedrooms and restaurant.

Annexe: 48 (1fb) CTV in all bedrooms ® T S% sB&B fr£27 dB&B fr£38 Continental breakfast

110P squash pool table

French V S% Lunch £7.95&alc Tea 65p Dinner £7.95&alc Wine £5 Last dinner 9.30pm

Credit cards 1 2 3 5 V

WITHERSLACK
Cumbria
Map **7** SD48

★ **OLD VICARAGE COUNTRY HOUSE, WITHERSLACK**

(ExecHotel) (044852) 381

Closed Xmas wk

This a charmingly converted Georgian vicarage set in three acres of attractive, well kept gardens and woodland in the unspoilt Winster Valley — an ideal spot for a peaceful break or walking holiday. It is run by two couples, Roger and Jill Burrington-Brown and Stanley and Irene Reeve, who combine to create a friendly and charming hotel. It is on a relatively small scale but none the worst for that: sunny sitting rooms are attractively decorated as are the comfortable bedrooms, which are spotlessly clean and provided with flowers. Take an aperitif in the cosy bar before the five course fixed price dinner which you are sure to enjoy. The cooking of first class ingredients is talented but you should be warned that there is no choice until the pudding stage. Luncheons are served by arrangement and the hearty breakfast deserves special commendation too: porridge with whisky, local Cumberland sausage and black pudding are among the items. It has been warmly recommended by our members and inspectors.

7rm(3 4) CTV in all bedrooms ® T sB&B £35—£39.50 dB&B £40—£59 B

15P nc10yrs

English & Continental Dinner £15.50 Wine £4.65 Last dinner 8pm

Credit cards 1 2 3 5

WITHYPOOL
Somerset
Map **3** SS83

★★ **Royal Oak Inn** Exford (064383) 236

Comfortable, well appointed inn whose restaurant specialises in local dishes.

8rm(2 2)(1fb) 1 CTV in 6 bedrooms ® sB&B £17—£19 sB&B £26—£28 dB&B £30—£34 dB&B £40—£44 B

20P nc10yrs

English & French V Bar lunch £2.50—£7 Dinner £13.50&alc Wine £5.80 Last dinner 9.30pm

Credit cards 1 2 3 5

★★🏨 **Westerclose Country House** ☎ Exford (064383) 302

Closed Dec—Feb

Small, privately owned and run hotel in extensive grounds which include stables.

8rm(7⇌)(1fb) 1🛏 CTV in 3 bedrooms sB&B£15 sB&B⇌£15 dB&B⇌£30—£36

14P ✿ U

English & French Bar lunch fr£5 Tea fr£1.50 High Tea fr£5 Dinner fr£10.50&alc Wine £4.50 Last dinner 9pm

Credit cards 1 2 3

WIVELISCOMBE
Somerset
Map **3** ST02

★ **LANGLEY HOUSE, WIVELISCOMBE**

Langley Marsh (1m N on unclass rd)
☎ (0984) 23318

Peter and Ann Wilson bought this hotel from the McCullocks and have certainly maintained the Red Star quality of this old house, which dates mainly from Georgian times. Set just outside the town, amid the folds of the Brendon Hills, it has 3 acres of delightful gardens. The public areas and bedrooms are comfortably furnished and prettily decorated. The two sitting rooms have pictures, ornaments, books, magazines and are fresh with flowers, sparkling silver and crystal. Mrs Wilson with her few helpers, will look after you with sociable warmth while Mr Wilson cooks. He provides a four course dinner without choice until the pudding, of what might best be termed country house cooking; it is basically refreshingly simple, but with interesting touches and makes use of fine ingredients. Bedrooms are well equipped with television, radio, books and plants, as well as superior toiletries; all much more than you would expect at this star classification. Peter Wilson is an experienced hotel-keeper; now doing his own thing, and it is no wonder that he is setting such

high standards so quickly. Our members who have known it under the past ownership think the standards of hospitality have improved, but more attention needs to be paid to the food in order to retrieve the rosette.

9rm(5⇌2🚿)(1fb) 1🛏 CTV in all bedrooms ✱sB&B£17.50—£22.50 sB&B⇌🚿£26.50—£29.25 dB&B⇌🚿£44—£53 B

16P 2 ✿ croquet nc7yrs *xmas*

✱Tea 75p—£1.50 Dinner £12.75—£14.75 Wine £6.75 Last dinner 9pm

Credit cards 1 2

WOBURN
Bedfordshire
Map **4** SP93

✿ XXX **Paris House** Woburn Park ☎ (052525) 692

Smart little restaurant in half timbered building (dating from 1878), set in the grounds of Woburn Park.

Closed Mon & Feb Dinner not served Sun

French **V** 40 seats ✱Lunch fr£12.50 Dinner fr£17 Wine £6.20 Last dinner 10pm 20p nc

Credit cards 1 2 3 5

X **Crispins** 22/23 Market Pl ☎ (052525) 516

This small, quaint, beamed restaurant provides generous portions of wholesome food, the menu featuring seasonal specialities and an extensive vegetarian section.

V 50 seats ✱Lunch £10.50—£11.50 Dinner £11.50—£12.50 Wine £5.50 Last dinner 9.30pm nc7yrs

Credit cards 1 2 3 5

WOKINGHAM
Berkshire
Map **4** SU86

★★ **Cantley House** Milton Rd ☎ (0734) 789912 Telex no 848210

Set 600 yards back from the road in its own grounds, a converted, late-Victorian, private house offers sound food and friendly, informal service.

19⇌(1fb) CTV in all bedrooms **T** ✱sB&B⇌£39 dB&B⇌£45

☾ ## 100P

✱Lunch £9.50&alc Dinner £9.50&alc Wine £4.50 Last dinner 9.30pm

Credit cards 1 2 3 4 5

WOLF'S CASTLE
Dyfed
Map **2** SM92

XX **Wolfscastle Country Hotel** ☎ Treffgarne (043787) 225

The country house restaurant provides friendly service and an interesting menu with good, fresh, home cooking standards. For the more energetic, tennis and squash courts are available on request.

Closed 5 days Xmas Lunch by reservation only

English & French **V** 60 seats ✱Dinner £10.50alc Wine £4.90 Last dinner 9pm 50P Live music wkly

Credit cards 1 2 3

WOLVERHAMPTON
West Midlands
Map **7** SO99

★★★ **Connaught** Tettenhall Rd ☎ (0902) 24433 Telex no 338490

63rm(55⇌8🚿)(2fb) CTV in all bedrooms **T** ✱sB&B⇌🚿£23.50 dB&B⇌🚿£32.50

Lift ☾ CTV 80P sauna bath solarium *xmas*

Continental ✱Lunch £5.50&alc Tea 50p High Tea £1.50 Dinner £7.50&alc Wine £4 Last dinner 10pm

Credit cards 1 2 3 4 5

★★★ **Goldthorn** Penn Rd ☎ (0902) 29216 Telex no 339516

Closed Xmas Day & Boxing Day

A large, privately-owned hotel offers a warm welcome and prompt, courteous service.

70rm(62⇌3🚿) Annexe: 12rm(8⇌4🚿)(2fb) 2🛏 CTV in all bedrooms ® **T** sB&B⇌🚿£38 dB&B£38 dB&B⇌🚿£38.50—£52.50 B

☾ 150P ♿

English & French **V** ✱Lunch £7.60—£9.15&alc Tea 75p Dinner £7.95—£9.50&alc Wine £4.75 Last dinner 9.30pm

Credit cards 1 2 3 5

★★★ **Mount** Mount Rd, Tettenhall Wood (2½m W off A454) (Embassy) ☎ (0902) 752055

Set in 4½ acres of landscaped gardens and located in a rural area, the hotel is nevertheless near enough to the centre of Wolverhampton to be popular with business people.

58⇌🚿(11fb) CTV in all bedrooms ® **T** S% sB⇌🚿£38.50—£41 dB⇌🚿£55—£60 B

☾ 250P CFA ✿ Live music & dancing Sat (Sep—May) *xmas*

English & French **V** S% Lunch £5.15—£6.40&alc Tea 65p Dinner £8.65&alc Wine £4.70 Last dinner 9.30pm

Credit cards 1 2 3 4 5 Ⓥ

★★★ **Park Hall** Park Dr, Goldthorn Park (2m S off A459) (Embassy) ☎ (0902) 331121

RS Xmas Day & Boxing Day

Once the home of the Earl of Dudley, this is now a modernised hotel.

57rm(17➡40⋒)(1fb) CTV in all bedrooms ®T S% *sB£21—£29 sB➡£23—£41 dB£38—£41 dB➡£38—£54 (room only) Ꞓ

☾400P CFA ✿ Live music & dancing Sat

English & French V S% *Lunch fr£8.25&alc Tea fr60p Dinner fr£8.25&alc Wine £5.10 Last dinner 9.45pm

Credit cards 1 2 3 4 5 Ⓥ

★★**Castlecroft** Castlecroft Rd ☎ (0902) 761264

The hotel, popular with a business clientele, stands in a residential area of the town, surrounded by well-kept gardens and local sports grounds.

16rm(7➡4⋒)(2fb) CTV in all bedrooms ® T *sB&B£25 sB&B➡⋒£28 dB&B£30 dB&B➡⋒£34 Ꞓ

60P ✿ solarium putting

International *Bar lunch 95p—£3.50 Dinner £7.95 Wine £4.90 Last dinner 10.30pm

Credit cards 1 3

★★**York** 138—140 Tettenhall Rd ☎ (0902) 758211

RS Xmas

Very busy, small but popular, personally run hotel.

16rm(11➡5⋒)(3fb) CTV in all bedrooms ®T S% sB&B➡⋒£21.50—£30 dB&B➡⋒£32—£42 Ꞓ

CTV 20P

S% Lunch £2.95—£5 Dinner £7.50—£8.90&alc Wine £4.50 Last dinner 9.45pm

Credit cards 1 2 3 5

★**Wulfrun** 37 Piper's Row ☎ (0902) 24017

Closed Xmas Day & Boxing Day

Small individually run hotel on a busy town centre junction.

14rm(2fb) sB&B£10 dB&B£18

CTV

Lunch £6.50alc Tea £1.50alc High tea £6.50alc Dinner £6.50alc Last dinner 6.15pm

Credit cards 1 2 3 5 Ⓥ

Wolverhampton — Woodford Bridge

WOOBURN COMMON
Buckinghamshire
Map **4** SU98

★★**Chequers Inn** Kiln Ln (1m W unclass towards Bourne End) ☎ Bourne End (06285) 29575 Telex no 849832

The bedrooms of this small, quality hotel are prettily decorated and have pine furnishings. A high standard of cuisine is maintained by a talented chef.

17rm(16➡1⋒)(1fb) 1 CTV in all bedrooms ®T sB&B➡⋒£38—£46 dB&B➡⋒£42—£52 Ꞓ

50P

V Lunch £3—£9&alc Tea fr£1.50 Dinner £5—£9&alc Wine £4.75 Last dinner 10pm

Credit cards 1 3 5

See advertisement under Beaconsfield

WOODBRIDGE
Suffolk
Map **5** TM24

★★★**Melton Grange** ☎ (03943) 4147

Spacious, fully-modernised country mansion set in 11 acres of grounds on the outskirts of Woodbridge.

37rm(33➡)(3fb) CTV in all bedrooms ®T S% sB&B£32.50—£35 sB&B➡£32.50—£35 dB&B£45—£48 dB&B➡£45—£48

CTV 100P ✿ Live music and dancing Sat *xmas*

English & French V Lunch £7&alc Dinner £9&alc Wine £5 Last dinner 9pm

Credit cards 1 2 3 5

★★★ *L* **Seckford Hall** ☎ (0394) 385678 Telex no 987446

Closed Xmas Day

Picturesque Elizabethan manor house, set amid gardens, parkland and lake.

24➡⋒ 4 CTV in all bedrooms ®T S% *sB&B£36 sB&B➡⋒£39—£42 dB&B➡⋒£52—£56 Ꞓ

100P 4 (£2 per night) ✿

English & French V S% *Lunch £6.95—£7.50&alc Dinner £13alc Wine £5.25 Last dinner 9.30pm

Credit cards 1 2 3 5

★★**Crown** Thorofare (Trusthouse Forte) ☎ (03943) 4242

Centrally situated, fully modernised old coaching inn, with parts dating from 1532.

8➡ Annexe: 10➡ CTV in all bedrooms ® sB&B➡£45.50 dB&B➡£63.50 Ꞓ

30P *xmas*

Last dinner 9pm

Credit cards 1 2 3 4 5

✕✕ ***Town House*** 13 Market Hill ☎ (03943) 2957

Dinner not served Sun

English & French V 60 seats Last dinner 10pm

Credit cards 1 2 3

WOODFORD
Greater Manchester
Map **7** SJ88

✕ **3 Gates Bistro** 547 Chester Rd ☎ 061-440 8715

A smart little bistro stands in rural surroundings, next to a country church. The friendly, informal atmosphere complements the enterprising cuisine with all dishes being individually cooked.

Closed Mon Lunch not served Sat Dinner not served Sun

English & French 46 seats *Lunch £9.50alc Dinner £10alc Wine £4.95 Last dinner 10pm 15P

Credit cards 1 2 3

WOODFORD BRIDGE
Devon
Map **2** SS31

★★★ *BL* **Woodford Bridge** ☎ Milton Damerel (040926) 481

This impressive thatched building, originally a 15th century inn, has been converted to a comfortable, high quality hotel. The bedrooms are beautifully furnished, and there is a pleasing dining room. Nine luxury cottages are situated →

W

in the grounds, and there is also a good leisure complex.

12rm(9⇌3⋒) Annexe: 9⇌(1fb) CTV in 9 bedrooms ® in 9 bedrooms **T** sB&B fr£24.40 sB&B⇌⋒ fr£32.50 dB&B fr£46.50 dB&B⇌⋒ fr£62 **B**

CTV 200P ✽ (heated) (hard) squash sauna bath solarium *xmas*

English & French Lunch fr£6 Tea fr£1 Dinner fr£13 Wine £5 Last dinner 9.30pm

Ⓥ

See advertisement under Bideford

Woodford Bridge — Woodstock

WOODFORD BRIDGE
Greater London
London plan 5 *F5* (page 447)

★★★ ***Prince Regent*** ☎ 01-504 7635

Tastefully furnished hotel with modern, well-equipped bedrooms and an enterprising restaurant.

10⇌⋒ CTV in all bedrooms ®

☾100P

English, French & Italian **V** Last dinner 10.30pm

Credit cards 1 2 3 4 5

WOODFORD GREEN
Greater London
London plan **5** *F5* (page 447)

★★★ **Woodford Moat House** Oak Hill (Queens Moat) ☎ 01-505 4511 Telex no 264428

Modern hotel with good restaurant and pleasant service.

99rm(69⇌30⋒) CTV in all bedrooms ® S% sB&B⇌⋒ £36—£46 dB&B⇌⋒ £48—£58 **B**

Lift ☾150P CFA

English & French **V** S% Lunch £10—£12&alc Tea fr£1 Dinner £10—£12&alc Wine £4.95 Last dinner 10.15pm

Credit cards 1 2 3 4 5

WOODHALL SPA
Lincolnshire
Map **8** TF16

★★★ **Golf** The Broadway ☎ (0526) 53535

Standing in spacious grounds close to the town centre, this aptly-named hotel is popular with golfers; bedrooms are modern and well equipped.

51rm(41⇌10⋒)(2fb) in 8 bedrooms CTV in all bedrooms ® sB&B⇌⋒ fr£35 dB&B⇌⋒ fr£45 **B**

☾CTV 100P ✽ pool table *xmas*

V Bar lunch £1.50—£4.95 Tea 70p Dinner £8.50—£15&alc Wine £4.50 Last dinner 9.15pm

Credit cards 1 2 3 5 Ⓥ

★★★ **Petwood** Stixwould Rd ☎ (0526) 52411

A large, attractive, Edwardian country house, set in four acres of wooded gardens and grounds, provides well-equipped accommodation and caters for tourists, businessmen and the conference/function trade.

28rm(21⇌)(8fb) 2 CTV in all bedrooms ® **T** ✱ sB&B £27 sB&B⇌ £33 dB&B £34 dB&B⇌ £44 **B**

Lift ☾100P ✽ billiards *xmas*

✱ Lunch £7.50&alc Dinner £9.50&alc Wine fr£5 Last dinner 9.30pm

Credit cards 1 2 3 5

WOODHOUSE EAVES
Leicestershire
Map **8** SK51

✕✕ **Cottage in the Wood** Maplewell Rd ☎ (0509) 890318

The village centre restaurant, convenient to the main A6 road, comprises a row of cottages with a modern extension at the rear.

Closed Mon & Tue Lunch not served Wed-Sat Dinner not served Sun

English & Continental **V** 100 seats Sun Lunch £6.95 Dinner £9.95—£13.95 Wine £5.50 Last dinner 9.30pm 20P

Credit cards 1 2 3 Ⓥ

WOODLANDS
Hampshire
Map **4** SU31

★★ **Busketts Lawn** 174 Woodlands Rd ☎ Ashurst (042129) 2272

Country hotel in woodland setting with all modern facilities.

15rm(8⇌7⋒)(2fb) CTV in all bedrooms ® **T** S% sB&B⇌⋒ £24—£48 dB&B⇌⋒ £48—£96 **B**

CTV 50P ✽ (heated) putting croquet Disco wkly Live music & dancing wkly *xmas*

English & Continental **V** S% Lunch £7 Tea £1.70—£1.90 High Tea £3.50 Dinner £9 Wine £6.10 Last dinner 8pm

Credit cards 1 2 3 5

See advertisement under Southampton

★★ **Woodlands Lodge** Bartley Rd ☎ Ashurst (042129) 2257

One of the original Forest Lodges with gardens and paddocks, quietly situated in the New Forest.

11rm(10⇌1⋒)(2fb) CTV in all bedrooms ® sB&B⇌⋒ £20—£25 dB&B⇌⋒ £40—£50 **B**

40P ✽ nc 3yrs

Bar lunch £1.50—£6 Tea £2—£3.50 Dinner £9—£11 Wine £4.65 Last dinner 8pm

Credit cards 1 3

WOODSTOCK
Oxfordshire
Map **4** SP41

★★★ *B* **Bear** Park St ☎ (0993) 811511 Telex no 837921

RS Xmas Day evening

This ancient coaching inn retains parts of the original 16th-century structure and a staircase of that date. Bedrooms are particularly comfortable and well-equipped, the lounge bar, with traditional features and log fire, is characteristic of an

W

old English inn and the comfortably-appointed, beamed restaurant offers à la carte and table d'hôte menus.

40rm(33⇌1⋒) 6⇌ CTV in all bedrooms ® T S% *sB⇌⋒£62.15—£75.30 dB⇌⋒£100.70—£132.75 (room only) B

☾40P CFA *xmas*

English & French V S% *Lunch £11.20—£14&alc High Tea £6alc Dinner £15.20&alc Wine £7.60 Last dinner 10.30pm

Credit cards 1 2 3 5

★★ **Feathers**

(see opposite)

★★ ***King's Arms*** (Best Western)

☎(0993) 811412 Telex no 437287

Closed 24—26 Dec

The small hotel incorporates the Wheelers Fish Restaurant, a new cocktail bar and modernised bedrooms.

10rm(5⇌5⋒)(1fb) 1⇌ CTV in all bedrooms ®T B

Live music & dancing Fri

French V Last dinner 10pm

Credit cards 1 2 3 5

★★

★★ FEATHERS, WOODSTOCK

Market St ☎(0993) 812291 Telex no 83138

Once the Dorchester Arms, its name was changed after extensive refurbishment by Patrick Campbell-Gray, the owner. It dates from the 17th century and in the centre of this showpiece village next to Blenheim Palace. The red brick-fronted building with its cobbled courtyard and small garden is picturesque. On entering, the impression one gains is of comfort and of standards much higher than its star classification would suggest, despite a certain attractive, rambling feeling. There is a bar, painted totally in green and two sitting rooms, one very atmospheric with its dark panelling, book shelves and open fire. Antiques, flowers, pictures and prints all add to the effect. The bedrooms vary in size — some are quite small but all are individually decorated with many extras for your comfort. The restaurant is elegantly appointed and conducive to one's enjoyment of the food, correctly and appetisingly cooked by the talented young chef. There is a fixed price luncheon which represents good value

and an à la caret menu at dinner. His style is influenced by the modern fashion. Our Red Star award has been popular with our members; not only have they enjoyed the food and comfort, but also the warmth of the hospitality.

16rm(13⇌3⋒) CTV in all bedrooms T S% sB&B⇌⋒£38—£58 dB&B⇌⋒£64—£88 B

xmas

English & French V S% Lunch £10.50—£12.50&alc Tea £3.50 Dinner £15.50—£16.50&alc Wine £6.50 Last dinner 9.45pm

Credit cards 1 2 3 5 Ⓥ

★★**Marlborough Arms** Oxford St (Best Western) ☎ (0993) 811227

Closed 24—27 Dec

Partly 16th-century coaching inn called the George Inn in Scott's 'Woodstock'.

14rm 1 CTV in all bedrooms T ® S% sB&B£24—£26 dB&B£36—£40 dB&B £44—£52 B

CTV 14P

French V S% Lunch fr£7.50 Tea £1.50—£1.75 Dinner fr£8.50&alc Wine £6 Last dinner 10pm

Credit cards 1 2 3 5 V

See advertisement under Oxford

WOODY BAY

Devon

Map **3** SS64

★★**Woody Bay** ☎ Parracombe (05983) 264

RS Dec-Feb

Pleasant hotel in woodland setting.

14rm(7 1)(1fb) 2 ® sB&B£13—£21 dB&B£26—£42 dB&B £32—£48 B

CTV 15P nc 6yrs *xmas*

English & French V Bar lunch 75p—£6 Tea 70p—£1.50 Dinner £9.50&alc Wine £4 Last dinner 9pm

Credit cards 1 3 V

WOOLACOMBE

Devon

Map **2** SS44

★★★**Watersmeet** ☎ (0271) 870333

Closed Nov—Etr

Traditional holiday hotel with a country house atmosphere in a superb situation.

26rm(19 1)(3fb) 1 CTV in 21 bedrooms T sB&B£13—£21 sB&B £24—£32 dB&B£26—£42 dB&B £42—£58 B

CTV 25P 20 (£2 per night) (heated) (grass)

English & French V Lunch £5.50—£7 Tea 70p Dinner £10.50—£14.50&alc Wine £4.90 Last dinner 8.30pm

Credit cards 1 2 3 5

Woodstock — Woolacombe

★★★**Woolacombe Bay** South St (Consort) ☎ (0271) 870388

Closed Jan

Well-appointed, privately owned hotel in a prime situation whose many facilities ideally cater for family holidays.

48 (26fb) 1 CTV in all bedrooms ® sB&B £30—£53(incl dinner) dB&B £60—£106(incl dinner)

Lift CTV 70P & (heated) (hard) squash snooker sauna bath solarium gymnasium Disco 3 nights wkly Live music and dancing 3 nights wkly Cabaret 3 nights wkly *xmas*

English & French V Lunch £5 Tea 60p High Tea £5 Dinner £9 Wine £5 Last dinner 9.45pm

Credit cards 1 3

★★*B* **Atlantic** Sunnyside Rd ☎ (0271) 870469

Closed Oct—Etr

Comfortable, friendly, privately owned holiday hotel, overlooking village and bay.

14rm(9 1)(8fb) ® sB&B£13—£17 sB&B £16—£20 dB&B£26—£34 dB&B £29—£37

CTV 14P games room

*Dinner fr£6.50 Wine £4 Last dinner 7.30pm

★★*HB* **Devon Beach** The Esplanade ☎ (0271) 870449

Closed Oct—Etr

Well-appointed, privately owned and personally-run holiday hotel.

36 (21fb) in all bedrooms CTV in all bedrooms ® sB&B£13—£20 sB&B £17—£24 dB&B£26—£40 dB&B £34—£48 B

28P 3 (£2.50 per night) (heated) solarium Disco Wed & Fri Live music and dancing Mon Cabaret Mon

English & French Bar lunch 90p—£2.90&alc Tea 80p—£1.20 Dinner £7.50—£9 Wine £4.50 Last dinner 8.30pm

V

★★**Little Beach** The Esplanade ☎ (0271) 870398

Closed Nov—Jan RS Feb

An Edwardian gentleman's residence by the sea features a relaxed atmosphere and imaginative, carefully-prepared food.

10rm(4 4)(1fb) sB&B£17—£22 sB&B £24—£29 dB&B £46—£66 B

CTV 8P sauna bath solarium

English & Continental Bar lunch £4alc Dinner £10.25 Wine £5

Credit cards 1 3

★★***Sands*** Bay View Rd ☎ (0271) 870550

Closed end Sep—mid May (except Xmas)

Spanish-style stucco building in a quiet road overlooking the sea and the beach.

23rm(7)(9fb) CTV in 18 bedrooms

CTV 19P 1 (charge) Disco wkly *xmas*

English & Continental V Last dinner 8.15pm

★★***Whin Bay*** Bay View Rd ☎ (0271) 870475

Closed Nov—Apr

The family-run holiday hotel, perched high above the bay, offers comfortable bedrooms with lovely views.

17rm(4 11) ® B

CTV 16P

Last dinner 9pm

Credit cards 1 2 3

★*H* **Crossways** The Esplanade ☎ (0271) 870395

Closed Oct—Feb

Bright, attractive hotel, personally run by the proprietors, provides accommodation in compact bedrooms which are attractively decorated and spotlessly clean. Lounge and dining room are comfortable, and residents can obtain lunchtime snacks in the feature bar.

8rm(4)(4fb) CTV in all bedrooms ® *sB&B£10.25—£13.50 dB&B£20.50—£26.50 dB&B £23.50—£31

9P

★**Headlands** Beach Rd ☎ (0271) 870320

Closed Nov—Feb

Family-run small hotel, specialising in family holidays.

10rm(1🛁4🚿)(6fb) 1⊟⚡ in 2 bedrooms S% sB&B£11—£15.50 sB&B🛁🚿£12.50—£17 dB&B£22—£31 dB&B🛁🚿£25—£34 B

CTV 16P *xmas*

English & Continental ⚱ ☕⚡ Lunch £2.50—£3.50 Tea 40p High Tea £1.50 Dinner £4.50—£5.50 Wine £3.25 Last dinner 7pm

Credit card [3] Ⓥ

★**Sunnyside** Sunnyside Rd ☎ (0271) 870267

Closed mid Sep—mid May

Pleasant family holiday hotel in a quiet position.

18rm(2🛁)(4fb) sB&B£13—£14 dB&B£26—£28 dB&B🛁£27.50—£29.50 B

CTV 12P ✿ Disco wkly

⚱ Dinner £6—£7 Wine £5 Last dinner 7.15pm

WOOLER

Northumberland
Map **12** NT92

★★***Tankerville Arms*** Cottage Rd ☎ (0668) 81581

The large, comfortable inn is managed by resident proprietors who maintain a high level of service.

16rm(4🛁1🚿)(1fb) B

CTV 100P ✿ ⛹

⚱ Last dinner 9pm

★**Ryecroft** Ryecroft Way (Guestaccom) ☎ (0668) 81459

RS 2—13 Nov & 23—25 Dec

A friendly, comfortable hotel offering sound, home made cuisine.

11rm(3fb) ® sB&B£16.50 dB&B£32 B

CTV 20P ✿

⚱ ☕ Lunch £5.50 Tea £2 Dinner £10 Wine £5 Last dinner 8pm

Credit cards [1] [3] Ⓥ

Woolacombe — Worcester

WOOLFARDISWORTHY

Devon
Map **2** SS32

★★**Manor House** ☎ Clovelly (02373) 380

Closed Jan

This privately-run Georgian manor, situated in a quiet village, provides vegetarian and traditional menus in a restaurant which is popular with visitors and locals alike.

7rm(6🛁1🚿)(5fb) CTV in all bedrooms ® sB&B🛁🚿£15.50—£21.50 dB&B🛁🚿£31—£43 B

CTV 28P (charge) ⊭ ✿ ⛱ (heated) games room ⛹ *xmas*

International **V** ⚱ ☕ ✱ Lunch £3.95—£14 Tea fr50p High Tea fr£1.95 Dinner fr£8.95&alc Wine £4.25 Last dinner 9.30pm

Credit cards [1] [3]

See advertisement under Clovelly

WOOLVERTON

Somerset
Map **3** ST75

★★**Woolverton House** ☎ Frome (0373) 830415

Closed 25 & 26 Dec

This comfortable small hotel, set in attractive grounds, offers interesting food and a relaxed, friendly atmosphere.

11🛁🚿 Annexe: 3🛁(1fb) CTV in all bedrooms ® T sB&B fr£29.50 sB&B🛁🚿 fr£29.50 dB&B fr£40 dB&B🛁🚿 fr£40 B

75P ⊭ ✿

English & French **V** ⚱ Lunch £6.95alc Dinner £10alc Wine £4.80 Last dinner 9pm

Credit cards [1] [3] [5]

WORCESTER

Hereford & Worcester
Map **3** SO85

★★★**Giffard** High St (Trusthouse Forte) ☎ (0905) 27155 Telex no 338869

Busy, modern hotel in the centre of Worcester, offering wide range of conference and banqueting facilities.

104🛁 CTV in all bedrooms ® sB&B🛁£53 dB&B🛁£70 B

Lift ☾ CFA *xmas*

⚱ ☕ Last dinner 10pm

Credit cards [1] [2] [3] [4] [5]

★★**Star** Foregate St (Wolverhampton & Dudley) ☎ (0905) 24308 Telex no 385075

Town-centre hotel, popular with business people.

45rm(20🛁1🚿)(5fb) CTV in all bedrooms ® T ✱ sB&B£20—£29 sB&B🛁🚿£29—£33.50 dB&B£33.50—£35 dB&B🛁🚿£35.50—£45 B

Lift ☾ CTV 80P ♿

English & French ⚱ ☕ ✱ Lunch 90p—£5.50 Dinner £5.50&alc Wine £4.70 Last dinner 9.30pm

Credit cards [1] [2] [3] Ⓥ

See advertisement on page 792

★★*B* **Ye Olde Talbot** Friar St (Whitbread) ☎ (0905) 23573

The bedrooms of this 13th-century coaching inn are of high quality, sympathetically furnished in keeping with the traditional standards maintained throughout the city-centre hotel.

17🛁🚿 CTV in all bedrooms ® T ✈ sB&B🛁🚿£37.50 dB&B🛁🚿£48 B

CTV P ⊭

Mainly grills **V** ⚱ Lunch £5.50—£6&alc Dinner £7.50&alc Wine £4.80 Last dinner 10pm

Credit cards [1] [2] [3] [5]

See advertisement on page 792

★**Park House** 12 Droitwich Rd ☎ (0905) 21816

Closed Xmas/New Year

A small, family-run hotel on the outskirts of the city offers a friendly, homely atmosphere. →

W

7rm(2fb) S% sB&Bfr£12.50 dB&Bfr£22
CTV 9P

V S% Lunch £2.95 Tea fr£1 Dinner fr£6.50 Wine £4.50 Last dinner 5.30pm
Ⓥ

★**Talbot** 8—10 Barbourne Rd ☎ (0905) 21206

Closed Xmas Day & Boxing Day

Small, popular, half timbered inn.

14rm(2fb) sB&B£13.50 dB&B£23

CTV 40P

V Lunch £5alc Tea 75palc High Tea £3alc Dinner £6alc Wine £3.65 Last dinner 10pm

✿XX**Brown's** The Old Cornmill, South Quay ☎ (0905) 26263

This splendidly restored riverside cornmill has won awards for both conservation and excellence of food. Diners can enjoy good views of the river as well as an impressive interior décor, and innovative, freshly-prepared food is served by attentive staff.

Closed Bank Hol's Lunch not served Sat

English & French 70 seats Lunch £10—£13.95 Dinner £10—£17.95 Wine £5.95 Last dinner 9.30pm nc8yrs

Credit cards 1 2 3

Worcester — Worfield

XX**King Charles II** New St ☎ (0905) 22449

This interesting building, whose interior dates back to the 16th century, features an equally interesting menu. Orders from the comprehensive a la carte or table d'hôte menus are taken in an intimate cocktail bar, and the well-prepared food is professionally served in a justifiably popular restaurant with lace cloths and open fires.

Closed Sun

International V 52 seats Lunch £7—£8.50&alc Dinner £15—£16&alc Wine £6.50 Last dinner 9.45pm

Credit cards 1 2 3 5

X**Sailors Return** Sailors Bank, Lower Broadheath (3m NW on B4204) ☎ (0905) 641120

Comfortable little restaurant where an enterprising menu offers French cuisine with modern innovations, largely based on local produce.

Closed Mon Lunch not served Tue—Sat

Dinner not served Sun

French V 36 seats Sun lunch £7.25 Dinner £14.95&alc Wine £4.25 Last dinner 9.30pm 18P nc12yrs

Credit cards 1 2 3

WORCESTER PARK
Greater London
Plan **5** *C1* (page 446)

X**Golden Tandoori** 208 Cheam Common Rd ☎ 01-337 5262

Closed Xmas day

North Indian V 50 seats ✱Lunch £7.95—£15&alc Dinner £11—£25&alc Wine £5.50 Last dinner 11.30pm 20P

Credit cards 1 2 3 5 Ⓥ

WORFIELD
Shropshire
Map **7** SJ40

★★ **Old Vicarage** ☎ (07464) 498 Telex no 35438

Fine red brick house combining Victorian character with modern facilities.

10rm(8⇌2⋒)(1fb) 1 CTV in all bedrooms ®T sB&B⇌⋒£33.50 dB&B⇌⋒£46 B

☾30P croquet

V Lunch £7.95—£9.95&alc Tea £2—£2.50 High Tea £2—£2.50 Dinner £11.95—£12.95&alc Wine £6.50 Last dinner 9pm

Credit cards 1 2 3 5 Ⓥ

W

WORKINGTON
Cumbria
Map **11** NX92

★★★**Cumberland Arms** Belle Isle St ☎(0900) 64401

Closed Xmas Day

Commercial, recently modernised hotel opposite the railway station.

29rm(27➡2⋒)(1fb) CTV in all bedrooms ⓇT ✱sB&B➡⋒£24 dB&B➡⋒£30 B

Lift ☾ CTV 60P pool table

☋English & French V ♁ ☕ ✱Lunch £7.50alc Tea 60p Dinner £6.95&alc Wine £5.05 Last dinner 10pm

Credit cards 1 2 3 5 Ⓥ

★★★**Westland** Braithwaite Rd ☎(0900) 4544 Telex no 64229

A modern hotel, 2m outside Workington, just off the A595.

50rm(40➡5⋒)(3fb) CTV in all bedrooms ⓇT ✱sB&B£20 sB&B➡£27.50 dB&B£29 dB&B➡£39 B

☾ 200P ✿ Disco Wed & Sat Live music and dancing Wed & Sat *xmas*

☋English & French ♁ ☕ ✱Bar lunch £2.45—£5.40 Tea fr£1.50 Dinner £7.50—£9.50&alc Wine £4.30 Last dinner 9.30pm

Credit cards 1 2 3 5

★★**Clifton** Great Clifton ☎(0900) 64616

RS Xmas Day

Modernised 18th century farm house that retains much original character.

14rm(8➡6⋒) CTV in all bedrooms ⓇT sB&B➡⋒£25—£27 dB&B➡⋒£37—£39 B

50P nc 12yrs

☋English, French & Chinese V ♁ Lunch £5.50 Dinner £7.75—£9.75&alc Wine £3.50 Last dinner 9pm

Credit cards 1 3

★★**Crossbarrow Motel** Little Clifton (3m E on A595) ☎(0900) 61443

A purpose-built complex with modern functional bedrooms.

37rm(29➡8⋒)(3fb) CTV in all bedrooms Ⓡ sB&B➡⋒£25.25 dB&B➡⋒£39.50

CTV 50P ✿

♁ Lunch £3.50alc Dinner £5.50alc Wine £3.90 Last dinner 9.30pm

Credit cards 1 3

★★**Green Dragon** Portland Sq ☎(0900) 3803

Situated in a quiet square, the hotel provides public areas which have been tastefully refurbished to combine comfort and character.

10rm(5➡3⋒) CTV in all bedrooms Ⓡ ✕ sB&B£15 sB&B➡⋒£18.50 dB&B£25 dB&B➡⋒£28.50 B P

☋International V ♁ Bar lunch £2.05—£3.70 Dinner £5.70—£10.05alc Wine £3.60 Last dinner 9pm

Credit cards 1 3 Ⓥ

Workington — Worthing

★★**Washington Central** Washington St ☎(0900) 65772

The modern hotel features a most interesting structure, everything being built round a central core, but the atmosphere is traditionally pleasant and friendly.

20➡⋒(2fb) CTV in all bedrooms ⓇT ✕ sB&B➡⋒£26 dB&B➡⋒£43 B

Lift ☾ CTV 20P Disco Wknds

V ♁ ☕ Lunch £4—£7 Tea £2—£3 High Tea £2—£4 Dinner £9—£10&alc Wine £5.40 Last dinner 9.30pm

Credit cards 1 2 3 Ⓥ

WORKSOP
Nottinghamshire
Map **8** SK57

★★**Regancy** Carlton Rd ☎(0909) 474108

Comfortable accommodation and friendly service is offered by its owners at this former railway hotel near the station.

12rm(7⋒)(1fb) Ⓡ ✱sB&B£12—£18.50 sB&B⋒£18.50 dB&B£20 dB&B⋒£32

CTV 14P 6

☋International ♁ ☕ ✱Lunch £2.50&alc Dinner £4.50&alc Wine £3.50 Last dinner 8pm

Credit cards 1 2 3 5

★★**Lion** 112 Bridge St ☎(0909) 477925

This town-centre inn, dating from the 15th century, has been extensively modernised to provide well-equipped, comfortable bedrooms and elegant public areas.

8⋒ CTV in all bedrooms Ⓡ ✕ ✱sB&B⋒£20 dB&B⋒£35

30P Live music & dancing twice mthly *xmas*

☋International ♁ ☕ ✱Lunch £5.25 Dinner £9.50 Wine £5 Last dinner 10.30pm

Credit cards 1 2 3 5

WORMIT
Fife
Map **11** NO32

★★**Sandford Hill** ☎ Newport-on-Tay (0382) 541802

Closed 1 & 2 Jan

Set off the A914, three miles south of the Tay Road Bridge, the country house hotel has a modern bedroom extension and a reputation for good food that makes it popular with the Dundee business sector.

15rm(13➡)(3fb) CTV in all bedrooms ⓇT sB&B£28 sB&B➡£34 dB&B£44 dB&B➡£54 B

CTV 50P ✿ (hard)

☋Scottish & Continental V ♁ ☕ Lunch £7.50—£8.50&alc Tea 65p High Tea £3.50—£5.50 Dinner £11.50—£13&alc Wine £5.50 Last dinner 9.30pm

Credit cards 1 2 3 5 Ⓥ

WORTHING
West Sussex
Map **4** TQ10

★★★*HL* **Beach** Marine Pde ☎(0903) 34001

Friendly seafront hotel with spacious lounge and well equipped bedrooms.

91rm(71➡9⋒)(3fb) CTV in all bedrooms T ✕ sB&B➡⋒£29—£31.50 dB&B➡⋒£44.50—£52.50 B

Lift ☾ 55P CFA nc 8yrs *xmas*

♁ ☕ Lunch £7.25&alc Tea 90p Dinner £9.25&alc Wine £5 Last dinner 8.45pm

Credit cards 1 2 3 4 5

See advertisement on page 794

★★★**Chatsworth** The Steyne ☎(0903) 36103 Telex no 877046

The hotel has an attractive Georgian frontage and overlooks Steyne Gardens and the sea.

105rm(83➡17⋒)(5fb) CTV in all bedrooms ⓇT S% sB&B➡⋒£35 dB&B➡⋒£54 B

Lift ☾ P CFA snooker *xmas*

☋English & Continental V Lunch £7.50&alc Dinner £8.75&alc Wine £5.40 Last dinner 8.30pm

Credit cards 1 2 3

★★★**Eardley** Marine Pde ☎(0903) 34444 Telex no 877046

Modernised Victorian seafront terraced house.

83rm(57➡7⋒) CTV in all bedrooms ⓇT sB&B£21—£22 sB&B➡⋒£28—£32 dB&B£34—£36 dB&B➡⋒£47—£52 B

Lift ☾ 20P CFA *xmas*

V ♁ ☕ Lunch £5.25—£6.50 Tea 90p—£1.60 Dinner £7.50—£8&alc Wine £4.25 Last dinner 9.30pm

Credit cards 1 3

★★***Ardington*** Steyne Gdns ☎(0903) 30451

Closed Xmas

Pleasantly situated hotel facing Steyne Gardens, close to the promenade and the shopping centre.

55rm(22➡22⋒)(4fb) CTV in all bedrooms Ⓡ B

☾ P

♁ ☕ Last dinner 8.15pm

Credit cards 1 2 3 5

★★**Beechwood Hall** Richmond Rd ☎(0903) 32872

Regency period house set in own wooded ground.

18rm(14➡2⋒) CTV in all bedrooms ⓇT sB&B➡⋒£25 dB&B➡⋒£37 B

☾ 60P ✿ *xmas*

☋English & French V ♁ ☕ Lunch £2.50—£6&alc Tea £1.50alc High Tea £1.50alc Dinner £7.50&alc Wine £4.50 Last dinner 9.45pm

Credit cards 1 2 3 Ⓥ

★★**Kingsway** Marine Pde ☏ (0903) 37542

Seafront hotel with luxurious lounges and good home cooking.

30rm(22 8)(1fb) CTV in all bedrooms ®T sB&B £28—£30 dB&B £28—£30

Lift ☾ 12P *xmas*

V Lunch £5.95 Tea fr85p Dinner £8.70—£8.90 Wine £4.95 Last dinner 9pm

Credit cards 1 2 3 5

✕✕**Paragon Continental** 9—10 Brunswick Rd ☏ (0903) 33367

Italian run international restaurant with good personal service.

Closed Sun & Bank Hol's

English & French 40 seats S% Lunch fr£8&alc Dinner fr£10.75&alc Wine £5.25 Last dinner 10pm

Credit cards 1 2 3 5

WRELTON

North Yorkshire
Map **8** SE78

✕***Huntsmans*** ☏ Pickering (0751) 72530

A converted farmhouse providing friendly homely surroundings.

Closed Mon Dinner not served Sun

English & Continental 45 seats Last dinner 9.30pm 25P

WREXHAM
Clwyd
Map **7** SJ34

★★★ **Llwyn Onn Hall** Cefn Rd ☎(0978) 261225

13rm(10⇌3⋒) 1 CTV in all bedrooms **T** ✻sB&B⇌⋒£40—£45 dB&B⇌⋒£55—£65

70P nc8yrs *xmas*

Lunch £7.50&alc Dinner £11&alc Last dinner 9pm

Credit cards 1 2 3 5

★★★ **Wynnstay Arms** High St/Yorke St (Consort) ☎(0978) 353431 Telex no 61674

Modern hotel, situated in the town centre.

75⇌⋒(10fb) in 4 bedrooms CTV in all bedrooms ®**T** S% sB⇌⋒£41.25 dB⇌⋒£55.50 (room only) **B**

Lift ☾ 50P 20 *xmas*

V Lunch £5.25—£5.95 Tea £1.20—£1.45 High Tea £5.25—£5.75 Dinner £9.85&alc wine £5.75 Last dinner 9.45pm

Credit cards 1 2 3 5 Ⓥ

★★ **Cross Lanes** Marchwiel (2m SE A525) ☎(0978) 780555

20rm(7⇌9⋒) 1 CTV in all bedrooms ® **T** S% sB&B fr£17 sB&B⇌⋒£20—£27.50 dB&B⇌⋒£35—£37.50 Continental breakfast **B**

☾ CTV 100P (heated) sauna bath

English & French **V** S% Lunch £5.95&alc Tea fr£1 High Tea fr£3.50 Dinner £5.95—£8.50&alc Wine £5 Last dinner 9.30pm

Credit cards 1 2 3 5 Ⓥ

WRIGHTINGTON
Lancashire
Map **7** SD51

✕✕ **High Moor** Highmoor Ln ☎ Appley Bridge (02575) 2364

This attractive, cottage style restaurant, with stone fireplaces and oak beams dating back to the 17th century, stands in a rural setting near Junction 27 of the M6. Chef/patron James Sines and his staff have made the former farmhouse a restaurant of acclaim, offering a style of nouvelle cuisine adapted to the local taste and featuring seasonal variations, including game. The interesting wine list contains a good selection of house wines.

Closed Mon, 1—7 Jan & 14—31 Aug Lunch not served Sat Dinner not served Sun

French **V** 50 seats Lunch £15—£16alc Dinner £15—£16alc Wine £6.50 Last dinner 9.45pm 35P

Credit cards 1 2 3 5

WROTHAM HEATH
Kent
Map **5** TQ65

★★★★ **Post House** London Rd (Trusthouse Forte) ☎ Borough Green (0732) 883311 Telex no 957309

After a meal in the carvery restaurant of this modern, very well equipped hotel, guests can visit the leisure complex or relax in comfortable lounges or on the patio; bedrooms are spacious, tastefully appointed and well equipped.

119⇌(19fb) CTV in all bedrooms ®**T** sB&B⇌£58.50 dB&B⇌£74.50 **B**

Lift ☾ 140P (heated) sauna bath solarium gymnasium *xmas*

Last dinner 10.30pm

Credit cards 1 2 3 4 5

See advertisement under Maidstone

WROXHAM
Norfolk
Map **9** TG31

★★ **Broads** Station Rd ☎(06053) 2869

19rm(10⇌)(3fb) ®sB&B£14 sB&B⇌£16 dB&B£24 dB&B⇌£27.50

CTV 18P

V ✻ Bar lunch 70p Tea 55p Dinner £5—£10 Wine £3.25 Last dinner 8pm

★★ **Hotel Wroxham** Broads Centre, Hoveton ☎(06053) 2061

This hotel's low, modern building forms part of a shopping complex in the centre of this Broads town. Many of its bedrooms have balconies overlooking the river and the bars and restaurant are popular with visitors.

18rm(14⇌)(2fb) CTV in all bedrooms ®**T** sB&B£22 sB&B⇌£30—£33 dB&B£34 dB&B⇌£42—£45 **B**

60P snooker solarium *xmas*

Hungarian **V** Lunch £5.75&alc Tea 75p Dinner £6.75&alc Wine £6 Last dinner 9.30pm

Credit cards 1 2 3 5 Ⓥ

WYE
Kent
Map **5** TR04

✕✕ **Wife of Bath** ☎(0233) 812540

Small cottage restaurant with low-ceilinged rooms.

Closed Sun, Mon & 24 Dec—1 Jan

French 50 seats ✻Lunch £13.90 Dinner £13.90 Wine £5.25 Last dinner 10pm 12P

Credit card 1

WYKEHAM (near Scarborough)
North Yorkshire
Map **8** SE98

★★ **Downe Arms** (Best Western) ☎ Scarborough (0723) 862471 Telex no 527192

Bedroom accommodation has recently been upgraded in this restored, eighteenth-century coaching inn, which also offers a lavish dining room.

9⋒ CTV in all bedrooms ®S% sB&B⋒fr£18 dB&B⋒fr£36 **B**

Lift 120P 2(charge) Disco Fri →

W

English & French V S% Lunch fr£5.25 Dinner fr£8.50&alc Wine £5 Last dinner 9pm

Credit cards 1 2 3 5 V

WYMONDHAM
Norfolk
Map 5 TG10

★★★**Sinclair** 28 Market St (0953) 606721

A family-run hotel offering a warm welcome in this newly converted Victorian building occupying central position in this historic market town.

12rm(4 8)(2fb) 1 in all bedrooms CTV in all bedrooms ® T *sB&B £29—£32 dB&B £40—£44 B

8P 1 *xmas*

V *Lunch £7.50—£8.50 Tea 40—50p Dinner £8—£10&alc Wine £5.25 Last dinner 9.30pm

Credit cards 1 2 3

★★***Abbey*** Church St (0953) 602148

Small, modernised hotel, part of which dates from the late 16th century, in a quiet location near Wymondham Abbey.

31rm(21 1)(4fb) CTV in all bedrooms ® B

Unlicensed Lift ☾ 4P

V Last dinner 8.30pm

Credit cards 1 2 3 5

X**Adlards** 16 Damgate St (0953) 603533

A former butcher's shop, part of a narrow row of terraced cottages off the main street, has been converted into a delightful little restaurant. The reputation of the cuisine, based on top-quality produce cooked lightly in the modern style and presented with flair, draws customers from a wide area.

Closed Sun & Mon Lunch not served

French 25 seats *Dinner £13—£14.50 Wine £5.25 Last dinner 9pm

V

YARM
Cleveland
Map 8 NZ41

XX**Santoro** 47 High St Eaglescliffe (0642) 781305

This modern, first-floor restaurant in the High Street features a spacious, open-plan area which includes an attractive dining room, small bar and comfortable lounge. The interesting menu shows both French and Italian influences and offers very good value.

Closed Sun & Bank Hol's Lunch not served Sat

English, French & Italian V 45 seats Lunch £4.50—£9.50 Dinner £10.50—£12.80&alc Wine £5.20 Last dinner 10.15pm 20P

Credit cards 1 2 3 5

YARMOUTH
Isle of Wight
See **Wight, Isle of**

YARMOUTH, GREAT
Norfolk
Map 5 TG50

★★★**Carlton** Marine Parade South (0493) 855234 Telex no 975642

91rm(68)CTV in all bedrooms ® T S% *sB&B fr£29.50 sB&B fr£35 dB&B fr£40.50 dB&B fr£50.25 B

Lift ☾ 20 CFA Live music & dancing nightly (Summer) Wkds (Winter) *xmas*

S% Lunch fr£1.75 Dinner fr£7.95&alc Wine £6.35 Last dinner 9.30pm

Credit cards 1 2 3 5

★★★*H* **Cliff** Gorleston on Sea (2m S A12) (Best Western) (0493) 662179 Telex no 987129

30rm(24 6)(5fb) 1 in 2 bedrooms CTV in all bedrooms T sB&B fr£32.50 dB&B fr£53 B

☾ 50P Disco wkly Live music and dancing wkly *xmas*

V Lunch £6—£6.75&alc Tea 70p High Tea £1.75 Dinner £8—£9&alc Wine £5 Last dinner 9.30pm

Credit cards 1 2 3 5 V

★★★**Dolphin** Albert Sq (0493) 855070 Telex no 975037

A commercial-style hotel in a tourist area, the Dolphin offers many amenities, including two restaurants. One of these, the Porthole, specialises in fresh fish dishes.

42(1fb) CTV in all bedrooms ® T S% dB £37.50—£68.50 (room only)

☾ CTV 12P 12 (heated) sauna bath solarium gymnasium pool table

V Last dinner 10pm

Credit cards 1 2 3 5

★★★**Sandringham** 74—75 Marine Pde (0493) 852427 Telex no 975037

24(3fb) CTV in all bedrooms ® T *sB&B fr£35 dB&B fr£50.95 B

☾ CTV Live music & dancing Fri

V *Lunch £7.15alc Tea £1.50alc Dinner £9alc Wine £4.65 Last dinner 10pm

Credit cards 1 2 3 5 V

★★**Burlington** North Dr (0493) 844568

Closed Nov—Feb

The family hotel is situated on the quieter North Drive, having views of the sea, gardens and tennis courts.

33rm(15 10)(5fb) CTV in all bedrooms ® T *sB&B £19—£34 B

Lift CTV CFA (heated) sauna bath solarium *xmas*

English & French V Lunch £6—£7.50 Tea 60p Dinner £8—£9.50 Wine £4.70 Last dinner 8pm

Credit cards 1 3 4 V

★★*B* **Imperial** North Dr (0493) 851113

Family run seafront hotel with modern, comfortable accommodation.

41rm(30 11)(8fb) CTV in all bedrooms ® T S% sB&B fr£35 dB&B fr£44 B

Lift ☾ CTV 50P CFA *xmas*

English & French *Lunch £9.20—£11.50&alc Tea fr£1.50 Dinner fr£9.20&alc Wine £6 Last dinner 10.30pm

Credit cards 1 2 3 4 5

★**Marine View** North Dr (0493) 842879

50rm(2 11)(16fb) CTV in all bedrooms sB&B fr£16 sB&B fr£19 dB&B fr£32 dB&B fr£38 B

Lift CTV 30P 8 solarium Live music & dancing Mon *xmas*

V Dinner fr£7 Wine £4.35 Last dinner 7.30pm

Credit cards 1 2 3 5 V

YATTENDON
Berkshire
Map 4 SU57

★★*H* **Royal Oak** The Square Hermitage (0635) 201325

RS Sun & 2 wks Jan/Feb

Very hospitable 16th-century inn with oak beams and log fires.

5rm(3) CTV in all bedrooms sB&B £37.50—£40 dB&B £52.50—£55 B

30P

English & French V Lunch £17.50—£20alc Tea £1.25alc Dinner £17.50—£20alc Wine £6.75 Last dinner 10pm

Credit cards 1 2 3

YELDHAM, GREAT
Essex
Map 5 TL73

XX**White Hart** (0787) 237250

A black and white, timbered building dating from the 15th-century is set in three acres of garden bordered by the River Colne. Both à la carte and table d'hôte menus make skilful use of fresh, local products in creating interesting dishes, and a young staff provides courteous, friendly service.

English & French V 75 seats *Lunch £9.95&alc Dinner £9.95&alc Wine £5.95 Last dinner 9.30pm 50P Live music Sat

Credit cards 1 2 3 4 5

W

Yelverton — York

YELVERTON
Devon
Map **2** SX56

★★★**Moorland Links** (Forest Dale)
☎ (0822) 852245 Telex no 45616
Closed Xmas wk
The two-storey, pre-war colonial-style hotel stands in its own grounds, and attractive public rooms include the Gun Room Bar and the Pheasant Restaurant, where a good menu is offered. Rooms in the new wing have been upgraded to a high standard, and the hotel is popular with business people.
31 in 4 bedrooms CTV in all bedrooms ®T sB&B fr£36 dB&B fr£46
100P CFA
V Lunch £6.65—£12.50 Dinner £10.45—£15 Wine £4.75 Last dinner 10pm
Credit cards 1 2 3 5

★***Saddlers Retreat Country House***
Tavistock Rd
☎ (0822) 852099
Small congenial quiet hotel.
9rm(2 1)(2fb) CTV in all bedrooms ®
40P *xmas*
V Last dinner 9pm
Credit cards 1 3 5
See advertisement under Plymouth

YEOVIL
Somerset
Map **3** ST51

★★★**Four Acres** West Coker (3m W A30) ☎ West Coker (093586) 2555 Telex no 46666
18rm(15 2) Annexe: 5 CTV in all bedrooms ®T ✱sB&B £32.50—£41 dB&B £45—£49
40P 5 table tennis pool table *xmas*
English & French ✱Lunch £9.25&alc Tea fr86p Dinner £9.25&alc Wine £4.95 Last dinner 9.30pm
Credit cards 1 2 3 5 V

★★★B **Manor Crest** Hendford (Crest)
☎ (0935) 23116 Telex no 46580
Well-appointed hotel in city centre. Bedrooms are particularly well equipped. The standard of food and service are especially worthy of a mention.
42rm(40 2)(3fb) in 4 bedrooms CTV in all bedrooms ®S%
✱sB £33.50—£43.50
dB £43.50—£53.50 (room only)
50P CFA *xmas*
English & French V S%
✱Lunch £6.50—£8.50&alc Tea 95palc High Tea £1.95alc Dinner £11.50&alc Wine £6.25 Last dinner 10pm
Credit cards 1 2 3 4 5

★**Preston** 64 Preston Rd ☎ (0935) 74400
A small, convivial hotel, family owned and run, is situated on the Taunton Road at the edge of the town and offers good parking.
7rm(1 2)(1fb) CTV in all bedrooms
✱sB&B £15 sB&B £19 dB&B £23 dB&B £28
19P
Mainly grills V ✱Bar lunch £4.50alc Dinner £7.50alc Wine £3.45 Last dinner 8.30pm
Credit cards 1 3 V

XX**Little Barwick House** (2m S off A37)
☎ (0935) 23902
This attractive, Georgian, country dower house stands in a tiny hamlet just outside Yeovil, off the Dorchester Road. It provides a relaxed atmosphere, good, interesting food and a reasonably priced wine list.
Closed Sun Lunch not served
English & French V 32 seats S% Dinner £14alc Wine £6 Last dinner 9pm P
Credit cards 1 2 3 5 V

YORK
North Yorkshire
Map **8** SE65

★★★★**Viking** North St (Queens Moat)
☎ (0904) 59822 Telex no 57937
The large, modern hotel is situated beside the River Ouse, in the heart of the city. With a choice of three restaurants, it caters for business people or for tourists.
188rm(176 12)(7fb) CTV in all bedrooms ®T S% ✱sB&B £55 dB&B £80
Lift 15P 80 sauna bath solarium gymnasium
English & French V S% ✱Lunch £4.50—£8.25 Dinner £8.25&alc Wine £4.95 Last dinner 10pm
Credit cards 1 2 3 5

★★★**Chase** Tadcaster Rd (Consort)
☎ (0904) 707171 Telex no 57582
Closed 25 & 26 Dec
A large, traditional hotel adjacent to the Race Course provides spacious public rooms and modern facilities. Bedrooms are well-fitted and cheerful.
80rm(63 17)(2fb) CTV in all bedrooms T (except guide dogs) S%
sB&B £36 dB&B £60
Lift CTV 100P 12 (charge) CFA putting Live music & dancing Sat (Nov—Etr)
English, French & Italian V Lunch £6 Tea fr75p Dinner fr£13 Wine £5 Last dinner 8.45pm
Credit cards 1 2 3 5

★★★**Dean Court** Duncombe Pl (Best Western) ☎ (0904) 25082 Telex no 57577
Converted merchants' house near Minster.
36rm(34 2) CTV in all bedrooms T
sB&B £42—£45 dB&B £78—£80
Lift 12P
English & French V Lunch £9—£11 Tea £1.50—£2 Dinner £13—£15 Wine £4.75 Last dinner 8.45pm
Credit cards 1 2 3 4 5

Y

★★★*BL* **Fairfield Manor** Shipton Rd, Skelton (Consort) ☎ (0904) 25621

An early Georgian mansion, with extensive lawns and gardens, lies three miles north of the city on the A19.

25rm(20⇌5⋔)(1fb) 2⊟ CTV in all bedrooms ® T ✗ sB&B⇌⋔£35—£44 dB&B⇌⋔£48—£58 ⊟

50P ✿ ⚑9 nc 5yrs *xmas*

English & French V ☕ Lunch £6.25—£6.75&alc Tea £3.25—£3.50 Dinner £8.75—£9.25&alc Last dinner 9.15pm

Credit cards 1 2 3 5

★★★**Ladbroke Abbey Park** The Mount (Ladbroke) ☎ (0904) 58301

Tourist and business hotel offering modern style accommodation.

84⇌(11fb) ⊁ in 5 bedrooms CTV in all bedrooms ® T sB&B⇌£49—£59 dB&B⇌£75—£85 ⊟

Lift ☾ 40P CFA *xmas*

V ☕ Lunch £6.75—£8 Tea £1 Dinner £9.95—£12 Last dinner 9.30pm

Credit cards 1 2 3 5 ⓥ

❀★★★**Middlethorpe Hall**
(see opposite)

★★★**Post House** Tadcaster Rd (Trusthouse Forte) ☎ (0904) 707921 Telex no 57798

This multi-storey hotel near the Race Course has spacious, attractive lounges, a dining room with a garden patio and well-fitted bedrooms.

147⇌(30fb) CTV in all bedrooms ® T sB&B⇌£53.50 dB&B⇌£73.50 ⊟

Lift ☾ 180P CFA ✿ *xmas*

Last dinner 10pm

Credit cards 1 2 3 4 5

★★**Abbot's Mews** 6 Marygate Ln, Bootham ☎ (0904) 34866 Telex no 5777

This hotel near the city centre was converted from a coachman's cottage and stables.

12⇌⋔ Annexe: 30rm(16⇌11⋔)(8fb) CTV in all bedrooms ® T ✗ S% sB&B£27—£34 sB&B⇌⋔£27—£34 dB&B⇌⋔£37—£52 ⊟

20P ✿ *xmas*

International V ☕ Lunch £5—£8 Tea £1—£1.50 Dinner £10&alc Wine £5.50 Last dinner 9.30pm

Credit cards 1 2 3 5 ⓥ

★★★

❀★★★MIDDLETHORPE HALL, YORK

Bishopthorpe Rd (Prestige) ☎ (0904) 641241 Telex no 57802

Architecturally, this is perhaps the most interesting of our country house hotels. In advance of its time (1699—1701) it is a beautifully proportioned Queen Anne style house of red brick with tuck-pointing, stone dressings, with, on the hipped roof, a parapet with carved stone festoons surmounted by an eagle. There are equally impressive features inside: a handsome doorcase separates the stone flagged lobby from the black and white marble floored entrance hall with a magnificant carved oak staircase supported by Ionic pillars. Historic House Hotels — owners of the Red Starred Bodysgallen Hall Hotel — have made a superb job of the restoration here, complete with good antiques of every description, portraits, rich hangings, gilded mirrors, and all fresh with flowers. Reception rooms include the library and the magnificently done drawing room as well as the atmospheric cellar cocktail bar. The dining room is in two sections: one panelled, the other with cornice and marble effect walls; both are beautifully appointed and include flowers and candles. Talented Aidan McCormack is the chef, and he uses fine ingredients to interesting effect on the mainly modern style menus. The fixed price luncheon including a half bottle of wine is a bargain; at dinner there is another fixed price menu and an à la carte. The young waiting staff are courteous and obliging as all the staff are. Bedrooms are appropriately done and well provided with extras like trouser presses, books, Malvern Water and biscuits. Our readers have been glad of our recommendation, finding it a most enjoyable place to stay in.

31⇌⋔(1fb) 1⊟ CTV in all bedrooms T ✗ S% sB&B⇌⋔fr£65 dB&B⇌⋔fr£88 Continental breakfast ⊟

Lift ☾ 70P ✿ croquet nc 9yrs *xmas*

V ☕ S% Lunch fr£12 Tea fr£6 Dinner fr£19.50&alc Wine £8 Last dinner 9.45pm

Credit cards 1 2 3 5

★★**Ashcroft** 294 Bishopthorpe Rd ☎ (0904) 59286

Closed Xmas & New Year

Large but quiet house with restful atmosphere and good home cooking.

11rm(10⇌1⋔) Annexe: 4rm(3⇌1⋔)(3fb) CTV in all bedrooms ® T sB&B⇌⋔fr£20 dB&B⇌⋔fr£40 ⊟

CTV 40P ✿

V ☕ Lunch £4.75&alc Tea fr65p High Tea fr£3.95 Dinner fr£7&alc Wine £5.40 Last dinner 8pm

Credit cards 1 2 3 5

★★**Beechwood Close** Shipton Rd ☎ (0904) 58378

Closed Xmas Day

A converted country house with its own gardens stands in a suburban area to the north of the city. It provides homely public areas, an attractive restaurant and the attention of friendly proprietors.

Y

14rm(8 6)(5fb) CTV in all bedrooms ® T sB&B £21.50—£23 dB&B £37—£39

CTV 36P putting

V Lunch £3.75—£4.50 Tea fr60p Dinner £7.95—£9.95 Wine £4.95 Last dinner 9pm

Credit cards 1 3 V

★★**Disraeli's** 140 Acomb Rd ☎ (0904) 781181 Telex no 57715

Closed 24 Dec—31 Jan

The gabled, brick-built hotel stands in its own grounds in the suburb of Acomb. It offers well-proportioned bedrooms, tastefully appointed, and an elegant restaurant.

9rm(8)(4fb) CTV in all bedrooms ® T sB&B £24—£29 dB&B £42

CTV 40P

Cosmopolitan V Lunch £6.50 Tea 50p High Tea £3 Dinner fr£9.50&alc Wine £4.85 Last dinner 9.45pm

Credit cards 1 2 3 5 V

See advertisement on page 800

York

★★***Heworth Court*** 76—78 Heworth Green ☎ (0904) 425156

Closed Xmas Day & Boxing Day

Comfortable hotel with modern facilities and pleasant dining area.

4 Annexe: 9rm(3 6) CTV in all bedrooms ® T

CTV 13P 1

V Last dinner 9pm

Credit cards 1 2 3 5

See advertisement on page 800

★ ★**The Hill** 60 York Rd, Acomb (Exec Hotel) ☎ (0904) 790777 Telex no 57567

Closed mid Dec—mid Jan

A modernised Georgian residence, suitably restored and renovated, lies in three-quarters of an acre of walled garden about two miles from the city centre. Well-appointed bedrooms and public rooms retain some original features, while modern bedrooms in the new wing are well equipped.

10 (1fb) 2 CTV in all bedrooms ® **T** sB&B £24.50—£29 dB&B £36—48 **B**

12P

York

Lunch £5—£8.50 Tea £1.50—£2.50 Dinner £9—£11 Wine £4.95 Last dinner 7.30pm

Credit cards 1 2 3 5

★ ★**Hudsons** 60 Bootham ☎ (0904) 21267 Telex no 57715

Closed 24 & 25 Dec

Large Victorian hotel of character, with modern facilities and new wing.

28rm (25 3)(2fb) 1 CTV in all bedrooms ® **T** sB&B £18—£32 dB&B £48—£56 **B**

Lift 35P

V Lunch £5.50 Tea £1.50 High Tea £2.50—£4 Dinner £10—£12.50 Wine £5.50 Last dinner 9.30pm

Credit cards 1 2 3 5

★ ★**Kilima** 129 Holgate Rd (Inter Hotel) ☎ (0904) 58844

This carefully restored and upgraded Victorian rectory stands about a mile outside the city walls and has its own car park. Victorian accessories add to the

Y

charm of the lower ground floor restaurant and lounge bar, whilst bedrooms are well equipped.

15rm(11 4)(1fb) 1 CTV in all bedrooms ®T sB&B £27.50—£35 dB&B £42—£45

20P *xmas*

English & French V Lunch £10alc Tea £2alc Dinner £10alc Wine £5.50 Last dinner 9.30pm

Credit cards 1 2 3 5 V

★★**Railway King** George Hudson St ☎(0904) 645161

22rm(6 16)(2fb) CTV in all bedrooms ®T S% ✱sB&B £29.50 dB&B fr£43.50

12P

V ✱Lunch £3.50alc Tea 75p Dinner £7alc Wine £4.45 Last dinner 9.45pm

Credit cards 1 2 3 5

★★**Sheppard** 63 Blossom St ☎(0904) 20500 Telex no 579

Four-storey town hotel, dating from 1834, on the A64.

20rm(16)(4fb) 1 CTV in all bedrooms ®T S% sB&B £17—£20.50 sB&B £23—£30 dB&B £24—£32 dB&B £37—£45

CTV 10P 4 (charge)

York

English & Continental V Lunch £4—£6&alc Dinner £6—£7.50&alc Wine £3.95 Last dinner 9.30pm

Credit cards 1 3 5 V

★★*L* **Town House** 100—104 Holgate Rd ☎(0904) 36171

Closed 24 Dec—31 Dec

Friendly, hospitable hotel with well appointed accommodation.

23rm(12 6)(5fb) CTV in all bedrooms T ✱sB&B £17 sB&B £25—£32 dB&B £30 dB&B £37—£39

23P

European ✱Bar lunch £1.20—£5.50 Tea fr£1 Dinner fr£7.25&alc Wine £5.55 Last dinner 9.30pm

Credit cards 1 2 3 5 V

See advertisement on page 802

★**Fairmount** 230 Tadcaster Rd, Mount Vale ☎(0904) 38298

7rm(1 4)(4fb) CTV in all bedrooms ® sB&B £13—£18 dB&B £34 dB&B £34

7P 2 (charged) *xmas*

International S% ✱Lunch £6—£8 Tea £1.50—£2 Dinner £7—£9 Wine £4.50 Last dinner 7.30pm

Credit cards 1 2 3 5

See advertisement on page 802

★**Moreland House** 106-108 Holgate Rd (Crest) ☎(0904) 35971

A pair of town houses has been combined and modified to create this friendly hotel. The accommodation is equipped to modern standards with a charm and character enhanced by the conservatory-style entrance lounge and cosy basement dining room.

13rm(3 4)(4fb) CTV in all bedrooms ✱sB&B £15—£17 dB&B £25 dB&B £28.50—£35

16P *xmas*

International V ✱Lunch £5—£8 Dinner £6.25—£10&alc Wine £4.50 Last dinner 9pm

Credit cards 1 3

★**Newington** 147 Mount Vale ☎(0904) 25173 due to change to 625173 Telex no 65430

Four town houses have been suitably converted to form this hotel on the A1036 (south) approach road into the city.

27rm(3 19)

Annexe: 15rm(1 14)(2fb) 2 CTV in all bedrooms ® →

Y

sB&B🛁🚿£25.95—£28.50
dB&B£36—£39
dB&B🛁🚿£43.90—£47.90 B

Lift CTV 32P 🏊(heated) sauna bath solarium Disco Sat *xmas*

V 🍷 ☕ Lunch £4—£5.95 Tea fr £1.50 Dinner £7.50—£7.95&alc Wine £4.95 Last dinner 8.30pm

Credit cards 1 2 3 5 V

○**York Crest** Cliffords Tower, Tower St (Crest) ☎(0904) 648111

130🛁🚿
Due to have opened Summer 1986

York

✕***Tony's*** 39 Tanner Row ☎(0904) 59622
This charming little restaurant has a cosy aperitif bar, and a warm, homely atmosphere prevails. Dishes are prepared by the chef/patron, and his family gives dedicated service.

Closed Sun & 2 wks Feb
Lunch not served Sat

🍽Greek 24 seats Lunch £5&alc Dinner £10alc Wine £4.50 Last dinner 10.30pm P

Credit cards 1 2 5 V

Overseas Offices of the British Tourist Authority

Australia

British Tourist Authority
Associated Midland House
171 Clarence St.
Sydney
N.S.W.
2000
T: (02) 9-8627

Belgium

British Tourist Authority
Rue de la Montagne 52 Bergstraat,
B2
1000 Brussels
T: 02/511.43.90

Brazil

British Tourist Authority
Edificio Vila Normanda
Avenida Ipiranga 318-A,
12° Andar, conj 1201
01046 São Paulo
= SP
T: 257-1834

Canada

British Tourist Authority
94 Cumberland Street, Suite 600
Toronto,
Ontario
M5R 3N3
T: (416) 925-6326

Denmark

British Tourist Authority
Møntergade 3
DK-1116 København
T: (01) 120793

France

British Tourist Authority
6 Place Vendôme
75001 Paris
T: 4296 4760

Germany

British Tourist Authority
Neue Mainzer Str. 22
6000 Frankfurt am Main 1
T: (0611) 2380 750

Ireland

British Tourist Authority
Clerys
O'Connell Street
Dublin 1

Italy

British Tourist Authority
Via S. Eufemia 5
00187 Roma
T: 678.4998 or 678.5548

Japan

British Tourist Authority
Tokyo Club Building
3-2-6 Kasumigaseki, Chiyoda-ku
Tokyo 100
T: (03) 581-3603

Mexico

British Tourist Authority
Edificio Alber
Paseo de la Reforma 332-5 Piso
06600 Mexico DF
T: 533 6375

Netherlands

British Travel Centre
Leidseplein 5
1017 PS
Amsterdam
T: (020) 23.46.67

New Zealand

British Tourist Authority
c/o Box 2402
Auckland

Norway

British Tourist Authority
Mariboes gt 11
0183 Oslo 1
T: (02) 41 1849

Singapore

British Tourist Authority
14 Collyer Quay 05-03
Singapore Rubber House
Singapore 0104
T: Singapore 2242966/7

South Africa

British Tourist Authority
7th Floor JBS Building
107 Commissioner Street
Johannesburg 2001
PO Box 6256
T: (011) 29 67 70

Spain

British Tourist Authority
Torre de Madrid 6/4
Plaza de España
Madrid 28008
T: (91) 241 1396

Sweden

British Tourist Authority
For visitors: Malmskillnadsg 42
1st Floor

For Mail: Box 7293
S-10390 Stockholm
T: 08-21 2444

Switzerland

British Tourist Authority
Limmatquai 78 8001 Zurich
T: 01/47 4277 or 47 4297

USA Chicago

British Tourist Authority
John Hancock Center Suite 3320
875 N. Michigan Avenue
Chicago Illinois 60611
T: (312) 787-0490

USA Dallas

British Tourist Authority
Plaza of the Americas
North Tower Suite 750
Dallas Texas 75201
T: (214) 720 4040

USA Los Angeles

British Tourist Authority
612 South Flower Street
Los Angeles CA 90017
T: (213) 623-8196

USA New York

British Tourist Authority
40 West 57th Street
New York N.Y. 10019
T: (212) 581-4700

Using hotels and restaurants -do's and don't's

Booking

Book as early as possible, particularly if accommodation is required during a holiday period (beginning of July — end September, plus public holidays and, in some parts of Scotland, during the skiing season). Some hotels, particularly in large towns and holiday centres, ask for a deposit, and some also ask for full payment in advance, especially for one-night bookings taken from chance callers. Not all hotels take advance bookings for bed and breakfast for only one or two nights, and some will not accept reservations from mid week.

Cancellation

Notify the hotel straight away if you are in any doubt about whether you can keep to your arrangements, once the booking has been confirmed. If the hotel cannot re-let your accommodation you may be liable to pay about two-thirds of the price you would have paid had you stayed there (your deposit will count towards this payment).

In Britain it is accepted that a legally binding contract has been made as soon as an intending guest accepts an offer of accommodation, either in writing or on the telephone. Illness is not accepted as a release from this contract. For these reasons you are advised to effect insurance cover, e.g. AA Travelsure against a possible cancellation.

Complaints

Members who wish to complain about food, services or facilities are urged to do so promptly on the spot. This should provide an opportunity for the hotelier or restaurateur to correct matters. If a personal approach fails, members should inform the AA regional office.

Dress

Some hotels and restaurants do not permit guests to enter the dining room or restaurant in informal or unconventional dress.

Fire precautions

As far as we can discover every hotel in Great Britain listed in this book has applied for, and not been refused a fire certificate. The Fire Precautions Act does not apply to the Channel Islands, or the Isle of Man, which exercise their own rules regarding fire precautions for hotels.

Licence to sell alcohol

All hotels and restaurants listed in this book are licensed for the sale and consumption of intoxicating liquor unless stated otherwise.

Children under 14 are not allowed in bars in England and Wales (including any place exclusively or mainly used for the sale and consumption of intoxicating liquor) during permitted hours (unless they are resident but not employed in the premises, or they are children of the licence-holder, or they are passing through the bar to some other part of the building which is not a bar, and from which there is no other convenient access or exit). This prohibition does not apply when a bar is usually set apart for serving table meals, and is then not used to sell intoxicating liquor except to those people taking table meals.

In licensed premises, alcoholic drinks may not be sold to, or purchased by people under the age of 18, neither may such people consume intoxicating liquor in a bar. 16-18 year olds may purchase beer, porter, cider or perry for consumption with a meal in a part of the premises (not a bar) set apart for the service of meals.

Basically similar laws apply in Scotland, but more details together with information pertaining to the Channel Islands, Isle of Man and Isles of Scilly may be found in AA leaflet HR192, *The Law about Licensing Hours and Children/Young Persons on Licensed Premises,* available from AA offices.

Licensing hours vary within the British Isles and details may be found in AA leaflet mentioned above.

Licensed hotels and restaurants are subject to separate rules from general licensing hours, although they normally follow them with extensions in certain circumstances and/or areas. Hotel residents may be served intoxicating liquor at any time, but special rules govern their guests. Children, if hotel guests, may sit in a bar (see above).

Club licences. At hotels which have registered clubs, membership cannot take effect, nor can drink be bought, until 48 hours after joining.

The contents of this section has been compiled by the AA on information available to it, as part of its service to members and the contents are believed correct as at March 1983. However, it should be noted that laws can change.

Meals

Unless otherwise stated, the terms quoted in the gazetteer section of this book are for full cooked breakfast. This is usually of three courses, including items like cereals with milk, eggs and bacon and toast with butter and marmalade. The items can vary considerably, however, and may feature regional specialities.

In some parts of Britain, particularly in Scotland, *high tea* (i.e. a savoury dish followed by bread and butter, scones, cakes, etc) is sometimes served instead of dinner which may, however, be available on request. The last time at which high tea or dinner may be ordered on weekdays is shown, but this may be varied at weekends.

On Sundays, some hotels serve the main meal at midday and provide only a cold supper in the evening. Some hotels serve meals only between stated hours, and the dining room is closed at other times.

Payment

Most hotels will only accept cheques in payment of accounts if notice is given and some form of identification (preferably a cheque card) is produced. Travellers' cheques issued by the leading banks and agencies are accepted by many hotels but not all. If a hotel accepts credit or charge cards, this is shown in its gazetteer entry (see page 55 for details).

Prices

The Hotel Industry voluntary Code of Booking Practice was revised in 1986, and the AA encourages its use in appropriate establishments. Its prime object is to ensure that the customer is clear about the precise services and facilities he is buying, and what price he will have to pay, before he commits himself to a contractually binding agreement. If the price has not been previously confirmed in writing, the guest should be handed a card at the time of registration, stipulating the total obligatory charge.

The Tourism (Sleeping Accommodation Price Display) Order 1977 compels hotels, motels, guesthouses, farmhouses, inns and self-catering accommodation with 4 or more letting bedrooms to display in entrance halls the minimum and maximum prices charged for each category of room. This order complements the voluntary Code of Booking Practice.

The tariffs quoted in the gazetteer of this book may be affected in the coming year by inflation, variations in the rate of VAT and many other factors. You should always ascertain the current prices before making a booking. Those given in this book have been provided by hoteliers and restaurateurs in good faith and must be accepted as indications rather than firm quotations. Where information about 1987 prices is not given, you are requested to make enquiries direct.

Bed and breakfast terms, which include a full cooked breakfast unless otherwise stated, are quoted in this guide. These show minimum and maximum prices for one and two persons, but charges may vary according to the time of year. Where a Continental breakfast is included in the price quoted, this is stated in the gazetteer.

Some hotels charge for bed, breakfast and dinner, whether dinner is taken or not. Many hotels, particularly in short-season holiday areas, accept period bookings only at full board rate.

For main meals served in hotel dining rooms and restaurants, minimum and maximum table d'hôte prices are given. Where an à la carte menu is available, the average price of a three course dinner and lunch is shown. Where establishments offer both types of menu, table d'hôte prices are the only ones shown but indicating that an à la carte menu is also available. All prices should include cover charge. The price of wine quoted is that of the cheapest full bottle (i.e. 70 cl.).

VAT is payable, in the United Kingdom and in the Isle of Man, on both basic prices and any service. VAT does not apply in the Channel Islands. With this exception, prices quoted in this guide are inclusive of VAT (and service where applicable).

Country-house hotels

Quiet, often secluded hotels are listed below. At an AA country-house hotel you should be assured of a restful night, together with a relaxed, informal atmosphere and personal welcome. On the other hand, some of the facilities may differ from those to be found in purpose-built, urban hotels of the same star rating.

It should be noted that not all rurally situated hotels are AA country-house hotels, neither are AA country-house hotels always located in an isolated situation.

See appropriate entry in gazetteer for other details including merit awards where these apply.

England

AVON

Town	Rating	Hotel
Bath	★★★	Combe Grove
Freshford	❀★★★	Homewood Park
Hunstrete	❀★★★	Hunstrete House
Lympsham	★★	Batch Farm Country
Rangeworthy	★	Rangeworthy Court
Thornbury	❀★★★	Thornbury Castle

BEDFORDSHIRE

Town	Rating	Hotel
Flitwick	❀★★★	Flitwick Manor

CHESHIRE

Town	Rating	Hotel
Nantwich	❀★★★	Rookery Hall
Tarporley	★★	Willington Hall

CLEVELAND

Town	Rating	Hotel
Easington	★★★	Grinkle Park

CORNWALL

Town	Rating	Hotel
Falmouth	★★★	Penmere Manor
Helland Bridge	★★★	Tredethy Country
Helston	★	Nansloe Manor Country
Lamorna Cove	★★★	Lamorna Cove
Liskeard	★★	Country Castle
Mawnan Smith	★★★	Meudon
Newquay	★★	Porth Veor Manor House
Penzance	★★★	Higher Faugan
Portscatho	★★	Roseland House
Ruan High Lanes	★★	Polsue Manor
St Agnes	★★	Rose in Vale Country House
St Austell	★★	Boscundle Manor
St Wenn	★	Wenn Manor
Talland Bay	★★★	Talland Bay

CUMBRIA

Town	Rating	Hotel
Alston	★★	Lovelady Shield
Ambleside	★★	Nanny Brow
Appleby-in-Westmorland	★★★	Appleby Manor
Bassenthwaite	★★★★	Armathwaite Hall
	★★	Overwater Hall
Blawith	★★	Highfield
Brampton	❀★★	Farlam Hall
Crosby-on-Eden	★★	Crosby Lodge
Grange-over-Sands	★★	Graythwaite Manor
Grasmere	❀★★	Michael's Nook
Hawkshead	★★★	Tarn Hows
Keswick	★★★	Underscar
	★★	Red House
Levens	★★	Heaves
Longtown	❀★	March Bank
Lorton	★	Hollin House
Loweswater	★★	Scale Hill
Pooley Bridge	❀❀★★★	Sharrow Bay
Thornthwaite	★★	Thwaite Howe
Underbarrow	★★	Greenriggs Country Hotel
Watermillock	★★★	Leeming Chase
	★	Old Church
Whitehaven	★★	Roseneath Country House
Windermere	★★★	Langdale Chase
	★★	Holbeck Ghyll
	★★	Lindeth Fell
	★★	Linthwaite
	★	Quarry Garth Country House
Witherslack	★	Old Vicarage Country House

DERBYSHIRE

Town	Rating	Hotel
Bakewell	★★	Croft Country House
Matlock	★★★	Riber Hall

DEVON

Town	Rating	Hotel
Ashburton	★★	Holne Chase
Barnstaple	★★	Downrew House
Bideford	★★	Yeoldon House
Bovey Tracey	★★	Edgemoor
Buckland in the Moor	★★	Buckland Hall Country House
Burrington	★★★	Northcote Manor
Chagford	❀★★★	Gidleigh Park
	★★★	Great Tree
	★★★	Mill End
	★★★	Teignworthy
Chittlehamholt	★★★	Highbullen
Clawton	★★	Court Barn Country House
Combeinteignhead	★★	Netherton House
Fairy Cross	★★★	Portledge
Gittisham	❀★★	Combe House
Haytor	★★★	Bel Alp House
Heddon's Mouth	★★	Heddon's Gate
Holbeton	★★★	Alston Hall
Honiton	★★★	Deer Park
Horns Cross	★★★	Foxdown Manor
Ilfracombe	★★	Langleigh Country
Kingsbridge	★★★	Buckland-Tout-Saints
Lee	★★	Lee Manor Country House Hotel & Restaurant
Lydford	★★	Lydford House
Lynmouth	★★	Beacon
Lynton	★★	Hewitts
	★	Combe Park
Martinhoe	★	Old Rectory
Mary Tavy	★★	Moorland Hall
Moretonhampstead	★★	Glebe House
Newton Ferrers	★★	Court House
Sidmouth	★★	Brownlands
South Brent	★★	Glazebrook House
Stoke Gabriel	★★★	Gabriel Court
Whimple	★★	Woodhayes

DORSET

Town	Rating	Hotel
Bridport	★	Little Wych Country House
Gillingham	❀★★	Stock Hill House
Milton Abbas	★★	Milton Manor
Studland	★★	Manor House

ESSEX

Town	Rating	Hotel
Dedham	❀★★★	Maison Talbooth

GLOUCESTERSHIRE

Town	Rating	Hotel
Bibury	★★	Bibury Court
Buckland	❀★★★	Buckland Manor
Cheltenham	❀★★★	Greenway
Coleford	★	Lambsquay
Lower Slaughter	★★★	Manor
Stroud	★★★	Burleigh Court
Tetbury	★★★	Calcot Manor
Upper Slaughter	★★★	Lords of the Manor

HAMPSHIRE

Town	Rating	Hotel
Brockenhurst	★★	Whitley Ridge Restaurant & Country House
Burley	★★	Moorhill House
Hurstbourne Tarrant	★★	Esseborne Manor
Lymington	★★★	Passford House
Lyndhurst	❀★★★	Parkhill
New Milton	❀❀★★★★	Chewton Glen
Rotherwick	★★★★	Tylney Hall
Winchester	★★★	Lainston House
Woodlands	★★	Woodlands Lodge

HEREFORD & WORCESTER

Town	Rating	Hotel
Abberley	❀★★★	Elms
Broadway	★★	Collin House
Ledbury	❀★★	Hope End Country House
Malvern	★★★	Cottage-in-the-Wood
	★★	Holdfast Cottage
Pencraig	★★	Pencraig Court

HUMBERSIDE

Town	Rating	Hotel
Driffield, Great	★★	Wold Country House

ISLE OF WIGHT

Town	Rating	Hotel
Bembridge	★★	Elm Country
Ventnor	★	Madeira Hall
Whippingham	★★	Padmore House

KENT

Town	Rating	Hotel
Ashford	❀★★★★	Eastwell Manor
Cranbrook	★★	Kennel Holt

LEICESTERSHIRE

Town	Rating	Hotel
Oakham	❀❀★★★	Hambleton Hall

MANCHESTER, GREATER

Town	Rating	Hotel
Bolton	★★★	Egerton House

NORFOLK
Bunwell ★★ Bunwell Manor
Grimston ❀★★★ Congham Hall Country House
Shipdham ★★ Shipdham Place
Thorpe Market ★★ Elderton Lodge
Witchingham, Great ★★ Lenwade House

NORTHUMBERLAND
Otterburn ★★ Otterburn Tower
Powburn ❀★★ Breamish House

OXFORDSHIRE
Horton-cum-Studley ★★★ Studley Priory
Milton, Gt ❀❀★★★ Le Manoir aux Quat' Saisons

SHROPSHIRE
Ellesmere ★★ Grange
Oswestry ★★ Sweeney Hall
Worfield ★★ Old Vicarage

SOMERSET
Dulverton ★★★ Carnarvon Arms
★★ Ashwick House
★★ Three Acres Captain's Country
Evercreech ★★ Maesmoor Glen
Holford ★★ Alfoxton Park
★★ Combe House
Shapwick ★★ Shapwick House
Shipham ★★ Daneswood House
Simonsbath ★★ Simonsbath House
Ston Easton ★★★ Ston Easton Park
Wheddon Cross ★★ Raleigh Manor Country House
Wincanton ★★ Holbrook House
Withypool ★★ Westerclose Country House

STAFFORDSHIRE
Rangemore ★★ Needwood Manor

SUFFOLK
Brome ★★ Oaksmere
Woodbridge ★★★ Seckford Hall

SURREY
Bagshot ★★★★ Pennyhill Park
Farnham ★★ Trevena House

SUSSEX, EAST
Battle ★★★ Netherfield Place
Rushlake Green ★★★ Priory Country House
Stone Cross ★★★ Glyndley Manor
Wadhurst ❀★★ Spindlewood

SUSSEX, WEST
Arundel ★ Burpham Country
Climping ★★★ Bailiffscourt
Cuckfield ★★ Hilton Park
East Grinstead ❀★★★ Gravetye Manor
Lower Beeding ❀★★★ South Lodge
Thakeham ❀★★★ Abingworth Hall

WARWICKSHIRE
Billesley ★★★ Billesley Manor
Ettington ❀★★ Chase Country House
Leamington Spa (Royal) ❀❀★★★ Mallory Court
Wishaw ★★★ Moxhull Hall

WILTSHIRE
Castle Combe ★★★ Manor House
Limpley Stoke ★★★ Cliffe
Malmesbury ★★★ Whatley Manor
Warminster ★★★★ Bishopstrow House

YORKSHIRE, NORTH
Arncliffe ★★ Amerdale House
Ayton, Great ❀★★★ Ayton Hall
Crathorne ★★★★ Crathorne Hall
Hackness ★★★ Hackness Grange
Kirkby Fleetham ★★★ Kirkby Fleetham Hall
Lastingham ★★ Lastingham Grange
Markington ★★★ Hob Green
Masham ★★ Jervaulx Hall
Monk Fryston ★★★ Monk Fryston Hall
Northallerton ★★★ Solberge Hall
Scarborough ★★ Wrea Head Country
Whitwell-on-the-Hill ★★★ Whitwell Hall Country House

YORKSHIRE, WEST
Wentbridge ★★★ Wentbridge House

Channel Islands

JERSEY
Rozel Bay ★★ Chateau la Chaire
St Saviour ❀★★★★ Longueville Manor

Wales

CLWYD
Llangollen ★★★ Bryn Howel

DYFED
Aberystwyth ★★★ Conrah
Crugybar ★★ Glanrannell Park
Eglwysfach ★★★ Ynyshir Hall
Hebron ★ Preseli Country House
Lamphey ★★★ Court
Llechryd ★★★ Castell Malgwyn
St Davids ★★★ Warpool Court

GWYNEDD
Aberdovey ★★★ Plas Penhelig
Abersoch ❀★★★ Porth Tocyn
Beddgelert ★ Bryn Eglwys
Betws-y-Coed ★★★ Plas Hall
Criccieth ★★★ Bron Eifion
★★ Parciau Manor
Llanbedr ★★ Cae Nest Hall
Llandderfel ★★★ Palé Hall
Llandudno ★★★ Bodysgallen Hall
Llanrwst ★★★ Plas Maenan
Pennal ★★ Llugwy Hall Country House
Rowen ★ Tir-y-Coed Country House
Talsarnau ★★ Maes-y-Neuadd

POWYS
Crickhowell ★★ Gliffaes
Llanfyllin ★★ Bodfach Hall
Llangammarch Wells ★★★ Lake

Scotland

BORDERS
Chirnside ★ Chirnside Country House
Dryburgh ★★★ Dryburgh Abbey
Ettrick Bridge ★★ Ettrickshaws
Greenlaw ★★ Purves Hall
Kelso ❀★★★ Sunlaws House
Peebles ★★ Cringletie House
★★ Venlaw Castle
St Boswells ★★★ Dryburgh Abbey
Walkerburn ★★ Tweed Valley

CENTRAL
Callander ❀★★★ Roman Camp
Dunblane ❀★★★ Cromlix House

DUMFRIES & GALLOWAY
Auchencairn ★★★ Balcary Bay
Borgue ★★ Senwick House
Colvend ★★ Clonyard House
Crossmichael ★★ Culgruff House
Newton Stewart ❀★★★ Kirroughtree
Portpatrick ❀★★ Knockinaam Lodge
Port William ★★★ Corsemalzie House
Rockcliffe ★★★ Baron's Craig
Ruthwell ★ Kirklands

FIFE
Letham ★★★ Fernie Castle

GRAMPIAN
Banchory ★★★ Banchory Lodge
★★★ Raemoir
Huntly ★★ Castle
Kildrummy ❀★★★ Kildrummy Castle
Rothes ★★★ Rothes Glen

HIGHLAND
Achnasheen ★★ Ledgowan Lodge
Arisaig ❀★★★ Arisaig House
Cannich ★★ Cozac Lodge
Drumnadrochit ❀★★ Polmaily House
Dulnain Bridge ★★ Muckrach Lodge
Fort William ❀❀★★★★ Inverlochy Castle
Glenborrodale ★★ Glenborrodale Castle
Invergarry ★★ Glengarry Castle
Inverness ★★★★ Culloden House
★★ Dunain Park
Isle Ornsay, (Skye, Isle of) ❀★★ Kinloch Lodge
Kentallen ❀★★ Ardsheal House
Leckmelm ★ Tir Aluinn
Muir of Ord ★★ Ord House
Nairn ★★★★ Newton
Skeabost Bridge (Skye, Isle of) ★★★ Skeabost House
Torridon ★★ Loch Torridon
Whitebridge ❀★★ Knockie Lodge

LOTHIAN
Aberlady ★★ Green Craig House
Bonnyrigg ★★★★ Dalhousie Castle
Gullane ❀★★★ Greywalls
Humbie ★★★ Johnstounburn House
Uphall ★★★ Houstoun House

STRATHCLYDE
Eriska ★★★ Isle of Eriska
Kilchrenan ❀★★★ Ardanaiseig
★★★ Taychreggan
Langbank ❀★★★ Gleddoch House
Skelmorlie ★★★ Manor Park
Stewarton ❀★★★ Chapeltoun House

TAYSIDE
Auchterhouse ★★★ Old Mansion House
Blairgowrie ❀★★★ Kinloch House
★★ Altamount House
Cleish ❀★★★ Nivingston House
Glenshee (Spital of) ★★ Dalmunzie
Kinclaven ★★★ Ballathie House
Meigle ★★ Kings of Kinloch
Perth ❀★★★ Balcraig House
Pitlochry ★★ Pine Trees
Strathtummel ★★ Port-an-Eilean

WESTERN ISLES
Scarista (Harris, Isle of) ❀★★ Scarista House

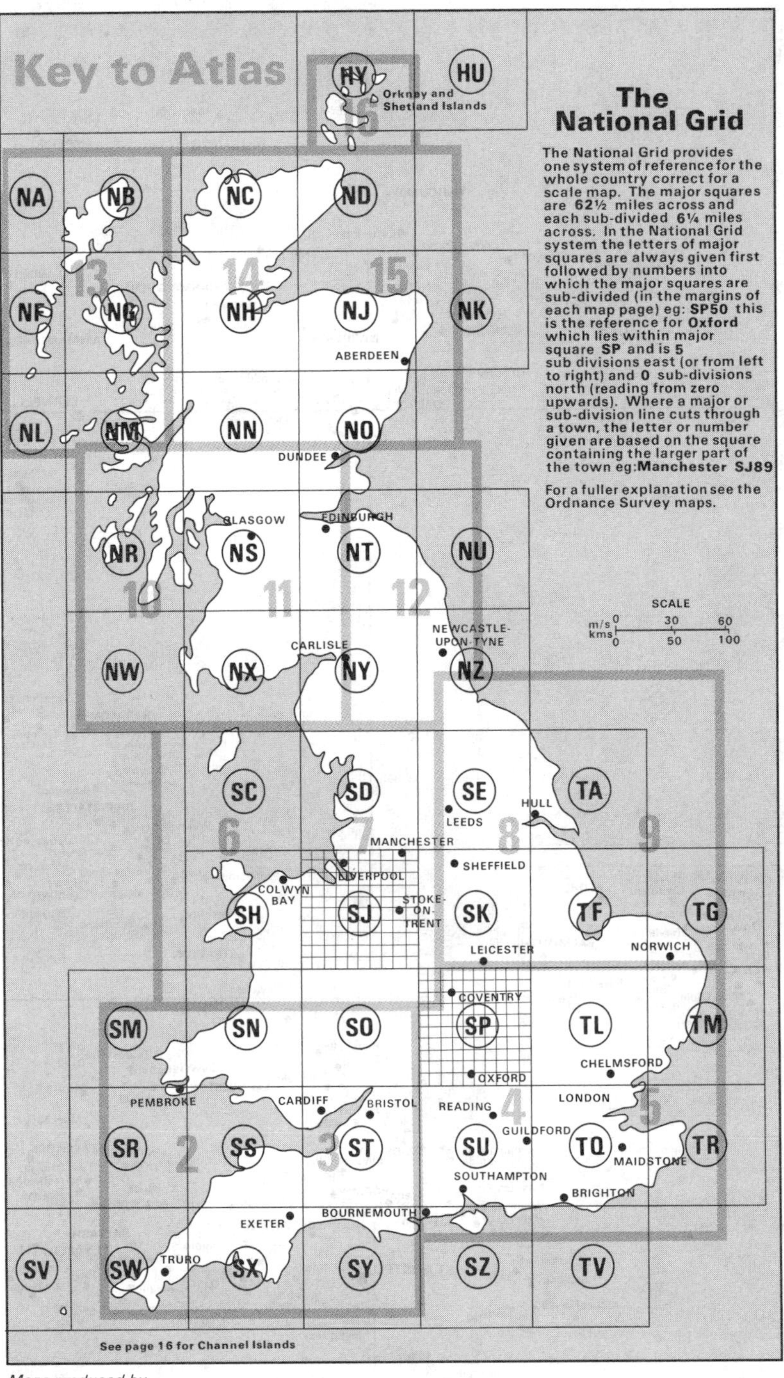

Key to Atlas
The National Grid
The National Grid provides one system of reference for the whole country correct for a scale map. The major squares are 62½ miles across and each sub-divided 6¼ miles across. In the National Grid system the letters of major squares are always given first followed by numbers into which the major squares are sub-divided (in the margins of each map page) eg: SP50 this is the reference for Oxford which lies within major square SP and is 5 sub divisions east (or from left to right) and 0 sub-divisions north (reading from zero upwards). Where a major or sub-division line cuts through a town, the letter or number given are based on the square containing the larger part of the town eg: Manchester SJ89
For a fuller explanation see the Ordnance Survey maps.
SCALE
m/s 0 30 60
kms 0 50 100
HY
HU
Orkney and Shetland Islands
16
NA
NB
NC
ND
13
14
15
NF
NG
NH
NJ
NK
ABERDEEN
NL
NM
NN
NO
DUNDEE
GLASGOW
EDINBURGH
NR
NS
NT
NU
10
11
12
NEWCASTLE-UPON-TYNE
CARLISLE
NW
NX
NY
NZ
SC
SD
SE
TA
LEEDS
HULL
6
7
8
9
MANCHESTER
SHEFFIELD
LIVERPOOL
COLWYN BAY
SH
SJ
STOKE-ON-TRENT
SK
TF
TG
NORWICH
LEICESTER
COVENTRY
SM
SN
SO
SP
TL
TM
CHELMSFORD
OXFORD
PEMBROKE
CARDIFF
BRISTOL
READING
4
LONDON
5
SR
SS
ST
SU
GUILDFORD
TQ
TR
2
3
MAIDSTONE
SOUTHAMPTON
BRIGHTON
EXETER
BOURNEMOUTH
SV
SW
TRURO
SX
SY
SZ
TV
See page 16 for Channel Islands

Maps produced by

The AA Cartographic Department (Publications Division), Fanum House, Basingstoke, Hampshire RG21 2EA

This atlas is for location purposes only: see member's Handbook for current road and AA road services information.

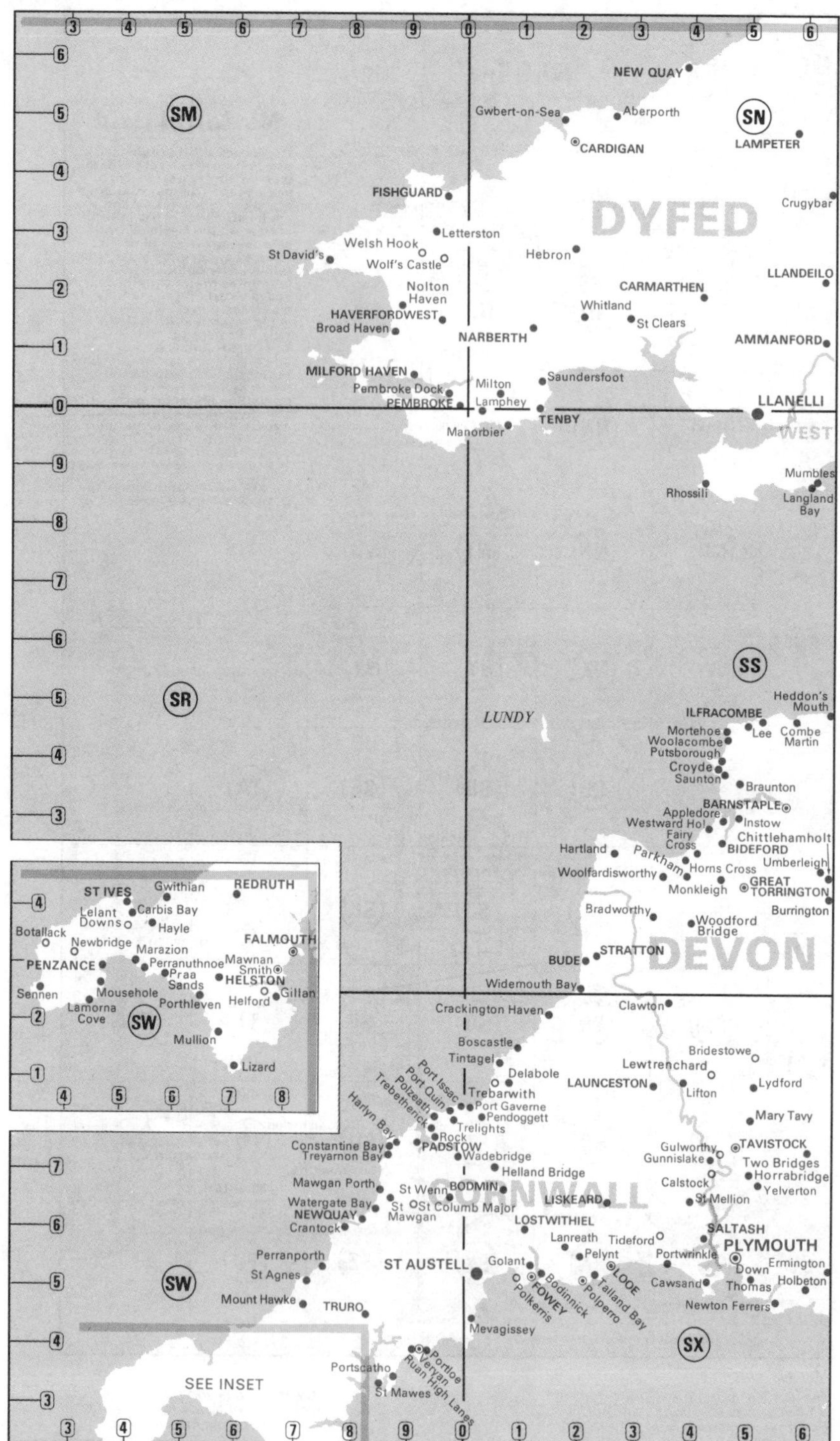

For continuation pages refer to numbered arrows

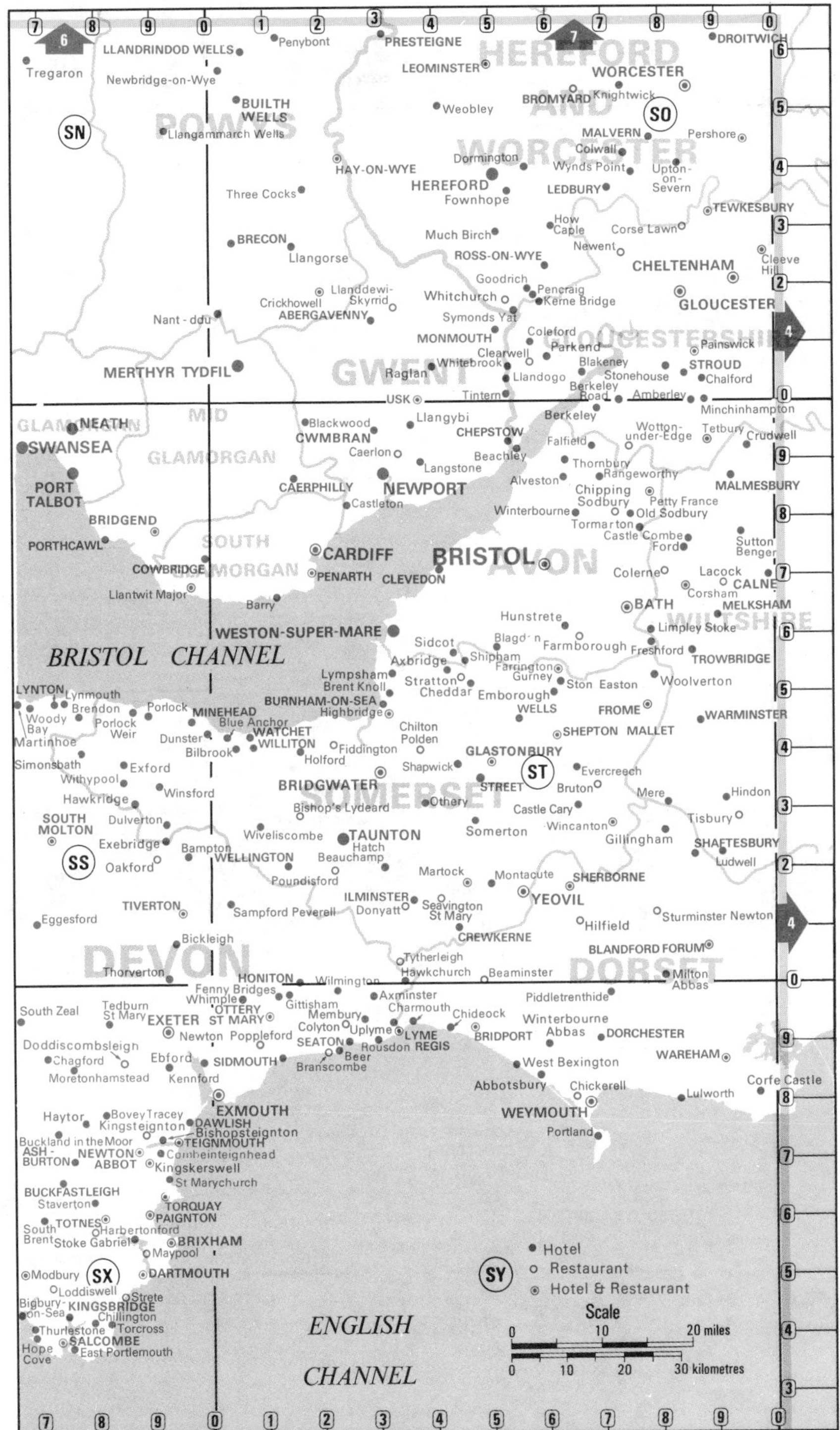

SN
SO
SS
ST
SX
SY
HEREFORD AND WORCESTER
POWYS
GWENT
GLOUCESTERSHIRE
MID GLAMORGAN
SOUTH GLAMORGAN
AVON
WILTSHIRE
SOMERSET
DEVON
DORSET
BRISTOL CHANNEL
ENGLISH CHANNEL
Tregaron
LLANDRINDOD WELLS
Penybont
PRESTEIGNE
LEOMINSTER
DROITWICH
Newbridge-on-Wye
WORCESTER
BROMYARD
Knightwick
BUILTH WELLS
Weobley
Llangammarch Wells
MALVERN
Pershore
Colwall
HAY-ON-WYE
Dormington
Wynds Point
Upton-on-Severn
HEREFORD
Fownhope
LEDBURY
Three Cocks
TEWKESBURY
How Caple
Corse Lawn
BRECON
Much Birch
Newent
Llangorse
ROSS-ON-WYE
CHELTENHAM
Cleeve Hill
Goodrich
Llanddewi-Skyrrid
Crickhowell
Whitchurch
Pencraig
Kerne Bridge
GLOUCESTER
ABERGAVENNY
Symonds Yat
Nant-ddu
Coleford
MONMOUTH
Parkend
Painswick
Clearwell
Blakeney
STROUD
MERTHYR TYDFIL
Whitebrook
Raglan
Llandogo
Stonehouse
Chalford
Tintern
Berkeley Road
Amberley
USK
Minchinhampton
NEATH
Blackwood
Llangybi
Berkeley
SWANSEA
CWMBRAN
CHEPSTOW
Wotton-under-Edge
Tetbury
Crudwell
Caerlon
Falfield
Beachley
Thornbury
PORT TALBOT
Langstone
Rangeworthy
CAERPHILLY
NEWPORT
Alveston
Chipping Sodbury
Petty France
MALMESBURY
Castleton
Winterbourne
Old Sodbury
BRIDGEND
Tormarton
Castle Combe
Sutton Benger
PORTHCAWL
Ford
CARDIFF
BRISTOL
COWBRIDGE
PENARTH
CLEVEDON
Colerne
Lacock
CALNE
Llantwit Major
Corsham
Barry
BATH
MELKSHAM
Hunstrete
WESTON-SUPER-MARE
Limpley Stoke
Sidcot
Farmborough
Freshford
Axbridge
Shipham
TROWBRIDGE
Farrington Gurney
Lympsham
Stratton
Woolverton
Brent Knoll
Cheddar
Emborough
Ston Easton
LYNTON
Lynmouth
BURNHAM-ON-SEA
Highbridge
WELLS
FROME
Brendon
Porlock
MINEHEAD
Woody Bay
Porlock Weir
Blue Anchor
Chilton Polden
WARMINSTER
Martinhoe
Dunster
WATCHET
SHEPTON MALLET
Bilbrook
WILLITON
Fiddington
Simonsbath
Holford
GLASTONBURY
Exford
Shapwick
Evercreech
Withypool
BRIDGWATER
STREET
Bruton
Winsford
Hindon
Hawkridge
Mere
Othery
Bishop's Lydeard
Castle Cary
Tisbury
SOUTH MOLTON
Dulverton
Wincanton
Wiveliscombe
Somerton
Gillingham
Exebridge
TAUNTON
SHAFTESBURY
Bampton
Hatch Beauchamp
Ludwell
WELLINGTON
Oakford
Martock
Montacute
SHERBORNE
Poundisford
TIVERTON
ILMINSTER
Donyatt
YEOVIL
Seavington St Mary
Sampford Peverell
Sturminster Newton
Eggesford
Hilfield
CREWKERNE
Bickleigh
BLANDFORD FORUM
Tytherleigh
Hawkchurch
Thorverton
Beaminster
HONITON
Milton Abbas
Wilmington
Fenny Bridges
Axminster
Piddletrenthide
Whimple
Gittisham
South Zeal
Tedburn St Mary
OTTERY ST MARY
Membury
Charmouth
Chideock
EXETER
Colyton
Uplyme
Winterbourne Abbas
LYME REGIS
Newton Poppleford
BRIDPORT
DORCHESTER
Doddiscombsleigh
SEATON
Rousdon
Chagford
Ebford
Beer
WAREHAM
SIDMOUTH
Branscombe
West Bexington
Moretonhampstead
Kenford
Corfe Castle
Abbotsbury
Chickerell
Lulworth
EXMOUTH
WEYMOUTH
Haytor
Bovey Tracey
DAWLISH
Portland
Kingsteignton
Bishopsteignton
Buckland in the Moor
TEIGNMOUTH
ASH-BURTON
NEWTON ABBOT
Combeinteignhead
Kingskerswell
St Marychurch
BUCKFASTLEIGH
Staverton
TORQUAY
PAIGNTON
TOTNES
South Brent
Harbertonford
Stoke Gabriel
BRIXHAM
Maypool
Modbury
DARTMOUTH
Loddiswell
Strete
Bigbury-on-Sea
KINGSBRIDGE
Chillington
Thurlestone
Torcross
SALCOMBE
Hope Cove
East Portlemouth
● Hotel
○ Restaurant
◉ Hotel & Restaurant
Scale
0 10 20 miles
0 10 20 30 kilometres

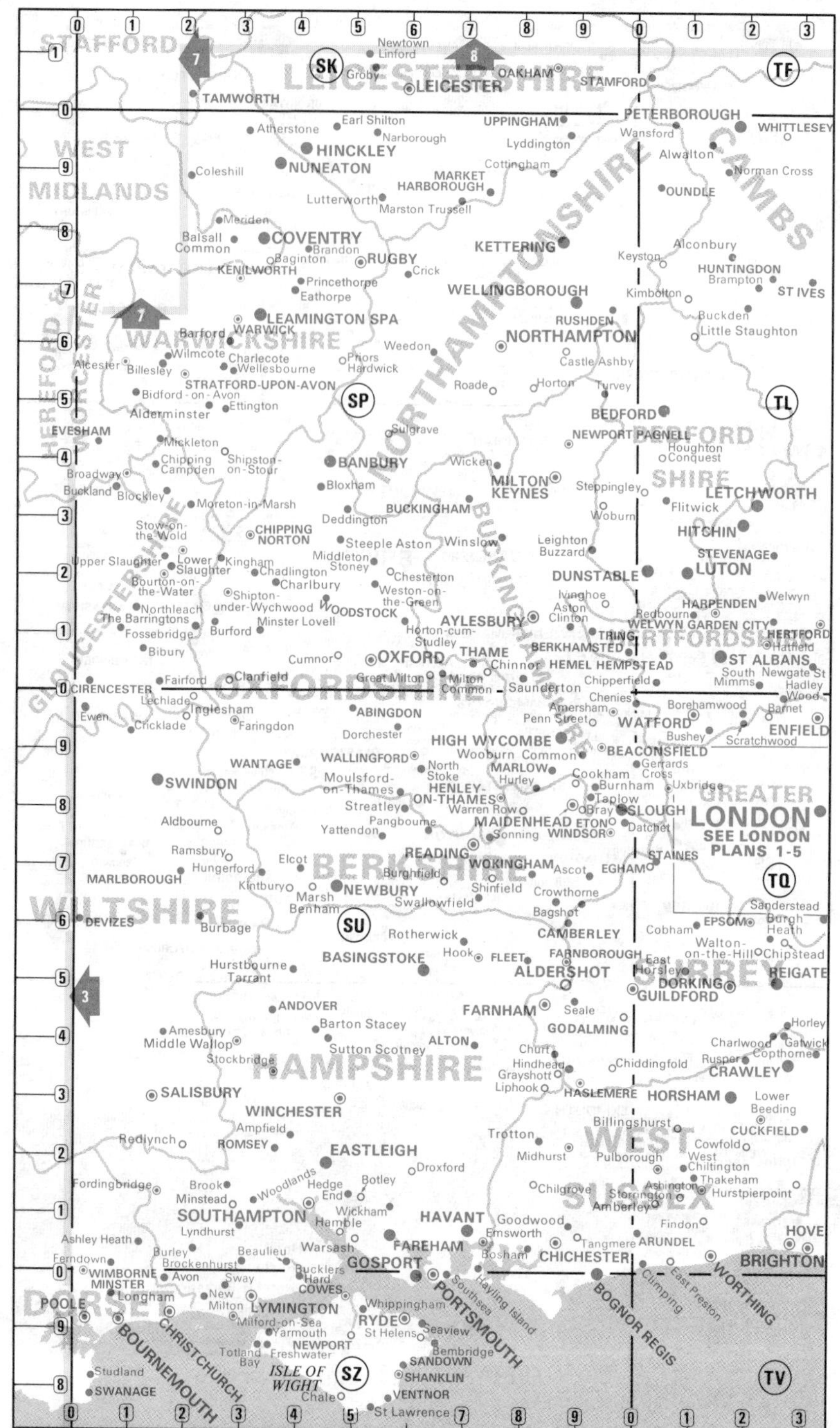

For continuation pages refer to numbered arrows

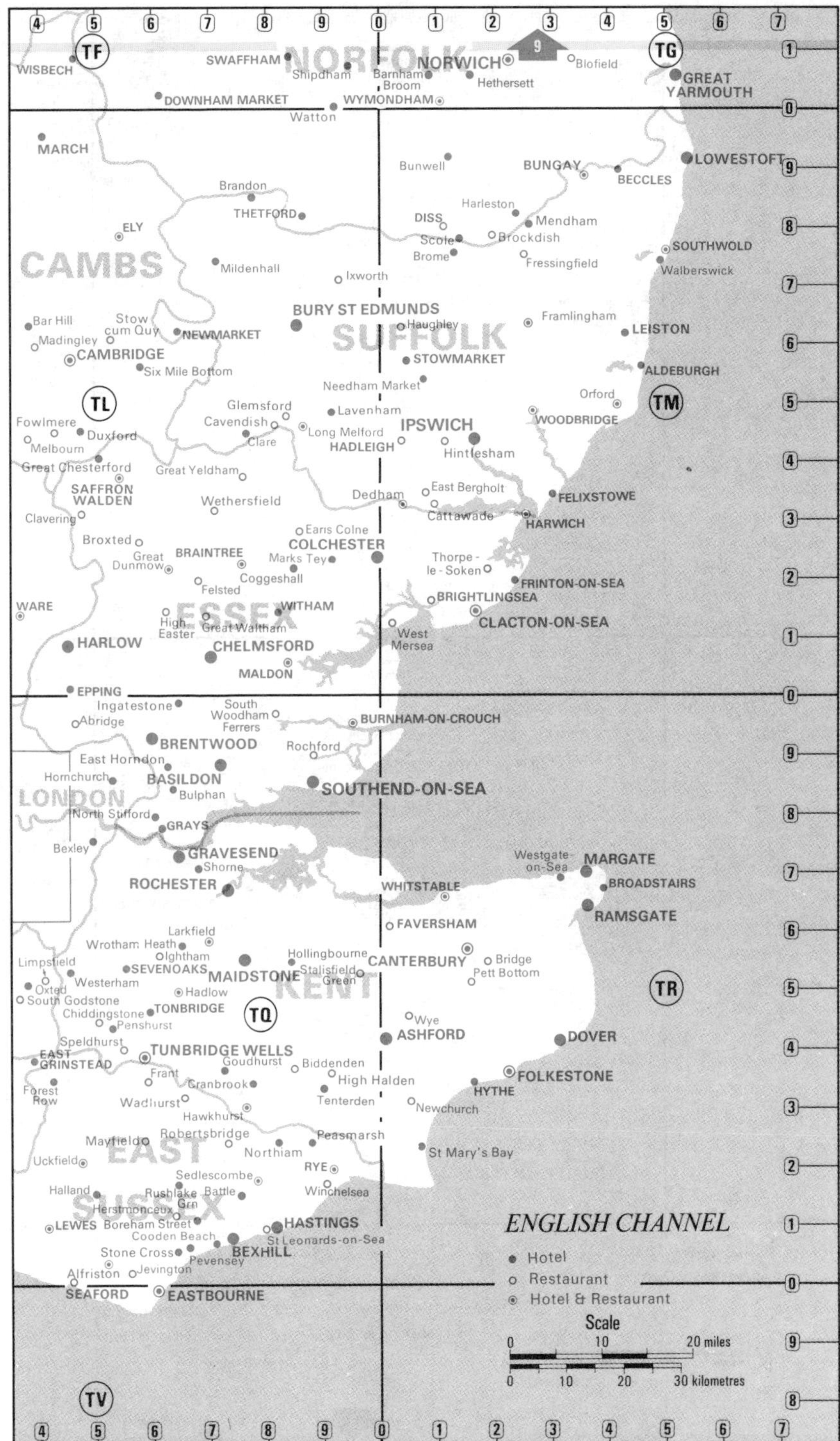

TF
TG
NORFOLK
WISBECH
SWAFFHAM
Shipdham
Barnham Broom
NORWICH
Hethersett
Blofield
GREAT YARMOUTH
DOWNHAM MARKET
WYMONDHAM
Watton
MARCH
Bunwell
BUNGAY
BECCLES
LOWESTOFT
Brandon
THETFORD
Harleston
DISS
Mendham
Scole
Brockdish
ELY
Brome
SOUTHWOLD
CAMBS
Mildenhall
Ixworth
Fressingfield
Walberswick
BURY ST EDMUNDS
Framlingham
Bar Hill
Stow cum Quy
Haughley
LEISTON
Madingley
NEWMARKET
SUFFOLK
CAMBRIDGE
STOWMARKET
Six Mile Bottom
ALDEBURGH
Needham Market
Orford
TL
Glemsford
TM
Lavenham
Cavendish
WOODBRIDGE
IPSWICH
Fowlmere
Duxford
Clare
Long Melford
Melbourn
HADLEIGH
Hintlesham
Great Chesterford
Great Yeldham
SAFFRON WALDEN
East Bergholt
Dedham
FELIXSTOWE
Wethersfield
Clavering
Cattawade
HARWICH
Earls Colne
Broxted
COLCHESTER
Great Dunmow
BRAINTREE
Marks Tey
Thorpe-le-Soken
Coggeshall
Felsted
FRINTON-ON-SEA
BRIGHTLINGSEA
WARE
ESSEX
WITHAM
High Easter
Great Waltham
West Mersea
CLACTON-ON-SEA
HARLOW
CHELMSFORD
MALDON
EPPING
Ingatestone
South Woodham Ferrers
Abridge
BURNHAM-ON-CROUCH
BRENTWOOD
Rochford
East Horndon
Hornchurch
BASILDON
SOUTHEND-ON-SEA
LONDON
Bulphan
North Stifford
GRAYS
Bexley
GRAVESEND
Shorne
Westgate-on-Sea
MARGATE
ROCHESTER
BROADSTAIRS
WHITSTABLE
RAMSGATE
FAVERSHAM
Larkfield
Wrotham Heath
Ightham
Hollingbourne
Limpsfield
CANTERBURY
Bridge
SEVENOAKS
MAIDSTONE
Stalisfield Green
Pett Bottom
Westerham
Oxted
Hadlow
KENT
South Godstone
TR
Chiddingstone
TONBRIDGE
TQ
Penshurst
Wye
Speldhurst
ASHFORD
DOVER
EAST GRINSTEAD
TUNBRIDGE WELLS
Goudhurst
Biddenden
Frant
FOLKESTONE
Forest Row
Cranbrook
High Halden
HYTHE
Wadhurst
Tenterden
Newchurch
Hawkhurst
Robertsbridge
Mayfield
Peasmarsh
EAST
Northiam
St Mary's Bay
Uckfield
RYE
Sedlescombe
Winchelsea
Halland
Rushlake Grn
Battle
SUSSEX
Herstmonceux
HASTINGS
ENGLISH CHANNEL
LEWES
Boreham Street
Cooden Beach
St Leonards-on-Sea
Stone Cross
BEXHILL
Pevensey
Alfriston
Jevington
SEAFORD
EASTBOURNE
TV
Hotel
Restaurant
Hotel & Restaurant
Scale
0 10 20 miles
0 10 20 30 kilometres
9
4 5 6 7 8 9 0 1 2 3 4 5 6 7
1 0 9 8 7 6 5 4 3 2 1 0 9 8 7 6 5 4 3 2 1 0 9 8

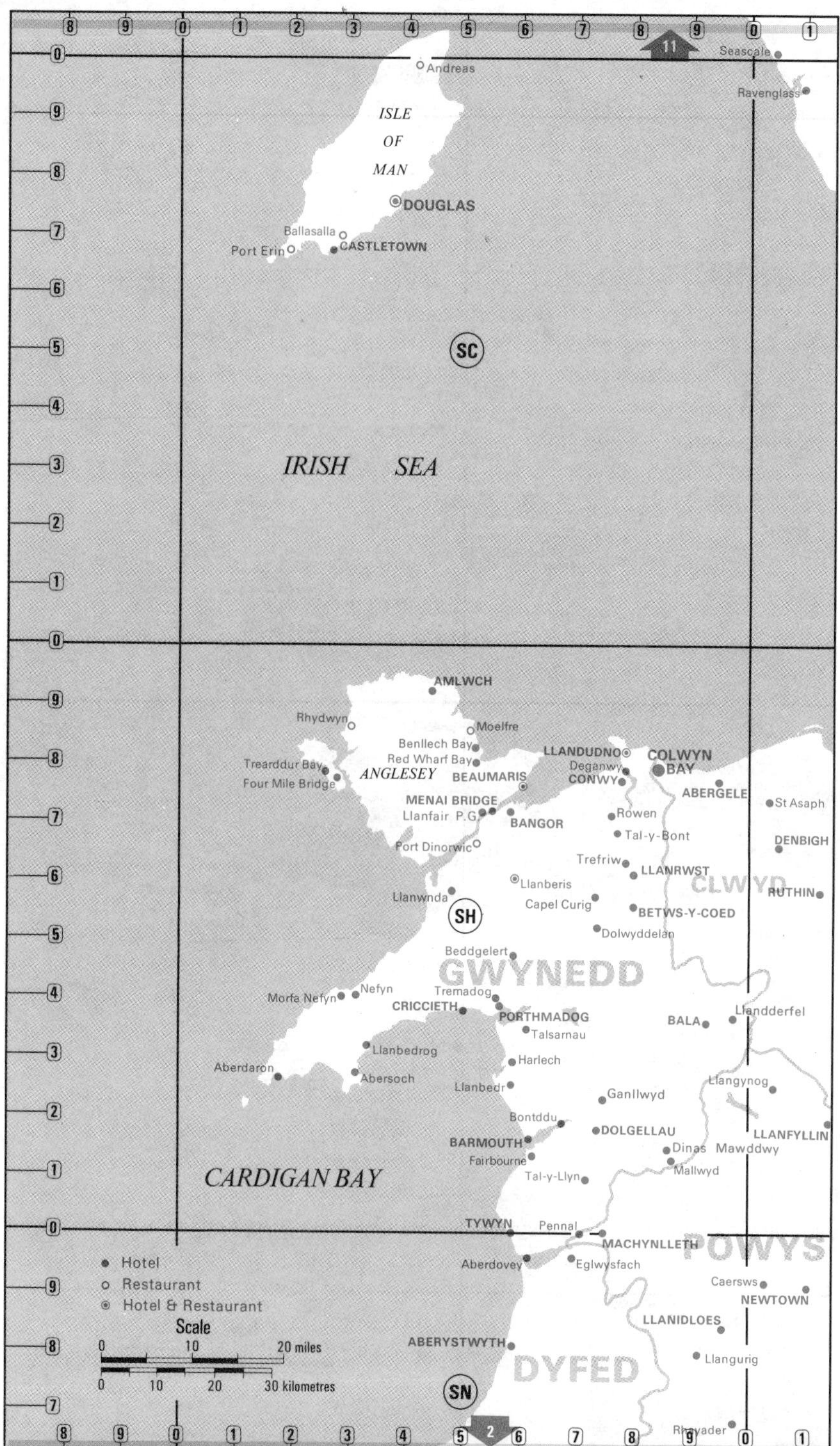

Seascale
Ravenglass
Andreas
ISLE OF MAN
DOUGLAS
Ballasalla
Port Erin
CASTLETOWN
SC
IRISH SEA
AMLWCH
Rhydwyn
Moelfre
Benllech Bay
Red Wharf Bay
Trearddur Bay
Four Mile Bridge
ANGLESEY
BEAUMARIS
LLANDUDNO
Deganwy
CONWY
COLWYN BAY
ABERGELE
St Asaph
MENAI BRIDGE
Llanfair P.G.
BANGOR
Rowen
Tal-y-Bont
DENBIGH
Port Dinorwic
Trefriw
LLANRWST
CLWYD
RUTHIN
Llanberis
Llanwnda
Capel Curig
BETWS-Y-COED
SH
Dolwyddelan
Beddgelert
GWYNEDD
Tremadog
Nefyn
Morfa Nefyn
CRICCIETH
PORTHMADOG
Talsarnau
BALA
Llandderfel
Llanbedrog
Harlech
Aberdaron
Abersoch
Llanbedr
Ganllwyd
Llangynog
Bontddu
DOLGELLAU
LLANFYLLIN
BARMOUTH
Fairbourne
Dinas Mawddwy
Mallwyd
Tal-y-Llyn
CARDIGAN BAY
TYWYN
Pennal
MACHYNLLETH
POWYS
Aberdovey
Eglwysfach
Caersws
NEWTOWN
LLANIDLOES
ABERYSTWYTH
Llangurig
DYFED
SN
Rhayader
11
2
• Hotel
o Restaurant
◉ Hotel & Restaurant
Scale
0 10 20 miles
0 10 20 30 kilometres

For continuation pages refer to numbered arrows

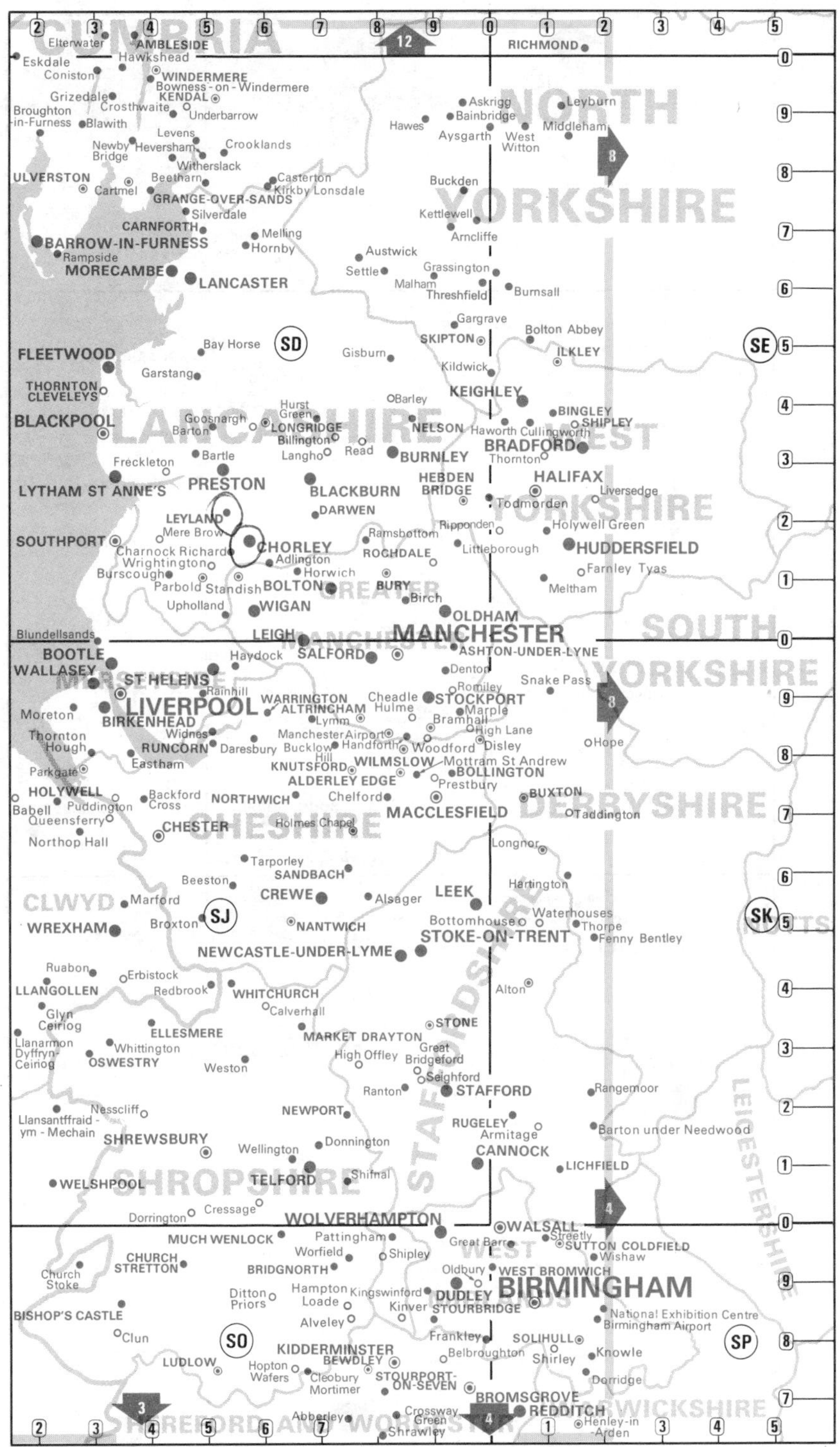
CUMBRIA
NORTH YORKSHIRE
LANCASHIRE
WEST YORKSHIRE
GREATER MANCHESTER
SOUTH YORKSHIRE
MERSEYSIDE
CHESHIRE
DERBYSHIRE
CLWYD
STAFFORDSHIRE
SHROPSHIRE
WEST MIDLANDS
HEREFORD AND WORCESTER
WARWICKSHIRE
LEICESTERSHIRE
NOTTS
12
8
8
4
3
4
SD
SE
SJ
SK
SO
SP
Elterwater
AMBLESIDE
Eskdale
Hawkshead
Coniston
WINDERMERE
Bowness-on-Windermere
Grizedale
KENDAL
Broughton -in-Furness
Crosthwaite
Underbarrow
Blawith
Levens
Newby Bridge
Heversham
Crooklands
Witherslack
ULVERSTON
Cartmel
Beetham
Casterton
Kirkby Lonsdale
GRANGE-OVER-SANDS
Silverdale
CARNFORTH
Melling
Hornby
BARROW-IN-FURNESS
Rampside
MORECAMBE
LANCASTER
RICHMOND
Askrigg
Leyburn
Bainbridge
Hawes
Aysgarth
West Witton
Middleham
Buckden
Kettlewell
Arncliffe
Austwick
Settle
Grassington
Malham
Threshfield
Burnsall
Gargrave
SKIPTON
Bolton Abbey
ILKLEY
Bay Horse
FLEETWOOD
Gisburn
Kildwick
Garstang
THORNTON CLEVELEYS
Barley
KEIGHLEY
BINGLEY
BLACKPOOL
Hurst Green
Goosnargh
Barton
LONGRIDGE
Billington
NELSON
Haworth
Cullingworth
SHIPLEY
BRADFORD
Freckleton
Bartle
Langho
Read
BURNLEY
Thornton
LYTHAM ST ANNE'S
PRESTON
BLACKBURN
HEBDEN BRIDGE
HALIFAX
Liversedge
LEYLAND
DARWEN
Todmorden
Mere Brow
Ramsbottom
Ripponden
Holywell Green
SOUTHPORT
CHORLEY
ROCHDALE
Littleborough
HUDDERSFIELD
Charnock Richard
Adlington
Wrightington
Horwich
Burscough
Farnley Tyas
Parbold
Standish
BOLTON
BURY
Meltham
Birch
Upholland
WIGAN
OLDHAM
Blundellsands
LEIGH
MANCHESTER
BOOTLE
SALFORD
ASHTON-UNDER-LYNE
WALLASEY
Haydock
Denton
ST HELENS
Romiley
Snake Pass
Rainhill
LIVERPOOL
WARRINGTON
Cheadle Hulme
STOCKPORT
ALTRINCHAM
Marple
Moreton
BIRKENHEAD
Lymm
Bramhall
Thornton Hough
Widnes
Manchester Airport
High Lane
Hope
RUNCORN
Daresbury
Bucklow Hill
Handforth
Woodford
Disley
Eastham
KNUTSFORD
WILMSLOW
Mottram St Andrew
Parkgate
ALDERLEY EDGE
BOLLINGTON
Prestbury
HOLYWELL
Backford Cross
NORTHWICH
Chelford
BUXTON
Babell
Puddington
MACCLESFIELD
Taddington
Queensferry
CHESTER
Holmes Chapel
Northop Hall
Longnor
Tarporley
Beeston
SANDBACH
Hartington
Marford
CREWE
Alsager
LEEK
Waterhouses
WREXHAM
Broxton
NANTWICH
Bottomhouse
Thorpe
STOKE-ON-TRENT
Fenny Bentley
NEWCASTLE-UNDER-LYME
Ruabon
Erbistock
LLANGOLLEN
Redbrook
WHITCHURCH
Alton
Glyn Ceiriog
Calverhall
STONE
ELLESMERE
MARKET DRAYTON
Llanarmon Dyffryn-Ceiriog
Whittington
Great Bridgeford
High Offley
OSWESTRY
Weston
Seighford
Ranton
STAFFORD
Rangemoor
Nesscliff
NEWPORT
Llansantffraid-ym-Mechain
RUGELEY
Armitage
Barton under Needwood
SHREWSBURY
Wellington
Donnington
CANNOCK
LICHFIELD
WELSHPOOL
TELFORD
Shifnal
Dorrington
Cressage
WOLVERHAMPTON
WALSALL
MUCH WENLOCK
Pattingham
Great Barr
Streetly
SUTTON COLDFIELD
Wishaw
Worfield
Shipley
CHURCH STRETTON
Church Stoke
BRIDGNORTH
Oldbury
WEST BROMWICH
Ditton Priors
Hampton Loade
Kingswinford
DUDLEY
BIRMINGHAM
Kinver
STOURBRIDGE
National Exhibition Centre
BISHOP'S CASTLE
Alveley
Birmingham Airport
Clun
Frankley
SOLIHULL
KIDDERMINSTER
Belbroughton
Shirley
Knowle
LUDLOW
Hopton Wafers
BEWDLEY
Cleobury Mortimer
STOURPORT-ON-SEVERN
Dorridge
BROMSGROVE
Abberley
Crossway Green
REDDITCH
Henley-in-Arden
Shrawley
2
3
4
5
6
7
8
9
0
1
2
3
4
5
0
9
8
7
6
5
4
3
2
1
0
9
8
7
6
5
4
3
2
1
0
9
8
7

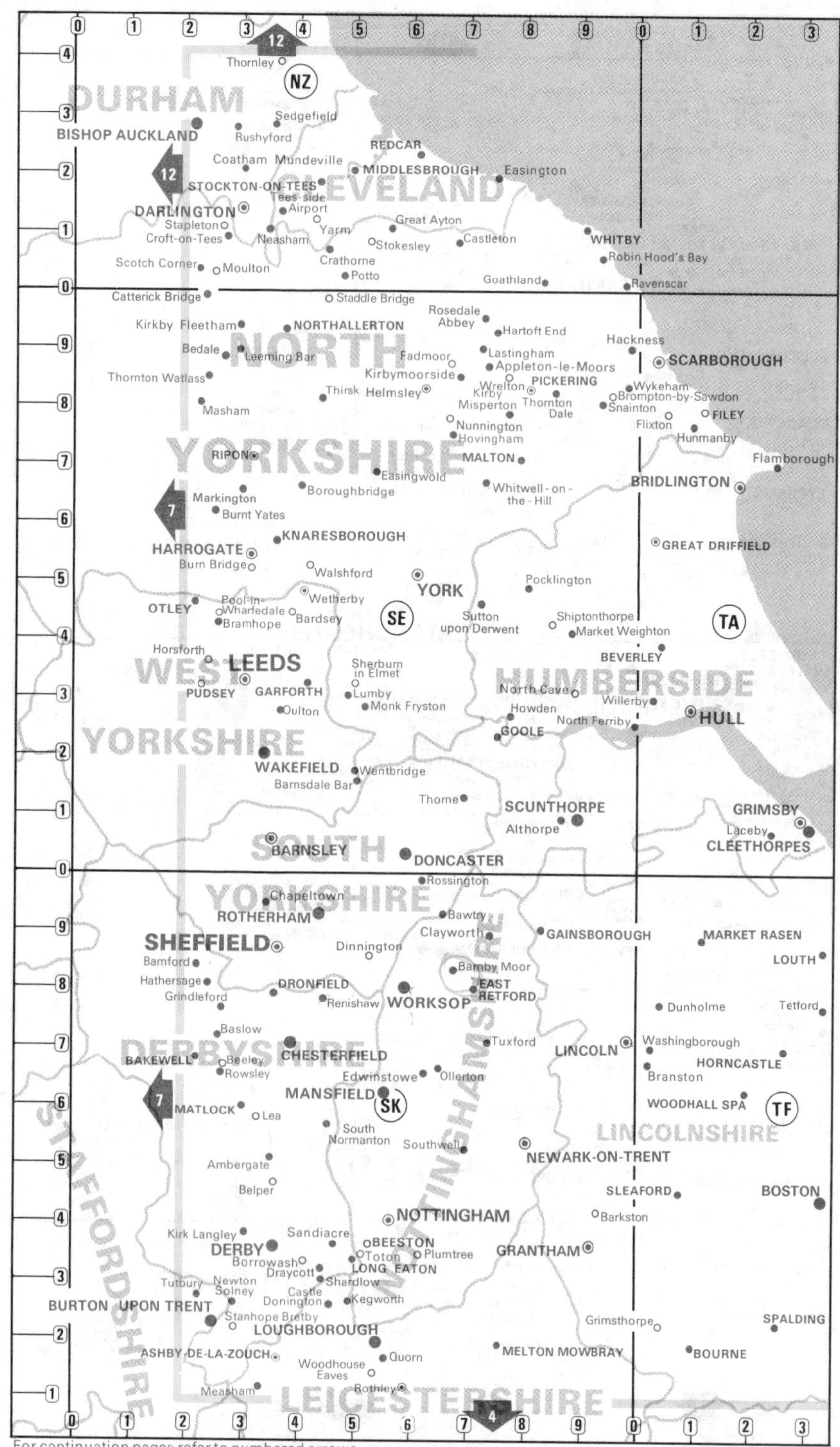

For continuation pages refer to numbered arrows

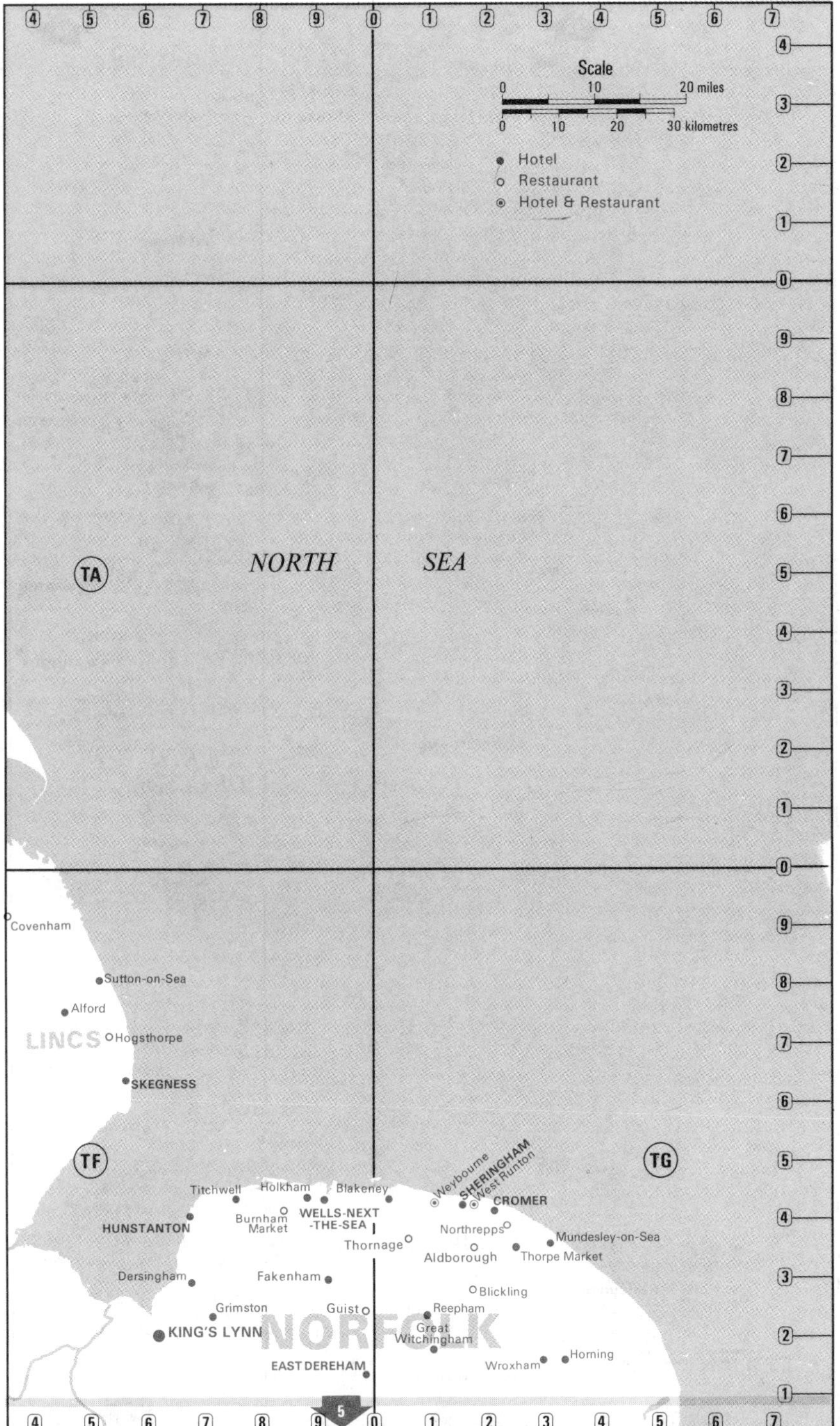
Scale
0
10
20 miles
0
10
20
30 kilometres
Hotel
Restaurant
Hotel & Restaurant
TA
NORTH
SEA
TF
TG
Covenham
Sutton-on-Sea
Alford
LINCS
Hogsthorpe
SKEGNESS
Titchwell
Holkham
Blakeney
Weybourne
SHERINGHAM
West Runton
CROMER
HUNSTANTON
Burnham Market
WELLS-NEXT-THE-SEA
Northrepps
Thornage
Aldborough
Mundesley-on-Sea
Thorpe Market
Dersingham
Fakenham
Blickling
Grimston
Guist
Reepham
KING'S LYNN
NORFOLK
Great Witchingham
EAST DEREHAM
Wroxham
Horning
5

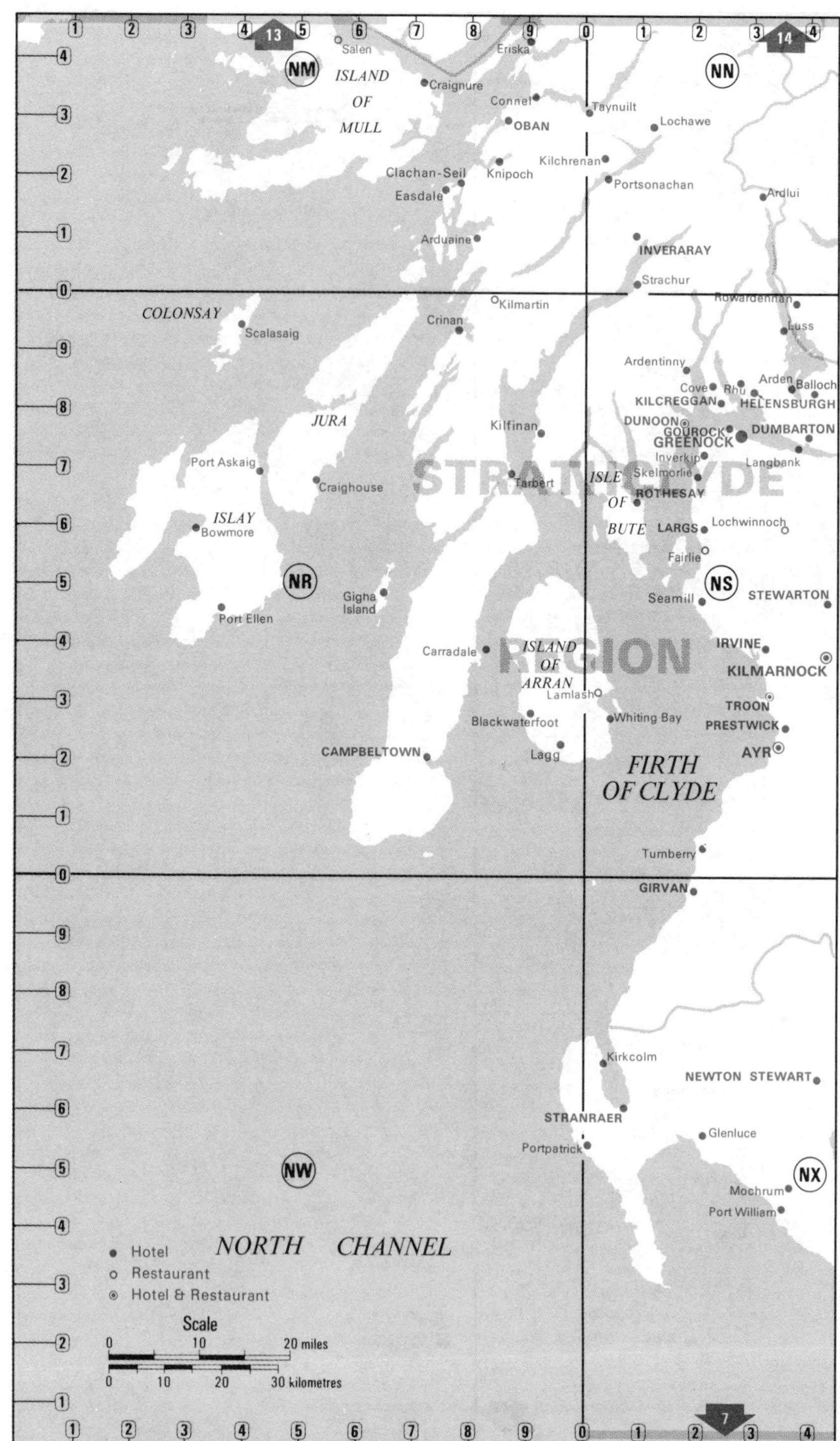

For continuation pages refer to numbered arrows

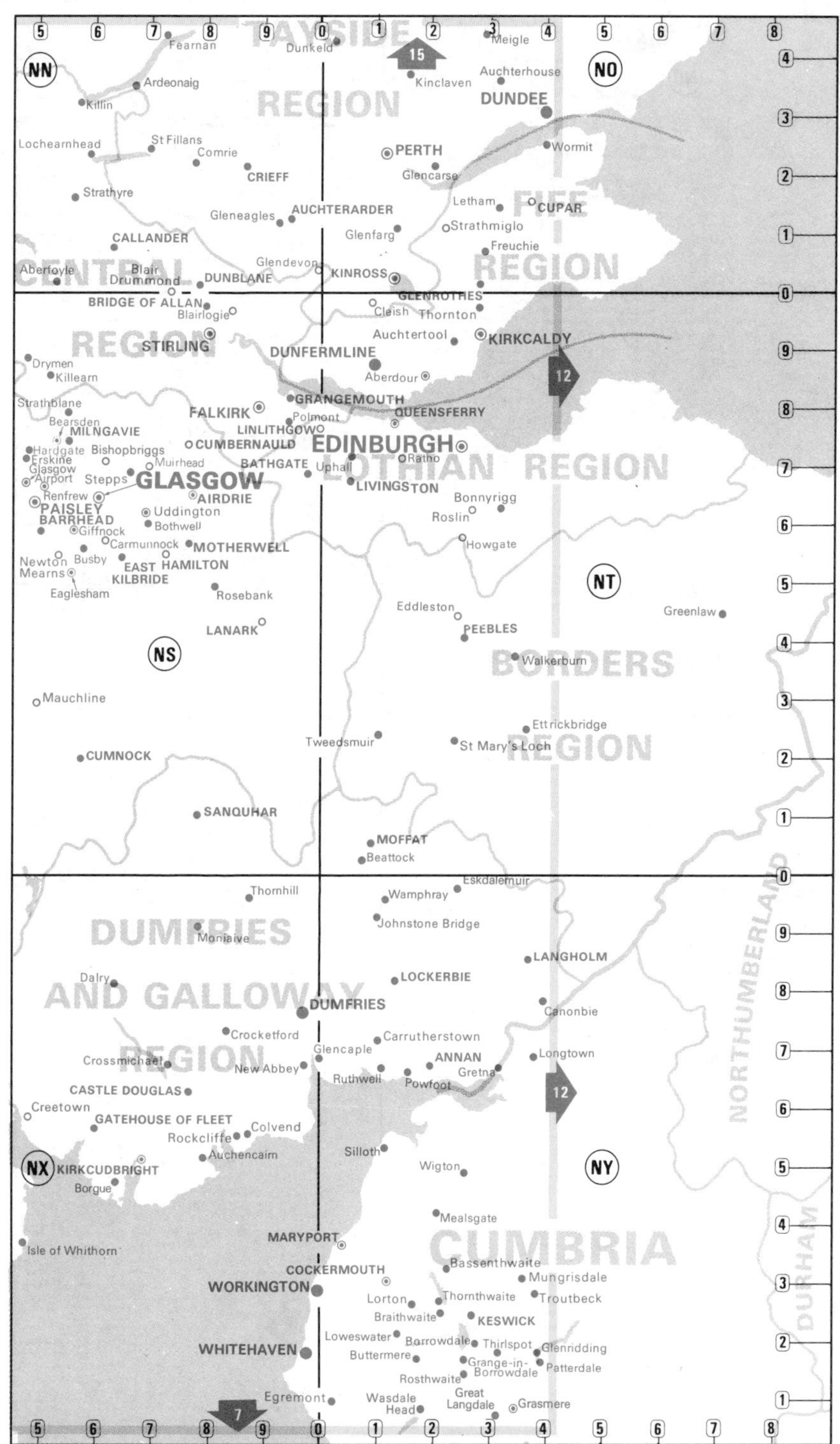
NN
NO
NS
NT
NX
NY
TAYSIDE REGION
CENTRAL REGION
FIFE REGION
LOTHIAN REGION
BORDERS REGION
DUMFRIES AND GALLOWAY REGION
CUMBRIA
NORTHUMBERLAND
DURHAM
15
12
7
Fearnan
Dunkeld
Meigle
Ardeonaig
Killin
Kinclaven
Auchterhouse
DUNDEE
Lochearnhead
St Fillans
Comrie
PERTH
Wormit
CRIEFF
Glencarse
Strathyre
Gleneagles
AUCHTERARDER
Letham
CUPAR
Strathmiglo
Glenfarg
CALLANDER
Freuchie
Glendevon
Aberfoyle
Blair Drummond
DUNBLANE
KINROSS
GLENROTHES
BRIDGE OF ALLAN
Cleish
Thornton
Blairlogie
Auchtertool
KIRKCALDY
STIRLING
DUNFERMLINE
Drymen
Killearn
Aberdour
Strathblane
GRANGEMOUTH
Bearsden
FALKIRK
Polmont
QUEENSFERRY
MILNGAVIE
LINLITHGOW
Hardgate
Bishopbriggs
CUMBERNAULD
EDINBURGH
Erskine
Ratho
Glasgow Airport
Muirhead
BATHGATE
Uphall
Stepps
GLASGOW
Renfrew
LIVINGSTON
Bonnyrigg
PAISLEY
AIRDRIE
Uddington
Roslin
BARRHEAD
Giffnock
Bothwell
Carmunnock
MOTHERWELL
Howgate
Newton Mearns
Busby
EAST KILBRIDE
HAMILTON
Eaglesham
Rosebank
Eddleston
Greenlaw
LANARK
PEEBLES
Walkerburn
Mauchline
Ettrickbridge
Tweedsmuir
St Mary's Loch
CUMNOCK
SANQUHAR
MOFFAT
Beattock
Eskdalemuir
Thornhill
Wamphray
Johnstone Bridge
Moniaive
LANGHOLM
Dalry
LOCKERBIE
DUMFRIES
Canonbie
Crocketford
Carrutherstown
Glencaple
Longtown
Crossmichael
ANNAN
New Abbey
Gretna
Ruthwell
Powfoot
CASTLE DOUGLAS
Creetown
GATEHOUSE OF FLEET
Colvend
Rockcliffe
Auchencairn
Silloth
KIRKCUDBRIGHT
Wigton
Borgue
Mealsgate
MARYPORT
Isle of Whithorn
COCKERMOUTH
Bassenthwaite
Mungrisdale
WORKINGTON
Lorton
Thornthwaite
Troutbeck
Braithwaite
KESWICK
Loweswater
Borrowdale
Thirlspot
Glenridding
WHITEHAVEN
Buttermere
Grange-in-Borrowdale
Patterdale
Rosthwaite
Egremont
Wasdale Head
Great Langdale
Grasmere

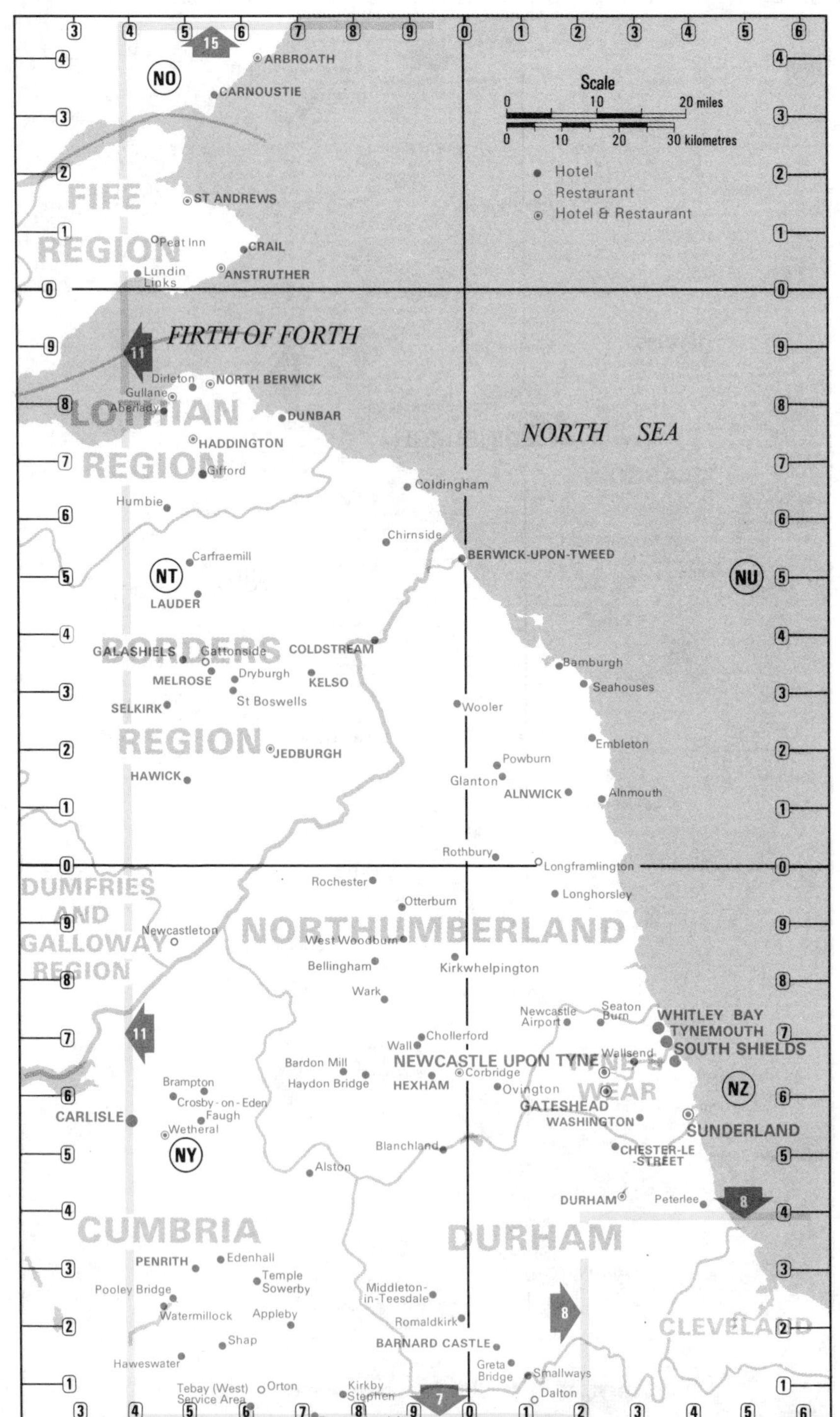

For continuation pages refer to numbered arrows

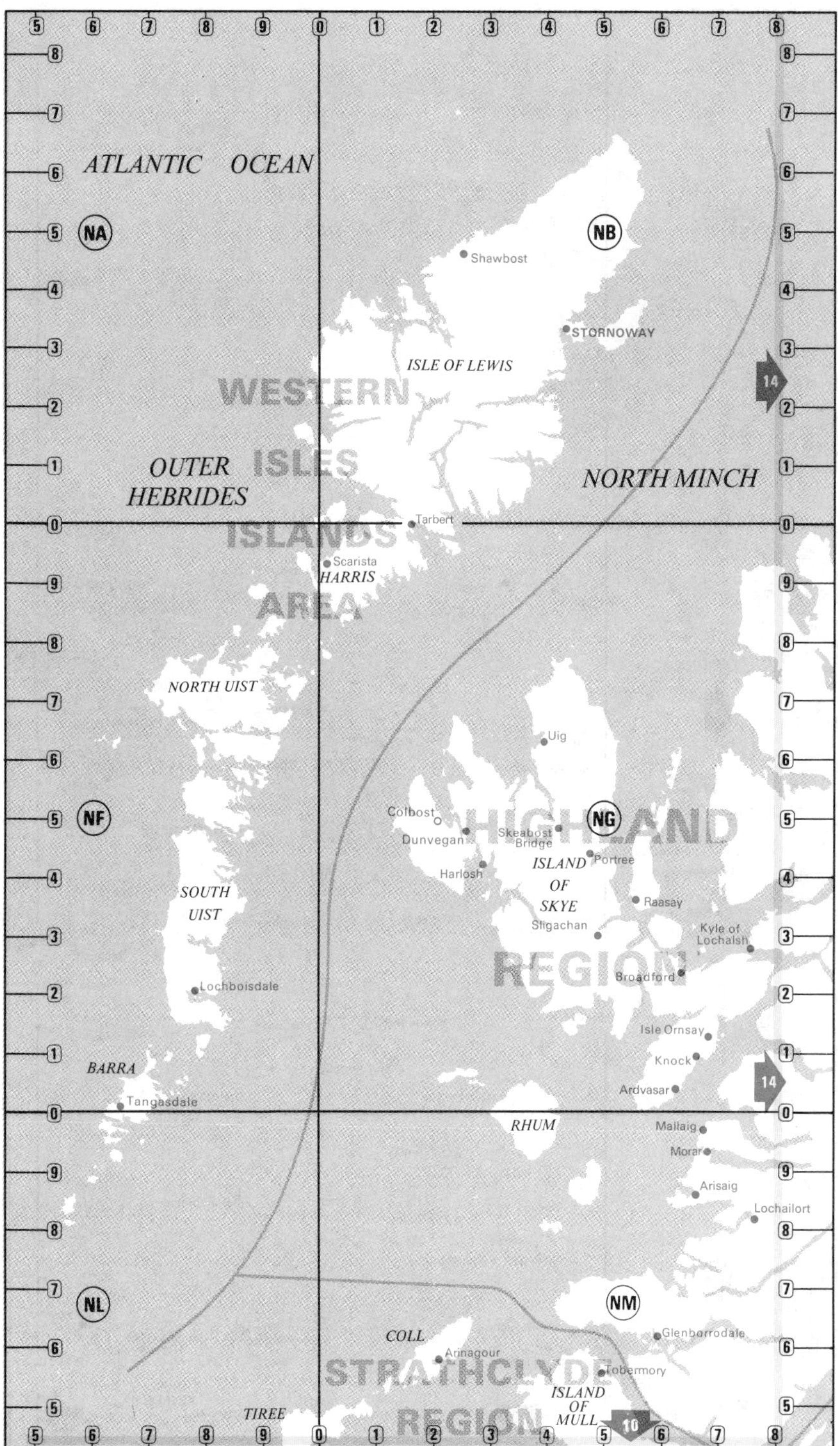
ATLANTIC OCEAN
NA
NB
Shawbost
STORNOWAY
ISLE OF LEWIS
WESTERN ISLES ISLANDS AREA
OUTER HEBRIDES
NORTH MINCH
14
Tarbert
Scarista
HARRIS
NORTH UIST
Uig
NF
Colbost
Dunvegan
Skeabost Bridge
NG
HIGHLAND REGION
Portree
ISLAND OF SKYE
Harlosh
SOUTH UIST
Raasay
Sligachan
Kyle of Lochalsh
Broadford
Lochboisdale
Isle Ornsay
Knock
BARRA
Ardvasar
Tangasdale
RHUM
Mallaig
Morar
Arisaig
Lochailort
NL
NM
COLL
Glenborrodale
Arinagour
STRATHCLYDE REGION
Tobermory
ISLAND OF MULL
TIREE
10

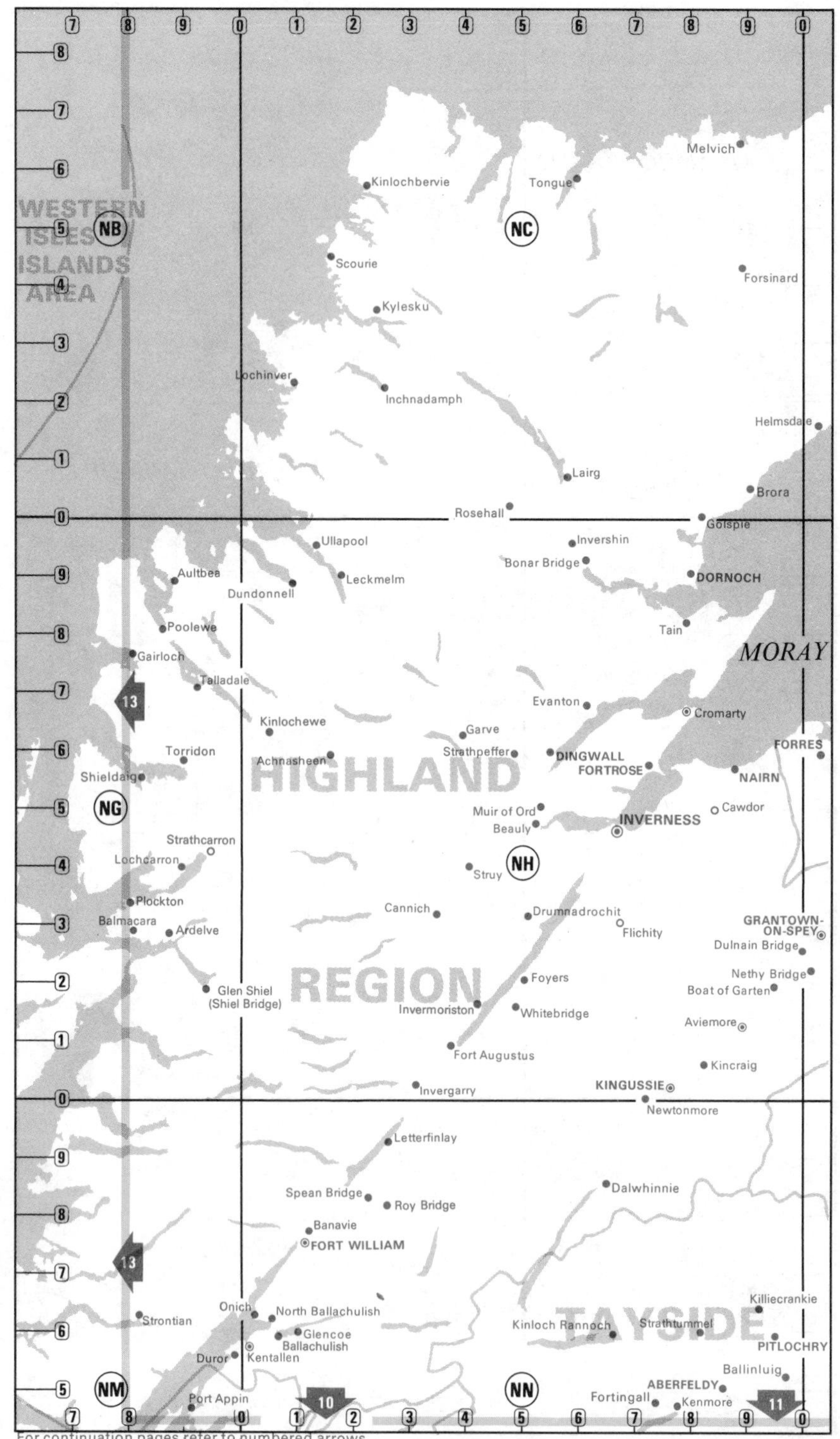

For continuation pages refer to numbered arrows

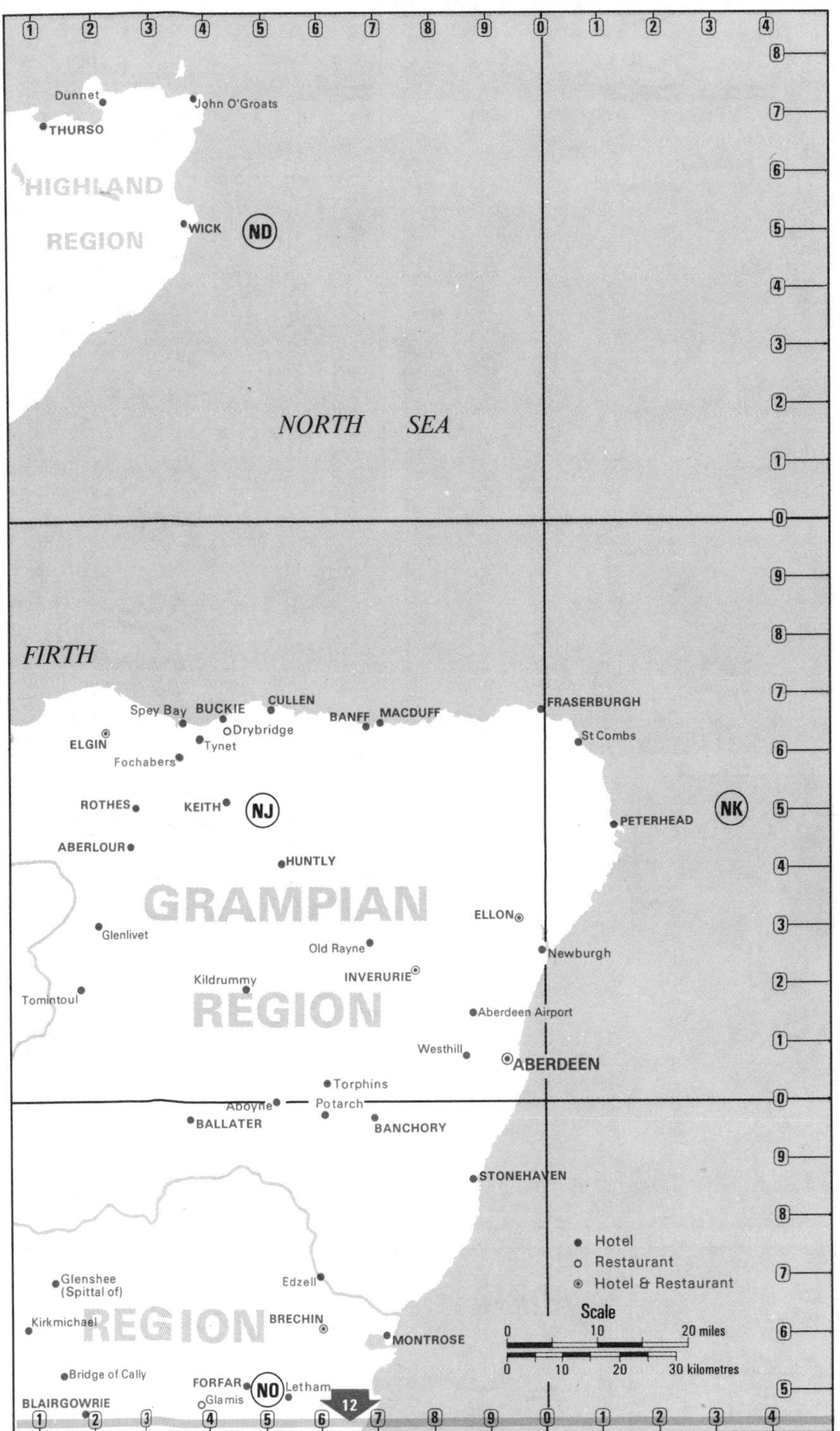
Dunnet
John O'Groats
THURSO
HIGHLAND
REGION
WICK
ND
NORTH SEA
FIRTH
Spey Bay
BUCKIE
CULLEN
Drybridge
BANFF
MACDUFF
FRASERBURGH
ELGIN
Tynet
St Combs
Fochabers
ROTHES
KEITH
NJ
NK
PETERHEAD
ABERLOUR
HUNTLY
GRAMPIAN
ELLON
Glenlivet
Old Rayne
Newburgh
Kildrummy
INVERURIE
Tomintoul
REGION
Aberdeen Airport
Westhill
ABERDEEN
Torphins
Aboyne
Potarch
BALLATER
BANCHORY
STONEHAVEN
Hotel
Restaurant
Hotel & Restaurant
Glenshee
(Spittal of)
Edzell
Scale
0
10
20 miles
Kirkmichael
REGION
BRECHIN
MONTROSE
0
10
20
30 kilometres
Bridge of Cally
FORFAR
NO
Letham
12
BLAIRGOWRIE
Glamis

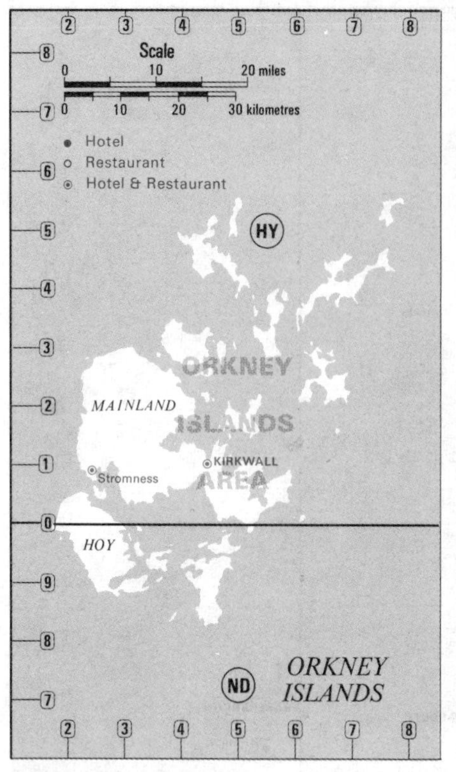

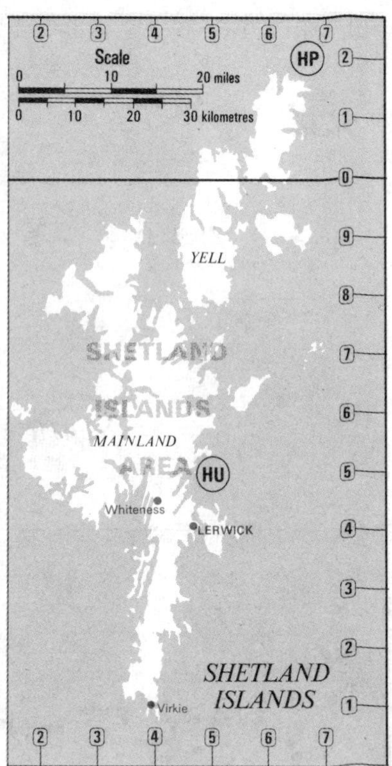

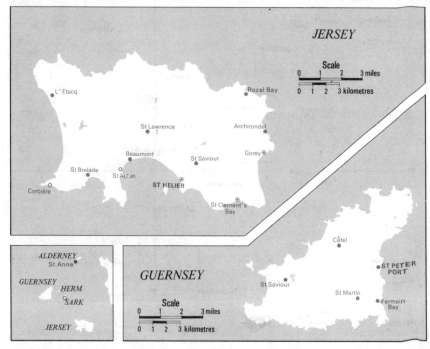

JERSEY

Scale
0 1 2 3 miles
0 1 2 3 kilometres

L' Etacq
Rozel Bay
St Lawrence
Archirondel
Gorey
Beaumont
St Saviour
St Brelade
St Aubin
ST HELIER
Corbière
St Clement's Bay

ALDERNEY
St Anne
GUERNSEY
HERM
SARK
JERSEY

GUERNSEY

Scale
0 1 2 3 miles
0 1 2 3 kilometres

Câtel
ST PETER PORT
St Saviour
St Martin
Fermain Bay